The United States Navy in World War II

THE UNITED
STATES MARINE
CORPS IN
WORLD WAR II

THE ONE-VOLUME HISTORY, FROM WAKE TO
TSINGTAO—BY THE MEN WHO FOUGHT IN
THE PACIFIC, AND BY DISTINGUISHED MARINE
EXPERTS, AUTHORS, AND NEWSPAPERMEN

THE UNITED STATES MARINE CORPS IN WORLD WAR II

T HE ONE-VOLUME HISTORY, FROM WAKE TO
TSINGTAO—BY THE MEN WHO FOUGHT IN THE
PACIFIC, AND BY DISTINGUISHED MARINE EXPERTS,
AUTHORS, AND NEWSPAPERMEN

Compiled and edited by S. E. Smith

With an Introduction by
Lieutenant General Julian C. Smith

 RANDOM HOUSE • NEW YORK

First Printing

1098765432

Copyright © 1969 by S. E. Smith

Library of Congress Catalog Card Number: 67-22643

Manufactured in the United States of America

All photographs are official Marine Corps photographs, provided by courtesy of the Department of Defense.

Grateful acknowledgment is made to the following for permission to reprint previously published material:

The Associated Press: an eyewitness article by Sgt. Jim Hurlburt which appeared in the November 11, 1942, issue of the *Washington Star.*

The Bobbs-Merrill Company, Inc.: from *Last Man Off Wake Island,* by Lt. Col. Walter L. J. Bayler as told to Cecil Carnes. Copyright 1943 by The Bobbs-Merrill Company, Inc.

Brandt & Brandt: from *Admiral Halsey's Story,* by Fleet Admiral William F. Halsey, USN and J. Bryan III, published by Whittlesey House, McGraw-Hill Book Company, Inc. Copyright 1947 by William F. Halsey. Copyright 1947 by The Curtis Publishing Company.

Thomas Y. Crowell Company Inc.: from *The Bloody Battle for Suribachi,* by Richard Wheeler. Copyright © 1965 by Richard Wheeler.

The Saturday Evening Post: "We Mopped Up Makin Island," by Lt. W. S. Le François; "Battle Without a Name," by Capt. Robert Blake; "Battle of Cibik's Ridge," by Capt. Steve Cibik as told to James D. Horan and Gerald Frank. Copyright 1943, 1944 by The Curtis Publishing Company.

E. P. Dutton & Co., Inc.: from the book *Joe Foss, Flying Marine,* by Capt. Joe Foss as told to Walter Simmons. Copyright 1943 by E. P. Dutton & Co., Inc.

Doubleday & Company, Inc.: from *On Valor's Side* and from *The Friendly Dead,* by T. Grady Gallant. Copyright © 1963, 1964 by T. Grady Gallant.

Exposition Press: from *Guest of the Rising Sun,* by Hans Whitney. Copyright 1951 by Hans Whitney.

Bernard Geis Associates: from *Yanks Don't Cry,* by Martin Boyle. Copyright © 1963 by Martin Boyle.

Blanche C. Gregory, Inc.: from *The Assault,* by Allen R. Matthews. Copyright 1947 by Allen R. Matthews.

Harper & Row Publishers: from pp. 135-144 in *Corregidor:* The Saga of a Fortress, by James H. Belote and William M. Belote. Copyright © 1967 by James H. Belote and William M. Belote. Abridgment of pp. 96-99, 103-109 in *Incredible Victory,* by Walter Lord. Copyright © 1967 by Walter Lord. From pp. 113-144 in *Coral Comes High,* by George P. Hunt. Copyright 1946 by George P. Hunt. From pp. 181-196 in *Devilbirds,* by John A. DeChant. Copyright 1947 by John A. DeChant.

Holt, Rinehart and Winston, Inc.: from *Iwo Jima,* by Richard F. Newcomb. Copyright © 1965 by Richard F. Newcomb. From *Last Chapter* by Ernie Pyle. Copyright 1945 by Scripps-Howard Newspaper Alliance. Copyright 1946 by Holt, Rinehart and Winston, Inc. From *A Ribbon and a Star,* by John Monks, Jr. Copyright 1945 by Holt, Rinehart and Winston, Inc.

Houghton Mifflin Company: from *Battle for Solomons,* by Ira Wolfert.

The Journal Herald: for an article by Pete Zurlinden in the November 25, 1943 edition.

Col. D. L. Dickson: for material from *Leatherneck* Magazine.

Life: from "Reminiscences" by General Douglas MacArthur, *Life* Magazine. Copyright © 1964 by Time, Inc.

Little, Brown and Co.: from *Marine at War,* by Russell Davis and Brent K. Ashabranner. Copyright © 1961 by Russell Davis and Brent K. Ashabranner. From *Marine,* by Burke Davis. Copyright © 1962 by Burke Davis. From *Wake Island Command,* by W. Scott Cunningham and Lydel Sims. Copyright © 1961 by Lydel Sims and W. Scott Cunningham.

Marine Corps Gazette: "Incident of the Blue Goose," by Captain John DeChant "Corry's Boys," by Brig. Gen. Samuel B. Griffith; "Last Days of the USS Quincy," by Major Warren P. Baker; "4th Marines at Corregidor," by Hanson W. Baldwin; "Marine Artillery on Guadalcanal," by Brig. Gen. Pedro A. DelValle; "Battle of the Tenaru," by Gen. Clifton B. Cates; "Ambush in China," by Captain Walter Mansfield; "Guam" by Robert "Petter" Martin; "First to Fight," by Gen. Thomas Holcomb; "Tanks on Guam." Copyright 1943, 1944, 1946, 1947, 1952 by the Marine Corps Association. For the painting of Tarawa by Thomas Lovell.

McIntosh and Otis, Inc.: from *They Call It Pacific,* by Clark Lee. Copyright 1943 by Clark Lee.

The New Yorker: "A Reporter at Large: D Day, Iwo Jima," and "A Reporter on Okinawa: I - Suicides & Bushwhackers, II - The Tomb Life," by John Lardner. Copyright 1945 by The New Yorker Magazine, Inc.

W. W. Norton & Company, Inc.: from *Once a Marine:* The Memoirs of a General, by A. A. Vandegrift, U.S.M.C., as told to Robert B. Asprey. Copyright © 1964 by A. A. Vandegrift and R. B. Asprey.

G. P. Putnam's Sons: from *Hell in the Heavens,* by John M. Foster. Copyright © 1961 by John M. Foster. From *The Sky Is My Witness,* by Captain Thomas Moore, Jr. Copyright 1943 by Thomas Moore, Jr. From *Baa Baa Blacksheep,* by Col. Gregory Boyington. Copyright © 1958 by Gregory Boyington. From *Betio Beachhead,* by Captain Earl J. Wilson, Jim Lucas, Samuel Shaffer and C. Peter Zurlinden. Copyright 1945 by War Orphans Scholarships, Inc.

Random House, Inc.: from *But Not in Shame,* by John Toland. Copyright © 1961 by John Toland. From *Guadalcanal Diary,* by Richard Tregaskis. Copyright 1943 by Random House, Inc. From *Strong Men Armed,* by Robert Leckie. Copyright © 1962 by Robert Leckie. From *Follow Me!,* by Richard W. Johnston. Copyright 1948 by Second Marine Division History Board. From *Helmet for My Pillow,* by Robert Leckie. Copyright © 1957 by Robert Leckie.

Alfred A. Knopf, Inc.: from *The Long and the Tall and the Short,* by Alvin M. Josephy, Jr. Copyright 1946 by Alfred A. Knopf, Inc.

Fleming H. Revell Company: from *The Leathernecks Come Through,* by W. Wyeth Willard. Copyright 1944 by Fleming H. Revell Company.

Charles Scribner's Sons: from *Coral and Brass,* pages 129 - 134, 168 - 174 and 267 - 275, by Holland M. Smith and Percy Finch. Copyright 1949 by Holland M. Smith.

Shipmate, a publication of the U.S. Naval Academy Alumni Association: "Nine to One over Guadalcanal," by Capt. M.E. Carl.

Stackpole Books: "The March to Viru Harbor," by Anthony P. Coulis, from *Purple Testament,* edited by Don M. Wolfe.

University of North Carolina Press: from *Marine from Virginia,* by David Tucker Brown.

Vanguard Press, Inc.: from *This Is It,* by Harry Davis, pp. 92-103. Copyright 1944 by Harry Davis.

CONTENTS

PART I   *WAKE TO MIDWAY: BEGINNING'S END*

PART II   *GUADALCANAL: OFFENSIVE IN THE SOLOMONS*

PART III   *MUNDA TO CAPE GLOUCESTER: REDUCTION OF RABAUL*

PART IV   *TARAWA TO PELELIU:*
          BATTERING THE EMPIRE

Part V   IWO JIMA TO OKINAWA: DEATH OF AN EMPIRE

LIST OF MAPS

LIST OF PHOTOGRAPHS

EDITOR'S NOTE

The United States is currently engaged in the fourth costliest war in its history. In eight years approximately 35,000 men of our armed forces have died in Vietnam, many of them sons of United States Marines who fought the Japanese in World War II. While the technology of war has been inordinately refined since the conclusion of that conflict nearly three decades ago, the killing power of a bullet remains unchanged—as inescapably unchanged as Marine Corps' *esprit* and pride of accomplishment. But beyond these hallmarks of service, marines are a unique breed of men—they excel. They did during the war years of 1941-45, and they do now in Vietnam, two wars later. This volume underscores that fact.

At Pearl Harbor, small detachments of marines were stationed aboard battleships and cruisers off Ford Island when the enemy struck the United States Pacific Fleet. Marine gunners contributed much that "day of infamy." But the Corps' real war began a day later, and here was the starting point of the present volume—the unalterable course through to the unique Japanese surrender in North China, when the Corps officially laid down its arms.

Thus the creation of this volume was clear-cut. Material issued from many sources, and the problem, if one can logically call it that, was one of selection from the writings of a large number of gifted men. However, barracks pieces and others of similar "slice of life" vein were shunted off with sincere regret. Hopefully, of course, the work itself will transport old marines back to the more colorful days of their youth. Indeed, the cocky gyrenes of my generation need no reminder of how it was on liberty in Brisbane, Australia, or even in Norfolk, Virginia, while awaiting a draft to the Pacific. But this was a lighter side of their war, and properly it has no place in this volume.

I owe a substantial debt of gratitude to many persons for their generous guidance and cooperation in assembling this project: General Lemuel C. Shepherd, Jr.; Lt. General Julian C. Smith (upon whose hospitality I imposed more times than were warranted); Col. Paul M. Moriarity; Col. Frank C. Caldwell; the late Col. James W. Hurlbut; Col. Donald L. Dickson; Col. Paul R. Hines; Col. Philip N. Pierce; Col. Robert D. Heinl, Jr. (whose definitive *Soldiers of the Sea* provided a running guide); Lt. Col. Gregory S. Prichard; Rowland P. Gill; Henry I. Shaw, Jr.; Lt. Col. Richard S. Stark; Benis M. Frank; and Robert D. Loomis, senior editor of Random House, who accompanied me on the long and frequently stormy passage into the war zone. Without them, surely this work would not have come to fruition.

S. E. SMITH

New York, N.Y.

INTRODUCTION

Julian C. Smith

LIEUTENANT GENERAL U.S.M.C. RETIRED

Here is a magnificent mosaic of the Marine Corps in World War II, a rich panoply of history and drama skillfully interwoven with heroic individual exploits. In war and peace, since the first landing operation in the Bahamas in 1776 when the Corps was less than six months old, marines have always been called upon to land on foreign shores to insure the nation's security or to protect the lives and rights of its citizens. Marines were with Stephen Decatur during the war with the Barbary States when his force boarded and destroyed the captured American warship *Philadelphia* in the harbor of Tripoli. These marines stormed the pirate fort of Derne and raised the Stars and Stripes for the first time on African soil.

During the Spanish-American War, a battalion of marines made the first landing in Cuba at Guantanamo Bay, and won a naval base for the United States Fleet operating against the Spanish Fleet under Admiral Cervesa in Santiago Harbor.

All landings were not marked by bloodshed, however, as for example the landings at Tokyo Bay in 1853. Marines provided a show of force for Commodore Perry when he landed near Tokyo to arrange for the opening of Japan to trade. Perry whimsically noted that during the negotiations the marines drilling onshore in their dress blues "impressed" the Japanese with their discipline and precision.

In our small "Banana Wars" marines went through tropical jungles, fought their way out of ambushes, stormed fortifications, took towns and cities, always against great numerical odds. In World War I marines took the full measure of Germany's best troops. In Shanghai and Peking a few faced many and their presence alone kept peace.

A study of the Marine Corps' activities prior to World War II gives an understanding of the morale and *esprit de corps* that were the foundation of its combat efficiency, but it does not show the study of command, staff and logistics and the tactical training that were equally responsible for successful marine assaults on the Japanese strongholds in the atolls of the Pacific.

The year 1933 marked a turning point for the Marine Corps. Major General John H. Russell, then Assistant Commandant, initiated the organization of the Fleet Marine Force and recommended that it be included in the fleet organization subject to orders of the Commander in Chief of the U.S. Fleet. Thus, the Marine Corps had finally committed itself to the doctrine that its paramount wartime mission was the seizure and defense of bases for naval operations.

The combined maneuvers of the Navy and Marine Corps in the late thirties revealed many deficiencies in equipment, especially in the types of small boats available to the landing forces with their combat equipment and the supplies. The result was the development of the alligator tractor, or LVT as it was known, and the troop-carrying landing craft medium called the LCM, with a retractable bow that could be let down as a ramp for the debarkation of troops. These two boats became the standard medium landing craft used by the United States forces during the war.

Marine Corps Aviation was developing at this same time. Beginning with a few hardy individuals who began their training as naval aviators, Marine Corps Aviation performed all peacetime chores assigned to it, and then pioneered the air support of ground troops in combat. In at least two actions, Ocotal and Quilili, Nicaragua, it turned the tide of battle for marines hard-pressed by greatly superior numbers, and performed miracles of communication, supply and evacuation for troops in remote jungle-bound areas. Thus, the beginning of World War II found the Marine Corps low in numbers—only 65,000—but high inefficiency, forming a nucleus ready to expand and meet its responsibilities in a large-scale modern war. But we will let S. E. Smith tell this side of the story in this book.

An accomplished historian, with the vitally necessary combat background, Smith has skillfully captured the spirit of the men who bore the brunt and took the casualties in the hard-fought battles of World War II. Instead of writing a history of the Marine Corps from the dispassionate historical view of twenty-five years after the events, Stan Smith has collected largely firsthand accounts by men who participated in or witnessed the actions recorded.

The result is a fascinating, historically accurate mosaic that takes the reader into the excitement of battle and the uncertainties of the "fog of war" enveloping the participants as they carried out missions, which at the time seemed to be producing only casualties instead of tangible results.

Indeed, Mr. Smith has produced a documentary of such value and interest that it is certain to become a most popular and enlightening history of the Marine Corps in World War II.

PART I

Wake to Midway: Beginning's End

Eight months before the United States entered World War II Admiral Husband E. Kimmel, Commander in Chief of the United States Pacific Fleet, perceptively noted that "one of the initial operations of the Japanese navy may be directed at Wake. If Wake be defended, then for the Japanese to reduce it would require extended operations in an area where we might be able to get at naval forces with naval forces." Thus, Kimmel stood behind the order which sent a handful of United States Marines to this strategic atoll, where was written in blood one of the most stirring chapters in the history of our nation.

Wake is a lonely, surf-swept cluster of islands far from the mid-Pacific shipping lanes. Actually it is the top of a submerged volcano, comprising about 2600 acres of land mass with a maximum elevation of 21 feet, covered sparsely by shrubs and dwarf trees. The entire coastline measures less than 20 nautical miles, and is shaped like a "V" pointing northwestward. Three islands make up the atoll: Peale, the northwest tip; Wilkes, the southwest tip; and Wake, the main body. Discovered in 1568 by the Spaniard Alverado Medana, Wake lay abandoned until the middle of the nineteenth century, when it was visited by the Wilkes Exploring Company. The United States formally claimed Wake in 1899. Commander E. D. Taussig of the gunboat *Bennington* came out, planted the American flag, fired his one-pounder and departed. Down through the years sailing masters sent their crews ashore to search in vain for fresh water, and Japanese plumage hunters came to kill seabirds. But the atoll had no military significance until 1939, when, because of the steadily deteriorating situation in the Pacific, the Government ordered a survey of Wake by the crew of the U.S.S. *Nitro.*

As the tempo of the war drums increased, Wake correspondingly assumed strategic importance as a fixed carrier base: 450 miles from Bikini; 620 miles from our future enemy's installations in the Marshalls; 764 miles from the Marcus chain; 1023 miles from Midway; and 1300 miles from Guam. We could ill afford to overlook it. On the recommendation of the Hepburn Board in 1940, Congress voted to give the Navy Department the appropriations to develop Midway and Wake as submarine and air bases. However, before a military establishment could be implemented on Wake, Pan American Airways installed a seaplane base and hotel on Peale as an overnight stop for its transpacific flights.

The first contingent of the 1st Defense Battalion—6 officers and 173 enlisted men—arrived at the atoll aboard the U.S.S. *Regulus* on August 19, 1941. The first of 1200 Pacific Naval Airbase workmen, civilians, came out a few days later. In October, Major James P. S. Devereux arrived from Pearl Harbor bringing the ordnance with which his command was to defend Wake during its ordeal: two 5-inch .51-caliber coastal guns (taken from old battleships); four 3-inch antiaircraft guns (with fire control for only one), two dozen .50-caliber and an undisclosed number of .30 caliber machine guns for beach defenses.

By November marines and workmen were hacking out a 5000 foot airstrip, mounting gun emplacements, bulldozing roads, revetments, constructing buildings and sheds, erecting storage tanks and dredging channels. Another 9 officers and 200 enlisted men arrived from Pearl on November 2, increasing the garrison's strength to 15 officers and 373 enlisted men—less than half of the battalion's rated complement. Commander Winfield Scott Cunningham, executive officer of the aircraft tender U.S.S. *Wright,* arrived on the twenty-eighth to replace Devereux as island commander, and he brought 9 officers and 58 bluejackets to service a naval air station. At this juncture the United States Army, with the help of marines hand-pumping gasoline at any hour of the day or night, staged flights of B-17s through to Guam. Crude as it was, and notwithstanding a dire shortage of marines and equipment (radars were still in Hawaii), Wake was a going concern.

On December 1, the day that the Imperial Council met in Tokyo to ratify General Tojo's decision to attack the United States, Great Britain and the Netherlands, Wake was on war alert and braced for attack despite a prevalent attitude that "the Japs are just bluffing again." Nevertheless, in a final attempt to beef up the atoll's fighting potential, 12 Grumman Wildcats, F4Fs under the command of Major Paul Putnam, were launched from the carrier *Enterprise* on the morn-

ing of the third. The planes roared over the Wake airstrip that afternoon to the great delight of all hands. Meanwhile, Devereux relentlessly drilled his marines, many of whom had only recently enlisted
in the Corps. He established an observation post atop a water tower
in Camp One, the marine base, but harbored little hope that lookouts would hear the drone of approaching aircraft over the pounding
of the surf. They never did.

Sunday, December 7 (east longitude), was the last day of peace on
Wake. Prophetically, Devereux rested his troops. It was their first
day off in two months, and the men swam, fished, played cards and
wrote letters. During the afternoon Pan American's *Philippine Clipper* arrived from the States bringing mail and the latest scuttlebutt of
the diplomatic crisis in Washington. Devereux made his rounds and
spent the better part of the afternoon in his tent. "There's no use fret-
ting," he wrote in his memoirs. "If you weren't stationed on this island, you'd be stationed on another."

The saga of the Marine Corps' magnificent holding action at the
onset of the Pacific conflict is told in six parts, the first by Colonel
Robert D. Heinl, Jr., former chief of Marine History and currently
the military editor of the Detroit *News*. A second lieutenant at the
time of the Japanese attack, Heinl, holder of a Legion of Merit, was
aboard U.S.S. *Tangier* with the 4th Defense Battalion during the
abortive Relief Expedition. Here, from his definitive monograph
of Wake written for the Marine Corps—undoubtedly the best and
most accurate work ever published—Heinl recounts the opening
days of the epochal battle.

• 1 • WAKE: THE ENEMY STRIKES

COLONEL ROBERT D. HEINL, JR.

The Pan American Airways *Philippine Clipper* embarked passengers shortly after sunrise on Monday morning, 8 December, taxied out into the calm green of the lagoon, took take-off position, and at 0655 soared outward toward Guam. Ashore on Wake the usual 0600 reveille had broken out the Marines, all of whom were well rested after their Sunday of holiday routine. Breakfast was being concluded in the mess halls, and many Marines were already squaring away their tents prior to falling out for the day's work. Major Devereux was shaving.

In the Army Airways Communications Service radio van set up by Captain Wilson near the airstrip, an operator was coming up on frequency with the base at Hickam Field on Oahu, when, at 0650, a frantic, uncoded, procedureless transmission cut through from Hickam: Oahu was under enemy air attack.

Wilson made for Major Devereux's tent, and delivered it to the defense commander. Devereux, after attempting unsuccessfully to reach Commander Cunningham by telephone, called the base communication shack, and learned that a coded priority transmission just in from Pearl was now being broken down. Without hesitating further, Devereux dropped the telephone, called for the field music on watch and ordered him to sound "Call to Arms."

Marines piled into the trucks which rolled to the battery areas in Camp 1 as gunnery sergeants broke out their men and checked to see that they had their rifles and ball ammunition. By 0735, all positions had reported manned and ready, a defense battalion officers' conference had been briefly held, and a watch had been established as previously planned atop the water tank OP in Camp 1.

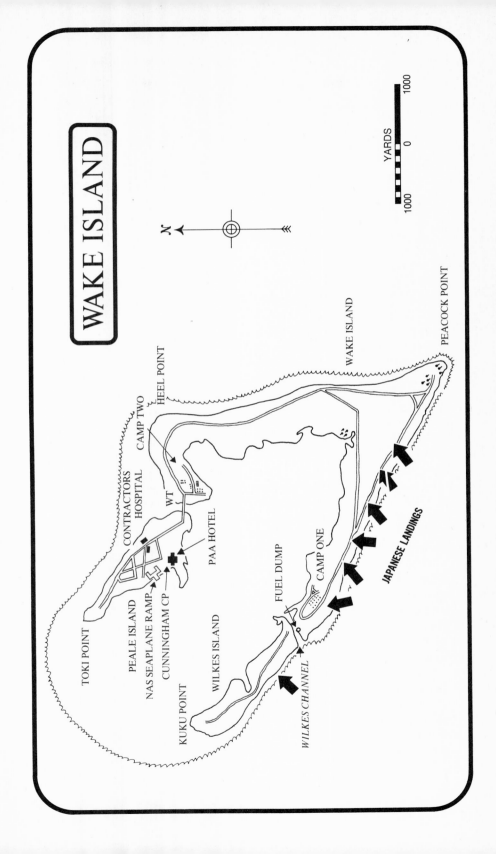

WAKE ISLAND

YARDS

1000   0   1000

TOKI POINT

PEALE ISLAND

NAS SEAPLANE RAMP

CUNNINGHAM CP

CONTRACTORS HOSPITAL

WT

CAMP TWO

HEEL POINT

PAA HOTEL

KUKU POINT

WILKES ISLAND

FUEL DUMP

CAMP ONE

WAKE ISLAND

JAPANESE LANDINGS

WILKES CHANNEL

PEACOCK POINT

Aviation, which already had the dawn patrol airborne prior to arrival of the news from Pearl, was initiating measures for the safety of the 12 new Wildcats as the *Philippine Clipper*, recalled only 10 minutes out of Wake, circled and let down into the lagoon. At the airstrip something close to consternation existed. VMF-211, which had been on Wake but four days, one a holiday, could hardly be said to have gotten established. Although dispersed aircraft revetments were being dozed up and would be ready by 1400 that day, the equally necessary net of access roads which, for the sake of the airplanes, had to be smoothly surfaced, was also uncompleted. The small size of the existing parking area prohibited dispersal beyond rather narrow limits . . .

Thus the primary morning activities of VMF-211's handful of pilots and mechanics were to disperse the aircraft as widely as possible in the open parking area and usable vicinity, to relocate the squadron radio installation from its original temporary site to one under cover, and, above all, to commence arming and servicing all aircraft for combat, in itself no light job.

At 0800, but a few hours after the gutted and blazing *Arizona*'s colors had been broken out aboard the dying ship, under a hail of enemy fire at Pearl Harbor, Morning Colors sounded on Wake, and the flag announced to all hands the garrison's determination and courage for the job ahead.

Defensive preparations hummed throughout Wake. Full allowances of ammunition were dropped off by truck at each unit; the few spare individual weapons in Marine storerooms were issued—as far as they went—to the unarmed AAF soldiers and to the naval air base bluejackets; gas masks and the old style World War I helmets, on hand only for Marines, were distributed to the battery positions. On order from Devereux, watches were set at fire-control instruments and guns, while the balance of personnel worked on fox holes, filled the few remaining sandbags at hand, and set about other measures of defensive fortification. The 3-inch antiaircraft batteries were specifically directed to keep one gun, plus all fire-control instruments, fully manned.

Initial command posts, not only for Marine units, but for the island commander, were hastily set up, in most instances for the time being resembling that of the 1st Defense Battalion detachment, which was simply a switchboard in the brush just east of Camp 1. Commander Cunningham's was located in Camp 2, and VMF-211's remained in the squadron office tent, personnel being unavailable from more pressing duties, such as belting extra ammunition and transferring bulk fuel into more dispersable drums.

At 0900, Putnam's four-plane combat air patrol returned to base, and after refueling and taking a smoke and stretch, the four pilots clambered back into F4F's 9 through 12, took off, executed their section rendezvous and climbed to 12,000 feet, scouting the most likely sectors for enemy approach south of Wake. Shortly afterward, the first pilot of the *Philippine Clipper,* Captain J. H. Hamilton, reported to Putnam at VMF-211's headquarters, with orders from the Island Commander to prepare to conduct a long-range southward search with fighter escort during the afternoon.

While VMF-211's combat air patrol was making a swing north of Wake at 12,000 feet, a half mile below them 36 twin-tailed Japanese bombers droned northward toward the atoll. This was Air Attack Force No. 1 of the Twenty-fourth Air Flotilla, based at Roi, 720 miles to the south. As the group leader signaled for a gliding let-down in his 10,000-foot approach, he noted that the south coast of the atoll was masked by a drifting rain squall at about 2,000 feet. The three divisions, in 12-plane V's, dropped rapidly down into the squall and emerged a few seconds later, almost on top of the Wake airstrip.

At 1158, First Lieutenant [Wallace] Lewis, commanding Battery E at Peacock Point, chanced to look skyward just in time to see a V of 12 strange aircraft heading over a point just midway between Camp 1 and Peacock Point. He jumped for a field telephone connected to the "J"-line as a spray of bright sparks began to sail through the air ahead of the formation, and, as one civilian exclaimed, "the wheels dropped off the airplanes." Japanese bombs were falling on Wake.

Lewis, an experienced antiaircraft artilleryman, had not only complied with the commanding officer's directive to keep one gun manned, but had added another for good measure, and, within a matter of seconds, two of Battery E's 3-inch guns were barking at the Japanese, using fire-control data supplied by Lewis's estimate. All along the south shore of Wake, as enemy incendiary bullets began to prickle and spit, .50 caliber antiaircraft machine guns opened fire.

A closed spaced pattern of 100-pound fragmentation bombs and 20-mm. incendiary bullets laced the entire VMF-211 area, where eight Grummanns were dispersed at approximately hundred-yard intervals. While two 12-plane enemy divisions continued to release bombs and to strafe Camp 2, one division broke off, swung back and approach Camp 1 and the airstrip from the westward over Kuku Point, and headed for the Pan American installations on Peale, which were likewise heavily attacked. By 1210, the enemy divisions had expended bombs and ammunition, turned away, rendezvoused and commenced their climb back to cruising altitude. "The pilots in every one of the planes were grinning widely. Everyone waggled his wings to signify 'BANZAI.'"

On the ground, despite prompt and fairly dense antiaircraft fire,

not only from Battery E but from D (3-inch, Peale) and from .50 calibers all over the atoll, the enemy attack had taken telling effect,
especially in and about the airstrip.

As pilots attempted to man their planes, seven of the eight F4F-
3's had been burned or blasted from tail to rudder, and the remaining one had sustained serious but not irreparable damage to its reserve fuel tank. Air-ground radio installation was severely damaged
by fragments and strafing, and the whole aviation area seemed a sea
of blazing gasoline from the 25,000-gallon avgas tank which had been
hit in the first strike; on all sides, as well, 50-gallon fuel drums popped
into flame. VMF-211's tentage, containing the squadron's scanty stock
of tools and spares, had been riddled and partially burned.

Worst of all, of 55 Marine aviation personnel then on the ground,
23 were killed outright or died of wounds before morning, and 11
more were wounded and survived. At one stroke, VMF-211 had sustained over 60 percent casualties. Two pilots (Lieutenants Graves
and Holden) were killed, Lieutenant Conderman would die before
daybreak, and another, Lieutenant Webb, was seriously wounded.
Three more pilots, Major Putnam, Captain Tharin and Staff Sergeant
Arthur, had received minor wounds but remained on their feet. Almost half of the ground-crews were dead.

In Camp 2 and the adjacent Pan American area, the luxurious hotel,
together with more important seaplane-base facilities, was afire, the
Philippine Clipper had received a few stray machine-gun bullets,
and some 10 Chamorro civilian employees of PAA had been killed.

So far as is known, the enemy escaped without the loss of a single
airplane, although several of the bombers sustained damage from
AA fire. The Marine combat air patrol, well above the raid and momentarily scouting to the north, had not made contact, and executed a
routine landing some minutes after the attack. To add the final stroke
of ill fortune, F4F number 9, piloted by Captain Elrod, was unable
while landing to avoid striking its propeller on a mass of bomb debris,
and it too was out of action with a bent propeller and a badly jarred
engine.

Admiral Inouye might well congratulate the Twenty-fourth Air
Flotilla for their devastating strike and upon their initial good fortune . . .

After the enemy had departed, the immediate problem was dam-
age-control at the airstrip. Casualties were despatched to the contractor's hospital, a one-story structure containing two wards, isolation facilities, an operating room and clinic which had been taken over as
the island aid station. Hardly less important than the human casualties were those inflicted by the Japanese on Major Putnam's "sleek
and fat" airplanes.

The intact three (numbers 10, 11, and 12) were immediately sent aloft on combat air patrol and to safeguard them against further surprise on the ground. Before the fires were completely out, the squadron commander had designated Second Lieutenant Kinney as the replacement Engineering Officer, vice First Lieutenant Graves, who had been killed. Kinney's principal assistant was Technical Sergeant Hamilton, an enlisted aviation pilot of many years' experience in all phases of Marine Corps aviation. Within a few hours, Kinney and Hamilton had commenced the ceaseless scavenging of burnt-out wreckage for salvageable tools and parts which was to mark outstandingly the maintenance in effective operation of the remnant of VMF-211 . . .

Throughout the atoll, the tempo of activity—except among the majority of contract workmen—already swift, had been accelerated perceptibly as a result of the first air raid, which had demonstrated so graphically the enemy's power to inflict damage.

At all battery positions, individual improvement of emplacements, fox holes, camouflage and all posisible defensive work was pursued. As a protection against any attempt by the enemy to force Wilkes channel, a Navy lighter, loaded with dynamite amid a stack of concrete blocks, was anchored directly in the channel. Telephone lines, exposed as they were above ground, had been pounded and whipped apart in the bombing. Steps were therefore initiated to double up key trunks and to attempt to dig the most important underground. Construction of more durable and permanent command posts and shelters was likewise initiated before the day closed in a cold drizzle.

As a final, somewhat macabre touch, the bodies of Wake's first dead were taken from the hospital, which had no mortuary, to an empty reefer box at Camp 2, and were placed there pending eventual burial.

During the night, working as best they could by black-out, aviation Marines, assisted by volunteer civilian equipment operators, followed a previous design experimentally worked out at Ewa by Marine Air Group 21, and completed eight blast-proof aircraft revetments. By next morning, 9 December, which dawned bright and clear, the four operational aircraft (including number 8 with the damaged reserve fuel tank) were therefore relatively safe. Plane 9, which required an engine overhaul and propeller repairs, was also being worked on within a bunker.

Forty-five minutes before dawn, at 0500, the day began with general quarters, following which the defense commander set Condition 1. This condition of readiness consisted of having all phones manned and circuits open; weapons and fire-control instruments fully manned; and battle-lookouts posted.

At 0545, after their morning warm-up, the four F4F-3's took off over Peacock Point, rendezvoused in section over the field and climbed upward to scout 60 to 80 mile sectors along the most probable routes of enemy approach. At 0700, by the time the fighters had finished their search and were close aboard homeward bound, the defense battalion detachment was released to Condition 2, which relaxed personnel readiness to permit only half the guns at each position to be manned, reduced fire-control instrument crews, and allowed circulation of Marines around positions while at work—of which there was ample amount.

At 0730 the Grummans returned with negative reports, and, at the airstrip, Lieutenant Kinney continued his tinkering with plane 9. With the squadron's engineering problem what it had become, it was evident that means must be established for hangar overhaul and night work by black-out. Considering these problems, Major Putnam determined to modify two of the new plane shelters by enlarging them, ramping down entrances from ground level, and roofing them over with I-beams, lumber and lightproof paulins. By this expedient it would be possible to conduct extensive overhaul and maintenance around the clock and always with maximum protection.

As the morning wore on, individuals tended to keep closer to their fox holes and peel a weather eye skyward. Based on the known distance to the mandated Marshalls, it had already been a simple matter to compute that, with a dawn take-off, Japanese bombers could reach Wake at any time after 1100.

At 1145, methodical almost to a fault, the Twenty-fourth Air Flotilla arrived over Wake from Roi. This time they were spotted by Marine Gunner H. C. Borth, who was in charge of the water tank OP. Within a few seconds after he had shouted his warning into the J-line, the air-ground radio (once more in operation with makeshift equipment obtained by Major Walter L. J. Bayler from the Naval Air Base), was telling the combat air patrol of the raid; on the ground, batteries were going to general quarters; and, all over the island burst of three shots, the now accepted air-raid alarm, were being fired to spread the word.

As the leading Japanese planes approached Peacock Point at 13,000 feet—a welcome change from the previous day—batteries opened fire from Peale and Peacock just before the first salvo of bombs was released. A few moments before, south of Wake, the combat air patrol had made contact with one flank of the line of division V's, and, while the enemy planes droned steadily on at 160 knots, Lieutenant David D. Kliewer and Technical Sergeant Hamilton managed to cut off a straggler despite hot return fire from a top turret. As the bomber nosed down into its final, flaming spin, 3-inch high-explosive shells began to burst in and around planes of the center division, and the fighters broke off.

Bombs began to strike the ground: first on Peacock strong-point, all about Battery E, one of the 3-inch batteries now in action, damaging a 3-inch gun and shattering the range-finder of closely adjacent Battery A (5-inch seacoast). Up the east leg of Wake Island traveled the strike of bombs; Camp 2 was next. The contractor's hospital received direct hits and burst into flames; civilian and Navy barracks; garage and blacksmith shop; advance-base storehouse and machine shop—all were destroyed within a few minutes by fire or explosion. The incomplete Naval Air Station, adjacent on Peale, despite the steady fire of Battery D's 3-inch guns, took destructive hits in the aerological building, hangar, and radio station, where a greater part of Wake's Navy radio gear was destroyed on the spot.

But the tight Japanese air discipline, excellent for defense against fighters, made their formations a well-aligned, carefully closed-up, massed target for antiaircraft guns, and, by the time bombs had hit Peale, five bombers were visibly smoking from the ground. A moment later, one of these burst into a sheet of flame and disintegrated in the air, Wake's second certain kill. The other four limped toward home somehow but were still smoking when the 24-power antiaircraft height-finder tracked them out of sight.

The resultant damage almost equaled that of the initial raid. The hospital, filled with wounded from the day before, burned to the ground while the two surgeons saved first the patients and then what medical supplies and equipment could be salvaged. Camp 2 and the Naval Air Station were now as badly off as the airstrip and VMF-211's area.

Four Marines and 55 civilians were killed.

Japanese aviation's performance this day, however, had conveyed some lessons to the defenders. Summing them up, from 9 December until the final carrier-strikes, Major Putnam would write:

> The original raid . . . was tactically well conceived and skillfully executed, but thereafter their tactics were stupid, and the best that can be said of their skill is that they had excellent flight discipline. The hour and altitude of their arrival over the island was almost constant and their method of attack invariable, so that it was a simple matter to meet them, and they never, after that first day, got through unopposed . . .

The afternoon of 9 December saw commencement of what would be a painfully familiar and laborious process on succeeding afternoons: the business of collecting wounded, of picking and salvaging for undamaged items amid blasted ruins, the relocation of undamaged installations in safer spots.

The Japanese attack on Peacock Point's antiaircraft battery (Battery E) suggested to Major Devereux that the enemy were working in a familiar and logical sequence. On the day before, they had struck at Wake's means of fighter defense. Today they had bombed not only the Naval Air Station but the 3-inch battery which had opened so promptly against their first raid. To protect his remaining nest-egg of AA weapons, the commanding officer of the defense detachment therefore ordered that Battery E evacuate its present position and displace to a new site some 600 yards east and north, from which the battery could carry out present antiair missions equally well. At the same time, to bring the battery up to its former effectiveness, Marine Gunner McKinstry was sent to Wilkes to pick up one of the unmanned Battery F 3-inch guns as a substitute for that knocked out by today's raid. The displacement was executed with care, one platoon (two guns) at a time, the first being set up and ready to fire at the new site before the second quit the old.

With the hospital destroyed, another pressing problem had arisen. That afternoon, therefore, the Island Commander directed that ammunition now stowed in Magazines 10 and 13—"igloos" of reinforced concrete and steel—be placed in the open to make way for two 21-bed underground wards. Interior dimensions of the erstwhile magazines were 20 by 40 feet on the sides, and, at the highest, a 15-foot overhead. Blacked-out operation of the new aid stations would of course be possible and electric lighting was to be provided by small gasoline generators. The shelters were located at the north and south ends, respectively, of a group of four such newly completed magazines. Separation of the two wards was intentional, for the sake of safety in dispersion, and medical supplies were equally divided between them. A Marine aid station, under Dr. Gustave M. Kahn, functioned in the southern shelter, and a Navy-civilian aid station was established in the northern one under Dr. Shank. By nightfall, both were in opperation.

All through the night the Marines of Battery E labored to complete displacement. Aided by contractor's trucks and almost a hundred civilian volunteers, the guns, sandbags (too valuable and scarce to be left at the old position), fire-control equipment and ammunition were removed to the new site where emplacements were dug, sandbags refilled and the guns set down again. By 0500, just in time for dawn general quarters, Battery E was in position and ready to fire.

On 10 December, after a morning of continued defensive activity, the Japanese confirmed the defenders' expectation that the previous day represented a fair sample of the prospective pattern of life (and death) on Wake. At 1045 or a short time after, 26 of the same bombers appeared, this time from the east. Again VMF-211 intercepted, and again the squadron scored. Captain Elrod, leading the combat-air patrol, personally shot down two more bombers while the 3-inch guns slammed away.

This day's raid again hit what luckily was now the empty original 3-inch battery position at Peacock Point, although Battery E's guns were firing on the enemy from their new site. Battery D, the other active 3-inch unit, on Peale, received two successive passes by one division. During the first, although the battery very inconveniently suffered a power-plant casualty at just the wrong moment and thus had to fire on barrage data, one enemy plane was seen to catch fire, and circled back, smoking badly.

On Wilkes, however, heretofore uninjured, the enemy scored a success which compensated for his bad bombing over Peale. One stick of bombs lit squarely on a construction dump of dynamite in which 125 tons were cached west of the "New Channel."

The explosion denuded the greater part of Wilkes of brush, set off all 3-inch and 5-inch ready ammunition at Batteries L and F (fortunately the latter was still not in full commission), and swept the seacoast battery (L) clean of accessories, light fittings and anything else in the least movable. To everyone's amazement, casualties on Wilkes amounted to but one Marine killed, four Marines wounded, and one civilian suffering—as well he might—from shock.

Damage to Battery L was serious if not crippling. When the dazed gunners picked themselves up, they found that all battery fire-control instruments (except the gun telescopes on Gun 2) had been destroyed, blown away or damaged beyond repair. The guns themselves, rugged pieces of naval ordnance built to stand long and hard lives at sea, were similarly battered. Gun tubes were dented, firing locks torn off, training and elevating racks burred and distorted.

Battery F, the hitherto unmanned 3-inch battery, had suffered similar but not quite so serious damage. One more gun (over and above the damaged weapon which had just been towed down from Peacock Point) had suffered serious injury from blast and flying debris. Marine Gunner McKinstry who, this very morning, had been directed by the defense detachment commander to form with these guns a scratch antiboat battery from sailors and civilian volunteers, had lost half his weapons before starting in. Finally, one 60-inch searchlight on Wilkes had been knocked end-over-end, with resultant major damage to the delicate arcs, bearings, and electronic fittings of the multi-million-candlepower light.

His judgment ratified that the enemy were definitely attempting to knock out Wake's antiaircraft defenses, Devereux again ordered Battery E, principal object of enemy attentions, to displace, this time to a position north of the airstrip in the interior angle of the lagoon. The dummy guns set up in the original Peacock Point antiaircraft emplacements, by now rather badly battered, were renewed during the afternoon of 10 December and the unmanned fourth gun of Battery E was detached from the battery for antiboat emplacement elsewhere. Reasoning which prompted selection of the site above the airstrip was subsequently explained by the battery commander:

> Most all bombing runs were made from the east or west and the bombs were dropped along the length of the island. In this position the Japanese must make a run for the battery alone and most of the bombs would be lost in the lagoon.

All night the Marines of Battery E sweated out a second displacement, and again before daylight the much displaced 3-inch battery was in position and ready to shoot.

And they, as well as the other Marines on Wake, might well now ask, "What next?"

❊ ❊ ❊ ❊

IN ACCORDANCE WITH THE PRECISE JAPANESE TIME-table for victory, Rear Admiral Sadachimi Kajioka, Commander Fourth Fleet, was now steaming in task force toward the atoll, confident his samurais had softened marine morale to the point where invasion presented no obstacles. John Toland, the celebrated journalist and author, recounts the crucial battle: Wake's finest hour was at hand.

·2· INVASION ATTEMPT

JOHN TOLAND

On December 11, at 1:50 A.M., 11 Japanese ships cautiously approached . . . Wake. They drew within 8000 yards, then stopped. This was the Wake Island Invasion Force—the light cruiser *Yubari,* 6 destroyers, 2 patrol craft, 2 transports and a landing party of 560 infantry-trained sailors. They had come from the Japanese-mandated Marshall Islands to the south.

Each patrol craft began lowering a single landing boat holding 80 armed men. Though the wind was brisk, they were safely launched. Now boats were carefully lowered from the two transports, but they banged dangerously against the steep sides of the old-fashioned ships and were quickly hauled back aboard. Word of this difficulty was flashed to the flagship, *Yubari,* and the overall commander, Rear Admiral Sadamichi Kajioka, postponed the landing until after sunrise.

A little before 3:00 A.M. the *Yubari* and 4 destroyers began to move toward the island. According to the latest intelligence report, the daily bombings of Wake had crippled at least half of the coastal guns and completely wiped out the air force. Kajioka was determined to bombard the remaining guns to rubble. There was still no sign of life ashore. The enemy, the admiral assumed, was asleep as usual.

But the Americans were well aware of the enemy off their southern shore. Major James Devereux was watching from the beach through night glasses . . . Devereux was faced with an almost bald defense position. The atoll's highest point was 21 feet and except for some dwarf trees and shrubbery there was no cover. He could use only four of his six 5-inch guns to defend the arm of the atoll now about to be invaded and all of these had been damaged partially by the bombings. Neither the two guns of Lieutenant Clarence Barninger at the apex of the V-shaped atoll, Peacock Point, nor the two of Lieutenant J. A. McAlister, on tiny Wilkes Island, had range finders.

As Devereux walked back to his dugout command post, which was about a mile inland of Peacock Point, he worked out his plan of defense. He telephoned McAlister and Barninger: "Don't fire until I give the word." Then he called Major Putnam of Marine Fighting Squadron 211 who was at the narrow airstrip. This was about 400 yards south of Devereux and ran east-west for a little more than a mile along the southern arm of the atoll. "How many planes do you have in commission?" asked the soft-spoken Devereux.

"Four."

"Don't take off until I open fire. I'm trying to draw them in, and the planes would give the show away."

"Okay. Good luck."

Just as the first faint daylight appeared, the *Yubari* headed directly for the apex of the atoll. When it was about 7000 yards off Peacock Point, it swung to the west closely followed by the 4 destroyers. All 5 ships opened fire about 5:30 A.M.

When *Yubari* reached Wilkes, the end of the atoll's left arm, she reversed, coming in a few hundred yards closer, and continued the bombardment of the southern shore. At Peacock Point she again reversed and moved in to 6000 yards. When there still was no answering fire, Kajioka was convinced the Wake guns were harmless.

On Wake, Devereux's phone was clamoring. Barninger and McAlister kept begging for permission to fire. "Under no circumstances fire until I give the word," he told his talker, Corporal Robert Brown.

"Hold your fire till the major gives the word," Brown relayed to the gunners.

"What does that little bastard want us to do?" one answered. "Let 'em run over us without even spitting back?"

But the major still refused to give the word as the Japanese moved closer with each pass. At 6:10 A.M., the invaders were only 4500 yards from Barninger's guns on Peacock Point.

"Commence firing," ordered Devereux.

There was a roar from Barninger's battery. The first salvo went over. The *Yubari,* stunned by the close miss, zigzagged out to sea. The next salvo from Barninger straddled the cruiser.

Destroyers darted wildly, trying to lay a smoke screen to protect the flagship. The two guns from Wilkes opened fire on the destroyer *Hayate.* After the third salvo a great cloud of smoke covered the ship. When the smoke cleared there was no sign of the *Hayate.*

McAlister's gunners yelled and cheered.

"Knock it off, you bastards," shouted Sergeant Henry Bedell. "Get back on the guns. What d'ya think this is, a ball game?"

By 6:15 A.M., Putnam and three other Marine pilots were 15,000 feet above Wake, waiting for an expected attack by carrier planes.

"Well, it looks as if there are no Nips in the air," said Putnam on the two-way radio. "Let's go down and join the party."

Putnam's Wildcat broke through the overcast. Anti-aircraft fire burst all around but he kept coming. At 3500 feet he began a steep dive. At 1500 feet his two 100-pound fragmentation bombs, slung under the plane with homemade lugs, dropped. They missed a destroyer by 200 yards.

Putnam dove on another destroyer. The crew had neglected to take down the glass from the bridge. Sun glistened as Putnam came head-on at bridge level. He got all four guns on the glass. The shattered splinters made a rainbow. Bombs and ammunition gone, Putnam headed back to reload.

Kajioka's force was wildly zigzagging trying to avoid the shells and bombs. A Wildcat swept down on the *Yubari,* its machine guns raking the bridge and narrowly missing Kajioka himself. The admiral ordered withdrawal. The flotilla turned south, but Fighting Squadron 211 followed.

At 7:37 A.M. Putnam, now on his fourth flight, saw a destroyer, the *Kisaragi,* lagging behind the main body. He hesitated, wondering if he should go after the cripple or follow the cruiser. Just as he decided to make a pass at the destroyer, the *Kisaragi* suddenly became a ball of fire. Moments later, at 7:42 A.M., Putnam could see no wreckage below. Just empty, sparkling ocean. Although some thought he had sunk the ship, Putnam guessed a bomb dropped earlier by Captain Henry "Baron" Elrod had started a fire that finally reached the magazines.

The first battle for Wake was over. The southern horizon was clean of ships. Back at Devereux's command post all was quiet. Reports of casualties came in: three men slightly wounded by shrapnel. Devereux was puzzled. Why hadn't the Japanese brought air cover? Why hadn't they bombarded thoroughly before moving in? Why hadn't they sent assault troops ashore in landing craft?

"It's been quite a day, Major, hasn't it?" said Corporal Brown to Devereux.

The little major nodded absently. He was already thinking of the next attack.

※   ※   ※   ※

IN HIS FIRST ADDRESS TO THE AMERICAN PEOPLE since the Pearl Harbor attack, President Franklin D. Roosevelt told of the courageous struggle taking place on Wake, and he prepared the nation for the fall of the beleagured garrison. Yet it was still possible that Major Devereux and his marines could hold out until the Wake Relief Expedition was organized. Here, then, was the perfect opportunity to test Admiral Kimmel's thesis of "naval forces against naval forces" at Wake. On December 13 such an expedition was organized under the command of Rear Admiral Frank Jack Fletcher, whose warships aggregated the carrier *Saratoga,* cruisers *Minneapolis, Astoria* and *San Francisco,* 9 destroyers, a fleet oiler, and the 4th Defense Battalion embarked in U.S.S. *Tangier.* As a necessary adjunct to the plan, *Enterprise* was to execute a diversionary raid on the Marshalls while *Lexington,* operating west of Johnston Island, offered protective screen for Oahu.

The Relief Expedition (with Marine Fighting Squadron 221 aboard) got under way from Pearl on December 13, lifting in explosives alone 9000 rounds of 5-inch, 12,000 rounds of 3-inch, and more than 3 million rounds of belted .50-caliber and .30-caliber machine gun ammunition, plus grenades, and antipersonnel mines.

Meanwhile the titanic struggle continued, and between the almost constant bombing raids, life went on. Twice winner of the Navy Cross, Winfield Scott "Spiv" Cunningham rose to rear admiral in retirement, and wrote one of the classic accounts of the fight for Wake. With collaborator Lydell Sims, he tells of typical days following the repulse of the Japanese fleet—when there was yet hope.

·3· ATTRITION

REAR ADMIRAL W. SCOTT CUNNINGHAM AND LYDELL SIMS

We were ready, after the exultation of our great day, for anything but what followed: boredom. It is a strange word to use, but it fits better than most. We waited. We spent hours, even days, in waiting. Then the planes flew over, the bombs fell, we made the repairs that could be made, and the waiting began all over again. Wake had become the Japs' favorite bull's-eye in the Pacific, and even peril, in time, can become monotonous.

Nine times during the next eight days the Japs hit us, and not at regular intervals as they had done at first, but spasmodically, at noon or by moonlight, singly or in masses of as many as forty-one bombers in a single raid.

An enemy four-engine flying boat came over early on the morning of the twelfth, a Friday, and was shot down by Captain Tharin of the fighter squadron. None came on Saturday. There were two raids on Sunday, one on Monday, two each on Tuesday and Wednesday, none on Thursday, one on Friday.

Despite the variations in time and number, despite the occasional loss of life, despite everything, it grew increasingly monotonous. Nerves remained tense for so long that they grew listless and flabby; the time came when we had to remind ourselves that our lives were the stakes in the tiresome game we were playing. I actually found myself nursing a small-boy resentment against the enemy one day because there was no raid to report to Pearl Harbor.

Bernard Lauff, one of my decoding officers, turned out to be a genius at repairing boat engines. He spent hours at the landing near Wilkes Channel, keeping our small boats in condition for their frequent runs to Wilkes. At the airstrip, work continued daily on the jigsaw task of arranging battered parts into planes that would fly. Two Wildcats were in working order on Friday; on Saturday Lieutenant Kinney's crew was able to get a third into the air, but on that same day a crash-landing brought the score back down to two. Sunday a bomb hit left only one effective; Tuesday we had two again; later in the week, briefly, three planes were flying. By Friday the nineteenth, the count was back down to one.

But aside from skilled work like this, most of the man-hours on the atoll during those eight days were spent in uneasy idleness. There was simply nothing to do the majority of the time but wait. The foxholes were all dug, the shelters covered and reinforced; the time that might have been spent in repairing damaged guns was cut to almost nothing because we had no parts for repairs.

One day, having nothing better to do, I went up to Peale and looked through the ruins of the bombed storehouse where my private possessions had been stored. The remains of my trunk were still there; inside I found my gold watch, which I had put away for minor repairs. It had melted flat like a surrealist painting. Fortunately the cheap biscuit-sized watch I had bought as a temporary replacement was serving me accurately, and would continue to do so until it was taken from me by a Japanese soldier.

As the days passed we grew contemptuous of the enemy's marksmanship, and often complained less about the bombers than about Wake Island's rats. The humpbacked little creatures crawled into foxholes, almost as if they were in search of companionship; they roamed the roads and scurried over the guns; in the communications dugout, where I now slept with my head pillowed on one of the sandbags that blocked the vacant doorway during the raids, they waked me now and then by ambling across my face.

Occasionally our nerves would tighten suddenly in reaction to the nightmare routine.

I was walking along the beach with one of my officers one day when he gave a startled: "Oh-oh!" I almost snapped a vertebra in my effort to see the bombers that must surely be approaching, but it turned out he had merely noticed some interesting object on the beach. For a moment I could have strangled him with pleasure.

Major Devereux had expressed dissatisfaction with the dugout prepared for him on the southern beach and I told him to move into one of the magazines on the east shore, just north of Lieutenant Kahn's hospital. One day after a raid I was touring the atoll's defense positions, as was my custom, and came to his new command post. Finding no one in the vicinity, I parked nearby, walked over to the big steel door, and knocked on it Devereux himself opened it a crack, looked past me at my truck, and cried out: "My God, Captain, get that truck out of here before those bombers come back and locate this place!" It wasn't likely, for they had never yet circled back once they had faded away in the distance; still, it was a possibility. I headed on down the road and checked the battalion CP later that day.

Paul Putnam could not shake off the terrible memory of the destruction that had visited his squadron on that first day. He continued to push himself relentlessly at the airstrip, trying to improve and extend the ground works, and increasingly he grew impatient with Wake's civilians. One day he came to me in an angry frame of mind.

"Captain," he asked, "will you give me authority to use some armed marines to round up these civilians and make them work? Dammit, they've got to hold up their end."

I turned him down. It was true that many of the civilians had taken to the bush and could not be found except when food was being distributed. And others, after being detailed to working parties, would fade away like old soldiers. There was even a report that one group of civilians had headed for the beach with their suitcases when the Japanese ships approached on the eleventh, determined to be the first to board what they thought were evacuation ships.

But the situation was not as simple as it appeared to Putnam.

For one thing, these men — or the great majority of them — had had no previous military training of any kind. They had not been drilled in that automatic response to discipline which is the first necessity of any fighting force. And they had no government insurance, no hope of veterans' benefits, no prospect of pensions in case of injury. Furthermore, they had been given to understand they would be evacuated, by some means that was never quite spelled out, before Wake was hit by the enemy. Many of them felt cheated and abandoned as the days rolled by and nothing was done about this pledge.

But when all this was considered, the fact remained that a surprisingly high number of them did pitch in and help, faithfully and at personal hazard—far more than Putnam could see from his limited vantage point at the airfield. Already they were stationed all over the atoll in support of the defense battalion's gun crews; they worked at filling sandbags, moving guns, delivering food and ammunition, operating heavy equipment to scoop out personnel shelters. At the airstrip itself they had accomplished much since the war began, bulldozing the surrounding area, making bunkers for the airplanes, helping to mine the landing strip, putting the radio station underground, assisting with personnel dugouts. And their group had suffered the highest number of casualties on the atoll.

And what, I wondered, could we accomplish if we shifted from voluntary to forced labor? What effect would such a step have on the morale of the men who were gladly putting out every effort to assist wherever they were needed? And what, in the final analysis, would armed marines do if they ran into civilians who defied them? Major Putnam did not suggest the answer to this, and neither alternative I could think of struck me as a happy one.

But the decision to overrule Paul Putnam on this point only served, in a way, to emphasize for me how fortunate I was generally in the devotion, skill and good judgment of the officers under my command.

It had always been my conviction that a commanding officer should allow his subordinates as much freedom of action and decision as was commensurate with his own responsibilities. The picture of a CO who threw his weight around simply to demonstrate that he was head man had never appealed to me—and indeed, in the increasing trend toward military specialization such an attitude would be dangerously wasteful.

The function of command, as I saw it, was to listen as well as act; to approve as well as disapprove; to let each specialist run his part of the show as long as he did a satisfactory job, and coordinate the over-all picture. Devereux knew the details of ground defense and artillery tactics better than I, just as some sergeant in his battalion no doubt knew how to operate a direction finder more skillfully than he. Putnam knew his planes and the men who operated them; Greey knew what was possible in the way of defense construction, in view of the limitations imposed by our situation; Keene, besides serving as my executive officer, had learned within a few days the complicated task of directing the distribution of food under security conditions, along with a dozen other essential jobs; Teters, who was the equivalent of a staff officer despite his civilian status, was the ideal liaison between Greey and Keene on the one hand and the construction workers on the other.

So I consulted with these men day after day, observed what they were doing, and almost invariably was satisfied with the results. Thus far I had overruled only two major requests, one involving the approaching task force and the other on the question of civilian cooperation, both of which had quite properly been put to me as matters I must decide and for which I must ultimately bear the responsibility. On the whole, I thought, it was a pretty good record for all concerned.

Meanwhile, we had begun to get messages from Pearl that indicated thought was being given to the problem of reinforcements. On the twelfth the office of the Pacific Commander in Chief, Admiral Kimmel, asked for a confidential report on the status of aviation materiel for maintaining planes. I replied that, while we could operate two squadrons under the physical setup, maintenance work was limited to the salvaging of spare parts from the wrecked planes. The same day we were asked for, and gave, a report on the ammunition situation, which was still reasonably good.

A silence followed these reports, and on Sunday the fourteenth I made a few requests of my own, listing some of the many supplies we so urgently needed. At the end of the list I added the one thing that, at the outset, we had needed most of all:

"One radar."

On Monday I gave a general report on the effects of the raids to date, and added a request for 300,000 sandbags. We had plenty of coral sand, but by now the crews of civilians and marines were having to put it in empty ammunition boxes for want of bags.

Still no word came from Pearl on what we could expect. We waited hopefully, and then on Wednesday we received a message whose unconscious irony was overwhelming:

HIGHLY DESIRABLE CONTINUE CHANNEL DREDGING, ADVISE FEASIBILITY UNDER PRESENT CONDITIONS WITH EXISTING EQUIPMENT, GIVE ESTIMATED DATE COMPLETION. . . .

I suppose I must have blown my top. I did not answer for almost twenty-four hours, except for a message reporting yet another raid—the twelfth since the war had begun—and when I did, it was with some heat.

TO DATE, I reported, HAVE BEEN CONCERNED ONLY WITH DEFENSE OF
ISLAND AND PRESERVATION OF LIFE, REPORTS SUBMITTED HAVE BEEN FROM
THAT VIEWPOINT. REGARD TO COMPLETION OF CHANNEL FOLLOWING CON-
DITIONS PREVAIL. NO WORK CAN BE CARRIED ON AT NIGHT DUE NECESSITY
FOR LIGHTS. DAYLIGHT HOURS FOR WORK LIMITED TO MAXIMUM OF SIX DUE
HEAVY RAIDS WHICH COME WITHOUT WARNING. HAVE NO RADAR. MEN
WORKING NOISY EQUIPMENT CANNOT BE WARNED IN TIME. EQUIPMENT
GREATLY REDUCED WITH NO REPAIR FACILITIES. WOULD REQUIRE IMME-
DIATE REPLENISHMENT DIESEL OIL AND DYNAMITE. MORALE CIVILIAN WORK-
MEN IN GENERAL VERY LOW. UNDER PRESENT CONDITIONS NO DATE COM-
PLETION CAN BE PREDICTED.

Looking it over, I added another sentence:

TO BE UNDERSTOOD THAT RELIEF FROM RAIDS WOULD IMPROVE OUTLOOK.

I turned it over to one of the coding officers and then, still steaming
with exasperation, sat down and added a postscript giving further
details of the damages we had suffered. It was the last time Pearl asked
about the status of construction.

After Tharin shot down the flying boat Friday morning, we enjoyed nearly forty-eight hours of peace, the longest stretch of relief
during Wake's defense. But we had no way of knowing when it would
end, of course; while a few dirty marines, sailors and civilians found
their way to the lagoon for a quick swim and wash, the time generally was given over to waiting.

The moonlight raid on Sunday morning gave us something new
to think about. These bombers were seaplanes. It appeared the Japs
were bringing up other weapons to assist in our reduction. Further
indication of a step-up came at 11 that morning, when forty-one bombers of the B-18 type came over. That day, in addition to the loss of an
airplane bombed on the ground, we added three more names to the
roll of our dead: Sergeant Robert F. Garr, Jr., and Corporal John F.
Double of the fighter squadron, and Coxswain George James Wolney
of the Naval Air Station detachment.

The seaplanes returned on Monday, six of them this time, and inflicted one civilian casualty. And on this day through an error, we
lost a chance to sink another Jap sub.

Major Putnam came in from patrol and reported he had found a
submarine on the surface, to the southwest of Wake, but had refrained
from attacking because he thought its markings indicated it was a
Dutch vessel.

For a moment this report irritated me mightily. The idea that a
Dutch sub might have been operating in waters near Wake without
letting us know was incredible, and the further likelihood that if it

was there it would risk surfacing in the daylight was simply fantastic. This was no time for hesitation; Lieutenant Kliewer had set the example three days before when he acted first and didn't even bother to ask questions afterward.

I was on the point of expressing myself rather bluntly on the subject when I realized that no one could have been more eager to sink a sub than Paul Putnam. If he had been bemused by strange markings, it was a mistake of judgment and not of will. Already he and the men of his squadron had proved their devotion and daring; they had earned the right to exemption from ordinary reprimands.

"From now on," I told him, "all submarines found will be attacked." We let it go at that.

Bryghte Godbold's battery of three-inch guns of Peale had claimed most of the enemy's attention in that day's raid. Most of the bombs had fallen into the lagoon, but the experience emphasized to the men of Battery D that they could profit from a large personnel shelter in lieu of individual foxholes. So after the raid was over, Teeters and Greey rounded up a working party of seventy-five civilians to help with the job. It continued that night and the next before it was completed, and it proved so comforting that later in the week another party set to work on a second shelter near the first one.

Another move was made on Monday, this one by Commander Keene. He and I had moved together into the communications magazine when our cottage finally became too dangerous to sleep in. Now Devereux suggested it might be a good idea for us to separate. It *was* a good idea; in the event of my death, Keene would become island commander as next senior officer, and as long as we shared the same quarters one bomb could kill us both. I told Keene to move into Teeters's dugout and take good care of himself.

We suffered more materiel losses on Tuesday. Thirty-one bombers, in an early afternoon raid, did considerable damage to Peale and the remains of Camp Two. Antiaircraft fire claimed one of the enemy. The day's other attack was by a single flying boat that strafed Battery D's position.

The *Tambor,* one of the two American submarines that had been operating in our waters, set out for Pearl Harbor that day for repairs. Now the *Triton* was our only offshore friend. Our contact with the submarines had been fragmentary at best, but it had given me a good feeling to know they were there. I hoped nothing would happen to force Pilly Lent and the *Triton* to pull out.

The Wednesday raids—bombers and seaplanes—produced damage chiefly on Wilkes, where a supply tank of diesel oil was set afire, and at Camp One, where virtually everything left standing after previous raids was flattened. The Friday raid, after our second attack-free day of the war, hit Camp One, the wreckage of the Pan American installation, and the fighter squadron area south of the airstrip.

It was about midway in this week that we first heard a strange and, in some ways, exasperating story from the home front. There were a number of short-wave radios on the atoll, private property of civilians and servicemen alike, and occasionally one of them brought us a creditably clear portion of a broadcast from America.

We had heard with pride that President Roosevelt himself had hailed Wake's resistance effort, and we had tried to discount as propaganda for enemy consumption the gloomy reports that relief for Wake could not be expected. But now we heard something that set our teeth on edge.

When Pearl Harbor asked the defenders of Wake if there was anything that could be done for them, the story went, an answer came back:

"Yes. Send us more Japs."

If there was anything we didn't need at Wake it was more Japs. I had sent no such message, and since the release of dispatches was at all times under my direct control, I dismissed the story as a reporter's dream, as did most of the others on the atoll who heard it.

Not until years later, in fact, did I learn through Bucky Henshaw, one of the decoding officers, how the story began. Bucky got it from his fellow-decoder, Bernard Lauff, when they met in Honolulu after the war, and so far as I know this is the first time the details have ever been published.

Part of the decoders' job was to "pad" messages with nonsense at the beginning and end as a device to throw off enemy code-breakers. Such padding was either entirely meaningless or, on occasion, something involving a private joke between Henshaw and Lauff on the one hand and their opposite numbers at Pearl Harbor on the other; it was not expected that the padding would be filed with the text of the message.

On the morning we turned back the invasion fleet, Lauff said, he had done the padding on my message. He had begun it:

SEND US STOP NOW IS THE TIME FOR ALL GOOD MEN TO COME TO THE AID OF THEIR PARTY STOP CUNNINGHAM MORE JAPS. . . .

So what the world took as a gesture of defiant heroism from Wake Island was actually nothing of the kind and was never intended to be. In fact, those of us on Wake realized as the days passed, the whole idea of heroism can be tremendously, even embarrassingly, misleading. The picture conjured up by the radio reports was as far removed from reality as Wake was from Pearl Harbor. And this, in a way, was inevitable; no man can completely understand what war is like until he has experienced it for himself.

We were doing our best, and we were proud of it, but our best seldom included that disregard for sanity that marks so many romantic visions of the thin red lines of heroes. When the bombers came over we sought cover—unless, as in the case of Gunner Hamas's trip across the channel to Wilkes, there was a tremendously important reason not to. Our gun emplacements were protected as thoroughly as possible. We wanted to live. We kept to our foxholes, our personnel shelters, our magazines.

On all Wake only a few hands had actually fired shots against the enemy. For this was not the kind of war our grandfathers had fought at Shiloh and Gettysburg; this was something vast and impersonal, a contest of machines assisted occasionally by men, a battle of statistics rather than personalities. The thought that anyone should leave the safety of cover and dash back and forth along the beaches, shouting defiance at the bombs as they fell, was ridiculous.

Only in the fighter squadron did men still come to grips with the enemy on an intensely personal basis. Only in the air over Wake did lone men face the choice between heroism and cowardice, between playing it safe with none the wiser and flinging their lives into the path of the enemy. This emphasis on the individual was part of the challenge that had drawn me to flying in the first place, but now I was denied the satisfaction—or would it have been the humiliation?—of learning how I would face it. Like the others whose jobs kept them on the ground, I observed the prescribed precautions while a little handful of men went up day after day to engage the enemy directly. If there were heroes, old-style, on Wake, these were the men who had been given a chance to prove it. And seldom in all history, I felt, had men responded with such abandon to the challenge.

So the battle continued, and each day we grew weaker. We had been returning shot for shot, and by now an impressive number of enemy planes lay under the waters off Wake along with the two ships we had sunk, but still they came back with more. Twenty-seven bombers were in the Friday raid.

The list of parts and supplies I had requested from Pearl was an indication of the gravity of our matériel needs. We were short on everything, from recoil fluid to range finders, from firing pins to height finders, in addition to the tremendous shortages with which we had begun—and by now I could have sent another list just as long as the first. Our personnel losses had been cut to almost nothing, but it was the machines of war rather than the men who served them that would finally settle the issue of Wake.

We went into our second Saturday of the war sleepy, lean, weary, confident of our ability to hold out unless the Japs threw still bigger blows at us, but wondering more and more whether Pearl had in truth written us off as beyond reach of relief.

❧ ❧ ❧ ❧

ON THE MORNING OF DECEMBER 20 A NAVY PBY (Catalina) landed on the atoll's green lagoon. Its cargo included guard mail, news of the Relief Expedition, and a set of orders for Major Walter L. J. Bayler, who had come out with the U.S.S. *Wright* contingent to establish a ground-air communications system for marine aircraft. Bayler was one of the Marine Corps' few specialists in communications at the time, and he was badly needed for the same job at Midway. He holds the unique distinction of being the last man off Wake. With noted author and war correspondent Cecil Carnes, Bayler relives his last week in the company of giants before departing December 21.

·4· LAST MAN OFF WAKE

COLONEL WALTER L. J. BAYLER
AND CECIL CARNES

I spent six nights in my rat-infested foxhole, and then my esthetic side rebelled. I moved for one night into a cozy little concrete bomb shelter and slept well, with nothing running over me or trying to make nests in my hair. The place was even rain- and tide-proof, so I woke up bone-dry for a mighty welcome change.

Paul Putnam, who was bunking in the Command Post, heard of my housing troubles and promptly invited me to move in with him. He didn't have to ask me twice. It was equivalent to swapping a hall bedroom in a bug-ridden rooming house for a bridal suite in a de luxe hotel. Lights—telephones—a radio—everything but breakfast in bed.

It is a fortunate thing that man can adjust himself to almost any drastic change of environment or circumstance; otherwise most of us would die of disease or go mad. By the time I got settled with Paul and the Command Post, life on our bombed and beleaguered island was proceeding according to a routine that might have been going on for ages.

I would wake up about 4:45, while it was still dark. Paul would be moving around too, and we'd grope for our shoes in the pitch-blackness. I would climb up on the revetment and make my toilet for the morning; that is, I would comb my hair by running my fingers through it, and if I thought my face was dirty I would go over it carefully with a handkerchief.

By then it would probably be light enough to see what was going on in the world. The post commanded a view of neighboring dugouts whose tousle-headed inhabitants would start creeping to the surface, reminding me invariably of a colony of ground hogs preparing for another busy day. Freuler and Kinney had a dugout near by; Kliewer and Davidson bunked in another by the edge of the woods; Duke Tharin and Baron Elrod lived in luxury becoming to the nobility; their hole-from-home had a sandbag revetment and it was common knowledge that they had stocked the larder with twelve cases of canned food and five five-gallon containers of water.

Sitting on top of his dugout would be Sergeant Bob Arthur keeping a critical eye on the preparations for dawn patrol. A little pickup truck would clatter into the ground-hog village, take aboard a pair of pilots, and push off again in a cloud of white dust. It would run them to the airplane revetment at the west end of the runway, where they would climb aboard the planes. Soon the coughing of cold engines would come to my ears.

Usually, in a few minutes the phone would ring. I would take the customary message from the hangar: "Sir, Number 16 won't 'take' this morning." I would relay the news to Putnam, who would order the other plane—by then our only good one—to go up alone.

Number 16 was our problem plane, a little beast with the temperament of a crab crossed in love. Its theme song was "Oh, how I hate to get up in the morning!" Later in the day, when the sun had warmed it through, it would almost go up of its own accord. My theory was that the critter had rheumatism, but that was too simple for our expert mechanics who went on installing new engines, new carburetors, new batteries and magnetos from the wreckage of previous crack-ups. Number 16 would just put back its ears and balk.

Life really began with breakfast. I would stroll to our open-air cafeteria and sit on a rock, talking with the boys, while our volunteer pot-walloper heated up the remainder of last night's coffee, or "boiler compound," as it was more commonly known. When that eye-opener was down, it would be time to line up with our plates and cups in readiness for the arrival of Dan Teeters's chuck wagon. There would be a liberal helping of stew from steaming kettles, fresh coffee, fresh bread, jam, and sometimes milk of the powdered variety; and the first finished, there was always a second and third helping for any who wanted them. There were lashings of food on the island, including candy and chewing gum, items often rare in military stores.

I'd always have three cups of coffee. Finally satisfied, I'd drop my dirty dishes in the common bucket and mosey off—usually picking my way through rocks, bomb craters, dugouts and furrows of coral rubble to the Command Post, where Paul and I would try to figure out which area would be hit that day by the raiders. While we talked, we'd police the premises, putting our bedding out to air—on the ground, if we had dark blankets; in the woods if they were conspicuously light in color.

I would push along then to my radio setup in its dugout, and talk with the boys there about equipment and possible improvements to sets, antennae, power supply, etc. Then on to the generator, also in a dugout, to make sure all was well. It used to be hot as hades, and I'd have to get out in a hurry, till I had a hole opened in the coral roof for ventilation.

Sometimes I'd walk through the woods to the south beach, where I would chat with a tall young first lieutenant who was in charge of the machine-gun battery at that point. Sometimes I'd go instead to Camp I, walking down the long road with an eye always open for shelter in case the Tojo Express should turn up ahead of its usual schedule.

Occasionally I walked on past the camp to Devereux's Command Post. Jimmy would be there with his executive officer and my classmate, Major George H. Potter, and other members of his staff. We'd chat a bit. Jimmy would be his usual quiet, reserved self, speaking seldom; but when he did say anything, it had stuff in it.

Back then, by way of the other side of the field, to our own Command Post. Now it would be time to stop, look and listen in real earnest. For this business I would remove my GI sun helmet because the wind would whistle through it, and that combined with the roar of the surf made it next to impossible to hear anything. Marines in every direction were doing the same, standing with their hats in their hands; it made them look as if they were gathered in reverence, but nothing could be farther from the truth. They and all of us were cursing Tojo and his bomber nuisances.

Finally, there would be the expected ringing of the telephone on the "battle" circuit. It would be the observer at Koki Point, or Peacock Point. "Sound of airplane motors, sir," and the direction from which the sound was coming. All eyes would turn to the indicated quarter; all ears would be straining to hear the planes. At last I'd see them, specks of light flashing in the sun. I would radio the news to the Grummans, high in the heavens. "Bandits—south of the field— about four miles off—flying high!"

Next I would draw my pistol and send three shots into the air, and I'd hear the signal repeated near and far.

Bob Arthur or I would kick the phones—there were three of them— into the dugout to protect them and to have them handy during the raid. We'd go below ourselves, pausing to peer up from the entrance to count the big brutes as they approached overhead—most often three divisions in lines of nine planes each—twenty-seven bombers in all. Somebody would say: "They're meaning to bomb the hell of a wide area this time! Let's duck!"

We would duck. There would be the swishing sound of bombs rushing through the air—terrific explosions and reverberations—noise —smoke—a storm of flying rubble.

We'd snatch the phones and report:

"Raid over with!"

We'd scramble topside hurriedly. All over the island men would be emerging from their shelters, thankful to have survived one more raid. I'd watch the devils make a wide sweep southward—homeward bound. Sometimes one or two would be smoking from machine-gun or antiaircraft fire; sometimes one or two of the twenty-seven would be missing! Paul and I would excitedly speculate on who shot down how many.

Then I would accompany Paul on a tour of inspection to note casualties or damage and to report anything of the kind to Spiv Cunningham. On several occasions it was my duty to write down the names of dead men and take them to Cunningham's Command Post so that the casualty list would be correct and up to date.

By now it would be about three o'clock. Our planes would come down—all two of them. Problem child Number 16 would have flown like an angel, up there in the sun. Paul and I would listen eagerly to the pilots' reports and log their adventures.

This was now all a matter of routine.

The raid and its results now matters of history, I would be free to go to the beach and take a bath, glad my tub was the Pacific Ocean and that there was plenty of water.

Generally I would do a bit of laundry while about it. I'd come out of the "tub" feeling refreshed and clean, put on the dry garments I'd brought with me and take back the wet ones to hang up in the woods.

Our Command Post was the social center of Groundhog Town.

The boys would come over and we'd "shoot the breeze" in long bull-fests. Conversation mostly revolved around the Jap and how best to remove him from the world. Air tactics were discussed and serious consideration given to the more approved methods of bringing down a bomber. Was the overhead pass better than the belly rip, or not? And what other good angles of approach might there be?

Then the talk would drift to various phases of the war. Pearl Harbor was an unfailing topic of interest. And our families in Honolulu—when would we hear news of them? And *when* would relief units turn up at Wake, now that it was common knowledge at home how few planes we had left?

I haven't mentioned lunch because there wasn't any. All unnecessary surface movement on the island was discouraged during the midday hours, and that included chuck wagons. If we got too hungry for comfort, we could visit one of the caches of dry food in the woods and have an alfresco snack. Hardtack and jam were available and very popular.

At dusk the Dan Teeters Catering Service would rattle up with a hot dinner, the menu practically the same as breakfast. We would go through the ritual of lining up, plates and cups in hand, and we could have all the chow we wanted. The water wagon would come along and supply our needs. We used the invaluable five-gallon tins for water; we threw the empty ones in the road, where they were refilled from the wagon and left for us in the edge of the woods.

If Dan Teeters was a good soldier even before December 8, he was a one-man army after it. He took over the food department for the whole island, and at dawn and dusk his chuck wagons, loaded with hot food, both nutritious and appetizing, would deliver the goods to every spot where marines might be stationed.

He tried to ascertain our every need and supply it. He threw open his stores to us, giving us food, clothing, candy—anything he had that we wanted. It was he who sent over large working parties to dig foxholes and construct shelters—and he supplied the timber, tools, nails and general equipment with which to do the various jobs.

And how well and fast those civilians could work! Ask for something and there it was, as if you had rubbed Aladdin's lamp.

We were deeply touched as it dawned on us that the men from Camp II not only admired the marines for their fighting qualities, but had a genuine affection for them as comrades and friends. It was manifest in the cheerful spirit with which they would tackle any task likely to aid or comfort us.

There was little we could do in return, except thank them from the bottom of our hearts. It was a source of lasting regret to us that we couldn't show them some tangible proof of what we were doing.

A busted bomber on the beach would have been fine, but every one of the nine brought down by the Grummans and the A-A batteries fell into the sea. A nice fresh corpse would have helped, but not one of the Japs who were drowned on December 11 had the grace to float ashore.

The enemy was keeping the heat turned on Wake. It was not their intention to let us feel neglected or forgotten for a moment.

At dawn on the fifteenth they sent over three patrol boats, just for a change. They put on a curious show, flying very high and dropping all their bombs in the lagoon, then turning and beating it for home as fast as they could. We were coldly critical of the performance. Connoisseurs of bombing raids by now, we decided these three could not be professional artists but were merely terrified amateurs.

At eleven o'clock the same morning the Tojo Express arrived, twenty-seven strong. That was a pretty tough raid. We had several men wounded, but our antiaircraft boys covered themselves with glory by shooting down two of the big bombers.

The antiaircraft gun crews on Wake Island were worthy of the highest praise. Their courage and morale were in keeping with the proudest traditions of the Marine Corps. While those of us who were not assigned to some specific duty were ingloriously hotfooting it for shelter, the A-A gunners were out in the open, fighting their pieces and taking everything the Japs could dish out in the way of hell. Bombs would burst all about them, machine-gun bullets would whine past their ears, but they stood to their guns and sent death hurtling at the foe.

And by some whim of the God of Battles only two of them had been killed or wounded up to the twentieth of December.

The sixteenth was a memorable day. There were forty-one planes in the raid which started at 12:30. We watched the arriving squadrons from the Command Post entrance, and saw the flight divide just before it reached the island. One section devoted its attention to us at the airport; the other crowd swerved away and poured it on civilian Camp II. There were no casualties to personnel in either area, but a lucky hit blew up a dynamite dump on Wilkes Island. The explosion was stunning.

That evening, just as twilight was deepening into dusk, we were surprised by a big, four-engined seaplane. Its pilot was a nervy devil, for after he had dropped his bombs he came lower in the teeth of a withering fire from antiaircraft and proceeded to strafe the airport with his machine guns.

Duke Tharin was up there somewhere in Problem Plane Number 16, carrying out the usual twilight patrol. The moment the lone Jap raider appeared I called Duke by radio and told him what was going on. He heard me all right, for his eager "Roger!" the word of acknowledgment—came to my ears ringing clear. I peered cautiously out of the Command Post entrance to see what would happen.

Nothing did. I couldn't see the Jap, but I knew where he was since he was firing tracer bullets that linked him to the earth by smoky ribbons. But there was no sign or sound of Duke Tharin, and our antiaircraft was still failing to connect.

The Jap's guns were suddenly silent and the luminous ribbons faded out.

Then Tharin struck like lightning. His bullets, fired at close range, ripped the seaplane from one end to the other. At last its starboard engines caught fire and it headed downward to make a forced landing on the sea. Tharin's excited voice sounded.

"He's down, Walt! I'm coming in for bombs and then I'll finish him off!"

Being on patrol only, he had no bombs with him. A few minutes later he hit the runway, and while the armorers were hoisting two bombs into place, he told me what he had done. He had figured we on the ground were holed up as usual and hardly likely to be struck, so he had hovered around at a distance, keeping clear himself of our antiaircraft stuff, till the Jap had emptied his guns. Then Tharin had coolly sailed in and torn him to pieces. It was excellent tactics, though he had worried us a bit.

He flew off with his bombs to where he had left the burning plane, but the *coup de grace* turned out to be unnecessary. He got to the spot just in time to see the charred wreckage sink beneath the surface. There was no sign of the pilot or crew.

That should have been enough incident for one day, but the crowded sixteenth had still another left.

We were routed out of bed that night by a sudden alert. One of the lookouts had spotted a concentration of ships approaching Wake, and it was "battle stations" for all hands in a hurry. Here was something we had been more than half expecting—an attempt at a night landing by the Japs.

Then came the crisp order from Putnam; our Aviation would be marshaled to fight as a ground force in repelling the invaders. The news thrilled us like a jolt from an electric battery. We turned out eagerly, every man overhauling his weapons to make sure pistol and tommy gun and rifle and knives and bayonets were ready for their job. We stood by in the dark, waiting till we knew at what point the Jap-laden surf boats would drive in . . .

We were sick to death of dodging bombs dropped from a height of three or four miles and against which we could do absolutely nothing. And though it had to be done, we were awfully tired of the undignified and humiliating necessity of diving into holes in the ground like a lot of mice escaping from a cat.

So Aviation was ready for action, and craving it, and it looked as if we were going to get it pronto.

We got a pain in the neck instead. The flotilla faded out into the night and was never seen or heard from again. We never knew what ships they were, or whose. They might have been a Jap task force passing Wake en route to some other objective. They could have been ships of our own.

Morosely we returned to bed.

And just by way of shattering our already broken slumbers, the Japs picked that night for a raid. I don't know how many planes were involved, but it was plenty. That was a truly ghastly affair. To go through a bombing by day is bad enough; somehow night makes it seem more terrible. And we had to wait anxiously for daylight before we could ascertain definitely what damage had been done. Nothing serious; we were inclined to believe the attack was aimed at our morale rather than more material targets.

The next day, the seventeenth, the Tojo Express was with us as usual. No casualties among the men, but bombs hit the Diesel oil depot on the other side of the island and set it afire. It burned the rest of the afternoon, sending up a towering column of heavy black smoke that mushroomed at the top and hung over Wake unpleasantly like a pall.

The Japs were always thinking up surprises for us. On the eighteenth, the surprise took the agreeable form of a respite. No bombers at all.

On the other hand, and very ominous in its implications, one lone plane appeared, flying high. It was an exceptionally clear, bright day, and as the plane flew the full length of the island without the slightest deviation to right or left, we knew what it meant. It was a reconnaissance plane taking pictures, and now Tojo would have a detailed aerial map of Wake.

That boded us no good, we were sure.

Besides the absence of bombs, the eighteenth lives in my memory for another very pleasant reason. Very early that morning, a civilian fishing for something interesting on his radio, picked up a news item that forthwith swept over the island like a tidal wave—a tidal wave of happiness and relief . . .

I had just finished breakfast on the morning of the nineteenth when Slim Jones, the civilian shell-ornament artist, appeared at the edge of the woods, caught my eye and beckoned to me. I went over to see what he wanted.

"I've found those three missing men," he said.

He was referring, of course, to the three Aviation boys who were absent and unaccounted for after the raid of December 9, ten days before. Their fate had been a continued matter of speculation; it seemed as if the only possible explanation was that they had literally been blown off the face of the earth. Whenever anybody thought of it and could spare the time, he would search through the woods in the hope of coming upon some trace of them.

Now Slim said he had found them, and the way he said it sounded as if the discovery had not been too pleasant.

I went with him to the spot, stumbling and tripping through the tangled undergrowth. The place was in a particularly heavy-wooded corner of the woods, down near the lagoon, where nobody ever went. That fact had occurred to Slim, who had been hunting off and on like the rest of us, and he had pushed his way into the jungle-like growth just on the off-chance of finding them.

The bodies lay in a big bomb crater in the center of a small clearing. Dampness, tropical heat and rats had been busy. I will not describe the condition they were in; I did not even try to describe it to the doctors whom I called up immediately after I returned to the Command Post. I just reported the location of Slim's find.

Kahn sent an ambulance and several attendants to the scene. The ambulance waited by the roadside while the men went in. They came out a bit later, so I heard, looking rather white. "We had to bury them right where they lay," was their brief report. I went over to Cunningham's office and saw that the notation was duly changed from missing to killed in action.

That brought the score for Aviation to twenty-eight dead and six wounded. Thirty-four casualties out of a detachment of sixty-one officers and men. Over fifty percent—a high rate in any man's army.

I didn't get those errands out of the way any too soon, for the raid turned up that morning at 10:30, nearly two hours in advance of the usual time. Twenty-seven planes droned over us—and I mean us, for Devereux's Camp I and our airport were the targets selected for the day. We sat it out according to habit, in the bowels of the earth; no geologist ever knew as much about the insides of a volcanic atoll as did the First Defense Battalion on Wake Island.

We woke next morning, the twentieth, to weather as unusual as any produced by Southern California. The sky was overcast, a chill wind was blowing, and a fine, penetrating drizzle, half mist and half rain, was saturating everything it touched.

A delightful morning. When my routine tour was made, I sat down, took out my notebook and wrote a few lines in the diary I keep for my wife—the same one in which I had described Wake Island as being so utterly *peaceful*. It was eleven o'clock and the weather getting more and more unusual.

I wrote: "Today, lots of rain in the sky so far." Then, with bombers in mind, I added: "I hope nothing else comes in the sky today!"

However, something did. Out of the gray mist, to drop on the surface of the lagoon as lightly as a gull, came a big Navy patrol boat piloted by Ensign Murphy, USN. He brought official mail for Devereux and Cunningham; he would take off again at dawn the next morning for Pearl Harbor, touching at Midway en route.

Midway? Putnam pricked up his ears when he heard that. He remembered me and my orders.

"We've an officer here who is needed at Midway and is under orders to proceed there as soon as possible. Have you room to take him?"

"Sure," said Murphy. "Plenty of room, and glad to have him."

So my destiny was arranged for me, and when Paul told me of the arrangement I had to hustle to get ready. Not that I had much packing to do—my thoughts went wistfully to the lovely lingerie draped on the trees and rocks of Wake—but there were other matters to be cleaned up.

I went to Spiv Cunningham's office for my orders, but he only shook his head and grinned sadly. My orders had been destroyed when his headquarters was bombed. He remembered what they were, however, so he directed me orally to proceed to Midway by this, the "first available air transport." That settled, I hurried back to the airport.

It was physically impossible for me to play Mercury to all marines and civilians, much as I would have liked to, but I decided I could take out messages for the wounded, and for some of those splendid medical men who were working so hard and so faithfully in the magazine hospital. It was late at night before I could tie up the loose ends of my radio job and get to the hospital, but none of the boys minded being awakened when he learned it meant an opportunity to send a word or two home. I told them the messages must be exceedingly brief, and promised to get them off by telegraph at the earliest moment . . .

To Mrs. J. R. Lanning, 320 D Street, National City, California: "OK, Chick."

To Mrs. Neil Gooding, of Gooding, Idaho: "OK from Boyce."

To H. O. Pace, Casa Grande, Arizona: "OK from John."

To V. F. Webb, 110 Military Street, Oxford, North Carolina: "OK, everything fine, from Gorham."

To Mrs. Luther Williams, of Stonewall, Mississippi: "Solon is OK. Tough fight—but OK."

To Mrs. C. E. Compton, 2419 Fernleaf, Los Angeles, California: "Just say Clair is OK."

To F. W. Reeves, 334 Hawthorne Avenue, Palo Alto, California: "OK from Wayne."

Spider Webb was still confined to his bed, but he was coming along nicely, in good spirits, and anxious to be up and at them again. He was rollicking in his bunk on his elbows for exercise and sport, demanding daily: *"When* can I get up for another crack at the bastards?"

Murphy was taking off at five in the morning, so I had no more than the merest catnap before hitting the deck again.

Paul gave me his report to date to take out. The pickup truck ran me to Devereux's Command Post. Jimmy was not yet there, but George Potter was waiting for me with a packet of official papers.

Time was flying. I hastened to the lagoon dock, where Murphy was already beginning to look from the eastern sky to his wrist watch and back again.

Not a few of the officers and men who had become my good friends during the past month were there to bid me good-by. A quick, hard handclasp, a few hurried words: "I'll be seeing you . . ."

Now the moment had come, I was sorry to be leaving this island of high adventure. The bombing raids were a nuisance, of course, but a sharp end would be put to them—and very soon, I was sure— when reinforcements arrived.

Meanwhile, there was nothing to worry about. There were ample supplies of everything a defense force could need—food, water, oil, gas, weapons and amunition. Good officers, also, to direct as fine a bunch of fighting men as ever lived.

I looked at our flag, still snapping in the breeze at the top of the pole where it had been hoisted on December 8. I looked at the cheerful, grinning faces and the confident bearing of the youngsters on the dock. As I waved a last good-by and took my seat in the plane, my smile was as cheerful as theirs . . .

❧   ❧   ❧   ❧

"WE CAN LICK THE LITTLE BASTARDS THE BEST DAY they ever lived!" Devereux heard these words many times from his bone-weary marines, and they sustained him during the darkest hours. The amazing fighting spirit of men who had virtually nothing left to fight with was something he would always remember. Now, however, it was not so dark on Wake. The news of the Relief Expedition had spread through the atoll like a grassfire. With bullets, bombs and planes it would be a different story, the marines grinned. But Wake's defenders did not learn until long after the battle had been forfeited that Task Force 14 was recalled to Pearl Harbor when less than 500 miles from its destination, and that the feeling of the marines on the ships was one of "shame and astonishment and anger." The blame was to be fixed at command level.

Devereux' almost private war raged on. After a midday raid on December 21, the marine commanding officer walked among his men inspecting the coastal guns, shifting battery positions and talking with the wounded. "I noticed a strange thing. It was an unspoken thing, intangible, but it was real as the sand or the guns or the graves . . . There seemed to grow a sort of stubborn pride that was more than just the word morale. . ." This day the last plane was gone, riddled with Japanese bullets, and the marines were down to their last few rounds. Devereux lay in his tent, too numb to think.

Born in Cuba in 1903 and educated in Switzerland, Devereux served as an enlisted man in Nicaragua and China. He received the Navy Cross for Wake, and was promoted upon retirement to brigadier general.

Let us join him.

·5· "THERE ARE JAPANESE IN THE BUSHES..."

COLONEL JAMES P. F. DEVEREUX

It was still early the night of December 22 when lookouts began reporting "a hell of a lot of lights" northwest of the island.

I went outside and climbed on top of the dugout to observe them. The lights were coming in vivid flashes from far beyond the horizon. We had seen occasional lights blinking at sea for a couple of nights, apparently signals between scouting elements of the Jap task force we knew was near the island, but now the flashes of light were so bright, so numerous, and continued so long that we began to think a naval battle was in progress.

Men argued the chances as we watched. The American task force coming to evacuate the civilians was not due until sometime December 24, but maybe it had come on ahead of schedule. Maybe the ships that were expected to bring us reinforcements had run into the Japanese force that had been bombing us for two days, softening us for a

landing. Maybe our necks were being saved by a sea battle fought too
far away for us to hear the guns.

Corporal Brown said, "I'll settle for that for Christmas."

Somebody said, "You and me both."

But if the flashes were not gunfire, if the lights were illumination
by the Japanese, it meant the enemy was there in great force and that
he was up to something. It meant, perhaps, that tonight he was coming.

Whatever was happening out there miles away from Wake, it was
fixing the odds on our chances of staying alive, only we couldn't read
them. The men watching in the dark could wonder what the flashes
meant or they could guess, but none of us could be sure of more than
the marine who said, "If that ain't a battle, it's sure a potfull of Japs."

We watched the flashes lessen and finally cease, and again there
was only darkness on the sea. If the enemy wanted to sneak in on us,
he had a good night for it. The weather was kicking up. The surf was
louder on the reefs. It would be hard to hear the motors of small boats
tonight. There should have been a moon, but the night was impene-
trably black, and wind and rain squalls swept the island.

It was late before I was able to stretch out for a nap. Corporal Brown
was on duty at the air raid warning phone, listening in on the network that was always kept open for simultaneous communication
between all positions. It seemed to me I had hardly closed my eyes
before Brown was calling me.

The enemy was reported landing on Toki Point. It was not quite
1:00 A.M., December 23.

"It came over the warning net," he said.

"Any confirmation?"

"No, sir."

But at each position, the marine listening in on the network had
heard the Toki Point report, and all over the island men were already
scrambling in the dark to man battle stations.

I phoned Lieutenant Kessler: What about the report of a landing
at Toki Point?

There were lights, he said. But no landing yet. Observers believed
small boats were close off the north shore of Peale Island. He was
manning beach defenses.

I told him, "That landing report came on the warning net. Check
up and make sure."

While I was talking to Kessler, Lieutenant Poindexter called from
his position near Camp One. He left a message that he had heard
the report on the warning net; that he was taking off by truck with
his "mobile reserve" to oppose the landing. He would have to pass
my CP, so I ordered a man outside to stop the truck. My order for

Poindexter was, "Stand by until the situation is clarified." Unless I had guessed entirely wrong, whatever was happening off Peale Island was at most a feint, and I didn't want Poindexter sucked out of the defense I had set up to meet the enemy's main attack. I still thought that the enemy would aim his heaviest blow at the beach between Peacock and Kuku points. That was the lee shore, in addition to everything else.

More reports were coming in: All batteries manned and ready. Machine guns manned along the shore. Such men as could be spared from gun crews were being deployed as infantry along the beaches. Small patrols—three or four men—were scouting the open sections of the long shoreline for signs of the enemy. They reported none except the lights north of the island.

Kessler was calling, "There are plenty of lights out there, but that's all."

"Any boats beached?"

"Negative."

I passed the word that the Toki Point landing was a false alarm. The enemy was there, all right, hidden by the darkness, probably in strong force, but he had not yet made his move. The enemy's continued failure to begin a preliminary bombardment and the opportunity for concealment offered him by the squally weather, made me more inclined to think his move might be a sneak landing, an attempt to slip ashore a landing force behind the curtain of darkness before we could discover what he was doing. In checking by phone with unit commanders, I stressed the need for extreme alertness, but no matter how alert a man may be or how much he may strain his eyes, he can't see through a wall. And the darkness around the island was a wall.

Then the enemy made his play.

At 1:15 A.M., "barges" were reported off Peacock Point. The "barges" were two destroyers, jam-packed with troops, but we didn't know that then. Then they were only darker blurs in the darkness.

Now reports were coming swiftly from all along the southern beach. Reports of "movement off shore." Reports of "some kind of craft close in." Whatever they were, they seemed to be moving in fast toward the beach.

At 1:20 A.M., machine guns on Wilkes Island opened fire.

Then everything started happening at once.

The Japs were coming ashore at four places. We had estimated correctly where they would hit, and now four landing groups were striking at that lee shore between Peacock and Kuku points.

The destroyers were heading for a spot about midway between Peacock Point and the west end of the airstrip. Between that spot and the channel, two landings were being made by troops in small boats. The fourth group was going in on Wilkes.

The Japanese plan for Wake proper was simple: the force from the destroyers would drive straight inland toward the airstrip. The next force down the beach would drive inland, turning the flank of any defenders attempting to hold up the main group. The third landing party, coming ashore near Camp One, would swing toward the channel, rolling back the marines holding that part of the beach, preventing them from moving to aid the defenders of the airfield.

Some of the landing craft were beached and the Japs were already moving across the shore before they were discovered, before machine gun fire began breaking out in spots along that blacked-out strip of beach. The most lightly held sector of the southern beach was between the airfield and Camp One, and I ordered Lieutenant Poindexter to go there with his "mobile reserve" and take command of the defense.

When the destroyers were first sighted, they were so close in that the 5-inch guns on Peacock Point and Wilkes Island could not be brought to bear. The only gun which could bear on them was the 3-inch AA gun which Lieutenant Lewis had left for beach defense when his battery was shifted from its original position, days before. The gun, emplaced between the beach road and the airstrip, was close to the point for which the destroyers were racing in the dark, but we had no crew for it.

Lieutenant Hanna, commanding the .50 caliber machine guns at the airfield, volunteered to man the gun himself. He could spare only one man from his .50's, so the pair of them—the lieutenant and Corporal Ralph J. Holewinski—stumbled through the dark to man the gun by themselves. Three civilians saw what they were trying to do and volunteered to help them. Lieutenant Hanna did not take time to request permission before using them. The civilians were Bob Bryan, Paul Gay and Eric Lehtola.

I could have ordered Lieutenant Lewis to send a crew to man the gun, and perhaps I should have done so, but I knew that daylight would bring the bombers and I wanted to hold Lewis' battery intact to oppose them. Except for machine guns, Lewis' guns were our only means of striking back at air attack.

I directed Major Putnam to place his aviation personnel as infantry between the 3-inch gun and the beach to protect Hanna while he fired. Major Putnam had Hank Elrod, Captain Tharin and perhaps twenty enlisted men.

I also pulled a squad from Godbold's battery, under Corporal Leon Graves, and when he reached my CP ordered him to proceed to Hanna's gun, but they never got there.

By the time Hanna reached the gun, the Japs were close aboard driving the destroyers straight into the reef. The first waves of Japanese were preparing to scramble off into the water, to wade ashore through pitch blackness and our almost blind machine gun fire.

Hanna's gun had no sights for him to use. The 3-inchers had electric repeaters for anti-aircraft fire, without sighting guides of any kind. It looked as though all he could do was point the gun in the general direction of the enemy, but that was the best we could do. Hanna opened the breech of the gun and peered through the bore, adjusting the gun until by looking through the bore he could see his target, the blurred blobs of black in blackness that were the grounded destroyers.

"Okay," he said—and opened fire.

The first shell was a hit. Hanna kept firing as fast as he could load, pouring shells into the crowded destroyers, breaking fire only long enough to sight through the bore when he shifted targets. He blasted the vessels, made a slaughter pen of the crowded decks, and the destroyers burst into flame. Now the marines could see the enemy. They could see Japs tumbling from the burning vessels into the water. The bonfire of the destroyers gave light enough for our machine gunners to sweep the crowded water, to pin down with fire the Japs who already had reached the shore.

Now the marines were not fighting blindfolded. Now they could see something to shoot at. Now the fighting was general all along the shore—where the Japs were wading in under Hanna's fire; where they were trying to push through Putnam's thin line to silence the gun; where Poindexter was fighting desperately to keep from being flanked. I had worked out data for beach barrages with Lewis days before, and now I ordered him to open fire.

To Pfc Wallace, watching from Peale Island, it looked like "a great big Fourth of July celebration." To the Japanese Navy Minister, Admiral Shimada, it was a battle "which would have made the gods weep." To the Japanese fighting on that beach, it was like this . . .

The marines had to give ground. They fell back slowly, step by step, stubbornly contesting every foot of the ground, sometimes fighting hand-to-hand in the darkness, but they had to fall back. There were just too many Japs. By this time, the enemy had fully a thousand troops ashore on Wake proper. In the sparse, broken line opposing them were eighty-five marines and perhaps fifteen civilians who fought without asking permission.

Meanwhile, Corporal Leon Graves had run into trouble. He commanded the squad I had pulled from Godbold's battery on Peale Island to reinforce Hanna at the start. The Japs were coming ashore by the time he got anywhere near the gun he was to man.

In that squad was Private Ralph Pickett. His mates called him "Hezzie" because, according to one explanation, he "hesitated" to make Pfc. Young Private Pickett had been up for Pfc three or four times before we came to Wake, but each time he had celebrated his impending promotion so enthusiastically that he always lost his stripe before he actually got it. He finally gave up, with the philosophical comment, "I started as a private and I'll get paid off as a private."

I think it was Private Pickett who started the joke about the Jap list. He claimed the Japs had a list with everybody graded. A man who didn't hurt the Japs was way down the list; a man who caused them trouble was up near the top. When a gun crew would hit a bomber, Private Pickett would inform them gravely that they were no longer No. 32 on the Jap list. They were No. 14. Maybe it was pointless, but the weary men got a laugh out of it and the whole battery made the Jap list a running gag through the battle. Private Pickett was a good man for morale.

Now as Corporal Graves led them forward, Private Pickett drawled, "What we doing, Graves? Making numbers on the Jap list?"

Somebody laughed. Corporal Graves told them to knock it off. They went forward in silence. A Jap machine gun opened up. They hit the deck, forming a firing line, squeezing off their shots at the flashes in the dark. Pfc Sammy Jackson said Hezzie Pickett never knew what hit him. "He just let out a little groan and rolled on his side."

Somebody said Hezzie Pickett had finally made promotion: "Yeah, No. 1 on the Jap list." But that was later. Up there in the darkness, they were too busy for wisecracks. They fought doggedly, trying to push forward to Hanna's gun, trying to creep forward, but they couldn't. They were pinned down.

Meanwhile, as reports of the fighting poured in, as the reports began to give me a clearer picture of our problem, I ordered Major Potter to set up a secondary line with the CP personnel—clerks, communications men and everybody else except two enlisted men. I kept those two with me at the CP, one on the switchboard and the other on the warning net. Major Potter had about thirty men to form his line straddling the road a hundred yards below my CP. I chose that position because if the Japs broke through from the beach, part of their advance would have to be across the open airfield to reach Potter's line.

Potter's line was formed, at least partly, by the time Corporal Graves's squad had to fall back, unable to get through to Hanna's gun. They took their place in Potter's line.

While all this was happening, communications were breaking down.

Just as the destroyers hit the reef, red flares had been observed. Small patrols were sent to search the lagoon shore, but they missed the enemy in the dark. We learned later that a number of Japanese had paddled into the lagoon in rubber boats and landed. Though we did not know it, they were behind us now, slipping about for a chance to snipe at us, searching for communications lines to cut. I do not know how much of our communications troubles were caused by these Japs or how much by mechanical failure, but the breaks in communications were a bitter handicap.

Communication with Wilkes was cut only a few minutes after the firing began. When Gunner McKinstry opened fire at the sound of the motor in the dark, Captain Platt requested permission to illuminate. Permission granted. A moment later, the searchlight on Wilkes lit up the beach. The searchlight had been badly damaged by bombing and now the light lasted less than a minute, but that was long enough to reveal a beached landing boat and Japs pouring ashore. A moment later, the telephone from Wilkes went dead. We tried to raise them on the warning network, but there was no answer. Other positions reported heavy firing on Wilkes. That was all we knew of what was happening there.

Now the enemy was shelling us with mortars and small guns from ships. Barninger reported machine gun fire was sweeping his position at Peacock Point but it was from a distance. There was no target on which his 5-inch guns could bear, but his crews were at the guns, crouching behind them for protection from the raking fire while they waited for a target. Barninger reported he was placing his range section with machine guns to hold the higher ground commanding his position. Then the line went dead.

West of the airfield, Poindexter's motley force of marines, sailors and a few civilians was being pushed back toward the channel. The last word from Poindexter was that he was being flanked. Then there was only the sound of firing in the dark to tell us what was happening.

The swarming Japs surrounded Putnam's little band, but the marines fought their way out of the ring. They fought their way back to Hanna's gun. Putnam was wounded, so weak from loss of blood that he would lose consciousness from time to time, but now he placed his men around the gun. He said, "This is as far as we go."

The Japs came in a screaming rush. The night exploded in fire around the gun, and some of the Japs broke through, but they were cut down, and the Japanese wave broke on that little rock of men who could be killed but would not step back. The Japs tried to crawl in close to the position so they could blast it with grenades, but they were met with fire; sent scuttering back into the dark. Now the position was surrounded, now the Japs were blasting them from all directions, but still they hung on, hardly twenty men against the hundreds; still they held in the center of the Japs' advance.

I didn't know what was happening to them. By this time, we had lost communication with all forward position except Lewis' battery and a .50 caliber machine gun position just east of the airstrip. That position should have been commanded by at least a sergeant, but we were so short handed on Wake that Corporal Winford J. McAnally was in command. He had only six marines and perhaps three or four civilians as the Japs poured in around him, but he acted like a man with an army.

McAnally still had communication with the machine guns north of Peacock Point as well as with my CP, and he kept reporting information from those positions as well as his own observations. That was about the only information I was getting as we tried vainly to restore communications with forward positions.

Corporal McAnally's position covered the road and he smashed a Jap attempt to advance along it. He took on himself the job of coordinating the fire of the machine guns north of Peacock, calling on them to fire or telling them to duck down because he was going to fire in their direction. He was closer to the Japs, in a better position to spot the enemy's movement in the dark, and he kept that area under such closely interlacing fire that the Japs could not push through.

The enemy spotted his position and tried to rush it. McAnally's crew beat them off. The enemy tried to crawl close enough for a grenade blast and a quick rush, but McAnally heard them. He held his fire until he couldn't miss—and then opened up with the machine gun and all the rifles he had.

But the Japs kept trying, and each time they drew closer; each time they were a little nearer to surrounding him. Once they did, it was all up with McAnally and his men. He called me for reinforcements.

"Sir, we got to have some help if we're going to hold this."

I had nobody to send. I told him he could withdraw.

"Well, sir," he said, "I reckon we can make out a little longer."

And he kept on fighting.

I was tempted to leave the CP and try to find out for myself what was happening. In a dugout, with communications crippled, with a thousand questions and no answers, you feel like a blindfolded man in a prize fight. Perhaps I should have made a personal reconnaissance, but Major Potter was out there setting up the secondary line and it seemed to me I had to stay where I was. There was not much I could learn wandering around in the dark, and the CP was where information came and control centered. It was where the officers would call for orders. So there I stuck, most of the time with a phone at each ear, trying to get through to the forward positions; trying to evaluate the information that dribbled back from McAnally, from Lewis, from Potter; trying to estimate what was happening out there in the dark.

Godbold and Kessler reported all quiet on Peale; only occasional lights off shore. I ordered Godbold to form his battery and .50 caliber personnel as infantry and proceed by truck to my CP. I did not now believe the enemy would attempt a landing on that windward side of the island. If they did, Kessler would just have to do the best he could. It was a risk I had to take to build up the secondary line that was our only chance of stopping the Japs if they broke through at the airfield.

Lewis reported mortar shells were falling on the airfield and that he was receiving rifle fire in his position. He requested permission to send out a gun crew as infantry to cover his battery. Permission granted. Sergeant Gragg's crew pushed out, but they were pinned down by enemy fire within fifty yards of the position.

Did that mean the enemy had broken through? Or was it only sniper fire? The intensity of the fire beyond the airfield, dwindling at times but always flaring up again, made me think that Putnam was still holding out. But I didn't know. A reconnaissance patrol sent out could not get through. I didn't know what was happening on Wilkes. Or what had happened to Poindexter after the last report that he was being flanked.

And what about Kliewer? If the Japs captured the airstrip, he was supposed to blow it up. The runway was mined with dynamite, and Lieutenant Kliewer had been assigned with three men to a generator near the west end of the strip to explode the dynamite if the time came. There had been fighting at that end of the field, but there had been no word from Kliewer. We couldn't contact him.

A wild-eyed civilian staggered in. He had been cut off when the Japs pushed Poindexter back. He had been playing hide-and-seek for his life in the dark and he didn't know what had happened to Poindexter. He said he saw the Japs knock out the machine guns west of the airfield. He said he saw the Japs bayonet the crews.

"They're killing 'em all," he said.

I tried to question him, but he was too shaken to tell much. He kept repeating that he had seen the Japanese stabbing men at the guns. There was still fighting down there, but maybe it was only the Japs mopping up the last isolated pockets of resistance. I tried to calculate the accuracy of the civilian's information. He was on the verge of collapse from fear and exhaustion, but he stuck to his story of what he said he'd seen. It was the first news we'd had of the battle west of the airport since the lines went dead, and there was no reason to doubt his story. I looked at my watch. It would be getting light in a little while. I was wondering how long it would take Godbold's men to arrive when Corporal Brown broke in.

"I've got something, sir." He was listening on the warning network. Somebody was whispering into one of the phones on the network. The voice kept whispering the same thing over and over:

"There are Japanese in the bushes . . . There are definitely Japanese in the bushes . . ."

Brown said, "Who's this? Where are you?" But the voice kept whispering:

"There are Japanese in the bushes . . ."

At other positions men were listening to the whispering on the network and one of them blurted, "For Christ's sake, where are you?"

The only answer was the whisper: "There are Japanese in the bushes . . ."

It was like hearing a dead man talk. He was speaking so carefully, so monotonously, over and over, every now and then repeating that word "definitely." Brown kept asking him who he was, where he was, but the whisperer's power of reception must have been gone. He could not even know that anyone was hearing his message. He could only whisper into a telephone, somewhere in the dark.

Trying to warn us before they got him. Trying to warn us before he died. But not remembering we could not tell on the network where he was calling from.

"There are definitely Japanese . . ."

There was a burst of sound, and Corporal Brown could not tell afterward whether it was a scream, but the whispering stopped . . .

The Japanese pressed their attack methodically. They had pushed inland to the road, before they swung to drive toward the channel. They kept pushing detachments farther inland, trying to turn Lieutenant Arthur R. Poindexter's flank, and he had to pull slowly back. He did not have the men to extend his line. He could not see what was happening in the dark. His odds-and-ends detachment was heavily outnumbered and fighting blind, trying to stop an enemy they could not see. Men could fire only at flashes or the empty dark or wait until shadows loomed up before them, sometimes almost close enough to touch. They were helped by the light from the burning destroyers down the beach, but mostly it was a battle in the dark. They fought all the way. They fought on the beach and in the brush and on the road, but they had to keep falling back to escape being flanked in the dark.

Then the darkness was fading. Men were beginning to see. Sergeant Elwood Smith reported Japanese on the lagoon side. There were only a few, probably landed from the rubber boats, but now they were prowling around trying to pick off marines behind the firing line.

A civilian named Gordon had sought shelter behind a chunk of coral. In the dim early light, a couple of these Japs spotted him. They began shooting at him. Mr. Gordon was clutching a grenade he had picked up, but he discreetly hugged the deck behind his chunk of coral. Mr. Gordon was a large man, however, and the lump of coral was not big enough to hide all of him. The Japs could still see his bottom sticking up. They kept firing at it, the bullets splatting into the sand beside him, until Mr. Gordon got angry. He raised up and threw his grenade. They say his form was lamentably unregulation, but the grenade landed between the two Japanese. They didn't do any more shooting at anybody.

Meanwhile, as he fell back, Poindexter had been picking up men and now others were able to see what was around them and make their way to join him. Sergeant Smith scraped together the last available men and moved up to the line. Poindexter now had some seventy marines and sailors. He said they'd do the shoving for a change. The Japs came on, but Poindexter was through retreating. He started forward. It was a dirty, bitter job, but they slowly fought their way back along the way they had come, pushing the enemy back toward the airfield.

But at the CP, we did not know this. Nor did we know what had happened to Lieutenant Kliewer and his detail assigned to blow up the airstrip if the time came.

The generator with which they were to explode the buried dynamite was at the west end of the runway. With Kliewer were Staff Sergeant J. F. Blandy and Sergeants R. E. Bourquin, Jr., and C. E. Trego. They were armed with two tommy guns, three pistols and two boxes of grenades. The Japanese moving in from the beach stumbled on them and were beaten off. By 2:00 A.M., their communications line was cut and the Japs were surrounding them.

The Japs tried a bayonet charge, but it was blasted with tommy-gun fire and grenades. Several times the Japs tried to rush them in the dark, but each time the four marines beat off the attack. In the lulls between attacks, they discussed whether they should blow up the field now and escape in the dark, but Lieutenant Kliewer said the orders were to blow it up only to keep the Japs from getting it. Their job was to hang on until they knew that was about to happen.

As the morning grew dimly light, the Japs made a concentrated attack. This time they were determined to sweep over the four men who had held them up for hours. The marines were firing as fast as they could, flinging grenades into the face of the charge, but there were too many Japs. This is it. This was the finish.

But at the west end of the airfield, 150 yards or so away, a machine gun crew was able to see the Japs in the early light. They caught the Japs with .50 caliber fire. It was like a sickle through grass. The charge ended in thickly scattered dead.

As it grew lighter, Kliewer was able to see Jap flags all along the shore. He could see Jap flags at numerous places farther inland, too. He decided it was time to blow up the airstrip.

"We'll set her off and then retreat to that .50 caliber position behind us," he said.

But the intermittent rain through the night had drowned the mechanism. And the Japs were attacking again. The .50 caliber gun again helped them beat off the attack, and then they worked on the generator, trying to get it started so they could explode the buried dynamite. They had to interrupt their work from time to time when Japs crawled too near or tried to rush them. They were almost surrounded now. If they waited much longer they wouldn't be able to retreat anywhere. But they kept working on the motor.

That was about the time Corporal McAnally met the "men from Mars" at the east end of the airstrip.

The marine who saw them first said, "What the hell's that?"

McAnally looked at the figures moving out of the brush. They had strange eyes and weired tanks on their backs.

"Looks like men from Mars," he said—and opened fire.

One of the weird-looking men dropped for cover behind a big chunk of coral, but the other was killed. He flopped with his feet sticking up. It looked as though he had webbed feet, but that was only the split-toed Jap shoes. The men from Mars were Japanese wearing big goggles and armed with flame throwers. They had been sent to burn out the positions still holding up the advance.

The Jap behind the big chunk of coral must have felt pretty safe, but Corporal McAnally sighted his machine gun on the center of the chunk and opened fire. The stream of bullets chipped through the coral like an ice pick. When the lump was chipped through, the hiding Japs got the bullets.

But of all this, of all that was happening from the airstrip to the sea, the only word I had was Corporal McAnally's report that he had killed Japanese armed with flame throwers.

Over on Peale Island, Pfc Wallace couldn't forget that he might still have been in Philadelphia if he'd kept his mouth shut when he had a few beers with his pal that night. He and Pfc Albert Breckenridge had been watching the fireworks of battle from their posts on the shore of the lagoon. It must have been quite a show from where they sat. Pfc Wallace remembered later that Pfc Breckenridge even forgot to boast about Dallas and Texas. He was rather thoughtful.

"I bet we never see the sun rise," he said.

Pfc Wallace said, "Nuts."

Then they climbed into trucks with the rest of Godbold's men to move to Wake. It was getting light when the last of them reached my CP. They climbed from the trucks and moved forward afoot to fill in Potter's line. I had finally been forced to withdraw Corporal McAnally's crew from the airstrip to save them from being cut off, and now Potter's line was beginning to receive scattered fire.

Breckenridge and Wallace were digging in as day came. Wallace stopped digging.

"You lost that bet," he said. "There's the sunrise."

Breckenridge was not convinced. He said, "Well, I bet we never see it set."

From his own hole, Pfc Verga heard the discussion. He also heard a bullet whine past them and yelled:

"Get down, you dopes! That ain't no hummingbird!"

They finished their holes from the inside, and by that time the enemy was appearing on the other side of the strip. By that time, Potter's men were getting something to shoot at.

In the brush near Lewis' battery, under sniper fire as they waited to defend the guns, Shorty Martin looked at Sergeant Gragg as the day came. The snipers were hitting closer, but Pfc Martin sounded as cheerful as ever:

"Good morning, Sergeant Gragg! I sincerely hope I can say the same thing tomorrow morning."

About then, dive bombers were sighted approaching the island. As they approached in formation, six thousand feet or more in the air, Lewis' battery engaged them until the formation split and the Japs went into their bombing glides.

Now it was light enough to see the Japanese fleet. It lay in a vast circle around the island, surrounding us, but far out of range of any gun we had. Men tried to count the ships—it was like counting their own chances of staying alive another day—but even now we do not know exactly the strength of that Japanese fleet. Major Potter reported sixteen men-of-war, light and heavy cruisers. Lieutenant Barninger counted twenty-seven ships of all kinds, and some of the enlisted men thought there were more. Lieutenant Kessler reported at least four of the Japanese vessels were battleships or "super-cruisers." But whatever force the enemy had in that far, slow moving circle, it was more than enough and every man of us knew it. At any moment the enemy wished, whenever they got the word from the Japs ashore so they would not kill their own men, their big guns could blow us out of the sea—and at that range our heaviest batteries were as useless as BB rifles.

Then Kessler was calling from Toki Point. Jap ships were in range: three destroyers closing in off Wilkes. He opened on the lead destroyer with 5-inch guns. The fourth salvo got her. She swerved sharply, badly hit. Kessler shifted fire to the next target, but the undamaged Japs escaped by running away. The wounded destroyer also tried to flee, but marines watching from the shore saw her sink. After that, the Jap ships discreetly remained out of range until after the surrender. We learned later that some of them thought we had 16-inch guns on the island, which was rather a compliment to the marines manning our 5-inch batteries.

Commander Cunningham left the conduct of the battle to me, but I was in constant touch by telephone with his CP dugout in the direction of Camp Two, reporting developments as I learned them through the hours of blind fighting in the dark. Now, about 7:00 A.M., I reported to Commander Cunningham the way the situation looked from my CP. We had no communication with Wilkes Island or any other forward position, so my estimate of the situation had to be based largely on guesswork and probabilities . . .

Jap flags were reported flying "all over Wilkes." In the absence of any indication to the contrary, I had to assume that Wilkes Island had fallen.

On Wake proper, all along the front of the Japanese advance, the enemy had pushed through to the airstrip and even beyond. The firing line set up by Major Potter—our secondary line—lay across the road only one hundred yards below my CP and now it was our first line. Now some of Potter's men were firing on the advancing Japs at three hundred yards or less. The enemy's return fire at that range was from light machine guns as well as rifles, and the marines could see increasing forward movement all along the enemy's front.

Major Potter had tried to close the gap between the right flank of his line and Lewis' 3-inch battery position on the lagoon side, but he could spare only a squad from his starvation-thin line for the attempt and the squad he sent to plug the hole was driven back after losing two men. Now Gunner Hamas reported that Potter's right flank was receiving fire from the lagoon side as well as from the front. And in the concealing brush on the lagoon side, in the crook of the horseshoe, Sergeant Gragg's crew defending Lewis' battery as infantry were still unable to push out far enough to prevent enemy rifle-fire into Lewis' position. Gragg's crew were still pinned down by unseen Jap fire near the battery.

By this time, Lieutenant Kliewer's detail should have blown up the airstrip and the demolition volunteer at the boat channel should long since have exploded his dynamite-laden barge to block the channel, but there had been no explosion and now the enemy was well past both positions.

From all this, I had to assume that our forward positions had been overrun or, at best, broken up and isolated in a few helpless "last stand" pockets that could do us no good. I had to report to Commander Cunningham that it looked to me as though the Japs had secured Wilkes Island, Camp One, the channel, the airstrip and probably Barninger's position as well, and that now the enemy was eating his way into the island with Potter's line as the next bite.

I said, "That's the best I can judge the picture on the dope I've got."

There was a long moment before he replied. Then:

"Well, I guess we'd better give it to them."

I could not believe he had said it. I had not contemplated even the possibility of surrender. If we could not hold the enemy at Potter's line, we could fall back and try again at another position, even though that probably would mean pulling over Kessler's battery as infantry, leaving Peale Island naked to a landing. I do not think any of us had thought further than trying to hold the enemy as long as possible at each position, buying time, for next day ships were scheduled to evacuate the civilians and we all felt sure those ships were part of a task force bringing reinforcements.

But now he was saying we had to surrender.

I said, "Isn't any help coming?"

"No," he said. "There are no friendly ships within twenty-four hours."

"Not even submarines?"

"Not even them."

I said, "Let me see if there isn't something I can do up here."

He didn't reply at once. I knew now he was considering the lives of the unarmed civilians, more than a thousand lives for which he was responsible. Then, quietly:

"All right, Jim."

I told him I needed riflemen desperately and I could not strip Peale except as a last-stand resort, but Commander Cunningham didn't have any to send me. The only riflemen guarding his CP were the five Army communications men I had armed when war began. Five men would not have helped much.

I tried to think of something—anything—we might do to keep going, but there wasn't anything. Even if we could stop the advance temporarily, even if we killed every Jap on the island, the enemy had only to pour ashore more men and still more until we were swamped. He had only to sit off there with his fleet in perfect safety and blast the island until his men could stroll ashore. And their dive bombers were still attacking. It was a numbing realization, bitter to take, but Commander Cunningham's decision to surrender was inevitable, beyond argument. We could keep on spending lives, but we could not buy anything with them.

So I said, "I'll pass the word."

I got up to do what I had to do as Gunner Hamas came in. He reported the last of Godbold's men had arrived on the line. What were my orders now?

I said, "It's too late, John. Commander Cunningham has ordered us to surrender. Fix up a white flag and pass the word to cease firing."

He looked at me as though I were crazy. John Hamas born in Zemplin-Humenne, in what became Czechoslovakia, was a veteran of World War I. He had served in the Austro-Hungarian army and won his commission as lieutenant in the Czech infantry before enlisting in the Marines in 1921. He had been a marine ever since, serving over the world, the kind of legendary character that men write stories about. He did such a job of fighting in Nicaragua that the President of the Republic offered him a colonel's commission if he would stay when the Marines pulled out. The pay was $900 a month, a giddy fortune to a sergeant of Marines, but Sergeant Hamas turned it down. As he put it, "They might change presidents on me in Nicaragua, but a marine is sure of his pension." Now he had to pass the order for marines to surrender. I think his reply to me was probably the hardest thing John Hamas ever made himself do. He said, "Yes, sir."

He went out, and from the doorway of the dugout I heard him shouting the order to cease fire. He sounded like a kid who was trying not to blubber.

"Major's orders! We're surrendering . . . Major's orders . . ."

I was told a long time later that I stepped to the entrance and yelled at him, "It's not my order, God damn it!"

Maybe I did, but I don't remember it. A lot of men must have forgotten things they said in that numbed time it took us to realize this was actually happening to us, this death of pride.

I was giving the word to all positions I could reach by phone when a call from Barninger's battery came through. They had managed to repair the line at last. They still held their position, ready for attack . . . But it was too late for anything except to repeat the word:

Cease firing. Destroy all weapons. The island is being surrendered.

Along Potter's scattered line, the order was passed from man to man, but some of them off in the brush didn't get the word and some wouldn't believe it when they did. They kept fighting on their own, mostly alone, one man with a rifle trying for one more shot at the enemy before they got him.

A corporal crawling along the line brought the news to Pfc Breckenridge and his pal, Pfc Wallace. Breckenridge had lost his bet that they would never see the sun rise and then he had bet they would never see it set. Now Wallace said, "Breck, I guess you're going to win that second bet."

They took the bolts from their rifles and flung them as far off into the brush as they could. If the Japs wanted to use those rifles, they'd have to do some hunting first.

They sat down to wait for the Japs to come for them. Pfc Wallace remembers he took out the letter he had carried through the battle, the letter from his girl in Pennsylvania telling him how happy she was that he was in the Pacific where he would not be in danger. He slowly tore it into little pieces and let them blow out of his hand. Neither of them said anything as they sat watching the tiny bits of paper scatter over the sand.

At the artillery positions, blankets were stuffed into the muzzles of the guns and the guns were fired. To make sure the enemy could never repair the damaged guns, marines then dropped grenades into the muzzles. They cut all cables, broke gun dials, destroyed the firing locks. Lieutenant Lewis' battery used twenty pistol shots to make sure their director and height-finder were damaged beyond repair. Sergeant Robert Box was firing his .45 into the height-finder when a bullet ricocheted and hit him. He turned the air blue with his comments on the luck that would bring a man through a battle — and let him wound himself when it was over.

When their weapons and equipment were wrecked, the marines on Peale Island and Peacock Point sat down to gorge themselves, to eat up as much as they could of their food supply before the Japs came for them. There was no sense saving food now and it might be their last meal.

About forty minutes after the first word to surrender had been given, Lieutenant Lewis marched his men to the CP and reported:

"Sir, the guns and fire control equipment of E Battery have been destroyed."

He kept his tired, streaked face expressionless, but his men stood staring at the white flag over the CP — a bedsheet nailed to a timber — and there was bewilderment and resentment in their faces. They could hear firing up ahead, the fight was still going on, and they had been ordered to destroy their guns and quit.

I told them, "I don't know whether any marines have ever surrendered before, but those are the orders and they'll be carried out."

As they relaxed, sitting down to wait for the Japs or sprawling wearily on the ground, somebody asked what the Japs would do with them.

Sergeant Gragg said, "If they don't shoot us, we'll probably go to Manchukuo and work in the salt mines."

A Pfc drawled, "Join the Marines and see the world—the hard way."

Somebody laughed. Somebody broke out a small supply of hoarded chocolate bars. They had to break the bars in half to make them go around, but there was no use saving them now. So they waited, munching candy, for the Japs to come.

Meanwhile, Platoon Sergeant Bernard Ketner came to the CP on an errand from the firing line. He must have stood watching me as I worked at the phone, but I did not notice him until he stepped up to me and stuck out his hand.

He said, "Don't worry, Major. You fought a good fight and did all you could."

We shook hands, and then the sergeant trudged back to the line and I picked up the telephone again.

I knew the enemy's advance units were near the military hospital, which was between my CP and the enemy. I had called Dr. Kahn, the Navy doctor, to raise a white flag and give word of the surrender to a Jap officer, if he could manage contact with one. Now my phone man turned from the switchboard:

"Sir, the hospital doesn't answer."

I spoke to a group, "Rig a white flag you can carry. We'll have to go down there."

A sergeant, Donald Malleck, volunteered and tied a white rag on a swab handle and the two of us started walking down the road toward the enemy.

We didn't know it, but the Japs already had captured the hospital. They celebrated the capture by firing into the crowded dugout, killing a civilian and wounding a naval officer. Then they herded the sick and wounded out of the hospital and prodded them into lines along the road.

Before Sergeant Malleck and I reached the hospital, we met the Japanese point, the leading man of their advance. We stopped in the middle of the road and Sergeant Malleck held up his white flag. The Jap came toward us with slow caution, covering us with his rifle, finger on the trigger. He stopped a few feet from us, his fixed bayonet ready to lunge, and peered at us. He could not help seeing the insignia of my rank on my shirt collar.

He motioned with his bayonet, making me understand I must drop my helmet and pistol belt and empty my pockets on the ground. He let me keep my handkerchief and wallet; nothing else.

He made Malleck do the same. He even made Malleck take off

his shirt and leave it on the ground. Then he stepped aside and motioned with his bayonet for us to precede him toward the Jap lines. He followed a few paces behind us.

We had gone only a few steps when we saw the second man of the Jap advance party waiting in the road. As we approached him, a rifle cracked in the brush. The Jap fell on his face.

I yelled, "The order has been given to cease firing, and damn it, you'll obey that order!"

The shot must have been fired by one of Potter's men who failed to get the word and failed to see our white flag in the brush. Our guard only motioned us to walk on to the fallen man. He stooped and rolled the body over. He saw the man was dead, but he showed neither pity nor anger. He simply motioned for us to move on.

The Japs had cleared the hospital when we reached it. There were about thirty Americans—wounded, sick and ablebodied—and all had been stripped down to their skivvies and shoes. Now they sat in four rows beside the road with eight machine guns at their backs. Their hands were lashed behind them with telephone wire and one end of the wire was noosed around each man's neck. If he tried to free his hands or even ease the strain of the wire cutting into his wrists, he would tighten the noose around his neck.

Several Japanese were standing at the hospital door, watching us approach. One of them was wearing a sword, so I knew he was an officer. I asked him, "Do you speak English?"

"Yes, a ritter."

"Well, we are surrendering."

His face lit up. He said something to his men and then gave me a cigarette. He was trying to act nonchalant, but I think he was only trying to hide his fear that our surrender was a trick.

I asked, "Where did you learn English?"

"Studied at schoor. A'so, was at San Francisco Wor'd Fair, 1939."

Somebody yelled excitedly, and we saw that a Japanese sentry had stopped one of our trucks. Commander Cunningham got out and walked toward us. I was surprised to see he had changed to his formal blue uniform. The Jap officer—a Navy lieutenant, junior grade— looked from Cunningham to me undecidedly.

"Who Number One?" he asked.

I pointed to Cunningham. I said that while he arranged the formal surrender, I would go around the island with Malleck to be sure that everybody got the word to surrender. The World's Fair jg and about twenty troops escorted us back to the CP where I made sure that all our men in the vicinity were disarmed. Then we started walking toward Camp One.

As we crossed the airstrip, we met the commander of the Jap landing force, a Navy captain. He had been wounded in the hand. He shook his head when I asked if he spoke English, but he handed me a pad and pencil. I knew many Japanese can read and write English without speaking it, so I scribbled: "I will stop the fighting." I left further explanation to the World's Fair jg.

Another Jap jg joined our party as we started on. I made the usual inquiry: Did he speak English? In perfect English, he replied:

"No, I do not speak English. Do you speak Japanese?"

He walked directly behind me. He kept swinging his sword as though anxious to use it.

It was about 9:30 A.M., seven hours since I had lost communication with my forward positions. Now we came to Hanna's gun, the 3-inch gun he had volunteered to man for beach defense when the enemy started landing.

When Major Putnam's sparse line defending the gun was broken by the irresistible force of numbers, thirteen marines and civilians rallied around Hanna's gun for a last stand. They were surrounded. The enemy swept the position with heavy fire. From the safe shelter of revetments built for our planes, the Japs dropped a pounding rain of rifle grenades on the defenders. Three of the thirteen defenders of the gun were killed and nine were wounded. Only Captain Tharin was still unhit, but he and the nine wounded men were still holding at bay at least two hundred Japanese when I climbed onto a revetment and yelled to them.

"This is Major Devereux! The island has been surrendered! Cease firing! Put down your weapons!"

There was no answer.

I shouted again and walked closer. Our men could see me now. I walked closer, calling that the island had surrendered. Now a few of them were coming out to meet me. Major Putnam looked like hell itself. He had been shot in the jaw. His face was a red smear.

He said, "Jimmy, I'm sorry, poor Hank is dead."

Elrod had been a fury. Men remember how one charge almost overwhelmed them and how Hank Elrod stood upright, blasting with a tommygun and broke the charge. Japs fell that time close enough for him to touch. A man remembers Elrod saying, "Kill the sons-a-bitches!" They remember he was standing up to throw a grenade when a Jap shot him. The Jap had crawled in among the enemy dead scattered thickly around the position and waited there for his chance. Somebody killed the Jap, but Elrod never knew it. He died instantly. Now he lay there with his eyes open, defiant, and the grenade still tightly clutched in his hand. With him at the gun died Robert Bryan and Paul Gay, civilian volunteers.

The Japs separated Major Putnam, Captain Tharin and Lieutenant

Hanna from the men and left both groups under guard while the rest of us walked on toward Camp One.

We stumbled on another siege at the generator pit where Lieutenant Kliewer and his three sergeants were still trying to blow up the airstrip. The four marines were still alternately beating off Jap attacks and working on their stalled generator, trying to get it started so they could explode the dynamite buried under the strip.

They held their fire when they saw me approaching with Malleck and the white flag. The Japs were a little behind us. I stopped and called to them that the island had been surrendered.

One of the sergeants grabbed Kliewer's arm. "Don't surrender, Lieutenant! It's a hoax. Marines never surrender."

But finally Kliewer shook his head and stood wearily up. The escort party took Kliewer's detail under guard and we went on. It occured to me to thank God in my heart that Kliewer had not succeeded in blowing up the airstrip while we were crossing it. Even if we had escaped the explosion, the Japs would have murdered us all for what they would have considered an act of treachery.

We gathered in the crews of two .50 caliber machine guns still holding out at the end of the airfield and then pushed on toward the sound of small arms fire in the direction of Camp One.

We came up behind fifty or sixty Japanese in a fire fight with troops we could not see. The Japs were getting the worst of it. They were giving ground when they saw us. Our white flag was flying plainly, but some of the Japs swung around and fired at us. A bunch of them— a couple of dozen maybe—charged us with bayonets.

The sword-swinging jg stepped forward, shouting at them until they stopped the charge, but then he let them jostle us around, pushing and pulling us, making us turn out our pockets. They didn't seem to want anything we had, not even as a souvenir. They just thumbed through our things and threw them away, money and everything else, among the rest my wallet containing my only photograph of my wife and my son.

Now we could see the marines who were pushing back the Japs: Poindexter and perhaps twenty of his "reserve." Poindexter's idea had been to fight his way back toward the airfield, driving the Japs before him, until he could hit the flank of the main Jap force driving inland toward the CP. Now he saw us standing there with the white flag and a bunch of Japs. He was grinning as he came down the road. He thought the Japs were our prisoners. The truth seemed to stun him. His reaction was like that of many men I have seen under emotion too strong for expression in any words.

He snapped his fingers and said, "Oh, shucks!"

We marched on, picking up prisoners in driblets. The guards were making us walk with our hands in the air, but the World's Fair jg told us, "Put them down." When he dropped back to the rear of the column, a guard rapped me sharply with his bayonet and motioned for me to put up my hands again. I obeyed, but the jg came back and told me to put them down. He and the guard argued back and forth, countermanding each other, while I wondered if this example of discipline was typical of the Japanese military. It was.

Our flag was still flying from the water tower at Camp One where we had hoisted the colors when the flagpole was shot down. When the Japs saw the flag, some of them broke into a run, cheering and yelling, and one of the Japs began climbing the tower. I looked at my men. They were staring at the Japs with burning eyes. Fists were clenching. They were at the breaking point, the crazy point where a man will go against a gun with bare hands.

I snapped, "Hold it! Keep your heads, all of you!"

They could only get themselves killed if they tried to stop the Japs. So we stood watching while the grinning Jap on the tower cut our colors down, stuffed them in a camouflage net and climbed back to the ground with his prize.

Platoon Sergeant Dave J. Rush did not know about the surrender when he caught sight of the Jap climbing the water tower to cut down the flag. Sergeant Rush told me later that he drew a perfect bead with a machine gun, on the climbing Jap, but fortunately held his fire for a few seconds—and then saw the surrender party. Otherwise, it would have been extremely embarrassing to us.

Gunnery Sergeant John Cemeris was at a .30 caliber machine gun near the small boat channel and didn't see us, either, but he did see a Jap dive bomber swooping in. Cemeris opened up with his gun. A .30 caliber is normally used for ground defense, but Cemeris bagged the Jap. I saw the Jap jettison his bombs and later we learned that the plane crashed. It was beautiful shooting, but it made things a little ticklish for us because our Jap escort also saw it, but they only prodded us on to the small boat channel.

I had been unable to order the dynamite-laden barge blown up in the channel after communications failed and the civilian volunteer assigned to the exploder had been unwilling to assume the responsibility of destroying the channel without orders. I told the sword-swinging lieutenant about the dynamite barge. Nothing could be gained now by trying to hide it and an accidental explosion might cause the Japs to massacre us . . .

※ ※ ※ ※

THE GREAT HOLDING ACTION WAS OVER, THE FINAL phase coming, when the Wilkes marines succumbed following a desperate struggle which lasted into the next day. In all, 470 officers and men of the Navy and Marine Corps, and 1146 civilians, became prisoners of the Japanese. But the enemy paid dearly for his victory: 820 killed and 333 wounded; 4 warships sunk and another 11 damaged; and 21 planes destroyed by pilots and antiaircraft.

On January 6, 1942, President Roosevelt offered fitting tribute to the marines of the 1st Defense Battalion. In his State of the Union message Roosevelt said: "When the survivors of this great fight are liberated and restored to their homes, they will learn that a hundred and thirty millions of their fellow citizens have been inspired to render their own full share of service and sacrifice . . ."

On January 11 the prisoners were marched aboard the transport *Nitti Maru* for shipment to POW camps. Hans Whitney, a civilian, recorded this moment of hell.

·6· "HARD, SQUARELY IN THE FACE"

HANS WHITNEY

At last, all but three hundred and fifty men were taken off the Island —I was in the first group to leave. We were taken in small boats to the barge that tied on to the port side of the *Nitti Maru,* one of the Japanese first-class passenger vessels.

From the barge we were herded through a door on the side of the ship. As we entered, we were told to put our hands over our heads and a Jap sprayed us with disinfectant . . . so we would not infect the lice, vermin, etc. we were to encounter in their unspeakable prison camps. Hands still up . . . we were marched down one aisle lined with guards, rifles alert, bayonets fixed. Hard and inhuman thugs, they looked and surely lived up to their appearance—eager and anxious to find any excuse at all to inflict summary and brutal punishment . . .

We were frisked. One man had his false teeth in his pocket—they found them, of course. The Jap looked at them with disgust and threw them to the floor. When the owner stooped to pick them up, a guard kicked him, *hard,* squarely in the face. Just a sample of what was to follow with fiendish variations.

We were handed the following regulations to guide us as to requirements for a happy sojourn in the Great Japanese Empire . . .:

1. The prisoners disobeying orders will be punished with immediate death.

    (a) Those disobeying orders and instructions.

    (b) Those showing a motion of antagonism and raising any sign of opposition.

    (c) Those disobeying the regulations by thinking only of themselves, such as rushing for their own goods, etc.

    (d) Those talking without permission and raising loud voices.

    (e) Those carrying unnecessary baggage on embarking.

    (f) Those walking and moving without orders.

    (g) Those resisting mutually.

    (h) Those touching the boats, materials, wire, electric lights, tools, switches, etc.

    (i) Those climbing ladders without orders.

    (j) Those showing action of running away from the room or boat.

    (k) Those trying to take more meal than given them.

    (l) Those using more than two blankets.

2. Since the boat is not well equipped, the inside being narrow, food being scarce and poor, you will feel uncomfortable during a short time on the boat. Those losing patience and not obeying regulations will be heavily punished for the reason of not being able to escort.

3. Be sure to finish your "nature calls"—evacuate the bowels and urinate—before embarking. Buckets to be used for toilets will be placed at the four corners of the room. When the buckets are filled the guard will appoint a prisoner, who will take them to the center of the room where they will be pulled up by a derrick and thrown away. Toilet paper will be furnished and everyone co-operate to keep the room sanitary.

4. Meals will be given twice a day. Only one plate to each prisoner. The prisoner called by the guard will pass the food out honestly and as quickly as possible. Anyone reaching for his plate without orders will be heavily punished. The same orders will apply in handling plates after meals.

5. The Navy of the Great Japanese Empire will not punish you all by *death* if you believe in the actions, obey all the rules and regula-

tions and the purpose of the Japanese Navy, and co-operate with Japan in constructing the New Order of the Great Asia, which leads to the world's peace.

Under these unique regulations we set sail.

❧ ❧ ❧ ❧

THE JAPANESE TOOK GUAM AT THEIR LEISURE, opening hostilities December 8 and sending in 5500 ground troops two days later. After a brief struggle at Duncas Beach and in the capital, Agana, the 153-man marine garrison commanded by Colonel William J. McNulty was overwhelmed. Among the prisoners was Private Martin Boyle, twenty, who remained in the Marine Corps after the war and rose to captain. As a guest of the Rising Sun, Boyle assiduously kept notes and many years later wrote a powerful chronicle of life behind barbed wire.

•7• POW FROM GUAM

MARTIN BOYLE

January 16, 1942—it was my first morning in enemy Japan, and I didn't want to wake up.

Sleep, though, was impossible. It was too cold. I could feel the harsh January wind as it whistled relentlessly through the loose boards of the clapboard barracks, and neither my summer uniform nor the thin, papery Japanese blankets offered much protection against the cold. I finally opened my eyes and was mildly surprised to find myself curled up next to Josh Mackery. Then I remembered the bitter cold that greeted us the night before when we had landed in Japan. To help get warm, most of us had doubled up for the night, throwing the lumpy straw mats together on the floor, trying to get the extra warmth of another body as well as the flimsy protection of another blanket.

I pulled the blankets tighter around my shoulders, and as I lay there in the cold, early morning gloom, the events of the past six weeks raced through my mind. The carefree days of Guam, the bombing . . . the capture, the first prison . . . the voyage to Japan. I could clearly remember almost everything, that is, but what happened between the time I came face to face with the Japanese patrol and the day we were herded aboard a ship bound for the homeland islands of Japan . . .

The Japanese didn't tell us where we were going that January morning. Japan? Saipan? Okinawa? The guards only shrugged and smiled. They just told us to pack up and get ready to leave. Pack up? I almost laughed. We didn't have anything left but the clothes on our backs. For most of the men this meant a pair of shoes, khaki trousers, and cotton shirt; but some of us were still in khaki shorts and T-shirts. We marched the six miles from Agana to Piti silently, hardly seeing a native. The few who did venture out to wave good-by to us were crying. When we got to Piti we saw that Apra Harbor was filled with Japanese ships. They were the ugliest, most unseaworthy-looking ships I'd ever seen. Some of us tried to crack a few jokes about our chances, but the jokes dried up in our throats when we left the dock in a small shore boat and got a closer look at the invasion fleet. None of the rusty buckets of bolts looked like they could outrun or outmaneuver a garbage scow—much less the American submarines that we suspected were laying in wait for us outside the reef.

Small jawbone bets were laid on what ship we would catch—and how long it would stay afloat. The saddest looking ships were the favorites, and I don't think anyone made a bet on the *Argentina Maru*. We didn't see her at first. From our approach she was half hidden behind some large troop transports, and we were surprised when our boat cleared the transports and headed in her direction. The *Argentina Maru* was a magnificent ship. I later learned that she was one of the fastest and plushest passenger liners then afloat, and that she had only recently been diverted from the lush Tokyo to Buenos Aires run to less glamorous duty in the war zone. She looked proud and sleek, and she was wearing a fresh coat of gray paint. Swinging gently at anchor in Apra Harbor—majestic among the dirty, drab ships of the Japanese fleet—she reminded me of a dignified San Francisco dowager among the riffraff of South Market Street.

We filed up the gangway to the gleaming quarter-deck and looked around us. Josh Mackery summed up all our feelings when he said that it looked to him like the Japs wanted to make sure they would get us to wherever we were going—and fast—otherwise we would have caught one of the really sad-looking tubs that blighted the beautiful harbor.

We weren't happy about leaving Guam. The way we had it figured, our people would come storming in within a couple of days, weeks at most, and we wanted to be on hand when they got there. Some of the guys had already lost a month's pay, in jawbone wagers, betting the Japs would be run off the island before New Year's Day, 1941, and the guys that had taken the bets grumbled a little because they didn't want to get too far away from the pay office. But, since we *were* leaving, the *Argentina Maru* looked like a pretty good way to go, and I didn't hear any squawks about the travel arrangements. We weren't exactly jaunty, but we perked up a bit as we walked between two rows of stolid-faced Japanese soldiers and glanced through the open doors of the staterooms and saw the rich paneling and full-length beds—real beds—not like the steel bunks we had at Guam—but real beds—like in a hotel. My shoes sunk into soft carpeting as the guards steered us through a large, luxurious lounge, but I almost fell on my keester when we walked across the highly polished hardwood floor of a fancy ballroom that was just aft of the main lounge. It was, as the saying goes, first class all the way.

Then the roof caved in. We left the ballroom behind and above and started down. First by way of a carpeted, winding staircase; then by one not quite so fancy; and another; then a regular ship's ladder; and finally a plain iron stepladder. I don't know how many decks we passed on our way down, but when we got to the point where there were no more ladders we found ourselves in a steerage hold. It was worse than the cramped steerage compartments shown in the movies about the immigrants who came over from the old country before the turn of the century. The hold was dirty. The air, what there was of it, was hot and musty, and it stank. A honeycomb of jury-rigged wooden shelves filled the entire hold, and it was plain that there would be no sharing a stateroom with a geisha girl on this voyage. But then, neither the geisha girl nor the tight quarters mattered very much because everyone was thinking about his belly. At least I was. I was hungry. We had had a rice ball about the size of a baseball for breakfast, and we hadn't had anything since. It was mid-afternoon before we entered the hold, and I could feel something pretty vicious chewing at my insides. I guess everyone else felt the same way because no one said much for the next couple of hours. We just lay on the hard wooden shelves, trying to guess where we were going. Later on, the ship got under way, and it was dark before we were given something to eat. I suppose it was dark outside, because a sickly light was turned on in the hold, and someone pushed a couple of buckets of plain white rice and a box of tin plates and chop sticks through a hatch.

I grabbed a plate of rice and climbed on a shelf alongside Mackery. I had never used chop sticks before, and they were hard for me to handle. The best I could do was dig into the rice and hope to get a few grains to balance on the sticks. I noticed something moving when I poked the rice. The movement wasn't caused by the roll of the ship—the rice was actually moving. I looked at it a little closer. There was something alive in the rice.

"What the hell kind of livestock is this?" I asked Josh.

"Worms," he volunteered.

"Worms!" I almost gagged. "By God they can jam it! I'll be damned if I'll eat their wormy rice!" I must not have been as hungry as I thought.

"Here, I'll take it!" someone hollered and grabbed for the plate.

"I'll give you a buck for it payday!" someone else offered.

I was tempted.

"Better eat it yourself, friend," Mackery said, "it may be a long time before that six-foot body of yours gets the next meal."

I started to take a bite but I could still see the worms wiggling around in the rice. I closed my eyes but that didn't help. Without another word I handed the plate to a pair of grasping hands whose owner promptly gobbled up the contents.

I didn't make it to the head before I began to dry heave.

That night . . . and the next day . . . and the days and nights after that passed slowly. It was hard to keep track of time. Some of the guys up forward in the hold could tell night from day through a small latticed hatch high above their heads. Since we didn't have much room to move around in, most of us took their word for it when they announced the end of another day. It was a hell of a lot better way to keep track of the time than trying to use the meals as a gauge. There was no set time for the meals. At irregular intervals, the hatch opened and the rice buckets were passed in. My best guess was that we were fed twice a day, and it didn't make much difference whether it was breakfast, lunch, or dinner because each meal was the same bowl of plain white rice. I didn't bother to inspect the rice after passing up my first shipboard meal because of my run-in with the worms. I wasn't about to make that same mistake twice.

We knew we were sailing north because each day was a little colder than the day before. The ship dropped anchor late in the afternoon of the fifth day at sea. The engines were shut down, and the ship lay dead in the water, the heat blowers silent. And with the silence, the cold seeped through the steel hull and clung to the bowels of the ship like an invisible blanket of ice. It was pitch dark when we marched stiffly out of the hold, and I don't think anyone paid any attention to the luxurious appointments of the *Argentina Maru* as we retraced our route to the main weather deck.

Once on the open deck, our bodies, the blood thinned out by the warm tropical weather of Guam, recoiled violently from the almost forgotten winter winds. A light snow was falling when we off-loaded into a scow, and those of us who huddled on the windward side of the small boat as she pitched her way through the choppy sea toward a cluster of lights were damned near frozen stiff by the time we reached the dock. I halfway expected to hear Eddie Lashio crack the old saw about being as cold as a well digger's ass in Alaska, but even Lashio wasn't in any mood for small talk. He looked at me with a twisted little grin on his face, just shook his head, and brushed back his dark curly hair, which he kept long—as long as regulations allowed.

We disembarked from the scow into the blinding glare of a battery of high-powered floodlights. The dock was lined with bayonet-wielding soldiers, but the welcoming committee was dominated by official-looking civilians and a platoon of Japanese Army brass. They made quite a production of our arrival. I was too numb from the cold to be impressed by the dockside ceremonies, but I wasn't too cold to notice that all the Japanese brass had on heavy greatcoats to protect themselves from the biting wind. A train ride of ten miles and a short march later, we arrived at what appeared to be a huge military barracks. Exhausted, we tumbled into the straw and tried to sleep away the cold and hunger.

And now it was the next morning. So many strange, unreal things had occurred during those past six weeks that I found it hard to believe they had ever happened. I pulled the blankets over my head and dug deeper into the straw. I tried to go back to sleep but I wasn't fooling myself. I knew that even if I did get back to sleep I wouldn't wake up later to laugh off a hell of a bad dream.

I propped myself up and looked around. About forty or fifty men were lying on the floor of the big room. Some of the guys were already up and a lot of the others were beginning to stir around. I could tell by the look in their eyes that they, too, were finding the whole damn thing hard to believe. Somebody asked about the Navy women, and we all wondered how they had managed the trip and where their quarters were.

The Japanese authorities got themselves organized before we did—a little matter that we would take care of as time went by. We were now official prisoners of war, *horios* as they called us in the Japanese language, and the camp staff had a field day with us those first forty-eight hours at Zentsuji. It was here that we were introduced to our first breakfast of rice and soup. We'd had plain rice for breakfast at the church and aboard the *Argentina Maru*. But it had never been laced with soup. I guess you would have to call it *daikon* soup since that was what it was made from. A *daikon* is a pulpy vegetable, something like a cucumber, but much larger and much flatter tasting. It doesn't make very good soup, but it's quick and easy to make. Just slice the *daikon* as thin as you can and boil in plain water! No salt or other seasoning is required, otherwise the flat, watery taste might be lost! It would be pretty hard to say that *daikon* soup was tasty or that it had any body—but it and a bowl of rice were to be our main meal for years to come—supplemented on rare occasions by a thin slice of fish or meat, or maybe even a dash of oil, and every now and then a bowl of beans. But no Japanese POW can ever forget the *daikon* soup. Anyway, the first Zentsuji breakfast wasn't very appetizing, but at least the soup was warm and there were no worms in the rice.

After breakfast we were lined up for an issue of winter clothes, and we had our first chuckle since December eight. Each prisoner was issued a discarded Japanese Army winter uniform—a shirt, jacket, cap and legging trousers. I inherited my first winter clothes from a soldier who must have been stunted. I couldn't button the pants, either at the waist or at the legs, and they struck me halfway to my knees. The shirt would have been a tight fit for me when I was in the seventh grade, and at that moment I stood 6'1" and weighed 180 pounds. Everyone else had a hard time getting into the uniforms too, but we didn't worry about the fit. Once we struggled into them, they were a hell of a lot warmer than our tropical cottons.

We were let outside after the uniform fitting, and we got our first look at a POW camp. We were in the middle of what appeared to be a large training area. Zentsuji POW camp itself was a run-down dilapidated complex of old wooden Army buildings hemmed in tightly by a heavy barbed-wire fence. One of the guards—most of them spoke a little English—told us that we were on Shikoku Island, the smallest of the four major islands that make up the Japanese homeland. Lying near the heart of the huge Inland Sea, about midway between Kyushu and the main island of Honshu, Shikoku has the appearance of a heavily wooded mountain top sticking up out of the water.

We were at Zentsuji for a couple of days before the camp commander showed an interest in our well-being. Prompted, no doubt, by the propaganda experts, he ordered us outside to a large barbed-wire enclosure for a session of organized calisthenics. The propaganda corps, naturally, had their cameras ready, and they set us up as the main subjects of a propaganda film. I have no doubt that they had good reason to make such a film—and get it in the theaters as soon

as possible. It would soothe the apprehension of a normally sedate
and unwarlike nation of civilians who, even in those times of great
Japanese glory, were biting their fingernails. Even then (and this
was to be proven later to our satisfaction) most of the Japanese civilians suspected that Tojo had made a fatal mistake when he pulled
the trigger at Pearl Harbor. In any event, we were to be in a propaganda film. It wasn't easy to get the proper reaction from us, and
it wasn't until a lot of us felt the butt end of a rifle that we agreed to
go through the motions. It didn't take any brains to realize that the
big, healthy gang of Americans would soon be featured in newsreels
throughout Japan as living proof that the American myth had indeed
been exploded. I could almost hear the narrator chortle, "Look! Here
are the enemies of the Emperor. Real, live Americans! Now, who
among the Emperor's people can ever say again that Nippon is not
a strong nation? Here's proof of our strength! Here are the Americans
that we captured when we defeated an American stronghold in the
Pacific! Banzai!"

It was a hell of a feeling to be part of the act.

A few days after the calisthenics bit, the Japanese expanded their
propaganda efforts—and this time they revealed a canny sense of
drama. It began simply enough. We were lined up in single file and
marched past a long row of low wooden tables. As we passed down
the line, a Japanese soldier at each table issued each of us a bar of
hard-water soap, a pair of wool socks, a small package of cookies, a
piece of rock candy, and a package of Japanese cigarettes. No small
item, the cigarettes. They proved to be a lethal weapon that could
destroy man's decency, his honor, and almost life itself.

The issue—the surprise party, as we called it—was a rousing success. The gifts were nothing less than luxuries. We hadn't had soap,
sweets, or a whole cigarette in almost two months. We all tried to show
restraint, and we did our damnedest to appear casual and nonchalant as the items were handed us. I know, though, that our faces lit
up like the faces of youngsters getting their first look at a Christmas
tree.

The pay-off was well timed. The cameras were hidden from our
view until after we had the cigarettes in our hands. By then it was
too late. The damage was done. Our foolishly grinning mugs had
already been recorded on film and would soon be graphic evidence
to the whole world that the Japanese were treating their prisoners
rather well—and the wild glow in our eyes shining above a mushy
grin would be clear proof that we were an appropriately subservi-
ent and grateful lot. We knew we'd had it. We had been duped, and
we felt like the rear end of a skunk—but we soon found out that the
picture taking wasn't the unhappiest episode in this little Nipponese

drama. As we shuffled out of camera range, around the corner of a building, other guards took away everything they had given us. The grinning little bastards didn't even give us time to light a cigarette. Our consolation prize was a quarter of a bar of soap and ten cigarettes split up between three men. I don't know what happened to the rest of the gear, but I could have suggested a good place where it would have been a nice tight fit.

Curiously, this incident was a turning point. Our morale picked up, and we began to appreciate the only ray of hope we had in the first two months of the war—our never-flagging, unwavering faith that the war would be over "tomorrow." At the worst, we were expecting to sweat it out for another month or so. While it was a tough spot to be in, I felt the same as every other American prisoner or war—I knew that we could survive anything for another month. We felt we could do it standing on our heads, if need be.

⁂   ⁂   ⁂   ⁂

IN THE UNITED STATES THERE WAS NO LACK OF patriotic fervor. Pearl Harbor and Wake had unified the nation. In Texas, a young newspaper reporter named Jim Lucas quit his job and enlisted. Here is the gifted Scripps-Howard columnist and Pulitzer Prize winner soon after being sworn in.

·8· BOOT CAMP DAYS

JIM LUCAS

The trip to Parris Island . . . was hot, tedious and endless, but interesting. A recruiting sergeant, transferred from Oklahoma City to Augusta, Georgia, was making the trip with me, and taking his bride. Later he was to visit me in boot camp, where acquaintance with a sergeant meant more prestige than a personal relationship with the President of the United States. I had never been through the South and was perfectly content to watch the scorched countryside of Tennessee, Alabama, Mississippi and Georgia slip past and then to spend a day in Memphis when I missed connections. My sergeant kept me interested with stories out of Nicaragua, Panama and China.

I met my first Marine recruits in Atlanta. Farm boys from Alabama, they had enlisted in Birmingham because it seemed the likely thing to do.

It was at Yemassee Junction, South Carolina, later to be celebrated by a picture story in *Time* as the military crossroads of the United States, that I met the Marine Corps. He was only a buck sergeant and about as big as Helen Hayes, but he had a voice that rang with authority and he scared hell out of me.

The trip from Augusta to Yemassee had been bedlam. More than 1,000 recruits, each bent on convincing all the others that his heart wasn't in his throat, had turned the car into a shambles. The old conductor, who had done this route daily for thirty-five years, was too wise to attempt to enforce order. He had let us riot.

"Have a good time," he had said. "It ends at Yemassee."

And then the sergeant came aboard.

"You WILL"—and it was the first time I was to hear that authoritative command—"remain in this car until you are told to dismount. You will not GET OUT of this car until I give you the word. You WILL remain in your seats. You WILL keep order."

Everyone was silent, down to and including the boy from Cincinnati who had done the most talking.

The sergeant walked to the end of the car and glared.

"The vacation's over," he barked. "You're in the old Marine Corps now."

We stayed in Yemassee indefinitely. The car grew hot in the South Carolina sun, than which there is none sunnier. The recruits grew restless. But the sergeant had spoken, and we remained in our seats. Another group of 700 recruits had a worse time of it. They stood for two hours before they came aboard. We could at least remain seated— we had to.

The old train finally snorted, puffed and headed for Port Royal, debarkation point for Parris Island. The recruit next to me said he'd heard we would take another physical examination there, and the thought of final rejection, after the build-up I'd given myself, chilled my heart. I wondered how I could explain my weak right eye. But I resolved I'd never go back to Tulsa in such disgrace. I'd become a vagabond and wander outside the boundaries of Oklahoma.

Our first sight of Parris Island was its barrage balloons, lazily floating overhead. After Tulsa, with its passionate but vain ambition to be bombed, they sent a real thrill down my spine. This was war!

Port Royal is not a place to fill a budding young combat correspondent with the impulse to write lyric prose. Our reception committee
was not composed of gentlemen to encourage a prolific pen.

The utter horror of my position engulfed me. I felt a wild desire
to run away from the whole damnable mess, to get back to Tulsa and
the security of the *Tribune* as swiftly as I could.

Like so many cattle, we were bundled off the train, lined up for
an inspection by a bunch of noncoms who left little doubt they considered the war all but lost if this was what the nation had to offer,
and told us we were "boots."

"Boot!" The tag clung to me like a wet shirt for the next eight weeks.
I was later to learn that the Marine Corps does not refer to its recruits
as "men"; we were always called "you people." I have never realized
that membership in the human race could be made to sound so triv-
ial and repulsive.

With what little baggage we had brought along, we were pushed,
shoved and jostled into a line of waiting trucks. Our clothing was
soggy and black. We had washed the night before and put on clean
shirts, but no trace of this tidying up was now visible.

I can report little of that trip to Parris Island. I had left Tulsa with
visions of a pleasant ocean cruise. Indeed, I had been told that Parris
Island was a converted pleasure resort. I found the island connected
with the mainland by a bridge, and I made the trip in the rear of a
truck whose canvas-covered bed gave me little chance to gather a
description of the scenery. That would come later, and it would not
be pretty.

"YOU'LL BE SORRY!" That was our introduction to Parris Island.

Boots in platoons along the sandy parade grounds stopped their
work to jeer and shout at us. I was to learn later that what is the standard form of welcome to the horrors of boot camp. It seemed a warning all too true and all too late.

Two days later, a veteran of Parris Island and its rigors, the *Tribune*
only a dream with no basis in reality, I too was to stand and yell at
the top of my voice:

"YOU'LL BE SORRY!"

Someone said we would be fed, and we were. Boiled ham, mashed
potatoes prepared before dawn, bread, and water which had never
known ice.

I stood on the steaming pavement outside the mess hall, jumping
whenever anyone shouted, and I can swear on oath that no one spoke
that day in anything less than a deafening roar. I seriously debated
the advisability of announcing myself a conscientious objector and a
pacifist who had gotten into this awful business while drunk. I thought
back to the pack of Jehovah's Witnesses I had interviewed just be-

fore I made the fatal leap, and wondered why I hadn't accepted their invitation to number myself among the faithful.

A three-day-old platoon marched by, smacking their rifles in a manner to scare the hell out of one who had never fired anything more powerful than a .22 rifle, and that with rabid distaste. A kid young enough to be a patrol leader in Boy Scout Troop 20 wiped the sweat off his brow and winked.

"I've been here three days," he said, "and it seems like three years." I felt an immediate kinship.

We were herded back into formation by another bunch of noncoms, who looked on us with horror so overwhelming I had begun to share it. We were herded at double time—I have yet to learn why everyone was in such a hurry—into a long reception room and pelted with questions by clerks who knew in advance we couldn't give a sane answer.

When my turn came, I expected the worst, and I got it.

The big boy behind the desk—he wore the two stripes of a corporal—flipped over my record book and fixed me with a glare.

"You," he accused, "are 5-b."

I was damned—completely and irrevocably.

Five-b, my classification, is reserved for specialists, and old-line marines hate with a purple passion all specialists. This corporal's hate was extreme even for a marine, because specialists upset his bookkeeping, required additional entries and extra mental gymnastics. I had done all this to him, and more.

"What the hell are you, a radio-man?" he asked. I did not need to inquire what the corporal thought of radio-men.

I don't know what I answered. Somehow I managed to get it out that I was a combat correspondent.

The corporal said that could not be. It was, he insisted, impossible, and the PFC (Private, First Class) at his side agreed with a vigorous nod of his head. I was too weak to argue. It was a trick, after all.

The corporal dismissed me abruptly. He'd take care of me later. I was too gratified to slip back into nonentity to protest. At the next desk a recruit had lost his traveling orders and was undergoing the tortures of the damned. It was quite apparent, even to a blind man, that the full wrath of the Navy Department was about to descend on his head and Secretary Knox soon would arrive to arrange for his court-martial and execution.

We were divided into four numbered groups—499, 500, 501 and 502. Each group contained approximately sixty men. I was in No. 501. In charge of us they placed a crusty veteran of thirteen years in the Marine Corps, one Corporal Fullmore. Corporal Fullmore faced his task with evident resignation. He'd seen a lot, his manner implied, but nothing so wretched and sordid as the human misfits fate had tossed into his lap this day. But he'd make men out of us if he killed seventy-five percent in the process—a prospect I am certain he enjoyed.

Someone gave us cigarettes. It seemed almost too much. I expected some noncom to yank them out of my hands and roar that I was not entitled to smoke. Fortunately, my brother (Sergeant J. Bob Lucas, now with the famed Rainbow Division, U. S. Army) had enlisted two weeks earlier, and on his first furlough had told me what was in store for recruits who throw their butts on the grass. Before I could pass on this valuable information to the rest of 501, the first offender had been caught. He was given to understand that it was only because Corporal Fullmore was a good church-going Baptist with a mother and a sister at home, and therefore a rarity among Marine Drill Instructors, that he was spared the firing squad. But even Corporal Fullmore's patience could be exhausted.

We were herded up five flights of stairs and told to carry out a pile of boxes which apparently had been accumulated over a period of the last ten years specifically for this occasion. What had come in those boxes, to this day I do not know, but I suspect it was spare parts for a battleship. But we cleared them out.

It was dusk when we got our bucket issue.

The bucket issue is a tradition of the Marine Corps. We were given a tin pail, cigarettes, soap, a brush, a pair of swimming trunks, and a few assorted odds and ends. We were, we were given to understand, to pay for this bucket issue out of our first check. Were there any objections? There were none.

I have never learned the name of the sergeant in charge of that issue, but I shall nourish an all-encompassing hatred for him as long as I live. He roared at us from the moment we appeared until the moment we left. Our bare existence, for which we were humbly apologetic, plagued him, and sent him into spasms of rage.

"Each man," he bellowed, "will take five packages. Now ____ you, I don't want some of you taking three or four. You WILL take five. Is that plain?"

It was.

When the cigarettes had been issued, the sergeant's face screwed itself into a black rage. There were, he said, three packages still in the box. Some blockhead had taken only four. Who was it?

We stood dumb, glued to the floor.

It was, we learned later, a practical joke, an attempt to edge some would-be profiteer into attempting to get a sixth package. Our failure to bite, the sergeant regarded as a personal affront. The recruits we're getting now, he complained bitterly, are "too blank, blank smart; a bunch of wise guys."

I shall not attempt to enumerate the gear I accumulated that day. We marched from one end of Parris Island to the other, always through burning sand, always under the impatient prodding of Corporal Fullmore. The sand burned through my civilian low-cuts, and I was never happier than when I changed them for the big field shoes I was to wear thereafter. We got blankets, helmets, cots, sea bags, shoes, socks, underwear (we learned to call them "skivvies"), shirts, trousers, dungarees, and more. It made a monumental load, and when we finally drew up in front of the row of Quonset huts that was to be our home, my strength was gone, my spirit broken.

Evening chow I cannot remember. If I ate at all, it was in a stupor. My principal memory of the Parris Island chow halls is that of a 240-pound recruit complaining bitterly that he was not used to eating at a table where everyone was so ill-mannered, and shoveling his food down with both hands.

But, of that evening, I recall one point. Corporal Fullmore "gave us the word" in an important detail.

"Most of you," he said, and I still suspect he is a mind reader, "came in expecting a set of blues [the Marines' swank dress uniform] and a furlough. You will get neither."

Most of us knew that Army selectees were getting one week's furlough at that time. Corporal Fullmore knew what we were thinking. "No one," he said, grinning, "made you become a marine. You enlisted." That settled that.

For some reason, unexplained to this day, I was made a squad leader. A more unfortunate choice was never made. I simply was not cut out to be a squad leader.

Hell descended on me the next morning. If reveille was blown, Squad Leader Lucas did not hear it. Neither did any other member of the first squad of 501. At 5:15 A.M., an ungodly hour, of course, for men to be sleeping, we were still in our cots. It was Assistant Drill Leader Dickey—a 19-year-old North Carolina mountaineer, with the one stripe of a PFC—who broke the spell.

I do not remember what Dickey said. It is sufficient to report that he said it, and that loudly. The first squad scrambled into its dungarees and rushed frantically to the platoon formation back of the head. My world was crumbling about my feet.

"Lucas!" Dickey roared.

Lucas died.

"Lucas," he roared, "I mean you, you ---- --- -- -----!"

I recognized the description and stepped forward.

Dickey was at his sarcastic best.

He dealt at length on the desire of the Marine Corps that I not be disturbed. He recognized, he said, that so delicate a flower must not be mistreated. He and Corporal Fullmore, he assured me, were only present to make my life comfortable. I shook hands with an ant that crawled past.

"AND NOW," he wound up, "don't let it happen again."

I slunk back to my spot. The first squad, ignoring the fact that not a man of them had awakened at reveille, regarded me as a moral leper. I was in disgrace.

It was Sunday. I inquired cautiously if I might go to church. To my dismay, I got a civil answer, something I was unprepared to receive. Not this Sunday, but next, I was told. Thereafter I never missed a service in Parris Island's tiny chapel. It was our sole contact with the life we had left.

That Sunday was the hottest I have ever endured. We marched, marched, marched. I learned that a marine spends ninety percent of his time standing in line. We marched to chow, we marched to the movies, we marched to the swimming pool. We continued to draw equipment, not the least important item of which was our rifle. While waiting to receive mine, two men in the platoon ahead dropped from the heat. Against orders, they had stolen a quantity of ice water from a nearby fountain. I did not know that, and resigned myself to death from sunstroke.

We were soon to learn water discipline, and to fight down the impulse to guzzle after a hard day. It was one of the toughest lessons of boot camp.

During the afternoon we cleaned our new rifles—we soon learned they were not "guns"—and found it a messy, stick job. I lived in the fear that I would fail in this first of all important tests, and wondered secretly what diabolical turn of mind invented the gum in which weapons are kept.

I went to bed that night hating Corporal Fullmore and PFC Dickey. Too tired to sleep, I lay awake planning fiendish means of doing them to death. Nothing too gentle or too swift. I wanted a lingering, horrible end, to fit their crimes. Something I'd once seen when Wallace Beery played Pancho Villa. Bury them in an ant hill and pour honey over their heads. That would do, I decided, until something better presented itself.

Our platoon was joined that Sunday by a bunch of late arrivals, all boys from Florida. One of them, Al Brown, became my closest friend—I still owe him $10. He gave me his sister's address, but I've lost it, and if Al ever reads this book, I am still ready to pay him.

Fifty percent of our platoon had come from Cleveland, Ohio, where the recruiting sergeants must have been working overtime, and that night we embarked upon a sport that was to keep us busy for the next eight weeks—fighting the Civil War. I recall at least two black eyes and three bloody noses as a result of the perpetual post-mortem. On another occasion we made so much noise after taps that Corporal Fullmore took us out at midnight for physical exercise under arms.

The next week was more hell. No. 501, it developed, was not the finest platoon Parris Island had ever developed. Corporal Fullmore, who told us he had the reputation of producing the best-drilled men on the island, foresaw the collapse of his fame. We were willing, we may even have been overanxious, but we were inept. We were wrong far more often than we were right. Fullmore punished us on the second Sunday by drilling us at double time until church. Life had become an unbearable burden, relieved only by my burning hatred of D.I.'s and their assistants. We wrote our own parodies to the ditty: "The G.I. DI from PI."

There were a few breaks in the clouds. Corporal Fullmore, discovering a few promising boxers in our ranks, seemed pleased at last. But I couldn't box. I was still among the great unwashed, but I stood by and cheered because I figured that was what the corporal would want.

And, occasionally, we went to swim. Usually I enjoyed it, for it was a bit of heaven in an otherwise uninterrupted hell, but I recall the day the sun produced a splitting headache and I tried to beg off from the swimming party. Fullmore would not hear of it.

"You WILL swim," he commanded. "That's an order."

Even our pleasure had become regimented.

Shortly after our arrival on Parris Island, we had been taken to the auditorium and given a series of intelligence tests. On the basis of some of them, a few of our men were sent to specialist schools. I remember I stood up and mentioned something about what I had enlisted to do, and cautiously inquired if it were necessary for me to go ahead with the exams. The answer chilled me, and, as far as I know, it was the last time I ever mentioned on Parris Island that I was to be a combat correspondent. And I took the tests.

No one ever tried harder than I did in those horrible eight weeks. But I was the source of constant amusement for the rest of my fellows. My weight, even though it was fast melting away, was all in my hips. I waddled. My only consolation was that Fred Rothermell, a Cleveland boy, was just ahead of me, and Fred waddled too. Others bounced. We soon became able to tell a man without looking him in the face, simply by watching his walk.

I was no longer squad leader, and was content far back in the ranks. In a burst of frankness, I had told Corporal Fullmore that I had a man-sized job on my hands taking care of myself and didn't want to be responsible for eight others. Fullmore, having watched me for three days, agreed wholeheartedly.

Fullmore, meanwhile, drilled us constantly, and demanded that we develop a pride in 501. Such a pride was showing itself. We were, we soon became confident, a much better bunch of men than 499, 500 and 502. Such clods!

A lot of those boot camp memories escape me, but there sticks in my mind the day we were lined up and told the name of the commandant of the United States Marine Corps.

"Holcomb," Fullmore roared. "Thomas A. Holcomb. Now, you ---- -----, if anyone asks you who your commandant is, what will you tell them?"

"Holcomb," the ranks murmured.

"Like hell you will," Fullmore grumbled. "You'll forget."

Like an oasis in a burning desert, there remains the memory of the day we were marched across a burning parade ground to a cool little shack and addressed by a PFC, who told us the whys and where-fores of the war. I was deeply interested, but too tired to listen. I fell asleep while PFC Paul Douglas, former professor of economics at the University of Chicago, had talked on. Later, Captain Paul Douglas was to sign my transportation orders when I went to New Georgia for that brutal campaign.

There were other pleasant interludes. There was the night PFC Dickey marched us to the auditorium to witness a stock production from New York. It was corny, it stunk, but we roared. Our faith in humanity, our fading belief in the existence of an outside world, was renewed.

By the end of the second week we were veterans. An all-day bat-tle problem in the boon docks had exacted its toll, sending thirty-two of us to sick bay with a mild sunstroke, but we had proved we were men by sticking it out. My resentment had crystallized into a bitter, passionate determination to show them I couldn't be broken.

We had a few more privileges. One man from each squad could now be sent to the post exchange at 5 P.M. to buy writing paper, candy, ice cream and novelties for the bunch. He usually came back look-ing like Santa Claus, and finally two, three and even four men went on this all-important errand.

We were getting letters from home, and an occasional package. The girls in the *Tribune* office did not let me go hungry. Incensed at my failure to get what I considered a fair share of the mail, I wrote a blistering letter to Tulsa, only to receive five letters that afternoon. A week later I was punished by a telegram tearfully protesting that they had written and suggesting that they had the wrong address. For two weeks I penned at least one abject apology each night.

At chow I had met James ("Hot") Dorris, a Nashville politician who had enlisted as a Marine Corps recruiting photographer. Dorris and I considered ourselves creatures apart. He was due for assignment in Atlanta, and I was to go to Washington. We became the envy of the platoon.

Corporal Fullmore wasn't so sure. In his books, the only marine worth his salt was the fighting line-soldier. Specialists were trash. Clerks were incompetents. I diplomatically avoided any mention of my future. Not so, Dorris. He constantly threw it up to Fullmore, who railed. Only the fact that "Hot" was probably the best marine in 501, and impervious to any ridicule, saved him many embarrassing moments.

Inspections were a terror. I recall now the night of the first. Our clothing was to be laid out in careful order on our bunks, each article in its place. In showing us how it was done, and in the confident assurance that we were too thick to follow his instructions, Corporal Fullmore used my bunk as a model. I left everything as he had put it, and slept on the floor. The next morning an outraged young second lieutenant generously tore it apart and insisted that not one piece was in its place. Corporal Fullmore remained discreetly silent, but he never forgot or forgave.

On our second inspection, a captain, the highest ranking officer I had ever met, insisted that my rifle was dirty. That was rank libel, for I'd spent three hours on it that morning, beginning before dawn and supplementing five hours' work on it the afternoon and night before.

"Look," he said, tossing it back to me.

I looked.

"See it?"

"No, sir," I replied.

That was heresy. "Look again!" the captain roared, while Corporal Fullmore went through the motions of jujitsu behind his back. "See it?"

"No, sir," I was stubborn. "It's clean."

"Clean it," the captain ordered, "and report to me at 1700 [5 P.M.]."

I got KP for that one.

Finally, slowly, painfully, I was fitting myself into boot camp. It was still hard, I still grated on the edges, but I was learning to be a boot.

There were still other painful episodes, though they are now amusing.

We were soon far enough advanced to be assigned to guard duty. This important chore involved walking slowly for four hours among the huts, warning other boots to shut their screen doors.

We carried rifles, but they were never loaded, though we slowly executed the Manual of Arms in shifting them from one aching shoulder to the other.

On the first stint, I was assigned to guard the latrines. I recall that my most auspicious moment arrived when I was able to bawl:

"Sergeant of the Guard! Post No. 7!"

The cry was taken up by Posts No. 6, 5, 4 and so on down the line.

The sergeant came on the dead run.

"Sir," I reported importantly, "Post No. 7 is out of toilet paper."

Latrine guarding struck me as funny. I was moderately confident that neither the Japs nor the Germans would have them. On one occasion I regaled the boots in my hut with a highly colorful, fictitious and interesting yarn of a Jap attack on my post, and my valiant defense of our latrines. Just as I had single-handedly repulsed all the invaders there was a dead silence. Turning, I faced Corporal Fullmore.

And then came the day we went on the range. This was the test, the making of a real marine. Boots were divided into two classes, those who had been to the range and those who had not. We were getting up in the world.

Our three-mile trek to the range was physical torture. It was celebrated by nature with a sandstorm and then a rain, which covered us first with silt and then with mud. Our huts leaked. It was 10 P.M. before we were settled for the night, and we were up at 4 A.M.

The Spanish Inquisition never offered anything so painful.

For three days we "snapped in." "Snapping in" involves getting into positions in which the Creator never intended a man to get himself, and then holding them for minutes that grow into hours. This is supposed to make you limber and to teach you how best to hold a rifle. The coaches were long since past feeling human pity or compassion. We ached in every joint, and went back the next morning for more.

From "snapping in" we went to the 22 range. To my surprise I qualified, not without my mishaps, of course. On one occasion I thought I had liberally sprayed my target, only to find I had been shooting at the one next to it. I drew zero.

Then followed the pistol course. Again I qualified. My self-respect increased by leaps and bounds. The *Tribune* considered my pistol exploits so remarkable they devoted quite a little of their space to it. Sheriff Garland Marrs wrote me that he'd like me for a deputy.

Now came the time for the rifle tests. My range coach was an Oklahoman, who told me no Sooner had ever failed to qualify. That record seemed certain to fall.

On preliminary day I nervously shot a miserable 148. At least 175 was necessary to qualify. That night Parris Island had a first-class cloudburst. Our carefully cleaned rifles were guarded against rust. I went back to the cleaning vats three times, once after dark.

Qualification day broke damp and dismal. There was a strong wind, enough to hamper expert riflemen, and 501 was still far out of championship class. Fullmore, who no longer was our boss, having been ordered to await transfer to the new Marine base at New River, N.C., came by and dropped some alarming hints.

I began badly. At 200 yards, standing, I shot a 28. Thirty-five was the required average.

Thereafter I performed better, but it was an uphill fight. I recall that my coach, who had developed a paternal interest in me, decided at one point, while I was shooting offhand (standing), to cheat in my favor. He gave me his shoulder for a brace. I fired, and drew a Maggie's Drawers, indicating a complete miss. He was furious.

"You and your conscience!" he growled at me.

On the final round, at 500 yards, I needed a 48 out of 50 to qualify. Eight bull's-eyes and two fours. Nothing less would do.

Somehow I did it. I shall never forget that last shot. I worked for five minutes before squeezing it off, and was rewarded with the white disc. I was the last man in 501 to complete the course, and my pals were lined up back of me, praying and pulling. A successful candidate for the presidency never got such an ovation, and certainly never strutted more nobly.

I was, at last, a marine.

❧　❧　❧　❧

HIROHITO'S SEEMINGLY INVINCIBLE JUGGERNAUT rolled on, and at the end of February three-quarters of the nations of the Pacific had either succumbed to her armed might or were about to. In the Philippines General Masahara Homma's forces were pushing down the spine of Bataan Peninsula. The last avenue of retreat was The Rock, fortress Corregidor, at the entrance to Manila Bay, where a conglomeration of half-starved American and Filipino armed forces under General MacArthur resolved to hold out to the bitter end. Here, too, was Colonel Samuel L. Howard's 4th Regiment, 44 officers and 728 enlisted men who had arrived from China six weeks before and were now under Army jurisdiction.

There was a mystique about these 4th Marines ("Tough, veteran troops," MacArthur), a *corps de elite* quite unlike any other in the world. This swaggering band of brothers, whose numbers would swell to 1400 following the fall of Bataan by the absorption of marine units from three other islands, were the guardians of The Rock's beach defenses and several of its batteries. But let us momentarily put aside the saga of Howard's troops to first give a clear picture of life on Corregidor, where men were expected to subsist on less than 1000 calories a day. Although large sums of money were offered to guerrillas to run the tight Japanese blockade, none risked an instant bullet-in-the-head, and consequently the ragged, bomb-and-shell-weary holdouts slowly starved.

Let us join MacArthur, who was awarded the Congressional Medal of Honor for his role in the Philippines. It is shortly before President Roosevelt has ordered him to Australia by PT boat. The enemy has intensified his pounding of the fortress, and from the skies a flow of surrender leaflets rains down daily. Surrender? The foxholes rock with laughter. More to the point is the fervent, unanswered prayer heard everywhere: "Give us this day our daily bread."

.9. MY DUTY

GENERAL OF THE ARMY
DOUGLAS MacARTHUR

Our headquarters, called "Topside," occupied the flattened summit of the highest hill on the island. It gave a perfect view of the whole panorama of the siege area. As always, I had to see the enemy or I could not fight him effectively. Reports, no matter how penetrating, have never been able to replace the picture shown to my eyes. The Filipinos, even as the smoke pillars of their burning villages dotted the land, were being told that Europe came first. Angry frustration, for citizens and soldiers alike, irritated bruised nerves and increased the sense of heartache and loss. And the enemy, night after night, in the seductive voice of "Tokyo Rose," rubbed raw the wounds by telling them over the radio that defeat and death were to be their fate while America's aid went elsewhere. President Quezon was stunned by the reports of the huge amounts of American supplies now being sent to Russia. His expression of bewildered anger was something I can never forget. As an evidence of assurance to these people suffering from deprivation, destruction, and despair, I deemed it advisable to locate headquarters as prominently as possible, notwithstanding exposure to enemy attack.

They came in a perfect formation of twin-engine bombers, glittering in the brilliant blue sky. Far-off, they looked like silver pieces thrown against the sun. But their currency was death and their appearance a deceit. These were deadly weapons of war and their bomb bays contained a terrible force of destruction. The long white main barracks, a concrete straight line, cracked and splintered like a glass box. The tin edges of the overhanging roof, under the impact of a thousand-pounder, were bent upward like the curvature of a Chinese pagoda. Pieces of the metal whirled through the air like bits of macabre confetti. A 500-pound burst took off the roof of my quarters. Telephone lines snapped and coiled to the ground. The sturdy rails and ties of the local streetcar line were loosed and looped up into meaningless form. The lawn became a gaping, smoking crater. Blue sky turned to dirty gray.

Then came strafing, and again the bombing. Always they followed the same pattern. Their own orders could not have enlightened me more. What I learned, I used to advantage later. They kept it up for three hours. The din was ferocious. The peaceful chirping of birds had been replaced by the shrill scream of dive bombers. The staccato of strafing was answered by the pounding of the anti-aircraft batteries. Machine guns chattered everywhere and ceaselessly. Then they left as shaking earth yielded under this pulverizing attack, and there rose a slow choking cover of dust and smoke and flame.

My new headquarters was located in an arm of the Malinta Tunnel. Carved deep in the rock, the central tunnel was actually the terminal point of a streetcar line. Other passages had been hewn out of the rock and these now housed hospital wards, storerooms, and ammunition magazines. The headquarters was bare, glaringly lighted, and contained only the essential furniture and equipment for administrative procedure. At the sound of the air alarm, an aide and I would make our way out through the crowded civilians seeking shelter in the main passageway, huddled silently in that hunched-down, age-old Oriental squat of patience and stolid resignation, onto the highway to watch the weaving pattern of the enemy's formations.

There was nothing of bravado in this. It was simply my duty. The gunners at the batteries, the men in the foxholes, they too were in the open. They liked to see me with them at such moments. The subtle corrosion of panic or fatigue, or the feeling of just being fed up, can only be arrested by the intervention of the leader. Leadership is often crystallized in some sort of public gesture. For example, in peace, such a gesture might be the breaking of bread as a symbol of hospitality, or with native Indians, the smoking of a peace pipe to show friendship. But in war, to be effective it must take the form of a fraternity of danger welded between a commander and his troops by the common denominator of sharing the risk of sudden death.

❦   ❦   ❦   ❦

CLARK LEE OF THE ASSOCIATED PRESS SAW THE Philippine war as did few civilians. In Manila at the outbreak of the conflict, he followed the Army in its steady retreat to Corregidor, and was one of the few to leave the fortress shortly before its collapse. In the following excerpt the durable Lee also speaks of life on The Rock, where much of his time was spent with old cronies of the 4th Marines.

·10· LIFE ON THE ROCK — BETWEEN BOMBS

CLARK LEE

When the planes weren't overhead life on Corregidor was not too unpleasant. For the first few days there were still some of the minor pleasures of peace time life in the big Army garrison—a little ice cream or a bottle of Coca-Cola; but they soon became major luxuries and then disappeared altogether.

I met a lot of old friends from Shanghai in the Fourth Marines, who were assigned to beach defenses of Corregidor after having been bomed out of Olangapo. Colonel Samuel Howard, the Marine commander, set up headquarters in the Navy tunnel. Lieutenant Colonel

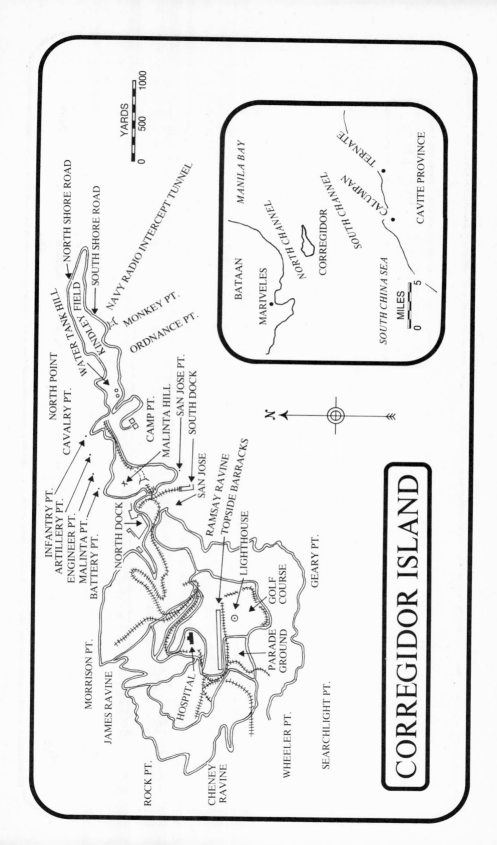

CORREGIDOR ISLAND

YARDS

0   500   1000

NORTH SHORE ROAD
NORTH SHORE ROAD
SOUTH SHORE ROAD
NAVY RADIO INTERCEPT TUNNEL
WATER TANK HILL
KINDLEY FIELD
MONKEY PT.
ORDNANCE PT.
NORTH POINT
CAVALRY PT.
INFANTRY PT.
ARTILLERY PT.
ENGINEER PT.
MALINTA PT.
BATTERY PT.
NORTH DOCK
CAMP PT.
MALINTA HILL
SAN JOSE PT.
SOUTH DOCK
SAN JOSE
RAMSAY RAVINE
TOPSIDE BARRACKS
LIGHTHOUSE
GOLF COURSE
PARADE GROUND
GEARY PT.
MORRISON PT.
JAMES RAVINE
HOSPITAL
ROCK PT.
CHENEY RAVINE
WHEELER PT.
SEARCHLIGHT PT.

N

MANILA BAY
BATAAN
MARIVELES
NORTH CHANNEL
CORREGIDOR
SOUTH CHANNEL
CALUMPAN
TERNATE
CAVITE PROVINCE
SOUTH CHINA SEA

MILES

0   5

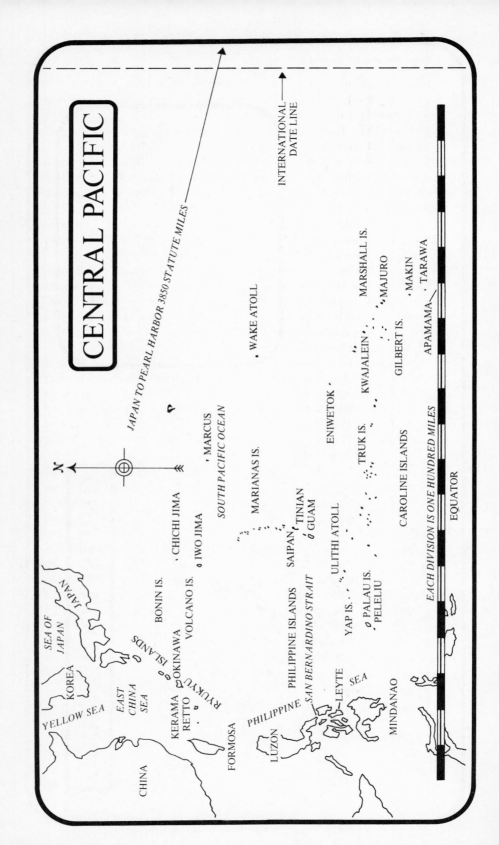

"Duke" Hamilton got me a pair of marine shoes to replace the China-made oxfords which had stood up during the hike from Baguio but were now decidedly down at heel. Corporal "Gabby" Kash of Los Angles gave the Jacobys and myself a half-dozen cans of salmon and a big can of tomato juice.

I asked Gabby, who had been a protege of radio announcer Carroll Alcott in Shanghai, how he accounted for the fine morale of the Marines and why they seemed to be less bothered by the bombing than the rest of the forces.

"Well," he said, "it's mostly because we have to live up to our traditions and reputation. Everybody expects us to be good—just a little bit better than anybody else—and so we just have to be good."

Sergeant White, star shortshop and rugby player of the Fourth Marines during their Shanghai days, lost a leg early in the Battle of Corregidor, but he was one of the most cheerful men on The Rock. I used to chat with him for a few minutes every day while he was in bed. Within ten days he was getting around easily on crutches.

I asked him if he wasn't in pain.

"I must have been," he said, "because they tell me I was delirious and pretty hard to get along with for a week. But I don't remember it at all. I'm all set now. They'll give me an artificial leg as good as new. I'll get preference for a civil service job that'll pay me one hundred and thirty dollars a month. In a couple of weeks our help will be here and we'll chase the Japs out of the islands and they'll take me to Australia in a hospital ship and then send me home."

It was a little cold sleeping in the trolley station, so Jacoby and I looked around for a place to live. Cabot Colville, former second secretary of the American Embassy in Tokyo and now a member of Sayre's staff, told us we could sleep on cots on the porch in the house assigned to Sayre, next door to General MacArthur's. Sayre, his wife, and her 12-year-old son were sleeping in the hospital tunnel. Annalee was also assigned a bed in the tunnel, over her strenuous objections. At Sayre's house we could get an occasional shower, when the bombs hadn't disrupted the water supply, and it also was high enough above the bay level to provide a good lookout post.

At night we could sit on the grass outside and watch our guns firing in Bataan. In the morning we would see our antiaircraft firing on the Japanese dive bombers which made almost daily raids on our improvised airfields at Cabcaben, on the southeastern tip of the peninsula. The house was handy to our first mess, which was driven out of Bottomside by the bombings and set up on a slope to the east of Malinta tunnel. We seldom made it for breakfast but the cooks would save us a cup of coffee. Later, after a couple of weeks, General Mac-

Arthur transferred us to the officers' mess which was just outside the eastern entrance to the tunnel.

There we ate more frequently but in lesser quantities than at the soldiers' mess. The officers were served a cup of coffee and piece of toast and sometimes a piece of bacon for breakfast; a cup of soup and a half sandwich at lunch; and for dinner some kind of salmon, canned vegetable, and dessert of rice pudding or something similar. The Chinese chef, Ah Fu, was an artist—but you could only do so many things with salmon and rice.

Social life in the evenings centered around the officers' mess and the mess for convalescent patients and hospital attendants outside the northern entrance to the hospital tunnel. It was cool, and the stars shone brightly above the bay, and we listened to San Francisco on the radio and to Tokyo, and to the puppet station in Manila. Later, USAFFE set up its own "Voice of Freedom" radio in Malinta tunnel with news broadcasts three times daily to the troops.

There was considerable grumbling the night Bing Crosby broadcast to Bataan, because the Japs jammed the music and dialogue—all except the cheese ads. There had been one of the worst bombings that day and nobody had had much more than a piece of bread and a cup of coffee. Our reaction was, "For God's sake, Americans, stop making cheese and make bullets and airplanes, because we need them fast."

Living next to General MacArthur had its disadvantages. If his phone rang in the night it would awaken us and we would know that some serious threat had developed in Bataan. In the mornings the general would walk around his lawn and circle our house with his long, purposeful strides. He never paid any attention to air raid alarms until the planes were actually overhead. To save face, we would have to ignore the warning too and stifle our inclination to dash for the safety of the tunnel. Many mornings we would walk along with him and get the latest news.

Getting news and getting it out was our first concern after our status on Corregidor became established, and for Jacoby and myself it was the toughest battle of the war. As early as the first day we told Colonel Diller, "We want to report this story."

Diller said, "Go ahead and write it." We wrote and wrote and wrote. We wrote of the last night in Manila, the fires and the destruction, we wrote about the bombing of Corregidor. But the censors wouldn't let the stories through. I spent a day with Lieutenant Jennings and some other Marine friends in a concrete trench during a heavy bombing raid and had one eardrum injured and nearly got killed—to get a story. I wrote about how it felt to be nearly killed by bombs, and Diller still said no. There were no facilities for press transmission.

There seemed to be no hope. We decided that unless we could do our jobs, it was up to us to move on and stop eating the food needed for someone who was doing a job.

$$\text{❧} \quad \text{❧} \quad \text{❧} \quad \text{❧}$$

AND WHAT OF THE DEFENDERS? HERE ARE THE distinguished brothers Belote—James H., a military analyst for the Government, and William M., an associate professor of history at the United States Naval Academy—whose book, *Corregidor* stands as the definitive work on the fortress.

·11· CORREGIDOR: PRELUDE TO INVASION

JAMES H. AND WILLIAM M. BELOTE

Colonel Howard's Beach Defense Command with too few trained infantry to fulfill its mission . . . had about 3,900 officers and men of whom only 1,500 were marines, members of his own 4th Marine Regiment. The remainder were from several score units of the Army, Navy, Philippine Army, and Philippine Scouts. Except for a handful of Bataan survivors, who were in poor physical condition, some aging World War I veterans, and a few leathernecks who had fought in Nicaragua in the 1920s, none had had prior combat experience. Even the marines had not trained in the field as a unit for years. Their pre-war station had been Shanghai, where they had served as garrison troops.

All of Howard's men had rifles and a respectable total of 225 .30 and .50 caliber machine guns as well as twenty light M-1916 37 mm. cannon, but they were woefully short of other support weapons. Their few converted Stokes mortars had no sights, they had no field howitzers, and their only antitank weapon was the "Molotov cocktail," a bottle of gasoline and oil with an igniting fuse. Ominously, there was no plan to support them with fire from seacoast batteries on Corregidor or the other forts.

For antiboat defense Howard had one 155 mm. gun, twenty-three British-type 75's of indifferent quality with large spoked wheels, a pair of Navy 3-inch landing guns, and three Navy 3-pounders. With the exception of the sailors who manned the Navy guns, all of the gunners were Scouts of the 91st and 92nd Coast Artillery Regiments. In the aggregate the guns totaled a respectable number, but when scattered in pairs all around Corregidor, they were spread quite thin, and along the north shore Japanese fire had knocked out all of them. Only on the extreme tail of the island two 75 mm. guns remained intact facing Bataan. These survived because of their location and because their commander, Lieutenant Ray G. Lawrence, U.S.A., had been ordered by General Moore not to reveal his position by firing back during the pre-invasion bombardment.

Colonel Howard had devised his defense plan at a time when the greatest threat to The Rock came from outside Manila Bay rather than from Bataan. Consequently, the bulk of his men were on Topside. There he had concentrated 2,035 men of the 2nd and 3rd Battalions, mainly in James, Cheney, and Ramsay ravines, backing them up with his regimental reserve of about six hundred officers and men stationed in Government ravine at Middleside. Only one battalion, his 1st, under Lieutenant Colonel Curtis T. Beecher, defended the entire tail of the island from Malinta Hill eastward. For reasons best known to himself Howard did not change his dispositions after Bataan's fall, even though it now was obvious the Japanese probably would mount from inside the bay, striking at his vulnerable 1st Battalion.

With over ten thousand yards of traversable beach to defend, and possessing neither a defense in depth nor a usable reserve, the 1st Battalion was a hollow shell. Once through its thinly manned lines the Japanese would encounter little opposition. It had only fifty-three officers and 1,024 men, and of these but twenty officers and 367 men were marines. The remainder consisted of Filipino aviation cadets, miscellaneous American and Filipino survivors of Bataan, Company A of the 803rd Engineers, 240 veterans Scouts of the 91st and 92nd CA Regiments manning the surviving beach defense guns, and even a number of retired Filipino mess boys of the U.S. Navy who had been recalled to active duty when war came.

Along the shattered north shore, where all wire and beach defenses had been destroyed, Beecher had merely a reinforced company and a platoon from Battalion headquarters, commanded by Captain Lewis H. Pickup. Just three platoons guarded the area where the Japanese actually landed, from North Point eastward to the tip of the tail. The other side of the island was defended by Company B under a young lieutenant, Alan S. Manning, who twice had been wounded by the bombardment, while the weapons company, D, under Captain Noel E. Castle, disposed its machine guns and 37's on either side of the tail. Beecher had a small battalion reserve under Lieutenant Robert F. Jenkins, Jr., but since it was occupying positions above possible landing beaches on either side of Malinta Hill, he had to leave it in place; consequently it never saw action.

All the members of the 1st Battalion were groggy from concussion and lack of sleep. Seven of the officers had been killed or wounded, including, as we have seen, the commanders of Companies A and B, whom Pickup and Manning had replaced. Many had suffered close calls; it was not uncommon for a marine or G.I. to have his rifle smashed from his hands by a shell fragment. Patches covered shrapnel holes in the jackets of some of the water-cooled machine guns. Considering the ferocity of the bombardment the wonder is not that units became entangled and the beach defense line ragged and intermittent as the men sought the deepest holes they could find; the wonder is that they remained on the exposed tail at all. Three days before the landing Beecher warned Colonel Howard that his command's battered condition made it "extremely unlikely" that he could beat off a Japanese attack.

To mount a counterattack if the Japanese won a lodgment Colonel Howard could muster only his ill-equipped reserve armed with Enfield rifles and Lewis machine guns. His two companies of headquarters troops, Companies O and P, totaling thirty-two officers and 276 men under Major Max W. Shaeffer, U.S.M.C., formed one-half of the reserve. This half was called the Regimental Reserve. The other half, commanded by Major Francis H. (Joe) Williams, U.S.M.C., consisted of 275 officers and men grandiloquently designated the 4th Battalion, 4th Marines. Both units were stationed along steep trails in Government ravine at Middleside, defiladed from the murderous Japanese artillery on Bataan.

Consisting mostly of veteran sailors, petty officers in the higher grades from the Navy's section base at Mariveles and the scuttled submarine tender U.S.S. *Canopus,* 4th Battalion was led by a heterogeneous collection of Navy and Army officers, of whom a few had seen combat on Bataan. First Lieutenant Otis E. Saalman, U.S.A., formerly of the Scout 57th Infantry, was perhaps the most experienced. Boasting that it was the "highest-paid marine unit in the world," because of the lucrative salaries of its enlisted specialists, the battalion also had the highest lettered companies anyone had ever heard of: Q, R, S, and T. The men "trained" by plinking at debris in the bay with their rifles and listening to lectures on combat tactics during lulls in the bombardment. All took the meager indoctrination seriously. "The chips were down," wrote Captain Harold E. Dalness, U.S.A., commanding Company R, "and there was no horseplay."

Each man had an Enfield rifle, but there were not enough helmets, cartridge belts, or canteens to go around. The equipment of Frank Gomez was typical.

> I had a World War I helmet, a white piece of line for my belt, a safety pin that was to hold my canteen to the line. A Filipino sailor gave me a big horse blanket. I stripped my gas mask bag . . . That was my ditty bag, just room for a change of clothing, soap, if any, and a few canned goods, like salmon or dry chocolate (unsweetened).

Effective use was not made of the coast artillery units, even though all had small arms and machine guns for their men and had trained as infantry and at counter-landing assignments. Instead of pulling them from their positions as their batteries were silenced, headquarters left them in place and merely assigned each a defense mission in its vicinity. It alerted four batteries for use as reserves on call of General Moore. In view of the heavy shelling, it may be that headquarters concluded that to do more would be impossible.

With his customary thoroughness Captain Ames of Battery Chicago had prepared a line of defenses across the forward slope of Morrision Hill, making certain by drills carried out under fire that each man would occupy his assigned foxhole when the order came to man the line. Denver, on the other hand, occupying what turned out to be the key to the American defense, a position atop Water Tank Hill, a ridge running west from Kindley Field, was so demoralized following the death of First Sergeant Dewey Brady on April 24, that its morale temporarily had collapsed. To revive the stricken battery Colonel Chase had assigned to command on May 1 Ames's able "exec," Captain Paul R. Cornwall, but time was too short for the young officer to restore the battery completely even though morale improved. Consequently, Cornwall was unable to carry out in full the defense plan, which called for Denver to establish a defense line across the crest of its hill, tying into the marine beach defenses on either side. He did, however, establish some positions across the top of the ridge near the two water towers and on a shoulder of the hill, admonishing the men to do their best should the Japanese attack.

As the morning of May 5 dawned, even the few remaining optimists sensed the inevitable end. No convoy from the States could help now. "A continuous pall of dust and debris hung over everything," wrote Captain Jack Gulick. "There was a feeling of doom mingled with wonder." To Lieutenant Commander T. C. Parker the whole island seemed ". . . beaten and burned to a crisp. It resembled a sponge . . ."

By now most of the fixed installations either were out of action or useless because of Japanese fire. The antiaircraft batteries were silent from cumulative damage to data transmission lines, weapons, directors, and height finders. Batteries Flint and Chicago each had one antiaircraft gun operative; Denver had none. The others, unable to direct their fire, lay silent. The unopposed Japanese pilots dipped so low that helpless observers on the ground could see them thumb their noses as they flew by. To be sure, most of the damage was repairable, but Corregidor needed a respite from the fierce shelling before much could be done.

Already General Moore had been deprived of a commander's most essential need—his power to communicate rapidly with his units. After April 29 all telephone lines on the island were regularly cut after a few hours, forcing reliance on runners until repair crews could fix them. This means of conveying orders was dangerous, slow, and unreliable. Crossing Bottomside on foot in the vicinity of the wrecked power plant was a particularly hazardous venture. Captain Rolly Ames of Battery Chicago traversed it nightly to have a wound dressed in the Tunnel. Although the Japanese slackened their fire at night, Ames still termed the area a "nasty place" where "one felt positively in the spotlight for artillery batteries on Bataan." The once-jungle-covered road along the north shore of the island was a seared, whitened scar along ground blasted bare. The time was rapidly approaching when repair of wire communications would be impossible, when movement would cease above ground by both day and night.

Getting enough water even for drinking purposes was already a serious problem for the more exposed units, especially Beecher's marines and attached troops on the tail. Chicago, with positions facing Bataan, had to manhandle its water from Middleside in cumbersome twelve-inch powder cans from a well equipped with its own pump. Mobile, with its platoons scattered along the tail and on Kindley Field, being refused water at Malinta Tunnel, had to send its only remaining truck to the well Chicago was using. Even Malinta Tunnel was running critically short; reserve stocks from which the post hospital drew had dwindled from a total of three million gallons on April 10 to but a few days' supply at normal consumption rates. Showers had stopped in the hospital on April 15, and the principal source of additional water for the entire tunnel complex was a well near the east portal served by a pump operated by a coughing diesel motor.

Corregidor still had plenty of water in the ground; the trick was to get it out. Most of the wells had auxiliary pumps and continued to supply water, although the Fort Mills power plant had been inoperative since the first week in April. But by May 5 the supply of diesel oil was sufficient for only another week of pumping operations.

Feeding the men outside the tunnels had become as difficult as getting them water. The marines, their attached troops, and the crews of the antiaircraft and roving gun batteries ate frugally twice a day, once shortly after dark when the shelling slackened, and again before dawn in the morning. Rice, bolstered by a little canned salmon and a few tidbits, was the ration. As Colonel Bunker, a dedicated meat-and-potatoes man, noted, "This rice diet fills you *temporarily* but it doesn't stick to your ribs." Some had less even than that. A section of Battery Mobile near Kindley Field had one can of tomatoes apiece per man in a thirty-six-hour period, supplemented by a monkey or two they found and killed.

By May 5 virtually all of the naval vessels were out of commission . . . the strafers had done her in. Other smaller craft were immobilized by a lack of bunker oil, the one major supply item to run out completely during the campaign. General Moore feared that when the Japanese landed he might get no warning and was reduced to positioning two small craft six hundred yards offshore of the east and west ends of the island to signal with a vertical sweep of their searchlights when the enemy came. "Damn that full moon!" he exclaimed on the evening of May 5 to Colonel Braly, his operations officer, "they'll probably come tonight." The night before, General Wainwright had estimated to General Marshall in Washington that if the Japanese landed, his chances of beating them off were "somewhat less than even."

A few lucky men and women had left the Rock. On April 29 two PBY's from Australia had glided in during darkness and alighted in the bay between Corregidor and Fort Hughes. To drown out their engines the crews of several naval launches had operated their motors without mufflers, making a terrific racket. With the Japanese unsuspecting, the PBY's took off safely with fifty passengers, including radio intercept specialists General MacArthur had specifically asked for, and several nurses. One made it to Australia, but the other hit a log on Lake Lanao on Mindanao, its staging point, and was disabled. The water runway ordinarily used had come under shell fire and the PBY's were forced into swamps. The damaged PBY later got away but its passengers eventually fell into Japanese hands.

The last submarine, the *Spearfish*, slipped in on the night of May 3 through a new passage swept in the Navy's contact mine field between Corregidor and the Cavite shore. It carried out fourteen more nurses, as many as could be accommodated, in addition to a few other carefully selected personnel. Colonel Irwin, General Wainwright's operations officer, and Colonel Hoyle, who had commanded the 45th Infantry on Bataan, went out, as did Colonel Jenks, the USFIP finance officer, Colonel Hill, the Inspector General, and Colonel Savage, the air officer. All these men held locked within themselves and within the records that accompanied them experience too precious to lose. General Moore offered Colonel Louis J. Bowler a berth on the sub, but the gentlemanly adjutant demurred. "No," he said, "send a nurse."

A complete roster of those still alive went, along with a list of recent promotions. In this way "Skinny" Wainwright and George Moore did their best for their men. Had promotion orders not gone, many would not have received credit, and the allotments of their dependents through three long years of captivity would have been substantially less.

What kept those going who stayed behind? The men themselves wondered. Considering the terrific punishment the Rock was taking and the weariness of the exposed units, cases of combat fatigue were surprisingly few. Colonel Wibb E. Cooper, the chief surgeon, and his fellow medical officers believed that this was because there was no escape from reality , no place to hide. What is more surprising is that morale held up adequately, although a decline became noticeable in the last few days when even the most sanguine finally realized that help would not come.

The combat leaders, commissioned and noncommissioned, were professional soldiers. War was their business, and so long as they could fight they would fight. Their men were for the most part volunteers, in the Philippines because they had elected to be. They took fierce pride in unit and country. The majority of the men on Corregidor did not then and do not now believe their sacrifice was in vain. Many remain certain that their stand saved Australia from Japanese invasion and was therefore militarily worth it. But they paid heavily in blood; by May 5 the casualty figure stood at about a thousand killed and wounded since the war began, and the worst was to come.

[That day] the Japanese took all four of the Fortified Islands of Manila Bay under heavy fire, concentrating most of the day on the batteries, probably as a deception measure. Planes roared constantly overhead at low altitudes without reply from the antiaircraft guns. Nevertheless, at General Wainwright's command, George Moore at 12:30 P.M. ordered Paul Bunker to fire a co-ordinated counterbattery with everything he had left. Crofton (14-inch gun) on Frank, Wilson (14-inch turret) on Drum, and Way (one 12-inch mortar), Cheney (one 12-inch gun), Wheeler (one 12-inch gun), and roving batteries Wright, Rose, and Gulick, all on Corregidor, roared defiance simultaneously, exploding three ammunition dumps and silencing several Japanese batteries, at least temporarily. A pinprick this was, a fine gesture of defiance, by men who knew their hours of freedom were numbered.

Air raid number 300 sounded at 2:47 P.M. with Fort Hughes the target. Dropping very low, the Japanese pilots were accurate, filling Craighill's mortar pits with debris and inflicting several casualties. By 6:30 P.M. all the harbor forts were being pounded "terrifically," and an ominous change had taken place in the fire directed at Corregidor. The Japanese had begun to shell the tail and beaches of the north shore, obviously in a pre-invasion bombardment. At 9:00 P.M. Colonel Howard ordered the beach defenses manned, the shelling having grown more intense rather than slackening, as it usually did after nightfall. The tip-off came at about 9:30 from the sound locators of the 60th's searchlight units. Amid the din of bursting shells their great mechanical ears picked up the unmistakable sound of many landing barges warming up in the vicinity of Limay. The operators flashed the word to the air defense headquarters, and from there Colonel Chase relayed it to H Station, General Moore's command post. At 10:30 Moore warned Colonel Howard, "Enemy landing attack indicated." The issue now was joined; the Japanese soon would be on their way.

※　※　※　※

BY APRIL 1 HOMMA WAS READY FOR HIS FINAL THRUST. With 14th Army, reinforced, and crack divisions from China and the Malay, he opened the drive April 3 with heavy bombers and multiple batteries of 240-millemeter howitzers, relentlessly keeping the pressure on for a continuous week. By the seventh the ragtag "Battling Bastards" under Wainwright (now lieutenant general and commander of all armed forces in the Philippines) were finished. Major General Edward P. King, his second, ordered his beleaguered troops to destroy all tanks and arms rather than risk seizure by the enemy. Immediately the American-Filipino troops blew up munitions and fuel dumps in Mariveles Harbor, and the explosions were so severe it sounded like an earthquake to those on Corregidor. An observer wrote: "The southern end of Bataan was a huge conflagration which resembled more than anything else a volcano in violent eruption . . . white-hot pieces of metal from exploded shells flared in great numbers and charged off on crazy courses much as a rocket which has run wild on the ground." Out of this holocaust emerged battered and weary troops—all who could walk or crawl. Many died in the waters of Manila Bay which were raked by enemy artillery. It was all over. The Japanese made no offer of surrender terms, merely unconditional surrender of 75,000 troops. King signed.

Homma now could taste the final victory, and from mid-April he subjected the fortress to a merciless pounding by no less than 9 bombing squadrons and 37 batteries (guns ranging from 75 to 240 millimeter) emplaced on Bataan. Homma's plan was to lead the attack with his 61st Infantry Regiment followed by tanks, artillery and mortar units. He chose the moonlit night of May 5 for landings.

The defenders of Corregidor waited . . . and the Japanese came exactly as anticipated. Hanson W. Baldwin, retired military editor and analyst of *The New York Times,* brilliantly recounts the defense on the beaches and at Water Tank Hill. A graduate of the Naval Academy and a Pulitzer Prize winner, Baldwin is the author of many authoritative books and articles about the armed services. The following excerpt is from his four-part series written for the *Marine Corps Gazette,* an unadorned account of the last fight of Howard's 4th Regiment.

·12· LAST STAND OF THE 4TH MARINES

HANSON W. BALDWIN

The enemy landed shortly after 11 P.M. (one hour before the moon rose) near North Point on the low tail of the island. Corregidor's topography favored a landing on the north shore, which faced Bataan, two miles away. There are good landing beaches around North Point and Cavalry Point, and the shore line curves to the southeast. The south shore's rocky cliffs rise almost straight up from narrow rocky beaches, and then curve toward the tadpole-shaped end of the island—Hooker Point.

"On the high ground between the shores," Lieutenant (now Lieutenant Colonel) Jenkins writes, "there was a small landing field—(Kindley Field) and on the ridge extending westward from the airfield there were several 3-inch AA batteries (among them Battery Denver) . . .

"The 1st Battalion was responsible for everything east of Malinta, a shore line of at least 10,000 yards." Company A with some help from Headquarters Company held the entire North shore from Malinta to Hooker Point; Company B had the South shore, and Company D tried to cover both shores with its mortars and machine guns.

On the Company A front, the 3d Platoon held the beach from North Point to the end of the island; the 2d Platoon from Cavalry Point to North Point, and the 1st Platoon took over the sector from Infantry Point to Cavalry Point.

Captain Lewis H. Pickup, an officer who had relieved Major Lang (killed) as CO of Company A, had just finished a partial inspection of his company positions and was eating supper with Marine Gunner Harold M. Ferrell when the enemy came in. The landing boats approached in echelon on the heels of the barrage; the marines manned their guns and waited. The boats in groups approached and then those directly in front of the company CP veered off and lay to. But further to the east, the enemy had made it, filtering through a hole in the thin defenses—then extending the breach and driving on over his dead. Not without losses; some of the barges were sunk and at least one of the landings was turned back. The remaining guns on the outlying islands—answering the call for help from Corregidor—blasted Jap troops and boat concentrations at Cabcaben on Bataan. Tracers flicked over North Point, Infantry Point, Artillery Point, and all the low tail of the island, and shell splashes rose white and shining from the dark waters of the North Channel.

But the enemy came on. Five or six landing boats grated on the beach between Cavalry Point and North Point and the enemy was on Corregidor. Captain Pickup sent Ferrell to Battery Denver (Army AA battery in the center of the island) to see if the flank of Company A was covered. The personnel of Battery Denver were to depress their AA guns and hold their battery position in the center of the island, while Companies A and B filled in the flanks and held a line across the island.

". . . Still bewildered that they could have possibly gotten ashore, (I) was in the battery (Denver) position," Ferrell reported, "when I heard voices, not American.

"Corporal O. O. Morris crept close enough to observe; the place seemed to have Japs all over it digging in."

Battery Denver had pulled back and A and B company's flanks were wide open. Ferrell didn't know it, but the first sergeant of Battery Denver had been killed by artillery fire and his men—without a leader

—had gone to pieces. The Japs got through the hole and in behind a platoon of Company A which was manning beach defense positions. It was a critical moment—a hole in the center of the line—and more Jap landings imminent at Artillery Point and elsewhere. The marines had no air support, virtually no artillery, and they were galled and raddled by an intense bombardment, which "walked" back and forth across their positions.

Lieutenant Mason F. Chronister organized a local counterattack. Gunnery Sergeant Dudley held up the trails of a 37 millimeter gun so it could be depressed enough to fire down the cliffs at Jap landing boats. Platoon Sergeant "Tex" Haynes met the enemy head on near his beach defense position. He emptied two pistols into their midst, grabbed up the rifle of a dead buddy, and then cradled a .30 caliber machine gun in his arms (the mount had been wrecked by shell fire) and fired two belts at the enemy until a grenade left him terribly wounded and one eye gone—there at his post.

Ferrell got some of his men—whose guns were out—pushed them on the hogback in the center of the island "to prevent the enemy from coming down on the backs of the men on the beaches."

Word got back to the 1st Battalion CP by runner—all other communications were out, and the battalion adjutant, Captain Clark, arrived on the double. Captain Noel O. Castle, CO of Company D, grabbed some D Company and Headquarters men and probed out toward that vital Battery Denver position. He pushed the Japs back— but not far enough—and he lost his life in the act of doing it.

Things were happening all over the eastern part of the island now and happening fast. The Jap artillery made the night hideous and slowed greatly the bringing up of reserves. The men on the hogback were reaching out toward each other in the dark, and down on the beaches some of the A Company platoons began to realize they were flanked. First Lieutenant (now Lieutenant Colonel) William Frederick Harris, who had a platoon of A Company, pulled his platoon off the beach and went into a position of all-around defense. The Japs—in the center—pushed 500 yards past him toward the west, and scattered outfits of Companies A and B were cut off and isolated from each other and from mutual support.

Captain Clark called upon Ferrell for mortar fire on the ridge, where the Japs still held what had been Battery Denver. Ferrell gave him 20 rounds and was told to cease firing "since the fire was too close to troops on either side . . .

"The mortars used were converted Stokes without sights, and an occasional round seemed to go astray . . ."

Back at Regimental Headquarters in Malinta Tunnel communications were bad; the wire to battalion was in and out; intermittent field radio, runners, and patrols were the sources of information. Colonel Howard, and Colonel Donald Curtis, his exec, and their staff—and General Moore, commander of the fortified islands—knew only that the Japs were ashore—perhaps 500 or 600 of them in the eastern end of the island. About midnight, they got a clearer picture; that hogback in the center was the key; at all costs the Japs must be kept clear of Malinta Hill. They ordered the reserves—at 11:45 A.M. Major Schaeffer's desperate platoons formed around the cadre of the headquarters and service company; and at 12:15 A.M. May 6, when Captain Castle's counterattack had been held—Major Williams joined with his blue-jackets from the USS *Canopus.*

It was time. The 2d and 3d Battalions were pinned down to their beach defense positions by the threat of another Jap landing, and the platoons of the 1st Battalion that were not engaged were repelling landings or enduring intensive Jap artillery. Lieutenant Jenkins' 2d Platoon, Company A (with some of its positions on Malinta Hill), took heavy casualties. Reserve squads furnished replacements but before the night was old there were more casualties than there were replacements.

"One squad leader came to me (Jenkins) and reported that he had two men left in his squad."

Major Schaeffer took his headquarters group into the Navy tunnel under Malinta.

Major Williams' 4th Battalion moved down to Malinta Tunnel about 0030. The men were loaded down with hand grenades and ammunition but they moved silently in two single-file columns on either side of the South Shore Road from their bivouac area down through Middleside—which was under desultory enemy shell fire—and then across the low ground of "Bottomside." The battalion was held up by an artillery barrage for about 15 minutes just before reaching "Bottomside." The silent men, moving out in the last forlorn hope passed through a "scene of utter desolation—thousands of shellholes, wrecked buildings, upturned automobiles," and entered the west entrance to Malinta Tunnel.

"Inside it was hot," Lieutenant (now Captain) Brooks recalls, "terribly hot, and the ventilation was so bad that we could hardly breathe."

Battalion Headquarters was set up in the eastern end of the tunnel near Lieutenant Colonel Beecher's 1st Battalion CP and after a company officer conference, the battalion prepared to file out of the tunnel to the attack.

It was to move out upon a confused and confusing battlefield.

Exactly what happened that night on the shell-shattered eastern slopes of Corregidor may never be known in full detail for many of the men who could tell are dead. And even those who live saw only segments of action; the fighting was inchoate, wild, vicious; the risen moon only served to confound confusion. Its light shone down on a battlefield after Goya, the bodies of the dead and wounded were shadowed by the torn trunks of uprooted trees.

The Jap landing and penetration through the Battery Denver position had split up elements of A and B Companies, and some were isolated behind the Jap lines in the Kindley Field area and to the east. The Japs had infiltrated our lines and a few of them had penetrated in the darkness up toward Malinta. American units were behind the Jap lines; Jap units were behind ours. It was a fire and grenade fight with the main lines only thirty yards apart; it was a barroom brawl and devil take the hindmost. So closely interwoven were the combatants in the darkness that when the Japs called for an artillery barrage, it bracketed both sides; the little yellow men had enough and sent up a rocket to halt their guns.

While the scrapping was going on for the hogback, the Jap barges, stuttering away in the North Channel like a fleet of B-17's, were coming in toward other beaches. Five or six of them came in toward Harris's outflanked men at Cavalry Point. The marines had only one .30 and one .50 caliber to meet them; they had lost six .30 caliber machine guns to Jap shells, and the emplacement of their single 37 millimeter had been damaged. But the marines were exultant. For four months they had been on the receiving end; now they had a chance to dish it out. They dropped hand grenades and 30-pound fragmentation bombs down on the beaches; they let the barges have it with point-blank fire. Many sons of Nippon never saw Fujiyama again.

There were other brushes along the north shore. One of the 75s that was still functioning (sited far beyond the main action) took some Jap landing craft under fire and sank a neat number of them. At dawn, the Japs approached the North Dock area, where a cable barrier and a string of twenty-one 500-pound TNT sea mines were awaiting them, but Corregidor's remaining artillery opened up and drove them off.

But the Japs still clung to the hogback reaching westward toward Malinta from Kindley Field and they had inched forward in the dark hours, leaving behind them isolated units of still fighting marines.

So Major Williams and his composite battalion smashed out in counterattack at 5 A.M.—in the last effort.

They moved out from Malinta—this last vain hope—in platoon columns—Companies Q, R, S, and T in that order. Schaeffer's men held the right flank, and S Company filled in a gap on the left. Scattered along the line were the decimated units of Companies A and B and the 1st Battalion reserve units—those of them that were not cut off behind the Jap lines. Captain Herman Hauck, USA, and some 60 men of a Coast Artillery battery were sent in on the left flank of S Company about 8 A.M. to stop some Japs infiltrating along the beach.

Schaeffer's outfit got its orders from Colonel Beecher, 1st Battalion commander, in Malinta Tunnel, while "the company and platoon commanders supervised the distribution of additional hand grenades and extra magazines for our Lewis machine guns.

"While awaiting the return of Major Schaeffer," Quartermaster Clerk F. W. Ferguson, CO of the 1st Platoon, Company O, recorded, "we also obtained the services of some volunteers to act as ammunition carriers . . .

"These men were marines and sailors on duty at Queen Tunnel ('Navy' Tunnel, the CP for all Naval and Marine Corps activities on the island) who should be commended for volunteering for this hazardous duty when they were neither officially nor morally obligated to do so. I am sorry that in the hustle and bustle of getting things done I was unable to obtain the names of these men. Some of them were to die a very few minutes later.

"Major Schaeffer soon returned with his orders and passed them on to the company and platoon commanders. We were to move out as quickly as possible and dislodge the enemy who had gotten ashore and so far as was known would be encountered near the landing field. P Company was to proceed ahead with D Company following and were to deploy when we contacted the enemy. P Company to the left and O Company to the right. My platoon was to deploy so as to contact P Company on my left and my right resting on the road that ran from Malinta to the eastern end of the island.

"The 3d Platoon under Quartermaster Sergeant John H. Haskins was to deploy to my right and the 2d Platoon was to be the company support taking position to the rear of the 1st Platoon.

"We had hardly cleared Malinta Tunnel before we observed some shadowy forms up on the ridge to our left. A couple of men took a quick shot or two at the forms but quickly learned their mistake when sulphurous oaths came back from the forms on the ridge. No Japs could talk like that. They were men from P Company who were attempting to dig out someone who had fired on them from that ridge.

"I saw a couple of white flares go up some distance ahead of us. Word was passed to the men to keep their eyes open for seeking immediate shelter for I suspected that the flares were a Jap signal for artillery support. My estimate was not wrong for almost immediately all hell broke loose. Although artillery barrages and bombings had become almost commonplace to us after having lived on Corregidor for over four months I must admit that this particular barrage was the most severe and concentrated I had ever come under. Since the Japanese had been holding 'target practice' for months with planes spotting for them they had their guns registered on every road right to the inch and they really gave us a good beating for what seemed a very long time but which probably did not last over 15 minutes.

"As soon as the barrage had lifted I got a report from all squad leaders and learned that I had only lost eight men. We immediately resumed our move to the east but we soon came under heavy enemy machine-gun fire being directed from a hill ahead of us on which we knew Battery Denver had been emplaced the last time we made a reconnaissance to that part of the Island. As previously ordered I deployed my platoon straight to the front with my right resting on the road and ordered the men on the left to extend their lines as far as possible to tie up with P Company. Sergeant Haskins' 3d Platoon was expected to deploy to my right down the southern slope and I presumed Snelling's (Quartermaster Clerk Herman L. Snelling) platoon (the 3d) was in my rear for support.

"We found the Japs already firmly set up within the heavily sandbagged gun positions that Battery Denver had formerly occupied. The Japs seemed to have a machine gun or other automatic weapon every few yards and so placed as to offer sympathetic support. We attempted to assault these positions three times and each time managed to advance a few yards but at heavy cost. Not hearing any firing on my right I investigated and found my right wide open. The only thing I could do was to place one automatic rifle and one Lewis machine gun in a position where they could cover the road toward the Jap lines and could also have a field of fire down the southern slopes on my right.

"A little later I learned why Haskin's platoon was not deployed to my right. The answer was simple. All but about five of his men had been killed or wounded when caught in the barrage just after leaving Malinta Tunnel. He came up with what he had left and reinforced my position. Since I still had no report to the effect that my left had contacted P Company I ordered Haskins to take his men and extend my line to the left and report when and if contact was established with P Company. Then Warrant Officer Snelling came up. He had four men left in his platoon to survive the Jap barrage that we had been caught in and Captain Robert Chambers, Jr. (CO of Company O) had decided to send his remaining men to me knowing the losses I had suffered in the barrage and on my three assault attempts. I realized I was in a precarious position as long as both my flanks were open so I sent Snelling's four men plus a few other stragglers from other units to the left. Soon word came back that P Company had been joined. My relief was great but not for long. Things were happening too fast for that. In one of our short gains up the hill we had retaken what was left of a tin shack. There was only one open end of this shack and that was toward the Jap positions. While shouting some orders I felt a stinging sensation in my right arm and at the same time the man on my left dropped mortally wounded. Since the Jap machine guns ahead of us were firing at us at the moment, I assumed I had been nipped by one of them. However, in the first faint light of dawn one of my men was peeping through one of the holes in the tin shack and was surprised to see two Japs lying inside the shack and they were breathing. They had been in there all night having been caught there when we advanced and had been unable to get back to their own lines. They would wait until their own machine guns would open fire then these Japs would fire through the walls of the shack by pointing their rifles by a sense of feel so to speak while peeping out through another bullet hole in the shack. In this way we could not see the flash from the muzzle of their rifles. In this way they had picked off several of my men during the night and had almost done the same thing to me. After they were spotted one of our automatic riflemen did a nice job of finishing their careers as loyal soldiers for His Imperial Majesty.

"Since the Japs had their line of resistance tied in with the old Battery Denver gun positions in which they had placed several machine guns I was in a quandary as to what to do. Frontal assault had proven foolish and the heaviest thing I had in the line of weapons were automatic rifles, Lewis machine guns, and hand grenades. Since the Jap and American lines had been no more than about 30 yards apart all night we had tried to rout them with hand grenades but the trees that had been felled by shell fire interfered with us in the use of grenades. However, Quartermaster Sergeant John H. Haskins and Sergeant Major Thomas F. Sweeney during the night had climbed to the top of an old water tower and were a little more successful from their vantage point. Haskins was later killed in attempting to reclimb the water tower to take some more grenades up to Sweeney. Sergeant Major Sweeney was also later killed atop the tank. They were very close friends in life and it was most fitting that they should go out together."

Schaeffer's outfit had shot its bolt; the deadly Jap barrage had bled it white.

But Major Williams' 4th Battalion, which followed Schaeffer's outfit through Malinta and swung into the attack on the left flank of Companies O and P, drove doggedly ahead.

The terrific Jap barrage, enfilading our positions from Bataan, harried the attackers and the enemy machine gun positions were well sited. Two guns—one in the ruins of a powder magazine, Carl E. Downing, acting sergeant major of the 4th Battalion reported, and the other to the right of a road leading to the North Point OP held up the advance, but by 0600 they had been knocked out. The line moved on, rooting out determined enemy resistance. But not for long. Sniper and machine-gun positions again bogged down the counterattack. Somebody—perhaps Sergeant Major Sweeney and

Quartermaster Sergeant Haskins, who Warrant Officer Ferguson mentioned—wiped out the snipers. These two old-timers—marines from their tough jaws to their big feet—apparently performed prodigies that last day of their lives, but the story of it—like the story of all that time—is confused and lost. But that they climbed the stone water tower under fire is certain—and one of them was wounded doing it. From the tower top they lobbed grenades into the Jap lines—and one of them apparently supplied the other with grenades—climbing up and down the tower—several times. One of them died at the bottom of the tower; at long last, the Japs got his friend on top.

"Long afterward," Lieutenant (now Captain) Brooks reported, "American prisoners of war working on Corregidor found his body on top of the tower. He was one of the great unsung heroes of the war. Also, long afterwards the Japs showed us a fictitious Japanese moving picture of the fall of Corregidor in which they showed a Japanese captain climb to the top of the same water tower and kill hundreds of Americans with hand grenades, which is a good example of the inaccuracy of their propaganda. At least they paid tribute to our sergeant by trying to claim his heroic act as their own."

The officers were an inspiration and example. Major Williams was everywhere, rifle and grenades in hand; he personally aided in wiping out many nests of resistance. Lieutenant Bethel B. Otter, USN, CO of Company T, and Ensign Lloyd, USNR, a company officer, were both killed in leading an attempt to wipe out a machine gun nest.

First Lieutenant Otis Edward Saalman together with Captain Harold Dalness, both of the Army, and a small hastily organized party silenced a Jap automatic rifle, located in the basement of a ruined structure. Corporal Scott, 4th Battalion clerk, voluntarily accompanied the battalion into action, and, acting as a "medic" dashed out several times in the face of heavy fire to carry wounded men to safety.

"Boatswain Harold Parks, USN, Carpenter Talmadge Smithey, USN; Lieutenant Charles P. Brooks, USN; Captain Calvin Chunn, USA; Captain Paul C. Moore, USA; Lieutenant Edward N. Little, USN; Ensign Andrew W. Long, USN; Sergeants Kenneth W. Mize, Carl Downing, Wardlow, McCormick, and Scott of the U. S. Marines . . . all were conducting themselves as soldiers and veterans with definite purpose in mind and a definite mission to accomplish . . ."

Sergeant Dennis, assigned a safe Headquarters job in Malinta, got permission to leave his paper job for an hour, and organized a voluntary patrol of clerks, typists, and telephone men. Dennis and his men got one machine gun and two snipers; then reported his return, and said: "I'm sorry I'm late, sir; it took me longer than I expected."

Thus, led by such men the line moved on; it moved in blood and anguish—and soon its progress slowed. The price was too high. The Jap shells were walking back and forth across our line; dive-bombers, now the day had risen over smoking wreckage of a fort, were leisurely pin-pointing their objectives. Machine guns, mortars, light artillery had been landed; the enemy came on in the thousands. For dead marines there were no replacements; behind the Japs were 250,000 more on Bataan. The hospital laterals of Malinta were filled with the wounded, and they lay now in the open beneath the shells.

The 4th Battalion and Major Schaeffer's outfit had been riddled. Otier and Lloyd were dead; Brook of the Navy, with a terrible leg wound, lay on the amputation table in Malinta; Captain Calvin Chunn of the Army, S-2 of the battalion, was wounded in the stomach; Lieutenant Edward N. Little, USN, CO of S Company, had a chest wound, and Ensign Andrew W. Long, USNR, was wounded in the arm. At least 90 of the men were dead; others wounded. And still the Japs came on.

Quartermaster Clerk Ferguson, who had gone out of Malinta as a platoon commander in Schaeffer's outfit, had found himself, as the full light of the tropic morning blazed down on the battlefield, attacking two Jap gun positions with one unwounded man—Corporal Alvin E. Steward of the 803d Army Engineers. The two men had picked off 20 Japs but the inevitable happened: Ferguson took two bullets in the face—("the first . . . had struck the cheek bone and had laid the right side of my face open to such an extent that some of the men thought part of my face had been shot away"). Ferguson staggered back on limp legs to Malinta, carrying with him to Colonel Howard, about 8:30 A.M. on 6 May 1942, Schaeffer's request for additional reinforcements.

But there were no more.

All reserves had been committed. Harris's platoon, cut off behind the Jap lines, had managed, when the counterattack came, to rejoin our own forces, but all the 1st Battalion's battered reserves had been fighting for hours; Schaeffer's out and Williams' 4th Battalion were spent and virtually shattered as fighting outfits, and Hauck's coast artillery men, backed by every gunner that could be scraped up, were pitifully few in number.

"In the daylight," Lieutenant Jenkins reported, "our sector had a new and grimly fantastic appearance. Where there had once been trees there were now tangled masses of shattered stumps and shell craters. Our barbed wire was wrecked. The foxhole in which we had stored our reserve rations was now a shell hole and the precious food was splattered in all directions. The shells were still pounding us fast and furiously."

The counterattack was spent—and still the Japs landed.

I The First Six Months: Wake to Midway

Wake's last stand. (From a painting by Albert Henning)

The graveyard at the end of the line for planes of VMF 211 on Wake. These are the remains of the Grumman Wildcats which defended the atoll until they could fly no more against an overpowering foe.

占領

開戦と共に、わが航空部隊が殖爆のウェーキ島めざし二十一日夜牛、特設陸戦隊は、荒れ狂ふ南海の怒濤を冒して果敢な敵前上陸を敢行し翌日これを占領、その名も大鳥島と改稱す。

Japanese flag-raising on Wake. (Photo taken from a Japanese picture book)

Japanese troops paying homage to a memorial erected to Unit Commander Uchida, killed in the Wake landing.

Three officers of the gallant garrison which defended Corregidor Island for weeks before its fall to the Japanese inspect defense positions during a respite from enemy attacks. Left to right: Lieutenant Colonel John P. Adams; Colonel Samuel L. Howard, Commander of the Marines on the Island; and Major General F. Moore, United States Army.

Lieutenant Colonel Herman Anderson, USMC, and staff, 2nd Battalion, Fourth Marines.

During a lull in the Japanese attacks on Corregidor these Marines laid aside their arms, sat back in their chairs, and read magazines.

Marines captured in the Philippines before the start of the infamous Death March from Bataan to Cabanatuan Prison Camp. (A Japanese photo)

Japanese attack on Midway Island, June 4–6, 1942.

Fresh Marines arriving before the decisive battle.

Attack plane on the way in.

In the aftermath of a Japanese attack—a damaged F4F Marine fighter.

U.S. attack on Wake Island, October 5–6, 1943, showing sunken Japanese freighter.

The enemy, as the morning drew on was still on the hogback—though he had yielded ground. That hole in the Battery Denver position had been the payoff.

"We needed mortars to jar their MGs loose," 1st Lieutenant William F. Hogaboom, CO of Company P, reported, and there were no mortars save the modified Stokes without sights.

"Sometime between 10:00 and 11:00 (my watch went out of action leaving me in doubt about time from dawn on) we noticed the right flank beginning to fall back in disorder," Hogaboom said. "I detected Major Williams attempting to stop the withdrawal and ran over to find out from him the cause. He told me that tanks had been brought into action and there were no antitank weapons available to stop them. (Acting Sergeant Major Carl E. Downing of the 4th Battalion had observed two tanks coming ashore from landing barges to the east of North Point about 10:45.) By then is was too late to reorganize the line previously held. The Major ordered a general retreat to the concrete trenches just east of Malinta Hill (the planned final defense line). I passed the word on down into the ravine. Men came streaming out, all dazed by the intense action but indicating resentment of the unexplained order to fall back. Orderly action was impossible. The area was being swept by machine-gun fire and by artillery fire. We had to pass through two 240 millimeter barrages to reach the road cut near the trenches. It was each man for himself. Casualties were heavy. Those of us who reached what had been the concrete trenches before the 240s worked them over prepared to set up a defensive line. Major Williams went to Malinta Tunnel to report the situation and obtain reinforcements. (There were none.) Lieutenant Harris (of Company A) joined me in the trench I had occupied with a couple of dozen of available men . . ."

It was to have been the final stand, but even as they occupied the battered position someone noticed a Japanese sniper had infiltrated on to the heights of Malinta behind them . . . heavy bombers with the meat ball insignia on their wings were filing leisurely across the sky; divebombers roaring to within a few hundred feet of the blasted hills. There was no answer, save the crack of marine rifles and the occasional staccato chatter of a Lewis gun as it fired a burst toward the enemy. Corregidor was all but silenced, and the last messages started to go out, from those dusty, hot and bomb-shaken tunnels of Malinta.

From the Navy—Captain K. M. Hoeffel: "One hundred and seventy-three officers and 2,317 men of the Navy reaffirm their loyalty and devotion to country, families and friends . . ."

From the Army—Sergeant Irving Strobing sending while the tunnel shook and the lights flickered and the sweat dropped from the sergeant's brow: ". . . We've got about one hour twenty minutes before . . . (Pause)

"We may have to give up by noon, we don't know yet. They are throwing men and shells at us and we may not be able to stand it. They have been shelling us faster than you can count . . ."

Back near the East entrance to Malinta Schaeffer and Williams and Beecher were looking for replacements and antitank guns and ammunition and water . . . and food, and men, just fighting men . . .

But Colonel Curtis told them it was no use. Wainwright had ordered surrender.

(At his headquarters on Bataan, Lieutenant General Masaharu Homma, commanding the Japanese Fourteenth Army, was moaning as he listened to reports of the fighting: "My God, I have failed in the assault!")

At 10:30 Regimental Headquarters had gotten the order from General Moore:

"Execute Pontiac; execute Pontiac."

It was the code name for that last bitter order which in their hearts they long had known would someday come. It was surrender as of twelve, noon, 6 May 1942.

It was Wainwright's decision but Colonel Howard agreed with it and so did "Don" Curtis, the able exec, who was a tower of strength until the end.

"All general reserves having been committed, the enemy was making additional landings, ammunition in East sector was practically exhausted and it was impossible to get any into the area. Practically all of our guns were destroyed and it became only a question of a few hours before our lines would be overrun," Colonel Howard reported.

The Jap tanks were within a few hundred yards of Malinta Tunnel and in its laterals were 150 nurses, more than 1,000 wounded. MacArthur had said to hold until he returned, but his return was still three long years and 90,000 lives away . . .

And so the messages went out. Strobing:

"We've got about 55 minutes and I feel sick at my stomach. I am really low down. They are around now smashing rifles. They bring in the wounded every minute. We will be waiting for you guys to help. This is the only thing I guess that can be done. General Wainwright is a right guy and we are willing to go on for him, but shells were dropping all night, faster than hell. Damage terrific. Too much for guys to take . . ."

At the Regimental Headquarters in the Navy tunnel Colonel Howard put his face in his hands and frankly wept.

"My God," he said to Colonel Curtis, "and I had to be the first Marine officer ever to surrender a regiment."

Colonel Curtis ordered Captain R. B. Moore, regimental adjutant, to burn the regimental and national colors. Captain Moore came back with a tear-streaked face, and all about him Filipinos were crying openly and unashamed.

The psychological and emotional tragedy of surrender, especially to a Corps with the pride of the Marines, is wracking. Particularly to the 2d and 3d Battalions defending the beaches of the central and western parts of the island, surrender was bitter anticlimax. For months, these men with the stoicism born of discipline, had been taking it, had seen some of their comrades blown to bits, had watched the gradual destruction of the fortress of Corregidor. At last the long siege was ended; at last, when the Japs landed, these men who had been taking it would have a chance to dish it out.

But it was not to be. The Japs landed in the 1st Battalion area, but the threats of new landings were sufficient to immobilize and pin down to their beach defense positions the men of the 2d and 3d Battalions. They scarcely fired a shot. Keyed up to great effort, the sudden ending of months of hardship left them dull with fatigue, blank with depression, weighed down by that awful leaden feeling of the mind and the heart and the stomach which the word "Surrender" means. To some, no doubt, the order was divine relief; they had done their best and this hell on earth that had been Corregidor these weeks past was unendurable.

But, as they waited for their last "zero" hour, they never forgot they were marines. All over the island dumps of ammunition and equipment were destroyed by the defenders; the few remaining guns were smashed; even rifle bolts were thrown into the bay. In the western and central parts of the island, where there were no Japs, the officers called their men together and made little talks.

Lieutenant Colonel William F. Prickett, then a captain and CO of Company I, said:

"I've lived pretty close with you men for the past five months and I've grown pretty fond of you all—and proud of you, too—mighty proud . . ."

He could not go on.

They washed—those who could—shaved, put on their cleanest uniforms and prepared to surrender with honor and with pride . . .

The 14-inch turrets of Fort Drum—the tiny "concrete battleship," which was a sub-post of Corregidor—were firing to within five minutes of the end. This was the one battery in all the fortified islands that was never out of action. Drum, on El Fraile Island, a pinpoint at the entrance to Manila Bay, was hammered by at least 1,000 shells in the last day—but the guns still fired.

But it did no good.

At noon, the white flags of surrender blossomed from the CPs and the caves and foxholes.

(At noon, as the white flag moved out from Malinta, General Homma was pacing his headquarters on Bataan, worried by the "fog of battle." Jap losses in the first attack had been excessive, and he expected a heavy counterattack.)

But Corregidor was finished. And in the final hour, as throughout much of the siege, the marines bore the burden of responsibility. Let Lieutenant Colonel A. C. Shofner (then a captain) who later escaped from the Japs tell the story as he got it from Captain Clark, the principal actor in the tragedy:

"The final hour of Corregidor brought to the Marines the honor or dishonor of surrendering the island. When the inevitable decision of surrender came from General Wainwright it was a Marine officer, Captain Golland L. Clark, Jr. (died aboard Jap prison ship at Formosa), who was assigned the mission of offering surrender to the Japanese commanding officer, and expressing General Wainwright's desire to confer with Lieutenant General Homma regarding terms. Captain Clark's party consisted of a music, a flag bearer, carrying a piece of white sheeting on a pole, and an interpreter; all were marines except the interpreter.

"The party left from Malinta Tunnel and proceeded east, about 700 yards to the front lines; numerous times the group was forced to seek cover momentarily due to the heavy Jap artillery and mortar fire, but realizing the importance of the mission rapidly continued forward, Captain Clark in the lead.

"As the party passed the last Marine outpost the music sounded off and the flag bearer waved the white standard. The party marched erect across the fireswept no-man's land and, unusual as it may seem, the Japanese did not intentionally direct fire at the group although many ricochets fell nearby. At this time Captain Clark's thoughts turned back five years to a lecture at the Marine Officers Basic School, the conduct of a *parlementaire* at a surrender. At the time of the lecture he never dreamed that he would be sent on a surrender mission, but now he strained his memory for all the details of procedure in order to assure the safety of his party and the men of General Wainwright's command.

"The first Jap soldier located was very amazed at this group of four, and after much parley, the soldier conducted the party to his corporal and eventually, after much searching by the guides, Captain Clark reached the senior Japanese officer alive on the island, a lieutenant colonel. The Jap lieutenant colonel contacted high headquarters on Bataan and arrangements were made for General Wainwright to proceed to Bataan about three o'clock that afternoon—thus ended the story of Corregidor."

Almost—but not quite. The negotiations for surrender were difficult and protracted. Most of the marines, the remnants of the naval battalion, and the army troops were huddled in Malinta or to the west of it, waiting for the Japs to come to them. Firing was stopped, white flags displayed, the marines made no attempt to maintain an organized defense line across the island. But the Jap shelling and bombing continued for two days stopping sporadically only to be resumed.

And in the eastern part of the island isolated and cut-off remnants of the 1st Battalion and perhaps some sections of other outfits, kept fighting to the last. They had received no word of the surrender, so in one's or two's or three's by sections or squads, they fought and died. That afternoon, when the shells were still falling, doctors attached to the 4th Regiment—went out under white flags, searching for the wounded—and they heard, as they looked, the sound of intermittent small arms fire to the east. Sergeant Catlow who had barricaded himself in a position on the south shore, when his outfit was cut off, fought on until word of the surrender finally reached him. Two men holed up in a wedge in the cliffs and were still fighting at 3:30. And days later, prisoners cleaning up the island found an American body in a foxhole with seven Nips piled up in front of him.

. . . And so the 4th Regiment surrendered, its colors dipped in defeat. But never in shame . . .

And forever the Fourth will be "proud to bear the title of 'Corregidor Marine.'"

※   ※   ※   ※

MAY 7. THE ROUNDUP OF AMERICAN AND FILIPINO prisoners began. Private Fred Stolley of Battery Denver gathered up his pack and walked out to surrender. A prolific writer, Stolley retired from the Marine Corps as a chief warrant officer and joined the staff of the United States Naval Institute. We learn of the tragic aftermath when beaten men were glad simply to be alive.

·13· POST MORTEM

FRED STOLLEY

We shouldered our packs and started up out of the ravine. At the first turn in the road we paused and looked back at what had been our home for five months—it was a scene of utter desolation.

Jagged stumps of trees stood out against the torn land, and timbers lay crazily askew over boulders. A fine patina of gray coral dust lay over all to give it a sand-table look of unreality.

Only one spot remained undefiled and was still jungle-green in its surroundings. We had built our head in a sheltered arm of the ravine—it still stood staunch . . . ready to serve.

We looked at it. A week before I had gone to burn it out and John Rice, our assistant paymaster, assisted in the rite. We dumped a quarter of a million in bright blue and red peso notes down it, added a little fuel oil and a match and it burned out clean.

John had invited me to help myself before we deep-sixed the money but I didn't figurre pesos would be a medium of exchange where I was going.

Sloan had followed my look around and grinned at me.

"A man could have sat the war out there and never got a scratch."

We hunched-up again under our packs and got going.

"What in hell are we supposed to do when we meet them?" Sloan mused. "Shake hands . . . like after a tennis match and congratulate them on winning?"

"Beats me," I told him. "The manual ain't been written on this one yet."

We rounded a turn at the rim of the ravine and saw the gray-clad figures before us. One was holding a rising-sun flag mounted atop a long bamboo pole. Another, behind him, was standing at ease, smoking a cigarette. Others crouched on either side of the road with rifles trained on us. We halted awkwardly and for a few seconds there was silence.

Instinctiively, we both raised our right hands, palms out, in the gesture the white settler always used to affirm his peaceful intentions toward the Red Man.

Suddenly a thought flashed through my mind.

"Suppose this don't mean the same to them as it does to us? Suppose this means 'up your bucket' in Japanese . . ."

But I guess they had seen enough Western movies to understand. They guy smoking the cigarette waved us forward. You could tell he was in command.

Everybody relaxed and grinned when we moved forward.

"Jeezelbub," Sloan said out of the corner of his mouth, "you suppose they were scared of us?"

I didn't think so, I told him back.

When we got up to the group we could see the cigarette-smoker was a captain. We had seen enough Japanese soldiers in Shanghai to recognize the top N.C.O. and officer rank, so we saluted him. He returned the salute courteously and waved an enlisted man forward.

This character was carrying a yellow ruled tablet like they used back in the third grade at the old Grayland School in Chicago. He thrust the pad toward us and on it was printed in block letters, "How many men down there?"

I was trying to figure out how to tell them in terms of fingers when Sloan spoke.

"*Nee yako, go ju.*"

I grunted in surprise; the troops hissed their amazement. But the captain just laughed and threw down his cigarette.

"You speak *Nippon-Go?*" he said, in English.

Sloan barked back at him and then I remembered that Sloan had picked up a bit of the language when we were in Shanghai just before the war.

I was so snowed hearing Sloan speak Japanese, I didn't realize the captain was speaking English. It was soon apparent that neither one would win a public speaking prize in the other's language but they managed to understand one another.

"There are about 250 men down there," Sloan told him, "many wounded. It will take them some time to get up."

The captain grunted some orders and a squad detached themselves from the main body and headed down into the ravine. Then he pulled a map out of his haversack and showed it to us. It was the best map I had ever seen of Corregidor.

"His objective is Topside Barracks," Sloan said. "He wants us to guide them up there."

"Well," I told him, "I had planned to stop off at the Middleside N.C.O. Club for a few cold brews, but he being a stranger here and all . . ."

All of a sudden I stopped. Here I was running off the mouth just like it was Saturday night in Cicero. Holey shmoley . . . these guys might just want to serve me up as the main course at the victory banquet.

But Sloan was grinning again.

"Come on. We got to lead the way. He thinks the road might be booby trapped."

On the way up, I got a good look at the troops. These were the guys the Stateside magazines and newspapers had derided for years. They said they were bowlegged illiterates who couldn't see to shoot and had no stamina. As a matter of fact, we had always considered them rather comic-opera type characters ourselves when we saw them in Shanghai.

But here I could see the difference between the occupation-type troops who did their four-on, eight-off on the Garden Ridge and these case-hardened combat troops who had gone through Singapore like shrapnel through a tin horn.

They moved right. They were crisp. Their uniforms were beat up but their rank insignia and weapons were clean. All of a sudden, I knew this was going to be a long war.

Considering the fact that the island was supposed to be surrendered, there was a hell of a lot of shooting going on. Incoming from Bataan batteries was swooshing in over our heads and exploding topside, and dive-bombers were active all over the place. I stopped and talked it over with Sloan.

"Let 'em walk into it," he said. "Let 'em all get killed by their own party."

"Wait a cotton-pickin' minute," I told him. "Whose side are you on? Let's not forget who's grand marshal in this parade."

The captain came up and wanted to know why we had stopped. He pointed to one of his wrist watches and indicated he had a time schedule to meet.

In pantomime that would have won me first prize in any game of charades, I told him why I was getting nervous in his service. He slapped his knee and laughed. Then he pulled me over to the side of the road and pointed at Bataan. The observation balloon was up. He barked a command at the trooper with the flag on the long bamboo pole and the trooper waved the flag back and forth. A heliograph blinked thrice on the balloon and I could see everything was under control.

"Excelsior," I quoted. But no one seemed interested nor did they pause to admire my educated tomfoolery. As a mattter of fact, the captain's orderly kicked me. We went on up.

"What the hell kind of a deal is this?" I asked myself. "We are surrendered. We are P.O.Ws. We should be in a compound telling some stern interrogator we will only give them our name, rank and serial number. What in the kite-flying-sky were we doing *leading* the enemy's advance party?"

Then it hit me. I didn't *know* my serial number. In those days, before the war, you were required to know your rifle number but no one gave a tinker's dam about your serial number. I remembered one time going in to see Bozo Duncan, our First Sergeant. "What's my serial number?" I asked him.

"What you want to know for?" he growled.

"No reason, just though I'd like to know what it was," I said.

"If'n I think you should know what your serial number is I'll tell you," he snapped. "Now, get out of here."

I picked up my pace and moved up alongside Sloan.

"I'm in bad shape," I said.

He was concerned.

"Heat getting to you?"

"No . . . not that . . . it's just that I don't know my serial number."

"Oh for cripes sakes . . . get with it, will you?"

I could see he didn't understand the problem, but before I could argue it out, we broke out into the Topside parade ground. After five months of continual bombing and artillery fire, Topside didn't look like much. A week before, the Japanese had made a direct hit on a 12-inch mortar battery magazine in Cheney Ravine and one of the mortars was blown all the way up to the middle of the parade ground. Other than that, the place was looking pretty drab.

The group was bunched up with the Japanese all examining the wreck of the huge mortar. Then I heard the spine-tingling sound of a plane homing in. Before I could locate it I heard the shoo-shoo of his bombs and knew they were going to hit close. I dove into the dust.

"There's always that 10 percent who don't get the word . . ." I muttered as I waited for the blast.

But the bomber was about 10 feet off. This sounds like pretty good shooting except on Corregidor. If you miss Topside by 10 feet the bombs land on Middleside which is a good 500 feet below.

I lay there for a minute and looked around. Everyone else had hit the deck except Sloan. He had been standing there smoking a cigarette when the plane came in and he never moved. After the bombs hit, he continued to smoke and he looked at us carefully as we got up and sheepishly brushed the dust off.

The captain was mad. He kicked his orderly and he kicked the flag bearer. Then he gave Sloan a long cool look and walked off toward what was left of the barracks. We followed.

There was a semblance of a roof left over the veranda at one corner of the barracks. The captain pointed, spoke a few words, and the entire company turned to cleaning up the place. First, a chair was hauled out of the rubble and set in the shade of the porch. The captain took it and relaxed.

At this point, his orderly became a little Napoleon and indicated he wanted us to take part in the police detail.

"You are dog's blood," Sloan told him in Chinese.

This was an error in judgment on Sloan's part, I thought, because Little Napoleon evidently understood him. Many of the Japanese, having served in China, had good reason to become familiar with a Chinese curse.

Little Nap drew his bayonet and made a banzai rush at Sloan.

"This is it," I told myself.

But before I could get into the act Little Nap was sent sprawling in the dust. The captain stood over him, picked him up once, knocked him down again, then stood him at attention and whacked him smartly across the face a half dozen times as he punctuated each point of the reprimand.

A few moments later we sitting in rattan chairs in the shade alongside of the captain and as near as I could come to it, Sloan and the captain were talking about how it was in the "Old Corps."

"What service?" the captain asked.

"Dykesentai," Sloan told him.

We had both shed our flat tin hats and were wearing our field hats with emblem. The captain admired the emblems and then tied us in with Shanghai.

"Garden Bridge . . ." he chortled. "Broadway Mansions . . . Majestic Cafe . . . Little Club . . ."

We were in rapport. We three had enjoyed Shanghai duty.

About this time Little Nap tried to make some of his numbers back. He came rushing up with a gallon jug . . . it was cider vinegar. He pointed to the apples on the label and gave the captain a cup. I was about to open my big fat mouth when Sloan stopped me.

"Let him go . . . vinegar won't kill him."

Little Nap poured out a big fat dollop into the captain's cup and stood back grinning, waiting for the captain's approval. It came fast. The captain took a big slug, his eyes popped out and then he spat it all, right in Little Nap's face.

"*Kuda*," he shouted, "*damme da na!*"

Later I learned the English equivalent. But it loses something in the translation.

The next thing I knew, the captain had a forage party lined up and I was in charge. I didn't really understand everything he was saying to me but I got the general idea. He wanted to throw a company party that night and we'd better come back with the works. Sloan, I found out, was to be the guest of honor because he showed up the whole company that afternoon during the bombing.

Well, what could you do? I was an N.C.O., the captain put me in charge of a detail, so what could I do but take charge? But I'll tell you one thing, if some bookie had offered me one million to one the day before that I would be in charge of a Japanese working party, I wouldn't have taken a peso's worth even if he had given me credit.

So off we went. Of course, there were food dumps all over the Rock and I knew we wouldn't have any trouble getting chow. Whiskey was not available but I knew that the N.C.O. club at Middleside must have had plenty of beer stashed away. We headed toward Middleside.

We got back some two hours later with the Japanese hauling me in a machine gun cart. Little Nap was second-in-charge of the detail and, being leery of making another mistake, he made me taste everything before he would OK it for the larder. I was making it all right through the Kosher pickles, early June peas, meat and beans routine but then we ran into the beer cache. Little Nap made me drink one can out of each case they took back.

You never saw such a party in all your life. By the time we got back they had cleared out the old messhall and set up tables. They had cooked up a slew of rice which was dished up in discarded helmets and five gallon tins. The rest of the stuff, most of it in #10 cans, was hacked open with bayonets and set on the table. There was plenty of beer but the most popular item was the big messhall-type cans of beef gravy.

It was kind of like a mess night. The captain called on each unit to render a song in turn and in between they sang national and regimental songs in unison. I had a little trouble with Sloan, who was from Atlanta, when they sang one of their national songs. The music, bar-for-bar, is the same as "Marching Through Georgia."

Finally, came the moment of truth. The captain insisted that we render our bit.

"What'll we do?" I asked Sloan.

"Sing the Hymn," he said.

"I only know the words of the first verse!"

"We'll sing it three times."

We did and we brought down the house. They demanded an encore.

"What now, wise guy?"

He had an answer to that one too. We sang "Down by the Old Mill Stream" and three choruses of "Sweet Adeline" before they let up. After assaying Sloan's barbed-wire baritone and my monotone I knew they were just being polite.

The next day we did nothing but sit with the captain. We had food, cigarettes and beer. We hadn't had it so good for six months. But we were uneasy. We saw no other Americans. We were worried about the fate of the company and the battalion. We queried the captain.

"Where they are is a very bad place. You are better off to stay with us," the captain told us.

Sloan and I had a talk that night.

"I think this guy wants to keep us with him as trophies," Sloan said.

"I think so, too. And if we stay with him we might wind up carrying rice sacks for his outfit in every campaign from now on."

"We gotta get back to the outfit," Sloan said.

The next morning we explained our position to the captain.

He was sympathetic.

"But," he said, "all *Horios* are in a compound of the 92d Garage area. There is little water, little food and much sickness. Why not rest with me until the confusion is straightened out?"

Sloan pushed the point and the captain finally agreed to let us go. First he called Little Nap and had him fill two canteens of water for each of us. Then he filled our packs with cigarettes and food.

"Goodbye," he said. "I cannot give you an escort. You have a long way to go and you will have trouble."

He was right, of course. I don't know what made us think we could walk from Topside all the way to the 92d Garage, through the entire Japanese Army without having trouble. But, I guess, half the battle is in not knowing that the job is impossible.

First we ran into a couple of privates who pushed us around a little, relieved us of our wrist watches, and then sent us on our way. The next episode was a little more hairy.

We got captured by a first lieutenant who started out being real friendly. He escorted us to his headquarters, which was in the shade, under what was left of an old house. Everything was going fine until he decided to go through our personal effects. When he got to the picture of the Japanese girl in Sloan's wallet he got real nasty. He pulled out a revolver, took out all but one of the rounds, spun the cylinder and held the muzzle up to Sloan's head.

I almost fainted but the hammer clicked on an empty chamber. He spun it again and held it up to my head but I was too numb to care. The game went on for another five minutes and then a runner came in and spoke to the lieutenant. He took us down to the road, pointed toward bottomside, and bowed to us. We went on our way.

"What kind of hand gun was that he had?" Sloan asked. "It was a good looking piece."

"I'm no gun nut," I said bitterly, "and I never will be one. Ain't that guy never heard anything about safety precautions?"

We never did hear why that lieutenant let us go so suddenly and I didn't ever have any inclination to go back and ask.

The rest of the way down wasn't exactly a breeze but we made it. At Malinta Tunnel a hydrant was running and we paused to fill our canteens. A little farther down the road we came to a long line of *Horios* herded along by several Japanese. They had containers of every type with them. It was evident the crying need at 92d Garage was for water.

The Garage was several acres in size. Flat, mostly concrete, it reflected the hot tropical sun. Thousands of American and Filipino prisoners were crowded into the space. One strand of barbed wire was strung loosely around the area and Japanese guards with fixed bayonets were spaced about every hundred yards. We walked by a guard at what we supposed was the main gate and he didn't even ask to see our credentials. Right then we knew we should have listened to the Japanese captain.

We were looking for someone to report to, when we heard someone yell.

"Sergeant Sloan . . . Sergeant Chipmunk . . ."

It was the Field Music.

"Where's the Command Post?" we asked him. "Who do we report to?"

"There's no C.P. . . . nobody to report to . . . I think the 'Top' is dead and nobody's seen the captain . . . everybody's over here."

We moved over and the outfit was in rough shape. The Japanese had herded them down en masse with long pauses in the hot sun. They had no food and very little water in forty-eight hours. *We* had been on a picnic!

Sloan got the Music started to rigging shelter with ponchos and I went around to the worst cases. Bozo Duncan was lying still as death, his face like putty. I didn't have a handkerchief so I tore off a piece of my skivvy shirt and wet it with water from one of my canteens. I swabbed his face with it and after soaking it again I forced open his teeth and jammed the cloth between them so it would drip into his mouth.

By sundown, things were fairly well organized. Bozo was set up in a shelter against a clay bank and was making out a muster roll. Sloan had collected all the chow and cigarettes and had established a supply dump . . . John Zimba and Ernie Bales were guarding it. Everyone was under shelter and there was a fire going. Sloan and I sat, backs propped up against the clay bank, and I felt pretty good about it. But not Sloan.

"We're out of water," he said, "and all we got to eat are Vienna sausages and 'C' rations . . . heavy in salt content . . . light in liquids. By noon tomorrow everybody will be raving maniacs."

There was one well next to what was left of the main motor pool building. I asked about it.

"They drained it this morning . . . it's been coming back in pure salt."

"There's a water detail going out tomorrow morning at 0800, we can get some men on it."

"I already got Stefanski in charge of that. Webber, Allender, and Musick are going with him . . . each one is gonna carry twelve canteens, but they're never going to make it to Malinta Tunnel unless they have a drink or two before they set out."

We smoked in silence but it didn't taste so good with our parched throats. Suddenly Sloan snapped his fingers.

"Come on," he grunted, "let's get some canteens."

I thought he'd flipped and was ready to swish a net over him, but I should have known better.

"This is the motor pool," he explained. "All those wrecked vehicles standing around have all got radiators . . . what is in radiators?"

"What . . .!" I breathed . . . "cool, cool, water!"

We had to move carefully over and around the sleeping thousands, all thirsty too. By morning our fingers were sore and our knuckles were torn and bleeding from opening the rusted drain cocks of the automobile radiators . . . but we had twelve canteens of water.

"Red with rust . . . but rich in iron!" was the way Sloan put it.

We got our water detail off that morning with a full canteen apiece and rat-holed the other ten canteens for emergencies. It was well we did. Refugees from the company and battalion kept floating in. All of them needed water.

The lieutenant came in . . . he was beat. The Japanese had had him on a burial detail for three days. The captain came in . . . the Japanese had had him showing them where all of our trip mines were located on the beach. We took care of them.

Everybody was in bad shape at 1400, so Sloan rationed out the rest of the water. Then we waited for the water detail to come back. It was hell-hot. The lieutenant said he knew where a big chow dump was located out on Monkey Point . . . nobody was interested.

Then about 1600 we saw a cloud of dust and knew the water detail was coming back. Sloan immediately kicked some men up. A dozen were picked to guard the company perimeter . . . we took another six down to guard our water detail back to the area.

In they came . . . we had to fight our way to the mob at the gate to get our detail but we made it. The stout Stefanski had managed to pick up two five-gallon tins and had them balanced on each end of a pole he carried over one shoulder. They were full of water as well as the twelve canteens he carried, also strung on the pole.

Everybody got a good slug of water, chatter started up and the troops started to move around. Four of them came up to the lieutenant and asked about the chow dump and, right after dark, they moved out between two of the sentries. They were back in an hour with sacks loaded with chow and cigarettes.

Late that night, surfeited with food, canned peaches and "C"-ration coffee, we sat around and talked about what we would do when the "Yanks and the Tanks" came. We were starting to live again.

I lay under a poncho shelter with my head cushioned on a piece of driftwood, enjoying a last smoke when Sloan came back. He had been visiting sentries. He kicked me gently before he turned in.

"You see," he said softly, "you worried for nothing. Nobody has asked you for your serial number yet!"

❋　❋　❋　❋

FEW MARINES MANAGED TO ESCAPE FROM CORREGI-dor, and fewer yet returned to fight again. One who did was Sergeant Reid Carlos Chamberlain of the 3rd Battalion, who sneaked down to the beach on the night of May 6 and found an abandoned boat. Somehow he managed to reach Mindanao, where he joined the intrepid guerrilla forces of Colonel Wendel Fertig, and was subsequently given a commission in the Army! Two years later the Marine Corps learned of this somewhat soldier and Chamberlain was lifted from the Philippines by submarine. In Washington, General Vandegrift pinned the Army Distinguished Service medal on him and offered him a spot commission in the Corps. Chamberlain declined. He preferred his old rank, sergeant, in Company A, 21st Marines. He was killed at Iwo Jima on March 1, 1945 . . . still a sergeant.

Let us follow him in a few passages of his diary.

·14· ESCAPE

SERGEANT REID
CARLOS CHAMBERLAIN

At 6 P.M. a motor launch pulled close to shore just off our position. We had no idea where the launch was going but it was leaving the Rock, and that was good enough for us. Army and I waded out to it and crawled aboard. There were three soldiers and one marine in the boat. But before the launch left, ten Filipinos waded out and boarded her. Nearly all the men from Cass Battery were on the beach. Several of them were yelling for us to come back, as it might mean our necks. The Japs had issued an order that no one was to attempt escape. I visualized these little men leering at us, laughing at us, subjecting us to indignities and humiliations. I knew I wouldn't be able to take that. Any fate was better than falling into their hands.

It was dark when the launch pulled across the channel, eight miles to the Cavite shore. There we found a deep bay and, in order to determine whether there were any Nips along the shore, made several runs toward the beach. As we neared shore we would quickly turn the launch around and head back toward the sea. In this way we hoped to draw fire at long range from any Japs in the area. No one fired at us, so, muffling the motor, we pulled close to the beach. About 100 yards from shore we turned the boat's nose to the sea and, as we slipped over the sides into the water, opened wide the throttle.

The water was cold and it was difficult swimming with our clothes and shoes on. I was glad when I got to water shallow enough to wade in. When I got to the beach, Army was the only person close by. We had become separated from the others.

We slowly crept through the nearby jungle, our clothes dripping wet, and climbed over the first small ridge. We had neither food nor weapons. In order to run as few risks as possible, we decided to hide in a thicket until daylight.

We arrived at a small barrio (town) after sailing three days and nights down the Luzon coast in a small sailboat, encountering considerable difficulty with reefs and unfavorable winds. We had been told by natives that a Spaniard, who was very friendly to Americans, would help us.

Shortly after landing we were approached by a middle-aged woman whose husband had been a member of the Philippine Army and was now in a Japanese concentration camp in Manila. She asked me seriously if it were true that the Japs had sunk the "Navy Department." I placed her mind at ease by telling her that was an impossibility, since the Navy Department was housed in a building situated on dry land. I also asked where she had learned that the Japs performed such miracles and she replied that she had read it in a Manila newspaper sponsored by the Japs and dedicated "to enlightening" the Filipino people.

She directed us to the friendly Spaniard's hacienda, where we learned that a Captain O. E. Vera was operating a guerrilla band which had its headquarters in the nearby mountains.

We arrived at Vera's headquarters shortly after noon. He was a meduim-sized, slender man with long, black, straight hair that he combed back in a sort of pompadour style. He had black flashing eyes and a narrow, long mustache. He looked like a movie version of a suave villain.

The captain appeared very glad to see us and to learn we desired to join his band. He brought out a quart of tuba, native liquor made from the juice of the heart of the coconut tree. Vera, his aide, Army and I proceeded to empty the bottle.

Army asked Vera how many men he had in his organization.

"Five hundred, perhaps 600," he replied. "My men, they wish me to hold a higher rank than captain but my intentions are purely patriotic, my friends, so I do not wish to assume a higher position."

I felt Vera was a liar and made up my mind I would remain with his band only long enough to procure his aid in moving further south. However, he was a genial host and the tuba was having its effect, making me feel in a very expansive mood.

"Captain Vera," I said, "you shouldn't be so modest. With 500 or 600 men you should be a lieutenant colonel, at least."

Army joined me in urging him to accept the position. Finally, after getting out another quart of tuba and taking a few more drinks, Vera graciously accepted the promotion. To show his gratitude to us for his elevation in rank, he immediately named me a first lieutenant and Army a second lieutenant.

Vera sent me out to the south in charge of a patrol of fifty men. I ordered thirty-five to remain with me at an old hacienda and sent fifteen others to kill two Japanese civilians. They had been causing the guerrillas trouble by informing the Nips of our activities. This had resulted in several of our men being ambushed.

A lookout reported that he saw a detail of twelve armed Japanese soldiers trudging up a path in the mountains. Colonel Vera gave me two dozen men and ordered me to lay an ambush.

I sent a scout in advance of our party to obtain their exact location. He reported back that they were three kilometers distant and were armed with rifles and one light machine gun.

We pushed forward to a point about a mile from where they were and I ordered the men to hide in the bushes along both sides of the path. Evidently they didn't know the guerrillas' headquarters was so near since they approached with no sign of being alert. When the Japanese reached the point where we were hiding, the guerrillas opened up with their rifles. We killed all twelve of the Nips. I don't believe they got off a single shot.

❀   ❀   ❀   ❀

SEVERAL MONTHS AFTER THE FALL OF CORREGIDOR, the American Red Cross delivered mail from survivors to their loved ones in the States. Captain John Clark of the 4th Marines poignantly tells of the tragic sequence of events from May 7. He died in a prison camp.

·15· AN OFFICER DETAILS HIS CAPTURE

CAPTAIN JOHN CLARK

Bilibid Prison
Manila, P.I.

My dear darling Lillian—and Johnny:

While I feel brim full of sentimentalities which I should exercise herein—I probably won't—the words come too hard and I'm sure you know how deeply I love you both—and how I long to be with you again. However, I do want to tell you my story . . . and hope that you will let . . . any others you wish read this . . .

The morning of the surrender I . . . beat my way to our headquarters' splinter-proof cement structure with shells bursting all around—little craters opening up in the ground right alongside of me. Remembering that I wonder why I should worry about what the future holds . . .

The surrender itself was a grim affair. Fighting did not stop immediately, for it was almost impossible to notify the engaged troops. Bombing and shelling continued, but later in the day the surrender seemed to have taken effect. For ourselves it was complete collapse. Command ceased, and naturally the nerves of everyone had been keyed high for five months—the let-down was terrific. For two or three days the Nips pushed us into the two big tunnels but finally more, some 10,000, including American and Filipino troops and Filipino laborers, down into an old dirigible hangar area approximately four acres in size. No drinking water and very little shelter was available from the scorching tropic sun, and sanitary facilities were nil. We spent two weeks there, in as great discomfort as anyone would want. We then were taken to Manila in Nip cargo boats (that is most of the white Americans were), and after wading ashore from the landing boats, were marched five or six miles to Bilibid prison, the same spot in which I am now writing this.

We carried on our backs, across our shoulders, or as best we could, what clothing and effects we had been able to save and once again the sun was blistering hot. Straggling out of line sometimes met with raps from non-coms' swords, although older men who collapsed later were picked up by truck. This march apparently had been publicized and Filipinos invited to witness the great parade—but I saw no expression of joy on any of the onlookers' faces. Most of the women were in tears, a fact which for some reason surprised me. I guess we were a pathetic looking crowd at that.

Bilibid was a blessed haven for a week. Plenty of running water, roofs over most of our heads; and an opportunity to get rested. The well men and officers started out in groups of 1500 each day by train for Cabanatuan. I and our group of Marine officers left the fifth day. The group ahead of us had hiked from Cabanatuan, the railhead, twenty kilometers into the foothills to establish at one of the former Philippine Army training camps. Our group, after spending a horrible night in a Cabanatuan school yard where a terrific thunderstorm thoroughly soaked us, hiked fifteen kilometers through another hot sun to another Philippine Army camp, carrying our possessions which of course became unbearably heavy. During the first phase of the march we had been advised that sick or weak who fell by the wayside would be picked up by truck, and this the guards permitted. Guards were changed about halfway—and these lads didn't "have the word."

Anyone who fell by the wayside was forced to his feet at the point of a prodding bayonet, well-aimed kicks, and other means, and no one was permitted to fall out of the line of march. Even so, there was fainting in the column from exhaustion or heat every twenty or thirty yards. It was a tough march—this on Memorial Day 1942. When we arrived at our camp, which was quite unprepared for us—in fact, no advance party there, either of Nips or Americans, we found no water, no cooking facilities. Fortunately, a rainstorm enabled all of us to fill our cups and canteens under the eaves of the buildings, and after many hours rice was gotten to us. After a day in this spot, the Nips decided to move us back toward Cabanatuan, to another Army Camp—nine kilometers from Cabanatuan . . .

The camp we ultimately settled in finally became Prison Camp No. 1 and at one time included close to 10,000 men, including hospital patients. (Those who had preceded us into the foothills were at Camp No. 3, and the camp we abandoned because of no water was Camp No. 2.) Later on, the Mindanao camp became No. 2. The group of 1000 officers which I accompanied was the first occupant of Camp No. 1—a large Philippine Army camp situated on the northeastern edge of the large Cabanatuan plain. Quarters were swali barracks—22 feet wide and about 55 feet long. The walls were of swali, a woven reed, with a nipa roof (which shed the rain well until typhoon winds ripped the "shingles" apart). Down the middle of the building lengthwise ran a five-foot alleyway, and on either side two "shelves" or sleeping platforms were built. The lower platform was about two feet higher than the deck of the alleyway. The upper platform was about five and a half feet above the deck. Upright timbers supporting the roof separated the platforms in five "bays," upper and lower along each side, and in these bays, we made our homes. The first night spent in one of these bays at Camp 2 saw seven big men with blanket rolls, haversacks and miscellaneous gear crowded into the 8 x 9 foot space. During the first few months at Camp No. 1, five men to a bay was the average, but as details were shipped off, gradually we got down to three men to a bay—which by comparison was comfortable.

Our new Camp No. 1 was built primarily in rice paddies which are designed to hold water and not for drainage. Coupled with that, there was but one water tap available for a long time—no bathing water and insufficient drinking water, for the rainy season also is very hot. Eventually an additional pump was installed and ultimately we had fair water supply. After our arrival at the camp, other large groups of prisoners started coming in from Camp O'Donnell, some distance away, where the Bataan prisoners had been quartered for almost two months. Fifteen hundred Americans and probably fifty Filipinos had died at this camp, and several thousand who joined us now were in the large part sick, starved and in generally bad health.

Sanitary facilities in Camp No. 1 to begin with were almost non-existent, and the Nips refused to provide tools or materials with which to alleviate this. As a result, diarrhea and dysentery ran rampant. During our first six months 2500 men died, generally from malnutrition and dysentery, although a typhoid epidemic took several. No medicines were available, or in insufficient quantities, which further made things difficult. I . . . was . . . in charge of working parties that went out beyond the camp in the morning to dig large graves. In the afternoon, another working party would carry as many as forty bodies out to be crudely buried in these holes. The situation was grim. Men lay dying in and under barracks—and there was nothing that could be done for them . . .

Surprisingly, the well people remained in fair spirits and there were constant rumors of American forces approaching the islands, provision for the exchange of prisoners, and multitudinous stories most welcome but all unfounded. A large book could be written of the feverish eagerness at which prisoners of war will grasp at any wild story—hoping against hope that there may be a morsel of truth in it . . .

༔ ༔ ༔ ༔

WHILE THE MARINE CORPS MOBILIZED AND DEPLOYED forces in the United States during March-May 1942, and sent the 4th Defense Battalion to occupy Efate, New Hebrides, another Pacific battle was in the making. Here, again, because of a piteous lack of proper equipment, the marine mission was almost total sacrifice.

At Midway—1135 miles west northwest of Pearl Harbor—marines under the command of Colonel Harold D. Shannon braced for a massive invasion at the onset of June. Japan needed Midway as bait to lure the United States Pacific Fleet into decisive engagement. Briefly, Japan's plan was to create a diversion in the Aleutians while her superior firepower waited at sea hoping to trap the U.S. fleet as it charged out in defense of Midway. Fleet Admiral Isoroku Yamamoto gambled everything on the assumption that we would not let "the sentinal for the Pacific" go by default, and in this respect he was quite right. What Yamamoto did not know, however, was that our Intelligence had compromised top-secret Japanese codes, and that battle forces under Admiral Chester

W. Nimitz, who relieved Admiral Kimmel, knew the enemy's composition and plans.

Nimitz strengthened Midway's defenses with everything that could fight, including Army B-17s and a squadron of PT boats. The atoll, 6 miles in diameter but very little of it dry land, consists of Sand (2 miles long) and Eastern Island (1 mile long) which lie nearby separated by a dredged channel. A barrier reef forms a breakwater protecting the islands, which themselves enclose a lagoon and navigable harbor. Midway was under the command of Navy Captain Cyril T. Simard, and it served as an important submarine and patrol plane base.

Marine defenses at Midway included 3-inch, 5-inch and 7-inch batteries; the 6th Defense Battalion and the greater part of the 3rd Defense Battalion; four infantry companies; and Marine Air Group 22 with fighting and dive-bombing squadrons (VMF-211 and VMSB-241) under Major Floyd B. Parks and Major Lofton R. Henderson. Unhappily, the fighters were obsolete Brewster "Buffalos" and were slow, fabric-covered aircraft; not even a bad match for the Japanese.

Yamamoto's armada aggregated more than 120 warships of every category, including battleships, carriers, cruisers, destroyers, submarines and ships of the train. The Midway Attack Force was sighted June 3 at 9 A.M. by a Navy PBY which radioed a contact report. Simard sent off the long-range B-17s. These planes found the enemy 570 miles from the atoll and made several attacks; Catalinas next located the transport group and attacked with torpedoes at 1:15 A.M., June 4. At 4:30 A.M., 108 Japanese fighters and bombers took off from four first-line carriers to strike the atoll. The battle was on.

For this first phase of Midway, we present the matchless Walter Lord, whose best-selling *Incredible Victory* is the story of the Battle of Midway. Lord spent three years interviewing American and Japanese survivors of the crucial engagement. When we join him the enemy strike is just coming in.

·16· MIDWAY STRIKE

WALTER LORD

On Sand Island the powerhouse whistle blasted away; the siren on Eastern added its wail. Private Love, just lining up for chow, dropped all thoughts of breakfast and raced for his antiaircraft battery. Lieutenant Donald Cooksey, 6th Battalion dental officer, rushed to his first-aid post, well aware of Colonel Shannon's sharp reminder, "A dead or wounded doctor is no damn good to me." In his Eastern Island dugout Captain W. M. Bell, platoon leader of I Battery, recalled an old Marine dictum that it was an officer's duty to look calm and well-groomed at all times. He carefully shaved, dressed, and sipped a glass of pineapple juice before going to his platoon.

Confusion was everywhere along the Eastern Island runway. When the first contact reports came in around 5:30, the Marine CP ordered all planes to start engines. Enemy bombers were said to be only 100 miles away. But when minutes went by and nothing appeared on radar, new orders went out: cut engines. Then at 5:53 Navy radar broke in: "MANY BOGEY AIRCRAFT BEARING 310°, DISTANCE 93."

This was it all right, and as the siren went off at 5:55 new orders went out to get going. But by now some of the pilots had cut engines; others were still warming up and couldn't hear the alarm. The CP truck raced along the runway, its own siren shrieking, Captain Bob Burns shouting to everyone to stand by for take-off.

At least the B-17s were no problem. They had gone out as usual at dawn, but instead of merely using up gas, this morning they had been ordered to attack the Japanese transports again. Now the new threat changed everything. Captain Simard radioed Colonel Sweeney to divert his bombers to the carriers sweeping down from the northwest. At the same time, orders went out to the PBYs on patrol: stay clear of Midway; after completing mission, go to French Frigate Shoals, or one of the outlying reefs.

But there were still 66 planes at Midway; none must be caught on the ground. At 6:00 the 26 fighters began taking off. One of them soon returned with engine trouble, but the other 25 climbed toward the northwest. Major Parks led the way with two divisions; Captain Kirk Armistead followed with the rest, heading out on a slightly different bearing as a hedge against radar error. About 30 miles out they were all ordered to orbit. They would not have long to wait: at 6:04 Navy radar put the "bogeys" only 74 miles away.

Next it was the six TBF's turn to take off. Captain Burns raced up in his jeep and spoke to Lieutenant Fieberling. The skipper sent a mechanic running to each plane; he scrambled on the wing and yelled above the roar of the motors, "320°, 150 miles out!" One by one the TBFs thundered down the runway, rising gracefully despite the torpedoes. It was 6:10, and radar had the Japanese 47 miles out.

Now the four B-26s. Major Jo K. Warner, the Army liaison man, drove up and gave Captain Collins the dope. But as the crews scrambled into their planes, Lieutenant Jim Muri still wasn't sure what this was all about. He only knew he had a torpedo, a position, and there was some "target" out there. Rolling down the runway, he hoped it would be a nice, fat, easy merchantman.

Only the Marine bombers were left. Major Benjamin Norris went first, taking out his 12 decrepit Vindicators. One immediately returned when a cowling blew off. The squadron's skipper Major Henderson brought up the rear, leading the relatively new SBDs. By now there was no field organization left—no radio, no briefing officer, no directions. Just a wild scramble to get into the air. But Joe Henderson somehow knew what to do, and his young pilots were more than willing to follow. At the last minute two of the SBDs broke down, but the other 16 took off. Colonel Kimes fixed the time at 6:15; some put it a few minutes later. In any case it was none too soon—at 6:16 the radar had the Japanese at 29 miles.

With the last planes gone, an overwhelming silence hung over Eastern Island. Men crouched quietly in the gun pits, the slit trenches, the observation posts—all eyes fixed on the empty blue sky to the northwest. It was almost hypnotizing, and at E Battery Captain James O'Halloran sharply reminded his lookouts that there were other sectors too—that the Japanese had been known to pull some surprises.

In the shelters and dugouts hundreds of other men quietly waited, hidden by sand and camouflage. As WO Bill Lucius hurried toward his slit trench near the mess hall, Major William Benson called out from the command post dugout: "Bill, I have the best dugout on the island, as well as the best communications equipment. Why don't you stay with me?"

"I was so scared at Pearl Harbor," Lucius replied, "that I hardly saw the Japanese planes; I don't want to miss them now."

From the piers and moorings a small flotilla of boats slipped into

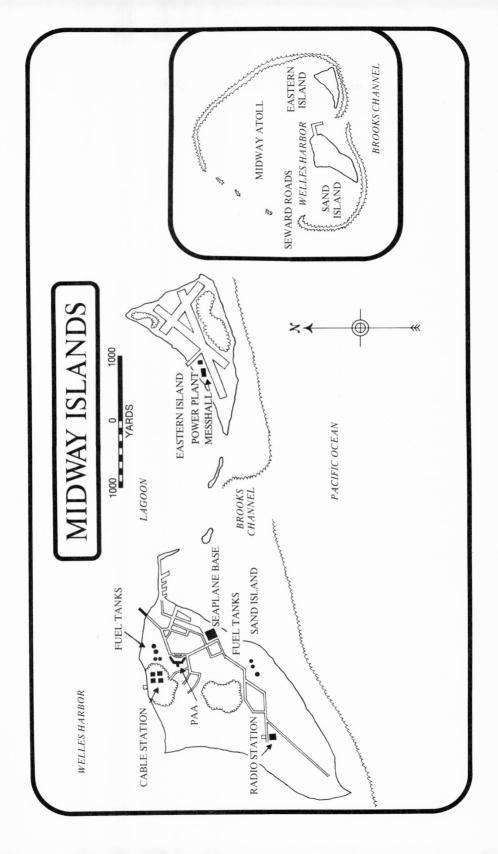

MIDWAY ISLANDS

LAGOON

EASTERN ISLAND
POWER PLANT
MESSHALL

BROOKS
CHANNEL

PACIFIC OCEAN

1000   0   1000
YARDS

N

WELLES HARBOR

FUEL TANKS

SEAPLANE BASE

CABLE STATION

PAA

FUEL TANKS

SAND ISLAND

RADIO STATION

MIDWAY ATOLL

SEWARD ROADS

WELLES HARBOR

SAND ISLAND

EASTERN ISLAND

BROOKS CHANNEL

the lagoon between Eastern and Sand. Lieutenant Clinton McKellar neatly dispersed his 11 PTs. Boatswain Olivier carefully positioned his collection of launches, all loaded with machine guns and rifles. Chief Boatswain's Mate Stanley Engels took his tug *Tamaha* and tied up to an old sunken scow that looked like the last thing the Japanese would want to bomb.

In the dugout hospital on Sand Island Pharmacist's Mate E. B. Miller began boiling coffee on a hot plate. It was far too strong to drink; he was making it for a "Murphy drip," an old-fashioned remedy used rectally in treating shock.

At the command post Captain Simard couldn't resist temptation. He should be in the dugout by now, but he hung back—fascinated like so many others—straining his eyes to the northwest. Logan Ramsey kept urging him to get under cover.

On the upper decks of the powerhouse Simard's "movie-ite" John Ford was searching the northwest too. He was now equipped with cameras, film, binoculars and a phone direct to the CP. His vantage point was perfect, but so far there was nothing to see. In fact Midway looked deserted—nothing moving—just a lazy, peaceful tropical island.

Outside Colonel Shannon's command post the Marine guard, Pfc. Ed. D. Winslow, stood watch by the doorway. It was a distracting assignment this morning. The radar station was hard by, and as the Japanese drew closer, someone kept calling out the miles. Inside, the radar operators watched closely as two sets of blips—one enemy, one friendly—swept together just beyond the horizon.

. . . To Pfc. Philip Clark at D Battery, they looked like three wisps of clouds far out on the horizon. To Pharmacist's Mate Miller, up from his dugout for a look, they seemed more stretched out in a single line. But there was no doubt they were coming on fast. At 6:29 the radar fixed them at eight miles . . . 6:30, Battalion said fire when within range . . . 6:31, all guns opened up.

A dozen black puffs erupted 200-300 yards behind the advancing planes. At D Battery Sergeant Evitts, who knew more about fire control than all the brass, cranked in an arbitrary adjustment. A single string of bursts left the main group and "walked through" the formation, setting one plane on fire. Then another blazed up, but kept flying in flames for an interminable period. As it fell a great cheer went up; even the men deep in the Navy command post could hear it. At the entrance Captain Simard watched transfixed, while Logan Ramsey urged him again and again to get under cover: "Skipper, this is no place for you to be."

At 6:34 the planes were directly overhead. On Sand Island Sergeant

Jay Koch studied them through the F Battery telescope as the bomb bay doors opened and the first bombs dropped out. He felt a moment of terror as he wondered where they were going to hit.

High in the powerhouse John Ford didn't see them unload, but assuming the seaplane hangar would be one of the first Japanese targets, he already had his camera trained on it. He was right. A stick of bombs hit home, spewing fragments in all directions. Ford not only filmed the scene, but perhaps too smart for his own good, he caught a load of shrapnel in his shoulder. Stunned for a moment, he was soon back on the job, shooting pictures and phoning his blow-by-blow account to Captain Simard's command post.

Another stick of bombs crashed down on D Battery. Captain Jean Buckner didn't see them coming . . . never knew what extra sense made him yell over the command phone, "take cover." But he did, and his men ducked just in time—except Corporal Osa Currie, hanging on at the exposed height finder. He fell fatally wounded.

Yet war is a matter of wild contrasts. The same moment on Eastern Island found Warrant Officer Lucius dodging a barrage of knives, forks, cigars and cigarettes, as the first bombs there smashed the PX and mess hall. And even before the dust settled, one old-timer ran out from his shelter and gathered in all the cans of beer he could carry.

Now it was 6:40, and the dive bombers' turn. To Carpenter's Mate William Schleis, battling a fire on the roof of the seaplane hangar, it looked as though every plane was diving directly for him. Huddling against a heavy beam, he put his hands over his face, but peeked through his fingers and saw how it came out. The bombs just missed.

No such luck at the powerhouse on Eastern. It was a small building, heavily bunkered, but that didn't help. A perfectly aimed bomb landed squarely on the roof, wiping out the inside completely.

Major Benson's command post got it next. Seeing it go, Warrant Officer Lucius thought of the Major's invitation to spend the attack there, where it was "safe." Now Lucius was untouched in his slit trench, and Benson's CP was lost in dust and smoke. He rushed over to help, but it was too late—his friend was already dead in the rubble.

In a way it was hardest on the men underground. They could only listen and wonder. In the first-aid dugout on Sand Island, Pharmacist's Mate Miller tried to concentrate on his Murphy drip, while the light bulb blinked and swayed. Smelling the coffee, Lieutenant Commander A. E. Ady, the doctor in charge, cheerily announced he would like some. It wasn't fit to drink, but this seemed a brave attempt to keep up morale; so Miller poured them each a cup. They stood up and solemnly toasted each other. Then hanging onto a stanchion as the dugout rocked with explosions, they tried to drink it down. Still going strong, Dr. Ady launched into a series of jokes. Miller—now as sick as he was nervous—vaguely heard him ramble on, "Well, that reminds me of the old fat woman in Arkansas . . ."

Outside, it was the Zeros' turn. In they swept—strafing the oil tanks, the gun pits, anything that moved. One fighter came so close to D Battery that Captain Buckner yearned for a full-choke shotgun. Another skimmed by F Battery as Sergeant Carl Fadick ducked low . . . but not low enough. A bullet smacked into the back of his helmet—then miraculously came out the front without even scratching him.

A man could be unlucky too. When a Zero swooped down on PT 23 out in the lagoon, a bullet entered the bell of the boat's bull horn, made a 370° turn, and hit a machine gunner in the back while he was shooting at the plane.

In Colonel Shannon's command post a phone began ringing. It was some quartermaster who noticed that in the confusion no one had yet raised the American flag—shouldn't it be up? It was a morning of a million problems, but here was one where the answer was easy. "Yes," said Captain McGlashan, "run her up!"

Pfc. Billecheck, a handful of others raced out to the pole . . . snapped on the flag . . . and heedless of the Zeros streaking by, raised the colors for all to see.

The men fought back with everything they had. Not just the regular antiaircraft guns, but small arms too. Anything. "Deacon" Arnold used a Browning automatic rifle. A sailor at the Sand Island Fire Station had a Colt .45. At E. Battery on Eastern, Pfc. Roger Eaton popped away with his 1903 Springfield.

Of course, they usually missed . . . but not always. A Zero staggered over the southwest tip of Sand Island, fell in a blazing heap 50 yards from H Company. A dive bomber caught another blast, careened wildly down—almost taking out the water tower—and crashed by the entrance to Captain Simard's command post.

But there was little anyone could do about the Zeros shooting at the few Marine fighters left. They were usually too far away. The men at E Battery watched helplessly as one Buffalo, returning with a badly sputtering engine, went after a circling strafer. The Marine, coming in quite low, tried to climb up under the Japanese. The Zero simply stood on its tail and executed a beautiful loop. A few short bursts, and the Buffalo fell in the ocean.

Two Zeros went after another Marine fighter off the northern edge of Eastern Island. The Buffalo began burning, and the pilot bailed out. The Zeros followed him all the way down, blazing away as he dangled in his chute . . . then strafing the sea where he landed.

Somehow a few of the Marine fighters limped home. Shot in both legs, Captain Carey "proved the hard way that you could fly an F4F with just the stick and no rudder." Lieutenant Canfield's flaps were

gone, and when he touched ground his landing gear collapsed. Sliding
to a stop, he dived into a trench while a Zero slashed away at the abandoned plane.

A crippled Buffalo came in low, a Zero in hot pursuit. With a last
effort the marine climbed a few feet, forcing the Japanese even lower.
Every gun on Eastern Island seemed to open up. The Zero wavered,
then slammed down burning on the runway. As it skidded along,
Pfc. Clester Scotten had a fleeting, indelible glimpse of the pilot throwing his arms over his face. Then he was lost from sight in the flames.

But the one they remembered best of all was the really "hot" pilot
who wasn't content with bombing and strafing. Sweeping in alone,
he turned bottoms-up and stunt-flew the runway upside down. He
nearly got away with it. For long seconds the marines watched in
amazement, too surprised even to fire. Then the spell broke, and guns
opened up everywhere. The antiaircraft finally got him, and he spun
off into the lagoon. . . . [The attack was over at 6:48.] A few Zeros lingered, perhaps looking for some last easy kill, but by 7:01 they too
were gone— disappearing, as they had come, into the northwest.

For Pfc. Morris McCoy at E Battery, the sudden silence was worse
than the bombs and the gunfire. Major Warner, the Air Force man,
had never known such an eerie quiet. No sound whatsoever, except
the occasional wail of a tern, or the mournful honk of a gooney bird.

In the dugouts the men waited . . . and waited . . . then cautiously
began to emerge, blinking in the bright morning sun. Almost the
first thing Ensign Jacoby saw was the wreckage of the Japanese plane
that crashed near the entrance of Captain Simard's command post.
The pilot's body was lying nearby, a symbolic Rising Sun flag tied
around his waist. It was the very first "enemy" Jacoby had ever seen,
but with the foe right before him, his mood was empty of hate. It was
just another man, whose teeth were pushed in the way his would have
been, had the tables been somehow reversed.

The all-clear sounded at 7:15, and Midway began to pick up the
pieces. On Eastern Island Colonel Kimes radioed his VMF-221 pilots: "Fighters land, refuel by divisions, 5th Division first."

There was no answer. Kimes tried again. Still no answer. After
trying several more times he began to understand, and new orders
were sent: "All fighters land and reservice."

One by one they straggled in—six altogether. Added to the four
that crash-landed during the raid, it meant only ten had survived
the fight . . . and only two of these were in shape to fly. VMF-221 was
virtually wiped out: of the 25 planes that took on the Japanese, 23
were shot down or put out of action.

"It is my belief," Captain Philip White observed in his action report, "that any commander that orders pilots out for combat in an F2A-3 [Brewster Buffalo] should consider the pilot as lost before leaving the ground." Understandably bitter, yet a commander must fight with what his country gives him.

In any case, VMF-221 was gone. Nor was that all. The thick black smoke rolling skyward told the story on Sand Island's fuel tanks, and the seaplane hangar was burning too. The Navy dispensary was a total loss; other buildings like the parachute loft were badly damaged. In the shell of the laundry, a five-gallon glass water cooler stood majestically intact amid the rubble and shredded shirts.

On Eastern the CP, the powerhouse, the mess hall and PX were all demolished, but what really hurt were the gas lines. True, they were always breaking down, but now some bomber had finished them for good—just when they were needed the most. Colonel Kimes shuddered to think of the bucket brigade he'd have to organize to refuel those thirsty B-17s.

Casualties were a happier story. Colonel Shannon's reproduction of the western front had paid off well. Thanks to all his sandbags and dugouts, they were only 11 dead and 18 wounded among the islands' defenders.

Best of all was the way they handled their planes. Only one was caught on the ground—an obsolete biplane used for utility work. The only other aircraft lost was a decoy plane made of packing crates and tin roofing. Dubbed the "JFU" ("Jap Fouler-Upper"), it played its role to perfection.

So they were still in business. But Midway's biggest fear lay in what was yet to come. When would the Japanese be back? What would they bring next time? Were the battleships and transports just over the horizon, waiting to close in? Even the cheerful Dr. Ady, casting aside his jokes and bad coffee, grabbed a Springfield rifle and headed for the beach . . .

※ ※ ※ ※

LET US TURN THE CLOCK BACK A FEW HOURS . . . HERE is Captain Thomas F. Moore, Jr., who participated in the marine action over the carrier *Agaki,* and was one of the few survivors of the air engagement.

We join him at the opening of this momentous day.

·17· "A RECTANGULAR PIECE OF ENEMY . . ."

CAPTAIN THOMAS F. MOORE, JR.

"C'mon, hit the deck! Hit the deck!"

The voice traveled miles through the fogs of sleep, and then, after a long time, I heard it and opened my eyes. Someone had switched on the light. I looked around. Major Henderson was out, and already Rollow, Ward, and Schlendering were dressing.

"What"—I yawned—"the hell! I'm sleepy."

Rollow, sitting in the bunk near mine, began to bang his shoe on a piece of iron pipe near my pillow. "Get up out of the flea bag!" he shouted above the din. "Get up! Get up! Get up!"

That noise was too much. I climbed out of my bunk and began to dress. Glancing at my watch, I found it to be only a few minutes past 3:00 A.M. Well, this must be it; this was not just another alert. The waiting was ended. Looking about the room, I could see that I was not alone in my opinion. Using a *Saturday Evening Post* across his knees as a desk, one of the boys was writing a letter. No one had written letters at three o'clock in the morning before . . .

When I had finished dressing, I made my way through pitch-black darkness to the mess hall. There I found the others of the dive-bombing and fighter squadrons already collected. I cannot recall the names or faces; I had seen them too often before to take notice of them now. But it seemed as though everyone had something to say. We were like people who keep talking all through a minor operation in order to keep their minds active on other things than what the doctor is doing. So while we chewed on thick slices of bread with marmalade and drank burning hot swallows of coffee, we talked and talked. Who listened, I'll never know.

It was still not yet dawn when we made our way in groups of threes and fours to where the planes were waiting in pits. Private Huber, my gunner, was already there checking his guns and ammunition and whatever else he had to do. I didn't know Huber very well, but in just a few hours I was to find out a great deal about him.

"Everything shipshape, Huber?"

"Everything shipshape, sir."

A 500-pound bomb was in place under the fuselage. It looked deadly even there. I climbed into my cockpit and started the engine to warm it up in case a quick take-off was necessary; then I tried the radio and intercom telephones. Everything was in order. Danny Iverson, who was in the pit next to mine, waved and I waved back. There was nothing to do now but wait.

Perhaps I should write a short note to Janet; it could be written by the light from the instrument panel. No, I decided against it. It was too late for that now. If I was to write I wanted it to be something meaningful and everlasting in case I didn't come back. I couldn't think of any such words now. I could think only of her, and of our unborn baby. What would the baby be like? A boy or girl? A boy, of course, and he would be named after my dad. Thomas F. Moore, III; it sounded almost like a king's name. What would he look like? Would he cry a lot? Sure! He'd cry just to show his spirit. How big would his fingers be? And his toes? *My* baby, *my* son. That was the hardest of all to imagine . . . *God, let me live long enough to see him!*

In the east, the sun was beginning to bayonet away the night. Morning was coming . . . An hour later it had arrived.

Major Henderson's plane started to taxi slowly along the runway that adjoined my position. As he approached, it appeared as though he were getting ready to take off on a routine patrol flight. Captain Zach Tyler ran out toward the moving plane, and when the Major saw him he stopped. Tyler bounced up on the wing and spoke a few words, then I saw Major Henderson's hand describe a slow, beckoning motion. Tyler ran back to his own plane and started getting ready. Then Danny Iverson began to move out on the runway. That was all I needed. Already the Major's plane was in the air.

"Okay, Huber, let's go!"

I gunned the engine and we moved out onto the runway. We headed into the wind, and then my hand pushed the throttle forward. We began to move faster and faster. The plane was straining to lift itself into the air when the engine started coughing and spitting. I knew I wasn't going to make it. I cut the throttle back sharply, intending to taxi the plane to the engineering shack and have the engine checked. Then I saw many more of my squadron mates taking off. I wanted to be with them. I decided to try it again. With some difficulty, we got into the air.

I had heard no formal command given, but our squadron was up.

For almost a minute and a half there was nothing but the steady drone of our engine, and a few idle remarks passing over the phones. I was wondering whether we would see any enemy when suddenly over the radio came the unbelievable words:

"Attention! Attention! Island is now under heavy attack! Island is now under heavy attack! . . ."

I glanced backward. It was true—bombs were bursting all over the island. All at once a sheet of flames streaked toward heaven and fell back. Thick palls of smoke were climbing upward from three different places. We rendezvoused at a predetermined point. We fell into a box formation as we flew. Above, the sky was very blue and clean of clouds. The wind from the propeller whipped around my goggled eyes and face, but otherwise the weather was mild. Then Dick Fleming's voice came on directing a change in our course.

Major Henderson was some distance off to our right, flying a roving patrol scouting the enemy. He felt he was more apt to spot them if he didn't have to concentrate on his place in the formation.

The enemy! What would they be like? How would it be to attack them? To kill them?

My watch—it was a high school graduation gift from Mother and Dad—was marking off minute after minute, sixty of them . . . sixty-one . . . sixty-two . . . still we flew on.

I wished I had written that letter to Janet. She knew I was at Midway. Already the news of the battle's beginning must be on its way back home . . . How would Janet react? How would Mother and Dad react? How would America react? It would depend on the outcome . . . I was scared, no doubt about it . . . What was Huber thinking?

"Everything okay, Huber?"

"Okay, sir."

I ordered him to recheck his guns and make sure they were in good working order. We'd be in this together, he and I. Rank had kept us apart; I hardly knew him. But if we died today, we'd remain beneath the sea through eternity no more than five feet apart. It was a rub . . .

My watch showed eighty-three minutes from time of take-off . . . eighty-four . . . eighty-five . . .

"Attention? Attention! All pilots, attention." It was Major Henderson's voice. "Two enemy carriers on our port bow! Enemy carriers on our port bow! . . ."

"Attack!" . . .

There they were! There were two and they were big. They left wakes that were two thin white lines upon the sea . . . These two big bastards —this was the enemy!

The sound of our engines, the booming within me—it was like a big bass drum beating like hell under my shirt.

" . . . Enemy aircraft! . . . Enemy aircraft!—"

Suddenly, off to the left appeared a score of trim little airplanes, buzzing mosquito-like toward our formation. On their short stubby wings was marked an oversized red ball. Japs—Zero fighters—was all that registered as I saw them roll and twist against the sky and the sun. At first they looked almost playful; then they came down upon us. Quickly they grew from mosquitoes to sparrows, from sparrows to hawks, and, as their distance from us closed to no distance at all, they became warplanes firing a hundred lines of gray-white tracers that webbed in the air.

Now, above the sound of engines, I could hear the brittle rattle of machine guns. I saw them sweep down on friends flying near me. I saw my friends respond to the attack valiantly, hopelessly. They fired fast at the faster moving Zeros. Burst after burst of gunfire raced from friend to Zero, from Zero to friend. A Jap Zero veered and turned a hundred feet from me, pilot and motor dead. I heard the thin whine of the wind as it passed over his wings. A helmeted head lolled from side to side as the plane wobbled out of control. Then like a struck match he burst into flame and fell burning into the sea.

Still they came on. Two of them roared up behind us. Little holes were racing across our right wing. Bullets whipped into the instrument panel before me, shattering glass in all directions, shattering the radio equipment. My first and only reaction to this was, "God, here comes part of the Sixth Avenue El!" Huber opened fire. I heard the sharp bark of our gun throwing bullet after bullet at the Japs. It was a good sound, a comforting sound. Already one of them had turned away. The other was still behind us. Huber would get him . . . All at once our gun stopped firing.

"My gun is jammed!" Huber yelled through the phones.

I was in no mood for this news. "For God's sake," I shouted back, "if you can't shoot the damn gun at least aim it at him! Make him think it's good! Scare him with it!"

I am not proud of that command, but there was nothing else to do. A bullet rang off the steel armored plate behind me. To hell with that sonofabitch! The sound of gunfire was now part of me. Its impression had been made and noted. I saw a friend ride into a blast of bullets that went in one side and passed out the other. I saw that friend begin to fall. A long trail of oily black smoke was bursting from beneath his engine like a ribbon unwinding from the tumbling plane.

Already many of the squadron had gone down upon the carriers. I was awaiting my turn. Though they could knock some of us to hell, they couldn't break our formation. We would dive only when ready or only when dead.

Again and again and again the bastards came down, zooming under us, over us. Sometimes they passed Huber and me with only six or eight feet clearance, their machine guns giggling. Several bullets tore in and out of the fuselage—

Then I saw Blaine go into his dive. Now it was my turn! I kicked left—left rudder, left aileron—stick forward. We began to dive. Damn it all to hell, here we come!

Everything I had every been taught about flying or bombing was cut so deep in me I never needed to think or remember. This was it! This was a live run! A real, live run! The bomb was armed; I checked it again and again. We were diving fast—as fast as three tons of dead weight tied to a thousand racing horses could dive. It was a sleigh ride, a damn belly-whopping sleigh ride.

Down, down, down from eight thousand feet to the enemy. Below, a thick cloud bank was racing upward to meet us. In a second we were inside it, feeling its dampness, its coolness. Then, another second, and we were free of it.

There was the water. And up and down inside my sights was a carrier, a rectangular piece of enemy! We were dead upon it. No need to change direction; the cross-hairs divided it evenly. I checked my bomb again. It was growing bigger and bigger, filling the sights, filling them and now overlapping them. The wind was whining and shrieking in an unending high G.

Pull out! Pull out! A voice was shouting through to me. *Drop the bomb and Pull out!*

I snapped back, glanced at the dials on the instrument panel. The needles were spinning crazily. The altimeter read five hundred feet and we still were diving straight on the target!

At four hundred feet I punched the bomb release and pulled the stick toward my stomach. The bomb fell clear. I never heard the explosion, but a wave of concussion smashed back at us, and we were thrown completely out of control.

For about five endless seconds I fought the drafts that gripped and tossed us down toward the sea. We dropped, climbed, and dropped again as the propeller spun and screamed. We were losing altitude— the water was less than forty short feet below—

Then, abruptly, we were free and clear again. Only twenty-five feet above the water, the airplane recovered its balance and motion. We began to skim the waves, gaining speed to regain altitude.

I looked back to see what damage our bomb had done to the carrier, and the view was suddenly blocked by the sight of three Jap fighters bearing down upon Huber and me—hell bent for destruction!

Futilely I pushed the throttle to its last advance notch, and the speed indicator needle began to climb to higher numbers; but the highest number on the dial was not high enough, not with the altimeter registering dangerously close to zero.

The Japs came on. Somewhere off in the sky ahead was a cloud bank, a refuge if I could reach it. But we would never make it in time; I knew we were going to get it and get it good. Still, it was a life ring, and I made my grab for it.

I heard the bastards warm their guns with a few short bursts of fire; they were estimating the range. I knew Huber was still positioning his gun. He was in a bad spot. He was helpless. Their guns began to rattle a jumbled tac-tac-tac-tac-tac-tac-tac-tac . . . Their many guns against—what? Against a nineteen-year-old kid behind a useless weapon. Tracers streaked by us on all sides. "____ 'em! ____ 'em!" I heard myself cry out a dozen times. The sound of their machine guns sounded above everything else, a sharp, angry noise. One of them was firing a long, long burst.

"I'M HIT!" Huber screamed. "I can't aim the gun any more . . ."

Hang on! Hang on! The cloud was closer now. I looked back at Huber. God! His face and chest were covered with splashes of blood. I thought he would soon die, and only two hours before—

Another burst, and another, and another. The bullets were close and deadly. They rang alarms as they struck all parts of the ship. The motor began to cough. It coughed four or five times and stopped. The propeller was turning in slower and slower circles. We started to nose down; I had to prepare for a water landing. The fuel line must be shot away. I switched tanks and grabbed for the wobble pump. I almost broke my hand reaching. From his rear seat Huber, wounded as he was, was already working it. The gasoline from the auxiliary tank was pressured to the engine. The motor coughed and caught; the propeller was spinning again. We were still flying!

Behind us the Japs had seen the engine quit, had seen us nose down toward the water. Two of them, thinking we were done, had pulled away. Now only one remained—that bastard!

He brought his plane into position above and before me; about two hundred yards separated us. I still pointed toward the cloud bank. Then the Jap turned and roared down toward us, thin little darts of flame spitting from his guns. When he had passed, he turned and came in from the rear. Another burst.

Then something stabbed and burned across my left index finger. I saw my blood start out across it in all directions, but I could tell at a glance it wasn't serious. Then another something seared and cut across the back of my head. I clapped my fingers to the wound and they came away with blood on them. How long would I live? That last wound was the end. I knew it; I felt it as I felt the blood coursing from my body. But that bastard—he would come with me!

Now that bullets had brought blood from my body, they scared me, and because they scared me I wanted to kill as I never wanted to kill before. That bastard kept firing and firing, and I wanted to smash out his brains against those guns with my bare hands.

He was up there again, still in the same position, safe from Huber's gun which he thought was still active, and beyond mine. He was preparing for another attack. This time when he turned upon us, I would turn upon him. If my guns didn't get him I would ram the bastard—he was coming with me!

He swung around to attack and I turned to meet him. Quickly he swerved out of range. Through the static of the broken phones, I heard Huber moan. Maybe I could still get the kid back to the base. But the Jap came back. He began to make another pass at us, and again I turned to meet him. He twisted into a loop, and then back into his former position. He was watching us like a vulture, waiting for me to turn for the clouds so that he could rake us again. For a hundred years—my watch must have moved but forty seconds—the game went on. Now he was at us again. I turned like the crack of a whip—I had him in my sights—he was gone with a diving turn. I wheeled for the clouds and, looking back as I entered them, I saw him turn away.

I was flying on instruments—on those that remained. Over my earphones Huber still moaned every now and then. I wanted to get him back. I wanted him to live. How long can the blood of a nineteen-year-old last when it runs out from bullet holes? The moaning had stopped. I didn't want to look back. The last time I had looked his blood-spattered baby face had made me weak.

I tried to contact Midway, but my set had been shattered to uselessness by hot lead. We were flying blind with little more than a compass to guide us. The clouds were thick, impenetrable. I had lost all track of drift figures and as we flew, longer and longer, the dread and helpless feeling that comes with being lost over the sea began to gnaw at what little spirit I still retained. Now and again Huber mumbled something, but I couldn't make out any of the words through the static and the droning of our engine. What was he saying, this nineteen year old, so close to heaven and so far from home?

I broke through the clouds at regular intervals, hoping to see one of my squadron mates to join on. Neither Midway nor even a landmark to Midway was in sight. There was just sea, broad and blue and endless. The gasoline would give out soon.

Then, *there was a reef!* It was Midway. I began to flash recognition signals so they would know it was a friend that was coming in. I came lower and lower—when all at once I came to the bitter realization that here was not Midway but either Hermes Reef or Kure Island. If it was the Pearl and Hermes Reef we didn't have enough gas to reach Midway. There was no choice to my guesswork. I flew on the supposition that it was Kure—if only it *was* Kure Island!

It is fifty-five miles from Kure to Midway and I flew those fifty-five miles, and when I was through Midway was not there. I had been wrong in my reckoning, fatally wrong. Half in hysteria I began to execute lefthand turns, trying to figure where I was. There was no reason to it, but nothing had reason any more. The gas would soon run out. It was running out now. Soon the motor would sputter and stop.

I was in another of those wild left turns when I felt Huber kicking the rudder bar in a righthand direction. I didn't want to look back at him, but I had to. Mutely and with feeble gestures he pointed to port, to what appeared to be nothing but a black cloud hanging over the water. It looked as if it might be a burning ship, but it would be a good idea to land close by. There would be life-boats down there. I headed toward the black smoke.

Just then a pair of Army Flying Fortresses swept by. I wanted to yell Hallelujah! That was the way I felt. I moved in behind them. They knew the way to Midway and in just a few minutes there it was!

Smoke was still columning up from it in several places. I spiraled down for a landing, when all at once I discovered that the shattered hydraulic system made it impossible to lower the wing flaps to break the speed when we approached the ground. I was getting ready to climb up again to lower the flaps with an emergency manual control, when Huber mumbled again.

Damn the flaps to hell!

We touched ground at high speed, bounced up into the air again, bounced down again, blew a tire, and after rolling a good distance we stopped. Field men dashed toward us, with a stretcher. Gently they lifted Huber from his seat. He was still conscious when they carried him away.

"Do you think he's got a chance?" I asked one of the men standing by.

The man shrugged. "Maybe; maybe not."

I was returning from the dressing station when I saw Jesse Rollow coming toward me. "Jesse," I called out, "how many got back?"

He fell in beside me. "I don't know, Tom," he replied in a shocked, toneless voice. "I just got back myself."

We lit cigarettes and stood watching the sky, waiting for friends to come home.

❈ ❈ ❈ ❈

A SECOND ATTACK ON MIDWAY DID NOT DEVELOP, for the dive bombers of Rear Admiral Raymond A. Spruance caught the Japanese planes at the precise moment when flight decks were full with planes refueling and taking on bombs. Down in flames went the invasion hopes of Yamamoto, along with four firstline carriers and the cream of her naval aviation. The enemy force turned back . . . and Japan never again mounted an offensive.

PART II

Guadalcanal: Offensive in the Solomons

With Japan's carrier-air striking power virtually nullified at Midway, the United States exploited a temporary advantage by moving into the offensive stage of the war at Guadalcanal and Tulagi of the Solomon Islands. Thus began the first campaign, a bloody, internecine struggle which cost the combatants thousands of fighting men and dozens of warships as Japan desperately attempted to oust the invasion from the South Pacific.

Briefly let us trace the background of the magnificent role played ·by the Marine Corps: unknown to Major General Alexander A. Vandegrift, his 1st Marine Division was selected to spearhead the attack on the 560-mile Solomons chain which lies northeast of Australia. Elements of the division were then in Wellington, New Zealand, operating under general instructions to prepare for undesignated assaults in about six months. But when on June 26 Vandegrift received word to report to Vice Admiral Robert L. Ghormley's headquarters at Auckland, marine standby status changed with dramatic abruptness. Ghormley, recently appointed Commander South Pacific Force and Area, handed Vandegrift a plan for the invasion of the Solomons to be executed in five weeks: Operation "Pestilence."

Vandegrift was stunned. ("I didn't even know the location of Guadalcanal. I knew only that my division was scattered over hell's half-acre.") His orders were to prepare an assault utilizing two combat teams of the 1st Marine Division, one combat team of the 2nd Marine Division (en route to the Fijis from Hawaii), the 1st Marine Battalion (in New Caledonia) and the 3rd Defense Battalion (in Pearl Harbor). The two men felt certain it was impossible to land anywhere by August 1, but they agreed to make the best of a bad situation until Ghormley could consult with higher authority.

What was known of the target areas? In effect, nothing, and particularly in the case of Guadalcanal. Despite the fact that a staff had been working on plans for about four months, the only existent maps of the target areas were German and pre-World War I. Before leaving Ghormley's headquarters, the division commander met with Brigadier General DeWitt Peck, Ghormley's plans officer who offered a few details: Vice Admiral Frank Jack Fletcher with three carriers was in command of the Expeditionary Force (TF 61); Rear Admiral Richmond Kelly Turner, the brilliant and scholarly tactician who masterminded all Pacific assaults, was in command of the South Pacific Amphibious Force (TF 62); Rear Admiral Victor A. C. Crutchley, RN, with eight heavy and light cruisers, was in command of the Screen (TF 62.2); and Rear Admiral John S. McCain at Efate in the New Hebrides was in command of shore-based aircraft. The presence of Crutchley, holder of a Victoria Cross, was easily explained: the primary purpose of the invasion was to protect our line of communication with Australia, and therefore British Empire representation in this first forward step signified total military and diplomatic rapprochement between the two nations.

When Vandegrift arrived at his headquarters he ordered Colonel Frank Goettge, G-2 (Intelligence), to depart for Australia in an effort to compile a dossier, however superficial, on the south Solomons. It was July, and considering the little time in which Goettge had to conduct a great number of interviews with ship masters, former copra plantation owners, Royal Navy personnel, retired missionaries and half-caste traders, Goettge did a creditable job. (Unfortunately, he was unable to contact the best possible source of information about Guadalcanal, Captain W. F. Martin Clemens, the daring British coastwatcher.)

Guadalcanal was discovered in 1568 by the Spaniard Alverado Medana, who stayed no longer than was necessary to fill water casks and plant the King's flag. Down through the centuries history has recorded a strange miscellany of explorers and adventurers who touched on the Solomons, including Jack London, who wrote of cannibals and generally described the jungle island as a fetid, malaria-ridden "place of death." Ninety miles long and 25 wide, the population of Guadalcanal at the time of our invasion was about 25,000 Melanesians, a few of whom had been organized into a British Constabulary Force. The average native was black, short, wooly-headed and fiercely loyal; an excellent man to go up with against the Japanese. Sergeant Major Vouza, Clemens No. 1, for example, received the Silver Star and George's Medal for extraordinary heroism in support of the marines.

Goettge learned that Guadalcanal was considered good grazing land for Tulagi cattle, and that gold was occasionally found in the alluvial sands of the 8000-foot mountain range; he heard of dense jungles and great plains where razor-sharp kunai grass grew to as high as eight feet; rain, heat and humidity characterized the weather. Goettge learned that the best beaches were just above Lunga on the northwest coast, and that the Tenaru River was not really a river but a trickle of muddy water except during the rainy season; he was also the recipient of misinformation which, fortunately, did not impede marine progress on D-Day; one plantation owner casually described "Grassy Knoll" as a hillock and it subsequently turned out to be "big as Mount Hood" to one of the assaulters.

Conversely, Goettge gleaned much invaluable information about Tulagi, which is separated by 20-mile-wide Sealark Channel. By comparison this island was the hallmark of civilization in the Solomons— or had been prior to the arrival of the "Co-Prosperity Sphere" in May when the enemy occupied the target areas of Guadalcanal and Tulagi. The latter, once the home of a British resident commissioner and an Anglican bishop who stayed there when not converting natives, was selected by the Royal Navy at the turn of the century as a fueling station because of its fine deepwater anchorage; thereafter it was given over to the Royal Australian Navy and in due course it became a seaplane base. With a population of Melanesian, Chinese and half-castes, Tulagi boasted two RAAF tennis courts, a Lever Brothers trading post, and a tin-roofed town complete with native saloon where a man who had counted too many coconuts could stay drunk for months. The original Chinese settlers arrived in 1865, the result of schooner *St. Paul* striking a reef offshore; they became the merchants of the quaint settlement. As of May, the population of the south Solomons had increased considerably: there were 2300 Japanese troops, of whom 1500 were laborers, on Tulagi; and 5000 troops, including a reinforced infantry regiment and an antiaircraft battalion on Guadalcanal. Goettge's rough sketch of the target areas was complete. He returned to Wellington.

General Vandegrift, meanwhile, had a good deal of trouble getting "Pestilence" properly launched. At Aotea Quay, with its impecunious five-ship capacity, stevedores ceased all loading operations, and he was forced to step in. Ordering Colonel C. G. Thomas to draw an operations plan, Vandegrift directed Lieutenant Colonel Randolph M. Pate to have the marines do their own combat loading on a round-the-clock basis rather than become embroiled in the city's internal affairs. Perhaps all might have gone well in another season—

but not now. This was the dead of the Anzac winter, and driving rain slanted down on the docks where the division worked three eight-hour shifts daily. Rain soaked supplies; flimsy cartons of cornflakes and cigarettes burst open at the seams. After a steady week of downpour the dock was a soggy mess underfoot: marines could survive without cornflakes, but the loss of smokes eventually hurt.

It was July 17, and in spite of Ghormley's pleas for more time, the Joint Chiefs of Staff granted an extension only to August 7, 1942: D-Day for the Solomons. Vandegrift, going over final details with Admiral Turner, wanted one last opportunity to secure intelligence about the target areas. He sent Lieutenant Colonel Merrill B. Twining and Major William B. McKean on a photo reconnaissance mission via Port Moresby, thence by B-17 out to the islands. During the course of the flight three Zero float planes came up from Tulagi and the B-17 was forced to take "violent evasive action"—shooting down two of the three—and Twining and McKean had the singular honor of being the first marines to see action in the Solomons. They photographed a crude airstrip on Guadalcanal, returning July 25. News of an airstrip was vital information and it galvanized "Pestilence" into a final burst of action. The marine plan was as follows:

Vandegrift was to exercise overall command from Guadalcanal, while Brigadier General William H. Rupertus was to command forces attacking Tulagi and the harbor islands of Florida, Gavutu and Tanambogo. The Guadalcanal attack was to be launched at Beach Red about 7000 yards northwest of the airfield, with Colonel LeRoy Hunt's 5th Marines penetrating inland to Grassy Knoll (Mount Austen) and Colonel Clifton B. Cates' 1st Marines moving southwest toward Lunga Point. The Tulagi attack was to be launched by Colonel Merritt A. Edson's 2nd Raider Battalion with an infantry battalion in support, and Major Robert H. Williams' 2nd Battalion, 2nd Marine Division, was to strike Gavutu and support Edson.

After dress rehearsals in the Fijis ("a complete bust"—Vandegrift) 956 officers and 18,146 enlisted men embarked in 23 transports screened by heavy cruisers *Quincy, Vincennes, Chicago* and *Astoria,* Australian heavy cruisers *Australia* and *Canberra,* light cruisers *Hobart* and *San Juan* (US), and steamed into the Koro Sea July 31. The first Expeditionary Force since 1898, and the first of World War II, was under way.

The story of the Solomons invasion through D-Day is told in five parts, the first by the distinguished journalist-author Richard Tregaskis, whose *Guadalcanal Diary* was a best seller during the early years of the war. A correspondent for the International News Service who covered both Atlantic and Pacific theaters until wounded in Italy, Tregaskis, like Ernie Pyle, was warmly regarded by officers and enlisted men alike. We meet him at sea on the Sabbath.

· 1 · UNDER WAY

RICHARD TREGASKIS

Sunday, August 2

Church services were crowded this morning, for the day of our landing is drawing close and more and more of the men aboard, "the Padre," Father Reardon, told me, want to settle themselves in some sort of spiritual self-understanding and be prepared for at least the possibility of death. The general feeling is that our landing will take place some time before next Sunday; that therefore this is the last Sunday for Communion and the straightening of souls.

I watched Father Reardon, his face pale in the flickering light of the votive candles, as he chanted the mass. He was kneeling, rising automatically as if mesmerized, with his eyes half shut and his lips moving only faintly, as in a dream.

I saw the marines filing out of services, stopping in the companionway to kneel against a bare wall which for the time being was a holy station. In another hour or two it would again become merely a wall, and the church would become the mess hall. I watched one particularly well-muscled fellow, whose broad, sinewy back and heavy arms gave the impression of tremendous physical power. His broad face was passive and dreamy as he knelt by the wall and made the sign of the crucifix.

After the Catholic ceremonies, came the Protestant, also crowded. There was a sermon, with a proper dash of science, on memory and its part in duty, delivered by a fat young man in blues. There were hymns, and, after the services, communion.

After lunch, I went into Hold No. 3 to watch the occupant of a neighboring cabin, Lieut. Donoghue (Lieut. James V. Donoghue of Jersey City, N.J.) telling his machine-gun platoon about the plans for landing. Today was the day on which, all over the ship, platoon leaders first passed the details of our attack plan along to their men. Donoghue's session was typical; his men are going ashore in the first wave of assault troops.

Under a yellow electric light in the dingy hold, Lieut. Donoghue, a huge, beefy fellow who used to play football for Notre Dame, unfolded an already well-worn map.

"Company B will land here at zero hour," he said, pointing with a stubby finger. "You know we'll be with 'em. We're in the first wave." There was no sound from the circle of men.

"We are the assault wave guide," continued Donoghue. "See, here's where we land, to the right here." Then he went through the details of the operation.

"I recommend you take along a change of underwear," he said, and that brought a laugh.

"Well," concluded the lieutenant, "that's the dope. You want to go in there expecting the worst. I expect the naval bombardment will soften the place up a lot. I'm depending on you to take things over if I get knocked off."

At 2:30 in the afternoon the leaders of the assault companies, Capt. Kaempfer of A Co., and Capt. Hawkins of B Co., met with their platoon leaders in the wardroom. For two hours they pored over plans. And that, they told me, was only the beginning. It will take days of study and mental drilling to get the facts of the planned operation down to the last buck private.

At 3:30, general quarters was sounded, but it was only a rehearsal. There was practice firing into the bright blue sky with our anti-aircraft machine guns and small cannon. It was pleasant to watch the streaks of tracer bullets branching up into the blue, and then, as they burned out, shrinking into bright glowing spots clustering like stars for a moment, and then fading.

Up on the bridge, I found a happy group of ship's officers and men. Now at least we are on our way directly toward our objective. The watch officer told me that our base course is pointed straight at the Solomons.

In the beautiful white sunlight on the open signal bridge at the top of the ship, I found Col. Hunt and his staff officers relaxing. The colonel, seated in a canvas chair under an awning, was reading a magazine with as much contentment and calm as if he had been sitting on his front porch of a Sunday afternoon back home.

At supper tonight, it was made known that the day of our landing is to be Friday, August 7th, five days hence. The zero hour is not yet known, but it will be in the early morning.

After supper, Maj. Milton V. "Mike" O'Connell (a former New York newspaperman and public relations counsel) gave a lecture to the officers on Japanese jungle-fighting tactics. Genial, portly "Mike" drew a laugh when he warned the lads to be as silent as possible while advancing against the Japs.

"We can beat the Japs at their own game of silence," he said, "if you don't yell back and forth. You know how the marines are; some marine'll yell to his buddy: 'Hey, Bill, is that C Company over there?'" Maj. O'Connell waved his short arms wildly, mimicking the enthusiasm of his typical marine.

"Don't let your men get curious and run over to see if B Company is over there, or what kind of chow (food) they've got. If your man gets too curious, he'll be chow himself."

The major warned of the Jap sniper's trick of tying himself in a tree, waiting until you have passed by, and then shooting you. "Don't take any chances," said the major, "it's better to shoot a few coconuts than miss a Jap egghead."

In our cabin tonight Capt. Hawkins and I talked over the coming offensive. He said the men were ready. All over the ship, he said, he had seen them sharpening their bayonets, oiling their knives, cleaning and sighting along their rifles. "And they do it without being told," he said, as if awed by the phenomenon.

Monday, August 3

After lunch today I walked out on the bow of the ship, where there were groups of marines scattered over the piled gear, boats, ropes, hatch covers, ammunition boxes and assorted machinery that filled the deck. The sunshine was bright and there was a pleasant cool breeze.

Some of the men were still whetting bayonets and knives, and others were cleaning and oiling their guns. Others were grouped around a four-handed game of cards. One little group of men lounged by the starboard rail, idly watching one of their numbers who was throwing half-dollars over the side. He had a big stack of them in his left hand.

"He's trying to make 'em skip on the waves," one of the group explained to me.

Now another marine, armed with a pile of half-dollars, also began to throw the money over the side. "I won't have no use for it anyhow," he explained.

"I've seen many a guy make liberty on as much money as they're throwin' away," suggested a sailor who was watching.

"Oh, hell," said one of the marines, "money don't mean a thing out here anyhow. Even if you stay alive, you can't buy anythin'."

Brownie, the sailors' dog, began to bark. On the bow some of the men were hosing down the decks, and they had excited him.

"Did you know Brownie got his tetanus shots, just like us?" asked one of the marines. "He's got a tag marked with his name and the date of his tetanus shot; and it says on there, 'Class, Dog.'"

By this time the crowd of marines and sailors in our particular group had increased in size. Spotting my "C" arm band, they knew I was a news correspondent and had come up with the pleasingly straightforward idea of getting their names in the paper.

I asked where the majority of the marines aboard came from. "Boston and New York," said one of the boys. "We take a poll every day. Right now Boston's leadin'."

As we were talking, a short, chubby boy with a shaved head came up and stood at the edge of our circle. "There's the youngest guy on the ship," said one of the marines. The lad told me he was just seventeen, and that his name was Sam Gearhart and he came from Allentown, Pa.

"You must have joined up before you were seventeen, Sam," I said.

"I did," he answered. "But they can't throw me out now."

An even younger-looking lad ambled by on the deck. I asked him how old he was. "Eighteen," he said. He looked about fifteen at the most. He said his name was Thomas H. Pilant and his home was in Harlan, Ky.

The other marines told me a story about Pvt. Pilant. "His face is so small," said one of them, "that he can't get into a regular gas mask. They won't let him go in with the assault wave."

The other, older marines, kidded Pilant about his fate. "That's all right," they said. "You'll go on galley duty."

Col. Hunt issued a mimeographed notice to his troops this afternoon. "The coming offensive in the Guadalcanal area," he wrote, "marks the first offensive of the war against the enemy, involving ground forces of the United States. The marines have been selected to initiate this action which will prove to be the forerunner of successive offensive actions that will end in ultimate victory for our cause. Our country expects nothing but victory from us and it shall have just that. The word failure shall not even be considered as being in our vocabulary.

"We have worked hard and trained faithfully for this action and I have every confidence in our ability and desire to force our will upon the enemy. We are meeting a tough and wily opponent but he is not sufficiently tough or wily to overcome us because We Are Marines [the capitals were the colonel's].

"Our commanding general and staff are counting upon us and will give us wholehearted support and assistance. Our contemporaries of the other Task Organizations are red-blooded marines like ourselves and are ably led. They too will be there at the final downfall of the enemy.

"Each of us has his assigned task. Let each vow to perform it to the utmost of his ability, with added effort for good measure.

"Good luck and God bless you and to hell with the Japs."

In the late afternoon, I listened while Lieut. Harold H. Babbin of New York City, a swarthy, cheerful fellow with a good Bronx accent, passed on his instructions to his platoon. Most of his talk centered around the Japanese tactics of jungle fighting. The circle of tough lads, many of them with unshaven faces, listened good-naturedly, interrupting occasionally, but not too often, with remarks.

Lieut. Babbin warned against booby-traps, such as helmets, bayonets, or other items of interest which the Japs might leave about with a rig of wiring to cause an explosion when they were picked up.

"When you see a .45 or something with beautiful pearl" (he pronounced it "poil") "on it and beautiful engraving, don't pick it up," he said. "It might blow up."

"The most beautiful poil in the woild," one of the lads mimicked. But Babbin was used to that. He smiled and went on.

"If a Jap jumped on you from a tree," he asked, "what would you do?"

"Kick him in the b----," answered a marine.

"That's right," said Babbin. "You hit the nail on the head."

"You might see a Jap sniper hanging from the top of a tree, lookin' dead," the lieutenant continued, "because they tie themselves in with ropes. He might be playin' possum. So, don't hesitate to throw another .30 up there, bounce him off the tree again. That's good stuff."

"Yeah," somebody piped up, "it might hurt him."

After the meeting was over, Babbin said to me, "They're a tough gang . . ."

Tuesday, August 4

This day went slowly. We are still plodding toward our goal, in the open sea, and there is little to do but recheck preparations already made. Capts. Hawkins and Kaempfer, leaders of the assault companies, were in a huddle with their N.C.O.'s for three hours this afternoon. They passed out sector maps which had been prepared yesterday, drilled the details of their plans into their own minds and those of their subordinates.

On deck the lads lounged about, still shooting the breeze, still sharpening knives. "I just want to kill a Jap, that's all," said one of them to me.

Some of the men tossed empty tin cans over the stern and shot at them with .45 automatics and sub-machine guns, until the officers ordered an end to the matter.

Many lads had written the word "Fight" in black ink on the backs of their jackets. Talk of ferocious designs on the Japs reached a new high.

On the forecastle, a group of men sat around a howitzer, lovingly occupied with cleaning and greasing the parts. Next to them, a poker game went fast and furiously, with stacks of bills blowing in the wind.

"A lot of the boys are putting money in the regimental safe to be sent home," a marine told me. "One put in $450 today, and me, I cracked away 125 bucks. I thought of getting into a crap game, but then I thought if I won, I wouldn't know what to do with the money."

Wednesday, August 5

This morning at breakfast, Lieut. Cory said, "Two days more to go." Forty-eight hours," said Lieut. Manterfield. And we all remarked that amazingly there are no cases of jitters evident anywhere. Except, somebody suggested, for one doctor. He, it was said, is scared to death. [Note. I was later to see this certain doctor acting with the greatest coolness and bravery under fire.]

"Scuttlebutt"—the navy and marine name for unfounded rumor—was rampant today. Naturally, it would be, for we are riding up to the climax of our expedition, and as yet there has been no action. We had expected some—and now busy imaginations are filling the gap.

One story was that one of our accompanying cruisers had found, and sunk, a Japanese submarine traveling on the surface. A marine told me he had seen the flashes of gunfire himself. I checked the story with the ship's executive officer. He laughed. "There was some heat lightning early this morning," he said, "behind that cruiser."

Another story told how we had discovered a lifeboat full of natives, the remnant of the crew of colored sailors from a merchant ship which had been sunk by a Jap destroyer. This story was equally easy to track down. It originated this morning, when our task force slowed for a few minutes for a motor whale-boat, carrying dispatches from one transport to another. It is not clear by what process the boat's crew became Negroes.

This morning, in the bright sunlight of the ship's upper deck, I watched Col. Hunt passing the time of day with his officers. He was in high spirits, going through the tap-dance routine he used to do, he said, when he was a student in Stanford University before the First World War. He sang his own accompaniment, a bass rendition of such tunes as "I Want a Girl Just Like the Girl That Married Dear Old Dad."

The colonel could still turn in a very passable buck and wing. He was excellent, too, at the exit with the lifted straw hat. I decided his youthful exuberance arose because now he was getting into the zone of action. He had been one of the heroes of the First World War.

At supper tonight there was a mimeographed message placed under each plate. "The _____ (name of ship) has been singularly honored to be entrusted with getting ashore the first assault wave of the first U.S. ground force offensive action in the present war," it said. "Our ship has a good name. I expect it to have an honored and revered name after this coming action." The message was signed by the captain. Another note was also printed on the sheet. "We may expect sudden attack from submarines or bombers at any time from now on."

In the cabin, I found Capt. Hawkins busily oiling his sub-machine gun and his cartridges. He did not seem nervous. In the course of conversation I asked him how he felt about being one of the leaders in the assault wave. "I don't feel funny about it," he said. "I don't feel any more nervous than if I were being sent out to do a tough job in civilian life—you know, like trying to sell a big order, when there's a lot of sales resistance." The captain had once sold groceries, wholesale, in Boston.

Thursday, August 6

It was easy to see that this was the day before the big event. Sailors were busy rigging big booms to the heaviest of our landing lighters, so that they could be quickly launched. At several parts of the ship, canned rations were being issued: concentrated coffee and biscuits, meat and beans, vegetable stew, chocolate bars—enough for two or three days' subsistence until field kitchens can be rigged on Guadalcanal.

In the ship's armorer's shop, working single-mindedly at the benches, giving their weapons a last-minute check of adjustment, were a crowd of officers and men.

At luncheon, one of my table-mates, Lieut. Patrick Jones of Kansas City, said that he expected to transfer to another ship tomorrow before going ashore. The ship, he said, is carrying our reserve of ammunition, and gasoline. It would be too bad if she were hit by a bomb or shell.

"As I fly over Kansas City," said Lieut. Jones, "I'll drop off a souvenir, saying 'From Pat.'"

We all wondered at the fact that our task force, now well within range of the Japs, was not attacked by submarine, plane or surface craft. But there was not even an alarm.

The weather has been greatly in our favor. All day today, there was a heavy overcast, and visibility was very short. Unless the Japs had come very close, they could not have spotted us. But still, we were amazed, and I, for one, wondered if the Japs might have prepared a trap for us to walk into.

Dr. Malcolm V. Pratt, the senior medical officer aboard, who won distinction in the First World War, told me an amusing story this afternoon.

"I went below to look around in the hold last night," he said, "expecting to find the kids praying, and instead I found 'em doing a native war dance. One of them had a towel for a loin cloth and a blacked face, and he was doing a cancan while another beat a tomtom. In one corner of the room, there were about four or five boys wrestling around, but no one paid any attention to them."

As the afternoon wore on, I saw marines tying up their packs, with blanket rolls neatly folded over the top, and standing the finished products in tidy rows along the bulkheads. Men carrying armfuls of black-cased hand grenades hurried up and down the companionways. On deck, working parties were breaking out medium-heavy artillery ammunition.

Tonight at dinner, some of the officers betrayed signs of nerves. One was sure he heard the anti-aircraft machine guns firing on our upper deck. Another said he could hear it too. But it was merely the sound of heavy drums being moved about.

It was announced tonight that breakfast will be served at 4:30 A.M. We will reach our launching point at about 6:20. The zero hour has not yet been set, but it will be somewhere near 8:30.

After dinner, I talked to Col. Hunt, in whose assault boat I will be going ashore. He said that Col. Maxwell and some of the other officers would be going in another boat. "No use putting all your eggs in one basket," he said, and that had an uncomfortably hazardous sound.

In the men's mess hall, center of most of their activities including church, I found a close-packed crowd of marines with a sprinkling of sailors. Most of them sat on the benches—talking loudly in order to be heard against the jazzy boom of a juke box, and filling the air with cigarette smoke. A marine jitterbug, minus his shirt, his torso shiny with sweat, cut racy jive steps near the juke box, while another marine danced the part of the girl. After a few moments two sailors joined in the fun, themselves cut a rug or two.

In the officers' wardroom, three groups of officers entertained themselves with three separate, polite games of hearts.

I walked the deck in the dark, damp night. There was no trace of a moon—fortunately. At 10 o'clock I came back to the men's mess hall and the officers' wardroom. The lights were out. All the life was gone from both places.

❊ ❊ ❊ ❊

NOW IT WAS D-MINUS-ONE, AND THE APPROACH TO the targets entered its critical stage. In the next few hours the great convoy would break up into attacking components, Xray Group (16 transports) moving into the Guadalcanal landing beaches while Yoke Group (7 transports) headed for Tulagi and the harbor islands. On *George F. Elliot* of the Guadalcanal component was Private Robert Leckie of H Company, 2nd Battalion, 1st Marines, a machine gunner and scout. One of the great combat writers to emerge from World War II, Leckie, author of *Strong Men Armed* and other powerful works concerned with the Marine Corps, saw the war from the authoritative perspective of the man on the front lines. Here is the incomparable Leckie, to conclude the voyage from Koro and tell of the first hours of invasion.

·2· D-DAY: THE LANDINGS

ROBERT LECKIE

"Darken ship. The smoking lamp is out on all weather decks. All troops below decks."

It had come for the last time, this order. It had been heard for many nights, by some men for months of nights, but it had never before possessed such capacity to chill hearts.

They went below, with little of the accustomed horseplay, without the usual ineffectual insults hurled at the bullhorn that had ordered them down. They descended to troopholds far below the water line, where five-tiered bunks were slung from bulkheads and the air could become one with the foul reek of the heads if the blowers should break down. Many of them took showers, in fresh water if they were lucky enough to be aboard a ship that could spare it, but generally in salt water which left their bodies sticky and unrefreshed. Some men gathered at final Protestant services, others went to confessions being heard by Catholic chaplains. Weapons were wiped free of excess oil that might gather sand and clog them. Packs were checked for the last time, filled with mess gear, clean socks and underwear, shaving gear, rations—here a Bible, there a pack of letters-from-home, an unfinished paperback book, a crumpled photo of a pin-up girl—all those individual extras which men put in their packs as whim and character might direct. Now the men were banging the chained bunks down from the bulkheads, crawling into them fully dressed—for no one removed his clothes that night. The showdown games had ended and the ultimate winners were choosing between stowing the money on their persons or sending it home via the ship's post office. Attempts at humor were falling flat and fading into tight-lipped silence, lights were going out below decks, and all was quiet save for the steady throbbing of the ships' motors. Lulled by this and the gentle rise and fall of the ships, the men of the First Marine Division sought sleep.

In the wardrooms above, lights still burned. Shadows formed grotesque patterns on big maps plastered to the bulkheads, and fell in long dark shafts across green-covered tables at which the officers sat with cards and chessboards. Aboard Admiral Turner's flagship *McCawley* both Turner and General Vandegrift were grateful for the darkness closing on them as they reached Guadalcanal's back door. They could not know, but they could suspect, that bad weather during the last two days had grounded enemy seaplanes at Tulagi, allowing them to sail along the southern coast of Guadalcanal undetected.

At two o'clock in the morning of August 7, by the light of a moon emerging just as the American force rounded Cape Esperance at Guadalcanal's northwestern tip, men on the weather decks could make out the bulk of Savo Island rising from the mists ahead.

Because of Savo, a round cone which sat like a brooding sentinel at the western mouth of Sealark Channel, the invasion fleet had to split in two. Ships carrying the main body turned immediately east or right to sail between Savo and Guadalcanal and take up stations off the Guadalcanal beaches. The other sailed north or above Savo before making their eastward turn, moving to stations off Tulagi, Florida and Guvutu-Tanambogo.

Both sections were in position before daylight.

Aboard the troopships the men were going to the galleys fully armed. They ate beans for breakfast and climbed the ladders topside.

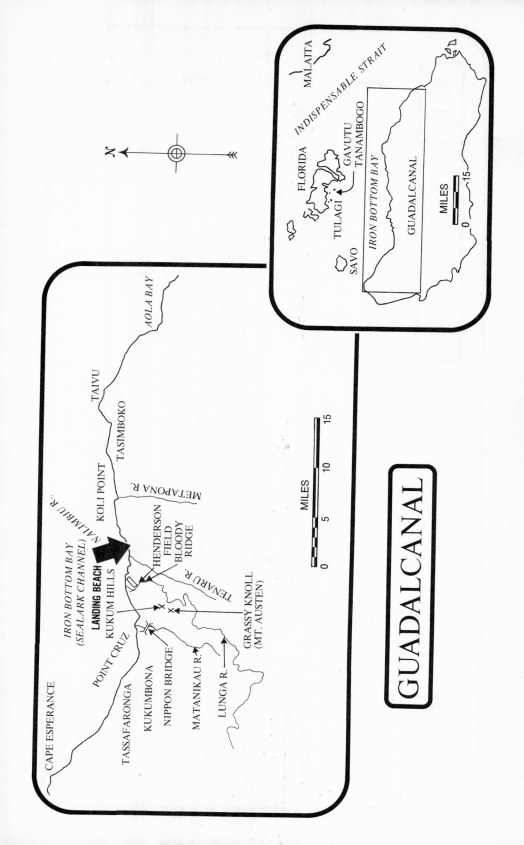

GUADALCANAL

Inset map labels:
MALAITA
INDISPENSABLE STRAIT
FLORIDA
GAVUTU
TANAMBOGO
TULAGI
SAVO
IRON BOTTOM BAY
GUADALCANAL
MILES
0   15

Main map labels:
CAPE ESPERANCE
AOLA BAY
TAIVU
KOLI POINT
TASIMBOKO
NALIMBIU R.
IRON BOTTOM BAY (SEALARK CHANNEL)
METAPONA R.
POINT CRUZ
LANDING BEACH
KUKUM HILLS
HENDERSON FIELD
BLOODY RIDGE
TENARU R.
TASSAFARONGA
KUKUMBONA
NIPPON BRIDGE
MATANIKAU R.
LUNGA R.
GRASSY KNOLL (MT. AUSTEN)

MILES
0   5   10   15

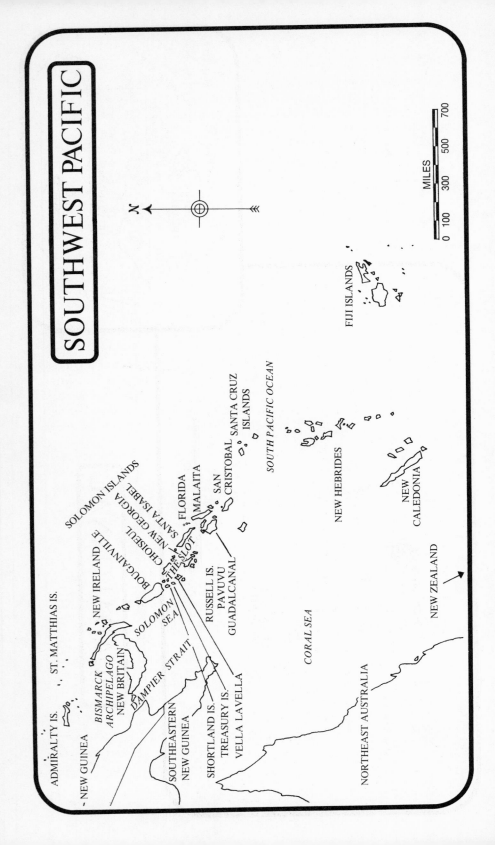

SOUTHWEST PACIFIC

MILES
0 100   300   500   700

ADMIRALTY IS.

ST. MATTHIAS IS.

- NEW GUINEA

BISMARCK
ARCHIPELAGO
NEW BRITAIN

NEW IRELAND

SOLOMON ISLANDS

BOUGAINVILLE

CHOISEUL

SANTA ISABEL

NEW GEORGIA

THE SLOT

SOLOMON
SEA

DAMPIER STRAIT

SOUTHEASTERN
NEW GUINEA

SHORTLAND IS.

TREASURY IS.

VELLA LAVELLA

RUSSELL IS.

PAVUVU

GUADALCANAL

FLORIDA

MALAITA

SAN
CRISTOBAL

SANTA CRUZ
ISLANDS

SOUTH PACIFIC OCEAN

NEW HEBRIDES

NEW
CALEDONIA

FIJI ISLANDS

CORAL SEA

NORTHEAST AUSTRALIA

NEW ZEALAND

They came on deck, blinking in what was now broad and sunny day, startled to hear the thundering of the American cruisers and destroyers or the crashing of bombs dropped by the warplanes of Admiral Fletcher's carriers.

The bombs fell on those Japanese on both sides of the channel who had awakened in terror to find their waters stuffed with enemy ships. Seaplanes in Tulagi Harbor were caught before they could rise, and were turned into floating torches. One of them tried to take off and was tumbled back into the water by a cruiser's guns. Fires were started on both sides of Sealark Channel. Marines moving to their battle stations gazed with satisfaction at flickering shorelines to north and south. At shortly after seven o'clock the assault troops of both sections were ready to launch simultaneous attacks.

"F Company stand by to disembark. First platoon stand by to disembark."

"All right, you men—down them cargo nets!"

Antlike they went over the side, clinging to the rough rope nets that swayed out and in against the warm steel sides of the ships. They stepped on the fingers of the men below them and felt their own hands squashed by men above. Rifles clanged against helmets. Men carrying heavy machine guns or mortar parts ground their teeth in the agony of descending to the waiting boats with 30 or 40 pounds of steel boring into their shoulders. And the boats rose and fell in the swells, now close in to the ships' sides, now three or four feet away.

The men jumped, landing in clanking heaps, then crouched beneath the gunwales while the loaded boats churned to the assembly areas, forming rings and circling, finally fanning out in a broad line at a few minutes before eight and speeding with hulls down and frothing wake straight for the shores of the enemy.

※   ※   ※   ※

GUADALCANAL WAS A MAMMOTH ANTICLIMAX, devoid of combat. The first wave stepped ashore at 9:10 A.M., but not a shot was fired by the enemy, who departed in haste when the bombardment began, leaving behind all manner of personal belongings, including rice bowls. After Vandegrift took a look at Grassy Knoll, he changed Cates's objective to the airfield while Hunt's outfit was ordered to Kukum, south of the Lunga River. Colonel Pedro A. del Valle's 11th Marines reached the airstrip by dusk and dug in along the east bank of the Lunga. Guadal's D-

Day casualties numbered one marine, who cut his hand on a machete opening a coconut.

In these initial hours of invasion, when fighting curiously bypassed Vandegrift's main force, marines in the harbor islands found war aplenty. With Edson's Raiders was (then) Lieutenant Colonel Samuel B. Griffith II, twice a Navy Cross winner, and one of the Corps' most eloquent spokesmen. A historian and widely read authority on guerrilla warfare, Griffith presents a brief panorama of the harbor Island fighting.

·3· FIRST BLOOD

BRIGADIER GENERAL
SAMUEL B. GRIFFITH II

On the Florida side . . . the most concentrated opposition was anticipated and here Vandegrift committed his most thoroughly trained and aggressive outfits, Edson's 1st Raiders to Tulagi, and Major Robert H. Williams's 1st Parachutists to the harbor islet of Gavutu.

To protect the left flank of the Raiders as they landed on Blue Beach at 8:00 A.M., Baker Company, 1st Battalion, Second Marines (Lieutenant Colonel Robert E. Hill) was previously to seize the Haleta promontory on neighboring Florida. To protect the Parachutists as they boated toward Gavutu for an 11:00 A.M. H hour, the remainder of Hill's battalion would before that time take a covering position on the tip of Halavo peninsula. This arrangement, not without complications, was phased to permit optimum use of naval gunfire and strike aircraft. Eight boats carrying Captain E. J. Crane's company beached at Haleta a few minutes before 8:00 A.M.; shortly thereafter the bulk of Hill's battalion seized the tip of Halavo. The first Americans to hit the beach in the Solomons landed without firing a shot. There were no Japanese in either place.

In the meantime, the 1st Raiders were debarking from the destroyer transports in which they had traveled from New Caledonia. They, too, had suffered from lack of exercise and crowded quarters, but unlike the troops who were to land on Guadalcanal an hour later, they were stripped down to minimum equipment for combat. Edson expected a tough fight. "Don't worry about the food," he had said to a company commander. "There's plenty there. Japs eat, too. All you have to do is get it."

At exactly eight o'clock two Raider companies—Baker and Dog—began wading ashore from Higgins boats grounded on coral shoals off Blue Beach, a landing area on the western end of the island selected in the hope that, because beaching seemed impossible, there would be no defenders. This hope was realized; no fire came from the jungle. As men struggled in waist-deep water to find footing on the slime-coated coral, many carrying heavy loads—mortar tubes, base plates and radio packs—went under. Yanked to their feet, they were propelled shoreward. Those who fell rose with hands bloodied by coral outcroppings, dungaree trousers ripped, and knees gory. Still, by 8:15, assault companies were ashore and the executive officer signaled Edson "Landing successful, no opposition." The remainder of the battalion followed quickly as first-wave boats returned to the APDs and embarked Companies Able and Cast.

The Raiders climbed the silent steep ridge to their front, wheeled to the right, and began to move to the southwest along the spine and sharply sloping sides of the island. On their heels, Lieutenant Colonel Harold E. Rosecrans's 2nd Battalion, Fifth Marines, landed over Blue Beach, crossed Tulagi and swept its northwest half without encountering any sign of the enemy. Rosecrans then collected his battalion and moved into position to support Edson.

Resistance first developed in the former Chinese settlement which hugged the Burns-Philp docks on the north coast opposite tiny Makambo Island. Here, just before noon on August 7, marines suffered their first battle casualties of the South Pacific campaign. In attempting to render aid to three seriously wounded men, Lieutenant (j.g.) Samuel Miles, a young Navy doctor, was killed, and a company commander critically hit. As Raiders moved warily toward the flimsy shacks, the Japanese brought light mortars into action. Progress slowed, and late in the afternoon Edson called a halt to consolidate for the night.

The marines held a line generally along rising ground from Carpenter's Wharf on the north to the spacious frame Residency in which the commissioner had lived until forced to flee the island in late April. On the south side of the Residency, a gently sloping finger fell off to a small golf club house near the beach. This defensive line was not organized; there was no time for that. Raiders dug shallow two- and three-man foxholes, and Rosecrans deployed his battalion to back up the forward positions.

The configuration of the ground favored the marines. The hogback they occupied sloped sharply down to a rectangular level area used in happier days for cricket matches and football games. The Japanese held positions on a rugged, rocky, brush-covered ridge which bounded the east side of the playing field. The afternoon's fighting had revealed that the defenders of Tulagi were liberally equipped with light mortars, grenade throwers, and heavy and light machine guns. The estimate was that there were between three and four hundred of them, and that they would attack during darkness.

They did—four times. But each assault was less impetuous than the one preceding, and all were repulsed. Some Japanese infiltrated; six crawled under the Residency porch and hid there. Just after first light on August 8 they killed three marines. Five minutes later they were grenaded to death.

In a foxhole in the center of the tenuous line he had done much to hold, Private First Class John Ahrens, an Able Company automatic rifleman, lay quietly, his eyes closed, breathing slowly. Ahrens was covered with blood. He was dying. Next to him lay a dead Japanese sergeant, and flung across his legs, a dead officer. Ahrens had been hit in the chest twice by bullets, and blood welled slowly from three deep puncture wounds inflicted by bayonets. Around this foxhole sprawled thirteen crumpled Japanese bodies. As Captain Lewis W. Walt gathered Ahrens into his arms to carry him to the Residency, the dying man, still clinging to his BAR, said, "Captain, they tried to come over me last night, but I don't think they made it."

"They didn't, Johnny," Walt replied softly. "They didn't."

The islet of Gavutu, connected to even smaller Tanambogo by a narrow causeway, proved a tougher D-day job than had Tulagi. Although defenders were fewer, so were the attacking Americans. Air bombardment of Gavutu, which measures about 500 yards in length and less than 300 in width, was brief and completely ineffective; hidden deep in reinforced dugouts and caves, the Japanese suffered only minor inconvenience, and set themselves to give the Parachutists a bloody reception.

As assault craft ran toward the shore, destroyers' guns neutralized defensive fire, but when boats grounded and marines scrambled out, this friendly fire ceased and the Japanese took charge. The Parachutists, momentarily disorganized by the hail of lead poured on them from invisible automatics, sought what cover they could find. There was not much. Before any progress had been made, Major Williams was hit; command devolved on Major Charles A. Miller. Men were dying on that thin strip of beach, but supporting destroyers, in uncharted waters, hesitated to close the range to deliver the pinpoint fire needed. The only escape was to move, and, in small groups, desperate men went toward the enemy. By midafternoon a squad gained the top of Hill 148, the highest point on the island. Here a marine broke the American flag. But a Rising Sun banner whipped defiantly above tiny Tanambogo, whose defenders were still very much alive. It was worth a man's life to expose himself near the causeway, periodically swept by bursts of automatic fire.

Obviously the Parachutists could not proceed with the capture of Tanambogo, originally assigned as their Phase Two objective. At the moment they were standing on top of a volcano which might erupt at any time, for under their feet some two dozen caves and dugouts harbored Japanese. These caves could be reduced only by explosive charges strapped to poles. Many were pushed into position by a huge, blond captain, Harry Torgerson. His trousers were ripped off by the first charge he detonated.

Thus, as the sun sank behind Savo, there remained the problem of Tanambogo. Rupertus called for air strikes on the islet, and directed Captain Crane, whose company had earlier withdrawn from undefended Haleta, to boat up and assault at dusk. The general's operations officer, Major William K. Enright, pointed out that this effort, concocted on the spur of the moment, promised small chance of success. Rupertus felt otherwise. As Enright had predicted, Crane's marines were met by murderous fire as the boats approached the landing point. Only one managed to beach; its occupants were shot to pieces. The other two, holed in half a dozen places, hastily withdrew to Gavutu.

This abortive attack did produce one lasting result, for it convinced Rupertus that he needed help. He appealed to Vandegrift, and at midnight Turner released Lieutenant Colonel Robert G. Hunt's battalion of the Second Marines, slated in the basic plan to occupy Ndeni. Rupertus ordered Hunt to land on Gavutu at dawn, relieve the Parachutists, and capture Tanambogo.

Night and rain brought no surcease to Gavutu. Individual Japanese crawled from caves to throw grenades or fire spasmodic bursts from light machine guns. The marines had no choice but to endure these attacks and to wait for dawn.

※　※　※　※

DEEP IN THE MOUNTAINS OF GUADALCANAL THE booming cacophony of invasion had been heard by one who "waited a lifetime" for our forces to come to the Solomons—Captain W. F. Martin Clemens, the coastwatcher. August 7 was a climactic day for the Britisher. Let us turn the clock back a few hours to recapture his jubilance.

·4· DIARY OF A COASTWATCHER

CAPTAIN W. F. MARTIN CLEMENS

Having gone to bed dinnerless on the night of the 6th, I slept pretty solidly; it was *not* the light of dawn that woke me up. It was the noise of a tremendous bombardment at Lunga Point! I was up in a flash, tired no longer. There was no doubt as to what it meant!

I could hardly realize that help had come at long last, and yet instinctively I knew that it had. A scout rushed down from Vungana and, breathlessly, gave out that the whole Jap fleet was at anchor between Lunga and Tulagi. I couldn't believe it, but for a moment my heart stood still. Luckily, I had just got the wireless receiver turned on and after swinging the dial madly for a few moments, I picked up the wavelength of the landing forces and I could hear intercommunication between ship and plane which made it pretty clear that not only Kookoom [Kukum] and Lunga, but also Tulagi and Gavutu were being attacked by Allied landing forces. It sounded as if they were mainly American. It was terrific.

I could hardly bear to sit quiet and listen. I wanted to get up and dance. I heard "Orange base" and "Purple base" calling various numbers. It reminded me of the "Red Sox" and the "Golden Bears." It didn't take long to deduce that these were two carriers, whose planes were supporting the landings. My diary entry said "Wizard!!!—Calloo, callay, oh! what a day." I heard targets being assigned to planes and lookouts kept coming in with reports of their pet objective at Lunga going off with a loud bang and a cloud of smoke. It was a "ba-amb to ba-amb" description. The Jap fuel dump, the ammo dump, and the power station on the river, all of which we had been at pains to describe, went up beautifully.

Over fifty ships had been counted in the channel, including two Australian cruisers. At five past twelve I picked up a message that marines had landed on Gavutu—so that's who they were. I had heard tell of the American Marines, but had never met them at close quarters . . .

Our own [Australian] planes passed overhead all day long. It was a nice change. A two-engined job, probably a Hudson, went past, fairly low just before lunch time with a damaged tail. Morale amongst the boys had gone up about 500% and we could not resist waving madly, and giving the chaps in the air a cheer. The morning shelling plastered the shore from Kookoom to Tasimboko and everyone hoped that the Tasimboko boys had been given a bit of hurry up. I picked up a message that several Jap guns had been knocked out and that the Japs were running madly in all directions.

It was great stuff, and in time to come there would be ample material for the "Records Broken Department" during the silly season, i.e., largest number of vessels seen in Indispensable Straits, off Tulagi, in Tulagi, near Tenaru, etc. In the middle of all this jubilation and excitement a message came in which sounded a more serious note, at least as far as I was concerned. It was a signal warning that we might be in danger from Japs retreating into the bush. It was not so good, but the boys' morale was so high that it raised a laugh. That day they would have walked through a whole division. The "powers that be" would also try and let us know when to come down. I remember wishing that they would send some shoes instead.

Late in the afternoon, Gavutu was reported to have been secured, but the Japs on Tanambogo were still holding out. Some dive bombers were told off to attack them. At a quarter to five Tulagi was under control, except for the Southeastern or hospital end of the island. I heard one of the dive bomber pilots asking permission to down a Jap flag on Makambo Island. "Permission granted," I heard, and shortly afterwards "assignment achieved." I heard another pilot put in the doghouse for dropping bombs without orders . . . It was as good as a football match, but I would have given practically anything for a beer and a grilled steak.

From Vungana, all day, came a continuous glowing account of din and destruction. Man and boy, they were all watching with eyes popping. I heard over the air, "I see a truck, I see two trucks, I see a hell of a lot of trucks! Sweep in low and you'll get a good haul."

. . . I couldn't stand it any longer . . . I just had to see what was going on, Japs or no Japs!

※   ※   ※   ※

ON RABAUL, THE ENEMY'S MIGHTY BASE NEAR THE headlands of the Solomons, a radio message was received from the Tulagi garrison at 6:30 that morning: "Tulagi under severe bombardment from air and sea. Enemy task force sighted. 1 battle-ship, 2 cruisers, 3 carriers, 15 destroyers and 30 to 40 transports." The message was delivered to Rear Admiral Gunichi Mikawa, Commander Eighth Fleet and Outer South Seas Force, who immediately saw the United States landings as a welcome opportunity to avenge the Imperial Navy's defeat at Midway. Initially, Mikawa's battle plan called for the 25th Air Flotilla to send down air strikes on the transports lifting Vandegrift's warstuffs. Much of the marine supplies and cargo was already piled on Beach Red, and the landing site was a scene of confusion which could only get worse as Imperial planes penetrated the radar screen to deliver blows at the transports.

By noon, shortly after the guns of the cruiser *San Juan* blasted Tulagi radio station to oblivion, Mikawa broke his two-starred flag in the heavy cruiser *Chokai* to lead a powerful eight-ship task force down through The Slot (the aptly named deepwater channel threading the parallel islands of the chain) in order to attack the invasion. Before setting sail, the admiral ordered 410 rifles of the crack Sasebo Special Naval Landing Force to embark in two destroyer-transports for Guadalcanal, and pulled two RO-boats (submarines) off war patrol in Australian sea lanes, ordering them to attack American transports. Mikawa, as the invasion sadly learned, was no caricature of the cross-eyed little Nip admiral; he was death itself, and one of the two toughest adversaries (Vice Admiral Raizo Tanaka—the "Tokyo Express"—the other) to confront the United States Navy in the Pacific.

It was almost dark now on Guadalcanal. During the afternoon carrier-air from *Essex, Wasp* and *Saratoga* had beaten off two severe attacks by the 25th Air Flotilla. On the beach marines were stripped to their waists unloading boxes and crates; a few yards off the sand Vandegrift's command post was set up under a shell-torn palm tree. Here he received word of heavy fighting in the harbor islands, with the enemy pinning down Williams' parachute battalion on the causeway between Gavutu and Tanambogo. Rupertus had called for a reserve battalion and Vandegrift had seen to it that the men were there. Now Vandegrift ate GI rations with his men and made plans for the next day. Meanwhile, trigger-happy marines, tense to the breaking point in some areas, let fly with small arms at every sound. One who fell this night was a Navy corpsman who failed to pronounce the password "Lilliputian" well enough to satisfy a sentry . . .

In the harbor islands the 2nd Division combat team was now

fully committed, fighting a tough, well-disciplined enemy. United Press International's Richard W. Johnston, unofficial historian of the 2nd Division, covered the battle. At present the editor of *Sports Afield,* Johnston takes us through this night to the first light of D-Plus-Two.

·5· THE TANAMBOGO — GAVUTU FIGHT

RICHARD W. JOHNSTON

Night had fallen, and under cover of darkness the company [B Company, 1st Battalion] began a desperate withdrawal. One boat, taking wounded, got away from the pier. The other was smashed. For the marines who were left, there was no escape except by wading or swimming, and there had to be covering fire. All through the fearful night a little knot of thirteen marines held the pier position, shooting back at the Japs, while their comrades made their way back to Gavutu. The thirteen did not escape until nearly daybreak. B Company had failed to take Tanambogo, but there was no word of blame from the Parachutists or from the Regiment.

Within twenty-four hours, the rest of the Second Division Marines were off the hot ships and into the hot fight. The balance of the First Battalion and the Second Battalion (2/2) were sent to Tulagi to reinforce Edson's hard-pressed Raiders. The Third Battalion (3/2) came to Gavutu, as did C Company of the Second Tank Battalion and A Company of the Second Amphibian Tractor Battalion. The Third Battalion of the Tenth Marines (3/10) dragged its pack howitzers ashore on both Tulagi and Gavutu. The Second Division Marines, who had been officially tagged as "reserve" for the First Marine Division, were now fully committed and at grips with the enemy on Tulagi, Gavutu, and Tanambogo, while on Guadalcanal, the First had scarcely established contact. These, of course, were the fortunes of war, but until Tarawa gave the Second Division a glory all its own, many a Second Division Marine bitterly resented the journalistic tendency to call the Solomons invasion a "First Division show."

The Second Regiment Marines who came to Gavutu and Tulagi

the morning of August 8 got a swift initiation into the rigors of war. Although they were not making an assault landing, the landing beaches were far from secure. Jap bullets whined around their boats, and on Gavutu enemy fire from Tanambogo was still pinking the old Lever Brothers' store, which had been taken over as an aid station for the wounded. On the steep hill that rose above the Gavutu beachhead, a Japanese flag still flew, although the Japs had been driven from their positions around it. This flag brought grief to K Company of the Third Battalion soon after the marines disembarked.

As the company reached the hilltop, an American plane dropped a fragmentation bomb on the Jap ensign. The bomb did not knock down the flag, but it killed and wounded several marines. The enraged survivors hauled down the "meatball" and Pfc. Edward Cooke of Missouri fished a small American flag out of his pack. K Company hoisted it, and for the first time the Stars and Strips fluttered over soil purchased from the enemy with blood.

The flag raising had symbolic value, but it probably had less effect on the marines than the careless gallantry of the sergeant who wrote: "What in hell's the use in worrying?" He was Sergeant Robert E. Bradley of Wisconsin, a member of M Company, 3/2. Bradley was perched on the upstairs balcony of the Lever Brothers' store building, manning a telephone circuit between the balcony OP and M Company mortarmen, when enemy fire tore away his larynx. It was a few minutes later, in the aid station below, that Bradley scribbled his immortal comment on a casualty tag supplied him by Dr. John N. Roberts, a Navy doctor from Arkansas.

But neither the flag raising nor Bradley's inspirational response changed the immediate military situation. The reduction of Tanambogo remained the imperative necessity. How best to do it? Lieutenant Colonel Robert Hunt, whose Third Battalion would have the job, worked out a plan of attack in the temporary command post he had established near the Lever store. He decided to send I Company, less its weapons platoon, by boat to the far end of Tanambogo for an amphibious landing. The attached platoon of C Company of the Second Tank Battalion—two light tanks—would accompany them in lighters. Simultaneously, a platoon of K Company would attempt to storm across the causeway, splitting the Jap defenses and clamping a pincers on the island. It was a good plan, and it worked, but it was not an easy way to take Tanambogo. Colonel Hunt didn't have enough marines and enough time to do it the easy way.

The climactic battle for this virulent little flyspeck of an island began in the early afternoon when a Navy destroyer emerged from the cluster of ships in the anchorage area and opened salvo fire on Tanambogo's defenses. On the Gavutu bluffs overlooking the causeway, members of M Company's machine-gun platoon had been busy for some hours digging in their .30 calibre weapons in positions that would cover K Company's charge. The day, like the day before and most of the days to come, was almost unbearably hot and moist, though clear.

At 1620 Captain William G. Tinsley, a tough Kentuckian, led I Company onto the oil-and-blood-stained beach and Lieutenant Robert Sweeney of Illinois shepherded his two light tanks ashore. At the same moment, the K Company platoon began inching down the long, exposed causeway. The Japs fought back on both fronts. Their machine guns swung back and forth across the causeway like flaming windshield wipers. One marine dropped and then another and another, but the survivors did not falter. The M Company gunners were answering the Jap fire, and Lieutenant J. J. Donahue kept his men moving forward. As the first few marines reached the Tanambogo end of the causeway, the Japs rose from their holes to meet them. For a moment the marines were engaged with bayonets, and the battle was hand to hand, man against man and steel against steel.

A few hundred yards away Tinsley's company was meeting the same kind of Banzai opposition. No Japanese expected or desired to survive. As Sweeney, the tank commander, drove his two eggshell monsters inland, screaming Japs ran at the tanks with pipes and crowbars to jam the treads. Sweeney's guns were all going, and so were the guns of his companion tank, but there was a painful lack of room to maneuver. Rising from the turret to reconnoiter, Sweeney took a bullet through the head. The tank stalled and the crew men fought their way out of it against Japs who were swinging knives and even a pitchfork. Meanwhile, the other tank had stuck between two coconut palms. Its trapped crew was confronted by an equally horrifying attack, with gruesome trimmings. The Japs fired the tank with gasoline and set upon the desperate marines with knives and bayonets. Two marines died and two others survived severe burns and multiple knife wounds. But the next day the bodies of forty-two Japs were counted within the sweep of the burned tank's guns.

Despite the loss of the tanks and heavy casualties in his own company, Tinsley held the beachhead and the K Company Marines, having successfully carried out the war's first bayonet charge, dug in for the night on the other end of the island. During the hours of darkness marine patrols filtered across the island and shot up the Jap warehouses that were concealed in the palm groves. In the first light of August 9, they completed the mop-up, with the help of marine artillery. The day before I Battery of 3/10 had got its guns emplaced on Gavutu. Now the weary Tanambogo marines were able to call for support from their own famed pack howitzers. These shells, hurled from Gavutu to Tanambogo, were the first fired offensively in the war, although II Battery of the same battalion was in action almost simultaneously, firing on the islet of Makambo.

While 3/2 was cleaning up Gavutu and Tanambogo (the Parachutists had been relieved from all but defensive missions), 1/2 and 2/2 had been catching hell on Tulagi, in support of the Raiders. No Japanese had surrendered. Instead, they drew into the honeycomb of caves patiently hollowed from the Tulagi bluffs and carried on a hopeless but relentless counter-fire. The Second Regiment battalions, under Lieutenant Colonel R. E. Hill and Lieutenant Colonel O. K. Pressley, had been landed to help dig the Japs out of these caves. It was slow and agonizing work. The marines had not yet developed the efficient flamethrower demolition teams that simplified the purification of strongpoints in later campaigns. On Tulagi the Japs were blasted out by frontal assault, or by satchel charges which members of the Second Pioneer Battalion attached to long poles.

After the fury of the first forty hours, the marines on Gavutu and Tanambogo were faced with a similar mop-up. The problem and its solution was typified by the activities of a lean Wisconsin gunnery sergeant named Orle S. Bergner. Sergeant Bergner, who happened to be on Tanambogo, moved almost casually among the Jap caves and emplacements, and systematically blew them in. Ignoring the snipers, intent only on his explosives, Bergner inspired his comrades and won from them the designation "the one-man stick of dynamite." He later was recommended for the Medal of Honor.

❧   ❧   ❧   ❧

ALTHOUGH TULAGI AND GAVUTU WERE technically "secured," the hard mop-up fighting was to go on for some days. One of Edson's stout mortarmen, gratified by the performance of his tube, scribbled a lasting tribute to his weapon:

> We have a weapon that nobody loves,
> They say our gun's a disgrace.
> You crank up 200, and 200 more,
> And it lands in the very same place.
> Oh, there's many a gunner who's blowing his top,
> Observers are all going mad,
> But our affection has lasted
> For this old pig-iron bastard,
> It's the best gun this world ever had.

Guadalcanal was still in a world of its own, however. The only fighting was the air war conducted by Fletcher's carrier planes versus bombing attempts by the 25th Air Flotilla. The previous afternoon enemy planes had streaked in low over Florida Island to attack the transports, but all had been driven off, and 17 were shot down. The transport, *George F. Elliot,* had been hit by a bomb and prematurely abandoned by her merchant crew. Despite the heightening frequency of air raids Saturday, things were going pretty well for Vandegrift. Hunt's force had attained its objective, Kukum, where large stores of enemy food were found. That night Vandegrift wrote a letter home, amusing in retrospect, in which he told of the ease in which the Guadalcanal part of the campaign had been won.

But about 10 P.M. Saturday the situation for our forces on Guadalcanal and Tulagi swiftly changed. Vandegrift was summoned to an emergency conference aboard Admiral Turner's flagship, *McCawley* ("Whacky Mac"), where he became aware of the first intimation of trouble. Turner and Crutchley were in the wardroom, waiting grimly. After telling the marine general and his operations officer, Jerry Thomas, of a sighting report of a Japanese fleet 150 miles northwest of Savo (a sighting made eight hours before but never acted upon because the pilot stopped for a cup of tea before reporting to his operations office), Turner handed Vandegrift a dispatch from Fletcher to Ghormley, intercepted a few hours before:

> Fighter-plane strength reduced from 99 to 78. In view of the large number of enemy torpedo planes and bombers in vicinity of this area, I recommend the immediate withdrawal of my carriers. Request tankers sent forward immediately as fuel running low.

Without waiting for a reply, Fletcher had removed his carriers from the area, and Turner, with no choice but to protect the transports, as Fletcher had set the precedent, told the marine general he would have to clear his transports in the morning. The only question now to be discussed was supplies. Vandegrift said the troops on Guadalcanal were in "fair shape," but he had no idea how Rupertus was holding up, as all fighting thus far had been in the latter's area. What needed to be done obviously was for Vandegrift to go out and talk with the other marine general. He did so after a short, spectacular trip aboard the minelayer *Southard.*

This was the moment when the Japanese force "about 150 miles northwest of Savo" entered the Sound, and Gunichi Mikawa began to make his presence felt. The admiral's eight-ship force amassed a total firepower of thirty-four 8-inch, ten 5.5-inch, twenty-seven 5-inch and 4.7-inch guns, and sixty-two torpedo tubes—a deadly sufficiency of firepower.

It was shortly after 1 A.M., August 10. Several minutes later four float planes from this force were sent aloft to signal the position of our warships patrolling in boxlike formations at the distant ends of Savo ("Ironbottom Sound"). After his planes reported in, Mikawa closed the first formation at 28 knots, and at 1:47 A.M. all Japanese ships came into gunnery range. Mikawa spat out the order *"Fire!"* and in a veritable orgy of shot and shell —guided by the jagged light of the transport *George F. Elliot*— enemy gunners loosed a devastating hammerblow on five cruisers, sinking *Astoria, Quincy, Canberra* and *Vincennes,* one destroyer, and damaging the cruiser *Chicago* with a total loss of 1024 Allied seamen. The worst defeat ever inflicted on the United States Navy required exactly forty-six minutes.

Aboard *Quincy* was Major Warren P. Baker, 11th Marines, temporarily attached to the heavy cruiser as an aerial observer. He briefly tells of the warship's death throes before he went over the side for five hours.

·6· ABOARD THE DOOMED *QUINCY*

MAJOR WARREN P. BAKER

A Jap plane was overhead dropping flares that illuminated the whole area. The flares were brighter than anything I have ever seen, seemingly brighter than daylight, and they appeared to be suspended in the air . . .

Almost immediately the secondary battery opened fire. The portside 5-inch guns had us directly in its beam, and as our ship turned starboard, all nine of the 8-inch guns blasted in its general direction. The searchlight went out.

By this time, the cruiser astern of us was ablaze. As its plane went up in smoke, the sky around us again lighted up so that the *Quincy* and its crew were silhouetted against the blackness of the night — perfect targets.

Our starboard plane was struck and burst into flames. The crew tried frantically but without success to control the fire. Then someone on the portside of the bridge yelled, "Shells are falling short about 100 yards . . ." Another salvo landed about 75 yards away from the starboard bow, and we all realized what a straddle meant. From this moment on, the *Quincy* received direct hits from stem to stern.

Our 5-inch gun crews were for the most part wiped out. One of the loaders stood with a star shell in his arms, ready to seat it in the chamber of the gun when a fragment from an enemy shell hit it and set it off. The man and most of the gun crew were killed instantly. Down on the main deck unrecognizable gun crewmen were lying dead, including a battery officer whose legs were cut off at the hips.

Suddenly the ship shook violently and literally leaped out of the ocean. The two torpedoes had connected with our port bow. Then came a series of explosions and one of the forward magazines blew up, and that part of the ship was aflame.

The sound of breaking glass, of steel hitting steel, the hissing of air from the compressed air line, the explosion of countless shells and the pitiful cries of the wounded all merged into one, and seemed to shout the doom of the *Quincy* . . .

As the flames began to lick at the bridge, Aldridge, Brilliant and I became separated. The flames blocked our exit to the main deck and the powder gas was so strong that we choked. My lungs seemed full of the stuff, but finally I managed to get down the small ladder at the end of the signal bridge.

Down on the main deck, the smoke wasn't as bad, but the sight of our men lying wounded and dead was ten times worse. I saw the radio crew and they knew we had been hit seriously as all of the radios had been destroyed, but were unaware of the ship's real distress . . . [Now] the ship began to list badly to port. I walked out on the main deck and saw that survivors were in the water clinging to the life nets . . . By the time I was ready to leave the ship, the normally vertical splinter shields around the 5-inch guns were then within a few degrees of being horizontal.

I climbed up on one of them, removed my shoes, and placed them on the steel plating. But my helmet, pistol and flashlight were still with me when a life net floated by and I jumped in. I no sooner reached the net than other survivors began to yell to get away from the ship so that we wouldn't be sucked under when she went down. A few minutes later the *Quincy* started down, and to our surprise we were pushed farther away from it instead of being pulled down.

I turned to watch the *Quincy* sink—her bow was down and her stern stuck out of the ocean. The propellors were still turning as she submerged. I looked at my watch; it was just 0235.

❧ ❧ ❧ ❧

WHILE BAKER STRUGGLED IN THE BLACK WATERS, and Vandegrift observed the pyrotechnics from a minesweeper, Corporal T. Grady Gallant of the 11th Marines, with a 37-mm howitzer platoon, watched from Guadalcanal. With his tense, untried men who felt the enemy was everywhere around them, we meet gifted author-newspaperman Gallant, city editor of the *Chattanooga Post,* and spend two eventful days with him.

·7· "SERIOUS, VERY SERIOUS . . ."

T. GRADY GALLANT

During early evening, a tropical drizzle began to fall. We wrapped ourselves in ponchos in an effort to keep as dry as we could. But ponchos aren't as effective as they should be. We slowly became wetter and wetter. The rain would stop occasionally, then start up again. For a while, sleep was impossible. But, finally, I managed to fall asleep, a blessing due to exhaustion. None of us had slept much since the afternoon of August 6, catching catnaps at odd moments.

We took turns on watch. One man in the squad would sit with an automatic weapon and guard the rest of us on a four-hour shift basis.

Several hours before dawn . . . Trenton shook me awake.

"Something is goin' on out on the ocean," he whispered. "You awake?"

I grunted, too tired to move.

"Looks like all hell has broke loose," Bellflower added.

Somehow, the thought occurred to my sleep-drenched mind if Bellflower was awake, something *must* be going on. I heard what sounded like distant thunder. With great effort, I got up and fought my eyes open.

I looked toward the ocean. We were back from the beach about a hundred feet and only a few inches above sea level. The rumbling continued, deep kettledrum-like sounds and flashes of light. Instantly, it came to my mind: This is a naval battle.

"I bet you it's a damn fight out there," Trenton said. "Look over there . . . over to the left, there."

I looked. The flashes were close-in, near Savo Island. Flashes like summer lightning were coming from many points. The sound rolled in seconds later. It was a strange sensation to watch in the darkness, wet and cold, and see these bursts of light, sometimes from one source, sometimes from several places at once, all scattered toward the horizon. The firing was in drumlike rolls with intervals of rapid beats alternated by single broadsides of fire. It was clear to us from the flashes, the ships were in rapid motion. The light would flower in great bursts in one spot, then would repeat at a new and different point at sea.

As the conflict continued, there were great and sudden bursts of huge red, cloudlike displays of glowing puffs that changed to a mixture of white, crimson, bluish, and blood-red mixtures before suddenly reducing themselves to smaller embers of color. We were positive such awesome flowerings marked the direct hit and sinking of an enemy vessel. The pyrotechnics were massive, even at the distance we viewed them. They came as cheering signs to us as we crouched in our foxholes, front-line troops witnessing a battle at sea. This, I think, was one of the few times in modern history a great naval battle had been witnessed by troops engaged in conflict on land.

We came to hope desperately for more evidence of sinking ships. We were now convinced beyond any doubt our warships were driving the enemy from the ocean. We knew the Japanese had been trapped by our Navy and were now being destroyed.

The great rumbling continued. Now much closer inshore and to our left as we looked toward the sea. Suddenly, there was a massive burst of crimson flecked with white that rose upward, expanding all the while and boiling as clouds do in a storm. We could hear explosions, faint and different in tone from the rumbles, as the fires leapt to great heights as a semicircular ball, intensely red in the center, then reduced itself in volume and soon disappeared.

"We got that one!" Trenton said excitedly. "That was a hit and the thing blew up. Boy, wasn't that a sight. It must have been a battleship, or something like that."

All of us were filled with excitement. We were like spectators in the days of Rome, turning our thumbs down, thirsty for the blood

of gladiators in the arena. We called for blood. There was a feeling
of exhilaration. We forgot our wet clothing and the dripping of the
rain, which now had become a series of large drops.

As we watched, the battle seemed to drift farther away, slowly, with
fainter and fainter rumblings that followed fewer and fewer flashes
of light, it faded and was gone. The sea was dark and quiet again.

"We'll know tomorrow what happened," I said. "I'm anxious to
know how many we sank."

Trenton yawned. "Me, too. That makes it a little better around
here. You know, makes it safer, and we can get unloaded."

"Uh-huh," I said.

Victory was sweet to us that night. We wrapped up again. Daylight
was not far away.

At dawn we were up, and after washing our faces in the sea, we ate
a breakfast of pineapple slices and coconut. In a foxhole, we built
a fire with paraffin-coated tubes in which our 37-mm shells were
packed. These waterproof containers made excellent fuel that burned
with a smokeless flame, a matter of some importance in concealment.
Such a fire heated water in our canteen cups quickly. To this we added
a brown powder which dissolved reluctantly to make a bitter liquid
identified by Headquarters, Marine Corps, as coffee. Though this
wasn't the best coffee known to mankind, it was brown and hot. The
desire for hot coffee is a passion with marines. I usually drank three
cups at breakfast. These were canteen cups, and they totaled three
pints. At the other two meals, I drank two cups, for a total of four more
cups—or seven pints of coffee a day.

Coffee at breakfast is a boost to morale in battle. It is usually all
there is, and without this simple beginning for the day, the world
seems to get off on the wrong foot. Cigarettes don't taste as good, and
there is a gnawing feeling something is missing. And, of course, what
is missing is the coffee. A steaming canteen cup of coffee warms the
bones after a night of damp cold.

Not long after coffee, we were ordered to work our way over to
the airstrip. We hooked the cannon to our truck, hopped in, and
bumped over a winding trail leading inland. The distance was not
great, and within a few minutes we were in the middle of civilization as
it was known on Guadalcanal. The airstrip area looked more urban
than anything we had seen since our arrival. There were some frame
structures; a few of these were rather large. Rambling, and low, they
resembled oversized chicken houses. We crossed Lunga River, a
shallow, rapid stream with a rocky bottom, commented upon the Japanese privies standing on stilts over the water, and approached the airfield.

Shellfire from our warships and bombs from Navy planes had caused some destruction, but all was not lost. The field itself didn't look too bad, though the runway was still rough and pocked with a few scattered craters. A Seabee unit was with us, and these professional construction men were to go to work on the field and other necessary construction as soon as possible. Now that we had it, it was vital the landing area be readied for our own planes.

Lieutenant Rose ordered the guns—there were three others in our unit—to set up across the width of the west end of the field and for us to dig in around them. This we did, stringing the cannon across the clearing, pointing them toward the end of the runway with the length of the field behind us. A tall grass, something like sagebrush, grew in this flat, cleared area. My gun was on the left side of the field, with the others in line to my right. Considerable distance separated us, but we could command the area to our front very easily. We dug the guns in, set them for immediate action, and threw nets over them. Into the nets we stuck the sagebrush, and the effect was very good, we thought, as the guns blended with the terrain.

To our left, was a small knoll covered with trees. It rose sharply from the field with a steep slope that was clear of underbrush. After we got our gun position set, Trenton and I made for the knoll to see how effective the camouflage was and to learn a little more about the terrain nearby. It is always something of a comfort to know before nightfall what lies near, what possible danger spots there are, whether or not other units are implaced, and landmarks of the immediate areas. It gives a certain advantage to know these things. It prevents confusion should there be a night attack. It prevents engaging your own units and it provides a mental map that becomes useful in the darkness. So, we made for the knoll. It was farther away than it appeared. As we walked we heard the throb of a plane. At first, we thought it was one of ours, and paid little attention. But as we looked up, we saw the Rising Sun—the Meatball—on its wings identifying it as Tojo-made. With that, we broke into a race for cover, making the hill in a matter of seconds. The plane seemed little interested in us after all, and we felt a little foolish. It flew in lazy circles, evidently on a mission of reconnaissance. The Jap pilot was fairly high, but not extremely so, and appeared to be interested chiefly in the airfield.

"Where are our fellows? Where are the good guys . . . could they still be at lunch?" Trenton asked.

I was still puffing from the sprint. I tried to catch my breath, looking up at our visitor. "Maybe they've gone home. Come to think of it, Trenton, I haven't seen the Navy in some time."

"Me, either."

We watched the Jap. He was rather arrogant, we thought. He just sailed about, his engine throbbing in the peculiar way the enemy engines had, taking his time.

"He must know our planes aren't around," Trenton said.

"If he doesn't, he's nuts," I agreed. "I wonder if he can see our gun out there."

"Can you?"

I looked for the first time since reaching the knoll. My full attention had been on the plane. I couldn't see the little cannon. Just a field of sagebrush. It looked very natural, as they say at funerals.

"Nope," I answered him. "We finished in the nick of time. He can't see the thing, even with his glasses on."

Trenton tilted back his helmet. The straps dangled. "He isn't goin' to do a damn thing. He's just lookin'."

We watched in silence. The Jap pilot was making oval passes from one end of the field to the other.

"Takin' pictures, you think?" I asked, watching the slow circles.

"Sure. They are tryin' to find out what hit 'em."

I lighted a cigarette. It was a Jap brand. All of us had run out of American brands. We had found these at a Jap dump and had loaded up with them.

Trenton took one, lighted it and blew out smoke, his eyes watering.

"Jesus," he moaned, "these are awful." He inhaled and coughed. "I think these things are dope . . . or manure."

"Can't you tell the difference?"

"If it's dope, it's cheap dope," he added. "But just think about it for a minute, now. Why, they could wreck this operation by getting us mad for these things. . . ."

"That'll never happen," I said. "You just said they are awful."

"Uh-huh, but they could have poppy leaves in 'em . . . or opium roots." He removed the cigarette and looked at it.

"Dried," I said.

"Dried?"

"Dried roots."

"Sure! They would dry 'em . . . Look at that Jap! Look at him!"

The Japanese plane was lower and heading for our hill.

"He sees these cigarettes and crazed for dope, he's going to try to get one," I said.

The plane had begun to circle short of our hiding place.

"I wouldn't put it past 'em . . . doping cigarettes." He took another drag. "God, these are awful."

I smoked my cigarette. The taste was dry and bitter. The smoke burned throat and nostrils.

"Nobody had shot at him. You noticed that?" Trenton asked.

"No use givin' away the gun positions. That's what he wants. He can't see anything he doesn't know already, anyway."

I nodded.

The plane continued to circle, gaining altitude. Finally, it droned off in the distance.

As it was growing dark, the major arrived with the captain and several other officers. He called all of us together at the edge of the airfield. His mustache tips were waxed. They stood out from his cheeks and pointed heavenward. He appeared distracted and waited impatiently for us to gather. Some of the men were at the guns. They had to be called in and one man left to keep an eye on things. This took a little time; not much, but some. The major appeared anxious to get on with the matter that had brought him.

"Now, men," he began without preliminaries, "we are in something of a spot. There may be a counterattack tonight, and if there is, you are to hold. If the Japs do attack, they will try to take this field. They will not succeed."

We were gathered in a little circle about him. He wasn't talking loud, as the enemy might be listening. I felt discouraged. News of an expected enemy attack tends to dampen the joy of battle. It is a defensive attitude. But there is always a possibility; when the possibility gets very good, then there is a special conference about it.

"We are in a serious position," the major continued. "The naval battle early this morning caused serious losses on our side. . . ."

Lord, we lost the damn thing! I thought with a cold chill. Those must have been our ships sinking . . . not Japs. My spirits became wringing wet.

The major cleared his throat. "The Navy has withdrawn and the carriers have gone. We have no air support, and will have none until we can get this airfield in shape. That may be several days . . ."

My spirits were now wading, knee deep, in gloom. The size of it was: We had gotten hell beat out of us at sea. Now here we were with no sea or air support, standing on an airfield we couldn't use.

The major continued: "Conserve ammunition. We may need all we have and more. Don't waste any. Don't fire unless you are engaged . . . None of this insurance firing . . . Go easy with your food supplies . . . Watch the water supply . . ." He paused.

The little knot of men shuffled. No one said a word. The news was rather shocking. We had thought the whole thing had been easy. Too easy, it was turning out. Hell, it was just beginning. In fact, it hadn't really begun.

"What about the transports?" one of the men said.

"They are going to be here in the morning, and we are going to get off all we can . . . everything we can. Then they will pull out. They can't stay long with no protection, except those old destroyers."

There was a murmur of low comment in the group. Little whisperings and sighs.

"Are they coming back, sir?"

"Oh, yes," the major said. "It is not certain just what day. It will be several days, several days. The destroyers may come in and out . . ."

Hell, I thought, we've lost control of the water. We are cut off and have just about been treed. That's probably why that Jap plane was so calm and collected today.

The major emphasized again to be on one hundred percent alert. "The situation is serious, very serious . . . but there is one good thing, one ray of light . . ." He hesitated, then went on in a low, soft tone, "The Navy at Pearl Harbor has broken the Japanese Naval code. We are intercepting their orders and translating them. You must not discuss this. But you should feel better. We still have an ace up our sleeve. . ."

This was an interesting bit of news. Hell, why didn't they know about the situation last night? We should have beaten them, if we were doing all this. But, then our ships did know the enemy was on his way. They knew that, evidently.

"How many ships did we lose, Major?" someone asked. "How many were lost in that battle?"

"I can't say . . . but it was serious. We didn't win it. They won. The situation is now acute. But I can't say how many. I don't think they are at all sure about it . . ."

This was quite a let-down from our false beliefs of early morning as we watched the crimson flashes and heard the rolling thunder of broadsides. Those had been our men sinking, being blown up, burning and lighting the night sky for miles around. We had cheered it in our hearts . . . we had wanted more. It had never occurred to us we could lose. That we could be beaten in a battle. Beaten again and again, from the very first day. Well, there had been exceptions; but they had been rare, these exceptions. The United States had been fighting brave defeats. Now here we were. What would be the outcome here? Would it be another defeat? More of the same? Would we be wiped out? Forced out? Or starved out in a blockade?

The major was beginning to move off. The group broke up. It was night. The moon was still down. The field was pretty dark. Trenton and I stumbled through the sagebrush. The rest of the squad moved along with us. We found our position. In the dark we located the foxholes. I got the squad together. We sat in the darkness by the gun.

"You guys be ready all night. Stay in your foxholes. Two of us will be on watch all the time. The rest of you can doze. If something cuts loose, I'll wake you with this cannon. When it goes off, do your jobs like we have always done it. No smoking. No noise. No talking above a whisper. If you hear anything, let me know and we'll try to figure it out. Get settled and stay settled. Bellflower, stay awake as much as you can."

We put a round of canister in the cannon and left the breech open. We got out some hand grenades and a couple of flare grenades.

"If I had known this sooner, we could have set up a trip wire for one of these flare grenades out front," I told Trenton.

"Too dark now," he said.

I agreed.

This was a good squad. We didn't have a full complement, but we had good men. Besides Bellflower, who was ammunition man; there was Gleason, the gunner; Maywell, loader; Thompkins, truck driver and machine gunner for the .50-caliber mounted on the truck; Flint, who was a young kid, rifleman and ammunition carrier; Trenton, who drove the jeep, carried messages and helped Lieutenant Rose locate gun positions ahead, which we later occupied, and myself. This was barely enough men to operate the weapons. About half as many as we should have had. Sometimes the lieutenant stayed with us, but usually he was with the platoon sergeant, who was with another gun.

It was a long night. The usual jungle sounds, with the exception of falling coconuts, which we had come to recognize, permeated the darkness. We were still too new on the island to be positive of our identification of complex noises, weird cries, and commotions. We knew, too, the Japanese were not above imitating such sounds. Sleep under such a situation was impossible. All sounds were danger signals. We tried to penetrate the night with our eyes. Quickly we learned we could see anyone walking, or crouching, by taking a low-level view. This put anything not flat on the ground in relief against the starlight. From this observation, we developed the technique of lying on our backs in a foxhole with our feet toward the enemy. Such a posture enabled one to see anything coming, even if there were no moon, and to fire without exposing one's body. It also prevented the Japs from stabbing one in the back. This way, you got stabbed in the chest. Nevertheless, it was a posture that allowed faster action—more rapid change from resting to fighting stance—than lying on the side or stomach. When in this position, you didn't have to pop your head up from the hole, like a turkey behind a log, to find out what was going on within a reasonable distance from the foxhole. . .

Dawn came. Nothing had happened. And we were worn out with it. Bone tired. Tension of past days began to be felt as a weight. The constant state of alert, the movement, excitement, physical work, eyestrain and tropical heat were burdens; indeed, shocks we had absorbed. Nature would remedy the situation. We would soon be so sleepy, we could sleep anytime, anywhere.

Battle creates a new order of living. It forms new blocks of time, erases the division between night and day, wipes out the meal hours, removes bedtime. The neat hours of an ordered civilian day are no longer in existence. Now the day is really twenty-four hours long with no discernible division between it and the day before, or the day following. Time is no longer morning, afternoon, or night; it is day or night. It is either daylight or darkness. Whether it is 8 A.M., or 11 A.M., or 3 P.M., means little; the important thing is that it is daylight. It is the same with the night, whose broad divisions are: getting dark, after dark, late, before daylight, and getting daylight. It's just as dark at 8 P.M. as it is at midnight, as far as night fighting may be concerned. The point is: It is either a long time to daylight, or it is almost daylight.

With the establishment of this new order of block time, the human machine is subjected to great and sudden change. There are no regular mealtimes. Food is eaten when available and when hunger is persistent enough to call itself to the attention of the mind. Hunger is always present, but in varying degrees. Thus, the stomach, intestines, kidneys, heart, lungs, legs, arms, feet, eyes, ears, and brain must adjust. Rhythms must change.

Fresh troops, new troops, cannot sleep. But as time wears on, as these troops become more and more adjusted to twenty-four-hour days, they become able to fall asleep instantly when the occasion presents itself.

Catnaps. Little slumbers. Dozes. These snatches of rest are taken in fits and starts, day and night, serving to keep all men going all the time—like the heartbeat, which rests briefly between pumps, but works day and night without stopping its vital function.

Such rest works out very well. No group of men sleeps at once; someone is awake all the time. By the same token, some are sleeping. If things are quiet, all are resting, some sleeping, some idle, some talking, some on watch; when the quiet is shattered by demands of war, all are in action.

As troops get more and more adjusted to block time, they can sleep through bombardments, air raids, small-arms fire—anything, provided the situation does not affect them directly and they are not needed, or provided they can do nothing about it—can neither fight back nor leave, as in the case of naval bombardment or aerial attack by bombers.

We had not established this routine. We did not know of it. It was forced upon us by circumstance. It came without plan or schedule. It became a way of life, the way men lived, the normal order of things, an adjustment of Nature, for such living is the wisdom of wild animals to whom life is war. Such animals live without knowledge of Time as civilization knows it, as men view it, for Time to beasts is the living instant without future or past. It is *now.* In this way we entered the kingdom of animals, fitted ourselves into Nature's pulsating movement of life without neat divisions, or smooth, polished, planned order. We were absorbed by our environment and the dangers we found in it.

As the sun appeared, a red mass that converted the heavy dew into steam and brought sweat rolling down our backs, Lieutenant Rose arrived bubbling with activity. Trenton had barely finished his coffee. I was washing my face in my helmet in preparation for breakfast. The rest of the squad was stumbling about, engaged in similar activity. The officer was surging through the brush when we first saw him, freshly shaved, pink of cheek.

"Good morning, men!" he cried, surging up to the cannon and placing a foot on the trail.

Trenton and I saluted; he returned the greeting.

"I trust you had a pleasant night, sir," I said, water dripping from my face and hands. I dried them on my dungaree sleeves.

"Excellent," he grinned. "A room with a view."

Trenton remained silent. It was evident he was thinking of how nice a beer would have tasted for breakfast. His eyes were not adjusted and appeared as small pools of red.

"Corporal Trenton," Lieutenant Rose said, "man the jeep. We are to move to Lunga Point. We have to find it and look it over."

"Yes, sir," Trenton replied, bending over to pick up his sub-machine gun.

"Secure this position, Corporal Gallant," the lieutenant said. The two started to move toward the jeep, which was covered with sagebrush about thirty feet behind our position.

"Yes, sir," I said, turning to the squad. "So be it," I told them. "Wake Bellflower up."

Flint, fresh-faced and looking very much as if he were ready to go to school, probed Bellflower with his boot. Bellflower was stretched on his back, mouth open, snoring softly.

"Hit the deck, Bellflower," Flint snorted, lifting Bellflower's leg and dropping it.

Bellflower opened his eyes. He looked even more vague than usual.

"Get up, Bellflower," I told him. "There's a war on. We are moving out to a better foxhole in the sky."

He yawned and got up. Sagebrush hung down from his helmet giving him the appearance of having dived through a bale of hay. He poured some water in his canteen cup and put the cup in the fire.

"Now that you've put on breakfast, let's get this gun secured while it's cookin'," I said.

We secured the gun, gathered up personal gear, made horseshoe rolls and buckled up our packs.

I turned to Thompkins. He was ready to go. "Get the truck and hook up this gun . . . get 'em off this open place. Put 'em over there in the edge of the trees and stay with 'em. Stick with the machine gun until we get over there with you. These guys can finish breakfast. When they get through, we'll all come over."

Thompkins got the truck, hooked the gun up with our help, we loaded on our packs, and he drove off, bumping over the field. He pulled into cover. It looked good. I didn't want the thing blown up by a Jap plane.

At mid-morning Trenton and the lieutenant reappeared. We moved out, heading toward the beach in a westerly direction. The road wound like a cowpath. We passed some broken-down shacks and plunged into the coconut grove. The other guns were ahead of us. We were bringing up the rear. We came to a house that faced the sea and had a chicken-wire fence in the backyard. Our truck stopped.

"Corporal," the lieutenant shouted from the jeep, "set up in this area." He pointed toward the house. The jeep moved away through the trees.

"Pull on toward the beach," I told Thompkins.

We moved ahead slowly. At the edge of the coconut grove, the beach dropped slightly. This was a gentle slope, shallow; not more than a foot or two. We stopped.

"Abandon ship," I said. We all got out. I looked around.

It was evident the U.S. Coast Guard was using the house. We could see some guardsmen moving around inside. The building was a white frame structure of modest size with a front porch. It was in good condition and looked like thousands of similar dwellings near railroad tracks in the States. The backyard, with its sagging chickenwire fence was a jumble of coops, boxes, and piles of weathered lumber, scrap wood actually. There was a large iron kettle of the type used in the deep South to boil clothes in the old days when Negro women earned extra money by "taking in washing." There were rusty cans scattered about, the evidence of a hasty departure. But, evidently, our ships had not hit the place during the shelling.

At a corner of the fence nearest to us was a small structure, a tool shed of some kind with a door hanging open. It had been built recently and didn't look completely finished. It was clean inside, though in disorder. The floor was covered with loose papers, some books, and torn pieces of equipment—part of a knapsack, a cloth belt, a dental mirror, note paper.

About ten feet from the shed was a large hole. It appeared the Japanese had been preparing to build a gun emplacement. The hole was fairly large, about four feet deep and maybe five feet square, but the sand at the corners had caved in, making the hole funnel-shaped. It had been covered with coconut logs, which were now scattered about; some of the logs had fallen in the hole, others had rolled to one side. There were several bundles of straw bags. Some of these were still tied together, other bundles had broken open and the sacks were loose. This was a light-colored straw; a bright tan reed of some sort woven into a container. They seemed pretty strong, and were new.

We started our gun position, locating it just in front of the coconut trees so we would have a clear field of fire toward the ocean and to the left and right, yet enjoy some protection of the palms. The frame house was to our right, and we were some hundred feet from it. At the same time, the gun was not far distant from the Jap excavation, which we had decided to convert into an air-raid shelter, since most of the hard work had been done for us by the enemy. This thought made us feel quite good. We unhooked the gun and rolled it to the spot selected earlier, smoothed the sand around it, dug in the trail, and set to work filling the woven sacks with sand. We stacked these sandbags at each side of the gun as low walls.

The air-raid shelter was easy. We rolled the logs back on top, filled sandbags and stacked them four deep on top the logs and on all sides, except at an entrance we constructed on the landward side. We decided any shells would come from the sea, so we discarded convenience for safety. This work took until almost dark. But inspection of the shelter convinced us it had been worth the effort.

During late afternoon, a tank lighter beached near us and brought off two wounded found on a raft in the channel. They were survivors of the night battle at sea. We put them in our truck and a corpsman appeared from somewhere. We never did know how he got there.

One of the men was badly burned. He was just a boy, actually; not more than eighteen years old. His burned arms and face had been exposed to the water, the tropical sun, and the abuse of a wave-tossed raft. Long strips of burned skin, detached from the seared flesh by salt water, hung from him. His eyes were puffed and swollen almost shut and his shoulders were alternate patches of black and livid red meat.

The other sailor, who was a little older, was not burned so badly, but he was also in serious condition.

"Can't you give him something to stop the pain?" Thompkins asked.

He was in the driver's seat, ready to take the injured back to the airstrip, where the field hospital had been set up in one of the Jap buildings.

The corpsman, a middle-aged careerman with a pot belly, had a small piece of cotton in his hand. He was looking at the arms of the boy who was so badly burned. "I can't seem to find a place that isn't burned," he said. "I think it would be better if I gave him the shot in an unburned area."

"Go on, give him something," I said. "He can't hurt any worse than he is now."

The boy was only semiconscious. He would try to open his eyes wider, but couldn't.

"Help me . . . oh, please . . . please . . . help me," he sobbed. His voice was very weak.

"We better get him back to the hospital," I said.

The corpsman gave the injection. The boy didn't seem to know anything had happened. He was muttering, but we couldn't understand him.

"Thompkins, go ahead," I said. "Drive easy, but get there as quick as you can."

He nodded and the truck moved away. The corpsman hopped in the back with Bellflower, who was riding shotgun.

Gleason, gunner on the 37-mm, turned to me. "God, that was awful," he said. Gleason was a quiet fellow, about twenty years old. He was from South Carolina. A small man with black hair and a large nose, he was a good gunner and liked by all of us. He kept pretty much to himself and was not much of a talker, though when he did say something he meant it.

The two sailors had upset me, too. I nodded agreement. "I hope that kid makes it; I hope he lives."

"I don't think he will . . . I don't thing he'll live . . . I don't see how he can."

"I don't think so, either; but I hope he can . . . I hope he can live. He's such a young fellow," I said.

"Awful young to die like that," Gleason said.

"Burned up."

"And then on that raft all this time."

I shook my head. I wanted to put the sight from my mind. But I couldn't. I kept seeing that pitiful hand with long strings of burned skin hanging from the wrists and fingers, and the blood-red, raw flesh of the arms and face . . . and the skin hanging from his chin and neck. I wanted to put this out of my mind. I couldn't. The vision was too fresh, too clear.

"I wish we could have done something. You know. Could have helped some," I said.

"We don't even know who he was," Gleason said.

"I know it. Just saw him like that . . . and that was all," I said . . . "That other fellow will make it."

"I don't see how they made it," Gleason said, looking out toward the ocean. "All that time. I don't see how they found 'em."

"I hear they were looking out as far as Savo for survivors, you know, searching with the Higgins boats and tank lighters."

"Sharks got most of 'em, I guess," Gleason said. "They are awful bad in these waters . . . awful bad."

Our truck appeared through the trees. Thompkins didn't look happy. We gathered around the truck when it stopped by the toolshed.

"He didn't make it," Thompkins said.

"He didn't? What happened?" I asked.

"He died before we got halfway. Just died."

"I guess it was best," Gleason said. "Burned up like that. . ."

"That other one . . . he's goin' to make it, though," Bellflower announced.

"How do you know?" Gleason asked.

Bellflower, with a grin, jumped off the truck and took off his helmet. "Doc said so."

"Well, I'm glad of that . . . I'm glad of that," Gleason said.

"Better pick out where you're going to sleep and tell me where you'll be," I said. "Let's get all that settled before dark."

Trenton came up in the jeep, cut the motor and hopped out. "Supper ready?" He was grinning broadly. "I've brought the cocktails." He turned and reached in the back of the jeep, withdrew a blanket and unrolled it with much ceremony while we stood in a circle around him. "See!" he cried, waving two large bottles.

"What th' hell?"

"Saki, or gook brew," he laughed. "There are damn near two quarts of the stuff."

What's it taste like?" I asked, astonished by the display, and somewhat weak, as I was both empty and dry.

"It is supposed to be good stuff, something like homebrew. They are giving a bottle to each squad and I found an extra one."

We examined the bottles.

"This is for after dinner. We'll have to spread a cloth and light candles and do this right," Trenton said.

"Guard the goods . . . and with your life," I said.

He put them in the air-raid shelter. "Say, that ain't bad," he observed as he came out.

"Nothing but the best around here," Thompkins laughed. "They dug a good hole."

We looked around the position and got the lay of the land while there was daylight.

"How far down the beach do our lines go?" I asked Trenton.

"Not far. The other three guns are on our left and they're about fifty yards apart . . . and there's a space, then the riflemen have a line inland. Not much behind us, either."

We were talking as we stood by the gun. Looking toward the water and toward the left, where the island curved out into the sea.

"Look at that," Trenton said. "That black thing there in the water." He pointed a little to the left of our gun.

I looked. There was a black, round object floating on the water. It appeared to be a small piece of wood.

"A piece of driftwood," I said. "Don't you think?"

"Well, it could be. But watch it and see if you still think that."

I watched it. It didn't bob up and down like a piece of wood does in the waves. "Maybe it's a post stuck in the water." It was out a couple hundred feet, but appeared close inshore.

"Somethin' funny about it." Trenton's voice carried a note of excitement. His eyes never left the black thing.

I looked. It just appeared the same. It stuck above the water about a foot.

"It's moving!" he cried.

I watched intently. It *was moving,* but very slowly. Since it stuck from the water like a post, it wasn't normal for it to move in such a position . . . not that high from the water.

"Why, the bastards," Trenton snorted, his eyes wide. "I got it . . . I know what the hell is wrong with that thing." He was about to burst with the excitement of his discovery. "You look now . . . !"

"Hell, I'm lookin'."

"Now, now . . . what's it doin'?"

"Movin'."

"Aw, crap! Which way? Which way is it goin'?"

"From left to right," I said, unable to get excited about a stick in the water.

"Right! An' which way is the current—the waves—which way is the flow? You just tell me, by God, now . . ."

"From right to left," I said in some excitement as it dawned on me the thing was drifting against the current; moving against the tide.

"That's a periscope," Trenton shouted, swinging to face me. "It's a gook sub . . . it ain't ours for sure!"

He was right. That's what it was. I had never seen one before, but now it was obvious to me. It was a periscope. A Japanese sub was slowly, silently checking the beach. Spying on us. Watching us with glittering eyes from the depths. I felt foolish. Here we were gawking into a periscope while the enemy must be filled with mirth as he watched from the other end. All the time we had been pointing and discussing the floating object they had been looking directly at us.

"I'll get a rifle and blast his glass," I said. "If he wants to poke it up, we can knock it off for him." We were unarmed. Everything but the cannon was back in the grove with the rest of the squad. But if I could get a rifle and get back without him suspecting me, I could hit him; it was an easy shot.

Trenton nodded. "Be careful. If he thinks we know what he is, he'll pull down under water."

I thought how silly all this was. Here was a whole tubful of Japs, practically at our feet, and we were trying to play cat and mouse. I was going to try to blind him with a .30-caliber rifle bullet. He was going to down scope the minute he caught on.

"I'll try to ease back as if we don't know the score," I said.

The periscope was still moving slowly through the water, cutting little ripples as it slipped through the tiny waves. I turned and started walking toward the grove. Trenton watched the scope. I entered the trees and broke into a run, charged up to the truck, pulled off a rifle and thundered back. As I reached the edge of the trees, the scope disappeared.

"Damned!" Trenton bellowed. "He saw you . . . he saw that rifle."

"Cowardly bastard," I puffed as I trotted up to Trenton. "After all, he had a five-inch gun, maybe bigger."

"He didn't want to go home with a busted glass," Trenton grinned. "He'd of had to surface and put in a new one, or else be blind."

"Aw, they have a spare on the conning tower," I argued. "You know they wouldn't be that stupid. Not have a spare."

"Well, he got away, by damn!" Trenton growled.

"Yep," I said, then remembered the Jap brew. "This calls for saki time. We need a drink after all that."

Trenton's face lighted up; his pace increased. We went back to the squad and opened the saki, divided it among the canteen cups of good men and true, and hashed over our failure to outwit the sub. We ate pineapples from a gallon can. There was hardtack and coffee. We had coconut for dessert. It all tasted pretty good. Especially the saki. It had a warm glow, a friendly approach; it tasted like beer, only better and stronger.

We sat in a little circle, weapons by our sides, helmets on, sweat dripping from our chins. There was a feeling of trust and strength in this small group. A sense of comradeship and security of belonging. We watched the fire in the hole in the sand as smokeless flames licked the sides of our canteen cups. It was the coffee hour.

The sun was beginning to touch the sea. A dull-red giant of a sun glaring through a cloudless sky. It appeared twice as large as back in the States. At this time of day, you could look at it as it sank with startling speed to be extinguished by the water far at sea. Night comes suddenly at this place and with forceful impact.

We covered the fire with sand. Darkness was now our cloak. To smoke, we had to take turns in the air-raid shelter, where no glow could be seen from outside. I divided up the watch. Flint, the young kid, was on first. This way he had company most of the time. Then Maywell, the loader, who was nervous at night. Then Bellflower and Gleason, and Thompkins and Trenton, and I took the last watch, plus the responsibility of checking on the other watches during the night. These watches consisted of staying awake, searching the beach and surf with glasses from our gun position, and insuring that strangers did not visit us during the night. It was a silent look and listen job. You stayed down, stayed quiet, and stayed alert. Anything suspicious meant waking me up. But there was no such thing as a night's sleep for anyone. Battle makes light sleepers.

I had dug an L-shaped foxhole along the chicken-wire fence line. This was what I considered a clever new foxhole design. There were few L-shaped foxholes in these early days, and I can safely say I was the originator of them. The length of the hole, which was quite shallow, was such that anyone wishing to get at me had to stick his head into the short end of the L. This put his neck in a convenient position for me to grab it and rip it open with a very keen hunting knife I had bought at Jacksonville. Before I had gotten the hunting knife, I had owned a hook knife used to butcher hogs, but it was stolen from me. It was too novel for anyone to resist. And it was not long in my possession. But the hunting knife that replaced this hook knife was adequate to any job, I felt, and I was proud of it. You cannot easily cut a throat with a bayonet; it was too dull. It is a stabbing weapon, anyway. So, most of us bought from our own funds various knives for emergencies, and for cooking. The bayonet was a can-opener, and a good one.

Over this L-shaped architectural triumph, I had placed some sheet iron similar to the galvanized tin roofing that is so romantic in a rainstorm, especially on honeymoons. This roof would offer about as much protection from gunfire as a window screen, but that was not the point. The purpose of the roof was to protect me from rain which had fallen upon us with unfailing regularity for varying periods each night.

Into this hole, I placed my poncho and blanket, settled the roof, and, with much struggle, falling sand, and head bumping, managed to back inside. Once underground—or under roof to be more exact—I discovered the place was cozy beyond my wildest expectations. It was dry. It muffled jungle noises. With my ear on the ground, I could detect footsteps at some distance. There was a feeling of security a nesting bullfinch must know, or a gopher in his hole. If necessary, I could spring erect, sheet iron falling to one side, or lie quietly to ambush unsuspecting Japs bent on bayonet drill. My blind side was protected by the sagging chicken-wire fence. It was a perfect place. I thought of writing Headquarters, Marine Corps, and suggesting they include the design in training manuals to replace the common straight foxhole, the spider hole, the shellhole and the zigzag trench. I was positive no creature could find me unless by accident.

By inching forward slightly, I could see the sky over my exit. In this way, I could detect the approach of an intruder. Should he put his head in the opening, I could nab him around the neck and pull his head underground, there to slit his throat while the rest of him threshed helplessly outside. He could not even hit me with a rifle bullet, if he should fire straight into the entrance. I thought about hand grenades. But, then, I could spring upward and the grenade would go off harmlessly in the crater I had just left.

I drifted into sleep.

It seemed I had been napping for only a few minutes when I was awakened by footsteps. Not fully alert, my mind focused in a blurred way on the sounds. The noises were disorganized. They seemed to be made by heedless running, stumbling, and falling. I moved into position to drag anyone who came close into the foxhole and cut his throat. My hunting knife in my hand, I waited. I was very calm, a state of being that surprised me considerably. I waited, quietly, trying to fathom what was going on. It is best to find out what the action is before revealing your position. This is a rule that has saved many lives. I waited, looking down the short end of the L and upward toward the sky. Anything near me would block out the sky. The movement was confused. It reflected either panic or total disregard for personal injury. It seemed to be whirling around the air-raid shelter.

Almost without warning the noise was at the entrance to my advanced L-shaped foxhole. The starlight suddenly was blacked out. The space between the earth and the roof over it was filled with heavy breathing, grunts, and unintelligible speech gasped out between puffs and moans.

This is it, I thought.

I reached out with my arm and clamped a human neck in its vise and anchored it by plunging my clamped fist to the soft earth. The result was as I had imagined it. The victim was completely helpless. His face was pressing into the earth. His neck was hung in my arm like a little boy's between pickets in a fence. Outside, his arms and feet pounded and threshed helplessly. He could do nothing. I had him on the hook ready for the knife. I tightened my grip on the hunting knife and shifted slightly so when I tilted his head back with my arm I could do an effective job of surgery across his throat.

It was evident that whoever I had caught in my trap was fighting for his life. His flops and tugs pulled at my arm much as a fish jerks the line. The fellow kept making noises with his mouth but they were muffled. Nevertheless, they struck me as being unlike Japanese, as spoken by a native, would sound.

"I am going to kill you, you son-of-a-bitch," I informed the gurgling specimen and raised my new hunting knife to his throat. I knew I would have to make the stroke swiftly then jump upward through my metal roof, else I would be sprayed with hot blood. I had no desire to have fresh blood squirted in my face or splattered all over my dungarees, as I had only two pairs, one of which I was wearing.

I lifted the unknown head, which I now fully intended to sever from its anchorage, and bent it backward to expose the throat and tighten the muscles and skin for a smooth sweep of the knife. It was dark as pitch in the foxhole, a disadvantage of the roof; in fact this was the only defect I had discovered in my design.

As I lifted the head from where I had originally clamped it, removing the now violently flopping body's face from the sand into which I had pressed it with the force of a man who thought he was fighting for his life, the words, "Please don't kill me," penetrated my consciousness.

Great God, he speaks English as good as I do, I thought. Then, I said to him, "I'm goin' to cut your damned throat."

"Oh, God!" he cried, "Please don't, it's me, Private Maywell."

I was stunned. "Who?" I bellowed.

"Maywell . . . Maywell . . . Please don't kill me, please don't."

I must be crazy, I thought. But, then, it *did* sound very much like Maywell.

"Back out slowly," I said. "And I won't kill you until I can see you better. But go slow."

He was frozen with fear. He backed out slowly. I held onto his neck and crawled slowly along with him. We got out of the L-shaped foxhole.

The starlight was very bright. I looked into the face of Maywell. "You crazy bastard," I growled. "What's the matter with you? I could have killed you . . . And who the hell would have been loader?"

"I got scared," he said. "I thought I heard something and I couldn't find your foxhole."

"The devil you couldn't," I said.

I felt a surge of pity and shame for Maywell. Poor guy. He had guts enough to admit he was scared. I was scared, too. The night was very lonely on Guadalcanal, and strange.

"We'll stay up together," I said. "You have ruined my damned night."

"I'm sorry," he said. "I know I did."

"But you proved I was right about the L-shaped foxhole — you can't beat it."

"Uh-huh," he said without enthusiasm.

I looked around in the night. Everybody was asleep. The Japs, evidently, could drive a herd of elephants through our squad and not disturb them.

Maywell and I went out to the gun position. I checked the sea with the binoculars. It was empty. We settled down on watch. The water whispered across the sand and the wind played among the palms. Somewhere behind us a Jap machine gun sputtered and paused. A Marine weapon coughed in reply. We sat in silence each comforted by the other's presence; tired, but attentive to every sound.

"This ain't too bad a place," Maywell whispered.

"No, I guess not . . . better than nothin'," I said.

We listened to the night and looked at the jeweled heavens. In the distance Savo Island was a dusky hump. The Coast Guard house was silent. Down the beach, the sand seemed to have a dull, white glow.

Isn't this silly, I thought to myself. Silly as the very devil.

A cockatoo began to stir. We knew what that meant.

"We better keep a lookout on that cockatoo, it may be a Jap," I said. Maywell nodded.

We sat in the sand and listened. Listened to the cockatoo. And watched the sea, the endless rolling sea.

※   ※   ※   ※

TWO DAYS AFTER HIS STUNNING VICTORY IN SAVO Sound, Admiral Mikawa (less cruiser *Kako* sunk by submarine S-44 off Kavieng) steamed into Rabaul with flags flying. Although he was criticized for not going after the United States transports, Mikawa was nowhere at fault. His flagship, *Chokai,* had taken a shell in her chartroom and that compartment had been destroyed. Mikawa now met Lieutenant General Haroushi Hyakutate, newly arrived from Tokyo to command the 17th Army composed of crack units from China, the Philippines, Singapore and Borneo. On paper 17th Army numbered about 50,000 troops, the most available of which was Colonel Kiyono Ichiki's 900-man detachment. Mikawa proposed to lift this force in five destroyer-transports escorted by a light cruiser, while a submarine squadron shelled Guadalcanal and Tulagi. Hyakutate agreed. He was a confirmed believer in the Imperial manual, and the manual suggested that very little was needed to make an American run: "The character of the American is simple and lacking in tenacity and battle leadership . . . If they have a setback they have a tendency to abandon one plan for another."

Intelligence informed the general that United States Marines on Guadalcanal numbered only 10,000 men. If Ichiki was not able to handle 10,000 marines, the general was prepared to call up two full divisions—the Sendai 2nd Division and the 38th—plus the heavily reinforced Kawaguchi Brigade, the 8th Tank Regiment and an Army artillery command. To Hyakutate's way of thinking now that reports of Mikawa's victory were filtering in from the islands, it was imperative to press home the attack. Perhaps, he thought, the Ichiki Detachment might alone retake the airfield if given night and day bombing support; he issued the necessary orders.

On Guadalcanal, General Vandegrift was in a bleak mood. The departure of the transports and gunships had left him, despite Turner's promise to return shortly, "bare ass." Worried about attacks on his flanks, Vandegrift pulled in Cates's 1st Marines, less a battalion, and ordered a dig-in commencing 600 yards inland and extending to the Lunga River. There, tied in with Hunt's 5th Marines the perimeter was carried to Kukum and around to the Lunga. To reinforce the 9600-yard perimeter, del Valle's 75-mm and 105-mm howitzers were given focal points which enabled gunfire to be pushed in any direction. North of the airstrip were 75-mm half-tracks with mobility to go in any direction, and behind them was an infantry battalion and tank company.

Simultaneously Vandegrift ordered supplies moved up from the beach and work to commence on the airstrip—now named Henderson Field in honor of Major Lofton R. Henderson, who died at Midway. In their haste to quit the area the Japanese had not bothered to remove their equipment. The result was inad-

vertent help for the airstrip marines—two small gasoline trains
with hoppers which proved a boon to engineers, who were frank
to say that without them it would have been impossible to move
7000 yards of cubic fill in a few days.

The placement of guns at Henderson Field was the responsibility of one of the Marine Corps' great warriors, the commanding officer of the 11th Marines, (then) Colonel Pedro A. del Valle.
Born in Puerto Rico and a graduate of the United States Naval
Academy, del Valle received the Legion of Merit for artillery
defense of the hotly contested Guadal airstrip. He speaks of his
command's preparation of howitzer positions.

·8· THE GUNS AT HENDERSON FIELD

LIEUTENANT GENERAL PEDRO A. DEL VALLE

On the morning of the 9th, the infantry cleared Henderson Field,
and the 2nd and 3d Battalions moved into positions previously selected . . . The 2nd Battalion was emplaced to cover the west flank
and the beaches west of the Lunga River in direct support of the 5th
Marines (Colonel L. P. Hunt), which defended that sector.

The command post of that battalion was in a wooded depression
directly west of the runway. The batteries were bivouacked just south
of the airfield and along the Lunga River where a slight depression
and heavy jungle growth gave concealment and some defilade. The
3d Battalion, 11th Marines, was bivouacked just south of the low ridge
which dominated the airfield from the south. Its batteries were emplaced on the edge of the woods covering the east flank of the position
and the beaches east of the Lunga River in direct support of Colonel
C. B. Cates's 1st Marines which defended that sector. The 5th Battalion, 11th Marines (Lieutenant Colonel E. H. Price), was emplaced
along the same ridge, facing generally north. Their right flank battery was contiguous to the left flank battery of the 3d Battalion and
their left flank battery was what was known as Edson's Ridge.

. . . The command posts of the 3d and 5th Battalions were in the
palm groves north of the clearing which was an extension of the air-

field. These were subsequently moved to the woods south of the field near the batteries. The regimental command post of the 11th Marines was set up about 200 yards east of the division command post in the woods close to the banks of the Lunga at the eastern end of a wooded, rocky formation which pointed like a finger toward the airfield, some 500 yards distant. The Special Weapons Battery was bivouacked in the wooded depression just north of this command post. An ammunition dump was established in the palm grove near the eastern end of the runway. The regiment employed its time in surveying and digging personnel shelters against enemy bombing. Registration on check points was initiated without delay. Numbered concentrations were prepared to cover our front and flanks.

The positions occupied by the Field Artillery at this time corresponded to the estimated situation. The Japanese had made two violent, but successful, air attacks against our transports since the landing. Our naval coverage to seaward had withdrawn after the Battle of Savo Island on the night of the 8th and 9th of August and the transports soon followed. Beach Red, the original landing beach, was still full of our supplies which were being gradually brought within the defenses of Henderson Field. They contained a separate garrison not including field artillery. We had knowledge of Japanese to the eastward of us and had made contact with the Japanese to the westward near the Matanikau River . . . It was logical to prepare fires in defense of the beach front and the two flanks as far back as practicable.

The jungle to the south of us was so dense that it was not believed the Japanese would make any determined attacks from that quarter for the time being. The infantry at our disposal being so limited, there was none to cover the rear of the field artillery in its position, and, at first, none to cover the east flank of the 3d Battalion, 11th Marines. The right flank of the 1st Marines, which covered the beach front and the right flank along the Tenaru, did not meet the east flank of the 3d Battalion, 11th Marines, by about 1,000 yards. Between them lay a flat known as the Tenaru Flat which was covered with kangaroo grass.

Almost immediately, the artillery began to receive fire from small parties of Japanese, especially in our rear and along our right flank. We were obliged to cover our own rear with machine gun posts situated at intervals. After two nights of almost continuous firing, the artillery commander obtained permission from the division commander to form patrols and send them into the jungle after the Japanese. There were nine patrols in all, each commanded by an officer. These left every morning at dawn on compass course south in paralleled columns with as much lateral communication and support as was practicable in the dense growth, and returned before dark within our own lines. Thus, the versatility of the marine, who never forgets his infantry training, was very useful indeed. These 11th Marines' patrols combed the jungle to the south of us so effectively that harassing tactics of the Japanese in that sector ceased almost entirely. A number of Japanese were killed and ninety-five prisoners were brought in.

Infiltration from the open areas on the right flank of the 3d Battalion, 11th Marines, was countered by having various units take up defensive positions along the flats aforementioned, between the right flank of the 1st Marines and the right flank of the 11th Marines. At first, the tanks covered it, and later units from the reserve battalion of the 1st Marines. We had now arrived at the conclusion that a perimeter defense must be maintained. As there was not sufficient infantry, the south front from the Lunga to the Tenaru had to be covered by the artillery. Accordingly, we constructed a fairly continuous line of machine-gun positions along this front and continued our patrolling as far as practicable.

. . . Headquarters, 11th Marines, made the necessary surveys, which were extended by the battalions. [Then] alternate positions were constructed covering the sectors to the south . . . It required considerable expenditure of effort, but the fires of the entire regiment, prepared and registered, could be directed at any target within range, at any point in the perimeter. This work and the preparation of a gridded map, made from the available aerial photographs supplemented by our own surveys, occupied our time very fully in . . . the defense of Henderson Field.

❧ ❧ ❧ ❧

GEORGE McMILLAN, AUTHOR OF *THE OLD BREED* AND a former reporter for the *Washington Post,* missed the Guadalcanal campaign. His first action with the 1st Marine Division was at Cape Gloucester. However, McMillan labored long to achieve his magnificent history of the division, and a brief excerpt from it reveals marine mood after the temporary departure of the Navy —and a sad introduction to Japanese treachery at the outset of the campaign.

·9· ALONE

GEORGE McMILLAN

The feeling of expendability is difficult to define. It is loneliness, it is a feeling of being abandoned, and it is something more, too: it is as if events over which you have no control have put a ridiculously low price-tag on your life.

When word got around Guadalcanal in the second week of August that the Navy had taken off and left the Marines, the feeling of expendability became a factor in the battle.

"I know I had a feeling," says a man who was there, "and I think a lot of others felt the same way, that we'd never get off that damned island alive. Nobody said this out loud at the time. I was afraid to say it for fear it'd come true."

"But," says a captain, "there was an awful lot of talk about Bataan."

"It was about this time," recalls a sergeant, "that the men of my platoon began to knock off a lot of their letter-writing."

"One of our battalion officers," remarks a second lieutenant, "used to sit around and mope a lot. I was called up to division CP once in a while, and every time I'd come back he'd pin me to a tree and want to know what scoop I'd picked up. At first I brought him all the rumors, but then I saw the way they affected him and I knocked it off. Why, he was getting so bad, so humped over with worry, I told him if he didn't stop his shoulders were gonna touch in front."

"I had it figured this way," says a private. "Our necks were out and it was just a question of how far down the Japanese were gonna chop."

If there was doubt anywhere that the Navy had really left, that doubt was dispelled when the Division went on short rations, when the chow was cut down to two meals a day, and most of that captured Japanese food.

"Fish and rice, fish and rice, fish and rice," is one distasteful recollection. "And black coffee without sugar, flat candy, dehydrated potatoes, cabbage and carrots. We finished off the meals with a Jap cigarette, using pasteboard holders provided with each pack so that the acid in the cheap paper wouldn't give up lip sores. Sometimes, the Jap diet was broken by a plate of beans, canned salmon, or a slab of beef from a Lever Brothers cow."

The air raids started immediately, for it did not take the Japanese more than a few hours to discover that we had no planes to oppose them—no planes and only a few 90 mm antiaircraft guns manned by the Defense Battalion. So they went into a routine, an arrogant, nasty, infuriating, frustrating routine.

Almost every afternoon—and the weather was good there in the Solomons in August—they'd come in, sending first a small group at noon or shortly after, dropping a few bombs as if to curdle a man's lunch. In mid-afternoon they'd come in greater strength, holding their tight formations. "It was a lovely sight, and the men used to watch, or at least they did until one came close," recalls a Guadalcanal veteran.

As soon as dark set in, a solitary plane would appear, cruise insolently overhead, sometimes caught in the Defense Battalion's searchlight. In its own good time, the plane would drop its bomb, cruise around a while longer, then disappear leisurely, only to be replaced by another. In such fashion the Japanese stayed over the Marine perimeter all night during mid-August. They truly harassed, and it is no wonder that the men personified the night patrol, calling all the planes that came over in darkness, "Washing Machine Charlie."

The men found some relief in wild stories. One patrol told their regimental intelligence officer they had come across the toilet articles of some Japanese women.

"I immediately phoned Division," the officer says, "and requested permission to to attack inland to free these women. The reply I got was: 'A lot of good it will do an old man like you. Stay where you are.'"

The facts challenged the fiction. On August 14, a lanky shorts-clad stranger appeared out of the jungle. He was Captain W. F. Martin Clemens, a British district officer, who had hidden himself through the Japanese occupation of the island.

"He arrived at our CP one afternoon with about twenty native carriers," says the officer who greeted him. "They were laden with all kinds of fruit, having hiked from up in the mountains. After drinking a bottle of brandy in nearly one gulp, Clemens had a few more drinks of Japanese sake, and he and Widdy [a British officer who landed with the Division] had a regular old home week. About 0300 I had to send them word to 'pipe down.' Although they had killed over two liters of sake, they didn't show any signs of it, except to talk loudly."

. . . There was the desire among the men—so much a part of Marine tradition—to close with the enemy. Defense was all right, but the idea of sitting on your dead duff and waiting for the Japs to come at you was not good.

So one day when a Jap naval rating was captured and told our intelligence people that some of his buddies up around the Matanikau would surrender if only we would go "liberate" them, the instinct was that it should be done. The fact that the Nip was surly only made his story seem more credible.

Also, some marine on patrol up that way claimed he saw a white flag flying above the Jap bivouac.

There was not a single 8-ball among the party organized to make the trip. Colonel Goettge himself (he was D-2) was to be in charge, and he selected twenty-five men, most of them scouts and intelligence specialists, to go along with him. He just about cleaned out the Division intelligence section, not to say a big hunk of the 5th Marines-2 section. Colonel Goettge felt that his men would, among other things, be acting in a humanitarian role: The Japs were said to be starving. He, therefore, took along the assistant division surgeon and a language officer, one of the few in the division, to help out.

These men showed off in a Higgins boat from Kukum shortly after dark on August 12, and put ashore opposite Matanikau village. Only three of them returned.

As far as the Division's records are concerned, the patrol disappeared into oblivion. There is no official record of what happened to the party after it left Kukum; indeed the historical monograph on the campaign says that the point where the patrol landed has never been fixed, and that no trace of the dead was ever found.

In an attempt to reconstruct the events of that night, the author of this book interviewed (May, 1948) Sergeant Charles C. (Monk) Arndt, one of the three survivors.

McMILLAN: Monk, start at the beginning and tell me about the Goettge patrol. Do you remember when you were first told about it?

ARNDT: They told us about it early in the afternoon of August 12, told us that there was a Japanese party in the Matanikau area that was willing to surrender. Our idea was that this was a reconnaissance patrol and that no fighting would take place unless absolutely necessary.

M: What did you carry?

A: We had ponchos, a belt, canteen with no cup, one can of C-rations, and one can of fish. We left the CP around six o'clock. We went to Green Beach where we got into lighters and we went down to the area at night. There were 25 men in one boat, 4 officers and 21 enlisted men, plus the Navy cox'n.

M: About what time was it when the cox'n let the ramp down?

A: He didn't let it down. He hit this sandbar and we waded ashore. Some of us tried to push the boat off the sandbar and I guess we made a lot of noise. I went on in.

M: How far in?

A: Up to the edge of the woods which was about twenty yards at least.

M: Were there native houses there?

A: Just a few grass huts. It was real dark, no moon or stars, it was a little cloudy that night. I couldn't see much.

M: And what did you do then?

A: We didn't dig foxholes. We sort of buried ourseleves in the sand. We all had a little conference there for a few minutes and then a few of them stepped through the little perimeter we made and were going to look for a place to sleep that night. Colonel Goettge was in the lead. He got hit.

M: Were you surprised?

A: All the men were surprised. No one knew exactly what was going on. Then a couple of other men were hit. One was Sergeant Custer. Commander Pratt, old Commander Pratt, one of the best doctors the Marine Corps ever had, was out there. He patched up Custer. Custer's left arm was bored a little by a bullet and he gave me his pistol and I threw away the lousy Reising [submachine gun] I had. Then the firing stopped for a minute and somebody crawled up to see if they could find the colonel. But first we called his name a couple of times. "Goettge, Goettge," somebody whispered. Then when there was no answer somebody crawled up to find him.

M: Did you find him?

A: Yes, Captain. . . . . .put his hand right into the colonel's face, where there was a big hole. Then, Hugh, who was right with the captain, got jumped by some Japs.

M: How close were you?

A: At his heels. I could touch his feet.

M: They didn't jump you?

A: No, they jumped him. I made no sound whatever. Only Hugh. He said, "They jumped me." And he was stabbed through the left chest and into the left arm. It went right through his chest and into the left arm. Then Hugh started cussing.

M: What about the others? Was anybody else hit?

A: Right after that the Jap machine guns opened up.

M: Did you have a machine gun?

A: No. And no BARs.

M: No grenades?

A: No, no grenades at all. Nothing like that.

M: When the Japs opened up, didn't they come on in at you?

A: No, they stayed back and fired close range, so close you could feel the air from the muzzles. About that time a corporal went out to the water's edge and started firing tracers, trying to get an SOS back. We didn't have a radio. The fighting went on until about 1 o'clock.

M: Do you remember anything you said?

A: No, we were all very quiet. Except for touching each other once in a while, and wondering what was going to happen next. About then old Commander Pratt was hit, first in the butt, later in the chest. He died a little while after that.

M: Wasn't there any cover? No coconut logs? Nothing?

A: No. Just the open beach.

M: When you were talking a minute ago you said something about 1 o'clock.

A: That's right. About one in the morning the captain said someone had to go back for reinforcements, and I was very close to the captain and I told him that if anybody could get through the line I thought I could.

M: Why did you think that?

A: Well, I was about the only senior scout in the group and I had taught those men everything they knew. I had more time in the service than they did.

M: So you volunteered to go back?

A: There was no chance to leave by land and I was a pretty good swimmer. I went in the water just like a snake, on stomach, hands and knees, and I went like this just as far as I could without swimming at all. Out for about thirty yards.

M: Didn't you take your shoes off?

A: That was one of the mistakes I made because as I tried to take my shoes off they tied in knots. As I waded out I did take my clothes off. I had all my clothes off except my shoes and socks, the only things I couldn't get off. And my helmet. I still had that on.

M: You couldn't swim with a helmet on?

A: Oh, yes. It was very easy with the breast stroke. Anyway, when I crossed that damned sandbar I must have made some noise. Somebody fired at me. I felt funny out there naked and them firing at me.

M: Did you swim far out?

A: No, right along the beach. Quiet, with the breast stroke. I'd go in to the beach once in a while and there was a lot of coral that I had to hold on to and I have scars yet on my hands and legs where I was pushing around this coral. I was crawling over the rocks awhile and swimming awhile.

M: This place where you were going through coral was all in Jap territory? I don't understand either about the coral.

A: It ran right into the water. Shallow coral underneath the water and once in a while you'd hit a patch, and stand up. Then you'd swim on to another patch.

M: Did you still have your pistol all this time?

A: I kept *that* all right.

M: How did you keep it dry?

A: I kept it up under my helmet, hooked the butt under my chin strap . . .

M: You kept that helmet on all that time? And you had your pistol inside your helmet?

A: I sort of stuck it up behind my ear, under the chin-strap.

M: Where did you keep ammo?

A: I had a good clip in the pistol and the other one was wet but I kept it just the same. Then I saw a man and shot him, and I heard no running away from where I shot.

M: Did you stop awhile then?

A: No, I took off, out into the water. I was afraid to go too far out. I was getting pretty tired. But I swam on a while, along the beach sort of, and then I saw a native boat beached. I crawled in it and felt around and saw one end of it was all full of bullet holes and I pushed out and got in the other end. There was an old plank in it. I paddled away until I got back down to the boat base and there everybody was challenging me. I didn't know the pass word so I kept yelling, "Million, million." That had a lot of "l's" in it. And when I hit the shore and guys started looking at me funny I realized I was bleeding all over. I was cut all the way to the hips from the coral. They told me later that the bones were sticking out from my fingers. Then they wrapped a blanket around me and I told them that I had to get word to Colonel Hunt, and they got him on the phone and I told him that the patrol was all cut up and was being shot all to pieces.

M: What were you thinking about, Monk, on the trip back? Can you remember?

A: It's just like a man is just exhausted completely and ready to give up and then I'd look back where the patrol was and see a tracer shoot up in the air and then I'd go on again. I was thinking about those men down there.

M: Go back to the patrol, now for a minute. Did anyone there say anything about . . . did they show any signs they knew they weren't going to get back?

A: No. No one showed any signs at all. In other words, they were gonna stay there and fight it out.

M: Nobody got panicky?

A: No.

M: Nobody wanted to run back to the water and try to swim out?

A: No, no one thought that because, I tell you, they were all men who had been with the outfit two years or more. They were seasoned and they knew what to expect.

Of the other men who got back, the last was a half-Indian. He did not leave until nearly daybreak, and as he splashed out into the water to start his swim to safety, he looked back to see (he told a correspondent) "swords flashing in the sun," the Japs hacking up the last of our people.

※　※　※　※

THE SLAUGHTER OF THE GOETTGE PATROL WAS avenged August 19 at Matanikau Village, seven miles northwest of Henderson Field, by Companies B, I and L of the 5th Marines. An account of this episode, in which 33 Japanese were killed, is presented by Corporal Nicholas Saleo of Captain Lymon Sperling's L Company, who was severely wounded in the action.

·10· "I FIRED FOUR TIMES AND GOT TWO OF THEM"

CORPORAL NICHOLAS SALEO

It was typical Guadalcanal weather, with the temperature far above the one hundred mark, and the humidity so high there was a blue mist in the air. We headed straight back into the island, so that we could circle through the mountains and come in on the village from the rear. Meanwhile, another platoon went straight up the beach, approaching the Japs' line of fortifications head on. This was a feint, by which we hoped to hold their attention while we came in behind them.

We marched in staggered lines spread along the mountainsides, going around them, never over them. This lopsided marching on the side of a mountain is an ordeal. Blisters form on your feet in ten minutes, burst in another ten minutes, and you march the rest of the way on raw feet. We were dressed in ragged dungarees, called fatigue dress, and in addition to helmet, gas mask, ammunition and rifle, each of us carried an entrenching tool. I carried a pick. Our clothes, often ripped in a dozen places and flapping because of missing buttons, were black with sweat in an hour. The heat got worse as the morning wore on. My face was flushed, and it was hard to get my breath. Everyone kept wiping his eyes, trying to keep the sweat out of them. We kept on, mountain after mountain, one foot always lower than the other, sliding on the loose dirt, our faces flaming.

By one o'clock, I was desperate for air, with my chest heaving up and down. Then the marine directly ahead of me caved in, and fell. I made the mistake of stopping beside him. When I stood still, my own body heat swept to my head and face. I gasped, and fainted.

We rested there for an hour, watching five Jap bombers over Henderson Field. We saw one of them shot down. Later, someone spotted three Japs watching us from the ridge of a hill opposite us. Private Steel, a Browning Automatic Rifleman from Tennessee, exchanged guns with me and, with another marine, went over after them. They were back in fifteen minutes, having shot two of the Japs. Much later in the Guadalcanal fighting, Steel was found wounded beside one of the three machine-gun nests he had succeeded in wiping out singlehanded.

We went on. By the middle of the afternoon, we were within three hills of the village. We quit marching, and began to crawl, standing up only when we were in the tall jungle growth in the valleys between the hills. The hills themselves are sparsely wooded with scrubby trees, affording very poor protection.

Late in the afternoon, there was the sharp crack of a rifle shot. A marine a few yards up the column from me was hit. He had been crawling on his stomach, and the bullet had struck his cartridge belt. He suffered a flesh wound. The marine thought it was a joke, laughing and cursing loudly. A corpsman, Pharmacist's Mate Coffee, rushed forward and dressed the wound.

Another man had seen the sniper's puff of smoke when he fired. Word passed along the line that the marine would fire a tracer at the spot, and that the rest of us were to fire after it. Every gun in the platoon barked. There was a faint yowl, shrill and animal-like, from the tree, but the body did not fall out. Jap snipers strap themselves to their trees and tie their rifles to their bodies, so that when they are killed the enemy will not know it. The idea is for the Americans to waste ammunition firing on a dead body. The Japs think of everything.

By nightfall, we were only two hills away from the village. We encamped for the night. Orders were whispered. Equipment was placed gingerly on the ground, and there was no talking or smoking. I stretched out on the ground and opened a can of Japanese crab meat. At this time all we had to eat was the food we had succeeded in capturing from the Japs. I had been on the island only twelve days, but I had already lost eight or ten pounds; I could tell by the slack in my pants. I ate the crab meat with my fingers; it was quite tasty.

The dew is as heavy as rain on Guadalcanal. An hour after nightfall, we were all soaked. I rested on the wet earth until midnight. My security was Private First Class Paraleck of Boston, Massachusetts. We were always in pairs on Guadalcanal. That was orders. If one wanted to rest, somebody had to stand by him and watch. Even on errands of the flesh, someone had to go along to stand guard. Paraleck, who was a BAR man, was one of the bravest men I ever knew. He was killed later.

At midnight, Paraleck and I relieved the company guard. We stood watch until three in the morning, Paraleck lying on his stomach, me sitting besike him. Most of the fighting on Guadalcanal was done on the stomach, but I was an exception. I was always nervous and uncomfortable in that position. I preferred to sit down with my legs

bent under me. I could move quicker this way, or at least I thought
I could. I am about six feet tall, and when I got all stretched out on
the ground I felt awkward and helpless.

I sat in the tall grass in the pitch dark, and listened for three hours.
We half-expected to be attacked, because we were almost certain that
some sniper or scout had spotted us and had reported our presence.
There was nothing to see, so I had to depend on my ears. A hundred
times I imagined I heard stealthy footsteps, and my heart would
thump and I would strain into the darkness. Once a parrot flapped by,
and I nearly aroused the whole platoon. Small animals would come up
in the dark, smell our presence, and stand there, watching us for a
moment, just long enough for my heart to stop beating when I saw
the fleeting glint of watching eyes.

By the time I was relieved at three o'clock, I imagined the whole
encampment was completely surrounded. I could almost feel them
creeping up on us, but this was all my imagination. The night passed
without trouble.

At dawn, the order to move on was whispered down the line. Paraleck shook me awake. I sat up and took a drink of water, which was all
we would have inside us that day. I started to crawl down the side
of the hill after the others. This was the day we would fight it out with
the Japs. As I crawled along in the wet grass, I blessed myself. I left
the rest to God. There was nothing else to do.

When we reached the gully between the two hills a sudden tropical squall blew up. It rained in torrents for five minutes, then stopped
just as suddenly. Right after the storm, it got furiously hot, even
though it was only about seven in the morning. We moved on across
the gully, crouching, heading for the next hill. Just then, another rifle
shot rang out, and I heard the bullet zip over my head.

"There he is!" Paraleck shouted, pointing to a tree on the hillside
facing us. We both fired at once. We saw a branch sag and bend, as
the Jap sniper slumped in his strap.

Before going up the next and last hill, my own squad was assigned
to the advance position. There were nine of us, and it was our job
to go ahead of the rest and establish contact with the enemy. Two
scouts led the squad, with me directly behind, acting as point. The
others were scattered directly back of me. Way up ahead somewhere
were three other men. They had gone out a day in advance of us to
scout the Jap position. One of them was a friend of mine, Staff Sergeant Branack.

With my squad leading, we continued up the hill, crawling very
cautiously through the mud, tall grass, and brambles. As we squirmed
along silently, I heard a rustle and the sound of heavy footsteps up
ahead. I watched the scout, who was waving back, warning us to take

cover. A moment later, two men broke through the thicket, carrying the upright body of a third marine between them on their crossed hands. It was the advance scouting party. The dead marine was Staff Sergeant Branack. They brought him on down the line. His eyes were open. I couldn't believe he was dead.

Paraleck, looking after them, said: "It's funny, but they seem to get all the good guys first." I couldn't answer him. We circled the hill near the top and started down, still crawling. Soon we were in sight of the village. I was sweating heavily; my heart was pounding. The brush got very heavy, and my fixed bayonet was slowing me down, getting entangled in the undergrowth. I jerked it off angrily, thinking I would replace it when we got to the edge of the village. I never did.

Looking down, the village seemed to be deserted. Then I spotted six or seven Japs lounging near one of the huts. The remainder of the force was on the far side of the village, facing down the beach toward Henderson Field.

Without being noticed, we got to the very edge of the village. At a motion from Corporal Meglien, who was now directly behind the scouts, we opened fire. At the first shot, the Japs darted swiftly into the jungle. One fell.

Everything happened with the speed of lightning after that. The scouts led the way, as we raced through the village, which was made up of fifteen or twenty straw huts. As we dashed through, I stumbled over a stalk of bananas in the road.

Our company was following about fifty feet behind. One of the scouts, reaching a small path leading toward the beach from the far end of the village, spotted the Japanese line. They had heard our shots, and were already swinging their guns around to face us. The scouts shouted a warning. A moment later we fell into a skirmish line. Both sides fired almost at once.

Our Colonel, meanwhile, ordered us back to the platoon line, but the order never reached us. The Japs, shrieking wildly, charged back toward us, shooting and throwing grenades as they came. There were nine of us and two hundred of them. I was on the extreme left of the line now, squatting on the beach protecting the left flank of the BAR man, Paraleck. Paraleck was hit almost immediately, although I didn't know it.

A second later, one of the scouts, Private Narcross, of Bridgeport, Connecticut, got a bullet in his chest. While the screaming and wild firing were still going on, Narcross crawled back along a small ridge on my right separating the jungle from the beach. Pharmacist's Mate Little, seeing him, began to crawl forward to meet him. Reaching his side, Little patched up his wound while they both crouched there under fire. Then Little sent him back to the rear. Just as Narcross crawled away, Little himself got a bullet in his head. He was killed instantly.

Meanwhile, I was sitting on the beach near a small clump of shrubbery. I had snatched a large palm leaf from a tree. I shoved one end of this into the top of my shirt, like a bib, for camouflage. So far the Japs hadn't broken through at my point on the beach. I sat there, clutching my rifle, waiting for them to come.

I couldn't hear the BAR man firing. I assumed he had been shot. I decided to close in, and cover his position. As I started to crawl across the beach, I saw Private Hornback, of Illinois, who had been in a central position beyond Paraleck, creeping back with a deep wound in his back. A grenade had got him.

Then, right behind him, came Paraleck with a great gash along the side of his head. Just then three rifle bullets whizzed directly over my head, and thudded into the sand in front of me. Involuntarily, I flattened. They had come from my rear, apparently from a sniper's rifle. I crept on.

Directly in the center of all this action was Corporal Charles Meglien, of Kearny, New Jersey, directing the fire of the squad. A braver man never lived. As the Japs charged, firing, he was shot in the leg. He fell, but pulled himself up again and returned the fire. A second later, four Japs swept in on him and bayoneted him in the stomach. The Jap wielding the bayonet was shot a moment afterward by fire coming from our rear. Meglien, still alive but mortally wounded, again got into firing position, and opened up on a second wave of Japs rushing in his direction. As they came on, he kept firing, getting two of them. They were firing point-blank at him now, but they couldn't kill him. His rifle was still blazing as they rushed him, swinging their rifle butts at his head. They beat him to death.

The squad, almost out of commission now, had not retreated. Private Larry Oliver, of Boston, was still on his feet. Private John McCarthy, of Concord, Massachusetts, a slight youngster of nineteen, was also in there somewhere, blazing away. Joe Boleniese (known as Murphy), of Brooklyn, was in the tough spot of being the man to whom the order to withdraw had been passed, but he could not relay it further, because everyone near him was dead or wounded. There was also another marine, a little fellow from Pennsylvania, who was still alive. I can't remember his name, but he had plenty of guts.

While the Japs were charging Meglien, I opened fire on six Japs who ran shrieking out of the jungle, zigzagging down the beach, intending to circle behind the squad. At first they did not see me. I raised my rifle, took careful aim, and fired. By a stroke of luck the first bullet hit three of them. They were running one behind the other.

They tumbled in a wild heap, and I had a momentary sense of angry pleasure as I noticed that one of them wore a United States marine's jacket. That Jap had obviously seen duty on Wake Island. The remaining three Japs swerved off, leaping and sprinting over the small ridge into the jungle.

I, too, raced into the jungle. Our squad was now behind the Jap lines, since their first charge had carried them through and beyond us. I had no hope of getting out alive. As I darted over the ridge into the undergrowth, I saw twenty Japs crawling away from me on their stomachs, heading toward our platoon, which was now in battle formation behind us. I dropped into my sitting position behind a clump of bushes, yanked out a grenade and was just ready to toss it when, only a few feet from me, I saw the three Japs from the beach running past me, bent over. We saw each other at the same instant. I fired from my armpit. I was close enough to see my own bullets penetrate their uniforms and bodies. I fired four times and got two of them.

My rifle was empty now and, furthermore, I had exposed my position. The Japs up ahead whirled around, saw me, and opened fire. I had no cover. The tree trunks were so small that to have attempted to hide behind them would have resulted in my being cut to ribbons. Running on their bowlegs, a dozen Japs rushed at me, firing as they came. I leaped up, and raced back to the beach. By instinct I was running back to the position I had just left, hoping to get some protection behind the clump of bushes and ridges in the beach.

I ran twenty feet without getting hit. Then a bullet struck me low in the stomach, paralyzing a leg. As I fell, another one plowed into my chest. "I am dead," flashed through my mind. I went down into the blackness. A few seconds later I regained consciousness. The Japs, thinking they had killed me, did not fire again.

My position was hopeless. I knew what the Japs were capable of doing to a wounded marine found behind their lines. I tried to move, thinking that maybe I could crawl away somewhere and hide. I couldn't move. I was numb and stunned. I got up onto one elbow and looked around. I saw a Jap race out of the jungle, and run directly toward me. He had seen me move and knew I wasn't dead. I recognized him. He was the one out of three I had just missed in the jungle. He came at me in a mad dash, and pointed the gun into my face. I managed to whirl onto my back and throw up a hand. He fired. It was as though the explosion went off inside my head.

When I came to, the firing and shouting was still going on. Almost immediately I passed out again. Then I came to again; I was lying on my face. One hand was under my throat, and the blood was spurting up around my face. The Jap bullet had been an explosive one. When I threw up my hand, the bullet had struck it and had exploded, tearing off some fingers, and ripping a hole in my throat. I could not feel anything in my hand. I assumed that I was bleeding to death at the throat. I fainted again, came out of it in a moment, then went off again. This continued for quite a while. I wished I would hurry up and die. I felt it coming slowly. It was a deep inward sinking. I blessed myself in my mind and, visualizing my father and mother, said good-by to them, then to my two sisters, Nancy and Frances.

I regained consciousness with a sound of running feet in my ears. Painfully I turned my head toward the ridge, expecting to see more Japs coming at me. I saw our men. The battle was still going on. I tried to shout, but not a sound came from me. As more and more men fought their way forward along the ridge, I tried over and over to make a noise. I could move only my head, so I tried to bob it up and down to attract attention. At last, a young marine, glancing down, saw the movement. I could see his face. It went ghastly white. I thought he was going to crumple up. He turned and staggered back out of sight. In a few minutes Pharmacist's Mate John Arnold, notified of my plight by the marine, left the platoon and raced across the beach, which was still under fire. Our corpsmen—Coffee, Little, Arnold—were among the most courageous men on Guadalcanal. These men walked many times into enemy fire to save a life, with nothing in their hands but a first-aid kit. To do that takes plenty of guts. Arnold patched me up a little, managing to slow the flow of surging blood. Then Sergeant McCullen came up and said: "Nice going, boy!" He had seen me shoot the two Japs in the jungle.

While I was being carried away to a Higgins boat, to be returned to Henderson Field, my company fought on, refusing to give an inch before the violent charges of the superior Jap force. When at last it was over, there were eighty-seven Jap dead. The rest were wounded. Our mission . . . had been successful.

❦ ❦ ❦ ❦

TO KEEP THE TORTUOUS GUADALCANAL OPERATION going was the big problem. The abrupt departure of Turner's transports on August 9 had left the marines with only a part of their supplies, guns and ammunition, and during this time there were continual raids by the 25th Air Flotilla. Guadalcanal was virtually indefensible, for while marine ingenuity could stretch GI rations and Japanese rice, it still took bullets and bombs to fight a war. However, Vandegrift's confidence in Turner was not misplaced, as the first increment of warstuffs arrived August 15, when destroyer-transports *Calhoun, Gregory, Little* and *McKean* dashed north from New Caledonia bringing 400 tons of avgas, 282 bombs, and 120 men of Cub One to service marine aircraft expected momentarily. Five days later a shipment of 120 tons of rations was received when the plucky little warships again sprinted into Guadalcanal, and that same signal day two marine squadrons, fighters and bombers, were flown off the deck of the "jeep" carrier *Long Island* for defense of the accursed island. As the planes roared over the strip, marines leaped into the air and cheered: "I actually saw tears of joy running down the cheeks of some of my youngsters," recalled one who was present.

While air marines were tooling up for their mission, let us look a bit closer at the eradication of the Japanese troops which had ambushed Goettge and his men. Contrary to initial thinking, this was no ordinary jungle patrol; these Japanese constituted the advance echelon of the Ichiki Detachment, and they were equipped with accurate maps of marine positions, charts, codes and diaries. The enemy revealed his numbers and identity when Sergeant Major Vouza stumbled on a large force near the Tenaru perimeter. The Japanese severely bayonetted the brave Melanesian, but Vouza, bleeding and half-dead, dragged himself to marine lines to spread the alarm.

It was shortly after midnight August 21, 1942. Colonel Edwin A. Pollack's 2nd Battalion, 1st Marines, were dug in, waiting. The classic story of the Battle of the Tenaru (Ilu) is told in four parts, the first by Private Robert Leckie, whom we have met.

·11· HERE WAS HELL

ROBERT LECKIE

The Tenaru River lay green and evil, like a serpent, across the palmy coastal plain. It was called a river, but it was not a river; like most of the streams of Oceania, it was a creek—not thirty yards wide.

Perhaps it was not even a creek, for it did not always flow and it seldom reached its destination, the sea. Where it might have emptied into Iron Bottom Bay, a spit of sand, some forty-feet wide, penned it up. The width of the sandspit varied with the tides, and sometimes the tide or the wind might cause the Tenaru to rise, when, slipping over the spit, it would fall into the bosom of the sea, its mother.

Normally, the Tenaru stood stagnant, its surface crested with scum and fungus; evil, I said, and green. If there are river gods, the Tenaru was inhabited by a baleful spirit.

Our section—two squads, one with the Gentleman as gunner, the other with Chuckler as gunner and me as assistant—took up position approximately three hundred yards upstream from the sandspit. As we dug, we had it partially in view; that is, what would be called the enemy side of the sandspit. For the Tenaru marked our lines. On our side, the west bank, was the extremity of the marine position; on the other, a no man's land of coconuts through which an attack against us would have to pass.

The Japanese would have to force the river to our front; or come over the narrow sandspit to our left, which was well defended by riflemen and a number of machine-gun posts and barbed wire; or else try our right flank, which extended only about a hundred yards south of us, before curving back north to the Tenaru's narrowest point, spanned by a wooden bridge.

The emplacement for the Gentleman's gun was excellently located to rake the coconut grove opposite. We dug it first, leaving Chuckler's and my gun standing some twenty yeards downstream, above the ground, protected by a single strand of barbed wire strung midway down the steeply sloping river bank. We would emplace it next day.

We dug the Gentleman's gun pit wide and deep—some ten-feet square and five-feet down—for we wanted the gunner to be able to stand while firing, and we wanted the pit to serve as a bomb shelter as well, for the bombs were falling fiercer.

But furiously as we worked, naked to the waist, sweat streaming so steadily our belts were turned sodden, we were unable to finish the pit on the first day. When night fell, only the excavation was done, plus a dirt shelf where the gun was placed. We would have to wait for the next day to roof it over with coconut logs.

We felt exposed in our half-finished fortifications, unsure. The dark made sinister humpbacks of the piles of soft red earth we had excavated, and on which we sat.

But, because we did not know real battle—its squallish trick of suddenness—we could not feel foreboding as we sat atop the soft mounds, concealing the telltale coals of our bitter Japanese cigarettes in cupped hands, softly smoking, softly talking. We were only uneasy in that shiftiness that came each night and disappeared each dawn.

No one went to bed. The stars were out, and this was enough to keep everyone up, unwilling to waste a bright night.

Suddenly in the river, upstream to our right, there appeared a widening, rippling V. It seemed to be moving steadily downstream. At the point of the V were two greenish lights, small, round, close together.

Jawgia whooped and fired his rifle at it.

To our right came a fusillade of shots. It was from G Company riflemen, shooting also at the V. More bullets hit the water. The V disappeared.

The stars vanished. The night darkened. Like our voices, the men began to trail off to bed, wrapping themselves in their ponchos and lying on the ground a few yards behind the pit. Only the Chuckler and myself were left, to stand watch.

Lights—swinging, bumping lights, like lanterns or headlights—glittered across the river in the grove. It was fantastic, a truck there, as though we might awake next morning and find a railroad station confronting us across that stagnant stream. The coconut grove was no man's land. The enemy had a right to be there, but, by all the experience of jungle warfare, it was inviting death to mark himself with lights, to let his truck wheels shout, "Here we are!"

"Who goes there?" the Chuckler bellowed.

The lights bumped and swung serenely on.

"Who goes there? Answer, or I'll let you have it!"

The lights went out.

This was too much. Everyone was awake. The mysterious V in the river and now these ghostly lights—it was too much! We jabbered excitedly, and once again warmed our souls in the heat of our voices.

Shattering machine gun fire broke out far to the left. As far down as the sandspit, perhaps. There came another burst. Again. Another. The sharply individual report of the rifle punctuated the uproar. There followed the "plop" of heavy mortars being launched behind us, then the crunching roar of their detonation across the Tenaru. The conflagration was sweeping toward us up the river, like a train of powder.

It was upon us in an instant, and then we were firing. We were so disorganized we had not the sense to disperse, clustering around that open pit as though we were born of it. Falsetto screeching rose directly opposite us and we were blasting away at it, sure that human intruders had provoked the cry of the birds. I helped the Gentleman fire his gun, although I was not his assistant. He concentrated on the river bank, firing burst after burst there, convinced that the Japs were preparing to swim the river. The screeching stopped.

The Gentleman spoke softly. "Tell those clucks to quite firing. Tell them to wait until they hear the birds making a clatter, 'cause a smart man'd try to move under cover of it. That's when they'll be moving."

I was glad he gave me this little order to execute. I was having no fun standing in the pit, watching the Gentleman fire. I crawled out and told everyone what he had said. They ignored it and kept banging away. There came a lull, and in that silent space, I, who had had no chance to fire my own weapon, blasted away with my pistol. I leaned over the mound and shoved my pistol-clenching hand into the dark and emptied the clip. There came a roar of anger from the Hoosier.

"Dammit, Lucky, ain't you get no better sense'n to go firing past a fellow's ear? You like to blow my head off, you Jersey jerk!"

I laughed at him, and the Chuckler crawled back from the bank and whispered, "C'mon, let's get our gun."

We snaked up the bank on our bellies, for the night was alive with the angry hum of bullets. The Chuckler took the gunner's spot and I crouched alongside in the position to keep the gun fed. We had plenty of ammunition, the long two hundred and fifty-round belts coiled wickedly in the light green boxes, those same sturdy boxes which you now see slung on the shoulders of shoe-shine boys.

The Chuckler fired and the gun slumped forward out of his hands, digging its snout into the dirt, knocking off the flash hider with a disturbing clatter, spraying our own area with bullets.

"That yellow-belly!" the Chuckler cursed.

He cursed a certain corporal who was not then distinguishing himself for bravery, and who had set up the gun and done it so sloppily that the tripod had collapsed at the first recoil.

I crawled down the slope and straightened it. I leaned hard on the clamps.

"She's tight," I told the Chuckler.

His answer was a searing burst that streaked past my nose.

A man says of the eruption of battle: "All hell broke loose." The first time he says it, it is true—wonderfully descriptive. The millionth time it is said, it has been worn into meaninglessness: it has gone the way of all good phrasing, it has become cliche.

But within five minutes of that first machine gun burst, of the appearance of that first enemy flare that suffused the battlefield in unearthly greenish light—and by its dying accentuated the re-enveloping night—within five minutes of this, all hell broke loose. Everyone was firing, every weapon was sounding voice; but this was no orchestration, no terribly beautiful symphony of death, as decadent rear-echelon observers write. Here was cacophony; here was dissonance; here was wildness; here was the absence of rhythm, the loss of limit, for everyone fires what, when and where he chooses; here was booming, sounding, shrieking, wailing, hissing, crashing, shaking, gibbering noise. Here was hell.

Yet each weapon has its own sound, and it is odd with what clarity the trained ear distinguishes each one and catalogues it, plucks it out of the general din, even though it be intermingled or coincidental with the voice of a dozen others, even though one's own machine gun spits and coughs and dances and shakes in choleric fury. The plop of the outgoing mortar with the crunch of its fall, the clatter of the machine guns and the lighter, faster rasp of the Browning Automatic Rifles, the hammering of fifty-caliber machine guns, the crash of seventy-five-millimeter howitzer shells, the crackling of rifle fire, the *wham* of thirty-seven-millimeter antitank guns firing point-blank canister at the charging enemy—each of these conveys a definite message, and sometimes meaning, to the understanding ear, even though that ear be filled with the total wail of battle.

So it was that our ears prickled at strange new sounds: the lighter, shingle-snapping crack of the Japanese rifle, the gargle of their extremely fast machine guns, the hiccup of their light mortars.

To our left, a stream of red tracers arched over to the enemy bank. Distance and the cacophony being raised around us seemed to invest them with silence, as though they were bullets fired in a deaf man's world.

"It's the Indian's gun," I whispered.

"Yeah. But those tracers are bad stuff. I'm glad we took 'em out of our belts. He keeps up that tracer stuff, and they'll spot him, sure."

They did.

They set up heavy machine guns in an abandoned amtrack on their side of the river and they killed the Indian.

Their slugs slammed through the sandbags. They ate their way up the water-jacket of his gun and they ate their way into his heart. They killed him, killed the Indian kid, the flat-faced, anonymous prize fighter from Pittsburgh. He froze on the trigger with their lead in his heart; he was dead, but he killed more of them. He wasn't anonymous, then; he wasn't a prelim boy, then.

They wounded his assistant. They blinded him. But he fought on. The Marines gave him the Navy Cross and Hollywood made a picture about him and the Tenaru Battle. I guess America wanted a hero fast, a live one; and the Indian was dead.

The other guy was a hero, make no mistake about it; but some of us felt sad that the poor Indian got nothing.

It was the first organized Japanese attack on Guadalcanal, the American fighting man's first challenge to the Japanese "superman." The "supermen" put bullets into the breast of the Indian, but he fired two hundred more rounds at them.

How could the Marines forget the Indian?

Now we had tracer trouble of a different kind. We had begun to take turns firing, and I was on the gun. The tracers came toward me, alongside me. Out of the river dark they came. You do not see them coming. They are not there; then, there they are, dancing around you on tiptoe; sparkles gay with the mirth of hell.

They came toward me, and time stretched out. There were but a few bursts, I am sure, but time was frozen while I leaned away from them.

"Chuckler," I whispered. "We'd better move. It looks like they've got the range. Maybe we ought to keep moving. They won't be able to get the range that way. And maybe they'll think we've got more guns that we really have."

Chuckler nodded. He unclamped the gun and I slipped it free of its socket in the tripod. Chuckler lay back and pulled the tripod over him. I lay back and supported the gun on my chest. We moved backward, like backstroke swimmers, almost as we had moved when we stole the case of beer out the North Carolina shanty, trying meanwhile, to avoid making noise that might occur during one of those odd and suspenseful times of silence that befall battles—noise which might attract fire from the opposite bank—if anyone was there.

For, you see, we never knew if there really was anyone there. We heard noises; we fired at them. We felt shells explode on our side and heard enemy bullets; but we could not be sure of their point of origin.

But, now, there was no enemy fire while we squirmed to our new position. We set up the gun once more and resumed firing, tripping our bursts at sounds of activity as before. We remained here fifteen minutes, then sought a new position. Thus we passed the remainder of the battle; moving and firing, moving and firing.

❧ ❧ ❧ ❧

TO THE LEFT OF LECKIE'S POSITION WAS CORPORAL Al Schmidt, with Lee Diamond and John Rivers. Roger Butterworth, former *Life* editor, detailed this battle in a wartime biography of Corporal Schmidt. For this action, in which he received multiple wounds and was blinded, Schmidt was awarded the Medal of Honor.

·12· LONG NIGHT ON THE TENARU

ROGER BUTTERWORTH

Lee Diamond was right beside him. Al heard him say, "Jesus Christ, I gotta get over there." They were both crawling as flat as they could.

The Japs really opened up then; the air got stiff with bullets a few inches over their heads. They crawled about halfway; they still had twenty or thirty feet to go, and Al said, "Let's make a run for it." Lee told him, "No, they'll cut us in two." Then he remembered Al's leg. He said, "You stay back, Smitty; your leg is bad."

"It doesn't hurt me any more," Al told him. It didn't either.

The lieutenant was lying there a few feet away and he hollered for Lee, to give him some orders. Lee went over to his hole and Al stood up and made a dive for the nest. He didn't quite make it; he landed on hands and knees behind a tree. Bullets were snipping the bark off. Somebody said, "Is that you, Smitty?" Al said, "That's me— here I come," and made another dive. He got halfway across the back window, which was just a row of sandbags. He yelled, "Pull me in," and they pulled him in. There was a belt in the gun already. Al got hold of the box and got set to feed the bullets in.

Lee came sliding in right behind him, yelling, "Come on, there's too many in here. Get going! Clear out!" Everybody got out but Lee and Al and Johnny. Johnny was there on the gun when it started; when Al came in, he said, "Okay, Smitty," and kept on staring across the river. It was dark in the hole. Al could see some of Johnny's face, under the helmet; he had his mouth screwed up in a funny grin, like when somebody socked him in a fight. He was watching the other side of the river.

The orders were to hold fire until the Japs started to cross. If they fired too soon it would give away their position, and the Japs would try to knock them out with mortars.

They held their fire. The Japs were coming closer, in the cocoanut grove over there. They were screaming in the high-pitched, hysterical way they had, when they wanted to get on your nerves. One of them would yell, "EEEE-YI," and fire off his rifle and the rest of them would do the same thing. Al could see the little white hunks of fire at the end of their rifle barrels, winking in the trees like fire-flies.

There were streams of incandescent tracer bullets coming across from the Jap machine guns; bullets were thudding into the sandbags in front of the nest. It was a bright night, with a big moon out over the river, but the trees on both sides threw inky shadows on the water.

Al thought: All right, you rotten buggers, you're going to get it.

He was scared and his heart was pounding. They were all scared. But that didn't mean anything. They knew what their job was; they knew each other; they had been sweating and working together a long time, just for this.

They strained their ears for little sounds near the nest—for Japs that might have sneaked across to come up on them from behind. Once Johnny thought he heard one, out there in the dark. He took his .45 and went out after him, but he didn't find anything. He came back and they crouched there, with just their eyes and their steel-hel-meted heads above the ground, and waited. There was hardly a foot of ground between the three of them.

The Japs had made a good-sized landing that night, under heavy Navy protection, about three miles east on the beach. They were fol-lowing almost the same route the marines had taken on the first day. They planned to crash through the marines' rear lines and grab the airfield before the marines could consolidate. There were eight hun-dred to a thousand Japs on the west bank of the Tenaru when the battle started. And on the east side, at the mouth of the river, there were about two hundred marines, with two machine guns and two 37-millimeter antitank guns.

About 1:30 the Japs started coming across. Al saw a dark, bobbing mass on the other side down near the river, right in front of the gun. It looked like a bunch of cows coming down to drink. The Japs down there were being very quiet, but they hadn't spotted the nest. Lee stood up and began pushing sandbags away from around the front of the gun; he pushed them down like they were confetti. He wanted to get clear so they could tilt the gun straight down and fire into the water if they had to.

He said "Fire!" and Johnny opened up. He raked the dark blob of Japs back and forth and it broke up into a lot of little shadows and shapes, screaming and running and flopping down in the water. Bull Warren's gun, a hundred yards to the right, opened up at the same time.

It sounded good to hear the deep, chut-chut-chut stutter of the Amer-ican guns. It made the Jap .25's sound like popguns.

Now the Japs had both Marine guns spotted and they gave them the works. They plastered them with everything they had—the firing before had been nothing. Bullets whizzed into the nest and threw chips of wood and dirt down the back of Al's shirt. Nobody was crouching down any more; they were standing up and working. Johnny watched for the spurts of fire on the other side and tried to douse them. The noise of the gun drowned out everything; Lee would punch Al on the arm, and Al would punch Johnny, and point to where he should fire next.

Bull Warren's gun suddenly stopped firing. Al thought: Maybe he's been hit. Then Johnny got it.

A string of slugs tore into his face and the blood spurted out as though you had turned on a faucet. He fell back in the trench without making a sound. Al's heart thumped; he felt the hate rising in him— hot, and then icy cold. He moved over and took the gun and Lee got in position to load. They didn't have to say anything. They were trained for this too.

Al didn't feel scared any more; he didn't even feel tired. He felt cool and confident and tough, swinging the gun back and forth with his left hand. It was Johnny who had always called him "Southpaw." He heard his bullets hissing through the water and banging into the Japs' helmets. He knew he was hitting something now; he was ramming lead and steel into the Japs' guts and slaughtering them to hell out there in the water. That made him feel better.

He was seething inside with unspoken curses for the Japs, things he didn't have time to say. He thought: Die, you bastards, die! when he heard them screaming and sobbing in the water.

They were still trying to come across, in several places at once. There was one Jap officer who kept screeching and barking commands at the others; he had a nasty shrill voice that stood out over all the firing. Al thought: I don't care if you're a general; I'll get you too, and fired a burst in the direction of the voice. It stopped a minute and then it started up again—jabber, jabber, jabber. Al tried several times but he never stopped that voice—he can still hear it sometimes, jabbering away in his dreams.

The Japs must have got rattled because they started coming over right where the moon was shining on the river; Al could practically see the buttons on their jackets. He waited till they were only fifty yards away and then he mowed them down like sitting ducks.

Once he looked at Johnny and thought he saw his elbow sort of twitch. The next time he looked there was a jacket over Johnny's face— Lee had put it there.

Lee was loading and helping direct the fire. Al would be shooting across the river to the left, and he would feel Lee hitting him on the arm—really *hitting* him—and pointing upstream. Al would swing the gun up there and hear the Japs yelling when his bullets ripped through them. A Jap machine-gunner got set up on the other side once and put a string of bullets through the water jacket of Al's gun, about three inches in front of his nose; the water spurted out over his lap and chest, and the gun started to crackle and sputter, like an empty kettle on a stove. The gun got red-hot, but for some reason it didn't jam the way it was supposed to when it didn't have water.

Lee spotted the Jap gunner who did it, and Al swung his gun around to his right hand and let go with a burst. It must have caught the Jap dead on because that was all they heard from him.

There was an old amphibious tank that the Marines had abandoned in the river on the first day; it was about a hundred yards upstream, just part way around the little bend the river made to the right. It was an ugly old thing that nobody ever thought much about until that night when a Jap gunner got in there and set up. He made a lot of trouble for Al because he could spot Al's position and Al couldn't quite spot his; there were some big trees there and they hid him in shadows. A mortar shell took care of him, though.

Once Lee thought he heard something scrambling around a few yards in front of the nest, he got his Reising gun in one hand, poked his head over the top and let go a few rounds. Later on they found three dead Japs down there.

A Jap bullet caught Lee on the arm and knocked him down; he fell partly across Al's feet. Al went on firing and loading for himself; he would look at the belt every few seconds, and when it got close to the end he would fire a short burst, rip open the magazine, and stick in a new belt. The sweat was pouring down his face like the day when he was grinding corn for Mr. Rosenbaum. He was talking out loud, sometimes, but he doesn't remember what he said; he just remembers hearing his own voice. He wasn't thinking, or worrying, or even feeling very much. He was killing Japs.

He kept it up for more than four hours, with and without help, while heavy Marine reinforcements came up behind him, and a strong force of marines went across the river upstream and swung down to catch the battered Japs from behind. The Japs were stopped cold at the Tenaru that night; their whole attack was a ghastly flop. Later on in the morning some Marine tanks went across and killed off all the Japs that were left in the cocoanut trees.

But somewhere one of them got through. There was a blinding flash and explosion and something hit Al a terrific wallop in the face. It was a hand grenade that exploded against the left stirrup of his gun. Al put his hand up and all he could feel was a wet sticky pulp, and warm blood pouring down through his fingers. It felt like somebody had cut off the front of his face with a hatchet.

He went down on his back in the trench. Lee was lying across his legs. Al heard himself say, "Goddam, they got me in the eyes." Then he could feel more pains, in his left shoulder and arm and hand. The shrapnel from the grenade had ripped him there too. His arm began giving him hell.

The Japs were still pouring bullets into the nest, and Al reached around to his holster and took out his .45. Lee heard him fussing with it and yelled, "Don't do it, Smitty, don't shoot yourself."

Al said, "Hell, don't worry about that. I'm going to get the first Jap that tries to come in here."

"But you can't see," Lee told him.

"That's all right," Al said. "Just tell me which way he's coming and I'll get him." Then he said, "I can smell the rotten buggers . . ."

After that he began to get kind of crazy. He kept asking, "How's Johnny," even though he knew all the time that Johnny was dead just a few inches away. Lee kept telling him "Johnny's all right." They were helpless, there in the hole, and it was getting to be daylight. There was a Jap sniper up in a tree across the river who was firing almost straight down at them. The only thing that protected them was the shelf where the machine gun stood; there was a ledge of dirt about two feet above their faces. The Jap's bullets kept hitting the edge of that ledge, knocking the dirt and sand down into Al's face. He knew the dirt was falling into his eyes, and he couldn't do anything about it.

He was gulping his own blood; he knew he was because he could taste it. It wasn't like when you cut a finger and put it in your mouth to suck it, either; it was like somebody broke your arm off, and let it run in a bucket, and then stuck your head in it. That's the way Al remembers it. He kept thinking: I'm drinking my own blood . . .

They were there a long time, probably an hour, when Whitney Jacobs, one of the boys in the squad, jumped down in the hole. Al was scared; he thought it was a Jap and he lifted his .45. He heard Jake say, "Where the hell are you, Smitty?" and he relaxed. Jake crawled around to where he was and said, "You'll be all right, Smitty—just got a little dirt in your eyes." Al said, "Hell, I got more than that in my eyes." Jake went to get him some water out of the spare can for the machine gun; it was full of rust and oil, but it was water. Al's steel helmet had been knocked off by the explosion and Jake poured the water in it. He lifted Al up a little and Al stuck his bloody face down in the helmet and drank sand, oil, blood, and everything. Jake lit him a cigarette and he took three puffs, but he couldn't smoke; his guts hurt too much from the concussion. He heard the lieutenant yell, "Jake, come on out of there; throw the gun out and come out." Jake called back, "I'm taking care of Diamond and Smitty," but a few minutes later he hopped out and ran back, ducking bullets that were singing all around. He was a game little guy.

The next Al knew they were taking him out on a blanket. He heard the lieutenant say, "Hey, Smitty," and he answered, "Whaddya say, boss?" and he knew the lieutenant was helping to carry him out. It took nerve to do that; the Japs were keeping up a steady machine-gun fire all around the nest. He said, "Are those our guns?" and the lieutenant said, "Sure, they're our guns." Al said, "Gwan—they're Jap guns—I know 'em." The lieutenant said. "Don't worry about it, Smitty. We're winning. It's in the bag."

They had to run quite a way to get out of there. When they got out Al felt himself drifting off. He thought: I'm going to kick the bucket now. He thought of Ruth, standing at the station. He still had his .45 in his hand.

He reached out with it toward the lieutenant. "I guess I won't need this any more," he said, and passed out.

❧ ❧ ❧ ❧

AT THE 1ST MARINE COMMAND POST, COLONEL Clifton B. Cates listened to the uproar of battle. This distinguished officer, who fought in the trenches of France during World War I and rose to Commandant of the Marine Corps (holder of thirty decorations), was eager to enter the fray. Let us join him, as the sky begins to lighten faintly but the sounds of conflict do not diminish.

·13· "LEAVE US ALONE, WE'RE TOO BUSY KILLING JAPS!"

GENERAL CLIFTON B. CATES

Finally day began to break . . . the battle continued. It was a gruesome sight on the sand-spit as it gradually became visible. Dead Japs were piled in a row from our gun positions eastward. Among them were some only wounded, who resumed fire after playing dead. Others had taken refuge under a two-foot sand embankment at the edge of the water, not forty yards from our lines.

The battle raged on and we soon realized that our fire had pinned them down. Now these questions arose:

How much of a force was behind them?

Was this their main body or was it an advance party of a larger force?

Where were their reserves?

At 0800, the 1st Battalion, First Marines, commanded by Lieutenant Colonel Leonard B. Cresswell, was released to me by Lieutenant Colonel Gerald C. Thomas, Operations Officer . . . He also attached "B" Company, 1st Tank Battalion, to our regiment for a proposed enveloping attack.

After a hasty conference, orders were issued for the 1st Battalion, with the company of tanks attached, to proceed southeast across the grassy field to the upper reaches of the Tenaru; to pass through the jungle area and, after crossing the branches of the river, to deploy and attack northward, keeping their right flank on the Block Four River. The mission: to envelop and attack the enemy from their rear, and to prevent their withdrawal and escape.

Due to the difficulty in getting through the dense jungle, the attack proper did not get under way until 0950 and the tanks never did get across the Tenaru branches.

After Cresswell had started his movement northward, he requested permission (telephone communications were maintained throughout the attack) to sweep eastward to the Ilu River, so as to be sure that a force wouldn't hit his open right flank. Leaving a small force to cut off any possible escape of the Jap force to the south, he advanced to the beach with his right flank on the Ilu.

No resistance prior to reaching the beach; but after executing a left turn and changing direction to the westward, he [Cresswell] soon struck heavy fire. But this was soon overcome and the advance through the coconut trees continued. The detachment from the south closed up and the Jap force was entirely surrounded.

. . . I ordered a platoon of five tanks to cross the Tenaru sand-strip at the beach and to assist the attack. With guns blazing they rolled across, right to the middle of the enemy positions and knocked out gun after gun. It was a great sight seeing them running along the beach, weaving through the coconut grove and chasing the fleeing Japs. Finally one tank had its track blown off by an antitank mine, but another tank rescued its crew.

About this time I ordered the tanks, by radio, to withdraw, but the reply I received was: "Leave us alone, we're too busy killing Japs."

The Japs, realizing that they were entirely surrounded, became panicky and about 250 of them ran and tried to jump into the ocean. Caught by fire from three sides, they dove into the ocean and tried to swim seaward. Pollock's men picked them off like ducks.

The tanks were withdrawn and the 1st Battalion closed in for the final mopping up. The whole attack was a beautiful example of perfectly coordinated effort, fire, and movement.

After receiving word that the Jap force had been entirely surrounded, I hopped into my jeep and went up on the Point to see the finale. As Strunk (my chauffeur) and I ran up to the forward gun position on the Point, the Jap fire was still ricocheting through the coconut trees and was plenty hot. Captain Harry Q. Findley, in command of my weapons' company, was standing watching the fireworks when he was hit in the chest by a sniper. What we thought was only a fairly serious wound later proved fatal to him.

By 1700 practically the entire enemy force of 1,000 had been annihilated. The sand-spit and coconut tree areas were a mass of dead and dying. Never . . . did I see such a congestion of dead.

※　※　※　※

THE CORRESPONDENT RICHARD TREGASKIS WAS awakened by gunfire during the night. He dressed and made his way to Cates command post, where he requested permission to go to the front. However early he arrived, he was still waiting impatiently for escort at 11:15 A.M., when two marines finally volunteered to take him to the battle.

·14· THE GROVE: MOP-UP

RICHARD TREGASKIS

Now we moved with even more caution than before, running bent from the waist as we made our way from tree to tree. Snipers were firing occasionally. We heard the crack of their guns, and bullets ricocheting among the trees. Our artillery was still ranging on the Jap positions on the far side of the Tenaru. And the Japs were throwing rifle grenades over to our side. We could see one of the bursts ahead, a spray of dirt rising where the explosive hit. Occasionally we heard the bursts of sharp-sounding Jap machine-gun fire: the light .25 calibers.

We pushed ahead, moving between bursts of firing, until we could see the river, and the long curving spit of gray sand which closed its outlet into the sea, and the shadowy cocoanut grove across the river where the Japs were.

We were crouching behind a tree when Col. Pollock, looking quite calm and walking erect, came over. "The prisoner's up there," he said. He pointed to a group of three or four men lying prone around a foxhole about fifty feet away.

We made a dash for the foxhole and flopped beside it. In the foxhole on his back, with one of his arms wrapped in a red-stained swath of bandage, lay the Jap prisoner. He looked dazed and unhappy.

Capt. Wolf immediately began talking to him in Japanese. But the prisoner's answers were slow and apparently not very satisfactory. A marine told me the prisoner had got up from a foxhole and walked across the intervening no man's land all alone. "Like a ghost," he said. "Or somebody walking in his sleep." Evidently it had been an awful spectacle.

The Jap said he did not think the others would surrender. When asked how the invaders had arrived on Guadalcanal, he was very vague. He either knew nothing or would say nothing about the ships on which they had arrived on Guadal. (One reason for his confusion became apparent later, when it was learned from other prisoners that the troops, new arrivals, were not told where they were or where they were going. Some of them did not even know they were on Guadalcanal.)

It was only about a hundred yards from the foxhole, where the prisoner lay, to the front line of the Tenaru River.

Snipers began to range on us from across the river. We heard the ping-ping-ping of their .25's, and bullets began to whir fairly close. I lay for a few moments while the firing continued, thinking what a wonderful target we were, gathered so close together in a small circle, and then two of the other onlookers and I got the same idea at the same moment; we headed for cover.

A pink-cheeked captain shared my cocoanut tree. He told me while we watched the shadowy woods across the river that it was his unit which had been doing the fighting in this particular sector. He said that his name was James F. Sherman, and that he came from Somerville, Mass. "Lots of Boston boys in the outfit," he said. Then we heard the crackling of a light .25 caliber machine gun, and it was no effort at all to duck and stop talking.

When the firing let up a little, the captain waved a hand at a point of land which marked the seaward extremity of the Tenaru's west bank. "That's Hell Point," he said. "That's where the Japs tried their crossing. Some of our men moved up onto the point to get a better field of fire, and the Japs put up flares that were as bright as daylight. We lost some people in there. But," he added, "we stopped the Japs."

One did not have to look hard to see that he was understating the case. I worked my way, crawling between volleys of firing, flopping close to the earth when a mortar shell or grenade burst, to Hell Point, and looked out on hundreds of Jap bodies strewn in piles.

It was easy to see what they had tried to do. A sandbar, about fifteen feet wide and ten feet above the water level at its crest, shut off the mouth of the Tenaru from the sea.

The Japs had tried to storm our positions on the west bank of the river by dashing across the sandbar. Many of them had come close to reaching their objective. But they had run into unexpected rows of barbed wire at Hell Point, on our side of the Tenaru.

"That wire maybe saved the day," said a marine lying next to me.

I looked across the river into the shadowy cocoanut groves, where only 150 yards from us the advance elements of the enemy were located. We could hear the crack of rifle and machine-gun fire from there, and the occasional crash of our own artillery shells falling among the Jap positions. But no Japs were visible—and that, I had learned, was a perfectly normal condition in this jungle warfare.

I heard the report of a sniper's rifle coming from the right very close, on our side of the river bank. The sound seemed to come from above. I saw a marine run, crouching from one tree to the foot of another, and stand peering up into the tree, with his rifle ready.

Then, silently as a ghost, he beckoned to another marine, who then zigzagged his way to the foot of the same tree. The second marine had a tommy gun. The first marine pointed up into the foliage, and the second followed the gesture. Then the marine with the tommy gun made his way to a nearby stump, and crouched behind it, watching the tree top. I resolved to watch him ferret out the sniper and bring him to earth, but my attention was distracted by the sound of a .25 caliber machine gun coming from the sandbar that closed the mouth of the Tenaru.

"There's a bunch of Japs on the lee side of the bar," said the marine next to me. "They open up every hour on the hour from behind it. We can't spot 'em."

I could see how it might be possible for Japs to hug the lee side of the bar without being seen by our people. The bar was curved in a gentle arc toward the sea, and the bar had steep shoulders like an old-fashioned road. The result of this combination of circumstances was that at certain places there was excellent cover.

The machine gun snapped out at us again in a long burst. "If we could spot that guy we could lay mortar fire right on him," said my informant.

The battlefield is full of distractions. Now I was distracted by heavy firing from our own rifles, coming from my left. I saw a line of marines, lying close together behind sandbags, firing out to sea.

Out in the glassy blue water I saw globs of water jump up where the bullets struck. "They've got a Jap out there," said my friend. "He's trying to swim around and get in behind us. We've killed a lot of 'em that way."

A veritable sheet of bullets was smacking into the water. The marines apparently were all anxious to shoot a Jap.

I worked my way back to Capt. Sherman, who was standing behind a tree with Col. Pollock. Pollock still looked calm and efficient as he trained his field glasses on the patterned rows of cocoanut trees across the river.

There were bright-yellow explosions in the grove now, a series of them. A haze of white smoke drifted among the trees. And apparently from the back of the grove came heavy fusillades of rifle and machine-gun fire.

Col. Pollock looked at his watch. "Probably Cresswell's coming in," he said.

Machine guns began to clatter on our right. "They must be trying to cross the river down there," said Capt. Sherman. He told me how, in the darkness of the early morning today, some of the Japs had tried to cross the Tenaru lagoon by swimming.

Some of them, he said, had reached our side and hidden themselves in an abandoned tank which lay on the sloping river bank. They had set up a machine-gun nest in the tank and it had taken some hours' effort to get them out. I could see the gray bulky shape of the tank up-angled on the slope.

"That machine gun in the tank made it tough for the marines to man that field piece," said Capt. Sherman. He pointed to an artillery piece on the river bank. "They could take that thing in cross fire," he said. "every time somebody moved into position to fire the gun, he got shot."

I remembered then that during the first heavy outburst of firing during the early morning I had heard the loud bang-bang-bang of the field piece, slower and heavier than the fire of a machine gun, and then not heard it again for an hour or two.

At about 1:15 Col. Pollock said, "Our people are coming in at the rear now. I can see 'em. Keep your fire down." He walked erect along our front firing line, saying, "Keep your fire down. Those are our people coming in the rear." Rifle and machine-gun fire still cracked on the other side of the river; grenades and mortar shells were still bursting among us, but Col. Pollock was as cool as if he were leading a parade-ground maneuver.

The volleys of machine-gun and rifle fire, from the depths of the grove across the river, grew louder. Col. Cresswell's people were rolling the Japs toward us.

Suddenly I saw the dark figures of men running on the strip of beach that bordered the palm grove. The figures were far off, possibly a half mile down the light ribbon of sand, but I could see from their squatness that they were Japs. There was no time for any other impression. In a few seconds the black, violently moving blobs were squashed down on the sand and we heard a fusillade of rifle fire. The Japs did not get up again. It was the first visible evidence that Cresswell's men were completing their maneuver of encirclement.

We knew that from this time on things were going to grow hotter along the Tenaru. It was possible that, as the Japs were pushed in from the rear, they might charge our positions on the west bank of the Tenaru, might again try to take the spit of sand across the Tenaru mouth.

Two ambulances had come up and stopped well back of our front line. The bearers were now picking up casualties on stretchers, loading them on the ambulances. Col. Pollock said to me: "The ambulances are going back. You can ride if you want to." I decided to stay and see the excitement.

The colonel passed the word along the line that there should be no firing unless a specific target was visible. The men had one of those a few moments later when a single Jap jumped out of the underbrush, just across the Tenaru in the edge of the cocoanut grove, and made a dash for the beach. A storm of firing burst from our line, and red streaks of tracers zipped around the Jap. He dropped to the ground, and for a moment the firing ceased, and then again he was up and running wildly for his life, and the firing was louder than ever. This time he fell violently, on the beach, and did not get up again.

Now the .25 caliber Jap machine gun which had been shooting at us for hours from the lee side of the Tenaru was opening up again. As usual, it had the effect of making us keep cover and to a certain extent pinning us down. But this time we spotted the Jap. A sharp-eyed marine saw a hand move above the level of the top of the sandbar, and made a mental note of the exact spot.

One of our mortars went into action. We heard the "thwung" sound of the piece discharging, waited the usual long seconds while the projectile arched into the air, then felt the ground shake as the explosive struck the sandbar and blew up.

We could hear a marine shouting, apparently giving the mortar crew directions on the matter of correcting their range. Then again, the "thwung" and the shattering explosion.

"That's better," called a marine. "Up fifteen."

The mortar went off again, and just after it was discharged, the figure of a Jap popped up from behind the spit of sand. He was less than 150 feet from me. I saw him take about three fast steps, and then the mortar shell landed almost directly on top of his helmet. The explosion of the shell was a canopy of dirty gray smoke and debris shedding over the Jap from above, and then swallowing him altogether.

The puff of the explosion expanded over the ground, and as it spread and thinned, we saw three more Japs, evidently members of the same machine-gun crew, leap up and start to run for the far end of the Tenaru sandspit.

They had gone only a few feet when they were in clear view of our troops, and bullets, including tracers from our machine guns, were winging all around them. Two of them fell as the fusillades of firing rang out and one kept running, then dived for cover.

But when he jumped up again, our men were waiting for him. Apparently he sensed this, for he ran desperately, turning in a fast hundred yards in his dash for the far end of the spit. Before he reached it, however, the bullets caught him and knocked him down. I was not sorry to see the end of the last of this machine-gun crew. War takes on a very personal flavor when other men are shooting at you, and you feel little sympathy at seeing them killed.

A rumbling of powerful motors came from behind us. We turned to find a group of four tanks moving down the trail through the cocoanut palms heading for the Tenaru and the spit of sand across its mouth.

The plan, evidently, was to send the tanks across the spit and into the Jap positions at the edge of the grove.

On our (west) bank of the Tenaru the tanks halted for a few moments, then plunged on across the sandspit, their treads rattling industriously. We watched these awful machines as they plunged across the spit and into the edge of the grove. It was fascinating to see them bustling amongst the trees, pivoting, turning, spitting sheets of yellow flame. It was like a comedy of toys, something unbelieveable, to see them knocking over palm trees which fell slowly, flushing the running figures of men from underneath their treads, following and firing at the fugitives. It was unbelievable to see men falling and being killed so close, to see the explosions of Jap grenades and mortars, black fountains and showers of dirt near the tanks, and see the flashes of explosions under their very treads.

We had not realized there were so many Japs in the grove.

Group after group was flushed out and shot down by the tanks' canister shells.

Several times we could see our tanks firing into clumps of underbrush where evidently Japanese machine-gun nests were located, for we could hear the rattling of the guns, in answer to the heavier banging of the tanks' cannon.

I saw a bright orange flash amidst a cloud of black smoke bursting directly under the treads of one of the tanks, saw the tank stop suddenly. It was crippled. The other tanks moved in protectively toward it. I learned later that they were taking off the crew, who escaped uninjured.

The three remaining tanks continued to roar and rattle amidst the palm grove for a time that seemed hours long. Everywhere they turned in their swiveling course, their cannon spewing sheets of orange flame. It seemed improbable that any life could exist under their assault.

I remember seeing one Jap in particular who was flushed out from under the treads of one of our tanks. I saw him jump up, and run hard toward the beach, with the tank following. I thought the tank would run him down or hit him with machine-gun fire, but it turned off quickly and headed back into the heart of the grove.

II Mounting the Offensive: Guadalcanal

The original Henderson Field on Guadalcanal soon after its capture from the Japanese. (Photo taken from a J2F)

Seventh Marines pushing forward after landing. (Photo by Sgt. McBride)

Corpsmen bring back Marine wounded while in patrol
ahead of front lines. (Photo by Pvt. J. E. Ely)

Commanding General of the First Marine Division and
part of his Division Staff. Most of these officers were
Regimental Commanders, Battalion Commanders, and
Executives of Regiments and Battalions.

1. Col. George R. Rowan	12. Lt. Col. F.C. Biebush	23. Maj. William Chalfant III	34. Maj. R. B. Luckey
2. Col. P.A. del Valle	13. Lt. Col. E.A. Pollock	24. Maj. D.W. Fuller	35. Lt. Col. Sam B. Taxis
3. Col. W.C. James	14. Lt. Col. E.J. Buckley	25. Maj. Forest C. Thompson	36. Lt. Col. E.H. Price
4. Maj. Gen. A.A. Vandegrift	15. Lt. Col. W.W. Barr	26. Maj. R.G. Ballance	37. Lt. Col. Merrill B. Twining
5. Lt. Col. G.C. Thomas	16. Lt. Col. R.P. Coffman	27. Maj. H.C. Buse	38. Lt. Col. W.A. Reaves
6. Col. C.B. Cates	17. Lt. Col. F.R. Geraci	28. Maj. J.C. Frazer	39. Lt. Col. J.D. Macklin
7. Col. R. McC. Pate	18. Lt. Col. W.E. Maxwell	29. Maj. H.H. Crockett	40. Lt. Col. Hawley C. Waterm
8. Cdr. W.T. Brown, USN	19. Lt. Col. E.G. Hagen	30. Lt. Col. L.B. Cresswell	41. Maj. James C. Murray
9. Col. W.C. Whaling	20. Lt. Col. W.N. McKelvy	31. Maj. R.O. Bowen	
10. Col. F.B. Goettge	21. Lt. Col. J.N. Frisbee	32. Lt. Col. J.A. Bemis	
11. Col. L.P. Hunt	22. Maj. M.V. McConnell	33. Col. K.W. Benner	

Japanese bombing planes attacking American transports off Guadalcanal on D plus 1.

The rising sun reveals the corpses of Japanese jungle-fighters half buried in the tidal sands of the Tenaru River, where they fell in their night attempt to dislodge the Marines from Guadalcanal.

These four Marines are rescuing their wounded comrade while under heavy sniper fire. As calmly as they would walk on their village green, they carry their buddy to safety.

Readying for the next attack: an unidentified Marine inspects his 8'03.

This pagoda was headquarters for Marine and Navy fliers at Henderson Field. After surviving numerous enemy bombings, the building was torn down following a near-miss which rendered it useless as a shelter.

Dogfight over the airstrip.

SBD Squadron warms up before Japanese strike.

Lieutenant Colonel Donald Dickson's conception of the typical beat-up Leatherneck, several weeks after the campaign opened.

Lieutenant General Thomas Holcomb, Commandant of the Marine Corps, sits up front with the chauffeur as Major General Alexander A. Vandegrift rides in the rear.

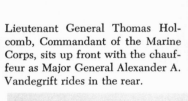

The Mantanikau, in its upper reaches, flows smoothly and tranquilly, belying its title "The Bloody River." (Photo by Sgt. Diet)

A raider battalion hikes over rugged terrain during operations. (Photo by Wright)

In their newly dug trench near the front lines two Marines wait beside their weapons for chow call.

Bombing raids permitting, there were movies once in a while . . . SRO.

Medal of Honor Men. From left to right: General A. A. Vandegrift, Brigadier General M. S. Edison, Lieutenant Mitchell Paige, Sergeant John Basilove.

Guadalcanal L'Envoi . . . taking along the last of the Japanese prisoners. (Photo by Menken)

The Jap, however, continued to run. He was heading for the beach. All along our front line, rifle fire banged and machine guns clattered; the tracers arched around the running Jap.

Then the Jap sank into the underbrush, took cover, and Col. Pollock shouted: "Don't shoot. You might hit our own tanks."

The Jap jumped up and ran another forty or fifty feet toward the shore, then sank down into cover again. Despite the warning, several rifle shots were fired at him. As usual, each marine was eager to kill his Jap.

"One man fire," shouted Capt. Sherman. He designated a grizzled, leather-faced marine to do the shooting. I noticed that the man wore the chamois elbow pad and fingerless shooting glove of a rifle-range marksman. The marines told me he was Gunnery Sgt. Charles E. Angus (of Nashville, Tenn.), a distinguished marksman who had won many a match in the States.

We watched Sgt. Angus, as if he were the spotlighted star of a play, when the Jap jumped up again and began to run. Angus was nervous. He fired several shots, working his bolt fast, and missed. He inserted another clip of cartridges, fired one of them. But then the Jap had sunk down into cover again.

It was a little disappointing—but only for the moment. The Jap had flopped on the beach. He was evidently heading for the sanctuary of the water, hoping to swim for it. But now he started to get up again—and that was as far as he got. He had reached only a crouch when Sgt. Angus, now quite calm, took careful aim and let one shot go. The Jap sank as if the ground had been jerked out from underneath him. It was a neat shot—at about 200 yards.

Now the tanks, their job finished, were rolling out of the grove, heading for the spit. There were only three of them now. One sat very still and dead in the grove.

In a few minutes the tanks were behind our line. I followed them back until they stopped a few hundred feet west of the Tenaru, and the tank captain, his face grimy and his shirt soaked with sweat, climbed out. He said his name was Lieut. Leo B. Case (of Syracuse, N.Y.).

Col. Pollock had come back to talk to Lieut. Case. The colonel said, "Man, you really had me worried." He laughed. "But what a job!"

The colonel told me that his orders to Lieut. Case had been only that the tanks should run up and down the beach, on the far side of the Tenaru, and do a sort of reconnaissance. Turning into the grove, where close-spaced trees made it difficult for tanks to maneuver, and blotting out the Jap positions with point-blank fire—this had been Lieut. Case's own idea.

I went back to our front line, for firing was growing heavy again.

Across the river Jap after Jap jumped up from the underbrush and dashed for the shore. It was their last hope for escape, with Col. Cresswell's troops coming in from behind. Most of the Japs were knocked down by our fire as they ran, long before they reached the beach. Some of them, however, reached the beach and tried to swim away. Their heads, small black dots amongst the waves, were difficult targets to hit. But our men relished the firing. Whenever we could see the head of a swimming man, a small storm of little waterspouts rose around him as our bullets smacked home.

Now we could distinctly see a few green-uniformed marines, noticeably bigger than the enemy, popping into view, then disappearing, in the grove across the river, far back among the even lanes of trees. And the sound of rifle and machine-gun fire accelerated, telling us that there must still be considerable Japanese resistance in the grove.

There were more of our troops on the beach at the edge of the grove, far down across the Tenaru. They were visible for a few seconds at a time, as they moved forward, then took cover, then repeated the process.

Our artillery fire, which had been pounding into the grove constantly in the earlier part of the day, had now halted. But Col. Cresswell's people were using mortars to finish off the Japs. The flashes of the explosions were like huge orange flowers scattered through the edge of the grove, just across the Tenaru. We simply kept our heads low and watched the excitement. There was no firing from our side of the river, for we were afraid of hitting our own men. And the Japs were too occupied with fighting our people closing in the rear to bother with those of us on the west bank of the Tenaru.

From time to time a live Jap stirred from among the dead piled on the Tenaru River spit and dived into the water. But at such point-blank range, these would-be escapers did not get far. From Hell Point, on Col. Pollock's end of the spit, volleys of firing sprang out and the Jap was killed as he swam; even the kindliest marine could not let the swimming Jap escape, for he would be apt then to swim around our rear and throw grenades as several Japs had done earlier in the day.

There was bitter fighting now in the grove across the Tenaru. We realized that the tanks had not "mopped up" completely, for we could still hear the snapping of Jap machine-gun and rifle fire. But Col. Cresswell's people were closing in fast. A large group of them advanced steadily but cautiously down the beach bordering the grove. Several groups moved simultaneously among the rows of palms scarcely 300 yards beyond the Tenaru. We kept our heads low, for the bullets of Cresswell's marines might accidentally strike among us.

And then the fighting, suddenly, seemed to have ended. We saw marines at the opposite end of the Tenaru spit, three of them, swiveling their heads about, stepping tensely with rifles at the ready—all set to kill any Japs who might try one last stealthy act of resistance.

Several times, as these three leaders moved across the spit, live Japs stirred among the piles of dead—I was told later that some of them tried to throw grenades at our people—and were killed for their trouble.

Jap dead are dangerous, for there are usually some among them alive enough to wait until you pass, then stab or shoot you. Our marines had by this time learned to take no chances. The dead were shot again, with rifles and pistols, to make sure.

More marines trickled out of the cocoanut grove, from the other side of the Tenaru, following the three leaders, advancing just as cautiously. More of our men moved out from our (Pollock's) side of the Tenaru to move across the spit and help in the brutal but necessary re-butchery of the dead. I watched our men standing in a shooting-gallery line, thumping bullets into the piles of Jap carcasses. The edge of the water grew brown and muddy. Some said the blood of the Jap carcasses was staining the ocean.

I followed our men out onto the Tenaru spit. At the far end I talked to some of Cresswell's men; they told me there were hundreds of Jap dead in the grove and beyond, and some wounded prisoners—a few.

Just then came a recrudescence of rifle fire rattling in the cocoanut grove, then a few of the unmistakable sharp cracks of a Jap .25. Snipers were still operating in the grove. We spread out a little on the spit. The strip of sand was not yet a safe meeting-ground.

But the Battle of the Tenaru was to all intents and purposes at an end. The detailed sequence of the fighting was not yet clear. But we knew that a major Japanese attempt to break through our lines and seize the airport had been stopped, and we knew too that this must have been one of the most crushing defeats the Japs had yet suffered. Our own casualties, I found, were only 100, twenty-eight killed and seventy-two wounded; whereas the Japs had lost an estimated 700 killed. (I found later that the actual count of the Jap bodies in the Tenaru battle area was 871.)

※   ※   ※   ※

BEFORE TURNING TO THE NEXT PHASE OF THE CAM-paign, let us see what happened to one of the diversions scheduled to coincide with the Guadalcanal landings: the highly publicized Makin Island (garrison of 250) raid by the 2nd Raider Battalion.

Lieutenant Evans F. Carlson (Navy Cross and Legion of Merit) was a devoutly religious and dedicated officer: "It is necessary that you live close to the men, study them and teach them not only military techniques and maneuvers, but basic, ethical doctrines as well." The marine officer began his military career in the enlisted ranks, serving in China for many years and then adopting the motto *Gung Ho* ("Work Together") for one of the toughest mobs of fighting men ever welded together into a marine combat unit. Carlson's executive officer was Major James Roosevelt, the President's eldest son.

The purpose of the raid on the Gilberts was manifold: the diversion effect, which failed; the destruction and annihilation of the garrison and all buildings on the island; and the gathering of intelligence information. On August 8, after a late start, Carlson's Raiders boarded submarines *Argonaut* and *Nautilus* at Pearl Harbor. Among the 222 marines was Lieutenant Wilfred S. Le Francois, another who came up through the ranks with service in the 4th Marines. Wounded in the ensuing action, for which he received the Navy Cross, we meet Le Francois on the night of August 16, 1942, after a long undersea voyage is over. His rubber boat is about to lead the way into the beach.

·15· CARLSON'S MAKIN RAID

LIEUTENANT W. S. LE FRANCOIS

At eleven P.M. the hatches were opened and we started climbing up. I carried a large ship's compass, and it clanked against the side of the sub until I felt sure that every Jap ashore would hear it. In the great swells, the sub sank deep into the sea; then, as it rose high, water poured from it in streams, a goodly portion going into our rubber boats and dreching our motors. The rubber boats bounced around like toys and looked very frail. Filled with water, they blended so

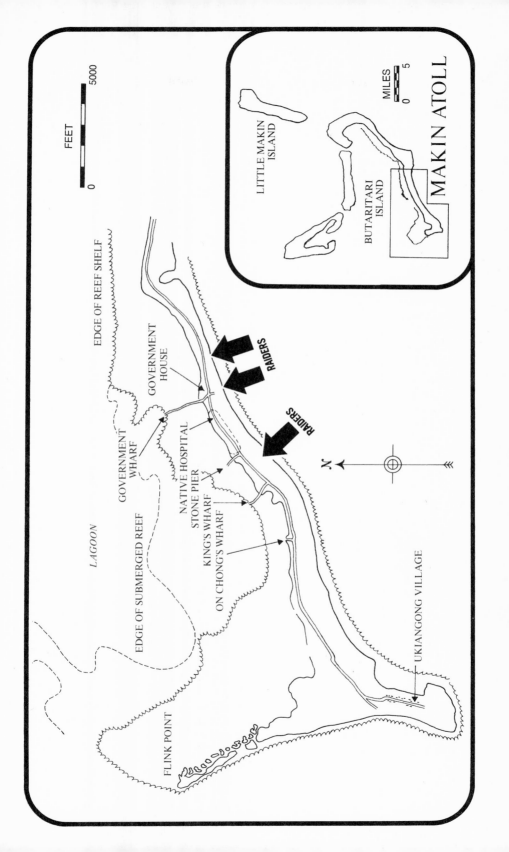

FEET

0   5000

MAKIN ATOLL

MILES

0   5

LITTLE MAKIN ISLAND

BUTARITARI ISLAND

EDGE OF REEF SHELF

LAGOON

EDGE OF SUBMERGED REEF

GOVERNMENT HOUSE

GOVERNMENT WHARF

NATIVE HOSPITAL

STONE PIER

KING'S WHARF

ON CHONG'S WHARF

RAIDERS

RAIDERS

N

FLINK POINT

UKIANGONG VILLAGE

well with the ocean that you wondered if you were going to hit anything at all when you jumped for one.

I had the lead boat. When we arose on the peak of a swell, I could see an outline of trees to our left. Together with our boats, the submarine was caught in a current which was taking us shore-side; and [the submarine skipper] . . . was compelled to move the sub out to sea. I grouped the boats as best I could, believing that in union there was strength. Since the swift current made it impossible for our boats to operate in two task groups, Colonel Carlson changed our plan for landing and passed the word along for all boats to follow his. This change was a lifesaver. We learned later from the natives that all Jap islands had been on the alert since the American attack on Guadalcanal on August seventh. As a result, on Makin the Japs were guarding the beach that I was to have landed on. At the very moment we were embarking on our rubber boats eight machine guns were emplaced on this beach.

The current began to help us and soon we heard the roar of the surf. With a terrific rush, a breaker hoisted us up and tried to spin us sideways and turn us over. But we kept our nose pointed toward shore, and by strong paddling finally landed on a sandy beach. Running the boat into the brush, we took up defensive positions. We were organizing those positions when the heavy growl of a Browning automatic rifle ripped the silence wide open. One of our men had let go with an accidental discharge and the enemy would now be alarmed. In my opinion, that accidental discharge really helped us. The alarm forced the immediate carrying out of a plan on our part, and, as it turned out, it caused the Japs to seek us. Now we could let them come and try to get us. They only tried.

Soon Lieutenant Plumley crawled up to us, asking for me. He told me the colonel wanted to know where we were, and that he wished us to contact the enemy and to keep as much distance as possible between our beached boats and the Japs. I could recognize Plum in spite of the intense blackness, which was eloquent proof of the value of the intensive night practice we had had.

Sergeant Thomason—Clyde Thomason, of Atlanta, Georgia—led the reconnoitering group across the island, following the course of a shallow ditch for cover. He was followed by the squads commanded by Corporals Pisker, Debosik and Witenburg. Corporal Young was at the head of the column, waiting my arrival before going farther. My water-soaked Reising gun had Japs to kill, and I squirted oil into its mechanism. As far as I was concerned, it was the weapon that was keeping the conquering hordes from my home town.

I sneaked along the line of men. Once in a while, the fellows guiding me whispered a wisecrack, and it aggravated me to think that they were thoroughly enjoying this adventure, which could easily mean our complete annihilation. Certainly it could cost my neck and the lives of many marines. I knew that the Japs were good at camouflage, and that one of their tricks was to let advance guards pass through them, so that they could pour their fire on the unsuspecting main body of our troops from prepared positions.

A haze barely outlining the bush and trees announced the dawn. Corporal Young went ahead, and I followed with my runner, Metcalf. Some of the men carried shotguns for close-in fighting, and, patting his beloved and extremely destructive weapon, Thomason followed with my detail. Another 100 yards and Young came back to report that he had located a long pier jutting out into the water. He had also found the island's flagpole. Thomason, Metcalf and I found the government house. It loomed up before us, and I reported our position, so Colonel Carlson could make plans. Thomason and I crept closer, and approached the place from the side opposite that on which our detail had taken its position.

We were doing fine when two blasts roared from the left and double-0 buckshot sprayed a wooden shack near us. Thomason shouted the password "Gung" to keep our men from shooting us in a cross fire. Then, to our amazement, the countersign "Ho" was shouted to us from our hostile left, and out came Charley Lamb with two men. He had taken our shadowy forms for those of Japs.

We all went rapidly through the government house. It was vacant. By this time it was quite bright and we could see things clearly, including a straight dirt road running the length of the island. The long government pier was evidently not in use, as sections of it were demolished and no boats were tied up there. We had landed at the best possible place for secrecy.

Lamb pointed up the road. A group of tall, well-built native men, women and children was coming down it, laughing and chattering. Apparently, they had taken our firing for Japanese practice maneuvers. When they saw us, they were startled, but quickly became friendly. A few of them spoke broken but intelligible English. They disliked the Japs and told us that eighty of them were living at the On Cheong pier. Lamb went back with this information. I was uneasy. I was thinking of a possible Jap ambush, and wanted to be on our way, alert for that kind of activity. Young and Pisker had found a Jap stormy-weather flag in a hut near the flagpole. They had a tussel over it, ending up with each of them owning half of the flag. It was one more example of the fact that none of these fellows seemed to worry about anything and took it for granted that the story was bound to have a happy ending.

Orders came to move up the road and establish contact with the enemy. Our main body was evidently now in shape to support any action our advance party got into. With his men, Young went scurrying all over the place, determined to rout out any hidden Japs. Metcalf and I followed. I was bareheaded. My helmet was slung on my back, so I could see anything and hear any sound. I carried my gun on "full automatic," with the safety catch off. Back of us came Thomason with the guard. I could only see our men here and there in the bush, but I knew that our raiders, in staggered groups, were following me, ready for the fight.

There was much dense vegetation, especially around small bogs. Our point and flankers thoroughly combed such hide-outs. We had just passed a group of fifteen shacks near a long house. The house had no walls but a very high, pointed roof. There were open spaces on each side of the road which offered a good field of fire.

Suddenly, the point hit the ground, and the rest of us followed suit. A truck had stopped way up the road. Japs jumped out of it and were joined by other Japs, a total of more than thirty in all. They planted a large rising-sun flag and ducked into the bushes beside the road. I knew this meant that they were operating from this spot as a focal point. I also knew that more troops were following, and that they were probably aware of our general location and were coming to get us. Their tree observers must have been watching us all the way and had been waiting for their troops to appear to tell them of our presence by signal. For the moment, they were lying low, waiting for the fight to start before commencing their sniping.

This was a much better place in which to meet an enemy than any I had seen. I called in the point, who made sure the fight would start then and there by letting the Japs have a burst. I signaled to Thomason to double-time his men up the road, and I moved toward them to a higher elevation which would afford the best field of fire on this side of the village. Without regard for his own safety, Thomason ran up and down the line, picking out good positions for the men, while I sent the command post information about our location.

I could see the Japs creeping toward us in bunches along the narrow 100-yard strip of trees and light brush between the road and the lagoon. They were perfect targets and were walking into a trap. Surely, I told myself, things like this didn't happen. No leader could be so lucky as I. I decided to swing our left flank closer to the point, so that this part of the line would form a sort of pocket with frontal and a flanking fire to welcome the Nips. It was a perfect setup. Thomason chuckled with glee and patted his shotgun. The Japs were advancing aggressively, but we had done a fast, sure job and were waiting for them.

Thomason shouted, "Let 'em have it!" and poured a barrage of double-0 buckshot into the enemy. Those sudden explosions came sooner than I had intended they should, but they were well-timed. There was about four minutes of inferno in which everybody in the area was blasting away at somebody or something. Anything out in the open was riddled. Then we realized we were the only ones making any noise, and let up. Later, I found our fire had been so deadly that this Jap combat group in its entirety had seen its last battle.

But there was activity down the road beyond the red-ball flag, and not 200 yards away a Jap heavy machine gun was peppering us and enemy snipers were taking a grim toll. One slug kicked up dirt into my mouth.

Metcalf yelled, "You'd better come over here near me! You won't live long there!"

I ran over and flopped down beside him. A bullet hit between the two of us as we lay about an inch apart.

I said, "I'm going back. Your Jap has too good a shooting eye. Mine misses by at least a couple of inches."

Then came a "thut," and Metcalf said, "They got Thomason."

I inched my way over to him and felt his pulse. There was no heartbeat.

Slowly, I returned to my post. The men on the left flank were sticking out like a sore thumb, and I shouted to them to work their way back on a line with us. Reluctantly, they snaked back. The confidence each raider had in his own ability to handle the whole situation by himself was supreme, almost colossal.

I felt sure that two of the enemy snipers were out to get me. I was trying to locate them when I heard several bursts of fire from a high-powered weapon on my right. "Killer" Wygal had located the sharp-shooters in their tree nests, had borrowed an automatic rifle to take the place of his own low-velocity weapon, and had ended my worries. He crawled around our right flank, along the shore line of the lagoon, and saw a lot of dead Japs—and the live ones he was after. Huddled back of a water-cooled machine gun, they were raking our lines. Using hand grenades, his pistol and his knife, Wygal sent those Nips to their ancestors.

Somebody shouted from my right, "Lieutenant Holton has been shot and is dying! He needs medical attention!" Then came, slowly, the words, "Never mind!"

I had been watching the fighting up the road back of the flag. I could see much commotion. Later I learned why. Lieutenant Peatross' boat had had a good motor, but not a good compass. They had become lost in the waves, finally landing by themselves at a point back of the Japanese lines. A Jap messenger had come up the road strenuously pedaling a bicycle. He saw two American marines, stopped, dismounted and started to take his rifle from its slung position on his shoulders. He was one dead man who must have known what hit him. Before they were done, Pete and his men had killed eleven Jap messengers on bicycles and one on a motorcycle. The Japs couldn't get a messenger back to their commander and didn't know where to turn. They came our way to follow out their original plan, preparing the way for their advance with shells from a mortar. I winced as I looked at the bog on which my vulnerable left flank rested. Shell after shell came over. They sounded terrifying and hellish. I asked the command post just what constituted our left security.

They replied, "It's ample. What are you doing about that mortar?"

One of the machine gunners must have heard that question, for the "ra-ta-ta-ta-tat" of his gun silenced that mortar.

Crouching low, I scurried over to a little ditch just off the cleared area on the edge of the dangerous bog. I reinforced my left flank with an additional automatic rifle and a rifle, and I had a gangster gun which could do a lot of damage at close range. I could see our men moving up from the rear and apparently making a strong point in the dense foliage on the other side of the bog. That bog was a loophole placed in our otherwise perfect firing line, but with luck it could be a death trap for the Japs too.

The Japs sounded two shrill notes on a bugle, and the little green-uniformed monkeys charged down the center of the island, running at full stride, holding their rifles over their heads with bayonets fixed, and shooting from that position without aiming. They came shouting, "*Banzai.*" It seemed that there was no end to them. It was an amazing and fantastic piece of showmanship, and we were so fascinated by this attempt to scare us into panicky flight that we waited until they were uncomfortably close before we mowed them down with a withering fire. Two of them emerged not twenty feet from my position and roused me into a frenzy of action. I poured almost twenty precious slugs into their bodies before I could control myself. The noise of our firing exceeded any noise I have ever heard. Next day, eighty-two dead Japs were counted in the area where that fatal charge took place.

Back of this Jap infantry wave followed four light machine guns and a flame thrower. Well camouflaged with foliage, the Jap machine-gun crews crept up to within thirty yards of our lines. Fortunately, the flame-thrower operator was killed by stray machine-gun bullets. We found his body with his wicked weapon still strapped to him.

I kept my eyes on the terrain and on the trees to our front. The Jap snipers never let up, and they were too clever to make any false moves. Corporal Earles was hit by a sniper, and it seemed to craze him. Blood ran from his mouth and the men kept begging him to lie still. Fred E. Kemp, of San Francisco, was hit in the cartridge belt by a bullet which set off one of his tracers. Smoke poured from him, and he tried to beat it out with his hands. Finally, he threw himself into the swamp. By that time Earles had become delirious.

He jumped up and shouted, "I'll get those heathens by myself! Show me where they are!"

He began to run through the thick brush, shooting dead and live Japs indiscriminately. Then the Jap machine guns, riflemen and the snipers opened up on him. I was never to find out how much damage Earles did before those guns murdered him.

Over on the extreme left, "Transport" Maghakian—Victor Maghakian, of Fresno, California—had been waving his arms around, giving directions. His right arm caught a bullet, but he wrapped it up and kept on directing a stream of lead on the enemy machine guns. Later, he gave directions in exactly the same manner on Guadalcanal, and was shot in the other arm.

I was one of the first ones shot when the deluge of lead from the four Jap machine guns hit us. There were five light machine-gun bullets embedded in my right arm and shoulder. One of them, an explosive bullet, exploded in my shoulder. None of them seemed to hurt me on impact, but my clothes and the ground were soon soaked with blood. I squeezed tight against the earth in a near-by ditch.

Corporal Young knocked off the machine gun which had shot me up. Back of it were two dead Jap officers and three enlisted men. In back of another of the Jap guns lay ten dead men, huddled close together, with one lying on the ground partly naked. For some reason, with the last ounce of his strength he had attempted to remove his clothing in order to go out of the world bare, as he had come in.

One of the boys crept up to me, took his belt off and tied my arm to my body. I tried to recognize this lad, but my mind was foggy. I knew that I was of no use any more, that I was bleeding to death and would soon be unconscious. My one chance was to get back to the doctors. To be killed instantly in such an attempt was much better than slow death from loss of blood. Besides, I had not yet seen those two-man tanks the Japs were said to have, and I wanted to have at least one look at those dreaded rolling forts before my number was up.

I rolled over and over to the cleared swamp to my right. The struggle was a painful one and my condition infuriated me. I was getting in a frame of mind to tackle the Mikado himself or just sit down in that swamp and stay there. Pulling myself up, I stumbled to the rear.

A Jap infantryman, gleeful over the fine target I made, stood up, took aim at me and was shot dead by one of my own men, Joe R. Bibby, of Dallas, Texas. Then that damned Jap bugle sounded again, and

I was sure I could hear the roar of advancing tanks. But the Japs never had any tanks at all on Makin Island. They only rumbled in our imagination. This second Jap attack was similar to the first one, but on a smaller scale. Our men knew the terrain better now, and had settled down. The attack turned out to be a long dogfight, with our troops on top.

In the huddle of shacks I met Plum and Colonel Carlson. They were much pleased with the job we had done so far.

Our reserve area, which contained our rear guard, the dressing station, the liaison group, the demolition outfit and the command post, was not more than 400 yards from the front lines. Major Roosevelt operated the command post while Colonel Carlson moved around to inspect various parts of the line and coordinate the action. The dressing station was situated in a large building with a cathedral-like roof. Here the Navy doctors were helping to take care of our wounded. I stumbled over to Dr. Arthur Cantrall, of Alpine, Arizona, who guided me to a straw mat on the dirt floor and got me ready for Doctor MacCracken.

Mac cleaned my wounds, packing them with sulfanilamide. He said, "Frankie, this isn't so bad as it looked at first. You just lie here and relax until we go back to the ships. Everything is going to be all right."

The "zing" of snipers' bullets resounded in that great hall-like building. I was weak, but my arm and back pained me only if I stood up or sat down. I could walk slowly and all my faculties were intact. I was even fairly happy, and eager to see a Jap fall out of a tree, especially those skunks trying to pick off our doctors. Wobbling into the open, I leaned against a post and watched the tops of the palms where the leaves bunched and the coconuts met in a great mass.

An automatic-weapon man came up to me and said, "Lieutenant, we have found most of the rats in the leaning palms. If you see anything suspicious, point to that tree and I'll give it the works."

This proved a tedious job, but we got our reward when my partner let out a whoop to indicate satisfactory results. Our score of one less Jap didn't compare with the success of Julius Cotten, of Canton, Mississippi. He was no larger than a Jap himself, but he stood under a tree, pulled the safety pin from a hand grenade, counted three and tossed it up into the palm leaves and the coconuts. It exploded on the count of five and blasted out three monkeys—two bucktooths and a real specimen.

Then, about midmorning, the roar of several big guns split the air. Somebody hollered, "The Jap fleet!" I made my way over to Major Roosevelt, who was in a clump of bush, his bald head shining like a polished grapefruit. It offered a good target, and the Japs hadn't failed to notice it. Bullets whistled around him and he turned constantly, trying to locate the snipers. Every once in a while he looked out into the lagoon, where lay a small Japanese transport loaded with troops. A Jap gunboat was dropping anchor close to it . . .

As best I could, I hurried toward a house projecting out into the lagoon, which made a swell grandstand. The Jap gunboat had opened up now, but, since it had no observer to check its fire, its shots were wild. Our sub scored two direct hits on the gunboat amidships, setting off its magazine in a sheet of flame and sending it to the bottom of the lagoon. The transport was sinking too.

Returning to the hospital, I lay down and was soon asleep. I had a rude awakening. Jap planes were scouting the island, probably from their base at Jaluit in the Marshall Islands. While they were overhead, we remained motionless under cover of dead palm leaves. The Jap troops probably sent them some kind of signal, for they went away, but we knew they would come back soon.

The native men and boys began to come out now and helped move the wounded. I was very tired and no longer angry at my fate. I just didn't care any more, and for the rest of the day the raid took second place in my mind to my own comfort and health. I had myself propped against logs in a little hollow filled with dry leaves and waited for the next aerial attack there. It came in four waves of three planes each. They strafed and bombed us, dropping sticks of antipersonnel bombs, but they missed us entirely. Word came back that they were bombing their own troops. This was too good to miss. A group of native boys pulled me to my feet and went with me all the way up to my impromptu grandstand. I could see no activity at all on the island, but out there on the lagoon was a sight for sore eyes. A four-motored transport had started to land on the water, and some of our machine guns and antitank guns, as well as a few rifles, opened up on it. The white tracers streamed across the water and lit squarely on the plane. It nosed up, caught fire, tipped to the left and sank swiftly out of sight . . .

. . . Quite a lot of firing opened up to my left. I think the Japs wanted us to return their fire, thereby disclosing our positions to their planes, but the planes had gone now and the Japs had started what turned out to be their last stand. I had a hard time seeing, and even reasoning things out, but the job of mopping up, burning and demolitions was next on the schedule, I figured . . .

We had picked out a small wooded promontory, so that when daylight came we could see everything, both seaward and landward. As far as we knew, we were the only marines ashore, and there were no boats.

The next morning we woke not long after dawn and scanned the land and sea. To my delight, our submarine was surfaced. They could not rescue us, so they must have expected us to get to them somehow. And that was exactly what was happening. We had not been the only ones left on the island. I saw two of our boats trying to get through the surf. One of them turned over. Major Roosevelt and Lieutenant Lamb were in that one. Lamb nearly drowned, and when a second attempt to reach the sub was made, he just pushed the boat off and remained behind, preferring to take his chances on the island rather than risk death in the sea. He stood there, waved to the major, and watched that boat fight its way straight through the surf and out to the submarine.

From our promontory, Chapman reconnoitered the beach and I looked over the adjacent area. To my amazement, I found exactly what I was searching for—a rubber boat completely equipped with a motor and an extra can of gasoline. It had been so thoroughly camouflaged that it had been passed over the night before. Soon there gathered before me the most disheartened, forlorn, bloody, ragged, disarmed group of men it had ever been my experience to look upon. Their heads hung low, and despair had frayed their spirits. Only one man, Olan C. Mitchell, of Houston, Texas, had a rifle.

I asked, "What's the matter with you people?"

One spoke up in a voice so low I could hardly hear him, "No weapons. No boats. What are we going to do?"

So that was it—a bunch of marines without their rifles.

"No weapons?" I said. "They are lying around with ammunition all over the island. No boats? Follow me."

I showed them the boat I had found, and they started to laugh, talk and get cocky again. "We can make the sub right now," they said. God knows, I was sold on making the attempt, but it was getting late, and if a Jap early-morning plane attack was coming it was due soon. One the other hand, I was in bad shape and needed medical care. I looked straight into Mitchell's eyes. He was calm, methodical and dependable. He knew what I was thinking about, and shook his head, meaning "No." That headshake saved our lives. I ordered the men to camouflage the boat and to take cover in the bush. They were dejected, but went quickly about the task.

In the center of the island lived the native chief. Some of the men had slept in the native-village shacks that night and one of them had struck up a friendship with an old man who could talk broken English and who knew the chief. There were pictures on the walls of the old man's home, including one of the Virgin Mary. He kept a prized silver crucifix in his little trunk box and was a devout Christian The marine carried a metal disk on which was stamped a cross. It had been given to him by his girl friend. He gave this disk to the old man, who interpreted the gesture to mean that they stood together, both believers in the Savior and both men of the Cross.

Seeking this old man, I went into the bush and found him alone in a little shack. He looked me over carefully, weighing every word I said. I asked him if I could see the chief. He gave me a flat refusal, but he handed me a clean, white, knitted cotton jacket to replace my bloodstained coat, together with a bowl of hot, bitter liquid which was really invigorating. Also, he saw to it that chow was taken to the raiders.

The cry "Planes!" rang out. I hurried to the shore and took cover there, wondering what progress the two rubber boats full of our raiders had made—the ones we had seen paddling subward. If we had started out for the sub when we had been tempted to, we would have been less than halfway to our objective by this time and would have been wiped out of existence by the Jap planes.

The planes concentrated on the sub. They flew low, hedge-hopping from the lagoon side of the island. The boatload of men in the water away from the sub was strafed and bombed. The submarine was bombed while in its crash dive. A huge geyser of water shot up into the air at the stern of the ship.

Someone near me said softly, "Poor gobs. There goes our transportation too."

I learned later what had happened. Major Roosevelt had made the ship safely, as had all the men in the boats, except one lone raider. But the sub crash-dived right under him. He climbed back into a rubber boat; then, seeing a plane bearing down on his craft, quickly and wisely swam away from it. Hearing the planes' guns, he dived under water. When he came to the surface, his boat was gone. Then he swam ashore. Another raider, Herbert H. Oliver, of Honey Grove, Texas, had swum all the way to the sub, only to have it dive out of sight as he came near it. He turned around and swam back to shore.

Shortly before the planes came over, five marines safe on the submarine, picturing their comrades ashore, hurt, with few firearms, no food and too weak to battle through the heavy surf, decided to take the boat that Lieutenant Peatross had used and try to get to the island with needed supplies. If they arrived in time, they could throw out a line and pull the motorless boats through the surf, one by one. It was a long chance, but they took it. The planes came in at them, flying low, and swooped down, spitting fire and death. If ever men gave their lives for their fellow men, those marines did.

The bomb that had hit the sub was an antipersonnel bomb and not a depth bomb. It did no damage at all, but only made a grand splash in the water.

Those of us left on Makin gathered together in the shacks and discussed possibilities while single Jap planes strafed us every once in a while. About eleven o'clock in the morning another batch of planes hit us, methodically strafing the beaches and bombing them, dropping five bombs at a time. I was sitting crosslegged in the middle of the floor with several of the boys, listening to Young describe how we could make our getaway that night from the lagoon side of the island. One stick of five bombs fell right in line with our shack, and the flimsy structure began to shake as one explosion after another tore the air in shreds. If there had been a sixth bomb, we would have been torn to pieces. The whole terrain around us looked as if it had been blasted clean and swept by a giant broom of concussion.

I looked around the shack. We were all scared, and some of the men had folded up into balls, but Mitchell was as cool as ever. I went outside with him and looked the situation over. At high tide that night, with no treacherous surf to contend with, we determined we would just pass out through the entrance of the lagoon directly into the swells, and so to the sub.

Back at the government house, Colonel Carlson was waiting for us. Captain Coyte, Doctor MacCracken, Lieutenant Lang and Captain Davis were all there. All told, we made a band of about seventy raiders. We knew that some Japs were still on the island, for they had had patrols out the previous night. A red-headed marine, Jess Hawkins, from South Gate, California, had broken up one of those patrols singlehanded, although he was shot up badly doing it.

Many of us had armed ourselves completely with Jap weapons and ammunition. I was rebandaged and given another shot of morphine. With the detail, I went back to find what boats I could locate. I ended up at the old native man's hut.

I asked him if we could get swimmers and outrigger canoes that night to help us, and he went to ask the chief about it. Captain Davis had been negotiating for those same outrigger canoes to transport the wounded, but he had no more success than I had in actually seeing the chief.

Then we returned to the government house. I had bled almost continuously, and was becoming weaker. The doctors and the medical corpsmen were exhausted, but still held their chins up.

Elterman worried and fretted over every case. He told me, "I never thought it would be as terrible as this. I can never go through anything like this again." But he did, on Guadalcanal.

Adam R. Dinges, of Sheridan, Arkansas, had an idea. Out in the lagoon lay a forty-foot sloop. He had talked to the owner, who said it had Diesel engines and oil, and was ready to go. It was ours for the taking and could furnish reliable transportation to the submarine that night. Howard Gurman, of Clarksdale, Missouri, knew

Diesel motors and could handle that end of it. I told the colonel. The colonel told Charley Lamb, and Lamb and our detail walked down to Stone Pier. A rowboat was selected for the trip, and the time was set for just before dusk.

We found a detail loading food and other comforts for our wounded. On this pier was a general store which carried good American corned beef in stock; also quantities of men's silk underwear, sky blue, baby pink, and so on, made in Japan. Soon our raiders were wearing this stuff, and they looked like a child's-picture-book version of a gang of pirates. Across from this store was the island's second radio station, a good-sized affair, now demolished by our forces.

Across the water lay King's Pier, at that moment defended by the last of the Japs. A group of raiders was already on its way to mop up this gang.

A Japanese field medical kit was captured on that pier. It was well-equipped with fine, German-made surgical instruments. Our doctor lost no time in transferring these to his own kit. Many of our men were trophy happy. In years, if not in experience, they were boys and, like all boys, wanted souvenirs. This is a sample of their talk:

"Hey, Ted, look at the Smirnoff sword I got from one of the monkeys."

"Samurai sword, Swede. That means that the bird who wore it was one of the four hundred or something."

"Oh, well, it's mine now and I can call it what I want. To me it's a genuine Smirnoff sword."

I was so weak from loss of blood that on the way back I lay down in a house on a hard plank bed with a little round Jap pillow underneath the back of my head. Lamb rested too.

In came "Filipino" McCall, all decked out in blue undershirt and Jap helmet, and carrying a Jap rifle.

"Lieutenant," he asked, "how would you like a nice cool quart bottle of Japanese beer?"

"Get out of here, McCall," I told him. "This is not the time for kidding."

"I ain't kidding and here's the beer."

He had raided a Jap officers' pantry. The Nips make good beer.

I got back to the government house in time to hear the putt-putt-putt of two outboard motors. The mechanical skill of Corporal Cotten and his detail, who had been working like galley slaves on those motors, had not failed us. Now we had a means of transportation.

The colonel was out burning Jap installations. We could see a huge cloud of black smoke up the island. It came from exploding gasoline and oil.

Coyte and Lamb were all for trying to escape from the lagoon at once. The problem was to get in touch somehow with the Navy and arrange to be met at the mouth of the lagoon instead of off the seaward side of the island. Once more I began to visualize a prolonged stay on this South Pacific island. Only two of our rubber boats had survived the strafing and bombing the planes had given the beaches. We repaired one more and carried those boats to the lagoon side of the island and hid them. Two large native boats were made ready. We were playing all our cards. We hoped for the big native sloop, but if, for some reason, we couldn't use it, we still had boats.

The wounded were spread out under the trees around the government house. Those who were not too badly wounded loaded magazines with ammunition and kept the weapons which were stored in the reserve area in good shape for outgoing details.

Lamb and his detail started for the Diesel sloop about an hour before sundown. Nearing it, they spotted a Jap aboard and chased him belowdeck with rifle fire, then finished him off with a grenade. But the sloop had been scuttled and was resting on the bottom, so they started the tiresome row back to shore.

This was our cue to go quietly to the various boats and launch them when darkness came, then paddle and row them to the rendezvous at the government pier. I had had another shot of morphine and my trip up the road was a hazy one. I had been searching for suitable boats all the afternoon, and here I stood on the side of the road, looking at dozens of them, all pulled up in a row on the beach. Captain Davis was coming up the road. I asked him over.

"Look at the boats waiting for us," I said. "Where did they come from?"

"Okay, Frankie," he told me. "Let's go look for them."

But they were gone from the beach where I had seen them. They had never been there. I was seeing things, so I staggered out on the pier to the section where the wounded lay. Many of the wounded men—Lamb, Lang, Donald D. Daniels, of Seattle, Washington, and others—never had to relax their efforts. The prompt, efficient and constant medical care they received from the moment they were injured kept them going. Lamb was directing the construction of a raft, at the same time grouping the men for boat assignment. He praised, begged and kidded them in a masterpiece of persuasion, and at last the job was done.

The raft was made up of three rubber boats tied together, with a seaworthy native fishing boat on either end, the whole thing being lashed securely together. The two good motors we had were on the end rubber boats. The oars of each native boat were manned by our strongest men. Our wounded occupied the center cross seats of the rubber boats. We took our places, wondering whether those motors would work and what would happen to us when we hit the great swells at sea.

Colonel Carlson had asked Captain Coyte to be on the seaward beach at seven P.M. Now they stood there together, anxiously looking for our sub. We owned the island now and could wait where and when we pleased. The welcome signal finally came, telling us the sub had surfaced. The colonel had signaled them to go to the south lagoon entrance, where we would meet them at eleven P.M. Commander Haines suspected Japanese treachery. He was satisfied that we had taken the island, but he thought that maybe some loose Japs were inveigling him within range of the coast guns they were reputed to have on the land points at the entrance to the lagoon. The colonel assured him that there were no such guns and asked for a "Roger" signal to make sure the commander had received the message and understood it, but at the end of every message from the commander came the question, "Who? Who? Who? Who?" Finally, the commander sent us this question, "Who followed my father and me fishing?"

There had been a good bit of banter and fun in the mess over an argument as to what officer had succeeded the commander's father, "Jockey" Haines, as Adjutant and Inspector of the Marine Corps. Someone said Rufus Lane, but the colonel insisted strongly it was Gen. "Squeegie" Long. The colonel figured the commander's message probably referred to this friendly argument, a dispute about which the Japs certainly had no knowledge.

So the colonel replied, "Squeegie."

The welcome answer came from the sub, "Roger."

Captain Coyte hurried across the island and took his place in our evacuation raft . . .

The colonel and his detail were the last men to reach the boats. Back of him, a red glare lit the whole sky, sending the flickering outlines of tall wavy trees streaking out over the water. He was tall and gaunt and sinewy, a man with a tremendous amount of endurance and a trigger-fast mind that made the right decisions in a split second. His men had followed him into this dangerous mission because they believed in him. He took a look at the raft, nodded his head in a satisfied manner and took his place, followed by the men of the patrol.

Lamb ordered, "Shove off. Start the motors."

The motors sputtered and stopped and the coxswains cursed under their breaths. We kept our fingers rigidly crossed. Again the motors went "sput-sput-sput" and "blup." We were tense and hardly breathing. All at once there came a steady purr from one motor and then from the other one. It was a sweet sound.

Behind us, occasional shots were still being fired on the island. It was our guess that the armed natives had decided to settle some old scores among themselves before the ammunition ran out. The warehouses on one of the piers made a towering blaze. A cliff stuck its jaw out at us to our left front. Then the great fires along the shore became smaller and smaller as we drew away from them, and their leaping tongues merged into balls of waving red.

One of the motors coughed and stopped. It was out of gas. We decided to refuel slowly and carefully, to let the motor cool and also to keep both motors from running out of fuel at the same time while bouncing around on the high seas. The sudden stoppage of one motor threw the raft to port, and it took clever co-ordination on the part of the oarsmen to straighten us out.

Came the word, "The colonel says keep headed for the star."

Back went the word, "That will take a little time. This is not a Higgins boat; in fact, it is the damnedest contraption ever floated."

But most of us thought pretty well of it. At least we were still on top of the water and moving slowly ahead, homeward bound. A flare burst beyond the small islands to our right. We wondered if it came from Jap destroyers convoying transports with a landing party. Or it might be our own Navy risking detection and taking that means of telling us they had arrived out there at the new rendezvous, and were awaiting our arrival. Knowing our naval officers as he did, the colonel finally decided in favor of the latter interpretation and we kept our course.

As we passed through the entrance, we saw blinker signals out in the blackness. We hurriedly flashed our answer, shouted, sang, jabbered and slapped one another on the back. We had only a couple more miles to go, but those two miles were packed with terror and fraught with agony. My previous forebodings about this part of the adventure were mild compared to the real thing. We hung on to one another and to the raft. It pitched and tossed, and the rubber boats groaned as they beat and tore against one another. Lines snapped and were replaced. The current twisted us in the wrong direction, and the oarsmen strained and pulled us back on the right course again. The two big outboard native boats transformed the waves from avalanches of water into great showers of spray. This and the fact that the boys had the motors well covered kept our power plants dry and operating.

How they ever did it, I don't know, but Jergens, Angel, Gurman and Captain Davis managed to refuel in that welter of salt water. Somehow they learned when to pour in the gasoline and when not to.

"Now pour . . . Hang on to everything . . . Grab the top of that can . . . Pour . . . Hold that rag over the hole. Don't let salt water get in there . . . Pour . . . Damn it, in there, not on me . . . Hold on to everything."

It had been some raid. Now it had boiled down to a piece of rubber in the form of a boat between me and eternity. Our shores will never be invaded in that way. The Jap can sneak and slither on his belly through swamp and jungle, but Japan has no men that could do this. Talk about overestimating the American! We have underestimated him! Ninety-nine percent of us have never really met ourselves.

The sub lay taking the sea to starboard, and we had to come aboard on the leeward side. They played their searchlights on us. I sat there utterly dazed; then somebody leaned heavily on my wounded shoulder and I was ready to fight again, this time either friend or foe. I clambered aboard into the hands of gobs who got me down the hatch into a clean soft white bunk. Soon we were headed full speed toward Hawaii.

The submarine officers gave up their cabins to the seriously wounded. For a whole day they gave up their wardroom, eating out of plates in the passageway, holding them up in the air, so men could get by. The wardroom was turned into an operating room. The mess table was made the operating table. Instruments were sterilized in a pan in the small galley.

After my operation, I was drugged, and I felt that the air was suffocating me. By special courtesy, a tube was installed from the ventilating system to my head, so that I could breathe to my heart's content . . .

. . . Back at Pearl Harbor, Colonel Carlson introduced me to Admiral Nimitz aboard our submarine soon after it docked. Bands were playing, the rails of the ships near by were manned and the crews were cheering.

Major Roosevelt stood near by, wearing a smile. The admiral was looking over the captured sword of the former Japanese commander of Makin Island. I was uneasy in his presence, but I figured that I was supposed to say something.

"I hope the admiral is pleased with the results of our efforts," I managed to get out.

"Very pleased," he told me. "Very pleased—a very successful raid."

❦   ❦   ❦   ❦

ON AUGUST 24 THE STORM WHICH HAD BEEN THREATening since Mikawa's sortie broke with devastating fury in the eastern Solomons. Under no less a personage than Yamamoto, who exercised strategic command from Truk, Japan's Operation "KA"—ousting the invasion in a showdown of naval forces— amassed 4 carriers, 3 battleships, 12 cruisers, 20 destroyers and 15 transports with train; also 160 land-based fighters and bombers of the 25th Air Flotilla. The Japanese plan in some respects was a variation of the Midway theme: the small carrier *Ryujo* was offered as bait to suck the big United States Navy carriers into fatal position, while landing forces under Raizo Tanaka were put ashore on Guadalcanal.

Fortunately, American naval intelligence had correctly deduced Japan's intentions—the major buildup of naval strength and the direction from which the strike would come. What we did not know was *when* Yamamoto planned to unleash this formidable power. Thus, not wishing to repeat the Savo debacle, Ghormley ordered Fletcher with 3 carriers, 1 battleship, 7 cruisers and 17 destroyers to cruise about 150 miles east of Henderson Field and take necessary safeguards.

At 6:30 A.M. on August 23, Fletcher launched 20 SBDs from *Enterprise* on a 200-mile arc search pattern. Simultaneously, McCain's land-based command ordered aloft a PBY on a long-range scouting mission.

Yamamoto might well have won the battle but for one of those freak accidents of war—the PBY flew 200 miles off course and in the process the pilot observed the massive Japanese fleet steaming toward Guadalcanal! At 10:17 A.M. the pilot radioed his contact report (he was shot down but survived), and a few minutes later American commanders were informed of the presence of a Japanese fleet only 281 miles from Fletcher's carriers. Immediately a strike of 31 SBDs and 6 TBFs was ordered up from *Saratoga,* while at Henderson Field Captain John L. Smith's VMF-223 met the joint *Ryujo*-25th Air Flotilla effort head-on, resulting in a loss of 21 enemy fighters and bombers to 3 marine planes.

Although *Saratoga's* air groups under Commander Harry Felt found and eventually bombed *Ryujo* under the waves, a Kawanichi patrol bomber spotted *Enterprise* and the enemy launched an air strike that came in on our carrier and hit her hard, thrice, killing and wounding 169 officers and men. However, during the course of this momentous day the enemy lost 82 planes. Toward dusk the commanders of the big Japanese carriers learned of *Ryujo's* fate, and not wishing the same, radically maneuvered out of range of American air strikes. (One consequence of the battle was the transfer of 11 SBDs under Commander Turner Caldwell from *Enterprise* to Henderson Field, where they fought for a month with Major Richard Mangrum's VSMB-232. In passing tribute to Caldwell, Mangrum later remarked, ". . . The best marines I ever saw in bell-bottomed trousers.")

With the Imperial Navy no longer able to furnish air cover for the transports, they were ordered into the Shortlands, where small ships were to lift the Kawaguchi Brigade (5000 troops) and the 5th Yokasuka Special Naval Landing Force (1000 troops) to Guadalcanal. But the next morning, August 25, Navy and Marine air groups from Henderson Field found these "uncovered" vessels with Tanaka's Support Force, and worked them over with a vengeance. *Jintsu,* Tanaka's cruiser flagship, was sunk, as was transport *Kinryu Maru,* carrying the bulk of the Yokasuka SNLF. One of the happiest of marines that morning was a shavetail, Second Lieutenant Larry Baldinus, who planted a 500-pound bomb between the flagship's forward turrets.

The Battle of the Eastern Solomons had been decisively won, and Guadalcanal earned a temporary respite. Air strength on the island stood at 64 planes—some Navy (Caldwell's SBDs), some Army (P-400s), and the two marine squadrons, VMF-224 and VMSB-231, fighters and dive-bombers.

On September 1 the 6th Naval Construction Battalion (392 Seabees) arrived, and happily brought two bulldozers. This gave Henderson Field three bulldozers, a measure of comfort to the air marines who had to get their field back in shape after almost every raid. Two days later they were further enriched by the arrival of Major General Roy S. Geiger, the exuberant, hard-fighting commander of the 1st Marine Air Wing, who established his headquarters a few hundred yards from the airstrip in a building formerly occupied by Japanese. On September 5 Marine Air Group 25, the precursor of the South Pacific Combat Air Transport Command (SCAT), arrived with candy and cigarettes, and departed shortly after with a cargo of wounded marines. In the first ten days of operations, Henderson Field aircraft had shot down 56 enemy aircraft and lost 11—an amazing record, considering the state of their airstrip, and the shortage of bullets and bombs.

Following a report on September 8 from Martin Clemens that the Japanese were landing reinforcements at Tasimboko, 20 miles north of Guadalcanal, General Vandegrift sent the surviving elements of the 1st Raiders and the Parachute Battalion out in destroyer-transports *Manley* and *McKean* for a reconnaissance. This 850-man force was commanded by Colonel Merritt Edson, and it landed soon after an apparent Japanese landing. After stealthily making its way to Tasimboko village, Edson's force surprised a Japanese concentration estimated at 1000 men and opened fire. The brief battle cost the enemy 27 dead and a vast store of supplies, including 75-mm cannon, 47-mm antitank guns and more than 500,000 rounds of small-arms ammunition. The marines destroyed the supplies, buried 3 of their comrades and departed: Vandegrift now knew for certain that trouble was coming.

Here is Colonel William McKennon of the Parachute Battalion to tell us of the Battle of Bloody Ridge in which McKennon, as a major and battalion commander, participated. This first meeting with the Kawaguchi Brigade (3450 troops) cost the enemy 600 killed outright and another 900 dead of wounds in the jungles; 40 marines were killed and 103 wounded. Colonel Merritt A. Edson, the battalion commander, received the Medal of Honor.

·16· BLOODY RIDGE

COLONEL WILLIAM McKENNON

By the middle of September we knew a lot about the Jap that was never contained between the covers of a military textbook. We knew that he was well equipped and outfitted for whatever task he was assigned to, with a curiously impressive attention to detail. He didn't go through the jungle in a G string and a singlet, as some people seem to have thought. Instead, he was equipped to meet the rank, clawing, clutching jungle growth with two pairs of trousers—not one—with heavy shirts, gloves, and cloth-covered helmets that made no sound when they brushed against tangled trees and vines. His shoe was a sort of cloven hoof of soft rubber. The Jap's big toe fitted into one compartment and, in his progress through the jungle, he could feel any object beneath his feet, avoiding stones that might roll or twigs that might snap and thus reveal his presence.

We knew Tojo lived well. Not on "a handful of rice a day"—although he could do that, too—but on good canned fish and beef, plenty of canned vegetables, and an unsavory variety of hard candy. In his leisure moments he stank himself up with cheap perfumery, smoked cigarettes from the East Indies, and drank a brand of liquor looted from the Philippines and known as "Old Whisky." His officers regaled themselves with sake.

. . . Japan's countermoves on Guadalcanal had been prompt and vicious. From the very beginning there was no holding back, no playing for time, no delay to await reinforcements. They hit us with whatever they had handy. And while they were cracking at us from the sea and sky they were reinforcing themselves on land. On one occasion, in fact, they could actually be seen from one of our ridges, engaged in disembarkation operations in broad daylight. They paid for this impertinence with hundreds of lives.

Heartening and discouraging events were crowded in equal mixture into those first five weeks of our occupation. A strong attack was repulsed from over the Tenaru River, and for a day or two we breathed easier. We made thrusts occasionally through the jungle, to find that the Jap had silently faded away. He is a master in the art of disappearing. We went in small expeditions down the coast and arrived to find his supposed concentration withdrawn jungleward. Often we returned empty-handed, but each day brought its lessons, some of them costly. The enemy, meanwhile, was constantly sliding in reinforcements of men and guns, and later of tanks. We needed no superintelligence to tell us that an all-out attack was brewing.

Throughout the week of September 6, the enemy stepped up his counteroffensive. The nightly bombardment, generally from midnight until two o'clock in the morning, grew more intense. The air squadrons made their daily visits in ever-increasing numbers.

An attack was launched on the night of September 12 by Jap infantry, which had landed far to the east of the Tenaru River, according to our belief at the time, and swung in a great arc through the jungle until they had reached a point to the west of Lunga Ridge. It was a combined sea and land attack, with Japanese naval units standing off the coast to the east and lobbing their shells directly over the ridge and into the jungle beyond in the general direction of Colonel Edson's outfit. On the whole, the naval action contributed little more than noise, and the land attack never reached full intensity, leading some of us to believe there had been some miscalculation by the Jap command—that they had intended a full-dress attack that night, but were hampered by failure of some of their contingents to arrive at their base, hence put on only half a show. They did succeed in penetrating our forward lines on the right flank between Lunga Ridge and the river, but no attack came that night on the left flank, where our battalion was holding the slopes of the ridge.

Dawn brought the usual retirement into the jungle by the attacking forces. The night had been but a prelude or rehearsal for the main show.

During the morning came orders for the counterattack. My company was ordered to follow one from another battalion in a joint penetration of the jungle, but our advance was almost instantly halted by concealed Japanese defenses which would have made further effort costly on this narrow front. We withdrew on order—for the moment—circled backward, and went in again, this time with artillery support. We found few snipers in the vicinity, and we succeeded in restoring our former lines.

At 3:30 we had our first meal of the day. The cooks had saved it for us. Since our regular evening meal was scheduled for 4:30, the men went around to the end of the line and began all over again on the second meal. Marines are like that.

The men had had practically no sleep for the past forty-eight hours, so we decided to let them turn in, maintaining a sufficient number on guard. At dusk, or around 6:30 in the evening, there were evidences of a renewal of the conflict. I could hear considerable artillery fire, but the shells were hitting far over the ridge and well forward. Even the thunder of the guns meant nothing just then. I dropped into a doze. I awoke to find a runner from battalion headquarters telling me I was wanted at the command post. I made my way through the dense jungle in the pitch darkness to headquarters and was advised there that the situation up front was threatening and that our company was called for at the ridge.

Word was passed by First Sergeant Marion LeNoir, a young man whose mild manner is a mask for a rugged character and good military toughness, and the men piled out through the rough jungle growth, shook themselves awake, and plodded toward the front.

Most of us realized this was to be the big night. Two days before this action Major James Murray, division adjutant, had said casually to me, "I don't want to worry you, but five thousand Japs are coming over to try to take the field." A few days later the Jap radio said that four thousand Japs had come over—which was an understatement—and that they had taken Henderson Airfield—which was wishful thinking.

In fighting of this nature, the marine generally takes any extra weapon he chooses—usually the one at which he is most expert. For heavier weapons we had some 30-caliber Browning light machine guns and some light mortars. The men carried 45-caliber submachine guns. Some of them also had new-type weapons; some relied on the old Springfield, other on the Browning automatic rifle (BAR). We took all the ammunition that could be packed in, plus case upon case of hand grenades. So we went up the slope on the jungle side of the road, loaded down like pack animals.

"I s'pose we get time and half for this, huh, captain," one of the boys said as he went by in the darkness.

Our orders were to stand by along the road until it could be determined where we were most needed. A few minutes later we were ordered across the road into a position along the upper side of the nose of the hill. There we were to tie in with another battalion, which was to hold the right flank. While we were trying to find the other outfit, all hell broke loose. Captain Harry Torgerson, battalion executive officer, and Captain Richard Johnson suddenly found mortar shells dropping too close for comfort and "a jungle full of Japs around them."

On another hill on their right, Captain Justin Duryea's company was being subjected to the special brand of terrorism that is the hallmark of a real Nipponese attack. The sky and jungle were blazing with fireworks and a hellish bedlam of howls. Firecrackers, a cheap imitation of machine-gun fire, exploded in front of, in, and behind their position. Parachute flares that burned brightly for an instant and then bobbed along and went out lighted the scene intermittently. And from the jungle below with the rhythmic accompaniment of the slapping of gun butts, came the chant: "U.S. Marines be dead tomorrow. U.S. Marines be dead tomorrow."

There is purpose behind this bizarre accompaniment of attack. It is designed to mark the pattern of the attack and, second, to terrorize the opponent, to demoralize and confuse him. A third aim is to mask an operation, assault, or sneak attack from another quarter. A fourth is the not unimportant one of arousing the Japs themselves to a fever pitch. Certainly the attack takes on something of the quality of a mad religious rite.

During this strange and horrible movement, other Japanese forces were milling around in the hollow between our hill and the one where Duryea's company was being attacked. There was danger that they might cut off or surround the other companies. They had set out smoke pots and when unholy clouds came rolling in, somebody yelled, "Gas!" It was probably a Jap.

Three thrusts were developing at this time. One had filtered through the jungle on our left, a second had been launched frontally against the hill to the south, and the third was coming from the southwest through the hollow. The last one was momentarily held up just around the corner of the hill, so close that we could hear the Japs jabbering while they organized for assault. They were perhaps seventy-five yards away.

In the uproar, the commanders of the companies on the advanced slopes were ordered to withdraw from their exposed positions to a point where the battalion could be consolidated and a stronger defense set up. In this situation I came upon Major Kenneth Bailey, one of the finest Marine Corps officers in the Solomons—or anywhere else—whose subsequent death was a tragic loss to us. Colonel Edson was on the crest of the ridge and we could not reach him at once. I told the major that my right flank was exposed and that we had no contact with the company with which I was supposed to tie in. All this was happening more rapidly than it can be told. It was obvious that the hill must be held at all cost. Once it was lost, the airfield itself would be gravely imperiled.

After some delay we reorganized the defense of the hill. I moved the company higher up on the slope, spreading them along a few yards from the top. My right flank swung around the nose of the hill and my left extended from the nose down toward the road. At this point, Captain Torgerson took over command of the battalion and, carrying out orders from Colonel Edson to counterattack, moved Duryea and Johnson's companies forward to a position paralleling our own.

One company took a position on our left flank, from the hill to the road. We had not had time enough to establish any solid defense— no time to dig in, to string barbed wire. We finally got one machine gun in position covering the right flank and had another at the center of our position on the military crest of the hill. A third was set up covering the left flank.

Meanwhile, the chattering Japs had completed their organization for assault. We could mark their coming by the progress of their flares. Above us, at the command post on the plateaulike summit of the hill, Colonel Edson was directing the general operations, and with him was a private named Watson, a cool hand with a positive genius for the work he was called upon to do. Throughout the night he acted as spotter for the artillery placed far to the rear of us. Our guns hurled their shells over us in a ceaseless bombardment of the advancing enemy forces, just where we needed them, right into the laps of the Japs. That night Watson was a private first class. The next day in the field he was made a second lieutenant.

The first assault came vomiting forth from a triangular patch of jungle directly on our left front. There was little rifle fire, but the Japs poured blast after blast of bullets from their Nambus—light machine guns—against our own machine-gun positions. A Nambu is hard to locate because it gives off no appreciable muzzle glare, and it is particularly effective in a night attack. But in fire power there is nothing like our own machine guns. The three we had set up poured it into the oncoming Japs, smashed them back, knocked them over, broke their assault. The guns never jammed. There were screams and bleating, and then comparative silence in the hollow. The firing had lasted perhaps five seconds. It seemed like hours.

The Nambus had located our machine guns and were trying desperately to knock them out. I went over to the right flank to check that gun. The gunners were yelling expressive epithets, of which the marines have a full vocabulary. We were beginning to lose men, but as fast as one machine-gun crew went down their places were taken by others. Sergeant Keith Perkins, the section leader, was finally handling the gun himself. The action cost him his life—and us a good man.

The attack was almost constant, like a rain that subsides for a moment and then pours the harder. In most of these assaults the Japs never reached our lines. I believe now that they had no definite plan other than the general order to attack, attack, and attack. When one wave was mowed down—and I mean mowed down—another followed it into death. Some of the Jap rushes carried them into our positions and there was ugly hand-to-hand fighting. But not one of our men, to my knowledge, met death that night by a Jap bayonet. Most of our casualties came from the Nambus, mortar shells, or hand grenades.

The Japanese light mortar, carried strapped to the soldier's leg, is a crude, simple weapon. The Japanese hand grenades were of the offensive type, designed to injure and stun the enemy, but lacking the force that would make them dangerous to the Jap soldier, who follows them closely in to come to grips with his stunned opponent. They can be used at short range. Our own pineapples, by contrast, are terrifically destructive, and the man who throws one must be far enough away or it will blast him and his antagonist at the same time. We were thankful for our own grenades. We used them constantly and with deadly effect. We took them out of their cases by hundreds, pulled the pins and rolled them downhill into the noise below. They wrought havoc and a shrill chorus of shrieking arose.

I had established a command post near the center machine gun. Too near, I guess. At any rate, LeNoir and I saw a grenade coming at the same instant. I say "saw" because a Jap grenade often gives a sputter of light from the fuse when it is on the wing. We ducked—the sergeant to the right and I to the left. And I swung neatly into the orbit of another one that I definitely did not see.

As I was rolling downhill I heard somebody yelling, "Don't roll down there!" I thought it was a little funny to be told not to do something I had to do. I don't think I was ever completely unconscious. I remember rolling to the road and—how long after I do not know, although it may have been a matter of seconds—someone's pulling me off the road. It was a private who had been knocked down the hill by the same or another grenade. We struggled to our feet, grog-gily got our bearings, and felt our way along the fringe of jungle to the collecting station. We met a corpsman from our battalion, who put us in a jeep and bounced us through to safety, barely escaping a hand grenade on the way. I was swabbed with sulfa and given a shot or morphine. The morphine killed the pain, but I lay awake trying to determine the progress of the battle by the sound of the guns. The conflict died at dawn.

First Sergeant LeNoir poked his head into the hospital the next day and grinned at me. "Did I ever thank you for stopping that gre-nade for me, captain?" he asked. Thereafter he got a tremendous kick out of thanking me almost every time he saw me.

Our casualties had been heavy and some of our best men were gone. But I would say that almost 85 percent of our casualties were saved for service again. Sulfanilamide is a wonderful thing.

In front of our positions, sprawled in grotesque caricatures of life, were nearly five hundred Japanese bodies. In the jungle, where our guns had blasted and riddled and laced through the thick growth, were many more. All the way back to their base our planes, pursu-ing them, harrying them, strafing them wherever they could be found, came across remnants of the five thousand. They seemed to have one idea—to get back to where they came from, stopping only to bathe their wounds in the river.

❧   ❧   ❧   ❧

HANSON W. BALDWIN WHOM WE HAVE MET, ARRIVED late at Guadalcanal, but not too late to draw an ingenuous word-picture of our enemy. In one of his initial columns filed from the South Pacific, the matchless correspondent speaks frankly of Japanese fighting ability and cites a case in point.

·17· "A RUTHLESS AND DANGEROUS FOE"

HANSON W. BALDWIN

The whistling of the "Marine Corps Hymn" and "Reveille" by Japanese soldiers in an attempt to deceive their opponents is the latest stratagem of the enemy in the jungles of Guadalcanal, in the Solomon Islands.

The Japanese are full of tricks, deceit and cunning; the unorthodox is their rule. Hard, ruthless, brave, well-equipped, they are the best jungle fighters in the world—judging from their operations in the Solomons and elsewhere in the Pacific. And many of our fighting men in the South Sea area—particularly those who have faced the Japanese—agree with former Ambassador Joseph C. Grew that they are the toughest of our foes.

The Japanese are never content with defense; they always try to attack. And to confuse and destroy their foes they try everything, from the strategy of terror to sniping, according to Marines who have fought them on Guadalcanal.

In jungle fighting opposing forces are often only a few yards apart, hidden from each other by a thick, leafy screen. Camouflage and concealment are of prime importance; if the enemy sees you before you see him you will probably never know what hit you. The Japanese, therefore, use all sorts of tricks—particularly at night—to entice the enemy to reveal his positions and to deceive him as to his opponents' whereabouts.

Some of the English-speaking Japanese—and their number is not small—have learned the names of some American officers or men, or use a common name like Smith or Brown. In the middle of the night a Marine on outpost duty in the jungle may hear a voice that sounds like that of his platoon or company commander. Or he may hear a voice calling "Smith, Smith," or directing American officers by name to move their men to a new position. If the Marines are incautious enough to expose themselves or to comply with the "orders," they will probably be killed.

The Japanese are also good at bird calls and animal cries, which they use at times to cover their rustling progress through the jungle or to distract the Marines' attention. When they want to be, the Japanese jungle fighters can be almost completely noiseless and invisible. Carefully camouflaged, they inch their way through the tall grass or wait motionless and supremely patient for hours, lashed to treetops or almost neck deep in swamps.

Another favorite stratagem is as old as warfare. One Japanese detachment, making a good deal of noise and chattering or yelling, advances toward the Marine lines from some distance away. The Marines may fire toward the group that has plainly given away its position. If they do they may find themselves sniped at and perhaps flanked and overpowered by another group of the enemy, close at hand, that has crept forward silently through the grass, its progress covered by the noise of the rear detachment.

The Japanese are supremely confident that they are foreordained to win. They expect their enemies to flee from them and they sometimes use the strategy of terror. This was tried on September 13 and 14 in the strong attack against the Marine lines at Guadalcanal. The Japanese led up to the Marine positions with calcium flares and advanced shouting and singing. Some of those who spoke English screamed: "American Marines, you die!"; others yelled "Banzai!" at the top of their lungs and threw hand grenades as they charged. At this juncture the foe is supposed to break and run. The Marines didn't, and the Japanese were mowed down.

The Japanese Army, unlike most armies, likes to attack at night, for night gives the best cover for their favorite infiltration tactics. Although some degree of control is lost by the commanding officer, each soldier knows his objective and makes his own way toward it— if necessary through the enemy lines. In dense jungles such tactics are hard to beat.

Japanese equipment in use on Guadalcanal is well adapted to war in the jungle. The Japanese have no artillery or tanks on the island, but they have mortars, automatic arms, rifle and hand grenades and knives. One ingenious little mortar or grenade-thrower—so light that it is easily carried by one man—can be propped on a soldier's knee and fired from that position. A spring takes some of the recoil. The Japanese also have flamethrowers.

The enemy's grenades are of considerable power and apparently are more effective than ours. Some of the Japanese rifle bullets are the small .25 caliber, which make small holes on entry into the body but mushroom out like dum-dum bullets and make great gaping wounds when they leave the body. The Japanese anti-tank grenades, or powerful charges of TNT, can be hung on any projection of an enemy tank by a soldier, who may often be killed in the resultant blast.

Many of the Japanese are equipped with tree spurs made of strong steel wire, which they use to shinny up the smooth boles of the palms to the fronded tops to get into position for sniping.

The Japanese have proved themselves ruthless, treacherous, fanatically brave and thoroughly skillful. As Major Gen. Alexander A. Vandegrift, commanding the Marines on the Solomons, said, "In order to meet them successfully in jungle fighting we shall have to throw away the rule books of war and go back to the French and Indian Wars again."

Our Japanese enemies are a ruthless and very dangerous foe. They never stop trying until they are killed or crushed. The Marines have stopped trying to help the Japanese wounded since the early days of the Guadalcanal fighting, when badly wounded Japanese, playing dead, suddenly flung hand grenades in the faces of Hospital Corpsmen who were trying to help them.

The war in the South Pacific, therefore, is a cold, hard, brutal war. The foe is supremely tough and supremely confident. But in the fighting on Guadalcanal he has shown at least one great weakness. Regardless of the circumstances, regardless of the hopelessness of a particular plan of action, regardless of the opposition, he has always strictly, stubbornly, face-savingly, fatalistically adhered to that plan; he has shown a definite inability to improvise a new plan on the spur of the moment in the midst of action.

He will keep coming until he is dead, but down here he won't or can't change his plan quickly. That is one reason why Japanese casualties have been heavy and why Japanese corpses have been piled high along the Tenaru River and opposite the Marine line in the Guadalcanal jungle.

A story of fighting on Guadalcanal was told yesterday from a hospital cot by Private Jack Morrison of Evansville, Ind., who has been a Marine since last December.

It was Sunday, and the little ward in the Niessen hut—with the breath of the Trades blowing through it—was quiet. Some of the island people, kind and compassionate, had used their tiny store of eggs and butter to bake cakes for the wounded and were distributing them.

Private Morrison had one—and tea. He spoke in phrases, haltingly, not because he had been shot through the arm and chest, for he was in no pain now, but as if his mind sought words to express his story and sufferings.

"There was firing all around us," he said, "and I looked around, and suddenly I felt something hit me in the side and I fell over."

He fell in some bushes with his body hidden but with his feet sticking out. He remembers some things dimly, others sharply, and some of the things he saw he will never forget.

The firing went on for a time, then dwindled—and "the Japs were all around me."

"There was this fellow—Private First Class Dunn—who stuck with me, and he was well hidden in some bushes and a fox hole so the Japs couldn't see him. I lay very quiet and played dead; I was scared they would see my feet sticking out."

There was "another fellow," apparently a wounded Marine, groaning and moaning behind a log. After a while a Japanese came out, leaped over the log and stuck a bayonet in him twice—and the moaning stopped. Somebody shot the Japanese.

Morrison had been hit at 3:30 o'clock in the afternoon. He lay there, with Dunn a few feet away and with Japanese jabbering around them, through the long hot hours. Now and again he was semiconscious, but often the full flood of consciousness—and pain—swept over him. He dared not move.

Slowly the hours passed and night shut down. Dunn crawled out of his fox hole and, quietly and carefully, dragged Morrison into a deep tangled thicket. He took off his shirt and tried to bind Morrison's wound, but the shirt became soaked with blood and he threw it away.

They had to have water. Dunn's canteen was empty. So was Morrison's. Dunn crept cautiously from the thicket—for the Japanese were all around—to the dead man behind the log. But his body had been looted; his canteen was gone.

They were on a bank of the Lunga River. Water was only twenty-five yards away. But Dunn didn't dare try it; there was an open stretch between them and the river and they could hear the Japanese.

So they lay there through the night and the next day. And still the Japanese jabbered and the dead lay unburied around them.

The second night came. The enemy moved off a little way. Dunn, slowly, carefully, dragged Morrison down to the river.

There was a log in the river. They inched their bodies into the water and hid their heads behind the log. And they drank.

"Then Dunn sort of got me on his back and started crawling down the river with me on his back," Morrison said.

The river was shallow; it varied between knee and shoulder depth. They tried to keep all but their heads under water.

"It took us all night," Morrison said. "We had to stop and rest a lot in the bushes at the side."

By morning they arrived at the river mouth. They crawled up the beach and reached the Marine lines and safety.

Morrison had lost a lot of blood but a plane took him off Guadal-canal to the Niessen hut and good medical attention.

"He's going to be all right," the doctor said, "but I guess he doesn't know yet the Lunga River is full of alligators."

※ ※ ※ ※

BETWEEN THE BATTLE OF THE RIDGE ON SEPTEMBER 13 and the first Battle of the Matanikau on September 27, great events took place on Guadalcanal — the first of which was the arrival of the 7th Marines from Samoa. To tell of this period of critical development and constant probing, we present Major General Alexander A. Vandegrift, who was awarded the Medal of Honor for his conduct of the campaign.

His citation for the nation's highest award reads, in part: With the adverse factors of weather, terrain and disease making his task a difficult and hazardous undertaking, and with his command eventually including sea, land, and air forces of the Army, Navy and Marine Corps, Major General Vandegrift achieved marked success in commanding the initial landings of the United States Forces in the Solomon Islands and in their subsequent leadership. His tenacity, courage and resourcefulness prevailed against a strong, determined and experienced enemy, and the gallant fighting spirit of the men under his inspirational leadership enabled them to withstand aerial, land and sea bombardment, to surmount all obstacles and leave a disorganized and ravaged enemy.

A Virginian, born in 1887 and commissioned second lieutenant at the age of twenty-two, Vandegrift became the first Marine Corps four-star general in 1945, shortly after he succeeded General Holcomb as Commandant. Here is the unpretentious marine leader in an excerpt from his powerful memoirs, written with collaborator Robert B. Asprey.

·18· "ARE YOU GOING TO HOLD THIS BEACHHEAD?"

GENERAL ALEXANDER A. VANDEGRIFT
AND ROBERT B. ASPREY

We had been on Guadalcanal for over five weeks. We were still eating two meals a day, mainly of Japanese rice. Many of us suffered from dysentery and fungus infections and more recently from malaria, a disease we had not known was endemic to the island. Against this dreaded fever we force-fed the troops with atabrine, a preventive pill that tinged the skin yellow, nauseated the stomach, and caused the ears to ring.

Day by day I watched my marines deteriorate in the flesh. Although lean marines are better than fat marines, these troops were becoming too lean. Some of my units were shot, certainly the parachutists, by now scarcely over a company, which I replaced with the 3d Battalion, 2d Marines, from Tulagi.

Shortly after the battle of the Ridge I received a welcome reinforcement—the 7th Marine Regiment, which sailed from Espiritu Santo on September 14. Kelly Turner's audacious move cost the Navy heavily. In only a few minutes a Jap submarine torpedoed the carrier *Wasp*, a battleship and a destroyer. On the same day enemy air and surface attacks hit us very hard.

But on September 15 enemy attacks against us suddenly ceased. Two days later I wrote home:

> Things have quieted down entirely and we all have gotten two nights of sleep which we severely needed ...

On the morning of September 18 Turner's transports, miraculously unscathed, began loading-off at Lunga Point. The bonanza included over 4,000 fresh marines complete with supporting units, motor transport, heavy engineer equipment and ammunition. A separate convoy landed a large amount of aviation gasoline sorely needed by Roy Geiger's fliers.

With considerable reluctance I ordered what was left of the para-chutists aboard these ships along with my other wounded. Although the parachutists were never to jump during the Pacific war, they rendered brave and invaluable service first at Gavutu, then on Gua-dalcanal, actions which together cost them over 50 percent casualties.

I now made a change in my command lineup, a very difficult task. Several weeks earlier General Holcomb had written that the Corps, now 157,000 strong, would reach 223,000 by the turn of the year. As one result we were promoting officers in wholesale batches. A recent list promoted nine of my lieutenant colonels to colonels, which put me seven colonels over strength—the Commandant directed me to return these senior officers to the States, where he needed them to organize and train new regiments . . .

The Commandant further directed me to send home other surplus officers. As I wrote Kelly Turner:

> I have gotten rid of some of the older lieutenant colonels and replaced them by younger lieutenant colonels and in some instances majors who are much younger and who have shown by their actions here an aggres-sive spirit and conduct in pushing patrols and handling their battalions in the jungle. I feel as we now stand, after the changes are made, that we are much stronger than we were before.

About this same time Admiral McCain also received orders to Wash-ington. I hastened to write him a fond letter of farewell:

> I think too much of you to congratulate you. I can think of nothing worse than to be in Washington at this time. Your friends here will miss you, but we will know we have a friend in court who will render a sympathetic ear when told that we need more fighter planes.

He replied:

> What I hate most is the breaking off of my close association with your-self and the tough eggs under you.

In a final paragraph he reminded me of all he had tried to do:

> The planes must find these ships that run in and hit you at night and must strike them before dark. Should I die now, those words will be found engraved on my heart.

McCain referred to the destroyers and barges called the Tokyo Express which almost nightly brought enemy reinforcements to Gua-dalcanal, movements which we did everything in our power to pre-vent. We were just not strong enough to stop them from landing troops at their will. Even if this will were confined to the night, the night was still ten hours long. Geiger worked miracles with his planes, asking and receiving more than we possibly could expect from our fliers.

Despite their exhausted condition, the pilots kept a keen sense of humor. One of their favorite stories concerned an F4F pilot cut off by a flock of Japanese Zeros. Undaunted the pilot radioed the rest of his flight: "Hey, fellows, come on over; I've got twelve of the bastards cornered."

Competition also ran high, particularly between fighter pilots. About this time our leading ace, Marion Carl, was shot down and presumed killed. We were pleasantly surprised five days later when he walked into the perimeter, a native scout having picked him up, succored him and returned him by small boat. When he reported for duty Geiger told him that in his absence Smith's tally had risen to fourteen enemy planes—two more than Carl's record. Carl looked at Geiger: "God damn it, General, you'll have to ground Smith for five days so I can catch up."

McCain's very able relief, Rear Admiral Aubrey Fitch, visited me on September 19. After a pleasant chat I turned him over to Roy Geiger and settled down to a long talk with Mr. Hanson Baldwin, the military correspondent for the *New York Times* whom I had known in Washington and who rode in with Fitch.

Hanson passed on some disconcerting information. The people of America, he told me, were not getting a true picture of Guadalcanal. As opposed to the tiny perimeter which we were defending and the rugged quality of our lives, which he instantly recognized, the American public saw us strongly entrenched, occupying most of the island. At the same time, he explained, it was no secret around Washington that top officials viewed our position with mounting alarm, a tone of defeatism which he heard more strongly expressed in Ghormley's headquarters.

I told Baldwin I could neither understand nor condone such an attitude. Within a month we had stopped Japan's march across the Pacific besides hurting her badly. Her air and surface fleets were suffering as much if not more than ours. I did not know Japan well but I doubted if her industrial capacity could begin to repair such losses as readily as our own.

Every indication, I continued, suggested that our advance into Guadalcanal had caught Japan away off guard. The messages intercepted by our intelligence pointed in certain cases to mass confusion at top command levels. More important was the confusion of her acts in fighting us. I told him of the blind, crazy assaults against our Tenaru position which revealed how fanaticism could produce tactical blindness. I explained the recent battle of the Ridge, pointing out the futility of the enemy's trying to hold a co-ordinated attack plan after spending days marching through jungle which often limited progress to less than a mile a day. I went over our present positions, telling what I could. I admitted our problems but claimed our strengths, particularly the fantastic esprit displayed by officers and men.

When I had finished he looked at me in the probing way of a professional journalist. "Are you going to hold this beachhead?" he asked. "Are you going to stay here?"

I answered, "Hell, yes. Why not?"

He seemed impressed with what he learned—to my surprise he termed it an exclusive story—and when Fitch left a short time later Hanson accompanied him. His subsequent stories in the *New York Times* began to enlighten the public vis-à-vis our true position as well as our determination to hold; much later the series won him a well-deserved Pulitzer prize.

Shortly after this visit Major General Harmon, USA, flew down to spend the night. I received him warmly because his visit concerned our eventual relief by an Army division which he hoped to have ready before too long. Harmon painted a bleak picture of life in the higher echelons. He said he would never place an Army division on Guadalcanal under Kelly Turner's command (and he never did). He abhorred the pessimism increasingly displayed by Ghormley and certain of his staff, and he vigorously criticized the supply situation in Noumea which Hanson Baldwin had described as chaotic.

Since he was a very capable professional officer, I was pleased when he agreed to my tactical dispositions. In talking through some of these I mentioned how a lack of cutting tools hindered our efforts. After a moment's thought he perhaps unwittingly put a verbal finger on the enormous changes wrought by this war: "We have plenty of cavalry sabers up at Noumea. I'll send you a shipment. You can sharpen them—they will make splendid machetes."

Shortly after Harmon's visit I wrote Kelly Turner my thoughts on our relief:

> I know you favored sending the Division to Noumea in event of an immediate relief as had been planned before the occupation. This, of course, has been no Russian front but the men have been, and I imagine will continue to be, under a constant strain of both aerial and surface craft bombardment—this, together with the hardships of the jungle, I feel warrants a change in the plan, and I earnestly recommend it. The Division will have to be entirely refitted in clothing, the equipment gone over, and rehabilitated before another offensive. The men will need to get to a place where there are recreational facilities and a real change of atmosphere. I do not feel that this is available at Noumea. It was found in the World War that units pulled out of the line and taken to a perfectly safe place with comforts and conveniences, but yet lacking in recreational and amuse-

ment facilities, were not near as fresh as those who went back to an area where those things were available. I realize that it is a long jaunt to Wellington or to Auckland, but I strongly recommend for your consideration that when and if this Division is pulled out of this place, it be sent to one of those two places so that we can rebuild and reequip. The Division will not need combat training while in this area but will need, after a prolonged period of living in foxholes, to have disciplinary drills, long marches, in order to weld together a compact, well-trained outfit.

With my forces numbering over 19,000 I felt an almost luxurious freedom of action. Wishing to enlarge the perimeter as far to the west as the Matanikau River, I approved a plan described to Kelly Turner on September 24:

> To the west we have patrols down as far as Matanikau River, coming back through a jungle path that the Japanese had cut about a mile and a half inland. This morning, at dawn, Lieutenant Colonel Puller is taking his battalion [1st Battalion, 7th Marines] and cutting his way to the southwest until he hits the large grassy mountain [Mt. Austen] which we have so often talked about and which was mentioned in our attack order. I am sure that there is an observation post about the center of that ridge, and he is to go down it until he gets to the western end of it. Tomorrow or next day I plan to send a battalion out to Kokumbona where they will dig themselves in for protection at night and operate from there, particularly to the westward and up the (Native Track) trail which leads from Kokumbona southward to Beaufort Bay. I don't of course intend to send them over the mountains at the present time. I do, though, want to scour the country from that trail eastward to our installations. Not only so that we will know there is no one in it, but also to familiarize ourselves with that country.
>
> With reference to the installation here and defense area, we are maintaining our right on the Tenaru as it is a strong and natural boundary. We are pushing our west boundary out to a ridge line which gives us a strong position, and our rear we have pushed out to another ridge line which makes us feel safe in that direction. We are handicapped by a lack of cutting tools but hope that some are on the *Betelgeuse* [a transport scheduled for early arrival]. We are making fine progress, I think, in cutting approaches through the jungle to our lines, and cutting a field of fire in front of the lines where such cutting is necessary. After our two experiences of the Tenaru and the attack on the rear, I feel confident that if we can have fifty to one hundred yards of clear space in front of us, well wired, mined, and booby-trapped, that our fire and grenades will stop any assault they can make, certainly long enough to throw in our reserves for a counterattack.
>
> Should they attack again, I feel certain it will be from the west and south, and perhaps with augmented personnel of the forces now in the vicinity of Cape Esperance. We are keeping them under constant observation by the P—400s, who daily visit them and strafe or bomb whatever is in sight.

This limited operation began on September 24 when Puller's battalion marched south to the upper foothills of Mt. Austen, fought a number of contact engagements and turned west to the Matanikau. Finding the river defended in considerable strength, he marched down its east bank to the coast.

Hoping to box in the force uncovered by Puller, I sent Sam Griffith's raiders south to the upper Matanikau, there to cross and come in behind the enemy while the 2d Battalion, 5th Marines, attacked across the bar at the mouth with Puller's battalion landing from boats on the other side of Point Cruz.

The action, commanded by Merritt Edson, backfired when the raiders ran into severe opposition. In the ensuing fire fight Ken Bailey, Griffith's executive officer who won the Medal of Honor at the battle of the Ridge, was killed. In an attempt to envelop the enemy later in the afternoon Griffith himself was severely wounded but refused to relinquish his command.

Believing the raiders had crossed the river and started to fight toward the coast, Edson sent the 2d Battalion across the bar of the Matanikau and simultaneously pushed Puller's battalion west for the Point Cruz landing. Both attacks ran into enemy concentrations which repulsed them with severe losses to us.

Back at division headquarters we held a fair idea of what was going on. When Edson radioed for air support to help the battalion that was all but surrounded at Point Cruz we hastened to comply. But now an air raid, the first since September 15, hit us very hard and temporarily knocked out communications. Puller, who stayed back to help Edson, fortunately got aboard a destroyer which steamed to Point Cruz and evacuated his battalion.

We concluded the action late on September 27. It taught me a big lesson: the danger of overconfidence. Obviously the Matanikau area held a far stronger enemy than I had suspected. I still wanted to move against him, and I would. But next time I would move more slowly and in much greater strength.

❧ ❧ ❧ ❧

OCTOBER 3: A QUIET DAY FOR GUADALCANAL. PILOTS of VMF 223 and 224 were beginning to think of a few hands of poker and sacktime when the siren erupted and there was word of 30 Zeros escorting a small group of bombers. To recount the events that afternoon, here is the ace Major Marion E. Carl (18 1/2 kills) of 223. In the following episode we see Lieutenant Colonel Harold "Joe" Bauer (11 kills), recipient of a posthumously awarded Medal of Honor, at work.

·19· NINE TO ONE

MAJOR MARION E. CARL

We finished noonday chow and gathered around to open a tattered package of out-dated magazines. But came the report . . . "Enemy approaching Henderson Field, 145 miles out at 12,000 feet." A hundred and forty-five miles is not much for a fast plane and everyone knew it. In seconds the whole scene was changed from one of peace and quiet to one of feverish activity for our fighter squadron. Our ground crew had our F4F—4's warmed and ready as we rushed onto the field.

As leader of VMF-223 I took off first. Right behind me were Second Lieutenants W. M. Watkins and K. D. Frazier. Lieutenant Colonel Bauer led the second section . . . We poured the throttle to those Grumman Wildcats to get upstairs in a hurry and succeeded in reaching 34,500 feet before the raid reached the vicinity of Henderson Field. Information was sent us that the Japs had split their formation about 100 miles out and what was probably a flight of 10 or more bombers had turned back to the northwest.

Disappointed, there was nothing [we could] do but go back. We began to lose altitude and had gone down to about 30,000. I looked to our port side and at about 10,000 I spotted 11 Zeros approaching the field. I turned into a loose spiral, leading the squadron down between the Zeros and the sun. When about 1,000 feet above the Zeros they made a 180 degree turn and high-tailed it back in the direction of their base. They had spotted us and apparently didn't want to mix it up, but we were determined that they wouldn't get out of our backyard. We were in position for a good attack and they knew it. I went after the first division of five Jap planes. Diving on the Zeros from about 30 degrees astern their group, I attacked the last plane on the starboard flank from about 100 yards. After a short burst the Zero exploded and plunged toward the sea, ablaze. All but one of my guns had jammed in the steep dive so I pulled up. Zeros were maneuvering violently all about me by this time. I let go with a couple of short bursts without effect and withdrew to recharge my guns.

Lieutenant Colonel Bauer was third in the column behind me. I saw him spot a very loose formation of six planes—three in front and three behind. He picked the plane on the far portside and made a high side rear attack. This Zero also burst into flames. Bauer zoomed up fast and made a run on the last plane in the column. The leader of the Japs by this time had gone into a climbing turn to the left and his pilots followed. Bauer, quick as a flash, pulled up inside the last Zero and shot him before reaching the stalling point. It was a bull's eye. This Zero also plummetted to the sea in flames.

At this point Bauer had only one gun in operation. He dived out, then up, and again made a run on what was now the last plane in the column. He liked to "work" on those planes in that tail-end spot. The Japs repeated their tactics, never making an effort to get on his tail. On one run Bauer's tracers tore into another Zero. The Jap's gun commenced to fire harmlessly into the open sky as the plane nosed up. It was apparent he had hit the pilot.

Bauer climbed into a cloud and rearmed his guns. Coming out from the other side he saw below him another Jap fighter. This Nip never knew what hit him. He also went blazing into the sea. Then, as Bauer made a high side run, he spotted two parachutes coming down along the northwest coast of Guadalcanal. A Jap fighter was strafing one of the chutes. A couple of Jap pilots probably had bailed out. The Jap turned quickly and headed home, but not before Bauer got in a good burst and started him smoking. The Colonel chased the Jap until he had to turn back because his fuel was running low. The Zero disappeared in the northwest at a low altitude, still smoking.

Winter, who made his dive behind us, had to pull up to avoid hitting three burning Zeros. The Jap squadron had started to scatter. One enemy fighter climbed up right in front of Winter and almost stalled. Winter flattened out on his tail and fired from about 100 yards but missed. To get out of the range of fire the Zero did a wing-over fall out, but Winter stayed with him and closed in to about 25 to 50 yards before he opened up with his guns. This time he connected. The Zero blew up and pieces of airplane literally filled the air for a few seconds. Seeing no more Zeros near, he dived down a few thousand feet and joined up with me.

Lynch did not see us spiral down and was alone up at 30,000 feet when he saw six or seven Zeros below in a column at about 14,000. Unseen by the Japs, he dived on the last man in the formation, making a high side attack. On the first run he missed but he flattened out behind another Zero, ran up on his tail and blew him apart from close range. He had to duck to avoid debris. Diving out and seeing no Grummans, he headed back up the beach to the field.

Frazier flew wing on my plane. He had been watching and waiting for the right opportunity to attack. This was the first time he had see Zeros flying formation which was loose and in sections of three and four planes. Suddenly I saw him go into a slow spiral downward, taking the men to his left. The Zero saw him coming and went into a climb in front of him. Frazier opened up at not over 50 yards. This Jap plane blew up, one wing falling. Frazier had to maneuver quickly to avoid hitting it, but one small piece hit his windshield, cracking it. Still carrying plenty of speed he cut upwards to the right for another run when he saw a Zero trying to get on the tail of one of our boys. The Jap saw Frazier coming and pulled up into a loop. Frazier was right behind him, shooting on the way over. Coming out of the loop and close on the Zero's tail, Frazier's guns went into action and this plane blew up into a thousand pieces.

As he headed toward a cloud several 20 mm's hit the bottom of his cockpit. He was successful in losing the pursuing Zeros but his engine had already started burning.

Frazier was over enemy territory so he headed out to sea. Two miles from land, he opened the cockpit to bail out. Unable to get free he pulled the nose up, rolled over, and dropped out of the plane while it was upside down. He reached for the rip cord, intending to wait until close to the surface, but the chute opened.

Just as he was approaching the water he heard the crackle of tracers. He saw a Zero diving at him. The fiery-tailed projectiles were passing within a few feet of his head and shoulders, when a Grumman streaked past from the south, giving the Zero a good burst. The Jap plane started smoking heavily, and pulled away. Frazier landed in the water safely and was seen and picked up by a friendly destroyer. A few hours later he was landed on the beach.

After we got back to the field we learned that at the same time we were tangling with the Zeros, another group of our fighters were engaging some Zeros eight to ten miles northwest of Henderson Field. Our boys apparently did pretty well in that skirmish. One Zero was shot down, and another went over the beach at a low altitude, smoking badly.

Our results were analyzed and tabulated. VMF-223 on that afternoon had definitely shot down nine planes. Two others were last seen faltering badly and smoking and it is quite likely they crashed because they were badly shot up. Nine safe hits out of eleven times at bat is pretty fair hitting in any league. Frazier's plane was our only loss.

❧ ❧ ❧ ❧

OUR FIRST PROBE OF THE MATANIKAU AREA HAD cost the 1st Marines 60 dead and 100 wounded. Worse yet, it presaged another bitter round of fighting. For it was only a few days after Colonel Lewis Puller had snatched his troops from the cauldron that Lieutenant General Maseo Maruyama's Sendai Division and a regiment of 150-mm howitzers got ashore. There was coincidentally another trouble sign at this juncture: daily patrols in the Grassy Knoll (Mount Austen) sector were encountering increasingly heavy resistance which required enlargement of patrols in order merely to stay in the area. Vandegrift's work was cut out.

The Army promised reinforcements, and the Navy came through with a few cruisers and PTs (the North African invasion required the bulk of our firepower); Vandegrift realized that he was to stay in his present impoverished state for some time to come—indeed, if his marines held on, it was attributable only to sheer determination. Japanese interest in the Matanikau piqued the marine general. Reconnaissance had observed tanks and other heavy equipment being ferried onto Guadalcanal. For the enemy to move such equipment to the airfield required crossing the Matanikau, a job in itself; however, once across, it was relatively simple to move artillery up to the perimeter and shell the airfield. Vandegrift expended little thought to determine Japanese intentions at this point: deny the marines use of Henderson Field together with heightened air, sea and artillery bombardment, and the invasion was in dire straits.

Now Vandegrift revamped his battle plans, and on October 7 he sent Edson with the 5th Marines to the enemy side of the Matanikau River to hold the right bank. Lieutenant Colonel W. J. Whaling with the 2nd Marines was to link up and wheel northward. Lastly, two battalions of the 7th Marines (Colonel Amor Sims) were to follow Whaling, extend his flank and strive for the sea. With the 2nd Battalion, 7th Marines, was John Hersey, then a young *Life* corresondent about to witness his first combat, which he vividly recorded in the following article.

·20· INTO THE VALLEY

JOHN HERSEY

The Battle of the Matanikau River on Gaudalcanal was a laboratory sample of the thousands of skirmishes our men are going to have to fight before the war is won. In terms of Stalingrad or Changsha or El Alamein, it was not a great clash. It flatters the action a little even to call it a battle. But it affords an example of how battle feels to men everywhere.

Few Americans have ever heard of the Matanikau River—to say nothing of its Third Battle. The river is a light brown stream winding through a jungle valley about five miles west of Henderson Field. When I arrived on Guadalcanal, our forces did not hold positions out to the Matanikau. The Japs were moving up in some strength, evidently to try to establish their bridgehead—the first in their series of heavy moves against our camp. It became imperative for our troops to push to the river and force the enemy back beyond it, before it was too late.

The first two battles of the Matanikau River had been earlier attempts to do just that. In the first one, the marines tried to do the job frontally; but their force was too small. In the second they tried a tactic of encirclement, but again not enough men were thrown into action. This third time, with the enemy constantly growing in strength, there could be no question of failing . . .

"Awright! Reveille! It's 6 o'clock. Come on, fellas, all out. Reveille!"

Although it was 6 o'clock and just barely light, it did not take much persuasion to start the men in Col. Amor Leroy Sims's camp stirring, wandering out to brush their teeth, shave, start cramming things into their packs, polish their already polished rifles.

Word was passed up through the encampment: "Mass at 6:30 for those who want it. Six-thirty mass." Attendance was pretty good that morning. While that religious rite was being carried out, there was also a pagan touch. Four buzzards flew over the camp. "To the right hand," said a young marine, like a Roman sage; "Our fortunes will be good."

One of the last orders we had heard Col. Sims give the evening before was to the officer of the mess: "Breakfast in the morning must be a good, solid, hot meal. And if we get back from starving ourselves for two or three days out there and find that you fellows who stay behind have been gourmandizing, some one'll be shot at dawn."

Breakfast was solid, all right—our last square meal for three days. On the table there were huge pans full of sliced pineapples, beans, creamed chipped beef, a rice-and-raisin stew, crackers, canned butter, jam, and coffee.

As the units began lining up to move out, the first artillery barrage broke out—75's and 105's coughing deeply, and then a minute later the answering coughs, far out. At 8:30 the column started to move. We had a good long hike ahead of us. Col. Sims's encampment was about eight miles from the Matanikau, but terrain would force the column to move at least 15 miles before contact.

Gradually the column fell into silence. The walking, which had been casual and purposely out of step, began to get stiffer and more formal, and finally much of the column was in step. On the engineers' crudely bulldozed roadway, there began to be a regular *crunch-crunch-crunch* that reminded me of all the newsreels I had seen of feet parading on asphalt, to a background of cheering and band music. As a matter of fact we had a band with us, but the bandsmen were equipped with first-aid equipment, stretchers and rifles.

For a time the column wound through thick jungle, then emerged on a grassy plain edged by a kind of Great Wall of steep, bare ridges. Just before we reached the first of the ridges, Col. Sims turned in his position at the head of the column and said: "Ten minute break. Get off the road, spread right out."

Lieut. Col Frisbie, Col. Sims's hulking executive officer, sat cross-legged in the grass and thundered at me: "Would you like to hear about our plan of operation? It is a very simple scheme," he explained. "We know that the Japs have moved up into positions on the other side of the mouth of the Matanikau. Perhaps some of them have already crossed to this side. Our aim is to cut off and kill or capture as many as we can. Those which we don't pocket we must drive back.

"Edson—that's Col. Merritt Edson, who trained the first Marine raiders—will push a holding attack to the river right at the mouth, and try to make the Japs think that we intend to force a crossing there. Whaling actually will force a crossing quite a little higher up, and then will wheel downstream beside the river, Hanneken will lead part of our force through behind Whaling, will go deeper than Whaling, and then cut right. If necessary another force will go around by sea and land behind the Japs to close the trap.

"This is very much like a plan Lee used at the Chickahominy, when he had Magruder make a demonstration south of the river, and send D. H. Hill, A. P. Hill and Longstreet across at successive bridges, with Jackson closing the trap at the rear. We aren't sending the units in with quite the same pattern, but it's the same general idea. The advantage of our scheme is that Whaling goes in, and if he finds the going impossible, we haven't yet committed Hanneken and Puller, and we can revise our tactics.

"I think it'll work."

"All up! Let's go!"

The column started sluggishly up again. As it wound up over the ridges, past a battery of 75's, through a gap in the double-apron barbed-wire barrier, and out into the beginnings of No Man's Land, it looked less like a drill-ground army than like a band of Western pioneers, or some gold prospectors, wary of Indians. Each man was armed to his own taste and heart's content. Most carried rugged old 1903 bolt-action Springfields. A few had Browning automatic rifles. Almost all carried knives, slung from their belts, fastened to their packs, or strapped to their legs. Several had field shovels. Many carried pistols. Pockets bulged with grenades. Some were not satisfied with one bayonet, but carried two. There were even a couple of Jap swords. But probably the greatest refinement was an ugly weapon I spotted in the tunic pocket of Cpl. Joseph Gagney, of Augusta, Me.—a 12-in. screwdriver.

I asked him how he happened to bring that along.

"Oh," he said, "just found it on my person."

"When do you expect to use it?"

"Never can tell, might lose my bayonet with some Japs in the neighborhood."

After we came out on the last and highest ridge, Col. Sims and I walked by a shortcut down to a coastwise road. We commandeered a jeep and rode forward as far as we could. This coast sector was where Col. Edson, past master of the bush, was staging his holding attack. We asked our way to his command post.

Col. Edson is not a fierce marine. In fact, he appears almost shy. Yet Col. Edson is probably among the five finest commanders in all the U.S. Armed Forces. "I hope the Japs will have some respect for American fighting men after this campaign," he says so quietly you have to lean forward to catch it all. "I certainly have learned respect for the Japs. What they have done is to take Indian warfare and apply it to the 20th Century. They use all the Indian tricks to demoralize their enemy. They're good, all right, but"—Col. Edson's voice trails off into an embarrassed whisper—"I think we're better."

Edson's forward command post stood in the last of the palm trees, and consisted of a foxhole and a field telephone slung on a coconut tree. As we came up, he was sitting on the ground, cross-legged, talking to one of his units on the phone.

When he was through phoning, Sims asked him what his situation was. "Only slight contact so far," he said. "We've met about a company of Japs on this side of the river, and they seem to be pretty well placed."

"I hope the muzzlers aren't pulling back," Sims said.

"Don't think so. They seem to have some mortars on the other side of the river, and I think they're pretty solid over there."

Here at Edson's C.P. I heard for the first time close at hand the tight-woven noise of war. The constant fabric of the noise is rifle fire. Like a knife tearing into the fabric, every once in a while, there would be a short burst of machine-gun fire. Forward we could hear bombs fumbling into the jungle, and the laughter of strafing P-39's. A mortar battery directly in front of us was doubly noisy, for its commander was an old-fashioned hollering marine. But weirdest of all was the sound of our artillery shells passing overhead. At this angle, probably just about under the zenith of their trajectory, they gave off a soft, fluttery sound, like a man blowing through a keyhole.

I inquired about the doubly noisy mortar battery. It belonged, I was told, to a character such as you would find only in the Marine Corps. This was Master Gunner Sergeant Lou Diamond, who is said to be approximately 200 years old. I saw him presently—a giant with a full gray beard, an admirable paunch, and the bearing of a man daring you to insult him. Lou is so old that there was some question whether to take him along on such a hazardous job as the Solomons campaign. He was getting too unwieldy to clamber up and down cargo nets. On one of the last days before embarking, Lou found out that they were debating about his antiquity, so he went out and directed loading operations with such violence that for a time he lost his voice entirely; the next morning he was told he could go along.

Now here he was, proving that even if he out-Methuselahed Methuselah, he would still be the best damn mortar man in the Marines. As we went by he was, as usual, out of patience. He wanted to keep on firing, and had been told to hold back. "Wait and wait and wait and wait," he roared. "God, some people around here'll fall on their ass from waiting . . ."

For the next two hours and more we were to witness some waiting which was nearly as disastrous. This was the watering of our force. The men had hiked more than ten miles under a broiling sun, and most had emptied their canteens. No one was certain when there would be another chance to get water—and water is the most precious commodity in human endurance. Therefore it was extremely important for the men to fill up.

The disaster was the way they filled up. The water source was a big trailer tank, which had been towed out from the camp by a truck. The tank had only one faucet, and each man had to file by, turn the faucet on, hold his canteen under it, and turn it off again. This took time, far too much time.

We turned off the beach road and cut up through a jungle defile parallel to the Matanikau. Now we were really moving into position, and word was passed that we must be on the lookout for snipers. The trail led us constantly upward. Occasionally we would break out onto a grassy knoll, then plunge back into the jungle. The jungle seemed alien, an almost poisonous place. It closed in tightly on either side of the trail, a tangle of nameless trees and vines.

By midafternoon our column had emerged on the crest of a broad and fairly high ridge which looked down over the whole area of battle. It was there that I came to understand the expression "the fog of war." We thought we knew where we were, then found we didn't, then found it wasn't too easy to locate ourselves. The Matanikau was hidden from our view by intervening ridges, so that we were not very sure of its course.

Fortunately we were high enough to see the coastline; we could figure out where we were by triangulation. One of the men took a bearing with a little field compass on Point Cruz, off to our left. Then he took a bearing on Lunga Point, back where the camp lay. He drew the two lines of bearing on the map, tangent to the tips of the points— and where the lines crossed was our position.

Lieut. Col. Puller's men were following us up the trail. When Col. Sims found where we were, he told Col. Puller that we would have to push on, even though darkness might shut down before we got to the prearranged bivouac. Now Col. Puller is one of the hardest Marine officers to restrain, once he gets started. He is as proud of his men as they are of him. And so when Col. Sims told him to move on, he threw out his chest, blew out his cheeks, and said: "That's fine. Couldn't be better. My men are prepared to spend the night right on the trail. And that's the best place to be if you want to move anywhere."

Col. Frisbie overheard this and couldn't resist giving The Puller a rib. "Gwan," he said, "we know your men are tough. The trouble with the trails along these ridges is that there's not enough horse dung for your men to use as pillows."

As we moved forward, the high flat snap of Jap snipers' rifles became more and more frequent. Once in a while, from nowhere, a lone bullet would sing over our heads like a supercharged bee, and hundreds of men would involuntarily duck, even though the bullet was long past. The worst seemed to come from a valley ahead and to the left of us. Down there Whaling was trying to force his way through to the river, and his men were meeting not only sniper fire but occasional machine-gun and mortar fire. When I looked at the faces of a handful of Col. Sims's young men, who by now were already friends of mine—C. B., Bill, Ralph, Irving, Ted—I saw that they were no longer boastful joking lads. The music in that valley made them almost elderly.

Our bivouac for the night was on a ridge right above that valley, and we had hardly had time to set up our radio equipment and to get the field telephone working when the walking wounded began to dribble up the awful incline out of the valley; young fellows with bandages wrapped scarf-like around their necks or with arms in slings, or with shirts off and a huge red and white patch on the chest. They struggled silently up that 60° slope, absolutely silent about what they had seen and how they felt, most with a cigarette dangling lifelessly, perhaps unlit, out of one corner of the mouth, their eyes varnished over with pain.

Near the equator, the sun rises at about 6 and sets at about 6 all year round. By a quarter past 6 that night, it was nearly dark. An overcast was settling down, it looked like rain.

Breakfast had been huge, but we had done quite a bit of work in twelve hours. We were famished. There were no niceties out here; no please-pass-the-salt and no sir-may-I-please-be-excused. We just flopped down wherever we happened to be and opened our rations and gulped them down. The main course was Ration C—15 oz. of meat and vegetable hash, straight from the can, cold but delicious. For dessert we had a bar of Ration D. At home this would have seemed most distastefully healthy; it sounded like a convalescent's formula: 4 oz. (equal to 600 calories) of chocolate, sugar, skim-milk powder, cocoa fat, oat flour, vanillin, and 250 International Units of thiamin hydrochloride (vitamin B_1). But out there it was mighty good.

Gradually our bivouac settled down for the night. The men snuggled down into whatever comfortable spots they could find. They couldn't find many, because Guadal's ridges came up, once upon a time, out of the sea, and their composition is nine-tenths crumbled coral—not the stuff of beauty-rest.

C. B. had had the sense, as I had not, to look for a comfortable bed before it got pitch dark. The spot he picked was at the military crest; not on top of the ridge, but a little down the side—so that we would not be silhouetted at dawn, and so that sniper fire from the opposite side of the ridge could not reach us. Somehow he had found a place about 12 ft. wide and 6 ft. long where the coral was quite finely crumbled. When he heard me stumbling around and cursing coral, he called me over. I took off my pack and canteen, folded my poncho double, and settled down. There was nothing to serve as pillow except either my pack, which was full of ration cans, or my steel helmet. I finally found that the most comfortable arrangement was to put my helmet on, and let it contend with the coral.

"Well, what do you think of the Marines?" C. B. asked.

I told him I was sold.

"They're a pretty fine bunch," he said. "Lots of this particular gang are pretty green, but they're willing and bright. There's no bitching among the privates in the Marine Corps for two reasons. The first is that they're all volunteers. If one of them starts talking back, the officer says: 'Nobody drafted you, Mac,' and every time the squawker stops squawking. The other thing is that these men are a really high type. In peacetime the Corps only accepted about 20 percent of the applicants. In fact, the only difference between our officers and our privates is luck. One fellow got a break that the other didn't happen to get, and so he had the advantage of position."

And suddenly, like a child falling off in the middle of a bedtime story, C. B. was breathing hard and regularly. From then on, the night was in my hands, and I didn't like it.

My bedroom was the hollow empty sky, and every once in a while a 105-mm. shell would scream in one window and out the other. There was nothing soft and fluffy about the noise here. We lay within 200 yd. of where the shells were landing, and we heard the peculiar drilling sound you get only on the receiving end of artillery fire. All through the night snipers took pot shots at our ridges.

It was 5 in the morning before I dropped off. At 5:30 it started raining, and I waked up again. So did all the marines. The poncho helped, but rain infiltrates better than the Japs. Soon a spot here, a patch there, got wet. With the damp came chills, and before long there were a lot of miserable marines. The only consolation was that across the way there were undoubtedly a lot of miserable Japs.

War is nine-tenths waiting—waiting in line for chow, waiting for promotion, waiting for mail, for an air raid, for dawn, for reinforcements, for orders, for the men in front to move, for relief. All that morning, while time seemed so important to a layman, we waited. The plan was for Whaling to force his crossing after which Sims's men, under Hanneken and Puller, would follow through.

The artillery and plane barrage that morning was a real show from our grandstand ridge. The climax of the show was when two TBF's, the Navy's most graceful planes, came over and dropped two strings of 100-lb. bombs. From our ridge we could see the bombs leave their bays, describe their parabola, and fall, terribly, exactly where they were intended to fall. All along our ridge and the next marines stood up and cheered.

When the barrage subsided, huge white birds circled in terror over the jungle across the way and we had visions of the Japs circling in terror underneath. Bill, evidently thinking of them, said quietly: "War is nice, but peace is nicer."

We settled down to wait for Whaling to have success. A few of us crept out on a knoll which towered above the river itself, we could look down on the area where Whaling's men were doing their bitter work, and we could hear the chatter of their guns, but we could see no movement, so dense was the growth. In midmorning we could see seven Japs running away up a burnt-off ridge across from us. A machine gun about 20 ft. from us snapped at their heels, and they dove for cover. "How do you like the sound of that gun?" crowed one of the gunners. "That's the best damn gun in the regiment—in the Corps, for that matter."

At 11:40 A.M. the first of Whaling's men appeared on the ridges across the river. A signalman semaphored back the identification of the unit, so that we would not fire on them. At 11:45 A.M. Whaling sent a message back that the crossing had been secured. Col. Hanneken's men began to move. It was time for me to join a unit and go down.

Captain Charles Alfred Rigaud, standing there in the drizzle about to lead his heavy machine-gun company forward, looked like anything except a killer who took no prisoners. He had a boy's face. There were large, dark circles of weariness and worry under his eyes. His mustache was not quite convincing.

We stood on a high grassy ridge above a 300-ft. cliff. In the valley below was a little stream, which ran into the Matanikau River. Captain Rigaud's mission was to clear the valley of snipers, push to the river, and force the crossing.

The crossing was supposed to be made easy by the fact that Whaling's force was working around behind the Japs on the other side of the river, so that the enemy would be trapped. But Whaling had run into trouble and been delayed. Therefore Captain Rigaud's mission was doomed before it started—but he had no way of knowing.

I asked Captain Rigaud if I could go along with him. "You may go if you want to," he said, as if anyone who would want to was crazy. My valor was certainly of ignorance: if I had had any understanding of what Company H might meet, I never would have gone along.

This was a company of veterans. They had been in every battle so far, and except perhaps for Edson's Raiders had been in all the toughest spots. The company had already lost 22 dead. They were tired. In the last war, men seldom stayed in the front lines more than two weeks. These men had been on Guadal two months. There were veterans, sure of themselves but surfeited with fighting.

We went down into the valley in single file. My position in line was immediately behind Captain Rigaud. About half the company was ahead of us, about half behind. The company's proper weapons were heavy machine guns, which the men carried broken down. Quite a few of the men carried ammunition boxes in both hands—a terrible load in such country. Some had rifles. Captain Rigaud and some of his platoon leaders had Browning automatic rifles.

After we had forded the stream once, the jungle suddenly became stiflingly thick. This was enemy territory in earnest. Our column moved in absolute silence. Captain Rigaud whispered to the man in front of him and to me that we should pass the word along for men to keep five paces apart, so as not to give snipers bunched targets. The message hissed forward and backward along the line in a whisper: "Keep five paces . . . keep five paces . . . keep five paces . . ."

It is impossible to describe the creepy sensation of walking through that empty-looking but crowded-seeming jungle. Parakeets and cockatoos screeched from nowhere. There was one bird with an altogether unmusical call which sounded exactly like a man whistling shrilly through his fingers three times—and then another, far off in Jap territory, would answer.

As we sneaked forward, the feeling of tenseness steadily increased. The next word to be passed back from the head of the line came slowly, in whispers, for it was a long message: "Keep sharp lookout to right and to left . . . keep sharp lookout to right and to left . . . keep sharp lookout to right and to left . . ."

As if we had to be told! After this word, another kind of message came back along the line: the tiny clicks of bullets being slipped into the chambers of weapons.

It was probably because I was a bad soldier, and looked at the ground rather than up in the trees, that I stumbled on my first really tangible evidence of the enemy. To the left of the trail, at the foot of a huge tree, I found a green headnet. It was small, and was made like some little minnow net. I picked it up, touched Captain Rigaud on the arm, and showed it to him.

Without changing his expression, he nodded, and shaped the soundless word "Jap" with his lips. Belatedly, it occurred to me to look up in the tree. There was nothing there.

A little farther along, I noticed a rifle lying in the stream. It had

a very short stock and a very long barrel—not like any U.S. type I
had seen. Again I touched Captain Rigaud's arm and pointed. He
nodded again, and shaped the word "Jap."

We were moving very slowly now. It seemed strange to me to be
walking erect. I had had visions of men in the jungle slithering along
on their bellies, or at least creeping on all fours, like animals. But
we didn't even stoop.

Up ahead, suddenly, three or four rifle shots—the high-pitched
Jap kind—broke the silence. Almost at once a message came canter-
ing back along the line: Hold it up . . . hold it up . . . hold it up . . ."

A strange little conversation followed. Several of us were bunched
together waiting to move—Captain Rigaud, Peppard, Calder, Brizard.
Suddenly one of them whispered: "Jesus, what I'd give for a piece
of blueberry pie!"

Another whispered: "Personally I perfer mince."

A third whispered: "Make mine apple with a few raisins in it and
lots of cinnamon; you know, Southern style."

The line started moving again without any more shots having been
fired and without the passing of an order. Now we knew definitely
that there were snipers ahead, and all along the line there were anxious upturned faces.

About a hundred yards farther along, I got a real shock. I had been
looking upward along with the rest when suddenly right by my feet
to the left of the trail I saw a dead marine. Captain Rigaud glanced
back at me. His lips did not shape any word this time, but his bitter
young face said, as plainly as if he had shouted it: "The Japs are bastards."

We kept on moving, crossing and recrossing the stream, which
got wider and more sluggish. We were apparently nearing the Matanikau. Up ahead, as a matter of fact, some of the men had already
crossed the river. There seemed to be no opposition; we had reason to
hope that Whaling had already cleaned out whatever had been on the
other side, and that our job would be a pushover. Just a sniper or two
to hunt down and kill.

The captain and I were about 75 ft. from the river when we found
out how wrong our hope was.

The signal was a single shot from a sniper. A couple of seconds
after it, snipers all around opened up on us. Machine guns from across
the river opened up. But the terrible thing was that Jap mortars over
there opened up, too.

The Japs had made their calculations perfectly. There were only
three or four natural crossings of the river. This was one of them.
And so they had set their trap. They had machine guns all set up ready
to pour stuff into the jungle bottleneck at the stream's junction with

the river. They had snipers scattered on both sides of the river. And they had their mortars all set to lob deadly explosions into the same area. Their plan was to hold their fire and let the enemy get well into the trap before snapping it, and this they had done with too much success.

Had we been infantry, the trap might not have worked. Brave men with rifles and grenades could have wiped out the enemy nests. Captain Rigaud's helplessness was that he could not bring his weapons to bear. Heavy machine guns take some time to be assembled and mounted. In that narrow defile his men, as brave as any, never succeeded in getting more than two guns firing. The mortar fire was what was terrifying. Beside it, the Japs' sniper fire and even machine-gun fire, with its high, small-sounding report, seemed a mere botheration. But each explosion of mortar fire was a visitation of death.

When the first bolts of this awful thunder began to fall among Rigaud's men, we hit the ground. We were like earthy insects with some great foot being set down in our midst, and we scurried for our little crannies—cavities under the roots of huge trees, little gullies, dead logs. Explosions were about ten seconds apart, and all around us, now 50 yd. away, now 20 ft. And all the while snipers and machine gunners wrote in their nasty punctuation. Our own guns answered from time to time with good, deep, rich sound, but not enough.

Individually the marines in that outfit were as brave as any fighters in any army in the world. But when fear began to be epidemic in that closed-in place, no one could resist it. The marines had been deeply enough indoctrinated so that even flight did not wipe out the formulas, and soon the word came whispering back along the line: "Withdraw . . . withdraw . . . withdraw . . ." Then they started moving back, slowly at first, then running wildly.

It was then that Charles Alfred Rigaud, the boy with tired circles under his eyes, showed himself to be a good officer and a grown man. Despite the snipers all around us, despite the machine guns and the mortar fire, he stood right up on his feet and shouted out: "Who in Christ's name gave that order?"

This was enough to freeze the men in their tracks.

Next, by a combination of blistering sarcasm, orders, and cajolery, he not only got the men back into position; he got them in a mood to fight again. I am certain that all along, Captain Rigaud was just as terrified as I was (i.e., plenty), for he was eminently human. And yet his rallying those men was as cool a performance as you can imagine.

When he had put them back into position, he immediately made preparations to get them out in an orderly fashion. He could see that the position was untenable; staying there would merely mean losing dozens of men who could live to fight successfully another day.

He could not get his weapons into play; obviously Whaling's force had not unsettled the enemy across the river. Therefore he beckoned to a runner, filled out a request for permission to withdraw on his yellow message pad, sent the runner off to the rear C. P., and then set about passing whispered orders for the withdrawal.

Now the heroism of the medical corpsmen and bandsmen showed itself. They went into the worst places and began moving the wounded. I joined them because, I guess, I just thought that was the fastest way to get the hell out of there.

I attached myself to a group who were wounded in a dreadful way. They had no open wounds; they shed no blood; they seemed merely to have been attacked by some mysterious germ of war that made them groan, hold their sides, limp, and stagger. They were shock and blast victims.

There were not enough corpsmen to assist more than the unconscious and leg-wounded men, so they had set these men to helping each other. It was like the blind leading the blind. I commandeered three unhurt privates, and we began to half-carry, half-drag the worst of these strange casualties.

The rain and trampling had made the trail so bad now that a sound man walking alone would occasionally fall, and in some steep places would have to crawl on hands and knees, pulling himself by exposed roots and leaning bamboo trunks. We slid, crept, walked, wallowed, waded and staggered, like drunken men. One man kept striking the sides of his befuddled skull with his fists. Another kept his hands over his ears. Several had badly battered legs, and behaved like football players with excruciating Charley horses.

The worst blast victim, who kept himself conscious only by his guts, was a boy whom I shall call John Smith, though that is not his name. Part of the time we had to carry him, part of the time he could drag his feet along while I supported him. Before we went very far, a corpsman, who saw what pain he was in, injected some morphine in his arm. Smith had a caved-in chest, and one of his legs was blasted almost out of use.

As we struggled along the trail he kept asking for his sergeant, whose name I shall change to Bill Johnson. "Don't leave Johnson," the wounded boy pleaded.

Gradually I pieced together what had happened. Smith and several of these others had been the crew of one of the machine guns which did get into action. Sergeant Johnson was in command of the gun. While they were approach-firing, a mortar-grenade went off near them, knocking the crew all over the place. Most of the men took cover. But Johnson crawled back to the gun just in time for another grenade to come much closer yet.

We asked around in the group to see if Johnson was with us, but he was not. "They got him sure," one said.

"He shouldn't have gone back," Smith said. "Why in hell did he have to go back?"

And all the way out of that valley of the shadow, John Smith mumbled about his friend Sergeant Johnson.

The farther we went, the harder the going seemed to be. We all became tired, and the hurt men slowed down considerably. There were some steep places where we had to sit Smith down in the mud, and slide him down 10 ft. to the stream. In other places, uphill, we had to form a chain of hands and work him up very slowly. It was almost dark when we got out of the jungle, and by the time we had negotiated the last steep ride, it was hard to tell the difference between the wounded men and the bearers. We turned the wounded over to Doc New, the Navy surgeon, who had an emergency dressing station set up on the crest of that last ridge.

While I talked with Captain Rigaud, who had led his men out by a shorter way and beaten us in, corpsmen and bandsmen hurried down for Johnson. It was pitch dark when those heroic boys found him. They were in territory, remember, where snipers had been all around, and where, if they betrayed themselves by the slightest sound, they would have mortar fire pouring down on them. They asked Johnson: "How do you feel, Mac?" He said: "I think I can make it." They fashioned a stretcher out of two rifles and a poncho, and started out. Johnson was in bad shape. He was conscious, but that was about all.

The only way they could find their path was to follow, hand over hand, a telephone wire which some wire stringer had carried down into that hot valley. In the darkness they had great difficulty making progress, and had to halt for long rests.

Men who are wounded do not talk rhetorically; famous last words are usually edited after the fact. Johnson's sentences to Sgt. Lewis W. Isaak and Private Clinton Logan Prater were simple requests: "Help me sit up, will you please, oh God my stomach" . . . Soon he said very softly: "I wish I could sleep." The wish was fulfilled: he dropped off in apparent peace. He gave a few short breaths and then just stopped breathing.

I never did find out exactly how many men were killed and how many wounded in that valley. But I do know that one less died than would have otherwise, if Doc New hadn't been mighty handy in an emergency.

A dying officer was brought to him. He was in absolute shock. He was gray as ashes in the face. His hands were cold. You could not feel his pulse. He had suffered a bad wound from mortar shrapnel in his left knee, and he had another shrapnel wound in his right hand. Doc

New realized that plasma, and lots of it, was all that could save this man.

He had to maintain blackout. He had also to try to keep the man warm. To serve both these ends, most of his corpsmen gave up their ponchos. Working feverishly, interposing such expressions as "Dadgummitdingwhiz," he covered first the wounded man, then his own head and shoulders, with ponchos. Before the first unit of 250 cc. was all in, the patient came out of his coma. By the time the second was in, he was able to speak. By morning he was able to talk to his C.P. on a field phone, stand the ride on a stretcher down to the beach road, and sit up in a jeep on the way back to the hospital.

The sunrise next morning, after the slop and terror of the day before, was one of the most beautiful things a lot of marines had ever seen. Bill said: "Anyone who can't see beauty in that doesn't deserve to live. My mother would like to see that. 'Dear Mom: You should've seen the sunrise this morning' . . ."

Operations now proceeded according to plan—the formal way of saying "with moderate but unspectacular success." By 10:20 A.M. the leading troops of the flanking units had reached the beach. They found that most of the Japs had withdrawn during the night, taking most of their wounded with them. Evidently they had pulled out in quite a hurry, for they left packs and other equipment behind. They left 200 dead on the field. The Marines lost 60 dead—their worst casualties in any single operation on Guadal up to that time.

Probably the bitterest clash of the whole battle occurred at the mouth of the Matanikau. For two whole days, Edson had been unable to root out that entrenched company of Japs on the east side of the river. Finally, on the second night, he called on his Raiders, the men who do or die in the true jams on Guadal. He put them between the Japs and the spit, their only avenue of escape.

* * * *

ANOTHER OF THE GREAT REPORTERS ON GUADAL-canal was John Graham Dowling of the *Washington Post,* at the front lines whenever he could get there. In the series of strikes which preceded the great Matanikau offensive, Dowling noted a broader picture than Hersey. He speaks of seeing some of Whaling's beaten men returning, but also speaks of the pulverizing attack by Edson's forces—an over-all week of action which cost the enemy 690 dead, as against 65 marine dead and 125 wounded.

·21· CORRESPONDENT AT THE MATANIKAU

JOHN GRAHAM DOWLING

First day, 8 A.M.—Artillery fire! We are sitting in the mess hall struggling through breakfast when the first blasting salvo gets off and we pause with our spoons halfway up to our faces, waiting, listening for the rounds to register on the Jap. They go crump-crump into the earth miles away and we sense a delicious satisfaction that it almost is evil in its pleasantness. Somebody says "hit him again," and the second salvo gets away. By this time we are out of the mess hall, running for the top of the ridge where we can see the big guns in action and enjoy their beautiful power.

They are spread all over the ridges and meadows beyond us, dug snug and squat into the earth against a background that reminds you of the cool hills of Africa. Their salvos hang about them on the air like a light mist. Crazy little figures, stripped to the waist, serve the guns—load and draw back and fire—load and draw back and fire. And their high catcalls come across to us standing in the bleachers on the ridge and between the intervals of thunder, "hit him again!" It's the same guy yelling, carrying on as though he were at a baseball game.

"Hit him again! Oh lay it into him brother!" And it goes on for 10 minutes and then stops as suddenly as it had started.

The silence is like something solid, like going through a curtain as you walk away. The baseball citizen says, "Wow! That was really something! I wonder if they feel as good about it when they're shelling us?" "Hell," another answers him, "them guys haven't got any feelings."

8:15 A.M.—Dive bomb and strafe!

During the barrage the Navy dive bombers and Army pursuit planes have taken the air and now we see them in the distance working back and forth over the Jap ground.

Theirs is a lonely show that the infantry is sort of out of. The airmen heckle the Japs for the rest of the day while our people get into position.

Second day, 1:30 P.M.—Jerry comes with the "peep" to drive us to the front. Something's going to happen soon, he says. We ride up to the front eating candy. It is Jap candy, captured peppermints in paper bags tasting like sugar mixed with chalk and the Jap characters on the bag say something about Vitamins A, B, C and D. The Japs are as bad as we are when it comes to patent medicines. Even their candy has to pretend to be health food.

Jerry, our peep driver, squats at the wheel in his pot helmet, looking like Charlie Chaplin with a New England accent. He is a philosophical chap who often refuses to drive us where we want to go, explaining with magnificent logic, "I don't mind getting killed for my country in the line of duty, but I ain't going to get bumped off driving a bunch of crazy newspapermen places where no soldier in his right mind would think of going."

That's the way he feels about today's venture. He is candidly unhappy about it. But we urge him on and finally he drives like an old stage coach character with his rifle cocked and resting across his lap. There are three of us in the peep with him, Francis McCarthy of United Press, Sherman Montrose of Acme, and myself.

We drive through the grey afternoon, away from Henderson Field into the tall coconut grove, the worn road winding like a puzzle toward the beach. We swing left and roll bumpily along the beach road in the direction of the Matanikau. The palms thin out and we reach the wire at the edge of our perimeter and pass through. The guards warn us that there are Jap snipers at work behind our front. Jerry steps on the gas and boils down the road as fast as the peep will go while we hang on, our eyes nervously scanning the undergrowth on our left.

One feels like a fool when there are snipers about. You recognize they are not too much of a menace and yet they make you nervous. There is always a chance they will let one fly at you and there is always a chance that—for a change—their aim will be true. It is beneath your dignity to fall on the ground and crawl, yet standing there you feel like a balloon in a shooting gallery. So we tear along the road until Jerry's nerves tell him the terrain is reasonably secure and then we take it slow and easy.

Again, up ahead, the peculiar blast of mortar fire is heard and the peep crawls cautiously through a strong Marine unit whose men are resting in the tall grass at each side of the road. Their tanned faces wear that drawn, resentful look that you have seen before on the faces of men going to battle and they pull in their feet from under the wheels of your car as you go by and say nothing. A little farther along we pull off the road to allow a creeping ambulance to pass through to the rear. More resentful eyes, wounded, now peep out at us from behind the flapping brown canvas and this is where you really begin to feel it. This is where the heart contracts and you begin to experience a little difficulty breathing. It is a curious form of excitement and the only experience comparable to it is lovemaking.

2 P.M.—We pull off the road at Colonel E's command post, which consists of a field telephone attached to a palm tree in a rather heavily undergrown area between the beach and a high, wooded ridge. It is the end of the palm grove. Up ahead the ground is wooded and in some places jungle, and ahead of that is the Matanikau River with the village of Matanikau on the other side.

Ahead of the command post are the heavy mortars and 100 yards ahead of them the light mortars. At intervals they let go with earcracking concussions. There also is Jap machine-gun fire up ahead sounding quite close.

Colonel E. lies on his back in the grass, the telephone to his ear while his aides, officers, and runners squat in a little group around him. We go up and join the circle, squatting like Indians. Montrose cracks open a coconut and digs into it with a penknife. He passes it around. It isn't good—overripe. I spit mine out, but Montrose seems to like it.

The colonel seems unhappy. It is the job of his outfit to advance to the Matanikau and hold the Jap on that front, occupying his time while another Marine unit goes around through the hills and comes in on his right flank. But the colonel seems unhappy.

2:45 P.M.—Rather heavy sniper and automatic rifle fire between us and our front lines. Artillery lets fly an occasional load into the Japs. Sergeant Jim Hurlbut of Arlington, Va., a Marine combat reporter, walks back from the front and joins us. He is covered with mud, streaked and mixed with sweat. We ask him how it goes and he stands there with the thousand-yard stare coming into his eyes. We understand. Everybody is quiet.

The marines in back of us start digging in. They start to do it without orders. The scuttlebutt has passed the word around that there are at least three Jap snipers up there in the woods just in front of us. At 5-minute intervals their bullets ping into the grove harmlessly, but you feel like a fool again and there seems to be a Jap machine gun about 200 yards ahead of us in the woods near the beach. Very annoying.

Colonel E. is annoyed. He waves an angry hand ahead of him and comments coldly, "They've been piddling around for five hours trying to go 150 yards. Every time a Jap fires a shot they dig a hole in the ground and stay there."

He studies the map a moment and says "Send a company to hold the beach flank in case the Jap tries to come in by boat. A company will be enough." The aide answers "Yes, sir," and moves to the phone while the rank and file turn their heads and stare at one another in silent understanding.

In this operation the company is slated as the reserve of the reserves. The colonel stands up and talks earnestly into the phone: "If they don't get those Nips out of this side of the river before dark they're going to be in for a hell of a lot of trouble tonight."

Whoever is at the other end of the phone talks for five minutes. The colonel listens in silence, biting his lip, and when the gentleman at the other end is through, the colonel says "You've got to take a chance on getting hurt. Somebody has to get hurt in these things. I want it done!" and he hangs up and you feel unhappy for the gentleman on the other end of the stick.

Third day, 9:15 A.M.—We are at the front. We find General A. A. Vandegrift and Colonel E. sitting on a log beside a "half-track" which is blasting at the Jap machine gun emplacement across the river. The Jap answers.

Whoever the citizen was who was told to do it apparently did it, and some people got hurt doing it. We hear the story on the way to the front. The Japs came through at night and cut one company to pieces before they were tossed back.

Jerry drives us along the muddy road that winds now between the walls of the jungle until we meet corpsmen coming out with a stretcher case. We turn the peep over to them and go ahead on foot. We pass the forward command post, a jungle hollow off the side of the road where some 20 men are huddled behind a huge banyan tree, cursing a sniper who keeps putting bullets among them. Finally three of them take off on their own to hunt the sniper down.

It is raining now and we stop to shoot the breeze with Joe C., a Brooklyn boy whom we met out on a patrol. We give him a bag of Japanese candy and congratulate him. We go forward again, feeling very unhappy about it, the three of us, Montrose with his camera and McCarthy and I.

As we tread on eggshells across an open space a sniper lets one fly at us and we hit the ground—one, two, three—plop-plop-plop. Then we try to rise. I cannot get up—I'm tangled up in my poncho and keep tripping on it and falling back into the mud.

I curse—"Dammit! Dammit!" feeling the sniper's eyes still on me. Finally I rip the poncho off and throw it away. I'd rather be wet than dead any time.

Forty yards behind the front, or river line, we come across General Vandegrift and Colonel E. squatted on a log in the rain. The general has his elbow on his knee and his chin in his palm. Directly ahead of us is the half-track, pumping shells into the Japs who are only 25 yards away across the river. The sound of the firing of each shell and its striking explosion are only a split second apart at this point-blank range. Shrapnel from its own shells passes back over the half-track which goes bo-boom, bo-boom, and on the other side the Jap sticks to his guns under this terrible fire and pops back tat-a-tat-tat-a-tat. From where we are sitting we are forced to admire his guts, an emotion which does not interfere with our determination to see him dead. The half-track runs out of ammunition and comes backing down the road. As it goes by the general waves at the crew and says, "Nice going. Are they still up there?"

A powder-burned gunner answers, "Yeah, I think there's a couple of them left. We'll be right back. It is quiet now. The Japs, if there are any of them left over there, are taking time out to sweat."

And the big droop Montrose is still laughing at my struggle to get off the ground after the sniper shot. He points to my correspondent's badge and says, "they get 25 extra points for getting a correspondent." I believe him. I rip the green badge off and stick it in my pocket. I'll take my chances now like a private or a general.

9:30 A.M. — The general converses on the beach by a tree trunk with members of the company. We have crossed the road and now are out on the gray beach standing behind a huge tree trunk peering over the top at where Point Cruz needles out into the water. That is where we want to get — Point Cruz, and it seems so near from here.

Four young privates of 15 of the unfortunate company that was on the line last night also are behind the tree trunk. They are a sad-looking bunch. Their clothes are ripped, their equipment is gone and one of them is still unable to talk. The general asks what happened to them and a young Tennessee boy standing wet and bedraggled in his torn undershirt appoints himself as spokesman.

"We don' rightly know what happen', Gen'l. They come at us in the dark and they don't stop to fight us — jus' go a-runnin' right on through us, and they was behind us and in front of us and all mixed up in amongst us. We don' know what happen'."

General Vandegrift speaks to the boy quietly. "What happened to your rifle, son? Why didn't you use that?"

"Warn't no use, Gen'l, we couldn't tell if we was shootin' marines or Japs."

"All right, son, you better get on back to the rear."

9:30 A.M. — It's raining like hell. We leave the beach and walk through drenching rain back to the forward command post by the banyan tree. General Vandegrift sits soaking in his peep and explains the maneuver to us using his stocky left hand as a map of the ground.

"My thumb is Point Cruz," he says, "and the fingers four ridges we have to cross to get into there."

My attention is diverted by the sight of a marine I know coming back down the road alone, holding his arm at the elbow while the blood runs down his arm and drips like the rain from his fingertips.

"I got a good one," he says as he goes by.

"Bad?" I call after him.

"I don't think so," he answers over his shoulder. "Ought to get me as far as Auckland, anyway."

Later I stand dripping by the banyan tree and watch the marines go into the line on the double. The word passes along. "There go the marines!" and the rank and file stop what they are doing to turn and watch the reserve of the reserves.

First on the flank and now into the front they go by, running with an easy confidence, their uniforms hanging from their shoulders in strips. And you turn away thinking that you have just seen an outfit that will go down in history alongside Rogers' Rangers and Morgan's Raiders. You feel that you have just had your finger on a moment in history.

Through the dismal twilight rain comes the sound of heavy stuff back in the hills to the west. The flanking force is making contact. The forces are committed. The battle is joined. The artillery continues through the night.

Fourth day, 9:55 A.M. — We're on the edge of the Matanikau River. Our boys signal us, "Men one-half mile away up the beach," while our mortars raise hell behind us. Terrible mess of dead Japs.

Colonel E. up there as usual. General Vandegrift on the phone. It is a clear, cool morning, fresh as victory and not yet turned to heat. We are at the mouth of the Matanikau where a spit of sand crosses over to the other side. It is the spot that is known on Guadalcanal as Hell's Corner, and at the moment is living up to its uncomplimentary name. It is a clearing 50 yards by 50 yards, at the edge of the jungle river. And in that little space, sprawled in the various awkward and grotesque postures that battle inflects on men, lie 103 dead Japs. Scattered among them are 16 dead marines, a little above the usual odds because it has been a dirty night fight.

The marines were holding the corner when the Japs, flushed by our flanking force, tried to get through to reach the sand spit to cross over the river in the dark. You can follow their hard passage now by looking at their bodies. The lieutenant estimates that perhaps two of the Japs got away. That is the way the marines fight!

One of the dead marines you find is Joe C. of Brooklyn. He is surrounded by five dead Japs and from the looks of it it was a hand-to-hand show. You are glad that you gave him the bag of candy yester-day. It is all you can do.

It is beginning to get hot. Colonel E. studies the other side of the river through his glasses while General Vandegrift worries over the telephone. By a tree he holds his helmet in his hand and bats the flies away with it. McCarthy collects souvenirs. We call him the "Ghoul of Guadalcanal." Montrose takes pictures. A Navy plane flies low overhead. A marine and I squat among the inanimate corpses, dis-cussing the politics of a certain newspaper publisher.

11 A.M.—Contact made across the river with a regiment. Their patrol can be seen weaving cautiously through the jungle until the lead man reaches the water. He looks across at us and lifts his arm in signal and smiles. General Vandegrift crosses the sand spit alone and at a walk Colonel E. and Photographer Montrose follow. Then I go across with McCarthy bringing up the rear. There are more Jap bodies on the beach, relics of previous skirmishes.

We turn off and enter the village of Matanikau. There is nothing left of it. Not even a stick. It's been smashed flat, obliterated.

12 noon—We are in Matanikau searching Jap knapsacks like ban-dits. We meet stronger units of the flanking regiment and find hun-dreds of Jap knapsacks. The field gives evidence of having been aban-doned in panic. We find bicycles, Jap machine guns, stores of rice, grenades and ammunition. We are burning most of it when the word comes up the line that an air raid is approaching. Our mission has been accomplished and all of us feel as one marine puts it, "Let's get the hell out of here."

1:05 P.M.—We are withdrawing from the outskirts of Matanikau. The air raid is still on and our artillery is throwing shells over our heads. We'll be pinned to the ground by the raid before we can get out of this place that was once a village. The Jap air raid catches us and we scatter to the cover of trees. Our fighters meet them overhead and trace their pattern of air battle in white lines in the sky for an hour before the "all clear" is given. We hear the bombs crunching back on our positions. Near the airport you feel nervous huddled by a tree behind the Jap lines while their planes boil up the sky over your head. If their ground people should decide to counterattack you are in a hell of a spot to receive it. You will feel better when you are back on the other side of the river. Then the order comes and we rise, reform ranks and struggle at a lope back to our own positions, and the battle, as far as we are concerned, is over.

We piece together the score, and the count is 571 known dead Japs and our lines have been advanced 3 miles to a more secure front. We return back to division in time for a dinner of cold meat balls and nobody is particularly happy. It takes something out of you and leaves you a little dry. It makes you unpleasant to be with for a while.

❀ ❀ ❀ ❀

GENERAL VANDEGRIFT'S URGENT NEED FOR REIN-forcements finally evoked action by Kelly Turner. On October 8 the Army's 164th Infantry Regiment (2850 troops; big, rawboned Scandinavians from North Dakota) was sent up from New Caledonia in transports screened by Rear Admiral Norman Scott. On the night of October 11 - 12 Scott's covering group was off Cape Esperance, the northwestern tip of Guadalcanal, when a raiding force of cruisers and destroyers under Rear Admiral Arimoto Goto steamed imperturbably southward. Their meeting, the Battle of Cape Esperance, resulted in a severe mauling for the enemy — with only one United States warship, *Duncan,* damaged, as against numerous major-caliber hits on all Japanese ships, with cruiser *Furitaka* and destroyer *Murakumo* sunk. Geiger's Air Wing completed the job the next day, sending two more destroyers to the bottom.

That night, following a surprise air attack by the 25th Flotilla, the Japanese were back with a vengeance. Now the full fury of the Imperial Navy was unleashed by Vice Admiral Takeo Kurita, with 2 battleships, 1 cruiser and 6 destroyers which pounded Henderson Field for 90 minutes, expending 700 rounds of 14-inch and 16-inch ammunition. Although newly arrived PTs came out from Tulagi, their sting did not bother *Haruna* and *Kongo,* whose guns fired steadily until 2:30 A.M. when they finished demolishing Henderson Field and 48 planes.

Major Walter L. J. Bayler, whom we met at Wake, and now an air officer on Guadalcanal, was one who survived the shelling and gloried in its aftermath.

·22· THE BOMBARDMENT

COLONEL WALTER L. J. BAYLER
AND CECIL CARNES

On the night of October 13 Guadalcanal was given a baptism of fire that none of us who was there will forget in a hurry. I think there must have been a spiritual angle to the baptism as well, for undoubtedly a lot of marines came out of the affair more thoughtful Christians than they had been since childhood.

Lieutenant Colonel Ray Scollin and myself were in the tent we were sharing at the moment on the lee slope of Pagoda Hill, both of us asleep, when we were fairly jolted from our cots by a series of tremendous shocks that jarred the earth. "Another quake!" I said, but knew I was wrong even before the notion registered on my mind. Earthquakes don't come with pyrotechnical displays, and we were conscious of a ghastly blaze of light, so brilliant it was almost blinding, outside our wigwam. Sound effects were provided by the scream of shells, a series of crashing, deafening explosions and, from somewhere upstairs, the drone of an airplane motor.

I grabbed my shoes, not with any idea of putting them on but just to take them with me as I got to my feet and half stumbled from the tent. Ray was right behind me as I headed for the nearest dugout, just outside the tent, and together we fell down into the muddy hole. Feeling a little more comfortable now that some parts of our bodies were sheltered, we peered with incredulous eyes at the show being staged on the field beside us.

It was provided by thousands of incendiary shells that were exploding with sharp, ear-cracking detonations and setting a lot of small fires. As each shell exploded it spewed forth hundreds of tiny cylinders, open at both ends and spitting fire. I think they must have been filled with some magnesium compound. The blazing stuff fell in streaks and splashes of brilliant fire, a spectacle that would have taken first prize in any show of fireworks.

In point of fact, those pretty little playthings were no more than a side attraction. It was their big brothers that really held our attention. Somewhere close inshore, battleships, cruisers and destroyers were tossing everything they had at us—and it seemed *us* to Ray and me. Included in the assorted hardware were some 14-inch shells which really left their mark on anything they hit. If our dugout had been shot from under us it wouldn't have mattered; there were plenty of fresh holes around, deep and spacious.

It was no place for a pair of quiet-loving gentlemen. At the first hint of a fancied lull in the storm—it was probably no more than an interval between salvos—we sprang convulsively from the dugout and put on a pretty good act of our own, imitating a pair of sprightly young kangaroos, as we headed for the Pagoda Tunnel.

The place was packed. There must have been at least one hundred and fifty men in the narrow passages leading to the operations room, and that too was packed by a mob of panting, sweating, cursing marines and Seabees. I hate to think what a direct hit from one of those 14-inchers would have done.

Every time a salvo of shells would hit Pagoda Hill on the north, or seaward, side the entire mound would shake like a bowlful of shivering Liz—Marine Corps Jello; dirt would rain down from the roof of the chamber, and often tunnels would be filled with dust and the acrid fumes of TNT pouring through from the entrance. The Pagoda itself was hit by at least six shells which snapped the coconut trunks like toothpicks.

The shelling ended about three in the morning. They had simply poured it onto us, like water from a bucket, for two and a half hours.

I came out of the tunnel to find fires burning everywhere in the black night. Those incendiary shells had done a nasty job. In the depths of the coconut grove great leaping torches of flame showed where drums of gasoline had been hit and set afire. They burned the rest of the night.

A 5-inch shell had cut a neat hole through the tent occupied by the pilots of Lieutenant Commander Roy Sempler's fighter squadron. It had then burst between that tent and the one evacuated so hurriedly, a few minutes before, by Scollin and me. It scooped out a huge hole in the soft earth, throwing large gobbets of mud and dirt, mixed with chunks of debris, all around the place.

The runway had caught it, too. I hopped into a jeep and made a dash the full length of it, counting thirteen shell craters. It was lamentably damn good shooting.

Throughout the shelling, our Colonel, Bill Wallace, was in a small sandbag revetment right on top of the Hill, smack in the line of fire from the ships. The shells that pierced the Pagoda must have come so close to Bill it was a wonder his hair had not been singed by their passage.

Down in the coconut grove, in the scout bomber bivouac area, the boys took a terrible pounding. Several of the pilots and a number of the ground personnel were killed by explosions *overhead* in the trees. Shells coming in at such a low trajectory splintered the palms, then exploded among them, and a roofless foxhole in the woods is no shelter against big shell fragments from directly above.

The entire floor of the grove was littered with fallen trees, palm fronds, coconuts whole and shredded, and assorted debris from tents and buildings.

Farther back in the woods, at a spot occupied by an artillery unit, several trees had been felled. One of the largest had dropped on a foxhole occupied by some Marines, its massive boughs pinioning their bodies to the earth. Another Marine saw the thing happen. He grabbed an axe, regardless of the shells bursting all over the area, and hewed away the crushing branches, freeing his injured comrades.

But heroes were a dime a dozen on Guadalcanal. Real heroes, too, for those fellows who risked and sometimes lost their lives didn't want to die any more than you or I or the next fellow.

This exceptionally heavy shelling left us with a deep conviction that the Japs were up to something special. We had taken an occasional pasting from destroyers and submarines, but this had been ominously different. Battleships and cruisers . . . We figured that the enemy, for some reason, didn't want our aviation to go up for awhile, so had centered their fire on runway and field.

They did not achieve their purpose. Although the runway was badly knocked about, our planes took off; first the overhead fighter patrol, then the scout bombers loaded for Jap. The idea was to find out where our overnight visitors had gone; whether they were still close by and menacing, or whether they had cashed in their chips and gone elsewhere. When the force was located, they were heading for the northwest—homeward bound through the passage on the north side of Santa Isabel Island, away from the beaten route of the usual channel.

Our planes discovered something else as well, and most fortunately. Down the alley toward Guadalcanal, fearsome and menacing, a fleet of six Jap transports, loaded with soldiers, escorted by fourteen destroyers, was steaming at full speed.

So *that* was it. An all-out nocturnal shelling, burned planes, incendiaries, a damaged runway, a sleepless night for our pilots—and then invasion. Tojo had thought it out cleverly; it showed how much he wanted our island back.

Well, we caught him at his dirty work and went after him. For all that the runway was damaged and now cluttered with a plucky arm of Seabees striving to effect repairs in a hurry, and for all that our striking force was crippled by the loss of five planes, our boys went up. They flew a smaller number of planes—but made up for it by flying them oftener.

Armed with thousand-pound bombs, and remarkably wide awake in spite of their sleepless night, our pilots flew up the alley, met the advancing foe, and threw their tons of destruction right in his teeth, braving the antiaircraft fire of the ships and the destroyer escort in order to get in close. Flight after flight took the air just as fast as the tireless ground crews could rearm them as they came back—with big bombs inscribed "Bundles for Tojo."

Our flights hammered those Japs all the way along the shores of Guadalcanal west of Henderson Field; hit and hit, over and over again, the battered fleet kept coming. Flying through a sky pock-marked with bursts of antiaircraft, with slugs whining and singing through every cubic yard of air, our fliers scored hit after hit on the transports till four of them were beached and burning.

Heavy black smoke drifted our way, bringing with it the unmistakable odor of burning flesh.

Japs were dying in satisfactory numbers, burning, drowning, or blown to fragments by bombs. I could see through my glasses the sea full of equipment-laden soldiers swimming desperately toward the island beaches. Some made it, but hundreds drowned and their bodies washed ashore—ghastly objects, swollen, torn and often eyeless.

※ ※ ※ ※

OCTOBER 15 WAS ALSO A SIGNAL DAY IN THE LIFE OF Major Jack Cram, skipper of the PBY5A Consolidated amphibian, the *Blue Goose*, which was lifting in a load of torpedoes for Torpedo Squadron VT8. This was the background of an aerial attack for which no PBY5A (the Lumbering Duck) was ever designed. The following account by Captain John DeChant, one of marine aviation's excellent historians, appeared in *Leatherneck*.

·23· THE BLUE GOOSE

CAPTAIN JOHN DeCHANT

In the weird light of the coming dusk, a lumbering PBY Catalina eased in over the shambles of Henderson Field. The darting, blood-shot eyes of the tired gunners watched it barely clear the trees. It spanked the end of the runway, and then moved on furtively as if afraid to lose speed. Down-field the Cat groaned painfully to the touch of a right brake and almost hurried off the strip.

The Blue Goose had just come back to that patch of hell wryly called a beachhead. This time it had ferried in two 2,000 pound torpedoes, one slung under each of its ungainly wings. Expertly, Jack Cram ran his fingers over the instrument panel. After the motors cut, his shoulders slumped a little in the loud silence. Wearily, automatical-ly, he wiped a hand over his forehead, peeling off the ball cap and earphones in the same motion. He slid down and out the hatch, bump-ing Hoffman's feet that still dangled from the engineer's tower.

Metz and Horton were waiting for him back at the starboard blis-ter. "They must have gotten the living hell kicked out of them again last night, Major. Look at that mess!" said young Horton.

"Yeah, but I think we still own the place, sir."

The Major kept his thoughts to himself. Then he told Metz to check the plane and see that the crew got chow in a hurry . . . wherever they could find it . . . but one man must stand by at all times.

Cram crawled slowly out the blister and down the black, oily lad-der. He could barely draw a breath in the smothering heat. Around him, the barrenness and havoc of the place made his last meal churn a little in his stomach. A scurrying jeep dropped him near Pagoda Hill. A crude Jap pagoda on the brow of the hill served General Roy Geiger and the rest of ComAirSols as a headquarters.

As he climbed the hill, Cram was madder than hell . . . and tired. He and his crew, Metz, Hoffman, Anderson, Kirby, and Horton, had flown 160 hours without a day's break. Done in himself, the Major knew how badly those men needed sleep. They flew all day and serviced the Blue Goose at night. It was maddening business. Into Henderson one day, back to Santos the next. Back and forth, back and forth. No fighting, no incentive, just the drone of motors, boring into your sanity.

"Great stuff," he thought. "I train ten years to fight. Then I get to be a General's pilot. Now I'm a glorified truck driver. Why doesn't the Old Man give me a break. The poor damn fighters and SBD pilots up here are so tired they can't stand up . . . at least I could fill for one of them . . ."

The eternally restless and eager Cram fell short of being tall. Lean of body and thin of face, the Major walked and moved with padded grace. His eyes laughed often. And he was a little whacky on the subject of exercise. Tropical heat or no, he ran several miles every day to keep in trim, a holdover from his Stateside days when he did a lot of cross-country running.

He was christened Jack Randolph back in the Pacific northwest about thirty-four years ago. His parents honored no ancestors with that handle. He insisted he was named after the meanest dog the family ever owned. Those around him were sure it must have been a bulldog. The Major had all the tenacity and unbridled courage of one.

Of what he was to do the morning after his walk up Pagoda Hill, one officer said: "If ever I saw a man with sheer guts, it was Jack Cram. He knew it would probably be his last flight but he jumped at the chance. As long as he had to, he was going out in a blaze of glory."

Before he got to see the General, Major Joe Renner filled him in on the situation. As he talked to Cram, he spoke with the clipped, haggard tension of a man who hadn't slept for seventy-two hours. "They've got our backs moulded into the wall. We've had a permanent condition red, all day, no sirens now unless at least fifteen Jap planes come in. The F4F's aren't scrambled to defend the field. We haven't enough gas or ammunition left to send them up each time . . .

"What did you bring in this time? Torpedoes? What in the hell good are they now? Every one of the TBF's got smashed up in the shelling last night. Good God, what a show that was! They must have had the whole bastardly fleet out there. It was like kicking a wounded guy in the groin time after time to see if he'd yell uncle.

"They frisked the place like a pickpocket. There was a BB out there in the channel with a flock of cruisers and destroyers in support. The insolent sons of bitches just stood off and plastered the place. Some walked searchlights up and down the shore, picking out targets. The rest of them went over the place with a fine-toothed rake. If they ever try to break through what's left today . . . God help us, Jack . . . it'll be bad."

Cram went on in to the General. "I brought up a couple of torpedoes, sir. The rear gunners you sent me for had shoved off in a transport by the time I got back. Yes sir, I know you didn't say anything about torpedoes, but I thought you needed 'em. May I try that attack tonight, sir. Maybe I can put a couple into that battleship. Aye, aye sir, I'll stand by."

Outside Renner, still functioning somehow after two and a half days without sleep, gave him the glad tidings. "There are twenty-two Bettys on their way down, Jack. We can't scramble the fighters, there isn't enough gas left."

Cram felt helpless and a little in the way.

"I'm going down to the beach for a swim, Joe, in case the Old Man wants me. It won't be so noisy there . . . for a while . . . and I haven't had a bath in a week."

That night the Jap fleet completed its trilogy of terror. It came back again, the third night in a row, to devastate the beachhead. To make it even more pleasant, "Washing Machine Charley" and about six of his friends came in at will every few minutes, dropping bombs and ghastly white flares to spot targets for the "Tokyo Express."

The shelling and bombing wasn't as bad as it had been the previous two nights, but that didn't alleviate its effect on bowstring nerves. It was like sitting through the same bad movie for the third time. Dawn might bring a major attempt at a breakthrough, but anything would be better than sitting and taking a beating . . . at least they'd have a chance to fight back!

At dawn, activity at the front lines remained sporadic. There was no attempted breakthrough. It was obvious then that the Japs were waiting for reinforcements. A convoy, loaded to the scuppers, was seen closing in yesterday. Immediate word was needed on its position.

A lone plane brought back the news. Six 8,000 ton transports were standing inshore between Doma Reef below Esperance and Kukumbona, just twelve miles up the beach.

"They have a destroyer screen . . . couldn't count accurately . . . between eleven and twenty DD's."

Air went to work on those transports with all it had left. Lone SBD's, as quickly as they were put in commission, went out one at a time to do what damage they could.

The runway at Henderson was rent and torn, the steel matting twisted and snarled as if a cyclone had hit it. There were nineteen shell craters in the 1,500 foot straightaway. Renner did the best he could. He marked out a weird path around the craters with flare pots at each hole.

Joe finally got one off by running in front of the plane, flagging the pilot through the tortuous path, to the takeoff position at 0430 on the morning of the 15th. The first one had failed to make it and crashed right in the middle of the field.

He took the third pilot in his jeep and drove him carefully down the runway, showing him each of the bad spots in turn by flashlight. By the grace of God, the third SBD got off the deck. His plane barely airborne, the pilot tried to haul his wheels up. They were frozen in place. Frantically he tried working the dive flaps. They were glued tight; the shelling had knocked out the hydraulic system.

Quietly, in the dawn, the pilot turned west and headed for the stark shadows of the transport. He laboriously climbed the circle for altitude, then pushed over in his dive. The rushing air played queer tricks with the wheels down; he corrected and weaved through the flak barraged from the destroyers and jerked the release. A direct hit on the first AK.

As fast as the ground crew could get the sieved planes in shape, the SBD's went off to do what damage they could . . . while they could.

First enemy plane to appear that morning was a lone photo-reconnaissance plane that brazenly circled the field at 11,000 feet. Twice it walked through the ack-ack but on the third pass, observers on the ground saw heavy stuff bursting close around it. Then, with the typical "It's all for the Emperor" attitude, it cut back and roared across the field less than three hundred feet in the air. Everyone within two miles cut loose at it with pistols, tommy-guns, rifles, and anything else that threw lead. One 105-mm pack howitzer fired five hopeful rounds. The bogey crashed in flames at the edge of the field.

At 0700, an umbrella of thirty Zeros took up station at 15,0000 feet over the landing area. Desperate as it had been before, it was madness now to send out lone bombers. General Geiger stopped all attacks. All hands were ordered to stand by.

The General decided on a coordinated attack with everything that could fly . . . a desperate measure for a desperate situation. Renner, as operations duty officer, was given the job of coordinating the attack.

After working on the "Old Man" all night, Cram finally got his way; the battleship he wanted to hit had not been sighted, but he was granted permission to make a torpedo attack on the transports under cover of the SBD attack.

Renner did his coordination by jeep. The communications system had been obliterated the night before. Cram rode with him.

The army fighter squadron promised to have four planes ready to fly at the designated takeoff time. They stopped at Radio to give them the word . . . then over to the ready room of Major Duke Davis' squadron who would furnish the balance of the fighter cover.

Colonel Al Cooley said he could have twelve SBD's ready for take-off at 1010. On the way back to the Blue Goose, Renner told Cram, "This will be the most screwed-up show in history . . . but there's no other choice. If it works, miracles are still with us."

Back at the PBY, the crew was ready. The Major had told them the night before to keep the engines warmed up for a possible night attack. "If that doesn't come off, we may try something unusual," he had told them.

The crew had tried sleeping in the plane and under its wings until the "Tokyo Express" started laying them in too close for comfort . . . or sleep.

That a PBY had never before in history made a daylight torpedo attack, nor the fact that he didn't have a co-pilot hadn't bothered Cram. Neither did the fact that he knew little or nothing about using torpedoes. Before Renner dropped him off, he got all the instruction he had time for from a fighter pilot whose brother flew TBF's. Getting that word took all of five minutes. None of the Cat's crew had ever been in combat before, but they took the word of the attack quietly. Their bitter frustration from the shelling outweighed any skeptical feelings they might have had.

They climbed aboard the lumbering old lady and took up stations. Kirby took over the .30 caliber in the bow; Metz and Horton shared the single .50's in the waist blisters, port and starboard; Hoffman monkeyed up into his radio perch. Anderson took the engineer's standby.

The Goose was first off. Cram nursed it down the shattered matting and sweated it grudgingly into the air . . . the one-ton load on each wing fighting to keep it on the ground.

Laboriously, the Major eased it upward, climbing for altitude inland, away from the beach. The assigned rendezvous area for the eight fighters and twelve SBD's was two miles east of the field away from the patrolling Zeros over Kukumbona.

As Cram pushed the ungainly ship higher and higher, the crew watched the furious movements around the transports, just a few miles away. Directly to the side, Duke Davis's Wildcats had joined the tail chase. Behind them the last of the SBD's had scrambled and were clawing for altitude. They had all taken off through a barrage from "Pistol Pete" that was raking the field.

While they watched, the thirty Zeros on station were relieved by thirty more that came down from the northwest. As they neared 9,000 feet, Metz, Horton, and Kirby test-fired their machine guns.

While the Blue Goose hung back like a lost soul, the F4F's and the

SBD's eased up-island to the west. The Zeros seemed to watch incredulously, but remained in their assigned patrol area.

In the mounting tension, as the last seconds ticked off, Jack Cram checked over the intercom. Each man rogered "Ready." Then to the west, the lurking SBD's exploded into action. The lead plane rolled over on its back, wings gleaming dully in the sunlight.

As it whipped down, the impending hell burst loose. Mud-brown Zeros peeled off for the kill. The two destroyers just outboard from the beach spewed up flak and the automatic guns on the AK's cut loose . . . this in a few frantic seconds.

Cram hunched forward . . . "This is it. Good luck" . . . and shoved the stick to the firewall. The surprised Cat went over on its nose and down in a vertical dive toward the first transport, a mile away. Built never to go over 160, the Blue Goose hit 270 miles an hour indicated in the dive. Cram fearfully watched the needle climb while the huge umbrella wings shrieked and groaned under the strain. They were literally flapping like an ancient crow's.

Afraid of what would happen, Cram hauled slowly back on the yoke. The Cat held together. He leveled out at 100 feet and went whistling past the first DD before they sighted him. Dead ahead the Japs on the transports were living and dying as frantically as ants while bombs from the SBD's gutted their ships.

After his dead level run at seventy-five feet, Cram screamed over the first and second AK's with his hand clutching the release toggle. Flak from the DD's flailed the plane like a steel whip; it bucked and shuddered from the impact. In the bow turret, Kirby leaned into the wind to keep his kicking gun on target while he strafed. At point blank range, Cram sighted in on the third transport. He lined it up amidships, sighting off his bow. Holding the plane steady with his left hand, he jerked back on the release toggle so viciously he almost tore it out of the panel.

The first torpedo splatted into the water and bored right toward the hull of the transport. Cram then grabbed the toggle on the left. A second later he yanked back the handle. The second torpedo dropped, porpoised for an instant, and followed the first one into the steel hide of the transport. Just as he pulled out of the run, flak from one of the DD's sheared off the PBY's navigator hatch.

In the melee overhead, five Zeros pulled away from the Wildcats and went down on the Catalina. Cram started to pull up, saw the Zeros, and stood the Goose on its left wing in a flipper turn that whipped the PBY around viciously and headed it in the direction of Henderson. As the plane pulled by the transport she was settling in the water.

Then the real hell of the morning caught up with the old Blue

Goose. Every one of the three guns on the plane opened up as the first Zero closed in from its dive. The Zero swung down, firing in an arc, and pulled up over the bow of the Cat. Young Kirby laced its engine with his .30.

Cram held her pointed toward Henderson as the plane jockeyed down through the gantlet of flak and Zeros. To make the plane as poor a target as possible, he jinked and rollercoastered it up and down hill, from just over the wavetops back up to 250 feet.

The Zero played tail chase in their eagerness to smash down this waddling crate. One after another they ran through the squirrel cage antics . . . dive . . . loop, and come back in . . . dive . . . loop, and come back in.

The twelve-mile run back to the field seemed to take an eternity. In the ventilated belly of the plane, Anderson, the engineer, stood by, waiting for word to switch tanks, should the gas run low. Metz and Horton and Kirby spewed out enough lead to keep it from being a slaughter.

The Cat barrelled in over the trees at the end of Henderson with a Zero on its tail. It was moving too fast to land there. Cram cut the throttle and prayed. The Zero's cannon and wing guns were playing at will over the Cat's fuselage.

Just in front of the Cat, Lieutenant Rog Haberman's smoking F4F was in the landing circle, wheels down. Haberman caught a quick look behind him and turned the Wildcat casually around. With his wheels still down, he finished his circle on the tail of the Zero. He stitched lead in its wing roots until it exploded. Then he calmly completed his traffic circle and landed.

Cram clipped off the treetops and brought the Blue Goose down on Fighter One . . . without an inch of runway to spare.

The excitement of their close shave still uppermost in their minds, Cram and the crew kidded one another about the last painful forty-five minutes. Though the Blue Goose looked like it had played host to a flatcar of lead, no one was hurt. The only damage suffered by the men was a few sudden grey hairs and a shrapnel scratch on Horton's leg. It was so minor he didn't even notice it until later. With a "God, was I lucky!" Cram reported back to Renner at Operations.

When the final reports came in, the attack which had been spawned in desperation had come off with almost incredible precision. Three of the transports were definitely sunk and the others damaged. Our losses were negligible in comparison.

Major Cram stood by to report to the General in his dugout. He was sure when he told the Old Man what was left of his prize Blue Goose, Portsmouth would be just around the corner.

Inside, the General was forewarned and prepared for his end of the show. Renner, Colonel Cooley, and several others stood around waiting for the fun.

Grimly, a very meek Jack Randolph Cram stepped up to make his report to a very straight-faced, stern-looking General, "Sir, I think I got one of them," and then before General Geiger could ask, Cram rattled off the damage to the plane:

"Sir, they hit us with everything in the house. There are at least 160 holes in the plane from 7.7, 20-mm cannon and shrapnel. The starboard engine was hit, both gas tanks have been punctured in several places, the starboard oil tank has several holes in it, the port propeller is punctured and both port struts are damaged. The port aileron torque tube is holed, and there are about twenty-three holes in the wing and eighteen in the hull. The rudder, vertical fin, horizontal stabilizer, and elevator tabs were almost shot off and will have to be replaced. The navigator's hatch is torn off, the port tire is punctured, and the port blister glass is broken . . . that's all, sir."

The General pretended to read him off and was doing well until a burst of half-stifled laughter from an onlooking officer broke up the show. Congratulations were followed by an invitation to lunch with the Commanding General at the Hotel de Gink.

Back at the field, the crew wistfully patched up what was left of the prize PBY with wire, rivets, putty, tape, and cloth. That afternoon, the Blue Goose limped proudly down the runway on a half inflated tire, and hiked herself into the air. She headed back to Espiritu Santo.

✾ ✾ ✾ ✾

THERE WAS NO RESPITE FOR THE FORCES ON GUADAL-canal. October 17 brought still another severe pounding by bombardment ships, covering a landing at Cape Esperance. This time the Japanese sent 752 8-inch shells crashing onto Henderson Field. The glimmer of hope shone faintly to the south, however, when on October 18 Vice Admiral William F. Halsey, who had been on the binnacle (sick) list since May, arrived in Noumea. As he stepped ashore, a courier handed him a dispatch: "You will take command of the South Pacific Area and Forces immediately." Halsey accepted the honor "with astonishment, apprehension and regret," as Admiral Ghormley was a close friend; nevertheless he immediately made plans to fly to Guadalcanal for a meeting with Vandegrift.

In Washington, October 19 was a dark day for Secretary of the Navy Frank Knox, who conducted a press conference regarding our invasion of the south Solomons. When asked the pointed question whether the United States Marines could hang on, Knox could only reply: "I hope so."

Admiral Halsey arrived at Guadalcanal a few hours later, and by now he was thoroughly apprised of the desperate situation confronting Vandegrift. The great fighting admiral recalls his initial meeting with the marines in an excerpt from his autobiography.

·24· THE ARGONNE CONFERENCE

FLEET ADMIRAL WILLIAM F. HALSEY AND J. BRYAN III

We met in my cabin on the *Argonne* on the night of October 20— Maj. Gen. A. Archer Vandegrift, commanding the 1st Marine Division; Maj. Gen. Alexander M. Patch, who later commanded the Army troops that took over from the Marines; and Maj. Gen. Millard F. Harmon, the senior Army officer in the South Pacific. Also present, in addition to my skeleton staff and Ghormley's subordinate commanders, were Lt. Gen. Thomas Holcomb, the Commandant of the Marine Corps, who happened to be in Nouméa on an inspection tour, and Maj. Gen. C. Barney Vogel, who had just arrived as Commander of the I Marine Amphibious Corps.

Archie Vandegrift and "Miff" Harmon told their bitter stories. It was quite late when they finished. I asked, "Are we going to evacuate or hold?"

Archie answered, "I can hold, but I've got to have more active support than I've been getting."

Rear Adm. Kelly Turner, commanding the Amphibious Forces Pacific, protested that the Navy was already doing its utmost. He correctly pointed out that the few bottoms we had were becoming fewer almost daily; we did not have the warships to protect them; there were no bases at Guadalcanal where they could shelter, no open water permitting evasive tactics; and enemy submarines were thick and active.

When Kelly had finished, Archie looked at me, waiting. What Kelly had said was of course true. It was also true that Guadalcanal *had* to be held.

I told Archie, "All right. Go on back. I'll promise you everything I've got."

. . . Within forty-eight hours after I took command, and despite my ignorance of the terrain, I had to make two important decisions. Supporting Guadalcanal was not one of them; here I was merely a willing mouthpiece for the Joint Chiefs of Staff. My first independent decision was whether or not we should proceed with construction of an airfield on the island of Ndeni, the largest of the Santa Cruz group. Not only was Henderson our sole advanced field, but it was at the weather's mercy as well as the enemy's; an hour's rain turned it into a marsh. Ndeni was 330 miles from Henderson, but at that it was 205 miles closer than our nearest field, on Espiritu. The plan for the Ndeni field had been approved, and Army troops were on their way to occupy the island, when the situation at Guadalcanal became so desperate that I intercepted them and rushed them into the defenses. This decision brought me considerable adverse criticism, but I never had reason to regret it; Ndeni's importance soon evaporated . . .

❧   ❧   ❧   ❧

BY MID-OCTOBER, GENERAL HYAKUTATE, ARCHITECT of the Japanese thrust to smash United States resistance on Guadalcanal, had steamed down to the scene of conflict to mastermind the final ouster of the invasion. One of the first things Hyakutate learned from Lieutenant General Masai Mayuyama and his intelligence officer, Lieutenant Colonel Matsumoto, was that it was becoming increasingly difficult to control the Grassy Knoll sector because of enlargement and frequency of the American patrols. Matsumoto, a fairly thorough individual, it was believed, happily displayed a map taken from a United States Marine officer who had recently been captured and beheaded. The map, clearly detailing the push-out of American lines, also indicated in footnote the precise strength of Vandegrift's forces. Hyakutate was impressed. He not only agreed that Matsumoto had gathered accurate information, but now, on the basis of it, made his final battle plans.

The essential feature of the Japanese advance was really a double penetration, an offensive at all points of Vandegrift's defenses by employing the 4th and 124th Regiments, which were supported by heavy artillery and tanks. The 124th was to cross and hold the American side of the Matanikau while the 4th overwhelmed enemy outposts; thereafter the initial attack was to be directed toward the capture of Henderson Field. At that juncture the 16th and 29th Regiments would follow in the second phase of the attack, push through the already gained positions, and after a heavy barrage attack the southern perimeter.

There was one small discrepancy in the plan: the United States Marine had relinquished a map which originally had been Japanese and was in substance an outline of suspected Japanese positions throughout Guadalcanal. How Matsumoto or Hyakutate could have possibly misinterpreted it has never been explained. Perhaps Hyakutate's order to his officers—that when General Vandegrift was captured, only he and an interpreter should be allowed to cross the Matanikau to sign the surrender—better explains the supreme overconfidence of the inscrutable Oriental accustomed to winning land campaigns.

On the other side of the perimeter, General Vandegrift was feeling a little better, owing to the arrival of reinforcements and the results of the Edson-Sims-Whaling expedition along the Matanikau. Although his troops had not been able to locate a 6-inch gun emplaced somewhere along the enemy line, and although shells were dropping into the marine positions every day, the airfield was reasonably operational and his pilots were acquitting themselves well. A map also figured in Vandegrift's thinking at this time: Japanese, showing what seemed to be the outline of a three-division attack emanating from behind the Matanikau, which the marine general already suspected was in the wind. The result was the emplacement of Lieutenant Colonel Lewis Puller's 1st Battalion, 7th Marines, in the line and the blooding of the 164th Regiment. (The Swedes were now fighting mad. They had been shelled repeatedly since coming onto the island; "Coffin Corner" gave them their chance to return fire.)

The Japanese attack was launched at 3 A.M. October 24 after an artillery bombardment and probes toward the Matanikau by the two enemy regiments. This, then, was the start of the big Japanese push which is now told in two parts; the first a panoramic view of the fighting with the 1st Battalion. A living legend and surely the epitome of a fighting marine (five times awarded the

Navy Cross and the Army's counterpart, the Distinguished Service Cross), "Chesty" Puller won forty decorations during a life-
span of combat from Nicaragua to Korea. Burke Davis, Puller's
biographer, recounts the initial phase of the second battle of
Edson's Ridge.

·25· "BLOOD FOR THE EMPEROR! MARINE, YOU DIE!"

BURKE DAVIS

Heavy rains swept the island almost daily and Japanese progress
was slow until, on October 22, a tank and infantry attack on the beach
struck the marines and was bloodily repulsed. This had an effect,
however, for to meet the threat, Hanneken's battalion was pulled
from its place beside Puller on October 24, and sent to a riverside
position. Puller's men spent the day in furious activity.

Puller now had to cover the whole sector of 2500 yards with his
understrength battalion, and he filled the hole left by Hanneken
by spreading his men and putting all except the mortars in line. He
had sent officers and noncoms among Hanneken's men before the
departure, and in an hour they learned more about the lay of the
land and the firing lanes than they could have learned in a day by
inspection. Holes were deepened and more machine guns were
put into position.

Puller had seen a couple of strands of barbed wire along a jeep
road in his rear and had that taken down for the front line; there were
no staples, and marines wrapped the wire around trees. The wire
was hung with tin cans filled with stones and grenades with their pins
half-pulled. There were no tripflares to warn of enemy approach
and light the area.

Puller walked the line most of the day, at each gun position asking
the man in charge to show him the field of fire; the Colonel checked
to see that the fire zones interlocked, and ordered improvements
at almost every point.

From left to right, the companies were: A, C and B. On the far left,
where Regan Fuller commanded, was the only spot of open land,

where A Company joined the 164th Army Infantry. During the day the field in front of the Army position was plowed, to slow attackers. At the edge of the field Regan Fuller placed a 37 millimeter gun and two 50-caliber machine guns. Otherwise, A Company had the worst of the battalion position, for their ground was low and the hill in their front was heavily wooded.

Men worked so hard in the day, carrying arms and ammunition, digging, filling sandbags and hanging wire, that many were asleep by late afternoon.

A Company was weaker by one platoon than the other companies, for despite the protest of Colonel Puller, there was an outpost of forty-six of its men some 3000 yards to their front, commanded by Sergeant Ralph Briggs, Jr., of Port Edwards, Wisconsin. These men had been out for several days, to warn of an enemy approach.

Colonel Puller was on the field phone often during the day of digging-in, trying to persuade his regimental commander to have headquarters withdraw Briggs and his patrol: "They're going to sacrifice those men—that's all. We don't need any bait on the hook, as you say. If they're coming, they're coming. It's foolishness to throw away that platoon."

Once, when it appeared that the commander had expressed agreement, officers in the CP heard Puller roar: "All right, then, if you think so, why don't you waltz your duff down to Division and get 'em back in here?"

The outpost remained in the hills to the south, out of sight, but connected with the main line by telephone.

Puller also called Pedro del Valle, of the 11th Artillery, several miles down the coast, and asked him to be ready to fire support during the night. Del Valle was reassuring: "I'll give you what you want. I know you won't be unreasonable. Just call for all you need."

At dusk, as usual, the artillerymen registered their guns, and shells exploded in the thick growth a few yards beyond Puller's lines.

In the afternoon there was a report of smoke in the hills beyond the outpost and a rumor spread that a Jap officer had been seen studying the position through field glasses. None of this intelligence came to Puller, but as night drew on, men in the CP with him saw that he expected trouble. Sergeant Major Frank Sheppard was beside him as daylight faded:

"Shep, we'll probably get mixed up in a scrap tonight. The weather is right, and the moon won't be much. It'll rain like hell—and Nips are out there."

The Colonel had the field phones opened down the line so that all companies and platoons could hear every message. He made a final check after dark, squatting in the dugout of his CP; there was no light in the place except for a flashlight occasionally used by the radioman.

First Battalion, Seventh Marines, was ready for its night of trial. Rain began to fall.

At 9:30 the phone rang in the battalion CP. Puller answered. It was Sergeant Briggs, whispering. The company communications men listened to the conversation:

"Colonel, there's about three thousand Japs between you and me."

"Are you sure?"

"Positive. They've been all around us, singing and smoking cigarettes, heading your way."

"All right, Briggs, but make damned sure. Take your men to your left—understand me? Go down and pass through the lines near the sea. I'll call 'em to let you in. Don't fail, and don't go in any other direction. I'll hold my fire as long as I can."

"Yes, sir."

Puller had hardly put down the telephone when the bell rang once more. A company in the line reported Japs were cutting the barbed wire in its front. Puller spoke to the circuit down the battalion line.

"All right," he said. "Let's get this straight. Hold fire until you get an order from me. The outpost must get clear before we open up. If the bastards break through, use the bayonet. And keep someone at every phone. Wait."

Puller looked at his watch. It was ten o'clock. Yells rolled from the right: Japanese voices shouting in English, "Blood for the Emperor! Marine, you die!"

A marine bellowed back: "To hell with your God-damned Emperor! Blood for Franklin and Eleanor!" Obscene shouts followed.

Puller got on the telephone and called loudly: "Commence firing."

The front erupted with blazing weapons, and over their heads the artillery shells soughed through the rainstorm. Explosions farther back in the jungle halted Japanese columns before they could move but the vanguard pressed against the wire along a narrow front. Grenades blew holes in the fencing and enemy troops ran into the fire of the massed machine guns. Puller had almost doubled the normal strength of machine gun companies, picking up the weapons at every opportunity. Their weight was felt now.

Sergeant Manila John Basilone's nest of guns was about the center of C Company, in the middle of the line, with a slight decline in his front; the enemy drove toward him so persistently that he covered the hill with their bodies and when the first fury of attack faded

he sent men to push down the wall of enemy bodies, to clear the fire
lane.

Calls for help came from several outposts and Puller sent men from
headquarters; often he left the CP himself, prowling among the companies. The attacks now came in waves, each high tide lasting for
about fifteen minutes, with increasing fury each time. There was at
least one attack every hour. Weapons began to give out.

Regan Fuller, on the low ground at the left, saw an enemy mass
in the edge of the field, crowding against the jungle for cover. His
37 anti-tank gun fired three rounds of canister and the column disappeared. Elsewhere in his front Fuller had every weapon blazing—
he had a rifle platoon, a heavy machine gun section with four 50-cali-
ber and six 30-caliber machine guns, two anti-tank guns, and a number
of extra pieces, including half a dozen old Lewis machine guns, most
of which jammed. There were eighteen BAR's and a 60 millimeter
mortar. The mortar fired 600 rounds during the night, until it was
red hot; at dawn the tube barely projected from the mud. The wire
before A Company was not broken and not a man was lost during
the hours of darkness. In the first light, Regan Fuller saw enemy
bodies stacked "like cordwood" in the edge of the jungle, and in the
field where his anti-tank guns had fired was a column of Japanese
dead, each rank lying half atop the one in its front in perfect formation
—a weapons company with machine guns, rifles, mines and dynamite
still held by its troops.

Puller called Del Valle again: "Give us all you've got. We're holding on by our toenails."

"I'll give you all you call for, Puller, but God knows what'll happen when the ammo we have is gone."

"If we don't need it now, we'll never need it. If they get through
here tonight there won't be a tomorrow."

"She's yours as long as she lasts."

John Basilone came scurrying to the CP several times during the
night, at lulls in the fighting. He reported some guns in trouble and
vanished, bearing heavy parts or ammunition on his back. He was
barefooted. Regan Fuller saw him once on the A Company front. Basilone reported his guns burning out, and such a serious lack of water
that men were urinating in the gun jackets to keep them firing.

From the rear, after a couple of hours, artillerymen reported the
barrels of their 105's were white-hot at the muzzles. No one knew how
long the big weapons could maintain their fire.

Puller had a surprise on one of his visits down the line, while tracers hissed through the rain; Private Hirsch, who was under arrest for his conduct on the crater operation, was lugging jars of coffee along the line, stopping at each position to offer hot drinks to the hard-pressed gunners, exposing himself without thought for his safety. Puller determined to have the court-martial papers torn up.

Regan Fuller called the CP from the flank:

"Colonel, I'm just about running out of ammo. I've used almost three and half units of fire."

"You got bayonets, haven't you, Fuller?"

"Sure. Yes, sir."

"All right, then. Hang on."

In the heaviest of the firing, when Puller had left the CP, regimental headquarters called for him.

"Not here sir," the wireman said. "Colonel Puller's up front."

"Find him. Get him on the phone."

After the crew had made several calls to the line position, Puller returned and talked with the regimental commander. The few remaining in the pit heard Puller's explosive reply:

"What d'ya mean, 'What's going on?' We're neck deep in a fire fight, and I've no time to stand here bullflinging. If you want to find out what's going on, come up and see." He growled angrily to Pennington and Sheppard: "Regiment is not convinced we are facing a major attack!"

Near 3:00 A.M., when six or eight separate attacks had built up and waned on his front, under almost constant fire, Puller again talked with regimental headquarters—this time with the exec, Colonel Julian Frisbie:

"Yeah, it looks pretty bad . . . Sure, we could use help. But if it's coming, for God's sake don't hold it back—send it on in."

The battalion was now down to about 500 men, Puller estimated. He had no way to guess the strength of the enemy waves. Japanese had infiltrated the lines by this hour, and men who could be spared were hunting them in the blackness. Frank Sheppard organized a small security party for the CP in an effort to protect Puller and his diminished staff; there were now two men left with the Colonel.

There were more talks with the regimental CP before reinforcements arrived, and some delay ensued when the fresh troops, the Third Battalion of the Army's 164th, were led to regimental headquarters, instead of coming directly to the front.

"Who's guiding them in?" Puller asked.

"A Navy chaplain here, Father Keough."

"Put him on."

Puller was soon satisfied that the priest, who had often visited the front positions, could lead the battalion through the rainswept jungles the mile or more to his position. He hung up the telephone and went into the downpour, accompanied only by a runner.

The jeep road was lower than the battalion line and perhaps a quarter of a mile to the rear. When Puller reached the road and stood in the rain, waiting, there was an occasional tracer over his head. Within a few minutes the head of relief column appeared. Puller shook hands with Father Keough.

"Here they are, Colonel."

"Father, we can use 'em."

Puller greeted the Army commander, Lieutenant Colonel Robert K. Hall: "Colonel, I'm glad to see you. I don't know who's senior to who right now, and I don't give a damn. I'll be in command until daylight, at least, because I know what's going on here, and you don't."

"That's fine with me," Hall said. "You lead on."

"I'm going to drop 'em off along this road," Puller said, "and send in a few to each platoon position. I want you to make it clear to your people that my men, even if they're only sergeants, will command in those holes when your officers and men arrive."

"I understand you. Let's go."

Puller, Keough and Hall led the file along the dark road in the rain with the thunder of fire growing to their left. Every hundred yards or so they met a runner who had come back through the undergrowth to lead in reinforcements. Puller halted at each runner and gave him a squad or more of men. When they came to the end of the line all the troops had been fed in, with guides to their positions, and were ready to help stand off the enemy.

In some of the holes marines took the fresh guns and ammunition of the Army troops and did much of the firing themselves—but other beleaguered veterans found the newcomers superb fighting material, though they did not know the ground. The Army men had the new M-1 rifles, the first the marines had seen. The mixed men fought well together, and as dawn approached beat off two or three more Japanese attacks.

Puller went to the CP with Keough and Hall when the men of 3/164 had been distributed. It was after 4:00 A.M. An hour later the enemy drove a wedge into the line, some seventy-five yards deep and perhaps fifty yards wide. As the first light of day came Puller sent mortarmen on either side of this break and with a flurry of fire cleaned up the salient. Marines counted thirty-seven Jap bodies in the small triangle when the line had been straightened.

Puller gave the Army colonel and the priest blankets and a meal

of C-rations, then left them to inspect his line. He later recommended Keough for the Silver Star for his work of the night; it was not
awarded.

Reports of trouble still came from the line. Sergeant Robert Cornely had lost several guns in his position, one because a steam condens-
er had exploded, and his men competed with others for spare gun
barrels in the morning. Dozens of automatic weapons had been fired
for so long that the rifling was worn smooth. Two of the three men
shot during the night in Cornely's position were killed by marines
in the confusion caused by Jap infiltrators in the rear.

Soon after dawn Puller was told that men had found a party of about
forty of the enemy, lying asleep near the 80 millimeter mortar position commanded by the great gunnery sergeant, Roy Fowle. The
sleeping Japs bore land mines and dynamite, evidently for an attack
on the mortarmen, whose fire had wrought such havoc on the Jap
columns. The sleeping invaders were soon wiped out.

There was one enemy prisoner, a sullen little warrant officer who
refused to talk when he was brought to Puller. The Colonel was so
stung by the insolence of the prisoner that he slapped him with the
flat of an entrenching tool; teeth spilled from the Jap's mouth, but
they were false teeth. He gave no information, even then.

A later prisoner talked freely with Puller:

"Why didn't you change your tactics when you saw you weren't
breaking our line? Why didn't you shift to a weaker spot?"

"That is not the Japanese way. The plan had been made. No one
would have dared to change it. It must go as it is written."

The commander of the Army's 164th Regiment, Colonel Bryant
E. Moore, sought Puller during the morning. "Colonel Puller, I want
you to know how happy I am to have had my men blooded under
you. No man in our outfit, including me, had ever seen action, and
I know our boys couldn't have had a better instructor. I wish you'd
break in my other battalions." Puller praised the men of the battalion in return: "They're almost as good as marines, Colonel."

His old friend, General R. S. Geiger, the aviation chief, also visited the front and walked over the torn terrain. He was astonished
by the windrows of Japanese bodies. Overhead, his planes were strafing and bombing the retreat of the enemy through the interior.

Sergeant Briggs and his men of the outpost had a hair-raising return to the lines. When the battle broke out Briggs led the way to
the area before the Army regiment, where most of them hid overnight. There was a close call on the way. As Briggs told the story:

"We gained cover in the woods where it was cold as hell, and the

Japs seemed to be all around us. We could hear them jabbering and walking so close that one Jap stepped on a marine's bayonet and another stepped on the helmet of a man hit by rifle fire.

"They filed by in squads, the most unreal sensation I ever had, but they didn't want to tangle with us for fear of betraying their position to the guns."

At daylight Briggs and the party crawled into the grass. Japs turned mortar and machine gun fire on them. Private Gerald White and another man made an heroic trek from this spot. When he remembered the machine gun he had left behind in the outpost, White crawled back some 600 yards to the spot, accompanied by his friend, and removed a bolt, making the gun unserviceable. In his absence Private Robert Potter gave his life to save his companions. When Jap fire became heavy in the field Potter leapt to his feet and dashed back and forth, drawing fire, shouting to his friends to run for American lines. Most of them escaped in that way. Potter was killed. Several remaining men of the party got back into the lines aboard a Bren gun carrier sent out by Regan Fuller. Only four of the outpost failed to return.

Puller's men found two hundred and fifty Japanese dead inside their lines during the day, about twenty-five of them officers—one a major who had committed suicide, leaving a final entry in his diary on the loss of his colors and troops: "I do not know what excuse to give. I apologize for what I have done . . . I am going to return my borrowed life today with short interest."

Puller's casualties for the battle were nineteen dead, thirty wounded and twelve missing. In his first report, the Colonel estimated that he had been attacked by a Japanese regiment with a strength of 2000 men. Captured documents revealed that his half-battalion had beaten off the suicidal attacks of three enemy regiments (the 16th, 29th and 230th), plus the remnant of a brigade—or the equivalent of a Japanese division. Two of the regiments admitted to carrying off 500 stretcher cases between them.

Two or three days later when the stench of bloated bodies in his front made his men retch, Puller persuaded Division to make a count of enemy casualties and bury the corpses. This burial detail counted 1462 bodies and spent two days at the grisly work. Bulldozers gouged holes and covered the enemy dead in great pits.

There was an attack on the night of October 26 following Puller's big fight . . . it was clear that, for the time being, 1/7, with the aid of Del Valle's artillery and the final support of the Army battalion, had saved the perimeter against almost staggering odds. It had cost the Japanese dearly to leave their artillery on the rugged trails and to confine their attacks to a narrow front. Guadalcanal saw no fighting more furious, by land, sea or air.

Puller added somber figures to his report: In the campaign thus far his battalion had lost twenty-four percent of its men and thirty-seven percent of its officers.

General Vandegrift sent the battalion a commendation for its "determined and vigorous defense against . . . numerically superior enemy forces . . . The high combat effectiveness demonstrated is a tribute to the courage, devotion to duty and high professional attainments of its commanding officer, Lieutenant Colonel Lewis B. Puller, and to the company commanders, Captains Charles W. Kelly, Jr., Regan Fuller, Robert H. Haggerty, Marshall W. Moore, and Robert J. Rodgers."

The company commanders won Silver Stars for the night's fighting, but Regan Fuller, for one, thought that Sergeant Briggs, Gerald White and Robert Potter should have been honored instead. Sergeant John Basilone won the Medal of Honor, the first Marine enlisted man to win the award in World War II.

Puller won a second gold star for his Navy Cross.

⁂   ⁂   ⁂   ⁂

OCTOBER 25 — A DAY THE MARINES WORKED FURIOUSLY patching up their perimeter, for lines had melted away and units had become inextricably mingled during the night. Some semblance of order was restored just in time for three companies of the 2nd Battalion, 7th Marines (F, G and E), to feel the full weight of the Japanese attack. The battle centered on another ridge and went on all night. F Company was wiped out. E Company was pushed back. But in a saddle between these units was a machine gun platoon which the enemy failed to knock out. It was manned by Sergeant Mitchell Paige, who won a field promotion to second lieutenant and the Medal of Honor for this fight. This is Paige's own account of the battle.

·26· "I PICKED UP A MACHINE GUN . . ."

SERGEANT MITCHELL PAIGE

Before we could get set up darkness came and it started raining like hell. It was too black to see anything, so I crawled along the ridge-front until it seemed I had come to the nose. To make sure I felt around with my hands and the ridge seemed to drop away on all sides. There we set up.

With the guns set up and the watches arranged, it was time for chow. I passed the word along for the one can of "Spam" and the one can of "borrowed peaches" that we had with us. Then we found out some jerk had dropped the can of peaches and it had rolled down the ridge into the jungle. He had been too scared to tell us what he had done. I shared out the "Spam" by feeling for a hand in the darkness and dropping into it. The next morning I sent out a couple of scouts to "look over the terrain." So we got our peaches back.

That night Smitty and I crawled out towards the edge of the nose and lay on our backs with the rain driving into our faces. Every so often I would lift up and call some of the boys by name to see if they were still awake and to reassure myself as well as them.

It must have been two o'clock in the morning when I heard a low mumbling. At once I got Smitty up. A few minutes later we heard the same noise again. I crawled over to the men and told them to stand by. I started figuring. The Japs might not know we were on the nose and might be preparing to charge us, or at any moment they might discover our positions. I decided to get it over with. As soon as the men heard the click of my pin coming out of the grenade, they let loose their grenades too.

Smitty was pulling out pins as I threw the grenades. The Japs screamed, so we knew we had hit them. We threw a few more grenades and then there was silence.

All that second day we dug in. We had no entrenching tools so we used bayonets. As night came I told the men we would have a hundred percent watch and they were not to fire until they saw a Jap.

About the same time as the night before we heard the Japs talking again. They were about a hundred yards from the nose. It was so damned quiet, you could hear anything. I crawled around to the men and told them to keep quiet, look forward and glue their ears to the ground. As the Japs advanced we could hear the bushes rustle. Suddenly all hell broke loose.

All of us must have seen the Japs at the same time. Grenades exploded everywhere on the ridge-nose, followed by shrieks and yells. It would have been death to fire the guns because muzzle flashes would have given away our positions and we could have been smothered and blasted by a hail of grenades. Stansbury, who was lying in the foxhole next to mine, was pulling out grenade-pins with his teeth and rolling the grenades down the side of the nose. Leipart, the smallest guy in the platoon, and my particular boy, was in his foxhole delivering grenades like a star pitcher.

Then I gave the word to fire. Machine guns and rifles let go and the whole line seemed to light up. Pettyjohn yelled to me that his gun was out of action. In the light from the firing I could see several Japs a few feet away from Leipart. Apparently he had been hit because he was down on one knee. I knocked off two Japs with a rifle but a third drove his bayonet into Leipart. Leipart was dead; seconds later, so was the Jap. After a few minutes, I wouldn't swear to how long it was, the blitz became a hand-to-hand battle. Gaston was having trouble with a Jap officer, I remember that much. Although his leg was nearly hacked off and his rifle all cut up, Gaston finally connected his boot with the Jap's chin. The result was one slopehead with one broken neck.

Firing died down a little, so evidently the first wave was a flop. I crawled over to Pettyjohn, and while he and Faust covered me I worked to remove a ruptured cartridge and change the belt-feed pawl. Just as I was getting ready to feed in a belt of ammo, I felt something hot on my hand and a sharp vibration. Some damned slopehead with a light machine gun had fired a full burst into the feeding mechanism and wrecked the gun.

Things got pretty bad on the second wave. The Japs penetrated our left flank, carried away all opposition and were possibly in a position to attack our ridge-nose from the rear. On the left, however, Grant, Payne and Hinson stood by. In the center, Lock, Swanek and McNabb got it and were carried away to the rear by corpsmen. The Navy boys did a wonderful job and patched up all the casualties, but they were still bleeding like hell and you couldn't tell what was wrong with them, so I sent them back. That meant that all my men were casualties and I was on my own. It was lonely up there with nothing but dead slopeheads for company, but I couldn't tell you what I was thinking about. I guess I was really worrying about the guns, shooting as fast as I could, and getting a bead on the next and nearest Jap.

One of the guns I couldn't find because it wasn't firing. I figured the guys had been hit and had put the gun out of action before leaving. I was always very insistent that if for any reason they had to leave a gun they would put it out of action so that the Japs wouldn't be able to use it. Being without a gun myself, I dodged over to the unit on my right to get another gun and give them the word on what was going on. Kelly and Totman helped me bring the gun back towards the nose of the ridge and we zig-zagged under an enemy fire that never seemed to stop. While I was on the right flank I borrowed some riflemen to form a skirmish line. I told them to fix bayonets and follow me. Kelly and Totman fed ammo as I sprayed every inch of terrain free of Japs. Dawn was beginning to break and in the half-light I saw my own machine gun still near the center of the nose. It was still in working order and some Japs were crawling towards it. We got there just in time. I left Kelly and Totman and ran over to it.

For too many moments it seemed as though the whole Japanese Army was firing at me. Nevertheless three men on the right flank thought I might be low on ammunition and volunteered to run it up to me. Stat brought one belt and he went down with a bullet in the stomach. Reilly came up with another belt. Just as he reached the gun, he was hit in the groin. His feet flew out and nearly knocked me off the gun. Then Jonjeck arrived with a belt and stopped a bullet in the shoulder. As I turned I saw a piece of flesh disappear from his neck. I told him to go back for medical aid, but he refused. He wanted to stay up there with me. There was not time to argue, so I tapped him on the chin, hard enough so that he went down. That convinced him that I wanted my order obeyed.

My ears rang when a Jap sighted in on me with his light machine gun but luckily he went away to my left. Anyway, I decided it was too unhealthy to stay in any one place for too long, so I would fire a burst and then move. Each time I shifted, grenades fell just where I had been. Over the nose of the ridge in the tall grass, which was later burned for security, I thought I saw some movement. Right off the nose, in the grass, thirty Japs stood up. One of them was looking at me through field glasses. I let them have it with a full burst and they peeled off like grass under a mowing machine.

After that, I guess I was so wound up that I couldn't stop. I rounded up the skirmish line, told them I was going to charge off the nose and I wanted them to be right behind me. I picked up the machine gun, and without noticing the burning hot water jacket, cradled it in my arms. Two belts of ammo I threw around my shoulders. The total weight was about a hundred and fifty pounds, but the way I felt

I could have carried three more without noticing it. I fed one of the belts off my shoulders into the gun, and then started forward. A colonel dropped about four feet in front of me with his yellow belly full of good American lead. In the meantime the skirmish line came over the nose, whooping like a bunch of wild Indians. We reached the edge of the clearing where the jungle began and there was nothing left either to holler at or shoot at. The battle was over with that strange sort of quietness that always follows.

The first thing I did was to sit down. I was soaked in perspiration and steam was rising in a cloud from my gun. My hand felt funny. I looked down and saw through my tattered shirt a blister which ran from my fingertips to my forearm. Captain Ditta came running up, slapped me on the back and gave me a drink from his canteen.

For three days after the battle, we camped around the nose. They estimated that there were a hundred and ten Japs dead in front of my sector. I don't know about that, but they started to smell so horribly that we had to bury them by blasting part of the ridge over on top of them. On the third day we marched twelve miles back to the airport. I never knew what day it was, and what's more I didn't care.

※ ※ ※ ※

WHY HAD GENERAL HYAKUTATE FAILED IN HIS offensive? For one thing, the Sendai was dog-tired when it went into battle. Japanese intelligence (which we already know left much to be desired) failed to determine the type of terrain Japanese troops would have to cross in order to get into attack position. Hyakutate's troops, additionally encumbered by fifty pounds of equipment per man, were forced to haul their artillery by ropes over deep gorges. But aside from human frailty, the multipronged attack was improperly coordinated. Colonel Oka's 124th Regiment was twenty-four hours late jumping off, and the best that singular character could do was to get his men slaughtered by United States Marines while he himself ran back across the Matanikau. What then of Maruyama's attack south of the airfield? After two postponements, Maruyama's troops launched an uncoordinated, half-hearted attack. It failed not because of poor leadership (Colonel Furiyama of the 29th himself penetrated the marine lines and wandered about lost for three days until he shot himself), but because of poor timing which could never be rectified once Japanese troops had gotten a taste of marine bullets. This ended the strongest enemy attack against General Vandegrift's forces: 3500 Japanese bodies were counted.

The following day, October 26, Admiral Halsey fought a major naval engagement in the Santa Cruz islands. Two Japanese carriers were knocked out of the war, while our carrier *Hornet* was sunk.

Five days later Vandegrift, who long wished to expand his perimeter, launched a general offensive with the 5th Marines, two battalions of the 2nd Division (1st and 2nd), the Whaling group, and the 3rd Battalion, 7th Marines, supported by three battalions of artillery, in order to push outward in a series of hotly contested actions which ultimately cost the Japanese 750 troops. With Lieutenant Colonel H. H. Hannekin's 2nd Battalion, 7th Marines, was Ira Wolfert of North American Newspaper Alliance, a Pulitzer Prize-winning reporter witnessing his first marine combat of which he writes in the following excerpt.

·27· THEY JUST WENT ON UP AND OVER

IRA WOLFERT

The jungle shore is withered and blistered with blackened clumps where the Japs held their line with what amounted to natural pillboxes. Artillery dug them out or plowed them under. The smell of dead bodies still hangs, in clouds and thick as smoke over these narrowly separated places where men who had traveled four thousand miles elected to stand and die. Huge trees which were felled or severed by shells are sticking up like gaunt, amputated limbs, like the wounded of the last war in Vienna who had turned beggers and used mutely to hold up their unbandaged stumps to passers-by.

Our fellows have elected to die here, too. Along the road pounded through by the wheels of our trucks lie several graves, one of a private. His friends have trimmed its mound pathetically with coconuts and fashioned a rude wooden cross for a headstone. A helmet with three holes in it, the holes as blank as dead eyes, tops the cross and on it is penciled, A Real Guy. Against the cross stands a photograph of a very pretty girl, staring silently. The sunlight is very bright here and you can see the brown color of the eyes in the photograph and seem to be able to look deep into them down past the look she gave the Dodge City, Kansas, photographer and his camera. Her dead man must have loved her truly, for he carried her picture into battle.

The flat shoreline runs only a short distance along the sea and then begins precipitously to climb up into ridges which mount rapidly into an eight-thousand-foot mountain range. Each ridge drops steeply into a ravine, known as a draw. The ridges are about five hundred yards apart and run from north to south. Since our advance is east to west, our troops have to go up and down steadily as if over waves. The jungle runs up along the sides of each ridge almost to the top, and then on the top there is bare grass, completely bare, not a tree or log or twig. The Japs stay down in the ravines and fire up at the bare space on top. That means our fellows going up and over after them are clearly outlined while the Japs have dense, actually impenetrable cover. Complicating the tactical problem even more is the fact that the jungle-covered sides of each ridge are pocked with naturally eroded coral caves which the Japs have enlarged and in which they entrench themselves obstinately. Flame-throwers are no good against these caves. The jungle, through which sunlight never penetrates and in which only lizards and red orchids flourish, is too damp to permit flame-throwers to function. The Japs either have to be interred in their caves or excavated by hand.

American troops, no doubt, will face more formidable opposition before this war is concluded, but never a more desperate terrain filled with more desperate men.

On the eastern front, tanks are used to flush the Japs out of the grass, and when they are flushed, they are shot down like running quail. But tanks are useless on the western side of Henderson Field. On the western side, it is all manual labor.

We sat on a ridge which had been won yesterday, then squatted to watch our marines move up to the next ridge about five hundred yards westward and start scooping out the succeeding ravine.

The second wave of marines worked their way forward slowly, flowing up the covered side of the ridge in the slow, purposeful uncertain-seeming way of raindrops on a window, stretcher-bearers coming slowly down among them from the top. There was a mingling of marines and corpsmen, and suddenly, in the midst of the mingle, flanking mortar fire dropped. Wham! The crack of it came back to us hard enough to sound like a hammer against the flesh of the brain. Then, wham again and wham! Three fifteen-pound shells in all, and the jungle's trees, all gnarled and burdened with parasitic creepers, bent and thrashed and groaned under the blasts. The Japs sent over only the three, evidently being short of heavy ammunition which they had been unable to drag with them in their retreat.

I think I closed my eyes when the first shell hit. It seemed too horrible, our men and the stretcher cases forming a cluster to cheer each other up and then becoming a bull's-eye for the Japs. When I opened my eyes, the ground was bare. There were three holes in it, very close together. I thought everybody there had been killed, and I sat there a moment thinking that. Then marines began to lift themselves from the earth to which they had dropped, and one by one, heads down, gathering up their rifles and gear as they went, resumed their slow, purposeful, upward flow. They never looked back. They just went on up and over.

Then down the other side, cautiously, probing, seeking to draw fire in order to locate Japs to shoot at. They drew fire all right—three machine-gun nests clustered so close together in the jungle that a grenade attack would most likely have been sufficient to wipe it out. But the marines now enjoy the luxury of artillery and nobody is wasting men around here—not our boys, not the kind of fellows we have here. So everybody waited for the big boys to go to work. They waited patiently, dug in one hundred yards from the nests.

It seemed as if it might be a long wait, and we scuttled through the sniper fire to the command post where Colonel John M. Arthur, of Union, South Carolina, directing operations on the whole front, Lieutenant Colonel Cornelius P. Van Ness and the artilleryman, Colonel William Keating, of Philadelphia, were ensconced. Fifteen Zeros, one of them burning, were working up some sort of hell in back of us back near the airport, at the same time that rifle and machine-gun fire was cracking all around us, and officers were trying to make themselves heard on the telephone above the din.

Captain Maxie Williams, a blondy, chunky, footballish young man, standing recklessly in the open trying to isolate the Jap harassing fire so it could be smothered and the command could be left to command in peace, called for three volunteers to swing around and work over to a certain tall tree. Sergeant Major Frank Regan, of Dallas, Texas, and combat reporter Sergeant Ned Burman, of San Francisco, crawled forth, Burman observing sallowly, "I forgot the first rule of the Marines—never volunteer for nothing."

I remarked to Captain Maxie that all this going-on reminded me of Harlan County, Kentucky, on election day, where politics are so mixed up that you cannot tell whether you are shooting a friend or a foe. And Captain Maxie leaned into the crater where we were hiding from the bullets to shout, "Sure ain't like Humphries County," he being from Waverly, Tennessee.

Through all the shooting, Colonel Keating directed the artillery fire toward the Jap machine guns holding up our advance. He worked like a surgeon probing for an ulcer. The first thing I heard him say—he had to shout over the rifle and machine-gun fire—was, "Now, just be calm and careful. We don't expect you to do any better than your best under the existing circumstances." He was talking to a boy in a forward artillery observation post whose job it was to direct the artillery fire. The boy, being so close to the target, was nervous.

He gave a target and Colonel Keating ordered one shell fired. We could hear this boom! like some brass-lunged giant clearing his throat, and then the feathered whistle of the shell. "It's passing right over- head now," said Colonel Keating. "Just watch for it. It ought to be there any minute." Then we heard the boom of the explosion.

Then the boy gave another target. Altogether, three ranging shots were fired. The fourth shot was right on the target. Colonel Keating asked the same battery to fire a salvo of five shells, and we heard the booms all run together and the feathered whistles all run together and the explosions like one long explosion. Then silence. "Do you want any more?" Colonel Keating asked the boy, and I could hear the boy's voice squeaking exultantly through the telephone. "That's enough, sir." he said.

All advances here are like that, inch by inch, slow and easy, and the Japs don't seem to have anything to stop them except another one of their combined-operations attacks—a fleet by sea, a fleet by air, forcing us to fall back on the airport and bury there the hell the Japs raise.

❀ ❀ ❀ ❀

LET US MOMENTARILY SHIFT OUR ATTENTION TO Henderson Field, where grueling aerial combat was an almost hourly occurrence. Here is Captain Joe Foss, second leading Ma- rine Corps ace with 26 kills. A Medal of Honor winner and for- mer governor of South Dakota, Foss (with collaborator Walter Simmons) speaks of momentous events of November 7 when his luck ran out after shooting down three Zeros in the ensuing action.

·28· "DOWN INSTANTLY, NOSE FIRST . . ."

CAPTAIN JOE FOSS AND WALTER SIMMONS

November 7. It began quietly . . . In the afternoon we were ordered to attack a small Japanese force of ten destroyers and a light cruiser, steaming toward us from about 150 miles to the north. Just as we sighted them, I saw six float Zeros in front of us, about a thousand feet below. They were going in the same direction we were, shooting at another flight of Wildcats led by Major Paul Fontana, of Sparks, Nevada. The funny thing about it was that Major Fontana, who did not know he was being fired on, was a couple of thousand feet above me. The Jap pilots were about 3,000 feet from their target, and I could see no sense in wasting ammunition at that range.

I called the boys and said, "Don't look now, but I think we have something here." We immediately started down for the attack. It was a mad race. All of us—we had seven planes on that flight—realized there were only six Zeros and somebody was going to get left out. On the way down everybody was trying to pull up, get in there, and get a shot.

Boot Furlow practically climbed under my wing. When I shot, the first short burst blew the Zero into a thousand pieces. The motor went off on a tangent and Boot, in order to avoid hitting it, had to do a Houdini.

I went in the other direction. As I came in again, Boot had already got on the tail of a second plane and shot it down flaming. I thought I would do a quick wingover and get another shot but by that time the six Zeros were all blown to pieces. Aside from dropping fragments—and chutes—we were alone in the sky.

Five of the chutes, strangely enough, were empty. Above me about 2,000 feet hung the sixth with an enemy pilot dangling in the harness. At that moment the Jap unbuckled himself and jumped out. He passed me on his back, falling headfirst at a little angle. Seconds later he hit the sea and threw up a big geyser of water.

The other five flyers had apparently done the same, although none of us actually saw them. The reasons for such suicidal tactics were a mystery. I never saw either side shoot at a parachuting man in the Guadalcanal area.

We went on with our attack, my boys joining up with Major Fontana's flight in reverse order, since we were going in to strafe the ships. That made me the tail-ender. Before I went down, I followed a useful custom and scanned the clouds. Caution paid dividends once more. The float of a scout plane was protruding from a cloud.

"You better get this baby so he won't follow you down in your dive and be dangerous," I told myself. I circled and made a diving run on him as if he had been a Zero. But he was a single-motored scout biplane, almost stationary up there high above the sea. Before I knew it, I was too close to shoot and had to worry about missing him.

I came down from behind, flipped over on my side, and squeezed by. As I passed, he turned over on his side too, and the rear gunner cut loose with his free gun. My plane was hit several times. One bullet splintered through the left side of the hood and out the curved part of the cockpit glass, right in front of my face.

This made a good-sized hole. The wind howling through it scared hell out of me. Seeing there was nothing specially wrong, however, I soon quieted down and circled for a diving belly shot.

My bullets hit the right wing just below the fuselage, sending the plane into a crazy spin. I left it. The last I saw it was hurtling toward the sea. A second craft of the same type—somewhat like our Navy SOCs—was coming in, not seeing me. I circled for position behind him, pulled up, and made an unhurried belly shot. He was an accommodating cuss—he burst into flames at once and went torching into the sea.

The planes of that day were later credited as numbers seventeen, eighteen, and nineteen on my list.

It was time to look for my boys. I had made the mistake of leaving my flight to get those last two planes and was afraid of being hopped by Zeros and shot down. The straggler is usually on his last mission unless he happens to be really lucky. I looked down at the ships in the vicinity. The Jap cruiser had been hit hard and was apparently in a bad way. A destroyer had also taken a beating. But there was no sign of our planes—they had done their chores and were long since gone.

Finally, though, I spotted another fighter. Pulling up alongside him, I gave the join-up signal. When he did not join up, I kept on going. I later learned he was having motor trouble and his plane could go no faster.

I was on the way home alone. Ahead were several rain squalls—just like waterfalls in the sky. Confident of the way, I didn't bother to check my compass. When I did, I was 30° off course. I saw a big squall directly ahead and figured if I went to the left of it, I would come right between the two big islands that stand as a gateway to Guadalcanal.

Instead, I should have gone to the right. The rain was covering the island I was aiming for. When the plane was turning and abreast of the rain squall, my motor started fading and throwing out clouds of smoke. I tried my best to push it along—you know, the way a child leans forward and pushes a kiddie car to get every foot. By this time it was apparent that the island wasn't anywhere near Guadalcanal. I was far off the route. In a moment the motor quit, caught hold again, then conked out cold. I tell you my hair stood up so straight it raised the helmet right off my head.

There was only one thing to do. I glided on, trying to make every inch I could toward the island. I could have turned at one point and landed close to shore, but I made a foolish circle in the wrong direction and landed between two and five miles offshore. That's a long way when you are strictly a fresh-water swimmer.

The tail hooked into the water, the plane skipped, hit with a solid smack the second time, nosed over like a brick, and went down instantly, nose first. Water poured in so fast it almost knocked me out. I had forgotten to pull the leg straps on the chute. When the water came in, the buoyancy of the chute and my Mae West floated me up. I was really buoyant. Trying to get the leg strap off, I bent my foot back, but it went under the seat and caught, so I was unable to get loose.

In my excitement I took in a couple of gulps of salt water. I stopped and thought the thing over there, thirty feet under the surface. "Listen, dope," I told myself, "if you don't quiet down, there isn't going to be any show." Using almost the last of my strength, I pulled down against the unwelcome buoyancy and managed to get my foot out. The water seemed to be crushing me as I shot to the surface.

Still the leg straps on the chute were buckled. They pulled me around and dumped me with my fanny up and my face down in the water. I had a tough time getting the straps unbuckled and the Mae West out of the way. In the process I swallowed several more gulps of sea water. The life jacket came up to my ears and almost got away.

By the time I had everything fixed okay, my shoes felt too heavy, so I pulled them off and let them sink. There I was, thrashing about in the water. I wasn't sure I stood any chance. It looked like it was about the end of the jig.

I don't say my thoughts would have made a three-dollar book, but plenty of things went through my mind as I looked toward shore. The current was so strong my best efforts only kept me in the same spot. I wondered what my wife would think when I didn't come back. I wondered if she would ever find out where I went and what became of me, and I wondered what the boys back at camp would say. I would swear that twice shark fins cut the water a few feet away. It was a horrible feeling.

I did more praying that afternoon out there than I ever did in my life. "Poor old Joe finally got it," I could imagine the boys saying. "He's shark bait." Every time I put out my arm to swim, I expected to draw back a stub. After a while I thought of the chlorine capsule in my pocket and broke it for protection. It seemed to keep the sharks —if any—away.

I continued splashing hopelessly. In an hour or so it was dark. I was heading for a point that looked close, but the longer I swam the farther away it seemed. In the dark I could see glowing phosphorescent patches in the water. I thought they were made by sharks' fins, and they nearly scared me to death.

After a while I could hear canoes coming toward me. There was the splash of paddles and a low mumble of conversation, but I could hear nothing else. Afraid of Japs, I kept still in the water as the canoes came straight toward me. I feared the paddlers would hear even my breath. They came so close I was between an outrigger and its canoe for a moment. As they missed me by inches I didn't move—just rolled my eyes in the dark, trying to make out who was in the canoes.

One man some distance away had a lantern. After the canoes had circled and hunted for about thirty minutes, the man with the lantern yelled, "Let's look over 'ere." Those were about the most welcome words I ever heard. "Yeah, over here!" I sang out. The men in the closest canoe just about bailed out, they were so surprised. The fellow with the lantern rowed over and circled, holding the light on me doubtfully and sizing me up. Silent faces in the shadows seemed to say, "If you turn out to be somebody we don't like, we'll bash your brains out." I did plenty of talking to convince them I was a good friend of theirs.

Finally they pulled me aboard, apparently satisfied, and whistled across the water to friends ashore. One of the men—a planter—had seen me land on the water.

I still had my chute with me. By this time its buoyancy was reduced to practically nothing. It was badly waterlogged and weighed several pounds. As the men pulled it into the boat with difficulty, one remarked, "You must be a superman to drag anything like that along with you."

They paddled rapidly and after a little bit swung into double time. I sat facing the man who had hauled me out—he turned out to be Tommy, a sawmill owner. He was holding his lantern up, when . . .

Bam! . . . something hit the lantern and dropped into the boat. It was a fish resembling a gar, about twenty inches long and with a long, sharp bill like a needle. Tommy quickly ducked the lantern. "I should have kept this thing down," he apologized, "but I guess I got a little excited. Plenty of men have lost their eyes at night because of holding lights. These jumping fish pierced their eyes." From then on in, I held my hands over my face and peeked through my fingers. I was in no mood to lose an eye.

Tommy said I was lucky not to reach the point I had been aiming for so unsuccessfully. I would have landed on a peninsula and walked across it, fording a stagnant stream to reach the mainland. That stream was filled with man-eating crocodiles. No doubt I would have walked right into the mouth of one of these cheerful customers.

This turned out to be Malaita Island, and there was a mission on it. All the padres were gathered on the beach as a welcoming committee. They had been out in canoes looking for me too. There were two bishops, four fathers, two brothers and eight sisters. Besides Tommy, the sawmill owner, there was a Norwegian planter. It was a regular League of Nations. One bishop was a Frenchman, the other a Russian. One father was from the Netherlands, another from Australia, still another from Norway. A brother was from Emmetsburg, Iowa, and another was from Italy. A sister was from Boston. The others came from as many different countries as the fathers.

They gave me some dry clothing. I gave my old clothes to the natives. Most of these missionaries had come here from other islands where the Japs were now in charge, and the same was true of the nuns. The Japs had an ugly habit of bayoneting missionaries through the throat.

That night I dined better than I ever had on Guadalcanal—steak (the first fresh meat I'd seen in weeks), eggs, papaya, pineapple. We sat up and talked till almost midnight. They wanted to know what was going on in the world, how the war was progressing, what was happening at Guadalcanal. Their only news came from Tommy, who had a little radio set aboard his scow. He tuned in the news every night, listened intently, and then came over to report. Though the war was going on right in their back yard, these people knew little except what they could see. One sister had been there forty years and had never seen an automobile. The first airplanes she saw were warplanes over the islands.

The missionaries had no tobacco other than that grown on the island, and this tasted like a poor brand of straw. I resolved to fly over with a sack of tobacco the first thing after returning to Guadalcanal. One of the fathers gave me his bed for the night. It was a woven job— thatch mat with a half-inch pad—and a pillow that resembled a hundred-pound sack of rock salt. But it was the best he had, and hard as it was I slept as if it had been a "Beautyrest" mattress. There was only one interruption. In the middle of the night I got up to be sick from the salt water I had swallowed.

Early the next morning, Sunday, I was awakened by singing. I got up and found my way to a little thatched church with a dirt floor. Services were under way, and the singing—a kind of weird howling would describe it better—was the chanting of the natives. It was an amazing thing. All the women were up in front and a padre was leading the song. I don't know what language he was using—I couldn't understand it. But it certainly sounded good. The altar was of bamboo and coconut shells. The natives, who were some of the orneriest characters in the entire Solomon Islands, wore red loincloths and their mouths were dripping red from betel nut.

After church I was placed on review—my first public appearance on any stage. The fathers asked me to stand in the covered areaway between two houses while the natives passed by and looked me over. They were great powerful brutes with bushy hair and savage faces, and they looked at me wonderingly, as if I were some strange animal. One of them was wearing my pants—given away the night before—and another was wearing my shirt.

A father explained their amazement. Many years before the war, an American schooner had stopped at Malaita with a crew of southern Negroes. They had told the natives they were Americans, so the natives expected to find me black.

We had a fine breakfast. Everything on the table was strictly the fat of the land, even though no supplies had been received for thirteen months. With arrival of the extra fathers and sisters, the food problem must have grown acute. But that morning we had eggs—a dessert to me—fresh goat's milk, and a dark bread that was really good, plus papaya and some delicious fruit I could not identify. In my honor we each had two slices of bread. Bread had been rationed, one slice per man.

The fathers pressed me to stay for two weeks. I agreed to stay maybe one week. In the midst of this unprecedented hospitality it looked as if I could get in some fishing, and then there were some wrecked Jap bombers and Zeros up in the hills that we intended to check over.

Through the jungle grapevine came word that on the previous day Marine raiders had made a surprise attack on a small Jap camp—a hundred miles away—on Malaita, killing twenty-four Japs and sending the twenty-fifth into the jungle with a slug in his chest.

After breakfast I went out and stretched my chute in the sun to dry. Shortly thereafter the natives started yelling that a plane was coming.

Sure enough, a Wildcat soon appeared overhead. The pilot, who turned out later to be Lieutenant Otto Brueggeman, twenty-four, of Lexington, Missouri, spotted the chute. We thought he did, anyway. Then the plane left.

Hours later as we were eating dinner in the dining hall—a small shack about ten feet long and eight feet wide, perched on stilts five or six feet above the ground—we heard the natives shrieking again. We jumped up and ran out. They were looking out under the trees far over the water and said there was a plane coming. Listening, we could neither see nor hear a plane.

But a PBY soon loafed into view. It came over, circled a couple of times, and landed in a little bayou in front of the mission. I hurriedly said my farewells, leaving the silk parachute for the nuns to work up into clothing, and jumped into a canoe powered by two huge natives. Everyone turned out to see me go. Even the nuns left their confines—something one of the fathers said he had never seen happen before.

The PBY was taxiing around in the bayou. Rowing wide open, the natives managed to catch it and I struggled aboard. Inside I found Major Charles Parker of New Orleans, Louisiana, an operations officer. Up ahead at the controls was my old friend, Major Jack Cram.

We took off and flew back to Guadalcanal—me wearing old socks, no shoes, a baggy pair of white pants, "b.v.d.'s" and a beard.

I went directly to the fighter ready tent and had a grand reunion with my boys. They told me fifteen Jap planes had been shot down the day I got three.

❅ ❅ ❅ ❅

WHILE THE MOP-UP OF GUADALCANAL WAS IN PROGress, Carlson's 2nd Raider Battalion (which arrived in October) was at Aola Bay, 40 miles east of Henderson Field. Since returning from the Makin Raid, the battalion had seen no action of the type in which it specialized. Now, however, the opportunity presented itself when an Aola airfield project failed to come to fruition. At Carlson's request, his raiders were temporarily detached for purposes of attacking an enemy force reported along the Gavaga, where the Army's 164th was fighting. Following inland trails, the marines began a series of month-long actions (November 8 - December 4), marched 150 miles, and killed 488 Japanese troops in a dozen private wars that rank as the greatest single patrol in the history of World War II.

Captain Herbert Merrillat, 1st Marine Division public relations officer and a former Rhodes scholar who wrote at length of the campaign, details one week of Carlson's month of fighting in which marine losses numbered but 16 dead and 18 wounded.

Let us join the patrol . . .

·29· JUNGLE PATROL

CAPTAIN HERBERT MERRILLAT

They lighted their fires in a driving rain and waited. A few miles west of them a similar party of Japanese waited in the darkness for their own landing force. The Japanese landed that night, but the Americans did not. From the beach at Aola the flames leapt up through the rain as the Japanese were busily unloading east of the Metapona. Fortunately, the enemy did not see the marines' signal fires, or perhaps they saw them, but did not know what to make of them. In any case, the fires burned out without drawing enemy fire.

The next night, during the early hours of November 4, the fires were lighted again. This time the American ships arrived, bringing two companies of the Second Raider Battalion under Lieutenant Colonel Evans F. Carlson, who were to secure the beachhead and cover the landing of naval construction workers and engineering equipment for work on the proposed airfield. After daybreak the Army units who were to guard the area after the Raiders withdrew began landing, and all day long the men, supplies, and equipment came ashore.

The Raiders had expected to leave with the ships after completing their mission of securing the beachhead during the original landing. The Japanese landing near the Metapona, however, gave them another mission. They received orders to push through the jungle to the west and help destroy the Japanese beachhead party. Four more companies of the battalion started for Guadalcanal to reinforce them.

November 6 the Raiders set out from Aola. They struck off through the jungle on a trail along the foothills, west to the Bokokimbo River about ten miles from Aola, and then headed north for the village of Reko. Across the river they surprised a foraging party of Japanese who had just killed a pig and were about to carve up their morsel. They killed two in the group of Japanese, who fired one volley and fled. The Raiders continued on to the Kema, scene of the First Raiders' landing when they had raided the Japanese beachhead at Tasimboko two months earlier. There the two companies divided, one going to the village of Tasimboko where they picked up food sent by Higgins boat from Aola, the other one pushing on to Tina.

November 9 the two companies of Raiders rejoined at Tina and advanced on to Bino on the Balesuna River, four miles from the coast. They had not yet had any major contact with the enemy. Lieutenant Colonel Carlson decided to use Bino as a base for future operations, since that was the westernmost village still occupied by natives. The village was, moreover, south of the pocket of Japanese now enveloped by the Seventh Marines and 164th Infantry, which the Raiders were to help mop up. The Raiders used Tetere as a beachhead for bringing in food from Aola.

November 11 the Raiders began to come into contact with the enemy. Part of the Japanese force trapped against the beach east of the Metopona had escaped through the ring of Marine and Army troops. As four Raider patrols fanned out from Bino on the 11th, they met the enemy detachments that had escaped. The southernmost patrol—Company C—ran into the main force about two miles from Asamana, a village on the Metapona four miles from its mouth. The company had crossed a grassy plain and just as they entered a patch of woods bordering the field, the Japanese opened up on them with machine guns, twenty-millimeter guns, rifles, and mortars. Company C lost five killed and three wounded in this clash. They quickly notified Lieutenant Colonel Carlson of the contact.

The Colonel ordered Company E, then two miles north of Asamana on the Metapona, to cross to the west bank of the river, move south, and hit the Japanese from the west. Company D was directed to move south along the east bank of the river and strike the enemy from the northwest. They, too, had to cross a grassy field and were hit as they entered the woods, losing two killed and three wounded. Meanwhile, Company E under Captain Washburn moved up the west bank of the Metapona, and just as they reached Asamana, surprised two companies of Japanese who were crossing the river from east to west. Some of the Japanese were stripped, swimming and bathing in the river. Others were wading across and passing supplies and equipment to the other side. As the Raiders came up and fired into the Japanese, enemy outposts opened up from good positions. A machine gun in the fork of a banyan tree was particularly effective and succeeded in pinning the Raiders down. Then Japanese forces began a flanking maneuver to get behind Captain Washburn's company. He withdrew to reorganize. The first attack had been led by the first platoon under Lieutenant Evans C. Carlson, the Colonel's son. When the Raiders withdrew, the Japanese apparently thought the attack was over and again began crossing the river.

Company E returned, however, with a fresh platoon—the second platoon under Lieutenant C. E. Early—in the lead. This time they knocked out the machine gun in the banyan tree, but as the Marines fired on the enemy soldiers in the river, the Japanese again began a flanking movement from two directions. As one force tried to work to the west of Washburn's company, six machine guns opened up on the Marines from the opposite bank. Washburn knew that Companies C and F were engaged two miles east of him, but the only line of withdrawal open to him was through a narrow gully to the north. The Raiders retired by this route, covered by a gunner at a machine gun who lost his life protecting the withdrawal of his company. The Raiders had killed one hundred and twenty Japanese at the river crossing.

When Lieutenant Colonel Carlson directed Companies D and E to move against the enemy engaged with Company C, he also had sent one platoon from Company B, his base security, directly to Company C as reinforcement. He also had recalled Company F from Tetere. When Company F arrived at Bino, Lieutenant Colonel Carlson moved with it to the scene of Company C's engagement to co-ordinate a concerted attack. The attack was executed by Company F and the platoon from Company B as darkness was falling. Aside from a few snipers, it was found that the enemy had evacuated to the south.

Leaving Company F on the scene of the action with orders to pick up the trail at daylight, Lieutenant Colonel Carlson returned to Bino with the rest of his force. Companies D and E had already arrived. The next morning (November 12) he led Companies B and E back to the scene of Company C's engagement. From Captain Schwerin (Company F) Colonel Carlson learned that the force he was covering had moved south for about three miles and crossed the Metapona to the west.

Company F was directed to return to Bino and relieve Company C as base security. Colonel Carlson then led Companies B and E to Asamana, where Washburn had dealt the enemy such a severe blow the preceding day. Here excellent positions for about a battalion were found on both sides of the river. Also notices in Japanese were found pinned on trees directing where various companies were to go. While Lieutenant Colonel Carlson was looking around, his out-guards shot two enemy messengers, one entering from the east and the other from the west. He decided that this was the rendezvous and disposed his companies in a defensive position from which they could cover by observation and fire the grassy fields which lay beyond the narrow strip of bush which bordered the river. Augmented by Company C, which arrived the night of the 12th, the Raiders occupied these positions for two days and two nights. During the first eighteen hours they shot twenty-five messengers and stragglers who attempted to enter the position. To quote Colonel Carlson: "It was like shooting ducks from a blind." He reported this success to Headquarters and added "still killing [strays]."

On the morning of the second day (November 13) it was discovered that the enemy force which had crossed the river below Asamana was in the woods to the south of Asamana, while the remnants of the force hit by Captain Washburn lay in the woods to the west and north. These forces began to get uneasy, probably because their messages had miscarried. They attempted to enter Asamana several times during the day, but their movements were never co-ordinated. The Raiders simply waited until the advance elements of a group approached within a hundred yards of their position, then opened fire on them with machine guns while throwing mortars back on the main body.

At one point a Marine lookout reported the remarkable news that a forest was moving toward the Raiders' position. Through field glasses Colonel Carlson saw that indeed Birnam Wood was moving to Dunsinane. A company of Japanese, in mass formation, was marching across a field of grass wearing cloaks of foliage and twigs. When within easy range the Raiders opened on the "forest" with mortars and watched it break up into "trees" which scattered in all directions.

On November 14, all being quiet on his front, Colonel Carlson returned to Bino with the three companies. During the two days at Asamana this group had accounted for one hundred and sixteen known Japanese dead without the loss of a man.

It was on the following day (November 15) that a scout reported the location of a small enemy base in a defile five miles south of Bino and west of the Balesuna River. A detachment of Company F under Captain Schwerin was sent to deal with it. The defile was so narrow that only three men could enter at a time. Waiting until the enemy sentry had been recalled for "chow," Captain Schwerin led an assault which resulted in the annihilation of the fifteen men in the enemy group and the capture of considerable arms, ammunition, and supplies without the loss of a man. Included in the captured matériel were the personal effects of Major General Kawaguchi, who had commanded the Japanese force that attacked Henderson Field in the Battle of the Ridge.

The First Battalion, Tenth Marines, a battalion of seventy-five-millimeter pack howitzers commanded by Lieutenant Colonel P. M. Rixey, supported Carlson in his operations against the Japanese around Asamana. The artillery had moved up with the Seventh Marines and 164th Infantry as they closed in on the enemy east of the Metapona. As Carlson's Raiders spotted "pockets of Nips," they requested artillery concentrations on those areas. The team of Raiders and artillery killed many and drove the rest farther inland . . .

※   ※   ※   ※

THE CLIMACTIC NAVAL ENGAGEMENT UPON WHICH hinged our very existence in the Solomons was at hand, and it resulted from reinforcement attempts by both sides almost simultaneously. In the small hours of Friday, November 13, following a reinforcement of Vandegrift by two transport groups, the screening warships under the command of Rear Admirals Daniel Callaghan (OTC) and Norman Scott fought the first phase of the decisive Naval Battle of Guadalcanal against a strong Japanese bombardment group commanded by Vice Admiral Hirotake Abe. During the ensuing melee, battleship *Hiyei* was severely damaged and lost propulsion; and the destroyers *Akatsuki* and *Yudachi* were sunk, the latter by naval gunfire shortly after conclusion of the main action. Our losses were far more grievous: two cruisers, *Atlanta* and *Juneau*, sunk, and 700 (including both admirals) killed. Shortly after daylight Navy and Marine Corps air groups, joining with torpedo bombers from carrier *Enterprise* (flown to Guadalcanal for Vandegrift's use) and Army B-17s, found the great cripple and in part exacted vengeance. At 10:20 A.M. the first torpedo was dropped, and thereafter dozens of hits were registered on "the unsinkable so-and-so" until at 6 P.M. the battleship went down stern-first.

Notwithstanding their losses, our brave foe sent down still another bombardment group the next night built around heavy cruisers *Maya* and *Suzuya* and succeeded in working over Henderson Field for thirty-seven minutes with 1000 8-inch shells.

Again, on November 14 Navy and Marine Corps planes made the enemy pay for his visit to Guadalcanal. Forty-two fighters and bombers spotted Tanaka's transport group and a cruiser formation steaming doggedly southward, distant about 150 miles. In a day of feverish air strikes, 7 of 11 transports were sunk; also 3 cruisers, including the heavy *Kinugasa*. But the enemy did not turn back.

Vice Admiral Kondo's Emergency Bombardment Group, aggregating battleship *Kirishima*, 2 cruisers and 14 destroyers, steamed southward from Ontong, Java, at 10 A.M., November 14. Admiral Halsey had anticipated something on this order, however, and while he was powerless to prevent the previous bombardment, he was ready for this one. About 100 miles south of Guadalcanal, and hoping to elude detection by Japanese "snooper" (scout) planes, Rear Admiral Willis Augustus Lee, with battleships *Washington* and *South Dakota* with five destroyers, waited for nightfall. The great clash, one of only four such slugfests of World War II, opened at 11:16 P.M. on November 14 when the two forces arrived at Guadalcanal simultaneously and Lee's destroyers spotted the loom of enemy warships first. During the ensuing action *Kirishima* was fatally battered by major-caliber fire (16-inch), while the two Japanese cruisers sustained damage which put them out of the war for some months. Our losses were 5 destroyers seriously damaged, *Benham* so badly that she was sunk by our own gunfire after the battle, and battleship *South Dakota* battered by 42 major-caliber hits. *Kirishima*, dying of her own internal explosions, sank at 3:20 A.M., November 15, 1942.

Witness to this historic engagement was the late Colonel James W. Hurlbut, foremost combat correspondent of the 1st Marine Division, and a widely read *Washington Post* reporter before his enlistment in the Marine Corps. Hurlbut, who rose through the ranks from private, was on Tulagi looking for a story when the battle commenced.

·30· EYEWITNESS TO HISTORY

SERGEANT JAMES W. HURLBUT

I climbed to an outpost on top of Tulagi's cliff. Three hours went by without incident.

Then one—two—three—four destroyers moved our way around the north end of Savo Island. After two minutes, battleships appeared.

A Navy signalman peered through binoculars. "They're ours, all right," he said.

"The destroyers are in the moonlight now," he added, after a pause. "They're going straight cross to Guadalcanal. There come the battle wagons. The PT boats are going up to them."

He continued:

"They're all over by Guadalcanal now. They're lined up from Lunga Point along the coast to the west."

He shifted the glasses.

"Wait a minute! Two more destroyers just came around Savo. A third one is coming down from the tip of Florida."

"Whose are they?"

"Well, they're not ours. They're long, lean, low jobs with the superstructure way forward."

"Jap destroyers!"

"Looks like it. They're moving out into the channel. The first one is in the moonlight. Now they're all in line. They must have seen something. They've all turned around and are going like hell for the west side of Savo."

We peered at the black outline of Guadalcanal. Nothing but darkness. We felt anxiety that the Japs were going to get away.

"Look at that!" A tremendous burst of light had split the gloom near Lunga Point.

"I think that was a salvo from a battle wagon," the Navy signalman declared. "There it goes again!"

This time the heavy turret fire was obvious. Then there was another blast, almost simultaneous with one a few hundred yards further west.

Three or four minutes later sharp stabs of white light even further west indicated action by our destroyers. So far there had been no return fire from the Japanese position.

Suddenly the sky lit up on the west side of Savo.

"The Nips are opening up," the signalman exclaimed.

The whole sky was ablaze with mushrooms of flames from battleship turrets.

Incredibly rapid white flashes came from our destroyers. Dull yellow flashes came from byond Savo. The firing from the Guadalcanal side was four times as heavy as that from the north. A red glow suddenly stained the clouds above Savo.

"There's a hit, damned good one, too," the signalman cried out. More firing. More firing. The battleships were moving steadily north and west. The big flashes were coming from the tip of Cape Esperance. Lines of red tracers pierced the low-hanging clouds.

"Must be some cruiser planes in the air. Yeah, there's one. Looks like they got him. He's coming down."

The powerful binoculars brought the battle close to the lookout. We couldn't see the falling plane, but as we looked there was another eruption of red flame. This time it was right at the south edge of Savo, and it didn't go out. A ship—apparently a Jap vessel—had been hit and set afire.

"She's burning pretty good," the lookout reported. The burning vessel moved slowly toward midchannel and then crept back toward Savo.

On the horizon a huge mountain of red flame rose slowly. Star shells flew out of the red mass at crazy angles. They seemed to hang there a full minute and then darkness began to envelop its bulk.

The burning ship was in the area where the Japs were located. It must have been one of theirs.

As though the blast had been the signal for the end of the first act, the firing stopped. The only light on the horizon was the burning ship.

"It looks like a heavy cruiser," the lookout said. "Flames are spreading out on the water. Probably oil."

Ten minutes later two heavy flashes blazed from the southwest end of Savo. Almost immediately there were heavy yellow blasts from the north. It was not destroyer fire—much too heavy for that. Then the whole sky beyond was lit up by scores of star shells. Twenty-five or thirty miles away, they were still bright enough to bathe our cliff in daylight.

The fighting was terrific. Every minute or so, a red flash signaled a hit. The two forces stood toe to toe and slugged it out.

There was hardly a pause between the second and third acts. Without any cessation in the fire from the ships on the south, the slugging match turned into a chase to the northwest. Each bright flash was further away.

"Well, the lookout said, "somebody's running—and it isn't us."

We watched the ship burning on the horizon for a few minutes and then trekked slowly down the hill to our bunks. It was 1:30 A.M. Sunday. For the third straight night, we had watched naval action in the Guadalcanal-Tulagi Channel.

We don't get news very quickly here, but the reports we have received seem to bear out our conviction that America has won the greatest naval victory of the war.

※　※　※　※

ALTHOUGH THE DECISIVE SEA BATTLE WAS CONcluded, the Japanese did not give up in their reinforcement attempts for another ten weeks, and during that time a great many servicemen on both sides paid with their lives. But it was by then clear even to Yamamoto that our invasion of the South Pacific was a *fait accompli* and our forward-march was not to be thwarted, no matter the sacrifice. The United States Marines had paid in blood for this initial step, backed by the inflexible determination and lives of our seamen. We were on Guadalcanal to stay.

Here is the prolific Fletcher Pratt, author of a dozen military histories and military editor of the New York *Post* during the war years, to analyze the campaign.

·31· THE CAMPAIGN ANALYZED

FLETCHER PRATT

. . . They [the Japanese] had put 42,000 men ashore and something less than 10,000 got away. The rest were dead, as was over half of the 38th Division in that butchery under the planes on 14 November. The American dead for the whole campaign were 1,979; the wounded approximately 6,000, a difference in the figures that is perfectly amazing when one considers the slenderness of General Vandegrift's resources during most of the campaign. The disproportion was so great that nobody on our side would believe it until we began to get into the Japanese records, and the consistent underestimate of the enemy's casualties ashore is even more striking than the consistent overestimate of his casualties on the sea.

. . . One obvious reason for the high enemy losses is that the Jap medical service broke down completely, while ours was very good. Of their huge casualties, well over 10,000, probably nearly 20,000, were medical—disease and wounded who died for lack of medicaments and care. But this itself looks back to another failure on their side. Why did the Japanese medical service break down? Partly at least because medical supplies did not get to the island; they were bombed out and burned out on the way in, chiefly by the planes which flew from the island itself. Partly also the medical failure was only a portion of the bad staff planning which distinguished, or failed to distinguish, the whole Japanese operation for the recovery of Guadalcanal.

The staff work on our side was by no means perfect and plans frequently did not succeed. This is what one expects in war, where every contact is the result of the impact between two mutually exclusive plans. But if there is any one thing that stands out in the whole campaign it is how well our cause was served by the twenty-year background of training, planning, and experience possessed by the Marines. General Vandegrift and some of his staff were . . . pretty much worried in the beginning by what they considered the lack of training among their men and there was a good deal of beefing afterward to the effect that more physical hardening was needed. But they were looking at it from a very high standpoint, the standpoint of the U.S. Marine Corps, professional soldiers who had long ago worked out the answers to most of the problems involved. Japanese commanders, to note only one small but significant detail, complained they could not get their men to use the latrines; but sanitation is one of the first things a U.S. Marine thinks of when going ashore, especially in the tropics.

At another point there is a marked difference between the two forces involved. One is struck by the fact that the Japanese leaders, naval and military, were always waiting for somebody else to do something —the Navy for the Army to take the airfield, Kawaguchi for Oka, Oka for the Navy to shell out the American planes. It was the tradition, almost the doctrine of the Marines that, being given a job, they should go ahead and do it without yelling copper to anybody. The thing was carried too far sometimes, as in the Puller-Edson attack at the Matanikau, where the forces were simply inadequate for the job those two very energetic marines tried to carry through. But the system has its bright side also; the dog-tired Raiders did not ask for help in the Battle of Edson's Ridge (except from the artillery, to which help they were normally entitled) and against all expectation, including that of General Vandegrift's staff, found they could hold the place.

In actual contacts, of course, much of the Japanese failure can be traced to the mystical belief that a man with Bushido and a knife is better than a man with a tommy gun and a bellyful of beans. This piece of irrationalism is fundamental; without it, or something like it, the Japanese would never have gone to war against a nation so superior in every material resource. But whether criticism really lies on this score can be questioned. Most acts of war, most of war itself, are not very rational, and the history of human conflict is full of instances where apparent material odds were overcome . . . at Edson's Ridge for example, and in Callaghan's desperate naval action. The true failure lies rather in that tenacity, that particular type of tenacity, of which the Japanese were so very proud—their persistence in error, their unwillingness to alter a plan once it had been set in operation. After Admiral Abe and then Mikawa had failed on successive nights to put the Guadalcanal planes out of business, one would naturally expect planners of even elementary intelligence to realize that the transports carrying the 38th Division were walking into the dragon's jaws.

In all the operations of the marines on the island there is only one case of a similar inflexibility on our side, the move at the Matanikau when Edson, Puller, and Griffith got into trouble. Even here there was the excuse that the Americans involved were acting on faulty intelligence. At first sight it would seem that for many of the Japanese failures a similar excuse could be made; that this is the only explanation of why they put in first the Ichiki Detachment, then the Kawaguchi Brigade, and finally the Sendais against forces that were always so much superior to them. But on examination the general plea of faulty intelligence on the Japanese side does not stand up very well. Their intelligence was often faulty, but not in any fundamental way. The original Japanese G-2 estimate of the number of marines on Guadalcanal was far more accurate than the intelligence on which General Vandegrift had to work when he made the landing. All through the operation the Japanese were exceedingly well served on the sea by both their submarines and their air scouts, and if their air reconnaissance ashore was distinctly faulty, their patrols and listening posts in the Grassy Knoll region covered everything so completely that General Vandegrift could hardly cut his fingernails without have it reported across the line. After the war it was revealed that the Japanese had been extremely acute about intercepting and making use of American radio messages.

The Japanese command simply chose to disregard the intelligence it received. It went right on making elaborate plans, like that for the attack of the Sendai, as though the whole thing were a sand-table problem, in which the enemy's action need not be taken into account, with no room for the unit commander to exercise his discretion. After the plan was once made it was never on any account altered, either from above or below. The last feature is sufficiently puzzling; and at least one high American officer who has studied the problem considers that some of the difficulty here may lie in the fundamental character of the Japanese language, a poor instrument for either ratiocination or the rapid communication of ideas.

But there is not only the question of why the Japanese lost; there is also that of why the marines won. The difference is pronounced when one sets procedures of the marines against the specific reasons for Japanese failure. Marine training, Marine doctrine, or, to add it up, Marine experience gained through the years of peace, said very clearly that war could be made only by giving subordinates a task in fairly general terms and then letting them alone. If the officer assigned proved unequal to his task he was relieved before he could mess anything else up—and in this connection it is interesting to note that officers who flopped on one job not infrequently panned out very well on another, different kind of task, or even under another leader, with whom they could establish a more effective rapport. The system that succeeded on Guadalcanal was in fact one of treating each campaign and each part of a campaign as a separate operation, to be solved by the men on the job with native intelligence and in the light of the peculiar special conditions surrounding the case. All war is, of course, made up of special conditions, but in practice this flexibility . . . can be attained only when men have worked together for a long time on similar tasks and understand much of what is to be done without specific and detailed orders.

❧   ❧   ❧   ❧

DECEMBER 1942. WHAT FIGHTING REMAINED ON Guadalcanal was about to become the task of General Patch's Americal Division. Marine combat was nearly over. To conclude this brilliant and epochal chapter in the history of the Corps—if, indeed, in the history of our nation—here again is General Vandegrift.

·32· VALIANT DEEDS BY GREAT MEN

GENERAL ALEXANDER A. VANDEGRIFT AND ROBERT B. ASPREY

Our time was now growing short . . .

By dispatch I learned that on December 9 the 5th Marines would embark with other units going out in increments of a few days' interval. On December 7 I issued my final division letter on Guadalcanal, one in which I tried to summarize our accomplishments in these long, brutal months:

In relinquishing command in the Cactus Area I hope that in some small measure I can convey to you my feeling of pride in your magnificent accomplishments and my thanks for the unbounded loyalty, limitless self-sacrifice and high courage which have made those accomplishments possible. To the soldiers and marines who have faced the enemy in the fierceness of night and combat; to the Cactus pilots, Army, Navy, and Marine, whose unbelievable achievements have made the name "Guadalcanal" a synonym for death and disaster in the language of our enemy; to those who have labored and sweated within the lines at all manner of prodigious and vital tasks; to the men of the torpedo boat command slashing at the enemy in night sorties; to our small band of devoted allies who have contributed so vastly in proportion to their numbers; to the surface forces of the Navy associated with us in signal triumphs of their own, I say that at all times you have faced without flinching the worst that the enemy could do to us and have thrown back the best that he could send against us. It may well be that this modest operation begun four months ago today has, through your efforts, been successful in thwarting the larger aims of our enemy in the Pacific. The fight for the Solomons is not yet won but "tide what may" I know that you, as brave men and men of good will, will hold your heads high and prevail in the future as you have in the past.

Two days later in an informal ceremony I passed command of Guadalcanal to General Patch. That day men of the 5th Marines embarked, some so weak they could scarcely climb the cargo nets draped over the sides of the fat transports. Two days later I walked to our small cemetery called Flanders Field to take my own farewell of the almost 700 officers and men of my command who died in this operation. I looked in silence on the rude crosses that bespoke valiant deeds by great men. The words of Robert E. Lee came to mind:

What a cruel thing is war; to separate and destroy families and friends, and mar the purest joys and happiness God has granted us in this world; to fill our hearts with hatred instead of love for our neighbors, and to devastate the fair face of the beautiful world.

PART III

Munda to Cape Gloucester: Reduction of Rabaul

United States forces moved up into the myriad of islands northwest of Guadalcanal in mid-summer 1943, slowly expanding the perimeter to the central and northern Solomons. The advance was plagued by heat, rain, swamp and jungle, and Japanese every step of the way. Rabaul, the enemy's citadel of the Pacific, was the objective.

Japan developed Rabaul in early 1942 as a nerve center for her newly occupied forward positions in the Solomons and New Guinea, from whence she hoped to move southwestward to Australia; garrisons and airfields had been established in an attempt to screen the great redoubt from attack from the south. One of these, Munda on New Georgia, assumed strategic importance when General Hiroishi Immamura, senior Army commander at Rabaul, was ordered by Imperial General Headquarters to evacuate survivors of Guadalcanal and prepare a line of defense through New Georgia. As we have noted, the evacuation was carried out with such skill and stealth that Tokyo Radio was able to announce on February 8, 1943, that Hyakutate's Seventeenth Army had been whisked away from under American noses.

Thus, Munda became the first order of business for Admiral Halsey and General MacArthur. But hampered by a lack of warships and without control of the skies, the concurrent drives of south and southwest forces (a double thrust up through the Solomons and New Guinea terminating at Rabaul) were restricted necessarily to the land-based bomber line.

Briefly, three considerations dictated the selection of Munda as the next big Solomons objective: New Georgia lay within the radius of Halsey's fighter planes, so that he could safely cover amphibious operations; he wanted a target near enough to Tulagi's harbor in the event that a strong Japanese task force came down from Rabaul (à la Mikawa); and, finally, it seemed possible to overcome with a minimum of troops and warships. Conversely, if the enemy was allowed to continue to use Munda's 4700 foot airstrip, his very presence in the area constituted a threat to our hard-won bases.

But in spite of Halsey's burning desire to capture Munda with one fell swoop, his staff prevailed on him to take an intermediate step: occupation of the Russells, 35 miles from Cape Esperance, although in seizure of these islands we faced the distinct possibility of a Japanese retaliation by sea force. Halsey and Army's Lieutenant General M. L. Harmon prepared for the worst, including a defense at the water's edge.

Combat units assigned to the operation were the 3rd Raider Battalion; 10th Battalion, Fleet Marine Force; a detachment of the 11th Defense Battalion; and Marine Air Group 21. Harmon committed the bulk of his 43rd Infantry Division. The marine target was Pavuvu, in the south; Army's, Banika, in the north.

At 11 P.M., February 20, 1943, Task Force 62 steamed out of Guadalcanal screened by a strong covering group of warships. Eight destroyers, towing small landing craft loaded to the gunwales, led the procession. Astern were 12 LCTs piled high with 700 tons of ammunition. The landings took place in the black hours the next morning.

Now an accredited combat correspondent with sergeant's stripes, Jim Lucas, details this first forward step from the 'Canal.

· 1 · OCCUPATION OF THE RUSSELLS

JIM LUCAS

We were due to hit at 5 A.M., before dawn. At 4:10 we cut our motors and began gliding into Paddy Bay.

I stood at the rail, my heart in my throat.

"There it is," said First Sergeant Staihr. He ought to know, I thought. He made the maps.

My knees began to tremble, and I sat down, bitterly ashamed of myself. But I couldn't help it. The suspense, I found later, is always harder than real combat.

Dark masses of land began slowly to materialize. This was Pavuvu. To the right was Bycee. We watched them, the suspense wearing us down. When would the firing start?

It was now 5 A.M., and still we moved. I felt the first surge of alarm. We were late!

We could now make out the outline of trees on the islands, and I saw a Jap back of every one of them.

Suddenly there was a plane overhead. I wilted. It was ours, but the discovery came too late to save me a nervous breakdown.

Dawn now was breaking, and we had stopped. We could see the outline of other ships in Paddy Bay—I can testify there is no more comforting feeling than the certainty that you are not alone—and the plantation buildings lining the waterfront.

There was another plane overhead. But it carried landing lights. It was also ours.

Still there was no firing. There was a weird, uncanny feeling about the whole business.

The first boats were in the water. They had gone over the side so quickly that I had missed it. I was surprised to see them manned and ready to start the dash to the beach.

"Those boys will catch hell," someone said.

Now it was our turn. We piled into a Higgins boat with the colonel. My entrenching tool, a shovel which I carried on the back of my pack, caught in the cargo net and I was dragged back as the boat moved away. The sergeant major freed me, but I was shaken. I thought again of the kid I'd seen drown the first day in Noumea.

We darted among the rubber boats, the colonel placing them in order. At the prow of one we saw Morang, busy with his oars. I grinned. Joe was working for this story.

The colonel's landing boat moved swiftly about the bay. Still there was no sound from shore. It could be a good sign or a bad one. No one was certain what lay ahead. My imagination, however, supplied the details. I began to wonder where I'd be within the hour, two hours, by nightfall, next week. The future offered many possibilities.

At 6:20 A.M. we headed for shore. We made three futile tries before we found a break through the coral, for Paddy Bay was full of the dangerous, treacherous nigger-heads for which the Solomons are notorious. As our boat nudged the sand, the first marines were on the beach, ready for trouble. Still burdened with too much gear, I struggled to the side of the boat, balancing myself precariously. As I stepped into the water to wade ashore, my automatic lifebelt inflated, giving me the appearance of an outraged toad.

Still there was no sound. Our assault waves moved inland fifty yards, and spread out in defensive formation. Others searched out the nineteen wharf buildings fronting the bay, with drawn bayonets. Not a Jap.

Colonel Liversedge came ashore and headed immediately for the abandoned plantation office where he was to set up headquarters. Captain Peters went with him, but I remained behind to assist in unloading supplies which were now coming in from the destroyers. Morang, in the rubber boat, had still to reach the beach. Thirty minutes later, thoroughly exhausted, he was to pull in, swearing that he had done more work than any man in the Russells campaign.

Waist-deep in water, I waded out to the first boatload of supplies and took my spot in the work chain. Interminably they came, boxes of ammunition, food, weapons.

"Swing them," someone yelled.

"I've got no swing left," I gasped.

Mott and Golub were busy with their cameras. Their pictures were later to appear in full-page spreads in most of the nation's big dailies. It was our first offensive since Guadalcanal.

An hour later I stumbled to Colonel Liversedge's command post to await orders. Mindful of the danger of air attacks, I began my first foxhole, staking out in a coconut grove to the rear of the plantation office.

It was a back-breaking job, for the soil of the Russells is three-fourths coral rock and one-fourth coconut root. I worked for thirty minutes without accomplishing a great deal. Captain Peters appeared and overruled my selection of a bivouac area, and I was glad of an excuse to stop.

The skies over Pavuvu were full of planes, but they were ours. We had been in the Russells three hours without sight of the enemy.

We began to feel an unreasonable, angry disappointment. We deserved more than this! Where were the 700 Japanese we had been promised?

Captain Peters went into conference to place us with the combat patrols. Joe, worn and tired, sat glumly on a coconut stump, disconsolately munching his K ration. I was too hot to eat.

Stavisky was ashore, and we watched him suspiciously.

The captain emerged and made his assignment. He and Joe were to go to Bycee, where there probably would be fighting. I was to accompany a second patrol to Mani. I was bitterly disappointed at missing possible action, but felt compensated because Mani was the nearest of the Russells to the big Japanese garrison on New Georgia. Vangunu, tip of the New Georgia chain, could be seen from the far end of Mani. Stavisky was to remain at Pavuvu. He took it all in good spirits, and appeared satisfied with his assignment.

Captain Peters and Joe left for Bycee, while my patrol fumbled with a balky outboard motor before leaving for Mani. An hour passed, and we called for a second boat. It, too, was jinxed. It was now mid-afternoon, and Mani was as yet unexplored. Alarm spread among the junior officers. It was possible, they knew, that reinforcements would be brought in from New Georgia, and Mani was the logical beachhead.

At 3 P.M. we got a boat and set out. Past the tip of Bycee, on which we could see an abandoned native village, we moved through Hooker Bay. Our luck held good, but off Bycee our motor stalled. Frantically the coxswains worked over it, while we sweltered in the sun and wondered if we'd spend the night at sea. Unable to help, we stripped and swam in the bay.

A mere spot on the horizon, someone spotted a canoe. Curious, we waited for it to come within range. It drew alongside, bearing five black natives, grinning their welcome to the Russell Islands.

I noted that each wore a small silver cross around his neck, and recalled that the Russells was a missionary outpost of the Church of England. New Georgia, on the other hand, was allotted to the Methodist Church under an unwritten gentlemen's agreement of the various missions.

Mott was busy with his camera.

One of the natives, obviously the leader, spoke. "I am Jappa," he said. "I am brother of Tami, the chief."

Jappa proved to be a find. He spoke our language with ease, and was a storehouse of information about the Russells. It was evident, however, that Tami, his brother and chief, was Jappa's perfect man. Quite frequently he would tell us, when he could not answer our questions, that the information was available if we would but ask Tami, who knew all things. This personage we were never to see. The Melanesians of the Russells jealously guard the persons of their chief and women, and were anxious that the white man see as little of them as possible.

We distributed cigarettes and ration chocolate, which the natives puffed and gulped hungrily. We had been warned to consume the highly concentrated chocolate bars slowly, and I was later to learn from bitter experience that too much, too quickly, can make a man deathly sick. But the black men wolfed it down, and I still wonder if there was not an epidemic of bellyaches among them that night.

Jappa told us that he had come to greet the white soldiers. His people, he said, were all on Leru, which accounted for the abandoned villages we saw then and later. They had gone there upon the arrival of the Japanese. On the whole, he said, the Japanese had treated the natives well, but the islands' tiny Chinese colony had fared badly.

"All Chinese boys shot dead," Jappa said. I recalled that the files in the plantation office had indicated a sizeable Chinese working class, and correspondence had ordered a strict observance of Chinese holidays.

Yes, Jappa had seen and talked with the Japanese. He frequently had gone from Leru to Pavuvu and Bycee, he said, to ask for food.

The Japanese, he said, had hastily departed the Russells two weeks before we arrived, apparently forewarned, or merely guessing at what was ahead. They had used the Russells as a staging point in their evacuation of Guadalcanal, and could hardly have been expected not to know that their position there was no longer tenable. But our disappointment was keen. We cursed our luck—and were secretly relieved, I feel certain.

"Leave in three big ships, big guns," Jappa said. We surmised they were cruisers, though they might have been oversized destroyers.

Jappa laughed quietly. I am sure this black man had developed a tolerance for the white and yellow men who insisted on killing each other when the mission books clearly said it was wrong.

But Jappa bore the Japanese one grudge. In leaving, he said, the enemy had destroyed all the natives' gardens, forcing them to replant. Since the Russell Islanders exist mainly on yams and taro roots, they were hard put to survive.

And the Japs, he said with unaccustomed bitterness, had killed their pigs. This, by all the rules of Melanesian good conduct, was unpardonable. Pigs are sacred.

Generously and, I hasten to add, with no authority from Washington, we promised to feed the natives. They grinned their appreciation. Other native canoes arrived, and we distributed more cigarettes and chocolates until they were exhausted. The stream of visitors ended abruptly.

Jappa and his party paddled away to visit the white men on Pavuvu, he said, his native crew making better time with their paddles than we had done with our balky outboard.

Stranded, we continued to labor with our motor. A Higgins boat rounded the point, and we hailed it. It was the colonel's craft, its mission to Bycee completed. I spotted Joe and Captain Peters in the crew. We hooked on, and were towed in a tour of the Russells. It was dusk when we returned.

There had been, the captain reported, no Japanese on Bycee, only signs of a hasty withdrawal. We complained anew, but with the same sense of relief.

After all, I reasoned, we had accomplished what we had set out to do. The Russells were now completely ours, for the Army had landed on Banka a few hours after we took over on Pavuvu, giving us a new base from which to continue our drive north. We were within sight of the Japanese on New Georgia. We had done all this in twenty-four hours, without the loss of a man.

"It's best," Joe counseled. "If there'd been opposition, there'd be a lot of American kids here tonight with holes in their bellies. There will be plenty of that soon enough."

Sure, I agreed, we've done it, and we're still in condition to fight. But it wasn't, I told myself, much of a story.

I went with the captain to inventory the plantation office. In an outhouse in the rear, I found a smashed short-wave radio set, and recalled that Jappa had told us that the first warning of the Jap occupation had been sent by the English plantation manager after the natives had spotted the ships. The office was wrecked. In the kitchen we found a half-empty bottle of Australian rum. Files had been sacked, and scattered over the floor. Apparently the Japs had searched and wrecked the office and then retired to Bycee to construct their defenses.

Joe Morang and I, now fast friends, retired early. We pitched our shelters in the coconut grove, brewed our synthetic coffee, and washed briefly off the pier. Joe cut himself on the coral and went to sick bay for treatment, because coral can cause a nasty infection. More conservative, I had bathed with my shoes on.

Dead tired, we were in our sack before 7:30. Joe had proved himself from the minute we left New Caledonia. Like an angry mother, he had sheltered me, shoving me into corners to protect me from the bombing, clucking at me excitedly when he thought I needlessly exposed myself to danger. I had completely revised my opinion of the big boy from China.

It began to rain, and again our shelter was inadequate. We were soaked to the skin, but it was not a new experience. Sleep came quickly, but during the night we were awakened by a loud explosion. Bombs! we thought. But it was only a clap of thunder, and we laughed at ourselves.

"There will certainly be an air raid tomorrow," Joe said, and I agreed.

At dawn Joe discovered that a company of marines had a mess tent in operation. Importantly he took pictures of the cooks while I bustled around with notebook and pencil. We were rewarded with an excellent meal, including hot fried apricot pies.

However, there had been no air raid. I began to growl. Come on, you Japs on New Georgia. Here we are. You know by now we're here. We've moved into your backyard and you won't fight.

At mid-morning I made a startling discovery. Our Tommy guns were missing. Excitedly I reported the theft to the sergeant major, who instituted a search. Joe's was found in some coconut husks in one of the warehouses, but mine was never located. I drew another Reising.

Soldiers who eventually were to take over the island had landed during the night. We had heard them marching through the rain, their heavy gear setting up a thunderous clatter. At dawn they were sleeping on the soggy ground, too tired to care. We walked among them. They did not stir.

Every night for a week thereafter new troops were to come ashore. Some of the soldiers we had met aboard the transport. Among them was the corporal who had been Joe Hardy's guard. They brought equipment, including the inevitable jeeps and heavy guns. We began to feel more secure.

Some of the Army units even brought cots, and Joe and I were later to steal a couple for our first good night's rest.

Shortly after dawn a Grumman roared low over the coconut groves. We stared. It returned, wigwagging. A third time, and it dropped a message. I retrieved it and ran to the command post.

"Boat stranded off Mani," it said.

A relief party quickly was organized. I piled in. Mott also went along.

The trip required two hours, and was tediously slow. Shortly after 10 A.M. we arrived off Mani. One of our Higgins boats, its motor out, had been shelved on the coral. Its crew had spent the night in sight of New Georgia without incident, although their nerves were frayed. We hooked on, and began the job of towing them back to Pavuvu.

Midway, we met another boat, this one bound for Hooker Bay to inspect a wrecked Zero. Mott and I changed boats and went along. The Zero was under water, but was hauled out. Caution paid dividends, for the cockpit had been armed with a booby trap. Our men dismantled it, and it exploded harmlessly. I learned a valuable lesson that day. The pilot, dead at least two weeks, was a skeleton. In Hooker Bay, at low tide, we saw a half-sunk Japanese destroyer, blasted in one of the battles around Guadalcanal.

That night we had a report that a Japanese patrol had landed on the far side of the island. It turned out to be a group of our own men. I recall, too, that one of our outlying observation posts was seen that night frantically signalling from another island. Deciphered, the message read:

"What's cooking?"

The boys narrowly avoided a serious jam, and it was never repeated.

We were by this time living off the Army. The Raiders had brought a minimum of supplies, and they were quickly exhausted. Our cooks drove hard bargains, for they were used to this sort of thing and the hard-bitten Raiders, I am afraid, treated the Army boys shamelessly. I like particularly the story of the soldiers guarding a chow dump near the beach who were approached by a squad of marines.

"Okay, boys," the marines said. "You're relieved. You can eat now."

Happily the soldiers took off. When they returned, the entire dump was missing, and so were their relief guards.

Joe and I moved that night into one of the plantation buildings, willing to risk bombs for a dry night's sleep. The housewife asserted itself in me, and I carefully swept down all the spider webs. Mosquitoes and flies, as a result, made sleep impossible, and Joe abused me roundly.

I soon found Morang a capable sleep talker. For weeks he was to amuse us with his outbursts. On this first night, he sat up, screaming:

"Lucas! Lucas! For God's sake, help me!"

I lost ten years' growth. Joe insisted the next morning that it never happened.

The inevitable all-day poker sessions began. Joe and Stavisky never missed a game, but I knew my limitations and stayed out. My own typewriter was missing, but Sam generously let me use his. I began to revise my estimate of our pet hate.

Across the poker table, Joe and Sam got together. Both claimed they could judge a man by the game he played, and by nightfall they were fast friends. That evening the three of us sat on the beach and sealed our friendship. I was never more wrong in my life than in my first impression of Sam Stavisky. But it was now water under the bridge.

The poker game continued for a full week, from daylight until dark. Our rations, meanwhile, had improved with arrival of the Army, and we were enjoying the stay.

On the fifth day Captain Peters left for Guadalcanal. He ran into a real air raid at Tulagi, more trouble than we'd had in a week at the front. In leaving he had hinted at a special mission for the colonel. I had wanted to go along, but had been turned down. I remained behind and continued my writing, interrupted only when we made a training film of rubber-boat landings on Mani.

Mott and Golub continued to do good work with their cameras. We soon learned to call our chubby New York corporal "Mother" Mott, for his careful attention to Golub was the butt of many jokes. On Guadalcanal, Walter had gone down with malaria. Mott had worn himself out doctoring his boy, demanding that he take his medicine, feeding him with a spoon. On the Russells, Mott cooked all the meals, made the beds, and watched after "Walluh" with an eagle eye.

"Mother" Mott was responsible for one of my best stories. On the third night, he hit on the idea of using their shelter halves for a hammock, strung between two coconut trees. It was an excellent idea, with only one drawback. It rained every night we were in the Russells.

They awoke at midnight to find that their hammocks had become bathtubs. Mott looked at Golub. Golub looked at Mott. They laughed. Stripped to the skin, they soaped off in their hammocks, and then stood in the rain to shower. It was the only fresh water bath I know of in the Russells.

On the fourth day I went to Bycee. A patrol had established itself in the abandoned native village. Far back in the jungles, we found the Jap bivouac area, so secluded that the enemy had marked their trails with vines. On the beaches we found abandoned Japanese honey, later to be tested by our doctors and added to our larder. There were Jap landing barges, stoves and hundreds of rounds of machine gun ammunition.

It was evident the Japs had left hurriedly.

On one of the abandoned camp sites, littered with Jap life preservers, clothing and rotting fish and rice, we found abandoned Japanese medical supplies, including hundreds of bottles of vitamin pills trademarked by the Dai Nippon Brewery, Tokyo, with instructions printed in English.

"With their diet," our doctor said, "they need them."

I found a souvenir postcard from Davao, in the Philippines.

"Well, we know where *these* bastards have been," commented the doctor.

I found several sets of chopsticks, my first authentic souvenirs of the Pacific war.

We admired the Japanese dugouts, for we have long since learned that the enemy is a past master at digging in. Cut in solid rock, beneath the roots of banyan trees, they were hard to spot until you were upon them. It must have taken the Nips several months to build such defenses, only to abandon them without a fight.

There were Japanese graves, some of them comparatively new, indicating that the enemy had been in the Russells some time before our arrival.

At the native church we found that the enemy had used for toilet paper the Church of England's song books, in which hymns were printed in pidgin English.

I returned laden with souvenirs, and the next day I met Martin Nelson.

Nelson was a Hollywood director's dream of a South Sea island beachcomber. Over seventy, with a long, drooping white mustache, soiled white linens and a huge white sun helmet, he strode onto the beach at Pavuvu out of nowhere.

When I met Martin Nelson in the Russells, he was a busy man. Manager of a trading post on Santa Isabelle Island, then still under the heel of the Japs, he had come to guide our boats through the coral reefs. For three days he had stood on the bridge of an American destroyer, finding little time to eat or sleep. He had been at breakfast when they called him to go ashore. Resolutely he had gone back to work.

We took Martin Nelson to our galley, where he wolfed down hot cakes and soggy bacon. He downed four cups of steaming coffee without a halt. I sat on the beach while he told me his story.

When the Japs had come to Santa Isabelle—it is now ours—Nelson had ample warning. Twelve hours before they arrived, his boys had brought him word. It was a simple matter for the old trader to fade back into the bush and disappear. The Japs had come, and at Rekata Bay had constructed one of their biggest seaplane bases.

"I just dropped back deep," Nelson said. "I saw the Japs often. They never saw me. If they had, I wouldn't be here."

Finally, with the invasion of the Russells imminent, Martin Nelson could become of use and made his way out to sea in a native canoe.

One of our PT boats picked him up. He had joined our forces, and helped to make occupation of the Russells possible.

Nelson was a native of Norway, but had spent most of his life in the Pacific in the British colonies. He hoped to die there.

While we talked, word came that Nelson had to go back to his destroyer. He downed his last cup of coffee and was away.

On the seventh day we had our first air raid. It came at noon, while the beach was loaded with supplies, and several boats were in Paddy Bay. In our quarters, we heard the planes roar in. I darted to the door to see the strafing start. I hit the ground while machine gun slugs cut the dirt around me. Seven men were killed, many of them in the warehouse at the end of the pier from which we used to swim in the bay. Miraculously a rubber boat returning from Bycee, while sunk, did not lose a man, for all of them went over the side and later swam to shore.

I scrambled to my feet and ran for the foxholes. But there was only one wave of attackers. Our fighters chased the Japs away, shooting down two of the five planes.

Stavisky, with the rest of us, went through the air raid calmly enough. That night, however, he spotted two large spiders hanging over his cot. With an unearthly howl, Sam was outside, and we could not induce him to come back inside. He slept outdoors for the rest of the Russells campaign. Bombs, yes; spiders, no.

Captain Peters returned. We were, he said, to go back to New Caledonia if we could find transportation. We were to become sea-going hitchhikers. Mott and Stavisky were to remain, but the rest of us would find our way home.

We left at noon the eighth day, aboard a tank lighter which took us to Banka. I have never seen anything so forlorn as Mott standing on the pier and waving good-by. "Walluh" was going along, and Mott was certain he would not receive the requisite care. That evening we were able to eat with a Marine defense battalion on Banka, and made arrangements to sleep in the hospital. We looked forward to a good night's rest, but were doomed to disappointment.

Captain Peters, meanwhile, had made arrangements to go aboard a destroyer at 2 A.M., and, fearful that we would miss connections, insisted that we sleep on the beach. There I discovered the wreckage of another Zero, and stripped off sufficient metal to make a bracelet later on. I lost that bracelet in the Gilberts. Rafael Garcia, a PFC (later a staff sergeant) from Laredo, Texas, entertained us with Mexican songs. His fine baritone voice soon drew a crowd, and we cheered happily until we drifted off to sleep.

At 1 A.M. we set out by Higgins boat. It was dark, and we feared we might be fired on by our own batteries. Two boats, unable to give

the recognition signal, had had that fate the night previous. Our coxswain told us he had been aboard our transport during our night
attack in February.

We were unable to pick up our can, which was to lie off Sunlight
Channel and wait for us. We moved out. Finally we saw it, a black
hulk looming up on the black sea. We drew alongside and scrambled
aboard.

The sailors treated us royally. We were given bunks, hot coffee
and sent to bed. At daylight there were fresh eggs, the first we had
seen since San Diego, and more coffee. They loaded us with cigarettes
and clothing.

By noon we were back at Guadalcanal, and left for shore. Captain
Peters went to arrange for transportation, and we waited on the beach.
A native sidled over.

"You here with Japs?" I asked.

"Me here," he said.

"You like Japs?" I asked.

"No, no, like Melicans," he replied. I gave him cigarettes, reflecting that the begger probably had told the Japs the same thing. I
learned later I was dead wrong, the natives of the Solomons were our
staunch allies.

We were in luck. Captain Peters was able to get us aboard a transport, which only recently had come to the Pacific from the North
African invasion. Better still, she was empty, and we would be the
only troops aboard. We drew quarters among the COP's, and looked
forward to a pleasant cruise.

It wasn't in the cards. The transport was shorthanded, and we were
given gun watches. I gained a new respect for sailors. I never slept
more than five hours at a time for the next five days. The sailors did
not seem to mind, but I was dead on my feet.

The second day out, the weather grew bad. I had never been in
a storm at sea, and confidently expected to go down. It broke, and
I was pleasantly surprised to find I could weather it. I enjoyed the
whole show, particularly those moments when we were relieved to
go below for a cup of hot coffee.

Standing there at the rail, my eyes peeled for the sight of danger,
I fancied myself the guardian of Democracy. My responsibilities
weighed heavily on my shoulders. The safety of this big ship, which
cost many millions of dollars, was mine.

When I relieved Joe on watch that first night, he reported:

"An enemy sub aft blinking to one forward."

I looked for four hours and saw nothing. Joe was indignant. He
felt that his veracity had been challenged.

The storm continued, hard and bitter. The radio room reported it was the tail end of one which had swept the Bismarck Sea. The Japs, you will remember, tried to ride it in to New Guinea, but it lifted and moved out to us in the Coral Sea.

Reports of the famous Battle of the Bismarck Sea began to come in. Systematically our bombers had destroyed 122 enemy ships in one convoy. We were elated. We could take bad weather if it meant this.

Just before we reached Noumea, the storm lifted. On that last day, standing at my post, I spotted two ships on the horizon. I reported them to the bridge.

"A cruiser and a destroyer, unidentified," came the report.

My excitement grew. But they were our own.

We made many friends aboard, including Father Foley, ship's chaplain, a first-rate person. It was good to see him striding about the decks in his wet slicker. The men liked and respected him.

Finally we were home, back to the Paris of the Pacific. Our first big adventure was over.

There was a delay in getting off, and we reached the docks after dark. Waiting for transportation, I walked over to a marine at the curb.

"Has there been any announcement about the Russells?" I asked.

"I heard a rumor we took it," he replied, "but I don't believe nothing."

I remained silent.

Back in Goettge, the boys greeted us joyfully. McDevitt shook hands, and we tore up my farewell notes. I had a stack of forty-two letters waiting for me, and I read each before going to bed.

That night, in my own sack, I regaled the boys with stories from the Russells. Across the way someone yelled: "Knock it off. We wanna sleep!"

I yelled back: "Listen, Mac" (every marine is "Mac" to another), "I've been with the Raiders in the Russells. Don't tell me what to do, you office soldier!"

The courthouse reporter had become a combat correspondent and a raider.

※   ※   ※   ※

WITH THE RUSSELLS SECURED, LET US BRIEFLY LEAVE the war zone. The Marine Corps, as all armed forces, urgently needed new officers as the youth of the country rushed to enlistment centers. For by now the Corps had reached the growth stage where it was no longer patronizingly regarded as "a band of brothers," in official quarters, but rather as a potent fighting machine which would put six full divisions in the field by the end of World War II.

At Quantico, Virginia, where Corps trained its officer candidates, Lieutenant General Thomas Holcomb, Seventeenth Commandant, addressed a graduation class of second lieutenants and spoke of the responsibilities and qualities of leadership that were expected of young men wearing shiny gold bars.

·2· THE COMMANDANT ADDRESSES NEW OFFICERS

LIEUTENANT GENERAL THOMAS HOLCOMB

It is no accident that you wear bars on your shoulders today. You earned them—and while they entitle you to certain privileges and recognition, they also place upon you a very definite responsibility. The manner in which you wear them will affect the reputation of the Marine Corps. If you wear them well, with courage, with intelligence, and with due humility, you will enhance our reputation. Reputation in the end is only a by-product of our acts. Reputation, to be real, like respect, must be earned—not demanded.

The Marine Corps has earned its reputation—it is not an accident. It comes from two sources—training and experience in combat—more than a hundred and sixty-seven years of both, as far as the Marine Corps is concerned. I repeat, our reputation and proficiency are not accidents.

Each of our previous operations has taught us lessons that are useful in succeeding operations. Warfare is continually changing in a tactical sense—that is, in its employment of new and ever-improving weapons. There can be little change in the strategical sense—that is, in the concentration of force where the enemy is weak, resolve to carry through and press an advantage, use of the element of surprise, meticulous planning in advance, gaining as much knowledge as possible of the enemies' strength, disposition, plans and habits, and a willingness and ability to change and improvise when the occasion demands it.

In the course of this war, on a scale which the world has never before seen, it is possible to lose sight of what your particular job is—of what the Marine Corps' job really is. The Marine Corps' primary function is to prepare the way for other troops. Ours is an amphibious operation—it has been recently called a "triphibious" operation. For that purpose we have trained for over a hundred and sixty-seven years. We are today, I believe, the most proficient amphibious military body in the world, and I say this with due modesty. We are so because of our experience and our training and our morale, which is a result of this experience and training.

It is no accident that the Marines are the First to Fight. They were the first U.S. troops to fight offensively in this war. They are the first because they must prepare the way. Because they are the first they must always be ready—you must be ready. With the many landings which will be required in the Pacific before Japan is finally conquered, many more opportunities will be presented us.

This specialized requirement of the Marine Corps requires specialized training. That is the reason for our schools, for this school. We are proud of our schools. We are confident they are the best in the world for our particular job. They not only give you the experience we have obtained in fighting under varying and every-changing conditions in many parts of the world, they give you also the most exhaustive research of landing operations of others throughout the world's written military history. And many of us have had the advantage, because of our peculiar amphibious job, of studying in the best of the Army and Navy Schools, an advantage that officers in other branches of the military profession do not often get.

This schooling, this training, however, does not make us better Army officers than the best Army officers or better Naval officers than the best Navy officers. They can run the Army far better than we can. They can run the Navy far better than we can. But by the same token, because of our specialized training, we can run amphibious and landing operations better than they can. With our tradition, experience, and our training, they could run amphibious operations as effectively as we can, but they do not spend their lives in this specialization. We do.

Now all this training, all this experience, will be of little avail unless it is built on the proper material, on men of the right character. We must have men who feel a sense of responsibility to their country, a sense of responsibility which makes them willing to take chances, to risk their lives if necessary, in dangerous and different tasks. We must have men who want to learn; men who realize that discipline is essential for the best results, who recognize they have a responsibility to the men under them as well as to those above them. We must have men who realize that teamwork is important, that it pays dividends. And finally, we must have men who realize that they must cultivate ingenuity, inventiveness for the occasion when those qualities are required.

A marine, you see, is therefore a man who disciplines himself and accepts discipline from others when required. He is a man who has practiced and learned self-control. Some of the best marines I have known are soft-spoken, quiet men. They are usually the qualities of the men with the most resolve and the most courage. Loud talkers are often those of little control, often the indication of an inferiority. Now this sounds as if our men are all the ideal—they are not—some have these qualities to a greater degree than others. The greater the degree to which we have them, the greater the success we shall have in the jobs assigned to each of us.

With the proper character and this training you will gain confidence—and confidence you must have—confidence, not cockiness, and confidence comes from knowing how to do your job. It comes from training, from experience—it comes only the hard way.

You officers will be leaders in our future operations. Leadership is not easy; it is not automatic. You must be possessed of those qualities of leadership which command respect and loyalty—which inspire in all hands the determination—and more important—the compelling desire to work together for a common end. No graph, no chart, no rules and regulations or other printed words can take the place of such leadership. May you have it to the greatest degree possible.

❧   ❧   ❧   ❧

BY MAY 1943, MARINE AIR GROUP 21 POUNDED AWAY steadily at Munda. Fighters and bombers hit the strip by day, and formidable Navy task forces worked it over by night. But always capable Japanese engineers repaired their installation (Henderson in reverse), and our firepower had little effect in blunting the fighting spirit of the island's garrison. Captain John Abney, an Intelligence officer, thumbed a ride on the so-called "milk run," and described his adventures in a powerful story which appeared in the *Marine Corps Gazette.*

·3· "WE ARE GOING TO DITCH . . ."

CAPTAIN JOHN ABNEY

Our mission was to bomb and strafe any buildings or positions the Japs might occupy along the beach of the little harbor or back in the plantation. We were in our attack formation headed in for the first run. Time: 0800 hours. The plane . . . was the second one in the formation. Since I had come along as an observer and hell raiser in general, I sat in the nose surrounded by plexiglass and the increasing roar of the plane's motors. I had a machine gun with which to put my two-bits' worth into the argument so everything was fine.

There was a lot of stuff ahead of us . . . a timid looking pier with a tired, old, rusty barge alongside, plenty of buildings and huts, a few boats under palm-leaf sheds and what appeared to be supply dumps scattered around the beach. The whole atmosphere seemed so serene and beautiful I almost forgot about the mission and what would be happening in the next minute or so. We were at 500 feet still coming down and perhaps a mile offshore. I charged my gun and flipped the safety catch off, then started lining up on the building just back of the pier. We were coming down fast. Eric, the pilot, called on the inter-phone to let me know about a bunch of Japs that were running from a hut near the water and cutting across the beach for the jungle. So we turned a few degrees off our course long enough to squirt a long burst at them and switched quickly back to the target.

Smoke from burnt gunpowder chokes you and makes your eyes water but you don't mind if you have a gun to jump around in your hands and can send your tracers out to probe at anything that may strike your fancy. And if you can see the tracers bouncing off or digging into a building or gun position, the smoke even acquires a delicate and celestial aroma.

Then everything began to stand up and move rapidly. Things never seem to get closer to me when we are low; they just get bigger. The timid pier that crouched in the water and the tired barge suddenly lurched and were beneath us, then buildings, huts, scattered oil drums and bomb craters that had filled with water. The sea of coconut palms and the crawling creek spilled together in a blur dotted and slashed by smoking tracers, bulged by sudden mushrooms of black smoke and wreckage. You couldn't see much because it was over too quickly. At three miles a minute it takes 20 seconds to cross a strip of land a mile wide and that isn't much time when you try to hit everything at once.

Then we were out over the water, climbing and circling for our second run. Planes were still scooting across the target that had now begun to take on the aspect of war. To me one of the most realistic pictures of destruction to be seen is that of huge geysers of smoke, dirt and debris belching skyward from a mass of flame and thunder and in the midst of it all, little planes darting along spitting tracers at the world in general.

Sure, the planes themselves are 15 tons of hell and wildcat, but they look like pee wees in the midst of all the destruction they spread. And once the bombs start falling there is no power, force or prayer that is going to prevent what will happen when they hit. All you can do is get flatter than you ever got before and hope.

Perhaps that is what makes the sight of an air raid a perfect picture of devastation. And that is what this was. The last plane had crossed the target and the mushrooms from her bombs had sprung up to take their places with the rest.

A heavy pall of black and grey hung over the whole target now and it looked as though we had really covered this end of it. But we had three more runs to make yet . . . one on this end and then two coming in from the other side and slightly above the spot we were hitting now. No one had seen any fire returned or any activity at all, for that matter, other than the monkeys running along the beach. But that was all right by me. You get over the Hollywood idea of wanting them to fight back after they do it a couple of times.

The armor plate door banged against my knee and Leo, the navigator, slid out of the crawlway to have a look around. The inter-phone buzzed and everyone reported ok on their respective stations. The tail gunner thought our bombs had hit the big building behind the pier but when you are low, turning and going fast, it is hard to tell.

Here we were again, headed in on about the same course but a little below the pier and almost to the beach. One run is about the same as another insofar as the scenery is concerned. Everything is very clear and gradually grows until you reach it, then it seems to leap at the plane and melts into the same mass of blurs and tracers with the spectacular blossoms of fire, smoke and wreckage to climax the run.

That is all the second one amounted to. We dumped our bombs ok and sprayed plenty of tracers around the buildings and landscape in general. Leo was kneeling beside me watching for any sort of activity, but as before, no one seemed to have noticed any. Either they were well hidden and not hitting back or we were too intent to see everything that was taking place.

We were a couple of hundred feet over the sea now, circling to come in on the other end of the target. The other planes behind us were still crossing their points and tearing up as much as they could. I looked out at the whole island and thought that once war comes, it really comes to stay.

There was a perfectly clear tropical sky, a calm and almost indifferent, freshly painted sea and a lush, green island that were a picture of paradise, untouched and unaffected by the small spot of rocking, twisted, torn, exploding hell in the midst of it all. Except for the one spot, it even looked peaceful.

I punched Leo in the ribs and told him to sit on the box so he could strafe with the gun the next time over. He slid forward and we changed places. The coastline darted past and Eric called all stations on the inter-phone to let them know we were coming in. Ahead was a queer, horseshoe-shaped hill that seemed to be all out of place away from the rest of the mountains; a listless, twisted river and beyond that the buildings scattered in clusters among the palms.

Leo charged his gun and fingered the trigger. I settled down just behind him and looked the place over pretty well. The other end of the target was smoky and hard to see, but this end might have been on the other side of the world for all appearances.

We were down low and the horseshoe hill looked as though it wanted-ed to push us right back when it jumped up and spilled beneath. We were almost within machine gun range now. I watched to the sides and ahead for muzzle flashes but saw none. There was the river. I punched Leo on the shoulder and pointed to the buildings ahead.

Eric opened up with all the guns and Leo started his going. Even when the Japs start shooting at you, the jarring of the plane, the smell of cordite, the mild thunder from the guns and the sight of the streams of tracers moving out ahead give you a feeling of security. But it is only a feeling.

So the tracers ripped on through the buildings and trees, then we were right over them and the bombs dropped. I leaned over to look out at the sight below. It was hard to pick up much because we were low and fast. There seemed to be some good buildings and some that were fairly well blasted from other raids but it was all indistinct.

There was a sound of gravel hitting suddenly on a metal roof; a half ripping, half sliding sound. It was loud but not shocking. Something stung my back, my left side and left leg. It lasted for a split second. I reacted more to sound than to the sense of touch because my first mental image was one of our props hitting a tree.

But wind whistled through the nose and tugged at hair and shirts in vicious blasts. The left side of my head stung a little. We were too high for trees. We were hit all over but it must have taken a full 10 seconds to realize it. Ten seconds is a long time when you are getting shot at.

There were three jagged holes in the left side along the level of the deck that you could roll a grapefruit through. There was very little glass left over us and what remained was filled with small uneven holes. I looked at Leo. He seemed a bit surprised and somehow unreal in the scene. I laughed and asked if he was ok. He didn't answer immediately.

Then in a moment he looked up and said, "The pilot has been shot." He just sat there and kept looking puzzled as though he could not understand what had happened. But he seemed to be all right so I told him to listen on the phones for instructions from the co-pilot, then slid back through the crawlway to see if I could help anyone.

Halfway back my foot caught in another hole. There was a strange heavy odor such as sweet celluloid, if there is such a thing. One of the ammo belts caught on my backside when I reached the end of the crawlway and started out. It always does that but this time I backed hard and broke it loose instead of tinkering around. The sweet celluloid was everywhere.

I stepped up into the pilots' compartment with one foot and looked at Eric. His head was rolled back, his mouth open with a small, thickish trickle of blood down his chin. It had stopped flowing. His eyes were closed; there was the same thick trickle of blood from each nostril. It had stopped flowing too.

Somewhere in the dim region of my mind sounded the echo, "Dead men don't bleed." I caught his right wrist to feel for a pulse. His arm was limp and fell back in his lap when I let go. I rolled his head over. Blood oozed out of his left ear and there were several holes in that side of his head. There was a heavy patch of blood on his left side just under his arm so I figured he caught some there too.

Two holes in his side of the plane showed where it had hit. Looked like small, explosive shells . . . probably 20 mm. I rolled his head back. There wasn't much question about his condition, but I was glad it had been quick for him and not drawn out.

"He's dead," I told the co-pilot. Ed nodded and kept on flying. I saw holes around him and asked if he was hit. He shook his head and kept on flying. He was watching instruments and listening to the motors. A scared or careless pilot would have killed us all. But I guess Ed didn't have time to be scared; he was too busy flying. Someone was standing back of me.

I looked around and saw the turret gunner. He looked inquiringly so I told him Eric was dead. He hesitated a moment, then turned and started to crawl back over all the gadgets to his position. I saw gas pouring all over the deck by the bucketful. The lines were cut and we were getting by on almost nothing. It couldn't keep us up and it wouldn't last much longer.

We were bleeding to death. I grabbed the boy's foot and pulled him back just as he started to climb over. He saw the gas and nodded. In the next minute or so it looked like we would blow up or hit the water and I wasn't especially sold on either one, but ditching was my choice. The whole place was shot up.

I asked Ed if he wanted me to do anything. He looked at me and shook his head: it meant "No, you can't" and "This damn thing won't fly any more." I felt Eric's throat to be sure. He was dead all right. God-damn every Jap. I wanted to see a bucktooth face leering before me right then. Eric's hand fell off his lap and dangled. I swore might-ily and hoped we had left some Japs in pieces but not to die quickly.

Perhaps it was a few seconds later, perhaps a minute, perhaps an hour; Ed leaned over and said, "We are going to ditch. Better get set." I said ok and settled down behind his seat with my back to him. He called on the inter-phone to all stations instructing them to stand by for ditching. We were up a couple of hundred feet now.

Right after we were hit, Ed had grabbed the controls and pushed us up as high as possible. We mushed along about five knots above stalling speed and a B-25 is no Piper Cub.

I motioned to the gunner and pointed down with my thumb. He understood and got set. I braced with my feet, arms and shoulders. There was a small axe for chopping out in case you got caught in a crackup. I kept my eyes on that. The motors were just about idling now. I reached up and caught the handle of the escape hatch above us and yanked it off. The wind came in with a hollow roar.

Ed was watching gauges and working the yoke back and forth with jerky little motions. I looked out of the window. The horizon was creeping up along Eric's profile and we seemed almost on the water. I had an urge to hang on to him so he wouldn't bump the instrument panel when we hit but remembered he was dead.

"Two shocks . . . the first one is slight and the second is hard." I had briefed my boys on that time and time again in their ditching procedure and I was glad now that I had. They knew it all better than I but it was coming back to me now and sometimes in a pinch you can use a little knowledge. Time lagged. The horizon kept creeping up and Eric looked natural except for the blood on his face. He prob-ably slept like that on long hops when Ed took over and he rested.

Out of the corner of my eye I saw Ed's hand flash across the switches and hit the feathering buttons to set the props so they wouldn't drag. I pushed my head hard against the seat and stiffened my neck so it wouldn't pop when we hit.

There was a slight bump and a sound of spray under terrific pressure. Then we hit. It wasn't too hard or jarring; just one of those powerful motions that you can't resist. Water poured in over us and held us down for a split second, then the nose seemed to be far under the surface. I shoved with my legs and pulled with my arms. Eric's head bobbed slightly as I shot past and out of the hatch. The water was a yellowish green so instinct must have told me we were not far under.

There was plenty of water around now. The nose of the plane went under when we hit and about the time I was coming up it apparently skidded to the side and came right back up. But I didn't hang around to see that. I thought it had gone down and I was sinking too. The cords on my Mae West were caught or twisted and it wouldn't blow up. My clothes were wet and heavy so I decided all time spent there was unnecessary.

I pounded like hell and came to the surface just in front of the port wing. The men were walking around on the plane getting the life raft inflated and in the water. One was helping Ed pull Eric out of the cockpit. I noticed the props were not bent. Then I reached the wing, climbed up and untangled the strings on my jacket. It came up with a quick and pleasant thud when I jerked.

Ed was lying on his side hanging down in the cockpit trying to get Eric's belt loose. I yelled at him but he didn't seem to hear. The plane was slowly settling and shudders kept passing through its body. Just like it knew it was going down shortly but didn't want to. So I got the men in the raft and told them to get away from the plane, then turned to Ed. He was standing up now on the top of the cockpit holding Eric, wet and limp, around the chest.

The plane lurched uncomfortably and I swore loudly at him. He jumped in the water with Eric and tried to swim but it was no use. Both their jackets had been ripped in getting out of the cockpit and could not be inflated. Eric was dead weight and kept Ed under the surface most of the time.

The crewmen yelled and I snapped out of it, jumped in and caught Ed by the shoulder. He kept hanging on but one jacket wouldn't hold the three of us up. Ed and I each weighed more than 200 pounds and I don't know how much Eric weighed. Ed was just about exhausted by now. Pulling a dead man out of a small place is tiring enough, but trying to swim with him, a lot of wet clothes and no support is too much. But he had just one idea in mind and was set on carrying that out.

"Let him go, Goddammit!" I shook Ed by the shoulder. "You can't help him now and you'll never make it if the plane takes you under. Let's get out of here." He seemed to realize for the first time what the score was and let Eric go. He hated to do it.

We stayed there for a moment until Ed caught his breath. The jacket held two of us up pretty well. I watched Eric sinking. The water was crystal clear and he seemed to be leaning forward, looking down and resting. I watched him until he was out of sight. He was a damn good boy.

We struck out for the raft. Ed caught his wind, beat me to it and climbed in. I swam around to the end and with the help of the crewmen, who kept making all sort of crude remarks about my backsides, managed to get in. Two of the boys had cuts on their faces and were a little bloody but otherwise all right.

One of them said he would paddle over and pick up some of the things that were floating away from the plane but Ed and I thought we had better get away from it before it sank. Besides, there was a fairly strong current taking us toward the shore and we didn't care to be placed in the embarrassing situation of landing in the Japs' back yard after all the bombing and strafing they had been taking. So we struck out for the open sea but paddling a raft isn't easy until you get accustomed to it.

The plane's nose was under and her tail lifting slowly. It shuddered, then sighed and slid under in a flurry of bubbles with a sound similar to squeezing air out of a wet sock; only much louder. It was a damn good plane. I looked up at our planes circling low over us. They would be radioing Dumbo (the rescue seaplane) like mad now so all we had to do was wait and stay away from the Japs.

Then someone asked, "Hey, where the hell's Leo?" We sat quietly for a wet and clammy moment and realized he was still in the plane. We looked at the spot where it went down but there were just a few cushions and a one-man raft still in its case floating around; nothing else. The last time I had seen him was in the nose. He seemed all right, but maybe he was hit and just didn't realize it or didn't mention it because he didn't have time.

Maybe he had passed out right after I left him or maybe he was knocked out or killed when we hit. We didn't know but the important thing was that he wasn't with us. I felt like hell. When things happen fast you generally act by instinct and don't have much time to think a lot. But after it is over you have plenty of time and can always figure out another way you could have done it so they would have worked out better.

Ed took the paddles from one of the crewmen and rowed us out while I took a canteen of water, some sulfa powder and fixed up the cut faces. I glanced at my watch; it was almost 0830. It seemed at first that the watch had stopped because I was sure somehow that it must be at least 1000 or 1030, but then I saw the second hand ticking along. The sea was calm and flat and there was no breeze.

There were more planes coming now. Fighters and dive bombers to take up where we had left off. We paddled. It was tough keeping the raft headed in the same direction all the time and rowing gets monotonous, especially if you want to watch the Japs get plastered some more. We figured we were probably a couple of miles offshore and wanted to get further out in case Dumbo took a long time in coming. Everyone was trying to paddle and watch the diving planes at the same time. The whole place was really a bed of giant mushrooms now. Everyone swore happily and hoped for the worst for the Japs. There was so much smoke over things we could see very little except the new explosions shooting skyward. Machine guns rattled in alternately high pitched and deep tones.

A big mountain loomed up a few miles to one side of us and in the general direction that the current was taking us. I thought if we didn't get picked up before we floated in we might land there. A lot of marines were on the other side. But we kept paddling. Our planes buzzed back and forth, coming down low to see who was in the raft and who wasn't. They would have to leave before very long to keep a safe margin on the gas supply. Anyhow, no Jappie would come nosing around in a boat as long as they were still there, Emperor or not.

Then one of the boys looked up the coast and spotted Dumbo lumbering placidly along toward us. She was pretty low and had a couple of fighters upstairs watching out. I told one of the men to put out a dye marker. We paddled hard to string it out. Only one of our planes remained now and he dived over us a couple of times so Dumbo could spot us.

Dumbo circled slowly and came over us dropping a smoke bomb. We threw kisses and broad grins all over the Pacific. Then she turned, landed, taxied up to within a few yards of us and cut her engines. We paddled over, got in, deflated the raft and pulled it in after us. I looked at my watch. It was a little past 0900. I thought it was a pretty good watch to keep running after all the water soaking.

Maybe it was worth 13 bucks after all. Inside Dumbo we looked each other over for cuts and bruises. The men got patched up again and we all sat down for some coffee and brandy. Dumbo took off and we circled a couple of times. Smoke was all over the target and it was hard to see anything. I was fine except for a good cigar that had got soaked but it was the only one I had brought along.

I looked down at the sea. The surface was flat and calm. There were some cushions and the one-man raft still floating around. Off beyond them was a long, green string of dye marker.

❧   ❧   ❧   ❧

CERTAIN FUNDAMENTAL ASPECTS OF THE CAMPAIGN in the New Georgia Islands now became apparent to Intelligence. Japan had dispersed her troops carefully through the island chain: on Kolombangara were about 7000 troops; on Munda, about 3000. But some of the lesser islands and reefs were garrisoned with as little as 20 or 30 men; and most significantly, no major Japanese warships had been seen operating in the target area.

Intelligence presented Halsey with a plan—"Toenails"—which envisioned the capture of Wickham and Viru Harbor as staging points for small craft plying between the Russells and Rendova, west of Munda. A reinforced regiment (less two battalions) was to seize Segi Plantation, at the southern tip of Munda, for construction of an airstrip capable of handling fighters in final attacks on Munda Airfield; we would grab off Rendova and build a motor torpedo boat base and staging area for future operations against other targets.

Army's Harmon determined that the 43rd Division under Major General Oscar W. Griswold's XIV Corps was to furnish troops for the operation; air support, the purview of Rear Admiral Marc A. ("Pete") Mitscher, Commander Air Solomons, was in turn assigned to Brigadier General Francis P. Mulcahy's 2nd Marine Air Wing for direct tactical support; and Admiral Turner again commanded the invasion.

With Halsey's Third Fleet providing gunfire support, Turner divided his forces as follows: Western Task Force (TF 31.1), under his command, was to seize Rendova, Munda and Bairoko. Eastern Landing Force (TF 31.2), under Rear Admiral George H. Fort, was to seize Wickham Anchorage, Segi Point and Viru Harbor.

The subdivision of forces was as follows: Western Landing Force (General John H. Hester) with the 43rd Division, 3rd Battalion of the 103rd Company, and the 136th Field Artillery from Army; and units of the 20th and 24th Naval Construction Battalions, 9th Marine Defense Battalion, Fleet Marine Force, and Company O of the 4th Marine Raider Battalion. The Eastern Landing Force (Colonel Daniel D. Handley) had the 103rd Infantry, 2nd Battalion of the 70th Coast Artillery, units of the 20th and 24th Naval Construction Battalions, and the 1st Marine Raider Regiment (less 2nd, 3rd and 4th Battalions) under Colonel Harry B. Liversedge.

Predicated on the assumption that the New Georgia landings could be effected without use of preinvasion bombardment. Turner's plan called for speedy and direct action. Simultaneous landings were to occur in the predawn of June 30. During D-Day antiaircraft guns on the warships and Army batteries were to protect the troops from air attack. Seabee detachments would then begin to construct an airstrip. The plan called for emplacements of 105-mm and 155-mm ("Long Toms") on lesser islands which commanded an overlook of Rendova Harbor. These big guns were to commence bombarding Munda Point, supporting the infantry advance upon landings. At this juncture, coastwatcher Sergeant Harry Wickham—with 20 natives in 18 canoes, and with a scouting party of marine raiders—was to reconnoiter and stake out a channel near Bana Island, about 1500 yards from New Georgia's south coast. In the meantime the 1st Raider Regiment would land in the Enogai-Bairoko area and immediately institute a series of reconnaissance patrols. Turner believed he could pull everything together and commence Army's full drive on Munda by July 4. However, he did not reckon with red tape and unexpected last-minute developments . . .

At Segi, coastwatcher Captain Donald Kennedy (he rescued more than 300 downed Allied airmen during the conflict) was faced with a problem requiring an immediate decision from Turner. He was being hemmed in by strong enemy patrols in eastern New Georgia, indicating a major buildup of Japanese strength. If he remained in the area he was sure to be captured and killed, and if he quit the area, invasion plans would go awry. This was certainly so, for General Saseki on Munda had decided to move his 229th Infantry Regiment from Kolombangara to Munda.

When Turner learned of Kennedy's predicament, he unhesitatingly went to the coastwatcher's aid. Not only would it mean taking a good man out of harm's way, but it would also give Turner an excellent opportunity to set up an advance base for operations against Viru and Vanguna: he issued orders sending the 4th Marine Raider Battalion (Colonel Michael S. Currin) to Kennedy's assistance. (Raiders were to be followed by another marine group and two companies of soldiers who would set up the advance base.)

Currin and his marines embarked in APD's *Dent* and *Waters* on the evening of June 20, and after a high-speed run the destroyers hove to off Segi at 5:30 A.M. the next morning. Twenty minutes later the marines were on the beach with Kennedy. For several days thereafter Currin's men conducted a series of reconnaissance patrols to determine the best way of attacking Viru Harbor. At 4 P.M., June 27, Currin made his judgment and radioed Admiral Fort requesting permission to land rubber boats at Regi, about one mile east of Nono (at the Choi River mouth, some three airmiles west of Segi). Permission was granted, and that night the marines paddled to Regi to begin their epochal march to Viru Harbor.

In Company P was Sergeant Anthony P. Coulis, twenty-one, one of those severely wounded in the ensuing action during which Raiders lost 13 men and killed 61 Japanese.

·4· THE MARCH TO VIRU HARBOR

ANTHONY P. COULIS

. . . It was a weird, ghostly trip on a moonless, tropical night. Like black shadows, the rubber boat convoy slipped silently through the many islets over glass-still water. We had strict orders. No smoking or talking. The only sound was the occasional cry of a seabird alarmed by our passage and the soft lap of the water. We became a little uneasy as a half moon gleamed down upon us through the thin layer of clouds. The channel and the surrounding islands lay exposed under its sickly bluish light. As if by a prearranged signal, everyone stopped paddling. A deathly silence . . . a sigh of relief as darker, heavier clouds covered the hellish moon glow. On and on we paddled till midnight. The native guides steered us to the deserted Regi village. Silently we reached shore.

Leaving the boats, we dispersed through the village. I motioned to my machine-gun squad to follow me and set up the gun to guard the approach to the village. It was cold and clammy and a poncho was the only protection we had as we settled down on the earthen floor till early morn. We each were to stand two-hour watches. Six-inch land crabs added to our discomfort . . .

At dawn of June 28, we began the march which was to become a nightmarish ordeal for us all. That day we hiked not quite six miles over those "good trails." It took us eleven hours, and every foot was a struggle. As we hiked out of Regi, gnawing on the chocolate ration bars which were breakfast, we plunged into a mangrove swamp . . .

Three hours later, we struck our first Japs! From somewhere behind there was a rifle shot. Then another, followed by the staccato chatter of a machine-gun. The rear guard had been hit. Five raiders were cut off by the enemy, but we later learned that they had traveled straight through the jungle, back to Segi Point, the Australian plantation where we had started the rubber boat trip.

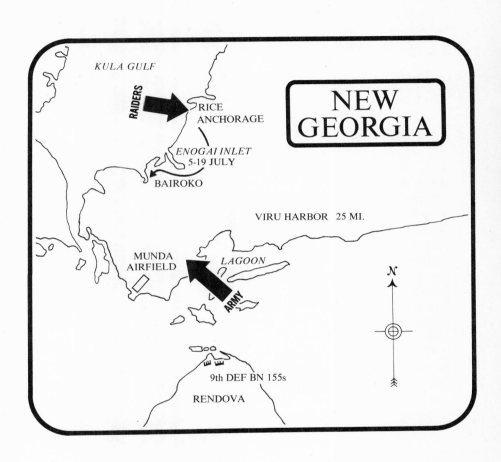

KULA GULF

RAIDERS

RICE
ANCHORAGE

ENOGAI INLET
5-19 JULY

BAIROKO

VIRU HARBOR 25 MI.

MUNDA
AIRFIELD

LAGOON

ARMY

9th DEF BN 155s

RENDOVA

NEW
GEORGIA

N

By 17:00 that night we reached a big river, a sullen, silent stream winding its way through a gash in the solid walls of the jungle. Night comes early in the bush, where even the days are shrouded in a green half light.

After the machine guns were emplaced on a tight defensive line around the bivouac area, we dug in for the night. Rain, that damned rain, started to fall, tormenting us further. Miserably we started a silent cursing streak. Crouching under our ponchos, we ate scraps of cheese from our C rations. A few minutes later I was asleep, despite the rain which poured down upon us all night long. I was tired, dead tired, and I didn't give a damn if my throat was slit as I lay sleeping, half lying, half sitting among the roots.

Late in the black jungle night I heard the muffled clatter of machine guns far away in distance. Next day, native scouts reported that the natives who were assigned the task of taking our rubber boats back to Segi Point had been discovered and massacred.

Before dawn of June 29, we resumed the forced march. This was destined to be a tougher day. We spent twelve hours, dawn to dusk, struggling through seven miles of wild jungle and swamp.

Shortly before noon, we were struck again, this time by a heavier force. Again I was fortunate to be at the head of the column. We lost five men—but we accounted for twenty Nips.

By midafternoon, we had reached the peak of physical exertion. We alternately crawled up and tobogganed down greasy ridges. We forded numerous jungle streams and swam three of them. The repeated torture of plunging into icy streams; the chopping away of endless underbrush and foliage; the continuous drizzle of rain; the days without hot food or drink; the mosquitoes tormenting us at night. It was sheer physical torture. The racking struggle of overtired muscles and empty bellies against the viciousness of the jungle itself. How I ever lived through that day, I'll never know. That night we didn't even stand guard. We plunged into the brush next to the trail and fell asleep with a prayer for protection on our lips.

The next day I heard men curse the jungle. I cursed, too. We cursed in hoarse, hysterical whispers. The snake-like roots that reached out to trip us; the damnable mud that sucked us down; the million and one vines and creepers which clawed at a man and threw him off balance. All this seems like a little thing to civilians. But too much of it could drive an exhausted, starving man mad.

That night we crawled over the crest into the flat top of a ridge and fell exhausted into the mud. I didn't even try to eat. In fact, I found out, to my dismay, that I was also out of drinking water. We flopped in the goo and slept like dead men. Tomorrow we were to attack!

At dawn we moved out. The worst of the trek was behind us. Swiftly, the order was given completely to encircle Viru, and by 9:00 A.M. we drove towards the Jap garrison.

There was a change in the men this day. We were men who would face the test for which we had been conditioned. The test of war!

The rain had begun again, a steady cold downpour. At a half run we moved up the trail. We had our gun assembled and ready for action. Suddenly the light and vicious spang of a Jap .25 pierced the silence. Two men in the point were hit. Automatically we fanned off into the thick underbrush. The attack began. That four-hour battle lives in my mind as a series of kaleidoscopic flashes. Things happened too fast. We advanced sporadically. This fight for Viru, one of the most vicious in the New Georgian campaign, really was a series of little battles, lasting from a minute to fifteen minutes. The jungle resounded with the chattering of machine-guns. The sharper crack of rifles and grenades would punctuate the racket and mingle with the screams and groans of men dying and fighting. We moved on, spitting on the blasted bodies of Japanese Imperial marines. Already the maggots had begun their work. Then all was silent. The silence of death. Suddenly we heard a queer, subhuman series of sounds: the screaming of Japanese, working themselves into a fanatical frenzy for a final desperate attempt to stop us. I was sweating feverishly. Then, at the climax, they charged. The staccato chatter of our guns began, smashing into the onrushing Japs. For two minutes the guns roared, then stopped. The howling began again, but this time it was different—the screams and groans of men mortally torn and ripped by American guns. The battle was won!

After the mopping up we searched for food and water. We found it and sat down to feast. We literally gulped down Japanese tinned salmon and clear, cold water. We relaxed, a job well done.

That night, we brought in our dead from the mud and slime of the jungle. There on that high bluff, overlooking the little harbor, the marines who died in the final attack on Viru were laid in shallow graves in a tiny clearing, amid the coconut palms. It was a fitting resting place for marines who . . . gave their lives in lonely, forgotten places of the world. May they rest in peace.

❀   ❀   ❀   ❀

THREE DAYS AFTER THE MARCH TO VIRU HARBOR, Army's B Company, 103rd Infantry, joined the marine outpost which had been set up by Currin's Raiders at the high ground near Munda Harbor. In the wake of their defeat the enemy had pulled back for the defense of Munda; 22 Americans had been killed in the skirmishing, but they cost the Japanese 102 dead.

But Rabaul was not concerned about these losses. Japan's air strength stood at its peak, and Admiral Kusaka and General Immamura (Eleventh Air Fleet and Fourth Air Army) were convinced they could stop any American threat. There were 200 aircraft of all types on hand, and replacements in pilots and planes were coming in from the homeland and other key areas of the Pacific at regular intervals. The two commanders were confident they could deploy a sufficiency of fighters and bombers to New Georgia to obliterate any landing.

But Turner struck June 30 at 2:30 A.M., and our troops reached the beach without opposition. Caught off-guard, Rabaul sent down three heavy air attacks during D-Day. Marine fighters downed 45 fighters and bombers before losing count; marine losses: 4 planes. The admiral's flagship, 7700 ton *McCawley,* which went to the bottom as the result of a late-afternoon torpedo-bomber strike that skimmed in undetected 20 feet above water, was the only real loss of the day. Thus began the campaign, primarily a tough Army operation in which the Marine Corps played only a supporting role, with the exception of two grueling weeks at Bairoko-Engoai.

Liversedge's regiment landed at Rice Anchorage, on the northwestern shore of New Georgia, to prevent an overland reinforcement of Munda, while Griffith's 1st Raider Battalion struck out for Enogai. On the ninth, after repelling an enemy attack, the latter's force hit Japanese outposts. Next day, in a furious attack on the village, raiders killed 350 enemy troops and captured four 140-mm guns. Liversedge, meanwhile, attacked Bairoko but took 236 casualties and fell back to Enogai to wait air support and flame throwers before attacking again.

One of the Marine Corps' great raconteurs, Griffith speaks of a brief interlude at Enogai. We have met the distinguished marine writer-historian before.

·5· CORRY'S BOYS

BRIGADIER GENERAL
SAMUEL B. GRIFFITH II

Corry was not a flying officer and had been commissioned in the RAAF because he had behind him many years of experience in dealing with South Pacific Islanders. So it fell to him in May and June . . . to organize a carrier company of about 150 New Georgians who were to lug ammunition and rations for the force commanded by Col. Harry (the Horse) Liversedge. The boys did more manual labor per capita per day than has ever been produced for the equivalent of one Australian shilling (hard money), a stick of trade tobacco, two bowls of rice, and tea.

In early July Col. Harry's force, after a night landing and a three day jungle march, had thrown the Japs out of Enogai and was trying to get itself pulled together for an assault on the Japanese position at Bairoko. It was at this time that Corry invited me to visit what he called "Corrigan's Christian Rest and Recreation Camp." After six successive nights of wakefulness induced by the operations of a Washing Machine Charlie from Kahili, I decided to accept. Charlie was never an accurate bombardier, but he admirably accomplished the Charlie mission of keeping people stumbling back and forth from sodden blankets to coral pits half full of rain water during most of the time the Lord meant for them to be asleep. Corry's camp, about a mile or so up river from Enogai, had received no attention from Charlie, who was apparently unaware of its existence. I badly needed eight uninterrupted hours in the hay and so one afternoon in late July I roused my man of all work, Eddie Wickham, and directed him to paddle over to Corrigan's Camp to find out whether or not there would be fresh fish for dinner that night.

Eddie, a sergeant in the Solomon Islands constabulary, was a fine looking man of about 25. He is a Christian quarter caste, swarthy, rugged, a good jungle scout and an accurate shot. Shortly after we arrived in New Georgia in early July, Eddie had reported to me as a handy man. He had travelled with one of the reconnaissance units sent to New Georgia in April and May and had killed five Japs with the carbine one of the officers of the patrol had given him. (He later ran his score to seven, but he was inclined to deprecate this achievement.) "Not very many, sir," he said to me once. "Frankie kill 17." Frankie was a New Georgia head man retained by Corrigan not to carry, but as a major-domo and a jungle scout. With Frankie, Jap-killing was purely a sideline from which he derived much pleasure but no profit. His daily rate of pay was two Australian shillings, two sticks of trade tobacco, a pound of rice and several ounces of tea. And Corry had promised him that when the show was over he would be rewarded with a bolt of cloth to take home to his "Mary." Eddie really knew how to cook rice, an accomplishment which very few Americans possess. Eddie cooked just about the best rice I have ever eaten: when he finished a mess it was beautifully dry, white and flaky. He brewed delicious tea in anything from a tin hat to an empty "C" ration can, and as a laundryman he had few peers. He is now a very fine provider for a Melanesian "Mary."

Eddie was quite happy at the prospect of getting over to Corrigan's for supper and a quiet night not only because he was as much in need of sleep as everyone else, but because he had not seen his friend for some time. He summoned his right hand man, a boy of about 17 who took care of him in exactly the same way he took care of me, and directed him forthwith to cease his labors on the roof of the bomb shelter and to grab his canoe paddle. In about an hour they returned with a note from Corrigan. We were welcome and there would be fish.

I picked up my helmet and pistol, Eddie bundled up the jungle hammock the padre had borrowed from an unobservant quartermaster, and we made off in the direction of the dock. In ten minutes we were up river and had landed on the beach below Corry's camp. Half a dozen canoes were hidden under the mangroves and a few of the boys were idly enjoying the sun and the feel of the warm ankle-deep mud. The path from the beach to the top of the bluff was steep and slick and even the vines that had been strung for hand lines could not prevent considerable stumbling, slipping and sliding (moral as well as physical).

Corry's housing development consisted of about 25 leaf-roofed lean-to's, each large enough to hold six or seven men, and though no real estate promoter could with truth have advertised them as cozy or homelike, they were at least dry, and in the jungles of the tropics one cannot ask for more. A raised platform served alike as floor and bed, and the leaf roof, about a foot or more thick, shed the rain. The towering trees of the forest hid the camp from the eyes of inquisitive enemy aviators.

The shack of the master of all this was no different from the rest except that it was slightly larger. In one end of it there was a portable radio transmitting and receiving set with which Corry tuned into the Coast Watcher circuit, a stack of old Sydney newspapers which he had brought along in lieu of extra shirts, a gallon tin labelled "Pure Alcohol," a pack of dirty cards and a case of grapefruit juice. This was obviously the library, bar, music room and dining room. At the other end of the shack Corrigan's assistant, a Marine sergeant clad in a battered felt hat, a short-sleeved shirt and a pair of ragged shorts, was sleeping peacefully. Everything was tranquil and secure; the waterproofed shacks with their beds of ferns impressed me as the utmost in luxurious appointments; I was at a loss for words when I thought of the reading material, the pack of cards and the gallon of alcohol. To find so many of the good things of life all gathered together was almost too much. Corry rose, smiling. He was a tallish, lean man, with slightly greying hair whose smile lit in his eyes. The Marine sergeant woke, sat up, adjusted his hat, spoke to me, lay down, and promptly went back to sleep.

"Get up," Corry said. "Get off your duff. It's your night to mix the drinks. I hope everybody in Montana isn't as lazy as you are." The sergeant wearily slid over to the bar end of the shack and began to open cans.

"I have 80 boys carrying stuff up to Shultz today," Corry said. "They took 60 cases of rations and 20 boxes of mortar shell. They have been gone since seven; should be back any time now."

I knew the trail up to Shultz's position. It was terrible going through swamps calf deep, up steep slopes to the tops of razor backed ridges, each of which fell inevitably and precipitately into another swamp. The day I had gone up we passed a column of about 60 boys, each with a case of ammunition, a bag of clothing, a reel of wire, or a box of rations on his shoulder. None of them were big men, but their brown bodies were wiry and their arm, leg and back muscles powerful. They wore gaudy cheap cotton lap-laps, or lava leaves wrapped around the waist. They didn't remind me of the sarong girls of Hollywood. Their broad flattish feet were incredibly tough with the skin perpetually wrinkled because it was perpetually wet. But none of them had the jungle sores on bodies or feet that the chafing of our clothes and shoes produced on our skins.

The boys hated the jungle as much as did the marines and GIs for they were not bush people but canoe people whose homes before the coming of the Japanese had been along the shores of coral enclosed lagoons. They had been rounded up for this show by the inexhaustible Kennedy, the coastwatcher at Segi who was the Colonial Office

"emperor" of the New Georgia group. (Kennedy had a fabulous reputation as a Jap killer, and the Japanese wanted his head in the worst
way. But his "subjects" were the most loyal in the world—as the presence of 150 of them with Corrigan was proof). There was never any
question in the minds of the boys about who was going to win the war,
and they were not lukewarm in the expression of hatred of the Japs,
who had destroyed the only way of life they knew.

The Marine sergeant, after much pouring, tasting, blending and
stirring, finally arrived at a concoction that met with his approval.
We raised the cups. "Cheers"; sipped slowly, and set them down carefully. As we sipped along, Corry told me that before he had come
to the Solomons in the spring of 1943, he had been in New Guinea.
In 1940 he had entered the RAAF, and in 1942 had been sent to Moresby to help get an airfield near there in shape. It was at this time that
the Japs were pushing over the Owen Stanley range, and things looked
their very worst.

Before the war he had been a planter and mine operator in New
Guinea. I was very vague on New Guinea and Corry got a piece of
paper and pencil and sketched as he talked, marking Port Moresby,
Buna, Gona, the Owen Stanley range, Finschafen, Madang, and
Wewak. He had been to all these places and many more and knew the
area around Madang and Wewak well . . .

And so we talked. Corry told me that most of his carriers were married and all of them were Christians, the majority of the Church of
England. There were a few Seventh-Day Adventists. It surprised
me to learn that natives of the latter persuasion did not use tobacco,
for the Melanesian as a rule will use tobacco in any conceivable form
in which it is offered to him. They particularly prefer a black trade
tobacco which comes in sticks or twists about four inches long, an
inch wide and a quarter inch thick. I felt myself somewhat of an authority on trade tobacco; . . . I had chewed it on Tulagi and Guadalcanal when the cigarette supply was low. I discovered that night that
I was no more able to enjoy it than I had been a year before. This
stuff is made either in Richmond or Petersburg, Virginia. The natives love it and the demand was then, and I suppose is now, absolutely unlimited.

Corry said that when the Japanese began moving south . . . from
New Britain along the Solomon chain the British Colonial officers
told the natives to leave their villages and, when the Japanese came
in the spring of 1942 to New Georgia, the "canoe" natives immediately "went bush." They took with them into the jungle hills their
"Marys," children, pigs, chickens, and what few crude household and
garden implements they possessed. They hid their precious canoes in

the mangroves that line the inlets and lagoons. Not a single "canoe" native on any island of the New Georgia group remained behind to cooperate with the Japanese, whose reputation had preceded them.

At about half past six Corry held his daily sick call. The afflicted lined up before the lean-to, some 10 of them shuffling shyly. Three of Corry's most trusted henchmen, Willy Pia, Johnny Tanisapa, and Frankie Talassasa, each equipped with a bottle of pills, placed themselves near Doctor Corrigan. Willie questioned the sufferers and translated into pidgin the saga of human woe poured into his ears. Corry listened attentively to the description of the symptoms, occasionally felt a forehead or poked a belly, then made up his mind and prescribed. "Two out of Johnny's bottle, one out of Frankie's bottle. Next man." A rapid conversation between Willie and the next suffered ensued and the symptoms were duly described in pidgin. "Three out of your bottle, Willie. Next man."

The sick call was over in 10 minutes to the satisfaction of everyone, the caps were screwed back on the bottles, the medicine stowed in Corry's kit and the three dispensers disappeared.

"It is alway either dysentery or malaria," Corry said. "I give them a bismuth and paregoric mixture for dysentery and quinine for malaria. They always get better. You can't kill them."

We finished our drink and the meal was brought on. The fish was superb, the rice perfect, and there was plenty of both. We drenched them liberally with soy-sauce (we had captured half a dozen huge tubs of it) and came back for more. For dessert we had dried apricots and raisins from a jungle ration pack, and the meal was topped off with tea.

"Frankie, Willie, and Johnny are the best boys I have," Corry said. He leaned around the corner of the shack and called to the cook: "Go get Frankie."

"Willie is head man of all the Roviana people. He is well educated. He went to mission school. Frankie is the best scout I have. Most of the boys are timid, but these three who help me run this show are not. When they talk, the boys jump."

Frankie appeared wearing a disreputable red lap-lap around his waist and an American tin hat that completely covered his small head and practically rested on his shoulders. He was about five feet three or four inches tall. He had a fine face, alert eyes, and he bore himself with dignity. Slung over his right shoulder was an Owen submachine gun which Corry had loaned him. With that gun Frankie had killed 17 Japanese. Corry told him to tell me about it.

Frankie was bashful, so we compromised on the story of how he had killed five Japs. He talked in pidgin, distinctly and slowly, and I caught most of it. He had seen a Japanese patrol of five men and he had followed the patrol, stalking it through the jungle for several days. Finally he had caught the five Japs where he wanted them, all of them sitting down on the trail, bunched up, jabbering and arguing while they ate pickled fish. He had set the Owen gun on "automatic" and shot into them. "Kill finish," he said, his eyes lighting up with pleasure.

Darkness does not fall in the jungle, it is dropped. When the sun sets, night begins and millions of insects start to buzz and hum. The mosquitoes began to go into action. Corry, the sergeant from Montana, and I sat on the edge of the floor of the lean-to batting ineffectually at the bugs with one hand and holding our canteen cups with the other.

"About time for Charlie," the sergeant observed.

"Not till 7:30," Corry said. "We have ten minutes yet."

Twelve minutes later the heavy antiaircraft batteries on Rendova suddenly opened up, first with a few sporadic ranging shots and then almost immediately with continuous heavy fire. The bursts blazed in the sky momentarily but it was seconds until the roar of their explosions reached us.

We could tell from the changing pattern of the flashes and the roar of exploding shells that Charlie was coming toward us and that the steel of the big guns was following him.

Corry reached for his tin hat and stood up. He took a leisurely drink and then called: "Condition Red." The Marine sergeant blew three sharp blast on his whistle. We could hear the boys scrambling for their foxholes. The shrapnel was screaming in the air above the trees. We put our canteen cups down gingerly just as a high-pitched shriek announced the passage of a piece of steel close by. Corry and I dove for the same foxhole at the same time. I made it first and he landed on top of me.

As soon as the antiaircraft let up, we could hear Charlie. There was only one of him, a single engined float plane. He usually carried five 100-pound bombs. He passed over us and went in toward the point across the river on a glide run. We got out of our holes, made motions at brushing ourselves off, picked up our canteen cups and sat down again. A few seconds later we counted five successive explosions. We could tell by the sound that they were well off to the east of the point.

"He's getting better," Corry said. "He only missed by about five hundred yards." We could hear Charlie fading off across Kula Gulf bound for his base at Kahili where he would report, as he did every night that he had sunk an American destroyer.

Some of the boys in the lean-to back of ours were singing Protestant hymns. I knew the tunes but could not make out the words, for they were singing in their own tongue. Eddie Wickam's strong voice dominated as the melancholy tune rose, fell, and died out.

We three sat silently, holding our canteen cups carefully and sipping now and then.

"The boys want to get back to their Marys," Corry said.

❧   ❧   ❧   ❧

THE ARMY HAD THE SITUATION WELL IN CONTROL during the first week at Rendova. The Marine role was one of waiting for a call to duty—any kind of duty. Robert W. Blake, who served with a tank platoon of the 9th Defense Battalion, wrote of a minor clash in a story which appeared in the *Saturday Evening Post*—the type of clash that never made headlines. Blake, who rose to the rank of major and received the Navy Cross for distinguished tank actions on Rendova during the ensuing days, is a former columnist of the *Cleveland Plain Dealer*.

·6· BATTLE WITHOUT A NAME

ROBERT W. BLAKE

. . . Now we nosed ashore, out of the evening twilight into the night; boxes and drums of fuel piled in the gloom. A tent with a red cross on a white flag. Cots containing quiet men. White bandages with huge dark splotches. A figure on a stretcher outside. A stack of stretchers against a tree. Nothing had changed since the last time; only the dot on the map.

There was no room for us inside the barbed-wire perimeter. Just outside, we pushed off the trail into the jungle on each side, forming a hollow circle. All guns loaded, trained and ready, pointing into the jungle night. "You cover the trail . . . You crossfire into that ravine . . . Everybody understand his station in case of an attack? Go to your places. Fire when ordered. Don't shoot at shadows. Let no shot be fired unless there's a dead Nip to show for it in the morning."

No time to dig in. Camp on the ground. Sleep on the briars, roots and stumps. Missed lunch, no time for supper. No appetite anyway with the knot at the pit of our stomachs. Silence now; no lights, no movement. Anything that moves is a Jap.

We lie down on a blanket or a strip of canvas, pistol in hand or rifle or tommy gun close against our ribs, finger in the trigger guard. Darkness, utter blackness. Silence among the resting men, but the jungle rustling with movement. There is a whistle in the night, repeated. The call is answered from the opposite direction. There is a call far away, then one very close. Now whistling is everywhere, on all sides. Clack! Clack! Clack! Sticks being pounded together. A branch cracks from a tree and falls thrashing through the foliage. You listen, breathless. There comes screeching in the trees and the heavy flap, flap of wings. Birds. You breathe again.

But something is crawling through the brush not six feet away. Slowly, you lift your head, straining your eyes into the darkness. You play with the idea that you may be blind; you move your spread fingers back and forth in front of your eyes, so close they brush your eyebrows. Nothing to be seen; probably a land crab crawling through the brush. You relax, laying your head down slowly, so as not to make the slightest sound.

Voices and the sound of a motor far up ahead. The noise grows louder. What can be moving at this hour? Near at hand among the men, you hear quiet clicks as hammers are drawn back on pistols and the bolts of rifles slide around into the chamber. Maybe the Nips have one of our jeeps and are trying to get through our lines by talking loudly and making a great racket. Down the trail they come. You can make out English words, "A little this way . . . Watch out for that tree." But the Nips often use English. The camp is still and black. We will let the strangers go right through, keeping our guns on them in case they discover us. Into our circle they come, into the crossing and crisscrossing lines of fire. No sound. They are passing through— a jeep and several men. There is the Jap odor of fish and smoke. "Hey, medics! Where are the medics! We have a wounded Jap! Someone tell us where the medics are!" They kept talking and calling out, but no one answered and they went on, never knowing they had passed through a camp.

We hear the jeep bouncing, tools and chains clanking as the incessant talking and exhortations fade out down the trail. There is no shooting at the wire. Evidently, the strangers knew the password and really did have a Jap bound for the hospital. But theirs had been a dangerous journey. Had one shot been fired as they passed our

camp, they would have been torn to ribbons, no one believing what
they said. But jungle-wise troops do not fire at night. They lie still
and kill with the knife. A rifle's flame only draws return fire.

Our artillery suddenly shakes land and sky with a salvo. Shells
rush overhead and pound into the ground. All other sounds are blotted out. The men take the opportunity to draw a full breath and shift
positions. The noise of moving is lost in the thunder of the guns.

The shelling lasted a long time. The noise was friendly. I fell asleep,
lulled by the swishing shells and the rocking crump as they hit.

Then suddenly I was aware that a noise was invading my consciousness. By the stir in the camp, I knew everyone was listening. From
above came the high-pitched drone of an enemy plane in a dive. We
flattened, waiting for the bombs. No bombs. The plane screamed
off in a wing-over and came pouring back over us. We expected strafing this time, but nothing came except the whine of the engine overhead.

Our artillery was silent with the plane above us. It was not long
before we realized what the plane was doing—spotting artillery fire
for the Japs. We heard the first Nip gun get its shell away, a distant
boom. Instantly there was a screeching over us and a shattering explosion behind. It sounded like a wreck, like a car throwing on the
brakes at high speed, followed by a gigantic crash. We lay pressed
against the ground, listening to the screeching shells and the jarring
blast. Some came close, but most of the projectiles carried beyond.
They were not aimed at us. The Nips could not possibly tell where
we were under the roof of the jungle.

Between blasts, we dozed until the plane circled away and could
be heard to throttle down as if for a landing. Probably a float plane
settling in some near-by lagoon. As soon as the engine noise died,
the whole world shook as battery after battery of our artillery tore
loose, answering from a dozen points with a double dozen shells for
every one the Nips threw over. The shells whined and swished overhead in one long, unending stream, like a rumbling freight train
passing.

Quickly, the airplane motor coughed up again and roared for a
take-off, frantic to get away before our shells found it. The drone
died out in the distance.

Floating in a half sleep for a time, I was electrified to stark consciousness by a cry, "Look out!" The camp hung in breathless silence, listening. Slowly, I moved my hand to my pistol. It felt massive and heavy
as I lifted it. I could not figure where the shout had come from. I knew
the direction, but I could not tell whether that direction was toward
our lines or behind us. I knew how we had parked, and I painfully
plotted out just how we were formed. I was sure my head pointed

out toward the front, but a rebellious compass in my brain refused to be rotated from the position in which it lodged when I awoke. It was like waking in a strange room and not being able to determine where you are.

I fell asleep still trying to orient myself, still trying to discover where the cry had come from, trying to imagine what had caused it.

A long time later, some movement again roused me with a start. I felt the muscles of my heart contract, shooting a cold fluid through my veins. Something was creeping along a little trail toward me. I peered through the night. The moon had risen, and bright white light, filtering through the jungle canopy, was mottling everything with brilliant patches. Where I lay was bathed in a stream of light. I felt that my face was glistening in the moonlight. Something invisible moved near by. Slowly, I raised my head, watching steadily. With a jab of freezing terror, I saw movement in a patch of moonlight. *This is it,* I thought. *I will never see morning. Why didn't I dig in, no matter how late? Only a fool sleeps above the surface of the ground.*

With the light bright upon me, I was afraid to raise my pistol, afraid to move. I strained to hold my head up and keep my eyes on the shadow. I was in no position to shoot. My pistol was in my hand by my side. I would have to bring it up to my head to fire. It was a long move. I would wait until the figure was in the middle of the moonlight, and then, with one move, throw out my pistol against him and fire. If only the figure did not see me, did not fire first.

Just then one of the men near by sighed in his sleep and turned over. At the sound, the figure on the trail grunted and went bouncing away. It had been some animal—a wild boar, a rat, a lizard or a coconut bear.

I relaxed and laughed to myself. But I was wide awake by then. I damned the long, long night and wondered if the darkness would ever end. I dug my wrist watch out of my pocket where I had put it to conceal the glare of its luminous dial. I stared at the tiny hands until my eyes could focus. It was only half past one.

When patches of dawn began to show through the trees, the tension of the night was broken and I fell asleep until the rattling of mess gear woke me as the first risers were preparing their breakfast. Getting up late—no use to hurry the war—I had a breakfast of pancakes and hot coffee at the hospital galley. Before I had finished, the sound of shots came from far up ahead, then the hammering of machine-gun fire, punctuated by the heavy blasts of cannon. The forward group of vehicles, on the island since the day before, were making their first attack.

Lieutenant B and I started forward in a jeep to see how the action was going. It was a long ride over roots, logs and rocky ground. The lane ended; we walked the rest of the way. The noise of firing pounded through the great jungle room—a hollow sound filled with distant echoes. We crept forward to the command post. An occasional shot snapped through the leaves. Soldiers sat in their foxholes, smoking, helmets off, rifles leaning against the walls. They smiled as they listened to the battle just ahead. It was roaring forward and no one was getting hurt. Everyone at the command post was happy. The colonel was beaming.

"The Japs are catching a bellyful this morning," he said. "Listen to that fire. I don't think we'll have any use for the rest of you." Those were good words to hear, but the colonel went on, "There may be a show for your group on another island near by. Bring your force up to the trail junction and we'll shoot you across as soon as we find some way of getting you there."

Another island. We did not mind the fight, but there seemed now to be no logical end, no place where we could stop and say the campaign was finished.

We moved the group to the vicinity of the forward ration dump and made camp. It would be several days before we were needed. We would take it easy. Up at the front, the sounds of firing stopped. Late in the afternoon, the battle commenced anew as the first group went in once more.

Lieutenant B and I hopped into a jeep and went to the front again to see how the battle was going. We were too late. Firing had practically ceased. Captain C's outfit was preparing to spend the night right on the trail where the forward movement had stopped. A dead Jap was sitting behind a machine gun at the base of a tree. A high-explosive shell had come along the barrel of his weapon and swept his head away. Only his lower jaw, full of teeth, sagged on his chest.

As we stood there talking over the day's action, a burst of machine-gun fire splattered against the side of the vehicle and clipped off leaves all around us. We dived for the ground. No one was hit.

"The Jap front line is out there about fifty yards in a little draw," Captain C explained. "Most of the Japs have been killed off, but the rest are just ahead."

It was practically dark when Lieutenant B and I reached our own camp. We ate some peanuts and dried prunes, and mixed up a chocolate drink out of water and powdered milk before climbing into our hammocks. Shots still rang out as darkness settled down.

The artillery duels of the night before began again. The Nip plane returned. One shell cut down a tree just outside our circle. Instantly, everyone was up, scrambling frantically for his vehicle. Shells screamed and pounded through the trees. We sat at our stations, feeling the earth heave. The shells screeched over in an unending stream.

As the sound commenced far away our muscles tightened, then hardened as the scream rose higher and higher, to terminate in a shattering blast. By the time the first had hit, another could be heard on its way.

Rain began to fall, lightly at first, then in a steady downpour. Water leaked in everywhere. We became soaked and cold. A high-velocity gun opened up. Sky bursts cracked over us. Slowly, the Jap shells moved off down the island and we crawled into our blankets, now soaked and muddy.

All night long we listened to the purring of barges coming and going among the near-by islands. Our artillery would roar out, smothering the sound of motors, but Jap shells would blast over in answer and the duel would be on again. When silence fell, the dull drone of Nip barges could be heard once more.

It was impossible to say what the enemy was up to. He was probably evacuating his forces, I thought. But at times it seemed that he was landing reinforcements.

The camp lay awake, listening intently for any movement around us. At last the sky through the trees showed gray. We were glad the night was over, glad to move around and get warm.

Up at the front, the attack got under way early. Reports coming back told of Captain C receiving tremendous fire, but all seemed to be going well. The firing slacked off about noon. Reports were still good. Shortly thereafter the ire was resumed—frantic and tumultuous machine-gun fire in long, breathless bursts.

An ambulance jeep eased through camp, creeping over the ruts and logs. Medicos stood on the sides, holding the stretchers on their racks. One figure was sitting in the back, both legs swathed in bandages. A man on a stretcher had his head and eyes bound up in a redstained bandage. Another was covered with a blanket to his chin. His eyes were closed, his skin had a greenish pallor that made his hair look blacker than it was. One of the medicos kept brushing the flies from his open mouth. The jeep paused and the man opened his eyes, staring straight up. He knew he was dying.

The battle had not gone well. The stretcher bearers said that Captain C's group had run into bad luck. Another soldier returning from the front reported that the Japs had launched a counterattack. He did not know what the situation was at present.

We waited until almost dark, getting only scraps of information. The news was bad. I preferred not to pry into the details. I would learn of them too soon. At dusk, we heard Captain C's group returning down the trail. The captain looked unutterably tired, his men serious and silent.

Yes, they had been stopped, and stopped hard. The Japs had strongly reinforced during the night. The attack ran into point-blank fire from some kind of heavy weapon. No, the captain did not know what it was, but it was big. Yes, there had been losses; he could not get them out; they were still in there where they had fallen. The Japs had "banzaied" and charged as soon as they scored the first hit. Our lines fell back. No man would have escaped had not a big blond Browning automatic rifleman stood his ground and kept his rifle pumping.

He cut down one Nip who was rushing forward with a bangalore torpedo to blow up one of the stricken vehicles and its crew. That BAR man piled up twelve Japs in front of him as they came on. Had it not been for him, all would have been lost. As the last crew man escaped, flames shot up over the treetops. The Nips reorganized and again rushed in, shouting "Banzai!" The lines sagged, but held. A third time the enemy came at the forward position, but the attack withered and fell back.

It was a somber evening as we drank our coffee and ate our cans of meat-and-vegetable stew. Tomorrow would mean another crack at the Jap line. The complexion of the battle had changed, for after today their morale would be high. They might launch an offensive. We had little idea where the gun was that hit us, nor how many there were. They would probably reinforce again overnight. I did not like to talk or think about it.

As usual, the night was filled with noise and vigilance. Jap barges could be heard moving across the strait. Spasmodically, our artillery boomed out, and the enemy, in answer, planted some shells near us again. Now and then came furious bursts of machine-gun fire from the front, echoing and re-echoing through the night.

I woke with a sense of dread. I had the feeling that today was a day that had come too soon, that something had to be done that I would rather not do. I lay in the hammock until late, knowing that I could not possibly miss what was in store. Whoever wanted me, would find me. At length I got up and drank a lot of coffee. I was not hungry for anything else.

The news of the night had been nerve-racking. The men did not know quite what to believe. They thought I knew all the facts and watched me to see if the situation was as bad as it seemed. I dared not betray how I felt. One man, feeling me out, asked, "A bit of bad luck yesterday, captain?"

"Oh, yeah, you can't win all the time."

"What's on the program for today, sir?"

"No word yet, but I hope they give us a chance to pay those slope-heads back." The statement rang so false in my heart that I wondered how anyone could fail to detect the lie.

"You don't mean we'll go in there blind against those guns!"

"Oh, we have a good idea where it is. Someone has to go in, and it may as well be us. You don't want to die of old age, do you?"

"The thing to do is get shot and get this war over with. Then you're either dead or evacuated."

"But think of what a hero you'll be. Your girl will think of you every time she kisses that defense worker."

Up the trail I heard the words that I had learned, in the long campaign, to dread as the prelude to overburdening responsibility, "Where is Captain Blake?" They never look you up to bring you good news. The knot twisted up in my stomach. I wanted to sit there and rest. Let them come to me.

They did: "Captain Blake, you're wanted on the phone at the ration dump right away."

This was it. I stood up, buckled on my pistol and picked up my tin hat. "Well, fellows, I'm going to get the dope," I said. "Be ready to roll by the time I get back." I strode off, thinking how restful it would be to slip into the jungle and hide. At the phone, I said, "Captain Blake speaking."

"Good morning, captain. This is Major S. How are you this morning?"

"First rate, major. How's it going? Are we winning the war?"

"It looks as though it depends on you today, captain. Are you ready to go in?"

"Oh, we're ready, but so are the Nips, I suppose. What about that gun—or guns?"

"We plan to outflank it to the right—and pray."

"I hope you're in good with the Lord."

Captain C, Lieutenant B and I drove up to the front. Action was stalemated. Something had to be done. By crawling a little way, we could see our casualties of the day before just in front of the Nip defenses. It was impossible to get to them. We did not like the idea of running into that gun again and piling up more casualties in no man's land. But we would never crack the Jap lines unless we tried.

As we lay looking, there seemed to be one possibility of success. The more we talked it over, the better the scheme seemed. Captain C, who could have easily stayed out of it, was eager to go in again. We would throw every weapon we had left into the attack. We would deploy them in a way never attempted before. What could the enemy do to stop us? If he had a dozen guns there, how could he hold us? Yes, it was an excellent plan. We passed from doubts to enthusiasm. We went back and told our men the plan. They agreed it ought to work. All misgivings vanished. They were ready to have a go at it.

As we moved into the forward area, we were sober and silent. Even with every assurance of success, there is always the chance that it may be you the reports speak of when they mention "negligible losses." The faint nausea returns to your stomach. You wish the battle were over. You wonder if they might not call it off at the last minute. But you are caught and enmeshed. The men in their foxholes are waiting for you; they are counting on you, and they watch as you draw up.

We get our crews together behind the lines and go over the plan. When everybody understands what he is going to do, it is: "Let's go and good luck." Slowly, maneuvering into position, the attack gets under way. The signal is given to open fire. One long, continuous wave of smoke and flame and thunder rolls through the jungle, plowing the ground, withering the foliage. A Jap helmet appears around the base of a banyan tree, eyes under the rim, peering. Suddenly, as if hit by an unseen hand, the helmet jerks and rolls into the open, a head covered with cropped black hair bows against the roots. Beyond, the underbrush rustles with movement. A helmet and a long barrel appear among the leaves. Tracers from a dozen guns converge on the spot. The movement becomes violent and terrified. Then it ceases. But the bullets, without mercy, keep ripping in.

Suddenly out of the green gloom a series of orange balls mushrooms toward us, one after the other, small at the start, but growing large as they hurtle past. Tracers like spray from a hose concentrate on the source of the fire. Leaves swirl and dance in the thrashing hail. A figure springs up out of the ground and starts to run, but is instantly caught in the blast and hurled into a tree, at the base of which he falls, his clothing blown and rippling with the bullets still tearing through him.

I shall never get used to the sight of the enemy. I shall always be amazed to see him there, peering at us, loping through the brush, working toward us. Sometimes I thought he did not know what was going on, the way he stood, took our shots and died. I shall never forget the triumphant shout of the observer: "There's one! At the end of the log! Get him! Get him!" Then, as a high-explosive shell found the target, "Good shot! You blew his head half off! Shoot him again; he's still kicking!"

Soon we moved up. "Anybody see anything? Any targets?"

"Hey, look at that! What the hell's he got?"

"For God's sake, don't shoot! It's one of our men!"

"Our man, hell! He's trying to mine us . . . Oh, I missed him! Give me a canister. Quick, he's getting away! . . . Forget it, too late. Son of a gun, now we'll have to kill him on some other island farther up the line."

"I couldn't find any more shells. We must be out of ammunition."

"No, there are a couple more rounds but save them . . . I see our men going forward over on the left. We've cracked their line! We've broken through!"

It was as easy as that. It was easy because we were in the right place at the right time, with the right equipment and the right idea.

The battle was won. All along the line, our troops were crawling forward unopposed. Captain C and I were anxious to get to the casualties of the day before. We moved into a deep draw and crawled up to the lip. Out on the flat, half hidden in the foliage, stood the cripples. We edged up toward them, crept alongside. Captain C raised up to take a look. Crack-thunk! Captain C dropped, hit.

After coming so far, to fall by so little, in the fraction of a second, hardly seems possible. A bullet is merciless and without discretion. But Captain C was not badly hurt. Maybe he is the lucky one, after all. It means a trip home. He promised to think of us as he lay healing in the arms of his ever-loving wife.

The enemy had been broken, thrown back. He fled without even a rear guard, leaving his dead and dying behind. Next day a patrol went out to find the Japs. We had a direct line with the patrol. We sat listening to reports of its progress: "One hundred yards, two hundred yards, five hundred yards. No opposition! A thousand yards, fifteen hundred yards. No resistance."

"They don't dare make another stand."

Relieved and happy, we sat there, our feet in a foxhole, drinking the morning coffee. Suddenly, far away, a long burst of machine-gun fire ripped the jungle silence.

Give me bombs and bursting shells. Those I can take, but I dread the sound of machine guns. A bomb or a shell usually explodes on empty ground, but machine-gun fire in the jungle means point-blank death for some kid who carried his girl's picture in his pocket and dreamed last night of going home.

It was a long time before we could get a voice at the other end of the wire. At last it came, tired and out of breath. "Enemy machine gun covering the trail at two hundred yards. We have two men hit and one man missing. Looked everywhere for him."

Late that night, from far ahead came an anguished cry for help and a splattering blast of machine-gun fire. They cry faded out. All who heard it knew what it was. But no one will ever know the horror of the death that man died, lost, alone and forsaken in the jungle darkness.

The next day we found him on the trail, face down in front of an abandoned machine-gun position. The campaign was over. He had been the last man to die. And he came so close to coming through alive. I cannot get him out of my mind.

❧ ❧ ❧ ❧

BY AUGUST 21 THE NEW GEORGIA CAMPAIGN WAS END-
ed and the marine fighters and bombers were using Munda airstrip to soften Bougainville. Captain John Foster, a fighter pilot
who had just arrived from Guadalcanal, details his first mission—
a long day in the give and take of war.

•7• FIRST MISSION

CAPTAIN JOHN M. FOSTER

I lifted up one edge of my mosquito netting. Swinging my feet I
located my heavy field shoes with my toes; then I lifted the wall of
net over my head and picked up my socks. I shined my flashlight on
and off to conserve the battery as I walked past the open foxhole to
the center pole and began the search for my flying suit. There was
only one nail on my side of the pole and it had about five different
articles on it—mine at the bottom. My flying suit still felt damp from
the perspiration it had absorbed the previous day as well as from
the high humidity of the atmosphere.

Outside, I poured some cold water from a bucket into a steel helmet and washed my face. Politely leaving the water in the helmet
for the next man, I tripped over tent ropes and returned once more
to the tent.

I slung the leather shoulder holster containing my 45-caliber automatic over my neck and buckled the belt, strung with my hunting
knife, first-aid kit, extra cartridges and canteen, around my waist.
After I had put my baseball cap on and grabbed my flying helmet,
goggles and gloves, I stumbled and slid my way fifty yards to Maud-
ie's Mansion for breakfast.

Two kerosene lamps glowed from the two vertical wooden poles
supporting the roof, while pilots on both sides of the aisle gulped
down the last of their coffee and ushered forkfuls of fried Spam to
their mouths, interspersing these with occasional bits of imitation
scrambled powdered eggs.

After breakfast, we climbed aboard one of the trucks provided to
haul pilots down to the landing strip. We waited until there was a
load—which meant stacking us in two layers—then jolted our way

down the winding road in the murky light of the coming dawn. Far away an air raid siren reached its triple crescendo monotonously. Another began its warning cry closer to us, followed immediately by others until the din swept past us to the area we had just left. The driver of our truck turned out the lights and we jumped out to find cover.

The high-pitched whine of an airplane became audible, increasingly so until it sounded as if it was heading directly for us. We crouched as low as we could in a drainage ditch. In a few seconds the plane was directly overhead. Now was the time that we should be hearing a bomb if any had been aimed at us. Nothing happened and we heaved a sigh of relief.

Five small red flashes appeared in the sky as our ack-ack went into action and seconds later we heard the *plop, plop* of the exploding shells.

The plane turned around and headed back for the landing strip. Then we heard the bomb. It was like a fluttering whistle as it fell, the sound increasing rapidly in its intensity and punctuated at the climax by a sharp, ground-shaking CRR-ACK.

The engine droned softly now and soon disappeared. The last red blossoms in the heavens died out.

We loaded ourselves into the truck again—glad to be alive—and wheeled down the road until we were out of the small hills and rolling across the slanting ground near the airfield.

On the road ahead of us we saw a parked jeep. A few yards away a few men were gathered together. "It looks like the bomb hit right over there," Witt remarked, pointing to a small crater not far from the men.

We were already late so we didn't stop to investigate. It was not until the afternoon that we learned what the little group of men had been clustered about. The driver of the jeep had stopped when the air raid alert sounded and had taken cover behind a tree stump. Unfortunately, he chose the wrong side of the tree. The bomb had burst close to him, spraying him fatally with shrapnel.

As soon as we arrived at the ready tent we were assigned to duty. A couple of the divisions took off on the moonbeam patrol (the code name for the dawn and dusk patrol). The rest of us got into a truck marked PILOT TRANSPORTATION ONLY and drove along the circular road through the airplane dispersal area. On each side we saw F4U's parked in sturdy stone revetments built by the Japanese. As we came to each airplane an enlisted man called out the name of the pilot who was to fly it and the truck stopped while he disembarked, loaded down by a parachute with a seat-type rubber lifeboat attached and a jungle pack, all weighing sixty-five pounds.

The first two planes I was assigned to each had something wrong with it. On the first one the left magneto was bad; the other had a broken generator. The third plane was satisfactory. After testing, I taxied the ship from its revetment to the end of the take-off string where the rest of the planes that were to be on scramble alert had been parked. I shut off the engine, prepared for a hasty take-off, then joined the otner pilots who were gathered under the wing of a Corsair.

Every half hour we started the engines up to warm them so we could take off immediately in case we were scrambled. After a couple of hours the transportation truck came by and eight pilots got out.

"Where do you think you're going?" I asked one, who was heading for my plane.

"They want us to go out on a barge hunt over near Choiseul."

"That's a hell of a note—here we sit on our duffs for hours and then when there's a chance for a little fun, they give it to you boys."

"Sorry, old man, but orders are orders and besides, you'll have plenty of time to catch up before we finish this tour."

As I helped the pilot into the cockpit and assisted him in fastening the shoulder straps I gave him a word of advice. "You want to watch these mechanics around here, Reid. The one on this plane didn't even know where to put the gas. Everything is all right now, though. I checked the gas and oil and the ammo. Some of these 'mechs' haven't touched a plane before. They have been pulled off their regular jobs to help out until we can get some trained men here. I notice the generator charges quite high; you'll have to keep an eye on it."

We got into the vacant truck and drove around the end of the landing strip to the ready tent, with little more than the width of the road between the strip and the ocean. We passed a shell hole containing hundreds of rounds of Jap 20-mm cannon shells, then a Jap three-pounder coastal defense gun.

A couple of hours later the pilots returned from their barge hunt. All of them tried to talk at once as they gathered around Gunner George Schaefer, our squadron intelligence officer, who had a wife and two children waiting for him in Los Angeles.

"Now, now, boys—take it easy," George said soothingly, "I can only handle one of you at a time. Now then, Gher, what do you have to say—did you see anything?"

"Sure did, George. Up along in here," the pilot said, pointing to a map of Choiseul, "we were fired on by some AA guns. Just around this bend, Moore noticed a barge hidden under some bushes along the shore. All the rest of us had passed by without even seeing it. He called us over the radio and we all went back and strafed. There was one measly ack-ack gun popping away at us, but we soon quieted him down. The barge was just a mass of smoke and flame when we left. It must have been loaded with barrels of oil."

After interviewing each pilot and finding the exact spot at which the barge had been found, as well as its length and appearance, who flew top cover to watch for Zeros and who did the strafing, George and Captain Terry telephoned headquarters and reported all the facts. They had a time limit of a half hour to report back to headquarters after each mission.

By this time it was nearly noon and the sun was beating down unmercifully. The canvas tents protected us from the direct rays, but even so, the humidity in the air prevented the escape of the heat to the outside. Consequently the tent became the lid to our oven.

"Okie's division—go over to chow now and come back as soon as you can, you've got to relieve the fellows out on scramble alert."

"Don't worry," Carl McLean replied in his best Ardmore, Oklahoma, drawl. "I won't be staying over there even long enough to eat if the food is anywhere near as bad as they say it is."

Four of us donned our shirts, which instantly clung to our wet, perspiring backs. We were joined by Ace Newland's division in the truck which drove us around the strip, along the taxi-way, past some wrecked Jap airplanes and up to Dysentery Chowhall.

Outside the low wooden frame building, the lower halves of three fifty-gallon barrels formed the dishwashing unit.

We opened the screen door and entered. The first sight to greet us was the seating arrangement. There wasn't any. Six rows of men stood side by side along both sides of waist-high tables which extended the length of the room.

We picked up metal trays which had been divided into compartments to prevent the peaches from mixing with the potatoes. Here we flyers were favored, because most of the enlisted men were eating from mess kits. There were no spoons or knives at the moment, so we got along as best we could with a fork. In a few minutes the supply of spoons and knives was replenished.

In the wall separating us from the kitchen were three large openings. From the first, a large spoonful of gritty spinach was dumped into my tray, followed by a heaping spoonful of dehydrated potatoes. I moved on to the next window for a slice of Spam. After a couple of stewed apricots had been splashed into the niche adjoining the meat, I moved on to the next window. Here my canteen cup was filled with what I called chocolate milk.

To all appearances the food was good, but the telling was in the tasting. The potatoes were so water-soaked that I had to force myself to eat them. The Spam was like all Spam. The spinach was so gritty that even the men who liked it ordinarily, rebelled at this gastronomical insult. The chocolate milk would be more aptly described by the name of watered cocoa. It tasted much the same. With the use of sugar it became drinkable, however. Its temperature was about the same as a human body, but fifteen minutes after drinking it, sweat came more profusely. There was only one enjoyable part of the food — the apricots.

In the days to come, many of us fasted at noontime, or else just ate the fruit the messhall had to offer — invariably apricots or peaches.

When we had finished eating we carried all our utensils out the back door. First we stopped at a barrel and emptied all the uneaten food into the garbage can. Then we slid our cup, knife, fork and spoon onto a wire which projected from one corner of the dirty eating tray. Holding the end of this wire, we dunked the whole shebang into the first tub of hot water. Next we dunked the utensils into the middle tub, which washed off the particles remaining from the previous rinse.

Fires built under the tubs of water kept them hot, although not always boiling as they should have been. It was an ingenious system the Seabees had rigged up to feed the fires with liquid fuel. Leaning over the hot, steaming tubs with the heat of the fire blasting from below and the sun blazing from above was almost suffocating.

After a third and final rinse in comparatively clean water we took our ware back into the messhall and left it on a table for the next shift. [Then] we carried our parachutes to the truck and were driven to the planes. Again we checked and made preparations for a hurried take-off. We sat in the cockpits this time, hoping for an order to scramble. Operations had given us special instructions to remain in the plane ready for an immediate take-off, evidently expecting some Jap activity. The sun was very hot and I remembered the old saying: "Mad dogs and Englishmen go out in the midday sun." The words, "United States Marines" should be inserted next to "mad dogs."

Finally, after one more midafternoon trip to the ready tent, the operations officer came in and asked, "Who wants to fly?"

My division leader, Okie, was the first to volunteer. We were to cover the withdrawal of some supply ships and their escorts, which had completed unloading at Vella Lavella and were anxious to get out of range of Jap dive bombers before darkness came with its "bomber's moon."

We took off and turned to our compass heading. As we left the vicinity of our base we each moved away from the leader to assume our battle formation on a line abreast, so that each pilot could watch the tails of the others and have space enough to turn into any enemy plane that might attack.

We were at ten thousand feet now, and climbing steadily. I picked up my oxygen mask and curled my legs around the control stick to keep the plane flying as smoothly as possible, while I struggled with the face mask. The elasticity of the rubber bands was nearly gone and a tiny clamp continuously came unfastened as I twisted my head from side to side, keeping an alert lookout for the Japs. The little clamp permitted the lower part of my mask to rest loosely against my face instead of snugly.

Ahead of us lay a small island, about fifteen miles distant, I took my map out of the knee pocket of my flying suit. Gizo Island, I thought to myself; and off to the left, that island rising like a hog's back from the sea for nearly fifteen miles must be Ganongga . . . Only a few miles of water separated Ganongga from the comparatively large island of Vella Lavella, which tucked tiny Baga in its side, much like a white corpuscle about to envelop a germ.

"Fox base from Red one leader. Over," crackled Okie's voice over the radio.

"Red one leader from Fox base, go ahead. Over." One of the destroyers, which we could see far below leaving a long white trail of foam behind, was replying to our call.

"Fox base from Red leader. Have arrived on station with three other chickens. Over." Okie was telling the destroyer that four fighter planes were now overhead and ready to relieve other planes in protecting it from Japanese aerial attack.

"This is Red one leader. Fly at angels ten. Wilco. Out." We began to climb up to angels ten, which happened to be 20,000 feet for that particular day. Several flights of fighter planes were covering the withdrawal of the supply force and were stacked up at altitudes assigned them by the fighter director officer on the destroyer, so that he had planes at all levels to intercept raiding Japs.

At 20,000 feet it is possible to see a lot of country. The land and the water spreads out beneath you as if you were perched high above a gigantic, varicolored map. I could make out the shore of Bougainville with the Shortlands this side of it. Farther toward the south I could see the long island of Choiseul and Santa Isabel . . .

My mind stopped concentrating on the past. For over two hours we had been on patrol. For two hours I had just been sitting in the cockpit, moving my hands and feet occasionally and twisting my neck constantly from side to side, like the rotor of a washing machine. We had strained our eyes for the sight of an unfamiliar speck that might materialize into a Jap plane. We had listened carefully to the radio to be sure we wouldn't miss any bogey reports. The radio popped and crackled and finally came to life and a voice told the destroyer that Red flight two had arrived on station. Fox base called our division, thanked us for our efforts and told us to return to base. We felt disappointed at leaving, because the Japs' favorite time of day for attacking was fast approaching.

We pointed the long smooth snouts of our Corsairs homeward and with a sun low in the sky at our backs we dived at a shallow angle, chopping the miles off the distance at the rate of one every twelve seconds.

We raced over the Munda airstrip, then one by one peeled away from the formation in three-count intervals with steep chandelles to the right. When we had lost sufficient speed we let our wheels down.

Never had I attempted to land a plane on a field as narrow and short as the Munda strip. It was about fifty feet wide. And of all fighter planes, the Corsair is perhaps the worst with which to attempt such a landing. The nose projects so far ahead of the pilot, without narrowing to a point as some fighter plane noses do, that when the plane is on the ground in a three-point attitude, forward visibility is nil.

I hoped for the best and swung in for my landing. The plane touched the ground gently and swished down the runway. Everything ahead was blotted from sight, except for a little triangular patch of the runway between the lead edge of the wing and the nose on each side. Unless I kept each of those patches the same width, I would run off the runway into deadly obstacles.

There was very little wind and my Corsair seemed unwilling to slow down as it should. A coral road went by on the left. I knew the end of the surfaced runway was fast approaching, so I applied the brakes, meanwhile keeping the plane rolling straight ahead. It soon slowed enough so that I was looking for the wide taxi road leading from the far end of the strip. In a few seconds I saw it, but I saw something else too—*mud!* Before I could unlock my tailwheel and turn off the runway, I felt the plane hit something and mush down, simultaneously coming almost to a stop. I felt like a fly stuck in molasses. I knew in a flash if the plane ever stopped rolling, a truck would be needed to pull it from the goo. I had to keep it rolling and try to plow through the mud. I shoved the throttle forward for more power and a fraction of a second later pulled the flap lever up so the mud wouldn't damage the flaps as the plane mired deep. I pulled back on the stick to lessen the tendency for the front wheels to dig in and flip me over on my back.

The plane slowed almost to a standstill, but I gave it more throttle and eased the stick forward to make the tail lighter, yet not so far as to endanger going over on my nose. The engine roared loudly and the plane shuddered with its mighty effort, but the wheels kept rolling as I gave it left rudder to get to the nearest solid ground and the taxi road.

Just as we reached the edge of the mud the plane slowed almost to its final stop. I quickly added more throttle and must have had nearly 2,000 horsepower to pull me up and onto the hard ground.

It had all happened in a period of fifteen seconds or less. I grinned and waved to a mechanic who was standing nearby, waiting for me to get stuck. He waved back and grasped both of his hands together in a handclasp and shook them over his head—just like a victorious prize fighter.

That night as we lay in bed, we heard piano music floating up to us from some place down the hill. Whoever was playing was an accomplished pianist with a strong resonant bass.

"Do you boys hear what I hear?" Leach asked us in that peculiar Mississippi drawl of his.

As if by one accord we all decided to play a little joke on him.

"Why no, Leach—I don't hear nothin'."

"What are you talking about, Leach?"

"I don't hear a sound, Jesse."

One after another we denied hearing anything. The music stopped as if the player was in our little game.

"Why, I coulda sworn that I heard somebody playing a piano just a few minutes ago. It's stopped now though," Leach said.

"Ace, you better go get Doc Brittingham over here. Poor ol' Jesse has been out in the sun too long today," I suggested.

When he heard that remark, Leach proclaimed adamantly, "I don't need no doctor—I'm as well as any man in here." He paused for a moment and added, "At least I think I am."

"That patrol was just too much for Jesse," piped up Hughes.

"Fools," drawled Leach, using his favorite invective, "there was somebody playing a piano, I am as sure of that as I am that I'm lying here next to Hughes."

"Oh, but you're not lying next to Hughes, old man, you happen to be lying next to me." Ace Newlands of Pasadena, California, interspersed that statement with one of his mock accents—this time an English twang. We all believed Ace was an escaped vaudeville comic, although he claimed to be a graduate of UCLA. He was as thin as a bean pole.

Leach was by now getting excited, judging from the rising inflection of his voice as it tried to surround the darkness shrouding our conversation. "Good Gawwd—what is this? Are you all ganging up against me or am I really going crazy?"

The music started again. Leach tried to call our attention to it and once more we denied hearing anything.

"Jesse, come to your senses and let us go to sleep. How in God's world would a piano ever get away up here at Munda, where they just cleaned the Japs out only a few days ago, let alone anybody around here that could play the damned thing like you claim he can?"

"That's what's worrying me. I just can't believe it could be true."

And so, with the mystery of the piano still unsolved, we dropped off to sleep.

A great noise spurred the air at 2330. My heart momentarily stopped beating. Without delay, I swung my feet over the cot and into my "air raid" shoes, which I had placed in such a position that my feet would fall into them every time I got up.

One chorus of antiaircraft guns was augmented by a second, very close to our tent. The bang of that gun caused me to drop my efforts at reaching for my steel helmet—and run. I took two steps and practically fell down the incline leading to our foxhole. I hit my head on the top of the foxhole doorway and was just ducking it lower for another try, when I felt somebody's feet land on my back. This bit of impetus sent me the remaining five feet into the dugout and I crashed into the opposite wall of our shelter. Dirt crumbled and slid down my back as I slumped to a crouching position.

"What's the idea of blocking the entrance, Zed?" asked Nugent right behind me.

"I couldn't help it, I hit my head. What's the idea of jumping on my anyhow?"

"Good hell, I didn't want to waste any time getting in here with old Washing Machine Charlie headed right this way and those guns shooting so fast."

There were three Johns in that one foxhole. John Witt of Wauwatosa, Wisconsin, was a dark-haired, rather stocky lad who was buddy-buddy with John Nugent, who hailed from Chicago. We called Nugent "The Face" because if there were any insects around, poison ivy or other skin maladies, they always got to him first. He was the same height as Witt, but not quite as heavy. I was the third foxhole John. With my shoes on I was almost six feet tall. My 10,000 odd brown hairs were cut short in the GI manner. I was nicknamed "Zed" because I was one of the three pilots in the squadron who had acted as Fighter Director Officer at Midway and in that capacity used Zed as my code name. I was soon to pick up another nickname, "Belts Foster," because of the jingling buckles of the three belts I wore every day—one to hold my trousers up, one to carry my knife, canteen, first-aid kit and extra cartridges, and the third to be accessible for a tourniquet in case I should get wounded badly in the air.

In front of our tent I found Ace Newlands, Leach and Hughes. They burst out laughing as I approached, thinking I looked funny in just a pair of shorts with my clodhoppers and steel helmet on. And we all laughed when we saw Jules Koetsch from Brooklyn. He was standing out there in the bright moonlight enjoying the air raid—

stark-naked with the exception of his meerschaum pipe. The moon made his balding head glisten.

Two of our veteran "sack" men—Texan Paul Pankhurst and Okie— hadn't stirred from their bunks during the entire aerial barrage.

We had just returned to our sacks for a few minutes when we heard the distinctive moan of a Jap airplane. Their engines had a high-pitched anemic roar compared to the deep, throaty resonance of American planes. Jap night raiders are called Washing Machine Charlie after the original pest that harassed our boys on Guadalcanal. At various times he had been called Louie the Louse, Maytag Charlie, and other names less printable.

Despite their impotent sound at night, the Jap bombers sometimes performed accurate bombings, but what was more remarkable was the small amount of damage they did compared to what they could have done.

This particular Louie the Louse was coming back for another try. The searchlights came on and caught a reflection.

"They've got him—they've got him in the lights," Nugent and I yelled. The rest of the men trouped out of the tent to see the sight.

Red polka-dots appeared on the black velvet of the sky. The orange flashes missed him by hundreds of feet. A fellow from the next tent shot his 45-caliber pistol into the sky at the Jap as a gesture of contempt for our AA.

We hit our foxhole just before the ground shook and dirt tumbled down from a near hit. Shrapnel chopped holes in our tent and rattled around in the trees. Then we returned to our still-warm sacks . . .

❧ ❧ ❧ ❧

HERE, AGAIN, IS MARINE TANK PLATOON LEADER (now Major) Robert Blake, a living legend during the New Georgia campaign. In the following unpublished present-tense narrative, we see him in action in this gripping reconstruction of a typical engagement.

·8· DEATH ON THE MUNDA TRAIL

ROBERT W. BLAKE

In a wedge of three tanks we push through our front lines and plow into the jungle beyond. Our guide, with rifle slung across his shoulder, is in front of the tank, backing up, waving us directions how to miss this tree and avoid that hole. I am still sitting, head and shoulders out of the turret, ducking vines and branches and phoning directions down to Amurri in the driver's seat.

We are creeping into an area where the foliage had been blasted and withered by shell fire. My eyes are on the guide. He is backing down a bank toward a shallow stream. Suddenly I look beyond him and freeze. There on the opposite bank, beneath a lip of foliage is a long, black slot.

"Look out," I yell, waving wildly at our guide. "You're backing into a pill box!"

I trip the seat lever and drop down behind the periscopic sight. I level the sight dot at the black slot and press the firing switch. WHAM, the gun bucks, a wad of smoke billows through the trees. The concealing branches are left raw and broken.

I can make out a rectangular shadow in the brush alongside the first. Another pill box! I blast into it.

Now everyone is yelling in the interphone. "Look, look, fresh earth under that pile of brush on our left!" "Hey, a pill box at the end of that log on our right!" Thetford's machine gun is hammering away in the bow. I blast into a row of dried palm fronds leaning against the bank. Another fire slot appears! There are pill boxes all over the opposite slope!

"Hey, Lieutenant, *Japs, Japs,*" Thetford is screaming through the tank.

"Where?" I jam my eyes into the periscope and swing the turret from side to side.

"They jumped up from beside us and ran across the stream through the brush! Couldn't turn this gun far enough to get them. They're gone now."

We crash forward to get a better view. On the far right a grass hut appears on the bank. We smash at it with canister. A second grass shack. We try to blow them up with shells or burn them with tracers, but give it up.

As yet we have received no return fire, not a shot. Except for the two that jumped and ran, we have seen no Japs, no signs, no movement.

Behind us our infantry covering squad is crouching in holes and behind trees. I jack up the turret seat and stick out my head. "Hey," I yell to the nearest man, "tell Major Carrigan that this place is deserted. Ask him to send the infantry in and we will push on." The man nods and starts to the rear.

From the top of the turret I eye the lush folds, the dark recesses of the jungle. It is too quiet.

I pull the sub-machine gun from its scabbard and begin to fire into everything in sight, into the black slots of the pill boxes, into the shades and thickets, into the clots of foliage in the trees encircling us. Still nothing to be seen, no Japs, no snipers. I empty the drum at coconuts in the trees overhead and drop back into the turret to put the gun away.

I am just sliding the tommy gun into its holster when, *rat-tat-tat-tat-tat,* something crashes against the tank. The armor vibrates, the metal rings. Smoke pours into the fighting compartment. It sounds like riveting, smells like welding, hot molten metal and scorched paint.

Another swift burst hammers against us. At once I am thrown forward, my head and shoulders stinging. Up goes my hand to my head. Instantly it is peppered with red hot burning fragments. I look at Hoban. He too is bent forward clutching the back of his neck. In a flash I realize; those open hatches. I look at Hoban. He looks at me.

Rat-tat-tat-tat-tat, we are lashed again with a hail of splinters, as machine gun slugs ricochet from the open hatches and shatter against the inside of the turret behind our heads. Have to close those hatches! But overhead shots pound by like one long explosion. I can visualize my arm evaporating in that stream of bullets. Suddenly a break in the firing. Out shoots my arm, slamming Hoban's hatch on the up stroke, crashing mine closed on the down.

Frantically I grind the turret back and forth, searching the jungle through the sights. I see nothing, no Japs, no gun, no smoke, no flashes.

Still the fire crashes against us, ringing the armor, shattering our nerves. Any moment I expect an anti-tank shell to come boring through our steel to erupt in our faces.

Those pill boxes! The Japs must still be manning them. As fast as Hoban can load, I splash high explosives into every one in sight. But it does not stifle the hammering of the enemy gun.

"Amurri, drive us out from behind these trees." He guns the engine. The tank twists forward. Instantly we are swept by a renewed hail of bullets.

"Hold it!" and the volley stops. I rotate the turret from side to side. Nothing but leaves and vines and trees.

"Well move on, Amurri," and again we are raked by a storm of slugs.

I radio the other tanks. "Does anyone see where that fire is coming from?"

"Can't see a thing. My periscope's shot out. Fixing it." It is Nobile in the tank beside me.

Ficket cuts in, "The shots are coming from down near the beach."

"You heard that. See if you can work us down there, Amurri."

The engine roars and we are lashed by another blast of bullets. Lead splashes in under the turret and flays against us.

"Hold it, Amurri!" I switch my thumb to the machine gun trigger and fire blindly into the brush, swinging the turret around as I do so. "I'll find that gun if I have to shoot down every leaf and tree to do it."

I pepper the jungle from the far right, across in front of us, and over toward the beach on our left. The gun jams. The turret swings on. I am still pouring through the sights. The gun is pointing at a clump of foliage not over fifty feet away. Suddenly there is a tiny flicker of flame among the leaves. A bolt of red flashes straight into my sights. I wince. A hail of machine gun bullets pounds against our armor.

"I see it, I see it," I yell and clamp down on the trigger of the cannon. WHAM, the gun kicks. A blast of smoke swirls between the trees. I watch as it clears. There is a hole ripped in the jungle, stripped of leaves, raw with broken branches.

I peer into the heart of the thicket for the slightest sign or movement. Slowly I traverse the turret back and forth. Suddenly at the very spot I am looking, flame spits out and bullets thrash against our armor.

"There he is!" Hoban and I shout at once.

Not over eight tank lengths away, at a V notch made by the end of an embankment and the base of a tree, protrudes the finned black barrel of a machine gun. Behind it a helmet moves, eyes peering underneath, sighting along the barrel.

"Canister, Hoban, quick, quick!" A live Jap! Strange wild excitement squirts through my veins. I had expected some nameless, faceless thing, seen only from far away. But there he is with mouth, and nose, and eyes, so close I could take his picture. A live target, after so long. I itch to fire at him, to kill him.

"Hurry, Hoban, before another tank shoots him!" And yet he looks so human, so much like one of us. But I can see him struggling with his gun, trying to load it. He would kill me if he could. Carefully I turn the traversing grip and twist the elevating handwheel, leveling the cannon full into the man's face. Instantly fire spurts from the muzzle of the Jap gun. A red streak hurtles toward my eyes to flail against the turret. Slowly my thumb bears down on the electrical switch. The tank jolts and a billow of smoke blows through the foliage. As it clears, the enemy gun is plainly visible. The man is writhing behind it.

A howl of triumph goes through the tank. "You got him, you got him!" "Shoot him again, he's still moving!"

"High explosive," yells Hoban as he slams a shell home.

I relay the gun on the writhing figure and squeeze the trigger button. Smoke bursts from the muzzle, dust and dirt blasts up at the target. When it settles the man behind the gun lies distorted and still.

Wild, insane excitement shakes us. We shout and pound each other on the back.

"Hey, Lieutenant, look, look," Amurri is shouting, "another Jap!"

Sure enough, another helmet moves in the foliage. A Jap is crawling along the embankment, not over fifty feet away. Head and shoulders appear. A figure in a gray-green jacket creeps over the body of the dead gunner and sits up behind the gun at which I am still aimed.

Everyone in the tank is shouting.

No need even to change the sights. His face is framed in the center circle. I depress the trigger. BLAM. When the fumes clear, the man's body is tangled with that of the former gunner.

Immediately, *rat-tat-tat-tat-tat,* new fire splashes against our armor. From another gun! I swing the turret off into the jungle, ripping at random into the brush. When I fire, the enemy fires. When I stop, he stops. It is impossible to tell where it is coming from.

"Move up, Amurri."

The engine roars and a new hail of bullets hits us.

"Hey, hey," Hoban nudges me, "a Jap is firing that same gun!"

"A little more, Amurri. I can't see him for the trees."

"Let me drive across the stream and run over him," Amurri pleads.

"No, we might bog down."

"Hell, everybody gets to shoot but me. A driver's got nothing to do but sit and watch."

The Jap is hunched over the gun, blasting at the tank behind us. I can see his face clearly, black brows frowning under the rim of his helmet, wide cheek bones, and a mouth drawn straight and thin with determination. I center the cannon on the bridge of his nose and squeeze the trigger. When the air clears, the head is gone. Slowly the torso flops back on the remains of the other gunners.

Even as I fire, another burst of machine gun fire sprays us. Impossible to see where it came from.

"A little closer to that embankment, Amurri."

The engine roars. Fire hits us. Slowly we twist between the trees. Suddenly a figure leaps from the foliage beyond the stream bank and lopes across the opening in front of the tank, and disappears behind the embankment beside the gun. So fast I could not put a gun on him.

"Look, they're working toward us!"

"Yeah, but don't stop here, Amurri. I can't swing the gun for the trees."

Instantly a second Jap, a little fellow in gray uniform, and wrap-around leggins, springs out of the brush and trots across to the same embankment, swinging his long rifle easily in his hand. Then another! And another!

"Hold it, Amurri!"

Nothing to be seen now. But there will probably be more Nips coming. I aim at a point between two trees past which each had run, and press the trigger. My tracers are high. I wind down the gun and fire several more bursts to bring my fire about knee high, and wait.

"There's one!" A helmet domes up over a sunken log, eyes appear, only to jerk back down when they spot the tanks staring at them.

The little Nip hides a long time. Then up pushes the helmet again and the eyes. The cannon is still pointing at him. Down he ducks. I stroke the trigger with my thumb. But still no shots, no movement. Up comes the helmet again, and then the eyes, slowly peering at the tanks, first one and then the other.

No one fires. The Nip takes confidence. Can't see out of those tanks, he thinks, and rises up behind his log and steps over it. Bending low, but without haste, he starts trotting for the embankment. My thumb quivers on the trigger. He reaches the first of the two trees. Down goes my thumb. *Tat-ah-ah-ah-ah,* tracers streak out, a long solid line of livid red in front of the Jap.

I have fired too soon. He can still dive or dodge or turn and run. But no, he never hesitates a step. On he lopes until he hits the dartling band of fire. His knees fly out sideways, smashed by bullets, and he sprawls headlong on the ground. I turn the traversing handle after him. Frantically the Jap scrambles on his hands to drag his broken legs the last few yards to the embankment.

His figure struggles in the aiming circle of the sights. I squeeze the trigger. Dirt spurts up short of the Jap. I turn the elevating wheel, and fire again. Burning tracers plunge into his ribs. The body jerks, the elbows buckle, the head bows forward. His shirt ripples in the storm of bullets, and the earth beyond spouts up. Slowly I turn the turret, stitching the length of him with tracers. Under the impact, the body pitches over, the helmet breaks and flies.

No sooner had I stopped firing, than a helmet pushes up behind the same log and, without a second look, the Jap leaps over the log and runs for the embankment. I do not even have to move the gun, just wait until he runs into the center of my sights, then depress the trigger. The first red burst sweeps into his knees. His momentum carries him forward, but his legs crumple under him. He comes to his knees, tries to run on them, falls forward on his hands to slither like a lizard on toward the safety of the embankment. I revolve the turret after him. The spitting red tracers curve toward him, catching him through the hips to fling him sideways into the base of a tree. Still he struggles forward on his elbows, dragging his body behind him.

"What's in the cannon, Hoban?"

"Canister."

I mash the cannon switch. The gun roars. The earth shoots up around the Jap. When it settles, the head and shoulders of the body are a shapeless mass.

"Let's creep a little closer to that embankment, Amurri."

The engine thunders and we clank slowly forward, stopping and backing and turning to squeeze between the trees. We have not gone far when, *rat-tat-tat-tat-tat* machine gun slugs slash into us again.

"There he is!" Everyone yells at once. About twenty feet beyond the first gun, right in the middle of a trail, a long, low, mean-looking heavy machine gun is set up, and bending over it, both hands on the grips, is a Jap. He has no cover, no protection, not even a bush to conceal himself. Up to now the trees had hidden him. But there he sits for the whole world to see. He glowers along the barrel of his gun. Flame flickers at the muzzle—no big flash, no smoke like ours make, just a bubble of light and the crash of bullets flattening against our armor.

The cannon breach clanks shut. "Canister," shouts Hoban, "let's see you smear him!"

I poise the aiming circle slightly above and to the left of the man's chest and clamp down on the trigger. WHAM. A storm of steel hurls the Jap from behind the gun and backs him into a tree, where he slumps like a pile of rags.

Even as I watch, another Jap crawls out of the mound of coral not far from the water's edge and makes his way on his stomach across the short open space toward the gun. Everybody is yelling again. Amurri wants to run over him with the tank. Thetford curses because the Jap is just beyond the traverse of his bow gun. Hoban begins to fumble (frantically) for ammunition. He finds a shell, flings it into the breach. "Canister," he yells.

By now the Jap, with the utmost caution has crawled to the middle of the trail, in plain view of the tank.

"No need to use canister on him, Hoban. It's a clear shot, not a leaf in the way. Let's see what high explosive will do to him."

Hoban opens the breach, takes out the canister, and slips a new round in.

The Jap has reached the gun and is flattened on the trail behind it. He lifts his head to have a cautious look. He is not going to sit up like the former gunner. He is going to fire from his belly. Slowly his hand goes up for the trigger. The upper part of his body lifts from the ground. I level the cannon at the soft of his stomach. I watch as he swings the barrel toward us. I wait until he sends a stream of lead against our armor, then press the trigger. BAMM. The projectile socks into the ground in front of the Jap and glances up into his exposed stomach. There is a sharp explosion and the top half of the enemy's body spins into the air—like a rag doll in a wild dance—then crumples over the breach of the machine gun.

A howl of triumph goes through the tank. "Best shot of the day!"

"You blew him in half!"

"Ah, hell," says Amurri, "a driver doesn't have any fun. Let me run over just one little old Jap."

"Take it easy, Amurri. We'll get jumped if we get too close."

Amurri does not say anything more, but I hear him rattling tools down in the driver's compartment. Probably fixing something or other.

I swing the turret off in search of new targets. Suddenly there is a burst of shots, not outside, but right inside the tank. Thetford screams.

"Good lord, he's been hit!"

Hoban and I both look at once—and relax. It is Amurri. He has wrenched the Cutts compensator from the muzzle of the tommy gun so he can stick it out the direct vision slot, and there he sits spraying the jungle with forty-five caliber slugs. The empty brass cases are flying from the gun in a steady stream across the tank and hitting Thetford who is doubled forward, clawing at his back, trying to dislodge a red hot shell that had gone down his neck.

"Hey, Lieutenant," Hoban nudges me, "one of those Japs is still alive! He's trying to reach the gun."

Sure enough. In the litter of bodies behind the embankment is an anguished, upturned face, and a trembling arm stretching for the trigger.

"High explosive," Hoban sings out, and a shell bangs into the breach.

I align the sight pipper on the Jap's shoulder and press the electric contact. When the smoke drifts off, the pile of Japs has blossomed out. An arm is lying on the trail.

Even as I search the littered remains for further signs of life, a helmet bobs along behind the embankment. I level my sights on the enemy gun, and wait. Without hesitating to look at the tanks, the Jap crawls quickly over the bodies of his comrades and takes his place behind the gun. I cannot believe it. His hands and knees must be sopping with their blood. He must be sitting in it!

Methodically he reaches out and slides another long clip of ammunition into the side of his gun, yanks the loading handle and sinks back to pepper us.

He is not over thirty feet away, thirty feet from three tanks and he rises up to challenge them, and with only a machine gun.

"Shoot him, shoot him," Hoban keeps banging my arm and shouting, as the bullets pound off our armor.

"There's no hurry."

A live Jap, so close I could almost touch him. He is wearing a quilted cover over his helmet, for camouflage. I can see the sparse growth of a moustache across his upper lip. What can he be thinking? It is frightening enough behind this armor. Think of the livid terror in that man's heart, knowing and waiting for the shell to come spinning into his face, to smash through his eyes and splash his brain like a gray paste on the leaves. What magnificent courage! But wasted. They probably think they can bait us in with that gun, and then jump us with mines.

The Jap lowers his eyes to check the lay of his gun, then straightens up to fire again.

I let him get his first shots away, then knuckle down on the trigger. When the smoke thins, he is sprawled on his back against the bodies of the other gunners, his heels pounding the ground and his arms clutching convulsively at the air.

"Look, that's a pill box they've been hiding behind!"

It is a large rectangular pile of coral. Coconuts have been placed to sprout among the rocks, covering it with thick foliage.

"A flock of Japs went in there and they have not all come out. Give me armor-piercing shells, I'll drill in after them."

The first shot and coral flies. The second shot, a deeper gouge. The third, and logs appear. The fourth shot, and I see the tracer twirling in a long arc out the other side across the water. Into the same hole I blast with high explosive. Smoke pours out.

The other two tanks take up the fire. If there are any Japs left alive in that pill box, they will be coming out and I want to be ready. I train my machine gun knee high between the same two trees as before, and wait.

"There's one!" A figure leaps from behind the pill box and runs back the way the other had come. He reaches the first tree. I squeeze the trigger. Nothing happens. I clamp down on it again. No shots. I beat on it, push and pull. No good. I sit helplessly and watch the Jap run through my sights, past all the lead dots, into the center circle, past the center dot and safely out the other side. The gun is jammed.

"Clear the 'thirty," I yell to Hoban, when out jumps another Jap, runs through my sights from one side to the other—right past the muzzles of our guns—and plunges into the jungle beyond.

"Clear," yells Hoban, and I jam down on the switch, peppering the spot in the foliage where the Jap disappeared. I chop away at it until the branches are frayed and leafless. I turn the turret back and forth and crank my fire up and down. He could not have gotten far. He may be hugging the ground, hoping I will shoot over him. I wind down my fire until it skims the earth causing the leaves to dance and whirl. I can imagine how terrified he is with machine gun slugs snarling through the brush after him.

Perhaps he is behind a log or in a hole and thinks he is safe. So I fire high explosives into the branches and through the trunks of trees to burst above the ground and lash the earth with fragments. Again and again I scour the surface with fire and pour it deep into the darkness beyond and wide on every side. When I feel sure there has been no escape, I spray the thicket another last time.

Half hidden in the brush behind the second gun we make out another pill box. We pound it full of holes. No Japs. We edge up to a single strand of barbed wire running between the trees. An observation shack appears on the shore. We shoot it down. As the foliage falls a tremendous pill box becomes visible with the yawning muzzle of at least a 75-mm gun protruding. My heart stops. We fire everything we have at that gun in desperation to keep it silent, before we realize that what had saved us from being blown up by that gun was its pill box which prevented it from being trained in the direction from which we were lucky enough to come. We receive no shots, see no Japs.

Ahead of the tanks, all along the stream bank, sticks have been pushed into the ground with strips of red cloth tied to them. Perhaps they mark anti-tank mines. I am wondering whether we ought to try to push across them when Hoban announces, "Only three rounds of thirty-seven ammo left." That settles it.

I open the rear pistol port and wave until an infantryman crawls up behind the tank. "Tell Major Carrigan that we have killed all the Japs in sight and shot up all the pill boxes. We're out of ammunition. We'll hold it here until the infantry can come up and take over."

At length a squad of men crawls up behind us. We watch a sergeant worm his way out in front of our tank. He wiggles on his stomach toward the first shore pill box. We see him pull a hand grenade out of his blouse, wrap his hand around it, and wrench out the pin. He gets up to a crouch, eyeing the screen of the jungle towering around him, and sprints the last few yards and flops against the side of the pill box. Quickly he reaches around front, flings in the grenade and springs back to hug the wall for the explosion.

We wait, and wait. I half expect the grenade to be thrown back out. Then the coral jumps slightly, smoke squirts out, a muffled crash. The sergeant springs out in front of the fire slot, ready with his carbine. *Bang, bang, bang, bang,* he fires as the smoke pours out. When it clears, he peers closely inside, leaps back and empties more shots at something he sees within.

All along the stream bank squads are working forward on their stomachs. Other men crawl up on the blind side of the pill boxes and pitch in grenades. I see a man on his haunches squinting into a pill box just ahead. He steps back a pace, takes deliberate aim and fires into the darkness.

I radio the other tanks to hold fast, and then grab my tommy gun and jump to the ground.

All the infantrymen are beaming. "We didn't lose a man today!" "Say, you tankmen are all right!" "Look what you did to the Japs, just look would you!" They point to the first machine gun. I see a jumbled heap of human shapes and go closer. The sight is horrible. There had been about eight Japs, but they are so blown and torn with such point blank fire that there is scarely a whole one left.

Scraps of flesh and tatters of clothing litter the ground. An arm lies on the trail. One Jap is shot through the face. Only the shell of his head remains, the face stretched and distorted like a rubber mask.

Here a torso is ripped open and entrails, a thin blue color, are spilling on the dirt. There a back is skinned by blast, exposing red, raw muscles in neat layers like the charts on doctors' walls. A crumpled leg with a white sliver of bone ripped through the flesh. A head of black hair hit by a fragment that entered over the temple and plowed down through the bone of the forehead and out the eye. A body, face down in the dirt, the shirt stitched with little wet patches where machine gun bullets left tiny holes.

Beyond is the second gun, and another tangle of Jap dead. The whole area smells of warm blood and raw meat, like a butcher shop, like the time I watched the farmer cut up a hog in the wagon shed. Already in the sticky silence of the jungle I can hear the flies swarming. I feel sick and start to turn away. Suddenly one of the red distorted figures in the pile groans, and moves.

"Good God, he's still alive!"

He lays propped against a tree, one knee tucked up under his chin, the other wrenched sideways on the ground.

Even as we watch, he groans again and his head rolls over on his shoulder in a twist of agony. His eyes open. He sees our feet. His head straightens up. He glowers at us with burning, blood-red eyes. All at once he jams his hand into a bulging pocket. I flick my tommy gun off safety, but before I can fire, a shot roars beside me, and the head smashes back against the tree.

I hurry on. In the shadows of each pill box I can make out arms and legs tangled across butchered bodies. On the ground behind the two grass shacks scores of Jap dead lie. Some are still in their blankets, their rifles and light machine guns jutting through the palm leaf walls, where they hoped to cut down our infantry as they emerged from the jungle across the stream. But our first few rounds of canister had plastered them where they lay.

At each sight and scent of mangled flesh, my horror and repugnance mounts. Only a matter of minutes ago and these were human beings like ourselves, with hearts and souls. We are not to blame for killing them. My blood boils against the monsters and the policies that have pitted us here against our fellow men. My heart goes out to those brave little men who stood and fought so gallantly against the tanks and died rather than retreat.

Anxious to leave the grisly sights behind, I return across the stream and am signaling Amurri how to back the tank between the trees to get turned around. On all sides of the slope I notice more Jap dead. The further I look, the more I see. It is strange that Jap dead should lie on our side of the stream.

I notice that some of the dead wear mottled jungle suits just like our own, and others wear our shoes, our helmets, and under some, our rifles. The Japs must be using captured American equipment. Then I step across a corpse a tank had run over on the way in. I bend down to look closer. It cannot be true! On a cord around the blackened neck dangle U.S. dog tags. Not Japs, but Americans are these, dozens of them, covering the jungle floor, lying where they fell, cut down in the battles two days ago by cross fire from the unseen pill boxes beyond.

Beside one tree, a machine gun tripod stands, and behind it, his bloated hands still on the legs, lays the body of the lad who put it there. Beside him is the gunner, the heavy Browning still cradled in his arms where he had crawled up under fire to put it into action. I hold my breath and hurry from the scene.

As I go I step across two more Americans. Between them is a folded stretcher, torn and splintered by machine gun fire. In a glance the

III   Northward Drive:
Russells to Bougainville

The Marines are unloading in a hurry after a bomb has struck between the two landing craft in the center at Rendova beach. (Photo by Sarno)

Raiders' landing force. Marines off troop transport awaiting transportation to camps.

Landing on Rendova Island from LSTs and lighter: a Marine aviation organization is on the move. Rough camp was quickly established by the pitching of pup tents. (Photo by Sgt. C. L. Smith)

This unusual photograph shows puffs of smoke rising from
Munda as huge American guns shell the enemy from
nearby Rendova Island. (Picture was taken with a telephoto lens by Sgt. C. L. Smith from a lookout tower on
Rendova)

Tankmen examine a Japanese flame-thrower, which was used against them during an attack. This equipment was captured at New Georgia. Captain Robert W. Blake, Leatherneck author and tank commander extraordinaire, is on the left. (Photo by Sgt. James H. McNamara)

Landing boats going toward the beach. (Photo by James)

Marines racing from landing boats across the beach to the jungle.

As the casualties are brought down to the beach, squads of riflemen accompany them in the event the enemy, attacking in overwhelming numbers, should penetrate the Marine line. (Photo by Ohman)

Members of the 1st Battalion, Third Marines, coming out of the jungle from the front lines. They were the first to hit the beach at Torekino Point, where the strongest opposition was met. (Photo by Pfc. Schwartz)

When the U.S. Navy Seabees named one of their miraculous roads on Bougainville "Marine Drive Hi-way" in honor of Marines who seized the ground from the Japanese, the Leathernecks responded with this sign. Shown shaking hands across the sign are Seabee Chief Boatswain's Mate Earl J. Cobb (left) and Marine Corporal Charles L. Marshall. (Photo by Capt. O'Sheel)

Marine infantry and tank in action. (Photo by Pfc. Phillip Scheer)

So when we reach the
"Isle of Japan"
With our caps at a
Jaunty tilt
We'll enter the city of Tokyo
On the roads the SEABEES
Built.

Third Marine
2ND Raider R

Marines moving and passing through mud on their way to
the Bougainville front lines.

Tents strung from trees in a jungle clearing served as the
command post for the Marines on Bougainville. (Photo by
Sgt. R. Robbins)

story tells itself. These two medics had heard the wounded scream and crawled out to bring them in. They got as far as this, when the Jap machine guns caught them and they too lay and bled and begged for help, until death came for them at last.

I have to turn from them and clench my teeth against revulsion. One upturned face is black and puffy. The eyes are open but the sockets empty. Flies crawl everywhere.

These are not just dead. They are Americans, lads who came over on the boat with us, stood in line with us for chow, and laughed with us at "Happy-Hour." In my heart the compassion I had felt for the Jap dead slips away and in its place a rage rears up and roars. That these Americans should have to come out here to fight and die and their bodies rot in this abysmal jungle just because a pack of international bandits wanted land that was not theirs.

The full impact of the crime the Japanese committed strikes me. They are to blame for all this death and anguish, they and their lust for empire. How I wish that I had shot that wounded Jap, hollowed out his skull point blank with my forty-five, or better, ripped him open with my pocket knife. I grit my teeth. I will kill them, kill them, kill them, a thousand lives for every one of ours! And if compassion ever tempts me, I will think of that field of blackened American corpses, of the dead gunner and his mate, of the riddled stretcher bearers, and of the wounded who lay and bled, and knew no help could come, and died, in agony, forsaken, and alone.

❁　❁　❁　❁

BOUGAINVILLE WAS NEXT. LYING ATHWART THE entrance to the Slot, this sprawling (30 miles wide by 125 long), fiddle-shaped French discovery was the closest land-based bomber hop to Rabaul. Bougainville was one of the key stepping stones of the advance to the northern Solomons, and its primary defenses were built around strongpoints in the Kahili Shortlands area, with large airfields at the southern end of the island; and the Buka area, with other airfields at the northwestern end. Rich, cultivated land and coconut plantations characterized the north coast, but as one moved in from the landing beaches on a west-east track, the land was pure swamp. The Japanese garrison numbered in the vicinity of 35,000, troops of the Seventeenth Army.

Pre-invasion bombardment was ruled out: we needed total surprise; however, there was adequate naval gunfire support

should it be required. Reconnaissance revealed light installations behind the beaches, and even more surprising, only about
1000 troops. General Vandegrift—recalled to the Solomons after
the death of Major General C. D. Barrett, who had been originally tabbed for this operation—again commanded the division.
The D-Day plan called for the 3rd Marine Division under Major General Allen H. Turnage, Jr., to secure the beachhead; then
the Army would take over. Twelve beaches were required for
the assault, all but one extending northwestward from Cape Torokina toward the Laruma River, and the 12th on the north (inner)
shoreline of Pulata Island, the larger of two islands off Cape Torokina. Three combat teams were to land abreast over these beaches, and given some degree of luck, some 14,000 marines would
be ashore D-Day.

The most imaginative feature of the Bougainville operation
was a diversionary raid on nearby Choiseul by Colonel Victor
A. Krulak, commanding the 2nd Parachute Battalion. On the
night of October 27 - 28 Krulak landed a 725-man force at Voza
on the southwest coast. In three days of raising particular hell,
Krulak's marines killed 72 enemy troops and simultaneously
struck at several strongpoints, including a barge facility which
they destroyed. Krulak withdrew November 3 with 11 dead and
14 wounded. But the most important product of this raid was
the supreme confusion it created in Japanese headquarters; Seventeenth Army prepared to defend against the marines at Choiseul, and hence our landings were lightly opposed . . . a perfect
diversion!

Despite poor targeting by four destroyers on D-Day, November, 1943, the 3rd Marine Division stormed ashore and was met
by a Japanese infantry company behind 18 pillboxes and case-
mated 75-mm gun. In the ensuing fight Sergeant Robert A. Owens,
Company A, 3rd Marines, seeing his comrades being swept by
machine gun in a pillbox, charged the box and blasted its occupants. He received fatal multiple wounds and was awarded a
Medal of Honor. That night the division and 6200 tons of supplies and equipment were on the beach, and Rear Admiral A.
Stanton Merrill made certain the marines were there to stay. With
our destroyers and cruisers posted and waiting, the unsuspecting Japanese naval command sent down a strong force bent on
destruction at the beachhead, but Merrill met it in a head-on
clash (what has become known as the Battle of Empress Augusta
Bay). The enemy lost one cruiser; one destroyer was sunk and
three destroyers damaged. Captain Arleigh A. ("31-Knot") Burke,
newly arrived in the war zone, had made his great fighting presence known by sinking three of those warships.

While the 3rd Division braced for counterattack, Captain John Monks of the 1st Battalion, 3rd Marines, was on the beach and dug in with his men. The brilliant playwright and novelist takes us through D-night and beyond.

·9· BOUGAINVILLE:
BEACHHEAD AND SWAMP

JOHN MONKS, JR.

The men had been up since 2:30 that morning. From H-hour until dark they had taken a physical beating. Fighting . . . swamp to the line of the first day's objective had been as exhausting as the fight for Cape Torokina. They had set up their defensive positions, dug their foxholes, cleaned their weapons, and wolfed their cold greasy rations in the rain. As night crept in around them, those not on the first watch took off their helmets, stuck their long-bladed knives into the side of their foxholes, wrapped themselves and their rifles in their ponchos, and snuggled down in four inches of water to try to get a few hours of rest. It would soon be their time to take the watch. They were tired.

And the men on watch were tired, too. But tired men can become dead men, for tired men grow careless. And they knew it. They strained to pierce the blank scrim of the jungle night, and listened intently to the million jungle noises—ground noises particularly, for they must learn to distinguish the sound of a lizard or a rat or a toad, or any one of the hundred little ground animals in the jungle, from the even belly-slide of a crawling Japanese jungle fighter. The men in the Third Marines were used to the jungle; but every jungle is different, and for the first time after all their training they were playing for keeps.

By six o'clock that night it was dark and every officer and man on the line and in the many C.P.s was in his foxhole. For these were trained men and they knew the law of the jungle: each man must be in his foxhole at dark and there he must stay until dawn. Anyone *out* of a foxhole during the hours of darkness was a Jap. Sudden death for the careless. From seven o'clock in the evening till dawn, with only centipedes and lizards and scorpions and mosquitoes begging to get acquainted—wet, cold, exhausted, but unable to sleep—you lay there and shivered and thought and hated and prayed. But you stayed there. You didn't cough, you didn't snore, you changed your position with the least amount of noise. For it was still great to be alive.

Not a light could be seen anywhere in the area, pitch-black darkness all along the beach, blacker still in the jungle. Though none were visible from the outside, lights were being used—flashlights mostly, under ponchos, inside blackout tents. Back at the Division C.P., the Regimental C.P., and the headquarters of the lower echelons, commanding officers and members of their staff worked over maps, written messages, and orders; and switchboard operators, already under ground, shunted messages to their important destinations.

There was another light, too—a very important one, shedding rays of mercy and hope: the light of Hippocrates. C Medical Company had landed early that morning. Doctor Glystine (the company's commanding officer) and Dr. Leo Koscinski had worked their way through the swamp searching for an island of dry land. They found a spot less than 200 yards in the rear of the front lines. With the help of two corpsmen they dug a hole ten feet square and three feet deep and covered it with canvas. Now, stripped to the waist, sweat pouring from their bodies, they crouched near a stretcher. A corpsman held a flashlight. Leo was administering the anesthetic. Dr. Sheppard, a Mayo-trained surgeon, was removing a bullet from the body of a wounded marine. He had been hit by a sniper late in the afternoon, too late to be evacuated. The ships had gone. Four buddies had fought the swamp and carried him to Bougainville's first hospital.

Major Steve Brody, acting Commander of the First Battalion, knelt in his foxhole and listened. His battalion C.P. was up forward near the front lines. He could hear the sound of men picking their way through the underbrush up ahead. Other men heard the sound, too—felt for their knives and waited. They knew what to expect. They knew there were Japs out in front of them. The operation order had accounted for at least a battalion less than twelve miles down the coast. An attack that night would be expected anywhere in the northeast sector, along the coast or through the swamp from the east. The sounds came closer. Steve waited. Those sounds could mean only one thing: a Jap patrol. The Japs would know this terrain well, but they wouldn't know the location of the Battalion's front lines or the position of the automatic weapons. They were out there to find out. Maybe a trigger-happy Marine gunner would open up, blaze away at a sound or a shadowy form, and reveal his position. That's what the Japs wanted. But the men in this outfit weren't raw recruits. They had had fire discipline shoved down their throats for months. They had patience and knowledge and self-control. Steve lay there and smiled. He was their commanding officer. They were his men. He was proud.

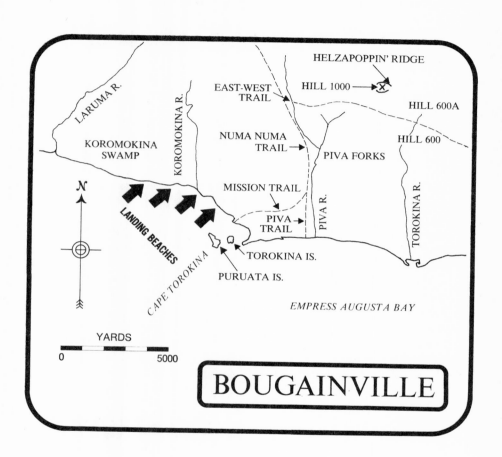

LARUMA R.

KOROMOKINA R.

HELZAPOPPIN' RIDGE

EAST-WEST
TRAIL

HILL 1000

HILL 600A

KOROMOKINA
SWAMP

NUMA NUMA
TRAIL

HILL 600

PIVA FORKS

MISSION TRAIL

N

PIVA R.

LANDING BEACHES

PIVA
TRAIL

TOROKINA R.

TOROKINA IS.

CAPE TOROKINA

PURUATA IS.

EMPRESS AUGUSTA BAY

YARDS

0   5000

BOUGAINVILLE

In about an hour the sound in the underbrush ceased. Some of the patrol might have crawled through the lines, might even be behind them. Let 'em crawl. They wouldn't see a thing in that darkness. There wasn't a human sound anywhere along the lines. Another hour went by. Nothing happened. Steve drove his knife into the bottom of his foxhole. It was a good knife; his brother had sent it to him in New Zealand. "Hope it comes in handy," he had written. The rain was letting up a bit but it was pretty cold. "Guess I'd better try to get some rest. Might even be able to sleep a little if I could get a little warmer," thought Steve. He reached over and straightened out his poncho, pulled the other half over him and looked up at the sky. A few stars were trying to come out, but it was still pretty cloudy. That was a break.

"The enemy will most certainly attack our beachhead with all the aircraft he has available. Air attacks can be expected at any time, day or night." Last night those had been just words in an operations order.

Planes were probably already warming up at Buka and Rabual. Steve thought about his former battalion commander, whom he had relieved. "Guess Spike was hurt pretty bad . . . they got him back to the ship . . . hope he'll make it O.K. . . . great guy, Spike. Well, no one let him down. That'll make him feel good . . . tell him all about it when I see him again." He closed his eyes—the first time in sixteen hours. It felt good . . .

"Jesus Christ—*Uhh*—Grab that son—Sam!"

Something had happened. *Damn*—a Jap had fallen into the foxhole of one of the men in the C.P. The Jap jumped out and started to run, tripped and fell on top of Dr. Sam Elmore, lying in a foxhole near by. Before Sam could recover from his surprise, the Jap was out of the hole. Steve, in a hole next to Sam, threw off his poncho with one hand and grabbed his knife with the other. He saw and smelled the Jap in the same moment—no mistaking that smell.

"*Watch* it, Steve—*Jap!*" Sam yelled.

The Jap plunged in again on top of Steve, and Steve was over him like a tent.

Sam crawled quickly over the edge of his foxhole and slid into Steve's. "Got him, Steve? You got him?"

Steve grunted as he hacked away with his knife. The Jap was screaming and crying at the same time. "No kill . . . no kill! I'm too . . . young . . . to . . . die!" wailed the Jap in high-pitched, terrified English.

"You're old enough," said Steve as he drove his knife into the Jap's back. They lifted up the bloody mess and dumped it out of the foxhole.

I Battery sounded off in the distance. A few seconds later they heard the shells pass over their heads, exploding a thousand yards in front of the lines. Japs were still dying.

On another section of the beach, a loading officer lay in a Japanese slit trench alongside one of the sand-covered Jap bunkers. He had had a busy day. His unloading party of marines and Seabees had handled cargo from two transports and one freighter. The surf up on the left flank had been too high for unloading on that section of the beach, and all of that additional cargo had been shunted down to his area. The supplies had been stacked above the high-water line, but dispersion had been impossible. Every inch of dry land and some of the swamp had been utilized. Ammunition, chow, and gasoline had been separated from one another, but each of the dumps was piled high. They had finished the last boatload at 5:30 in the afternoon. There was just enough light left to dig foxholes. The officer found his pack, grabbed a shovel, and started inland. He hadn't eaten since early morning, but there wasn't time now.

"The Japs will really work the beach over tonight," he thought. "If he hits that ammo dump, they won't even find our dog tags. Better obey the rules and dig a hole in the swamp. Going to be awful wet, though."

He found a spot about a hundred yards inland, cleared away the wall of thick vines, and started to dig. It was an exhausting job. Before he had finished a third of it his muscles refused to work. His head felt as if someone were beating on it with an ax. He leaned against a tree and vomited. Then he tried to dig some more, but the maze of vine roots was too tough; he didn't have enough strength to cut through them. Every time he lifted his shovel, the roots would grab it and the dirt would be spilled back in the hole. The brush was thick, and it was now dark in the jungle.

"The hell with it!" He picked up his pack and shovel and went back to the beach.

The damp sand was soft. He had scooped out a hollow for his hips and it felt wonderful. He didn't even mind the lingering stench of Japs emanating from the bunker. The ammunition dump with canister upon canister of high explosive mortar shells was less than thirty yards away. It was dangerous and stupid . . . but it was comfortable. "What the hell! Maybe they won't hit the dump. This is war. Gotta take some chances," he rationalized.

Five feet away, the shore-party commander was talking in a projected whisper over a field 'phone "Condition Red," he whispered.

A few minutes later, the loading officer heard the drone of Jap planes. They had to be Jap—we didn't have any night fighters in the area. He had been bombed many times on Guadalcanal and he could recognize that pulsating hum of unsynchronized Jap motors anywhere. For a long time the planes circled the bay and beachhead area.

Then, one by one, they would dive, drop a stick of bombs, and circle again.

"I wish those bastards would run out of gas," he said to the Commander.

"They've got plenty of gas."

"Did you ever sleep in a subway station, Commander?"

"Once."

"Wasn't it peaceful?"

Most of the bombs had dropped up at the other end of the beach; nothing had been hit. Now they circled closer.

"Why didn't I finish that foxhole back in the jungle and get off this damn beach?" the loading officer asked himself. "Too tired. Screw it . . . all a matter of luck, anyhow." Then he addressed his thoughts to the Jap flyers. "Drop your God-damned bombs and go home. You bother me. I want to get some sleep. Unh-hunh—must have heard me." One of the planes off to the left had gone into his dive The screaming motor came closer and closer. The officer rolled over, humped his belly off the ground, and rested his weight on his knees and elbows. It was a good position: too bad it had to be wasted on such an enterprise. *Wish . . . uh wish . . . uh wish . . . uh wish . . . uh wish . . .*

"Here they come!"

Raah voomb! . . . Uh wish . . . uh wish . . . uh wish . . . uh wish . . . Raah voomb! . . . Uh wish . . . uh wish . . . Raah voomb! Raah voomb!

One of the bombs landed close to the beach, the rest of them back in the swamp. The officer rolled over on his back and let out a sigh of relief. All of a sudden courageous, he called after the departing planes: "You couldn't hit the broad side of a bull's ass with a spade, you slant-eyed bastard! Go home and lie your head off! 'Flames could be seen for fifty miles'—and you didn't hit a God-damned thing!" The plane droned off in the distance.

"Have to go back when it's light and see whether a bomb fell near that foxhole I was digging," thought the officer. He did, early the next morning. No bomb crater anywhere near, but—lying right on the surface of the ground not five feet from where he had finished digging—was a Japanese land mine.

Later that night it started to rain again. When it rains in the tropics, it never kids around about it—it's always real heart-and-soul stuff. A machine-gunner in one of the many emplacements along the beach leaned up against the sandbags and cursed his luck.

"It is estimated that the enemy can attack our forces in the Cape Torokina area with two battalions coming from the Buin-South Augusta Bay area by sea on the night of D-day." That order had stressed the imminence of enemy action during the first night. Well, this would be the perfect night to hit us: tired troops, defenses only partially organized, bad visibility.

The machine-gunner had just relieved his assistant and had taken over the watch. Of all the lousy nights he had spent in the South Pacific, this one took the ribbon. "The poorhouse wasn't tough enough—they had to put a hill in front of it." A landing boat could be up on shore before you could even see it. Even the dark forms of the two islands silhouetted against a lighter background could no longer be seen. He looked at his watch. It was almost midnight; plenty of darkness left. Then in the distance far out to sea he saw flashes followed by a deep bass rumble. Lightning, maybe. There had been a thunderstorm that afternoon. The flashes came pretty close together. The phone rang softly. He reached over and answered it.

"Condition Black—enemy landing expected. You may expect shelling from enemy ships followed by counter invasion."

That wasn't lightning. "Let 'em come," he thought. He could feel a twinge of excitement, but it was a good excitement—not fright, not the fear of the unknown or of being unsure of oneself. He knew what was expected of him, what to do, and how he'd do it. "I'm the best God-damned machine-gunner in the Marine Corps. We've got 40 and 20 millimeters, 37's, and half-tracks all along the beach—that's before they ever get to the machine-guns. I'll keep this son-of-a-bitch firing till I burn out the barrel. And we've got two dozen hand grenades. Between the two of us, that's a lot of Japs," he thought. He could still see the flashes. The rain was letting up a little. Things were looking better. He smiled and reached over to wake his buddy. The rest of the night the two stood watch at the same time, talking their way through a dozen invasions after which it would take at least three days to bury the Jap dead.

The flashes and the rumbling lasted for over an hour. Then it was black again.

"Hope the Navy hasn't let us down," said the gunner.

"The Navy stinks," his buddy replied.

"I don't mean the Navy on transports. I mean the shooting Navy."

"I wouldn't know. I was never sea-goin'."

The Navy didn't let them down. A strong task force had put out from Rabaul and was headed for Empress Augusta Bay. The Navy was waiting with a reception committee far offshore. Four Japanese cruisers went to the bottom. The Japanese task force returned to Rabaul. The sea off the south coast of Bougainville no longer belonged to the Mikado.

Dawn broke at about 5:30. Morning was never more welcome. No one had slept, muscles were stiff from the day before, bones ached from lying on stones in soaking wet dungarees—but it was light and you could see what you were doing. In a little while the sun would be up. It would be hot and you could dry out. We had been bombed on and off all during the night but with no casualties. The expected enemy naval shelling had not materialized. The company of Raiders at the road block up the trail had been hit by a strong combat patrol. Four of five men had knife wounds, but still more Jap dead had to be buried. I Battery had laid down harassing fire in front of the First Battalion, thwarting any attack from the east. Snipers had pinged away during the night at the Raiders on the island, but these Nips were only tapping out their swan song.

The earliest action of D-plus-one-day occurred at daybreak. One of the men on the Cape started to leave his foxhole and was greeted by a Jap, stark naked, walking down the trail a few yards from him; he had probably swum over from the smaller island. The two saw each other at the same time. As the marine reached for his rifle, the Jap darted into the underbrush out of sight. A small patrol was quickly organized and overtook him about a hundred yards away. He had an M-1 rifle which he must have picked up on the beach. He didn't want to be taken prisoner, so one of the more obliging members of the patrol, with the aid of a Tommygun, helped him to die for the Emperor.

It didn't take anyone very long to test the fuel possibilities of the waxed cover of a K-ration box. One box torn into small pieces provided enough heat for a canteen cup of coffee. Many had already learned that a hand-grenade canister made an excellent waterproof cigarette case that would hold about three packs of cigarettes, so there were smokes with the coffee. Some of the men on the Cape were even luckier. The Japs have an excellent canned heat that they carry with their field ration. Four or five boxes of these cans had been found in the rustic Japanese storehouse. We never have been able to understand why our rations were not equipped with some type of canned heat such as Sterno. The little white heat tabs that are furnished are about as effective as a large fish fork in a soup storm.

The men on the beach were faring best. They had regular little stoves. All along the beach small groups of men were brewing coffee over small cans that had had holes punched in the sides, half filled with sand and then soaked with gasoline. Gasoline is used to clean a machine-gun. Most of it. A guy's got to have his coffee.

Daylight ushered in a certain freshness. Everyone anticipated a tough day ahead, but the strain of that first night had been relieved. There were enough hints of combat about as a reminder of more to come. Unburied Jap bodies furnished the olfactory evidence, and the sound of the higher-pitched rapid fire of a Jap machine-gun intermingled with the sound of our own weapons on Puruata Island was convincing proof that the Raiders weren't holding an early morning skeet shoot. But it was light—a man could see what he was doing, could clean his weapon, relieve his bowels, wash his face, and talk out loud.

Now it was 7 A.M. It had been light for an hour and a half. Commander Bruce, commanding officer of the medical battalion, trudged along up the beach in the direction of the Division C.P. He had been one of New York City's prominent eye specialists before he had joined the Navy and was assigned to the Marines. Now he was an expert on every branch of field medicine, from diagnosing and treating rare tropical diseases to methods of evacuating wounded from the swamp to the field hospitals, to the beach, to a ship. He knew men and he knew them well, all of them—marines, corpsmen, doctors, and officers. He understood the problems of the military as well as the medical, and he knew how to solve them and make the two separate departments dovetail. A big man with a boyish face smiling its love of humanity, he has a rapid-thinking brain, a witty tongue, and a feeling for the incongruous. Everyone knew him and was anxious to hear the latest scuttlebutt rendered in his inimitable style. But today he had to supervise the installation of three medical company field hospitals and had time only for a greeting and a few short plants for future reference. Bull-session time would soon come again and he would have some juicy contributions. Commander Bruce had a great imagination and he knew how to tell a story.

"Hiya, Brucie, where have you been?" called an officer on the beach.

"Morning, Hank. Been down on the Cape. Went down to give the boys a hand. Willets and Sam pretty busy. Got right in between the fire of two machine-guns. Should have seen me hit the deck!"

"It was pretty hot down there all right," Hank answered.

"Damn near had my butt shot off," grinned the Commander. "How's it going?"

"Pretty good. Lousy beach. Heard Steve stabbed a Jap." Hank wanted to hear the story.

"Yeah—cut him to ribbons. Big fella. I damn near had my butt shot off. Tell you all about it later." The Commander started up the beach.

"S'long, Brucie. Take it easy!"

The Commander raised his hand—then stopped, turned, and with the old mischievous twinkle in his eye called back, "Did you hear about the woman sniper?"

"Heard something about it," lied Hank. He'd heard about the woman sniper ever since he'd been in the Pacific; so had the Commander. "Did they really find one?"

"Tell you all about it when I see you." The Commander grinned and puffed on up the beach. Too bad there wasn't more time. In every campaign there had always been a woman sniper. Sometimes she had been found chained to a tree—sometimes she had been a Chinese woman—sometimes she had been a Japanese, but dressed exactly like a soldier. No one had ever actually seen her, but everybody knew someone who had. Now Hank knew there hadn't been one on the Cape, but Brucie's story would still be a good one.

A number of stories have sprung up from the island campaigns. Some are pure fabrication, many actually happened, and those of the "didn't happen but could have" variety are so probable that it doesn't really matter. One of the last variety is about a Marine Sergeant who was a machine-gun section leader. His section was attached to a combat patrol which had been beating the bush all day long without running into even a rumor of a Jap. Now a machine-gun is not something you can take or leave alone. You're either not interested, or you're a confirmed fanatic. You have to be. In weight alone, there is a considerable difference between an M-1 rifle and the gun with its tripod and ammunition supply, even in easy going country. In the jungle it is comparable to the difference between pickabacking your neighbor's six-year-old son and the kid who has just become eligible to join the Boy Scouts. This Marine Sergeant, off to one flank, was separated from the rest of his section by heavy underbrush. Nearing the crest of a hill, he halted, cautiously crept along the top, and looked down on a small valley on the other side. The vision before him made his mouth water. Less than 300 yards in front of him stood a whole Jap company lined up for chow. He had dreamed about a target like this for fifteen years. The Sergeant was an expert, and he knew in an instant where to lay his guns and the range and the number of bursts it would take to massacre everyone in the Nip company. He turned toward the underbrush where he knew the rest of the section would be and called excitedly: "Charlie—bring the guns over and lay them on the left."

A voice answered from the brush: "No—be better keep them on the right."

There wasn't even a field of fire on the right. His squad leader must be crazy. Now more excited than ever and growing madder by the second, he shouted his order again:

"Goddammit, Charlie—Japs! Bring those guns over here on the double and lay them on the left."

Same voice, same answer: "No—be better . . . keep them on the right."

Now there comes an end to every sergeant's patience. There are periods in his life when he even forgets the Golden Rule. This one sprang to his feet and tore through the underbrush. Here was one corporal who had disobeyed his last order. By God, he'd beat him down to parade rest . . . But as soon as he had cleared the bush his eyes fell upon a diminutive, toothy, English-speaking Jap squatting in a clearing. Still white with rage, he dashed up to the Jap and shook a finger in his face and barked: "Listen, you little son-of-a-bitch. You run your outfit and I'll run mine!"

E Company was trudging its weary way back from the Cape. Imagine yourself rising at 2:30 in the morning, unloading a transport all that day, hiking 3000 yards through loose sand with nothing on your stomach since early morning, digging foxholes at the end of the journey, being bombed all night as you waited in reserve to be thrown against a land attack or a counterinvasion, cleaning out left-over snipers the next morning, then—after a quick meal of a can of cold C ration and a lukewarm cup of coffee—hiking back along that same stretch of loose sand to join your outfit, which by this time will be over 800 yards away in the swampy jungle. Then grab the next marine you see with a Pacific ribbon on his blouse, take him into the nearest good bar, and buy him a drink. Marines hate to drink alone . . . and it'll make you feel better.

Captain George Coupe and Lieutenant Dick Maxwell were at the head of the column. Here was another crack company of the Third Marines. Coupe had been with the company since it had been formed over eighteen months before, and he knew the age, life history, and fighting potential of every one of his men. Maxie—an end from the famous Georgia football team of 1930, expert swimmer, fine baseball player, great boxer in and out of barrooms—was also one of the best instructors the men had ever known. He had taught every officer and noncom in the Third Marines when they had done their stretch in a rugged jungle school at Samoa. There wasn't a subject in the manual at which Max wasn't an expert, and at one time or another he taught them all: the compass, map-reading, scouting and patrolling, demolitions, hand grenades, Molotov cocktails, barbed-wire defenses, bayonet, knife-fighting, judo, gas camouflage, every weapon. He stood six feet two and had a forearm as large as the average man's leg. A deep scar from a Kansas City gangster's knife slash crossed his face from the corner of one eye to his ear. He had the charm of a matinee idol, a quiet, kind Southern drawl, and the straight right of a Jack Dempsey.

Max had come up from the ranks, had been commissioned, was finally given a platoon of his own just before the Third had shoved off from Samoa, and now was second in command of a rifle company. To every officer in the regiment he was a true buddy; to every enlisted man, a rugged hero. It was difficult to conceive of any living thing big enough to beat him—and there wasn't, not in the South Pacific. But there was something small enough: a little mosquito—and he contracted filariasis. He had lain on his bunk for three weeks before he shoved off from our staging area, refusing to turn in. "If I went home without killing a Jap, my daddy wouldn't let me in the house," Maxie told us. He was carried on the transport. He skipped the landing operations, and the three weeks' rest aboard the ship had reduced his swelling and given him back his strength. So he said. He knew how much his being with them meant to the men. He wouldn't go near a doctor. But that day of unloading and the succeeding exertion had brought the trouble back. The company had halted and was taking a ten-minute break. Maxie limped away from the company out of earshot of the men and flopped down under a tree.

"What's the matter, Maxie?" an officer asked him. "You look like a death's head at the feast."

"Can't keep anything on my stomach."

"Mumu?" asked the officer, using the native name for the first stage of filariasis.

"Yeah. Thought I'd licked it."

"Hurt pretty bad?"

"Like I'd been kicked in a football game and hadn't worn a jock." Pain was written all over Maxie's face. He was really suffering.

"You'd better turn in, Maxie—you'll never lick it on your feet."

"I can't let George down."

"You *are* letting him down. Give him a chance, Maxie. He's got to break somebody else in. How long do you think you'll last? About two more days. Then they'll carry you in."

"I know . . ." Tears were forming in the tough guy's eyes. He wiped his face on the sleeve of his dungaree.

"On your feet!" shouted Coupe.

Maxie pulled his body off the sand. "On your feet!" he barked. "There's a lot of water and chow waiting up ahead." He limped to the head of the weary column. The company started down the beach.

Three days later, Maxie collapsed in the field hospital. They evacuated him by stretcher. An arm, a leg, and his testicles were twice normal size. It was not only filariasis—soon, in hospital, he was in the first stages of elephantiasis, and further stages were to follow. Before Pearl Harbor we hadn't paid much attention to tropical diseases. But then, before Pearl Harbor, there were a lot of things we hadn't paid much attention to.

On another part of the beach a canvas fly had been rigged underneath a tree on the edge of the jungle, in the bivouac area of a Seabee working party. Inside the tent a piece of white target cloth had been thrown over a large wooden crate. On the top of this counter there was a half bottle of methiolate, a couple of bandages, and a bottle of C.C. pills. Though inadequately equipped, one might suspect that this tent was some kind of temporary first-aid shelter or sick bay, but a sign over the entrance removed all speculation. It read:

BOUGAINVILLE'S LEADING DRUGGIST

Work had been resumed in earnest. Bougainville's first highway had already been started, although at the moment it rated slightly less than a short dotted line on any road map. But when the Seabees go to work, a start is a promise. Groups of these beavers were cutting logs and brush and hauling them to the trail leading off the beach just west of the Cape to the northeast. A power shovel was operating on the beach filling trucks with sand. The trucks would deposit their load over the recently laid logs on the trail; then a bulldozer, that beloved prince of all invasion equipment, would smooth it out. Another bulldozer, hauling three wooden sledges of equipment, would follow immediately. In this way, an impassable swampy lagoon between the beach and an island of dry land would have been bridged and another dump for valuable equipment established. More logs, more sand, and the road would grow a few yards longer. Finally, a short stretch of the road would be solid enough for trucks to pass. More supplies would be dispersed, and equipment for another field hospital would be hauled up to a group of corpsmen busy clearing away the undergrowth on a small patch island of solid land, digging dugouts, and pitching tents.

Farther along the other side of the trail a Marine fighter control group was clearing the ground and digging in their installations. A little farther on, a motor park was being established. Dry land at a premium, and every inch of it being utilized for bivouac and operational areas. Get off the beach, disperse, become operative. The road would be torn up and a truck would mire down. A bulldozer would come to the rescue; the truck would be hauled out. Then more logs, a deeper drainage ditch along the side, more sand, more work for the bulldozer—then another line of overloaded trucks and sledges would crawl farther up the trail.

In the midst of this activity a sniper's bullet would ricochet off the side of a truck. Sniper patrols would soon spot the source of this temporary aggravation, and a few of the younger Seabees to relieve the monotony would sneak off with the patrols. A tall tree would be spotted, surrounded by the patrol, and another foolish Nip would have committed suicide. But the work went feverishly on. No one even bothered to take cover. Everyone was too busy.

Farther west along the beach, Marine Engineers and Amphibian Tractor men were pushing a cat trail through the swamp to the Second

Battalion's front lines. Still farther along Lieutenant Joe Gehring and his I Company Seabees were constructing a road to the Third Battalion. No outfit can advance too far beyond the base of its supplies. D-plus-two-days called for the further advance of 600 yards. Every yard of advance by the troops meant one more yard of swamp separating them from the beach . . . and the beach was the only base of supplies. Ammunition must be brought up, and men must eat. It would be weeks before roads over which even the lightest of vehicles might travel could be constructed through this thick jungle swamp, a great portion of which was below sea level.

How could this very important supply nightmare be licked without delaying the advance? But it *was* licked: by marines and Seabees, by bush knives and axes, by hours of sweating toil, and by a special type of transportation, the only vehicle that could negotiate the swamp—the amphibian tractor. Until D-day almost everyone, except a few broad-minded souls and the specialists themselves, despised these awkward, wallowing, noisy monsters. Every ship loading officer cursed them to the skies. All his vehicle problems would be solved— and then he would be given a consignment of amphibian tractors to load. There would be only one boom on the ship large enough to lift them; then either the hatch under the boom would be too small or the clearance of the upper 'tween decks too low. They would end up in the bottom of the hold, loaded in the tank lighters, or else on the only open fresh-air space for the troops on the deck. They were the cause of more arguments with the ship's cargo officer, more readjustments in loading plans, more bad feelings all around, than any other single item of cargo. In a noncombat movement from one place in the Pacific to another, we would try to get the use of them to facilitate the movement of cargo from the ship to the beach, and permission would always be refused: "The life of a tractor is limited . . . can't waste them . . . got to save them for combat."

"What good will they be in combat? They're only made of aluminum. A machine-gun'll cut them to ribbons," we'd answer.

"They can go places where other vehicles can't go. We've got machine-guns too. What do you think we'll be doing while they're trying to cut us to ribbons?" from the tractor marine.

"Treading water and hollering for a Higgins boat to save your butt —or getting in everybody's way on the beach."

"Yeah? It's a damn fine piece of machinery!"

"So is the Twentieth Century Limited, and it doesn't make as much noise."

"These tractors will come in handy."

"Let me know. I'll get a rhyming dictionary and write a poem about 'em."

But after D-day on Bougainville we wanted to bite our tongues off. No one worked harder or longer than the amphibian tractor crews. The tractors were used to haul supplies from one part of the beach to another, to crush through the thick undergrowth, bowl over trees and make trails, haul ammunition, chow, gear and medical supplies, and evacuate the wounded. Not once but all through the campaign the amphibian tractor bridged the vital gap between life and death, available rations and gnawing hunger, victory and defeat. They roamed their triumphant way all over the beachhead. They ruined roads, tore down communication lines, revealed our combat positions to the enemy—but everywhere they were welcome.

Major Grant Crane, Major Whitman, Captain McDonald, Captain John Winford, Quartermaster Clerk Bill Pollack, Lieutenant Breen, Gunner Greer, Lieutenant Duke Shananan, and all the quartermaster and supply units, men and officers, on the beach worked like Trojans to sort out supplies, obtain the transportation, and find the means of getting chow, medical supplies, and ammunition through the swamp and up to the troops. They knew these supplies were the life blood of the Regiment. They had to keep the ticker pumping. And when the fighting men of the Regiment needed that chow, when the doctors needed medical supplies, when units of fire had to be replenished, these officers and their men had them there.

"Condition Red."

The bogeys were at it again. Work ceased. Everyone ducked for his foxhole. Two of the planes came in low to strafe the beach and were greeted by an overture of machine-gun fire. It felt good to let it go—the barrels had been cooling for a long time and trigger fingers needed exercise. But the gunners on this second day on the beach failed to take the proper leads. The planes climbed swiftly back into the sky preparing to make another run. This time they would be able to do a better job. They had the limits of the working section of the beach clearly marked. They could take their time in judging the distance, peel off, dive at one end, and rake the beach unmolested. So they thought . . .

But high in the sky, circling around and around on station, were six Marine fighters. They had been there at daylight, they would stay there for the limit of their gas time, then be relieved by another six from our air base at Munda. These in turn would be relieved by another six, and so on all during the daylight hours. They were our daylight fighter coverage. And so just at the moment when the Jap falcon began to drool at the mouth, the Marine flyers roared from their high perch and dove at their unsuspecting prey. It was a beautiful sight—these roaring silver streaks flashing through the sky and spitting leaden death at the bogeys. It was more beautiful still to watch the columns of smoke spiral downward from the sky and pierce their watery graveyard in a splash of flame. The Marine flyers rolled in salute to their grateful buddies on the ground, and then soared back into their commanding haven high in the sky. More raids followed intermittently all during the day, but the Nip soon got the word: the daylight air above Empress Augusta Bay also belonged to the United States Marines.

Up on the lines, a muddy, wet marine pulled himself to his feet, stretched the kinks from his stiff body, and took a look around. Streaks of daylight were beginning to filter through and around the large banyan trees in the jungle. His buddy was still curled up in his poncho. He kicked the protruding bulge halfheartedly. His buddy opened his eyes.

"Hey, eight-ball. Get your ass out of the sack."

"What for?" his buddy yawned.

"Time to go to the office."

"What time is it?"

"Five-thirty."

"Too friggin' early."

"Get any sleep?"

"What sleep?" He threw back his poncho, climbed out of his muddy foxhole, pulled back the operating handle of his rifle, ejecting the round from the chamber, pressed the clip release, caught the clip of cartridges, picked up the ejected round from where it had fallen on the deck, wiped off the mud, put it back in the clip, tapped the noses of the rounds in the clip against the sole of one of his boondockers, and laid the clip on the top of his pack. Then he held the receiver of his rifle toward the light, inserted his forefinger in it to reflect the light, and looked down the barrel. "Who can sleep with a snoring bastard like you around?"

"You never talked like that when we were first married, you sourpuss eight-ball." The first marine had already disassembled his piece and was brushing off the grit that had gathered on the bolt with a cut-down paintbrush. A small bottle labeled "Mosquito Repellent," which now contained oil, half of an old skivvy shirt, a cut-down toothbrush, a thong with a small weight on the end of it, and a half-dozen gun patches, lay strewn out on half of the poncho; the various parts of the field-stripped rifle lay together on the other half.

The second marine pulled his poncho out of his hole and spread it out on the ground. Then he went over to his pack, stuck the clip in his belt, opened his pack, pulled out his cleaning kit and a can of ration, left the can sitting on the outside of his pack, went back to the poncho, and started to strip his rifle. When both had finished they walked off a short distance in the jungle away from the rest of the troops. Both carried their rifles, and one of them carried an entrenching shovel; one would cover for the other, who in turn would indulge in the early-morning luxury common to all mankind.

All along the line the men were climbing out of their holes, shaking off the mud, opening their packs. Each greeted the welcome morning in much the same way and each, without even thinking about it—before any part of his toilet was attended to, before he washed his face from the cleaner water drained into his helmet from one of the large cupped jungle leaves, before he brushed his teeth—he instinctively field-stripped and thoroughly cleaned his rifle. In less than an hour after he had rolled out of his sack he had his rifle in shape for immediate action, had smoked a cigarette, had changed his socks (he still had a clean pair this first morning), had cleaned himself up as well as possible, had moved his bowels, eaten his ration (some trying to heat a canteen cup of coffee, other sparingly drinking part of the remaining water in their canteens), had folded his poncho and put it back in his pack, and was fastening the straps when the word starting the day's action passed down the line: "Prepare to move out!" In less than five minutes he would be starting through the jungle. Before he had gone ten feet and shot his second azimuth with his compass, he would be up to his knees in mud; but for a moment—a precious, luxurious moment—before the beginning of another long, arduous, steaming-hot hike through the thick wall of vines and tangled bush, he was clean—at least a little cleaner, a trifle fresher, a bit more comfortable than he had been for hours.

Then came the bogeys. Word down the line:

"Condition Red!"

"Enemy planes!"

"Get . . . in . . . your . . . foxholes!"

Not back in those stinking, slimy, muddy foxholes? The planes could be heard circling over the area, but none seemed at the moment to be directly overhead. Maybe just squat near the hole . . . right on the edge . . . you can hear a bomb fall . . . still time enough to tumble in that mud. Now the planes seemed closer, but they couldn't be seen through the thick jungle ceiling. They wouldn't be able to spot us either, but they knew we were somewhere within a perimeter off the beach; if they could estimate the size of the perimeter, they would know the position of our front lines. A bomb anywhere along that irregular line was bound to hit someone. *Wish . . . uh uh wish . . . uh wish . . . uh wish . . . uh wish . . .*

"Here they come! Hit . . . the . . . deck!"

Two men made a dive for the same foxhole. One of them made it.

"Hey, Mac—that's my foxhole!" yelled the unlucky one.

"Semper Fidelis, Mac," from the man who had gotten there first. Which, translated literally, means "Always Faithful"; but it is commonly used by marines, as occasion demands, for "Frig you, Mac— I got mine," or "Pull up the ladder, Mac—I'm aboard."

No one needed any further coaxing to "hit the deck"! That familiar, unmistakable sound of a bomb falling through the air meant "positively."

Everyone had plunged back into the mud and was lying on his elbows and knees waiting for the ground to tremble, for the sound of splintering trees, the roar of the explosion, and the shove of high-explosive concussion. They closed their eyes, gritted their teeth, held their breath. *Uh wish . . . uh wish . . . uh wish . . . uh wish . . .* No bomb takes that long to fall. The sound continued; then it got louder; then it was a different sound. It belonged to the jungle. A string of pornographic oaths—unprintable but in keeping with the highest traditions of a marine's vocabulary—was justifiably hurled from every hole. A new, eagle-size type of jungle bird, flying low and flapping its wings loudly, gunned its way through the bush . . .

The men lay in their holes cursing Bougainville's wild life, and the mud, and the swamp, and the war, and Fate. The water once again seeped through their utility clothes, making them thoroughly miserable. Then the raid was over. Word was passed again.

"Condition green. Moving out."

The men moved to their respective places in their squads and platoons. Squad leaders shot an azimuth with their compasses, scouts moved out, the men took the necessary interval for dispersion— though close enough to remain at all times in sight contact with one another; then they started to cut their way through the jungle swamp towards the second day's objective 600 yards farther from the beach.

As a company moves forward in combat formation, it lays its combat communication wire connecting it with the Battalion C.P. Whenever a phase line is reached (a phase line being an imaginary line on a map of the terrain so many yards or at such-and-such a time interval from the starting point or last phase line), the order to halt is issued and passed to the front of the formation by means of arm and hand signals. All orders are issued in this manner in the jungle when contact with the enemy is imminent. Then the men halt, take cover, and remain silently alert. A 'phone is tapped in on the combat wire, and each company commander re-establishes contact with his battalion commander. On the move the companies will be out of 'phone communication until it reaches a phase line. When this is reached, the company commander checks in: "Buck calling Joe."

"What's the situation, Buck?"

And the company commander makes his report and receives any change in orders.

All during this second day, at every phase line, the battalion commander tried to talk his company commander into an optimistic report of dry land, rising ground, the end of the swamp.

"How's the terrain, Buck?"

"Swamp."

"How about over on your right?"

"Swamp."

"Does it look like there might be dry land up ahead?"

"Swamp."

"There must be *some* dry ground up there?"

"Swamp."

"O.K.—move out at 1320."

The company commander laid the 'phone down and whispered his orders to the platoon runners, and they started off toward their platoon leaders. Then after a few moments of relaxation, the company commander checked his direction of march, glanced at his watch, and at 1320 signaled to move out. The word had passed from platoons to squads, and the men, already on their feet, pushed off through the bush toward the next phase line.

By midafternoon the battalions had reached the line of the second day's objective. Again defenses were set up. Sketches of the terrain and their defensive positions were drawn and dispatched to their battalion C.P.s' carrying parties were sent back through the swamp to the terminus of the axis of supply for water, rations, and ammunition; communication lines to the battalion C.P. were tied in by lateral lines connecting each company; and foxholes for the night had already been started.

Again the men dug through the mud. Even those who were fortunate enough to be located on a small island of dry terrain found water at the eight-inch level. Some of the men had made up their minds that they were going to get one good night's rest, flooded foxholes notwithstanding. They constructed small shelters out of sapling and broad jungle leaves on the edge of their holes. Here they would sleep until enemy planes overhead would force them to roll over the edge of their foxholes onto the water-covered decks below the dangerous surface of the ground. Then, as on the preceding day, at three o'clock, the sluice gates in the sky opened up, a torrential downpound tearing through their leaf-covered shelters and flooding the foxholes and machine-gun emplacements. The dream of a warmer and more comfortable night faded with the last rays of daylight.

While the Second and Third Battalions were moving up to the new line and the First Battalion was consolidating its position east of the Cape, the Regimental C.P. had moved farther inland and was being dug in behind the right flank of the Third Battalion. By late afternoon communication lines had been laid to the Battalions; strength and unit reports from these units had been 'phoned in to the Adjutant; overlays of the Battalions' positions had been brought in by runner and were being plotted on the situation map; requests for supplies had been made to the Quartermaster; the Operation Officer had been out all day checking positions and trying to close the gap between the right flank of the Second Battalion and the Second Raiders, and was now getting the reports from the battalion operation officers. The Regimental Commander had been brought up to date by the reports from these various members of his staff, had made his report to the Division Commander, had received his orders from the same source together with all the latest enemy information which Division Headquarters was able to supply, and was now able to issue his orders for that night and the next day's advance.

A patrol on the way to the small native village up the trail to the northeast had located a platoon of Japs. Information from the one wounded Jap prisoner taken on D-day had substantiated the prior-to-landing reports of a Jap battalion fifteen miles down the coast to the east and two battalions ten miles farther down. They were equipped with enough barges to attack from the sea that night.

The First Battalion had had only sniper action during the day, and the Second and Third Battalions had met no enemy resistance. The beachhead at Empress Augusta Bay was now 1200 yards in depth. Each unit along the perimeter line was set up for hasty defense. All units attached to the Regiment were in direct telephonic communication with Regimental Headquarters and with each other.

The Jap bombers returned shortly after dark and pasted the beach and beachhead area all during the night. But expansion had increased the space between jungle targets, and the work of beach crews had broken down the heaping piles of supplies into smaller, better-dispersed, camouflaged dumps. The cold rain and droning planes were a ceaseless exasperation to the weary men. It was another miserable, sleepless night. But the skies were dark, the targets small, and the Japs' aim poor. No damage occurred and no casualties were inflicted. D-plus-one-day had been operationally smooth and thoroughly successful.

Two down, many more to go—but we were getting stronger all the time. The Jap was wasting valuable time. He shouldn't have done that.

※   ※   ※   ※

MARINES TOOK THEIR WOUNDED OFF TOROKINA IN APDs, destroyer-transports, whose minuscule sick bays had been converted to operating rooms. Captain Milton Sperling, a gifted Hollywood producer and playwright, and then a press officer for the 3rd Division, was aboard one of the vessels of mercy. When Sperling found his warm human-interest story, landing craft carrying the wounded were just beginning to pull alongside.

·10· EVACUATING THE WOUNDED

CAPTAIN MILTON SPERLING

. . . I was helping gingerly lift the wounded from the small boats to the deck of the ship. They had been evacuated from the beach by launch, their stretchers lying somewhat precariously over iron chains slung broadside across the small craft. Their wounds hastily dressed with enormous gauze patches, their torn "zoot suits" stained a fresh coat of red, the injured were on the initial leg of a swift passage to safety and treatment.

Down in the hot 'tween deck of this attack passenger destroyer, a chunky, red-faced, hairy-chested, balding doctor worked the sick-bay shuttle from Bougainville to Guadalcanal. Here under the dim, sticky battle lights, the wounded received their first promise of relief in the cocky, wisecracking banter of Lieutenant William S. Gevurtz, Medical Corps, USNR.

"They like rugged talk—their kind of rugged," he confided to me. "So I give it to them—in spades."

Stripped to the waist, sweating, swearing noisily at the improbable places a Jap missile can tear into a boy's anatomy, the doctor reigned over a compactly cluttered domain of precise medicine, rule-of-thumb psychiatry, home remedies, and prayer.

"I'm a chest man—studied the diseases of lungs for five years. Now I'm running a first-aid station." He sighed and waved his hand in the direction of the male nurses known in the Navy as hospital corpsmen. They were busily engaged in disrobing the wounded and stowing them neatly in bunks. "Without these wonderful kids I'd go nuts."

He pointed to a blond, scrawny youth carefully undressing a lacerated back. "See that one? I picked him up off a gun crew. Came to me and said he'd like to help out. Look at him. You'd think he was that guy's mother." Then he squinted down the long compartment and raised his voice sharply. "You fellows ready for me yet?"

A corpsman hurried up the aisle, unscrewing his fountain pen. He took up a handful of hospital identification tags.

"All set, doctor."

"Okay. Let's go."

I followed him into the main compartment.

The APDs are 1918-class, four-stacker destroyers converted to two stacks and armed with 3-inch rifles, 20-millimeter cannon, and 50-caliber machine guns—all aircraft defensive armament. "They're falling apart" was the universal crew opinion, but they still squeezed out twenty-seven knots. As jacks of all trades in forward waters, they carried troops, supplies, and fire power to combat areas and evacuated wounded to base hospitals. Number One engine room had been torn out to make space for passengers and crew, and in the vacated area originally intended for ship's personnel were the wounded.

The compartment was not quite filled to capacity. Six long rows of three-tiered, blanket-covered, iron-springed bunks suspended on chains, supported the now entirely naked, grubby, bandaged men. We started at the far end. The doctor was joined by another corpsman.

"Get their names, serial numbers, diagnosis, and prescribed treatment."

"Yes, sir," nodded the corpsman with the pen and tags. The doctor sighed to me, "The Navy still runs on paper. Got to get everything down."

He stopped at the end top bunk. The corpsmen gathered on his flank. I stood back.

The boy in the bunk hung over the side expectantly. His head was cropped almost to the scalp in prescribed battle fashion. It made him seem even younger than he was. He smiled and nodded vigorously at us.

"Hi, ya, doc!"

He thrust a hand out, then let it dangle in front of the doctor's face. The index finger was a reddened gauze patch. The doctor cradled the hand.

"My, my. How'd this happen?"

"Sniper got me," the boy announced—rather proudly, I thought.

"Did you get him?"

"Nope."

The doctor snorted. "Hell! You're no marine. You're supposed to get three of them."

The boy looked indignant.

"I got my three before they got me! Would have got more except this is my trigger finger."

The doctor laughed. "Let's take off the bandage and see what's under there."

He reached a hand behind him and a corpsman slipped a pair of surgical scissors into it. Deftly he snipped the soiled rags, then gently began lifting the basic gauze pad.

"Now this is going to hurt like hell, so yell if you want to."

The boy tightened his jaws and watched the doctor apprehensively. Ever so slowly, the pad came away. The ugly wound was exposed. The boy blanched and turned his head away, sick.

"Hey, don't let that scare you," soothed the doctor. "That green color isn't you. That's what the medicine did." Without looking around he called, "Sulfa powder." A paper packet was torn open and slipped into the doctor's fingers. He shook its entire contents into the wound.

"See, now it's white. This stuff is great for you. Makes you feel like a million bucks. Here, let me see your muscle." The arm came farther out of the bunk. "Flashlight," the doctor ordered. He switched it on to see better in the gloom. "You must be a hard hitter, kid. Look at those biceps. Ah, there they are. Little bumps."

He nodded to me to come closer. I peered at the arm. There were indeed little bumps all up and down the forearm. His face turned solemn for a moment as his lips formed the words "blood poisoning." Then he stepped back into the jovial role. He turned to the corpsmen.

"I'm sorry, but I've got a crummy detail for you." He glanced back at the patient. "Not you—them. We'll make 'em work for their pay. Massive hot packs constantly. Forty-five grains sulfadiazine right away." The corpsmen groaned.

"I told you I'm sorry, but it's got to be done. Get going. See you later, son." The doctor nodded to the recording corpsman. "Tag him."

He crouched on the deck to get to the lowest man in the tier. "What's cookin', kid?"

A head and shoulders struggled into view. The eyes were bitter as they looked out over the lumpy bandages beneath them.

"What a hell of a place to get hit," the mouth said. "In the face! Son of a bitch!"

"What you worried about, pretty boy?" the doctor caroled cheerily. "Scars? What do you think you've been paying twenty cents a month to the Marine Corps for since you got in? Uncle Sam will fix you up like new."

The boy's eyes flew up with surprise and suspicion.

"Like new?"

"Better than new. Hell, you'll be knocking off those babes like nothing. Sit still while I get this off you."

The tedious business of removing the bandages got under way. A running conversation about "dames" cracked through the proceedings. The boy's spirits were on the upswing until the last moment when the final dressing came off.

"How's it look?" he asked in a strained voice.

It looked terrible.

The doctor assumed a thoughtful expression as though working out the solution to a puzzle.

"Well, I'll tell you," he pontificated. "It looks like some Jap tried to kill you with a hand grenade—but he muffed. Those bastards can't pitch worth a damn."

The kid's Adam's apple bobbed as he swallowed hard.

"Yeah. They stink."

The doctor barked out orders. "Sulfa power—battle dressing—a big one—two grains of phenobarbital."

He held up the big dressing and exhibited it to the boy. "Do you know who made this dressing? Some doll sitting back in the States. When you have nothing else to do write a letter to the Red Cross telling them you got their bandage. Maybe you'll even meet the babe. Who knows?"

The bandage was being deftly applied. Finally the doctor straightened up from his squatting position and flexed his legs.

"Okay, Mac. See you later. Take it easy."

Our group moved up the aisle. A round red face and a chubby pair of shoulders appeared overhead.

"What's your trouble, lad?"

"Gee, doc. I got asthma!" The round face showed surprise and bewilderment at its own statement. The doctor reflected it instantly.

"Asthma? You come seventy-five hundred miles from the U.S. to get asthma? You must be nuts!"

Everyone laughed.

"They'll take care of you down south." The doctor waved away the asthma case. He was already eyeing another boy.

"Where'd you catch it?"

A pale, tired face looked up from the middle bunk. "In the gut, doc."

"Why'd you let him do that to you?" He went to work on him quickly.

"I could see him up in the tree shootin' at me."

"Did you kill him?"

"Sure did. Killed him dead."

"Kicked his teeth out?"

"Well . . ." he hesitated apologetically, "I was feelin' pretty sick by then . . ."

"Sure. Hell with him." A new dressing had been applied and the ubiquitous sleeping potion was being administered. The patient gulped it down and made a face. The doctor wrinkled his nose in sympathy.

"Sleep tight, my boy. When you wake up a nurse will be looking after you."

The kid's eyes opened wide.

"A girl nurse?"

"Sure. They got them at the hospital now. You'll have to shave that beard."

The boy grinned dreamily. "Nurses! Well, what do you know?"

The perspiration was running in streams down our backs. The doctor paused at the cooler for some more water. Over the cup he mumbled at me: "Christ, they're young. They're so goddam young!" He shook his head and clucked his tongue.

I asked him if he ever had any doubts about his treatment.

"You mean do I make mistakes?" He reflected soberly. "I guess so, but I make as few of them as possible—and I never make the same one twice. My grandfather used to say: 'When a man cheats me in business once, shame on him. When he cheats me twice, shame on me.' It's the same thing."

We started down another aisle. A dejected boy sat on top of a bunk sucking hungrily at a cigarette. There wasn't a mark on him, but he was trembling violently.

"What's your complaint?" the doctor asked him.

"Nerves," the boy stated almost inaudibly. He turned his head away. He looked whipped and ashamed.

The doctor laid his hand on the boy's belly. "You're pretty warm. I'll tell you what we'll do. We'll give you a nice, cool sponge bath and then you'll go to sleep. What do you say?" The boy didn't answer. The doctor patted his knee, then nodded to the corpsman. "Take care of him."

He walked off a few steps, then turned a harried visage to me.

"Those combat fatigue cases get me. I don't know how to handle them. The first one I talked to. I made him cry. So now I leave them alone. I guess I'm no psychologist."

We moved along, the corpsman trailing us. A neat round hole in a thigh confronted us.

"What you got there, kid? A leg?"

"Yeah—and I don't like it."

"I know. I was shot once and it was lousy. Flashlight."

The boy watched him gravely as the doctor examined the leg.

"Is it bad?" he asked. His voice shook a little.

The doctor assumed a professorial manner.

"It's never bad when there are two holes. One is bad. Two is good. Remember that." He turned to a corpsman. "Okay. Wrap her up and take 'er away."

The procession carried on. Amoebic dysentery was laughed off with outhouse humor and an enormous dose of sulfathiazole. Dozens of tiny shrapnel fragments were dug out of a buttock to the accompaniment of ribald kidding. Sponge baths were administered like decorations for good conduct. Jokes were exchanged and repeated with each set of patients. Repetition didn't matter. The jokes were good, even the third time.

An officer appeared, cool and pressed in his khakis, obviously straight from the bridge. He held out a board with some papers clasped to it.

"I've got some bad news for you, doc. We just received these messages."

The doctor groaned. "On top of everything else I have to be the coding officer. Can't someone else do it? I'm snowed down here. Tell the skipper I'm too busy, will you, Henry?" His voice wheedled with the last phrase.

The officer nodded his head wearily. "I expected to do it again, but you can't blame me for trying." He smiled. The doctor shoved him playfully and turned to the next patient.

This was a six-footer, square and rangy. He had the long taut muscles of a first-rate swimmer. A homemade eye patch hung from his forehead, and he was fiddling nervously with the strings of his life preserver. When the doctor approached he leaped out of bed and addressed him tensely.

"Doc, you tell me the truth. Am I going to go blind?"

The doctor regarded him suavely.

"How'd you know I was the doctor?"

"Why—why—"

"You could see me, couldn't you? Then what the hell are you talking about?"

The boy rocked on his feet, then continued persistently: "Out of only one eye, though. And the other one's getting dim. I've heard of it happening before. One eye goes bad, then the other one blacks out. I can't afford to go blind, doctor. That'd be bad. Very bad!"

The doctor pushed him gently back on his bunk. "Let me take a look."

He stripped off the eye patch, shone the flashlight into the injured eye.

"Now I tell you what you do. Close the good one and tell me how many fingers you see." He held up one finger and waggled it back and forth. The boy strained at the vision. I could feel his passion to see—to be right in what he saw. Finally he blurted out the answer: "Four."

The doctor clenched his fist quickly. "Pretty close," he said triumphantly.

"There were five, weren't there? I thought there were five, but I couldn't make out the thumb very clearly. There were five, weren't there?"

"That'd be telling. I'm going to try this test on you later again. You don't want to know the answer, do you? Now let's wash out that eye."

Carefully he swabbed the eye with boric acid.

"How's that feel now? Can you see better?"

The boy squinted up at the electric light bulb.

"Yes—a little," he replied uncertainly.

"Okay. Now I'm going to cross you up. I fixed it so you could see a little—now I'm going to make it so you can't see nothing. Let's have the eye dropper, Ted."

Midway in the operation, the boy jerked back. He looked at the doctor beseechingly.

"Am I going to lose this eye, doctor? I've got to know. Please tell me."

The doctor sighed. "Look, son, you've got a hundred-to-one chance of losing your eye. It's a great gamble—but you'd gamble me anything at a hundred to one, wouldn't you?"

He pulled the boy's head back toward the light and applied a neat new patch. The boy closed his good eye tightly. His lips trembled. He seemed ready to cry. The doctor grabbed his shoulders fiercely.

"Now listen, dammit! Don't you know you've got the best doctors in the world looking after you? Do you think when you get back to the Canal you'll have some punk from Podunk taking care of you? You'll have the best damn eye specialist in America working on you. And I just gave him a head start. Now cut it out or I'll drop you over the side."

The boy stared at the doctor, shaken by the anger in his voice. Then he seemed to relax all over. He spoke very quietly. "I'm sorry, doctor. I guess a lot of fellows got it worse than me."

"That's a good boy. Now lie down and get some sleep." He turned away, then twisted his head around and spoke confidentially. "If it starts to get you down, yell for me. I'll fix you up."

We went to the cooler. We all consumed quarts of ice water.

"This heat's murdering me. I'm forty-two pounds too heavy for the Navy and I can't sweat it off. Maybe I ought to go back to Oregon."

He turned to his corpsman. "Is that all of them?"

The corpsman consulted his pad before handing it to the doctor.

"Check," he said, "except for those two appendicitis cases you looked at before."

"They're not hot, but keep 'em on ice." He frowned at me. "You know, sometimes a kid gets scared and he wants to get out bad, so he develops a pain—appendicitis. The doctors on the beach have no way of testing it, and they can't take a chance, the kid might really have a hot appendix, so they ship him out. I'm taking no risks either. They get ice packs every hour." He wagged his head despairingly. "It's that damn psychology again."

He hung up the board on a hook next to him, and breathed out noisily. "Well, that's that!"

I glanced at my watch. We had left Empress Augusta Bay only two hours ago. "Going to get a little sleep now?" I asked him.

He snorted. "Sleep! I haven't been to sleep since—" He paused and considered a minute. "Hey, Ted, what day is this?"

The corpsman wrinkled his face with concentration.

"Isn't it Wednesday?"

"Wednesday? It's Saturday!" Then uncertainly: "Or is it Friday?" He returned impatiently to me. "I haven't been in a bed for a hell of a long time and I'm pooped. I get letters from my partner back in The Dalles—that's just outside of Portland where I practiced—telling me how exciting it must be for me and how he envies me." He dropped into a brooding silence. "I'm a chest man. Worked for years at the State Tuberculosis Hospital. That's my field and I'm going back to it. I studied under the best lung man in the world. I can use a bronchoscope like you can drive a car. I have a collection of trophies I took out of lungs that would amaze you. It was interesting and it was my business. Now I'd sell my soul to get an inch of shrapnel out of some kid's knee."

A long, low whistle sounded from over our heads. We looked up. The combat fatigue case was snoring profoundly under his opiate. The doctor regarded me mournfully.

"Those nerve cases," he complained. "They're the one thing that gets me down. I don't know how to handle them. I'm just no damn good at psychology. Let's go up on deck."

❧   ❧   ❧   ❧

THE MOST IMMEDIATE REACTION OF RABAUL (210 miles distant) to the invasion was the transit of a 475-man battalion which counterlanded on the west flank of the 3rd Division perimeter. Somehow these troops avoided contact with the marines until November 7, and then in a series of stiff skirmishes with the 3rd Battalion, 9th Marines, and subsequently with the 1st Battalion, 3rd Marines, in swamps and fetid jungles, the Japanese were isolated. The end for them came when Colonel John Wilson of the 12th Marines let fly an artillery barrage: 377 enemy dead as against 47 marines killed and wounded.

Action against the enemy now moved to the Piva (Numa Numa) Trail, the only overland approach to Torokina, where our forces were in almost constant battle with the Japanese 23rd Infantry. The 2nd Raiders had outposted the trail on D-Day, and within a week they began a twelve-day series of battalion-scale skirmishes along the trail calculated to clear the perimeter area. On November 17 a count of enemy dead stood at 540, and the 1st and 2nd Battalions, 9th Marines, plus the 2nd Battalion, 21st Marines, still had in front of them Japanese troops who stoutly refused to quit. At Piva Forks, the junction of the Piva Trail and the East-West Trail, the 3rd Marines and the 23rd Infantry clashed a half dozen times. The results were always the same: many dead Japanese and a lot left who were still full of ginger.

Next the Japanese tried an outflanking movement, and failing this, attempted combined sniper and mortar fire. Other unavailing skirmishes followed. On the twentieth the marines' luck finally turned when a platoon led by Lieutenant Steve Cibik of the 21st Marines stumbled onto high ground which had eluded previous patrols. About 400 feet high, the ridge was strategic in that it overlooked Empress Augusta Bay and dominated the trails in the area—an ideal place for artillery and an observation post.

With collaborators Gerold Frank and James D. Horan, here is Lieutenant Steve Cibik (Silver Star) speaking of the fight to hold the ridge—probably the most precious piece of real estate on Bougainville. It is a few moments after one of Cibik's men— Lieutenant William Kay ("The Fox")—has located the high ground . . .

·11· CIBIK'S RIDGE

LIEUTENANT STEVE CIBIK
WITH GEROLD FRANK
AND JAMES D. HORAN

It was The Fox who found the ridge. A lesser man would never have seen it, for it was a geographical freak, a knob of stone and earth lost in the green fury of the Bougainville jungle. The Fox—Lt. William Kay, of Baltimore, a scout's scout, a wizard in bushcraft—came trudging out of a wall of rain, his sharp nose sniffing, his thin utility almost transparent with water as it clung to his lean body. "You going up the ridge?" he asked, shaking the water from his eyes like a dog. "O.K., Steve; come along."

It was late afternoon . . . Only a few minutes before, our battalion had taken time out to rest. The odor of the jungle, warm and humid, was in our nostrils when Maj. Donald C. Schmuck, of California, appeared, coming up the line.

"Steve," he said without preface, "there's a knoll up ahead. Lieutenant Kay found it. He'll lead you to it. Take your men and occupy it for the night." He spat water and grinned. "We don't want the Japs to get on top of us tonight, and there are plenty of them out there. Keep your fingers crossed."

Then he was gone, and The Fox was emerging from the curtain of rain. I turned to my platoon sergeant, Charles B. Kenneday, of Winter Garden, Florida, and said, "Let's go."

We were a veteran company, with Guadalcanal behind us, and we thought we knew jungle. But here on Bougainville we were battling jungle such as we had never dreamed of. For nineteen days we struggled in miasmal swamps, fought vines that wrapped themselves about our necks like a whip, birds that dived at us like screaming Stukas, bats whose wings whirred like falling artillery shells, and snakes, lizards and insects without name or number. For nineteen days we attacked this natural enemy with our machetes and knives, hacking our way through almost solid barricades of vegetation run riot.

It rained daily from noon to dusk—fierce, pounding tropical rains.

If we had been lucky to hit fairly dry ground, we slept in foxholes six or eight inches deep. During the night, water seeped up through the earth. We invariably awoke drenched. Snakes ten feet long, with brown and sickly yellow markings, came out of the jungle one night to be our bedfellows, curling up with us for warmth. Next morning was loud with shouts of "Snakes! Snakes!" and the sound of thuds and thumpings as the men frantically beat them to death.

Now, on the twentieth day, we moved single file along the trail in the downpour and gathering darkness.

"What kind of a knoll is it?" I asked Kay.

"I've never been up there. I spotted it by luck," he said over his shoulder. "Stand fifty yards in front of it and you don't see it. We'll hit there in a few minutes."

We moved slowly, fifty-one of us in all, and at the tail end of the column our sixteen machine gunners struggled and swore under the weight of their two machine guns and ammunition cans. I carried a telephone, and behind me two scouts carefully let out a spool of combat wire for communication with our commanding officer, Lt. Col. Hector de Zayas. We pushed on, and after a while the rain stopped.

Shortly before 6:30, The Fox halted. He pointed to the left. "See it?" he asked.

I stood at his side and followed his finger. I made out a slight rise in the terrain.

It was the ridge. Nature had camouflaged it with surpassing skill; if it had not been for a nakedly white tree, it would have escaped us completely.

"That's it," he said. "All yours. *To-fa!*" he said cheerily, and with that Samoan good-by, he turned back.

We moved on. Suddenly I was brought up sharply against a wall of hard earth. I hacked at it with my knife, and the blade struck rock. It was an almost perpendicular wall with an outcropping of stone, impossible to climb. We had reached the base of the ridge. Moving like blind men, we investigated. Finally we found a good layer of earth covering the rock. I gripped a tangle of roots as thick as my wrist, and began to climb. After half an hour's heartbreaking work, we reached a small saddle where the ridge leveled off for a distance of fifteen feet, just as our communication wire gave out. We threw ourselves down to rest.

Better dig in here for the night, I thought. *No knowing how much farther we have. And then, are we climbing into a trap? Are the Japs up there, hearing us, waiting?*

I nudged Kenneday. "Tell them to dig in," I said. "We'll pull out before dawn." I heard Kenneday's whispered order go down the line.

The men set to work in the darkness, scooping up the soggy earth with their knives and helmets. I cranked the telephone and whispered "CP. CP."

I had to inform Colonel de Zayas that we were pitching in here for the night. Our artillery had been hammering this ridge with everything it had. If they opened up before we left, we would be wiped out. "CP. CP," I repeated.

No answer.

After ten minutes of fruitless calling, I turned the phone over to the man next to me and began to dig my own foxhole. The whispered "CP. CP." went on. I had the men take over the phone in turn. It grew deadly quiet. In this lull, even nature seemed to be listening, as we were, for that voice, to be reassured that we were in communication somehow with our front line. At five A.M. I told Kenneday to take an eight-man patrol and see how far it was to the summit. He and his men vanished. There was nothing to do but wait. A splatter of mud announced Kenneday's return. It was at least 200 more feet to the summit, he told us, and there, on a small knoll hardly big enough to turn around in, he'd found more than a dozen Jap foxholes. He'd seen no Japs, but they couldn't be far away. I woke my men. One by one they climbed out of their foxholes, rubbing their red-rimmed eyes, moving stiffened bodies. We started up once more.

As we climbed, the jungle awoke too. We heard the raucous caw of the bird that screeched for all the world like wood being sawed, the weird womanlike scream of the "banana cat"—half cat, half anteater, as near as we could make out—and the endless buzzing and whirring of insects.

We climbed for nearly two hours, dragging ourselves up by the vines, and lashing ropes around our guns to pull them up, like Alpine climbers. Finally we reached the summit and lay there, our hearts pounding. There were fifteen foxholes. Some were well constructed, large enough to hold four men, covered with a lean-to of bamboo, thatched with banana leaves. We found chopsticks, cigarette butts, scraps of paper, food cans, the remains of fire. Apparently the Japs used the crest as an observation post by day, and at night retired to their bivouac area at the base of the far side of the hill, to get away from our artillery fire.

I walked to the edge of the ridge and almost gasped. What a view of Bougainville! We were on the tip of a thumb of earth 500 feet high, an oasis in a sea of mist-covered jungle, the only high ground for miles around. In the distance towered the Emperor Mountain Range, and in its center, marked by wisps of dark, curling smoke, brooded the volcano of Mt. Bagana, and far out across the jungle roof top were the sparkling waters of Empress Augusta Bay.

We moved about the ridge slowly, examining our position.

"Look here!" called Kenneday suddenly. He was standing at the head of a narrow trail which led down into the concealed depths of the gorge below. Twenty yards away, we stumbled on a second trail. One led north, the other east. Both had been used recently. Kenneday and I talked things over.

What was our job now, and what had we to do it with? Our forces were small—there were fifty-one of us—we had only eleven belts of machine-gun ammunition, which would be used up in a few minutes of concerted fighting. We'd have to depend principally upon the BAR's [Browning automatic rifles] and rifles. Each of us had three hand grenades, and in emergency we would have to make the best use of these. We had no food. But no matter what the cost, we had to hold this ridge. Five hundred yards behind us were our front lines. In the valley below, on the other side of the Piva River, were several thousand Jap troops. We all knew that a big battle must be fought when the two forces met at the river's fork. When we attacked, this ridge would be invaluable. From here, we could spot Jap positions and direct our heavy-artillery fire; from here, we could drive down into the valley, engaging the Japs while our main forces fought their way across the river. On the other hand, were the Japs in control of this ridge, the tables would be turned. This ridge could be the key to success or failure in this phase of the battle of Bougainville.

We had to hold it. We established the two machine guns, each with a crew of six men; one covering the east trail, under Sgt. Richard Murphy, of New York, who had grown a reddish beard that gave him an appearance of raffish gaiety; the other, covering the north trail, under Slim Tierney, a taciturn Westerner who wanted to kill Japs more than anything else in the world. I had only one order to give the boys: "Don't fire until you must. We're saving all the ammunition we can."

We started to construct a perimeter defense, using the foxholes the Japs had already dug. Suddenly, as I scooped up a double handful of earth, I heard pounding feet. I wheeled around. Murphy was racing up the trail, BAR in his right hand, signaling frantically. He had heard the Japs working their way upward, apparently ignorant that the hill had changed hands.

We flung ourselves in our holes and waited. From behind the shelter of a huge banyan tree, I made out the first Japs. I waited until they were within range.

"Let 'em have it!" I shouted.

Our BAR's came to life; our riflemen, forced to sit up to aim because the hill was so steep, fired like a picked team of marksmen. The Japs screamed and vanished into the jungle. But they left behind them four still bodies. That was four for our side.

Kenneday grunted. "Might as well sit around till they come back again," he said.

I knew they would too. The Japs must have known every blade of grass, every quivering leaf here. They'd make good use of the terrain. If they succeeded in destroying the two guns, we'd be lost.

Ducking low, I ran back to Murphy's machine-gun nest, leaping the last few feet and landing in their midst. Murphy, a rugged, stocky, ex-baseball player from the Ohio sandlots, was sitting behind his gun, peering into the jungle below.

"Have the boys move this gun about twenty feet to the left, Murph," I said. "If the Nips come back, let's be where they ain't."

He nodded assent, and I made it back to my foxhole. The men redoubled their digging. As the morning wore on, the heat grew. It must now have been nearly 100 degrees. The men worked, drenched to the skin by perspiration. They were drinking water at an alarming rate, and I passed the word to go easy. Each man had only what remained in his canteen.

At noon, our artillery began. The first shell burst less than 100 yards from us on the Jap side of the ridge. The earth shook and the shrapnel whistled through the air. We lay in the foxholes and prayed that our artillery would not shorten range. If they did—one well-placed shell could wipe us all out.

The shelling lasted fully half an hour, and when it stopped we climbed cautiously out of our foxholes.

Kenneday prowled about and returned to announce, "Nobody hurt. So far, so good."

Suddenly a figure appeared low on the crest of the ridge. I jumped for my rifle, only to discover that it was Lieutenant Kay, unperturbed as ever.

He crouched there, a coil of wire strung over his left shoulder, and drawled, "You sure moved since the last time I saw you!" He moved carefully to the edge of the ridge and whistled. "Hell, Steve, this is wonderful. I didn't think my ridge was this good."

I didn't have any time to agree with him. I grabbed the coil, and the three of us climbed down the ridge to the saddle where we'd spent the night before. What we saw made us pause.

Kenneday pointed. "Look at that!" he said.

It was as though a cyclone had whirled through what had once been our foxholes. The earth was churned and plowed by direct shellbursts. Had we remained there, we would have been blasted to bits.

We *had* been bracketed by our own fire!

I hunted for the phone and found it covered with earth. We spliced the wire quickly and paid it out as we climbed back to the knoll. I plugged in the phone, cranked it, pressed the butterfly, and said, "CP! CP!"

A voice answered sharply, "Hello?"

I took a deep breath. "This is Cibik," I said. "Give me—"

A cool voice broke in, "Hello, Steve!" It was Colonel de Zayas himself. "Damn glad to hear you."

Kay grinned at me, and I grinned back.

"We're sitting on the top of the world, sir," I replied. "This ridge is a wonderful observation post. It's the only high land in the entire area."

"Very good, Steve," he said. "Now—" He had no sooner said "now" than our artillery opened up again. Shells tore over our heads, screaming like banshees. Fragments of steel nipped and tore at vegetation. A shower of splintered bark, broken twigs, ripped vines, tatters of banana leaves descended on us. It was impossible to talk while the thunder of shells rolled over the valley. I took advantage of a brief pause.

"Hear that, sir?" I said. "We're right in the middle of that barrage."

Colonel de Zayas was still on the phone. "What's your height?"

I had never made guesses for artillery before, but I tried it. "About four hundred feet, sir."

"We'll take care of it. Anything else?"

Again the thunder of Jap fire. "Yes, sir. We need more ammunition. We've only eleven belts. If they attack in force, we're sunk. And we need food, sir."

"We'll send the ammunition and food up as soon as we get some down here, Steve," he said.

There was a click and silence.

Kay pushed his cap to one side. "Well, I guess you're all taken care of now. I have to get back. I'll pass the word to hustle up that ammunition. *To-fa,*" he said, and vanished over the side of the ridge.

Suddenly, one of Murphy's BAR men dashed up. "Japs coming up again, Steve," he said, and I saw the bush trembling about 100 yards away.

"We'll do it with rifle fire and grenades," I ordered. I waited half a minute more, then yelled, "Now!" pulling the pin of my own grenade and lobbing it over.

At the same time, Kenneday's men opened with rifle fire. The brush was peppered. There were screams and the sound of men rushing down the trail. Then a pause, and from everywhere below, the Japs answered us with furious rifle fire. They were there in force. All that long morning we heard the shrill chatter of Jap voices and even the clanging of their shovels and the sound of wood being sawed. They were apparently preparing some sort of defensive position.

Through the early afternoon we heard the battle orchestration from the valley—the spatter of rifle fire, the tat-a-tat of Jap Nambu light machine guns, merging with the hoarse staccato of our machine guns and the cough of our mortars.

It was now about three o'clock. A blue haze covered the valley, at once luminous and pale, and suddenly I realized it was raining down there. But here on our little knob, our waiting army was still dry. In the hope that the rain clouds would blow over us, the boys made cups of banana leaves and placed them on the rims of the foxholes. But only the valley lay drenched and steaming, and no rain fell for us.

An hour and a half before dusk, our reinforcements arrived—ten men under Lt. Herbert G. Young, with three mortars and enough C-rations to go around once for every man.

Lieutenant Young, a tall, matter-of-fact virtuoso of the mortar, dropped his field telephone and announced, "Well, general, here we are. Where are your Japs?"

"I'll show you the Japs, but let's have some of these rations."

We distributed them around and the men had their first food in fifty hours. After we had licked the cans clean, I turned to Lieutenant Young and waved toward the north trail.

"Listen," I said.

Faintly, we heard the echoes of chopping and sawing.

"O.K.," he said, and he and his men swiftly set up their mortars and unloaded the miniature torpedo-like shells.

At five P.M., Lieutenant Young's men went into action with an ear-splitting cacophony of sound. The pom! pom! pom! of the mortars punctuated the hot afternoon, and it continued while the swift twilight rushed across the sky and darkness fell. Then the rain came and the temperature dropped. Somehow, despite the cold and the wet and the acute discomfort, some of us slept.

Those of us who could not sleep lay wondering. Would we be alive tomorrow? Would we get food and ammunition? If the Japs attacked in force, could we hold them? Thank God we had got that telephone in.

I thought of Logan Avenue in Leechburg, that quiet, leafy street upon which I grew up. High school . . . mother and dad—a thousand details of form and color surged through my mind. I was homesick. The steak mother used to prepare, and how it looked, crackling with goodness, as it came from the broiler . . . the very color and design of the kitchen linoleum . . . the apple pie she made so well, sweetened to my taste, but too sweet for the rest of the family . . . the radio at my bedroom window—

My thoughts were interrupted by a new sound—the sound made by two bamboo branches struck together. Then a rustling. I glanced at my watch; a globule of rain lingered on the crystal, making the figure "3" grotesquely large. It was nearly four A.M. I crept through the cream-smooth mud to Kenneday. He was awake too. "Japs." He formed the word with his lips. I nodded. They were down the trail, waiting for us to give ourselves away.

The night passed, and as dawn lit up our bivouac on the morning of the twenty-second, the rain stopped.

At 8:05 A.M. Sergeant Murphy suddenly raced up the trail, yelling, "Japs! Japs!" We stiffened into position, and a moment later the voice of Pfc. Steve Rider came.

"I'm hit!" he cried. A burst of Jap fire punctuated his words.

Corporal Jeffra, standing next to me, swore under his breath. "I'll go down after him," he said.

I looked at him. "Go ahead," I said.

He vanished down the north trail, and it was a long three minutes before he reappeared, helping Rider through the underbrush. Rider was limping.

"They're out there, Steve," he said. "A whole shebang of them."

Blood showed faintly on his right thigh. I ripped the leg of his utility and uncovered a small black puncture. A corpsman came up on the double, examined the wound, sprinkled sulfa powder on it and covered it with a battle dressing. I sent a man to accompany him back to our own lines.

Sgt. Peter Henzi, a tall youngster with a thick black beard, who hailed from Union City, New Jersey, was in earnest conversation with Lieutenant Young a few yards away. After Rider left, he hurried over to me.

"Suppose I go down there and spot the mortar fire," he suggested.

Tierney, still eager for a Jap, chimed in. "I'll go with you," he said. There was a gleam in his eye and the lines of his jaw were hard.

I said it was all right with me. They picked up Lieutenant Young's field phone and crawled toward the Jap lines. I took up a careful position in my foxhole.

About fifteen minutes later, Pete's voice came over the wire, clear and calm. "I'm hooked up and in position now, Steve," he said. "Let's have one on the range." I turned to Lieutenant Young, who was directly behind me, and repeated, "Fire one round; same range—"

There was a violent, ripping explosion.

Pete's voice came over again, "Bring it over twenty-five yards."

Again the roar.

"Right twenty-five yards."

Young and his men worked fast. The shell was dropped in and the men stepped aside.

Henzi's voice, "Getting closer. Make it twenty-five again."

This time I heard the crash of the explosion come tinnily over the wire. A moment later, Pete's voice, "Right in there, Steve! You hit so close, Tierney got it in the hand."

"Pull out, Pete," I told him. "We want to lay down a concentration there."

"O.K.," he said.

Ten minutes passed, and then we saw Tierney and Henzi coming toward us from the east trail. Tierney had been hit in the left wrist.

Now Lieutenant Young and his men were pouring a steady stream of shells into the Jap position. Tierney refused to leave, and because he was a good man, I kept him with me. Henzi explained that he'd got within fifty feet of the Japs and our shells then almost grazed their heads as they came over.

Above the bursts of our fire, the Jap machine guns sounded. The screaming commands of the Jap officers came faintly to our ears. It was a hot, steady exchange. Presently, the firing died down to a few ragged rifle shots.

Kenneday climbed out of his foxhole. There wasn't much ammunition left, he said. I rang up Colonel de Zayas and asked again for ammunition. As I spoke, the Jap snipers began pinging. The men stared watchfully from their foxholes. They showed the effects of twenty-two days on Bougainville. They were dirty, bearded and hollow-eyed. Those who were too weary to sit or lie down stood about; sorry figures, their arms hanging limply, their shoulders drooping. They expressed fatigue in every limb.

Shortly after noon, the sniping died down. And with the heat, the air brought us the sickening odor of Jap bodies—those who had been killed in the first attack during our first few hours on the ridge. By midafternoon, it was almost nauseating.

Finally, Kenneday said, "I can't stand it any longer. I'm going down and see what I can do about those dead Japs."

He was back shortly, his clothes reeking. He shook his head ruefully.

"I feel like a morgue keeper," he said. Give me some hunks of wire."

He went back with six men, and when he returned the second time, he was white under his stubble of black beard.

"They're spread all over the place," he said. "They must have walked right into our fire."

He and his patrol had carefully examined the Jap graveyard. They found machine guns ripped apart by shrapnel. The Japs were coming up the ridge to make a stand. Some of them apparently were trying to put their guns in place not only on the ridge but in trees. Had they succeeded, their troops could have advanced under a sheltering umbrella of their fire, and our situation would have been perilous.

Kenneday and his men used the wire to drag some of the bodies into a large foxhole and used that as a common grave. They'd found a small black book with a tan paper cover, post cards with nature scenes, and photographs of Japanese pin-up girls.

Kenneday produced what appeared to be a mechanical pencil. "Look at this," he said. "I was going to open it, but I figured it might be a booby trap."

We decided that the wisest thing was to send everything down to the Intelligence officers behind our lines. It was a good idea. We learned later that the pencil contained sufficient explosives to blow up a squad of men.

Before dawn we had reinforcements, drifting in by twos and threes. I spread them along the crest of the ridge, closing the gaps in our defensive line. They hadn't come a minute too soon. The Japs attacked with knee mortars and artillery fire. It was a full-scale offensive, with Jap infantry advancing steadily toward us in the face of everything we could hurl at them. Our guns never paused for breath. Shell after shell whistled over, moaning and crashing across the ridge, while we crouched below, pinned under a murderous crossfire. The brassy cordite was bitter in our mouths. Discretion was the better part of valor, I decided, and grabbed the phone. "CP! CP!"

A voice answered.

I shouted, "Tell the colonel to raise the elevation fifty feet, will you? Listen to it!"

A shell roared overhead. I held up the phone, so that the shell's whine wailed into the mouthpiece.

There was a quick "O.K., fella," from the other end. "We'll take care of it."

All that night, I was constantly on the phone, directing the fire. The shelling ceased at dawn. At nine o'clock, the phone rang.

It was Colonel de Zayas. "Can you move in fifteen minutes?" he demanded.

"Yes, sir," I said.

"Fine," he said. "At ten A.M., your mortars and X Company's mortars will lay a five-minute concentration on the Japs' strong point at the base of the ridge. At ten-five, your platoon will attack down the east trail and move along the base of the ridge and join X Company." He paused, and then he added, "Steve, if it gets too hot, pull out. Don't lose too many boys. Pull back to the ridge. We need you and your men tomorrow when we hit the Piva River."

I hung up and looked about for Lieutenant Young. He was examining one of his mortars. "How much stuff you got?" I asked.

"About nineteen rounds," he said. "What's the scoop?"

"We've got to start moving," I said. "They want us to attack the Japs at the base. We've only got thirteen minutes left."

I outlined the plan of attack swiftly. The men gathered around, listening quietly. I singled out Mitchum, told him to build up a firing line and spot targets while we moved down. "Pass the word along, so the men know exactly what we're doing."

Then we went over the side and down, crawling through thick vegetation, smelling the Jap dead before we saw them. The signs of our artillery shelling were everywhere. Finally, we reached a point of vantage. At the stroke of ten o'clock, we heard the first mortar roar down below us. Again and again, our shells hit the Jap position. I counted them—sixteen, seventeen, eighteen, nineteen. Lieutenant Young had no more shells. It was now 10:18. Company X's mortars had not yet opened fire. For a moment, I hesitated. If we went down, we might be caught in X's fire. Thirty seconds passed. No fire. We had to advance. We moved on cautiously, made about forty yards, and then the Japs struck, just as I gained the protection of a large banyan tree. I huddled at its base as Jap rifle and machine-gun fire from what we later learned were scores of machine-gun nests buried in tangled banyan roots, raked the trees over our heads. To my left, Pfc. L., a huge fellow so quiet that he was hardly ever noticed, gasped and moaned, and seemed to fold up. Mitchum, to my right, started to crawl toward him. I gauged the distance to the wounded man. I was about ten feet from L., but that area was almost completely denuded by shellfire. He was on one side of a square clearing, and the three of us, Mitchum, Mathews and myself, began to converge on him from the three other sides. Jap lead spattered all about us. L. slowly began dragging himself back up the ridge, his right thigh a mass of bloody flesh. A Jap machine-gun burst had nearly ripped off his leg. He made no sound, but under the grime and perspiration, his face was white as chalk. As he pulled himself along, he left a red trail on the matted jungle floor. Painfully, he began to crawl across the edge of the clearing less than four feet from me, when another machine-gun burst sounded above the sharp snapping of rifle fire. He was caught directly in the chest. He slumped over and lay still. Mitchum stared at me, and I shook my head helplessly. Mathews stopped and said nothing.

A Nambu light machine gun suddenly chattered alarmingly near. The Japs had succeeded in getting one of their light machine guns up into a tree, and were spraying us. The bullets grazed our heads. We'd have to pull out. I crawled to Mitchum, who was working his gun furiously.

"Mitch—" I began, and he uttered a sharp cry.

"I'm hit!" Blood poured from a wound in his wrist.

"Get back to the ridge," I said. Mathews now sat like an avenging Buddha with his BAR, waiting for a Jap burst from one of the trees.

We had to get back up the ridge. The wounded had to be brought up. I had to cross that clearing. I said to myself, *Steve, perhaps your number's up now,* and with that I rose and leaped across it. Bullets kicked up the earth before and behind me in that endless second, but I fell unhurt at Mathews' side.

"Get back," I said. "Get away from this clearing."

Another burst of gunfire. Mathews grunted. He rolled over on his back for an instant, the breast of his utility torn and bloody, and on his face was a look of surprise. His body remained in that curious position for a moment.

"Are you hit, boy?" I shouted. "Are you hit?"

His body began rolling over and over down the steep slope. And as it rolled, Jap fire riddled it as though it were a cloth dummy rolling down a hill and this was rifle practice.

Rage rose in me. I wanted to charge screaming down the hill, firing my rifle until it could fire no more. I wanted to kill Japs, to plunge my knife into their bodies, to strangle them with my bare hands. My face was covered with grime, perspiration burned in my eyes, my nostrils smarted with the acrid fumes of gunpowder. A hand touched mine. It was Pfc. Charles M. Skinner, of Franklin, Ohio, a BAR man, and while the rest of us worked our way upward, Skinner sat with his BAR, keeping the barrel of his gun hot as he covered our retreat. He deliberately drew the Jap fire upon himself.

To the first man I saw above, I said, "Send word back to get three BAR men down here, so we can get our wounded."

The BAR men came. They sat up, guns to their shoulders, and fired. The first gun jammed. So did the second. The two men swore.

The third was Arkansas Rowe, a tall, gangling Westerner with a wad of tobacco in his cheek.

"Give it a try!" I said. "Spray 'em!"

Rowe squinted into the jungle, twisted his face to one side, let go a stream of yellow tobacco juice, and aimed. His BAR chattered and stopped.

He turned around, cool as ice. "I didn't think this damn thing was going to work either," he drawled, and returned to his firing. Under his protection, our men began to crawl back up the slope. But Mitchum was still down there.

I sent word up for a machine-gun crew, and Sergeant Murphy showed up, dragging his weapon after him.

"Keep up a steady fire," I said. "We're going to try to reach Mitchum." Then we set off, but, after a few yards, came upon Pfc. Jacob Solomon, helping a bloody figure stagger along. It was Skinner, and he was badly hurt, his eyes glassy.

Solomon, scarcely able to walk himself, managed to gasp, "I found this guy firing even after the Japs got him. They hit him in the leg and one of the bullets went up the back of his helmet, made a circle right around his scalp, and then fell out."

I helped carry Skinner up to the crest, and there we laid him down. He needed plasma. Solomon left without a word to bring back Mitchum, going down the slope in the face of Jap fire. I knelt beside Skinner. He was breathing hard. His face was pale. His hair was plastered against his forehead.

A corpsman hurried over, ripped off Skinner's pants leg and sprinkled sulfa into the gaping wound. He dressed it swiftly. Then he raised Skinner's head and gently removed his helmet. Sure enough, there was a bloody, telltale crease about the boy's head, cut cleanly by the bullet.

I took Skinner's hand; it was cold and clammy. He was trying to whisper. I leaned over to catch his words. "I'm sorry, Steve," he was saying. "I tell you, I couldn't help it. Damn, I'm sorry I couldn't do better."

All I could say was, "You did a great job down there, fella! A real job!"

Now Solomon was back with Mitchum, who lay gasping, weak from loss of blood. But he managed to say, "I'm OK, Steve."

The runner came, out of breath, with the plasma. As it flowed into Skinner's veins, life seemed to creep back into his body. He smiled weakly when one of the men leaned down to wipe the perspiration from his face, and when a corpsman came up with a bottle of brandy, which he put to Skinner's lips, Skinner swallowed a few drops and even managed a feeble joke.

"That's swell," he whispered, licking his lips. "Let's have more of that medicine."

Two corpsmen placed him carefully in a stretcher and set off with him toward our lines. I found my foxhole and slid back into it. Kenneday wandered over. He offered me a cigarette from a dirty pack. It had been rain-soaked and now the cigarettes were dry and brittle. I inhaled deeply.

"Guess we'll be relieved this afternoon," he said.

"I hope so," I said.

We smoked in silence. The firing had died down, save for the occasional snap of a sniper's rifle. We seemed all right. With our reinforcements, the Japs would have a tough fight to dislodge us.

In midafternoon, the phone rang. It was Colonel de Zayas.

"All right, Steve," he said. "Move your men back down here. We want you in tomorrow's attack."

I gathered my men together and we moved off the ridge the way we had come. The men who followed me in single file were shaky scarecrows, fouled with mud, stained with sweat and gunpowder, their eyes sunken from lack of sleep, their skin showing through their tattered utilities. We climbed down almost as circumspectly as we had climbed up, and finally reached the original trail. Someone was coming up it. It was The Fox. He held a short bowie knife in his hand.

"Hiya," he said. "Congratulations. You boys did a swell job." I felt a strong hand clasp mine. "Here," said The Fox. "This is for you." He gave me the knife.

I looked at it, then at him. "What's this for?"

He pointed to the handle. He'd carved on it, "From The Fox to Steve."

"Hell," he said, "maybe you can use it."

We walked together to our bivouac, and some of the first men I met were from our own company. "Welcome back," somebody said, and "Damn glad to see you."

Henzi said, "Steve, you did a good job," and we shook hands. I was embarrassed, but at that moment I thought, *These fellows mean as much to me now as my own family. We're together. We're part of a brotherhood born in blood and battle.* I don't know if I thought this in these words, but I felt it strongly.

It was now six o'clock of November twenty-third. We had been on the ridge since 6:30 P.M. the night of November twentieth. Our executive officer greeted me, and led us to the area assigned to us.

Now a detail came up with cans of grapefruit and pineapple juice. Much as I hated rations, I went through four cans—ham and eggs, cheese and crackers, beef and vegetable stew.

At the command post, I found Colonel de Zayas poring over several maps. "Hello there, Steve," he said. "You and your men certainly did a good job up there. Tell me just what happened."

I sat down and outlined our experiences.

When I finished, he said, "Good enough. Now better get some sleep. We need your men tomorrow."

※ ※ ※ ※

BY DECEMBER 17, MARINE AIR WAS READY TO WORK on our ultimate objective, Rabaul, and more than 100 Corsairs, Hellcats and P-40s were flown in to participate in operations; the first plane off Bougainville was piloted by Lieutenant Colonel Gregory S. Boyington, who became the Marine Corps' ace of aces with 28 confirmed kills. A complex, deeply introspective man with a paradoxical flair for flamboyance, Boyington led his squadron on December 23 in an attack on 60 enemy planes, 20 of which fell in flames. Boyington himself shot down four Zeroes in the fight he now recounts—an action that brought him the Medal of Honor.

·12· "GOOD WILL TO ALL MEN . . . "

COLONEL GREGORY S. BOYINGTON

. . . On Christmas, on the peace-on-earth-good-will-to-all-men day, I went around the skies slaughtering people. Don't ask me why it had to be on a Christmas Day, for he who can answer such a question can also answer why there have to be wars, and who starts them, and why men in machines kill other men in machines. I had not started this war, and if it were possible to write a different sort of Christmas story I would prefer to record it, or at least to have it occur on a different day . . .

There was undoubtedly some basis for my feelings this day, for as far back as I could remember Christmas Day was repulsive to me. Ever since my childhood, it had always been the same. Relatives were forever coming to our house and kissing my brother and me with those real wet kisses children dread so much, and making a number of well-wishing compliments that none of them ever seemed to believe.

And then it started after everybody had a snout full of firewater, fighting and speaking their true thoughts. All Christmases were alike, my brother Bill and I ending up going to a movie. And even after I was old enough to protect myself, I did the same damn thing, leaving the house and celebrating the occasion with people I didn't know, in some bar.

I was leading a fighter patrol that was intended to intercept any enemy fighters that followed our bombers, which had preceded us to Rabaul. We saw them returning from their strike at a distance, and saw that Major Marion Carl's squadron was very capably warding off some Zeros, and before we got within range I witnessed three go up in flames from the .50-calibers triggered by Carl's pilots.

We caught a dozen or so of these fighters that had been heckling our bombers, B-24s. The Nips dove away and ran for home, Rabaul for they must have been short of gasoline. They had been fighting some distance from their base, with no extra fuel because they wore no belly tanks. They had not expected us to follow, but we were not escort planes and didn't have to stay with our bombers.

Nosing over after one of these homebound Nips, I closed the distance between us gradually, keeping directly behind his tail, first a thousand yards, then five hundred, finally closing in directly behind to fifty feet. Knowing the little rascal couldn't have any idea he was being followed, I was going to make certain this one didn't get away. Never before had I been so deliberate and cold about what I was doing. He was on his way home, but already I knew he would not get there.

Nonchalantly I trimmed my rudder and stabilizer tabs. Nonchalantly I checked my gun chargers. As long as he could not see me, as long as he didn't even know I was following him, I was going to take my time. I knew that my shot would be no-deflection and slowly wavered my gun sight until it rested directly upon the cross formed by his vertical tail and horizontal wings. The little Nip was a doomed man even before I fired. I knew it and could feel it, and it was I who condemned him from ever reaching home—and it was Christmas.

One short burst was all that was needed. With this short burst flames flew from the cockpit, a yellow chute opened, and down the pilot glided into the Pacific. I saw the splash.

Using my diving speed with additional power, I climbed, and as I climbed I could see off to my right two more enemy planes heading for Rabaul. One was throwing smoke. I closed in on the wounded plane, and it dove. His mate pulled off to one side to maneuver against me, but I let the smoker have it—one burst that set the plane on fire— and again the pilot bailed out.

His mate then dove in from above and to the side upon my own tail to get me, but it was simple to nose down and dive away temporarily from him. From a new position I watched the pilot from the burning plane drift slowly down to the water, the same as the other had done. This time his flying mate slowly circled him as he descended, possibly as a needless protection.

I remember the whole picture with a harsh distinction—and on Christmas—one Japanese pilot descending while his pal kept circling him. And then, after the pilot landed in the water, I went after the circling pal. I closed in on him from the sun side and nailed him about a hundred feet over the water. His Zero made a half roll and plunked out of sight into the sea. No doubt his swimming comrade saw me coming but could only watch.

This low altitude certainly was no place for me to be in enemy territory, so I climbed, but after searching for a half-hour I saw no more of the little fellows in this vicinity.

I next decided, since I was so close, to circle the harbor of Rabaul so that I could make a report on our recent bombings there. Smoke was coming from two ships. Another had only the bow protruding from the water, and there were numerous circles all around that had been created by exploding bombs.

While I was looking at all this, and preparing mental notes, I happened to see far below a nine-plane Nip patrol coming up in sections of threes. Maneuvering my plane so that I would be flying at them from the sun side again, I eased toward the rear and fired at the tail-end-Charlie in the third "V." The fire chopped him to bits, and apparently the surprise was so great in the rest of the patrol that the eight planes appeared to jump all over the sky. They happened to be Tony's, the only Nip planes that could outdive us. One of them started after my tail and began closing in on it slowly, but he gave up the chase after a few minutes. The others had gotten reorganized, and it was time for me to be getting home.

On the way back I saw something on the surface of the water that made me curious. At first I thought it was one boat towing another but it wasn't. It was a Japanese submarine surfacing. Nosing my Corsair over a little steeper, I made a run at the submarine, and sent a long burst into her conning tower. Almost immediately it disappeared, but I saw no oil streaks or anything else that is supposed to happen when one is destroyed, so I knew I had not sunk her.

My only thought at this time was what a hell of a thing for one guy to do to another guy on Christmas.

※ ※ ※ ※

BOUGAINVILLE TAUGHT THE MARINES A LESSON IN survival: how to live in swamps, jungle, mud and rain with little more than K-rations, some aspirin and atabrine tablets. The omnipresent Jap was there, too, and he was proud of being able to fight in these miasmic surroundings. Here, dry socks and dry underwear were luxuries: "The best deal was to sleep with a buddy and share ponchos—one above and one below. If you could keep the water out, you had it made." On rare occasions when the combat situation and the bivouac areas allowed, marines got together over stews of C-rations, bouillon soup and tomato juice heated

in a helmet over a fire. In terms of weapons, marines of the 3rd
Division learned something of the tools of their trade: 60-mm
mortars could be registered within 25 yards of their positions;
81-mm mortars and 75-mm pack howitzers within 50 yards; and
100-mm howitzers within 150 yards. But BAR and riflemen had
to get within 10 yards, so well concealed and bunkered was the
enemy.

The battle for Bougainville continued through to the hill mass
between Piva and Torokina, when marine air contributed to the
success of the mission by providing close support. On December 10, the 2nd Battalion, 21st Marines, took up positions on Hill
600 to the right flank of what came to be known as Hellzapoppin'
Ridge, between Cibik's Ridge and the Torokina River. Here
the Japanese elected to make their last stand until December 18,
and it was a good one. Artillery and mortar were unable to dislodge the enemy, and it was not until Major A. C. Robertson of
VTMB-34 led an attack of six torpedo-bombers to within "yards"
of the front lines that the Japanese were beaten back: 48 100-pound
bombs crashed into enemy positions within 75 yards of the 21st
Marines. The second strike was the crusher, and it was at this
juncture that the 1st Battalion, with bayonets and grenades,
charged—and Hellzapoppin' was American.

On December 23 the Army relieved the 3rd Division to commence mop-up chores. This island, next to last of the Solomons
stepping stones, had cost the lives of 423 marines, and 1418 were
wounded. But it rendered inevitable the fall of Rabaul.

Our final objective was New Britain in the Bismarck Archipelago, assaulted December 26, 1943, by the 1st Marine Division
under Major General William H. Rupertus. New Britain blocked
the Army's drive on the Philippines, and it was necessary therefore to control the straits—Viatiz and Dampier—which lay between the nothern tip of New Guinea and Cape Gloucester, at
the western tip of New Britain. This Cape Gloucester—"everything that Bougainville was, only more so"—possessed an airfield and 9501 troops of the Japanese 65th Brigade.

With General George C. Kenney's V Air Force providing air
support and Navy offering LCI gunboats, a recent innovation,
the landing plan of the 1st Marine Division was to put troops
ashore east and west of the airfields. The beachhead was to be
held by the 7th Marines, while Colonel Whaling's 1st Marines
moved into a swamp on the right and advanced on the airfield.
It was a perfectly executed D-Day, and a memorably wet one.

Sergeant George McMillan, whom we have met, writes of the
capture of New Britain in which the Corps losses came to 310

killed and 1085 wounded. It was the first action for the division since Guadalcanal.

·13· THE STRUGGLE FOR BORGEN BAY: FIRST PHASE

GEORGE McMILLAN

. . . Whatever its approach to perfection, the assault phase of the Cape Gloucester campaign was the only one of the four major landings made by the First Marine Division during which things happened—as nearly as can ever be expected in war—when they were supposed to happen. The landing went according to plan.

And the plan was the very same one for which the Division staff had held out during the summer, and which it had finally had its way about in the late fall. That is, two regiments (not one) in assault, both ready to meet trouble if trouble should appear on D-day. When and if these two secured a beachhead, one of them would then turn quickly to the right and march toward, and as quickly as possible seize, the Cape Gloucester airfield, the principal tactical objective of the campaign. A single battalion (2/1) was to make a diversionary landing at Tauali.

That, to somewhat oversimplify the case, is what happened. The two regiments were the 7th and the 1st Marines; the third of the Division's regiments, the 5th, stood by at Oro Bay ready to go aboard ship on call.

The 7th landed first, striking at a point called Silimati, midway between the two areas—the airstrip on the western tip and the series of commanding hills behind Borgen Bay—where Japanese strength was thought to be concentrated. At 0746, 3/7 hit the narrow beach, followed two minutes later by 1/7. The reserve battalion, 2/7, was ashore by 0805.

As soon as they were ashore, the men of 1/7 pushed painfully through the swamp toward Target Hill, a 450-foot mound behind and commanding the landing beach area. The early morning aerial bombardment had left Target Hill a barren, pocked and blackened mass, and as the troops moved on it they coughed from the acrid, lung-irritating phosphorous smoke which still enshrouded the hill. When they reached Target Hill, the captain of the assault company sent two of his platoons around the hill, one on each side, and himself led a third to the top. By 1200, he and his men stood there unopposed.

Only one thing was needed for the security of the beachhead. This was a perimeter, a line of positions to oppose counterattacks. The 2d Battalion followed the 1st through the swamp, ran into enemy outposts seven hundred yards inland and began—1,500 yards in—a sharp fight that was not to end for five days. Private Albion Sanderson of this outfit probably killed the first Japanese on Cape Gloucester in the following unglamorous fashion: Sanderson crawled atop a pillbox, looked through the aperture, saw a Jap staring back at him. Deliberately, Sanderson placed the muzzle of his M-1 against the Nip's forehead and pulled the trigger. The battalion also discovered a Jap supply dump hidden in the swamp so that when they stopped for the night the sergeant-major lined his foxhole with the boards of what had been a Japanese lean-to, smoked a Jap cigarette, and pulled a Jap rainproof about him as he brewed a cup of coffee with a tin of Jap canned heat.

With such shenanigans characteristic of D-day, it was obvious that the 1st Marines (less the 2d Battalion, which had landed unopposed at Tauali), whose assignment it was to capture the airfield, should turn in that direction once they were ashore, without, pausing within the 7th's perimeter. They were only an hour behind the 7th (landing at 0830) and they turned immediately westward toward the airfield, moving along the coastal track.

Here the reception was different. No sooner had the leading elements turned than they ran into a roadblock, well disguised in the jungle. Two captains walked unsuspectingly into the Japanese lane of fire and were killed immediately. An amtrac was brought up, but got stuck between two trees and the Japanese swarmed it. They shot one gunner, dragged the other over the side and beat and knifed him to death.

One of the amtrac men killed, Private Leslie E. Hansen, left his twin brother, Paul, aboard as a survivor. When General Rupertus learned that they were sons of a widow who had already lost an older son in the war, he ordered the surviving brother to be sent Stateside immediately.

Two Sherman tanks arrived soon after the amtrac was extricated and the infantrymen joined in a brief skirmish to destroy the bunkers. By nightfall, the troops moving on the airfield had reached their assigned phase line for D-day.

The one Japanese threat to the Division's D-day scheme turned out to be less than serious to the ground troops. The Japanese air

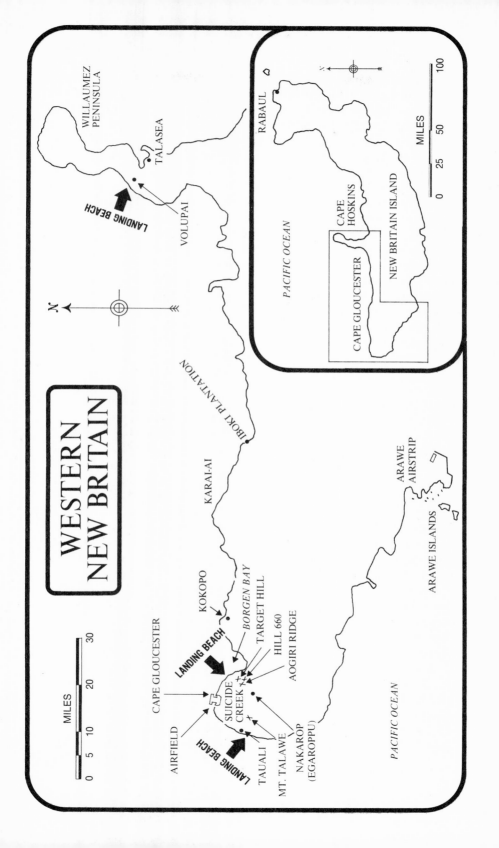

force in the Southwest Pacific was still not one to be sneezed at, and some formidable number (probably more than two hundred) of planes were sent to bomb the landing force. Fifth Air Force fighters intercepted them while they were still at sea and shot down fifty-nine. What is described as "a small number of enemy medium and dive bombers" did manage to get through at 1445, making their strike from low altitude, passing through a few American B-25s. Our ships' antiaircraft shot down two friendly planes in the confusion, and the Japanese sank one destroyer and damaged an LST.

While the deployments inland and the air fights at sea had been going on, the engineers in the shore party had made herculean efforts at the narrow beach, had unloaded fourteen LSTs of all vehicles (preloaded with supplies) as well as fifty-five per cent of the bulk cargo they carried, some 2,100 deadweight tons.

Altogether, December 26 at Cape Gloucester had been a most surprising D-day, with our casualties 21 killed and 23 wounded and with only some 50 of the enemy killed.

The rainforest claimed one of the casualties. The falling of those giant, rotted trees described by the naturalist, was accelerated by the shell fire and explosions. The trees began to fall on D-day, and one of them caught and crippled a man under its trunk, presaging the nearly fifty casualties to be suffered from this cause during the Cape Gloucester campaign.

There was some uncertainty throughout the ranks as the 1st Marines started their move toward the airfield on the second day. The only hindrance to the 500-yard front they pushed along the coast was the jungle: "because of rugged terrain and swamp areas along the shore," says the Division action report, "progress was difficult," and the front "finally was reduced to one company which advanced along the coastal track."

With the narrower front, the regiment passed phase lines as if they were roadside jingles, gaining at 0845 the line they were supposed to have reached only by the end of the second day. They moved on and, about an hour later, ran into some scattered bunkers, deployed, fought briefly and successfully, and moved on again. When they got to the phase line for the third day at 1210, they paused, still somewhat bewildered by the lack of resistance, to reorganize. They started forward again at 1335, not to halt for the night until 1720, when they rested their lines on the fourth day's objective.

Casualties for the day (December 27) in the First Marine Division were just 8 killed and 45 wounded. Most of these were suffered by the 7th Marines which had, in some further moves to strengthen the perimeter, run into sturdy Japanese resistance.

As much because of the uncertainty which continued to trouble the staff as for any other reason, word was sent before the day ended for the 5th Marines to go aboard ship and to come on up prepared to fight on arrival.

For the first few hours of the third day — D plus 2 (December 28) — the 1st Marines moved along much as they had on the second day, until, when they ran into a congregation of Japs at 1400, they found the presence of the enemy almost reassuring. The advance quickly halted and the support company (K) of the 3d Battalion was brought forward with a platoon of tanks to destroy the 75mm field pieces, anti-tank guns, mines, and machine-gun bunkers which were holding them up.

The tank platoon commander remembers how surprised the Japanese were by the strength of the Sherman armor.

"We turned a corner and ran right into a Jap 75," he said. "I saw one Jap walk calmly over and pull the lanyard. The shell, it was HE, hardly scratched the tank. They were so astonished they just stood there while we mowed 'em down and smashed the piece."

The tanks rumbled around through the Japanese bunkers (buttressed mainly with coconut logs and coral-filled oil drums), firing point-blank until the surviving Japanese ran out. Then the men of K company killed them with rifle fire. In less than four hours all the Japanese were dead, the action (the battle of Hell's Point) was over, and the 1st moved on again, halting for the night at 1730, in position to move onto the cleared airfield area.

The strongest and most determined Japanese charge since H-hour hit the 2d Battalion, 7th Marines, the same afternoon at 1413. More than a company of Japs sprang at the perimeter from well camouflaged bunkers, and there was a brief but fierce fight in the swampy area behind the beach, with the 7th holding its ground, killing 466 Japanese against losses of 25 killed and 75 wounded in Marine ranks.

The fourth day, D plus 3 (December 29), was more a day of maneuver than of fighting. With the arrival of the 5th Marines in the morning, it was decided to take the airfield in a coordinated drive with the 5th Marines moving on it from the south and the 1st Marines moving on it from the east. This meant that the 1st sat waiting for the newly arrived 5th to march from the beachhead up to the kunai-covered ridges south of, and overlooking, the airfield. The schedule called for the two units to start together at noon, and while the 5th was getting into position there was an artillery and air bombardment of the airfield.

The jungle slowed the two battalions (1st and 2d) of the 5th that were to take part, and they were not in position and ready to attack until 1500. When word was given for the drive to start, the 1st Marines went forward rapidly and were on the strip at 1755. When the 5th, however, started down the ridges toward the airfield, they ran into a series of bunkers in a ravine formed by a junction of two streams just south of the airfield. The men of the assault battalion, the 2d, closed in, hurling grenades, and when there was no reply they scurried up to look into the bunkers, only to find them empty. The battalion then turned on toward the airfield, reached it at 1925, after dark.

The 1st Battalion of the 5th, trailing the 2d, lost contact in the darkness and dug in on a ridge overlooking the field, only some 1,200 yards from the regiment's line of departure for the day, a day which had resulted in 5 killed and 38 wounded in the scattered fighting.

That night (December 29), the action shifted to Tauali where the 2d Battalion, 1st Marines (Lieutenant Colonel James M. Masters, Sr.) stood off what one historian has called "as futile an action as was ever fought; yet, acting without plan or imagination, the Japanese fought stubbornly, persistently, savagely."

Although the battalion had come ashore without opposition, the men had begun to feel the tension of their isolation for the battalion was, as Masters has said, "in radio defilade," unable to make contact with Division at Gloucester. Principally for morale effect, patrols were sent far beyond what would have been considered necessary for normal security, as far north as Dorf Point, as far south as Sag Sag Bay. What encounters there were showed that the Japs were not alert. One patrol, says Masters, "found a bunch of Japs 'flemished' out beside a trail, sound asleep with no security. My men killed twenty-three of them."

When the Japs came at Masters' all-around perimeter near Tauali Village on the night of December 29, they struck, as they so often had at Guadalcanal, on a narrow front, and a few broke through. The commotion awakened a gunnery sergeant who grabbed a light machine gun and rushed forward, gun blazing, toward the point of penetration. This halted the attack temporarily. Through the rest of the night the Japanese, in small groups, tried to come through. Next morning, December 30, a shallow saddle in front of the battalion's lines overflowed with Jap bodies, and the battle of Coffin Corner was over.

First thing the next morning back at the airfield, the 5th Marines sent a patrol out to establish contact with its trailing battalion, still up in the hills. The Japs, overnight, had moved back into the bunkers in the ravine, and there soon developed one of those typically nasty and intimate small actions, with each squad on its own and with a high degree of improvisation becoming the order of the encounter. The patrol sent word back and waited for reinforcements, which came in the form of a platoon from Company F. The job soon turned out to be too big for a platoon, and the rest of F came up, led by a captain who hummed his University of Illinois school song, recalls a member of the company.

As the morning wore on, with close-in fighting, tanks assisting where they could, the company grew short of ammunition. A private rigged semaphore flags out of dirty handkerchiefs, and when this failed to attract attention he went back himself to lead ammo carriers up.

"Nice going," somebody said to him when he returned.

"I only went down for my pipe," the private deprecatingly answered.

More help was needed, and the 5th asked the 1st, now comparatively unengaged in its positions on the other side of the airfield, to send over a company to help F. This was Company I, 3d Battalion, and the two fought on through the afternoon of December 30 and into the next day before the last of the Japanese was killed. But it was an isolated body of Japanese that had offered the day's resistance on December 30, and the main elements of the two Division regiments secured the airfield.

At 1300, December 30, General Rupertus sent the following dispatch to the Commanding General, Sixth Army:

"First Marine Division presents to you as an early New Year gift the complete airdrome of Cape Gloucester. Situation well in hand due to fighting spirit of troops, the usual Marine luck and the help of God . . . Rupertus grinning to Krueger."

Next day at 1200, the United States flag was raised over Cape Gloucester airfield.

* * * *

IMMEDIATELY AFTER THE FIGHT FOR THE AIRFIELD, General Rupertus began to think about three hills which rimmed Borgen Bay: Hill 150, Aogiri Ridge and Hill 600. He ordered Brigadier General Lemuel C. Shepherd, Jr. (later to command the 6th Division), to clear the enemy from this area in order to extend his perimeter. At 10 A.M. on New Year's Day the 7th Regiment and the 3rd Battalion, 5th Marines, began its advance through swamp toward the hills. The marines had penetrated only about 300 yards when they came to a broad shallow stream. Scouts crossed. Nothing happened. Then the first platoon crossed . . .

The distinguished magazine writer and combat correspondent Asa Bordages was attached to the 3rd Battalion, 5th Marines. He gave wartime readers of the *Saturday Evening Post* a grim story of the swamp battle.

·14· SUICIDE CREEK

ASA BORDAGES

They came to "Suicide Creek." It had no name and it was not on the map, but that is what the marines called it after they had fought two days in vain to win a crossing. The creek is swift, two or three feet deep, perhaps twenty feet across at the widest, twisting between steep banks. It flows over rocks that make footing difficult, and here and there a tree had fallen into the stream. The banks rise steeply from ten to twenty feet, up the little ridges in the jungle of Cape Gloucester.

The marines didn't know the creek was a moat before an enemy strong point. They couldn't see that the heavy growth across the creek was salted with pillboxes—machine-gun emplacements armored with dirt and logs, some of them dug several stories deep, all carefully spotted so they could sweep the slope and both banks of the stream with interlacing fire.

Only snipers shot at the Marine scouts who crossed the creek, feeling their way through the thickets. More marines followed, down into the creek, up the steep bank, on into the jungle. Then they got it. The jungle exploded in their faces. They hit the deck, trying to deploy in the bullet-lashed brush and strike back. Marines died there, firing blindly, cursing because they couldn't see the men who were killing them. Or not saying anything—just dying. The others could only hug the ground as bullets cut the brush just above their heads, like a sweeping blade of fire. They couldn't even help the wounded.

Snipers picked off some of them as they lay there. It's perfect for snipers when machine guns are firing; you can't hear the single pop above the heavier fire. You don't know you're a target until you're hit.

From the American side of Suicide Creek, marines gave the trapped platoon overhead fire. The idea is to fling such a volume of fire at the enemy's position that he must hug cover and slacken his fire. The overhead fire spread an umbrella of bullets above the pinned-down platoon, enabling them to crawl out and crawl back across the creek, pulling out their wounded.

That's how it went all day as Marine detachments felt for a gap or a soft spot in the enemy's positions along the creek. They would be hit and pull back, and then detachments would push across the creek at other points. They'd be blasted by invisible machine guns, and leave a few more marines dead in the brush as they fell back across the creek. Then they'd do it all over again.

There was nothing else they could do. There is no other way to fight a jungle battle—not in such terrain, when the enemy is dug in and your orders are to advance. You don't know where the enemy is. His pillboxes are so camouflaged thaw you can usually find them only when they fire on you. So you push out scouts and small patrols, until they're fired on. Then you push out patrols from different directions until they too draw fire. Thus you locate the enemy. Then you have to take the emplacements, the pillboxes, one by one in desperate little battles.

Private First Class Calvin B. King, of Pen Mar, Pennsylvania, remembers his platoon crossed the creek four times in a single day and four times had to stumble back under enemy fire. And not until the last time did they see a Jap.

"That time we got maybe a hundred and fifty feet into the brush and then we saw them coming at us," he said. "They had slipped around and were coming in from our flank to wipe us out. There were a lot of 'em. I don't know how many. It looked like they was everywhere.

"They didn't make a sound. They were just coming at us through the trees. We were firing, but they kept coming at us. There were too many of them to stop. We had to pull out. Machine guns were shooting at us from everywhere. And all them Japs coming. We'd pull back a little way and stop and fire, and then we'd fall back a little more.

"Somebody was saying, 'Steady . . . Steady there . . .' But I don't know who it was. I just kept firing. You don't think about nothing. You just shoot. Guys were getting hit. We had to pull them along with us. You can't leave a wounded guy for the Japs to get. The things they do to 'em . . ."

There was a private first class from Oakland, California. He was blinded by powder burns. He couldn't know it was only temporary. All he knew was that he was blind in the middle of a battle. He was saying, "I can't see." He was fumbling around, trying to feel his way in the brush. The bullets were cutting all around, but he didn't ask anybody to stop fighting to help him. He just hung onto his rifle, like they tell you to, and tried to crawl out, though he couldn't see where to crawl. Corporal Lawrence E. Oliveria, of Fall River, Massachusetts, grabbed the blind boy by the arm, pulling him along as they withdrew. He'd pause to fire, and the blind marine would wait beside him, and then Corporal Oliveria would lead him back a little farther. "The boy didn't moan or pray or nothing. He just kept saying, every now and then, 'I can't see.'"

By the time they got back to the creek, the Japanese were close on them, charging now. But the marines had machine guns at the creek. They piled the Jap dead in the brush and broke the charge.

Another platoon tried crossing the creek at another point. Near the head of the line was "the Swede," a private first class from some place out west. He was a big guy, built like a truck, the last man in the world you'd ever suspect of being sentimental. His big ambition was to send his kid sister through college. It took some doing, but he was doing it on his service pay. The Swede was just stepping into the creek when he got it.

"You could hear the bullet hit him in the stomach," said Platoon Sergeant John M. White. "He just stood there a minute. He said, 'Them dirty bastards!' Then he fell down. He was dead.

"When we got across the creek, the fire was so hot we couldn't do a thing. You couldn't see a single Jap. All you could see was where the bullets were hitting around us. And men getting hit. But no matter how bad it got, I never saw one of the boys pass up a wounded man."

Private First Class Charles Conger, of Ventura, California, was one of those hit. A machine gun cut his legs from under him. Nobody saw him. Nobody could have heard him if he'd yelled—the firing was too heavy. He was as alone as a man can be. It was slow, painful, dragging through the brush, crawling head first down the bank, dragging limp legs. He had to pull himself on by inches, then belly down the bank sprayed with bullets as thick as rice thrown at a bride. He tumbled into the creek. The rocks were sharp. He was gasping in the swift water, struggling across against the force of the stream. It was only blind luck that White saw him. White was too far away to help, but he stopped and waved his arms to attract attention, ignoring cover until two marines who were nearer saw the wounded man in the creek. Those marines were almost across. Safety lay just ahead. They didn't have to stop. But they went sloshing through the water to the wounded man. They half carried, half dragged him with them.

The battalion tried all day to win a crossing at the creek. In the end, they could only withdraw to the ridge on the American side and dig in for the night. It was getting dusk as one machine-gun platoon finished its gun emplacements. Then the men began digging their foxholes. Most of them were stripped to the waist and they laid aside their weapons as they dug.

That was the moment the enemy chose to charge. They must have slipped across the stream and up the slope and watched the digging. They must have seen that if they could reach those emplacements and get those machine guns, they could swing them and smash the infantry company holding the next section of the line. That is why the Japanese, perhaps fifty of them, did not yell and did not fire a shot. They rushed with bayonets.

Down among his infantrymen, Captain Andrew A. Haldane, of Methuen, Massachusetts, was talking with First Lieutenant Andrew Chisick, of Newark, New Jersey. They heard a marine yell. They looked up and saw the Japs racing toward the emplacements, and weaponless marines scattering out of the way. Some had no chance of getting to their weapons. The Japs were hardly thirty yards from the nearest gun and closing fast.

Then more marines were firing, but its wasn't enough to stop the charge. The nearest Japs were hardly ten feet from the guns. Captain Haldane ran toward the guns, firing as he ran. Lieutenant Chisick ran with him. Others joined the charge, some with bare hands, some with clubs or entrenching tools snatched up from the ground. The Japs reached one gun and swung it to enfilade the line. A Jap was in the gunner's seat. The marines' charge hit the gun before he could fire a shot. He got a bayonet through the chest. The enemy broke, and the marines cut them down. More than twenty dead Japs were scattered in the brush by the time it was quiet again.

The marines were bombed that night. Dive bombers. The enemy set up a heavy fire of tracer bullets to show the bombers where their own lines were and where they should drop their bombs in the dark. Nobody will ever be able to describe a bombing. You can't describe hell. You can only go through it.

The marines had to take the bombing after a day of battle, without any way of hitting back. The next morning, January 3, they attacked again. The enemy threw mortar shells. Sergeant White saw a shell explode, and ducked down the line to see if anyone was hit. "A kid was sitting there in his foxhole. He didn't have any head. He just had a neck with dog tags on it."

All through that second day, the marines pushed small units across the creek at different points, still trying to find a soft spot in the Japanese defenses. Each time they were hit. They knocked out some of the machine guns, but each time, in the end, they had to fall back across the creek.

There was a boy firing from behind a log. His face was gray. He stopped firing and looked around. His eyes were dull, without hope.

"It don't do any good," he said. His voice was flat. He wasn't speaking to anybody. He was just saying it. "I got three of 'em, but it don't do any good."

Platoon Sergeant Casimir Polakowski—known as Ski—said, "What the hell are you beefing about? You get paid for it, don't you?"

The kid managed a grin. As Ski crawled on down the line, the boy was fighting again, squeezing them off.

A platoon was pinned down in the jungle on their flank. They could neither go forward nor withdraw. They could only lie in the brush, held there by a crisscross net of machine-gun fire, while snipers took pot shots at them. Ski's platoon was ordered to lend a hand. They were bone-tired, but Ski said, "Let's get going," and they got.

Three of them were Denham, Melville, and O'Grady. Private Harry Denham, of Nashville, Tennessee, was called "Pee Wee" because he was so small. They say he went to "some fancy military school." But he didn't ask favors of anybody and he wouldn't back down before the biggest man in the regiment. Just a bantam rooster of a kid who'd take on anything that walked. Private First Class John O'Grady, of Ogdensburg, New York, left the talking for the trio to Denham and Melville. He was a quiet guy who never had much to say to anybody, but he seemed to talk plenty when the three of them were off by themselves. Maybe he told them what he wanted to be after the war. The kids all think about that. It's something to look forward to—and a guy needs something to look forward to. Private First Class John William Melville was called "Pete," but nobody seemed to know why. His home was Lynn, Massachusetts. He was twenty-six, almost an old man. He quit a white-collar job with the General Electric Company in Boston to join the Marines Corps.

Denham, Melville, and O'Grady—and Levy, Jones, and Brown— flung themselves at the enemy's flank so he'd have to break the fire that had the other platoon caught. Men dropped, but they kept going forward, fighting from tree to tree. They pushed the enemy back and held him long enough for the trapped platoon to pull out. That was long enough for the marines to form a line so they couldn't be rolled up by counterattack.

Another lull then. The jungle was still. First Sergeant Selvitelle asked Ski how it was going. Ski was smoking a cigarette. His voice sounded tired.

"They got Denham, Melville, and O'Grady," he said. They were lying out there in the brush somewhere and he was smoking a cigarette.

The word came to move up. There was firing ahead. Maybe an hour later Ski was behind a tree when he saw a wounded marine lying in the open. A sniper was shooting at the boy. Ski could see the dirt flung up when the bullets hit. The boy was trying to crawl away, but he couldn't.

Ski ran from cover and pulled him to a tree. The sniper saw him. All the sniper had to do was wait until Ski started to return to his post. Then he shot Ski in the back.

That was about the time Tommy Harvard's platoon crossed Suicide Creek, lugging their heavy machine guns. "Tommy Harvard" was the code name for First Lieutenant Elisha Atkins, who played football at Harvard, belonged to the Dekes and the Owls, and got his B.A. in 1942. "Very quiet and polite as hell" is the way a sergeant described him.

The enemy let First Lieutenant Atkins and about half his men cross the creek before they opened up. Six automatic weapons blasted them at point-blank range. There were at least three machine guns with perfect fields of fire. It happened too quickly for anybody to duck.

Sergeant Wills says, "I saw a man ahead of us and just as I saw he wasn't a marine they all let fly."

Marines were hit. Somebody was screaming. Corporal John R. Hyland of Greenwich, Connecticut, was frowning as he tried to knock out the nearest machine-gun nest with rifle fire. The screaming man stopped.

Corporal Hyland said, "We ought to get the hell out of here." But he didn't move to go. He kept his place, still shooting at the spot of jungle where he guessed the gunport was, until the order was passed to withdraw.

The machine guns swept the brush just higher than a man lying flat. The trapped marines rolled down the bank or pushed backward on their bellies until they could tumble into the creek. The screening bush was their only protection against the snipers perched in trees. As they rolled into the stream, they hunkered down as low as they could in the water. Some got down so only their faces showed above the water. All of them pressed against the Japanese bank as bullets slashed through the undergrowth above them, splattering the creek and the American bank beyond.

Two of the marines had fallen on a big log lying in the creek. One of them was hit in the leg and couldn't move, but he was near enough for Sergeant Wills to pull him into the creek. Other marines dragged him up against the brush-choked bank; but they couldn't reach the other boy on the log. He lay too far out in the field of fire. He'd caught a full machine-gun burst. He must have had twenty holes in him, but he was still alive. He was hung over the log, partly in the water. He was calling weakly, "Here I am, Wills . . . over here . . ."

They couldn't help him. They could only listen to him.

"Wills . . . I'm here . . . Wills . . ."

There were other wounded in the creek above them. They couldn't help them either. Most of those crouching in the bushes against the bank were wounded, too. The kid on the log was getting weaker. Just listening was harder than anything Sergeant Wills ever had to take.

"He was calling me, and I couldn't help him. All of them were guys we knew, but we couldn't do a thing. We had to lay in the water and listen to them. It was the coldest damn water I ever saw. Their blood kept flowing into our faces."

Their only chance was to creep downstream close against the bank and then make a dash, one by one, for the American shore. A little way down the twisting stream there was a spot where a man would have a chance to make it. Most places, he would have to stop to climb the bank. Only a man who wanted to commit suicide would try that.

It was slow work for the men in the creek, crawling downstream in the racing water, hampered by the thick tangles of vines and brush. Men caught in the vines struggled helplessly.

"Everybody had to cut everybody else loose as we went along," says Private First Class Luther J. Raschke, of Harvard, Illinois.

He found young Tommy Harvard tangled in the vines and cut him loose. "I tried to help him along, but he wouldn't come. He'd been hit three times. A slug had smashed his shoulder. He was losing blood pretty fast. But he wouldn't leave. He was trying to see that everybody got out first. He told me, 'Go on, go on!' He wouldn't let anybody stop for him. He said, 'Keep the line moving!' He made us leave him there."

They made their dash; got safely out and reached the line of foxholes to which the battalion had fallen back again after that second day.

But Raschke couldn't forget the wounded officer they'd left in the creek. He said, "I guess everybody else is out."

"Yeah," said Corporal Alexander Caldwell, of Nashville, Tennessee.

"Well . . ."

"Yeah," said Corporal Caldwell.

So they got permission to go back into no man's land to hunt for their platoon leader. Corporal Caldwell took along two more volunteers, for they might have to carry Lieutenant Atkins, if they found him, and they might have to fight their way out. They were Louis J. Sievers, of Johnstown, Pennsylvania, and Joseph V. Brown, of Middletown, New York, both privates first class.

It was getting hard to see when they crawled down to the creek. Raschke stopped. They lay listening, but they could hear nothing except the rushing stream and, now and then, the sound of the Japanese talking. They had to make their choice then. They could go back without the lieutenant. Or they could risk calling. Nobody would blame them if they went back. Nobody would know they hadn't done everything they could do to find him.

Raschke lay on the edge of the stream and he remembers clearer than anything else how close the water was under his nose. The others were in the bush, rifles ready to fire if the enemy discovered him. Not that it would do any good. He'd be dead. For that matter, if the machine guns opened up, they'd all be dead.

"I was scared stiff," Raschke says. "I called as softly as I could, 'Tommy Harvard . . . Tommy Harvard . . .'

"A voice said, 'I'm down here.'

"It sounded weak, but we figured it might be a trap. So I said, 'What's your real name?'

"The voice said, 'Elisha Atkins.' So we knew it was him. We crawled down and pulled him out. He said, 'God! Am I glad to see you!'"

He was shaking from hours in the chill water, weak from loss of blood, but still calmly Harvard as they carried him to the rear.

During the two days the 3rd Battalion had been fighting vainly to win the crossing of Suicide Creek, the outfit on its left had been trying as stubbornly and as vainly to get across its segment of the stream.

During those two days, Marine Pioneers were toiling to build a corduroy road through the swamp in their rear so that tanks could be moved up to the line. The tanks finally reached the outfit on the 3rd Battalion's left, but they found the banks of the creek too steep for crossing. The gully formed a natural tank trap. So a Marine bulldozer was called to cut down the banks of the creek and make a fill in the stream so that the tanks could cross against the enemy.

The Japanese saw their danger. They concentrated fire on the bulldozer. Man after man was shot from the driver's seat—some killed, some wounded. But there was always a marine to jump in the seat. He had no shield, no protection at all. He sat up in the open like a shooting-gallery target for all the enemy's fire. But the Marine bulldozer kept on till the fill was made and the tanks were rolling across the creek.

The advance of the tanks made the positions of the enemy opposing the 3rd Battalion untenable. If they tried to hold against the frontal attack of the 3rd Battalion, they would be hit by tanks and infantry from the flank. They'd be a nut in a nutcracker. They had to retreat or be crushed, and they retreated . . .

❦   ❦   ❦   ❦

THE NEXT BATTLE FOR CAPE GLOUCESTER TOOK place January 9 - 10 on Aogiri Ridge, where the Japanese defended their supply route extending inland from Borgen Bay. Here, the enemy had built thirty-seven mutually supporting bunkers interlaced with tunnels, and he made a stand that stopped the 3rd Battalion, 5th Marines, dead in its tracks. Despite a herculean effort by Colonel Lew Walt (he dragged a 37-mm up and fired it alone), five strong night counterattacks kept the marines in virtually the same spot. It required the massed artillery of Captain Joseph E. Buckley's Weapons Company (tanks, half-tracks, infantry weapons) to attain the key Japanese overlook, Hill 660 commanding Borgen Bay. The battle ended there, atop a slimy crag, with a clear view of the water.

In January and February General Shepherd instituted search and destroy patrols on the western side of New Britain. The essential purpose of these was to locate the headquarters of General Matsuda, the garrison's senior officer, and to learn where the enemy was withdrawing. Under the talented hand of Chesty Puller, the 1st and 5th Marines explored the interior of the island to a depth of 60 miles inland. Until February 19, the largest patrol (384 men) of World War II chased and destroyed Japanese; once it was determined that Matsuda was retreating to Rabaul, small amphibious parties leapfrogged ahead to cut off his escape. However, the Japanese got through. There were other clashes in the next few days, but to all intents and purposes the Marine Corps' job was done. New Britain was ours at a price of 310 marines killed and 1083 wounded.

In fitting tribute, General MacArthur observed: "You know, in Central Pacific, the 1st Marine Division will be just another of one of six Marine Divisions. If it stayed here, it would be *my* division."

Now, finally, Rabaul was encircled and slowly cut off, its air fleets destroyed and its last hopes shattered beyond salvation. On February 15, 1944, the Army landed in the Green Islands, 120 miles from the fortress, and the rest was academic. Marine air groups played a decisive role in the defeat of the mighty enemy redoubt—flying 14,718 sortie (twice as many as Army or Navy), dropping 7142 tons of bombs, and shooting down more than 200 planes. The Corps had suffered and fought its way to victory on this terrible northwest drive, where on every island and jungle and swamp were marine dead.

Among the victims of the drive for Rabaul was Lieutenant Colonel Boyington, shot down January 3 while leading a fighter sweep.

Here he details his last dogfight: severely wounded, Boyington was picked up by a Japanese submarine and spent the duration of the conflict in a POW camp.

·15· "ON A ROWBOAT AT RABAUL ..."

COLONEL GREGORY S. BOYINGTON

January 3, 1944 . . . I was having baked beans for breakfast at the edge of the airstrip the Seabees had built, after the Marines had taken a small chunk of land on the beach. As I ate the beans, I glanced over at row after row of white crosses, too far away and too dark to read the names. But I didn't have to. I knew that each cross marked the final resting place of some marine who had gone as far as he was able in this mortal world of ours.

Before taking off, everything seemed to be wrong that morning. My plane wasn't ready and I had to switch to another. At the last minute the ground crew got my original plane in order and I scampered back into that. I was to lead a fighter sweep over Rabaul, meaning two hundred miles over enemy waters and territory again.

We coasted over at about twenty thousand feet to Rabaul. A few hazy clouds and cloud banks were hanging around—not much different from a lot of other days.

The fellow flying my wing was Captain George Ashmun, New York City. He had told me before the mission: "You go ahead and shoot all you want, Gramps. All I'll do is keep them off your tail."

This boy was another who wanted me to beat that record, and was offering to stick his neck way out in the bargain.

I spotted a few planes coming up through the loosely scattered clouds and signaled to the pilots in back of me: "Go down and get to work."

George and I dove first. I poured a long burst into the first enemy plane that approached, and a fraction of a second later saw the Nip pilot catapult out and the plane itself break into fire.

George screamed over the radio: "Gramps, you got a flamer!"

Then he and I went down lower into the fight after the rest of the enemy planes. We figured that the whole pack of our planes was going to follow us down, but the clouds must have obscured us from their view. Anyway, George and I were not paying too much attention, just figuring that the rest of the boys would be with us in a few seconds, as usually was the case.

Finding approximately ten enemy planes, George and I commenced firing. What we saw coming from above we thought were our own planes—but they were not. We were being jumped by about twenty planes.

George and I scissored in the conventional thatch-weave way, protecting each other's blank spots, the rear ends of our fighters. In doing this I saw George shoot a burst into a plane and it turned away from us, plunging downward, all on fire. A second later I did the same to another plane. But it was then that I saw George's plane start to throw smoke, and down he went in a half glide. I sensed something was horribly wrong with him. I screamed at him: "For God's sake, George, dive!"

Our planes could dive away from practically anything the Nips had out there at the time, except perhaps a Tony. But apparently George never heard me or could do nothing about it if he had. He just kept going down in a half glide.

Time and time again I screamed at him: "For God's sake, George, dive straight down!" But he didn't even flutter an aileron in answer to me.

I climbed in behind the Nip planes that were plugging at him on the way down to the water. There were so many of them I wasn't even bothering to use my electric gun sight consciously, but continued to seesaw back and forth on my rudder pedals, trying to spray them all in general, trying to get them off George to give him a chance to bail out or dive—or do something at least.

But the same thing that was happening to him was now happening to me. I could feel the impact of the enemy fire against my armor plate, behind my back, like hail on a tin roof. I could see enemy shots progressing along my wing tips, making patterns.

George's plane burst into flames and a moment later crashed into the water. At that point there was nothing left for me to do. I had done everything I could. I decided to get the hell away from the Nips. I threw everything in the cockpit all the way forward—this means full speed ahead—and nosed my plane over to pick up extra speed until I was forced by the water to level off. I had gone practically a half mile at a speed of about four hundred knots, when all of a sudden my main gas tank went up in flames in front of my very eyes. The sensation was much the same as opening the door of a furnace and sticking one's head into the thing.

Though I was about a hundred feet off the water, I didn't have a chance of trying to gain altitude. I was fully aware that if I tried to gain altitude for a bail-out I would be fried in a few more seconds.

At first, being kind of stunned, I thought: "Well, you finally got it, didn't you, wise guy?" and then I thought: "Oh, no you didn't!" There was only one thing left to do. I reached for the rip cord with my right hand and released the safety belt with my left, putting both feet on the stick and kicking it all the way forward with all my strength. My body was given centrifugal force when I kicked the stick in this manner. My body for an instant weighed well over a ton, I imagine. If I had had a third hand I could have opened the canopy. But all I could do was to give myself this propulsion. It either jettisoned me right up through the canopy or tore the canopy off. I don't know which.

There was a jerk that snapped my head and I knew my chute had caught—what a relief. Then I felt an awful slam on my side—no time to pendulum—just boom-boom and I was in the water.

The cool water around my face sort of took the stunned sensation away from my head. Looking up, I could see a flight of four Japanese Zeros. They had started a game of tag with me in the water. And by playing tag, I mean they began taking turns strafing me.

I started diving, making soundings in the old St. George Channel. At first I could dive about six feet, but this lessened to four, and gradually I lost so much of my strength that, when the Zeros made their strafing runs at me, I could just barely duck my head under the water. I think they ran out of ammunition, for after a while they left me. Or my efforts in the water became so feeble that maybe they figured they had killed me.

The best thing to do, I thought, was to tread water until nightfall. I had a little package with a rubber raft in it. But I didn't want to take a chance on opening it for fear they might go back to Rabaul, rearm, and return to strafe the raft. Then I would have been a goner for certain.

I was having such a difficult time treading water, getting weaker and weaker, that I realized something else would have to be done real quickly. My "Mae West" wouldn't work at all, so I shed all my clothes while I was treading away; shoes, fatigues, and everything else. But after two hours of this I knew that I couldn't keep it up any longer. It would have to be the life raft or nothing. And if the life raft didn't work—if it too should prove all shot full of holes—then I decided: "It's au revoir. That's all there is to it."

I pulled the cord on the raft, the cord that released the bottle of compressed air, and the little raft popped right up and filled. I was able to climb aboard, and after getting aboard I started looking around, sort of taking inventory.

I looked at my Mae West. If the Nips came back and strafed me again, I wanted to be darned sure that it would be in working order. If I had that, I could dive around under the water while they were strafing me, and would not need the raft. I had noticed some tears in the jacket, which I fully intended to get busy and patch up, but the patching equipment that came with the raft contained patches for about twenty-five holes.

"It would be better first, though," I decided, "to count the holes in this darned jacket." I counted, and there were more than two hundred.

"I'm going to save these patches for something better than this." With that I tossed the jacket overboard to the fish. It was of no use to me.

Then for the first time—and this may seem strange—I noticed that I was wounded, not just a little bit, but a whole lot. I hadn't noticed it while in the water, but here in the raft I certainly noticed it now. Pieces of my scalp, with hair on the pieces, were hanging down in front of my face.

My left ear was almost torn off. My arms and shoulders contained holes and shrapnel. I looked at my legs. My left ankle was shattered from a twenty-millimeter-cannon shot. The calf of my left leg had, I surmised, a 7.7 bullet through it. In my groin I had been shot completely through the leg by twenty-millimeter shrapnel. Inside of my leg was a gash bigger than my fist.

"I'll get out my first-aid equipment from my jungle pack. I'd better start patching this stuff up."

I kept talking to myself like that. I had lots of time. The Pacific would wait.

Even to my watch, which was smashed, I talked also. The impact had crushed it at a quarter to eight on the early morning raid. But I said to it: "I'll have a nice long day to fix you up."

I didn't, though. Instead, I spent about two hours trying to bandage myself. It was difficult getting out these bandages, for the waves that day in the old South Pacific were about seven feet or so long. They are hard enough to ride on a comparatively calm day, and the day wasn't calm.

After I had bandaged myself as well as I could, I started looking around to see if I could tell where I was or where I was drifting. I found that my raft contained only one paddle instead of the customary two. So this one little paddle, which fitted over the hand much like an odd sort of glove, was not of much use to me.

Talking to myself, I said: "This is like being up shit creek without a paddle."

Far off to the south, as I drifted, I could see the distant shore of

New Britain. Far to the north were the shores of New Ireland. Maybe in time I could have made one or the other of these islands. I don't know. But there is something odd about drifting that I may as well record. All of us have read, or have been told, the thoughts that have gone through other men under similar circumstances. But in my case it was a little tune that Moon Mullin had originated. And now it kept going through my mind, bothering me, and I couldn't forget it. It was always there, running on and on:

> On a rowboat at Rabaul,
> On a rowboat at Rabaul . . .

The waves continued singing it to me as they slapped my rubber boat. It could have been much the same, perhaps, as when riding on a train, and the rails and the wheels clicking away, pounding out some tune, over and over, and never stopping.

The waves against this little rubber boat, against the bottom of it, against the sides of it, continued pounding out:

> . . . On a rowboat at Rabaul,
> You're not behind a plow . . .

PART IV

Tarawa to Peleliu: Battering the Empire

The westward advance of the Marine Corps began at Tarawa, a coral sandspit synonymous with determination and sacrifice. Initially, Tarawa came into the Corps lexicon in August 1943 when Admiral Raymond A. Spruance flew to Wellington, New Zealand, where elements of the 2nd Marine Division were resting after the Guadalcanal campaign. The man Spruance conferred with was Major General Julian C. Smith, a combat-seasoned trooper, who pronounced his outfit ready for assignment although it was still fairly riddled with malaria. The admiral explained that Operation "Galvanic" was the two-phase seizure of the Gilbert Islands, with the Army's 27th Infantry Division committed to taking Makin, and the 2nd Marine Division, Tarawa. Tarawa, described as the front door of the Japanese Empire, was one of the more heavily fortified enemy outposts in the Central Pacific.

General Smith and his staff studied the target, a triangular-shaped atoll which lies somewhat north of the equator and about 100 miles south of Makin Island. The eastern and southern legs of the triangle are seventeen and twelve miles long, respectively; the base is a reef enclosing a lagoon with entrance approximately in the center. Overall, Betio is about two miles long and one-half mile wide, and is the largest of a string of coral islets which comprise Tarawa Atoll.

Situated at the southwest corner, Betio contained a 4000 foot airstrip which was the primary target of the invasion. Smith, suspecting that the island's southern and western beaches were bolstered by flanking shore batteries, wisely chose the lagoon side for landings.

This precious lump of coral (code name "Helen Island") now posed a monumental challenge to the commander of the 2nd Division. This was to be the first time for a landing across a reef in the face of opposition; the first time amphibious tractors (LVTs) were to be used in carrying troops; the first time both air and naval gunfire were to be called upon to support a landing; and the first time tanks were to be introduced in an amphibious landing. A lesser man than fifty-eight-year-old "General Julian" might have had grave misgivings about such an assault. Not Smith, whose combat days ranged back to the colorful "banana wars" in Haiti, Veracruz, and Nicaragua (where he won the Navy Cross).

But 2nd Division marines were to learn in due course that they had taken on a very potent piece of Japanese realty. Built up over several years, Tarawa's fortifications included formidable beach defenses and a run of obstacles including barbed wire and mines protecting reinforced bunkers of loopholed six-feet-thick coconut logs; in these soon would be found 4836 naval troops whose guns ranged down from 8-inch coastal guns to 1-pounders and dual-purpose .51-caliber anti-aircraft guns. According to the sole Japanese officer who survived the Tarawa invasion, Betio had been designed "to withstand assault by a million men for a hundred years."

Smith's staff gathered every shred of information about the atoll, including interviews with members of the Royal New Zealand Navy, one of whom had been a schoolteacher on Betio before he was driven off by the Japanese. There was a great deal of talk about unpredictably low neap tides, and how these would affect an amphibious landing—talk which ultimately proved meaningless when the amtracs came ashore, battalions abreast, on beaches Red 1, 2 and 3 of Betio's lagoon side.

On October 31, after dress rehearsals, "Galvanic"—composed of northern (Makin) and southern (Tarawa) attack forces under the command of Rear Admiral Richmond Kelly Turner—got under way. Rear Admiral Harry W. Hill commanded the Southern Attack Force from the battleship *Maryland,* supported by the Southern Carrier Group under Rear Admiral A. E. Montgomery. In all, warships bound for Tarawa aggregated 3 battleships, 5 cruisers, 5 escort carriers, 21 destroyers, 1 LSD (with tanks), and 16 transports embarking 18,600 marines. Julian Smith and staff were aboard the flagship *Maryland.*

On November 14, when the convoy was well at sea, Admiral Hill gave all hands a long-awaited general picture of the projected operation. "Just six days from today at 0830 we're going to hit Tarawa Atoll in the Gilbert Islands. We're going to land on this island at the end of the atoll, the natives call it Betio. Before we land on the place, we're going to pound it with naval shellfire and dive bombers. We're going to steamroller that place until hell wouldn't have it."

After the news of their destination made the rounds of the convoy and life settled down again to shipboard routines, some of the men were under the impression that they were to be held in floating reserve and would never get into action. (As time would prove, they worried needlessly.) Reading material, always at a premium, was passed from hand to hand. Cribbage games, poker and pinochle occupied the greater part of their time aboard ship. One statistically-minded marine tabulated his days in convoy thusly:

Played 215 consecutive games of gin rummy
Bought and smoked six cartons of cigarettes and one box of cigars
Drank 93 cups of coffee
Obtained one crew haircut
Washed same pair of socks and same underwear 11 different times
Read two religious essays
Read 19 mystery stories and one something-or-other called *The Haunted Pajamas*

The heat below decks was stifling. Marines gathered in the "heads" during rigidly enforced "watering" hours to wash and shave; showers in salt water were permitted at any hour. In the evening they wandered topside. There was a quarter moon, and a moon under most any circumstances, then as now, evoked talk of home, wife or sweetheart.

Shortly before the convoy arrived at Tarawa a press conference was held aboard the flagship. Smith listened with ill-concealed impatience as a naval commander spoke of bringing his warship to within 1000 yards of the beach for saturation gunfire; his armor, he said, rendered him practically invulnerable. Another spoke up and declared his armor was lighter and tougher, permitting him to get in even closer. Finally, when General Smith had heard enough he rose from his chair and stared around the room. "Gentlemen," he said softly, "when the marines meet the enemy at bayonet point, the only armor a marine will have is his khaki shirt."

On D-Minus-One this veteran of many wars read a deeply moving and inspirational message to his 2nd Division.

• 1 • "WHAT WE DO HERE"

MAJOR GENERAL JULIAN C. SMITH

To the Officers and Men of the Second Marine Division:

A great offensive to destroy the enemy in the Central Pacific has begun. American air, sea and land forces, of which this Division is a part, initiate this offensive by seizing Japanese-held atolls in the Gilbert Islands, which will be used as bases for future operations. The task assigned to us is to capture the atolls of Tarawa and Apemama. Army units of our Fifth Amphibious Corps are simultaneously attacking Makin, 105 miles north of Tarawa.

For the past three days, Army, Navy and Marine Corps aircraft have been carrying out bombardment attacks on our objectives. They are neutralizing and will continue to neutralize other Japanese air bases adjacent to the Gilbert Islands. Early this morning combatant ships of our Navy bombarded Tarawa. Our Navy screens our operations and will support our attack tomorrow morning with the greatest concentration of aerial bombardment and naval gunfire in the history of warfare. It will remain with us until our objective is secured and our defenses are established. Garrison forces are already en route to relieve us as soon as we have completed our job of clearing our objectives of Japanese forces.

This Division was specially chosen by the high command for the assault of Tarawa because of its battle experience and its combat efficiency. Their confidence in us will not be betrayed. We are the first American troops to attack a defended atoll. What we do here will set a standard for all future operations in the Central Pacific area. Observers from other Marine Divisions and from other branches of our armed services, as well as those of our Allies, have been detailed to witness our operations. Representatives of the press are present. Our people back home are eagerly awaiting news of victories.

I know that you are well trained and fit for the tasks assigned to you. You will quickly overrun the Japanese forces; you will decisively defeat and destroy the treacherous enemies of our country; your success will add new laurels to the glorious traditions of our Corps.

Good luck and God bless you all.

※　※　※　※

THE LAND BATTLE FOR BETIO BEGAN AT 9:10 A.M., November 20, 1943. It ended seventy-six hours later. The marines killed 4690 enemy troops. Marine casualties numbered 3301, of whom 980 were dead. Richard W. Johnston, whom we have met, covered the invasion and compared it with the Little Big Horn, the Alamo and Belleau Wood. Johnston came to Betio aboard the transport *Haywood* to give the American public some of the best war reportage ever written.

·2· FIRST DAY

RICHARD W. JOHNSTON

The Japs fired the first shot. At 0441 they sent up a red star cluster, and less than a half-hour later they suddenly opened fire with the big eight-inch guns that they had taken from Singapore. Soon after 0300 the transports had started dropping marines into the Higgins boats. Now, as Jap shells cracked around and over the thin-skinned ships, they hurried north to get out of the way. The battleships *Maryland* and *Colorado* were ready to answer the enemy challenge with counter-battery fire. The LCVP's trailed along behind the transports, taking great baths of brine over their square bows and making some of their passengers seasick. The marines knew now that Betio had not been evacuated.

The U.S. battleships and cruisers outgunned the Jap shore artillerymen. The exchange of fire dwindled as members of the first three assault waves began the difficult transfer—made especially hazardous by the high seas—from LCVP's to alligators. The sun was not yet up, but the eastern sky was red as a cluster of roses. "Red sky in the morning, sailor take warning." Marine take warning? You bet! Between 0500 and 0600 a naval airstrike was due. When it failed (unaccountably) to come in, the Japs took advantage of the lifting of surface fire to blast at the transports.

All of this action occurred outside the lagoon, off the open side of the atoll where a channel cut through the submerged reef. Around 0700 two minesweepers, the *Requisite* and *Pursuit,* moved through the channel to clear the lagoon of mines. They were met by fire from Jap gunners undismayed by the naval shelling and the air attack (which finally had arrived, a half-hour late). The destroyers *Ringgold* and *Dashiell* raced up to support the sweeps, and then followed them into the lagoon, where the *Ringgold* took three hits but did not retreat.

The inside of the lagoon was like a smoldering volcano. The long, flat island was canopied in smoke, its splintered palms looking like the broken teeth of a comb. At many points orange fire studded the haze, and at dead center a great spiral of black smoke curled up from a pulsing blaze that now was red, but at first had been white and hot as a magnesium flare. An ammunition dump. All morning the wind had been fresh, fresh from the southeast. It blew the smoke of the burning island toward the small craft moving in, and the smoke helped hide the condition of the reef and the Jap defenses.

Out in the open sea, aboard the *Maryland,* General Julian Smith could not see the target for the clouds of smoke. But radio reports from the minesweepers led him to delay H-Hour, first to 0845 and then to 0900. The Jap shelling of the transports had slowed us up. In the meantime, out of the crazy chaos of bobbing boats near the line of departure—an imaginary line 6,000 yards out, marked by the sweeps, which had found no mines—a few craft loaded with specialists headed in toward Betio. They were about fifteen minutes ahead of the first assault wave of forty-two amtracs, carrying the storm troops of 2/2, 3/2 and 2/8.

These specialists were marines of the Second Regiment Scout and Sniper platoon, under Lieutenant William Deane Hawkins of Texas, and engineers under Lieutenant Alan Leslie of Oregon. Their mission was to land on the end of the pier that reached 500 yards into the lagoon and clean out all Japs—Japs who might enfilade the assault waves. They made the pier, at 0855—the first Americans to land in the Gilberts, the first men ashore in the Central Pacific offensive

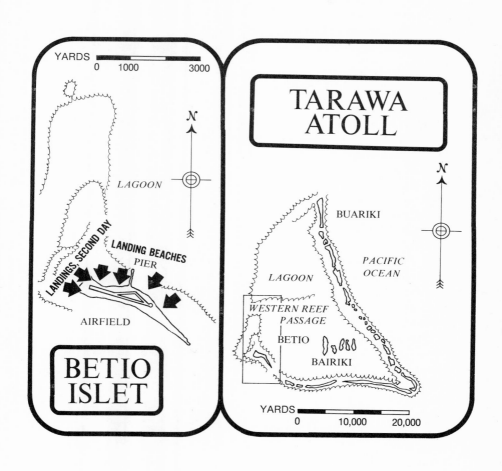

YARDS

0   1000   3000

N

LAGOON

LANDINGS, SECOND DAY

LANDING BEACHES

PIER

AIRFIELD

BETIO ISLET

TARAWA ATOLL

N

BUARIKI

PACIFIC OCEAN

LAGOON

WESTERN REEF PASSAGE

BETIO

BAIRIKI

YARDS

0   10,000   20,000

(if the pier could be called shore). On the way in, they learned a terrible truth: instead of the usually low neap tide which had been taken into account, we had an even lower "dodging tide," and the reef was almost bare. It would not float the shallow-draft Higgins boats. Only the amphibious tractors could be assured of reaching land. They learned something else, too. There were plenty of Japs left on Betio, and they were shooting with rifles, machine guns, anti-boat guns and mountain guns. Coral Kiska, indeed!

The first wave of amtracs got the word when it was 3,000 yards out, churning slowly toward the beach against the strong headwind. A sort of St. Elmo's fire began to flicker overhead, and something that felt like hot sand brushed the marines hunched low in the alligators. Air bursts, too highly charged to do much damage—but evidence enough that there were Japs ashore . . . At 2,000 yards the amtracs began to get bullets from long-range machine guns. At 800 yards the marines encountered the reef. The "little boats with wheels"—as the Japs called them—waddled up onto the coral. Their drivers gunned them toward the beach in a grim, nightmarish turtle race.

Landing Team 3/2 won the race. At 0910 the tractors, most of them hit but none as yet disabled, crawled the last few yards out of the water onto the coral of Red Beach 1. The marines piled out into the furnace of fire. Some of them hit the sand, a few on the far tip of the island broke across the four-foot-high sea wall. Seven minutes later LT 2/8 reached shore. Here, too, there was a coconut log sea wall. Like 3/2, 2/8 had experienced heavy fire all the way in, but had been helped by the close support of the two destroyers, the *Ringgold* and *Dashiell,* which whammed away at the Jap defenses until the first wave was less than ten minutes from shore. Last to land was LT 2/2, and for good reason. Moving in east of the long pier to the middle beach—Red Beach 2—they encountered the island's heaviest and most effective anti-boat and machine-gun fire. Worst of all, they tangled up in a spiny barricade of barbed wire the Japs had strung across the reef, a web that stopped some tractors and disabled others. The wading had begun, and on Beach 2 many marines died as they stumbled in from their wrecked machines.

Most of the three assault waves got ashore, one way or another. Casualties actually were not heavy for the whole group. But the tractors had taken a severe beating. Out of the eighty-seven that started from the line of departure, eight were knocked out on the way in, a good many more were disabled as they attempted to wheel and return for more troops, and an estimated fifteen sank the moment they reached deep water. The remaining waves of the landing teams would, for the most part, have to cross the reef on foot. They were eager to do so, for even from 6,000 yards they could sense the fury of the fight. Before the first amtrac returned, a Marine radioman got this message from the beach: "Have landed. Unusually heavy opposition. Causalties 70 per cent. Can't hold!" The impatient marines started for shore in the flimsy boats. With them came the General Sherman tanks, their turrets visible above the sides of the lighters.

With the battle for Betio less than an hour old, we had landed not more than 2,000 marines on the island's northern shore. They were badly disorganized. Only two companies had reached Red Beach 1. On Red Beach 2, one company had come straight in but another had been deflected toward the opposite flank and one platoon had been driven all the way to Red Beach 1. Only on Red Beach 3 was the Landing Team more or less intact, and under full command control. But if Combat Team 2 was disorganized, its members were not immobilized. After the battle Colonel Edson said: "It is my opinion that the reason we won this show was the ability of the junior officers and noncoms to take command of small groups of six to eight or ten men, regardless of where those men came from, and to organize and lead them as a fighting team."

This was a particularly precious ability in the light of command casualties. Only one of the three LT commanders reached the beach during the assault. This was Major Crowe of 2/8. Lieutenant Colonel Herbert Amey, the big Pennsylvanian who commanded LT 2/2, was cut down by machine-gun fire when his amtrac stalled and he attempted to wade to the sands of Red Beach 2. Amey's exec, Major Howard Rice, was in one of the tractors deflected to Red Beach 1. On Red Beach 1, where Major "Mike" Ryan, a company commander of LT 3/2, had taken impromptu command, the battalion leader, Major John Schoettel, had been halted at the reef by intense fire. And, finally, Major Henry J. Drewes of New Jersey, commanding the amtrac battalion, was killed in one of his tractors as he directed them in their first drive toward the beach.

Despite the confusion and chaos, against and beyond the sea wall, around the coral boulders and among the splintered palms, the marines were fighting—not for their lives, for all normal caution urged . . . take cover!—but for the Second Marine Division, and the United States Marine Corps. A civilian correspondent who made the landing wrote of that first morning: "In those hellish hours, the heroism of the marines, officers and enlisted men alike, was beyond belief. Time after time, they unflinchingly charged Japanese positions, ignoring the deadly fire and refusing to halt until wounded beyond human ability to carry on."

On Red Beach 3 the marines somehow had manhandled their 37mm guns across the reef, after the boats carrying them were sunk. Two were dragged to the left flank, but because there was no break in the seawall, it now appeared impossible to get them inshore. Suddenly a marine spotted two Jap tanks rolling toward the beach, and the gun crews yelled: "Lift 'em over!" This cry was answered by many willing hands, and the two 900-pound guns fairly soared over the seawall. Quickly placed in position, they knocked out one of the approaching tanks and forced the other to retire.

Only on the narrow ribbon of sand directly under the seawall, under the Jap guns, was there even a vestige of protection. And on the sand plateau above the wall, the Japs had erected defenses unlike anything the marines had ever seen. There were big blockhouses and small pillboxes and worst of all, row on row of protected machine-gun nests, staggered in support of each other, made into tiny fortresses by sandbags and concrete and coconut logs—fortresses which withstood rifle fire and grenades, and had to be reduced by explosives and flamethrowers. It was not an exaggeration to say that there was not a square yard, or even a square foot, of land within Marine control which was either safe or secure. If not actually hand to hand (and the Japs were wise enough to fight from inside their forts), the combatants were hardly more than a rifle length apart, and a man could stretch a hand above the seawall and get it shot off.

Behind the desperately engaged assault waves, in the warm, chalky water, made opaque by bomb and shell bursts that had powdered the coral reef, the marines of the fourth, fifth, and sixth waves were stumbling to the assistance of LT's 2/2, 3/2, and 2/8. Some of them came in along the pier, which still had a few snipers' nests. But more walked directly toward the shore, a 500- to 800-yard walk in most cases in water that at first was waist deep and then only knee deep and finally only something slopping about the ankles, pulling at the ankles and slowing eager steps. "Spread out! Spread out!" their officers cried, as the Jap machine guns racketed viciously and the water was laced with ripples. The marines walked steadily, their rifles held high at first to keep them clear of the water. Sometimes they slipped down into the treacherous coral potholes, sometimes they tripped over invisible obstacles. Sometimes they zigzagged, but there was little point in zigzagging. Off Red Beach 1 there was direct fire. Off Red Beach 2 there was enfilade machine-gun and sniper fire from a few nests still remaining in the pier. Off Red Beach 3 were both of these and something more—flank fire from the stubby Burns-Philp wharf some 400 yards west of the pier.

Some of the marines died in the deep water, sinking quickly under the weight of their equipment. Some of them died close in, lying half-exposed in the gentle surf. Some of them died horribly in the barbed wire off Red Beach 2; and on the eastern sector of that terrible beach, where the seawall was loop-holed, the machine guns looked straight out from the level of the sand and clusters of five and six marines fell face down, making a fan of bodies at the very muzzles of the guns. Overhead, the Kingfisher observation plane from the *Maryland* flew back and forth, acting as eyes for Admiral Hill and General Smith. Its pilot, Lieutenant Commander Robert A. MacPherson, watched the marines in the frightful long wade and wrote in his log: "The water seemed never clear of tiny men, their rifles held over their heads, slowly wading beachward. I wanted to cry."

The commander of Combat Team 2, Colonel David Shoup, had planned to follow the assault waves into Red 2 and set up his Regimental CP. Shortly before 1000, he was waiting off the reef with a party that included Lieutenant Colonel Evans F. Carlson, the Marine raider who was along as an observer, and Lieutenant Colonel Presley M. Rixey of Virginia, commander of 1/10, who hoped to land his pack howitzers before the day was over. Shoup was in touch with some of the assault elements by radio, and also with the *Maryland.* All the news was bad, and many units could not report at all — their inefficient TBY sets had become watersoaked and would not work. Within forty-five minutes of the landing, as the messages reiterated that "the issue is in doubt!", Shoup decided reinforcements must be hurried ashore if Betio was to hold. He ordered Major Wood B. Kyle of California to take his CT2 reserve landing team, 1/2, into Red Beach 2, where Lieutenant Colonel Walter I. Jordan, an observer, had assumed command after Amey's death. Almost at the same moment, General Smith released Major Robert H. Ruud's 3/8 — part of the Division reserve — to Shoup for use as he saw fit. Shoup directed Ruud to take his men ashore on Beach 3. The colonel and his own party landed on the fire-swept pier to begin inching their way to the beach.

The news that help was coming electrified the marines on Beaches 2 and 3. They needed more than men — ammunition was getting dangerously short, and so was plasma. Under the seawall on Beach 3 the line of wounded now stretched nearly fifty yards, and only those too badly hurt to move were there — the "walking wounded" were still fighting. There was even less protection — and even more casualties — on Beach 2. But balanced against this great need was the frightful problem of how to get help ashore reasonably intact. The tractor battalion had lost many of its machines and many of its men, particularly the .50-caliber machine-gunners who had tried to answer the superior Jap fire. Now there were only enough amtracs to take two companies of 1/2, and there were none at all for 3/8. A little after 1100 the two battalions started in, Ruud's men in the flimsy Higgins boats.

The members of 1/2 got there first, crawling across the reef in the alligators and taking concentrated machine-gun and anti-boat fire as they neared the sand. One group was deflected, as others had been earlier, to Red Beach 1. But a company got through, despite the fusillade, and the smoke-smeared, bloodshot veterans of 2/2 took heart. It was a different story on Beach 3. Some of the smoke had drifted away, the clouds had lifted and beyond the chalky surf of the blue lagoon danced in the sunlight. The little blue Higgins boats of 3/8's leading wave came churning in, five abreast. There was no fire until they were almost within spitting distance of the reef. Then, as their ramps came down—"Whang!" The sound, on the beach, was like a steel girder hitting concrete. It pierced the ears, above the howling fury of the battle, and it echoed for seconds. Out in the blue water, the westernmost Higgins boat disappeared. Quite literally. It had been there and suddenly it was not. In its place, for a split second, there was a blur in the air, and then there was nothing. "Whang!" A second boat vanished. It was a terrifying and heartbreaking sight. And there was nothing to be done about it, nothing that could be done fast enough to do any good. The Japs had gotten one of their 4.7 dual-purpose guns back in working order, beyond reach toward the tail of the island, and they had the exact and absolute range. On the shore marines who had fought tight-lipped all morning wept now and beat on the sands with their burned fists. In the remaining boats there was further disaster.

A coxswain some distance from the reef screamed: "This is as far as I go!" He let the ramp down, and a boatload of marines, heavily laden with packs, tumbled into fifteen feet of water and many drowned. Other boats were raked with machine-gun fire. They straggled toward the pier, where Shoup was desperately motioning them, and their dazed occupants jumped into the chest-deep water only to face more fire, fire which could not be kept off the logs and sand of the long dock. There was hardly enough left of 3/8's leading waves to land. Many officers were dead, and many men were dead or so badly wounded they needed quick evacuation. The Japs' dual-purpose gun was knocked out by destroyer fire after about twelve shots—and after it had done its damage.

The afternoon of D Day was a jumble that saw confusion compounded. One thing was clear after the disastrous approach of 3/8: unless the few marines ashore could get at the Japs' anti-boat guns, and the long-range machine guns, there was little hope of reinforcement across the reef. About noon Shoup and his command party reached Red Beach 2 from the pier and established CT2 headquarters behind a big Jap bunker (on D plus 2 twelve Japs were killed inside it). But communications were fragmentary. The CP was entirely out of touch with Major Ryan and his by-now composite LT on Red Beach 1. One thing was frighteningly clear both to the Regimental command and to Julian Smith on the *Maryland*—the Division had committed everything it had except one battalion, Major Lawrence Hays' 1/8, and it was not going to be enough. At 1330 Julian Smith radioed Major General Holland Smith, commander of the Fifth Amphibious Corps, asking him to release the Sixth Marine Regiment from Corps Reserve. Holland Smith answered in the affirmative—the Army had flushed only 836 Japs on Makin. This meant that 1/8 could be sent into action without further delay. Smith instructed Colonel Elmer E. Hall to take his Regimental Command and Hays' battalion to the line of departure and await further orders. At 1458 Major Schoettel radioed Shoup that his boat was still off the reef and added: "Have lost contact with assault elements." Schoettel landed on Red Beach 2, and ultimately reached 3/2 overland.

About 1500 Smith messaged Shoup: "Do you consider a night landing by LT 1/8 suitable and practicable on Beach Green? [the alternate landing beach on the western shore] If not, can reinforcements land on Beaches Red 2 and 3 after dark?" The message failed to get through. An hour later Smith radioed Hall to land 1/8 and all remaining elements of CT8 on the tapering eastern tip of Betio and attack northwest, in order to prevent a Jap counterattack on the left flank of 2/8. Once again the message vanished in the air, and 1/8 remained at the line of departure.

Nothing much happened on the beach during the afternoon. Nothing much, except that maybe 1,000 marines, maybe more, performed acts that would have got them the Navy Cross in any other battle. On Red Beach 1 the mixed marines of LT 2/2 and LT 3/2 were making better progress than anyone knew, but the point was no one knew. Now and then the engineers blew up a Jap pillbox. Everybody threw an occasional grenade, or blasted at places where Japs must be because so much fire was coming back. The Navy sent its carrier planes down to strafe, when asked, and out in the lagoon the destroyers banged away at hillock of coral, logs and concrete on the left flank of Red Beach 3. On Red 2 Shoup was trying to make sense of the battle and fight it at the same time. Out at the end of the pier, the Japs still had so many bullets going home that marines there since morning could not move in. Part of the pier was afire, a blaze set by one of Lieutenant Leslie's flame-throwing engineers before the landing. The Navy corpsmen and the members of the Division band climbed up and down over the wall or raced between the blasted pillboxes, bringing back the wounded. There were no more morphine syrettes, no more plasma, not much water, no food, not many bullets. The sunset was pretty, though. It was especially pretty because it seemed likely to be the last for any marine on Betio. On each of the three beachheads the commanders set up the best lines they could and then dug their men in as much as they could, to wait for the Japs' night counter-attack. All along the beaches marines died slowly, white-faced and in great pain, but uttering not a sound.

In some ways, the real situation on Betio at nightfall of D Day was not quite as bad as it seemed; in others, it was worse. The casualties, while high, were much lower than anyone believed at the time. Each of the Landing Teams held more ground than the others imagined they did. The Japs, although far from "annihilated," were much more disorganized than we supposed. On the debit side, we had failed to land an overpowering force and were scarcely better than even with the Japs in manpower. We were short of ammunition, had no food, and, worst of all, we had almost no valuable positions. The beaches and the gouges in from them were wide open, while the Nips were still encased in their armored pillboxes. Finally, we had only the most uncertain of communications—everybody was still "lost," and almost nobody really knew what had happened on D Day, in terms of anything larger than a squad or company.

What had?

Let's start with Red Beach 1.

As previously noted, the two companies of 3/2 which got ashore on the western tip of the island—the "bird's beak"—landed under savage fire. When less than an hour later, L Company, a few engineers and the mortar platoon of M Company, waded ashore from grounded Higgins boats, they took 35 per cent casualties. Luckily, Major Ryan, the commander of L Company, was not among the dead or wounded. He organized the survivors of I and K Companies, and, supported by two Sherman tanks which had crept across the reef, launched an immediate attack. From the beginning it was clear that the Japs had a ferocious defense stronghold in the curve of sand between Beaches Red 1 and Red 2. Instead of fruitlessly attempting to storm this fortress, Ryan led his marines through the only slightly less deadly pillboxes along the western shore—the shore that had been designated as "Green Beach." While this isolated 3/2, it flanked the Japs. By late afternoon, reinforced accidentally by several units of 2/2 and some of 1/2 which had been deflected to Red 1 by heavy fire, 3/2 had carved out a beachhead 500 yards deep along Beach Green and 150 yards wide. That night Ryan pulled back a little, to establish a 300-yard perimeter and await the inevitable Jap counterattack.

Between Ryan's composite LT and the marines on Red Beach 2 was nearly 600 yards of Jap-held island. This meant that 1/2 and 2/2, on the center beach, also had a flank to guard. In the morning their own casualties plus the lack of adequate cover had slowed down 2/2. When 1/2 landed, before noon, the remnants of these two teams combined to push as far inland as the diagonal taxiway of the airfield.

In the afternoon, in frightful fighting, this slim hold was expanded to the area inside the airstrip-taxiway triangle. By nightfall, the battalions held a "line" (it was hardly a line, but only a series of blown-up pillboxes, captured trenches, and shell holes) roughly 200 yards inshore from the beach. Kyle's Marines, of 1/2, also were deployed among wrecked and smoking Jap defenses on the right of Red Beach 2, to meet any night flanking attack by the enemy troops in the hot pocket to the west.

In the initial hours Crowe's 2/8 had made faster progress than any other LT, partly by virtue of naval support (from the two destroyers), partly because the command got ashore intact, and partly because it suffered the least casualties on the reef. F Company was sent immediately to the left to establish the flanking line across the island's tail. E and G Companies smashed directly inland. Crowe's executive officer, Major William Chamberlin of Chicago, had command of the flank, with Crowe directing the forward assault. The Japs fought as fiercely here as elsewhere, but 2/8 got across the corner of the taxiway quickly and then had to battle for every inch, paying dearly and in blood. The remnants of 3/8 straggled in during the afternoon and went into instant action, but despite repeated and heroic attacks the sunset line was no more than 200 yards inshore, and the flank line curved away from huge Jap defenses behind the Burns-Philp wharf.

The riflemen of the three assault battalions and the LT's which came in to reinforce them shared the glories—and the disasters—of D Day with a number of special units, each of which contributed a great deal to the fight. There can be no question of assessing the relative contribution of these outfits; let it suffice that without any one of them, the struggle would have been immeasurably harder and perhaps impossible.

We have mentioned the two tanks which provided fire power for 3/2's push on Red Beach 1. They were, of course, from C Company, Corps Tank Battalion—manned by marines who had trained in Noumea and joined the Division at Efate. Early in the morning of D Day, fourteen of the Shermans floated out of the LSD *Ashland* in their own lighters and moved to the line of departure. The plan called for six of them to land on Red Beach 1, in support of 3/2; four on Red Beach 2, in support of 2/2; and four on Red Beach 3, in support of 2/8. There were the first, second and third platoons, respectively. Shortly before 1000 the six lighters assigned to the First Platoon lowered their ramps and dumped the Shermans on the reef off Red 1, 800 yards from shore. The tanks started rumbling ashore under their own power, through water that came nearly to their turrets. Tank reconnaissance men splashed ahead of them, marking potholes in the coral with flags, and disregarding the intense Jap machine-gun fire.

In attempting to avoid running over dead and wounded marines, who littered the beach and the shallow reef near it, four of the tanks dropped into reefholes and were stalled. Two got ashore. One of them was *China Gal* (like bomber crews, tankers are partial to naming their craft), commanding by Lieutenant Edward Bale of Texas. In 3/2's push along Green Beach, the tanks played an all-important role. Their 75's and machine guns were a partial substitute for the marines' lack of artillery. *China Gal* outdueled a Jap tank in the course of the advance, and together the two Shermans smashed in numerous pillboxes and emplacements. One of them finally was badly hit, caught fire and burned. But as night fell *China Gal,* though damaged, was still operating, and Major Mike Ryan established her on his exposed flank.

The other Shermans, with one exception, landed on Red Beach 3 (according to plan). Less than fifty yards from the beach one of them dropped into a pothole and had to be abandoned. This tank was from the Second Platoon, destined for Beach 2. The three survivors climbed through a hole blown in the sea wall by the engineers and moved rapidly west to a prearranged assembly area. They wheeled to assist the marines of 2/2 in their desperate drive against the airdrome infield—the area between the taxiway and the airstrip. Meanwhile, the four Shermans assigned to Crowe's battalion—the Third Platoon— had crawled up on Beach 3, paused for orders, and then climbed the barricade. They struck due south, parrallel to the Second Platoon.

The tanks of both the Second and Third Platoons moved out more or less on their own, with instructions to "knock out all enemy positions encountered." They did well—as long as they lasted. But the penalties of operating blind (visibility is limited from the inside of a tank) were soon imposed. In the Second Platoon two tanks were knocked out by another Jap 4.7mm DP gun. In the Third platoon, one tank was wrecked tragically. At nightfall the only survivor on Red Beach 3 was *Colorado,* smoky, battered, but still in fierce and effective operation under Lietutenant Louis Largey of California. As Ryan had done on Beach 1, Crowe established *Colorado* on the sandy flank of Beach 3, to await the uncertainties of the night.

During the first hours of the assault, a few halftracks from the Regimental Weapons company had bumped and jolted and splashed their way across the reef, but despite the valor of their exposed crews they could not be kept in operation. One fell into an underwater shellhole before it ever reached the shore; another got in and fired effectively, but in changing position also became bogged down.

Long before the halftracks and tanks came, the Division's smallest but most spectacular band of specialists was on its way to Marine Corps immortality. This was the Scout and Sniper platoon under Lieutenant Hawkins, which had landed (as noted earlier) on the tip of the pier fifteen minutes ahead of the assault waves. The Japs had had a seaplane ramp near the end of the pier, and Hawkins (accompanied by four enlisted men and Lieutenant Leslie of the Engineers) got up on the ramp and went to work with grenades, rifles, and flame-throwers. They burned two Jap houses, cleaned out a Jap machine-gun emplacement, and worked their way along the pier until Hawkins was satisfied that it offered no major danger to landing troops. He then took his company ashore, and during the afternoon of D Day the Scout-Snipers and Engineers, still working together, were a major factor in blasting enemy forces out of the beach emplacements. The next day Hawkins would die, and in dying win the Congressional Medal of Honor, but that story belongs in the next chapter.

There is another fabulous story connected with the capture of the pier, involving the enterprise and heroism of a young Higgins boat coxswain named Stokes from the APA *Zeilin.* Stokes came back to his ship after delivering a group of marines to the reef with his boat riddled by Jap fire. He had a plan—and he fought his way all the way up the chain of command to Commodore J. B. McGovern to propose it. What he needed was a new boat. What he wanted to do with it was this: take a Marine flame-thrower team down the channel beside the pier to knock out the remaining Jap machine-gun nests. The marines had volunteered and were standing by. McGovern gave young Stokes his boat, and the mission was carried out with—surprisingly enough—only minor casualties.

In the later phases of the battle for Guadalcanal marines from the Eighteenth Regiment had experimented with flame-throwers and assault demolition. Betio was the perfect laboratory for their fiery and explosive specialty. Besides the unit under Lieutenant Leslie, which accompanied Hawkins, two twenty-man sections from the First Platoon, A Company, 1/18, went ashore with LT 2/2. One of these sections suffered 100 per cent casualties in the landing; the other had enough survivors to destroy six enemy positions before nightfall. On Red Beach 1 the Engineers (this was the Third Platoon of the same company) shared the heavy casualties of 3/2; even so, they got enough men ashore to attack five Jap positions with flame-throwers and several others with explosives . . .

The heroism of the Engineers in the D Day fight is exemplified in the story of Staff Sergeant William J. Bordelon of Texas, a member of the assault platoon of 1/18. The Japs got Bordelon's amtrac right in their sights, and he was one of four men who survived the trip across the reef. Ashore, Bordelon instantly went into action. In a matter of a few minutes he had made up two demolition charges and personally disposed of two enemy pillboxes. As he attacked a third position, he was hit by Jap machine-gun fire, but he did not fall.

Instead, Bordelon caught up a rifle and covered another group of marines who were scaling the seawall.

Corpsmen tried to give the seriously wounded sergeant first aid but he waved them away and presently splashed out into the water to rescue another demolition man who was injured and calling for help. He rescued two, spotting a second as he helped the first man to the beach. By this time Bordelon had done his duty and a good deal more, but he was not satisfied. Bleeding from his wounds but apparently oblivious to them, he prepared another dynamite charge and without assistance or cover attempted to blast a fourth pillbox. The Japs caught him in a volley of bullets, and the valiant sergeant died instantly. He was the first of four Division members to win the Medal of Honor at Betio.

One more word for the Engineers. On D Day afternoon elements of the shore party landed on the end of the pier, to begin preparing it for the receipt of supplies. Under constant Jap mortar and sniper fire, they extinguished the fire started by the pre-H-Hour flame-thrower team and at midnight began repairing the fire damage. There was no more cover there than anywhere else, and many marines—wearing the striped-trouser uniforms of the shore party group—lay dead on the splintered planks before the job was done.

Throughout D Day Lieutenant Colonel Rixey, the commander of 1/10, had eagerly sought an opportunity to land his pack howitzers and get them into effective support. He was frustrated by the simple fact that there was no place to put them—no position area from which to deliver normal fires. The "pack" crews waited, off the reef. In their stead, the marines had the assistance of Navy air and the two destroyers which had remained in the lagoon all day long, firing when requested. Requests—for both air strikers and ship's fire—were relayed by radio (when the radios were working). The men who did the job were young naval lieutenants and young marines—Navy in the case of air, Marine for the surface fire. These liaison officers were with each battalion, and their functions were vital. They had the delicate responsibility of obtaining fire where it was needed, but keeping it off our own men. They stuck at their posts, kept the radios going, and got results. The Navy Hellcats came in for a dozen or more strafing missions during the afternoon, their racketing guns sounding like sticks drawn over giant washboards. The destroyers put heavy five-inch fire on the Japanese every time there was a serious threat from the left flank of Red Beach 3.

The air liaison officers were not the only Navy men on the beach. The doctors and corpsmen had heartbreaking and terrifying assignments. We had long since learned that the Japs did not respect the Red Cross. The young corpsmen went among the pillboxes unarmed and unmarked, bringing in the wounded. Many of them were hit, some were killed. On the narrow beach strips that functioned as aid stations, the doctors did everything that could humanly be done—and cursed the lack of drugs, plasma and bandages as the day wore on.

Finally, there were the mortarmen. Some members of the M Company mortar platoon got ashore on Red 2 and got their 81mm mortars into operation. Near the base of the pier, between Beaches 2 and 3, another mortar was set up. The shells soared away, and all too often the men who fired them sank down and bled and died. One team, manning the pier mortar, was wiped out in a few seconds by a deadly accurate Jap sniper. But others took their places. There were no vacuums on Betio—whenever a man fell, be he rifleman, mortarman, corpsman, engineer, or tanker, another stepped up to replace and avenge him.

What we had won, in a day of dreadful carnage, heroic endeavor and selfless sacrifice, was less than one-tenth of a square mile of stinking coral, blown to useless bits and stained with great draughts of American blood. But it was one-tenth of a mile such as few men had ever won before, one-tenth of a mile with more fortifications than the borders of most nations, jampacked with fanatic enemy troops who not only were willing but eager to die. If, in the dreadful night ahead, every marine died defending that one-tenth of a mile, the valor of 20 November would still be sung in the Marine Corps for 100 or 1,000 years. Seldom in the history of any nation had the mantle of heroism fallen over so many shoulders.

❅   ❅   ❅   ❅

SERGEANT JIM LUCAS LANDED ON BETIO SHORTLY before midnight, D-Day, after a fifteen-hour wait at the line of departure. We meet him shortly before his LCVP moves inshore. In the darkness a command boat roars up and a man yells, "What do you carry?" Lucas' boat yells back, "Personnel and a truck." The voice growls, "To hell with the truck! Do you have ammunition?" Again, a negative reply, and the command boat moves off. Lucas and his buddies settle down, suddenly aware of how the battle is going. Dark as it is for us, thinks the combat correspondent, it is darker still for the Japanese. Here, with all the poignance and sensitivity a Pulitzer Prize-winning reporter can summon, is the remainder of that night into the morning of D-Plus-One.

·3· "TOGETHER WE PRAYED OVER OUR FRIEND"

JIM LUCAS

An hour later the command boat was back. "Do you have assault troops?" we were asked.

"We carry military police and combat correspondents."

I felt the sickening guilt which sometimes comes to specialists among fighting men.

I was to take the watch at midnight and I had not yet been awakened by the man who had the 8 to 12, so I know it was sometime before midnight when Matty shook me.

"We're going in," he said.

Four boats were following the command vessel, which was edging toward the pier. For a moment I feared we might land among the Japs. The danger was not as real as it appeared then, for Colonel Shoup since has assured me that our men held a beachhead of considerable length on that first night.

We drew fire—I swore then it came from the bulk of a small Japanese merchantman that had been blasted by our bombing of September 4 and was beached just beside the pier. Fortunately the fire, wherever it came from, passed over our heads.

Shortly before midnight—fifteen hours after we had left our transport—our landing craft drew up alongside the partially wrecked pier.

We were not fooling ourselves. After our first abortive attempt to get in, Matty and I knew our chances were none too good, no better than fifty-fifty. Matty took out his fountain pen and wrote: *Mrs. E. A. Matthews, Jr., 501 Sixth Street, Dallas, Texas.*

"Let her know how it happened," he said.

I nodded and gave him Ashleigh's address in Wellington. I had written letters to my own family and left them behind to be mailed if "anything," as I had said, "happens to me."

I had later to write Virginia Matthews and tell her how Matty died. It was one of the hardest jobs I ever tackled.

Matty was the first man out of our boat. He helped me onto the pier.

As I stepped on the pier I saw a marine directly under foot. I thought he was a wounded man, and cautioned Matjasic to be careful.

"He's dead," Matty said.

He was a kid of not more than eighteen. The white stripe on his dungaree trousers meant that he was a member of the shore party and had come to Betio to help in the unloading. He had died, in all probability, without firing a shot . . .

We had moved down the dock less than ten feet when the Japanese opened up with a hateful 40-mm barrage. The first shell hit the water and exploded not ten feet away, and we fell flat—not a difficult thing to do under fire.

The pier was crowded, for several hundred men lay crouched there waiting for the next shell to hit. My gas mask, strapped to my side, prevented my getting as low as I though the circumstances demanded, and I detached it. A great deal of my weight is in my hips, and one of the most frequent questions I was asked, when I returned to the States recently, was how I had kept from suffering an embarrassing wound. I could only reply that I was conscious of my exposure, and took pains to safeguard it.

Matty was on the outside, with Matjasic next to him. I was next to Matjasic. The three of us did not cover four feet of the pier.

The second shell hit directly beneath the pier. I was stunned, and drenched by salt water. I heard Ray scream. Matty moaned.

Ray and I jumped to our feet and ran to the opposite side, expecting the next to be a direct hit.

Matty did not move. I called to him, loudly, but he did not answer. I ran back and begged him to get up. Marines shouted at me to get down, and I was sorely tempted. I do not know when I have been as badly frightened. I tried to drag Matty, but he collapsed in a heap. The third shell, at this moment, hit farther out in the water, and I yelled for Matjasic.

Stunned by the blast, he had been lifted three feet in the air and thrown back on the wooden pier. He had disappeared.

Ray suddenly materialized out of nowhere.

"Who is it?" he asked.

"Matty," I replied.

Ray began to cry, and disappeared again.

I begged a marine to help me. I got Matty to the other side, and lay down beside him. The shelling lifted, and I began a frantic search for help. Finding a hospital corpsman, I asked him to come with me.

"Man," he said helplessly, "I've got 500 men hurt since 9 o'clock this morning. All I can tell you to do is put him on a stretcher, try to get him onto a boat, if you can find a boat going back, and send him out to one of the ships."

Meanwhile I had found Ray again.

"How's Matty?" he asked.

"I'm afraid he's dead."

We waylaid a second corpsman—a tow-headed kid who ought to have been back home teasing the girls in the junior play—and brought him to our lieutenant.

He felt of Matty's pulse and stood up.

"He's gone," he said.

Ray is a Catholic and I am a Protestant. Ray had attended confession aboard ship, and I had prayed with men of my own faith.

Together, we fell on our knees. Together, we prayed over our friend.

I stood up. A watching marine asked quietly: "Your buddy?"

I could only nod.

"They got my kid brother this morning," he said.

I have never felt so much alone as at that moment. It was difficult to leave Matty, but we had no choice. I have since learned that ten or fifteen marines who knew us both were in the area, but I did not see a one that night.

In his pack Matty had several stories I had written aboard ship. He was also wearing one of my shirts. This gave rise to a report that I had been killed, and I was to hear it many times after the fighting was over . . .

Ray and I covered Matty's body and began our slow trek. Many of Matty's friends, coming ashore later, saw him there.

We had only moved a few feet when snipers opened up from the left. We dropped to the floor of the pier, waited until the firing ceased, and went on. Ahead there lay a strip of 100 yards of white coral. And there was a moon. Back home it might have been beautiful. Out here we cursed it, for it made us perfect targets.

We reached the edge of the coral and waited. I abandoned my typewriter, and Ray took his camera from its bulky case. We threw off our packs, and went on with only our weapons and our ammunition.

We had gone only five yards when the ever-active snipers opened up. Three of our men, perhaps four, I cannot say definitely, fell. We dropped. Ahead someone grunted: "We can't stay here. They'll shell us, and we'll be done for."

An officer took command and shouted: "Move five feet apart and keep going."

Slowly we moved down the pier. We would drop when a man was hit, freeze until the firing ceased, and then move forward. It is impossible to describe one's feelings. I have tried many times to analyze how I felt. It is as much a mystery to me today as it probably will be to most readers of this book. Few of us had ever gone through such an experience, and I had, throughout, the suspicion that it wasn't really happening. And there was but one choice—keep moving.

It was morning before we reached the beach. I asked for the command post. Someone pointed indefinitely—so indefinitely that we paid no attention to the gesture.

On the beach fighting still was heavy. In the still-smouldering ruins of a beach warehouse, we spotted a gutted Jap steam roller and edged toward it, trying to put its bulk between us and the Japanese lines. It looked as good a place as any to spend the night, and we dug in the hot sand, still alive with red coals. There the two of us spent the night . . .

❀ ❀ ❀ ❀

NOT ALL OF THE FLOATING RESERVE UNITS MADE it ashore D-Day. Sergeant Gene Ward, the distinguished and gifted columnist of the New York *Daily News,* was still out at the line of departure until almost dawn of the second day. After the war, he wrote an occasional chapter on the Battle of Tarawa but did little more than throw it into an old suitcase in his attic. From a great newspaperman's unpublished memoirs of Betio, here is Ward detailing the end of his long wait when he closed his eyes for a nap.

·4· "THE DEAD WERE TOO CLOSE AROUND US"

SERGEANT GENE WARD

An ungentle tug at my shoulder. It was light. I pulled myself out of my cramped position to look toward Helen Island. She appeared for all the world like a derelict in the water with the blackened, denuded palm stumps as countless masts.

"We're going in," Sergeant Jack Combs said, and sure enough, the Higgins boats in our wave had swung out of their rings and were heading for shore, ours among the front-runners. We all tightened our belts instinctively, adjusted packs and slipped a cartridge into the chambers of our weapons. The boats surged toward the land, alternately racing with a wave and then falling back in a trough. We strained our eyes on the upsweeps. Nothing seemed to be moving but ourselves . . . Then, abruptly, someone shouted to "get down, you guys, they're shooting at us . . ."

"Tell 'em to knock off that stuff," said Combs, who thought it was some trigger-happy coxswain in one of the other boats.

"No, the Japs," somebody said.

I was just behind the coxswain and craning my neck. We were well off the 1800-foot pier and just as I was thinking we had a helluva way to go yet, something smacked the water beside us. At the same time the boat rolled and grated to a stop atop the coral. The coxswain gunned her, but that was as far as we went on that line.

The ramp went down. The men spilled and scrambled forward to stumble out into chin-deep water. Almost at once some of them were hit. Others, apparently from a boat which had sloughed into this coral patch just before us, were calling for corpsmen and struggling to get into our boat. They were the wounded.

I was pinned behind the coxswain and had to climb onto the motor shield, over it and down the length of the tilted boat. When I hit the tepid water I first became aware of the wasplike sound of the bullets and the sharp slap they made biting the water around me. Ahead toward the shore I could see wrecked amtracs; behind me an upended Higgins boat. I struggled forward and the water became shallower. At the same time the fire became heavier. Like others around me I kept only my eyes and right hand, which clutched my carbine, above water.

Gradually, by some laborious thought process, it dawned on me we were caught between machine-gun crossfire. One gun, obviously, was set up somewhere on or under the pier. This you could tell from the angle of the bullets as they made skipping patterns across the yellow-green surface. The other, a heavy-caliber job, seemed to be coming from a rusty-red derelict hull to our right and out a hundred yards or so. Every fourth or fifth bullet was a tracer and you could see 'em coming. They sort of blazed and hissed like large, angry fireflies. But the worst of it was, you couldn't be just certain where that winged death was coming from.

Over on my left came an incessant, plaintive call for a corpsman. I could see one marine with a machine-gun tripod across his shoulder attempting to lift another man. My pack, gas mask and dispatch case were becoming thoroughly waterlogged. I tried to unhook the mask but it was tightly fastened under my pack straps. Someone up ahead shouted back for the men to spread out, so some of us switched our line of crawl to the right, aiming at a point down the beach. The machine gun in the derelict kept talking. We were almost opposite its bow now.

The water had shallowed so I was worming along on my belly. I recalled then that coral cuts badly and I kept looking at my hands and wrists. They were bloody but I couldn't feel anything. Two of our tortured little group around me were hit. One crept back past me and I asked him if he was okay . . . "I'll make it," was all he said.

In all that hell I don't recall one man going back unless he was wounded and even several of them continued the struggle for the beach.

I was about halfway in when Navy dive bombers laid egg after egg around the Jap machine-gun nest in the rusty-red hull. But it was several minutes before a slower pontoon job scored a direct hit. By then I was near exhaustion. But as my body tired my mind grew clearer. I seem to recall the last half of what proved to be close to 900 yards of slow, desperate crawling with far more clarity than the first half. It was as if I had suddenly become detached from the general scene and was there merely as a matterless observer of all that transpired.

A grey, square plank, apparently a door off a landing craft of some sort, floated past me and I used it awhile as a raft on which to push my carbine and dispatch case in front of me. Indians used to do it this way, I thought to myself. Two men were up ahead a few yards. Just as I came up one was hit in the chest and his blood stained the water. A moment later a bullet hit just in front of my chin and then a whole hail of lead hit all around the two of us—the dead marine and I. The other man was moving as rapidly as he could out of range. I had tugged loose my gas mask finally and now, in staggering, crawling and wallowing out of that cone of fire, my dispatch case slipped away and sank in the befouled water. Then my cartridge belt loosened and both my canteens went with it.

For a brief spell I thought of groping for the case, as it contained all my notebooks, some stories I hadn't had the opportunity of filing, a new Hamilton wrist watch, my favorite snapshot of "Red," my wife, and a prized collection of articles like my short-snorter bill and my shellback certification for crossing the equator.

Mentally, I tabulated each of these items in a split second of time, but my body kept crawling away.

I was headed back toward the pier at this point but decided to turn again and make straight for the beach where I could see some tank traps about thirty-five yards off shore. On my left I still could hear that pleading call for a corpsman. I struck a soft body in the water.

About ten yards in front of these traps, pyramid-shaped concrete piles rising out of the water, was a string of barbed wire. I stood up-right and dove over into a pool of deeper water; then belly-flopped into the partial shelter of the trap. But here the snipers' fire was no less intense. A man behind the next trap exposed a shoulder and was shot, the bullet coming out through his chest. It was the marine who'd carried in the machine-gun tripod, the one I saw helping a buddy. The 55-pound tripod still was on his shoulder. He died there.

I told the men huddled behind the trap that I was going to make a dash for it. Lieutenant Fred Holmes said I'd better wait until I caught my breath but I lurched off and made the beach, falling twice, the last time in a pool in which I went completely under. The beach was strewn with dead marines. I picked my way between the bodies and threw myself down beside a battered amtrac which had upended it-self on the seawall the morning before in that initial and so futile attack.

I was dead beat. I never remember being so completely exhausted. All of us lay prone, as still as the dead men around us. Beside me was Mike Spear, a gunnery sergeant from Hammond, Indiana, I knew well. With his good hand—he'd been shot through the other arm—he offered me a cigarette. I hadn't the strength or the inclination to smoke it. I remember thinking that those certain cigarette ads always had sounded screwy anyway.

The snipers' bullets whirred overhead and every so often one clipped off a piece of palm frond.

One by one marines wove their way up from the water's edge to throw themselves under the partial protection of the seawall. Sev-eral times I watched one pick himself off the coral sand and run back into the water to help the wounded or the weak. I thought then what pure guts it takes to be brave when you're tired and miserable. Along with several others I finally began to wipe the coral grit from the mechanism of my carbine. I cleaned it as best I was able, carefully wiping each bullet in the magazines. Then I hitched my way atop the seawall behind a splintered piece of palm trunk.

I looked back at the stretch of hell those marines had come through. I tried to estimate how long we'd been in the water. I still don't know. I only know and always will remember how those marines kept going through that hail of fire to Betio.

It was a horrible Sunday scene . . . during the remainder of that first day . . . There were bodies everywhere; some, such as that of the marine inside the amphibious tractor by which I had first thrown myself, still held a spark of life. He had been shot in the back; had been there since the initial attack the day before. Three of us lifted him out onto an improvised poncho stretcher. Four others in the amtrac were dead. A box of cigars lay untouched amid the debris.

And so it was, up and down the beach—the bodies, the exhausted and wounded marines hugging the seawall, the cast-off equipment and the general rubbish. As the tide came in the remains of marines and Japs were mixed together in a giant potpourri of death.

The front line still was the beach, with all else a vast no-man's-land, the heaviest resistance concentrated in fortifications on the eastern extremity and a thick, deep vein of pillboxes toward the west. Snipers had the top of the seawall under fire all through the day and several men, one a doctor, were picked off around the first-aid station just to the right of the pier, supposedly one of the safer havens. Little posses were formed for sniper hunts from time to time. These were composed of remnants of the second and third battalions, Second Marines, and the second battalion, Eighth Marines, the units which finally had formed the D-Day initial assault wave. Also mixed in were the survivors of our own first battalion.

The bombing and the strafing never ceased. Plane after plane dumped its load and climbed into the sun. The island rocked. Still, the Jap machine guns chattered; their mortars thudded and their snipers chipped away the lives of our men.

As yet the deep-dug rifle barricades and pillboxes which bordered the seawall hadn't been cleaned out completely—and around noon I heard a faint mewing as if from a kitten. It came out of the sunken, covered pit behind which I had been crouched, peering for snipers. It was a wounded Jap and a Lieutenant Brooks put a slug into him twice before he died. Other Japs, several unmarked by bombing, barrage or bullet, were pried out of these covered entrenchments along the shore all Sunday, Monday and Tuesday.

Later . . . a regimental command post under Colonel Elmer E. Hall . . . was set up just off the beach to the right of the pier. There I caught a smattering of information as it drifted in and watched some semblance of order established under the snipers' fire. I have never seen a cooler officer in action than this tall, iron-grey former mining engineer. He sat there in the open on an ammunition case, listening attentively to the trickling reports and giving calm commands while the snipers wove a leaden canopy above his head . . .

Somehow, Sunday and Monday became telescoped together and are so fused in my mind as to be one long nightmare.

I dug a shallow foxhole behind a machine-gun outpost and rolled in. I remember a little white chicken with one wing blown off wobbling by just before my eyes closed shut. And I slept with the sand-crabs and through the Jap bombs which fell in the night from the bellies of their raiders.

I awoke to the shelling from our destroyers which were laying 'em in down at the eastern tip of Helen. Someone said some Japs had attempted to escape during darkness but that the tincan had stopped the bid cold. A Lieutenant Paul Hospodar . . . received permission from Colonel Hall to search for Jap papers and maps in the large pillbox next to the command post. Suddenly, we heard the muffled barks of his forty-five. There had been five Japs practically sleeping with us all night. One had bayoneted a trouser leg off Corporal Fred Mischuk . . . before Hospodar's bullet finished him.

About that time some of our shells hit the jackpot in the form of a Jap ammunition dump a couple of hundred yards to the east of the command post. It went off for almost an hour with the sound of Chinese firecrackers magnified a hundred or a thousand times. I watched from behind a bullet-riddled tank of some sort which sat at a crazy angle beside a huge crater. The administration building, or what was left of it, slumped on the edge of the airfield just thirty yards away and as I started over, ducking low for the snipers still were going strong, suddenly a pair of hamlike hands grabbed me.

It was Chaplain Willard. As he mauled me he gave out with a torrent of speech . . . "thought you dead sure . . . found helmet name Ward on it . . . sure figured you a goner . . ."

His boat, it seems, had been hung up on an outer reef and he had returned to the task force commodore to commandeer a ride in on an amtrac. Now he was off to bury the dead. And later in the day I saw him and his two assistants at their sad duties, exposed to a sniper's bullet that, at any moment, could have laid them in that same shallow grave on which they were laboring.

The stench along the beach and in the seawall barricades was awful. Yet, somehow, we managed to disregard the olfactory and visual assaults. The marines ate and slept amid it all; carried on and found the strength to fight. I ran into Sergeant Jim Lucas . . . and learned one of our mutual friends had been killed by a mortar shell. It didn't seem so very tragic then . . . the dead were too close around us. One young blond marine, only a few feet away, was draped over a United States-made cement mixer. He lay sprawled just as he had fallen on D-Day, his rifle at his side. Perhaps he had gone farther than any marine in that initial wave for he had died there almost on the edge of the airfield.

I wish I knew his name. But there was no identification and his dog tags were missing . . .

❈   ❈   ❈   ❈

WAR CORRESPONDENT ROBERT SHERROD OF TIME-
Life, who escaped from the Japanese at the onset of the war,
probably witnessed more invasions than most marines. He arrived at this one by way of transport *Zeilin,* and went ashore the
first day. His particular time in hell is magnificently detailed
in his best-selling *Tarawa, the Story of a Battle,* written during
the war years. Sherrod picks up the thread of bloody Betio on
the morning of the second day.

·5· SECOND AND THIRD DAYS

ROBERT SHERROD

1100: Finally at Colonel Shoup's headquarters. And what a headquarters! Fifteen yards inland from the beach, it is a hole dug in the
sand back of a huge pillbox that probably was some kind of Japanese
headquarters. The pillbox is forty feet long, eight feet wide, and ten
feet high. It is constructed of heavy coconut logs, six and eight inches
in diameter. The walls of the pillbox are two tiers of coconut logs,
about three feet apart. The logs are joined together by eight-inch
steel spikes, shaped like a block letter C. In between the two tiers of
logs are three feet of sand, and covering the whole pillbox several
more feet of sand are heaped. No wonder our bombs and shells hadn't
destroyed these pillboxes! Two-thousand-pound bombs hitting directly on them might have partially destroyed them, but bombing
is not that accurate—not even dive bombing—on as many pillboxes
as the Japs have on Betio. And when bombs hit beside such structures
they only throw up more sand on top of them.

Colonel Shoup is nervous. The telephone shakes in his hand. "We
are in a mighty tight spot," he is saying. Then he lays down the phone
and turns to me. "Division has just asked me whether we've got
enough troops to do the job. I told them no. They are sending the
Sixth Marines, who will start landing right away." Says a nearby officer: "That damned Sixth is cocky enough already. Now they'll come in
and claim they won the battle."

From his battalion commanders Colonel Shoup receives regular
telephone reports. One of them is now asking for air bombardment

on a Jap strongpoint on the other side of the airfield, which we can see a few hundred feet from regimental headquarters. "All right," says the colonel, putting down the telephone. "Air liaison officer!" he calls, "tell them to drop some bombs on the southwest edge of 229 and the southeast edge of 231. There's some Japs in there giving us hell." The numbers refer to the keyed blocks on the map of the island. It seems less than ten minutes before four dive bombers appear overhead, then scream toward the earth with their bombs, which explode gruffly: *ka-whump, ka-whump, ka-whump, ka-whump.* Even nearer than the bombs, destroyer shells in salvos of four are bursting within ten minutes after a naval liaison officer has sent directions by radio.

Next to regimental quarters rises a big, uncompleted barracks building, which withstood our bombing and shelling very well. There are only a few small holes in the roof and wooden sides of the building. Five-foot tiers of coconut logs surround the building, to protect it against shrapnel. I run the thirty feet from Colonel Shoup's command post eastward to the tier and leap over it. Some marines are in the unfloored building, lying on the ground, returning a Jap sniper's fire which comes from we know not where. Says a marine: "That goddamn smokeless powder they've got beats anything we ever had." Then I cross the interior of the building, go through a hole in the wall and sit down beside some marines who are in the alleyway between the wooden building and the tier of coconut logs.

"This gets monotonous," says a marine as a bullet whistles through the alley. We are comparatively safe, sitting here, because we are leaning against the inside of the log tier, and the vertical logs that act as braces are big enough for us to squeeze behind. The problem is to flatten one's legs against the ground so that they are not exposed to the sniper's fire.

1130: These marines are from H Company, the heavy-weapons company of the battalion I came with. "We've already had fifteen men killed, more in twenty-four hours than we had on Guadalcanal in six months," said the marine sitting next to me, "and I don't know how many wounded.

"We started in in one amphib, and it go so hot the driver drove off before he had unloaded all of us. Then the amphib sank—it had been hit—and another one picked us up and brought us ashore."

Where had they landed? "Right over there by that pillbox with the four Japs in it," he replies, pointing to the spot near which Bill Hipple and I had dug our foxhole. "You know who killed those Japs? Lieutenant Doyle of G Company did it—that's P. J. Doyle from Neola, Iowa—he just tossed a grenade in, then he jumped in with the Japs and shot them all with his carbine before they could shoot him."

By now it is fairly raining sniper bullets through our alley, as if the sniper is desperate because he isn't hitting anybody. The sniper is evidently a couple of hundred yards away, because there is a clear space that is far back from the open end of the alley. Japs can hide behind a coconut log without being seen all day, but nobody ever heard of one hiding behind a grain of sand.

A bullet ricochets off the side of the barracks building and hits the leg of the private who is second down the line. "I'm glad that one was spent," he says, picking up the .303 caliber copper bullet, which is bent near the end of the nose. I reach out for the bullet and he hands it to me. I drop it quickly because it is almost as hot as a live coal. The marines all laugh.

These marines calmly accept being shot at. They've grown used to it by now, and I suddenly realize that it is to me no longer the novelty it was. It seems quite comfortable here, just bulling. But I am careful to stay behind the upright coconut log which is my protection against the sniper.

Into the alleyway walks a marine who doesn't bother to seek the protection of the coconut logs. He is the dirtiest man I have seen on the island—men get dirty very quickly in battle, but this one has a good quarter inch of gray-black dust on his beardless face and his dungarees are caked. A lock of blond hair sticks out from under his helmet.

"Somebody gimme some cigarettes," he says. "That machine-gun crew is out there in a shellhole across the airfield and there's not a cigarette in the crowd." One of the marines throws him a pack of Camels.

The new arrival grins. "I just got me another sniper. That's six today, and me a cripple." I ask if he has been shot. "Hell, no," he says, "I busted my ankle stepping into a shellhole yesterday." His name? "Pfc. Adrian Strange." His home? "Knox City, Texas." Age? "Twenty."

Pfc. Adrian Strange stands for a few minutes, fully exposed to the sniper who has been pecking at us. Then the sniper opens up again, the bullets rattling against the coconut logs.

Pfc. Strange sings out, "Shoot me down, you son-of-a-bitch." Then he leisurely turns around and walks back across the airfield, carrying his carbine and the pack of cigarettes.

"That boy Strange," says the marine next to me, "he just don't give a damn."

1200: Colonel Shoup has good news. Major Ryan's shorthanded battalion has crossed the western end of the island (the bird's head), and the entire eight-hundred-yard beach up there is now ours. There are plenty of Japs just inside the beach, and the fortifications on the third of the island between Shoup's command post and Ryan's beach are very strong. And the entire south shore of the island, where there are even stronger pillboxes than there were on the north, remains to be cleaned out. That is the job of the Sixth Regiment, which will land this afternoon.

A young major comes up to the colonel in tears. "Colonel, my men can't advance. They are being held up by a machine gun." Shoup spits, "Goddlemighty, one machine gun."

1215: Here the marines have been sitting in back of this pillbox (Shoup's headquarters) for twenty-four hours. And a Jap just reached out from an air vent near the top and shot Corporal Oliver in the leg. In other words, there have been Japs within three feet—the thickness of the wall—of the Marines' island commander all that time. Three Japs had been killed in the pillbox yesterday, and we thought that was all there were.

There is very bad news about Lieutenant Hawkins. He may die from his three wounds. He didn't pay much attention to the shrapnel wound he got yesterday, but he has been shot twice this morning. He wouldn't be evacuated when he got a bullet through one shoulder. "I came here to kill Japs; I didn't come here to be evacuated," he said. But a while ago he got a bullet through the other shoulder, and lower down. He lost a lot of blood from both wounds.

Said the corporal who told me this, "I think the Scout and Sniper platoon has got more guts than anybody else on the island. We were out front and Morgan (Sergeant Francis P. Morgan of Salem, Oregon) was shot in the throat. He was bleeding like hell, and saying in a low voice, 'Help me, help me.' I had to turn my head."

Lieutenant Paine, who had been nicked in the rear as he stood talking to us—"I'll be damned. I stay out front four hours, then I come back to the command post and get shot"—has more news about Hawkins. "He is a madman," says Paine. "He cleaned out six machine-gun nests, with two to six Japs in each nest. I'll never forget the picture of him standing on that amphtrack, riding around with a million bullets a minute whistling by his ears, just shooting Japs. I never saw such a man in my life."

The young major whose men were held up by a single machine gun was back again. "Colonel, there are a thousand god-damn marines out there on that beach, and not one will follow me across to the air strip," he cries desperately. Colonel Jordon, who by this time was back at his old job as observer, our battalion having been merged with Major Wood Kyle's reinforcing first battalion, speaks up, "I had the same trouble. Most of them are brave men, but some are yellow." I recall something a very wise general once told me, "In any battle you'll find the fighting men up front. Then you'll find others who will linger behind, or find some excuse to come back. It has always been that way, and it always will. The hell of it is that in any battle you lose a high percentage of your best men."

Says Colonel Shoup, "You've got to say, 'Who'll follow me?' and if only ten follow you, that's the best you can do, but it's better than nothing."

1300: Now they are bringing up the dead for burial near the command post. There are seven laid out about ten yards from where I sit. They are covered with green and brown ponchos, only their feet sticking out. I think: what big feet most American soldiers and marines have! None of those looks smaller than a size eleven. The stench of the dead, as the burial detail brings them past and lines them up on the ground, is very heavy now.

Somebody brings in the story of a Jap sniper whose palm-tree roost was sprayed repeatedly. But he kept on firing, somehow. Finally, in disgust, a sergeant took a machine gun and fired it until he had cut the tree in two, near the top. The fall is supposed to have killed the Jap.

1430: Things look better now. The amphtracks—those that are left— are bringing stuff ashore and carrying the wounded regularly, and they get shot at only occasionally when they head back into the water. Major Ryan and his crowd are doing very well at the western end of the island, and the Sixth Marines are about to land there and start down the south shore. We've got another company of light tanks ashore, and they are going up as close as possible to the Jap pillboxes and firing high explosives into the slits. The improved situation is reflected in everyone's face around headquarters.

1600: Bill Hipple and I head east along the beach to Major Crowe's headquarters. By this time we are so confident that the battle is running in our favor that we do not even crouch down, as we walk four feet apart, one ahead of another. After we cross the base of the pier the inevitable sniper's bullet sings by. "Jesus," says Hipple, "do you know that damned bullet went between us?" We crouch down under the protection of the seawall during the rest of the journey.

That tough, old-time marine, Jim Crowe, is having a tough time yet, but he is still as cool as icebox lettuce. "We kill 'em and more come filtering up from the tail of the island," he says. I ask him about his casualties. "Already had about three hundred in my battalion," he says.

A young tank officer, Lieutenant L. E. Larbey, reports to the major as we are talking to him. "I just killed a marine, Major Crowe," he says bitterly. "Fragments from my 75 splintered against a tree and ricochetted off. God damn, I hated for that to happen."

"Too bad," mutters Crowe, "but it sometimes happens. Fortunes of war."

The heavy tanks are being used against the pillboxes. They have tried crushing them, but even a thirty-two-ton tank is not very effective against these fortifications. "We got a prisoner last night," said Crowe, "and we have four more, temporarily, sealed up in a pillbox. I suppose they'll kill themselves before we get 'em out."

The strafing planes are coming overhead in waves now and the grease-popping sound of their guns is long and steady. "Don't know how much good they do," says Crowe, "but we know their bullets will kill men if they hit anything. One fifty-caliber slug hit one of my men—went through his shoulder, on down through his lung and liver. He lived about four minutes. Well, anyway, if a Jap ever sticks his head out of his pillbox the planes may kill him."

1630: Crowe is talking on the phone, apparently to Colonel Shoup: "I suggest we hold a line across from the Burns-Philp pier tonight." That means his men have advanced about two hundred yards to the east, toward the tall of the island, and he believes they can hold a line all the way across the island, which is about six hundred yards at that point. Meantime, my old battalion, plus the reinforcements, are cleaning out the center of the island, Major Ryan's battalion is holding the western end, and a battalion of the Sixth Marines is landing to start down the southern shore (the Betio bird's back). We can see the light now. We are winning, but we've still got to dig out every last Jap from every last pillbox, and that will cost us a lot of marines. I reflect: isn't that true of our whole war against the Japs? They haven't got a chance and they know it, unless we get fainthearted and agree to some kind of peace with them. But, in an effort to make us grow sick of our losses, they will hang on under their fortifications, like so many bedbugs. They don't care how many men *they* lose—human life being a minor consideration to them. The Japs' only chance is our getting soft, as they predicated their whole war on our being too luxury-loving to fight.

Of this much I am certain: the Marines are not too soft to fight. More than three thousand of them are by this time assaulting pillboxes full of the loathsome bugs, digging them out.

1700: Hipple and I are surprised to see two more correspondents— we had long since decided that none others were alive. But Dick Johnston, a young, pencil-thin U.P. man, and Frank ("Fearless") Filan, A.P. photographer, had also managed to land with the assault waves. "Filan, here," says Johnston, "is a hero. The marine next to him was shot as they waded in. Filan started helping him back to the boat. But then a sniper opened up on the boat from the side. The marine beat Filan to the shore. And Filan ruined all his cameras and equipment helping the marine." The two correspondents report that at least one more correspondent arrived this morning. Don Senick, the newsreelman. "His boat was turned back yesterday," says Johnston, "but they got ashore this morning. Senick ought to get the Purple Heart. He was sitting under a coconut tree. A bullet hit above his head and dropped on his leg. It bruised him."

Lieutenant Larbey sits down beside us. "Were you ever inside a tank when it got hit?" he asks. "The spot inside the tank where the shell hits turns a bright yellow, like a sunrise. My tank got two hits a while ago." Larbey walks back to his iron horse. Says Johnston, "That guy is a genius at keeping his tanks running. He repairs the guns, refuels them somehow, and reloads them with ammunition."

A tall, grinning marine is here at headquarters getting ammunition. He has a bandage on his arm, and a casualty tag around his neck like those the corpsmen put on every man they treat—in case he collapses later from his wound.

"Get shot in the arm?" asks Jim Crowe.

"Yes, sir," says Morgan.

"What'd you do, stick your arm out of a foxhole, eh?"

"No, sir, I was walking alongside a tank." And Morgan goes on about his business, gathering ammunition. Crowe looks looks up at the sky, which is full of planes. "Look at them god-damn strafing planes. They haven't killed fifty Japs in two days," he growls.

A grimy marine seated alongside us muses: "I wonder what our transport did with those sixteen hundred half pints of ice cream that was to be sent ashore yesterday after the battle was over."

An officer comes in and reports to Major Crowe that a sniper is raising hell with the people working on supplies at the end of the pier. By this time we are stacking great piles of supplies on the end of the pier. The officer thinks the fire is coming, not from the beach, but from a light tank that is half sunk in the water. It is the same tank that I saw the naked figure dive into as I came ashore. These devilish Japs!

A destroyer standing so close to shore that it must be scraping bottom has been ordered to fire at a big concrete blockhouse a couple of hundred yards away from us. First, it fires single rounds—five or six of them. Then, when the range is found, it opens up with four guns at a time and to us it seems that all bedlam has broken loose. After about eighty rounds it stops. "They never hit it squarely," says Major Crowe, "but almost."

1803: Now, at three minutes past six, the first two American jeeps roll down the pier, towing 37-mm. guns. "If a sign of certain victory were needed," I note, "this is it. The jeeps have arrived."

1900: Back at regimental headquarters, Colonel Shoup wipes his red forehead with his grimy sleeve and says, "Well, I think we are winning, but the bastards have got a lot of bullets left." I ask him how much longer it would last. "I believe we'll clean up the entire western end of the island tomorrow, maybe more. It will take a day or two more to root them all out of the tail end of the island."

A surgeon grunts and rises from where he has been working feverishly over a dozen wounded marines who lie on the beach. His blood-plasma containers hang from a line strung between a pole and a bayoneted rifle stuck upright into the ground. Four deathly pale marines are receiving the plasma through tubes in their arms. "These four will be all right," the doctor thinks, "but there are a lot more up the beach that we probably can't save." He continues, "This battle has been hell on the medical profession. I've got only three doctors out of the whole regiment. The rest are casualties, or they have been lost or isolated. By now nearly all the corpsmen have been shot, it seems to me."

Lieutenant Colonel Presley M. Rixey, a blue-eyed, mustachioed Virginian who commands the artillery attached to Colonel Shoup's regimental combat team, is the first man I have heard pick the turning point of the battle, "I thought up until one o'clock today it was touch and go. Then I knew we would win. It's not over yet, but we've got 'em." Supplies are beginning to flow over the pier in quantity now. The last of Colonel Rixey's 37's and 75's are being landed, "at long last," he says.

"You know what," says Colonel Rixey, "I'll bet these are the heaviest casualties in Marine Corps history. I believe we're already lost more than ten percent of the division and we haven't landed all of it." Until now I haven't considered Tarawa in the light of history. It has only seemed like a brawl—which it is—that we might easily have lost, but for the superb courage of the Marines. But, I conclude, Colonel Rixey may have something there. Maybe this is history.

1930: Hipple and I begin digging our foxhole for the night—this time a hundred yards further up the beach, next to Amphtrack No. 10. "This one came in on the first wave," says a nearby marine, "there were twenty men in it, and all but three of them were killed."

As we dig deeper, the smell from our foxhole becomes oppressive. "Not all the Japs used those privies over the water," I commented. Hipple has finished digging with the shovel, and now he begins smoothing the foxhole with his hands—all foxholes should be finished by hand. The smell is so oppressive we throw a few shovelfuls of sand back into the hole to cover at least some of the odor.

Then we lie down to sleep. It has been more than sixty hours since we closed our eyes and the danger of a night attack has been all but eliminated, so we sleep soundly.

2400: We are rudely awakened after three hours' sleep. The tide has come up and flooded our foxhole. This is unusual, because the tide has not been this high since we reached the island. We sit on a bank of sand, wide-awake and knowing that there will be no more sleep tonight. Besides, Washing Machine Charley will be due soon and nobody can sleep while being bombed.

0500: Washing Machine Charley was over at four o'clock. He dropped eight bombs in his two runs over the island. Said Keith Wheeler, later, "He was absolutely impartial; he dropped half his bombs on us and half on the Japs." Water or no water, we lay face down in our foxhole as he came over. As the bombs hit, there was a blinding flash a couple of hundred yards up the beach, to the west. A few minutes later a marine came running up the beach, shouting, "There are a lot of men hurt bad up here. Where are the corpsmen and the stretchers?" He was directed to a pile of stretchers nearby. Soon the stretcher bearers returned, silhouetted by the bright half-moon as they walked along the beach. Washing Machine Charley had killed one man, had wounded seven or eight.

0530: At first light, Bill Hipple looks at what had been our foxhole. Then he learns that the odor was caused, not by Jap excrement, but by the body of a dead man who had been buried beside the foxhole. Bill had been clawing the face of a dead man as he put the finishing touches on the foxhole . . .

. . . Our line across the island had held during the night, preventing any fresh Japs from filtering toward the scenes of the toughest fighting. On the third day the question was not, "How long will it take to kill them all?" but, "How few men can we expect to lose before killing the rest of the Japs?"

But probably the biggest factor on the third day was Major William Jones' first battalion of the Sixth Marines, who jumped off at dawn from their landing point on the southwestern tip of the island and marched straight up the beach that is the Betio bird's back. The Sixth took heavy casualties—the fortifications on this south beach were even stronger than those on the lagoon side of the island—but they swung ahead quickly and violently, like men who are anxious to get it over with. Lieutenant Colonel McLeod's third battalion of the Sixth landed on the western beach in the early morning and marched through Major Ryan's depleted forces, cleaning out huge fortifications as they went along, walking beside medium tanks which bored into the fading Japs.

Commented Lieutenant Colonel Evans Carlson in midmorning, "These marines are in the groove today." Lieutenant Colonel Jordan, who had been distressed earlier because some of the marines hung back on the beaches, was proud of these same men today. "Tell you something interesting. Once we got those men off the beaches and up front, they were good. They waded into the Japs and proved they could fight just as well as anybody."

During the day I saw the first five of many Japs I saw who committed suicide rather than fight to the end. In one hole, under a pile of rubble, supported by a tin roof, four of them had removed the split-toed, rubber-soled jungle shoes from their right feet, had placed the barrels of their .303 rifles against their foreheads, then had pulled the triggers with their big toes. The other had chosen the same method some five hundred Japs chose on Attu: holding a hand grenade against his chest, thus blowing out the chest and blowing off the right hand. From the time he was a baby the Jap had been told that he was superior to the white man, and all he had to do to win was to fight aggressively. When he found that this was not true, and the white man could fight aggressively, too, he became frustrated. He had never been taught to improvise and his reflexes were hopelessly slow; if his plan of battle failed, as the Jap plan on Tarawa failed when the first marines made the shore, he was likely, under pressure, to commit suicide. He didn't know what else to do.

This is the way I recorded what I saw on Betio the third day:

0600: The destroyers opened up on the tail end of the island from very close range. Their targets are immense concrete blockhouses, which they are determined to penetrate if it takes dozens of five-inch rounds in the same precise spot on the wall. It is reported that three hundred Japs are in one of these blockhouses. The 75 howitzers, firing rapidly, are concentrating on the same area and the noise is greater than it has been before. The captain of A Battery is reported dead—shot through the head by a sniper.

Two dead Japs in a crater just behind our last night's foxholes have been discovered wearing Marine helmets, jungle dungarees and boondockers.

A corpsman comes by and sits down to chat. He found a dead marine under the edge of the pier, in a position where he might not have been discovered for days. From the dead marine's pack the corpsman had taken two cans of corned beef, two wet packs of Lucky Strikes, a soaked wallet containing a letter and some airmail stamps and an identification card: "William F. Pasco . . . born March, 1923." The corpsman knows he shouldn't have removed a dead man's identification—because of the confusion that might result if the corpsman himself is killed or wounded later—but like so many well-meaning soldiers and marines . . . "I thought I'd send the stuff home to his folks."

0630: Now the destroyers have let up momentarily and the dive bombers and strafing fighters are vying with each other to see who can tear up the tail end of the island. This goes on unceasingly for a half hour, with probably more than two hundred planes taking part. The isolated Japs on the end of the island must know that our determination to take Betio has not weakened. By now our own troops are dispersed so widely over the island that the bombers concentrate only on the tail-end third. When the planes have finished, the destroyers and artillery open up more furiously than ever. Sometimes the whole island shakes until it seems ready to disappear into the ocean—as the battleship gunnery officers threatened it would. But we doubt that it will.

0700: Here, a hundred yards inland from the beach, is the type of fortification that has withstood this awful pounding for two days, and it is no wonder! Double thicknesses of eight-inch-thick coconut logs, hooked together with steel spikes, buttressed by upright logs driven far into the ground, covered by three feet of shrapnel-absorbing sand. The pillbox cannot be built altogether underground because water lies only four to six feet under the surface on Betio, so it is half underground and half above ground. Dick Johnston, the U.P. correspondent, marvels at the almost impregnable construction when a Marine engineer comes along and says, "You've got to give them credit. They've got a good engineer somewhere in this Jap Navy." At the sunken entrance to the pillbox two marines are warming a can of C ration on a folding field stove over a Sterno flame. We put a can of the C ration—vegetable and beef hash—over the flame and eat a heavy breakfast of our own. For the first time it occurs to me that I haven't eaten in two days.

Nearby there is a chicken yard containing about twenty chickens, including two dead ones, and a coop inhabited by two small black and white ducks. Although the area is still under sniper fire a boyish marine chases an escaped chicken, then dives heartily after the bird, but misses. The two marines eating with us guffaw. Says one, "I almost opened up on a pig last night."

Johnston is tempted to take a flashlight, go into one of the pillboxes to hunt souvenirs. But the smell at the entrance is so oppressive he is easily dissuaded. Some marines tell us that there are twelve dead Japs inside. An apocryphal story going the rounds concerns the marine who had thrown several charges of TNT into a pillbox, but could still hear one Jap moving around. The marines is supposed to have yelled, "Come on out and surrender, you Jap bastard!" And the Jap allegedly answered, "Go to hell, you souvenir-hunting Yankee son-of-a-bitch!"

0730: Back at Colonel Shoup's headquarters, his redheaded operations officer, Major Tom Culhane, croaks happily, "We got 'em by the eyeballs now!" Major Culhane has shouted orders over the telephone, above the dine of battle, for nearly forty-eight hours, until he sounds like Mr. Wendell Willkie shortly after he opened his 1940 presidential campaign. Somebody asked the major whether he thought his voice would last until the battle ended. He answered, "I didn't think so last night, but we are going so fast now I believe I'll finish in a whisper."

There is good news, too, about Major Rice and the rest of the battalion staff I last saw as we started ashore. Major Rice's amphtrack landed far up the beach and his men have been fighting with Major Ryan's heroic piece of a battalion. Rice himself has maintained communications for Ryan.

The single saddest tragedy on Betio is reported—not that one American's death is sadder than any other, but because we thought for a while this death might have been averted—Lieutenant Hawkins, the nonpareil Texan, died during the night. One of the high-ranking officers comments in a low voice, "It's not often that you can credit a first lieutenant with winning a battle, but Hawkins came as near to it as any man could. He was truly an inspiration."

Several officers sit under a palm tree. They have watched the battle from its dark beginning to its present bright hopes of an early end. Says Colonel Carlson, the old Marine Raider, "Did you see three-eight (third battalion Eighth Marines) and one-eight wading in? They were mowed down like flies. I believe one-eight had a hundred casualties in less than a minute."

Said Colonel Edson, the hero of Guadalcanal, "This is the first beachhead they have really defended. They had no choice but to defend here—they had no interior position to retreat to; it was all exterior. Anyway," he smiles, "it won't last as long as Guadalcanal."

Captain "Frenchy" Moore, the Navy doctor who is division surgeon, shakes his head. "I was on Guadalcanal. And it was duck soup."

One of the officers off a transport comments, "I was at the Sicily landing. It was a pink-tea party, with ninety percent girls and ten percent boys."

Carlson: "This was not only worse than Guadalcanal. It was the damnedest fight I've seen in thirty years of this business."

It occurs to me that perhaps this Tarawa battle is going to be history, after all.

0800: Dr. Moore reports that six hundred wounded had been evacuated to the ships by last night, including four wounded who were floated out of a disabled tank lighter through a hole in its side. Up to now thirty-six have been buried at sea from the ships.

Preparations are being made for burying our own nearby dead, many of whom have been in the water for two days. It is a gruesome sight, even to men who have become hardened to anything, including the past two days' omnipresent sight and smell of death. Thirty-one marines are now laid out in a line beyond the command post. Some are bloated, some have already turned a sickly green. Some have no faces, one's guts are hanging out of his body. The eyeballs of another have turned to a jellied mass, after so long a time in the water.

The corpsmen and burial parties continue to bring in the dead from the coral flats, now that those flats are subject to but little sniper fire. One dead American wears a soggy, blue, kapok life preserver—he probably cussed because all the rubber, inflating-type, life preservers had been passed out before his turn came. Here come four more waterlogged, lifeless bodies. All of them wear knives which they never got to use.

The bulldozer scoops a long trench, three feet deep. Its Seabee driver pays scant attention to the sniper who fires at him occasionally. The bodies, not even covered by a blanket or poncho, are brought over and placed in the trench, side by side, while Chaplains MacQueen and Kelly supervise their identification and last rites. This is no dignified burial—a man's last ceremony should be dignified, but this isn't. The bulldozer pushes some more dirt in the marines' faces and that is all there is to it. Then the bulldozer starts digging a second trench.

Lines of corpsmen are bringing in the bodies as fast as they can find stretchers and wade into the shallow water. One marine is brought in who has suffered the greatest indignity of all. His head has been blown off completely. His left arm is gone, and only a few shreds of skin hang from his shoulders. I thought I had become inured to anything, but I am nauseated by this sight. I turn to the big red-bearded Marine gunner who is standing beside me and say, "What a hell of a way to die!" The gunner looks me in the eye and says, "You can't pick a better way."

1000: For the first time a good view of the battle is available. There is a five-foot-high lumber pile beyond the incompleted barracks building. It is possible to stand behind this lumber and watch the battle that is being waged across the airfield and to the eastward—by now bombs and artillery and naval gunfire and mortars have sheared the fronds off most of the coconut palms, and Betio is nearly bare except for the stumps of the trees.

To the awful symphony of the big guns is added the crackling rifle fire of hundreds of marines and several pillboxes full of well-hidden Japs. Marines dart across the expanse of the airfield while machine guns and snipers' rifles kick up dust around them. They dodge from shellhole to shellhole as they advance toward the enemy. One marine is wounded but drags himself the remaining ten feet to a shellhole, where eager hands pull him out of further danger. On the other side of the runway a medium tank, looking like a great, clumsy bug, lumbers up to a pillbox and begins blasting away, from less than fifty feet, round after round of 75-mm. shells. A Jap, naked except for his white cloth G-string, runs out of the pillbox and throws himself under the tread of the tank. There is a small explosion as the Jap's hand grenade goes off, but his suicide nets him nothing except his idea of a warrior's heaven. The grenade does not even blow the tank's tread off. The tank lumbers over the Jap, still firing. Further down the field, marines carrying mortar containers and boxes of ammunition walk across the open area. There are three of them. They do not even bother to try to run, though bullets spitting into the dust of the runway down this way plainly demonstrate that they are being fired at.

One of the destroyer shells finds a hitherto undiscovered oil dump in the middle of the island and the flames reach up very high. The destroyer gloatingly increases its firing until an area more than a hundred feet square is a roaring mass of flame and smoke. The island thumps and quivers, and flame and dust and curtains of smoke blend into the medley of unearthly noise.

1030: A dozen of us are standing around, or leaning against the big pillbox that protects Colonel Shoup's headquarters from frontal fire. All of a sudden a sniper who has apparently worked his way around to the side opens up. The bullets whiz through the command post, past the new ammunition dump we have started. Marines who are working on the dump start running. All of us at headquarters hit the dirt. All except rocklike Dave Shoup. He stands, fully exposed, arms akimbo, and bellows, "Stop! God damn it! What are you running for? Take cover, then move on up and kill the bastard." The marines sheepishly work themselves back westward. One who was hit on the side of the face by a bullet is bandaged and led off.

Five prisoners, naked except for their split-toed shoes, are marched into headquarters by Captain John T. O'Neill of Somerville, Massachusetts, and two enlisted men armed with tommy guns. The prisoners sit around a coconut palm on their haunches, looking up and frowning curiously as if they wonder what on earth will happen to them. They are short, but well-muscled and apparently well-fed. Only one has been wounded: his left hand is bandaged. An intelligence officer questions them briefly in Japanese, then Colonel Shoup orders them sent out to the ship which is receiving prisoners. "Korean laborers," says the intelligence officer. "They are mighty glad to get captured." A few minutes later another prisoner is led in, but this one, also a husky Korean, has been allowed to retain his short, civilian-gray pants. He wears a bandage on his neck, another on his arm. He tells the intelligence officer he had arrived on Betio only a few days ago—he had been cutting coconut logs on another island further up the atoll; these logs were shipped down to Betio, whose concealing foliage had been only slightly disturbed until the American battle-ships started working on it—D Day.

1130: Back of the incompleted barracks building is a big tinsmith shop. The sheets of tin and galvanized iron tell us that the Japs had plans to continue building up Betio. Many of the sheets are just so much twisted and perforated metal, but some are still serviceable. Of them the marines build shelter from the noonday equatorial sun. Beside the mass of tin there is a big pile of twisted steel pipe. Marines who are bringing in more guns have trouble wheeling the 37's over it. Some of the marines have already collected the long .303 Jap rifles. The newer rifles have a straight-shanked bayonet instead of the bay-onet with the half loop at the hilt (for catching the enemy's bayonet and twisting his gun of his hand). Japs on Attu and Guadalcanal had bayonets with loops at the hilt.

Along this area atop the seawall there are half-sunken machine-gun emplacements every five yards. These little coconut-log fortresses are shaped like a Y with the top half-closed, covered with sand which is covered by palm fronds. To look at row upon row of these pillboxes facing the sea, it seems impossible that the marines ever got ashore D Day. But, in one of them, somewhat larger than most along here, I think I find the answer. Inside the pillbox there are four dead Japs and two dead marines. Enough of those men in the first wave got ashore, jumped in with the Japs and killed them. Thus they knocked out enough machine guns so that others in later waves might live and win. Looking down on these two marines, I can say, "These men gave their lives for me. I can understand it, because this machine gun cov-ered the part of the water I had to wade through. They also gave their lives for one hundred and thirty million other Americans who realize it, I fear, only dimly." My feeling is one of deep humility and of re-spect for such brave men—God rest their souls. How much every man in battle owes to every other man! How easy to see on the bat-tlefield that we are all in this thing together!

1200: The pillbox which contained the four Japs Lieutenant Doyle killed has been cleaned out. It is now a communication center, and a switchboard is functioning inside it. Lieutenant Charlie Lowry of Valdosta, Georgia, who has an 81-mm. mortar platoon, has stopped inside the log-barricaded entrance. "I've lost about a fourth of my men," he says. "That's just the number of casualties we've had," says George T. Olson of Jackson, Mississippi, staff sergeant of the regi-mental communicators. "Ten out of forty."

There is still some sniping, and a bullet whizzes overhead now and then. After one furious burst, Sergeant Olson says, "It doesn't do much good to duck unless you're in direct line of fire. You might duck the wrong way and get a stray bullet anyhow."

"You sure can tell the difference between new men and those who have been through it before," Olson continues. "One kid was shaking all over this morning because he had to cross the air strip. I didn't send him. But two of my men have been walking through the line of fire all day. They don't seem to mind it." Across the strip we could see from this rear entrance to the pillbox four ammunition carriers calmy walking along, as if they were strolling through Central Park, completely unmindful of a dozen popping machine guns, the crash of artillery and naval gunfire, and the pall of smoke and fire.

"This morning some of the natives were brought over from one of the other islands," says the sergeant. "They said the Japs had told their men a million Americans couldn't take Tarawa. I guess we are doing all right."

1230: In a shellhole with two marines. Sniper fire is still rather severe—sometimes we surround a sniper, pass him, and assume somebody has killed him when all of a sudden he lets go a flock of bullets. Then we cannot find him under his log or in his hole. One is shooting at something beyond us, and his soprano bullets sing over our heads. Says one grinning marine, "I have only one regret—that John L. Lewis is not beside me." Says the other, "He wouldn't be alive if he was beside me. I don't mean the Japs would kill him. I would."

I had noticed this savage attitude toward labor grow steadily for a long time. It was particularly obvious during the bitter battle of Attu, which was fought during a coal strike. The man who is risking his life rarely stops to consider that there may be justice on the side of the striker, if such a thing is possible in wartime, or that other interests greedily force the laborer's cost of living toward an inflationary point. He simply figures that (1) a soldier gets fifty dollars a month for leading the most dangerous, most miserable life this side of hell, and (2) the laborer living in the faraway dream-world of the United States should be willing to forego a few extra cents an hour if it will help get material to the soldier to help him win the war. Only a man who has been on a battlefield can realize how wide is the maw of war. The amount of material required to fight a battle is probably beyond the civilian conception, the soldier figures. When the soldier sees how small a dent he and his comrades have made against the Japanese, and how much more material is necessary to win the Pacific war, he goes red-eyed at the mention of a strike. Oddly, the soldiers bitterest against labor are often labor-union members themselves.

To the soldier this is all a part of the gap between civilian conception of war and the realities of war—something the soldier himself does not bridge until he has been in a bloody, stinking, unromantic battle. He is likely to grow angry at the Army and Navy publicity men who are forever telling the folks back home how well Joe is treated. He gets mad at the "goddamn U.S.O. soldiers" who are stationed safely in the United States. He often scorns the newspapers and radio, particularly those "rear-area people" who rewrite and pump up the drily factual communique until it reads pretty and sparkles optimistically and sells more copies of the evening newspaper. The soldier wants the people back home to know that "we don't knock hell out of 'em" every day of every battle. He wants the people to understand that war is tough and war is horrible. He thinks labor's tendency to strike is a part of this misconception on the part of his own people at home—surely, no sane man would dream of striking against his own soldiers if he understood what war was like. I often speculate on whether or not labor did not set itself back ten hard-won years in the last ten giddy months of 1943, because I know labor will have one day to account to some ten million angry men—minus those killed in action fighting labor's war.

1300: I haven't seen a man killed today.

1330: Back of the seawall, fifty yards farther westward than I have ventured previously, nine dead marines have been gathered from the interior of the island and placed in a row. Some are covered with ponchos, some with a convenient palm frond. Nearby there is a cheap, cardboard Japanese suitcase, it contents scattered. All the Jap civilian's underclothing and shirts are silk. The shirt may have been captured. It is marked: "British produce—M. K. Mills. Size 36." Nearby there are thirteen dead Jap soldiers, dressed in the green wool Navy Landing Force uniform and wrap-around leggings such as U.S. soldiers wore uncomfortably in World War I. Burial parties are beginning to bury the Japs a little farther inland, because the smell of dead is becoming overpowering after three days. If any sign were needed that victory is ours, this is it: we have started burying the Japs.

A light tank stops at a fuel dump and four grimy, black-faced marines hop out. The tank gunner is an Iowa farm boy named Lowell Richman. I ask him how many Japs he has killed today and he gives the modest marine's answer, "I don't know." His pal says, "He's killed plenty. We are really knocking them off now." Says Richman, "We get 'em mostly by running up to the hole of the pillbox and dropping in some high explosive. If they run out we empty the canister into them."

A hundred yards farther up the beach I run into a conversation which has material in it for a sermon. Two marines from the Third Battalion, Second Regiment, evidently old friends, are standing behind the seawall—there is considerable sniper fire hereabouts. One marine is from Brooklyn, he tells me. He is fed up with the war. "I want to get back home now," he says. "I want to quit the Marines next year when I am nineteen—my four years will be up. I joined up because I didn't know any better and I stayed in because of patriotism— I got malaria at Guadalcanal and I could have gone home. But now I want to go stateside." His companion, another Iowa farm boy—he had married a New Zealand girl—attempted to quiet his friend, "Hell, if you don't stay out here and get shot at, somebody else will have to come out here and get shot at. Somebody's got to win the war. I could have gone back—I had malaria, too. But now I don't want to go back till it's over. You're not fighting just for yourself; you're fighting for the whole United States."

1400: It is quiet around this pillbox, although there is some fire two hundred yards ahead. Six medical corpsmen and a doctor use this pillbox for collecting the wounded, but they have not been busy this afternoon—not nearly as busy as when they arrived yesterday. One of them tells of a marine from Utica, New York. He was wounded on D Day, shrapnel in his head, arms, and legs, as the amphtrack approached the shore. "Everybody in the amphtrack was killed except him and his buddy," say a corpsman, "and his buddy lasted only one day. Then he spent two and a half days in that amphtrack in the broiling sun. His eyes were clotted over, his throat scratched inside like a piece of tin. He tried to commit suicide last night, he was in such agony, but he was too weak to pull the trigger. When we got to him he just said, 'Pour some water over my face, will you?' Plasma picked him up, and he's going to be all right, we think."

Said another corpsman, "These marines don't complain when they are wounded. I certainly have got a lot of respect for them. I guess they must be the best fighting men in the world."

Outside, there was some discussion as to whether a dead man was a Jap or a marine. He had been badly mutilated by shrapnel, and his body had turned a dark green. Most of his face had been blown off. He looked Japanese, but he wore Marine Corps outer clothing, "civvies" instead of the Jap G-string, and he had a lot of hair on his chest. Finally, the burial detail found his name on the inside of his belt, and took him away to be buried with the Americans.

The Japs around this pillbox, in this big hole, are bigger than any I have seen; three of the four are six feet tall and they are all heavy, even before bloating. The three dead marines, who apparently had knocked out the pillbox and its machine gun, are about the same size. The sun has raised blisters as big as half dollars on the skin of brown men and white men alike.

Best unofficial estimate of our casualties: six hundred dead, twelve hundred wounded.

1500: Two concrete mixers evidence further the Japs' intention of holding Tarawa. Here is what looks like a fence made of steel grating, six feet high, surrounding a squared area on a concrete base. The Japs had got as far as installing the reinforcing steel, but they had not poured the concrete walls when we arrived. Here is a concrete bomb shelter, about twenty by thirty feet. Marines say there is a dead Jap officer inside. He apparently had been wounded two days ago, had crawled inside to die. They drag him out and search the tomb-like structure, finding boxes full of what appear to be payroll books and war-saving stamps. The walls of this shelter, which have barely been nicked by bombs and shells, measure fifty-five inches thick.

1530: From behind the bomb shelter we can see a half-track fifty yards ahead working on a Jap pillbox. The marines pour round after round of 75-mm. shells into the entrance of the pillbox. Five or six Japs run out, straight into the withering heat of a flamethrower that is waiting for them.

These marines are from the first battalion of the Eighth, which took such heavy casualties in the water yesterday morning. Pfc. James Collins of Spartanburg, South Carolina, recalls, "The water was red with blood. All around me men were screaming and moaning. I never prayed so hard in all my life. Only three men out of twenty-four in my boat ever got ashore that I know of." Collins carried one wounded man back to the Higgins boat. Then he started back with another, a corpsman who had been hit in the shoulder. On the way the corpsman was hit again, half his head blown off while Collins held him in his arms. A preliminary check shows that B Company got ninety men ashore out of 199. Pfc. William Coady of Minersville, Pennsylvania, says he carried ten wounded men back to the Higgins boat before he finally made shore. A marine from the regimental weapons platoon says his outfit didn't fare so badly—only one man had been killed and two wounded out of thirty-six.

1730: Major General Julian Smith has arrived from the battleship on which he maintained headquarters with Admiral Hill—but, even on the third day, the Japs kept a sharp lookout for new arrivals. The general's amphtrack, which also contained two brigadier generals, was fired upon as it rounded the west end of the island, and its driver was wounded. Rumors, later proved exaggerated, are prevalent, even at headquarters. One officer reports that only 140 men remain out of the first and second battalions of the Eighth Marines, and that more than fifty percent of the officers have been killed or wounded out of the six assaulting battalions which faced enemy fire as they came in.

1800: By now all the war correspondents are accounted for. Keith Wheeler of the Chicago *Times* and John Henry of I.N.S. reached headquarters today after landing yesterday to the west, their amph-track having been turned back the first day, causing them to spend a night bobbing around in the lagoon. It is a miracle that none of the civilian correspondents was killed—they are the only "unit" which has suffered no casualties. Not one of the newsmen who accompanied the assault battalions as they waded ashore failed to see men killed around him. It is comforting to know that they all came through Tarawa, the toughest of them all, because in two years I have lost friends and colleagues all the way from New Guinea and Australia to Berlin.

But few war correspondents have experienced the horror which Gil Bundy, the artist, went through on his first assignment. He got into a landing boat with some of the regimental command on D Day. Bundy's boat received a direct hit about seventy-five yards from shore, probably from a Jap 90-mm. mortar. All others in it were killed or blown out of the boat, but Bundy miraculously was unharmed. That was only the beginning of his troubles. He jumped from his disabled boat, intending to swim to another boat. But a swift current carried him several hundred yards out to sea. Finally, he managed to pull up panting to another disabled boat. Several dead men were in it, but by then it was dark and Bundy had no choice but to spend the night with the dead marines. Early on the morning of the second day a boat which was returning from the beach stopped by Bundy's morgue. Captain Harry Lawrence of Albany, Georgia, the officer in charge of the amphtrack company, almost shot Bundy for a Jap—during the night Japs had swum out and manned some of the amphtracks. Bundy, rescued, was taken back to a transport. Until today we had assumed that Bundy had been killed. His identification papers had been found in his original boat, and several marines had reported having seen his lifeless body, as men in battle often report things they are ninety percent certain of.

1830: Two-thirds of the island's area is now ours. Lieutenant Commander Fabian, the beachmaster charged with unloading the hundreds of tons of supplies now pouring over the pier, says, yes, he thinks he knows the quickest way to get to a nearby ship which might lend the reporters typewriters. Wading through enemy fire carrying a typewriter is not standard procedure for war correspondents, who are usually dependent on the Navy for the loan of materials. Mr. Fabian introduces me and Dick Johnston and Keith Wheeler to a transport skipper, Captain Claton McLaughlin, who says, "Sure, come with me. I'm just returning to my ship."

The ship is a new AK—part transport, part cargo ship. The ship's crew is anxious for news of the battle. They grin when they hear that the last round is beginning. Says a sailor, "I'd have given anything in the world if I could have been over there on land to help out." The young junior-grade lieutenant who is the ship's supply officer opens up his ship's store to procure razors, tooth brushes, and soap. He will not accept pay—one of the correspondents had somehow retained some money. "It's the first time I've had a chance to do anything, and the battle only two thousand yards away," he says, bitterly. In the wardroom the hovering Negro mess steward brings in extra, afterhours helpings of ham and iced tea and coffee. The captain turns over his quarters to the correspondents, including a blessed freshwater shower bath (but it will take many baths to purge the grime of Betio from the skin pores). The yeoman in the ship's office finds typewriters and onion-skin paper which is necessary to take the many carbon copies the rules say a correspondent must turn in.

This desire to lend a helping hand is one of the most touching things in and around a battle, where every man wants to help every other man. I have seen men, when asked for a cigarette, feel the inside of the pack, find only one left. They bulge out the pack, proffer the last cigarette, then pocket the empty pack so the other man will not know that he is accepting the last one. On Betio the drinking water is almost undrinkable—the five-gallon cans had been filled in New Zealand many weeks before and the heat of the South Pacific had caused some of the enamel lining to dissolve into the water. Thus, the only palatable water was that which each man brought in his two canteens from his transport. Yet I have seen several men give their last drink of water to a comrade, with the untrue remark, "Oh, I've got some more in my other canteen." What a pity Americans at home cannot display the same unselfish attitude toward each other and toward the men who fight for them!

Within an hour after the correspondents left the island the Japs staged their twilight counterattack. All day Major Bill Jones' first battalion of the Sixth Marines had marched gallantly down the south shore of Betio. The tanks went down the beach first, except for those incredibly brave marines who went ahead and spotted for the tanks. The tanks poured high explosives into the seaward openings of the mighty coconut log and sand pillboxes. Then the Marine riflemen fired into those openings to kill whatever Japs were left. The flamethrowers did the rest. By dusk the Sixth had been able to travel slightly more than halfway down the south shore. There the marines dug in for the night, with wounded Captain Krueger's Company B, now in command of Lieutenant Norman K. Thomas, holding the front line. The Japs from the tail end of the island, despite three days of merciless pounding, were able to stage their *"Banzai!"* attack. Having cautiously stayed hidden in their holes for three days, the emperor-worshiping brown men now threw away all caution in anticipation of inevitable death. Screaming "Marine, you die!" and "Japanese drink Marines' blood!" they rushed Company B in what seemed like overpowering numbers. The line wavered, and in one place it cracked momentarily. Lieutenant Thomas telephoned Major Jones, "We are killing them as fast as they come at us, but we can't hold much longer; we need reinforcements." Said Jones, "We haven't got them to send you; you've got to hold." Company B held. At least three hundred Japs died in their fanatical charge. Company B's feat was one of the most heroic on Betio. The red-eyed, grime-coated marines who stumbled out of the front line next morning, more dead than alive, muttered, "They told us we had to hold . . . and, by God, we held." That line, I reflected, might be added to the Marine Corps hymn . . .

❀   ❀   ❀   ❀

SERGEANT C. PETER ZURLINDEN OF THE *DAYTON Journal-Herald* did not get ashore until well into the third day of fighting. But he arrived in sufficient time to file several dozen columns, and to find a small, almost private war.

·6· "SO I DROPPED MY PACK"

SERGEANT C. PETER ZURLINDEN

Burial parties were hard at work. Those not burying the dead were digging foxholes while Jap sniper bullets spatted all around. I first encountered members of my combat intelligence section and Lieutenant Sid Wallace, one of my officers, looked at me in amazement.

"My God," he said, "where the hell have you been? We'd given you up."

It's silly now, but I guess I wanted to be melodramatic. "You know better than that," said I. "They couldn't hit me with a double barreled shotgun at point-blank range."

Immediately afterward I superstitiously rued that comeback. Maybe, I told myself, you're asking for trouble. Bullets, I soon was to discover, play no favorites. They're indiscriminate, deadly little things that sneak up on you without warning and when one's headed your direction there's no way of turning it aside.

But I had been out in the water two days and two nights and all I could think about was that I surely must be the last newsman ashore and in my frantic mind I could see everybody back home reading the first Tarawa dispatches and our Washington Marine brass scowling over a desk and hollering:

"Where the hell is Zurlinden's stuff?"

So I dropped my pack, including one bullet-punctured typewriter, and darted off to the command post to get a quick summary of what had been going on in my absence.

I picked up a couple of stories a few minutes later, then made up my mind to have a look around the beach. I selected a sparsely wooded section where everything was quiet and strolled down it, swinging my little carbine easily in my fist.

The action must be over, I thought, for there was a temporary lull at the time. As I walked past groups of our men sitting and smoking in beach foxholes, I thought perhaps only the landing had been hazardous.

I kept on walking and somehow got into that quiet sector. It looked on the beach as though the Japs had caught hell here. Their dead were littered all about, their bodies giving off the death stench and already beginning to decompose.

Just then the sand at my feet began to spurt up in a distinct pattern of machine-gun fire. I'd only seen it in the movies before, but I could hear the staccato reports and I knew what it was.

I dropped flush into that group of stinking, rotting Japs and crawled around until I found myself a vantage point. Then I raised my head to have a look. The machine-gun opened up.

I thought I saw Mr. Squint-eyes' tree so I tried to fire my own weapon. But the sea water had fouled it up and it would not operate. Then I saw a Marine rifle, loaded, nearby and got it.

While I was creeping after it, some part of my body must have shown because the machine-gun chattered again. I then crawled back and poked the rifle over a dead Jap's shoulder and fired until the clip emptied.

I don't know whether I had the right tree or not. You couldn't really tell at any time.

But if I had killed that one, his brother or somebody took over because a machine-gun started working on me and bullets thudded into those Jap bodies—and you can bet I got down as close to the coral sand as possible.

I don't know how long I was there, but I noticed marines working up the beach toward my position and figured a dead reporter wouldn't be any good to anybody, so I laid low. About thirty minutes later a machine-gun crew set up about 25 yards away and I felt pretty good.

But the Jap apparently had stopped firing, waiting for me to get up, so I stuck my rifle up in the air and he let go with a burst. Then my buddies, bless 'em, raked his area, and ten minutes later I was on my way back to the command post.

When I got a little distance off, I said to a marine walking my way: "There's still a few Japs left in that quiet section back there."

He looked at me like I was crazy, saying, "Where, there?" and pointing to the area from whence I'd come.

"Yeah," I replied.

"Hell, man," he said, "we haven't even got started down there yet."

❉ ❉ ❉ ❉

NOW IT WAS AFTERNOON, NOVEMBER 22, AND THE Battle of Tarawa was over. But the marines did not rest. The beach was a scene of activity, with slit trenches being dug, wounded being prepared for evacuation, order emerging from the chaos of conflict. General Julian C. Smith's public information officer, Captain Earl J. Wilson, was a former *Washington Post* reporter who became the chief combat correspondent of the 2nd Marine Division. In the following excerpt Wilson, in collaboration with other noted combat correspondents, tells us of the aftermath of battle.

•7• MOP-UP

CAPTAIN EARL J. WILSON AND MASTER TECHNICAL SERGEANTS JIM G. LUCAS, SAMUEL SHAFFER AND C. PETER ZURLINDEN

. . . Betio, that afternoon, did not rest. Men who had become separated from their outfits walked all over the shell-torn islets looking for their buddies. When they ran into friends whom they hadn't seen since leaving the transports they shook hands or pounded each other on the back, happy at finding the other still alive.

The wounded who were able to stay on their feet put up palm fronds to keep the molten sun from the eyes of men who were more severely wounded than themselves. Some with one arm in a sling would use their good hand to wave flies away from the tired gray faces of the men on the stretchers.

First sergeants in all companies set up offices in shell holes and worked over their rosters to get out casualty reports. Regimental sergeant majors sent out runners to the top kicks to tell them to "get the hell on with their reports."

Slit trenches were dug for latrines. Many men had not moved their bowels in the three and half days of battle.

Men widened and smoothed the sides and floors of their foxholes, so that they would have a comfortable berth when night came. They would have to sleep in foxholes as long as they remained on Betio. At their best, foxholes put up no competition with inner-spring mattresses. The soft coral of Tarawa had the additional disadvantage that, if a bomb did burst, its concussion would cascade sand into the men's eyes and hair while they tried to sleep. It would get inside their sweat-stained dungarees and every time they moved the clothes rubbed their skin like sandpaper.

Word was passed that mail would be sent out by plane within twenty-four hours. Men were told they could write their families that they were on Tarawa, a relaxation of the usually stringent censorship regulations that came as a happy surprise.

Men dug up scraps of paper, pencil stubs, and envelopes. Some of them used Japanese stationery, which caused one boy's mother to think he was a Jap prisoner. They sharpened their pencils with the knives they had used during the night. They wrote to their parents, to their wives, and to their girls back home.

"Dear Mom: Just a few lines to let you know that I'm on Tarawa and that I'm all right . . ."

One marine wrote his wife: " . . . All I can think of right now is coming home to you. Pray that it will be soon."

Major General Julian Smith's command post took on the aspect of the Times Square subway station during a six o'clock rush hour. Battalion and regimental commanders showed up. Admiral Hill and Major General Holland Smith and their aides came ashore to extend their congratulations.

General Julian Smith walked among his men. There were tears in his eyes. One youngster showed him a dent in his helmet put there by a Jap bullet. He was very proud of the dent. The general told him to keep the helmet always.

Near the general's command post, in a corner of a wrecked Japanese warehouse, the "Tarawa Press Club" set up its headquarters. Press representatives and Marine Corps combat correspondents, using water cans for chairs and a Japanese torpeodo for a desk, pounded away at their typewriters on a story that was to electrify the nation. They hurried to finish their stories in time to make the first plane out: a flying boat that had landed in the lagoon a few hours earlier.

Several feet away from them intelligence officers questioned prisoners. Wounded marines lay on stretchers, waiting to be taken to the transports. Chaplains moved among them, cheering them up. In another part of the warehouse the ordnance section repaired rifles and machine guns, covered with rust and dirt, that had been salvaged. Many had been reclaimed from the reef.

A post exchange was set up on empty crates. Men lined up to buy cigarettes, pogey bait (candy), soap, shaving cream, and razor blades. The marines behind the crates refused to take any money. They said to those who held it out: "Keep it, Mac. What the hell would we do with money here? Charge it to Uncle Sam."

By afternoon the men had set up their beach defenses. Antiaircraft batteries were landed and their guns placed in position. Washing-Machine Charlie's unmolested raids on Betio were finished. Seabees were driving bulldozers on the airstrip, getting the field ready for the first American planes which were due the next morning.

Men explored. They came back loaded down with bottles of Japanese beer and saki, or with brand new white Jap sailor uniforms. They liked the beer, but usually passed up the saki after a few torrid swallows.

Some put on the Japanese sailor suits. The sleeves about reached their elbows and the trousers just a little below the knees. The effect was anything but svelte. It wasn't meant to be. The suits were clean. General Julian Smith shortly issued orders against the practice because of the danger that marines wearing them ran the risk of being shot after dark by their own sentries. The men put their filthy, battle-stained dungarees on again.

Radio Tokyo broadcast its private version of the battle. It made fascinating listening. Radio Tokyo claimed:

1. That five thousand marines were sent to the bottom of the Pacific when their transports were sunk.

2. That subsequently the Japs sank three large aircraft carriers, one battleship, one cruiser, and shot down eighty-nine planes.

3. That heavy fighting still raged on the beach at Tarawa.

Radio Tokyo has its moments of unreliability.

Night fell and the "smoking lamp" was extinguished all over Betio, meaning that smoking was prohibited. Sentries were posted in pairs around every bivouac area to guard against Jap snipers still alive. The precautions were well taken.

Singly, or in small groups, Japs came out of pillboxes where many of them had hidden under the bodies of their own dead. They drifted through the darkness, crept up on the marines in their foxholes. Some men were killed during the night by Japs who managed to crawl past the sentries.

The stillness was frequently broken with sudden, sharp shouts of "Halt," followed by rifle reports. Three of the Jap snipers were killed on the lip of the shell hole which contained the Sixth Regiment's command post. The sentry who shot them was heard to complain: "Why don't somebody tell those bastards that the war's over?"

✿ ✿ ✿ ✿

FEW MARINES COVERED MORE OF BETIO'S BLOODY acres than did big, gentle Chaplain W. Wyeth Willard, a native of Cape Cod. Like so many others, Willard wrote a book about the invasion. Here he speaks of the inevitably saddest of duties.

•8• DIARY OF A CHAPLAIN

CAPTAIN W. WYETH WILLARD, CH. C.

The chaplains conferred . . . and decided to bury the dead immediately. In the rear of the divisional CP a site was selected for the first Naval and Marine Cemetery to be established in the Tarawa atoll. The bulldozer began to excavate three long trenches, in which the dead could be placed side by side. Under the circumstances, the command decided that individual graves were out of the question. The main thing was to identify and bury our departed comrades with as much reverence as possible. But even with these arrangements, the engineers who operated the bulldozer risked their lives. Every now and then, Jap snipers fired at them. They would crouch behind

IV Central Pacific: Tarawa to Peleliu

Tarawa: Close-up of an approach to hell.

Taking cover behind seawall on Red Beach #3.

Two men drag badly hurt Marine back to cover of the wall.

Marines stalking and capturing a light machine gun pillbox.

Marines move out from the beachhead into Japanese smoke-covered airstrip.

Getting set to throw a hand grenade at a Japanese pillbox as the smoke of battle rolls back over the hastily thrown-up sandbag entrenchment.

Literally inch-by-inch.

Behind the slim protection that a blasted tree affords, this Marine picks off the Japanese in a pillbox. A very small target, the Japanese must be shot through the opening the Marine uses to sight through.

Quiet reigned when this picture was made of the lagoon on Tarawa Island, but a few hours earlier it was an inferno. Bodies float in the water along with amphibious tractors, and one tractor still hangs on the seawall.

When the word was passed to take a Japanese position on Tarawa, these Marines did not waste any time in scrambling out of their hastily dug trench and carrying out their orders.

Their job completed, these Marines march toward the pier on Tarawa to board the ships that brought them to the strongly fortified Japanese outpost. On the left are other Marines who remained to hold what they fought for.

Marines wounded in the landing on Tarawa are towed out to larger craft on a rubber landing boat by their buddies. The larger vessels took them to base hospitals for expert medical care.

General Robert Richardson, Admiral Nimitz, General Julian Smith, Colonel Edson. On Tarawa, November 29, 1943.

A wounded Marine receives a transfusion on the beach of Tarawa. The blood plasma flows from a flask on a rifle that has been upended on a bayonet. Following the transfusion—to lessen shock and restore blood lost by bleeding—the Leatherneck was removed to a base hospital for treatment.

Inspection tour: taking a look at battered Japanese pillboxes are General Julian Smith (leading), Admiral Nimitz,
and (climbing up the pillbox) General Richardson.

As the smoke of battle cleared, Marines on Tarawa raised
the Stars and Stripes on a palm tree they pressed into
service as a flagpole.

Tarawa—the gratitude which can be expressed only with silent admiration is mirrored on the face of Reverend Sister Raphael, of the Order of the Sacred Heart, as she visited the grave of an unknown Marine. Sister Raphael, stationed at various times at Tarawa, Apiang, and Apamama, was suspected by the Japanese of having harbored American bombing crews who had been forced to land near Tarawa atoll. On one occasion a Japanese soldier held a bayonet against her back and she was stood in front of a Japanese machine gun while being questioned about the location of downed Yankee flyers. (Photo by W/O R. L. Chapel)

The best public relations setup of any outfit . . . During the brief Marshalls campaign, Lieutenant Colonel Donald L. Dickson and Captain Eugene A. McNerny (right) are pictured on the beach making battle sketches to be released to syndicates and newspapers. Combat correspondents did the rest.

Craft landing on Palau. (Photo by McBride)

Marines of the First Division, pinned down by heavy enemy fire, remain near their equipment as they hit Orange Beach #3 on Peleliu.

In the bitter struggle to establish the Peleliu beachhead, infantrymen carry on the fight from the shelter of the amphibious tractor which brought them ashore. (Photo by Roemer)

Firing on snipers just off the airfield on Peleliu. (Photo by Vasicek)

A wounded Marine, while waiting for the stretcher bearers to come for him, is given a drink of water from the canteen of his buddy. (Photo by J. D. Wasden)

Man's best friend proved his worth in battle. Here a dog arrives and a handler receives and reads a message. (Photo by West)

Tanks move up, off beach. (Photo by Vasicek)

Smoke caused by aerial bombings and artillery shellfire casts a pall over a ridge on Peleliu. First Division Marines move up the sides and across the top. (Photo by Sgt. John E. Morgan)

Pinned down. (Photo by Pfc. John Smith)

Bottoms' up: "Molotov Cocktail" time on Suicide Ridge.

A hospital corpsman taking information on a wounded Marine. (Photo by Siderman)

The chow line—such as it was. (Photo by McElroy)

the machine for a few moments, and then hurry into the saddle to go on with the work.

Chaplain Kelly had charge of the bodies after they were brought to the cemetery. The rest of us went out with working parties to search out the dead. Many bodies of personal friends in the Second and Eighth Regiments—men whom I had known intimately—were brought in and laid to rest. There was Lieutenant Colonel Herbert R. Amey, of Ambler, Pennsylvania. We had attended an officer's party together at the Kersley's home in Lower Hutt, New Zealand. He had been killed as he led his men into battle. One of my former tent mates on Guadalcanal, Lieutenant W. D. Hawkins, of El Paso, Texas, had died a hero. Later on, the airfield on Betio was named in his memory. Soon the cemetery was filled with one hundred and twelve marines—our friends . . .

. . . And now it was up to each chaplain, carrying on his work in different sectors of the island, to select his own site for a cemetery . . . I wondered why I was not one of the corpses so abundant on that small island. I had been hit on a shoulder by a small piece of shrapnel . . . the flat surface of the two-inch fragment had struck the collarbone, saving me from a serious wound. With my right hand, I had reached up to my left shoulder, expecting to find a hole there. I looked at my fingers, which I thought would be crimson with blood. But no! A Jap hand grenade had exploded a few yards from me. Once again my life had been spared. On several occasions bullets had whistled through the air around me. "Why was not someone planning to bury me?" I thought, as I set about the sad task of burying my comrades . . .

Our own regimental adjutant, Captain Cleland B. Early, an extremely active and vigorous young Texan . . . had set up a CP adjacent to that of the Second Regiment. Captain Early assisted me in the task of selecting a site for Tarawa's Navy and Marine Corps Cemetery 2.

Colonel Merritt A. Edson informed me that I had the right to order any stray marine to help me. First Lieutenant Paul B. Govedare, of Wheaton, Illinois, with a group of engineers, was assigned to assist in the task. The bulldozer went to work excavating two long furrows.

A few yards from where I had been attempting to rest the night before, I noticed the body of an American marine curled up in death. I went over with my helpers to prepare him for burial. His helmet bore the name "W. C. Culp." There he lay, my friend, my former assistant for three months in the Solomons! When he had nursed me back to health, after an attack of dysentery, I had called him "my Angel." And now he was with the angels! Down in New Zealand he had been commissioned as a second lieutenant in the Marine Corps. He had led his platoon in the opening attack on Tarawa, and had given a good account of himself before he fell, mortally wounded. "Oh, my Lord!" were his last words. Five out of the six officers in his company were killed. Dear old Bill, as I used to call him! He had been one of the best personal workers, one of the finest soul-winners I had ever known. His signet ring and fountain pen were removed from his body, later to be sent to his sister in the States. Tenderly we laid him away to rest.

Soon after, my men discovered the body of Colonel D. K. Claude, of Orange, Virginia. We placed his remains in the common grave, near those of Bill.

We removed what personal effects we could, since we thought that these might be of some comfort to the bereaved families. On the body of one marine we found a card which contained a code whereby he had intended to let his beloved know his whereabouts. It was arranged with the following salutations and their interpretations:

My darling — Australia
Darling — New Zealand
My dearest — East Indies
Dearest — China
My dearest Violet — Rabaul
My dear Violet — Africa
Violet — Burma
Honey — Hawaii
Sweetheart — Solomons
My darling Violet — Truk
Violet darling — New Britain
Violet dearest — New Guinea
My dearest Darling — Salamaua
Precious — Aboard Ship
Princess — New Caledonia

Only we could let Violet know that her friend had landed on Tarawa . . . and would not come back.

Our men worked hard all day long. The bodies of sixty-six officers and enlisted men were interred. Some of them could not be identified, such as the lad whose grave we marked, "Just a pair of legs," or "Burned to death." There were many shipmates and other friends to whom we bade farewell.

The next morning at about 0600, I walked around by Beach Red 1. Along the shore I counted the remains of seventy-six marines, staring up at me, half in, half out of the water. A little further on, I came on officers and men from the battalion with which I had left the States.

"Where's Thaxton?" I inquired, wondering whether or not my

former assistant had been killed. His prayer of August 6 [the day before the landings at Guadalcanal], in the presence of more than a dozen others on board our transport, in which he had offered to give up his life because he knew Christ as his own personal Saviour, if in so doing God would spare some other marine who did not know Christ, had made him a marked figure, not only in the Marine Corps, but also back in the States. To my joy, I learned how Corporal Thaxton had led his machine-gun squad ashore during the initial assault on Betio. Thaxton had not only surged through the bullet-ridden surf with his M-1 rifle and other gear, but also had carried a heavy box of machine-gun ammunition. The marine beside Thaxton was bringing in the tripod, without which the machine-gun would be useless. A Jap bullet got him. He fell dead beneath the waves, bearing the tripod down with him. After some of the unit had reached shore, without orders from anyone, Thaxton waded out into the perilous waters, rescued the tripod, and then set up the machine-gun, thus saving many lives. How glad I was to see him. But many others of my friends in that battalion had fallen . . . my comrades Captain George R. Wentzel, Jr., Captain William E. Tatom, and Captain Clinton N. Dunahoe. Wentzel had roomed next to me on the transport coming from the States. Tatom had been my partner in several domino games on that same transport. Dunahoe had lived for a time in my little hut on Tulagi. Of the forty officers who were with that battalion, excluding those of attached units, when we left the States in 1942, only seven remained. The rest either had been returned to the States, for one reason or another, or had been killed.

But I was not to bury those men whose bodies I saw that morning as they hugged the sands on Beach Red 1. The division chaplain had taken over the supervision of burying our dead. Reinforcements had arrived. Our regiment had been ordered to move out. With a little hatchet I purchased in New Zealand (for what purpose I knew not at the time), my assistants Gonzales and Rosenberg hastily hacked out sixty-six crude wooden crosses. As we could not find any paint on the island, the name of each fallen comrade was written upon the cross placed at the head of his grave. As a means of further identification, each man's metal tag, inscribed with name and serial number, was hung from the cross.

We packed our gear and wearily moved down toward the wharf. The replacements looked fresh and clean. Our men, hollow-cheeked, with their faces unwashed and bewhiskered, dragged tired, aching bodies toward the pier . . .

※　※　※　※

ONE OF THE IRONIES OF TARAWA WAS THE CONSPIC-
uous absence of Major General Holland M. Smith, holder of a
Distinguished Service Medal and the Navy Cross, acknowledged
champion of the Fleet Marine Force, whose career was a magnificent span of service dating from Haiti and Nicaragua. At the time
of the Tarawa attack Smith was aboard Admiral Turner's flagship *Pennsylvania,* supervising the assault of Makin—and fum-
ing ("fighting dragged out . . . and chained me to this insignificant skirmish") despite a succession of battle reports from his
colleague, Major General Julian Smith. However, when Makin
was secured, "Howlin' Mad" succeeded in getting to Tarawa,
and he came ashore. But Tarawa, too, was secured.

The crusty marine gives us his reaction to Tarawa and his valued analysis of the battle.

·9· TARAWA: OBSERVATION AND ANALYSIS

LIEUTENANT GENERAL HOLLAND M. SMITH

. . . On my way to Julian Smith's Command Post, I passed boys
who had lived yesterday a thousand times and looked older than
their fathers. Dirty, unshaven, with gaunt, almost sightless eyes, they
had survived the ordeal but it had chilled their souls. They found
it hard to believe they were actually alive. There were no smiles on
these ancient, youthful faces; only passive relief among the dead.

I haven't the slightest recollection of what I said to Julian Smith
when I met him in the battered Japanese shack he called his headquarters, although I remember vividly the faces of the boys on the
beach. I do remember clasping his hand warmly and I must have
congratulated him on his fine conduct of the campaign. He was elated
over victory but, like myself, distressed by the casualties. We both
knew the Marines would be criticized by the people back home, to
whom the high price paid for Tarawa must come as a shock. I do remember that later I extended congratulations to members of his staff
and to officers of the Second Division—that is, those who survived.
Among 3,301 casualties at Tarawa were 57 officers killed and 111

wounded. The ratio of dead to wounded—about one to two—was probably the highest in any battle of World War II.

With Julian Smith I made a tour of the western and central portions of the island, where the enemy had built his strongest pillboxes and blockhouses. My pride in the invincible spirit of the Marines was never greater. Only men with the highest morale and willingness to die rather than be defeated could have captured this well-nigh impregnable chain of fortifications. Japanese prisoners told me their officers boasted Betio defenses were so strong that a million men could not take the island.

Turning to Major Woodrum, I said, "I don't see how they ever took Tarawa. It's the most completely defended island I have ever seen."

That inspection trip left other impressions on my mind—impressions of our own inadequacies. Before the Marines landed and the Navy laid down the final bombardment, one of the Admirals messaged the Southern Attack Force:

> It is not our intention to wreck the island. We do not intend to destroy it. Gentlemen, we will obliterate it.

Obliterate it? I entered every pillbox and blockhouse on the western end of the island and found only one had even been hit by naval gunfire. Not one had been destroyed. All of them had to be destroyed by the Marines with explosive charges and hand grenades. Dead Japanese lay everywhere but they were killed by marines, not by Naval gunfire.

Instead of three days' preliminary bombardment, Betio needed at least ten. After that amount of fire, the marines would not have faced guns that should have been knocked out before they landed. They would not have had to capture, almost barehanded, positions the Japanese had fortified for 15 months. The strength of the blockhouses was tremendous. Concrete was five feet thick and superimposed were 8-inch coconut palm logs, reinforced with angle iron and railroad spikes. The Japanese then piled ten feet of coral or soil on this structure. Nothing but a direct hit with a 16-inch shell, or a 2,000-pound bomb, could cave them in.

The Second Division had initiated a request to Major General Willis A. Hale, commanding the Army's Seventh Air Force, that 2,000-pound bombs be dropped on Betio. For some unexplained reason, this request was ignored so there was nothing left for the marines to do but take the blockhouses by frontal attack.

The Japanese Command Post was a case in point. On the low-lying coral island it reared against the skyline like a two-story house, a massive building of reinforced concrete, coconut logs and sandbags. A Kingfisher reconnaissance plane from the U.S.S. *Maryland,* Hill's flagship, spotted it intact long after it was supposed to have been knocked out. He radioed his discovery to the task force and his message was acknowledged. But it was not knocked out.

Once more, the Marines took the blockhouse their own way. Bulldozers were moved up, the drivers sheltering behind the blades, and buried the entrance in coral and dirt. As the height of the rubble increased, gunports and other apertures were closed, immobilizing all Japanese resistance and completing the process of entombment. Marines then climbed on top of the blockhouses and poured gasoline down the air vents. A few hand grenades, and incineration followed. Rear Admiral Keijai Shibashi, the island commander, was the principal victim of this holocaust. The marines took out 300 bodies. It was a grim procedure but the only course left to the marines if they wanted to survive . . .

. . . Tarawa taught us the necessity for more naval gunfire and more air bombing before we undertook a landing. What was considered by the Navy a paralyzing amount of fire was directed at Betio, in our first wedding of naval guns and airplane bombs in the reduction of a fortified atoll, but until after Tarawa we could not calculate accurately the result of this type of attack on concentrated fortifications such as the Japanese had constructed. Moreover, the Navy was inclined to exaggerate the destructive effect of gunfire and this failing really amounted to a job imperfectly done. The marines discovered this fact only when they tried to land. Air assistance was no better gauged than naval support and the strikes were poorly co-ordinated. The planes were not there when needed. The secret of amphibious warfare is concentration of your forces and meticulous co-ordination of all elements, plus as much naval gunfire and air bombardment as you can pour into enemy positions.

An island as small as Betio made it impossible to establish a beachhead as we understand the term in amphibious parlance. There was no depth beyond the beaches for landing supplies and organizing attacks. With every yard accurately and carefully covered by enemy fire, we had first to get a toehold and proceed to take the island all in one piece. This was the first time we had made an assault across a fringing reef covered by an uncertain depth of water and our calculations on water depth were badly in error. The Japanese were fully aware of the defensive possibilities of that reef from the vantage of their pre-sited guns, and they were helped by the inexplicably low tide which held for two days.

Another lesson the Navy should have learned was the need for better co-operation between all units. An Admiral should confine himself to the job of carrying the troops safely to the objective and then helping to protect them. He should leave details of landing and assault to the troop commander.

The reef at Tarawa emphasized the value of amphibian vehicles. The operation was as much a test of our technical equipment as it was of our landing technique. We should have had more amtracks for employment in the initial landing, with adequate reserves for vehicles knocked out by enemy guns or incapacitated by mechanical difficulties. The two or three types used stood up well. The average mechanical life of an amtrack is 200 hours; some of those used at Tarawa had already run 400 hours.

After Tarawa I made up my mind that all future landings would be spearheaded by amphibious vehicles, either the open-decked amtrack, of which a new improved model was already being made available, or amphibian tanks, carrying heavier guns, which were in production. This decision did not mean discarding Higgins boats. These craft could be used on unobstructed beaches, or through reef channels—as the work horse of amphibious landings—but for impassable reefs the solution was the amphibious vehicle.

Tarawa taught other lessons. It stimulated our desire to learn. It taught us more about the character of the enemy than all the textbooks and intelligence reports at staff disposal. In the strategical scheme for the Central Pacific offensive, it taught me that the instrument of high policy known as the Joint Chiefs of Staff was not infallible.

※　※　※　※

THERE WAS A COMBINED CATHOLIC, PROTESTANT and Jewish service in the Betio cemetery, and an epitaph was dedicated to those who fell in the historic struggle.

> So let them rest on their sun-scorched atoll,
> The wind for their watcher, the waves for their shroud,
> Where palm and pandanus shall forever whisper
> A requiem fitting for Heroes so proud.

One who visited Betio at this time was Admiral Chester W. Nimitz, Commander in Chief Pacific Fleet, who had come to meet the men responsible for this signal victory. Visibly touched, Nimitz said little except to make note of those who had distinguished themselves under fire and gaze on the awesome havoc of battle. Several weeks later the admiral awarded a dozen Navy

Crosses, the Medal of Honor to Lieutenant Colonel David M.
Shoup, and the Distinguished Service Medal to Major General
Julian C. Smith. In a few well-chosen words, Nimitz echoed the
sentiments of a grateful nation.

·10· THE NATION'S GRATITUDE

FLEET ADMIRAL
CHESTER W. NIMITZ

We have assembled today to honor those among your number who
have particularly distinguished themselves in battle against our enemy in the Pacific. The whole world knows of the gallant performance
and achievements of the men who fought at Tarawa. Nothing can
sufficiently express the nation's gratitude for the deeds of its sons
in battle. There is no yardstick to measure your sacrifice and no tangible remembrance which would be adequate reflection of your country's appreciation.

The capture of the Gilbert Islands paved the way for our more
recent successes in the Marshalls. At Tarawa American forces knocked
down the front door to the whole Japanese defensive system in the
Central Pacific. All the men who took part in this action have earned
for themselves a permanent niche in the hall of military fame.

The memory of those who died at Tarawa and Makin so inspired
your brothers-in-arms of the Army and Marine Corps that they quickly wrested Kwajalein and Eniwetok atolls from the enemy. From Hawkins Field at Tarawa—named in honor of your own Lieutenant Hawkins who heroically gave his life—sprang many of the planes which
supported the Marshalls action with an avenging fury.

The Second Marine Division has unstintingly carried out its tasks
in the drive which has eliminated enemy control of the sea over thousands of square miles and brought us measurably closer to the Japanese homeland. You shared in the historic beginnings of the ocean
highways we are opening across the Pacific. Most of you will share in
our future progress along that road until our combined power has
brought about the unconditional surrender of Japan . . .

I now present these awards in the name of the President of the United States who, were it possible, would have the keenest pleasure in pinning these medals on you. I want each of you to consider that your medal has been presented to you by the commander in chief.

✿ ✿ ✿ ✿

TARAWA WAS AN EXPENSIVE LESSON TO TEACH US the need for adequate softening of a target before invasion. Thus it was that Navy and Marine Corps ranking officers set up an air bombardment range at Kahoolawe Island, Hawaii, where gunnery officers concentrated on shore batteries and carrier pilots trained intensively in pinpoint bombardment. This training was vital, for it was now January 1944 and time for the Marshalls invasion, where the newly activated 4th Marine Division was blooded. Our objective was Kwajalein Atoll, the world's largest lagoon (66 miles long). This simultaneous Army-Marine Corps venture envisioned V Amphibious Corps landing on Kwajalein Island at the south end of the lagoon, and assaulting Roi-Namur and Eniwetok at the north end with the 4th Marine Division.

Colonel Robert D. Heinl, whom we have met tells us of this operation.

·11· OPERATION FLINTLOCK

COLONEL ROBERT D. HEINL, JR.

All during the planning and execution of the Gilberts operation, preparations were going forward for a larger, far more complicated, and—most feared—even more costly operation. Operation "Flintlock," the invasion of the Marshalls, had been planned ever since mid-1943, and, at higher levels, the work was almost completed when the 2d Marine Division took Tarawa . . .

On 6 December 1943 . . . Admiral Nimitz assembled his top sub-ordinates and presented them with a bombshell: earlier objectives should be abandoned and past plans junked. The new objective which Nimitz boldly proposed was Kwajalein, the world's largest lagoon, located deep inside the hard outer crust of defended islands which were the original targets. Kwajalein would be simpler to take than the earlier objectives; once captured, it would be a better base, and it was the strategic heart of the Marshalls. After they recovered from their surprise ("I, for one, was startled," recalled Admiral Turner), the planners acceded. A few days later, with JCS approval, Nimitz announced the new plan. The V Amphibious Corps would land si-multaneously on Kwajalein Island, at the south end of the lagoon, and on Roi-Namur, in the north. In addition, a small force of sol-diers would secure unoccupied Majuro Atoll as a supporting base. After various postponements, the D-day finally selected was 31 Janu-ary 1944, which barely allowed time enough to complete preparations.

Meanwhile, all hands made a concentrated effort to take advan-tage of the lessons so abruptly learned at Betio. Typical of this effort was Admiral Turner's blunt report, "Lessons Learned at Tarawa." This penetrating study, mainly of mistakes, was responsible for and foreshadowed many of the successful innovations which were to ap-pear in the Marshalls.

One particularly important development, among many, was es-tablishment, under control of the V Amphibious Corps, of an air and shore bombardment range on Kahoolawe Island, Hawaii. There, Marine and Navy gunnery officers began the painstaking training of carrier pilots and each fire-support ship in accurate methods in-tended to pinpoint and destroy individual beach defenses and bat-teries. A reproduction of a section of Betio's beach defenses provided targets.

Kwajalein and Roi-Namur (the latter a pair of adjacent islets joined by a causeway) are typical Central Pacific coral islands forming part of Kwajalein Atoll. Each commands a deep-water entrance into the lagoon, and, in 1943, each had a Japanese air base and defending gar-rison. Since the capture of Kwajalein Island was assigned by General [Holland M.] Smith to an Army force, the 7th Infantry Division under Major General C. H. Corlett, USA, whereas Roi-Namur went to the new 4th Marine Division (Major General Harry Schmidt), we shall focus on the latter.

Although not fully realized at the time, the defenses of both Kwaja-lein and Roi-Namur were not nearly as strong or as well developed as those on Betio or in the outer Marshalls. Here was a dividend of Nimitz's decision to strike the center rather than the edges. There were, nevertheless, 3,000 defenders, all Japanese Navy aviation or

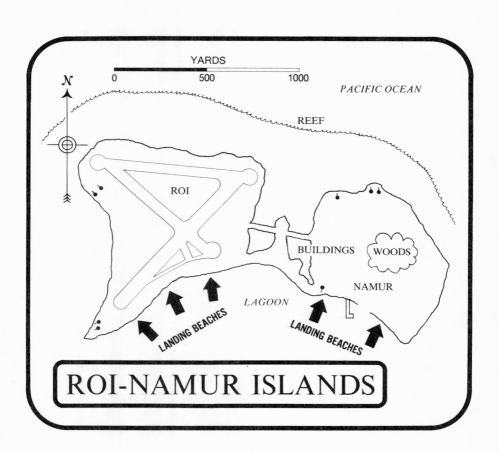

ROI-NAMUR ISLANDS

base-defense troops, on Roi-Namur. The defenses themselves included two coast-defense batteries each containing two twin-mount 5.5-inch dual-purpose naval guns, plus two 37-mm. antiaircraft guns. There were, in addition, 28 twin-mount 20-mm. and 13-mm. machine guns of the kind that had been so deadly at Tarawa, and 19 beach pillboxes mounting 7.7-mm. machine guns. Except for four massive concrete blockhouses, there was a general lack of heavy underground construction. Barbed wire and good grade concrete were not available, because American submarines were sinking or damaging two out of every three cargo ships carrying such essential cargoes. On the lagoon face of the islands, there were no underwater obstacles or mines, and beach defenses were weak.

Taking full advantage of the lessons of Tarawa, the general plan for the seizure of Roi-Namur was evolved. After two days of heavy, deliberate pounding of the main objectives by precision naval gunfire and air, adjacent lightly held islets would be secured, and the 4th Division's artillery (the 14th Marines, Colonel Louis G. DeHaven) would land. Next day, supported by overwhelming naval gunfire, artillery, and air, one regiment, the 23d Marines, would assault Roi, while the other, the 24th, landed on Namur. All assault landings were to be from inside the lagoon, in amphibian tractors, which, as a result of Tarawa, were being run off the assembly lines at a rate of 500 a month.

The naval attack force, headed by a newcomer to the Pacific campaign, Rear Admiral R. L. Conolly, included three old battleships, three escort carriers for close-support air, five cruisers, and 19 destroyers. Among the innovations presented by Admiral Conolly's force were: USS *Appalachian,* one of the new specially designed headquarters ships; LCI-gunboats, such as had been tried out in the Treasury Islands and at New Britain; and naval swimmers organized for the discovery and destruction of beach obstacles, the underwater demolition teams, or UDTs, as they soon were known. Admiral Conolly had played an outstanding role in the capture of Sicily and was destined to be respected and admired by all marines with whom he served. Unfortunately his amphibious group, particularly the transport and landing ship officers and men, were green and unskilled. For an inexperienced naval force to land an inexperienced division was asking for headaches.

One problem which vexed General Smith was a succession of attempts to subordinate the V Amphibious Corps to Admiral Turner, a matter which had already been settled (in the other direction) by Admiral King's 1942 decision that the landing force and naval amphibious commanders should occupy parallel status. When Nimitz in August 1943 had placed Smith's headquarters under Turner, King had countermanded the order within 48 hours. A month later, Turner had proposed to Admiral Spruance that he, Turner ("who always had suppressed ambitions to be a General," growled Smith), should be given control over training the V Amphibious Corps for future operations. Spruance had turned down the suggestion, but, within a month, when the command organization for Galvanic had appeared from the mimeograph machines, General Smith's headquarters had been missing, and the troops of the V Amphibious Corps had been parceled out under Navy commanders. Once again, as only he could, "Howling Mad" Smith had protested and had won his point. Finally, after the same thing had recurred in the Flintlock plan, Admiral Nimitz had imposed a final compromise: (1) during plans and training, landing force and naval commanders would be coequal; (2) during operations, the naval commander would have over-all operational control; but (3) when ready to do so, the landing force commander would land and assume full control of fighting ashore. This was not exactly what General Smith had wanted, but it could be lived with.

But V Amphibious Corps came under attack from another quarter as well. On 27 December, Lieutenant General R. C. Richardson, USA, senior Army commander in the Central Pacific, delivered a private memorandum to Admiral Nimitz. Richardson reminded Nimitz that he had questioned all along the wisdom of employing a Marine headquarters to command amphibious troops in the operations ahead. He suggested instead that Nimitz request the assignment of an Army corps headquarters to replace that of Holland Smith (whose individual competence he questioned), adding (in a refrain familiar to marines) that Marine officers did not possess the requisite experience and training for the duties of a corps staff and that the V Amphibious Corps staff was "inexperienced and untrained."

Nimitz, always neutral in inter-Service matters, simply forwarded Richardson's memorandum to Admiral King, who, in concert with General Vandegrift, made short work of it. . . .

Although the main object was quite simple—namely, to place four battalions of artillery on islets from which they could support the forthcoming assault—the operations required on D-day as preliminaries to the capture of Roi and Namur were highly complicated. Units of the 25th Marines under Colonel S. C. Cumming, plus the division scout company, had to make five separate landings to secure the entrance to the lagoon and six islands commanding the approaches to Roi and Namur. The 14th Marines, whose howitzers had to support the morrow's assault on Roi-Namur, and all the myriad supporting units (including more than a battalion of amphibian tractors and the new gun-carrying armored amphibians) were grouped with the 25th Marines under the assistant division commander, Brigadier

General J. L. Underhill. Underhill's group included as many am-tracs as the entire 2d Division had had at Tarawa only ten weeks ear-lier. The 4th Division as a whole had 240 LCTs and 75 armored am-phibians.

During the preceding 48 hours the Navy had poured thousands of tons of shells onto the Marshalls in a crushing but deliberate and carefully aimed bombardment (by the end of D-day the tonnage was 6,919). Repeated attacks by carrier and shore-based air had destroyed Roi's once powerful 24th Air Flotilla, and thus had partially avenged Wake. All these measures reflected Admiral Turner's determination to capitalize upon the lessons of Tarawa.

With such resources and support, the principal problems encoun-tered on D-day came from the inherent complications of the plan and the inexperience of all concerned, especially the landing ship and amphibian tractor crews. The intricately phased movement of the tractors into the lagoon broke down when the primary control vessel, a destroyer, had to abandon her duties in order to provide covering fire for minesweepers, leaving the LVTs leaderless. Com-munications were abominable. The early model, low freeboard am-tracs had power pumps with no manual auxiliary for use when gas was low or gone, and refueling boats failed to show up as ordered inside the lagoon. To worsen the situation, LST skippers refused to refuel or even salvage sinking tractors, on the jurisdictional grounds that they had been originally launched from other ships.

Nevertheless, all five landings were made somehow. During the forenoon the 1st Battalion, 25th Marines, secured Mellu and Ennueb-ing Islands, southwest of Roi, to the tune of carrier air support, naval gunfire, and rockets from the new LCI-gunboats. Of the 35 Japanese who outposted the two islands, 30 were killed, and five dazed pris-oners were taken. In midafternoon, following strenuous efforts to assemble and organize enough amtracs to make the landings, the 2d Battalion, 25th Marines, captured Ennubirr and Obella Islands, southeast of Namur. On Ennubirr, where the Japanese main radio station was located, an enemy platoon put up a fight: 24 Japanese were killed at a cost of seven Marine casualties. While this action was in progress, the 3d Battalion, 25th Marines, landed on Ennumennet, just north of Ennubirr, where ten enemy were killed. The final oper-ation of the day was the capture of Ennugarret Island, immediately adjacent to Namur itself, by an attack from Ennumennet. This task was complicated; twilight was falling and only four operable LVTs remained to Lieutenant Colonel J. M. Chambers, commanding the 3d Battalion. Nonetheless, by compressing 120 men into his first and only wave, Chambers, no man to abandon a mission, managed to establish a beachhead while the defenders withdrew to Namur.

During this day when little went according to plan, except the final results, the Navy continued to pound Roi and Namur. Huge fires and magazine explosions punctuated the deliberate drumbeat of bombardment. Whatever happened, Admiral Conolly was exerting every effort to prepare the main objectives and to ease the next day's assault. In the process, Conolly acquired a nickname. Dissatisfied with the positioning of the USS *Maryland* for her bombardment duties, the admiral ordered, "Move really close in." From that moment forward, he was "Close-In" Conolly and a marked man among marines.

The stage was set, to an extent, for the capture of Roi and Namur on the following day, 1 February. Colonel Louis Jones's 23d Marines, on the left, were to seize Roi, which was almost all airfield, while Colonel F. A. Hart, commanding the 24th Marines, would assault Namur on which the Japanese had most of their supply installations including—as the 24th Marines would soon discover—huge quantities of ammunition and explosives. The 23d Marines were to land in as yet uncommitted LVTs from the 4th Amphibian Tractor Battalion; the 24th would have to depend on the depleted remainder of the amtracs used the day before to secure the outlying islands. Trying to tidy up the previous day's legacy of confusion, Admiral Conolly and General Schmidt postponed the hour of landing until 1100 in order to permit the assault regiments to find tractors and embark and form up.

At the appointed hour, the 23d Marines, embarked by a fresh tractor battalion, were ready to go. The 24th, despite efforts since daylight, still were unable to marshal enough amtracs for the assault.

Never one to wait long, Colonel Jones chafed impatiently. Moments after W-hour he demanded to be released, and the control vessel acceded. The 23d Marines churned toward Roi, while the 24th milled desperately.

Moving in close on the heels of ships' gunfire, rockets, and strafing aircraft, which loosed a final string of eighteen 2,000-pound bombs along the beach when the leading wave was only 500 yards offshore, the 23d Marines encountered virtually no opposition on the beach. Every enemy pillbox was destroyed or neutralized. The few living Japanese in sight were dazed and groggy. As the marines surged forward across the debris-strewn airfield, Colonel Jones radioed to General Schmidt: "This is a pip X no opposition . . ." And so it proved. Although the whole day was consumed in getting the regiment across the island in an orderly fashion and in mopping up confused enemy survivors, there was no organized resistance. By nightfall, Roi was secure and safe, except for several trigger-happy outbursts among the 23d Marines. The landing had cost only 86 casualties.

Out of 110 amtracs originally allocated for their landing on Namur, the 24th Marines could only round up 62, but, as Colonel Jones headed for Roi, the leading waves of the 24th Marines attacked, too.

On Namur the bombardment had done its work as well as it had on Roi. Here, however, the clutter of debris, fallen buildings, and vegetation made co-ordination more difficult and aided the few active Japanese in their defense. Even so, the attack worked forward in good style. Then, at 1305, occurred one of the memorable mishaps of the Pacific war. Mopping up a large concrete blockhouse, an assault team of the 2d Battalion, 24th Marines, hurled a satchel charge inside. Seconds later there was an explosion which shook the entire island. The blockhouse had been chock full of torpedo warheads. On station above the beaches, a 4th Division air observer, Major C. F. Duchein, felt the shock, saw the explosion, and radioed, "Great God Almighty! The whole damn island's blown up!" From a mushroom cloud that towered thousands of feet skyward, rained huge concrete chunks, a few unexploded warheads, and all manner of other debris. One company suffered 57 casualties from this explosion alone; the 2d Battalion as a whole counted 120 including its commanding officer (who refused to be evacuated). For the moment the battalion was virtually out of the fight.

Profiting by the stunning explosion, the Japanese, who were already about as disorganized as possible, began to resist more stubbornly, and, instead of pushing across Namur in a few hours, like the 23d Marines on Roi, the 24th encountered more of a fight. By nightfall (when General Schmidt had landed and set up his command post on the beach), two-thirds of the island had been taken. In the darkness, occasionally lightened by Navy star shells, small groups of Japanese attempted to infiltrate, but, save for one determined attack at dawn, which required tank support to stop, achieved nothing. Next morning, with tanks and half-tracks, the 24th Marines launched a co-ordinated sweep which reached Namur's extremity at noon; two hours later the island was declared secured, and the 15th Defense Battalion (Colonel F. B. Loomis) slowly began the tedious job of organizing and digging in.

The score in casualties made Roi-Namur the counterfoil to Betio. One hundred and ninety-five marines were killed and 545 wounded — less than one-quarter of the cost of Tarawa. From the Japanese garrison, 3,472 were buried, and 91 prisoners were shipped back to Pearl. Among the Marine dead were Private First Class Stephen Hopkins, son of Harry Hopkins, President Roosevelt's confidant and special assistant, and Lieutenant Colonel Aquilla J. Dyess, shot down in the forefront of his battalion's final assault on Namur. For his bravery and leadership, Dyess received a posthumous Medal of Honor.

Of the Namur assault in particular, Colonel Walter Rogers, General Schmidt's incisive, energetic chief of staff, had this to say:

> The attack was seriously hampered by the failure of the tractors to get to the line of departure on time. I think the 24th Marines would have overrun Namur during the first hour or two if their assault troops had all landed as originally planned.

. . . The rapid and effective seizure of Roi-Namur and of Kwajalein (which Army troops secured on 4 February) whetted the planners' appetites for more. According to Admiral Spruance:

> The Kwajalein operation went through so quickly and with such small losses that Admiral Nimitz sent me a radio asking my recommendation on going ahead as soon as possible with the capture of Eniwetok . . .

The same idea, that of employing the joint expeditionary force reserve which had not been needed at Kwajalein for the capture of Eniwetok, had already occurred independently to Holland Smith. Accordingly, when Admiral Turner broached Nimitz's suggestion, the general simply reached into his desk and produced a plan whereby the V Amphibious Corps reserve, 22d Marines and 106th Infantry (less 2d Battalion), would be grouped under Brigadier General T. E. Watson to seize Eniwetok Atoll. Admiral Hill, who had commanded the attack force at Tarawa, was designated as General Watson's opposite number. D-day was 17 February, less than three weeks after the original landings in the Marshalls.

Three principal islands had to be taken in order to control the atoll and its magnificent lagoon: Engebi, at the northern end, containing an airfield, and Eniwetok and Parry Islands, at the southern end, commanding the wide channel entrance. Aside from a small security detachment and base development personnel, the atoll was not garrisoned by the Japanese until early January 1944, when 2,586 troops of the 1st Amphibious Brigade (Army) arrived from Manchuria. Therefore the brigade's organic weapons, including a few tanks, plus two fixed Navy 120-mm. guns on Engebi, constituted the entire defensive armament of the atoll, a welcome change from Tarawa and Kwajalein. Although the Japanese immediately began an energetic program of field fortifications, including some concrete pillboxes, their efforts were doomed to be overtaken by events.

Already pummeled by carrier air-strikes, the islands were to receive more of the same, and, beginning with the arrival of Admiral Hill's group, three old battleships and three heavy cruisers would provide the main fire support for the assault. As at Roi-Namur, artillery would be established on offshore islets to support the assault.

Engebi, thought to be the most strongly held, was to be taken first, by the 22d Marines; then would follow, in order, Eniwetok and Parry, assigned to the 106th Infantry. The 10th Defense Battalion (Lieutenant Colonel Wallace O. Thompson) would then take over. For the 22d Marines, who had been garrisoning Western Samoa since mid-1942, this was to be a maiden operation. Under Colonel John T. ("Johnny") Walker, the regiment had been trained to a fine edge. For the 106th Infantry also, Operation "Catchpole" (the code-name for Eniwetok) was the first. All told, General Watson's group totaled 10,376, of whom 5,820 were marines. Although properly a strong brigade in organization and supporting troops, nobody took time to designate it as such: "Tactical Group 1" was all the title the force ever had. Since only a fortnight elapsed between General Watson's first news of the operation and D-day itself, the hard-pressed planners had no time for niceties.

At daylight on 17 February Admiral Hill's ships and planes began bombarding Engebi and the other islands, while minesweepers, working with secret Japanese charts captured by a Marine reconnaissance unit on Kwajalein, cleared a channel into the lagoon. By early afternoon, following a 20-mile run up toward Engebi, Hill had put the V Amphibious Corps Reconnaissance Company ashore on two unoccupied neighboring islets, and the Marine and Army light artillery battalions were on their way in. When night fell, they had registered and began making night hideous for the 1,200 defenders of Engebi.

Next morning, reinforced by a company of medium tanks and supported by a two-hour naval bombardment, the 22d Marines landed on Engebi's lagoon shore. The ship-to-shore movement was executed smartly and precisely by Army LVTs of the 708th Amphibian Tank Battalion, a competent and experienced unit whose performance considerably outshone the green amtrac battalions at Roi-Namur. With two battalions in assault and the third mopping up behind them, the 22d Marines attacked straight across the island. Although the advance was rapid and spirited, the mopping up was tough because of the enemy "spider-hole" emplacements—central holes with radiating tunnels running out to well-camouflaged rifle pits. Even so, by 1450, Engebi was officially declared secure, although appreciable mopping up and a highly unsettled night remained ahead.

During the afternoon of D-day General Watson's intelligence officer reported bad news: captured documents showed that there were at least 800 Japanese, previously undisclosed, dug in on Eniwetok and Parry. There were, in fact, 908 enemy on the former, and 1,347 on the latter.

The capture of Eniwetok Island by the 106th Infantry, ultimately reinforced by the 3d Battalion, 22d Marines, consumed three days commencing 19 February. As it turned out, the Marine battalion, acting in lieu of the 106th Infantry's missing 2d Battalion, became involved in the hardest fighting and, in the words of the official history, "bore the brunt of the operation." While Eniwetok was being slowly taken, artillery was landed so as to be able to support the final landing, that on Parry, located northeast of Eniwetok.

Displeased by the slowness with which Eniwetok had been secured, General Watson decided to substitute the 22d Marines for the 106th Infantry in the landings on Parry, now set for the morning of George Washington's 212th birthday. During the preceding days, Admiral Hill's ships pounded Parry with more than 900 tons of naval gunfire, about four times as much as had been accorded to Eniwetok. Moreover, the Marine pack howitzer battalion was moved down to Japtan Island, an unoccupied spit north of Parry, from which the attack could be supported. To give the tired 22d a reserve, General Watson ordered the 10th Defense Battalion to organize a 500-man provisional infantry battalion, a measure that cheered the hearts of the base-defenders.

Promptly at 0900 on 22 February, the 22d Marines made their landing. One battalion, the 2d, attacked straight to the front and secured the north end of Parry Island. The 1st Battalion, despite having been landed 300 yards south of its assigned beaches (and thus encountering some "friendly" naval gunfire), likewise crossed the island and wheeled right to sweep southward. Behind the two assault battalions came the 3d, which also wheeled right beside the 1st. At 1300, the 1st and 3d Battalions jumped off. Though the Japanese attempted no counterattack or maneuver, they fought hard; at one time, their mortar and machine-gun fire even forced the USS *Pennsylvania* to shift station. After overrunning the main enemy center of resistance, in the zone of the 3d Battalion, 22d Marines, the attackers pushed rapidly ahead despite enemy minefields. By evening all but the 400-yard tip of Parry was in the hands of the 22d Marines, and the island was declared taken. General Watson, not generous with his compliments, thereupon radioed Colonel Walker:

> Well done, Johnny. My sincere congratulations to the 22d Marines and their supporting units. You have done a magnificent job.

And so they had. With only a fortnight's notice and few specific preparations for the job in hand, the 22d had, in their first campaign, stormed two well-defended islands manned by veteran enemy troops from the Manchurian ("Kwantung") army, and had played a stellar role in the capture of a third. At a cost of 254 dead and 555 wounded, the 22d Marines, assisted by the Army, had . . . advanced the strategic timetable of the war by almost half a year.

❈   ❈   ❈   ❈

ON MARCH 12, 1944, THE JOINT CHIEFS OF STAFF endorsed a plan for the invasion of the Mariana Islands, key to Japan's "Inner South Seas Empire," based on the assumption that whoever controlled that chain of islands also controlled Japan's line of communication. Other fundamental reasons were a need for a B-29 base from which we planned to launch attacks on the Japanese homeland, and a desire to reclaim Guam and to capture Saipan, points from which we hoped to develop advance bases to attack the Palaus, and Leyte or Formosa. The Joint Chiefs of Staff directed Admiral Nimitz to assault the Marianas—Saipan, Tinian and Guam, in that order—by June 15, 1944. This was Operation "Forager," a massive invasion lifting two divisions of Army, three divisions of Marine Corps and a reinforced marine brigade on a voyage of 1017 miles. Command of the massive armada in which were embarked 127,521 troops, two-thirds of whom were Marine Corps, devolved on Rear Admiral Richmond Kelly Turner, with (now) Lieutenant General Holland M. Smith in command of garrison and landing forces of the Joint Expeditionary Force.

Smith wore three other hats: administrative chief of V Amphibious Corps; commander of the 2nd and 4th Marine Divisions; and strategic commander of the 3rd Marine Division and the 1st Marine Provisional Brigade. The plan called for the Northern Task Force (2nd and 4th Divisions) to attack Saipan and Tinian, and the Southern Task Force (3rd Division and 1st Brigade), Guam.

The Marine Corps thus far had fought on two types of terrain: dense jungle and coral atoll. Now the shift of war to another Pacific area brought a third type, a topography of mountains dotted with caves. These islands loomed big to the Joint Chiefs of Staff— a prize from which the United States hoped to launch mighty offensives during the final phase of the war.

The fifteen Marianas lie directly in the shipping route to the Orient, extending in a southward arc for 425 miles along the 145th meridian, east longitude. Significantly, the islands are only 325 miles from Iwo Jima (as measured from Farallon de Pajaros, the northernmost island of the chain) and 250 miles north of the Carolines (as measured from Guam, the southernmost), and thus they are of intrinsic military value. Japan, in control of Saipan since 1920 when the League of Nations awarded her a mandate over the island, developed Saipan's potential. In 1941 the island produced a crop of sugar, wine, lumber, cattle and considerable Scotch, for a polyglot population of Japanese, Chinese, Chamorro and Filipino, and was generally regarded as the heart of the Marianas.

The United States was installed on Guam, south of Saipan, as the result of diplomatic negotiations with Spain in the 1880s when that nation was disposing of her empire. In 1887 Commander Edward Taussig of the U.S.S. *Bennington* arrived at Guam and set up the basis of a military rule. The United States wanted Guam to serve as a coaling station for vessels bound for the Orient, but other than to appoint naval officers as administrators and to build up the small naval facility there, we did nothing to stimulate Guam's development. Tinian, in much the same straits as Guam, was neglected until the Japanese saw fit to acquire it and erect sugar mills and, later, several airstrips in preparation for war.

In 1941 the population of Saipan was about 25,000; three years later, with the addition of the Japanese Army and Navy forces, it stood at nearly 60,000. The island was under the command of Lieutenant General Yoshitsugu Saito, whose troops were essentially composed of the 43rd Division and 47th Independent Mixed Brigade, Army. Overall naval command was exercised by Vice Admiral Chuichi Nagumo, the hero of Pearl Harbor. At the time of our invasion, Saipan's defenses were built around four 8-inch guns, eight 6-inch, nine 5.5-inch, and eight 5-inch dual-purpose guns, four 200-millimeter mortars and several blockhouses. (After the island was secured by our forces it was noted that Japan had made elaborate preparations for emplacing other guns and adding lines of trenches along the beach—all of which underscored the wisdom of the JCS in targeting the invasion for early June.)

Air operations began against Saipan and Tinian on June 11 and 12, followed by an intense naval bombardment from a battleship-cruiser force whose mission was reinforced by the memory of what had happened at Tarawa. However, this was no flat-trajectory range, and the thousands of tons of 16-inch and 5-inch rounds that pummeled the targets did a job as designed.

The Marine Corps plan of attack was as follows. Along Saipan's west shore, off beaches designated Red, Yellow and Blue, the 2nd and 4th Marine Divisions were to come ashore in 700 amtracs mounting new 75-millimeter guns, while the floating reserve was to create a diversion at Tanapag Harbor, a few miles to the north. But, as we shall see, this diversion failed to fool General Saito, who kept his main forces behind the Charon Kanoa beaches and let the marines have it.

June 15, 1944—D-Day—dawned clear and windless; blue skies and calm seas. Fifteen warships ranging from battleship to destroyer stood arrayed off the beaches and began firing almost steadily at 4:30 A.M. At 6:30, carriers began launching a series of air strikes for a half hour, after which the naval bombardment started anew. Now, at 8:00, marines of the four initial regiments—the 6th, 8th, 23rd and 25th—climbed into amtracs to wait the departure signal from the flagship; their LD was 5500 yards from the beach. The marine advance was preceded by an advance of 24 LCI gunboats covered by strafing carrier aircraft. The front was nearly four miles long.

These marines were veterans of Tarawa and the Marshalls, blooded and grimly resolute as they watched in speechless fascination the pillars of dense black smoke which shrouded crescent-shaped bluffs behind the landing beaches. Everywhere there were gun flashes and explosions. At 8:40, Admiral Turner signaled, "Land the Landing Force," and fourteen minutes later the first amphibians toppled over the reef. Simultaneously a well-emplaced, disciplined enemy opened enfilading fire from Afetna and Agingan points, while his machine guns flayed the open water ahead of the onrushing landing craft. This was to be a costly D-Day: 2000 casualties. In the 2nd Division alone, 553 were to be killed and 1022 wounded.

The story of the Saipan landings is told in two parts, the first by Sergeant David Dempsey, a gifted combat correspondent and graduate of the Yale Drama School who served on the staff of the *Christian Science Monitor* before enlisting.

·12· SAIPAN'S BLUE BEACH

SERGEANT DAVID DEMPSEY

Boated at daybreak, transferring from our transports to an LSD—a formidable-looking ship, the stern of which lowered to decant a holdful of amphibious tractors. Down this ramp we plunged into a sea churlish with the wakes of deploying ships. Our "amtrac" was a command boat and had radio communication with the air observers who hovered over the shimmering white beach and the chalky hills of the island. A young major passed around sticks of chewing gum and warned us to make sure that our cartridge belts were unfastened, in case we were hit and had to swim for it. Our boat would go in with the second wave of second battalion to land.

A pilot who had bombed Saipan the day before told me later that the soldiers on the island had gone into what appeared to be a sort of ceremonial fit when it became evident that we were going to invade, staging huge war dances, and in general carrying on like an Irish wake that had got out of hand. He said they appeared to relish the idea of the coming battle, which is more than I can say for ourselves. Our bombers tried to accommodate them by starting fires. They promptly danced around these when the planes began to leave.

Nosed out a hundred yards or so from the ship and rendezvoused, waiting for the waves to form. Ahead, the control boat bobbed just seaward of the reef, bedecked with signal flags that would send us across the line of departure. Idling there, we had a grandstand seat for the show our warships were putting on as a curtain raiser to the landing. We watched the shells bite into the coral sand and shred the palm trees that lined the shore. After an hour the fire was lifted and dive bombers went in for the final strike. They wheeled in formation high over our heads, peeled off, and plummeted savagely down, dropping their bombs a few hundred feet from the ground. As they began their climb the explosions threw bursts of fire, rubble, and a talcum-fine dust into the air. In a few minutes the beach was obscured.

MARPI POINT

TANAPAG PLAIN

TANAPAG HARBOR

GARAPAN

MT. TAPOTCHAU

MT. TIPO PALE

AFETNA POINT

CHARAN KANOA

KAGMAN PENINSULA

LAKE SUSUPE

MAGICIENNE BAY

MT. FINA SUSU

ASLITO AIRFIELD

AGINGAN POINT

NAFUTAN POINT

YARDS

0   2000   4000

.1000   1000   3000   5000

SAIPAN

Ahead, the first assault wave—cannon-bearing amphibious tanks—lined up along the line of departure, like nervous horses jockeying for position. At H hour minus 30 the control vessel waved them across the line. They moved in toward the reef and became tiny specks riding deep in the water, their tracks leaving a wake like a stern-wheeler. At H minus 20 the planes stopped bombing and went into a strafing attack. They flew at treetop height and raked the beach, diving at a 45-degree angle from the seaward side and opening fire while still over the water. A friend of mine in one of the first waves told me later that this threw their boat into a dither, as the planes appeared to be firing on them. Empty shell casings were plopping into the water all around them and falling, red hot, into the boat.

Our radioman, his headphones clamped tightly over his ears and the receiver buttoned up inside his poncho, picked up an aerial observer circling jauntily in his small plane. The noise of the amtrac's motor made conversation practically impossible, so his message—that the first wave had landed on schedule—had to be shouted from ear to ear around the boat.

We readied into position. The flag on the control vessel went up and five minutes later the ensign, dressed in oilskins and balancing himself neatly on the deck, waved us over the line. The speed of the tractor plunged us deeper into the sea, cascading a steady spray of water on us; we were thoroughly soaked within five minutes.

Our plane observer had been in the invasion of the Marshalls, where we had overrun our initial objective within a few hours. Now he radioed: "This is not at all like the Marshalls. Not at all." The radioman shouted this into the ear of the marine next to him, and he in turned passed it on. We looked at each other, and our glances formed a common pool of anxiety. I was conscious of a tightening in my stomach and I knew that if I had been alone I would have been afraid.

Half an hour was to elapse before we hit the beach. Some of the boys tried to read a little paper-bound Navy "expendable." One man was seasick and lowered himself to the deck and vomited.

We were halfway in when word was radioed to land on Blue Beach Two, instead of Blue Beach One, as originally planned. Fire on Blue One was too heavy. We changed our course and headed for Blue Two, about a thousand yards south. In a few minutes our tractor grumbled up onto the reef, lurching tipsily as we crawled over it, giving us the feeling, for that moment, that we were very naked and exposed. We were squatting in the bottom of the tractor and a marine near me stood up, out of curiosity, and looked over the gunwale. His eye caught a streak of flashing steel not more than three or four feet from his face, and he did a sudden flop on the deck. A moment later this apparition exploded in the water of our stern. He had had the rare, if somewhat unenviable, privilege of actually seeing a shell in transit.

Later, approaching the beach, a few more of us braved our heads over the side. Some of the amtracs had been hit and were flopped over like pancakes on a griddle. There was no small-arms fire in our sector. Except for the beachmaster waving the amtracs inland and a group of wounded awaiting transportation back to the ships, the beach was deserted. There certainly were no Japs. I think most of us would have felt better about it if there had been a few, preferably dead, just to reassure us that they had tried to stop us and hadn't succeeded. Our machine gunner, who had his weapon trained on trees that looked like good nesting places for snipers, turned to me and said, "It gives me the creeps. Like fighting a bunch of ghosts." It gave me the creeps, too, although I didn't tell him.

We advanced inland a few yards, detouring around the trees that had been blown down, and snaked single file along the road to Charon Kanoa. This was a village of white concrete one-story buildings, and ablaze with bougainvillaeas in bloom. For the sake of the record I should like to say that Japanese towns are not made of bamboo and paper—at least not the towns in the Marianas—and from what I could determine they were just a little less strongly put together than Parkchester, and their military fortifications are about as solid as the Croton Dam.

The town had been pretty well messed up by our naval gunfire, yet even the wreckage seemed tidy and intimate, the way the Japanese there had lived. Our tractor rolled down what had been the main street, and it was about all we could do to squeeze through. It obviously had not been constructed with an eye to accommodating amphibious tractors and from what we could discover later even the Japanese had lost their tempers when two trucks tried to pass. We went on to what should have been the town square, but was actually an American baseball diamond. A Buddhist temple stood across the street on one side and the town club was on the other.

Our unit was to pass through Charon Kanoa, mop up any resistance, and join the attack pressing toward the ridge about a mile inland. Before we had gone very far word came back that our forward elements were held up, and we debarked and began to advance on foot. I remember looking up and seeing a pair of men's drawers impaled on the limb of a tree. There was no sign of its owner, however, or any other living Japanese, and for perhaps half an hour quiet and a caressing sun lay over the town like a soft blanket.

Then a shell crashed thunderously in the wooded area just ahead of us. Another came down. And another. There was no time to dig foxholes, so we flattened ourselves behind trees and in the shelter of buildings that were still standing. Two lieutenants had dived into a small shellhole and were arguing the possibility of the shells' being short rounds from our own warships. Then one crashed very close by. There was an emphatic silence, until one of the lieutenants settled the argument in his familiar Harvard accent. "Definitely hostile," he announced.

A scout and I backed across the road and got into a Japanese stand-up foxhole; together we deepened and widened it and in so doing came across a case of port wine and some papers that had been cached there. We drank a bottle of the wine, which was mild and sweet, and in a short time had passed the remainder out among the command post. We crouched in the foxhole for some time. The shells were falling closer, and more of our men were being hit. Yet there was no panic and very little real fear. Somehow you figured they would never get you. Anyway, the tension was lifted when somebody behind me stood up and said, "Aw, knock it off, Shorty." We laughed for the first time that morning.

At the same time we were sure that our sector had been picked out by the enemy as a special target and when my buddy and I were ordered back to the regimental CP we both felt a sense of relief. We were under the impression that it would be safer. Actually, shells were falling more thickly on that part of the beach than in the town.

A medical aid station next to the CP was overloaded with casualties, and some of us volunteered to dig foxholes for the wounded and help load them on the tractors going back to the ships. One man was brought in with his leg almost blown off between the hip and the knee; the doctor amputated it without removing him from the stretcher. The shell-shock cases began to come in, too—boys who had "cracked up" under very heavy fire at the front and had to be led or carried in. They hid behind trees and cowered at each new shell burst. Some could not remember their names.

We were loading the wounded into tractors later when a private first class stretcher case expressed the desire to relieve himself. A corpsman handed him the helmet of a near-by sergeant, who was also a casualty. The sergeant lay there and watched in horrified fascination as his helmet was subjected to its ultimate indignity. "That I should live to see the day," he groaned, "when a pfc should do that in my helmet."

The shelling went on all night and its pattern became almost predictable; the barrage would last for about fifteen minutes and then let up for half an hour as the batteries were switched to some other target area. These interludes were almost harder to bear than the periods of shelling, creating suspense rather than relief. We went about pretty much as though our lives were charmed, although it was clear from the casualties coming in that a lot of lives weren't. After a while we could estimate where the shells were going to land by the sound of their whistles, and we dived into our foxholes only when the interval between the scream overhead and the "whop!" of the explosion narrowed to a second or less.

❧ ❧ ❧ ❧

HAVING ACCOMPANIED THE MARINES TO BLUE Beach, let us join professional journalist Robert Sherrod with General Merritt Edson, heading into Green Beach after a wait of several hours at the line of departure.

·13· GREEN BEACH LANDINGS

ROBERT SHERROD

At noon, just after a report said, "Heavy mortar and artillery fire throughout Red and Green beach areas," General Edson asked, via radio, the division commander's permission to land. Superfluously, Edson turned to me and asked: "Been on her long enough?" I swallowed and said, "Any time, think we'll leave soon?" He said, "Wouldn't be surprised." We moved over toward the Green control boat, but the four amphtracs we had requested to take us ashore were misplaced somewhere in the confusion of battle. The line of boats steadily plowing alongside of us were filled with artillery and ammunition. After some of the most effective swearing I ever heard, General Edson preempted four amphtracs. We piled into them.

Bobbing into the water, we saw, every now and then, artillery fire in the water around us. The sharp crack of detonation on the water, following the soft "whoosh" through the air, was almost deafening as we reached the reef, which was about 1,000 yards offshore at our point of crossing. Fifty yards to our portside an amphtrac had just been hit, and men were swimming in the breakers, some trying to make the shore, some struggling seaward whence they had come. Others undoubtedly were beyond movement of any kind.

As we closed in toward the shore Edson ordered everybody in our boat (Number 410) to get down, though he himself continued to stand and look ahead. I noticed that I was crouching on boxes containing 81-mm. mortar shells, and I figured a direct hit on this boat would preclude the necessity of deciding which way to swim. Actually, no shell hit closer to us than fifty yards as we approached the beach.

It was 1430 when the amphtracs crunched ashore; that is, three of them went ashore. The fourth landed somewhere farther up the beach, and was not heard from for a long time. We in the general's amphtrac jumped over the side, and ran to a tank trap a few yards inland. We had arrived on Saipan, 1,500 miles from Japan.

Whether we should ever leave there alive was in considerable doubt for the rest of the day and night. An artillery shell or a mortar shell— I have never found anyone who could definitely tell them apart as they exploded—landed near us every three seconds for the first twenty minutes. Most of them were in the water, 100 yards and more offshore, but some of them hit the beach itself. None hit inside the seven-foot-deep trap which the Japs had built for their protection and which we were now using for our protection.

Inside the trap the battalion aid station for 2/8 (Lieut. Colonel H. P. Crowe) had been set up. There were a half dozen men lying on the sand; they were already bloodily bandaged and awaiting evacuation by amphtracs. On the inshore edge of the trap there were five dead Jap soldiers lying beside their dismantled machine gun, which they apparently had been moving inland when they were hit. As the artillery and/or mortar fire continued heavily, a medical corpsman said, "Hell, I'm going back up front; it's safer." "Up front" meant about 500 yards across the incompleted coral strip which was just beyond the tank trap.

With General Edson, I walked a few yards south. There, in a shell-hole, lay the battalion commander, "Jim" Crowe himself, the old, red-mustached Jim who had been a legend in the Marine Corps for twenty years. Jim was breathing hard, but his steely blue eyes were bright as ever. Around his chest there was a wide bandage. On his left arm there were five smaller bandages. He had been shot through the lung by a machine gun bullet. Mortar shells which had killed a corpsman and wounded a doctor had done the rest. Now Doctor Otto Henry Jantan was finishing the patching, and giving Jim morphine. Jantan shook his head and murmured, aside, "Not much chance, I'm afraid." But there was nothing defeatist about 44-year-old Jim, no more than there was when I landed on his section of hell at

Tarawa. Said Jim, "I hate like hell for this to happen, general, but I'll be all right." The crack of an exploding shell sounded behind us. "Keep your head down, general." Then he shifted his eyes toward me, and said: "I'll see you stateside. We'll throw a whizdinger." As we turned away Edson said, "No man in the shape he's in has a right to look so well and talk so normally." As a matter of fact, the report spread throughout Saipan that Jim Crowe was dead, and the report was accepted as fact by all but old marines, who insisted, "You can't kill Jim Crowe gradually: if he's got a fighting chance he'll come through." The last time I heard of him, in the spring of 1945, he had completed his months-long tour in the San Diego hospital, had taken a rousing trip around the United States, and had returned to duty overseas.

Crowe's battalion was taken over by his executive officer, Major William C. Chamberlin, a reserve officer who resembled Crowe about as much as a bullfrog resembles a blue heron. Big Jim Crowe was rip-roaring and profane; one of the world's finest rifle shots, and a great Marine football player until he got so old he could make only half the tackles on his side of the line. Bill Chamberlin was 28 years old. Bespectacled, soft-voiced, he had been an economics teacher at Northwestern University until he went on active duty in the Marine Corps in 1940. Both Crowe and Chamberlin had received the Navy Cross for Tarawa.

Back at Colonel Wallace's regimental command post, just beyond the tank trap, we heard that the line in front of us was reported 600 yards inland. Wallace walked over to a corpsman who was removing the bayonet from a dead Jap's scabbard. He stormed: "You'll get yourself mixed up with a booby-trap. Now, God damn it, leave him alone." Somebody shoveled sand over the dead Nips, who were beginning to smell. The most cheering sight I had seen since arriving was a line of our tanks moving in through the water, one medium and 18 lights. A marine with a badly shattered leg was brought in and blood plasma was given to him. Colonel Wallace put down his telephone, and turned to the surgeon, "Doctor, the third battalion is badly in need of litters and litter bearers." The Japs opened up again, and the artillery shells "whooshed" overhead like hot blasts that ended when they burst on the water. Fortunately, nearly all went into the water, but even there I did not see another amphtrac hit all afternoon. On Saipan the Japs had not learned much about the proper use of artillery.

I looked around to see what my corner of Saipan looked like. Along the beach, between the sand and the coral airstrip, there were many small trees which looked like pines and scrub oak. Occasionally there was a flame tree in brilliant orange. Beyond the airstrip the small trees, including some palms, fresh fruit trees and pandanus, were even more dense, but nowhere was there anything resembling a jungle. Saipan was semi-tropical, but there was nothing of the South Pacific; in fact, the map showed that Saipan was almost as far north as Hawaii. I decided it might be a nice place if it were properly fixed up by the Seabees and the engineers.

About four o'clock I was sitting in the ditch next to the dead Japs, talking to a marine who said his name was David Swanson; he was a captain from Iowa. "I'm a 155 man," he said, "and I'm waiting for my guns. Let's take a walk up the beach." Swanson's LVT had been hit as it reached the beach. Of his own four men, three were lost; one killed, one wounded, one "went batty." We started south along the water's edge, but the mortar fire was very intense, so we retraced our steps and walked about a mile north.

We saw two dead marines lying on the sand, then two dead Japs. A third marine, a few feet farther north, had had the top of his head neatly carved out, evidently by a shell fragment, and his brains had run out on the sand. Near one of our 1,000-pound bomb duds there were three Japs. A marine named Robert Forsberg, a Catholic whose blood had been Type O, according to the dogtag which lay on his chest, had died of many wounds; he was bandaged in fifteen places. A little farther on, H. R. Walters was unconscious, but he was still breathing. Beyond him another marine lay in a position I had seen many times at Tarawa; when death struck him down he had been charging forward across the beach; his legs were still in a sprinter's crouch, and his M-1 rifle was still held in his extended right arm. Scattered along the beach were numerous Japanese "tape-measure" mines, discs about ten inches in diameter.

An amphtrac named "Beast of Denver" had been knocked out ten feet inland. A small white goat had taken cover under its curved bow. A Jap 75-mm. pack howitzer, mounted on wagon wheels, sat a few feet farther inland, beside two small ammunition wagons. Not far away was a marine who had had his leg blow off at the hip. Beyond the "Beast of Denver" another amphtrac, curiously named "Abattoir," lay in the water's edge. In the 300 yards separating the two vehicles I counted 17 dead marines. Several others who had been treated by corpsmen lay quietly, awaiting evacuation to transports where they would be hospitalized.

Near the invisible line dividing the 6th and 8th Marines, W. J. Worblewski (according to the name stamped on his canteen cover) had given his life toward his country's capture of Saipan. He had captured the 15 feet of sand which lay between the water and the spot where fate caught up with him. Two more dead lay next to amphtrac Number A-36, which was still burning with a color which strangely matched that of the exotic flame tree nearby. Under a small tree that looked like a cedar someone had planted a tiny American flag, which fluttered bravely in the breeze. The sight of it brought a hard lump to my throat, because I could see, all around me, men who had made the ultimate payment so that the little piece of bright cloth might wave there. And I knew already that many others within my view would also die before the Japs stopped contesting our presence on this island.

The 29th Marines were advancing across the airstrip, to pass through a battalion already fighting on the other side. Three amphtracs had been knocked out over there, and the sharp staccato of rifle and machine-gun fire told us that the battle was not far beyond the strip. In a big shellhole next to the airstrip the Japs had evidently registered a powerful direct hit, killing about six marines who had taken cover there. Their bodies were sprawled about the hole. They were terribly mangled; no more than half of any one man was left. One man's hand, ten feet from the hole, still held the trigger of his piece. Said Captain Swanson, "That man loved his rifle."

We walked back to the division CP, part of the way along the airstrip, part of the way on the sand. I was amazed to note how many men evidently had been wounded, only to be killed by a second or a third explosion. Two intelligence officers were questioning the first live Jap I had seen, a gold-toothed little fellow with a bullet hole in his leg. Near some blasted amphtracs a big Marine officer was shouting orders, though he had a thick, blood-stained bandage slung around his chin, which made shouting difficult.

A dozen wounded now lay in the aid station-tank trap where I had landed, and the puddle of water which had seeped through the sand was dark brown with the blood of many men. The amphtracs were evacuating the wounded as fast as possible, but they had difficulty in keeping up with the stretcher bearers who were bringing men from the front line back across the airstrip every few minutes. As I began to dig my foxhole for the night, I estimated that I had seen in this piece of the battleground about 100 dead marines, and only about 20 dead Japs; the last one had been killed a few minutes before, not far from where I was digging.

That first night was a succession of artillery and mortar shells in my particular area. From 8 until 9, from 11 until 1, and from 4 until 5, the shells burst on the beach and in patterns for 500 yards inland, one shell every five seconds. Around the old command post—General Watson moved the CP 1,000 yards north during the night, but I stayed in my original foxhole—perhaps 20 shells burst with 25 yards, but so far as I could find out, nobody was hit in the immediate vicinity of it. Men in holes are hard to hit.

For me there was none of the terror of the first night on Tarawa. Patly, I told myself, this was because I had become used to getting shot at; any man in combat begins to adopt a sort of "Is it mine or ain't it?" philosophy, after a while. But, also, we kept the front lines lit up with star shells, so that we could anticipate Jap counterattacks. Most of the night was like daylight; even the Japs used star shells. And there was a solid 500 yards between the front lines and my hole in the sand. That was better than the 20 feet we had at Tarawa. This time I got a few hours of sleep . . .

By returning to ship I missed the first real tank attack the Japs had ever mounted against the Marines . . . a spectacular affair. I was able to reconstruct it later: We had expected the Japs to use tanks on Saipan, perhaps 100 of them, maybe 200. The 6th Marines had destroyed four tanks on D Day, but the counterattack that night was an infantry charge. On this early morning of D plus 2 the Japs decided to try another counterattack, this time with tanks. Just why they had not tried a co-ordinated push in the first place was one of those inexplicable things about Japs. Maybe naval gunfire kept them under cover on D night.

B Company of 1/6 bore the full weight of the tank attack, aided only by a bazooka team from A Company, and, in the mop-up, by men from K Company and some halftracks from Regimental Special Weapons. Captain Rollen of B Company reported at 0330 that tanks were coming toward him from the hills which sloped off Tapotchau; the Japs evidently expected to gain surprise by avoiding the road from Garapan.

Within a few minutes, the tanks were upon the front lines of B Company. One of the company's 60-mm. mortar positions was overrun. Another 60-mm. position was overrun by a tank that was leaking oil; a Marine in the foxhole had oil-covered dungarees to show for it. Captain Rollen rose from his foxhole and fired his carbine, which was equipped with a grenade launcher. The tank kept going past him. The confusion that attends any battle was multiplied a hundredfold in the B Company area, where star shells lit up the sky, tracer bullets arched overhead, the clanging of Jap tanks was mixed with the explosion of anti-tank grenades and bazooka hits. Captain Rollen had his ear drum burst by an explosion, but he continued to direct his company until his relief was ordered and he was evacuated. Captain Norman Thomas, his relief, a hero of Tarawa, was himself killed before the relief was effected.

What did the men of B Company do? They stayed there and took it. Some men waited in their foxholes ("well built holes, they were") until the Jap tanks rolled over them; then they hit the tanks in the vulnerable rears with bazooka rockets and anti-tank grenades. Private Robert S. Reed of Cabot, Arkansas, according to his Navy Cross citation "accounted for four hits on four different tanks with his rocket launcher, and, then after running out of rockets, climbed upon a fifth tank and, with utter disregard for his own personal safety, dropped an incendiary grenade in the turret, thereby disabling the tank."

Pfc. John Kounk, of Sheboygan, Wisconsin, in spite of heavy enemy fire, moved among the tanks, firing his bazooka at very short range. He and his teammate, Pfc. Horace Narveson, of Oberon, North Dakota, hit three tanks with four bazooka charges. Corporal John E. Watson, of Lake Charles, Louisiana, threw two incendiary grenades into a tank, then killed the Japs as they tried to escape from it. Despite intense machine-gun fire from another tank, Watson carried a wounded pal to safety. Sergeant Alex B. Smith, of Lake Providence, Louisiana, directed the fire of his machine-gun squad against three tanks, but it was ineffective. So Smith took his carbine - grenade launcher, moved to a more advantageous (but more dangerous) position and put all three tanks out of action.

Perhaps two first-class privates, Charles D. Merritt of Greenville, South Carolina, and Herbert J. Hodges, of Anchorage, Kentucky, established some kind of world's record: They got out of their foxholes, moved first to the right and fired their bazooka there, then to the left and fired again. Time after time they repeated this. The Jap tank gunners and riflemen who followed the tanks were shooting all the time, but they did not faze Merritt and Hodges. Their score: Tanks fired at, 7; number of shots, 7; tanks hit, 7.

Partially, the Japs' tank losses were due to their own ineptness. The tanks were followed by some infantry, mostly after the second wave. But B Company's four heavy machine guns cut them down. Then the tanks, both blind and confused, ambled aimlessly toward the beach instead of penetrating B Company's lines farther, until the bazookas or anti-tank grenades stopped them. One of the marines told me later about the enemy antics: "The Nips would halt, then jump out of their tanks. Then they would sing songs and wave swords. Finally, one of them would blow a bugle, jump back into the tanks, if they hadn't been hit already. Then we would let them have it with a bazooka."

Not all the tanks had been knocked out by the hits scored on them. K Company of the Third Battalion helped to finish off seven tanks after it relieved B Company at daylight. The Regimental Special Weapons Company's halftracks were also called out, and their 75-mm. guns polished off the cripples or caught the remnants which were attempting to flee back to the hills. About 0700 one last tank was seen struggling back toward the Jap lines. A destroyer fired 20 salvos. The tanks burned all day. A total of 29 Jap tanks had been accounted for, and, in the words of General Watson: "I don't think we have to fear Jap tanks any more on Saipan. We've got their number." At 0735 the 6th Marines, including B Company, jumped off in the attack up the slopes of Tapotchau.

About noon of the 17th I got in a small boat and went over to the *Rocky Mount* to find out how things looked from the command ship. Lieut. General Holland Smith's wall chart was incomplete, but it told enough: Casualties in the assault battalions were marked; 2/8 and 3/8, 40 percent; 2/6 and 3/6, 197 enlisted men and seven officers; 23d and 24th Marines, "very heavy, especially in the 23d." The latter regiment had rapidly seized the area near the sugar mill, but had been driven back during D night. It was reported that two patrols of 12 to 15 men had been sent out that night to make contact with the Second Division, and no man had been heard of since. The Twenty-seventh Division had been called in from reserve; the 165th Regiment, which had taken Makin, had started landing behind the Fourth Division on D plus 1 night, and the 105th and 106th Regiments were being ordered to land. The invasion of Guam, scheduled for tomorrow, had been postponed because nobody had any idea how much this Saipan thing might cost before it was finished, whenever that might be.

At 1430, when I landed alongside the coveted pier at Charon-Kanoa, the sugar mill had long since been retaken by the 23d Marines. It was a mass of rubble, pounded by hundreds of tons of high explosives, its vats stinking in the sun and drawing millions of flies. The big smokestack had been pierced a thousand times, but it still stood. A small refinery next door (wistfully designated as a probable rum distillery by a marine) was as completely wrecked.

I walked a mile south from the little town, down the road that was already a foot deep in dust which had been ground to fine powder by tanks, trucks, and jeeps. At General Schmidt's Fourth Division CP, a deep sandbagged dugout of two rooms, there was no spirit of pessimism. The Fourth's casualties were 2,200 men. Eighty-six men had been buried, 70 more awaited burial, though collection of the dead had hardly begun. Even the artillerymen had been hit fairly hard; six guns had been knocked out the first day by counter-battery fire. By now four had been repaired. Lieut. Colonel Maynard Schultz, commanding the First Battalion, 24th Marines, had been killed. But troops of the division had almost crossed the island. Aslito Airfield had been partially captured on D Day, but the Marines had pulled back to a defensive line for the night, and now they were bypassing the airfield on its northern side, leaving its capture and the securing of the southern part of the island to the Army troops which were

already fighting their way back to the field. After the Fourth had
crossed the island it would swing north on the eastern side as the Second swung north on the western side. The Army division's troops
would come up the center, along the eastern slopes of Tapotchau.

Captain William McCahill, public relations officer of the Fourth,
had set up headquarters in foxholes between General Schmidt's CP
and the beach. "Have a foxhole," he said, passing the shovel, and
I begin digging alongside Frank Kelley of the New York *Herald
Tribune.* When the word "Condition Red!" was passed (meaning that
Jap planes were on their way), Kelley and I, slow diggers, found
refuge in a poncho-covered foxhole with the division provost marshal,
Lieut. Colonel Melvin Krulewitch of Albany, New York. The colonel
found—of all things—a bottle of bourbon.

※   ※   ※   ※

ON D-PLUS-TWO THE ENEMY WAS STILL LAUNCHING
strong counterattacks over a wide front, and one of these was directed at Hill 500 which had recently come into American hands.
If regained, Hill 500 (from which Colonel Oka, commanding
the 47th Brigade, had been ousted) would give the Japanese an
overlook of the airdrome and the entire southern portion of the
island. The following account by an anonymous combat correspondent details how a few brave marines defended that strategic position.

·14· HILL 500

ANONYMOUS

Nobody on Hill 500 expected an attack. The nearest Japs . . . except
perhaps for a stray sniper or so, were more than a mile away, being
steadily and relentlessly pushed back by marines determined to take
Mount Tapotchau.

There were Japs down on the Nafutan Point peninsula a couple of miles to the south and a little east of the hill. But they were bottled up by the Army, cut off from their own forces and facing extermination.

Two PFCs in a foxhole about 50 yards from the CP first knew the Japs were there. In the darkness, the enemy had set up a heavy machine-gun nest within spitting distance of the foxhole, one of five heavies and two light machine guns which formed an enemy line pointing into the rear of the CP.

Apparently the first flush of dawn revealed Pfc. Tom B. McQuabe and Pfc. Bill Cramford to the Japs who had escaped from the Nafutan Point trap. McQuabe, a strapping Buffalo, New York, lad, and Cramford, from Long Beach, California, had paired off on the beach more than a week before. They had worked together since, taking turns during those nights when the battalion had been on the front lines at standing guard while the other slept. Both were BAR-men and their rifles lay at their sides.

Something warned the two marines, maybe instinct.

Both of them reached for their rifles just as the Jap threw the grenade. It was a bad throw but the explosion hit McQuabe before he could get his weapon aimed. Cramford, however, opened up on full automatic, firing quick bursts. The Japs around the machine gun all went down.

That started it off. For the next fifteen minutes a fierce fire fight raged in the half dawn out back of the CP. It was a miniature banzai attack on the part of the Japs, who knew their only value was to take as many marines with them as possible before they went down.

Not one burst was ever fired from the enemy machine guns that had been set up so carefully. The fighting was hand-to-hand, and weapons were anything handy. Pfc. James Davie went down under a blow from a Jap wielding a shovel. When Pfc. Rayburn couldn't get his carbine to work he threw a pick mattock at a Jap rushing him with a bayonet.

Two Ohio PFCs, James Ferguson of Cleveland and Ed Martin of Cincinnati, were in a hole with a sheet of tin over it when the scrap started. Ferguson knocked the cover aside with the muzzle of his Tommy gun, saw a Jap staring down at him. He shot him while still pushing the cover. A Jap bayoneted Pfc. Robert Postal, who had been hit on the beach and had rejoined his outfit only the day before. Postal shot the Jap as he withdrew the bayonet.

The fight was over as abruptly as it started. They counted a total of 53 Japs within an arc of about 75 yards back of the CP. Cramford, whose BAR bursts had been the first shots fired, was hit himself near the end of the action. Another grenade stopped him after he had fired three clips. He was credited with at least seven Japs.

The battalion had been back at the CP for two days when the Jap breakthrough occurred. They had been pulled back to front lines during which they had pushed all the way to the foothills of Mount Tapotchau. It had been nasty going all of the way.

Actually, of course, they weren't really Raiders. The Raiders, as separate units, had been disbanded. They were just a battalion of the Fourth Marine Division.

But they were a cocky, self-sure lot and the "Old Man", Lieutenant Colonel J. M. Chambers, had been a captain with Edson's Raiders on Tulagi. So, in the weeks of training between Namur and Saipan they had dubbed themselves "Chambers' Raiders." And on Saipan they made the title stick—so well, in fact, that Lieutenant Colonel Evans Carlson, who was with them a good bit of the time until he was hit, called them the equal of any battalion he'd ever seen.

. . . At Saipan, they drew the reserve position coming in to the beach below Charon Kanoa about midmorning of D-Day.

The beach wasn't a healthy place to be: the white sand was alive with mortar shells which the Japs were lobbing over from behind the first hills, and with bigger stuff which came from the artillery holed up in the rocky cliffs back toward the center of the island. Every square yard of that beach had been carefully taped for mortar and artillery fire, which meant that the barrage was uncomfortably accurate. There was a saying, afterward, that four marines in a group were safe on the beach but that five or more were sure to draw fire.

It was obvious that the only way out was forward, so Chambers' Raiders moved up. They organized behind the embankment that carried Saipan's toylike narrow-gauge railroad around the western side of the island, and dug in for the night. The embankment provided an excellent haven. The law of trajectory made it virtually a blind spot for Jap artillery.

The story of Chambers' Raiders might have ended the next day. Company after company of the outfit was called forward to plug gaps in the line up front where the Jap was holed in. The colonel, at the CP, fretted the morning away, watching his outfit disintegrating.

He reminded you of a pirate as he stalked about, except that he was a strapping big fellow. On his hip was a .38-caliber pistol, carried in a specially made snap-draw holster. From under his armpit peeked another pistol, a .45, and dangling from his belt he carried a wicked-looking knife that had been cut down from a bayonet on Tulagi.

Finally, when only his headquarters staff was left under his command, the colonel couldn't stand it any longer. He sent a runner back with a plea that his battalion be put into the lines as a unit.

"I'm tired of being a company commander," he explained.

Headquarters said okay, so the battalion was reformed on the 01 Ridge, beyond Aslito town and north of the airport. It wasn't just that simple, however—they had their first real skirmish with the Japs before they made it.

They had to cross a large field and skirt the north edge of the airfield to get there. Chambers started through the field to find a rendezvous area. With him were Pfc. Vito "Vic" Cassaro, a blond New Yorker with a walkie-talkie on his back; Pfc. George O'Neill, an ex-Cleveland photo-studio worker, and Pfc. L. D. Rogers, two of the colonel's "shadows"; and several others.

A couple of snipers opened up when the group had inched out only a short distance. They kept going. Then a machine gun spit out an angry tattoo which kicked up the dust at their feet. They dove for cover—Chambers and Cassaro banging heads behind the same stump.

That was when they sent for Sergeant Hamilton Gibson, the Arkansas hillbilly, and his anti-sniper platoon. The colonel asked for tanks, too, and the demolition men, and sent word for the battalion to follow along behind the rough-stuff boys. The Japs really opened up then. Snipers and machine gun pockets were as thick as the flies which on Saipan are everywhere.

It was slow, tedious work, cleaning out that field and the little village. Gibson, with Pfc. Berthieume, who had served in Edson's Raiders with the Colonel, came upon a mound with a hole in the top. A Jap stuck his head out. Berthieume's rifle jammed but Gibson got in a burst and the Jap dropped back into the hole. They tossed a couple of grenades in just to be sure. A machine gun opened up off to the left. They thought it was firing at the others. Then another m.g. began chattering and Gibson knew it wasn't firing at the others. He felt a stinging burn in his right heel.

Pfc. Robert Bowman, another of the anti-snipers, sneaked his way into one of the houses that day and came out with a Jap machine gun to supplement his carbine.

O'Neill, with Pfc. L. D. Rogers, was all over the area in a jeep during the afternoon. Once they even were on the airport runway. In one of the houses which appeared to have been used as a barracks, they found several cases of beer and canned apricots. The booty was stowed aboard and the pair toured the bivouac area after things had quieted down, distributing their load. The apricots were a real delicacy to men who had had nothing but field-pack rations for three days. O'Neill's reward was the nickname of "Scavenger."

O'Neill achieved his major combat ambition on Saipan—to snipe the sniper. It was Hill 500. The Jap sniper was lying prone, lining up his sights on a marine on the next ridge. O'Neill came up from the sniper's flank and shot him through the head.

Hill 500 is perhaps the biggest prize to the credit of Chambers' Raiders. It's a clifflike collection of jagged rock peaks which looks like a pyramid of giant razor-back hogs and it juts up at the southwestern end of Saipan's mountain chain. From it the Japs could overlook the airdrome and the entire southern portion of the island. The enemy's southern defense hinged on that peak.

The assault of Hill 500 started with a barrage from the battalion's 37s. Supporting artillery, mortar, and rocket fire pulverized the Jap positions for an hour before Chambers' men started forward. The barrage kicked up a cloud of white rock-dust that coated the men, making them look like someone had dumped a sack of dirty flour over their heads.

The artillery shattered the Jap defenses but there was still a lot of infighting to be done as the colonel's men scaled the hill. They made the summit by midafternoon and set up a defense line for the night, before starting down.

But the Japs knew they had lost this hinge to their defenses. During the night a few snipers made themselves a nuisance. But more of the enemy committed hari-kari. Every few minutes, the blackness would be punctuated by the mournful sounds of someone intoning a native chant. Then a grenade would explode and there'd be a scream or a moan.

"Awful spooky," Scavenger O'Neill spoke up once, "but every one means one less to get tomorrow."

There were plenty of Japs left the next day, however. The day is one Chambers' Raiders will remember a long time. It started quietly enough, with the battalion moving through the gullies beyond Hill 500 on toward the foothills of Mount Tapotchau. They crossed a couple of ridges and had reached a third one with only minor incident.

Beyond the third ridge stretched a narrow valley ending in a wooded rise. On the left was a sheer cliff. On the right was another ridge, at right angles to the one they were on.

Colonel Carlson, who had joined the battalion for the Hill 500 action, and Colonel Chambers moved forward cautiously with the point of the line. O'Neill and Cassaro were with them. Everything seemed serene on the ridge. It looked like a trap. And it was.

The battalion was well into the valley before the machine guns started spitting from the cliff of caves. More guns echoed from the ridge on the right, and rifle fire and mortars splattered out from the woods ahead. It reminded you of Tennyson's famous lines about the charge of the light brigade. Only it was:

> Machine guns to the left of them,
> Machine guns to the right of them,
> Rifles and mortars in front of them
> Chattered and spit.

Cassaro was hit by an early burst of fire. The two colonels had picked him up to carry him back when Carlson caught the bullet that shattered his arm. The bullet whizzed past inches above Cassaro's stomach. The ex-Raider CO didn't even drop his charge. All he said was: "I'm hit."

Chambers' Raiders lost a number of men that day in the valley pocket. One company had three COs in less than an hour. A marine on the right flank went down before a burst of m.g. fire. He wasn't dead and the Japs kept firing at him. A tank lumbered over, rolled over the spot where the marine lay and when it passed he was no longer there. The tank crew had pulled the wounded man inside.

The tanks moved up to the front of the advancing lines. The mobile 37s and half-tracks also plowed in and the entrenched Nips turned panicky.

They began blowing up their ammunition dumps just ahead of the marines. One of these explosions knocked Colonel Chambers to the ground. He was stunned and shaken but otherwise unhurt. He was taken back to the aid station and Major James Taul, the exec, took over.

That night, after eight days in the front lines, the battalion was ordered back to Hill 500 for a rest. Fresh troops moved up to the foothills of the mountain to carry on the drive. The colonel rejoined them the next morning and for two full days those who were left relaxed on the peak they had captured only a short time before.

They could still hear the sound of battle up ahead but, except for that, it was calm on the hill. Men cleaned their weapons and those who were lucky put on fresh socks and sometimes scivvies. From somewhere cards appeared and a couple of games of the outfit's favorite pastime—pinochle with a double deck—got under way. Players came and went but the game went on so long as there was enough light.

The interruption caused by the Japs from Nafutan Point ended their rest. But it was scheduled to end that day, anyway. Orders had come through the previous night to return to the front the next day.

On the way back they stopped to watch a Jap bomber trying to dodge our ack-ack. Little black puffs made polka dots in the sky around the plane with the red ball. Suddenly it began to smoke.

"Blow up, you s.o.b.," yelled a marine watching from the valley.

As if in answer, the big bomber did explode a second later. The Japs should have heard, even in Tokyo, the cheers from those marines moving back into the lines.

❊ ❊ ❊ ❊

THE IMPERIAL NAVY'S COUNTERATTACK ON THE SAI-
pan invasion was launched June 18, and it was spearheaded by
Japan's remaining carrier-air striking power. Next day the Fifth
Fleet under Spruance fought the prelude to the Battle of the
Philippine Sea, the "Turkey Shoot," in which 346 enemy planes
were downed, while Vice Admiral Jisaburo Ozawa's main forces
were engaged on June 20. The latter action resulted in the loss of
carriers *Taiho*, *Shokaku* and *Hiyo* from a combined carrier-sub-
marine punch. Often criticized for not mopping up the shattered
Japanese fleet, Spruance returned to Saipan, whose protection, in
his valued opinion, was more important than another sea battle.
And at that juncture, according to a Japanese historian, "The
Mariana garrison resembled fish caught in a casting net."

On Saipan, the V Amphibious Corps was stretched out on an
arc facing north and its ultimate objective was Mount Tapotchau,
with the 2nd Marine Division on the left flank and the 4th Marine
Division on the right. Next day, because of the hard fighting now
encountered, Holland Smith advised the 27th Infantry Division
it was going to the line between the two marine divisions. The
slow advance of the 27th began with eighteen battalions of artillery in support, and additional help from naval and air bombardments. But slow advances irritated "Howlin' Mad," and he was
not loathe to keep his impatience a secret. In the following excerpt the marine general discusses a controversy which rankles
in some precincts even today.

·15· THE RELIEF OF MAJOR GENERAL RALPH SMITH

LIEUTENANT GENERAL HOLLAND M. SMITH

The attack opened on June 22. I put the Twenty-seventh in the
center of the line. As a precautionary measure, I formed two temporary Marine battalions, one from Corps headquarters and the other
from the shore party. At that time my headquarters in Charon-Kanoa
was protected by a company of 120 men of the V Amphibious Corps
Reconnaissance Company, in command of Captain James L. Jones,

whose Pacific island reconnaissance exploits are unique. These troops I ordered to reconnoiter assigned battle positions in the rear because I felt that, if the Japanese counterattacked, I would have two battalions to cover any unfavorable development.

After my experience with the Twenty-seventh at Makin and Eniwetok, I was reluctant to use them again in the Marianas, but when the operation was planned they were the only troops available in Hawaii and I had to take them.

The trouble with the Twenty-seventh Division was, if I may coin a word, "militia-itis." As originally mobilized, the division had come entirely from the New York National Guard, with a good record and tradition from World War I. Much of its leadership, as was the case throughout the New York Guard, stemmed from a gentlemen's club known as the Seventh Regiment, traditionally New York's "silk stocking" outfit, and likewise a worthy unit, *per se,* with an impeccable reputation for annual balls, banquets and shipshape summer camps. Any division, however, springing from such sources and maintained intact after mobilization, contains the entangled roots of home town loyalties, ambitions and intrigues. Employer-noncommissioned officers in the Twenty-seventh were sometimes commanded, if that is the word, by employee-officers; there was sometimes a gentlemanly reluctance on the part of officers to offend Old Seventh messmates through harsh criticism or rigorous measures; in the eyes of many, especially the ambitious, there were reputations—New York reputations—to be made or broken; and behind all there was Albany, where the State Adjutant General's office allocated peacetime plums.

A machine like the National Guard is an admirable and a truly constitutional machine for peacetime training. It is in a position to capitalize on all the values of local allegiance, but after mobilization these same allegiances become barnacles on the hull. The War Department must have realized this, especially in so clear-cut a case as that of the Twenty-seventh, which had been posing "political" problems to Washington ever since mobilization. These were, if anything, intensified by the fact that some of the higher-ups in the War Department were important in the Militia. Congressman "Jim" Wadsworth, who incidentally spurred on the anti-Marine Corps faction during the merger drives of 1946 and 1947, was an influential New Yorker of much military background and firm National Guard connections.

In such an atmosphere there could have been only one square-cut solution for the War Department: to disband the division after mobilization, or at the very least, too transfer its original personnel far and wide, and replace them with anyone on earth but former members of the New York Guard. What is more, such a widespread transfer would probably have benefited the entire Army, because, man for man, the New York National Guard enjoys an excellent reputation for individual peacetime training.

That such a shakeup was never made—especially after the showings of the Twenty-seventh Division regiments at Makin and Eniwetok—reflects broadly upon the War Department, and more particularly on its senior Pacific representative, Richardson, who, had he been willing to open his eyes and swallow inter-service stiff-neckedness, could have broken up a military combination which could do only harm to the traditions of the Army and to those of a fine state.

A lot has been written about the differences between Army and Marine methods in action. The two services use the same weapons and the same tactical manual and, therefore, I do not propose to enter into an unprofitable discussion here, but only to summarize the facts of the case concerning the Twenty-seventh Division on Saipan.

On the first day of the Tapotchau attack, the Second Division advanced 1,000 yards and the Fourth 2,000 yards. The Twenty-seventh was directed to pass through the Fourth and join a coordinated continuation of the attack on the morning of June 23. The Second and the Fourth, on the flanks, jumped off according to schedule.

The attack by the Twenty-seventh was late starting. According to reports to me, one battalion moved 50 minutes late, other elements moved even later and the 106th Infantry was unable to start forward until three hours and fifteen minutes after H-hour. I considered the two Marine divisions on the flank were jeopardized by the sagging in the center of the line and I plugged the gaps between them and the Twenty-seventh. We made little headway that day. By nightfall my maps showed our lines as a deep U, with the Twenty-seventh very little ahead of its departure point and still occupying the bottom of the U, and the two Marine divisions holding the flanks.

Furthermore, the 2nd Battalion, 105th Infantry, a Twenty-seventh Division unit, assisted by tanks, had been given the mission of cleaning up Nafutan Point, a broken peninsula jutting out of the southeast corner of Saipan, which was now in our rear. In order that our attack northward could progress with safety, I wanted this cleanup done as aggressively and rapidly as possible. The area contained 500 to 600 Japanese troops, plus battlefield jetsam of civilian refugees and a good many wounded, who had holed up to die in the caves. It has since been claimed that more than 1,200 enemy troops were on Nafutan, but a captured Japanese operation order which came to our headquarters later showed that, as of June 26, there were only 500 effective, unwounded personnel, and the 1,200 count comes unsubstantiated from one who was a party in interest to the subsequent controversy over this little operation.

The battalion from the 105th Infantry (which was subsequently awarded the Army's Distinguished Unit Citation for its performance on Saipan) failed to show the aggressiveness which its mission demanded, and it even permitted, on the night of June 26, a column of some 500 well-armed and organized Japanese, the last such on the Point, to march, *in column of twos,* right through its lines with hardly a shot fired. All these Japanese had to be killed before daybreak by Marine cannoneers and riflemen from the 14th and 25th Marines. The alibi for this performance claims that the frontage assigned this battalion (some 2,000 yards, according to the contemporary periodic reports) was excessive. What is not taken into consideration, however, is that, due to the taper of Nafutan Point, a single advance of less than 200 yards on the battalion's left would have shortened the total frontage by almost a thousand yards.

As Major General George W. Griner, USA, who later came into command of the Twenty-seventh Division, officially reported to me concerning the Nafutan Point operations about this time, " . . . a faint-hearted attack was made. The means were available for complete success, had a determined attack been made." Griner, incidentally, eventually had this battalion commander relieved.

It was in this context of all-round poor performance by the Twenty-seventh that, on the afternoon of June 23, I sought the help of Major General Sanderford Jarman, who was to assume the post of Island Commander when we captured Saipan. I asked him to see Ralph Smith and appeal to him, as one Army man to another, on the grounds that the reputation of the Army was suffering through a lack of offensive spirit. Before Ralph Smith went into the line, I had impressed upon him the need for strong, offensive action on Saipan. The Japanese were on the run, I told him, and in order to lick them we had to keep them moving. As my admonition had failed, I hoped that Jarman could influence him.

Shortly afterward, Jarman returned and reported that Ralph Smith had promised to do better the next day. Jarman also reported that Ralph Smith said if he did not do better he deserved to be relieved.

In a communication to Richardson, produced at the subsequent Army investigation by the Buckner Board—named after Lieutenant General Simon Bolivar Buckner, who presided—Jarman reported that, on June 23:

> I found that General [Ralph] Smith had been up to the front lines all afternoon and was thoroughly familiar with the situation. I talked to General Smith and explained the situation as I saw it and that I felt from reports from the Corps Commander that his division was not carrying its full share. He immediately replied that such was true; that he was in no way satisfied with what his regimental commanders had done during the

day and that he had been with them and had pointed out to them the situation. He further indicated to me that he was going to be present tomorrow, June 24, with this division when it made its jump-off and he would personally see to it that the division went forward. I explained my interest in the matter was that I was senior Army commander present and was anxious to see that the Army did its job as it should be done.

There was no improvement the next day. What had promised to be a swift, effective movement degenerated into a laggard action that almost came to a standstill. The two Marine flanks had to advance slowly to prevent the widening of the gaps between themselves and the Twenty-seventh in the center.

I took my map and went on board the *Rocky Mount* to discuss the situation with Kelly Turner. We both went on board the *Indianapolis* to see Spruance, who was in overall command of the operation. I told him the facts and said that the situation demanded a change in command. He asked me what should be done.

"Ralph Smith has shown that he lacks aggressive spirit," I replied, "and his division is slowing down our advance. He should be relieved." I suggested that Jarman take over the Twenty-seventh Division as a supplementary duty until another commanding officer was appointed. Turner supported me and Spruance agreed.

On June 24, the following message was despatched from Spruance as Commander, Fifth Fleet, to me as Commander, Northern Troops and Landing Force, and circulated to others concerned for information:

> You are authorized and directed to relieve Major General Ralph Smith from command of the Twenty-seventh Division, U.S. Army, and place Major General Jarman in command of this division. This action is taken in order that the offensive on Saipan may proceed in accordance with the plans and orders of the Commander, Northern Troops and Landing Force.

Accordingly, Ralph Smith was relieved and returned to Honolulu and Jarman succeeded him. Relieving Ralph Smith was one of the most disagreeable tasks I have ever been forced to perform. Personally, I always regarded Ralph Smith as a likable and professionally knowledgeable man. However, there are times in battle when the responsibility of the commander to his country and to his troops requires hard measures. Smith's division was not fighting as it should, and its failure to perform was endangering Amercan lives. As Napoleon has said, "There are no bad regiments, only bad colonels," and the basic remedy for the defective performance of the Twenty-seventh Division was to find a leader who could make it toe the mark. Ralph Smith had been only too conscious of what was wrong, as he was the first to admit to Jarman, but he had been incapable of strong and necessary action. I realized at the time, as I in turn said to Jarman, that the relief of Smith would stir up the hornet's nest because of its inter-Service implications, and because I knew how Richardson would make capital of such a situation; but in the face of the enemy, I felt that we were all Americans, and that victory was more important than any Service's prestige.

❊ ❊ ❊ ❊

IN THE MOUNT TIPO PALE FIGHTING OF JUNE 24, CAPtain John Magruder and his rifle company were showered with grenades during a night-long counterattack. Many of his men were killed. Magruder speaks of the aftermath in this brief, moving passage.

·16· EPITAPH

JOHN A. MAGRUDER

Heavy enemy mortar fire had caused numerous casualties in our front lines during the night. Now, in the morning, I was walking along the road when I saw some of the dead being loaded gently into the backs of several trucks that had been drawn up to take bodies to the division cemetery. I looked to see if I recognized any of the dead marines. There were half a dozen stretched out, some on their backs and several face down. One of the latter was a young, fair-haired private who had only recently arrived as a replacement, full of exuberance at finally being a full-fledged marine on the battle front.

As I looked down at him, I saw something which I think I shall never forget. Sticking from his back trouser pocket was a yellow pocket edition of a book he had evidently been reading in his spare moments. Only the title was visible—*Our Hearts Were Young and Gay*.

❊ ❊ ❊ ❊

THE SUCCESSFUL STORMING OF MOUNT TAPOTCHAU
under cover of smoke by the 1st Battalion, 29th Regiment, commanded by Lieutenant Colonel R. M. Tompkins and supported
by the 3rd Battalion, 8th Marines, broke the spirit of the enemy.
General Saito logically wired Tokyo: "There is no hope for victory." For by now the V Amphibious Corps was firmly in possession of Kagman Peninsula and Tapotchau, and surviving Japanese forces were being compressed into northern Saipan. (As
of June 28 the cost of this fight was 2116 marines killed and missing; another 6337 marines wounded; and 1023 casualties. However, as the battle for Saipan entered its final stage the toll mounted sharply). By July 6 when the Japanese launched a ferocious
counterattack with little more than sheer courage to go on, the 2nd
Marine Division had taken Garapan and Mucho Point, and the
4th Marines had captured Mount Petosukura. The attack was
initially directed at the 27th Division which was then on Tanapag Plain, braced for a banzai charge; marine intelligence had
learned one was coming and enemy commanders had exhorted
their men each to kill ten Americans.

At 4:45 A.M. Japanese troops screaming *"Banzai"* and *"Tenno
Heika"* (ten lives for the Emperor)—most of them armed with
only bayonets lashed to sticks—smashed into Lieutenant Colonel William J. O'Brien's 105th RCT. That officer was last seen
manning a .50-caliber machine gun mounted on a jeep and firing into the screaming enemy. Two batteries of the 3rd Battalion, 10th Marines, with twelve 105-mm. rifles slowed down the
attack but did not stop it. Major William L. Crouch commanded
these batteries and was killed; and 35 others were wounded, as
marines cut fuzes short and fired point-blank at the Japanese
horde now coming four abreast in a furious lunge. Hours after
the carnage was ended Robert Sherrod inspected the scene and
noted: "The whole area seemed to be a mass of dead bodies, stinking guts and brains." We had lost 406 Americans in the crazy
charge, against a Japanese loss of 4300. Next day, General Saito sat
down on a rock in prophetically named Paradise Valley and performed the rites of a doomed Japanese warrior, hara-kiri. He
opened an artery in his stomach and then an aide shot him in the
head, later cremating his body. Not far away, Pearl Harbor hero
Admiral Nagumo also took his own life, but with benefit of the
traditional ceremonial sword—he simply blew a hole in his head
and was cremated. The battle for Saipan was over.

We had suffered 16,525 casualties, of whom 12,935 were marines. The 2nd and 4th Marine Divisions alone had lost 2363 killed
in action. A second but ineffectual banzai charge materialized

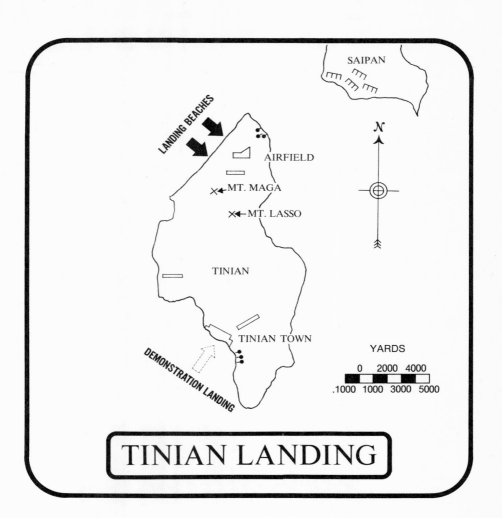

SAIPAN

LANDING BEACHES

N

AIRFIELD

MT. MAGA

MT. LASSO

TINIAN

TINIAN TOWN

YARDS

0   2000 4000

.1000 1000 3000 5000

DEMONSTRATION LANDING

TINIAN LANDING

even as the dead were being counted, but was driven off. Finally, on July 10, 1944, the American flag went up on General Smith's headquarters at Charon Kanoa, and from that point Japanese troops gave up. In due course they succumbed to hunger and surrendered, committed suicide or fell victim to marine patrols. In any case, Saipan was ours.

"Saipan," commented General Smith, "was the decisive battle of the Pacific offensive . . . Japan's Pearl Harbor."

Across a three-mile-wide channel from Saipan's Agingan Point lies Tinian. By the end of June marine artillery had begun to expend some 30,000 rounds of ammunition on it, and not a day passed that naval air and firepower missed an opportunity to flail away. By rights Tinian should have been properly softened by "J-Day," July 24, 1944. But it was not. The island was defended by 9000 Japanese Army and Navy troops, of which Colonel Hiyoshi Ogata's 50th Infantry Regiment, 29th Division, stood out as blooded veterans of the Manchurian campaign.

After frogmen had reconnoitered Tinian's beaches, marine planners decided to land on the northwest coast opposite Uishi Airfield, on beaches designated White 1 and White 2. The unhappy situation now was the width of the landing spaces—about 60 yards and 180 yards respectively—which did not permit entry by more than four LVTs or landing craft at one time. Although this did not present an insurmountable obstacle when the test came, it did give Major General Harry Schmidt's staff some anxious moments. The assault division—the 4th Marine Regiment commanded by Major General Clifton B. Cates—embarked from Tanapag Harbor on July 23 in 37 LSTs with amtracs aboard, followed by four LSTs which were lifting four 75-mm. battalions. Tanks were preloaded in LCMs and LCTs. The 2nd Division, in 16 transports, waited at Charon Kanoa while a third regiment of the division waited for the return of the LSTs from Tinian. Invasion procedure was essentially the same as at Saipan: a preliminary bombardment and diversion. However, diversion worked so well this time that Colonel Ogata shifted the main body of his forces to Tinian Town, and he never fully recovered from the shift. Unquestionably this had everything to do with the fact that 15,614 marines were on *terra firma* by nightfall, at a cost of only 15 killed and 225 wounded—the result of a few sporadic rounds of enemy artillery fire from Mount Lasso and rifle fire from the airfield.

Japanese reaction developed slowly because Ogata faced the serious dilemma of how to redeploy his forces, having on hand only two infantry divisions, twelve tanks and naval ground troops. Yet he elected to counterattack with these make-do forces in the early hours of July 25. A black night . . . showers . . . easy for the cat-eyed Jap to move in stealth. But this time it was a different ball game for the marines. They had learned how to handle the enemy on his own terrain, and they had learned well.

The first banzai charge came in on the left at 2 A.M., and when it did, the warships standing offshore opened up with star-shell illumination, lighting some 600 Japanese naval troops in white uniforms. After that everything from rifles and machine guns to pack howitzers cut down the attackers like a scythe. It was slaughter. In the dawn, bleary marines counted 476 dead Japanese piled within 100 yards of their perimeter.

The center attack commenced about 2:30, and briefly it seemed as if the attackers would penetrate the line. But, despite casualties, it held: another 500 Japanese in front of the perimeter at dawn. The final attack came just before dawn and was kicked off by five of the enemy's remaining tanks. The 23rd Marines opened up with bazookas, antitank guns and half-tracks. One observer reported: "The three lead tanks broke through our wall of fire. One began to glow blood-red, turned crazily on its tracks, and careened into a ditch. A second, mortally wounded, turned its machine gun on its tormentors, firing into the ditches in a last desperate effort to fight its way free. One hundred yards more and it stopped dead in its tracks. The third tried frantically to turn and then retreat, but our men closed in, literally blasting it apart. Bazookas knocked out the fourth tank with a direct hit which killed the driver. The rest of the crew piled out of the turret, screaming. The fifth tank, completely surrounded, attempted to flee. Bazookas made short work of it. Another hit set it afire, and its crew was cremated."

In the morning Ogata lost his taste for marines.

J-Plus-One found the marines moving inland, the 4th Division expanding the beachhead and preparing to mount an offensive against Mount Lasso, while the 2nd landed and went into the line. The advance was so swift, so devastating, that Ogata gave up the idea of a main attack entirely. On that day marines simultaneously reached the coast and overran Mount Lasso. On July 26 Uishi Airfield was taken, and by August 1 all of Tinian was in American hands. "The perfect amphibious invasion" (in the estimation of Holland Smith) had cost the Marine Corps 328 wounded and 1571 dead.

Guam, invaded July 21, 1944, was the last of our objectives in the Marianas, and from the standpoint of national pride the most important. Not unlike Saipan, Guam is, however, bigger (40 miles long as opposed to 10), with small mountains in the southerly portion and dense, rolling jungle in the north. The east coast, on which Pago Bay is situated, is comprised of a series of sheer cliffs and rivulets; altogether not a very good site for an invasion. Thus, the west coast was chosen by General Geiger's III Amphibious Corps because of its good beaches, which lie north and south of Orote Peninsula, and on both sides of Apra Harbor, the navigable port used by the Japanese.

Guam's Chamorro population had always been loyal to the United States, and particularly so after the arrival of the "Co-Prosperity Sphere," when the Japanese renamed the island Omiya Jima ("Great Shrine Island") and gave the people a choice of slave labor or death.

Soon after the Emperor's forces overwhelmed the United States Marine garrison on December 10, 1941, the enemy reinforced the island with 19,000 troops—blooded veterans of the China campaigns—under Lieutenant General Takeshi Takeshima. Their weapons included nineteen 8-inch guns, eight 6-inch, twenty-two 5-inch dual-purpose, six 3-inch, eight 75-mm. AA guns, 81 pieces of field artillery, two tank companies and 86 antitank guns. Many weapons were knocked out, however, as a result of the intensely accurate thirteen-day preinvasion bombardment—wrote a Japanese diarist: "wherever one goes the shells follow"—conducted by Rear Admiral Richard L. ("Close In") Conolly with a cruiser-battleship force which fired 28,000 shells into the target. The invasion was also the beneficiary of Navy and Marine Corps photo-reconnaissance delivered on a round-the-clock basis, as well as a great deal of underwater demolition work by Commander Draper L. Kauffman's frogmen. For three successive days and nights under Japanese guns, Kauffman's brave swimmers detonated mines and cut away underwater obstacles along the landing beaches; a number of them died in the process. But when Geiger's forces hit the beach on W-Day, the frogmen left behind tangible evidence of their operation. A huge sign posted to a tree read, "Welcome Marines! USO that way!"

The plan for Operation "Stevedore" called for the 1st Provisional Brigade, which had been created by adding the 12th Marines and the 4th Marines to the 22nd Marines (reinforced), to go ashore on Asan beaches, north of Apra Harbor (north of Orote Peninsula). The Brigade was under the command of Brigadier General Lemuel C. Shepherd, Jr., recently up from New Britain and raring for a fight. Geiger's III Amphibious Corps (Major General Allen H. Turnage with the 3rd Marine Division, and Major General A. D. Bruce with the Army's 77th Infantry Division) was to go ashore at Agat beaches, south of Apra Harbor (south of Orote Peninsula).

On W-Day—after softening by scores of Navy and Marine Corps fighter-bomber groups, and by LCI rocket launchers which fired 9072 missiles into the island, plus 22,000 rounds of naval gunfire—the marines landed on their respective beaches against stiff opposition. Fierce fighting was encountered on both fronts all day, resulting in 697 casualties. That night Japan's 38th Infantry launched a mighty counterattack against the 3rd Division. Meanwhile the 1st Brigade was well along in the reduction of Orote Peninsula, its aim to link up with the 3rd Division, after which both forces would wheel left up the length of the island.

For days, as the division and brigade fought against heavy opposition, Navy radiomen monitored the dialogue of marine tanks engaged in the struggle for Orote Peninsula. The following unexpurgated dialogue between a tank commander and his Shermans was recorded offshore against a background of machine-gun fire; the voices of men ranged from flat and authoritative, with moments of acid stress, to almost unbelievable male soprano during peaks of excitement.

·17· TANK BATTLE

A TRANSCRIPT

"This is Red One. Blue Two and Blue Three, move left a little but be careful of the swamp."

"This is Red Two, Red One. Heartburn says that he is ready to start shooting at those pillboxes."

"Tell Heartburn I can't receive him. You will have to relay. Tell him to give us a signal and we'll spot for him."

"Red Two, wilco."

"Heartburn, raise your fire. You're right into us."

"That's not Heartburn, Red Two. That's a high velocity gun from our left rear. I heard it whistle. Red One, out."

"Red Three, this is Red One. Can you see that gun that's shooting at us?"

"Red One, I think that's our own gunfire."

"Goddammit, it's not, I tell you. It's a high-velocity gun and not a howitzer. Investigate over there on you left. But watch out for the infantry; they're right in there somewhere. Red Two, tell Heartburn 'Down Fifty, Left Fifty.'"

"Red Two, wilco."

"Red Three, what are you doing? Go southwest."

"I am heading southwest, Red One."

"For Christ's sake, get oriented. I can see you, Red Three. You are heading northeast. Fox Love with hard left brake. Cross the road and go back up behind that house."

"But . . ."

"I don't know why I bother with you, Red Three. Yellow One, take charge of Red Three and get him squared away. And get that gun; it's too close."

"Red One from Red Two. Heartburn wants to know if we are the front lines."

"Tell him, 'Christ, yes.' We're plenty front right now."

"This is Red Two. Artillery on the way."

"Red One, wilco."

"Red One from Yellow One. I can see some Japs setting up a machine gun about a hundred yards to my right."

"Those are our troops, Yellow One. Don't shoot in there."

"The man at my telephone—I think he's an officer—says we have no troops in there."

"Yellow Two, go over there and investigate. Don't shoot at them; that man at your telephone probably doesn't know where the troops are. If they're Japs, run over them."

"Yellow Two, wilco."

"Go ahead, Yellow Two. What in God's name are you waiting for?"

"I'm up as far as I can go and still depress my machine guns."

"The hell with the machine guns. I told you to run over them. Run over them, goddammit, obey your orders."

"Yellow Two, wilco."

"Green Two, do a right flank and go up to the top of that hill. Keep in defilade. Red Two and Yellow One, open out a little more. Guide Right. Move out, now. And watch very closely; these troops are in a position to get into the same sort of trouble that they did yesterday. They're all screwed up, so be ready to move, immediately."

"Green Three, where are you?"

"I'm to the left of the road, Red One; just below Green Two."

"Raise the muzzle of your gun so I can spot you."

"Green Three, wilco."

"I thought so. Open out some more. I can't tell whether you or Green One is at fault, but you are too close."

"Move over, Green Three. You're within ten yards of me, now."

"O.K., O.K., Green One. I'm movin'."

"Red One from Green Two. I'm getting mortar fire. One landed about twenty-five yards to my right."

"All right, move out of there. Do a Fox Love and come down the slope a little. A Left Flank, Fox Love, goddammit. That's better. Now swing around some more and back out."

"Yellow One, what have you to report on that machine gun?"

"Red One, a Jap stood up and threw a hand grenade at us so I gave him a squirt."

"Did you run over that gun like I told you?"

"No, Red One, we put an HE [heavy explosive] in it and wrecked it."

"Chee-rist, won't you people ever learn to conserve your ammunition?"

"Red One from Green Two. I'm stuck between two trees."

"Green Three stand by him. After the Infantry has cleared up around there, get your assistant driver out and tow him clear."

"Green Three, wilco."

"While you're waiting, Green Three, keep an eye on that house on your right. I see troops coming out of there stuffing bottles in their shirts."

"Can I send my assistant driver over to investigate?"

"Stay in your tank. That's only saki."

"Yellow One from Red Three, where are you going?"

"You're a fine one to be asking such questions, Red Three. Red One, out."

"Red Two, can you still see the artillery splashes?"

"Affirmative, Red One. They're all right in deflection but they're all spread out in range."

"Red One, wilco. Keep spotting them on and have them put a couple of volleys of HE in that box."

"Red Two, wilco."

"Hairless, this is Red One. Have your infantry move through us and advance to that ridge. If they receive any fire, we'll move ahead of them."

"This is Hairless. We'll move around you."

"No, not around us; through us."

"Hairless, wilco."

"Red One, there's a man behind your tank."

"Red One, wilco."

"This is Red One. You Red and Yellow tanks are not to move until that mine field is cleared. Heartburn is going to put some smoke down at that crossroad to cover the engineers and you tanks give them support. Red Two, you will spot for Heartburn. I am going to move up with the Green and Blue tanks and we'll form a right echelon. All right, Green and Blue tanks, move out."

"Green Two, can you see if there is a gun behind those bushes? It looks like one from here."

"Green Two, wilco."

"Red One, there's a lot of sniper fire from over there but no guns or mortars that I could see. We gave them a spray, anyhow."

"Red One, this is Yellow Two. I am under mortar fire."

"All right, Yellow Two; move out if it's too hot for you. Don't back up. Stop, Yellow Two. Stop, Yellow Two. The infantry are right behind you. Move out ahead. Stop shooting that bow gun; the infantry are ahead of you and to your left, now. Be careful, Yellow Two."

"All tanks, move out. Guide right and open out the interval to one hundred yards. Red Two and Red Three, you are too close. Open out to the left flank . . . Red Three, Fox Love and move out to your left; you are too close to Red Two. Guide Right, all the Blue tanks. Move slowly and keep an eye on the infantry behind you. Green Four, not so fast; guide is right. Red One, out."

"Red One from Green Four. I am moving out to take a pillbox the infantry pointed out. I will take care of it and let them catch up."

"Where is it, Green Four?"

"In that clump of bushes to my right. Can you see it? Is it all right to fire?"

"Wait Green Four."

"Green Four, wilco."

"Green Four, you'd better not fire. The Fourth Marines are over there somewhere. Run up on the box and turn around on it."

"It's one of those coconut log things. It looks like it might be too strong to squash. Is it all right if I fire in the slit?"

"Affirmative. But be careful."

"Wilco."

"See that mortar over there, Hap?"

"No I don't, Fuzzy. Where?"

"To your right. I'm squirtin' at it now."

"O.K. Fuz, I got it."

"Red One, this is Blue Two. I just passed six AA guns looked like they was in pretty good shape and just been deserted. I destroyed 'em, anyhow."

"O.K. Blue Two. Wilco."

"Hairless, this is Red One. What are we waiting for, now?"

"Red One, they're waiting for you to move."

"For me to move. Christ, we ran away from them and had to stop."

"It's on the right flank, I just found out. The Fourth are doing some shooting and we are waiting for them to move."

"How about the left flank? We can move ahead there, can't we?"

"I guess so. We'll get them started."

"Red One, this is Hairless. We've got some Japs bottled up in two caves in Target Area Four Baker. We'd like you to leave two tanks to watch them."

"You know damn well that's the infantry's work. We're a mobile outfit, not watchdogs. Put your saki drinkers in there."

"O.K., Harry."

"Red One, out."

"All tanks, start 'em up. Move out now. Guide Right and form a shallow right echelon. As soon as we hit the flat ground around the airfield, spread out to 150-yard interval. All right, move out, move out."

❀   ❀   ❀   ❀

UNTIL JULY 29 WHEN THE AMERICAN FLAG WAS raised over the old marine barracks at Agana in an impressive color guard ceremony witnessed by Generals Smith, Shepherd, Geiger, and Admiral Spruance, marines encountered some of the wildest hand-to-hand fighting of the campaign. The worst banzai charge developed July 26 at 4 A.M. on a cliff held by the 21st Marines. A battalion of Japanese swarmed down on marine positions, and one of them screamed: "Wake up and die, marine!" In kind, a marine responded: "Come on, you bastards, and we'll see who dies!" Another attack was launched at the 2nd Battalion, 9th Marines, and raged throughout the night. Mortarmen got down to six rounds per tube, riflemen down to two clips per man; then

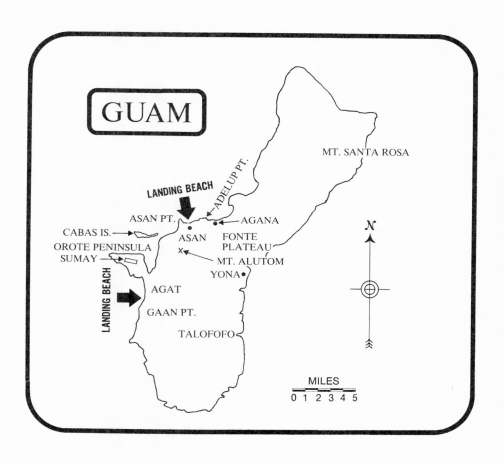

a tank laden with ammunition arrived at the critical moment and the battle slowly turned. In this action a company commander, Captain Louis H. Walton (Medal of Honor), although wounded seven times, maintained his nearly buckled position and saved several wounded men. Other units similarly distinguished themselves as support areas became battlefields, and hospital patients, shore parties and motor transport personnel lobbed grenades and fired pieces until the furious assault was beaten down.

On July 29 marines took their first bath, washed their clothes and shaved. The swift campaign which cost the Corps some 7800 casualties to Japan's 16,526 moved into its final phase. The next day Robert "Pepper" Martin, *Time* correspondent, joined the 3rd Marine Division for the balance of the fighting in and around the unsealed northern portion of the island. The following is his splendid account of the action to the final point, when Guam again became American.

·18· GUAM FINALE

ROBERT MARTIN

July 30, 1944—With bitter humor the marines named the squarish, vertical bluff Sugar Ridge because, as one burly, sweating sergeant explained, "It is a sweet place for the Japs to defend." It was sweet, but not to the marines. Those who survived will never forget the excruciating hours they spent probing its grim face.

Sugar Ridge lifts its almost perpendicular, 550-foot face from Adelup Point, whose tiny caves, crammed with mortars, had been stormed on D-day by flame-throwing marines. By D-night they had topped the 300-foot slopes of Chonito Cliff overlooking our long, flat beachhead. This flank was one of the major keys to the success of the Guam operations. To the left lies Agana, Guam's largest town, whose pulverized white buildings glint defiantly against green verdant background. Directly southward, steep ridges fall away in seemingly unending succession from the Pacific, caves in their rugged bluffs containing Jap mortars which had rained explosives on our beachhead, observation posts, and pillboxes—caves manned by suicide squads, machinegunners, and riflemen.

It was imperative that the marines clean out Sugar Ridge and connecting saddles. Otherwise our beachhead would remain shaky and our center and other flank held down. The Japs fought bitterly and unceasingly as the marines advanced down the coastal highway between Piti and Agana, their bodies littering highways, crumbled shoulders, and angling gulches. Finally the Japs broke and the marines, pressing their advantage, found the front overextended at nightfall. That regiment's right flank was nailed securely to a steep ridge while the left flank was anchored at Adelup Point. But there were wide gaps in positions where Jap fire, combined with almost inaccessible ridges, prevented continuous contact between advanced elements.

Jap reserves poured into the area from Tumon Bay, slashing down from the highlands to Adelup Point. Deep in one gulch, battalion headquarters was isolated and surrounded. Marines holding Chonita Cliff—a bare, reddish clay pinnacle from which ugly six-inch coast defense guns threatened any sea approach until our planes destroyed them before they fired a single shot—were also encircled during the night. Red-eyed, weary, thirsty marines threw back almost unceasing attacks.

When dawn broke, the Japs held positions 400 yards behind our lines, and one company was completely isolated on a ridgeside barren as a billiar ball, unable to advance, retreat, or move either flank because the Japs were looking down their throats.

Lieutenant Colonel Ralph Houser, slender, hard-bitten, and incisive, drew his battalion back, reversed the attack direction and hit a Jap breakthrough gap at their rear, utterly wiping out the Jap penetration. He again reversed, swinging into a position facing out from our perimeter.

Throughout Saturday, while Jap mortars plastered the beachhead, marines struggled up hills so steep that supplies were brought to the front on ropes dangling over cliff faces. Water was scarce and the slack-jawed marines cursed bitterly at their empty canteens and at sweating comrades struggling to carry precious five-gallon cans up the ridge.

The marines shifted weight from left to right and then center, attacked under cover of dive-bombers, naval gunfire, field artillery. The Japs were neutralized by the intensive barrage—but recovered before the marines could reach the crest. Twice the marines reached within grasping distance, only to fall back under withering machine-gun fire and grenade blasts from the entrenched Japs. It was tragic to watch those failing, desperate charges, but each time the marines

V Marianas Mop-Up: Saipan to Guam

Under cover of a naval and air bombardment by supporting units, these Marines, in various types of landing craft, form the first wave to hit the beach at Saipan in the Marianas.

The first wave to hit the Saipan beach takes cover behind a sand dune, while waiting for the following three waves to come in. (Photo by Sgt. James Burns)

It appears that one gyrene is relieving another on the beach at Saipan, but they are really crawling, under enemy fire, to their assigned positions. The wet Leatherneck (closest to camera) took a ducking when the landing craft he came in on was hit by Japanese mortar fire. (Photo by Sgt. James Burns)

Digging on the beach at Saipan in preparation for the attack on Japanese positions inland. In the background one of the amphibious tractors used by the first-wave assault troops burns furiously. (Photo by Sgt. J. L. Burns)

The rays of the morning sun show Marines digging in on the beach at Saipan, where they were securing their first toehold on that island. (Photo by Pfc. C. H. Walker)

Marines crouch low while Japanese shells hit nearby. Note the tenseness of all the men who have been fighting since D-Day, June 15, and have now reached almost to the extreme end of the island.

Second Marines advancing on the city of Garapan. (Photo by Cpl. A. Robertson)

Viewed through the window of a wrecked building: a gun crew set up behind an abandoned enemy truck fires at Japanese hidden in the debris of the town of Garapan, administrative center of Saipan. (Photo by Cpl. E. G. Wilbert)

Marines wait, in what was once somebody's backyard, for the word to advance against the Japanese entrenched in Garapan. (Photo by Cpl. A. Robertson)

Take cover! (Photo by Warnecke)

In a setting of aspen-like trees on the front lines, Marines, using an ammunition cart, haul supplies and equipment to a gun position. (Photo by Sgt. James Burns)

Flame-throwing tanks highballing it into action. (Photo by Opper)

A hand grenade, tossed by a Marine, sails through the air toward a nest of Japanese. Another Marine gets to heave his smoking grenade in the same direction.

Infantrymen move fast to take up new positions in Garapan, principal city of Saipan. Japanese buildings and installations were set afire by supporting infantry and artillery.

Jeeping with the brass; Admiral King (front jeep seat), Lieutenant General Holland M. Smith (standing in jeep), and Admiral Nimitz as Naval Officer toured Saipan after American forces had secured the island.

Crewmen of a night fighter squadron of the Fourth Marine Air Wing respond without hesitation to mail call—one of the first since they landed here to participate in the campaign. (Photo by S/Sgt. Cockran)

Marines, just back from the Saipan front, take advantage
of fresh water from a cistern near a Japanese barracks to
wash their tired, burning, and aching feet.

Marines who landed in the first wave at Saipan bid farewell to fallen comrades who have been prepared for burial.
(Photo by S/Sgt. R. E. Olund)

Marines hit the beach at Guam, literally and figuratively, as they jump from an amphibious tractor and scramble for cover behind a sand dune. (Photo by Ball)

More wet feet, more damn islands—Marines get their feet wet again as they charge down the ramp of a landing barge and onto the beach at Guam.

Marines crouch on beach as Japanese land mines knock out a couple of their tanks. Moving Marines keep low to duck sniper fire. (Photo by T/Sgt. G. R. Gass)

This Japanese airfield on Orote Peninsula, Guam, was one of the prime objectives of assaulting Marines.

Relieved by fresher troops, these tired, battle-stained Marines move back to a rest area on Guam.

Not the spoils of victory, but the rough duty en route...A machine gunner strains up a steep hill carrying the tripod of his gun, while a second machine gunner carries the barrel, and other members of the gun crew bear the ammunition. (Photo by T/Sgt. J. A. Mundell)

Three communications men of a signal company stand by
to receive word that another line has been put through.
(Photo by T/Sgt. James A. Mundell)

Machine guns at work.

Flame-thrower in the hands of an expert. (Photo by Carroll)

Enemy tanks knocked out by fire from Marine tanks, about 300 yards from the peninsula on the road to Sumay and the old Marine barracks on Guam.

Pl/Sgt. Ivan Hamilton taking a bath in the accepted manner on Guam. The tub was found in the ruins of Agana; it proved a boon to the Marines, who had known only the comforts of a steel helmet. (Photo by Cpl. K. W. Altfather)

Once again, after more than two years, Marines raise the American flag over recaptured Marine barracks. These same men took part in the historic action a few hours before, officially writing finis to the "perfect" campaign.

fell back a shorter distance. On the third attempt the Japs broke and ran and the marines crossed the ridge—156 survivors from rifle companies which started the attack.

Sunday I joined marines ordered to capture Sugar Ridge, which still dominated the ridges the marines had secured on Saturday (July 29). The assembly area was a shambles of reddish, churned clay, littered with half-destroyed equipment, Japs grinning balefully and obscenely in their death agony, neatly covered rows of dead marines; the inevitable flotsam of war: snapshots of young mothers and children who would never again see their marine husbands and fathers, a New Testament shredded by a bullet, a punctured canteen, half-eaten field rations scattered about.

We turned up a narrow, seven-foot-wide, shale-covered highway winding up the side of Chonito Cliff, where reserves were already moving to the front, their sergeants shouting hoarsely, "C'mon, c'mon, move up, keep your distance, watch that mortar fire." The battalion command post was a single foxhole, covered with a half-shelter, where men panted in the heat but ignored the stench of thirty dead Japs lying within a few yards of the C.P., where they had died the previous night during abortive attacks. Colonel Houser crunched off the road into the C.P. shouting, "Get water to X Company before they shove off. That's top priority."

Bedraggled marines grinned cheerfully when they saw the division's pert assistant commander, Brigadier General Alfred Noble, his deputy chief of staff, rugged and tough Lieutenant Colonel George O. Van Orden, onetime battalion commander of this same regiment, en route to the front to watch the attack.

We moved cautiously up the winding road because the Japs had the uncomfortable habit of firing mortars which ranged on the road. But we finally reached the chewed-off heights of the Chonito Cliff. Marines moved up behind us around the crest to the jumping-off point for the attack. From a hastily constructed clay revetment, with machineguns guarding all approaches and filled to the bursting point with grenades, we had our first closeup glimpse of the Jap lines two hundred yards distant, delineated by camouflaged blockhouses, a few slit trenches. No-man's-land was a grey-brown expanse devoid of cover except for occasional clumps of dying bushes. For a moment war seemed remote in that stillness, although one felt sharply the electric expectancy in the still air. Far below us, the Pacific was filled as far as I could see with transports, while incredible numbers of landing vehicles, resembling unnatural, large ants, churned the reef-broken water to froth and kicked up sand storms on the beachhead, bringing war's necessities to Guam.

General Noble peered across the ridge and then quietly remarked to the machinegunner: "I bet the bastards pulled out of there. Have you had a chance to look at them yet over your sights?" The gunner drawled, in tones reserved for front lines where rank counts comparatively little, "Naw, not since last night."

Then word passed up from below: "Get down, get down." We adjusted our helmets firmly on our heads and dug our noses in the crumbling clay. U.S. destroyers unloaded salvo after salvo, and then the dive-bombers came in. From the beach below, our mortars and 75s barked. For a moment I though our pinnacle had been torn loose from the earth by those tons of high explosives and we were churning madly in mid-air. The bombardment was almost on top of us, centered along a rectangle only two hundred yards distant. Then our machineguns began to snarl, and through a mental daze I heard Noble grunt contentedly, "By golly, they're right in there. That's nice accurate shooting."

The barrage lifted as suddenly as it began, and a column of marines crossed behind and to our left, striking toward the ridge heights. Another column moved cautiously along the ridge base, paralleling the first column in quick, nervous moves like the tentacles of a giant octopus groping for its prey. Noble chewed at his fingernails nervously, muttering: "Damn it, they should have moved faster. You've got to hit the enemy the moment the barrage lifts, before he can recover."

Soon the hill was alive with marines perfectly deployed, inching forward with marionette precision toward the Jap pillboxes. Then the peaceful silence was broken by the ping of a Jap rifle and a moment later two geysers of black smoke hurtled toward the sky, where a moment before only the marines were discernible. The Japs had opened up with grenades and mortars. A lone figure moved to the rear, holding his shoulder, which oozed crimson. The marines hugged the ground, pinned by Jap fire, but the machineguns on our right and left and the riflemen opened up. Van Orden joined the battle, grabbing an M-1 rifle and shouting "Goddamn it, those marines need help." Then our mortars again went into action, plastering the ridges and gulleys extending far to the rear of the Japs. The jungle undergrowth in the valleys and the bare ridges above were soon smothered in a smoke curtain, and the marines again began slowly to advance. As the smoke lifted, we could see wounded and dead marines rolling down the hill. One marine, his shirt torn, bleeding profusely from wounds, lay on his back and began sliding down the hillside toward the rear lines and medical aid. Out there it was each man for himself, each trying to reach the ridge top and bring momentary respite from the fear and agony which could be felt even in the comparative safety of our lines.

The Japs were concentrated in the narrow draw which bisected the ridge and like jack rabbits would pop out of the foxholes and take quick shots and then fall back. As the marines neared the crest and began blasting Jap defenses, the Japs ran out and staggered to the rear until marine marksmen picked them off. Some escaped but not many. Soon the marines had gained the first objective and the tanks were moving up to spearhead thrusts at the ridges extending far beyond.

August 7—The Japs had abandoned their magnificent Tumon Bay defenses in the jungles along eastern Guam's surf-beaten cliffs. Marines romped gaily through the jungles north of newly captured Tiyan airfield, collecting tons of supplies and pounds of souvenirs which the Japs had abandoned in their mad rush to the interior. It looked as if the Japs were in complete confusion, demoralized, and unable to concentrate for attack.

Last night the picture changed abruptly. The moonlight was brilliant, but rays filtered thinly through a massive umbrella of interwoven coconut trees and other growth. A regimental weapons company, tired by the day's advance, slept fitfully. At 2230 three Jap heavy tanks (the first heavies seen on Guam) charged down the road from Dedeo. Gunners hit the lead tank, but it kept going. Tanks overran our positions, firing as they moved full speed down the highway. One tank twisted the tail of a light field gun, injuring two men. Then the Japs broke contact, fleeing up a side road and back through our lines in a curving, roseate blaze of fire from the marines. Jap infantry was out there, too, but this battalion, commanded by Major Henry Aplington, was unable to establish contact. Fitfully the two forces waited. After an hour and forty-five minutes, the Japs mustered courage for a Banzai charge. This time the marines were ready, and our fire cut down between forty and fifty Japs. Three Americans were wounded before the Jap attack collapsed and they fled.

This morning the marines began to move forward again, but cautiously, against increasing Jap resistance. I went to the front, accompanying Lieutenant Colonel George O. Van Orden, who should remain at headquarters but insists on hunting for battle with his own private arsenal of pistol, carbine and Johnson light machinegun in order to get "one last crack at the Japs." We found the front quiet, with marines moving along the highway and into the underbrush beyond. We jeeped across desolate meadowland behind a coconut grove four hundred yards distant. Later we learned the Japs were concentrating inside the grove for an attack. We drove up a steep hillside on a new road gouged out by our dozers. A wounded Marine private staggered onto the road, and we stopped to assist him. He adjusted the bandage around his head and then grinned: "I was sure as hell glad I wore my helmet."

The road angled off toward the Jap lines from the brow of the hill, so we got out and walked, following a trail through the jungle, where mid-morning is like dusk. We stumbled over little groups of men— smoking, talking in hushed tones, or just resting—awaiting orders to move up to attack. We half slid, half crawled down a steep hillside to the battalion command post where Lieutenant Colonel Wendell H. Duplantis, slender, blond commander, was talking over the telephone, asking for mortar artillery support.

Duplantis smoked nervously but chuckled as he recounted the night's adventures. They had moved forward at dusk to the assembly area in an open field, but two companies got lost in the jungle night. Duplantis established a defense position and, with patrols, finally located all the men. He halted the search for the field until dawn. The battalion moved out this morning and finally found the assembly area. But the Japs were there, and when the fire fight was over his men had knocked out two Jap rifle positions and one "Nambu" pillbox. Said Duplantis, "That would have been damned rugged if we had bumped into them last night."

We prepared to move back, and then the hill trembled under the weight of steel clawing at its vitals. The Japs had swung their right flank around and hit—hit straight down the valley to our left. Our artillery mortars opened up while we hugged the ground. Planes flew low around the hill, then began to strafe directly below us in rhythm with our machineguns, chattering the unmusical song of death for the advancing Japs. Unlike many battles, this involved only one small front, and on every hillside marines could look down into the valley and see Japs advancing cautiously across strips of clearing or sidling among trees, seeking to get at American throats.

It looked as if it might be an all-day battle, so Van Orden and I worked our way to the rear to a road where we found a jeep waiting. We looked quizzically at the hand and bemused face of a dead Jap sticking half out of a trench, then ate our cold field rations and discussed what to do. The road over which we had come was under Jap fire. The same road to the right led to Jap lines, and Jap patrols were beginning to work in behind us. It looked as if we were at the narrowing apex of a triangle, with the Japs moving down the two legs. Reconnaissance to the right might show us the best way out, but sitting tight was safer. Van Orden doesn't like safety, so he drove the jeep over the hill. Halfway down, two logs jutted out from each side of the road, only a few yards apart. It was a typical Jap road block, which forces all approaching vehicles to slow down. Van Orden slammed on the brakes and, despite his bulk, went over the side with the easy effort of a pole vaulter. The jeep rolled to a halt in the ditch. Only half-armed (his Johnson was in the jeep), Van Orden cautiously scouted the logs, inching through the dense brush with agility gained from many years of boondocking in Haiti, Samoa, Guadalcanal, Bougainville. There were no Japs. As an anticlimax a column of marines filed out of the underbrush and up the road. We asked where they came from and they replied: "About fifty feet in the bush." With the marines once more moving on the flanks and the Japs retreating, we returned to the rear.

The marines poked effortlessly through the mutilated coconut grove, found 116 Japs stilled by that devastating machinegun fire. Fifty-five were discovered in the rear, victims of artillery blasting. The marines cornered twenty-six Japs in one huge bunker and six in another; wiped them out with flame throwers and grenades. Bottle after bottle of saki was discovered, which the Japs had been drinking before their charge. Whether it was an effort to gain courage or a last salute to the emperor, we never knew.

August 7 — Two gold-red statues of saints looked mutely out from the desolate roadside shrine, resting shakily on three pitted pedestals. A fourth was destroyed. But the marine standing respectfully by the side of the highway was not mute. He glanced at the graveyards, the once even rows of graves now obscenely scarred by two huge shell craters, the uniform neatness marred by half-toppling crosses. Said the marine, "Even the dead can't rest in peace."

That was Agana on Monday, July 31, the day we captured Guam's largest city.

The final assault started two days ago. The Third Division moved its outpost to the city's rim, after driving the Japs deep inland across the angling ridge, down the deep cleft valleys from our now solidly held beachhead. While artillery observers directed the barrage from newly won highland positions, our field artillery, rocket-firing gunboats, and mortars hammered the city, which resembles a rough rectangle approximately a mile long and four hundred yards wide. Sunday, our patrols penetrated the city and discovered the Japs had abandoned the area, whose two-hundred-foot cliffs on the southern edge could have provided a natural defense bastion, sweeping every approach.

This morning Sherman tanks, followed by wary marines, rumbled down the dusty highway from Adelup Point and entered the ruins where twelve thousand civilians once lived. Late this afternoon we occupied the entire city. Numerous white rags fluttered in the streets to show where mines were uncovered.

It was a near bloodless conquest (only two machinegun positions fought the advance) but we gained little except further tightening of the cordon across Guam and the inevitable squeezing of Japs in the ever-narrowing area.

The cathedral and churches were gutted by shells and fires. It was not wanton destruction but incidental to the overall necessity of neutralizing Agana, which the Japs had made into one of their chief supply bivouac areas.

Power lines were stripped, but the steel poles reached gauntly toward the sky. Virtually every building was a shambles, most of them beyond recognition. The coconut trees which once shaded the streets had broken like snapped twigs withered by fires, while debris littered every foot of the once beautiful Plaza Espagna in the city's heart.

While jeeps rolled through the streets, bulldozers filled in shell craters and a few hardier marines rummaged through huge stock piles of Jap goods or dug foxholes in the shade. Or they stood on the steps of Spanish style houses, whose only remaining color was red hibiscus. One marine created a homelike atmosphere with potted plants, which miraculously withstood the bombardment. Another whooped as he rode through the streets on a Jap bicycle. Still another challenged a buddy to a tennis match.

The lush green valley was shaped like a broken saucer, its broken edge formed by sharp, bare ridges which bore inland from Guam's beachheads. At the far side two figures could be discerned: a green-clad marine giving hand and arm signals to his mottled black-brown dog. They were hunting not birds but Japs, and the marines, who otherwise would be pecking cautiously at each bush, cave, and ground depression, could follow at ease, saving energy for the kill.

Dogs thus became a recognized Marine fighting arm. Raider battalions had experimented with them and they received some battle experience at Bougainville. They became warriors with thoughtful, sturdy tradition at Guam.

The journey to battle with the dogs is an education; here animal instincts, sharpened by training, have triumphed over science's dominance of the war. Most of the Marine dogs on Guam are Doberman Pinschers. Said one sergeant handler: "They are a mean dog and we make them meaner." Some scout dogs indicate the presence of human beings by pointing or growling, and the marines must determine the nationality of those discovered. Others can distinguish between Japs and Americans by their odor. All are trained to attack and kill on signal. Their skill at ferreting Japs from caves has terrorized the enemy. One dog chased four Japs into a cave where they committed suicide with grenades rather than fight.

Each night, while star shells, flares, mortars, and naval guns flicker fantastically against clouds overhanging Guam, faint barks can be heard from the perimeter defenses. The dogs alert the outposts whenever there is movement. Then our sentries open fire, and almost invariably dead Japs are found in the morning. During daylight the dogs roam the hills, cliffsides, and jungles, searching for Japs. They are death to snipers, whose chief defense is their ability to remain screened from sight but who have not yet discovered a method for eliminating human odor.

Other dogs are trained as messengers, and their speed through the jungles and mountains is almost fabulous. In a jungle test prior to the Guam invasion, one messenger dog sprinted sixteen hundred yards through heavy jungle in four and one-half minutes, beating a runner over the same terrain by eleven minutes. They are taught that their only friends in the world are their handlers, and the result is that they avoid all others, whether friend or enemy, while carrying messages. They fight any hindrance. Some follow trails they have earlier traversed en route from command posts to forward areas, while others have such a keen sense of direction that they go cross-country. They return to the front where a handler awaits them, trailing him by scent. If necessary, a dog can carry a hundred and fifty rounds of ammunition back to the front on a saddle pack.

The dogs have had heavy casualties on Guam: three dead, one missing, one wounded. (Handlers' losses: two killed and six wounded.) "Kurt" was hit by a mortar while hunting a sniper. "Babe," who was brought especially for that purpose, furnished blood for transfusion, but the dog died from shock. A mortar hit a foxhole which "Tippy" was guarding, blowing him six feet into the air, killing a marine and wounding another in a foxhole. But the dog suffered only stiffened hindquarters. The saddest casualty was a dog whose handler was killed by a sniper. Marines spent thirty minutes dragging the grieving dog from the body.

The favorite story of grinning Sergeant Bill Baldwin is about "Bobby," half Cocker but mostly "just dog," who is the outfit's mascot. Bobby is just barely beyond the puppy stage, but apparently he took the training of others seriously. One dark night Bobby tumbled out of a foxhole and chased a Jap around the command post. Bobby failed to catch the Jap, but Marine patrols found him hiding the next morning. The Jap is dead.

August 7—Valor finds expression in many forms. On Guam's bloody Orote peninsula a curly-haired, baby-faced Marine private, celebrating his twentieth birthday, watched as the marines reeled back under a bold frontal attack spearheaded by five Jap tankettes. The youngster seized a bazooka, and in the face of withering Jap fire knocked out the Jap lead tank with his first shot, at a range of twenty yards. His second shot exploded the second Jap tankette. Then a Jap bullet squarely in the head ended the boy's gallant stand. But the marines, who previously were hanging on by their eyelids, rallied and knocked out the three remaining tankettes and the Jap charge crumpled.

Lieutenant Paul Dorse, a former photographer and topnotch Hollywood still man, now a Marine Combat Photographer, grinned sardonically and heaved another grenade at a Jap strongpoint only a few yards distant. He muttered, "All photographers are crazy," referring to W. (Wonderful) Eugene Smith of *Life* and Universal's quiet, humorous, Australian Damien Parer. They were crawling through front lines, taking closeup shots of marines under fire. Smith got a souvenir that day: a smoking but spent Jap rifle bullet which came to rest on his back pocket.

In the first ten days, four Marine Combat Photographers and one Combat Correspondent were killed in action, one Combat Photographer and two Combat Correspondents were wounded. This is the heaviest casualty list of photographers and correspondents for any operation in the Pacific war.

❀　❀　❀　❀

SIXTY MILES NORTH OF GUADALCANAL ARE THE Russell Islands, of which Pavuvu stands out as the most maligned outpost ever visited by the 1st Marine Division. Unless you happened to be one of those depressed, mentally fatigued marines who came to Pavuvu after the Cape Gloucester campaign to "rest" in preparation for the invasion of Peleliu, the lyric sensuality of that South Pacific name might well conjure up visions of hulas and swaying palms. But such a vision belonged to American Samoa—not Pavuvu, where there were no hulas, and where the swaying palms had all rotted.

Pavuvu was the place for the 1st Marine Division to get accustomed to the idea that it was about to embark on another campaign—initially described by some headquarters evangelist as "a piece of cake," but which instead turned out to be one of the toughest nuts ever experienced in the history of the Corps. Pavuvu was literally one in a million: mud, rain, rotted coconuts, jungle fever, depression. There were no lights on the island, not even in the Division command post. Logically, the only thing to do on the island was write letters, and many hundreds of thousands were written during the "training" period before the men took off for Peleliu. But before going into the military aspects of the next campaign, let us present one of the Pavuvu letters. The author was a gifted and sensitive young North Carolinian, Lieutenant David Brown, who was killed on Iwo Jima. Brown's mother collected the letters he wrote to her and to his friends, and published them after the war.

·19· "A SENSE OF IMPIETY"

LIEUTENANT DAVID M. BROWN

Dear Ned:

This is just my weekly letter to let you know I am still alive, and . . . pretty well settled here. Yes, Col. Lou Puller is with the Division. I saw him (don't know him personally) at our mess the other day.

. . . It has been raining hard this morning, and during the first downpour I was going about my tent, improving ditches to divert the flood, picking up things from the deck near the eaves, and so on. Then I saw it creeping through the wet grass—the burglar, who had rummaged through my papers and possessions each night, often leaving a few torn papers or other clues in his wake. It was a grey field mouse, fair sized, striped lightly with russet brown. I watched it go to its hole, then come back into the grass under the tent eave. It seemed to be making a nest there, to keep dry and warm. I seized a small board, and crept up silently, one foot at a time laid stealthily in the gravel. The rain beating down muffled any sound I may have made, and so, as I knelt down with my board poised, it still rustled away placidly, tidying the nest. I stalked as unperceived as fate, towering overhead like a giant. Then down, down with the board! repeatedly I struck, stamping this nuisance out of existence. I rolled it over, dead, and then I saw that fate was darker, far more cunning than I'd thought. There in the warm nest lay two babes, helpless white puppets, still stirring feebly. The mother had brought them up out of the hole to save them from drowning. Now she lay still on her back, with her grey tongue thrust out through the little brute mouth. I was seized with remorse at the scene, like Burns. Undone, I was no longer a stalking god, but a mere blind instrument. So I killed the two babes and beat them out with their dam, as fate prescribed.

It is strange that you can have pity for a mouse. You do not naturally take human life, but you have no qualms against shooting a man, who confronts you, armed himself with a weapon and with an intention to put you out of the way. All men go to war knowing the chance, so there is nothing distinctly offensive in this inevitable killing. But this mouse pursued blindly its unobtrusive life. It knew no wrong in rummaging through my papers, eating my candy. When the flood came, according to nature, she solicitously cared for her young. Thus provided for, her race would go on quietly, in accordance with an ancient decree, and a will of which she was ignorant, yet docilely obeyed. One had a sense of impiety in interfering with this decree, with this great solicitude for something so small. It made the worthless even precious.

Still, a man may pity a mouse. I reckon this pity arises, in part, from an instinctive dread of cutting off a race; any race, a peculiar and marvelous creation which we could not reproduce, once destroyed. And in part it is that we see, as in a mirror, the frail trust that all life is. When I pity the mother mouse I pity, in an inadequate and dumb degree, the mothers who die with their children in a ruined or shell racked city, the young girl who loses her only child.

Forgive my spending half a morning elegizing, or philosophizing, over a mouse! But philosophy is an amusement, among the few we have. And it steadies the mind, when you have nothing much to think about except the details of daily routine. The prospect of a bottle of beer is a matter of interest and speculation to us here. One lad wrote in his letter of the things he bought at a recently opened PX—ink and a comb and handkerchiefs and shoelaces, chewing gum and a towel you could get at the meanest ten-cent store. "They are beautiful!" he says. And they are—as fascinating and novel as Robinson Crusoe's carpenter chest. Men make necklaces out of sea shells and rings out of Japanese planes—little things become important, and the tragedy befalling a family of vermin can be a matter of intense excitement to while away a morning!

I shall write again soon. I am very well off, with a good bunch of men. In this company I am again a platoon leader . . .

DAVID

❊   ❊   ❊   ❊

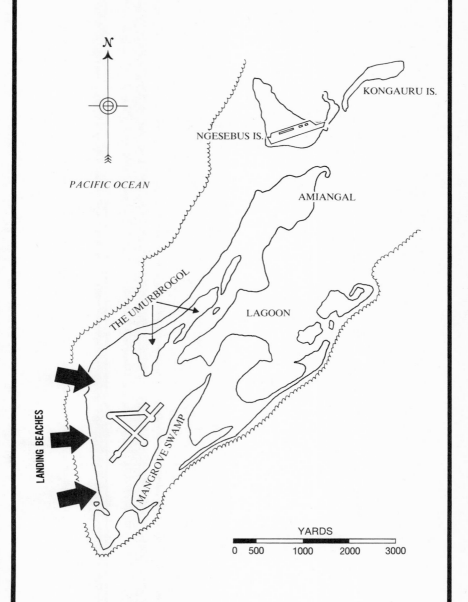

PELELIU

N

PACIFIC OCEAN

KONGAURU IS.

NGESEBUS IS.

AMIANGAL

THE UMURBROGOL

LAGOON

LANDING BEACHES

MANGROVE SWAMP

YARDS

0   500   1000   2000   3000

IN THE CONTEXT OF THE PACIFIC SCRIPT, AS MAC-
Arthur prepared his advance on Leyte and the ring around Japan
closed ever tighter, the Palau Islands assumed strategic importance because they lie only 470 miles east of Mindanao in the Philippines. Without prior neutralization, MacArthur's push to the
Philippines surely would not have been feasible. Thus it was up to
the marines to pave the way, and they did so in a costly operation,
aptly named "Stalemate." The Army's 81st Division was to capture
Angaur, south of Peleliu, and the 1st Marine Division was to capture Peleliu (six miles long and two wide), in what General William H. Rupertus overoptimistically called "a quickie. Rough but
fast." It was not fast, but it was certainly rough.

Naval aerial reconnaissance had taken photographs of the target
the previous March which, because of the enemy's adroit use
of camouflage, revealed the island to be low and flat when in reality it was a combination of topographies encountered at Saipan
and Tarawa—limestone and low, but also ridge-type and perforated with deep caves. General Rupertus' plan of attack was
to land three regiments abreast over five beaches paralleling
a small airstrip with Colonel Lewis "Chesty" Puller's 1st Marines
going in on beaches White 1 and White 2, the northernmost beaches, and wheeling northward along the spine of the island; Colonel Harold D. "Bucky" Harris' 5th Marines going in on beaches Orange 1 and Orange 2, the middle beaches, crossing the island
and capturing the airstrip; and Colonel Herman D. Hannekin's
7th Marines going in on beach Orange 3, south of the airstrip,
and cleaning up the southern tip of the island.

Although Major General Geiger (III Amphibious Corps) and
Major General Julian C. Smith (now with provisional headquarters) both suggested that Rupertus add a reserve unit to the 1st
Marines, Rupertus insisted it was not necessary. To compound
these difficulties of command, Rear Admiral George H. Fort
allegedly brought insufficient bombardment ammunition and
an inexperienced bombardment staff. However, even from the
beginning on Pavuvu there were problems: administrative, personnel, training, equipment and weapons.

The 1st Marine Division was now facing 10,700 Japanese troops,
and they were about equally divided into army and navy components. Their army was an outgrowth of the famed 14th Army,
and its men were psychologically geared to expect an invasion.
The naval troops were naval guard force, well-trained and tough
fighters. There were tanks and artillery. Peleliu's tactical command was in the hands of Colonel Kunio Nakagawa, a pragma-
tist who exhorted his men to desist from banzai attacks. He was
responsible for building a network of tunnels, in some instanc-

es six stories deep, with fireports and steel doors. Unlike other Japanese commanders faced with American invasion, Nakagawa chose to make his stand away from the beach. He chose to fight on his own best terms: inland, where his strongholds were deep limestone caves and ridges. Nothing—not even a daily bombardment of 1200 tons of ammunition from five battleships, eight cruisers and twenty-one destroyers—could dislodge Nakagawa.

For noted *Life* illustrator and correspondent Tom Lea, in Guadalcanal looking for a story, Peleliu seemed like the perfect invasion. Short and sweet, he was told. In 1946 Lea privately printed a manuscript entitled *Peleliu Landing,* a two-day journal embellished with his own matchless art: a strong and moving document of the landing and its bloody aftermath. We meet Lea as he wakes on D-Day.

·20· PELELIU LANDING

TOM LEA

My watch said 0340 when I woke up on the blacked-out weatherdeck below the bridge. Barefooted and in my skivvies, I got off my cot and stood by the rail rubbing grit from my eyes. Dead ahead, framed between the forward kingposts, there was flickering light on the black horizon. Sick yellow balls of fire flashed low in the clouds like heat lightning, but continuous. It was the Navy shelling Peleliu with the final punch before we landed. The black silhouette of a seaman on watch by the rail turned to me and said, "Them Japs are catching hell for breakfast."

Dawn came dim with low overcast. In the first gray light I saw the sea filled with an awe-inspiring company of strangers to our troop ships. Out to the horizon in every direction were lean men-of-war, fat transports, stubby landing craft, gathered around us like magic in the growing light. It was D-Day.

We ate our last meal together, dressed in baggy green dungarees, on the plank benches of the troop officers' mess. We washed the food down our dry throats with big mugs of coffee, and put all the oranges in our pockets. Getting up to go, Captain Farrell repeated his instructions for Martin and me, the two correspondents, "Be at Number Three Net, starboard side, at 0600."

Growing dawn had brought the ship violently to life. Power winches rumbled, hoisting out landing craft over the side. The marines, after long captivity in their crowded holds, moved at last to their stations by the rail, battle gear buckled, the last oil in the gun, the last whet to the knife. I felt some almost palpable spirit walking the emptying holds and passageways and along the crowded decks, with a word for every man.

In the corner where I kept my gear I checked it carefully and finally. There was the belt with the two filled canteens, first-aid kit and long black-bladed knife; and the pack with the poncho and shovel, the gloves, headnet and K-ration, the waterproofed cigarettes and matches and candy bar—and my sketch book and pencils and camera and films wrapped in the target balloon. All set. I checked my pockets for my watch and identification wrapped in rubbers—and my grizzly coin for luck.

Martin and I buckled our belts, slung our packs and put on our helmets. Inching along through the marines, we found Farrell and his men standing shoulder to shoulder with all their gear on the jam-packed maindeck near the rail over Number Three Net. The maindeck looked queer without the landing craft that had loomed overhead on the long convoy days, making shade for marine card games. Now these boats were down in the water ready for the loads.

"Free Boat Two," bellowed the squawkbox on the bridge and Farrell said, "That's us. Let's go."

We gave a hitch to our packs, hoisted our legs over the rail and went down the rope net, down the scaly side of our sea-bitten ship by swinging handgrips and tricky footholds between the swaying knots, down to where the bobbing net met the pitching deck of our little iron tub. When we were loaded the coxswain gunned our engine in a blue stink of smoke and we cast off.

Our ship seemed to fall away from us and grow small as we moved out; there was a kind of finality about leaving it. Yet final or not, there was relief in action, and release from morbid imagination. For a moment we even partook of the gaiety of our bobbing tub on the foam-tracked sea. Emotions of an hour ago seemed suddenly unimportant as we looked back at the transport and remembered the parting words we posted on the bulletin board in the Ship's Officers' Wardroom:

A MESSAGE OF THANKS
From: Marines aboard U.S.S. *Repulsive*
To: Officers and Men aboard U.S.S. *Repulsive*

1. It gives us great pleasure at this time to extend our sincere thanks to all members of the crew for their kind and considerate treatment of Marines during this cruise.

2. We non-combatants realize that the brave and stalwart members of the crew are winning the war in the Pacific. You Navy people even go within

ten miles of a Japanese island, thereby risking your precious lives. Oh how courageous you are! Oh how our piles bleed for you.

3. Because of your actions during this voyage it is our heartfelt wish that:

a. The U.S.S. *Repulsive* receives a Jap torpedo immediately after debarkation of all troops.

b. The crew of the U.S.S. *Repulsive* is stranded on Beach Orange Three where Marine units which sailed aboard the ship may repay in some measure the good fellowship extended by the crew and officers during the trip.

4. In conclusion we Marines wish to say to all you dear, dear boys in the Navy: "Bugger you, you bloody bastards!"

Sixteen thousand yards off the beach the LCVPs circled at the sides of their transports, awaiting H-Hour. From the air the big vessels must have seemed like a flock of fat ducks with broods of iron ducklings playing ring-around-the-rosy at their mothers' sides.

We circled until 0714 when our signal came to straighten out and head for the transfer line just outside the reef. The circles of iron ducklings suddenly unwound into parallel files of LCVPs gray with the seriousness of war, heading full speed for the flame.

For an hour we plowed toward the beach, the sun above us coming down through the overcast like a silver burning ball. Peleliu was veiled with the smoke of our shelling. New hits against that veil made brown and gray pillars like graceful ghost-trees by Claude Lorrain. As we drew abreast of our battleships and cruisers 1000 yards outside the reef, the sound of their firing changed from dooming booms to the slamming of huge doors.

At 0747 the carrier planes, hundreds of them, noiseless in the roar of gunfire, started pouring death. I counted 96 over my head at once. I saw one flash and fall in a long slow arc of flame.

Over the gunwale of a craft abreast of us I saw a marine, his face painted for the jungle, his eyes set for the beach, his mouth set for murder, his big hands quiet now in the last moments before the tough tendons drew up to kill.

At 0759 I noticed the amphibious tanks and tractors, the LVTAs and LVTs that would carry us over the reef, being spewed from the maws of LSTs. Sending twin plumes of foam from their tracks aft, they made their way to the transfer line.

At 0800 the rockets from LCI gunboats flashed pink and soared in flaming curves, by salvoes, into the wall of smoke on the beach.

At 0830 we wallowed aft the control boat on the transfer line, the reef a hundred yards ahead, and beyond the edge of the reef 700 yards of green shallow water thick with black niggerheads of coral. The first Jap mortar burst hit just inside the reef as our coxswain worked us up alongside an LVT for transfer. While the two craft bobbed and smashed at each other, we numbly piled ourselves and our gear into the LVT. The coxswain of the LCVP waved, backed his craft clear, and headed seaward.

The iron bulkheads of the LVT came above our heads—we could see only the sky. Farrell climbed on a pile of gear to see out, preparatory to giving our new coxswain the signal for heading in over the reef. Standing on a field radio case forward, I managed to poke my head up so I could see the first wave of LVTs go in. As I watched, the silence came into my consciousness; our shelling had ceased. Only our tank treads churning the water marred the quietness.

Then on the lip of the beach we saw many pink flashes—the Japs, coming out from under our shelling, were opening up with mortar and artillery fire on the first wave. Dead ahead there was a brighter flash. Looking through his binoculars, Farrell told us, "They hit an LVT."

As our coxswain watched the amphitracks toiling through the black obstructions on the reef, I heard him say to Farrell he doubted if it were possible to get us to our precise point on the far right of Beach Orange Three, and Farrell answered, "Well, take us as close as you can."

Mortar bursts began to plume up all over the reef and walk along the edge of the beach. Farrell, who could have waited another hour to take our Free Boat (not belonging to a specific assault wave) into the beach, abruptly put down his glasses, cupped his hands at the gunner by the coxswain, and bawled, "Let's quit this farting around. Tell him to take us in!"

The clatter of our treads rose to the pitch of a rock crusher and our hell ride began. In that clanking hearse it was impossible to stand without holding on to something, impossible to sit on the deck without the risk of fracturing our tailbones. So we grabbed and lurched and swore. Suddenly there was a cracking rattle of shrapnel on the bulkhead and dousing water on our necks.

"Get down! Squat!" yelled Farrell, and we bent down on our hunkers, grasping at each other's shoulders, at the bulkheads, at anything. That was the first mortar that came close. There were two more, and then the ping and whine of small arms in the air over us.

"Keep down!" yelled Farrell, with his head up over the bulkhead peering at the beach, "Still 300 yards to go."

We ground to a stop, after a thousand years, on the coarse coral. The ramp aft, seaward, cranked down fast and we tightened our holds on our gear. The air cracked and roared, filled our ears and guts with its sound while Farrell bellowed, "OK! Pile out! Scatter! But follow me to the right! The right, goddammit, remember!" And we ran down the ramp and came around the end of the LVT, splashing ankle-deep up the surf to the white beach.

Suddenly I was completely alone. Each man drew into himself when he ran down that ramp, into that flame. Those marines flattened in the sand on that beach were dark and huddled like wet rats in death as I threw my body down among them. There was a rattle and roar under my helmet while I undid the chin strap and smelled the flaming oil and popping ammunition from the burning LVTs around us. Men of the first wave had penetrated about 25 yards inland as I looked up the sandy slope.

Then I ran—to the right—slanting up the beach for cover, half bent over. Off balance, I fell flat on my face just as I heard the *whishhh* of a mortar I knew was too close. A red flash stabbed at my eyeballs. About fifteen yards away, on the upper edge of the beach, it smashed down four men from our boat. One figure seemed to fly to pieces. With terrible clarity I saw the head and one leg sail into the air. Captain Farrell, near the burst, never dodged nor hesitated but kept running, screaming at his men to follow him to their objective down the beach.

I got up to follow him, ran a few steps, and fell into a small shell hole as another mortar burst threw dirt on me. Lying there in terror looking longingly up the slope to better cover, I saw a wounded man near me, staggering in the direction of LVTs. His face was half bloody pulp and the mangled shreds of what was left of an arm hung down like a stick, as he bent over in his stumbling, shock-crazy walk. The half of his face that was still human had the most terrifying look of abject patience I have ever seen. He fell behind me, in a red puddle on the white sand.

I ran farther to the right, angling up the slope. Suddenly I recognized Martin's big back (he was unarmed like myself) under a three-foot ledge on the upper rim of the beach where vegetation started. I made a final dash to throw myself under the ledge at Martin's side. The exertion was so great I fell down almost unconscious. When I opened my eyes again my throat burned, yet I was cold with sweat. We were lying with our heads to the ledge, not four feet from the aperture of a Jap "spider trap," a small machine-gun nest built into the face of the ledge with coco logs. Loose sand shovelled away from the aperture in two widening banks at either side made the trough in which we lay and gave additional cover. I wondered how well I could use my knife if a live Jap suddenly should poke an ugly face out at me from the opening formed by the logs.

Mortar shells whished and whapped through the air over our heads. They hit without apparent pattern on the beach and in the reef at our backs. Turning my head seaward I saw a direct center hit on an LVT. Pieces of iron and men seemed to sail slow-motion into the air. As bursts began to creep steadily from the reef in toward the beach, the shells from one mortar rustled through the air directly over our heads at intervals of a few seconds, bursting closer, closer. Then a flat cracking flash nearly buried me with sand. Wriggling out, and trying to wipe the sharp grains from my sweating eyelids, I saw in the clinging gray smoke that a burst had hit about six feet from my left foot, beyond the bank of loose sand at my side. In almost burying me, this sand had also saved me from shrapnel, except for one small spent piece that burned my left shin—which I did not know until later. I yelled to Martin, but he lay with face down, and did not answer. I could see no blood but I thought he was hit. A moment later he raised his head—I shouted, but he could not hear me. The blast had deafened him. Burst followed burst, creeping out to the reef and then back into the beach again. We hugged the earth and hung on.

Abruptly from close by, from over the ledge at our heads came a shuddering explosion, then a wild popping of .50-caliber shells. Later when we got up, we discovered an LVT on fire in the brush above us. It had run over a mine.

A different kind of shellburst began to come at us from a new direction. We judged it was 75-mm. artillery from a Jap battery down the beach on a peninsula to our right. We saw hits on five or six LVTs as they came jolting in over the reef. As I looked over my shoulder a burst smashed into a file of marines wading toward our beach from a smoking LVT. Jap machine guns lashed the reef with white lines and marines fell with bloody splashes into the green water. The survivors seemed so slow and small and patient coming in, out there.

Our carrier planes were swarming the sky again. Fighters roared in low over our heads almost continuously, strafing beyond our perimeter inland. Dive bombers peeled off by sections, dropping their 1000-pounders, and TBFs made their roaring rocket runs, finishing off with bellies full of 100-pounders for the Japs. We had it all our way in the sky over Peleliu; there was not a Jap plane in the air. Airmen gave marines on Peleliu great support. Martin and I realized their efficiency and close contact with the ground command when we saw dive bombers making runs over the peninsula to our right. The Jap 75's were silenced.

For some reason mortar and sniper fire slackened too, and left us on our lonely beach in comparative quiet. We knew our lines were well toward the airstrip now.

Martin and I lay there weak, grateful and still, in the lull. Suddenly we were conscious of someone crawling up behind us from the beach and we turned our heads. It was a corpsman. As we moved around to see him, he grinned and rasped, "Christ, I thought you were a couple of corpses!" We agreed.

The delicious lack of bursts in our immediate vicinity was like a life-renewing elixir. Tension broke for a few moments, and we lit cigarettes, the three of us. For myself, I was sampling the sheer joy of being alive.

The sector of the beach we could see from our trough in the sand was empty of living creatures. Two dead bodies and five wrecked LVTs were our closest company. I stared at the sand bank above my head and saw against the smoking sky the tangled, broken wrecks of coco palms and tropical trees with their big leaves hanging burned and dead. Two birds with long bills and short bodies lighted on a smashed palm frond and cried. Then the mortars started again.

Hugging the ground and turning our heads seaward, we watched the next wave of LVTs come in. They had good luck. I saw no hits. The amphitracks crawled in, pushed their snouts against the sand, and the men came up from the surf. Most of them streamed off to our right along the rim of the beach at the edge of the broken trees. Mortar fire shifted far to our left, and there was only the occasional zing of a sniper's bullet. Four men carrying posts and orange beach markers walked by, and another wave of LVTs discharged men along the whole length of the beach. We got up and started walking to our right. I remember the strange quietness, the dead marines in the white sand, the men with heavy loads trudging along in the smoke of the LVTs. Two rows of land mines, sown about six feet apart, lined our beach. The Japs had not tended them well; they were easy to see. We stepped carefully around their rusty bellies and forked horns.

Behind us came a burly man walking fast, as if on eggs. He bawled at the men he passed, "Where's the Seventh's CP?" and always got the reply, "Up that way, Colonel." We recognized him as the CO of our regiment, and fell in behind him, to find Farrell's bunch. When snipers' bullets and occasional mortar shells went over our heads on their way out to the reef, I instinctively pulled in my neck—though I could judge by now when they would be really close. It was interesting to watch the colonel ahead. He never bobbled nor missed a pace, but there was plenty in his stiff stride—almost an expression on the back of his neck—to describe the trouble in his mind.

We followed him inland from the beach, plunging into the burned and twisted jungle trees. We stumbled through debris into an open space where four LVTAs were parked, and thirty paces further into the trees we found our CP being set up in a trench dug by the Japs. It was six feet deep and about twenty yards long. Under our naval shelling the Japs had given it up just before we landed. Farrell had found it, cleared it of Jap machine-gun fire, and had it functioning as a command post when his superiors arrived. It was full of marines now, taking cover from sniper fire and mortars. A burst hit close at our backs just as Martin and I slid down into the trench. There was a yell for corpsmen—somebody was hit.

We sat in the trench, getting our breath. My legs trembled from exertion, but I felt very relieved, very secure. Out some 200 yards ahead, our front line inched forward and our perimeter grew more solid. Firing on our area slackened gradually.

By this time it was 1300. Some of us climbed out of the trench and walked back in the smashed trees to stretch our cramped legs. Disposal squads were working through the area, digging out dud rockets, bombs and shells. When a projectile could not be disarmed with tools, disposal men would explode it. They would clear the necessary area, pass the word loudly to get down, and let 'er go—*blump!* All through the broken trees we found crude booby traps. Details were busy marking them and the land mines with red tape. Telephone linemen were unrolling their heavy spools of wire. Scout observation planes from warships wheeled high above our heads, directing naval gunfire. Occasionally they would go into a shallow dive and have awkward fun strafing.

Before noon the sun had bitten through the overcast of early morning and burned away all but a few white puffy clouds. Our planes were working against a background of bright, sharp blue. And as the sun, seven degrees above the equator, struck down upon us, it turned Peleliu into a bitter furnace.

Three of us had each carried a can of beer ashore in his pack. Giving each other the high-sign, we gathered behind a broken palm log, punched holes with our knives in the three cans, and drank a toast, *To the Marines on Peleliu*. The beer was hot, foamy and wonderful. When it was gone, we were still dry-mouthed. And not a bit hungry.

About thirty paces back of the Jap trench a sick bay had been established in a big shell crater made by one of our battleship guns. Lying around it were pieces of shrapnel over a foot long. In the center of the crater at the bottom a doctor was working on the worst of the stretcher cases. Corpsmen, four to a stretcher, came in continually with their bloody loads. The doctor had attached plasma bottles to the top of a broken tree stump and was giving transfusions as fast as he could after rough surgery. Corpsmen applied tourniquets, sulpha, morphine, and handled the walking wounded and lighter cases with first aid.

The padre stood by with two canteens and a Bible, helping. He was deeply and visibly moved by the patient suffering and death. He looked very lonely, very close to God, as he bent over the shattered men so far from home. Corpsmen put a poncho, a shirt, a rag,

anything handy, over the gray faces of the dead and carried them
to a line on the beach, under a tarpaulin, to await the digging of
graves.

It is hard to remember how the minutes ticked away, while the sun
climbed down from the top of the blazing sky. The battle pounded
on ahead of us. During flurries of fire I slid down into the trench;
during the lulls I tried to find shade from the sun. I was without emotion of any kind. I saw everything around me in sharp focus, yet it
no longer crashed into my consciousness. My mind blanked itself
for my body's sake.

Our front advanced slowly, if at all; the radio in our trench picked
up few reports, and the inactivity began to pall on Martin and me
as we grew more and more curious about the battle's progress in other
sectors. We had no access to the messages runners brought in to the
colonel.

Farrell was sending two men to establish contact with the Division
command post which was supposed to be far down the beach to our
left. Martin asked if we could go along and get news from the Division command. We buckled our canteen belts and joined the two marines.

It is hard to walk through a jungle that has been subjected to saturation bombing and bombardment for a week. Jagged holes in the
scattered stone and dirty sand, splintered trees and tangled vines
made a churned, burned wilderness. Strewn through this chaos were
not only the remnants and remainders of the marines' advance, but
also the new men and new gear that had poured ashore to back up
the front line. These men were digging in, making holes for themselves for the long night ahead when the Japs would surely counterattack. We jumped over foxholes, climbed over and around smashed
trees, sidestepped tapes denoting mines and booby traps, walked
gingerly around those yet unmarked. Telephone wires in crazy crisscross mazes were stretched along the broken ground. Scattered everywhere were discarded packs, helmets, rifles, boxes, clothes, rubber
life belts—the rubbish of battle. Lying on the seared leaves and hot
sand were dead bodies yet ungathered by corpsmen, the flesh bluish gray as the pitiless sun began to bring the peculiar and intoler-
able stench of human dead.

Planes came in strafing over our heads; the whump and chatter
of firing to our right made a constant churning of sound. Sweat ran
in streams from under our helmets which, without cloth covers, were
burning to the touch. Our dungarees, wet with sweat, stuck to our
legs and backs. The sand under our clothes scratched like sandpaper.

When we had snaked our way along for about 300 yards, the two
marines with us began to ask the men we met where the Division com-

mand post was. Nobody knew. We hunted for an hour, and never did find it. Intolerably hot and thirsty, Martin and I left the marines to their search. We turned left and walked down to the edge of the beach, planning to make our way back to our own CP by walking along the beach, the way we had first gotten there. The water's edge was crowded with men bringing equipment ashore.

We had walked fifty paces along the sand, dodging around LVTs, when we heard a mortar shell whirr over us and saw it send up its column of gray water about sixty yards out on the reef. That was the first of several salvoes. They began to get hot.

We were passing by a big hole dug in the sand with a sign above it reading "Shore Party CP" when a burst hit about 25 yards down the beach at the water's edge, where we had been, and set an LVT on fire. We flopped into the very crowded Shore Party CP. The mortar fire lasted for about ten minutes, with most of the hits on that part of the beach we had just traversed. Later that evening we learned from the two marine messengers that in their further search for the Division CP they had been directly under this fire and had four men killed in the same hole with them. They came back shaken and no longer eager.

Meanwhile we lay packed in the hole with the shore party. The supply officer in charge was stretched flat on his belly and holding a telephone in his hand. He wanted to make a call, but he would not get up to crank the box to get the operator. So I cranked it for him, as I was right by it. By the time he got an answer, and I had cranked and cranked, the mortar bursts were hitting further down the beach away from us.

Some guy buried deep in the sand hole stuck his head up and began to gripe, "Goddammit, what are all you bastards in this hole for? Them bursts are a mile off. Scatter, you punks!" Just then a shell came whapping over and hit very close, and the guy buried his head again and said no more. Somebody grunted, "You're a brave son of a bitch walking around out there ain't you?"

In a few minutes Martin and I got up and continued our way down the beach through the welter of men, vehicles and ammunition cases. In some places things were so jammed up that we had to wade out into the surf to get around. The Jap mortars were far from silent, and direct hits on this kind of concentration really played hell. Yet regardless of fire, the marines were pouring everything they could get on the beach before nightfall and the expected counterattack. We watched sweating crews lift light artillery out of the amphitracks and haul them ashore. Martin muttered, "The more of those damn guns they put on here tonight the better I'll feel."

Turning in from the beach toward our CP we found the area thick-

er than ever with marines digging in for the night. There were foxholes every three or four feet, most of them barricaded with coral
stones and logs moved around to help deepen and strengthen the
cover. The men worked at their places for the night earnestly, without much conversation except short declarations of fact: "It's the ferk-
ing night time I don't like, when them little ferkers come sneakin'
into your lap." They dug in the dirt and cleaned their guns.

I saw a big redheaded sergeant I knew, lying in a hole with his eyes
closed. It was his first action, and the day's events had bitten too deeply into his mind. At noon, I had seen him sink down on the ground
with his hands over his face and cry.

We found our CP. The trench was twice as wide at the bottom as
it had been, and cleared of broken tree limbs and big rocks. As we
came up a bomb disposal officer was carrying out a dud rocket he
had dug from the side of the trench. Improvements were going on.
Marines were filling new gunnysacks, making sandbags to pile around
the radio set and around the section of the trench where the colonel
would spend the night. Men were hacking roots from the sides of
the trench and smoothing out bumps, making places to rest their
backs. Others were cutting poles from broken trees, laying them cross-
wise over their part of the trench, and tying their ponchos across the
poles. It was getting cosy around the CP.

We asked Farrell if we could spend the night in the trench and he
told us he had a place for us down at the extreme left end where he
would be.

Very heavy firing suddenly started on our left. The radio operator got busy. When he finished writing out the message he showed
it to us before he passed it down the trench to the colonel. It said our
center was under heavy counterattack, the enemy using tanks. We
knew we had three Shermans ashore, and sat there listening and hoping they would be enough. Gradually the firing died down. The attack stalled after the Shermans had knocked out eleven Jap tanks.
A lull settled over us, as both sides prepared for the night.

About sundown we settled into our places at the end of the trench.
The low sun cast a sulphurous yellow light through the smoke, then
faded. Somewhat to the left and behind us two batteries of 75-mm.
were placed. They fired a few rounds over our heads and the crack
and blast made me jump. Then there was almost silence in the growing dusk. Our planes left the sky, heading out for their carriers. I
got the orange and candy bar out of my pack, ate the candy, split the
orange three ways to share with Martin and Farrell. Warm water from
my nearly empty canteen was dessert. Word was passed that the
"smoking lamp" would be out all night, that if anybody wanted a ciga-

rette this was the last chance before morning. So we sat smoking in the dusk.

Martin and I spread a poncho under us and I hung my knife on a tree root over my head where I could reach it easily. We settled down to sleep, as close into Mother Earth as we could get. Mosquitoes began to swarm and bite. Like everyone else, I finally rummaged in my pack, found my headnet and gloves, and put them on.

We had expected that it might cool off after sundown, but we were wrong. With our headnets over our helmets and tied at the bottom around our necks, and with our gritty gloves on, we sat and steamed in puddles of sweat. Gun flashes occasionally silhouetted the top of the trench against the sky . . . A deep and numb kind of weariness both of body and of mind made the trench and the battle, the anxiety and uncertainty unreal, without the power of fact. I did not give a damn. I accepted each moment as it came, as if watching the paying out of a coiled cable, not being able to see when the end would suddenly come, time's end, world's end. Meanwhile the cable unwound. I was neither contented nor disturbed.

꽃 꽃 꽃 꽃

NOBODY WAS IMMUNE TO FEAR THAT FIRST NIGHT. Private Russell Davis, who wrote a book about Peleliu because his three sons asked him to, was huddled in a hollow behind the beachhead following a sharp Japanese counterattack. Many years later Davis astutely observed that "it is very hard for a father not to make himself braver and wiser than he really is . . ."

·21· "PUT ME DOWN FOR LAST WATCH"

RUSSELL DAVIS

They were the first Negro Marines I had seen in the war. They were carrying water and ammunition in from the beach, led by a huge sergeant who carried a box of ammunition on each shoulder. They dumped their supplies at the foot of the bank, and just as they did the Japanese fired a twilight salvo in on the line and everybody scattered for their holes. One of the carriers dived into a hollow between Buck and me, and the three of us lay there while the Japs larruped the line with every gun they had. The dirt of the bank began to slide down, and I turned my face from it and looked into the white eyeballs of the carrier who was right beside me. I heard him say, "Man, man, this is no good. This is real bad."

The barrage began to let up and darkness was full down on the line. The carrier sat up and said: "Where they at? My party, I mean."

"Scattered all over the place," Buck said. "You better not move now."

"This hole taken?" the carrier asked.

"You got it," Buck told him. "There won't be any more heavy fire now because we'd spot their flashes. But it would be very dangerous to move."

"I'm staying right here," the carrier said. "Right in this nice place here."

It was completely dark. I couldn't even see the carrier's white eyeballs. Something popped overhead and everything lit up in a weird shade of green. The ships of the line had started to fire night flares. More flares popped, thrown up by the mortars behind us. They were green, too, the most frightening shade of green I had ever seen. When I turned toward the carrier he looked like a character out of a horror movie, and I must have looked as bad to him because he gasped and said: "Man, that doesn't make you look good at all. I knew people came black and white but I never expected to see any green ones."

He rolled over and said to Buck: "What you think I ought to do? I don't hear my people nowhere abouts."

"Do what you want," Buck said, "but if I was you I'd stay right here until morning. You can't do any carrying now dark has come. Everything shuts down."

"Reckon I better stay," the carrier said. "You mind?"

"Glad to have you," Buck said. "You can take the second watch. I'll wake you."

From somewhere in the darkness John laughed. "You can't stop Buck," he said. "If he can't fill his watch list, he recruits guys. Put me down for last watch." I remember very little of the details of the night. Buck must have stayed awake through all the watches. He never could seem to sleep well on the line. Not that anyone did. Every time a flare broke or a shell rumbled in close I almost choked on my own heart. The line at night has its own curious pattern of sound. There are long lulls when even the small-arms fire dies. When this happens and darkness is all around, the war is far away and you drop off into exhausted sleep. But then comes one shot, sometimes ours, sometimes theirs. A spatter of fire follows, at first rifle fire and then a few bursts from a BAR, and finally the full clatter of a machine gun. Then there is furious exchange as both sides wake up and hammer away in anger. Men call all along the line and flares pop and the shadows rush across the front of the line until you swear that the enemy is attacking in force. Tracers go pumping out into the dark. The mortar men wake and begin to fire a few. The artillery is called down, and the war is on. Then there is a lull, a few embarrassed rounds are fired, and things settle. Sometimes the harsh cry for the corpsman goes up and men ask along the line: "Who got hit? Who was it?"

"Just a guy in the machine guns," a rifleman tells another.

"Just a rifle guy in the first platoon," a machine-gunner tells another.

I woke up many times as short fire-fights flared up. I lay and listened to the fire from both sides. It was easy to pick out the different weapons, just as the different instruments in a symphony orchestra can be identified. It was easy to tell their weapons from ours. Their rifles had a lighter sound and a higher crack. Their machine guns fired faster than ours. Their artillery was more wobbly in flight than ours.

Despite the sounds and the endless, nervous conversation of Buck and the carrier, I managed to fall asleep.

Some time in the night I felt a hand that seemed to be tearing away my shoulder to get at my throat. I had curled up asleep in a ball and when the hand fell on me I unwound and reared up with my rifle pushed out in front of me and my knife in the other hand.

A voice behind the hand said: "Sorry to scare you, man. I tried yellin' but I couldn't make no headway against this other noise around here."

I recognized the carrier's voice and relaxed. It was my turn to go on watch. I rubbed my shoulder. "You got strong hands," I told him. "I think you ripped the arm right off my shoulder."

"Jes' nervous," he said. "Hope I didn't hurt you."

"All quiet?" I asked.

"Never quiet. But we're still livin'."

"I got the duty," I told him. "Relax and go to sleep."

I rolled over on my stomach and faced out toward the airport. I could see our front line foxholes but nobody moved out there. When the flares came up the view was stark and bleak, and when they died everything seemed to move in the running shadows. For a moment I had the feeling that everybody out in front of me had been killed. I turned back from the airport view and it was comforting to hear Buck and the carrier having a low-voiced conversation about automobiles. I called: "John . . . John." But there was no answer.

"He's asleep," Buck told me.

"How's he do that?" the carrier wondered.

"I'd like to know myself," Buck said.

I turned back to watch the airport. Suddenly, during a lull, a voice called out: "Amelicans. Amelicans. Pigs . . . Dogs . . . Amelican pigs and dogs." The voice must have come through a megaphone or a bullhorn. It was louder than life. I jumped and almost opened fire.

"That's a Jap," Buck said. "Some stinkin' miserable clown is crawling around out there. Don't fire. That's what he wants."

"Amelican pig," came the voice. "You die. You die. You die."

Just as the line had opened up to answer rifle fire, they opened up to answer the infiltrator, wherever he was. The language that volleyed out of the seemingly deserted foxholes almost lit the sky. Buck listened to it and chuckled. It was the first time he had relaxed since nightfall.

"They won't out-yell those guys," Buck said. "Nobody could."

"Hey, Shambo," some rifleman called. "Come on in and see what we did to your tanks. We're using them to pack fish in."

"Drop dead, you lousy Jap," someone said, "and save us the trouble of knocking you off."

Worse things followed, some in simple English and some in Japanese. One of the machine-gunners had been born in Japan and he was busy furnishing bad words in Japanese.

"Hey, Tom," someone called. "How do you say '____'?"

Tom would furnish the word or its equivalent. Back would go the word to the infiltrator. "Die! Die! Die!" the infiltrator yelled. The infiltrator had learned his English out of a book and he didn't have either a large or lurid vocabulary. He kept repeating "pig" and "dog"—and this was no match for the words that Tom furnished. The exchange lasted a few minutes and then the officers silenced the men. The Japanese used the trick to get a fix on the positions along the line. The whole exchange ended in a burst of rifle and machine-gun fire.

"I never knew they was so close," the carrier said to Buck.

"Usually they send out a more insulting guy," Buck said. "Some of them, especially the ones born in the States, can really bait you. That one didn't have the vocabulary."

Things quieted down except for a big fire-fight that flamed up over in the third battalion area. My watch was over and I woke John. I just had to touch his shoulder and he was awake and mumbling. I lay back down and tried to sleep, and a burst of fire came from the swamp behind us. That brought everyone awake and everyone was calling to everyone else. We grabbed our weapons and faced toward the rear and waited. The word was passed along the line. "It wasn't any Jap. Some kid cracked up and began to run around. Somebody shot him."

I lay back down again and tried to sleep. I was almost asleep when a terrible call sounded above even the sound of small-arms fire. The scream started high, went higher, gurgled and then rattled and then died. It brought every one of us awake, and the carrier muttered "Lord, lord, lord."

"Relax," John said, "it's only The Screamer back in the CP." The Screamer was a man who had terrible nightmares and who had been having them and screaming his way through them for three campaigns.

"Someday he'll get shot," Buck said. "I mean some night. The guy would drive you crazy if you didn't know about it."

"Go to sleep," John said. "I got the watch."

Finally I did sleep, fitfully, until just before dawn when the first heavy salvos came in with the new light. "Morning call," John said. "Wake, greet the new day, but don't get up or you'll get your block knocked off."

That morning we got ready to attack across the airport. The rations, water and ammunition that the carriers brought up, were doled out to the men. Orders were passed and a barrage was laid down on the other side of the airstrip. The riflemen got ready in their holes.

At the bottom of the bank we built a quick fire, using an explosive they called "Composition C," and put coffee water on to boil. "We'll go out in about fifteen minutes," Buck said. He used his knife in the handleslit to lift the canteen cup from the fire. He laid out our cups and one for the carrier and made four equal portions of coffee. The carrier said: "I liked you boys fine. But I'm not sorry that I get off here."

"I don't blame you," Buck said. "This attack is going across ground with no cover at all." He looked up toward the ridges where the naval guns were clawing away with fiery hands.

Overhead an air strike came screaming in, bombing and rocketing and dropping fire. The preparation for the attack had started. The tremors from the hills rolled all the way back to the ground where we sat. We could feel the shock in the seat of our pants. The whole island was wriggling.

The Japanese began to answer our fire, trying to jab our attack off balance. We scattered back to our holes to wait. Instead of Buck being pessimistic, John was. He said: "We jump off over about three hundred yards of open ground. Directly ahead are the pillboxes and the blockhouses. Above these are hills full of caves full of Japs and guns. May God have mercy on us. The Japs aren't going to . . ." He touched my arm. "Well, here we go."

Buck stood up and walked over the top of the bank and waved his hand ahead. "Just walk ahead as far as you can," he told me. "Let's move out!"

. . . As we moved, just behind the assault companies, the airport clouded over with dust and smoke and wriggling waves of heat. Beneath the arms of the riflemen appeared halfmoons of dark sweat, and just below their packs their dungarees showed dark and sometimes white from the salt. It was going to be a very hot day. Already sweat fretted in the open wound on my forehead, and my eyes blurred and stung, and the smell of powder and dust and burning things was everywhere mixed. There was also that peculiar odor that came from fetid pillboxes in which the Japanese lived and died. Buck called it "the stink of death." Perhaps it was.

We were maintaining a floating Observation Post just behind the assault companies, and our contact runner was the pudgy German named Larry, who looked too fat to run; but he could run very well. He seemed too baby-faced to be a combat man; but he was without fear. The only sign of stress he showed was in his face that flushed redder and redder as things got bad. And they got bad.

At first we walked into the humming mist, and ahead of us moved the long skirmish line of riflemen, scything forward all the way to the Fifth Marine lines. The line ambled, then quick-stepped, then trotted, then drove into the smoke, running hard. Before them, the shelling built a wall of spurting earth and flaming explosion and vicious, whirring shrapnel. Gaps opened in the line. Men bunched up and then spread out; and finally one long segment of the line folded down, as the riflemen went to the ground and returned fire on the pillboxes. A howling series of shellfire came in, and there was no longer any line at all—only broken bodies and a few men wriggling ahead on their own, without orders or control.

We dived into a shellhole and lay still, timing the mortars which walked all around us. I lay next to John. Larry and Buck were farther out. When the shellfire hit and the ground shimmied, John clamped down hard on his helmet top to keep the concussion from tearing it away. I saw him grimace and spit into the dust, and he was turned toward me, shouting something which was swallowed by the sound around us. I saw his lips and I could catch his message. He said: "This is a bad one. This will be a bad one for me." I had never heard John say such a thing before, and it frightened me, even though I didn't know then that he was right.

The fire built and built until my ears refused to receive more sound, and it was maddening, because even the ground was not steady. The whole field rocked. All around came the cry: "Corpsman!" No matter how loud the sound, that call came through. I felt that the artillery was trying to shake us loose from the earth itself, and I sprawled full length and dug into the dirt with my fingers. I was afraid if I let go I would slip down into some tremendous hole. I had always been afraid of falling; I had always been afraid of caves and mines and the combined fear of them made me scream. But everything else around me was screaming and it didn't matter. There was no one to hear it.

John knelt above me. He shouted something. He waved toward something off on the right. I couldn't understand him and I had no wish to. I put my head down and bellowed with the fear I felt. Then I felt fearful pain in my fingers. The pain made me jerk my fingers free from the holes I had dug with them, and when the fingers were free I was up and running, off to the right. I supposed, later, that John had stamped on my fingers to pull me out of my panic; but he never spoke of it then, or during the brief time afterwards he was to live.

I was running. Showers of dirt went up in my face and I was blinded by flash and dust, but I was running to the right, the direction John had ordered. Everything else had closed down on me again and my one thought was to get to the end of our battalion front and see what had happened. Men swirled around. I flopped and ran, flopped and ran, while great trains of artillery poured down and scrambled the ground under me. I dived into shellholes and rolled out of them and ran on. The air was thickly seeded with small-arms fire which meant nothing. At last I rolled down a bank and into a ditch, and other marines were there. A captain, a stranger to me, squatted at the edge of the ditch and tried to see ahead. Behind him was a company radioman, set up and ready to transmit. Riflemen had clustered there.

"I can't see," the captain complained to the radioman and the riflemen behind him. "I can't see, so how can I tell? It's coming in from everywhere in the pillbox area. Tell 'em never mind co-ordinates. Tell 'em just to fire and fire. For Pete's sake . . . the whole front is a target. Put it onto them." The radioman cuddled his set under him and put his mouth close to his speaker, and began his call, but there was no way to hear what he said in that noise.

I rolled close to a rifleman and shouted. "Is this the Fifth Marines?"

He was sprawled out on his face and for a moment I thought he was dead. But he rolled over and I yelled against his ear. He nodded his head. "It's the First Battalion, Fifth."

"Where does the First Regiment end?" I asked.

He shook his head. I didn't know at first whether it meant no, or that he couldn't hear me. Finally he said: "I don't rightly know about the First." He hitched up the side of the ditch. "Cap'n, where's the First at?"

The question annoyed the captain. "I don't know," he said desperately. "I don't even know for sure where the Fifth is. We're supposed to be the left-flank company. But it's scrambled. I mean mixed. If we could get the rest of the way over and lie up in those blockhouses there we might get some cover. But out here . . . Well, let's try. Come on!"

He stood up and waved, and his men crept out after him and disappeared somewhere beyond the flaming curtain that flapped in our faces. I worked back along the line toward center, and already I had learned how to move through the worst of it. Anything can be learned, and when life is the motivation it is learned quickly and well. The infantryman's basic trade is either learned or not learned in a day on the line. To be an expert takes months.

The first marine I recognized from the Second Battalion, First, was lying in a hole, dead. He had been bowled over on his back from the blast and, in death, he seemed to be posed for a picture with the caption HOW TO LOOK VERY DEAD. Just beyond him were a pair of live marines, a BAR man and his assistant. They said they were from the Second Battalion, First; and one of them said: "We don't know where the rest of 'em are at. Either ahead or back some."

"We oughta go back," the BAR man said.

"Or ahead maybe," the assistant suggested. "There's no cover at all behind us."

"Whatsa difference?" the BAR man said. They began to wriggle ahead and I followed them. The fire had not slackened. Headfirst we crawled into a hornet's nest, until the BAR man clapped his hand to his thigh and I saw blood welling through his fingers. "I'm hit," he said.

"You hit, Freddie?" his assistant said.

"Yeah, I'm hit. I'm going back if I can get there. You want this?" He pushed the BAR along the ground toward his assistant.

The assistant said: "I guess I'm supposed to take it. You ain't hit bad, are you, Freddie?"

"Naw. Do I look it?" He made a gesture toward the smoke and flames of the blockhouse area. "That's what they can do with this war," he said. He went back, dragging his damaged leg behind him. It must have hurt him, but he looked happy enough for me to envy him.

I lost the assistant—now the BAR—in the smoke somewhere. The texture of the ground under my hands and knees had changed. I could feel it biting, and when I looked down I saw sharp fragments of concrete—I had arrived in the blockhouse area. All the first line of pillboxes had been leveled and the fragments spread like a jagged carpet along the ground. I ran against a torn concrete wall with iron reinforcing rods twisted out on all sides. Against it I rested and wondered if anyone else had come across the airport with me. I felt very lonely; but there was no good in calling out, even if my voice could have carried above the din. Finally, I moved beyond the wall, and there was a lieutenant I knew very well. He and three riflemen were firing over a second low wall. The lieutenant had a BAR which he didn't use very well.

"I'm across," he said. "And these men are. But I don't know about the rest. I think they're lying all around, through here." He waved vaguely. "We got hit real bad on the field . . . squads all ripped up . . . we weren't half across."

Two men slid into our position between the walls and the lieutenant tried to grab them and place them. They had a light machine gun.

One of the machine-gunners said: "Look, sir, I got to see to fire, and I can't see nothin' in here." The lieutenant nodded. The machine-gunners went over behind a high pile of rubble and pegged their gun down and began to fire.

A sergeant came tumbling in beside the lieutenant. The sergeant wore his chevrons painted in black on his sleeve. "He's bringing it up," the sergeant said. "The stuff is coming."

"Good," the lieutenant said. "We can't move until we cave in that gun-slit. Seen any flame-throwers?"

"None. Only one got across, and that don't work."

The dark dynamiter I had seen in the trench near the beach rolled down into the hole beside the lieutenant. The demolitionist still wore the pack with DANGER stenciled below the skull and crossbones.

He was thick and hairy and had a face like an old lion. When he got into the ditch he stretched toward the sun, thrusting his thick arms toward the sky and throwing out his huge chest. I expected to hear him roar. "You got the stuff?" the lieutenant asked. He meant demolitions.

The dynamiter yawned again. Again I expected a lion's roar to come out of his corded throat. "I got it. I throw away my socks and food before I ditch this." He patted his pack. "I got it all made up. You give me a little rifle cover and I stick it right in that Jap's ear." He opened his pack and displayed a shaped charge of plastic explosive, fuzed and set to go. The lieutenant moved away from it. The dynamiter fussed with his bundle, pulling on the fuzes and patting the mold. "Oh, baby," he said. "When this rolls in on him!"

The lieutenant made a motion toward the machine-gunners. "Lay it on that slit." He waved at two riflemen. "Get out and flank that baby." The demolitionist lit the stub of an Italian cigar that was like a piece of black rope.

"Gimme lotsa cover," he said to the riflemen. He patted his big stomach. "Lotsa macaroni to roll in close. I bust 'em."

The lieutenant poked his head over the wall. The riflemen wriggled out to the flanks. The machine-gunners made their chatter. The dynamiter stubbed out his Italian stogie and moved ponderously toward the wall. He stowed the cigar in his pack so it wouldn't be wet by his own sweat. He held the charge in his two hands like a priest making an offering. I moved up beside him and he grinned at me. He was fingering a silver medal on his neck chain. He sweated but otherwise was rock steady. Perhaps he always sweated. He muttered something in Italian—probably a prayer. Then he made a gesture with one hand and said: "Hey, Rocco, gimme a break, hey?"

The lieutenant said: "His ears are in. Go get 'em!" The dynamiter wriggled out from behind the wall and, for a thick-bodied man, he could move on his stomach. He was in close to the pillbox, pushing up his charge and then wriggling back, and all the while the machine-gunners and two BAR men poured fire over him until he was lost in the rock dust they kicked up.

He came out of the dust like a surfacing whale. "Fire in the hole," he said, and pulled the lieutenant and me down behind the wall.

The concussion slammed us against the iron rods and, for an instant, we rode a pitching and bucking world. The dynamiter clenched his fist and shoved it toward the place where the pillbox had been. "Eat dust," he snarled. "Eat that and see how it goes." He nudged me in the ribs. "Pasquale give it to 'em—right in the old La Bonza!"

He fished the butt of his cigar out of his pack. He lit it and smoked.

He had expected to be alive, and he was. The next day he got killed, but by then he had probably finished his cigar.

I was working my way back through the rubble toward the airport, and men were still running both ways on the open field. When I got to the edge of the field I made two starts at running out, but both times I turned back and hugged the side of a pillbox. The field was still swept with fire as the Japanese tried to keep us from sending over reinforcements to hold our line. There were shellbursts all over the field, but men still ran through them. I had only to run back, but I couldn't. I hugged the pillbox wall until my fingers were stiff. Then I let go and clubbed at my legs with my clenched fist. But they were useless. I knew then what "paralyzed with fear" meant. It was something out of a dream. I wanted to run. I couldn't. I wanted to walk and I couldn't.

I crawled. Cut hands and bruised knees and all, I crawled until the great *whoosh* of a mortar came in. I was flipped over by concussion to lie under the clanging of great bells. Then I rolled over and was sick. Then I crawled until I thought I heard another *whoosh*. This time the effect was different. I jumped up and ran. I ran and ran, and only John stopped me on the other side of the airport. He got my collar and pulled me in as though I were a wild horse. Then he smashed me in the face and I calmed down. John was capable of intelligent cruelty when it would accomplish something. He knew just how to kill my kind of panic.

I reported to the colonel who had lost touch with his assault companies on the radios. I showed him on the map and on the ground where we were. I estimated we had the survivors of two companies across the airfield. The colonel called the good news back to Regiment, who relayed it back to Division.

John made me a lemon drink in his canteen cup and Buck lit me a cigarette. Larry came in from his side of the line where things were better because the companies had a narrower strip of field to cross. Larry had spent most of his time carrying in a wounded buddy. He had very little idea where the companies were or how many men were across in his sector. Buck, who had been bringing up tanks, bawled Larry out, but it didn't make any impression on him.

"When a buddy of mine is hit," Larry said, "I'm going to bring him in, and they can jam this war for all I care."

"Stupid," Buck said. "If everybody stopped to pick up the pieces, the war would last forever."

Word came in that two more of our company scouts had been hit. Bob was missing and we believed that he had been blown to bits somewhere on the airfield. This bothered me because he was, or had been back in the rest area, my buddy. I went all along the airport looking for him, and Buck didn't call me "stupid," because Bob was one of the section and Buck had a fierce loyalty to whatever small group he happened to belong. I searched out through the airfield, and each time I turned over the body of a marine I was ready to cry. I didn't find Bob.

At high noon I was sitting in the lee of a smashed blockhouse, my back against the steaming concrete that seemed ready to crack with the heat. Beside me was a big Polish man with half of his dungarees cut away—his left arm wasn't there at all, and his white chest and shoulders above the stump were beginning to burn under the sun. The stump oozed but did not bleed and he was so strong that he still could speak. He said—and shock and pain could not make him any less the man he was—"Look at that! Not much blood at all. No blood I can see. Maybe just a little."

I had just pulled him in and the shock was so fresh, or the wound so bad, that it had sealed in, and, in truth, it didn't bleed then. I waited with him for a corpsman who never came—at least while he was still alive. The arm never did bleed.

In the afternoon we were still slugging through the ruined blockhouses, but we were swinging to our left and making toward the nearest point of the scalded hills. The forward observer for the naval guns —a madcap lieutenant called "Mac"—and I were working out on the left end of the line, within sight of the first point of the ridges. A lot of men, from time to time, joked in combat, but Mac was one of the few who could keep up the patter no matter how bad the going got. When Mac called down a salvo from the guns out on the ships of the line, he invariably said: "This will stimulate the bidding up in the card room of the Jap Command Post."

Mac insisted that the Japanese general played bridge all through the campaign. As Mac pictured it, the high command sat deep in a cave, huddled over their cards, while the battle raged over their heads. It doesn't sound so funny now, but at the time and in the place it seemed hilarious, and Mac could always get a laugh out of me. When the shelling came in heavy on us, Mac would wriggle up close to me and shout: "Here it comes. Now we'll catch it. The artillery commander plays Goren, and his partner, the Chief of Staff, plays Culbertson. The partner just bid him out of a slam hand and now the artillery man is dummy, and boy, will he give it to us! . . . Slam, slam, slam!"

We brought Mac out so he could set up his Observation Post, but cautious Buck chose a safe place, and Mac wanted high ground, no matter how unsafe it was. We were just behind the assault companies and the fire was heavy all around.

"I don't care if I have to stand on the shoulders of a tall Jap," Mac told Buck. "I've got to have a high, clear spot to see from."

We had flopped down behind a pile of concrete chunks while Mac and Buck argued it out. The JASCO (Joint Assault Signal Company) radio man and I listened. Buck wanted to run left to more cover; Mac wanted to charge straight through the barrage.

"If we get out beyond this area where they're registered, we might see something," Mac argued. "Too much dust and smoke flying." That was all that bothered Mac about the opposition artillery: it made it hard to see. The shrapnel and explosion meant nothing to him. "I have to see to do my job, Sergeant."

"You'll see something, all right," Buck agreed grimly. "You'll see Japs."

"That's what I came out to see," Mac said, and before we could stop him he was up and running directly into the barrage.

He ran like a knock-kneed duck. I ran behind him, and Buck, cursing both of us, followed. The poor radioman humped along under his set, in the rear. We ran right through the rubble, across a road, and into a clearing where the artillery had torn down the palm trees and left a few standing, shredded of every branch and frond. Running into that same clearing from the opposite side was half a squad of Japanese riflemen. We saw them just as they saw us, and Mac and I dived into a pile of brush, between two tree trunks. There followed one of the most ridiculous scenes I ever witnessed in combat.

Mac unslung his carbine after a great deal of fussing and found that it wasn't loaded. The two extra clips he carried, in a pocket attached to the stock, had been knocked off while we were running. Mac raised his rifle, clicked it, and said: "Bang, bang. I pass." He turned a sweet grin on me and waited for me to fire John's Tommy gun which I was carrying then. I swung up my weapon and squeezed the trigger. Nothing happened. I squeezed harder, but still there was no action. Then I screamed: "Buck—Buck, my Tommy is jammed." Only a ridiculous remark by Mac saved me from throwing down my useless weapon and running for the rear.

Mac said: "Well, partner, if you don't have the cards you can't play them."

Buck saw no humor in the situation at all. He was convinced Mac was crazy, anyway. Buck was between two trees just behind us, and he opened up with his Tommy gun. The very rapid rip of it came right over our heads.

"Keep down," Buck snarled.

He ripped off another burst. There was no answering fire from the Japanese, also lying in the brush among the felled trees. We waited. We were in the eye of the artillery storm. Our fire went overhead to the ridges, and their fire went overhead into the pillbox area. The little bare wood lot was fairly quiet, and only the whispering overhead kept the war from disappearing altogether.

I began to get panicky. "What if they charge in?" I asked Buck.

"They won't charge. Just lie still and don't talk. They're down in the brush somewhere. They're as scared as we are; maybe more. But don't talk. You sound like a scared kid whistling in the dark. They can sense that."

We lay in the whispering clearing. I didn't believe the Japs were scared. Until I had personal friends among the Japanese after the war, I didn't believe that Japanese even felt fear.

Mac and I lay very still. We were quiet. At least I was. He said: "I think they're cutting for the deal. Do you know any bad words in Japanese? At least we could go down doing something nasty in the best Marine tradition."

He had picked up a big chunk of coral, and I think he meant to throw it if the Japanese charged us. He was the best forward observer on big guns I ever saw, intelligent and without fear, but outside of his specialty the rest of the war was a mystery to him. I tried my weapon again, but it wouldn't do anything. Then Buck crawled in near us.

"Is the bolt back on your Tommy gun?" he asked. I looked. The bolt was forward. I eased the bolt back so Buck wouldn't hear the noise. Mac winked at me. In my panic I had done a very stupid thing. The Tommy gun does not fire with the bolt forward. I had forgotten that. I stood up and poured a long burst at the Japs ahead.

Buck said: "It's firing O.K. now."

"I got it cleared," I lied. Mac went on grinning, but he never did tell Buck.

We lay still for a few more minutes. Then Buck stood up. Two rifles popped at him and he dived down again and lay there panting.

The three of us lay still some more. It was already late in the day, and I wondered if Buck was going to wait it out until dark came. Going back would be dangerous. We were in front of our own lines, or in a gap between them.

"I'd like to get set up before dark," Mac complained. "I can't hit what I can't see."

"Well, just stand up," Buck told him. "That will settle your problem."

And Mac did. He stood up and, in fact, stood up high on a palm branch. The Jap, who must have been crawling in close to lob a grenade on us, was so startled at the sight of Mac's red face that he stood up himself. He fired at Mac and missed. Buck stood up and fired.

Buck rarely missed. The heavy Tommy gun slugs knocked the Jap backwards into the bushes. There was no more firing. We waited.

"Shall we try again?" Mac asked, "I think it's about Dave's turn to be the test target." Buck nodded. Reluctantly, I straightened up and stood with my head and shoulders above the branches. When nothing happened, I showed more of myself. Nothing happened again. I stood clear, balancing on a branch. Nothing happened.

"Let's get out of here," Buck said, "before they sign us up in the Jap Marines."

We turned tail and scooted back through the bushes, across the road and into the rubble area. There Mac found a big pile of rubble on top of the dome of a pillbox. "Here is the spot," he said. "On this mighty rock I will build my Observation Post." But he didn't. In the excitement we had lost the radioman. If Mac did sight targets, he had no way to send them back.

"Let's go home before it gets dark," Buck said.

There was nothing else to do. With Mac urging us, we made a half-search for the radioman, but we didn't find him. As we started in, a platoon from the First Battalion had swung over to close the gap in the lines; they saw us and opened fire. One BAR man poured a full magazine over our heads while Buck lay behind a rock and cursed him. The firing stopped and Buck's terrible language sounded above everything else.

One of the riflemen yelled: "Who are you?"

"We're a mixed lot," Mac called. "We were sent out to find the Japanese golf course and blow up the clubhouse. The mission successful. There is no clubhouse standing on this island."

One of the officers, who knew Mac, laughed. "Let 'em by, boys. You're liable to meet anything out here."

When we talked to the lieutenant, we learned that a gap had opened up and we had been in it, holding it with sheer stupidity and luck. Mac thought that was a fine joke, but Buck couldn't see it.

Mac said: "Lieutenant, I now turn command of this sector of the line over to you. My men and I will go rearwards forthwith."

"I'm no bloody man of yours," Buck said sourly.

On that second night, we set up near the Battalion Command Post— which was among some low, sandy ridges near the edge of the air-field. The area resembled an old sand pit. It started as a noisy and nervous night. Buck was jumpy, as he always was after dark. Fire-fights raged all along the line, and green flares were overhead constantly. The Japanese were sifting through the gaps in the barracks area just ahead, and the colonel had ordered an all-round perimeter guard on the Command Post. The battalion scout section was put in holes on the outer edge of the perimeter. Buck and I were in one; the map keeper and Milt, the journal keeper, were in another. John was in a hole by himself. He said he was tired and wanted to sleep.

I drew third watch and, shelling or not, I slept through the early watches. In the middle of the night, Buck's hand came down hard on my shoulder and I awoke to hear firing all around us. Buck was crouched near the top of our hole, and his Tommy gun was unslung and ready for use.

"What is it?" I whispered.

"Beats me," Buck muttered. "They seem to be all around us."

As usual, the minute there was real danger, Buck was perfectly calm and ready. He only worried when things were quiet at night and just before nightfall. I could see tracers shooting through the darkness and in with the small-arms fire came the crack of hand grenades and the whine and sting of their fragmentation.

Then it all stopped and somebody was groaning in the darkness. Milt called to me, and we called the company scouts who were beyond us. Everybody answered—except John. Everybody was yelling at everybody else. The map man said: "I didn't hear anything from John. We better go look." The map man and I crawled out toward the sound of the groaning. It came from the direction where John had been. I was scared for him.

We found John about five yards from his hole, lying on his back. When we held a shielded match close to him we saw that he had been shot many times, so many we couldn't even tell where he was hit worst. While we knelt above him, the groaning stopped and the map man said: "He's dead. Or near it."

Word went around the Command Post that John was dead. Up in the center of the perimeter near the executive officer's hole, somebody began to weep and scream. He screamed and cried and blubbered. The exec yelled at him: "Shut up! Shut up! Your blubbering won't bring him back."

"I killed him," the man blubbered on. "I killed John."

And he had. For some reason, John, "the loner," had grown restless in the night. He had moved out of his hole and the other man had been trigger-happy and he had poured a clip into John, without challenging him, without ever giving him a chance. John, a fine man, who had survived four campaigns and dozens of battles as a rifle squad leader, had been killed by one scared man back in the relative safety of the Battalion Command Post.

It seemed very unfair, one of the millions of sour jokes that happen in a war. Mostly it was caused by the cowardice of the man who fired without challenging John. But it also came from the fact John was a "loner," without any real close buddy or companion. At night, the "loner" must be a very strong man in order to control his own fear, without help from a friend. John was a strong man, but he hadn't been that strong.

I crept back into my hole. Buck said: "I'm too tired and scared to move out of my hole now. But when daylight comes, I'm going to kill that guy. That lousy coward . . . So help me God, I'm going to give it to him the same way he give it to John. I'll put the whole clip right into him."

I think then Buck began to cry to himself. I know I did.

※ ※ ※ ※

BY 10 P.M., SEPTEMBER 16 (D-PLUS-ONE), CAPTAIN George Hunt's K Company, Third Battalion, had already beaten off several attacks, the last with captured enemy machine guns. But casualties were heavy, and by morning K Company's strength would be down to 75 men, or about a third of the number who made the landing. A Navy Cross winner for this battle, George Hunt (managing editor of *Life*) braced himself as 350 Japanese with mortar and artillery support lunged for his position.

·22· CORAL COMES HIGH

GEORGE HUNT

. . . When white naval flares burst in front of our lines the silhouettes of gnarled tree trunks reminded me of a picture of Stonehenge in the moonlight. There was the same chilly light, the same sentinel shapes. Haggerty said that it looked like a petrified forest. There was a dim mist which swirled around these forms rendering an almost supernatural effect. In the light I could see its movement, curling wisps of nearly transparent tails.

"Would you like a stretcher to sleep on, that is if you're not superstitious?" Giddons asked me. "I know a man who fell asleep on a stretcher and died on it without ever waking up."

"That's a cheerful thought," I said.

"I wouldn't sleep on a stretcher if I was paid to, unless it's by necessity," remarked Haggerty.

"I think I'll take a chance on it," I said. "It'll be better than the stones." I placed the stretcher on the most level spot I could find under a tree and lay down on it on my back. I saw the trunk of the tree rising up about thirty feet where it became a shapeless web of shattered branches.

"You know, Skipper," said Haggerty, "when I went back this morning to get help those people back there looked at me as though they had seen a ghost. They had just about crossed us off the list."

"We had a close call all right, but it'll be different tonight; we're well prepared for 'em."

It would be our turn to throw heavy stuff: mortars and artillery. We had seven machine guns on the line and thirty more men. Radios were working, and there were two telephone lines to Battalion. For the first time since we landed I felt secure. Let the Japs come ——

Five hours ago—the remaining ten men of my second platoon had joined me. Young Wiginton's round face was wreathed in a smile. He was the first to step out of the tractor.

"Gawsh! Captain," he said, "we're sure glad to see you. We was worried about you all up here and heard that you had been killed."

"We were worried about you too, Wiggie, you must have had a rough time."

"Yes sir, we got shot up pretty bad."

Tractors were rolling up to us all day along the reef. They brought my mortar section from up the beach, big men, with the tubes and base plates over their shoulders and clover leaf after clover leaf of shells, who set up their guns among the rocks and organized a chain gang to lug the ammunition from the water's edge. They brought up Lieutenant Klopf with his artillery observation team and a radio to communicate to his gun batteries which were located several thousand yards to the rear. He pulled a map from his dispatch case, and we figured out the correct concentrations to cover the area in front of our lines up to six hundred yards.

"We'll put as much explosive in there as you ask for," he said.

"You're liable to have a busy night," I told him. "The Japs want this Point."

"Just say the word and I'll ——"

The chattering of machine-gun fire on our right interrupted our conversation. I called Sellers: "What's going on on the right?"

"That's B Company tryin' to push into the gap. They're havin' a hell of a time. The Japs are still as thick as flies in there." That was the third company that had tried to fill up that hole and make contact with me. I heard the booming of tanks ____

"I'd hate to be isolated up here for another night, Klopf."

Then I saw First Sergeant Schmittou stalking up the beach, gaunt and glowering. I waved to him, and in return he swung a long arm over his head. Drops of perspiration had caught in the stubble of his day and a half's growth, and his eyes gleamed jet black.

"Glad to see you, Schmittou, I heard you had been stuck with a bayonet."

"Stuck with a bayonet!" he shouted. "It'd take more'n a goddam bayonet to get me. But them mortars nearly did it. Them bastards had me straddled to ten yards."

"Any of you hurt?"

"Wal, jest Mr. Stramel and I got outa there. The others'd been picked off before by snipers. I was layin' there jest where you left me, behind the bush. Mr. Stramel was back in the hole. Then this mortar drops twenty yards to my left, then twenty yards to my right, and I says to myself: Schmittou, the next 'un's got your number on it, and that son of a bitch lands ten yards in front of me. Before I knew it I'm jest about buried by sand and I looks back to see if Mr. Stramel's OK and his face is stickin' outa the sand just as gray as I've seen, but he wasn't touched."

"How have the others made out back there?" I asked.

"Little 'Smitty' is dead, and Haber got it in the legs. The cooks were all wounded when their tractor was hit by a forty millimeter, and Sutkaitus was run over by his tractor and had his legs crushed."

"Did he die?"

"Yeah, he died. I seen a bunch a our guys lyin' on the beach. Seemed that most of 'em were from K Company."

The men in the tractors brought cheerful word. Swiftly it passed along the line spreading encouragement. "They say the airfield's been taken."

Sniper fire bothered us all day. Japs were sneaking around our lines and occasionally I heard the burst of a grenade. McComas, deciding to catch some sleep, told his men to keep a careful watch, lay down and closed his eyes. When he woke up an hour later he found a man who had fallen into a doze. He kicked him in the foot.

"Goddammit!" he bellowed, "you cork off like that and some Jap will sneak up on ye. How d'ya know there aren't any Japs around here?" He swept his arm in a broad gesture. By chance it stopped when it pointed at a clump of bushes twenty yards out. Looking down his arm, he continued: "I'll run you up fer ____" He stopped, staring at the bushes. "Well Jesus," he said, speaking slowly with a tone of amazement, "there *are* some Japs in those bushes." He crouched forward searching the spot intently with sharp eyes, and without saying another word slipped off into the woods. Three cracks of a rifle and a grenade burst followed very shortly. McComas returned with two more Japs to his credit.

Sporadically mortar shells dropped into us. When they pounded along the line they never failed to clip someone. Rarely was the rocky ledge down at the water clear of wounded men with blood-soaked bandages awaiting the next tractor. I remembered Humplik, pale as a sheet, splattered across the chest and arms by shrapnel, murmuring as if in a dream: "G'ese it's hot, g'ese it's hot, fan me, Mac, fan me, fan me, it's hot as hell." Schmittou fanned him across the face with a folded map.

"Fan me more, Mac, fan me more, I'm on fire. Fan me harder."

I had seen so many of my men killed or wounded that I was left benumbed. Seeing them fall right and left had become a regular part of a day's work. Death was as common as head colds, and the wounded were simply ineffectives who must be replaced and carried off the field at once. My own actions had become those of a machine, as though my muscles and mind had been trained and co-ordinated since my birth to perform mechanically the activities of fighting, at the mere fall of a switch. I had long since forgotten about fatigue, the soreness of my eyes, the sun blisters on my lips, the heat, the blinding glare of the rocks, and the fantastic nearness of death which I accepted as I would the danger of crossing a city street.

Down by that ledge I kept my radio. Lockhead, the operator, a young, smooth-faced kid with freckles, moved twenty yards down the beach with it seeking clearer reception, when the heaviest mortar barrage since early morning thundered about us; and Lockhead was caught out there on the sand. Lyons was yelling at him:

"Run back here, chicken, come on back!" The impact of the explosions shook the cliff, and loose coral tumbled down to the water's edge.

I was on the phone talking to the colonel. Trouble shooters had fixed the break in the line.

"Heavy mortars falling—coming from about three hundred yards to our front."

"OK, George, I'm calling for planes now."

Lyons was shouting again:

"Get the hell back here, Lockhead!"

Behind me was the pillbox which Willis and Anderson had knocked out. The Japs inside were fried black, and the whites of their eyes shone in the dark like phosphorus. The forty-millimeter gun was twisted and yanked cockeyed from its mount. The flame had scorched its blued surface to a dull gray. Lockhead had not heard Lyons and had remained there huddled behind a round stone. I saw his mouth moving as he pressed it against the mouthpiece of the radio. The mortars were still falling ____

I heard the deep hum of engines approaching nearer, increasing to a roar. Gray planes with stars on their wings zoomed low over our heads, skimming the treetops. I heard the crackling of their guns spitting bullets which snapped above us and strafed the ground three hundred yards in front of our lines. The earth trembled with the impact of bombs ____

Then the mortars ceased; Lockhead was miraculously unhurt, but once again I heard the cry, "Corpsman!" echoing among the rocks.

It was in the early afternoon that I sent out Daily and Hahn with their squads to patrol in front of our lines and attempt to discover the Jap strength and activities. They had moved only a hundred yards when the Japs, swarming out of the caves among the ridges, opened up with grenades and rifles.

Standing on the line anxiously watching the fight which ensued I felt ridiculously helpless. To commit more troops would weaken my flank on the right, exposing us to an attack from that direction, and I did not want to engage all my men in a pitched battle out there where the Japs had the advantage. We could not fire from the line for fear of hitting our own men.

"Cover those men," I shouted to the machine-gun crews, "but do not fire!" That was all I could do. It was not much.

Again I heard the rattling of rifle fire and the popping of grenades. Japs were bobbing in and out of the rocks—I could see their flat, brown helmets. At times it was hard to distinguish them from my men, so quick were the movements. Daily was running back, dodging from tree to tree, his leg soaked with blood and his trousers ripped. He was bringing his squad back man by man. So was Hahn on the right, with his arm dripping red.

Daily's dark, heavy-browed face was chalk-white when he spoke to me. He knelt down supporting himself with his arms pushed stiffly into the ground. He talked in gasps.

"There's a mess of 'em in the caves—take a hell of a lot of men to rout 'em out. Cushman's dead out there—got it in the head—had to leave him—got the others back all right."

"Good job!" I said, and told him to get in the Alligator which, fortunately, was just pulling up on the beach.

And Hahn brought his men back with one other casualty outside of himself. A corpsman cut the sleeve off his jacket. His atabrine complexion had paled, and his eyes had dark rims around them.

"The boys are bringin' Jack down the beach—he's all right, I think—grenades and bullets flyin' all over the place. Looks like the Japs are concentrating around them knolls and gullies." Hahn followed Daily into the tractor.

I rang the phone. "Hello, Colonel, still plenty of Japs up front of us—seem to be gathering for something—maybe a night attack—I'm going to harass them with mortars and artillery."

"All right, all right—has B Company made contact with you?"

"Not yet."

"Hell, they should have been up there by now."

One hour after this conversation a patrol reported that friendly troops were closing in on us, and by nightfall my right was firmly spliced to B Company's left. After thirty hours we were no longer isolated.

Lying on my back on that stretcher and thinking about the day that had just passed, I became more aware than ever of how close we had come to complete annihilation. In the early morning we had been reduced to about eighteen men, surrounded on three sides, with our backs to the ocean. If the Japs, who outnumbered us twenty to one, had rushed us—I shuddered at the thought. The Point would have been lost and the beach would have been at the mercy of the Jap guns. I was sure that some unknown power must have been on our side. And I was mighty proud of my men and their sheer guts and stamina.

I was wondering if Anita realized somehow where I was and what I was doing. I knew she was worried because she would not have received a letter from me for several weeks, and that always meant I was going into battle. Her fight against anxiety must be worse than mine against the Japs. It is frightening never to know—for sure—I thought of her, laughing and curling up her nose and shaking her long hair, her eyes aglow with a rich, contagious joy of living, her skin very white and a suggestion of freckles across the top of her cheeks —freckles—she disliked them—said the sun brought them out—and her voice, musical, speaking the purest English—said "rahsberry" for "raspberry"—I liked to kid her about that—we were riding on the Long Island Railroad—the click and clack of the wheels on the track—the murmuring of voices in the car—the smell of cigar smoke, of fresh newspapers—the conductor opening the door to call out the next station—we were talking or sitting very quietly—peacefully—watching—thinking—always peacefully—and the houses and the tree-lined roads and the bridges and the street lights and the track crossings and the busses and the schools at recess and the automobiles which were going our way and seemed to be motionless and the beer joints and the switches and the stations with gold and yellow signs and the red-tiled roofs—all were sequestered and quiet and peaceful—then they drifted away from me into mist that grew thicker and thicker—swirling and turning and sweeping these images with it in circles which became confused and senselessly intermingled ____

I heard rustling at my head—crabs again, coming out of the rocks to annoy me—scratching at the stones and the thorny weeds—time went on, and I was unaware of it—I thought I heard the rustling—no—it was sharper that night—a creaking—louder ____

That noise! it sliced into my thoughts and my half sleep. It had a meaning. Something had warned me—that creaking—more than that—a splintering ____

Then I saw. I was paralyzed. Not to move meant sure death, but I couldn't. Some appalling vise had gripped me. That tree with the shapeless web of branches was falling! I strained and swung my left leg over my right and rolled with all my might off the stretcher onto the ground. At that very instant the tree crashed lengthwise along the stretcher exactly where I had been lying.

Breathless I lay there, astonished at the closeness of my escape. Had I realized what was happening one split second later I would have been mashed to pulp.

"What happened?" exclaimed Haggerty abruptly sitting upright.

"This tree nearly killed me. Look at the stretcher. It's crushed and almost buried under the trunk."

"Someone must be doing a lot of prayin' for you, Skipper."

"Yes," I said musingly, "there's several prayin' for me. I'm beginning to think it must do some good."

"Do you think you'll ever sleep on a stretcher again?" put in Giddons with a short chuckle.

"No, I guess I won't, unless I absolutely have to."

"I hate to say I told you so," remarked Haggerty, grinning, "but those things are strictly taboo."

I could not help laughing as the affair assumed a comical aspect. I began scratching away stones to make a new bed when I was startled by a figure climbing over the rocks.

"Who's that?"

"Adams."

"Password?"

"Chevrolet."

"What do you want?"

"I want to speak to the captain."

I went over to him and saw that he was one of the replacements who came up in the morning. He was nervous about something.

"What's the matter, Adams?"

"Well, we've been hearin' voices just in front of our positions, and a kind of squirming and gagging as though someone was being stabbed. We think the Japs grabbed a guy who went out to see what the score was."

"He went out to see what the score was," I repeated, surprised. "Who was it?"

"I don't know, but that's what the fellas all say. And we could use a couple of more men around that BAR position. Ain't many of us there."

"OK, Adams, let's take a look."

We wound through the rocks about ten yards and entered the coral basin where the line jutted outward, following the course of the rocks. The coral glowed ghostly white and threw a gray tone on the faces and clothes of the men who crouched behind the boulders with their weapons resting on top. Their helmets cast black shadows over their eyes as though they were wearing masks.

"Goddam this rockpile," Adams muttered as he stumbled on the stones.

"Shut up there"—a loud whisper.

Toller was squatting behind his machine gun, peering over the barrel into the woods which rose against the sky in thick clumps like balls of black wool.

"Have you heard anything out there?" I asked him in a hushed voice.

"Not yet, but further along on the left the boys say they can. Think we'll get an attack?"

"I believe so. It's dark enough for one."

"We're ready for 'em; plenty of ammo and grenades."

Stretched on the coral were dead men who had stiffened in rigid positions. Dark liquid, which I knew was blood, lay in pools around them.

I picked my way through the stones along the line with Adams following me.

"Hear anything?" I whispered to a man I couldn't recognize in the shadows.

"Think I did—sort of excited jabbering."

"Ssssh ____" Belizna, next to him, was whispering. There was a stirring to my left, and I saw an arm thrown forward, heard the snap of the grenade pin and then the explosion which reverberated in

the woods. The noises were more distinct now—whispered gibber-
ish and low squeals of pain. The grenade must have hit some of them.

"They're there all right and pretty damn near," I heard someone
murmur.

"Keep throwing grenades at 'em and don't open up with your guns
till you can see 'em," I said softly and followed along the line to where
Willis was sleeping very soundly.

"Wake up, Will." I shook him by the shoulder.

He sat up quickly, looking around.

"Yeah, yeah, what's the matter?"

"Japs milling around in front of our center position. Shift a couple of men over there to strengthen it."

"OK."

I heard Schmittou talking over the phone. "It's damn quiet up here.
Feels like somethin's gwanna happen."

I woke Stramel. "Better check your guns, Ray," and told Haggerty
to call his gun position and have the crews stand by.

I sent a runner over to Klopf with the word to be ready to cut loose
his artillery; and up behind a big rock I could see LaCoy, restless,
and waiting to lay in with his mortars.

There was nothing to do now but wait for the attack, if it was to
come. I thought of the tree that nearly crushed me, an ominous beginning of a night's work.

The battle broke with a tremendous, angry roar as though a fiendish blast had shattered the doors of hell and exposed to human ears
the horrible turmoil which bawled and writhed within. At the one
hoarse cry, "There they are! They're comin' in on us!" the entire line
opened up simultaneously, bursting into an uncontrolled din that
stirred the most furious, savage instincts of a man. I found myself
bellowing until I thought my lungs would crack.

"Give 'em hell! Kill every one of the bastards!"

The Japs were answering with grenades and mortars and rifles.
Again I heard the whirring of shrapnel and the whine of bullets, many
of which were smacking into the rocks, ricocheting and burning crazy
trails in the air. The Japs were assaulting us with stampeding fury,
wave after wave, charging blindly into our lines and the hail of bullets and shrapnel which we poured into them. Above the uproar I
heard their devilish screams, "Banzai, banzai!"

"Klopf!" I yelled, "cut loose! Fire until I tell you to stop!"

"LaCoy! LaCoy!"

"Yes!"

"Let 'em have it! Traverse the whole line and keep firing!"

"OK!"

I went to Haggerty. "Red, put as many rounds in there as you can pump out." He was on the phone in an instant, shouting his fire order.

Now we had the power. We were on the giving end of this stick— seventy-five millimeter artillery, sixty and eighty-one millimeter mortars, firing at will.

The earth shook under this new weight.

Shells crashed into the rushing Japanese and against the trees, spreading deadly chunks of shrapnel. The violent concussions rocked my senses. Barrage after barrage drummed a ruthless rhythm to the steady roar of machine guns and BAR's and the sharp popping of grenades.

"Artillery falling short!" The cry made me shiver— Rounds were landing twenty-five yards in front of the line—too close—I saw the fiery blasts as they struck.

"Goddammit, Klopf! Lift the range two hundred yards!"

"Short rounds! We're raising it now!"

It was all right. Klopf was doing a fine job.

I ran over next to LaCoy and heard him shouting into his radio. "Range 150, right 50, fire for effect. How many rounds did I say?—Fire until I tell you to stop!"

A voice in front of me was challenging someone: "Who's there?"

"It's LaBerge, it's LaBerge."

"Who's there, I say? I'll shoot."

"It's LaBerge, goddammit, don't you know me? I'm LaBerge!"

Bang! I heard the report.

LaBerge roared. "Are you satisfied now, you son of a bitch, you did shoot me?"

Dammit, I said to myself—confusion—some nervous kid—probably one of today's replacements who doesn't know anybody here— shot LaBerge through the shoulder.

A cruiser was throwing out flares, but the smoke of our firing hung around us and obscured our vision. The noise of the battle thundered on with greater momentum. The stench of the powder stung my throat making it raw. I suddenly realized I was soaked with sweat that was itching my eyes. The palms of my hands were wet.

I heard ferocious cries on the left at the water's edge. By the white light of a flare I saw the silhouettes of two figures, dim and queerly distorted in the battle fog, struggling against each other on the crest of the cliff. Their arms were swinging wildly, their heads lowered and legs intertwined. The largest figure seemed to heave forward with his entire right side. The knees of the other bent back, he turned sideways and losing his balance tumbled off the cliff. Then it was dark ⸺

Henn ran in front of me shouting: "They're comin' around the flank in the water. Bring that gun down to the beach!"

"LaCoy!" I yelled, "drop some rounds along the beach fifty yards in front of us."

Shadowy figures moved swiftly by me carrying a machine gun and disappeared down the cut to the beach.

The artillery and mortars were still firing into the woods; the artillery further out now, more distant and rumbling. I heard no wild Jap victory screaming, only howls of pain rising out of the smoky night like animal noises. The firing along the center and right of our line had dwindled, but on the left, as it countered a new threat, it picked up with new strength.

The Japs were cut down as they attempted to attack in the water along the reef. They were driven into the niches which indented the rocky cliff. There they were protected from hand grenades and bullets, so we threw thermite grenades into the indentures. The Japs caught fire and screeching horribly, with the ammunition in their belts exploding like strings of fire crackers, ran into the water and rolled over and over attempting to extinguish the flames which clung to them relentlessly. But that did no good, and they burned in the water, crackling human bonfires that lit up the night. Their shrill screams resounded so piercingly that I realized that the noise of battle had suddenly ceased.

Susinka came running over to LaCoy. "There's a pocket of Japs in a gully about fifty yards in front of me." He pointed with his arm. "I can hear them talking in there. They've got a mortar that's been firing at us."

"I'll put out a few more rounds."

Again that hollow pop as the shell left the tube, the vicious snap of the impact on the ground and the resounding explosion; one following another in rapid succession. After the last burst we heard squealing and sobs of pain which lingered for a few moments and then died out. We listened for other Japanese sounds, a shout, a rustling, a jabbering, a scraping of feet on the rocks. We heard nothing.

Our line was quiet and once more seemed to be smoldering under the powder smoke. Again I heard the water lapping against the rocks at the foot of the cliff. The battle had ended almost as abruptly as it had started. In front of us the woods were dead.

Now, when the artillery had ceased firing and the mortar men were resting by their guns and the men on the line were watching for any other movement, a stillness fell over us, a stillness of waiting for the dawn.

It came very soon. Gray and stark, the daylight crept over the woods and rocks. Flat streaks of black clouds stretched across the sky like steel bands, and the ocean, reflecting the mood of the new day, was somber. The air, still mingled with the smell of gunpowder, dripped with murk.

On the beach some of the men with their jackets off were cupping the salt water in their hands and throwing it over their faces and chests. Others were fumbling with cans of meat and beans and eating the mushy contents with their hunting knives. The watches on the line were sitting on the rocks with their rifles across their knees looking into the woods at the devastation which lay there.

The movements of the men, as they opened "C" ration cans, washed themselves, or poured water from the water barrels into their canteen cups, were slow and almost benumbed. They walked and moved their arms in a dazed way, and their minds seemed barely able to control the motions of their limbs. They preserved the calm that they had shown the first morning; the same quiet and rocklike attitude toward suffering and death; the same sturdy, undemonstrative feeling of pride and satisfaction in themselves and their company; the same loyalty, that they had not let themselves or each other down; the same bitterness over the losses of their friends.

That night we had suffered less than before. The wounded were lying on the beach waiting for the tractor which I could see was making its way toward us. I counted the men I had left. Out of the original 235 who had landed there were only 78 who had not been either killed or wounded. The Japs had accounted for 157 of us, but they were thoroughly beaten, and out in the water, on the beach, in the woods and on the rocks we counted over five hundred of them—dead.

Along the shore Jap dead washed in with the tide and bled on the sand. Out further on the reef we could see them floating and bobbing aimlessly with the motion of the water, some of them caught on the obstacle stakes they had driven there.

In the countless gullies and basins in the coral Jap dead lay four deep, and on the level stretches they were scattered in one layer. They sprawled in ghastly attitudes with their faces frozen and lips curled in apish grins that showed their widely separated teeth and blackened gums. Their eyes were slimy with the green film of death through which I could see an expression of horror and incredibility. Many of them were huddled with their arms around each other as though they had futilely tried to protect themselves from our fire. They were horribly mutilated; riddled by bullets and torn by shrapnel until their entrails popped out; legs and arms and heads and torsos littered the rocks and in some places were lodged grotesquely in the treetops. I noticed one Jap in particular with both legs and one arm shot off, blasted naked, and a pair of horn-rimmed spectacles still resting on his flat nose; and another one who was a major, sitting placidly on

a rock in the attitude of Rodin's "Thinker." He must have been net-
tled by the tactical situation which had developed, and while he had
been trying to think it out, a bullet had penetrated his skull.

A sickening, putrid stench was emanating from the ones we had
killed yesterday. Their yellow skin was beginning to turn brown,
and their fly-ridden corpses still free of maggots were already cracked
and bloated like rotten melons. Along the trail which led directly
to our lines was a forty-millimeter gun half falling out of a crate and
surrounded by the mangled remains of bodies. Blood had dripped
on the barrel which was shining dully in the dreary light filtering
through the trees. Seeing this I could think of no more scathing and
ironic symbol of their disastrous efforts to drive us from the Point.

I was opening a can of rations when Lyons appeared and told me
I was wanted on the phone.

The colonel's voice crackled over the wire.

"I Company will take over your positions at eight o'clock and continue the advance. You will go into reserve and get a rest."

Reserve!—rest!—the words sounded too good to be true.

The wounded were being carried into the tractor which had just
arrived. Among them was Duke who had wrestled with the Jap on
the edge of the cliff and hurled him down on the ragged rocks below.
His leg had been slashed by a samurai sword. He had been lying in
his foxhole when he had suddenly felt this hacking on his leg. Then
a bullet had pierced his arm. He had roared with pain and rage and
had jumped up engaging the Jap in the fierce conflict which I had
seen momentarily through the battle smoke. There was Fox who had
been stabbed in the shoulder and clubbed on the head by a Jap who
had sneaked behind him among the rocks. In the nick of time he had
swung his rifle around and drilled through the chest the Jap whose
arm had been raised for the finishing blow. He had lain in the water,
bleeding, stunned, until at the crack of dawn Byrnes waded over the
reef and pulled him back to safety.

And I heard about Belizna who had felt something solid and pointed smack him in the chest. He had thought he was shot, but he could
feel no blood, no sharp pain. When dawn broke he saw a dud grenade
lying at his feet in front of him.

I could see more tractors heading toward us and troops moving
up the beach. Around me I was aware of increased activity. Another
tractor was unloading pots of hot coffee, sandwiches, beans and fresh
apples. The men were forming in a chow line taking the food in canteen cups and empty "K" ration boxes. I heard the first sergeant.

"Now goddammit! if you people can't stay in line and keep spread
out ye won't git any chow!"

At the foot of the cliff I saw Willis and Panarese stretching out in the water. I chuckled—guess they did not mind the dead Japs. Lees brought me a cup of coffee and some doughnuts and an apple. I smoked a cigarette, and it felt cool and relaxing.

The colonel and his staff arrived, and the doctor pressed a small bottle of brandy in my hand and a large can of alcohol to give to my men. Schmittou rationed it out at the end of the chow line. The brandy slipped down my throat hot and invigorating.

I Company moved in and man by man took over our positions. I began to feel a weariness that made me want to lie down and sleep and forget. The sun, burning through the sulphurous cloud bank, made me drowsy. My eyelids were heavy. I heard the word "Move out!" passed along I Company's line and saw a blurred image of them advancing through the Jap dead and disappearing over the ground rise two hundred yards away, toward 0-2. Many of my men had already found beds on the coral and had fallen asleep in the first postures they had happened to assume. Some were carrying our dead to the beach where they laid them down respectfully in a straight row. There were no sheets to cover them.

Vaguely I heard the colonel talking over the radio.

"We have moved out—my companies are now at ____" The words drifted off—indistinguishable and fading—Stramel brought more sandwiches and coffee. He gave me a ham sandwich which tasted deliciously cool and fresh—from some LST he said.

I sat down and leaned back against a smooth boulder—surprisingly comfortable, I thought. I shut my eyes and listened sleepily to the sounds around me, feet scraping and scuffling on the loose coral, low voices that droned monotonously, the occasional distant boom of a naval gun, all mingling into gentle, lazy, lulling tones. Softly they stole away from me and hummed into murmuring echoes that were soon lost.

＊ ＊ ＊ ＊

IN ONE WEEK OF FIGHTING, CHESTY PULLER'S 1st MArines was virtually out of commission, with 1749 killed and wounded. This outfit had taken on the worst of the Peleliu assignment, for upon landing west of the airstrip it had wheeled northward to assault the Japanese dug in along the Umurbrogol "Hills"—in reality a series of coral ridges with an average height of 200 feet which extend almost the length of the island. Rupertus originally estimated that the Peleliu fight would last two days—a slight miscalculation. It would last two months, or considerably after Puller's gallant regiment had been hacked to pieces and General Geiger had called in the Army's capable 321st Infantry. A private who fought with Puller was Russell Davis, scout, whom we have met. Let us join him. It is D-Plus-Three.

·23· THE BLOODY RIDGES

RUSSELL DAVIS

The first night on the ridge was a night of terror. Mac pulled fire right in on top of us. He even fired behind us. To control the fire of ships miles away and to fire into the dark on the word of an observer who couldn't see the man in the next hole was a job which required complete confidence and courage. Mac had both. There would be a whispered word from the nervous radioman: "Under way, sir."

"All rightee," Mac would say. "Let's see where this one lands."

Buck and I, our knees pressing together and our hands on our heads, would wait, while the big bird came screeching up out of the darkness behind us. Orange flamed out in a star with a hundred points and the smash of the hit was like a blow from a dark fist, as all the ground shook. There was a terrible silence while we waited for the cry for corpsmen to come from our riflemen. But no cry came. Instead a flare popped overhead. In the ghastly light Mac grinned at us. He seemed some terrible Irish ha'nt as he said: "Sure, the man who had my job before, poor lad, tried this blessed same thing one night. For the life of me I can't remember what he did wrong exactly. Well, we need not worry at all. It will come to me."

Buck had little sense of humor at best, and no sense of humor at night. He muttered, loud enough for Mac to hear: "That miserable, crazy Mick will kill us all."

Insults, even from enlisted men, never bothered Mac.

"Now, now, Sergeant," he cautioned Buck. "I've been on this job almost three days and I've never lost an observer team." To the radioman, he said: "Let's bring that fire in a bit. Where are we?"

Late that night we went back to our holes and Buck was close to collapse. He lay down behind his shallow barricade of splintered wood and coral, got his body down as far as he could get it into the shallow depression we had made in the coral, muttered a few curses on Mac, began to mutter his prayers, and fell dead asleep. It was the first time, that I knew of, that Buck had slept since the landing.

The fourth day got lost in a blaze of heat. Men let the camouflage covers of their helmets down to shade their necks from the sun and to protect them from the sting of the rock dust that was everywhere. The riflemen looked like desert soldiers. Dark men grew darker, and light-complexioned men suffered the tortures of broiled faces, cracked lips, and almost sightless eyes. Many men threw away their helmets and wore only the old, soft, floppy fatigue caps of the Army. The round hat was a favorite in the First Division. It could be bent into any shape and serve against the rain or the sun.

There seemed to be no morning to that fourth day. While the sun blazed, we swung to the right of the first ridge, crossed a road that led nowhere, and came up against a sheer cliff. Down from this cliff, steep and studded with caves and holes, came Japanese fire. Only by hugging the base of it could we move. Machine-gunners were set up across the road, and the riflemen were assembled at the base of the cliff. The orders were to take the cliff. It was a stupid order.

While the riflemen were being assembled, the fire landed on E Company machine guns, and their screams came to our ears and racked our nerves. Buck, who had been hugging the cliff in terror, reacted as he usually did when there was something to be done. He walked out across the road and stood up on a rock while mortars poured down around him. Buck and a sergeant from E Company organized a team of riflemen snipers and they began to pick off the mortar observers who were up on the forward slope of the ridge. They also got a bazooka man to fire into a nest of mortars. Then they called in the company and battalion mortars and the Japanese fire dried up and died. When it did, Buck ambled back to the protection of the ridge, and, once he was there, he showed fear again. Our companies started up the cliff.

We had lost heavily, ever since the beach, but I had not realized how bad the losses were until our companies moved out on the cliff. Clawing and crawling up the cliff went platoons that were no more than squads, and companies that were no more than large platoons. I counted one platoon. It mustered eighteen men on that push. But they went up.

From the base of the cliff, we could pick out each man and follow him until he got hit, went to ground, or climbed to the top. Not many made the top. As they toiled, caves and gulleys and holes opened up and Japanese dashed out to roll grenades down on them, and sometimes to lock, body to body, in desperate wrestling matches. Knives and bayonets flashed on the hillside. I saw one man bend, straighten, and club and kick at something that attacked his legs like a mad dog. He reached and heaved, and a Japanese soldier came end-over-end down the hill. The machine-gunners yelled encouragement.

As the riflemen climbed higher they grew fewer, until only a handful of men still climbed in the lead squads. These were the pick of the bunch—the few men who would go forward, no matter what was ahead. There were only a few. Of the thousands who land with a division and the hundreds who go up with a company of the line, there are only a few who manage to live and have enough courage to go through anything. They are the bone structure of a fighting outfit. All the rest is so much weight and sometimes merely flab. There aren't more than a few dozen in every thousand men, even in the Marines. They clawed and clubbed and stabbed their way up. The rest of us watched.

Watching them go up, Buck, the old rifleman, said: "Take a look at that sight and remember it. Those are riflemen, boy, and there ain't many like them. I was one once."

I looked up the cliff, but everything had changed. There was no longer anyone in sight. Our men who had gone up were either in holes near the top, dead, or lying out wounded and cooking in the sun. Another wave of riflemen got ready to go up, but before they could move out, heavy fire fell again, tearing apart the command posts and scattering machine-gunners and even dropping in behind the low ridge beyond the road, on the company mortar men. Once more, Buck moved out in it and called targets. This time I went with him, out of shame.

We could see Japanese observers, scurrying around near the top of the ridge line. We put everything we had in on them and Buck even yelled: "I wish that crazy officer was here with his big guns."

Before I could answer, a mortar whooshed in and blasted us both from the rock on which we stood. I landed on my feet and ran head-down for the base of the ridge. There, safe under an overhanging ledge, I sat, sobbing with an effort to get my breath. I saw Buck pick himself up, dust himself off, and climb back onto the rock. I sat for ten minutes, and then, ashamed of myself, I went out and relieved Buck. If he knew that I had run, he said nothing about it.

In the afternoon we went out on a long patrol, swinging around the nose of the cliff in a sweep to our right. We still had a few men up on the cliff, but we had learned something. Beyond that cliff was a deep gorge. After fighting up to it, we found ourselves isolated, with no chance to go ahead. So we went around. I went out with Larry and a platoon leader and a dozen men and we got a long way out until we were pinned into a blockhouse by heavy fire from the hills ahead.

The lieutenant decided that somebody had to go back and report, and the job fell to Larry and me.

We moved to the steps of the dugout and stood there while the fire thundered down overhead. It was a very tough blockhouse. The roof creaked and mortar and sand sifted down on us, but it didn't breach. We took off out of the blockhouse, running. On the way in, everything happened. We hit a Japanese patrol and were pinned down and chased. Then we were spotted from the ridge and pinned down with mortars. Then our own naval guns made a wall of fire which blocked us off. Probably, Mac was calling those shots. When we hit the naval guns, Larry said: "We best run for it. Good luck to you!"

We ran for it. I got in but I don't remember arriving or reporting. I remember Buck dumping pineapple juice into my mouth from his canteen cup. The fruit juice had been sent in from the ships of the line, and never was there a more welcome gift. Men were dropping from dehydration and sun. Larry and I drew two cans each and I drank myself sick, but after the sun went down I could walk again. I even helped Buck prepare our position for the night.

The next morning I got up and joined the line, which was already moving off to our right along the route we had taken the day before. We got all the way to the bunker before we were stopped by fire from ridges which lay beyond a road and a causeway. The colonel took over the bunker as the battalion command post. Later, the regimental command post moved in. It was the best cover in the area. For me, it was like home. When I ran in from the causeway or the swamps, which were off to our right, the bunker was a welcome sight. Once inside, no matter what was coming in overhead, I felt secure. I knew every chink and crack in that foul and damp tomb, but it was home. It was a domed-roof pillbox, two steps down into the ground, concrete on top, steel reinforced, and concrete inside. It took direct hits until the mortar was all shaken out of the chinks between the clocks. But it held.

We were moved over toward a narrow causeway that ran through the swamp toward the road and the ridges. "Hold here," the lieutenant said.

Up on the causeway a memorable thing happened. A marine came dashing out along it, moving toward the ridge. He was hit and knocked flat. I remember his muddy fingers stretched toward where we lay. He was clenching and unclenching his hand, either from pain or through some death reflex beyond his control. A second man, unable to stand the pitiful sight of that hand, clambered up onto the causeway and drove toward the wounded man. The second man was shot to a skidding stop. He lay on his back, without a twitch. A corpsman, who had seen it, said, "Shove this, I'm gonna get those guys."

He rolled up onto the bank, got to his knees and never did stand up. The sniper shot him as he still knelt.

A fourth man, a squat and burly ape of a man with extra-long arms, reached up over the edge of the causeway and began to pull the men in. He exposed no more than his long, thick arm, and he must have had phenomenal strength to drag the weight he pulled with one arm. I could see him straining and sweating as he began to bug the first of the wounded men over the edge of the bank. The sniper poured fire in at that thick, heavy arm that seemed to reach up out of the swamp like the tentacle of some hidden monster. Mortars harrumphed and clopped into the mud but the man pulled all three wounded men to safety.

Late in the afternoon, they began to patch the line companies with every able-bodied man they could send up from the rear. In came men from the war-dog platoons, the military police, the division band, the division laundry platoon, regimental headquarters men and battalion clerks. I was assigned to take these men, each of them carrying a load of ammunition, out through the swamp and into the lines. Most of them were quiet and good men who were scared but not too scared to do what they were told. But a few of them had never visited the front lines and had no intention of going out there. They felt that the riflemen were a special breed, created to do all the suffering and dying for the division.

A fat clerk complained to me: "I haven't been trained for this. What good will I do?"

I had neither pity nor sympathy for him. "You'll do fine, Fatty," I told him. "You will probably stop two bullets and save two good men."

That fat clerk hated me long before we got into the swamp. Twice I caught him lagging back and looking for a chance to duck. Both times he had dumped his ammunition so he could run better. He finally did bolt when we got into the high grass, and I never saw him again.

At the time I was watching another man who was trying to duck out. He had a good reason, too. He was a heavy winner in the division poker game. He said his pack was stuffed with thousands of dollars in winnings and he offered me a small piece of his money to let him run to the rear. He wasn't worried about himself as much as he was about the money.

"What if I got hit?" he asked. "Some grave-robbing thief would clean my pack."

"I'll see that they bury it right with you," I promised. "Get those belts of machine-gun ammo around your neck and move out."

"I'm a sergeant," he told me.

"That's fine, Sergeant," I said. "I'm a private. Let's go."

We had easy going until we were in the high grass. There it was rough. The men with the belts of machine-gun ammunition couldn't run and they couldn't get down. The men carrying rifle ammunition in ponchos had a worse time. Nobody panicked until the first carrier was shot and killed instantly. His partner, carrying the other corner of the poncho, put down his load and howled like a dog, and that noise unnerved everyone in the party. Of the twenty, I got nine men to the lines. Probably no more than one other man had been hit. The rest either ran back or scattered to hide in holes in the grass. I had no time to flush them out of their cover.

After we got the ammunition out to the line, we couldn't find anybody to take it. Once more the companies were milling around, some men retreating and some attacking, but most of them were just lying there, hoping to get out alive. I dumped my ammunition in a company command post and went back to the bunker. It was like coming home to a house in the suburbs after a hot and hard day in the city.

I spent that last night on the line almost entirely out of the bunker. At dusk, as we were boiling coffee water at the entrance steps, a tremendous fall of artillery came down, and two old machine-gunners— who had transferred into the quartermaster section for safety—were hit and blown down the steps of the bunker. We never did make that coffee. We dragged the wounded men down into the darkened tomb and held matches while a corpsman tried to stop the bleeding. The floor of the bunker was soaked with blood. The salty smell of it was everywhere. When Mac came by looking for an escort out to the line, I was glad to go, and we went out of the company command post.

The remnants of our second battalion spent a terrible night up there. But, for the few men up on the higher ridge—mostly from C Company, First Battalion—it was far worse. All through the night we could hear them screaming for illumination or for corpsmen, as the Japs came at them from caves which were all around them on the hillside. Men were hit up there and we could hear them crying and pleading for help, but nobody could help them. The remains of the first and second battalions and the division scout section had been thrown in together, and most of the men were strangers to each other. Two or three men were killed by their own mates that night. Grenades slammed and the stinging sound of the shrapnel came down the hill. The cries of American and Japanese were all mixed together. It unstrung even Mac.

"I think we ought to get up there," he told the company commander.

"Stay put," the company commander snarled. "Those are some of my kids catching hell up there. How do you think I feel?" He listened to the whimpering calls from the hills, and his head was down between his knees and he cursed monotonously. But he was right. We would have done them no good. "This will be a long, long night," he said.

"A long night," Mac echoed. "I think I'll say a prayer for those kids. Naval gunfire can't help them, God knows."

Of the sixth and last day on Peleliu, I have no connected memory. Short sequences like bad dreams are all that I can recall.

There was a squat, black-bearded rifleman who spoke with a New Orleans accent. He carried nothing but a rifle and a bandolier of ammunition. His shirt was black with sweat and plastered to him, skintight, and he looked like a pirate. The colonel was talking to him as he got ready to lead his squad up the hill.

The rifleman said: "Colonel, we can go up there. We been up there before. And we'll go on up again until there's nobody left. But we can't hold that ridge, Colonel. We can't hold it unless there's more of us, sir. We can't hold it at all, sir. I mean ___."

The colonel turned away without answering. He was on the verge of exhaustion himself.

I remember, too, an old sergeant with an ugly, Irish face. Perhaps he was only thirty or so but he looked like a hundred-year-old dwarf, red-faced, red beard, undershot jaw, bandy-legged—a wee and ugly gnome. The advance had been signaled, and the sergeant stood up on his twisted legs and waved the men forward toward the hill. A few men stumbled out of their holes. Some could not move. At least they didn't. They leaned on their weapons and looked sick with dread. The sergeant looked at the men. He turned away and his face twisted with sudden grief and tears came down his bearded cheeks. He waved his hand and rubbed his dirty face with his sleeve.

"Let's get killed up on that high ground there," he said. "It ain't no good to get it down here." As the men stumbled out for him, he said, "That's the good lads."

There were few platoon leaders and few sergeants. The young officers had been hit and the sergeants had been hit or they had folded, and the "duty" fell on those who would take it. Rank meant nothing. Privates who had something left led sergeants who didn't have it any more, but who would follow, even if they wouldn't order other men to. One big Italian man moved forward, dragging his blanket, unwilling to part with it, even though it tangled in his legs. Another man had his head covered with a poncho, so that only his eyes showed. The eyes were like those of a small burrowing animal driven to ground and cornered. A small Jewish man, who carried a company radio, moved around in a circle. He was determined to move, but he was too damaged by shock and fatigue to get his bearings. A scout, who walked near him, pointed him toward the hill and the two of them staggered out.

The whole motley lot—a fighting outfit only in the minds of a few officers in the First Regiment and in the First Division—started up the hill. I have never understood why. Not one of them refused. They were the hard core—the men who couldn't or wouldn't quit. They would go up a thousand blazing hills and through a hundred blasted valleys, as long as their legs would carry them. They were Marine riflemen.

A machine-gunner, a Lithuanian, sat calmly at his gun, alone and beyond the causeway. Fire threw rock dust and powder and shrapnel all around him, but he did not move and he did not even flinch. He made no effort to protect himself. His gun was neatly set and laid in to cover the break in the ridge through which any counterattack would come.

He said to me: "I can't go up that hill again. I got no legs now. But no Japs will come through that hole while I'm here." He was sharp-faced and clean, even in the middle of the barrage. I remember that.

In a swamp, an old sergeant crouched in his hole. He had been away from his outfit for two days and his were the motions of a hunted animal. "I got nothing more inside," he said. "Nothing. I don't even know anybody who is still alive. They're all gone, boy. Done, the whole lash-up."

I never found out what we were doing, tactically, on the sixth day. At first, I did what they told me to do, but no more. I ran around to the jumbled messes that were called companies and I tried to help our colonel keep some control of the scattered survivors of many outfits that made the last push up the ridges. Things started bad and got worse and, finally, hopeless. I quit.

I picked up the rifle of a dead marine and I went up the hill. I remember no more than a few yards of scarred hillside, blasted white with shellfire and hot to touch. I didn't worry about death any more. I had resigned from the human race. I only wanted to be as far forward as any man when my turn came. My fingers were smashed and burned, but I felt no pain. I crawled and scrambled forward and lay still, without any feeling toward any human thing. In the next hole was a rifleman. He peered at me through red and painful eyes. Then we both looked away. I didn't care about him. He didn't care about me. I thought he was a fool and he probably thought I was the same. We had both resigned from the human club. As a fighting outfit, the First Marine Regiment was finished. We were no longer even human beings. I fired at anything that moved in front of me. Friend or foe. I had no friends. I just wanted to kill.

❧   ❧   ❧   ❧

TO CONCLUDE THE BATTLE OF PELELIU, A PYRRHIC
victory for the 1st Marine Division, we again meet the elegant
combat correspondent Sergeant George McMillan.

·24· PELELIU CONCLUDED

GEORGE McMILLAN

On the sixth day of the campaign for Peleliu the situation was this:
One-third of the First Marine Division's fighting strength was destroyed, unfit for further combat on the island. The two-thirds that
remained, the 5th and 7th Marines, were far understrength, had each
suffered heavy losses—the 5th in landing and crossing the airfield,
the 7th in its point-blank encounter with the Japanese in the southern tip of Peleliu.

The Japanese, still organized, still in stout strength, held most of
the commanding terrain on the island. The northern peninsula, the
coral crags and crevices of Umurbrogol Mountain that lay behind
the face that was Bloody Nose, was still unbreached.

What was needed was a fresh regiment, a fourth regiment—on this
there seems to have been agreement among all the echelons of command, ashore and afloat. Ashore of course General Rupertus and
his staff. Afloat was a rather complicated command. Immediately
above Rupertus was General Geiger who had returned to the Guadalcanal area from Guam a few days before the Palau expeditionary force
departed for its target. And above General Geiger was General Julian
C. Smith, expeditionary troop commander, the same Smith who had
commanded the Second Marine Division at Tarawa. Smith's role
in the task force was anomalous, made so by the fact that the whole
operation had been diminished in scope. He was to have commanded
a much larger force including elements of the Army XXIV Corps
which were to have landed on Yap, in the Carolines.

It was Geiger, brusque and aggressive, who began to press Rupertus
to use a regiment from the Army 81st Infantry Division which had
landed at Angaur against lighter opposition. One of the 81st's regiments had indeed been set aside as Corps reserve.

General Rupertus argued against taking one of the Army regiments.
It was not so much, testifies an officer who was close to Rupertus, that

he had a blind objection to getting help from another branch of the service—he did not think that Bloody Nose was the proper place to blood a green regiment. The 81st Division was having its first taste of combat in the Palaus. But General Geiger directed that an Army regiment be attached to the First Division.

There was relief among enlisted ranks the day the long, thin line of Army reinforcements came wading through the shallow water up onto the beach at Peleliu.

They were welcome.

By September 20 all of the 7th Marines was committed to the fight for the high ground, elements of that outfit having been put into the lines of the 1st piecemeal since the end of the third day, September 17. Thus the fight for the ridge was begun by a second one of the Division's regiments. The 7th took up where the 1st left off, a mission embodied in the first field order issued at Peleliu . . .

What this regiment had to do was probably one of the most thankless tasks of the Pacific war. A fairly accurate sketch map of the Umurbrogol Mountain area, made later, looks like the kind of drawing a child might make if it were locked in a room for an hour with only a single piece of paper and a pencil. Except for the road drawn along the boundary, there is not a single straight line on the map. And the curve marking the elevations runs voluptuously here and there for an inch or two, then breaks into pinched, sway-backed uneven lines, and finally repeats the pattern.

In military parlance this kind of terrain is called "cross-compartmentation." But that hardly did for the spine of Peleliu's northern peninsula. Criss-cross-compartmentation would have been better.

As at Guadalcanal, and as at Gloucester (though there for different reasons), here again large-unit tactics were worthless. Maneuver in anything larger than company strength was impossible. Improvisation was highly valued, and even coincidence played its role.

Lieutenant Colonel Spencer S. Berger, commanding the 2d Battalion of the 7th, had his command post on a coral cliff, directly above a Japanese cave system. The odor of the boiled rice drifting up to Berger's nose tried the patience of his not-too-well filled stomach. "It was damned provoking smelling that Jap food," Berger told a fellow officer. He ordered his men to try to pick off the Japs when they came out of the cave, and his men got a few of them in this fashion. But still the food smells rose all around him. Whereupon Berger ordered his men to tie a charge of TNT to a rope which they then swung back and forth until they got it in position to swing into the cave mouth. They thus scored a hit and closed the cave.

Of course Berger and his men had more conventional objectives than that of a Japanese stew pot. Having discovered before the end of September that the high ground was not to be taken in frontal assault from the south, Division decided to use the 7th to encircle the pocket of the Umurbrogol, searching as the men moved—painfully slipped and slid around its coral faults—for some easier way to take the high ground than Puller had found.

After a brief period of holding while the Army moved up the western coastal road on past the pocket to the flat ground in the north beyond it, two battalions of the 7th were sent along the sides of the pocket: Berger (2d Battalion, 7th) and his men went up the east coast road while Lieutenant Colonel John J. Gormley (1st Battalion, 7th) and his men went up the west coast road and cut inland behind the ridge to relieve elements of the Army which had worked down toward the ridge from the north. First the 1st Battalion, 7th, and then the 3d Battalion, 7th, attacked from the north while the 2d Battalion, 7th, attacked from the west.

By October 3, a junction of the 2d Battalion of the 7th and the 3d Battalion of the 7th had been made and each had captured an important hill mass in the northeastern area of Umurbrogol. On the west coast and on the south, the airfield was protected by "infantillery," artillery troops who had been handed rifles, as well as by amtrac crewmen and headquarters folk.

On October 4, Major Hurst (3/7) had his eye set on a ridge that protruded from the northern side of Umurbrogol, called later, "Baldy Ridge." But to reach Baldy he had to take three small hills, each about ninety feet high, as well as get up on a butte of Baldy, Hill 120.

Hurst recalls that he did not expect to get Baldy on the 4th. But when his men got on the three small hills easily, he decided to send them on to Hill 120, and to put a holding force on the three small hills.

What happened then is described by Marine Combat Correspondent Jeremiah A. O'Leary.

At 1415 forty-eight men of L Company moved out of their lines to seize a 100-foot peak called "Knob Three," according to O'Leary's report.

Commanded by 230-pound 2d Lieutenant James E. Dunn, of Duluth, Minnesota, the platoon encircled the butte by moving through a ravine with 100-foot walls into which a tank had tried to advance during the morning. Already K Company was on the sharp ridge to the left.

Dunn and his men drew their first fire from Japanese who were in another draw, one that ran perpendicular to the one through which they were moving. Two men were hit and sent to the rear and the rest of the platoon dashed across in twos and threes to the base of Knob Three.

There were three ways that the platoon could scale it: up the gradual slope exposed to Japanese fire that would come inevitably from another and higher ridge called Baldy; abruptly up the face of the butte; or along a ledge that ran parallel to K Company.

"Men went up all three routes," wrote O'Leary, "clinging to roots and vines, clambering over rock faults and crevices." When they reached the top they "lay on their bellies on the sharp, serrated coral, scattered here and there with scrub brush . . .

"All around them was a forest of spires and crags as high, or higher, than the height they occupied. Old Baldy looked down on them menacingly. Uncharted ravines isolated them on all sides from the rest of Umurbrogol. On one side only, the southeast, were friends . . ."

As they started to scout the top of the bluff, each man's mind was turning over the thought, the surprising fact, that they had reached the top unscathed, when suddenly one of them was shot through the head. The Jap who did that damage was quickly found and killed.

Then, looking around they saw a large cave in another cliff, a fact that surprised no one, for on Umurbrogol you had only to look, turn away, and look again to discover some Japanese position you had not seen before. The men of the platoon sprayed the cave and K Company joined in from its cliff, and it all sounded very much like a serious fire fight, so much so that two men from K tried to cross the ravine and come up Knob Three to help.

These sounds and this activity did not escape Japanese notice.

At 1630 as many of the Japanese fire ports as could bear in on the isolated platoon opened, especially a group directly under K Company, from the face of the same cliff on which K stood. Three men were killed instantly.

A Pfc went down the sharp side of the butte to try to find one of the caves and began a duel with a Japanese machine gunner. He covered the men who were lugging stretchers down the butte until he was wounded and himself had to be carried to the rear.

The Japanese stepped up the tempo of their fire and, "Men were getting hit all over the face of the hill. The heavy chug-chug-chug of the antitank guns was punctuated by the swift rattle of Nambus."

Lieutenant Dunn fell: "bullets tore him from his grip on the cliffside where he was trying to withdraw his men to safer positions, and he fell to his death on the ravine floor many feet below."

The platoon was trapped. As the men pulled back in one direction, shots hit them from behind. Company K tried to help, firing at every Jap position they could see and at many they could only suspect existed, and the beleaguered men tried to crawl over under K's protecting fire.

"The wounded crawled behind rocks or just lay motionless, bullets hitting them again and again," wrote O'Leary. "Others cried piti-

fully for help and begged their comrades not to leave them there."
Medical corpsmen worked bravely and efficiently, each of them dragging men to the ledge. One of them stood up to cry, "Take it easy!
Bandage each other. Get out a few at a time . . ." He was shot and
killed.

Those men who could move threw away their weapons because
they couldn't climb down the cliff speedily without using both hands.
And as they climbed down, some were hit and fell to the ravine floor.
Others slipped and fell, suffering severe cuts from the jagged and
sharp coral.

All this was enacted in plain sight of the company commander,
Captain James V. (Jamo) Shanley who had won a Navy Cross for himself at New Britain. As he saw his men falling to their death he cried
out to K Company.

"For God's sakes, smoke up that hill!"

And he called for a tank which went into the ravine as far as it could
and then stood helpless to find targets from where it stopped.

When the smoke grenades began to burst in the ravine, and a billow of phosphorus covered the ledge on which more and more men
were moving, some of them simply dropped themselves from it, taking the chance of injury from the fall. Five did this and escaped to
the safety of the tank. But there were still six wounded and four dead
on the ledge, with three other infantrymen and a medical corpsman
standing by them. Up higher, still on the crest of Knob Three, there
were three men whom the Japanese must have thought dead.

The wounded on the ledge urged those who stood uninjured by
them to jump. "You've done all you can for us," one of the wounded
sobbed, "get outta here."

When the next smoke grenades covered the ledge, the unwounded
took the measure of the moment's hazards and did what otherwise
might have seemed a cruel thing; they rolled the wounded off the
ledge.

One man's foot caught in a vine and he hung upside down helpless and exposed until one of the unwounded kicked at it until the
wounded man fell freely.

The three men who had been flat on the crest of the ridge among
the constantly ricocheting Japanese bullets now tried to come down.
One of them was killed instantly when he arose, but the other two
made it down to the ledge.

One of the wounded who lay on the floor of the ravine tried to help
another across the open draw to the safety of the tank. The lesser
wounded put his arms around the other and the two hobbled across
the open draw. They could not make it. They dropped helpless there
in the open draw, and the Japanese opened fire on them.

This was more than Shanley could stand. Although a lieutenant tried to hold him, Jamo ran out from cover into the draw, swept one of the men into his arms, carried him back to the tank, laid him down tenderly in the tank's lee and ran out into the fire-swept open ground again for the other. He did not reach him. A mortar shell fell before Captain Shanley got there. Shrapnel tore through Shanley, wounding him mortally.

When he saw Shanley fall, a second lieutenant, Shanley's exec, rushed out. He had just reached Jamo when the chug-chug of an anti-tank gun was heard. He fell at Jamo's side, dead.

Now some of the unwounded on the ledge tried to come down. Only a few of them made it across the open draw. Two of those who reached safety immediately volunteered to go back to the foot of the ledge with stretchers for the wounded. Both of them were killed.

By 1730, three hours and fifteen minutes after they had started into the draws and ridges of Umurbrogol, there were 11 men left out of the 48 who had gone in.

By the time the 7th Marines was relieved on October 6, after sixteen days on Umurbrogol, its casualties were approximately those of the 1st Marines.

Well before the 7th had shot its wad at Umurbrogol, a land that had come to look to one Marine like "the face of the moon defended by Jap troglodytes," plans were drawn for a new scheme for the seizure of that benighted area.

These were to involve the last of the Division's regiments which had not yet fought at Umurbrogol, the 5th, and as well the Army's 321st Infantry.

A brief look at the Division's field orders for the third week in September shows the evolution of staff thinking about Umurbrogol, the increasing respect with which that area was treated. Field Order No. 1 (September 20) had simply put the 7th in the line with the 1st. Field Order No. 2 (September 21) was intended to put the 5th into the line to relieve the 1st, thus creating a line of the 5th and 7th Marines. This order's intent was forestalled by the decision to use the Army 321st Infantry, and the order itself was rescinded the next day, September 22, by Field Order No. 3 which called for the 321st rather than the 5th to relieve the 1st.

The 321st went in on the left, along the beach, advanced to Garekoro, then faced eastward and probed into the ridges. The 7th fought on into the ridges.

Three days later, September 25, Field Order No. 4 was issued, and it was this one which called for the 5th to execute the new scheme of maneuver. The order noted that "intelligence reports give every indication that a swift move to the northern portion of Peleliu would be successful . . ." and if it did succeed "all that would remain would be a small area in the vicinity of Umurbrogol Mountain, with the enemy surrounded therein."

The 5th Marines were chosen to move through the Army regiment at Garekoro and march up the narrow coastal flat to the end of the island.

Evidently the new decision was hurriedly reached. The 5th was directed to pack and move out of its bivouac within three hours.

This the 5th did, and a new phase of the Peleliu campaign began as truckloads of men rumbled across the still rubbled airfield from the eastern side of the island to the dangerous west on the afternoon of D plus 10.

What happened then must have surprised everyone—not to say the Japanese.

The tradition-laden 5th, a fine regiment under a fine commander, disembarked from its trucks early in the afternoon, marched directly through the Army lines, and set out with amazing ease and few casualties to move that day more than half the distance to the northern tip of the island, led by tanks and flame throwers mounted upon amtracs.

At nightfall Colonel Harris made a bold decision. He cut his lines back to the Army and Marine perimeter, and rested his flanks upon the beach. There the men dug in for the night.

This was an invitation the Japanese could not decline. They first stayed in their caves and fired viciously with 70mm guns, shooting from cave mouths as near as three hundred yards from the 5th's lines, as well as with concentrated small-arms fire which fell on the advance battalion. And then they came pouring out in local counterattacks that brought heavy Marine casualties. But the Marines held, and started forward again on D plus 11, September 26, assaulting a hill formation that commanded the northern part of Peleliu. When the charge did not carry the last enemy positions at the top, another attack was launched, by-passing the hill. This worked and the regiment moved on, using tanks and flame throwers to full advantage.

As they moved north they began to come under fire from Ngesebus, an island separated from the northern tip of Peleliu by only a few hundred yards of shallow water. The Japanese had cleared away a fighter landing strip on it, besides what other emplacements the 5th could only at the time estimate. And considerable fire was coming in from a phosphate mine and factory on Peleliu itself. It was apparent the Japanese had turned the factory, with its concrete walls, into a blockhouse. There were snipers everywhere. Altogether the 5th's position was peculiarly exposed, and its security called for full coordination of all the weapons available to a regimental commander. It is to Harris's credit that he used them all: calling naval gunfire and artillery in on Ngesebus as well as other points that stood in his regiment's way. "Harris," said one Division staff officer, "used supporting fires more fully and more wisely than any of our regimental commanders at Peleliu."

And Harris in turn credited the supporting fire: "Only by all echelons of command repeatedly employing this same high degree of skill in coordinating fire and maneuver was the complex enemy defense system in northern Peleliu cracked and then destroyed."

How strong the Japanese system was could be seen when tanks fired point-blank into caves and tunnels without causing the Japanese to cease fire even temporarily. One-hundred-pound demolition charges failed to close the tunnels, and eventually they were closed by bulldozer tanks, medium tanks with an earth-moving blade on the front.

The final hill system in the north was flanked by an encirclement of it by the 5th's battalions so neat and so well executed that, by D plus 14 (September 29) not only all of northern Peleliu was taken, but also all of Ngesebus (D-day, September 28) and Kongauru, the latter two islands in a swift amphibious assault by 3/5 (Major John Gustafson) from amtracs with low-flying Marine air support. The small islands were lightly defended, and the extraordinarily well planned show in which fighter planes and dive bombers from Marine squadrons took part is recalled with satisfaction by the Division's planning officers.

With amphibian tanks in advance, the first wave of assault troops shoved off in LVT's at 0905, crossed the few hundred yards of shallow reef in six minutes and hit the beach at 0911 against weak resistance. The first tanks arrived twelve minutes later, and by 0930 tanks (three were lost in potholes) and troop carriers were ashore. After that, however, events were rather in the nature of anticlimax, at least judged by the kind of fighting that had been going on at Peleliu. By 1700 all except the northwestern tip of Ngesebus was secure.

Ngesebus taken, the 5th turned back south into Umurbrogol. Surrounded now though they might be, the Japanese were still there, still willing to fight, able to kill.

The battle had become, in final contradiction of the pre-invasion prophecy, "a battle of attrition—a slow, slugging, yard-by-yard struggle to blast the enemy from his last remaining stronghold in the high ground." These are the words of the Division's report.

In the last few days of September welcome rains began to fall. But barely had they taken the parched taste from the mouths of the fighting men before they turned to squalls. By October 2 high winds had whipped the squalls into a typhoon. By October 4 high seas were running off Purple Beach, now the Division's main supply artery. Two LSTs, tied up at the Seabee-built causeway off Beach Orange 3, were driven ashore, and no other craft could safely reach the beach from larger, or smaller, supply ships.

The rains had a glooming effect. The lightless sky turned the whole island gray. Dust-coated dungarees turned stiff, hard and unpliable when they dried out, and when they were wet they were very heavy.

There were rations for only four days on the island, and as at Guadalcanal, the Division was reduced to two meals a day.

A hurry call was sent to Guam for food, and Marine Air Group 11 answered by flying in 42,000 10-in-1 rations.

"The rugged ground in which the troops had to operate caused more wear and tear on clothing than we had anticipated," writes a staff officer, and clothing, too, was flown in from Guam: 1,000 suits of dungarees, 5,000 pairs of socks and 1,000 pairs of boondockers.

And by the end of September two worlds were compressed into the narrow, tiny confines of the island. There was, of course, the world of battle up in the ridges, but there was as well the workaday world of the rear echelons going about their business on the airfield and in the south of the island. The blackened, pocked muzzle that was the forward face called Bloody Nose, marked the boundary between the two. Within a hundred yards of it on the south, men went about their tasks obliviously. The post office was less than three hundred yards south. A movie was set up not very much farther away, and the sound was constantly out-voiced by the rumble of heavy artillery going ahead, bound for the ridges. One night, because of the interruptions of an ammo dump blowing up nearby, and other explosions, the feature film did not finish until 0200.

On the airfield itself, hundreds of Seabees, bare to the waist, covered only by green pith helmets, piloted slow grading and levelling machinery. Maintenance men and pilots for squadrons of Marine fighter aircraft now based on the field pitched their shelter halves along the borders of the strips.

The Division CP displaced forward (September 24) from the beach to the two-story Japanese administration building at the northern end of the airfield, less than three hundred yards away from the high ground, and there on September 27, when the 5th had reached the northern end of the island, there was a flag-raising ceremony, with General Rupertus and a scattering of brass and some CP enlisted men in attendance.

In the broadest tactical sense the island was secure. Only a small pocket was left, that and Japanese scattered throughout the caves on the high ground, totalling nobody knew exactly how many.

But while the flag was being raised there was the clear and unmistakable wham of mortar shells, the sporadic rattle of machine-gun fire. DUKWs loaded with wounded rumbled by, and at one moment, a thin line of haggard men stumbled along a road that circled the flagpole, coming back from the ridges.

Some of the men who lived in the workaday world could not quite avoid the feeling that things were not so bad up in the ridges, as they were made to seem. A few went north looking for souvenirs—and were abruptly shanghaied into the lines, this by order. Joe Buckley, now a major in the 7th, was one of those who filled out his lines with souvenir hunters. He was promoted from captain during the second week of Peleliu and looked upon his exalted rank with the awe of an ex-enlisted man. "Imagine me a f___ Major," he went around exclaiming.

So constricted seemed the fighting area that some of the most experienced Marines could not resist the temptation to go up and take a pot shot at the Japs. Such a one was Colonel Joseph Hankins who was dissatisfied with his role as Division Provost Marshal.

"Colonel Hankins approached me," recalls one of his friend, "and suggested that we get our sniping rifles and go up the west side road to 'Dead Man's Curve.' At that place the limestone cliffs were approximately fifty yards from the road. The cliff was perforated with cave entrances in which the Japs secreted themselves and sniped at the traffic moving up and down the road.

"Because the time was approximately 1600 I told Joe that I could not accompany him and tried to persuade him to send up a fire team from the military police detail. However, he took his binoculars and his rifle, went up, disembarked from the jeep and stood in complete view to anyone who was on the cliffs, and was promptly shot through the heart."

Division in its wisdom might know that the island was "secure" and raise a flag to symbolize its knowledge. But a few hundred yards away from the staff and its paraphernalia of command there was another wisdom, another truth. To the men of the 5th Marines, stabbing into the final pocket (now only 400 by 900 yards), insecurity was the reality.

The 5th's overlay of its actions from October 6 through October 15 shows a crazy-quilt of arrows, pointing now in this direction, now in the opposite. There was a cliff called "The China Wall," ridges called "Baldy," "Waddie," a group called "The Five Brothers," and another called "The Five Sisters."

What they seized, actually took and held, was this:

1. They pierced a 100-yard salient into the hills that arose from Dead Man's Curve, the place where Colonel Hankins had been killed, making the road safe.

2. They slugged their way up Baldy, the peak that had arisen above Knob Three where L Company of the 7th had been decimated, put-

ting Baldy at last into American hands. With Baldy, the 5th also secured an adjoining peak called Hill 140.

When Hill 140 was captured a prodigious effort was made to get a heavy weapon up there. And when the 75mm and its carriage and ammunition were up, some way had to be found to protect it on the exposed plateau. The coral was too rugged to break, so sand bags were brought up although the sand to fill them had to be carried all the way from the beach.

The Japanese constantly counterattacked the 5th. Small parties would approach near enough to throw hand grenades, and then close in with knives or bayonets.

In defense, a group of Marines on a forward slope worked out a solution by covering their foxholes with downward-sloped ponchos. When they heard the Japanese, and the thump of grenades on the roofs, they waited until the grenades rolled off back down toward the Japs, exploded, then they threw off the ponchos, hurled a grenade themselves and went out to finish the job.

An unorthodox technique of air support had already been devised. The bombing run made by Marine Corsair fighters from the airstrip to their Umurbrogol targets was probably the shortest of World War II. The airlift was often a thousand yards, and it was seldom more than two thousand. The planes hardly got off the field before they were over their targets. They had to circle and come back. And so small was the target area, so sure were the Japs to retake any sector even temporarily abandoned, that the Marines had to stand ready far nearer the blast than was normally considered safe.

To allow the plane time to get away before the explosion, bombs were armed with delayed action fuses.

Some planes dropped unfused tanks of Napalm. As soon as the aircraft cleared the area and dipped its wings in signal that the strike was completed, the Marines fired white phosphorus shells into the target to ignite the fuel.

Tank-infantry sorties were routine. The tanks would go forward with a group of infantrymen following. It was a move of provocation, and if the Japs took the bait, the tank would move up to fire point-blank on the rash Japanese. When the tank had made rubble of the cave entrance, the infantrymen closed in with flame throwers and bazookas.

An observer, writing of a sortie he witnessed, said he saw tanks run up into a ravine, and the infantrymen sit down in their lees and light cigarettes, waiting for the tanks to advance. "It is a common observance," the witness said, "that in a long campaign men tend to get more careless about taking cover as the campaign progresses, partly due to fatigue and partly, I suppose, to fatalism."

More than two weeks after the flag was raised to symbolize the capture of Peleliu, Admiral Fort, on October 12, declared that "assault" operations were officially over. Two days later the 5th Marines were relieved by Army units of the 81st Division, and five days after that Major General P. J. Mueller, commanding the 81st, relieved General Rupertus of responsibility for the southern Palau sector.

But the Japanese did not get the word.

Not until November 25 did the senior Japanese officer on Peleliu burn his colors, and message his superior on Babelthuap: "All is over on Peleliu."

Two years and eight months later, on April 21, 1947, long after the Japanese nation had surrendered, twenty-six Japanese soldiers and sailors, led by a lieutenant, formally surrendered to the naval island commander of Peleliu. The news picture of the surrender showed the Japanese lieutenant bending low before an American naval officer, with his obviously well-fed command standing at rigid attention behind him.

But by then, by the end of the war, American intelligence had figured out what had happened at Peleliu: the Japanese had thought that we were going to hit it before, and not after, we hit the Marianas. While the Americans in the Pacific in the spring of 1944 were putting priority on Saipan and Guam plans, the Japanese were putting priority of defense on the Palaus. They sent one of their best men down to the Palaus, a Lieutenant General Sadae Inoue. He arrived in March, 1944, gave his men some reassuring words, cautioning them not to be concerned "with the great explosive bursts or the strong local effect of naval firing," and telling them that "if the situation becomes bad, we will maintain a firm hold on the high ground . . ."

Inoue's subordinate at Peleliu, Colonel Nakagawa, commanding the 2d Infantry, outlined what at that time was an original plan for a Japanese commander, ordering that a last-stand defense was not to be made at the beach line, but rather in the high ground.

And then he put his men to work. They build a cave system the like of which Americans had never before encountered in the Pacific war, one that was never excelled, even at Iwo Jima and Okinawa, carving and channeling into the northern peninsula of Peleliu more than five hundred caves, most of which had entrances on more than one level. Many had five or six stories, with living quarters. Some had sliding armored doors. All were mutually supporting.

And his units were proud, bearing honors from the Russo-Japanese war, and many other Asiatic expeditions. The units were: the 2d Infantry Regiment, nearly two battalions of the 15th Infantry, a battalion of the 54th Independent Mixed Brigade, a naval guard force, and a battalion of tanks.

Nor need any of them be ashamed of what they did at Peleliu.

They exacted the following casualties from the First Marine Division: 1,121 killed in action; 5,142 wounded in action; and 73 missing in action—a total of 6,336.

What the First Marine Division alone expended in ammunition is a further tribute to General Inoue and his men:

    13,319,488 rounds of .30-caliber (carbine, rifle, BAR)
     1,524,300 rounds of .45-caliber (pistol and submachine gun)
      693,657 rounds of .50-caliber (machine gun)
       97,596 rounds of 60mm mortar
       55,264 rounds of 81mm mortar
       13,500 rifle grenades
      116,262 hand grenades

Nor does this count the artillery:

    65,000 rounds 75mm pack howitzer
    55,000 rounds 105mm howitzer
     8,000 rounds 155mm howitzer
     5,000 rounds 155mm gun

To kill each of the ten thousand Japanese soldiers on Peleliu then, it took:

    1,331 rounds of .30-caliber
      152 rounds of .45-caliber
       69 rounds of .50-caliber
        9 rounds of 60mm mortar
        5 rounds of 81mm mortar
        1 rifle grenade
       10 hand grenades
        6 rounds of 75mm pack howitzer
        5 rounds of 105mm howitzer
        1 round of 155mm howitzer
    1/2 round of 155mm gun

It took a statistical average of 1,589 rounds of heavy and light ammunition to kill a Japanese soldier on Peleliu.

Steel of course was not enough. The Presidential Unit Citation awarded to the reinforced Division for Peleliu notes that the Japanese were "thoroughly disciplined, veteran troops . . ." and that they were "heavily entrenched in caves and in reinforced concrete pillboxes," and then points to the "undiminished spirit and courage" of the Marines who fought on "despite heavy losses, exhausting heat, and difficult terrain."

Looking back on Peleliu, an officer who holds a high place in Marine peacetime councils had said:

"The casualties there came from the terrain and the Japs—no amount of pessimism or numbers of reinforcements would have materially reduced the overall number of casualties."

※   ※   ※   ※

BY OCTOBER 19, 1944, THE UNITED STATES NAVY HAD lifted General Douglas MacArthur and two Army Corps to the Philippines. Thereafter for the next week the Navy repulsed Japan's greatest effort (Operation "Sho") to wreck our invasion with a series of major naval engagements during which the greater part of the remaining Japanese fleet was sunk.

On October 25, the Marine Corps went into action on Mac-Arthur's behalf when General Ralph Mitchell's First Air Wing came in and began its monumental contribution to the Philippines campaign. For this final phase of 1944, a year in which the Marine Corps had been largely instrumental in turning the tide of the Pacific war, here, again, is Captain John DeChant.

·25· MARINE AIR GROUPS AT LEYTE

CAPTAIN JOHN DeCHANT

The first Marine air activity of the Leyte landing was credited to General Mitchell himself. He went ashore on S-Day as an observer on MacArthur's staff. (Air units in the original landings were the Air Section, Corps Artillery, Fifth Amphibious Corps, serving two battalions of Marine 155-mm. artillery and an air liaison section of the Marine Corps 2nd and 3rd Joint Assault Signal Companies.)

When some 40-odd Navy planes were forced to land on bomb-pocked Tacloban field after their escort carrier had been sunk during the sea battle, Mitchell grabbed a pair of signal flags, ran to the end of the strip, and acted as landing-signal officer, wagging in each plane safely. Mitchell reported in the early assault phases that, while he had spent a good deal of his Solomons duty in foxholes, Leyte set a new record. He dived into a foxhole 26 times in a single day as Jap planes raided the area.

Another sidelight on Leyte which Marines will long remember was the task assigned to a Marine dive-bomber pilot serving as an air support adviser on a carrier flagship. He flew the first official Marine air mission of the invasion, dropping not bombs, but a cargo of leaflets carrying the slogan "I have returned" to announce General MacArthur's arrival to the Filipinos.

The first Marine squadron to land at Leyte was VMF (N) 541, a night fighter unit commanded by Lieutenant Colonel Peter D. Lambrecht. Originally attached to the Second Wing at Peleliu, this F6F unit was called in hurriedly because the Army P-61 night fighters lacked range, climb, and pilots with experience to cope with the Japanese night bombers. For several weeks after its landing on December 3, Lambrecht's squadron did not operate as a true radar night fighter unit. Local commanders didn't believe in using fighters throughout the night to hunt intruders by radar. Instead, they were confined generally to dusk and predawn operations.

During the month VMF (N) 541 operated at Leyte, it found the dusk and dawn hunting excellent, shooting down 22 planes, sinking 4 small surface vessels, and destroying 6 planes on the ground. Four of these air kills were credited to Technical Sergeant John W. Andre, one of the few Marine enlisted pilots then still flying in the Pacific.

Andre scored twice in one night by casually joining up on two Japanese "Jacks" returning to their base on Luzon after a raid near Tacloban Field. The Japanese pilots failed to notice Andre. Over their home field, they turned on their lights, and went into their landing approach. Andre slid in behind one, fired, and it burst into flames. He gunned up behind the second plane, firing a long burst. That enemy plane smashed into the field, spewing fire in all directions as its gas tanks exploded. The Hellcat followed up with six strafing passes over the enemy field, burning at least three planes on the ground.

On December 3, four Marine squadrons added their Corsairs to the jam at Tacloban strip. For several weeks, this airfield was called the most crowded in the world.

Four days after arriving, these fight-bomber units of MAG 12 (VMF 115, 211, 218 and 313) made their first major contact with Japanese shipping convoys. In this attack and in subsequent ones on December 11 and 12 in the Leyte-Ormoc-Mindoro areas, 14 enemy ships were sunk and 5 damaged.

Japanese air activity lessened considerably during December. Of the 26 planes which Marines shot down during that period, 11 were destroyed on December 11.

MAG 12 fighter-bombers covered the landing of the Army's 77th Division at Ormoc and joined VMF (N) 541 and carrier pilots in supporting landings by elements of the Sixth Army on Mindoro Island, several hundred miles northwest of Leyte. In early January the Corsairs made a long run north to join the air cover for the Army landings on Luzon Island.

The Marines flew routine fighter missions and operated regularly against land targets in the Central Philippines during January in attacks which netted numerous vehicles, buildings, bridges, freight cars, and assorted Japanese installations.

Infantry-support missions for the F4U's became common in early February during extensive operations with the Filipino guerillas in the Visayan Islands and on Mindoro. Although native leaders made enthusiastic reports from time to time on the air strikes, few results were reported because of a lack of good communications.

Support missions for the guerillas continued during February while MAG 12 prepared for another campaign. Meanwhile, another fighter-bomber group was in action near by.

Marine Air Group 14 and its four squadrons, VMF 212, 222, 223, and 251, began operating from Guiuan on Samar in early January, after staging in from the South Pacific. During their first weeks of action, MAG 14 planes flew a heavy schedule of air patrols, convoy cover, and tactical air missions, but had little contact with the Japanese air force which, by then, had judiciously vanished from the area.

In April, the tactical situation in the Philippines was such that the major fighter squadron assignment was supporting the 8th Army (which had relieved the 6th) and the guerillas in mopping-up and expansion campaigns. The majority of the Corsair missions were flown against targets on Cebu and Negros Islands. MAG 14 squadrons were commended regularly for "very effective close support" strikes which rapidly became routine and, as the weeks passed, of little note because of the lack of suitable enemy targets in the areas under attack.

During their months of operation in the Central Philippines, the Corsair groups had enjoyed little wholesale contact with the Japanese, but they had thoroughly established the effectiveness of the fast Corsair as a more-than-adequate infantry air support weapon.

While the two First Wing fighter groups were holding forth on Leyte and Samar, the two dive-bomber groups were in action on a new front. On December 11, the ground echelons left the South Pacific by ship for the Philippines. About a week later, the flight echelons began their hazardous journey. With Marine Douglas transports navigating and carrying key personnel, the SBD's followed behind like broods of chicks in the wake of mother hens. They flew into action via Emirau, Owi, Biak, Peleliu, and Leyte. Their destination was the Lingayen beachhead.

On January 9, Krueger's Sixth Army, now composed of the First and Fourteenth Corps, went ashore at Lingayen Gulf and by nightfall had established a 15-mile beachhead against negligible opposition. Krueger left a strong force to seal off the enemy forces in the north and concentrated his offensive on a drive to the south and Manila. Yamashita made several attempts to bottle up the Army on the Luzon plain, but failed. His divisions either arrived too late or not at all. He took the only obvious course and retreated slowly into the foothills and the mountains. The troops of the XI Corps (Eighth Army) went ashore on the west coast on Luzon near Subic Bay on January 29 and moved eastward against light opposition to cut off Bataan Peninsula.

The Marine dive-bombers landed at Luzon on January 25 and began operations two days later as Marine Air Groups, Dagupan, under Colonel Jerome. To the infantry and the war correspondents, this combined enterprise was known as "The Diving Devildogs of Luzon."

The seven SBD squadrons operated under colorful nicknames: Flying Eggbeaters (VMSB 133), Wild Hares (VMSB 142), Sons of Satan (VMSB 241), Black Panthers (VMSB 235), Flying Goldbricks (VMSB 243), Bombing Banshees (VMSB 244), and the Torrid Turtles (VMSB 341). Their strip at Mangaldan airdrome in Pangasinan Province was a temporary field out in the rice paddies. Low dikes separating the paddies had been bulldozed and scraped flat, but there were few other improvements. Any of the usual heavy Philippine rains left the 6,500-foot runway a morass.

On January 27 Major Ben Manchester led the first air strike of the dive-bombers, an 18-plane attack on San Fernando La Union. This and other early missions against targets in Southwest Tarlac, Neuva Ecija, Bulacan and Cayagan Provinces, and in the vicinity of Clark Field near Manila were a disappointment because they were not of the close-support variety. The only resemblance they bore to the intensive training on Bougainville was that the strikes had to clear through the SAP regardless of the closeness of enemy troops. Little by little, however, as Army confidence in Marine accuracy grew, the targets moved closer to our own front lines.

SBD missions in January destroyed two small towns, 90 huts and storage buildings and two barracks areas. In return, one Japanese bomber raided Mangaldan Field but did no damage to the Marines.

At dawn on February 1, Jerome's bombers began their celebrated mission of supporting the 100-mile dash of Mudge's First Cavalry

Division, down Highway Three to Manila. In a tactic with few if any major precedents in the history of air-ground warfare, the SBD's were responsible for covering and guarding Mudge's left flank from the air. A flight of nine SBD's was on constant patrol from dawn to dusk over the flank and searching for enemy strongpoints ahead.

By evening of the first day, the advance column forded the river opposite the town of Cabanatuan. Reconnaissance flights by the SBD's indicated the disposition of enemy troops south of the town and permitted the First Brigade to continue its rapid advance. VMSB 142 had nine bombers harassing advance targets principally at the town of Angat. Fording the Pampanga River at dawn of the second day, the Brigade moved south. The SBD's were in constant patrol on its left flank, clearing the area for 20 miles behind and 30 miles ahead.

At dusk on February 2, the infantry column reached Balinag on the Angat River, where it met with the 37th Division. The dive-bombers, meanwhile, hit targets at San Isidro and Neuva Ecija. Next day, the infantry advance continued across the river and swung east to the near-by foothills with dive-bomber support so precise that General Chase commented, "I have never seen such able, close, and accurate support as the Marine fliers are giving us."

While some units covered the First Cavalry, other Marine bombing and strafing missions were sent out against a wide variety of targets close to and behind the enemy front lines. During the period from February 8 to 14, the two Marine groups attacked some 34 name-targets in addition to those hit as targets of opportunity. The SBD's rained down their loads on Corregidor Island where the Fourth Marine infantry regiment had been the unpublicized bulwark of the island's defense during its last days in 1942; and on Fort McKinley, Nichols Field, Balete Pass, Mount Oror, Rosario, Fort Stotsenburg, Antipolo Wawa, and other points. Highlights of the period were the annihilation of two ammunition dumps and Japanese Military Police headquarters and barracks at Baguio on February 11, and close-support missions on the same date near the Labauyug River in which all designated targets were destroyed. Two days later the Marines hit antiaircraft positions and personnel in the Malago River valley. This enemy strongpoint was hidden in a position 100 yards long and a few feet wide. After the bombing and strafing, the Army liaison party radioed the SBD's "area blasted, supplies demolished, and gun positions destroyed."

Throughout this "trial" period with the Army infantry in February, the Marine pilots flew an exhausting variety of missions to prove that their air-support weapon was a workable combination of flying artillery and sniping.

One incident among the many which helped sell Marine air support to the Army ground forces occurred when a patrol of the Sixth Division was stranded after falling down a cliff. The officer-in-charge was dying and three other men seriously wounded. The remaining 12 men refused to abandon their position, although their food was exhausted and a Japanese position was only 300 yards away. Attempts were made to relieve the patrol, but failed because of fire from the enemy position.

A flight of Dauntlesses was assigned to wipe out the Japanese strongpoint, even though the Army Colonel in charge of the relief effort was afraid of possible injury to friendly troops. The Colonel requested the flight leader to make a dummy run. It was right on. He requested the leader to drop one of his wing bombs. It hit the target. Then the SBD flight was cleared for the attack. Of the nine planes making runs, one dropped 80 yards from the target. The other bombs were within a 30-yard circle, all bull's-eyes. Next night, the Colonel evacuated his stranded patrol without interference.

Generally, the planes of MAG 24 and 32 operated under two types of tactical situations in handling these close-support missions. In the "ground alert" condition, the bombers were at their field, loaded and ready to take off the moment an order came from the Support Air Commander. The "air alert" provided for planes to be continuously on station in the air orbiting a stand-by point designated by the Air Coordinator.

A typical close-support situation shaped up in this fashion:

The infantry company or battalion commander bumps into an enemy strongpoint. With him on the front lines are his artillery observer and the Marine Air Liaison party. It is decided that the Jap position can't be handled by the artillery because of the time element involved or because the position is on the reverse side of a ridge and unreachable. The infantry request for planes is relayed back over the air network to the Support Air Commander, giving full details including the position of friendly troops, the enemy target, the number of planes and the type of bombs required.

If the condition is "ground alert," the SAC briefs the pilots thoroughly. They take off and arrive over the designated target at the prescribed time. If the condition is "air alert," this information is relayed to the Air Coordinator overhead. Usually, if the attack calls for precision, the planes are told to report to the Marine ALP on the front lines. In this case, the ALP radio jeep marks its own position by a panel or reports it in relation to a landmark easily visible from the air. Then the air-ground conversation starts, with "K-ration" as the radio jeep and "Red Dog" as the leader of the dive-bombers overhead:

"K-ration to Red Dog. Do you have my position spotted? Over."

"Red Dog to K-ration. Roger. Out."

"K-ration to Red Dog. We will mark our target with one burst of William Peter. Watch for it, 500 yards due north of us." (William Peter is phonetic for WP, meaning white phosphorous.)

"K-ration to Red Dog. William Peter on its way." (A mortar or howitzer had fired the phosphorous shell.)

"Red Dog to K-ration. I see William Peter. Over."

"K-ration to Red Dog. Roger. Make one dummy run on William Peter." (The infantry commander and the ALP watch critically as the little plane breaks out of formation at 9,000 feet and dives.)

"K-ration to Red Dog. Roger. You are right on. You may make your runs."

"Red Dog to K-ration. Roger and Wilco (Will comply)." (The bombers make their separate runs on the marked target. If one deviates slightly, the ALP radios an immediate correction to the next plane coming down. Finally all bombs are dropped and a strafing run follows.)

"K-ration to Red Dog. Well hit. That smears them nicely. Thanks again."

"Red Dog to K-ration. Anytime, Mac. Over and out."

The code calls for the planes changed frequently, but all the Marine ALP radio jeeps were "K-ration," plus an identifying number to distinguish them from other ALP's operating near by. This code call was supposedly devised by Captain "Frisco" Godolphin, who pointed out that the three components of the packaged K-ration were supper, breakfast, and dinner, or "SBD." Since the jeeps were directing SBD's, their code call properly should be "K-ration."

The use of white phosphorous was general throughout the campaign except in areas unreachable by artillery or mortars or where strong wind might dissipate the marker smoke. Colored smoke was used, but it proved hard to see from the high altitudes where the dive-bombers began their runs.

Sometimes the Japs tried confusing the issue by dropping smoke shells of their own on Army lines to make the Marines bomb friendly troops. In one instance, the enemy dropped a shell close to an ALP jeep.

Over the radio, the Marine ALP queried, quite unperturbed, "K-ration to Blue Boar. Do you see that William Peter?"

"Roger, I see it."

"Hit just 1500 yards north of it. Got it?"

"Roger. Coming down."

Occasionally, as they had in the South Pacific, the Japs broke into our radio channels to give the SBD pilots misleading instructions.

But the meticulous Japanese lacked a knowledge of American idiom and their efforts were usually without success, except in two recorded instances near Baguio, summer capital of the Philippines.

Nine SBD's requested permission to hit Baguio when they were unable to reach their target at Balete Pass because of weather. Permission was given and the bombing attack was successful except for AA which hit two planes. After the strafing run, the flight leader received a message purporting to come from his Support Air Party: "You are bombing and strafing friendly troops." The SBD's immediately returned to base to verify the charge, but found that there was no record of the message ever having been sent. Sometime later, another SBD strike was halted by a message to return to base with their bombs. Returning, they discovered no such message had been issued.

Without Jap planes to bother them, the dive-bomber pilots met their only opposition from enemy antiaircraft fire which ranged from intensive but inaccurate to light and ineffective. Air casualties during the month of February for more than 4,000 Marine combat sorties were only two pilots and one gunner. This was in spite of the fact that the SBD's were boring in low to get pin-point accuracy on bomb runs and then strafing in their slow planes at low altitudes. (Bomb loadings for the Dauntless varied with the targets assigned. The usual load per plane was one 500-pound bomb on the belly rack plus either two 250-pound or two 100-pound bombs on the wing racks. When a 1,000-pound bomb was carried, it usually constituted the entire load. The average SBD attack was made at an indicated air-speed of between 240 and 260 knots, at an angle approaching 70 degrees. Release was made between 2,500 and 1,500 feet. The planes pulled out of their steep dives at between 2,000 and 1,000 feet.)

Tactically, the biggest problem of the air support missions was target location. Maps were all too frequently incomplete and the aerial photos, at first, were outdated. Even when maps were finally complete and accurate, they were not of much use except for the general orientation of the pilots unless their target was some prominent landmark. The Air Liaison Party in the K-ration jeep proved to be the best possible method of target designation when working at the front, because the air liaison officer could see usually both the target and planes.

Mission after mission of SBD's winged out from the Dagupan strip, ranging in size from the usual 9 planes to as high as 81 aircraft. Relations with the Army infantry and its commanders improved daily. Colonel Jerome received an increasing number of commendations from the infantry commanders either by personal letter or via official channels as commendations. The official reports regularly carried unsolicited written or oral comments by ground observers on the air support efforts of the dive-bombers. These were terse tributes to their effectiveness:

February 11: Enemy position on ridge near Labauyug; SAP reported, "Target blasted."

February 12: Specified target in O'Donnel area; SAP reported, "Very satisfactory results."

February 13: AA east of Nichols Field; SAP reported, "Good coverage."

February 14: Enemy concentration; report, "Japs in disorder, you have killed a mess of them with your bombing and strafing."

February 16: Gun revetments and fuel dumps near Marakina; "Very good coverage of assigned area.

February 17: Troop concentration in a ravine; SAP reported, "All bombs in target area, good job."

February 20: Enemy troops and artillery positions; SAP reported, "Area well covered with bombs excellently dropped. Damage estimated as terrific." Barges on Taytay Esterpo River; "You have done more damage than you think."

February 21: Hilltop 4,000 yards south of Lumboy; SAP reported, "Bodies, guns, papers blown all over the place. Kisses from Commanding Officer of adjacent ground units."

February 23: Enemy entrenchments on hilltop; "Accuracy excellent."

These communications were of immense value to the airmen's morale, since for the pilot or rear-gunner, close support had many disadvantages. Though a precision task, it was one of the easiest they were called upon to do, particularly with ground fire at a minimum as it was in most of the Philippine campaigning. Close support offers no excitement or no special glory.

Major Ben Manchester, squadron leader, said: "It's dull as hell for a pilot. Remember, he hardly ever sees what he hits. To him, the target is either a hunk of ground or a hunk of brush, unless it happens to be a building of some kind. The pilot hits it and that's all there is to it. Unless the ground forces take the trouble to tell him the results, he never knows whether he has done any good for all his sweating."

But right down to the last private, the Marines agreed that operations in the Philippines were paradise compared to the aerial strangulation chore in the South Pacific. At least they saw towns and roads and other signs of civilization, even if they had to destroy them. The ragged but ecstatic Filipinos welcomed them noisily wherever they moved up. With these compensations and the incentive of offensive war, the "Diving Devildogs" kept hammering away at the Japanese.

It was many weeks, however, before it was thought fitting to let the enemy and the American public know via the medium of the communiques that the Marine air groups were in action there. But that was an old story to the Air Arm, as it had been to the Fourth Regiment on Corregidor years before. Though it was hardly so intended, this lack of any recognition in the communiques exasperated the Marines to even greater effort.

As the campaign progressed, air-ground integration was intensified and more air personnel were assigned to serve with the front-line infantry units. Section-leader pilots worked with the ALP radio jeeps on a weekly rotation basis and came back to their squadrons very much aware of the infantry's problems and the need for even greater precision teamwork.

Notable among the ACI (Air Combat Intelligence) officers who did front-line duty with the infantry was 42-year-old Captain Francis R. B. "Frisco" Godolphin, a veteran of four major Pacific campaigns. (A professor of Greek and Latin at Princeton University, Godolphin volunteered for the Marine Corps at 40 because both he and the president of the university felt there would be a serious need on the post-war faculty for a professor with combat experience who could really understand the problems of servicemen returning to college.)

Godolphin was in the front lines for 38 days as a Support Air Party officer. Marine Combat Correspondent Staff Sergeant David Stephenson reported several of Godolphin's exploits:

"During the early part of February, the Seventh Regiment had captured the Balera water-filter plant northeast of Manila. The Japs, determined to destroy the plant and pollute Manila's water supply, had been directing mortar and machine-gun fire at the building from four positions. Finally they brought up rockets.

"The rocket attack began at midnight. Captain Godolphin went to the roof of the plant with a sextant to determine the azimuth of the rocket position. Six enemy rockets landed within 40 yards of his CP, but Captain 'Frisco' got out alive with enough data to pinpoint the target for the SBD's the next morning. On another occasion, Godolphin and his party were studying a situation map when the enemy sneaked in close with a machine gun and wounded two of the men and destroyed the map.

"The largest Marine strike which the Captain helped direct on Luzon was an 81-plane attack east of the Marakina River. In preparation for it, the SAP sent a guerilla lieutenant—a civil engineer graduate of the University of the Philippines—into the area to be bombed. The officer, disguised as a native civilian, sketched and plotted the Jap position by night. After sufficient information had been obtained, Godolphin called in the dive-bombers. He radioed his data to Major Manchester, the air coordinator, who was circling the target, picking out each point of attack as it was described to him. Then Manchester sent his planes down for the kill.

"In the last strike which Godolphin directed, two waves of nine planes each were to drop 1,000-pounders 250 to 300 yards in advance of the First Cavalry troops. The first wave came in and dropped its load. All nine bombs were duds. The Captain recalled 'You should have seen the looks of discouragement on the faces of the infantrymen!' Then the second wave came over and all nine bombs exploded right on the target."

Among the unusual close-support missions performed by the dive-bombers while holding the Cavalry's left flank was one which occurred northeast of Manila. The advance had rolled to a stop before a cave-infested hillside where intensive Japanese fire pinned the infantry to the ground. The mission of blasting out the caves was assigned to the "Torrid Turtles" squadron.

Nine of its planes on station listened to instructions from the ALP radio. They were told to be particularly careful because the enemy position was less than 200 yards from friendly troops. The strike leader, Captain Jack Canaan, peeled off and came down. His 1,000 pounds of assorted bombs scored a direct hit.

The Air Liaison Party grunted satisfaction, then radioed: "Don't bomb another foot north. The concussion is bouncing our troops around. Confine your hits within 30 yards to the south." The remaining planes did just that and the soldiers moved forward again.

It was about this time that Lieutenant Ewing Crutchfield, a dive-bomber pilot, got his radio jeep assignment to another Army division, on the right flank of the First Cavalry.

He reported in and was told by the commanding general: "We don't believe in close air support. As a matter of fact, the closest air support we want is 1,000 yards from our troops." Somewhat discouraged, Crutchfield went to work flying a tiny Stinson observation plane as a spotter for the artillery. He helped remove a postoffice and several big gun emplacements by directing gunfire and air strikes. But because of the local opinion of air support, he left shortly after to join Captain Godolphin's unit.

At that time, the First Cavalrymen had occupied high land west of the Pasig River and had taken the Balera water plant. They were opposing Jap forces on a ridge in front of the Marakina River. The enemy positions on the ridge were causing considerable trouble with their heavy machine-gun and mortar fire. The Japs had also launched several abortive "Banzai" attacks, making the infantry's situation generally uncomfortable.

When Crutchfield arrived, Godolphin was working in the water tower at which the enemy fired frequently, but without much accuracy. Godolphin had run wire from the tower to his radio jeep and was doing his broadcasting only 150 yards from the Japanese ridge. General Mudge called a strike regardless of the close quarters.

When the air strike arrived, Godolphin had some prominent spectators in the tower, both General Mudge and the doubting commander of the right flank division. Manchester, the strike leader, was instructed to hit the ridge on its further slope because an explosion on the near side would have sent bomb fragments whistling into the Army infantry. While a lively firefight went on below, Manchester made his run with only a patch of scrub brush to hit.

His bomb bounced just off the crest of the ridge, on the Japanese side. His wingman followed in, cloaking the ridge in smoke and flying debris. The cavalrymen cheered the performance as though it were a touchdown in a football game. One of the Army patrols moved up at once, walking over the ridge with no opposition. They found 8 machine-gun positions and 15 mortar emplacements. There were dead Japanese about, but no live ones. The enemy survivors were bandy-legging it in retreat to a point more than half a mile away across the Marakina River.

The doubting General, now convinced, asked Godolphin how soon his own division could have the same kind of air support. General Mudge reminded his infantry cohort that the planes would have to bomb a lot closer than 1,000 yards, to which the once-doubting General replied: "I don't give a damn how close they hit!"

Some of the Marine K-ration jeeps remained with the handful of Army troops keeping Mudge's left flank secure over an 18-mile line from Laguna de Bay to Montalban. Here, the air support situation ran into difficulty because of the length and nature of the chain-of-command. If air support was needed, the request had to go from company to battalion, from battalion to regiment to division, from division to corps and from corps to the Sixth Army. These proper authorities took it up with the 308th Army Bombardment Wing under which the Marines were operating. The Wing then ordered the mission, and sent an O.K. grinding back down the same channels. This procedure often took as long as two days.

Captain Godolphin was beset by this red-tape menace in trying to knock out a portable rocket-launcher with which the Japanese were making local conditions extremely unpleasant. The launcher would be spotted or bracketed at night. Then a strike was ordered. By the time the planes arrived, two days later, the launcher had moved to an unidentified position.

The Marine captain sang his tale of woe to General Mudge. He was told promptly, "When planes report on station, you tell them what you want hit. Never mind what they have been briefed for. I'll accept full responsibility."

Next morning, when the SBD's came over, expecting to hit elsewhere, Godolphin directed them to a clump of brush at one end of the Jap-held Marakina airstrip where the rocket-launcher had taken its latest stand. Shortly, a pilot reported seeing the twisted wreckage of the rocket rack after his bomb had hit. Its remains were later found by the infantry.

This incident was of great value to the success of the air support operation, because the practice from then on was to use the planes on targets as needed, and usually without prior briefing, unless the situation was fairly static. In such cases, detailed briefing produced uniformly excellent results, as in the case against a target west of Antipolo.

Beyond the town was a double bend in the road, forming a winding M where the Japanese had bored industriously into the near-by hills, emplacing artillery positions and antitank guns. These enemy defenses stalled the infantry advance for several days, causing heavy casualties and knocking out two American tanks.

Enlarged photographs of the M were used to brief the pilots of 54 SBD's assigned to the mission. So complete were their instructions that they merely reported on station and went to work, singly, starting at one end of the road and working up. Reports from the infantry said later that the dust clouds raised by the Marine bomb blasts went along like the dust track of one fast moving truck. The caves were sealed and the gun positions eliminated. The greatest bomb miss was only 50 yards from the aiming point and most bombs were directly on. This was a startling demonstration of accuracy, even for experienced SBD pilots. The troops passed through the strongpoint without casualties.

In connection with dive-bomber accuracy, some comments were made by captured Japanese AA gunners. Their antiaircraft was fairly intense in some areas and planes were lost by Army fighter outfits and medium and heavy bomber squadrons. The Marines, however, were not shot at quite so often because the Japanese had no intention of divulging their position to "the little planes that dive." The Jap gunners were frankly afraid that a few shots might anger the dive-bomber pilots into retaliation. They had heard what could happen to AA positions when the SBD's came down.

Advance infantry elements from Lingayen entered Manila on February 4, meeting little early opposition and liberating war prisoners along the way. It looked as though the city would fall easily and cheaply, particularly since it had been supposedly declared an "open city" by General Yamashita. But the sullen Japs fell back slowly across the Pasig River, which winds through Manila proper, blowing up bridges and city landmarks one after another. For three savage weeks, the Japs defended Manila as American infantry cleaned them out of one big structure after another, fighting from floor to floor and often engaging in point-blank artillery duels down the corridors of buildings. When the enemy was routed finally, after heavy casualties among Filipino civilians and the infantry, the city of Manila, once regarded as the showplace of the Orient, was a desolate shambles.

Some Japanese moved from their crime at Manila to strongpoints beyond the city, but generally they retreated to the mountains in the north. A fast series of amphibious and airborne landings then bottled up the enemy positions or eliminated them. Four thousand Japanese died trying to hold Corregidor against a combined sea-air invasion which had been preceded by a mighty naval and air bombardment, participated in by Marine squadrons.

Marine planes covered infantry and guerilla landings at Burias Island, Masbete, Capul, Biri, and Nasugou. On March 10, the Corsairs joined in the air support for the landing of the 41st Division at San Mateo on Mindanao, second largest island in the Philippines. The Marines were in support during the Basilian landing in the Sulu Archipelago. The performance was repeated in the landing on Panay on March 18. Five fighter squadrons covered the landing on Cebu. This action was followed by constant close-air support missions throughout the Cebu and Negros island operations.

V-MB 611, a medium-bomber unit up from the Solomons, joined Marine and other air units in covering landings in April at Sanga Sanga, Bongao, and Jolo in the Sulu group. Marine fighters and bombers also provided air cover for invasion operations at Malabang, Parang, Cotabato, and Dumaguete in the Philippines.

Meanwhile the divisions of the Sixth Army met fanatical enemy resistance in the mountain ranges between Baguio and Balete Pass.

At Balete Pass, the Japanese were fighting a rear-guard action in a mountain fortress. The heavy crossfire from their cave positions disputed any entrance into the Pass, though artillery batteries had blanketed the area for days.

General Mitchell's pilots, already staging for another campaign, were called in. For five days of constant bombing, the SBD's pinpointed the enemy positions. Then the infantry moved in against feeble resistance. Japanese dead, hundreds of them, littered the target area, and many more bodies were found where the dive-bombers had caught a Jap reinforcement column moving up the Pass from Baguio.

The raids against the mountain targets wound up the assignments on Luzon for the SBD groups, which had moved from field to field behind the advancing infantry they were supporting. Before the Marines left, General Krueger of the Sixth Army sent his farewell message to them. It concluded:

"The war record of the First Marine Aircraft Wing is emblazoned with one success after another, from the bitter days of Guadalcanal, where they won the Presidential Unit Citation, to Luzon, where their record speaks for itself and from praises uttered by men of the Sixth Army who have done the land fighting."

❀ ❀ ❀ ❀

PART V

Iwo Jima to Okinawa: Death of an Empire

Where lay the next target in the strategic concept of the war? The question had been put before the Joint Chiefs of Staff as early as July 1944, and the target was tentatively identified: Iwo Jima, two hours flying time from the Japanese mainland and 660 miles south of Tokyo. Three months later, when it seemed reasonable to assume that nothing could deter the Army from its appointed task in the Philippines, nor Saipan-based B-29s from staging forays into the heart of the Empire, the Joint Chiefs directed Admiral Nimitz to prepare an invasion of Iwo for February 1945.

Saipan had proved something less than the ideal interim base for Major General Curtis E. LeMay's 21st Bomber Command, however. With the exception of the first strike launched from Saipan (the Tokyo raid of November 27, 1944, which was successful because complete surprise was achieved), succeeding missions were "chewed to pieces" by enemy fighter interception scrambled from homeland bases. Moreover, Japanese retaliatory raids from Saipan to Iwo underscored the urgency of invasion. Indeed, until we secured our next target (Iwo), a fixed base from which we could both stage B-29 raids with adequate fighter cover, and provide bullets, bombs and fuel,

and succor damaged aircraft, the toll of American aircrews and bombers was expected to mount precipitously. It did. After several weeks
of Saipan-based "Superfort" operations, LeMay was forced to remark:
"This outfit has been getting a lot of publicity lately without have
accomplished a hell of a lot in bombing results."

Iwo, described by a young marine as "not worth fifty cents at a sheriff's sale," was a small prize at first glance. Shaped like a porkchop
or a snake's head and tapering body, the island is only two and a half
miles wide by five miles long, with a volcano at its southern end. Iwo
is covered over with coarse gray-black volcanic ash, beneath which
is a crust of hardened lava; walking is difficult and running, impossible. In 1830, this center island of the Bonin chain attracted two New
Englanders who saw in it a potential coaling and provisioning station
for steamships. However, their action was repudiated by our government, and Japan seized the strategic chain without opposition. Until
the Marine Corps assaulted Iwo Jima, Japan quite properly regarded
it as an integral part of her inner defense system and garrisoned it
accordingly.

In 1945, Iwo Jima was under the command of Lieutenant General
Tadamichi Kuribayashi, a former chief of the Imperial Guard and
one of the most respected officers in the Emperor's service. (Holland
Smith called him "redoubtable." Other marine officers said they
hoped Japan had no more like him.) If Peleliu was formidable, then
certainly Iwo was beyond belief. It was, in point of fact, the greatest
fortress encountered by the Marine Corps in World War II, and its
depth, intricacy and elaborate planning were a tribute to the military
genius who spared no effort to render it almost impregnable: Kuribayashi.

The Japanese general's troops numbered 20,000, of which about
one third were naval components under Rear Admiral Takinosuke
Ichimara. The rest were units built around the veteran 145th Independent Mixed Brigade and five antitank battalions. The island had
over 750 installations, including 120 guns larger than 75 millimeter,
90 large mortars and rocket launchers (of the latter, 12 were of 320
millimeter and fired 550-pound rockets), 130 howitzers, 69 antitank
guns, and 240 machine guns of 20 millimeter and larger. There were
24 tanks. Beach defenses, numbering 201 installations, included 21
blockhouses so sited as to be mutually supporting, 6-inch and 4.7-inch
gun emplacements with five-foot-thick concrete walls and four-foot
average overheads; 13,000 yards of tunneling, concrete-lined and
many-tiered; and, finally, behind the landing beaches were 92 concrete pillboxes and 32 covered artillery emplacements with antitank
guns buried in pits and vulnerable only to direct hit.

Many of these guns were on the slopes of Mount Suribachi (560
feet above sea level), and so situated that an onrushing attack launched

from potential landing beaches would be opposed by maximum fire. In short, there was very little that could be done to impair the efficacy of Kuribayashi's fighting machine, and no sustained air and sea bombardment could possibly neutralize it. In September 1944, when Kuribayashi's defense plans crystallized, he instructed his troops to focus on "a gradual depletion of the enemy's attack forces, and even if the situation gets out of hand, defend a corner of the island to the death."

He drew his plans based on a conglomeration of battle reports accumulated over three years. But Saipan was really the criterion by which he decided that a water's edge stand was too brittle; that invasion also taught him the value of an in-depth defense. In short, allow the enemy to gain a slender foothold on the beaches and try to keep him there while hacking him to pieces with artillery and mortar; and failing this, allow him to penetrate inland where fixed gun positions would annihilate him. Kuribayashi issued orders against counterattacking except in the case of enemy tanks, and to this end all troops were thoroughly instructed in the handling of antitank mines and grenades; artillery was ordered to give these targets priority.

While Kuribayashi fine-tuned his defense, American submarines in the area were sinking convoys, and many a bedraggled survivor was brought to Iwo and absorbed into Ichimara's command. The Imperial Navy wanted no repeat of Guadalcanal, however, and after the loss of a few important convoys, reinforcements and the conveniences of home stopped coming. Yet it spite of virtual isolation and a gloomy intelligence report circulated about the first of the year that Iwo was soon to be invaded by three divisions of United States Marines screened by 18 destroyers and 1 battleship, Japanese troops faced the inevitability of death without complaint.

On December 8, 1944, the "softening" of Iwo Jima began when 164 B-24s and B-29s flew over and delivered their payloads. A few hours later Rear Admiral Allen E. "Hoke" Smith with three cruisers followed this up with a naval bombardment. Despite the shellacking (naval gunfire alone aggregated 6800 rounds of 8-inch and 5-inch shells), aerial reconnaissance revealed that the island was "more or less" intact. Between that first strike and February 15—four days before D-Day—Iwo Jima was additionally softened by a daily VII AAF bombing run which dropped a grand total of 1200 tons on the target; preinvasion naval bombardments in December and January delivered 203 rounds of 16-inch, 6472 rounds of 8-inch, and 12,250 rounds of 5-inch explosives. Notwithstanding, additional photoreconnaissance in January revealed several new installations amid the ruins.

Had Japanese moral been shattered by this prolonged battering? The Marine Corps did not think so. Holland Smith estimated 20,000 casualties (Kelly Turner even more), and this arbitary figure was considerably strengthened by the events of D-Minus-Two, when 12 LCI rocket launchers screening Navy frogmen came under intense and havoc-raising fire off the beaches. Simultaneously, a battery at the base of Mount Suribachi opened a huge vent in the cuiser *Pensacola,* killing 17 men and wounding 98; the nearby destroyer *Leutze* sustained light hits, and LCI 474 capsized. The only compensation for this severe mauling was the fact that Kuribayashi, believing the invasion had begun, unmasked several concealed batteries, one of them a four-gun, and the battleship *Idaho* took it under fire on D-Minus-One and knocked it out.

Marine planning did not involve conning or strategem; merely brute force applied to pressure points. In command of the assault troops which applied this force were the two officers who had largely masterminded the Marine Corps advance across the Pacific: Holland Smith and Kelly Turner. In command of the preinvasion bombardment forces was Rear Admiral H. W. P. "Spike" Blandy, a gunnery specialist out of the top drawer, and he had with him Colonel Donald Weller, the best gunnery officer in the Corps. The naval bombardment they laid down was the heaviest of the war: 6 battleships and 5 cruisers belched 14,000 rounds of 8-inch and 14-inch shells.

Major General Harry Schmidt and Rear Admiral Harry Hill commanded the assault and naval forces, and to them goes the credit for executing a devastating five-hour D-Day bombardment: 5000 tons of ammunition from 5-inch to 16-inch shells, plus the contribution of LCI gunboats and rocket ships and naval air with a 102-plane *Essex* strike (48 of the planes of VMF 124 under Colonel William P. Millington) in order to rake the beaches with napalm, machine guns and rockets. While Iwo, masked in dense black smoke, reeled under the impact of this terrible bombardment, the 4th Marine Division under Major General Clifton B. Cates and the 5th Marine Division under Major General Keller M. Rockey would storm ashore; the 3rd Marine Division under Major General Graves B. Erskine would wait in reserve.

The assault was planned thusly: 28th Marines (Colonel H. B. "Harry the Horse" Liversedge), 27th Marines (Colonel T. A. Wornham), 23rd Marines (Colonel W. W. Wensinger), and 25th Marines (Colonel J. R. Lanigan) would land abreast, left to right, on the east beaches, with Mount Suribachi on the left and cliffs and a quarry on the right. In reserve from the two divisions were the 24th Marines (Colonel W. I. Jordan) and 26th Marines (Colonel C. C. Graham), along with the 21st Marines (Colonel H. J. Withers), held in reserve as the forward element of the 3rd Division. When the beachhead was secure, these reserve regiments would wheel right, northward, against steep cliffs and a quarry demarking the high ground. The primary task of the 5th Division was to isolate the southern portion of the island by capturing Mount Suribachi and an airfield, Motoyama No. 1, while the 4th Division was to secure the high ground between the southern airfield and Motoyama No. 2 Airfield to the north. The 3rd Division, held in reserve until D-Plus-Five, was to drive up through the center of Kuribayashi's cross-island defenses.

Richard Newcomb, author and newspaperman, belongs to a small cadre of military writers whose specialty is dramatic recreation of a battle. He interviewed many of the participants and tracked down the stories of those who did not survive, to give his own taut version of Iwo Jima. In the following excerpt, the landing craft are lined up waiting for the signal to head into the beaches. It is 7:30 A.M. of a clear, crisp February 19, 1945.

• 1 • INVASION

RICHARD NEWCOMB

The Line of Departure, LD, was established . . . 2 miles offshore and parallel to the beach, a control vessel marking either end. Along the line, tiny vessels marked out the boat lanes, and the Assistant Division Commanders went to the line as observers, Brigadier General Hart for the Fourth and Brigadier General Hermle for the Fifth. The LST's opened their bow doors, and assault marines launched in their LVT's, armored amphibious tanks armed with 75-mm. howitzers and three machine guns. They would climb 50 yards inland and form a ring of fire for the following waves.

Boated and circling, the first three waves were ready at the line by 8:15 A.M. From the air they looked like water bugs, trailing white-plumed wakes. The sun was stronger now, and the island was many shades of brown and yellow. In a smart breeze, tiny pennants snapped from hundred of mastheads. It was a fine day.

The Central Control vessel dipped her pennant exactly at 8:30 A.M., releasing the first wave of assault troops, and the battle was on. Sixty-eight LVT (A)'s of the 2nd Armored Amphibian Battalion crossed the line and headed in, naval shells still whistling overhead. The LCI's moved in for the last mortar barrage of 20,000 rounds, and the second assault wave crossed the line, 1,360 marines in LVT's. Eight more waves formed behind them, ready to land at five-minute intervals. In less than forty-five minutes there should be 9,000 men ashore.

Just as the air observer overhead called out "Leading wave 400 yards from shore," the naval shelling lifted to move inland and the last air assault came down. This was Millington's bellyscraper mission and it roared over the beaches just off the sand.

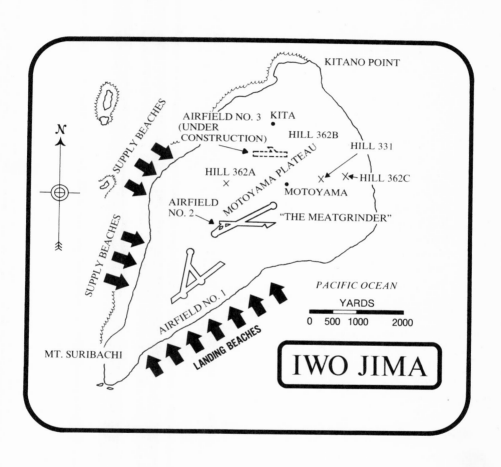

The first LVT (A)'s hit the sand on Red 1 at 8:59 A.M., one minute ahead of time, and in the next three minutes on every beach from Suribachi to the cliffs, except Blue 2. Before them, only a few feet inland and rising nearly straight up, was the first terrace, from 10 to 15 feet high and composed only of loose sand. It was quickly apparent that only tracked vehicles could make it, and not all of them. The amphtracs attacked it, and some got to the first plateau, grinding up the face in showers of sand. Some churned 50 to 75 yards inland on the center and north beaches, but down near Suribachi the cliff was impassable. The LVT (A)'s plopped back into the water, swam out, and turned to fire from the sea.

For the first few minutes there was no fire from the defenders, and the leading waves of troops scrambled from their LVT's and began to climb the terrace. It was like climbing a waterfall. Loaded down with equipment, from the 51 pounds carried by a corpsman to the 122 pounds saddled onto a mortarman, the men "swam" up the sea of volcanic sand, fighting to reach the harder ground of the first plateau. There was, as yet, no fire against them. Kuribayashi's plan was holding up well; let them swarm onto the plain and then annihilate them.

The third wave, with 1,200 men, beached at 9:07 A.M., and five minutes later nearly 1,600 men came in on the fourth wave. Other waves of men were right behind, ready to fall on the shore almost as regularly as the surf. Kuribayashi's time had almost come. A desultory rattle of small-arms fire began to come from the nearest lines.

As strength ashore began to build, Colonel John R. Lanigan's 25th Regiment formed and started to move inland, turning to the right toward the Quarry. Colonel Walter Wensinger's 23rd moved straight in toward Airfield No. 1. Next to them to the south, Colonel Thomas A. Wornham's 27th Regiment drove inland to curve around west of the airfield. The 28th of Colonel Harry B. Liversedge raced straight ahead with three jobs: to cut across the narrowest part of the island, turn south to take Suribachi, and turn north to help take Airfield No. 1. The first of these jobs fell to the 28th's 1st Battalion, Lieutenant Colonel Jackson B. Butterfield; the second to the 2nd Battalion, Lieutenant Colonel Chandler W. Johnson; and the third to the 3rd Battalion, Lieutenant Colonel Charles E. Shapard, Jr.

Nearest Suribachi, Captain Osada's 312th Independent Infantry Battalion was waiting. Major Matsushita's 10th Independent Anti-Tank Battalion lay behind Yellow 1, in front of the slope leading to the main runway of Airfield No. 1. Just north of that, behind Yellow 2, was Captain Awatsu's 309th Independent Infantry Battalion. It is no longer possible to say how many were still alive, but of Matsushita's 300 men, 6 were alive when the battle ended. The 312th and the 309th had each started out about 800 strong. Of the 1,600 men, 42 survived the battle.

One of these was Superior Private Nosaro Fuji, thirty-one, a devout Buddhist. The rolling naval barrage struck the 309th squarely, and of the 40 men in his company, only 10 men were left at the end of one minute. Fuji had been fighting since 1936, and he longed to return to his candy store in the Town of Miyazaki on the island of Kyushu. He stumbled north, fleeing the barrage, and found a cave in the crook of the runways at Airfield No. 2. There he stayed for nineteen days, as the war passed over his head.

As the landing progressed, the 312th gave ground slowly toward Suribachi. They fought all day and well into the night. Nine men of the battalion, about one in a hundred, lived through the battle.

On the morning of February 19, Private Shigeru Yoshida did not go outside. There was nothing more he could do.

For nearly a year he had been working at the top of the terrace, overlooking the east beaches. Each day, as he was told, he had laid up stones to make ammunition pits and shelters in the ground. On this February morning, Private Yoshida stayed in his cave at the foot of Suribachi. Around him he spread his gas mask, ointment for mustard gas, and bleaching powder to clear gassed areas. He brewed tea near a fumarole and waited.

The first thirty minutes ashore were surprising. And occasional mortar shell burst on the beach, and there was a light haze of small-arms fire, almost like a breeze on the prairie.

Lieutenant Wesley C. Bates of the 28th scrambled to the top of the terrace and lay there, exhausted and sick to his stomach. The battle was not ten minutes old, and so far was like nothing he had been led to expect. The twenty-four-year-old Texan (he'd celebrated his birthday a month before) had the 2nd Platoon of C Company. To his right, he knew, was Second Lieutenant Fred J. Huckler, with the 1st Platoon, and to his left was (or should be) Lieutenant Frank J. Wright of Pittsburgh with the 1st Platoon of B Company. For a moment, Bates allowed himself to hope that the Japanese had secretly withdrawn from the island.

Sergeant Thorborn M. Thostenson and a corporal ran to the first pillbox. They threw three or four grenades, and the corporal ran inside. He came out with his bayonet dripping blood, trotted to a second pillbox, and jumped on top of it. Fire from another pillbox killed him. Bates' dream was shattered.

Leapfrogging forward in little bunches, the men began to pass the pillboxes, blowing some and bypassing others. The sun was getting hot, and so was the mortar and small-arms fire.

Private First Class John H. Henning, twenty, of Guthrie, Oklahoma, arrived out of breath. He'd been chasing his squad leader, Sergeant J. D. Dawson, twenty-five, of Odessa, Texas, across the island. When they came to a pillbox with no way around it, they went over it. ("There was nothing I could do about it," Henning said.) Private First Class Paul Adams had stuffed his field jacket in his pack— machine-gun fire chewed it off his back. Private First Class James B. Treadway, twenty-three, of Walnut Creek, California, had a bump on his head where a bullet had traveled right across his skull, in one side of his helmet and out the other.

Lieutenant Wright reached the western shore about 10:30 A.M. He had started as a platoon leader with sixty men. The only men still with him were Private First Class Remo Bechelli, twenty-six, of Detroit and Private First Class Lee H. Zuck, twenty-two, of Scranton, Arkansas. On the way across, Zuck had leaped to the top of a 20-mm. gun emplacement and killed eight Japanese, one after the other, as they ran out the back door.

Bates reached the shore at nearly the same time as Wright. It had taken just ninety minutes to cross the isthmus, but only four or five men remained with him. The island could not yet be called cut in half. Turning back to look for his platoon sergeant, Lewis G. Pickens, Bates walked erect with a rifle in his left hand, unaware for the moment of any opposition.

As he came in sight of his company, some less than 150 yards in from the landing beach, Bates waved for them to come on. They waved him back, and almost instantly he knew why. A machine gun to his left opened fire, and a bullet broke his left forearm. Even as he fell he thought, "Oh, oh, Purple Heart." Then he saw a private, beating his bleeding head against his rifle butt and eating sand. A corpsman was running to help the private, and that was all Bates remembered for a while.

When his head cleared, he got up and rallied some men near him. The fire was intense now, and the noise and detonation of big shells all around was nearly suffocating. The Lieutenant was afraid for a moment that they were cut off on the western side. But men were coming through, incredible though it was.

Gunnery Sergeant Harry L. Mowery crouched in a hole near the center of the island. As men passed in either direction, he found out what they knew and passed the information on to the next party. No wire men were out yet, and everything was word of mouth.

Bates slowly learned where his men were. Pickens was wounded, and Sergeant Michael R. Kost, leader of the third squad, was dead. His runner, Private First Class Francis R. De Wendt, Jr., was wounded, and Private First Class Lloyd Tudor, a quiet boy, had slowly bled to death from a leg wound. But still the men came on. Platoon Sergeant Jesse J. Sutfin came in with the remnants of A Company's third squad.

Captain Dwayne E. Mears of Bakersfield, California, had the idea that blockhouses could be attacked with pistols. Time after time he did it, smashing forward across the island. Just as he reached the west coast, a bullet pierced his throat and blood spurted out. He lay still, but a private began to cover him with sand. Bobo Mears cried, "Get the hell out of here! I'm all right." In the late afternoon they got him to a ship, but he died the next morning.

There was only one company commander of 1/28 left in action. Captain Aaron G. Wilkins had held A Company near the beach until the 2nd Battalion, massing for the assault toward Suribachi, was ready. Then Wilkins started his men for the west side. Driving across in high excitement, the men sometimes watched Tony Stein. He was twenty-four and had been at Guadalcanal, Bougainville, and Vella Lavella. For this one, he had a special weapon, a "stinger." Tony had been a toolmaker in North Dayton, Ohio, and had fashioned a hand machine gun from the wing gun of a wrecked Navy fighter.

He was the first man out when A Company moved, and he ran for a pillbox. Right behind him came Sergeant Merritt M. Savage, a demolitions expert, and Corporal Frederick J. Tabert. With only his stinger, Corporal Stein attacked one pillbox after another, Tabert and Savage close after him. In the first hour Stein killed at least twenty Japanese. Then he did a strange thing. He took off his helmet and shoes and ran for the beach to get more ammunition. He made eight trips in all that day, and twice his stinger was shot from his hands, but at the end of the day he was still firing it. As his Yugoslavian mother always said, "He's a tough one, that Tony."

Taking Suribachi had been drilled into 2/28 until they thought it would mean the end of the war, and they piled ashore on Green Beach with fierce determination. It was after 9:30 A.M., and the Japanese in the mountain had now recovered. Heavy mortar fire was falling, and the gunfire came in short, purposeful bursts—no target, no fire. Some LVT's made it to the beach, others barely got through the surf line, and none could climb the terraces. The men piled out and scrambled for cover, splayed flat against the terraces, in shell holes, and realizing, suddenly, that others were being hit. The beach was jammed with men, waiting, it seemed, for leadership—and then it came. Up the beach, erect and contemptuous of the fire, strode a short, fat man shouting "Okay, you bastards, let's get the hell off this beach!" It was the battalion commander, Lieutenant Colonel Chandler W. Johnson, and by the sheer force of his personality, the men were lifted off the beach and started inland for Suribachi.

Right behind Johnson ran the battalion adjutant, Second Lieutenant G. Greeley Wells, a map case bobbing at his belt. In the case, for a very good reason, was an American flag. At rehearsals, each officer stood and recited his duties, and Wells always ended with the phrase " . . . and I carry the flag." Johnson would growl, "Why?" and Wells would reply, "Because it says so here." It became something of a joke in the battalion. At Guam, just before the battalion transferred from the *Missoula* to its LST, Wells had gotten his flag from the transport's office, and he had it with him now.

Lieutenant Charles F. Suver climbed to the top of an LVT in the tank deck of LST 634. It was 5:30 A.M. and time to say Mass, for he was a Jesuit and a chaplain of the 2nd Battalion. Afterward, the men stood quietly near their vehicles, eating sandwiches and coffee, and Father Suver, in his Jesuit way, mused on the difference between courage and fearlessness. "A courageous man," he decided, "goes on fulfilling his duty despite the fear gnawing away inside. Many men are fearless, for many different reasons, but fewer are courageous. I hope I have courage, for I will never again be fearless." They went in with the ninth wave—Suver, Captain Arthur H. Naylor, Second Lieutenant George W. Haynes, and a lot of others. The chaplain remembered now that, some days before, Wells had said he was going to get a flag from the transport. Haynes said, "You get the flag and I'll get it up to the top of Suribachi." Father Suver added: "You get it up and I'll say Mass under it."

On the next beach to the north, Major John W. Antonelli took Companies E and F of 2/27 in over Red Beach 1 in the first waves. Private First Class Harold L. Pedersen, a machine gunner from Williston, North Dakota, had no trouble remembering the date, it was his twenty-second birthday. Thirty-eight days later he walked off the island, carrying the only gun left of the dozen his company started out with. He also carried thirty-eight days of beard and was a good deal older than twenty-two years and thirty-eight days.

The 1st Battalion of the 27th went into action alongside the 2nd, landing on Red 2, led by Lieutenant Colonel John A. Butler. But the confusion was beginning. Company B went in on the left of Company C, instead of the right. There was no time to rectify this, so Company A was thrown in where Company B should have been, and the battalion quickly advanced across the southern end of Airfield No. 1. En route, the regimental exec, Colonel Louis C. Plain, was shot in the arm but finished an inspection and report before being evacuated. Crossing the beach, unreeling wire as he ran, Corporal Robert M. Blankenship 3rd, of Company A, smiled to himself. He remembered his sergeant's last words as they boated up on LST 756. Goldblatt, who had been in every invasion, it seemed, turned to his men and said: "I'll kill the first son of a bitch that says 'This is it.'" No one did.

Leading a machine-gun platoon of 1/27 past the southern end of the airfield, heading for the west coast, was a big-eared Italian boy, handsome and dark. It was Manila John or, more formally, Gunner Sergeant John Basilone, and there were few things he liked better than soldiering. He never tried high school, but he did a hitch in the Army, and by 1940 was in the Marines. One night on Guadalcanal in October, 1942, he held off a Japanese assault with two machine guns and a pistol, hauling his own ammunition. His Medal of Honor was the first won by an enlisted marine in World War II, and now he was back doing what he liked best. "I'm a plain soldier. I want to stay one," he said, turning down a commission. Behind him was that afternoon in 1943, when 30,000 people turned out to honor him on Doris Duke's estate near his home in Raritan, New Jersey. He'd been kissed by a starlet, had his portrait unveiled in the town hall, and been given a $5,000 bond.

For Manila John there was now only one objective, the west coast, and he ran for it, his men behind him. It was barely 10:30 A.M. A mortar shell thudded and burst, and five men were dead, one of them Manila John. As he lay on his face, his arms sprawled in front of him, one could almost see the tattoo on his left arm—"Death Before Dishonor." The Navy Cross was awarded to him posthumously.

Navy Lieutenant Louis H. Valbracht, a Lutheran chaplain with the 27th Regiment, was amazed at the humor in men about to face death. On the way in, a private hung over the side of the landing craft, watching the shells splash all around. "Boy, what a place to go fishing," he said. "Look at those babies jump." Another kid cried in mock hysteria: "Someone lied to me. The natives on this island *ain't* friendly."

Running for the terrace when his boat beached, Valbracht met a corporal from the previous boat, limping back. Shrapnel had torn off one of his shoes and several toes.

"Short war, no?" he said. He limped past the chaplain and into a boat for the ride to a hospital ship.

As the 27th turned north beyond the airfield, it came up against Major Tatsumi's 311th Independent Infantry Battalion. Of the 700 men, half survived D-Day; 23 lived through the battle.

In the ships . . . it looked like a World Series broadcast; knots of men were gathered wherever they could find a radio.

"We're in 50 yards," said a marine sitting in a jeep on the deck of a transport. "Tanks are up a hundred yards," he called out a minute later, and the sailors cheered again.

In radio rooms on the warships, men on watch got only fragments of the battle.

"Let's have some naval gunfire in Target Area 181."

"Air observer Fifth Division reports six friendly tanks on southern end of Airfield No. 1. Have stopped there."

"Air observer Fourth Division reports enemy gun position in TA 166 C-D (the Quarry)."

"Mission 11, enemy gun and mortar positions in TA 183 W-Q-D (behind Quarry) will be attacked by bombs, rockets, and machine-gun fire as soon as possible. 305 Lucky (16 planes) will expend all ammunition on this attack."

"Three torpedo planes with propaganda leaflets are now orbiting Point Sugar awaiting instructions."

Over the aerial observer frequency, a lot of men heard Ray Dollings singing. The Major, spotting for the Fifth Division, sang:

> Oh what a beautiful morning,
> Oh what a beautiful day,
> I've got a terrible feeling,
> Everything's coming my way.

After a moment of silence, the plane spiraled from the sky and crashed in the water among the assault boats coming in. One of the boats picked up Major Dollins' body and that of his pilot. The major's first child, a daughter, had been born eight days before.

Halfway across the island, Valbracht sank down at the foot of a shattered pillbox. As he lit a cigarette, his eye fell on a foot—a bare white foot, all by itself. The chaplain turned his head slowly to the right. In a shell hole 20 yards away, lay the tangled remains of four marines, their uniforms still smoldering. One of them was missing a foot.

The Fourth Division's beaches were the hottest. Before the first boat touched down, General Cates, watching the bluffs through glasses from the rail of his transport, shook his head gravely. "If I knew," he said, "the name of the man on the extreme right of the right-hand squad of the right-hand company of 3/25 I'd recommend him for a medal right now."

Guns and mortars on the heights had had the range for weeks, but there was no fire at first. The leading wave landed without trouble. "There's something screwy here," said Corporal Leone (Frenchy) Olivier, remembering the first wave at Tarawa. 1/23 and 2/23 were across Yellow 1 and 2 without a shot. Then it began. Fire poured in from the front and the flanks, from pillboxes, ditches, and spider-traps. In front of the 23rd were two huge blockhouses and at least fifty pillboxes. The blockhouses were partly wrecked, but fire still came from them. Lieutenant Colonel Ralph Haas sent out the first call for artillery and tanks.

But Sergeant Darrell Cole of 1/23 wouldn't wait. He led his machine-gun squad against the pillboxes, firing into the slits as he passed. When his gun jammed, he ran behind the pillboxes, one after another, tossing grenades into them. Twice he ran back for more grenades, but on the third trip a Japanese grenade fell at his feet. Cole was killed instantly, but he had started his platoon off that murderous beach.

The day started off badly for Company A, 1/23. Captain John J. Kalen took them in on the third wave, landing over Yellow 1, and, almost immediately, his radioman was wounded. As the captain crawled toward him, he, too, was hit. His men, held in their holes by incessant fire, watched in agony for forty-five minutes as Kalen slowly bled to death.

Fifteen hundred yards offshore, Lieutenant Commander Robert L. Kalen, gunnery officer of the *Chester,* directed the cruiser's main-battery fire inland, trying to clear a path for the marines. It was not until a month later that he learned his brother had died before the battle was an hour old.

First Lieutenant William E. Worsham took over Company A, and the 2nd platoon made it 250 yards inland, the 3rd platoon holding up a hundred yards back. Machine-gun fire from pillboxes ahead made it impossible to advance, and Worsham decided to make a run to the left around Company B. A moment later he was killed, and First Lieutenant Frank S. Deyoe, Jr., platoon leader of the 60-mm. mortars, took over. A bullet drilled him through the left shoulder, but the maneuver began. First Lieutenant Arthur W. Zimmerman led the men around Company B and up toward Airfield No. 1.

A blockhouse stood in the way, and Zimmerman went back to the beach for a tank. It was obvious that nothing else would do. He coaxed the Sherman into position, and its 75-mm. gun opened fire at close range. As the blockhouse fell silent, Zimmerman's men rushed it with demolition charges, and the platoon rolled over it. Through the afternoon they pushed on, and toward nightfall paused near the airfield to regroup. Zimmerman knew Kalen was dead, but he had not seen Worsham all day. Through the twilight came a gaunt figure, his left arm dangling. It was Deyoe, still in action. "I just wanted to tell you," Deyoe said, "that you've been in command for two hours." Zimmerman, a twenty-five-year-old Montanan, veteran of Roi-Namur and Saipan, smiled wryly. "I'm glad to know it's legal," he said. Deyoe turned and headed back for the beach. What was left of Company A, with its fourth commander in one day, began tying in for the night.

Also dead somewhere on that first wild day, was the 23rd's Lieutenant Howard W. Johnson, the Fourth Division's football star. At Camp Maui they named the baseball field "Smiley Johnson Field" in his honor.

On the beaches, trouble began almost immediately. As the enemy fire rose, so did the surf. Within twenty minutes the beaches began to clog up as the LVT's bogged down or were hit. Then came the LCVP's and real trouble. The light boats hit the beach hard and the surf broke over them, broaching some and swamping others. Other boats, some already disabled, piled in behind them and were hurled onto the beach by the waves. If this kept up, the beaches would soon be impassable.

On Blue 1, farthest north under the cliff, 1/25 came ashore and scrambled to get off the beach. Lieutenant Colonel Hollis Mustain rallied the men, and they struck out for the airfield to circle around and take the top of the Quarry. This was the key move of the whole day. The heights must be captured to stop that terrible fire on the beaches. Early progress was surprisingly good.

Calls for tanks went out before the men had been ashore a half hour. The LSM's, far sooner than planned, were called in and three of them hit the Yellow Beaches soon after 10 A.M., landing sixteen Shermans for the Fourth Division. The Fifth Division sent its first tanks ashore in LCT's. Two of them made it, but the third fell into the water as a wave threw the landing craft off the beach. Lieutenant Henry Morgan radioed his superior: "Horrible Hank sank." The rest of the Fifth's tanks came in in LSM's. . . .

❧ ❧ ❧ ❧

JOHN LARDNER COVERED THE INVASION FOR THE *New Yorker* and wrote one of the fine D-Day stories. Having come ashore with Colonel Thomas A. Wornham's 27th Marines, Lardner was in the thick of fighting within a few moments of landing between fiery Red 1 and Red 2 at 9 A.M. We meet a superb reporter just as the sand shelves up under the bottom of his LVT, and Wornham growls, "All right, be ready to bail out of here goddam fast!"

·2· A CORRESPONDENT AT THE BATTLE

JOHN LARDNER

. . . The landing ramp slapped down on the beach and the passengers bustled out with their loads and disappeared behind the first low hummock in the sand. I was on the point of disembarking, second to last, just ahead of the Colonel, when I realized that I had forgotten my gear, and in the moment it took to turn and pick it/up piecemeal, Wornham whizzed by me and was gone. I slogged up the beach across one wind-made ridge and trench and then another. Loose, dark sand came up to the tops of my high combat boots at each step, and my breathing was sharp and painful. I made it to the third and deepest trench, some thirty yards in from the shore, and fell to my face there alongside Lee [Alwyn Lee, an Australian war correspondent] and several men of the command-post detail. When you stopped running or slogging, you became conscious of the whine and bang of mortar shells dropping and bursting near you. All up and down Red Beaches One and Two, men were lying in trenches like ours, listening to shells and digging or pressing their bodies closer into the sand around them.

We were legitimately pinned down for about forty minutes. That is to say, the mortar fire was probably heavy enough and close enough during that time to make it impractical to go farther. However, there is such a thing as wishful pinned-down thinking, and it can become a more dangerous state of mind than any other in an area that is being shelled. A man tends to cling to his trench, even if it is in the center of a target, when the sensible thing is to proceed out of the target as quickly as possible, using his own best judgment about when it's prudent to dive for cover again. It seems to take about twenty minutes under shellfire to adjust your nerves and evolve a working formula by which you can make progress and gauge, very roughly, the nearness of hits and the pattern of fire.

Lee and I, by agreement, finally left our gear in a trench near the shore (we planned to salvage it later, if possible) and worked our way up the beach in the wake of Wornham and his men. There were marines on all sides of us doing the same thing. Each man had a different method of progress. One, carbine in hand, walked along steadily, pausing and dropping to one kneee only when something about the sound of the shells seemed to confuse him. Another made a high-hurdling jump into every trench or hole he used. At one point I listened to a frail Nisei interpreter arguing with an officer who wanted to help carry his pack. Again, at a moment when Lee and I were catching our breath, something stirred beside the dune just behind us. A wounded man, his face blackened by sand and powder, had roused himself from the lethargy in which he lay and noticed us. Shell fragments had hit him in one arm, one leg, the buttocks, and one eye. His eye, a red circle in his dark-stained face, worried him most. He wanted to know if there were any medical corpsmen with a litter nearby. He had been so deafened by the explosion of the shell that I had to go very close to make him hear me. There were no corpsmen or litters about. In fact, the enemy fire on the beach made it hard to get help to wounded men for the first two days, and then the process of evacuating them in boats, which had to bump their way through a high surf, was incredibly rough and painful. I promised this man to report him and get him help as soon as possible.

The next marine we passed was dead, and so were a number of others on our diagonal course over the beach to the upland, but I didn't see a dead Japanese soldier until we got near the edge of the plateau. "That's the third one we've found on Red beach today so far," said a soldier who sat near the mouth of a Jap concrete pillbox, which gave off a faint, foul smell. This pillbox, with walls three feet thick and built on a frame of metal tubing, was a good specimen of the Jap defenses on Iwo Jima, but in the days that followed I saw others even more substantial, with walls four to five feet thick, revolving gun turrets, and two or more approaches lined with neat stairs.

It seemed clear, by the time we reached Wornham's command post, now at least several minutes old, in a broad shellhole above the beach, that the Japs had quickly abandoned the beaches, after losing a few men, and had taken most of their dead with them. This worried Wornham, because he figured that it meant heavy counterattacks in the next night or two, and he was also worried, as regimental commanders are everywhere in battle, by the problem of keeping his combat battalions in communication with each other and with him. Sitting in his shellhole, along with a couple of dozen staff men, medical officers, messengers, radio operators, and stray visitors who just wanted to be in a hole with other people, we followed, by radio and courier, the adventures of three battalions a few hundred yards away. The battalions were known in Wornham's shellhole by their commanders' names—Robbie, Tony, and Butler. "Tony says he's ready to make his turn up the west beach," Wornham said fretfully, looking at a message in his hand. "I gotta get him." Now and then he looked around his hole and said plaintively, "Come on, let's break this up. Let's have some room here." At these words, a few of the strays would drift away in one direction or another, and a few minutes later others would take their places. The shells dropped more rarely in that neighborhood, but they were close enough. Tanks began to rumble up from the beach, at long intervals, and angle and stutter their way through a gap at the top of the ridge nearby. Purple Heart Louis came to the edge of the command post and had his right arm bandaged by a doctor to whom we had already reported the position of the wounded marine on the beach. "I knew Louis would get it again," said a young captain. "Right where he deals the cards, too. I hope it will be a lesson to him."

We heard of death after death of men we had been with on the transport. One divisional surgeon had been killed and another had already had a breakdown from overwork. Visible Japanese dead were still scarce, even though one company had found a nest of Japs and killed a hundred. "Here's a report from F Company colonel, sir," said an aide. "He says the presence of a lot of flies in a trench suggests the Japs buried some dead there."

There were live Japs near enough, for whenever the Navy's Grumman fighter planes dived at a point just to our right, near the airfield, they drew machine-gun fire. Looking around, I had the leisure for the first time to think what a miserable piece of real estate Iwo Jima is. Later, when I had seen nearly all the island, I knew that there were no extenuating features. This place where thousands of men of two nations have been killed or wounded in less than three weeks' time has no water, few birds, no butterflies, no discernible animal life— nothing but sand and clay, humpbacked hills, stunted trees, knifeedged kuna grass in which mites who carry scrub typhus live, and a steady, dusty wind.

[Now] . . . Lee and I were ready to send our first dispatches. We decided that the only way to get them off quickly was to make for the flagship, several miles offshore. We did not feel very good about the prospect. The mortar fire on the beaches was as steady as ever and the surf was running higher than it had been in the morning. We reluctantly started down toward the shore, threading our way through a column of silent, apologetic-looking reinforcement troops, climbing uphill with boxes of ammunition from the beach. Occasionally a soldier stepped out of line and asked us if we knew where this column was bound. I don't know why the people going downhill inspired more confidence or looked better-informed than the leaders of the column moving uphill, unless it was that the very direction of our progress suggested that we were Iwo Jima tenants of long standing—five or six hours, perhaps—possessed of sweeping oracular powers and the ability to speak words that would restore confidence and banish fear and confusion. This was certainly untrue. Lee and I paused in a hole halfway down the beach to argue about where we had left our packs and typewriters. I thought it was somewhere to the left, but every time I pointed, a shell was dropped on the exact spot I had in mind. Shells were now also chasing amtracks, ducks, and other craft some little way out from the shore.

Lee said he thought we should head toward a place where we could see some boats bunching and where there might be a chance of our getting a ride. We started off, and a few minutes later we tumbled into a trench practically on top of our gear. There were a lot of men in this refuge now. Two Negro soldiers carrying supplies had stopped to give some water to a pair of marines who were lying quietly at one end. The marines had been hit by shrapnel and were waiting for litter bearers. After they drank the water, their only movement was a slight, mechanical stirring of their heads each time a shell burst close by. By now almost everyone on the beaches, even those not killed or wounded, had had some sort of direct contact with Japanese shells, if only to the extent of having tiny spent fragments, still burning hot, drop onto their clothing or into the sand right beside them.

By the time we reached a hole by the water's edge, near where we had landed, we had lost our sense of urgency and entered that stage, which comes after a certain amount of time in a shelled area, when you can no longer bring yourself to duck and run constantly, even when you are moving in the open. But the men in the boats along the shoreline immediately aroused us. Since they came into the fire zone only at intervals and remained as briefly as possible, they had no time to lose their awareness of danger. It suddenly seemed to us a matter of desperate importance to get out of there at once. An ammunition dump was beginning to grow up around us, and the shelling did not abate.

We went up to a boat whose ramp was slapping the waves a few feet out from the shoreline and whose coxswain was trying to hold her to shore by keeping her engine running. There we encountered a marine named Connell, who for the next half hour gave the most spectacular demonstration of energy I have ever seen. Though he moved with great speed and fervor, there seemed to be no fear in him. He had been helping moor and unload supply boats all afternoon. He was stripped down to his green Marine shorts, and he spent as much time in the water as out of it, his lank, blond hair plastered to his skull. When we wanted to salvage a piece of equipment from the water, he made a long, flat power dive over the surf. His problem at the moment was to make this boat fast, so that the ammunition aboard her could be unloaded. With the coxswain's permission, we got into the boat and stowed our packs in the stern. It was quickly obvious that the crew of the boat, though they remained calm, were of no help to Connell whatever and considered the odds against unloading at this time overwhelming and the situation irremediable. Connell shouted orders or suggestions at them, but they simply stared at him and then stared up and down the beach at the shellbursts. Connell got hold of a rope, made it fast to the boat, then darted up the beach to tie the other end to a tractor, whose driver surveyed him curiously from the top of the vehicle. Connell persuaded the driver to start his engine and try to pull the boat in. The rope broke. Connell tied it again and it broke again. He swam out to get another rope, but by the time he returned to the beach the driver and tractor had disappeared. Swimming furiously, he then approached Lee and me, at the stern of the boat, and called out the courteous suggestion that we get ashore. "This is going to take a long time," he shouted over the sound of the surf, "and you fellows will do better somewhere else!" He never once showed the slightest sign of temper or desperation. He appeared to regard the wild scene and his own mighty efforts and constant frustrations as wholly rational and what was to be expected. He was wrong about the boat's being there a long time. A few minutes after Lee and I swam and struggled to shore—Connell made three personal amphibious trips to help us with our gear—the boat withdrew to sea, with its cargo still aboard, possibly to try a landing somewhere else. The last we saw of Connell, he was racing down the beach to grasp a mooring rope on another boat thirty yards away.

※　※　※　※

THE 4TH DIVISION BEACHES BORE THE HEAVIEST casualties. On Red 1, the maelstrom of mortar and artillery shells engulfing them pinned down marines in an area of 200 yards. (Sherrod: "Many were squarely cut in half. Legs and arms lay 40 feet from any body. In one spot in the sand, far from the nearest cluster of dead, I saw a string of guts 15 feet long. Only legs were easy to identify.") One who survived this terrible carnage was Sergeant T. Grady Gallant of the 25th Marines, formerly of the 11th Marines, with whom we spent two days on Guadalcanal.

Sergeant Gallant was a squad leader whose job was setting up a 37-mm. gun. Unlike most who wrote of Iwo Jima, Gallant chose to tell his magnificent account in the third person.

·3· THE FRIENDLY DEAD

T. GRADY GALLANT

A sergeant of the line and his corporal scrambled up the bank and viewed the desolation of the first terrace. They saw no movement, friendly or enemy—no human body; yet they knew two earlier waves of men were before them; two thin lines of men, but by now probably merged into one twisted and curving strand stretched the length of the assault beach.

Behind the two Marine NCOs no landing boats were discharging, no assault line was approaching; no wave of landing craft was moving toward them. But along the beach, scattered in a random way, as accident and chance scatter machines, in the direction of Mount Suribachi were broken amphibious tractors, wrecked and riddled with holes, some overturned and smoking, others flooded and listing with waves breaking against them, splashing them and then running back into the deep.

Out to sea were clusters of boats milling about in twos and threes, and mostly heading out to sea, though some craft were adrift, tossed by the waves and dead in the water. In these wallowing boats and amphibious tractors, sailors bailed with helmets or prepared to abandon ship as the crippled vessels shipped water and slowly sank in the swells.

Standing close inshore was a battleship, its bow headed toward the volcano, its guns depressed and aimed at the barren mass where heavy coastal artillery was known to be emplaced. Smoke drifted from the mountain's sides and the winking of enemy gunfire was visible at every level.

The view toward the cliff, rising sharply above the sergeant and corporal, was grim, for the smooth beach gave way to rock formations that formed a maze that could be populated by hundreds of Japanese, though no living person was visible.

"It's too far to swim back," the corporal remarked, for the transports were fifteen miles out to sea and below the horizon, as a safety measure against the big guns on the mountain and cliff.

The sergeant did not reply but searched the beach again with his eyes, shocked by its emptiness, its grimy, garbage-pit-like landscape, and the dreariness of the ash heap upon which Marine equipment burned and the blood of marines drained in increasing torrents.

Nothing moved along the beach, and the sergeant saw no other men on the bank, or along the shore. This absence of human life in the midst of such fevered gunfire and explosions increased the grim unearthliness presented by the wrinkled terrain. Only the sea-wet beach, the tilted bank of gravel, the maniacal, glittering mountain and the seething pillars of smoke that rose from the burning flatland seemed to live. Yet, there was no doubt in the minds of the sergeant and the corporal that nearby there crawled and burrowed fellow marines—and that the enemy watched from ambush in narrow holes, from beneath rocks, and from prepared nests and bunkers and tunnel openings.

The corporal slid down from the top of the bank and rolled over on his back. He was a short thick-set man with eyes that were accustomed to the sun and the wind. Their corners were crinkled and etched with fine lines from squinting against glare and distance. These eyes had seen too much war, and before that they had seen too much hardship. They had grown hard with such scenes, and were cold and steady. And when the corporal laughed, the eyes did not grow warm and soft; they did not laugh.

The corporal struggled up on one elbow, his arm sinking into the soft, yielding soil he already hated. "We are by ourselves, by God," he said quietly, and began to push himself up to the top of the bank again, gravel pouring over his chest as he moved. At the top of the bank, he held his head low to the ground, his chin buried in the cinders, and studied the terrace ahead. "It looks pretty clean." He paused and stared a moment longer, turning his head very slowly from left to right. "Not a goddamned soul. Nothin'." He did not take his eyes from the terrain ahead as he spoke, but swept the area again. "You see anything?" he asked the sergeant.

The sergeant pushed to the top and looked. There was pock-marked gravel. Gravel tossed into mounds by high explosives that had formed shell holes which were cone-shaped, because of the looseness of the soil. The gravel was furrowed to form waves of dry earth. It was a sea of earth. Earth that was frozen into dry waves and troughs and swept by a storm of bullets, and whipped by shellfire.

"Nothin'," the sergeant replied quietly, for the scene was bleak and strangely depressing, as a cemetery is bleak and foreboding, even though it is filled with bodies and one is not alone.

The two marines considered the terrace for a few minutes. They continued to examine it, square foot by square foot, with their emotionless eyes. The terrace was a problem: Could it be crossed at this time? If crossed, what would be the gain? Should their lives be staked on crossing it . . . just to look over the next bank?

They turned the problem over within their minds, silently; neither had mentioned the problem. They searched—probed for the solution—without enthusiasm. They did not believe they would find a solution. There was no answer to such a problem. They knew they would cross the terrace, all the terraces, all the island—if they did not die somewhere in between. So, they examined the terrace and the problem it presented. They sought an answer—a *reasonable* answer—that did not exist.

In battle, when faced with such a problem, it is sometimes best to wait—attentively, patiently, and allow the problem to rock back and forth. After a while the problem fades away. Bigger problems with longer questions take their places. They keep the mind occupied. They are question about life and death, about whether to stand and move forward, or to sit and die there, on that particular spot, or to die over there on another rise of ground—or in between, on the flat place. Which would be best? There is no answer. The problem of life and death remains. It sits within the mind and rocks quietly back and forth as it has done from the moment of birth, but now, in battle, for the first time it weighs upon the mind.

The two marines tried to dig in midway up the bank in case mortar fire began to drop on the beach behind them, or above their heads at the edge of the bank. A depression in the gravel would help. It might mean the difference between life and death. The marines used their hands and feet, pushing the gravel away from their bodies, without standing. They were on their sides, digging in this way. But as they pushed and dug at the gravel, it poured back into the holes they made, drizzled into their pockets and shoes. It was quite impossible to dig a hole. The gravel was too slippery, too shifting and powder-light, too formless; it was a dry quicksand that sucked at anything touching it, filling every hole as soon as it was formed.

They quit.

"Let's look over the next bank," the sergeant said. "The line ought to be there . . . there ought to be contact there . . . over the next bank."

"Well," the corporal said.

They waited for a moment, then crawled up the bank, ran across the terrace it formed toward the sloping cinders of the second bank, crouching low and moving as fast as they could. They hit the second bank on their bellies, working their feet at the same time to push themselves to the top and look over.

The flat was the same in appearance as the one they had just crossed

—about as wide, fifteen or twenty feet, and walled by a third sloping bank farther inland.

The sergeant wiped the sweat from his chin with the back of his hand. "This is a hell of a place," he said, an edge to his voice. "Just nothin'."

The corporal held his hand close to his cheek and pointed with his index finger toward the third bank . . . pointed off to the right slightly. "There are some guys . . . see? To the right over there." He wiggled his finger around.

"Where?"

"There."

"Don't wiggle your goddamned finger . . . point."

The corporal grunted and shifted in the gravel. "Along that next bank . . . down at the bottom of it some. You blind? Along the bottom."

The sergeant gazed to the right front, following the bottom of the bank with his eyes. "Uh-huh," he said. "Ten or twelve or so. That's some of the second wave bunch, you think?"

"Twelve guys," the corporal said. "They act like they're down against mortar fire . . . but I don't see none."

"Pushed up pretty close to that dirt, ain't they?"

"I don't see no puffs ahead of 'em."

"Me either."

"But who knows?"

The marines ahead were pressed against the gravel. Their bodies against the bank, but they were not near the top of it. They were flat on their stomachs, heads down against the earth, faces into the ground.

"Must be hot there," the corporal said.

There were a few random bursts of mortar fire along the terrace directly to the front, but small shells.

"They are just catchin' their breath," the sergeant said.

The two marines watched, searching for movement among the men ahead.

The corporal lighted a cigarette, cupping it in his hand as he pulled on it, and blowing the smoke between himself and the ground to dissolve it in the air.

"Gimme a drag," the sergeant said.

"Why don't we get the dope from them? They ought to know where the line is."

The sergeant nodded, his head close to the earth as he took several fast drags from the cigarette. He handed it back.

They searched the second terrace carefully. It was fairly clear of mortar bursts. They made another dash, kicking up gravel as they moved. They dived and hit the third bank, joining the marines crouched against the shelter it offered.

The arrival brought no comment. No one moved or spoke. The twelve lay still, pressed against the ground . . . silent.

"You know . . . you know somethin'?" the corporal asked in a low, disturbed tone.

"What?" the sergeant asked, uneasy within himself at the voice, sensing nervousness in his companion.

"These guys is all dead!"

"The hell they are?" The sergeant raised up, looking over the corporal, who was nearest the men.

"The whole damned line of 'em," the corporal said. "Dead as hell."

The sergeant stared at the line of men. They were dead as hell. Little holes were stitched along their backs; small round holes in the cloth of their dungarees and in their combat packs.

"Automatic fire," the sergeant said.

"Killed while they was waitin' to move on," the corporal agreed.

It was obvious the squad had had no warning. They had been killed so quickly, so suddenly, every man had died in position. None had had time to turn, or roll, or scatter, or face the fire that had killed them. Now they lay as they had died, faces in the gravel, their bodies held up by the angle of the bank.

After a long pause, the sergeant took a deep breath and blew it out through his lips with a hissing sound. "The Japs let 'em pass," he said, "then shot hell out of 'em."

"An' you know what?" The corporal's voice was low, urgent. "They . . ."

"Yeah," the sergeant answered. "Yeah . . ."

They both rose, turned, waited a second to sweep the route with their eyes, then crouched and ran back . . . back to the first bank. After what seemed to be a very long time, they reached it, gasping for air, utterly exhausted, aching with fatigue and a sense of hopelessness.

"Hell of a thing," the corporal said, his chest heaving as he lay against the bank.

The sergeant rubbed sweat from his forehead with a gravel-spotted sleeve. He was silent. There was nothing to say; there was no answer. No answer that made any sense.

The sergeant and the corporal were the extremity of the right flank. The Japanese, invisible but very much alive, were to their own right, and to their front. But the marines did not know where the next man to their left was located, and they had not found marines ahead, other than the dead.

They moved off the bank and down the beach, toward Mount Suribachi, following the base of the bank, which gave some protection from the inland side of the island, but none from any other direction. They moved at a slow trot, holding carbines in their hands, and bent at the waist. After above one hundred fifty feet, they turned inland and climbed the bank.

"That looks good," the corporal said, indicating a shell hole with his carbine. The hole had been made by a bomb, or a battleship shell. It was cone-shaped and large enough for a half-dozen men. The NCOs moved over the bank and ran for the crater, dropping into it with a landslide of gravel that covered their shoes and ankles.

They looked about them. Two privates were seated on the opposite side, their knees drawn up under their chins, their M-1 rifles cradled under their right arms with the fixed bayonets plunged into the earth.

Neither private spoke. They stared at the new arrivals with an idle interest but without much attention.

"What's the situation?" the sergeant asked the younger of the two privates, who appeared to be not more than nineteen.

"We don't know," the boy said with a drawl. "It's a mess."

The corporal nodded. "You got the picture, lad."

They sat in silence. The corporal and sergeant lighted cigarettes. There was a sense of security. Occasional bullets kicked gravel into the hole, or hummed overhead. But these were comfortably outside. The tobacco burned with a delicate aroma; a good, rich smell of fresh, moist cigarettes—not dry and stale. The sergeant watched the end of his cigarette glow and cover itself with a light gray ash. He blew off the powdery substance, and the end glowed a cherry red. It was very comforting. He took two long drags, allowing the smoke to pour from his nostrils as he inhaled the second puff. It was very restful. This was a delightful place, he thought—very comfortable.

A corpsman appeared at the edge of the shell hole. Gravel poured down the sides in a stream, filling the bottom and rising along the bayonets stuck in the ground.

"We need a guy to help carry a stretcher," he announced to the group in general.

No one answered. The group remained seated, heads tilted back, looking up at the corpsman, seeing his face chin first under the helmet.

"We got three guys to carry it. We need one more."

No one said anything. "It's some photographer, an' he's shot up pretty bad."

The group in the shell hole sat.

"We got to move him to the beach. It won't take long . . . he ain't heavy."

"How far off is he?" one of the privates asked in a vague tone.

"He ain't far . . . just over here a ways. Hell, come on!"

"How far?" the corporal asked.

"Just over the next bank. It won't take three minutes to get him to the beach. He's got to be evacuated."

"He shouldn't of been takin' pictures this early in the day," the corporal observed. "Is he nuts?" He spat. "We ain't got the beach hardly yet. By God, we ain't connected up the line. That sonofabitch is out takin' pictures."

"Headquarters wants to know how it all looks," the sergeant said. "The bastards."

They ought to come out and see . . . they think we're a bunch of tourists, or somethin'?" The corporal was almost angry. His face was beet-red and he scowled at the corpsman.

"Aw, come on you guys, I ain't got all day," the corpsman shouted. "This ain't no discussion group. God damn it, I'll show you where he is. We could of got him by now. We can get him to the beach." The corpsman turned, causing another landslide into the shell hole, and left.

"If he comes back again, it'll bury us," the corporal growled, kicking gravel off his feet.

The older private got up and climbed out. There was another landslide. He disappeared in the direction taken by the corpsman.

"That's the kind of thing that gets you killed," the sergeant said. "It makes a good target."

"What?" the corporal grunted, shifting to allow gravel to fall from his lap. He rubbed his nose on his sleeve.

"You got a cold?" the sergeant asked.

"Naw. Just itch." He rubbed his nose again. "What makes a good target . . . you was sayin' somethin' about somethin' makin' a good target."

"Yeah."

"What, by God?"

"Stretchers bein' carried over open terrain like this. Makes a damned good target. Get picked off easy. Shoot the guy on the stretcher first, then start on the guys carryin' it."

"That's right." The corporal reflected on this. "I don't ever volunteer . . . too much like askin' for it . . . like sayin': 'Come an' get me . . . here I am standing here holdin' this goddamned stretcher.'"

"That's right," the private chimed in.

"It's the volunteer who gets it every time . . . turns out that way. You ever volunteered to help somebody? Don't do it. Somethin' goes wrong and the bastard will hate your guts the rest of your life . . . he'll be the first to turn on you. Never seen it to fail. People hate people who help people."

"They figure they're nuts," the sergeant said.

The corporal nodded. "They are."

"Uh-huh, they are," the private declared firmly.

"I get the works every time I volunteer for anything," the corporal emphasized with a sweeping gesture of his hand. Every time, without fail . . . an' you don't get no medals for it."

"That's right," the private nodded.

"You just get the short end of the stick."

"An' they let you hold it," the sergeant added.

"Yeah, they let you hold it on the damp end . . . you don't think they're goin' to hold it themselves, do you? That's why people hate people who are runnin' around doin' good . . . you know . . . helpin' hand out . . . they are always lookin' for somebody to do the work for them."

"Come to think of it, you're right," the private said. "They don't do nothin'—they get somebody else to do it. Like them blood drives . . . they get somebody else's blood, you know."

"Same way with them doughnuts and all that crap," the corporal said.

"Suckers . . . they're just lookin' for suckers."

The sergeant nodded. "They tell you not to halt and fool with the wounded, but they don't say what to do when you are already halted—but halted somewhere else."

"Volunteer," the corporal said.

"It's not the answer," the sergeant said firmly.

The three men sat. The shell hole was comfortable.

There was a crunching of gravel which amplified in the shell hole into sound of footsteps approaching. The corporal flicked off the safety of his carbine. Four marines carrying a stretcher passed along the edge of the shell hole. The occupants could see the man they carried: his profile, his stomach, his feet. His camera was on his stomach. He was holding it there with one hand.

"Must have been shot in the leg or somewhere," the corporal said.

"It ain't his stomach, or that camera would get ruined. Did you notice they was all in step?" the private asked. "Bouncing hell out of him. I wouldn't let that damned bunch carry me. They ought to be out of step, an' then he wouldn't bounce so much."

The little group disappeared from view.

"Let's take another look at the beach," the sergeant said. "We'll never get anywhere in here."

"They might drop one in here, anyway," the corporal said as he shifted to his feet.

"Come on," the sergeant said.

They looked over the side of the shell hole briefly, then climbed out and disappeared.

The private sat alone. A landslide of gravel poured into the hole. He spat, tilted his chin, and looked at the sky.

So they had run for the beach. Their investigations had come to very little: a visit with the friendly dead, a respite in a shell hole. They knew no more now than when they first jumped over the severed corpse and embraced the first bank of gravel.

How long had that been? How long ago? An hour ago, or less. Not long. The morning had just begun; yet, it had already lasted many lifetimes.

The sergeant and corporal slid down the bank to the beach, happy to have reached it, and found themselves in a small knot of marines. Three or four men; not more than a half dozen.

"Hey, Butler!" the corporal shouted, moving toward a dirty, wretched-looking Pfc, who was standing at the fringe of the group.

Butler was small, seemingly lost inside large dungarees. He peered at the new arrivals from beneath his helmet, his scraggly neck and protruding Adam's apply rising from the depths of his dungaree collar. His eyes squinted, deep-sunk and almost lost beneath long, tangle eyebrows which bordered on a thin bridge of a nose that extended into a flat expanse just above chapped lips cracked by the salt air. The nose had been skinned on the tip, and this injury was stuck with cinders—a decoration that did not enhance his appearance as a hero image.

Butler swung around. "What the hell?" he cried, moving quickly to join the sergeant and corporal. "You yardbirds lost?"

The corporal grinned.

Butler bummed a cigarette.

Only a few feet away were a dozen stretchers. Each occupied by a marine. Some were unconscious. But most of them were aware of their helplessness and lay quietly. A few smoked.

"What's this . . . an aid station. Hell of a place for one," the corporal inquired.

"Kind of," Butler said. "They're waitin' for an LST to haul 'em out. We ain't got nothin' . . . just beach . . . an' it ain't much, by God. This is the only place they can bring these guys. It sure ain't much . . . no cover."

"No cover anywheres," the corporal agreed.

Butler shook his head. It moved as a loose knob riding his dungaree collar, which was turned up and almost touching his ear lobes. "We just got a toe-hold on this place. It's hit the fan good."

"We'll be lucky as hell to secure this dump," the corporal said.

"You been shot?" the sergeant asked, pointing to his bandage hand.

"Aw, naw! Not that lucky . . . I got cut. Divin'. Dove in a shell hole and they was a piece of metal, shrapnel, I guess, in it . . . I kinda swan dove in that hole. An' I hit my hand on that metal. But it ain't much of a cut. Not deep, or nothin'. I was helpin' them corpsmen lug back a stretcher"—he nodded his head toward the stretcher—"after I done it . . . after I cut my hand . . . an' I bummed a field bandage. I didn't want to open mine up . . . forgot to steal some toilet paper out on board ship, an' I might need some in a day or two, I guess."

"It may be a week, if we don't move faster than this . . . all the holes is occupied," the corporal said.

"Nothin' is organized," the sergeant said.

"The corps ain't every organized," Butler agreed. "Looks like at a time like this, they could get organized."

"Sure does," the corporal nodded.

"You guys hear about Doc?"

"Hell no," the sergeant said.

"He got it."

"Aw, naw?" the corporal breathed in a shocked tone. "You don't say so?"

"Yeah, I do," Butler emphasized.

"He's dead?" the sergeant asked.

"As a bottle of stale beer," Butler replied in a matter-of-fact voice.

The doctor had come in on the same tank lighter with these three men. It was his first assault landing. He was talkative. Uneasy, but not worried about what was to come. He had explained it all to these three marines. He had figured it out. The Japanese, he had said, wouldn't shoot a doctor. They were a fine people who had been misled by a dominant military clique in Japan. The Japanese people themselves really didn't realize what had been done to them by their war lords. The doctor said he felt sorry for the Japanese people, but not for the war lords who had misled them.

The three marines had listened attentively.

Anyway, the doctor had told them, he would be busy on the beach. He would do what he could for the wounded. It wouldn't be much different, really, from work he had been doing as an intern in the emergency room of the hospital: minor wounds, severe wounds—people torn up by automobiles, fights, and shootings. He said he had seen it all. He worked on all kinds: the clean and the dirty, drunks, drys, and the insane. This would about be the same, except every one of his patients would be sober.

The three marines had laughed at this. And the four of them had smoked and talked as the landing craft pushed its way to Iwo Jima.

The doctor told them he had married just before shipping overseas. His wife was a nurse and was still working in a hospital—gave her something to do while he was gone, he said. The extra money helped some, too. Anyway, she wanted to.

He laughed about his wedding. It had been a small affair at his mother's house. She lived on a farm. Lots of beef cattle, the doctor said—and the place was pretty far out of town, off on a country road from the main highway. The wedding party had gotten lost . . . some of it had: the preacher, best man, and a couple of friends of his wife. He and the bride had been left standing at the altar for a while. He enjoyed telling about that, and he told the story well. The three marines could picture it all, and they listened with close attention.

The delay had been rough, he said, because he just had a seventy-two-hour pass . . . and he knew he was going overseas. Time was important. But only a couple of hours had been lost, and after the brief honeymoon, he left his bride. Now he was here.

He told these things without having seen these three marines before. But they knew his mind and heart were back home. They listened and nodded at the right places. They laughed with him as he drew closer all the things he knew and loved and wanted so much. Without really knowing it—or, possibly, knowing it, but not realizing that they knew it, too—he reached across all those thousands of miles of sea and land and touched all those things so precious to him: his mother's house, his bride, the hospital, and all the things he knew and loved and that had been good to him in his life. These memories sustained him. The three marines shared in them.

That's why the news blurted out by Butler had shocked the corporal and the sergeant. Doc had been a friend. Now they carried his memories for him. Maybe that is why he had talked about all those things to them: he wanted to give those memories to someone for safe keeping, just in case, so he gave his memories to these three marines, and they kept them for him.

"He got shot?" the corporal asked.

"Artillery, about the time we hit the beach," Butler said. He moved closer to his friends. "I seen it . . . well, I almost seen it." He turned slightly to his right and pointed. "See that beached wreck? . . . that Jap barge, or whatever it is?"

"Uh-huh," the corporal grunted.

The hulk was a much bombed vessel about the size of an ocean-going tug.

"He was standin' near that. Gettin' ready to set up his stuff, I guess."

"That's right . . . that's what he'd be doin'," the sergeant interrupted.

"I was about here, right where we are now . . . oh, maybe a little farther away . . . six or eight feet, or so. But I was lookin' toward that wreck. Wasn't lookin' at Doc. Not at him . . . but, you know, I knowed he was there. I was kinda lookin' over that wreck. I had just looked at him, then looked on past. You know how you do when you ain't payin' much attention to any particular thing?"

The three of them stood and looked at the Jap wreck in silence. There wasn't much to see. It was a small craft chewed by bombs and shells. It tilted on its portside, stern in the surf.

The corporal cleared his throat. "What happened?"

Butler touched the tip of his nose with the tip of his index finger, feeling carefully with little pats of the fingertip. "This bleedin'? . . . feels wettish."

"Naw, looks good," the sergeant said impatiently. "Don't mess with it. You'll get it infected with them filthy hands. It's coated with a bunch of stuff . . . cinders and blood, it looks like."

"Feels funny as hell . . . rough and numb."

"Them cinders," the corporal assured Butler.

"Looks good," the sergeant repeated.

"I always get skinned up," Butler said with some disgust. "When I was a kid, I always had skinned knees and stubbed toes and cut heels and tore fingers. I was bleedin' all the time . . . a damned walkin' skinned place."

"You're okay now," the sergeant advised him.

"Wonder I didn't kill my fool self. Into somethin' *all* the time."

"You look good now," the corporal said without conviction.

"When I was just in the second grade I stepped on a rusty nail. It was one of them long finishin' nails, an' I hit it runnin'. It was hell pullin' it out, but I done it as a matter of manhood . . . hopped to the tool shed and got a pair of pliers an' clamped down in it . . . by God, it was jammed right even with the sole of my foot and poking out the top of it . . . drove clear through. I got them pliers and clamped down . . . I could just get a holt . . . counted to three an' yanked like hell . . . and out it come. I was a dumb bastard—but brave, by God."

"I'm touched as hell," the corporal growled. "But I ain't interested in your lousy knees and feet." He paused to allow this to sink in, but Butler was still feeling gently about the clump of cinders on the tip of his nose and seemed to miss the implication of the corporal's remark. "You said you was lookin' at Doc when he got it . . . now, by God, what happened?"

"Nothin' much. Hell, it was over quick. Like I said, I was kinda lookin' past him, an' there was this blast. I jumped and swan dove to the deck. It was pretty loud . . . an' close, it seemed to me. I thought I'd had it."

Butler cleared his throat and spat. He coughed and snorted. Several drawn-out gurgles were climaxed with more spitting. He covered the results with the toe of his shoe, and pressed down until gravel covered the tip, and swung his heel back and forth. "Sounded bigger than a mortar . . . wasn't that. Must have been an artillery shell, one of them guns on the mountain. The angle is about right. It wasn't no mortar shell. Too much noise and smoke."

He paused.

The sergeant and corporal were disgusted with the narration, but said nothing.

"Well, I seen it landed near Doc. When I swan dove, I remember thinkin' it was mighty near Doc. I thought: By God, that's mighty near Doc. It flashed through my mind that way. Mighty near Doc, I thought."

He fell silent while he explored the tip of his nose. He tapped the skinned place with the knuckle of his index finger. Then he wiped the side of his nose with the back of his hand. "The smoke was pretty thick at first . . . when it first happened . . . but was blowin' out right fast. By the time I got off the deck and got movin', it was pretty well cleared out."

"Was he alive when you got there?" the sergeant asked.

Butler spat. "He was easin' on in when I come up. He didn't know nothin'. Concussion slapped him good. Best thing that could of happened . . . knocked him out. An' he was dyin' . . . if he had to get it . . . it was the best way . . . didn't know it."

"Was he tore up?" the corporal asked.

"Bad."

"Damn," the sergeant said.

"Head?"

"Oh, naw. His head was still on. It was his legs."

"Legs?"

"Blowed off. He didn't have no legs from the knees down. Cut clean off. An' he had it in the guts, too."

The corporal grunted. "Cut off . . . goddamned shame."

"He didn't know it," Butler assured them.

"What the hell can a doctor do on an assault wave in the first place?" the sergeant asked. "He can't do a damn thing."

"Nothin' I can't do," Butler agreed. "Give 'em a shot and slap on a bandage."

"Doc could have waited aboard ship for a while, then come in," the corporal said. "It'd done more good."

"His orders didn't read that way," Butler reminded him. "He didn't have nothin' to do with it. Just like us. We don't have nothin' to do with it . . . we ain't done nothin' . . ."

"'Cept get shot at," the corporal said.

"Hell, we can't get off the beach. Everybody is holed up . . . them Japs can see every move we make . . . this place ain't goin' to be so healthy in a few minutes . . . too many damned people." Butler waved his arm in a half circle.

"Well, it's too bad about Doc," the corporal said softly.

Butler nodded. "I'll never forget it . . . like that damn nail in my foot . . . pullin' it out, an' . . ."

"We better shove off," the sergeant said. "We better get back where we were."

"Okay," the corporal agreed. "Butler, we're just down here a ways . . . toward them rocks. We'll see you . . . keep your nose clean."

While they had been talking—not more than two or three minutes—
a steady flow of stretchers had been brought to the beach and placed
alongside the ones awaiting evacuation. As the two marines started
to trot down the smooth, narrow path that separated the water's edge
from the first bank, they suddenly found themselves jumping over
stretchers. They were involved in a maze before they knew it. They
couldn't stop their forward motion without falling over one of the
wounded men. They tried to dodge, but each jump and turn brought
them into contact with another of the wounded. They jumped over
some of them, drizzling gravel on their bodies.

"Hell, boys, we didn't see you," the corporal shouted, twisting and
leaping through the rows of stretchers. The sergeant was doing the
same. They cleared the area without tripping and moved back to
their original spot on the bank. They crawled to the top and looked
over, noticing shell fire was much heavier on the first terrace. Bursts
were flowering in widely scattered sections, raking the place with
a rain of explosions.

"They are about to pin us down," the corporal observed. "We are
goin' to play hell takin' this lousy, stinkin' place."

The sergeant made no reply. He didn't want to think about it . . .
and he prayed the enemy would not work the bank with artillery.
He felt naked and alone. He was afraid and frustrated . . . and a feeling of helplessness and horror descended upon him. He had been
on Iwo Jima less than two hours. Less than twenty feet inland was
under Marine control . . . his control and the corporal's control . . . in
this particular place. The enemy was firing from both flanks—from
the front—and from above. Just ahead walked bursts of artillery fire.

The sergeant closed his eyes tightly. You are in a hell of a mess,
he thought. A hell of a mess. Somewhere deep inside—inside his brain
somewhere, wherever that voice is that talks when one is alone and
in deep trouble—in that inner room of the mind, from that dark,
mysterious place, the voice said to him: "Carnage."

The word, just that one word, nothing else, formed inside his mind
as clearly and precisely as a word is formed on a printed page. The
word repeated itself, and the sergeant listened in astonishment, for
the whole thing was an involuntary act, and a feeling of that word—
its presence; a feeling of that word being there, as the presence of
danger, or death, is felt.

The voice said nothing else. And the word, which had filled his
mind with such clear, definitive splendor, suddenly was gone. It was
such a strange thing. An event of only an instant. An accidental
glimpse of the mind making an effort to label all the messages of
horror and terror and danger it had received in its dark prison.

It had searched within the cluttered files of memory contained in the chemistry of its own living cells and in some mysterious way—without conscious effort or thought—the precise word was found. The exact word that told all that was happening on this morning at this miserable place. There was no other word for it. This was the right word. And the word was *carnage*.

The first enemy artillery shell to miss the terrace and strike the beach in this sector crashed just beyond the stretchers. It was not a large-caliber shell. Its blast did not tear the ground and throw cinders high into the air. It snarled as it drew near, then barked with a shrill, sharp noise and ripped itself to pieces, flinging metallic razors of burning steel through the air.

A small puff of dirty-gray smoke marked the point of impact. Smoke drifted close to the ground toward the sea, slowly fading into bluish wisps as it moved over the rippling surf.

"See that?" the corporal grunted.

"Small," the sergeant answered. "Didn't kick much of a hole."

"Maybe it's just off register. Maybe it was supposed to hit the terrace and missed."

"We can move up a terrace . . . we can move up with them bodies, if it gets too hot here."

There was a rain of shells on the first terrace.

The two marines watched. "We can damn well try," the sergeant said. "We can't stay here if they work over the beach."

They waited to see if another shell hit the beach. Another one did.

The second artillery shell struck among the wounded. It struck the gravel between two rows of stretchers. Gravel rose several feet into the air and rained down upon the wounded. It was a larger-caliber shell. The noise was sharper, louder.

"Oh, God!" the corporal moaned.

The sergeant could say nothing. He stared in horror. He felt desperate, trapped, as an animal must feel as the hunter approaches step by step to finish the chase, to end the hunt, to bleed the flesh and drain it—to extinguish that mysterious spark that marks life and separates it from clay.

Shells now arrived one after another, sighing at their work, slamming great metal doors, venting smoke, crashing and flinging bits and parts over the heads of the men. The shells beat against the beach. Gravel pattered over the silent, strangely motionless bodies of the wounded, who lay on their backs facing the sky.

As the shells burst, as they crashed and shrieked, one of the wounded rose from his stretcher. He rose slowly, bending at the waist. His head was bare and his arms were straight and rigid at his sides. He sat up, his legs straight in front of him, his hands gripping the two stretcher poles, his arms as two tent stakes at the sides of his body. The knuckles of his hands . . . the bones of his hands . . . almost cut through the skin.

He sat upright and tilted his chin upward, tilted it high, so that the flesh of his neck pulled taut from the chin all the way down to his shoulders and chest. The tendons of his neck were ropes tugging near their breaking point. The Adam's apple pressed out the skin as if it would tear through it.

He sat this way. Shells bursting all around him. Then he opened his mouth as wide as he could. His eyes were staring and fixed upon the sky, his forehead deeply furrowed and his eyebrows lifted, pulling at his eyelids, almost.

He sat this way—taut and stiff and straining every muscle of his body. He sat, his mouth wide open, stretched white at the sides . . . and screamed . . . and screamed . . . and screamed.

"Oh, my God, my God . . . Great God Almighty!" the corporal sobbed into the dirt. And the lips of the sergeant echoed the words, "My God . . . My God!"

The screams followed one after the other. They filled the minds of the sergeant and the corporal. The screams ran madly into their skulls, echoing in great gushes of sound. The two men clamped their teeth, as if to shut out the sound that way. But the animal shrieks seemed to run as blood into their eyes, blinding them, and filling their being with horror.

A shell exploded at the foot of the stretcher, boiling in the sand between the stretcher poles, flinging smoke and dirt and bits of metal into the screaming face. But the wounded man did not fall back, or die. He sat there, upright and rigid, his head tilted far, far back between his shoulders, his chin aimed at the sky, his mouth wide open, screaming.

The wind moved his hair as it blew on him. He faced into the wind, his eyes closed tightly, his teeth bared and white in the sun that was upon him. And another shell burst in almost exactly the same place on the sand at the foot of his stretcher, between the stretcher poles. But he did not fall.

"Why don't he fall?" the corporal asked. "Why don't he get killed? What's the matter with the sonofabitch? Goddamned."

"That stuff must be goin' straight up and not spreadin' out much until it gets pretty high," the sergeant replied. "If it wasn't, he'd be cut in half by now." But he didn't know why he wasn't dead, why he didn't die.

The sergeant and corporal wanted the man to die, quickly. But he wouldn't. He wouldn't die. He screamed and screamed. He screamed as he sat there surrounded by wounded men lying on their stretchers and getting killed by shell bursts. He was the only one sitting up. But he wouldn't die. He sat there and screamed.

The sergeant and corporal began to get angry with him and to hate him. It was a passionate and deep hatred that seared their souls and blinded them, for the wounded man sitting there compounded the slaughter before them . . . a butchery they could not halt. The screams cut deeply and hurt, and they began to hate him with a boiling, raging hate.

He made too much noise.

Why couldn't he lie quietly . . . like the others? Why did he have to sit up like a fool and scream like a madman? Oh no, he couldn't do that. It was too easy. Too civilized. He filled the air with screams. And they hated him for it.

The bastard should be dead . . . and quiet. He wasn't. He defied all logic, all reason. He defied civilization. He was loud and persistent and long lived and alive with the shells bursting around him, evil bouquets of smeared orange-red flame.

He sat there.

The sergeant and corporal glared at him through the smoke and flame of shell bursts and hated him. They cursed long, foul strings of rotten words, but they did not curse him. They hated what he stood for—the helplessness. He stood for that, and he would not be quiet about it. The sergeant and corporal did not understand him. He was not real or normal. He would not die, or shut up, or fall over. He sat there on his damned little stretcher with shells bursting all around him, and screamed.

The shells continued to land, one after another. The dirt and cinders, black pellets the size of buckshot, flew in his face, coating it with volcanic grime, blinding him. He looked neither right nor left. He faced inland toward the slanting bank, head far back between his shoulders . . . screaming. He screamed with an animal howl, a primordial sound, hoarse, wild bellows and shrieks that followed each other in an endless chain and filled the air with livid, raw bloody claws of sheer terror.

He seemed indestructible. Nothing could kill him. He would sit there for eternity wild and screaming, alone in hell, framed by stretchers, lighted by flames of burning wreckage on the beach, and shells bursting all around him; shells opening to bloom poisonously then to rot in a second into a swirl of unclean vapor.

None of the other wounded ever sat up. He was the only one. The others knew that to sit up was to invite certain death—just as they knew to lie there was to die. But knowing they were certain to die, they did not sit up, or scream.

But he sat as the center of a rough circle, a jagged circle filled with living and dying flesh, howling and bellowing as the shells threw cinders in his face, and on the bodies around him.

Finally, reluctantly . . . slowly . . . he fell backward. He was not dead . . . not yet; he had been struck down and he stopped screaming as he fell, but he was not dead. He lay on the canvas, moving his head from side to side, very slowly, very painfully, very deliberately in agonizing effort. All the while the shells slammed and puffed, falling within the circle of stretchers, never going over them, never falling short, but always there, always among them.

Then, once again, he struggled upward. Fighting his way. Falling back . . . then moving an inch at a time . . . blind and soiled with blood and dirt . . . slowly he lifted himself. He got upright again. Sometimes framed by bursts in front and behind him, sometimes obscured by debris, he sat with his legs straight in front of him . . . as they had been before. He cried out again. Long guttural sounds and sobs and choking moans . . . strangling sounds, liquid, sickening gurgles of sound chopped to pieces by the noise of the shells . . . came from deep inside him. Inhuman, wild, animal cries wracked him.

He swayed, dropped his chin to his chest, still upright. While obscured by a blast, he straightened his back, lifting his chin to the sky as smoke drifted around him—around his shoulders and head as if he were smoldering with some hidden fire—and when the fumes cleared, he was wide-mouthed, his teeth showing and the skin of his lips stretched as hide is stretched to dry. As the shells pelted him with cinders and metal, his elbows bent slightly . . . then more and more . . . and he fell with great deliberation, appearing to shrink and dissolve into the canvas of his stretcher. He fell on his right shoulder, rolling to his back, and was still and quiet on the coarse cloth—all of him, even his hands.

He had died and no longer moved. He was quiet and still and the battle was no longer his battle. Others had died with him. He had screamed for them all. The others had died quietly, but he had protested; he had been their advocate. He had argued their cause, and had protested the injustice, the cruelty, and the helplessness of the trial they had undergone.

He had lost.

They had all died with dirt in their faces, between the land and the sea. They had died as amphibious creatures die: not far inland, not far from the sea.

And now in the swirl of the sea fifty feet or more from shore, where it had been dumped from a tank lighter, there stood a 37-mm antitank gun, waves breaking over its muzzle and its wheels bogged in the sand.

Eight marines gathered around it. While two men lifted the weapon's trail, the other six cursed, pushed, and heaved against the sluggish wheels weighted by the steel that was the gun, and fought against the ocean for its possession. Waves beat against their abdomens, striking their ammunition belts with flat slaps, flinging brine into their eyes as their heavy shoes sank into the slush of the sea floor. They cursed and grunted and strained against the stubborn metal sunk in the sea, mired in the tenacious paste of cinders, sand, and volcanic ash. They slipped and fell, rammed their feet into the muck, and fought the gun, the undertow, the waves, and the grasping, clinging, sucking glue of the bottom.

The gun moved slowly, an inch . . . two inches . . . at a time, and as the men goddamned the weapon, fell and clawed against the awkward, silly contraption, it moved—and bit by bit they drew it from the sea.

The Battle of Iwo Jima had been in progress for one hour and forty-seven minutes. It was 10:47 A.M. when the eight wet and panting marines hauled the weapon on to the beach, dropped its dripping trail to the earth and fell, gasping for breath, against the first bank to recover from the task. Down the beach they noticed corpsmen moving stretchers, sorting them for some reason. Otherwise, there was very little activity visible. As they watched, an occasional landing craft would slowly poke its way through the burning wreckage of earlier machines, but there was a lull, and the beach was almost deserted.

A lieutenant colonel approached. He was armed with a .45-caliber pistol and was smoking a cigarette. Rather stocky in build, his stomach caused the pistol belt to sag beneath it and served as an undergirding for the paunch which forced itself against his dungarees. He stood near the water's edge and stared at the cliff.

In a few minutes, as the lieutenant colonel studied the terrain he was joined by a second lieutenant, who carried a carbine and who was soaking wet, his dungarees covered with cinders that had stuck to the wet cloth. The lieutenant, his face a dull, burned red, fumbled inside a back pocket, finally withdrawing a plug of chewing tobacco. He carefully pulled the wrapping from one end, bit off a chew, and restored the plug to the pocket.

"Get that gun up on that terrace," the lieutenant colonel said, "and lay down some fire toward that cliff." He pointed vaguely toward the towering elevation.

The second lieutenant spat quietly, turning his head and splashing the juice into the surf.

"Any particular place?" he asked, staring at the cliffside, searching for enemy emplacements. He saw none.

"No," the lieutenant colonel said. "The Japs are there, and to the front, but you can do better firing at the cliff. These banks cut you off to the front."

The second lieutenant motioned to a platoon sergeant on the bank. The marine trotted over. "Move that gun up on that first terrace and have them lay down some fire on the cliff . . . along the side of it."

"Any particular area?" the platoon sergeant asked, searching the cliff.

"No," the second lieutenant said. "Shoot at the cliff."

The platoon sergeant returned to the bank. "Get this gun on this first terrace and open fire on that cliff," he told the eight men who had dragged the weapon from the sea.

"Any special target?" the buck sergeant asked, pushing his helmet back on his head and looking up at the cliff.

"No," the platoon sergeant said. "Just shoot at the goddamned thing. You're bound to hit it."

"I don't think this gun will knock it down, though," the buck sergeant said. "It would be better to shoot at some target on it."

"Have you seen anything to shoot at on it?"

The buck sergeant shook his head. "No."

"Well, then . . . neither has anybody else around here. The bastards are dug in and covered up. Shoot at the cliff and maybe you'll hit something."

The buck sergeant motioned for his men. They got up and met him at the gun. "Get this thing up on that terrace," he said.

Two marines picked up the trail of the weapon. The other six gathered around it, finding places at the shield and muzzle.

"It'll have to go up trail first," the sergeant said. "That bank's too steep to go muzzle first . . . it'd plow into the dirt."

The men swung the gun around, pointing the trail toward the bank.

The buck sergeant grabbed the ring on the end of the trail. "Ready?" he asked. "All right, let's go." They pushed. The wheels hit the bank, sank into the gravel. The trail was elevated and the gun muzzle touched the beach. They pushed. The gun was immobile.

"This ain't goin' up thisaway," a private puffed from his position at the gun's shield.

The buck sergeant said, "Try it again . . . ready? . . . heave!"

The men pushed and pulled. The gun remained motionless.

"Once more . . . ready? . . . heave . . . push . . . push . . . push, goddamit." The men struggled, gradually going to their knees as the cinders gave way beneath them, covering their legs.

"Ease off," the sergeant said.

The men relaxed, breathing heavily.

The sergeant stared down the beach as he squatted by the tip of the gun trail.

The driver of the amphibious tractor considered himself lucky after he had unloaded and had had a chance to take a quick glance inland. He had been too busy until now, and he looked around a little before he headed back out to sea. The island was a mess. Desolate and dead-looking. Here and there he could see clusters of marines in shell holes or pressed against the banks, but there weren't many. Their few numbers served only to make the desolation more keenly felt.

The driver glanced toward the mountain. He could see the enemy muzzle blasts, and, lower—near the base of the mountain—he saw the liquid stream of a flamethrower spurting thick, black smoke at a target beyond his vision. But mostly he saw only a sea of cinders pockmarked and dotted with bursting shells. He couldn't hear the explosions because of the noise the tractor made. He was glad of this, in a way, because shell bursts were not as terrifying when they were noiseless.

He glanced at the shore. Too much wreckage to get out here. He'd have to drive down the beach and go around it. He gunned his engine. It sounded fine. He rolled down the beach toward the cliff, moving at a brisk clip and bouncing a little in his seat when the treads hit rough sand. He cleared the wreckage and took one last look inland as he edged toward the surf. His eye caught a group of marines against the bank by an artillery piece. One of them was waving his arms over his head, then bringing them down, pointing at the gun. The driver slowed and brought the tractor to a halt. A marine detached himself from the group and ran toward him. The driver let the engine idle, and leaned over the side of the vehicle.

The marine began shouting something before he reached the tractor. The driver shook his head, cupping a hand to his ear to show he couldn't hear the words. The marine trotted closer and shouted again. The driver nodded vigorously. They needed help getting the gun up the bank. He grinned. It would be nothing . . . easy . . . and would take only a minute. He turned, going into the surf a little way, then backing toward the gun. As he backed, he saw the marines swinging the weapon around, and holding the trail up so it could be attached to the tractor.

He backed right up to them and they had the gun hooked up in a second.

"Where to?" he yelled.

A buck sergeant came up and shouted: "On the terrace . . . get it up the bank for us, and we'll unhook it."

The driver nodded his head up and down, gunned his engine to get everyone clear, then moved in a wide circle to get headed straight into the bank. He gunned the engine and watched the front of the tractor rise as the treads moved the machine up the incline. Then the front dropped, jolting the driver as the forward treads struck the earth and the machine was level again. He swung the machine parallel to the next bank and stopped. In a minute the sergeant appeared again. "Thanks," he shouted. The driver nodded and grinned down at the marine as the tractor began to move again.

As the tractor moved along the first terrace, the driver saw a narrow road that curved inland just beyond the first terrace. He headed for it. He could get on the road and turn around on it. It would be easier, and there would be less chance of getting stuck during the turning process. He headed for the narrow, dirt road. As soon as he could turn around, he would head back out to sea. Ahead he saw a puff of smoke, then another. That damned artillery, he thought. He shook his head. It was odd, in a way, but he had never been afraid a shell would drop in his tractor. He just didn't consider it possible . . . oh, of course, it *was* possible, but, hell, it would have to be one chance in a million. It would be pretty hard to sit way off somewhere and drop a shell into a moving vehicle, even a pretty big one, like an amphibious tractor.

So, the puffs of smoke didn't worry him. He headed for the road. When he felt the treads grip the clay, he swung the machine and headed inland, down the road. He needed a little room to turn, and just ahead he saw a good spot. The road was a little wider there, and the cinders along the side were fairly smooth. That would be the spot. He'd turn around there.

The sergeant waved as the tractor moved off, then turned to his men. "Let's get it out from that bank, an' move it where we can see what we are doin' . . . the piece is too near that bank to swing the muzzle."

He lifted the trail, and the men began to push the gun. It moved slowly in the loose soil, getting stuck frequently . . . every foot or so . . . requiring maximum effort on the part of the marines as they staggered and strained against the dead weight of the weapon. The silent struggle continued for a minute or two.

"Hold it," the sergeant said. "That left wheel is bogged down. Hold off a minute, goddamit."

The men ceased their struggle. A marine nearest the bogged wheel began digging it out with his hand. The whine of bullets was more intense, and the marines moved apart in order not to present a crowded scene to the Japanese while they waited for the wheel to be cleared.

As they stood, they glanced in the direction of the tractor, attracted by its engine sounds. As they watched, the driver swung off to one side, halted and began to turn. As he did, there was the thunder of an explosion. Smoke gushed from beneath the vehicle. Crimson flames flashed, and there was the dull *whoosh* of gasoline igniting explosively. The amphibious tractor rose from the earth several feet . . . six or eight feet, it seemed . . . its treads parallel with the ground, just as if it had been lifted by an invisible hoist. Then it fell flat on its treads, flames and smoke swirling around it.

"He's hit a land mine, he's hit a land mine! See him?" one of the gun crew shouted.

"Great God, look up there," the sergeant cried, pointing toward the sky above the burning tractor.

The men looked. They followed the smoke of the tractor, higher and higher, and then they saw it. It was the driver. His body was rising, turning slowly in a circle as it rose. His arms were straight out, his legs flung wide apart, his back to the earth. It was a strange, unearthly sight, this body high in the air . . . and it continued to rise as the marines watched it.

"*Look* at him," one of the marines breathed. "Hell, he must be seventy-five feet up."

"An' still goin'." the sergeant said.

They watched, fascinated. The body began to slow in its ascent; finally, high in the air . . . at least a hundred feet above the battlefield . . . it stopped, and for one long moment hung suspended. Then the body, still turning in slow circles, still with its back to the earth, began its return to earth, moving slowly, reluctantly, at first, then with rapidly increasing speed.

It struck the earth near the burning tractor. The marines could hear the impact.

"That must have been one hell of a mine. He went up like he was shot from a cannon. I never seen anything to equal that," a private said.

"Lifted that damned tractor eight or ten feet straight up, too. Flung him out like a baseball."

"He's dead," the sergeant said. "That wheel unstuck? Okay, let's move it . . . ready?" the sergeant asked. "Now, heave."

They moved the gun to the middle of the terrace. They opened the trail and got the weapon ready to fire. As they did, a shell burst just in front of the gun. They ignored it. A second shell burst, a little closer. Shrapnel whined about them. A third shell followed closely, exploding to the right of the gun.

"Back off . . . back off . . . chop-chop, goddamit, the bastards ought to hit it with the next one," the sergeant shouted.

The men scattered, running for the bank and throwing themselves against it.

Shells began to fall one after another, striking all around the gun. A wheel was blown off. An explosion at the breech block took off the sight.

The marines watched from the bank.

"All that damned work for nothin'. They been sittin' up there watchin' and waitin' . . . wonder they didn't drop one right in the middle of us," a private said.

"Well, by God, that solves the problem of what to shoot at," the sergeant said. "We ain't goin' to shoot at nothin' with that gun."

"I bet it'd have burned that tractor driver up to know that," the private said.

"Yeah, I bet it would, too. If he'd know that, I bet he'd said to hell with it. But he don't know it . . . he don't know *nothin'*," the sergeant said.

It's a good thing," the private said. "It's a good thing he don't know it. Got blowed up for nothin'."

"Yeah . . . it'd have made him mad as hell," the sergeant said.

※   ※   ※   ※

THERE ARE SOME WHO ARE MAKING PROGRESS THIS D-Day. It is now shortly after noon and Easy Company, 3rd Platoon, 1st Battalion, 28th Marines, has reached the west coast of the island after a fast jump-off. This outfit—the one that will plant the flag on Mount Suribachi—is steadily moving toward the fire-swept mountain. One of the men in Easy Company is Corporal Richard Wheeler, who was wounded shortly before his regiment attained its objective.

Wheeler's chronicle of Iwo Jima, *The Bloody Battle for Suribachi,* is considerably more than an excellent personal narrative—it is a precisely documented history. In it Wheeler speaks of his buddies, men such as Corporal Leone "Frenchy" Olivier, probably the only marine to come to Iwo Jima with an old Springfield rifle. Having used the weapon at Tarawa, Olivier considers it an indispensable good-luck accoutrement, and nothing anyone can say can convince him to use the newer, lighter Garand.

Nearby, another marine who is superstitious about his piece is Corporal Tony Stein of A Company, of whom we have read.

Armed with a "stinger," an air-cooled machine gun taken from a wrecked Navy plane, Stein will win a Medal of Honor for his bravery under fire . . . single-handedly wiping out several pillboxes that barred the way of the 28th. Each time his stinger is emptied, Stein returns to the beach for ammo and brings with him a wounded comrade. He will keep this up until killed.

Here is Corporal Wheeler speaking of the first afternoon and night as his outfit advances south behind its Sherman tanks.

·4· "THOSE SONS-OF-BITCHES KILLED MY BUDDY!"

RICHARD WHEELER

The 1st Battalion had now crossed the island in force, and it was time for our company to start pushing into the scrubwood to occupy the captured ground . . . As an observation plane wheeled overhead we began another plodding advance across the yielding sand. But this move soon attracted machine gun fire from the volcano. Rapid bursts started to snap about our feet, some of the bullets ricocheting away with a highpitched buzz . . .

Howard Snyder and I, who had been moving abreast, dived on our stomachs in a skimpy depression. But we shortly realized we were exposed on the side facing the gun, for a burst struck so close to our heads it splashed sand in our faces.

"You okay?" I asked Snyder.

"Yeah," he answered. "But let's get out of here!"

We scrambled for new positions, and this time I jumped into a shell hole. It was a very shallow one, and I had to bend low to be safe.

Presently I heard our lieutenant announce, from a sand pocket a few yards away, "I'm going to leave my pack and gas mask here, and you fellows had better do the same. We'll come back for the stuff later. Right now we've got to be able to move!"

This was an agreeable suggestion, but as I sat up to take off my pack another burst of machine gun bullets danced about me. I quickly ducked low again, and the pack straps I couldn't disengage from my cartridge belt in this cramped position I cut with my combat knife.

It was a relief to shed the pack and mask. Together they probably weighed no more than twenty pounds, but their bulk made them unwieldy. Our remaining gear consisted of more immediate necessities. My own trappings were a helmet, a rifle, a bayonet, two fragmentation grenades, one thermite grenade, a cartridge belt, a knife, two canteens and a first aid kit—still a good 25-pound load.

"Okay, let's go!" Wells soon ordered.

I held my breath as I rose, but nothing happened. The machine gun had either been silenced or had changed targets. We were able to step faster now, and a short time later we entered a hummocky area that gave us a little concealment.

While picking our way among the rises in a southwesterly direction we came upon a lone wounded marine. He was lying on his back with his head resting on his folded poncho, and there was a blood-soaked bandage about his bared abdomen.

"Hey, Mac!" he called as I was going by. "Do you know whether there's a stretcher on the way for me?"

I hadn't seen any stretcher bearers since we'd left the beach, but I felt obliged to answer, "Yeah, I think there is."

I told this lie partly to ease the wounded man's mind and partly to avoid the possibility of having to deal with a request to go back and get help for him. We had been taught to leave the wounded to the medical teams. This seemingly forgotten marine would probably soon be found by stretcher bearers who would take him to an aid station. That he hadn't been found already was undoubtedly due to the trouble our evacuation setup was being caused by the chaos on the beach.

We were soon in the open again and were now only about seventy-five yards from the scrubwood. Dead ahead of us stood one of the area's outlying fortifications. It appeared at first to be merely a large pile of sand, but the slope that faced us held a dark rectangular aperture that told us we were approaching a reinforced concrete gun emplacement. Its covering sand served both to camouflage it and to give it extra protection. We eyed the sinister-looking mound nervously but continued to move toward it. If it offered no resistance we would assume it had been reduced by the 1st Battalion and would cut around it into the scrubwood.

Then the black aperture began to spurt fire, and machine gun bullets once more whipped among us. We lunged for cover, some of us finding craters or depressions and others falling behind a foot-high terrace that extended part way across our path. Again all of us somehow escaped being hit.

Our lieutenant at this point came into contact with his first dead Japanese. The corpse was lying on its back in a shell hole and its abdominal organs had been laid bare by shrapnel. In his jump for concealment Wells landed on the man in such a way that his knees squashed into the exposed organs. He said later: "After that my pants legs smelled so bad that at one time I almost cut them off."

Since we had all taken the closest available cover, many of us were poorly shielded. We pressed ourselves as flat as possible, and our hearts pounded against the sand. Those of us who were seeing our first combat had suddenly learned what it meant to be pinned down by an enemy pillbox.

Up to this time our platoon had been fortunate. Since we had lost Bert Freedman and John Fredotovich on the beach we had covered five hundred dangerous yards without incurring another casualty. But now it seemed as though our run of good luck had ended.

We all knew how a rifle platoon was supposed to handle a problem like this. While one man semicircled his way to the pillbox with a demolitions charge, the rest were to deliver a concentrated fire at the aperture and make it impossible for the gun crew to operate. When the demolitions man was close enough to make a dash for the aperture and push his charge inside, the others were to cease firing—but only long enough for the man to make his play. The moment he turned away, the firing was to be resumed so the charge couldn't be expelled. We had executed this maneuver numerous times in training, using live rifle ammunition and actual charges of TNT. The importance of close support for the exposed attacker had been strongly emphasized. In the case of one of our regiment's platoons this had been overdone. A demolitions man was shot and killed in the act of placing his charge.

As we lay in our places of skimpy concealment and considered the obstacle before us, the prescribed method of dealing with pillboxes seemed suddenly unfeasible. Few of us felt like poking our heads up high enough to fire our rifles, and the idea of a man's rising and venturing across that barren sand seemed absurd. But if Wells gave the order the measure would be tried.

Then we heard a shell explode about fifty yards to our right. We looked in that direction in time to see another burst raise a tall jet of sand. Our first thought was that this fire was meant for us and would shortly be coming closer. Then we realized what the enemy was aiming at. Two beautiful olive-green Sherman tanks were clattering around our flank. The column of armor had at last been able to get through from the beach. Four machines had already been put out of commission by antitank fire, but the column was still strong and was now ready to help mop up the scrubwood. We were very happy to see the two leaders head straight for the pillbox that had us pinned down. With their 75-millimeter guns booming, the dynamic machines rolled into point-blank range. The reduction was soon accomplished. As the tanks ceased firing and started toward the scrubwood, the pillbox took on a tomblike stillness And a tomb, of course, is what the structure had become.

We resumed our advance and shortly reached the first fringe of brush. There we received a gratifying surprise. The scrubwood's defenses included an extensive network of trenches and antitank ditches, and since the 1st Battalion had routed most of the Japanese from these excavations we would be able to use them for cover.

Falling into single file with Wells in the lead, we entered one of the roomy antitank ditches and began to thread our way toward the west coast. Our orders called for us to go all the way across. We would maintain our single-filed formation, sticking as much as we could to the ditches and trenches, for the whole 400-yard trip. Our progress was slow, since we stopped often for extended periods while Wells and Ernest Thomas reconnoitered and made decisions as to the best route to follow.

We moved among numerous bunkers and pillboxes, some of which had been reduced and some of which appeared untouched but were quiet. All of the structures were well covered with sand. This gave some an almost-conic appearance, while others were closer to being igloo-shaped. The camouflaging effect of the sand was often enhanced by patches of grass and other low vegetation. Several of the mounds we saw were smoking as the result of flame thrower assaults, and we passed close by one whose interior was venting a firecracker-like series of snaps and pops as its ammunition supply exploded. Since the unassaulted structures didn't resist our advance we left them alone. They would be blown by men of the 5th Engineer Battalion, a unit that would aid our regiment importantly in its conquest of Suribachi.

There were groups of 1st Battalion wounded scattered through the antitank ditches. These men had been given first aid by their unit corpsmen and were waiting evacuation. Their position was most unenviable, since the area still held live Japanese. Some of the bandaged and bloodstained men were lying with their eyes closed, while others watched us pass. The watchers remained silent, and we did the same. I found myself disliking to pay the wounded too much attention. Thinking about them increased my awareness that I might at any moment be sharing their plight.

We saw few of the 1st Battalion's Japanese victims. There were several sprawled in open gun emplacements, but most were inside the assaulted bunkers and pillboxes. It's possible that some had fallen in the ditches and trenches but had been furtively dragged into concealment by their surviving comrades. This policy of Iwo's defenders would not only make it hard for us to estimate their remaining strength but would tug at our morale. For the first few days the battle would seem painfully one-sided. We would see many of our own casualties, but there would be little indication the Japanese were being destroyed in substantial numbers.

That the scrubwood still held live defenders was demonstrated to a group of us while we were moving through a waist-deep trench.

There was an antitank ditch running parallel to the trench about fifty feet to our right, and we suddenly heard a jumble of excited Japanese voices coming from its depth. Our company executive officer, 1st Lieutenant Harold G. Schrier, was traveling with us at the time, and he quickly cautioned us to get down and be quiet. We dropped to our knees, tense and breathless, our weapons poised for action. But the voices shortly began to recede and in a few moments had faded entirely.

At one point Lieutenant Wells, while leading us into a shallow trough between two sand ridges, almost tripped a partly exposed mine. He had been studying the battered fuselage of a fallen Japanese plane up ahead, and he noticed the mine just in time. Before going on he placed Ernest Thomas at the spot to guide us around it.

It was late afternoon when we approached the defense perimeter the 1st Battalion had set up along the high ground overlooking the western beach. Enemy shellfire had caused a gap to be left in the line, and it was this gap we were ordered to occupy. Happily the fire was lifting as we started moving in. The area held several of the now-familiar mounds that were bunkers and pillboxes.

At the base of one of the larger mounds lay two marines who were dying of multiple bullet wounds. Their platoon leader, a young 2nd lieutenant, was sitting with them. Our own lieutenant's attention was drawn to the mound. It hadn't been reduced, and he realized it was big enough to hold an artillery piece. Its concrete doors were closed and it was altogether silent, but he felt that with night coming on it should be attended to without delay. He judged it to be a threat to the perimeter.

Deciding to blow the structure, he ordered Pfc. Clarence R. Hipp, of Brownwood, Texas, to ready a demolitions charge. If it was to be used, however, the two fatally wounded marines would have to be moved. When Wells asked the young officer to have them carried away, an argument resulted. Wells, though, was the more persistent, and the officer finally summoned several of his men. The dying pair didn't complain when they were lifted, but there was anguish in their pallid faces.

Wells and Hipp now prepared to use the charge. But a 1st Battalion captain who had been walking along the perimeter and had heard the argument chose to interfere.

"Don't waste your charge on that one," he said. "I'm sure it's only a supply house. It's been quiet all day."

Our lieutenant was outranked this time, and the captain was determined that we bypass the mound. So we moved ahead about twenty-five yards and began to set up our defense line. But we faced in the direction of the "supply house" and its companion mounds, and not toward the slope that led to the beach. The former area was by far the more formidable.

As soon as we had our line established, Wells decided to investigate the patches of brush along our immediate front. We had given these only a quick look as we passed them. The lieutenant took with him Pfc. Donald Ruhl, our platoon malcontent. Wells had his Thompson submachine gun and Ruhl his Garand rifle, to which he'd attached his bayonet. Ruhl had much earlier discarded the helmet he hated and was wearing only a fatigue cap.

While the two were kicking around in the brush, the bypassed mound suddenly came to life. The concrete door on its right flank rolled open, and a three-inch fieldpiece, flashing orange, began to boom shells along the perimeter toward the southwest.

Wells was about to alert our platoon for an attack on the bunker when he saw that a 1st Battalion squad was already moving against it. Led by a strapping 2nd lieutenant, the men closed in swiftly, their maneuver partly screened by a scattering of bushes. Then the bunker began to spit machine gun bullets, and the advance halted as one of the leading marines crumpled and died. But the squad soon swung around to the right, out of the machine gun's field of fire. From there a man rushed the bunker with a shape charge. He scrambled to the top of the mound, scratched away an area of sand, planted the charge, then bounded for safety. A loud blast followed, and a hole was driven down through the concrete and into the bunker. The measure wasn't strong enough to finish the occupants, but it made them hasten to close the doorway they had been firing through. Another marine now climbed the mound and dropped a thermite grenade through the shape-charge hole.

During the foregoing action Wells and Ruhl had been working their way closer to the bunker. And now, as the thermite grenade started to generate intense heat and smoke within, they became an important part of the assault. The concrete door that faced our lines was pushed open, and a cloud of white smoke billowed out. A huddle of green sneakers appeared at its base, and the two men opened fire. Wells let go an entire 40-round Thompson clip, and Ruhl emptied his eight-shot Garand. Three Japanese stumbled out of the smoke and fell to the ground. One made a feeble attempt to rise, and Ruhl hurried forward to finish the job with his bayonet.

A moment later Wells saw a hand grenade arc toward Ruhl from a thicket several yards to the left. At the lieutenant's cry, "Look out—grenade!" Ruhl dropped flat, and the fragments lashed out harmlessly.

Wells slammed a fresh clip into his Thompson and ran toward the thicket. He was staking his life on the probability that the Japanese, since he'd done no shooting, was without a firearm. The lieutenant crouched low as he entered the brush. Dusk was setting in, and he knew his best chance of locating his quarry lay in his spotting a silhouette against the sky. But a complete search convinced him the grenadier was no longer there.

Returning to the bunker, Wells found Ruhl involved in a struggle with one of the 1st Battalion Marines who had made the assault. The man was temporarily deranged and was trying to wrest away Ruhl's bayoneted rifle, apparently wanting to use it to mutilate the fallen Japanese.

"Give it to me!" he yelled, his eyes blurred with tears. "Those sons-of-bitches killed my buddy!"

"Take it easy! Take it easy!" Ruhl pleaded, straining to break the man's grip on his weapon. Ruhl himself had done what bayoneting he considered necessary, and all three of the Japanese were dead.

Two of the crazed marine's friends hastened toward the scuffling pair and pulled the offender away. He calmed down as they led him back toward their unit's section of the perimeter . . .

Darkness was now beginning to settle over the island, and the dreaded blanket seemed almost to have an actual physical weight. Its effect on our vision increased the threat to our lives. The ground we occupied was completely unfamiliar to us, while our adversaries knew it intimately. Perhaps they had even been trained to deal with the very problem our presence had created.

The Japanese were stealthy night fighters. Skilled at infiltration tactics, they often crawled about amid their enemies and tried to kill them as they slept. It was said among the marines that a night-creeping Japanese would sometimes feel about in a foxhole very carefully until he had touched a body, his purpose being to make sure it was warm, lest he waste a hand grenade on a corpse. Whether this particular story was true or not, it typified the audacity of the Japanese soldier. His daring sometimes went beyond the understanding of our Western minds, and we were quick to call him fanatical. We attributed his seeming fearlessness to a psychology based on a blind belief in his religion. But regardless of what one is taught he can't help but have an instinctive fear of violent death. So in the final analysis the "fanaticism" the Japanese displayed must have been prompted chiefly by courage and devotion to duty.

The Navy soon began to send up illuminating shells, and this measure would be continued until dawn. Because of the brush around us the dim light wouldn't aid our vision greatly but would cast moving shadows that gave us a start when we mistook them for skulking enemy soldiers.

We had been told to stay in our positions and keep down, since there was considerable danger of our shooting one another. A challenge-and-countersign system had been prearranged to cover the contingency of emergency movement. The challenger was to call out the name of an American automobile, any make, and if the challenged didn't respond immediately with the name of another make, the challenger was to shoot.

We men of Howard Snyder's squad had been assigned to the left flank of our platoon's sector. Snyder had picked a spot where two thigh-deep enemy trenches crossed each other, and we had taken cover in three segments of this junction. The fourth led toward the bunker area, and Snyder had instructed Pfc. Edward S. Kurelik, a curly headed Chicagoan, to cover its dark void with his BAR. Louie Adrian and I were in the north segment, close to the intersection. Just to our left were fireteam-leader Harold Keller and his two men, Pfc. James Robeson and Pfc. Raymond A. Strahm.

Corporal Keller was mentioned earlier as being one of our platoon's former raiders, and Robeson as being our youngest member. They made an unusual pair. One was sturdy and strong-featured, mature and calm, the very image of a fighting man, while the other was slim and animated and had a sunny, snub-nosed, whiskerless face that made him look like a typical well-favored high school student. Whereas Keller had seen extensive action, Robeson had joined the platoon straight from boot camp. The youth, however, was eager to learn and respectful of experience, and his assignment to the steady ex-raider had worked out to his advantage. Keller had advised him sensibly and patiently, and as a result he had got the most from our training program. Though Keller and the rest of us had fallen into the habit of calling Robeson "Chick" with a kind of paternal superiority, we knew that behind his boyish features there was manly resolution.

Raymond Strahm was a former paratrooper whose home was in Illinois. Several of his friends called him "Little Raymond" for a reason I never learned. He was neither little nor especially tall. Six weeks before the assault he had won the platoon's regard through a very generous act. While our regiment was aboard ship in Pearl Harbor, waiting the order to sail for its staging area, the platoon's poker players got together, and Strahm had an amazing run of luck. He broke about a dozen of us in a few hours. Soon after the game we got word that we'd be granted one final liberty in Honolulu before sailing time. But it seemed that we penniless gamblers would have to forego this pleasure. Strahm, however, promptly lent each of us ten dollars, even though he knew he'd probably never see any of the money again, since a platoon going into action has an uncertain future. We felt warmly grateful as we joined Strahm and the unit's non-gamblers in "doing the town" one more time. I myself spent part of the loan on a hula show that featured a group of chubby matrons and skinny high school girls.

(One day several years after the war I came across Strahm's home address in one of my service notebooks. Suddenly troubled about the money I owed him, I dispatched a letter in an effort to re-establish contact. The reply I received was from Strahm's wife, who informed me that my generous friend had survived the war only to die in an automobile accident soon after returning home.)

As our squad began its first fearful night on Iwo, Howard Snyder assigned us watches so at least one man would be awake and alert at all times. But there really wasn't any need for this arrangement, for most of would think twice before we even blinked.

It soon became uncomfortably cool, the temperature dropping to about 60 degrees. As the chill penetrated our thin dungarees we began to wish we had the packs and blanket rolls we'd discarded while crossing the island. The rations in our packs, however, didn't bother us. Though I myself had eaten nothing all day except the fruit bar at noon, I hadn't the least desire for food.

Soon after dark a group of 1st Battalion Marines came walking along the perimeter from the south and passed close behind our platoon's position. These men were talking to one another in deliberately loud tones, their reason doubtless being that they didn't want to be shot by friendly troops. I wondered what sort of emergency had prompted them to make this highly dangerous move. The voices soon faded in the darkness north of us, and the group didn't return.

The naval illuminating shells enabled us to catch glimpses of Mount Suribachi through breaks in the brush. It stood about a third of a mile to our right, and was now a combination of ghostly highlights and deep shadows. Our regiment's afternoon attack on this objective had accomplished very little. The openness of the terrain, the treachery of the sand and the stubbornness of the enemy were an alliance that proved temporarily unbeatable. Originally scheduled for 3:45, the attack had been delayed by organizing difficulties until nearly 5:00 o'clock, and it had stalled soon after it was launched.

Our platoon was closer to Suribachi than it had been for most of the day, but the night's limited visibility and the clusters of brush that screened us made the volcano seem less ominous. There were two men, however, who found its presence as disturbing as ever. Corporal Robert Leader and his BAR man, Pfc. Leo Rozek, had been ordered by their squad leader, Sergeant Katie Midkiff, to occupy a barren knob that thrust itself above the bushes. Their placement was a sound tactical move, since the spot commanded a good view of the enemy areas about our platoon. But the men found themselves in a most trying situation, particularly since the knob was too solid for foxhole digging. In the fluctuating light of the illuminating shells they pressed themselves as flat as possible and imagined themselves to be the constant object of enemy observations, both from the volcano and the ground close around them. Every now and then during the long night they would make another desperate attempt to dig in, but they would be unable to do much more than scratch the knob's surface.

The detonative noises that had been so much a part of the day continued through the night but were less sustained. Volleys of small-arms fire and concentrations of shellfire, both enemy and friendly, sounded intermittently from various parts of the island. The battalion our platoon was attached to received its share of enemy shells, but our own line was overlooked.

It was believed the Japanese would launch a counterattack against the whole of our beachhead in the darkness. They were known to have a large reserve force of infantry and tanks, and this first night seemed the most likely time for the force to hit us, since we were still only shakily established on the island. But a large-scale counterattack failed to develop. At one time during the night, however, the 27th Marines, entrenched just to the north of our own regiment, discovered the enemy to be organizing along a line about five hundred yards to their front. This effort was soon broken up by artillery fire laid down by the 1st and 2nd Battalions of the 13th Marines.

Another noisy incident took place not far from our platoon. The enemy tried a barge landing on the west coast between our location and Suribachi—probably having set out from the volcano's flank—and the barge was spotted by a 1st Battalion unit that took it under fire and killed about twenty-five of its occupants.

In keeping with their reputation, the Japanese also made many individual attempts to infiltrate our lines. My squad was among those hit.

The night was dragging wretchedly. As I lay in my segment of the trench, with my rifle in my hands and my combat knife stuck into the sand within easy reach, I shivered often. The 60-degree chill seemed now to have penetrated to my bones, and the anxiety I felt increased my muscular tension. Everything, as the saying goes, is relative. The day had been bad, but its terrors dimmed when compared with those of the night. Through the daylight hours I had often thought: "What a relief it will be to see this madness end." Now, as I shuddered in the darkness, my foremost thought was this: "What a relief it will be to see daylight come." My worries were increased by the fact that the side of my trench that faced the bunker area had been blown away by a shell, and instead of having a vertical wall for protection I had only a slope. I seldom took my eyes off the slope's summit, and I expected momentarily to see a Japanese silhouette loom above it.

But when the Japanese came, during the early morning hours, he didn't come over my summit. With a hand grenade in readiness, he came creeping up the trench Ed Kurelik was covering with his BAR. I was joltingly warned of his presence by Kurelik's sharp challenge, "Studebaker!" This was immediately followed by an exclamation in Japanese and a flashing explosion in our midst. Two men were hit—Kurelik and Pfc. Phillip E. Christman, one of our Californians. The rest of us sprang up with raised rifles as our assailant darted away. Several men fired into the shadows, and Snyder threw two hand grenades that exploded brightly and peppered the brush with shrapnel. But we had no reason to believe the Japanese had been downed.

As the brief incident ended I discovered that my teeth were chattering. The sudden scare, coming as it did after I had spent seven or eight hours chilled to the bone and tensely watchful, had tested me severely. Sitting down in my trench with my back against its solid side, I clamped my jaws together firmly until the spasm passed.

Only one of our wounded men had been hit seriously. Ed Kurelik had an egg-sized hole in his thigh and a foot injury that probably involved a fracture. Phil Christman had taken fine fragments on various parts of his body. The wounds were negligible, and he would stay in the fight.

One of our platoon corpsmen, John Bradley, who was dug in some yards from our squad, made his way to the men on his hands and knees, first letting us know he was coming so we wouldn't shoot him.

Kurelik seemed to feel that the Japanese hadn't quite played fair. While Corpsman Bradley treated him he said complainingly in his pronounced Chicago accent: "I heard somebody comin' up the trench and I hollered, 'Studebaker!' And then that Jap t'rew a hand grenade!"

Kurelik seemed to be implying that if the Japanese had been a good sport he would have merely done something like holler back, "Cadillac!"

But the Chicagoan's words were also proof of his courage. Many men, after such an experience, wouldn't have expressed displeasure with the enemy's methods but only anguish at being so badly hurt.

With daylight still two or three hours away, Snyder expected more trouble and placed a second BAR man, Chick Robeson, at the danger point, telling him he was to forget about challenging and was to open fire at anything he saw moving in the trench. Most of the rest of us initiated our own nervous watch on the trench area. But the remainder of the night passed without incident.

❊ ❊ ❊ ❊

LET US LEAVE THE SOUTHWARD DRIVE FOR A BRIEF recounting of events in the great convoy offshore, where men labored furiously to unload equipment and pile it into landing boats. Captain Raymond Henri, 5th Division public affairs officer, speaks of this little-discussed phase of the battle.

·5· LOGISTICS AFLOAT

CAPTAIN RAYMOND HENRI

In the convoy that had drawn up off the shores of Iwo . . . there had been a flotilla of LSTs and LSMs loaded with rations, water, ammunition, landing equipment—"hot cargo" that would be needed on the beaches during the assault phase of the battle. Farther out were regular cargo vessels, to be unloaded when the beach was secure. There were no reefs around the island and it was expected that the LSTs and LSMs would be able to come right up to the beach, lower their ramps, and unload their supplies—and this at least by the afternoon of D-day.

In the hold of each LST were amphibian tractors, themselves loaded with top priority cargo—supplies that would be needed to win the battle of the beach. They would leave the mother ships soon after the assault troops landed and precede the big vessels to the shore by several hours.

The LSMs (Landing Ships, Medium, used for the first time in a Marine operation) were carrying tanks, trucks, bulldozers and other heavy equipment, and would beach sometime between the landing of the amphtracs and the arrival of the LSTs. Much of this equipment would be needed to unload the LSTs when they came in.

The crews of these, the landing ships, the cargo vessels, the tractors, would fight the battle of supply, a battle often less spectacular but no less important to the outcome of the fighting, than that fought by the infantry. To supply an initial 40,000 men—later to become 60,000—on a hostile island 7000 miles from the United States and 750 miles from the nearest base, was the task confronting the supply officers and units.

Like a lot of other things on Iwo, the battle of supply didn't go according to plan. Some newspaper correspondent called Iwo the "Anzio of the Pacific," for few islands have been supplied under such hazards and with such losses in equipment. At no time were our beaches out of range of enemy artillery. The heavy surf, the soft sand, steep sides of the terraces, all worked against us.

Yet with few exceptions no marine went hungry or thirsty, or ran out of ammunition because of a breakdown in supply.

For three days, beginning on D-day, a lot of marines would have given odds they would be going without plenty of things for an indefinite time. The ships' beach parties, which had gone in with the assault waves to set up their direction system for landing men and supplies, were then pinned down and scarcely able to function. Some were put completely out of action and evacuated. When Seabees came in later they had to set up their own supply system. Primarily a construction battalion, they found themselves dug in right behind rifles and 37 mm. guns.

LSMs zigzagged in under intense fire. On Yellow Beach all but one got direct hits. One LSM lowered its ramp only to have a shell drop in the open maw of its cargo compartment. Quickly it raised its ramp and shoved off, as if it had come in for the sole purpose of collecting this souvenir of enemy defiance.

Some of these vessels unloaded their equipment, but others, still fully loaded, had to sail back out of range. Fire kept on increasing in intensity and accuracy during the day and it was decided not to try to bring in the LSTs.

Instead, supplies dribbled in on amphtracs that skittered from point to point along the beach until they found a spot where the shelling wasn't so heavy. Ammunition early became critical and Seabees volunteered to carry it by hand from the beach to the troops inland. Ducks, carrying artillery, sunk to their hubs in the sand, and the big guns had to be manhandled into position, often for hundreds of yards. Some Ducks, pounded by the heavy surf, capsized. Higgins type landing boats broached so that the sides became easy targets for the Jap gunners. By late afternoon of D-day so many landing boats had been wrecked that amphtracs and Ducks couldn't land along great stretches of the beach. Looking back from the upslope on which they were still fighting, marines could see amphibian tractors flopped upside down where they had run over mines; derricks tilted at insane angles by shells, jeeps and antitank guns mired down and smashed. Scattered among them were dead marines who had been buried in the sand as the tide came in.

At that moment it did look as if the battle of supply might be lost. That it wasn't is due to the determination of the amphtracs and Duck drivers, to the Seabees and beach parties, and to the marines on the beach who restored order amid confusion. Army, Navy and Marines together won the supply fight.

Somehow, bulldozers and caterpillars—the ones that were still un-damaged—carved passageways up through the sides of the terraces, and packed the sand down into the semblance of roads. Metal mats were laid on the beach. Beachmasters—traffic cops of the invasion—set up their loud speakers and boomed orders amid the crash of shells. Shore parties set up radio transmitters and established communication with the ships at sea.

Sometimes getting supplies to the troops was just a matter of sheer bravery. On Yellow Beach One a mortar section of the 23rd Regiment ran too low on ammunition. The section leader, Gunnery Sergeant Raphael E. "Jumbo" Kearns (Mobile, Alabama), finally went back to the beach himself. But he couldn't find any shore party person-nel to call the ammunition ashore.

Kearns then saw an amphibian tractor in the water with a load of shells. With dozens of vehicles already bogged down on the beach, the driver saw little chance of finding a route inland. He bobbed in the surf not knowing what to do. Kearns waded into the heavy surf, climbed aboard, and directed the driver to a point where the beach was hard enough to take the vehicle. Then Kearns took over the trac-tor himself and despite the danger of mines drove it until it bogged down.

It seemed as if Kearns' mortars just couldn't get enough ammuni-tion. So "Jumbo" made several more trips to the beach, locating shells that had been dumped there earlier. During the whole day, his guns never stopped their barking for lack of shells.

Whenever possible, amphibian tractors brought ammunition and supplies from the ships to the front lines. Some struck mines; some caught Jap shells; some threw their tracks in the sea of sand; some ran out of fuel in the water and drifted miles away, to be located later by planes and picked up by destroyers. One damaged tractor tried to reach a transport but sank just alongside. A crew member was dragged down by the suction of the ship's propellers and came up under the screw itself, which cracked him on the head as it sucked him out of the water again. But he had on his helmet. When he was hauled aboard he discovered that the vessel was the flagship and that Admiral Turner had been an interested spectator of what had happened to him.

Whatever happened the amphtracs kept coming—they kept coming in all night. They were the only link between the 40,000 men ashore and the ships. They *had* to keep coming. One tractor, on its way to the front with ammunition, was diverted into action by a Marine patrol held up by some Japs protecting an artillery position. When the Japs attacked with hand grenades the amphtrac crew fought them off with their machine gun, but not until a grenade had landed in the tractor and wounded one of the marines. The crew killed eight of the enemy and occupied the position, turned it over to the infantry, and went on its way.

Many of all the amphibian tractors at Iwo were put out of action on D-day. With the Ducks—amphibious trucks—they assumed the whole burden of getting cargo to the beaches during the first two days. And on their return trips they evacuated the greater part of the wounded. At night they patrolled the beaches against the possibility of an enemy counterlanding behind our lines.

On D plus 2 enemy artillery fire decreased sufficiently for the LSMs and LSTs to carry out their program of unloading supplies directly onto the beaches. Then we began to build up dumps. The artillery was still eating up vast quantities of ammunition but we were over the hump. The first and most critical phase of the supply battle had been won.

If marines were to nominate individual heroes in the supply battle on Iwo they would be the beachmasters and shore party commanders who controlled the ship-to-shore-to-interior set-up on the beach. Lieutenant Commander G. A. Hebert (Culver City, Calif.), a veteran of the First World War, and First Lieutenant Carl C. Gabel (Chicago, Ill.) worked Yellow Beach One. For the first five days and nights they had practically no sleep. "Hebert," wrote Bryce Walton, a Coast Guard combat correspondent, "had the responsibility of bringing in boats to the beach, handling them on the beach, keeping it clear of wrecked craft, maintaining salvage parties; responsibility for evacuation of all wounded from the beach seaward, for building traffic roads along the beach, and for rebuilding the shoreline when it became disfigured by the surf.

"Lieutenant Gabel's job began where Hebert's left off, the job of getting supplies from the beach inland, and getting inland casualties to the beach, of directing some 2000 Seabees and maintaining their lines of communication and supply. Perhaps the most useful and colorful parts of this set-up were the public address systems. They could be heard a quarter of a mile away.

"'LVT. LVT. Are you empty?'

"A signalman waved yes.

"'Stay right where you are. Stand by to evacuate casualties.'

"The loudspeaker blared again, making Lieutenant Gabel's whisper thunder.

"'Report right down here. Right down here to evacuate casualties.'

"'All right there,' Hebert said, 'get on the ball. Wave the LCM off! We can't take any more small boats on this beach at this time. Is that LST unloaded yet?'

"'No. hr. 728, have you got any rockets on you?'

"'We need a crane,' said Gabel over the loudspeaker. 'Get one of those LSMs coming in. You! Wave in the LCVP!'

"Then, and all the time, came shivering, thumping explosions. Men were running, scattering, frantic for cover. There would be a cloud of dirt, spray, and pieces of tractor going 50 feet into the air. Seabees, everyone, ran for cover.

"But the loudspeaker, inspired either by Hebert or Gabel, never stopped. They both stood out in the open talking into their phones.

"'Comfortable lying out there, isn't it, boys?' said Hebert.

"'Yeah,' said Gabel. 'They're getting that all the time up in the front line . . . About every five minutes, or maybe five every minute. They get machine-gun fire up there, too.'

"Then everyone went back to his job."

For 26 days these barkers on the beach directed the battle of supply.

As more troops came ashore, and the supply lines lengthened, the problem became more complex. The two-mile-long beach became so congested with traffic that, in the words of one Chicagoan, "It looked like State and Madison." The surf continued heavy. The island provided no real defilade for supply dumps and more than one dump went up in flames during an enemy barrage. Roads leading to the interior had been destroyed by our own shelling and had to be rebuilt. After the intense enemy barrages of the first few days, our beach was shelled at least once a day right up until a week or so before the end of the battle.

Yet when our troops did reach the northern end of the island they could look back from the hills and ridges there and see a whole new civilization springing into being. Motoyama Airfield No. 1 had been repaired and was already in use. Airfield No. 2 was under repair, even though it was within rifle shot of the enemy. Giant bulldozers, graders, sprinklers rumbled up and down the island carving roads. Mess kitchens went up. A field hospital was built.

Salvage work began; weapons and helmets of casualties were collected and reissued. Rows of white slabs and crosses indicated our cemeteries—the only thing on the island not a drab brown or green. Sometimes the men burying the dead were caught by an enemy shell, and were buried in the grave they had just dug.

By the end of the battle, more than 80,000 Americans were ashore on Iwo—three Marine divisions had thousands of Air Force and Army service troops. Imagine a city the size of Sioux City, Iowa; Saginaw, Michigan; or Stockton, Calif., springing up in a few days and dependent for its food, water, clothing supplies (to say nothing of tons and tons of ammunition, which a city would not require) on sources entirely outside of it. Then you have an idea of the magnitude of the logistics problem . . .

❈   ❈   ❈   ❈

TWENTY-FOUR HOURS AFTER THE INVASION OPENED, all six regiments and tanks of the 4th and 5th Divisions were ashore. Although there had been some attempts to infiltrate marine lines during the night, no real counterattack developed. During the ensuing two days and nights the 4th Division made very little progress in the area north of the quarry—it had already reached Kuribayashi's main position.

In the 24th Marines we find combat correspondent Allen R. Matthews, a gifted writer who set down his memoirs of the battle several years later. It was his first battle. At dawn of D-Plus-Two we find Private Matthews rising up from his poncho as a sergeant prods him awake.

•6• "CORPSMAN! CORPSMAN!"

ALLEN R. MATTHEWS

"Pass the word along to stand by to move out."

We repeated the sentence to the hole on our left and heard it being repeated down the hill toward the beach, fading to sibilants in the distance.

The two marines with their loot from the dead Jap darted out toward their own shelter and the members of my squad entered ours and began donning their gear. I assembled my rifle hurriedly, thinking this is the way it always happens; you get started on something and you immediately get the word to move out. But I was only dramatizing a fancied plight for my own entertainment because it was the first time such a thing had happened to me.

I rolled my poncho and the brilliant orange front line panels into a tight and compact bundle which I suspended from the rear of my cartridge belt by heavy twine, and I shrugged my way again into the suspenders which held the belt. I ducked low in the hole and removed my helmet and the fatigue cap beneath it, so that I could slip my gas mask carrier over my head and onto the back of my shoulders. I replaced the headgear and reflected that this made only the second time in more than twenty-four hours that it had been off my head. The first time had been last night when I removed the carrier. The helmet had become almost a part of me so that I felt naked and uncomfortable when I removed it.

I replaced the assistant BAR-man's belt on my left side, examined the grenades which I had shoved into the deep sand near my head last night, and put them into the makeshift carrier which I had contrived from the belt. When I had donned the bandoliers which hung crossed over my chest I was ready to move out at a moment's notice and I sat down in the hole, raised the gas mask carrier until the back of my neck fitted against it comfortably, leaned back, and lighted a cigarette.

We talked little but were content to take it easy. None of us had slept much the night before and we rested, relaxed in our minds as well as in our bodies. The Japanese mortars and artillery were beginning to fall again but the shells were not striking close to our lines. Our own artillery, which the veterans explained was pack howitzers, was firing over our heads and the shells fell far forward along the taxiway. I remembered the admonition of Sergeant Summers who had advised me to learn as quickly as possible the difference between the Japanese and our own artillery and I listened closely.

Our guns, several hundred yards to the rear, fired in batteries of four at a time. The discharges came not quite simultaneously so that we heard first the long, drawn out sizzling, then the faint flat chunk of the muzzle discharges followed closely by the smashing roar of the four explosions ahead of us.

But the sizzling continued, for by the time the projectiles from the first battery had fallen a second battery had fired and the shells were passing overhead, one after the other.

The veterans looked up and grinned. They were proud of the 75-millimeter weapons which had proved invaluable in previous campaigns.

"But just you wait," one of them said, "until the one-oh-fives come in and get going. They'll heckle the Jap artillery into a duel and then you'll see something.

"On Saipan they came ashore late the first day. The next day they fired at the Japs until a Jap artillery piece would answer and then — wham! they'd knock the hell out of it. They didn't waste any time about it, either."

Our naval vessels were also firing heavily again, and I had not yet learned to identify their fire. I still ducked involuntarily when they fired because they seemed to be almost in the hole with me. Their projectiles had so much more velocity than the artillery's that there was no sound of the intermediate sizzle; there was just a crack of the discharge and then the roar of the explosion as the projectiles struck their targets.

And I flinched violently, at the discharge of our rockets which were fired from the very beginning of the campaign from ships and planes. Even now the planes were over our heads, diving down on the cliffs one at a time, with the vicious sibilance of their rockets being followed by the grinding snarl of machine guns as they ended their dives with strafing runs.

The rockets from the ships came sometimes in strings of perhaps hundreds and turned the face of the cliffs into a seething, boiling mass of debris and smoke.

The plane rockets, usually fired in burst of six from each fighter, were even more terrifying because they were nearer to us.

Now the whole angry chorus was being sung over and about us. But it was mostly our song and the sound of it was sweet in our ears. We were almost jovial when we spoke, although we spoke seldom.

But even the small talk of our hole died down as the minutes dragged into an hour and we had not moved. What was causing the hold-up? We did not know and our uncertainty made us nervous.

And then came the electrifying cry:

"Stand by for a tank attack!"

Stand by for a tank attack stand by for a tank attack stand by stand by tanks tanks tanks, the words screamed and whispered their way down the hill and we stood up in our holes and milled thoughtlessly, for we were in no position to meet tanks and we knew it.

An officer strode swiftly by and spoke to our platoon noncommissioned officers and the sight of him quieted the troops who nevertheless continued to stand.

"The platoon is going to pull back here," one of the noncommissioned officers said, and he pointed to another terrace about thirty yards to the rear. "We are going to post spotters along this ridge, and the rest of us are going to set up our lines back here."

He glanced about.

"Koon! Matthews! You get up here on the right and watch everything ahead of you and to the right. There'll be somebody else to watch the left. For God's sake keep your eyes open. If you see anything coming give us the word and then run like hell. Do you understand?"

I nodded mutely.

"Get up there now," he repeated, "and keep your eyes open."

I walked slowly up the bank and my legs felt stiff and foreign to my body. I scooped out a hollow on the right side of the incline almost directly above the spot where the dead Jap lay and I sat with my back to him watching the ground which was level for approximately a hundred yards in front of me. Beyond that it gave way to a series of abrupt low hills which were covered with scrub trees of a kind which I could not determine at the distance.

Koon had climbed the bank at the same time I had and he sat in the foxhole which had been occupied the night before by Seiden, Laramie, and Rice. He was about five yards from me. Approximately twenty-five yards to our left I could see two other spotters from our platoon, Sergeant Adams and Corporal Degliequi. They stood together on the ridge line which lay behind me, and the upper half of their bodies stood out plainly.

Corporal Sibisky of the first platoon, looking extremely small and thin in his heavy gear, scrambled up the terrace back of me and

crawled into the hole with Koon. They chatted together for a few minutes and then Sibisky turned and, crouching low, ran to the place occupied by the other spotters. I left my hole on the side of the embankment and raced over to join Koon.

As I dropped into the foxhole which was shallow and wide I felt
water on the side of my face. Another drop struck me and then it began
to rain slowly and steadily. A chill wind blew across the open ground
and the rain beat in our faces and I buttoned my combat jacket around
my neck. I lowered my face against the rain and then, realizing I could
not maintain a watch with my eyes to the ground, I lifted my head
and the water trickled to the tip of my nose where it clung coldly.
I blew upward and spattered it, but another drop formed in its place
and then fell aggravatingly. I tried to brush it away with my hands
but they were covered with sand which transferred to my face, making me more uncomfortable than ever. And I noticed that where my
hands had touched my rifle the sand and dust from my hands had
been transformed into a thin mud which the rain was dissolving and
spreading along the hand guard and operating rod. I was angry and
nervous, for it looked as if I might need the weapon soon, and I cursed
but there was nothing I could do about it. I wiped each hand under
the opposite armpit and dabbed ineffectually at my rifle with the
dry underside of my right forearm.

And as I sat I turned cold. I was sitting in an almost squatting position with my heels pressed tight against my buttocks and the rain
dampened and then drenched my dungarees along my thighs and
the water seeped through and trickled down my upturned legs to
my crotch. I shivered and stretched my legs in front of me and the
wet trousers which had not heretofore touched below my knees settled and clung to them. My faint shivers turned to violent tremors
like those which I had experienced during the killing of the Jap soldier at night and I clenched my fingers about the stock of my rifle to
keep the trembling from showing.

But I noticed then that Koon was trembling also and that his lips
had turned a blue-gray. I unbuttoned my combat jacket and brought
out a cigarette and lighted it. He took one and I held out my cigarette to give him a light and we both trembled so violently that we
missed contact. I laughed.

"This would be funny as hell," I said, "if it weren't so damned un-
funny."

He smiled.

"You ain't kiddin'." He paused. "How'd you like a good hot cup
of joe?"

"How'd *you* like a good hot tom 'n' jerry?" I replied.

"And how'd you like a rifle butt in the mouth?"

We laughed and felt better, for the laughter had relaxed our nerves. But we still shivered and now we knew we shook from the cold.

"Last night," I said, "I couldn't make up my mind whether I was shaking from the cold of the weather or from the heat of the action."

He said he'd been the same and we chatted briefly but our talk died, for over our heads came the sizzling of our battery fire and the hills before us shook and spewed smoke and dirt high in the air. The sizzling continued, a full scale barrage in which the ships, now moved close to the shore under the cliffs, joined. And our mortars, also firing in batteries, became active, cleaving the air behind us with their s-s-s-schunk-s-s-s-schunk ... chunk-chunk-s-s-s and the ground vibrated as the barrage moved in from the hills toward us and then moved back again so that the shells fell out of sight beyond the rise in the ground.

And we nudged each other and pointed gleefully as a column of black smoke built up solidly beyond the hills, for in our mind's eye we could see a tank burning and we said to ourselves that's one of the bastards out of the way. But in truth we saw no tanks and, for that matter, no Japs, although Koon started suddenly and swore he had seen a soldier tumble down inside a shell hole about two hundred yards from us. He even professed to see footprints down the side of the hole. It was on an incline so that we could see into it and I imagined I could see them too.

But we were silenced suddenly as the barrage came back across the hills and dug at the open space before us, some of the shells striking within fifty yards of us and we burrowed as deep as possible into the foxhole, lifting our heads to continue our watch only when the sizzling of the falling shells stopped and the whine of the shrapnel died away.

The sand in front of our hole danced and spat with our own shrapnel and the unintentional barrage was as dangerous to us atop the crest as if it had been thrown down by the Japanese. But it moved away again and Koon and I sat up and looked about.

The spotters to our left were gone. The hill was bare except for us.

"Wait here and I'll see what the scoop is," Koon said. He sprinted out the hole and down the embankment and I turned again to watch the front. He reappeared in a short while.

"Come on down," he shouted and returned to the platoon's positions. I followed him.

"Adams has been hit," he said. "In the face. Pretty bad, I think."

The sergeant, his helmet off, lay on his left side on the rear embankment. About him clustered four or five friends, the platoon leader, and Scala the corpsman. Adam's face was as gray as the sand on which he lay and his eyelids fluttered feebly. A great flow of blood seeped from his cheek and neck and pooled into the ground under his chin. The corpsman was preparing an injection of blood plasma and another man had been sent for litter bearers when I turned toward my squad.

The rain had stopped but the clouds still hung low and heavy and the squad lay huddled in twos and threes just below the crest of the bank. The groups were spread about ten yards apart and most of them had dug shallow pits against the slope. About thirty yards to the left the terrace made an L-turn to the rear, and below us, under the protection of this declivity, was a tank. Members of the crew in their helmets stood by or walked slowly about the vehicle, eyeing and fingering holes in the armor plating along the sides and rear. The tank was out of commission and had been brought to this position for repairs.

I scooped a hole out of the side of the bank and lay in it, face to the rear. I could see others from our platoon clustered on top of the embankments behind our last night's position.

As I watched, our artillery and mortar barrage against the Jap lines across the taxiway dwindled and died away. Suddenly the air sizzled again and I thought we're still at it, for it was obvious that this was battery fire, but as I watched to our rear the ground spouted up in a line from the airport down to a point near where our platoon had advanced inland from the beach. This time it was Japanese fire; their guns, too, were being used in batteries.

And the thought struck me that the enemy had spotted this tank below us and was trying to destroy it and I unbuckled my entrenching tool which was fastened to my cartridge belt and widened and deepened my hole so that nothing short of a direct hit in the hole or on top of the tank would endanger me. But suddenly I knew I had figured wrong for the next salvo, and the next, hit in approximately the same location and it became obvious that the enemy, stung by our barrage, was seeking out not this tank but our artillery. I sat up in my hole and looked about.

Apparently most of fhe men thought as I did that we were in no immediate danger. But the man on my right continued to dig, stopping when the air above us was quiet but renewing his work when the sizzling occurred until finally, under a heavy outburst, he dropped his entrenching tool and, bending down, frantically scooped at the ground with his hands, flinging the sand, dog-fashion, between his legs. I pitied him because he obviously needed to learn about artillery fire even more than I did.

But the mortars did find us and they probed inquisitive fingers about for the tank until our platoon leaders gave the word for us to scatter away from the area surrounding the vehicle. We moved toward an embankment to our right and lay flat against the side of this hill.

I was there when Matchunis walked over and sat beside me. He was troubled.

"I guess you know that Lieutenant H____ has been killed?"

I had not heard this and I was sorry, for the lieutenant was known throughout our company as a fine officer. A huge, blond man with an emotionless face, he had been unpopular when he first joined the company, for he was, the men complained, too GI—a stickler for spit and polish. But after the Saipan-Tinian operations he was admired as much as he previously was disliked; there he proved himself to be a fair and fearless man.

"Captain Harshbarger got it, too," Matchunis continued. "Not too badly, I think, but he had to turn in.

"Matty," he continued. "I think I've got a charmed life."

"How's that?"

"Yesterday I was running with another feller for a shell hole. We both dived for the hole just as a shell burst near us. I made it, but he didn't. He had an arm blown off. I wasn't scratched.

"And then I was standing between two other guys when a mortar shell hit close to us. Both of them got it pretty bad but again I wasn't scratched. That was twice in one day.

"Our c.p. was hit earlier today and the top got it," (that also was news to me) "and then they set up another temporary c.p. near some tanks and the Japs started hitting at those and that's when Lieutenant H____ and Captain Harshbarger got it. I was standing right next to H____ when he was hit and I didn't get touched. But I'm afraid my luck is going to play out on me."

"How about the top; was he hurt badly?"

"Yeh. I hear he may lose an arm and a leg."

Matchunis rose to his feet and started away.

"Take it easy," I said.

Take it easy. It was the universal *vale* of this operation: a farewell clothed in concern but decorated with an air of calm carelessness. It was affected by everyone. What it meant, of course—and we all knew it—was just the opposite of what it said. For we didn't mean take it easy. We meant, instead, keep your tail down and your eyes open and run like hell . . .

[But] we moved cautiously; we were in territory new to us and we were afraid of mines. A demolitions outfit had gone through ahead of us at some previous time and had marked the mine fields but the mines still were there and in the growing dusk of the late afternoon it was difficult to see the tatters of cloth on the sticks marking the explosives.

And because we were uncertain of our territory we not only walked cautiously but we talked in the same manner. We were firm believers in passing the word and now the information and the warnings passed down the line slowly, working their way stumblingly from man to man.

"Heads down—open space up forward," it ran and the soft hisses of the s's slithered up to you and resolved themselves into words, then faded meaninglessly as they passed by you and to the men in the rear.

"Stay in the trenches—mines ahead," and the muscles tightened in our legs and our arms and our stomachs.

Our rules of quiet were broken only in emergencies and the entire line screamed in anxious, wrathful indignation when we saw three men unconcernedly walking across the fields which we had so carefully skirted. Our words were an invisible wall in front of them with their unconcern turning to bounding fright when they realized the meaning of the cloth-covered sticks past which they had been walking.

Like our words our steps ranged from the silent and cautious to the pounding and impetuous and we stormed in twos and threes and fours across the open spaces, taking advantage of each shell hole. It was in one of those, occupied temporarily by members of my platoon, that I came across the second Japanese I had seen on the island. Like the first he was dead, and in the same manner. His arms were mutilated and his hands missing but the cavity in his body from the blast of his grenade was lower—across his belly so that portions of his intestines hung over his legs.

"Watch the mine," someone said and I saw almost at the Jap's feet a wooden, box-like affair bound with cloth tape and with a detonator protruding from a hole in the wood. It was not until later that I learned this was no mine but an aerial bomb with an exposed detonator buried in the hole which the enemy believed large enough to attract a sizable unit of Americans. I stepped across the body of the dead soldier and sprinted for the next crater.

I paused there for breath and asked, "What's the scoop?" but the only thing anyone could tell me was that our outfit was moving down to the far right and we were going into the line at that position. Night was not far off and speed was essential so that we could find the lines and dig in before darkness enveloped us.

The column in which we traveled turned abruptly to the left and began slowly to curl its way from the beach onto the high ground

again and even as I darted across a slight knoll into a communications trench I heard the rattle of a machine gun in front of me and
I hurled my body against the wall of the trench.

Spurred from the rear, the remainder of the company continued
to overrun the communications trench and we shouted back for the
others to hold up, but on they came and we cursed and writhed and
waved our arms to stop them for fear that the overcrowded shelter
would draw fire from the enemy mortars. But more dove in with us
and the only thing we could do was to dash for holes ahead, which
we did in small, angry groups.

The sharp, light crack of enemy rifles joined in the fire against
us, punctuated occasionally by the shrill whine of hand grenades
and knee mortars. We flattened ourselves against the ground.

"God damn it," someone to my left growled. "They told us we were
going into the front lines. Hell, we *are* the front lines."

It was true. We had been staging a push without knowing it. But
we knew it now and we knew that enemy pillboxes lay in front of us.

And we heard shouts ahead of us and rose to our knees to watch.
Sergeant Summers and Corporal Degliequi from the second squad
were forward of us and had joined battle against one of the emplacements. Behind them and, we thought, engaged in the same action,
other members of the squad could be seen.

We heard the steady burst of our semi-automatic rifles followed
by the sudden dull discharge of a rifle grenade. We ducked as the
fragments flew back over our heads.

As we flinched the ground rose and hit us and the sides of our shell
hole fell in about us, pouring sand across our helmets, and the air
was heavy with sound.

We looked up to see a black column of smoke and we caught the
sight of fragments of some solid material flying even higher than
the smoke cloud.

"Demolitions," the man on my left said aloud but he was not talking to me or to anyone other than himself.

"Jesus!" another said. "They really poured it into them then. I wonder what size charge they used? I'll bet there's nothing left of that pillbox."

But there was. When we looked again we saw smoke still issuing
into the air and we saw the position of the emplacement clearly for
the first time. The squad moved farther up the hill and then split,
three men turning to the right and the remainder going directly to
the front. The three moved slowly and cautiously toward the pillbox,
which appeared to be only a slight rise in the ground. They almost
circled it before they stopped and pressed close against its side. The
man in front leaned his rifle against the wall and we could see that he

was disengaging the pin in the safety lever of a grenade. He lurched forward, threw hard to his left with an underhand motion and the three men scrambled to the near side of the rise and pressed against the ground. We heard an explosion and dust flew from the left of the mound.

The men rose and another one of the three, whom I recognized as Corporal Martel, repeated the performance. Again they raced to safety and this time the explosion was followed by the issuance of thick white smoke from what evidently was the embrasure.

"Phosphorus," said the man at my left.

The remainder of the squad was near the crest of the ridge and the members of it suddenly flattened themselves. Now the singing of enemy grenade fragments was clear but distant to us and we saw their origin. Another Japanese pillbox, also distinguished by little more than a slight rise in the ground, lay at the crest. As we watched, amazed, a Jap jumped high in the air from the rear of the shelter and we saw the arc of his arm as he threw. He was gone from sight before the squad's rifles cracked. And we could hear the angry cries.

"Grenade! Grenade!"

"Get 'im! Get 'im! Get the son of a bitch!"

"Watch him if he tries that again."

"Duke! Get down! That was a Jap grenade."

And the voice of Duke, who had been one of the three attacking the previous emplacement:

"God damn it! Why don't you tell somebody what's going on?"

But he continued to stand, his rifle held as if he were expecting a covey of quail to rise in front of him. The head and arm of the Jap appeared again and four rifles barked but once more the enemy had gone before the rifles were fired. The men of the squad, directly in front of the pillbox now, continued to stand, as cool as if they, too, were hunting small game, until the grenade struck in front of them and rolled toward them. They dropped to the ground as the missile exploded and then, unharmed, they rose to their knees. The force of a grenade's explosion against the ground is such that most of the fragments are thrown outward and upward; thus a man flattened against the ground a few yards away has at least a fair chance of escaping injury.

A marine in the center of the line twisted at the ring of his grenade. He threw with a quick overhand snap of the wrist, like a baseball catcher. The grenade disappeared just over the back of the pillbox. Almost immediately the Jap's head and arm appeared again and the grenade flew back into the open and the squad ducked hurriedly, knowing it would explode almost immediately. It did, sounding heavier and more violent than the Jap's.

And the angry cries rose on the tail of the whining of the fragments as the marines jumped to their feet again.

"Let's get that bastard this time!"

"Watch him!"

"Shoot the son of a bitch!"

Four of the attackers stood side by side in front of the pillbox and others moved to the right and to the left about it. There was no apparent haste nor, except in words, agitation. The attack went forward as it might have in maneuvers except that in practice, exposure such as this ahead of me would have brought instant condemnation from any observing officer.

The faint burst and the shrill crying fragments of another enemy grenade came, and then another, and with them the call:

"Corpsman! Corpsman!"

Someone was hit. I could not see who it was and the voices died as rifle fire exploded again.

It was obvious then that several Japs occupied the pillbox and that the emplacement itself was only one of a series of such defenses which were mutually supporting. This one was protected from the far side of the ridge so that the present small-scale flanking attack was useless. The men to the right and left came slowly down from the ridge and the squad as a whole pulled back to the main body of our troops.

Later we found out that Sergeant Summers, in an effort to overrun the pillbox before darkness, had asked for additional troops but the word had never reached those in the rear. Similarly, the destruction of the first strongpoint had been accomplished almost solely by Summers and Corporal Degliequi simply because the remainder of the platoon had not realized what was occurring. Summers had stumbled on the enemy who, from the shelter of a communications trench, were watching us move up. He was joined by Degliequi who forced the enemy into the pillbox through use of a rifle grenade. There one of them, wounded by Summers, blew himself up. That was the "demolition" charge which had shaken us. But the break in our down-the-line communications system which we had tried so vigorously to maintain had been costly in time and, perhaps, in men.

※　※　※　※

THE MOST HAZARDOUS DUTY OF ALL WAS THAT OF the scouts-snipers platoon, the advance men, a few of whom we are now privileged to meet in the following excerpt by Bryce Walton. The multiplicity of duties performed by this elite group of the 4th Division (24th Marines) took a severe toll of their gallant numbers.

·7· SCOUTS-SNIPERS PLATOON

BRYCE WALTON

They dodged from cave to cave. In one they found much ammunition and weapons, some Molotov cocktails for knocking out our tanks, machine guns and grenades. The place was reinforced heavily with concrete and stone and parts of wrecked aircraft. Sizemore looked back out of the hole just in time to see one of our amphibious tanks hit a land mine. The tank was blown to pieces.

They left a few grenades in the cave. The grenades exploded behind them setting off some stored Jap ammo. They went back to the C.P. to relax.

Pvt. Carl Rothrock of Clemmons, N.C., and Cpl. Ben Bernal of Tucson, Ariz., were sent up to a dump to get some rations. They, too, got their first Iwo Jap. As they approached the entrance to a dump, Bernal saw a Jap standing in the opening.

Bernal quickly lifted a .45 and shot the Jap twice. The man toppled backward into the hole. Bernal ran around to the other side of the cave to cover any opening there through which other Japs might leak out. Rothrock, with an M-1, advanced up to the opening and peered inside. The Japanese was trying to crawl off into a dark corner. Rothrock shot him.

They found rations and brought them back to the command post. They ate the stuff, then burrowed into the mushy black sand with ponchos over them. They couldn't sleep much, so, whenever they got a chance, they dug their foxholes deeper.

It seemed dull the next day until an artillery shell came over from the other side of the ridge. It made a direct hit on the battalion aid station. Four men were killed and 10 wounded.

All night long the scouts-snipers worked as litter bearers.

The next morning they still were waiting for orders. Meanwhile they did work they could never forget. They gathered together the bodies of dead marines for identification and marking. They worked through the consistent mortar and artillery fire.

The only break in the restless waiting came when a Jap shell hit an ammo dump less than 100 yards away. Sgt. Ralph Jones of Fort Madison, Ia., saw it go off as he dropped into a foxhole. There was a shaking concussion, and shrapnel hit everywhere, wounding several including Sgt. Elmer G. Smith of Cawker City, Kan., first of the scouts' casualties. He was struck on the arm by a hurtling 74 mm. shell and was evacuated.

The scouts' restlessness and nervousness grew as they kept on waiting, shelled constantly by mortars and artillery. Their waiting ended on the twenty-third when they moved up. [Lieutenant William] Holder was a little man who looked almost too young to be an officer. He had won the Silver Star at Saipan. McFall and Pfc. Anthony J. Ranfas stepped up as the lieutenant called them.

Holder, Ranfas and McFall scouted ahead to determine what course to follow toward the ridge. Ranfas returned and led the platoon up to their positions. As they advanced through the sand up onto rocky, rising ground, they knew why the looks on the faces of Holder, Ranfas, and Sgt. McFall had been so worn and grim when they came back.

The sand area broke suddenly into rocky ledges leading up into a no man's land that formed the right side of the bulk of the island, which the 4th Div. was slated to take. It was a broken area of death traps, blasted holes, undermined with winding labyrinths of caves. Piles of shattered concrete emplacements torn by aerial and Navy bombardment lay around. Japs still hid in their holes. Every pile of sandstone, dirt and concrete concealed a sniper, machine gunner, or mortar.

At the bottom of the first sharp uprising of brown cliff, a runner from K Company met McFall with a report as to position for digging in. The scouts-snipers' job the rest of that day and night was security for the C.P. and mortar section, which was just to their rear.

The runner from K Company rubbed his beared, dirt-caked face. "This is different," he said to Jones, as they hugged the ground and burrowed up against the sandstone walls of their dugout. "Those cookies up there are the best. Those snipers don't miss a thing if they see it. Not like the snipers on Saipan and Tinian. And their machine gunners rake the ground and unless you're behind rock they get you in the head."

Standing security watch for the C.P. that night, they came to know the meaning of fear. Not fear of the Jap, but fear of the unknown. The nightmare terrain, the bent dwarf trees and jumbles of rock seemed to take on life. Everything seemed to move and shift. When they sent up mortar flares, the shadows weaved through the defiles and across the broken places.

In the surrounding area were many caves and emplacements sus-

pected of containing Japs. Jones got orders from Holder to take out
a scouting party to clean them out. This was the job for which the
scouts had been trained. In caves to which they could see both entrances, they threw grenades. When only one entrance was visible,
they sealed it up with demolition charges, trapping the Japs inside
who had refused to come out. In these patrols were Doerner, Rindfleisch, Seissinger, Sizemore, Derhammer, Ragland, Bernal, Rothrock, and Pfc.s Charles De Celles of Harlem, Mont., and William
North of Brown's Center, Clearwater, Fla.

They had crawled up out of their foxholes, moving in a skirmish
line, when there was a sudden intense barrage of mortar fire that
seemed to burst all around them, raining chunks of shell fragment and
blasted rock. Again they sought cover.

Ragland was trying to find a position behind a rock ledge when
a piece of shrapnel caught him in the leg. Jones crawled over and
put on a quick battle dressing. They looked around and saw Bernal
holding his arm and looking dazed. Blood was seeping out around
his fingers.

Bernal stumbled down between high croppings of rock toward
the distant beach.

"You're going, too," Jones said to Ragland.

Ragland's dirt-encrusted face cracked in that tooth-spaced grin.

"Nah-huh," he said. "Just a scratch."

When the scouts-snipers came back to the C.P. they had worked
hard under fire all day, but Maj. Jim Miller, Company K commander,
wasn't satisfied. "It's bad enough having them as thick as flies in front
of you without having 'em crawling up in back," he said.

So, Holder led a mopping up squad consisting of Pvt. George Miller
of Maspeth, L.I., Huff, Ranfas, Pvt. David Owens of Charleston, S.C.
and Pfc. LaRue Stevenson of Pottsville, Pa.

That night the scouts-snipers got their final orders. A dangerous
gap had been eaten out of the area between K Company of the 3rd
Bn. and E Company of the 2nd Bn. The scouts-snipers would have
to move in to fill this gap as front line riflemen.

Of the platoon, only 9 had seen close fighting before. The rest were
to know a baptism of fire that set an all time precedent.

The weather had cleared. It was perfect—for the Jap. The terrain
seemed more menacing in the clear light but one still couldn't see
the Japs; but, moving up, he could see you.

They went up, two squads abreast, in a skirmish line. Pfc. Jack
Stearn of Woonsocket, R.I., as mapreader; Pfc. John Pluta of North
Rose, N.Y., and Owens, as runners; all led by McFall.

Jap fire seemed to come from everywhere, and nowhere.

They managed to wedge through for 150 yards. Huff heard a muffled groan. He went down on one knee as he twisted around. Stearn was down and gripping his right shoulder from which blood from a sniper's bullet ran freely. Huff ran back, sprinkled sulpha in the wound and put on a battle dressing.

Stearn's face showed no pain as he got to his feet and went back toward the evacuation station.

They dug in for the night, using abandoned Jap holes. Soon they were joined by a machine gun section. One machine gun was set up on either flank. There were 3 men to a foxhole. Three men, Huff, Owens, and Pluta were in a rear guard watch.

McFall was on watch when, at 9 o'clock, he heard what he assumed were Japs just in front of his position. Looking into the shadows of the weird shrubbery and grotesque rock formation you could assume almost anything. Then McFall began laughing a little to himself with the relief of being able to open up on something tangible. He had heard the familiar Jap jabbering, and fired 40 rounds into the Japs with his Tommy gun.

Huff's eyes were bloodshot with strain as he kept up his rear guard watch for bypassed Japs infiltrating from the back. Everything, to Huff, seemed to be moving, shifting. He couldn't seem to tell which was real and which was a gruesome part of his imagination.

Then suddenly he knew the difference. A chattering, bundled-up squad of Japs were jumping toward Huff over the rocks and among the twisted trees. "Halt!" said Huff, reflexively, after he began raking them with his Tommy gun. A few shadowed shapes seemed to fall. Others, instead of ducking or running back, ran parallel to the front lines. Then everyone began to throw hand grenades. The place was a kaleidoscope of shattered rock, shell fragments, and pieces of Jap bodies. After that episode, the following hours before dawn, in spite of the continuous mortar, artillery and machine gun fire from the Jap, seemed almost peaceful.

Jones was the first marine out of his hole and on his feet that morning. He had received the Silver Star for bravery under fire in the Marshalls. He was tall, blonde and rugged, and his speech was swift and clipped short. That's the way his actions were.

Jones crawled over into Huff's foxhole. "Give me your Tommy gun a minute," he said quickly. Huff complied. Jones went directly to a shell hole a few feet away, down behind a pile of torn rock. Ragland limped along after him, covering him with a BAR.

After searching around, Jones went back to his foxhole just in time to miss a mortar shell. He opened up some K-rations marked breakfast. Ragland and the two men with him had dug their hole about 12 inches from a shell crater. As Ragland started to duck back into his own dugout he noticed a dead Jap leaning against the stones of the next one.

"So help me!" yelled Ragland, "It's a Jap with a red goatee."

Word came down the line that they would advance at 0930.

Three half-tracks, 75 mm.'s, laid down a thundering barrage. Eighty-one mm.'s opened up on the immediate Jap positions. When the barrage lifted at 0930 the line went forward against withering cross-fire from more enemy snipers and machine guns.

A sharp cliff, dirty brown in color, rose up ahead. It contained a mass of hidden sniper and machine gun nests and it was about 100 yards from the base of this cliff that the Japs really opened up.

Holder stumbled, went down a sharp defile and rolled behind some rock. Another man pitched forward just after Holder fell.

Huff crept up, trying to stay beneath the path of machine gun fire, to Holder's side. Corpsmen ran in and took care of the wounded officer. Huff left them there and ran back toward his men, who were still trying to move against the cliff.

Huff now was in command of the platoon. An insurance agent before his enlistment, he had been a trainer back in the States. This was his first time in combat.

An explosion on Huff's left marked the end of that Marine machine gun. Their right flank machine gun was still in action. Huff ran up further to gain the edge of a high rock dugout to direct his platoon.

Ragland was up front, working his BAR. Beside him was Rothrock trying to find something to shoot at with his M-1, and Sgt. Jones.

"You're too naked up there," yelled Huff. He motioned them to drop back into his foxhole which was deeper and gave more protection.

Rothrock, keeping low, ran back.

Jones stood up, without regard for his own safety, exposed to the murderous cross-fire, and covered Rothrock and Ragland and Huff, while the former two worked their way toward a dugout. Then, after the three were down out of imminent danger, Jones sent a last round at the side of the cliff. Then he spun around as a return hail of machine gun fire found him.

Jones was dead as he fell, close to the three he had covered.

Huff crouched beside Ragland who had dropped his BAR and was firing an M-1. Another mortar explosion marked the end of their left flank machine gun.

"See if you can find any of our men over there," Huff told Ragland. "I'll cover you."

Ragland grinned stiffly and crawled up over the rocks toward the left. It was too hot to crawl. He got up in a half crouch and ran. He did a long frantic flying leap into a hole. Beside him were two more scouts-snipers. One, North, was dead, shot through the head. The other was Rindfleisch, whose arm was injured badly.

McFall appeared beside Ragland, dragging another slow-moving, dazed figure beside him. It was Seissinger. A close mortar blast had sent him into the "shock" list.

In spite of his injured arm, Rindfleisch managed to take Seissinger with him back of the lines.

Ragland and McFall scuttled through the open area to Huff, and the still body of Jones.

It seemed a couple of years later that Huff got most of his remaining men together, most of them in and around a large hole surrounded by plenty of sandstone. They kept down out of the path of Jap machine guns. Ragland was placed in command of the second squad.

All the time, McFall, a worried expression on his face, was wrapped around his walkie-talkie trying to establish contact with the regimental C.P. Finally he got a response. He looked up, swallowed painfully at the remaining scouts-snipers. Their faces, bearded with whiskers, dirt and blood, looked silently at McFall.

"We resume the attack," McFall said simply. "At 1330."

They all glanced at Huff. "Okay," he said. "If we could only see the bastards."

Machine gun fire kept them pinned down.

"We need that right flank machine gun working," said Huff. "I think the gun's okay. The men are gone, that's all."

Huff went up out of the hole and ran for the machine gun emplacement. Others had the same idea as Huff. Marines came in beside him dragging ammo. Maj. Miller came up to the scouts' position and talked to Huff. "There's a gap in the lines there 75 yards wide with only 12 men to cover it."

The major told Huff to report with him to the company C.P. a little behind the front lines for orders. It was a long run. They never stopped for cover. They just staggered, crouched and ran low when they could.

A sniper had grazed Huff's side with a bullet and the slug got the major in the shoulder.

Huff stayed in the C.P. until some tanks were ready to move up. He had been told that he wouldn't have to shift his platoon's position; that others would close in to fill up the gap. Meanwhile McFall's walkie-talkie had given out and Huff went back to his platoon's position. His return sprint was more perilous than before as the Japs seemed to know another advance was gathering, and were intensifying their fire.

When Huff reached his men this time, he said quickly: "Spread out. We're going to attack." At that minute a runner came up and told Huff that their orders were changed a bit. They were to advance, closing in against the platoon to their right. As Huff got up and started to place his men, a line of machine gun fire hit him. He could feel a blow against his back like a hammer. He saw Pfc. James McCollick of Bristol, Pa., flattened in a little hole and Huff yelled, "I'm hit!"

McFall heard Huff's cry. He said, "I'll get him." Ragland, who had been beside McFall, caught McFall's walkie-talkie as it was tossed to him. McFall crawled toward where Huff had fallen into a foxhole, dragging the butt of a Tommy gun along beside him.

Ragland tried to yell as he saw little puffs of dust and splintered rock run along across the ground toward McFall. Then the path of bullets traveled across the small of McFall's back. The sergeant raised up, mumbling something toward the Jap lines, and fell backwards firing his Tommy gun blindly.

McCollick got to Huff's side, and the latter thought McCollick was trying to administer first aid as he fumbled around behind him. McCollick's hand came out holding a blunted Jap bullet. "What's that?" mumbled Huff.

"It got your poncho, tore it to pieces," said McCollick, "but it didn't touch you."

Huff felt sick.

"It got your field glasses, too," added McCollick.

Huff felt a big emptiness in his belly as he thought of McFall who had died trying to save him because of a wound he didn't even have.

There was a 50-yard gap there and his men couldn't fill it. Pvt.'s Marion Saucerman of Sullivan, Ind., Pat Rion of Clemmons, N.C., and Frederick McCarthy of South Portland, Mich., were the only three men left in front of Huff.

Huff pondered on what action to take. Machine guns and snipers covered them. No one could seem to locate any of the nests. And, if they did, while you tried to advance on them with guns, grenades and flamethrowers, you were caught in the cross-fire from other emplacements. This was what the 4th Div. faced along the island's right flank.

Huff got orders to edge up to the right. McCarthy moved up front to pick up Rion and Saucerman. He gave them the orders and, as he tried to run back, a sniper got him in the right arm. The bullet caught him in midair as he jumped toward a foxhole.

The scouts crept through fire and the scarred, body-strewn area toward the right and found some deep holes. A mortar exploded close to a hole which Pvt. Henry Sellers of Wilmington, N.C., had dug into. He was injured, badly, by the mortar and Huff and Ragland applied 12 battle dressings. A shell fragment from the same mortar

wounded Cpl. Robert Pounders of Birmingham, Ala., in the back.
Huff sent Sellers out on a stretcher carried by Rion and McCollick.
Pounders managed to walk with them toward the evacuation station.
Nine were left on the line . . .

❧ ❧ ❧ ❧

IT HAD BECOME INCREASINGLY CLEAR IN TWO DAYS
of fighting that we were being opposed by an enemy whose leadership was brilliant, and whose troops were brave, determined,
well armed and intelligent. Witness the fact that it took the 4th
Division twenty-four days to go from Motoyama No. 1 Airfield
to the east coast just above Tachiiwa Point—a distance of three
miles. Marines were now aware that they were fighting a savage
enemy who simply retired into a labyrinth of tunnels honeycomb-
ing the island, and there waited for the propitious moment before rising and firing with mortar, rocket, machine gun and artillery. Typical of the grueling action was the experience of the
24th Regiment, which had been held up by six pillboxes. Two
tanks were brought up but were quickly destroyed by mines. Marine Gunner Ira Davidson and six of his buddies came into the
breach dragging a 37-mm. gun, but before these men could get set
up, three of them were out of action and one was dead. Somehow,
Davidson and the survivors managed to fire the gun and knocked
out the Japanese opposition. The infantry moved up.

It was equally rough going for those marines of Keller Rockey's
5th Division who turned north to move along the spine of the
island; for what they missed on the beaches they more than found
inland along the route of Kuribayashi's primary defenses. This
was the day when two Division men won the Medal of Honor.
In face of heavy enemy fire Captain Robert H. Dunlap of C Company, 26th Marines, crawled on his stomach to locate enemy guns
pinning down the advance. Then Dunlap returned to his own
lines and passed along information that resulted in an ear-shat-
tering bombardment by artillery and naval gunfire, while Dunlap imperturbably directed the shoot from an exposed position
until resistance stopped. Another who did credit to the Corps
was Private First Class Jacklyn H. Lucas who, while leading a
few men in an attack, was surrounded and taken under heavy
fire by a large enemy force. A shower of grenades engulfed the
marines, and one bounced into their midst. Without hesitation

Lucas threw himself on the missile and smothered it with his chest, taking the full force of the explosion. He lived, miraculously, and his men eventually fought their way out of the box.

D-Plus-One found the beaches ever hot, but those named Green 1 and Green 2 were both hot and wet. Huge surf piling into the shore since late the previous day made front line delivery of war stuffs impossible. The wreckage of gutted hulks was scattered over an area of two miles, so thick it looked as if nothing would ever get in. But one truck even at this time rolled off a ramp and the driver, a young Negro, got his vehicle out of the water and off the soft sand while Japanese gunners leisurely zeroed in. The truck was an ammo carrier. If hit it was likely the whole beach would go up. The driver called for help and men raced forward to roll the vehicle a distance of several hundred yards. But by now shells had begun to pummel the truck and it caught fire. Everybody scattered except the driver who finally jumped clear when he moved the truck to higher ground—it blew up with a colossal roar in a few moments. No harm came to those at the water's edge.

Meanwhile the 28th Marines was inexorably pushing south toward Mount Suribachi, gaining less than 400 yards a day. Liversedge's troops moved slowly and steadily, knocking out a succession of pillboxes and caves barring their way to the base of the mountain. By the close of D-Plus-Two the 28th had sustained losses of 11 officers and 185 men killed or wounded, and only 5 of its tanks were in action. But the ineluctable Liversedge kept up the pace. Next day three landing teams abreast continued the attack behind flamethrowers. That was when Corporal Daniel R. McCarthy acquired the name "Killer": he had a BAR and used it until 20 Japanese were piled up before him. In one of the caves in the area a troubled Japanese diarist noted: "Today is a most important day. Today we annihilate those who have landed. There are no reinforcements for us—are we not losing the battle?"

The stuff of which legends are made was evident that day. A captain, severely wounded in the head, led an attack on six pillboxes and knocked them out before losing consciousness. First Sergeant Edward R. Swain, heedless of the blood spilling from a deep gash in his back, cleaned out several caves with his machine gun. Another marine took on a sword-swinging Japanese officer who charged from a cave, wrestled the sword away with his bare hands, then cut the other's head off. By the close of the third day the 28th Marines had surrounded the base of Suribachi, but another 5 officers and 101 men were dead. Among the last to fall that rainy, gray afternoon was regimental surgeon Lieutenant Commander Daniel McCarthy. "At dawn," Liversedge told his officers, "we climb. We keep on climbing till we reach the top of that stinking mountain."

Here again is Sergeant David Dempsey, who tells of the capture of Mount Suribachi.

·8· THE FALL OF SURIBACHI

SERGEANT DAVID DEMPSEY

Early on D plus 4 four men from LT 2/28's F Company started to scale the gutted slopes of Suribachi. The patrol leader, Sergeant Sherman Watson, kept reporting as he went along that the Japanese still were holed up. Lieutenant Colonel Johnson, the battalion CO, made his decision. He threw together a forty-man combat patrol—remnants of the 3d Platoon of E Company, and a handful of men from battalion headquarters, and put in command Lieutenant Harold G. Schrier, the E Company executive officer.

"If you reach the top," Johnson told him, "secure and hold it. And take this along." "This" was an American flag which Lieutenant George G. Wells, the battalion adjutant, had brought ashore in his map case from the transport *Missoula*.

The patrol filed through reeking battle debris and blasted gunpits and started up the northern face of Suribachi, sometimes walking, sometimes crawling on hands and knees as the slope became steeper. Higher and higher the patrol picked its way, avoiding heavily mined trails and keeping men out on the flanks to protect the main body from ambush.

"Those guys," observed a marine below, "ought to be getting flight pay."

As the men neared the top they spread out around the rim of the crater. Schrier signalled. The patrol charged over the top and met— nothing, nothing but a deep, yawning lava pit.

Suribachi had fallen!

One marine ran up with a piece of hollow pipe. On it went the flag. At 1035, while Sergeant Louis Lowery, a *Leatherneck Magazine* photographer, photographed the event, Lieutenant Schrier, Platoon Sergeant Ernest I. Thomas, Sergeant Henry Hanson, Corporal Charles W. Lindberg, and Private First Class James Michaels raised the colors.

Hovering over a nearby cave, little sixteen-year-old Private First Class James Robeson refused to be included in the picture. "Hollywood Marines," he snorted and watched intently for a crack at anyone who might object to the flag-raising.

Several did. An enraged Japanese soldier hiding nearby pitched a grenade at the flag party and another charged, brandishing a Samurai sword. Both died quickly.

On the beachhead below, thousands of marines saw the tiny flag, but for every cheer that went up, a hundred got only as far as a tight, lumpy throat. Most marines simply stood silently watching the volcano, and they went on about whatever they had been doing. (Four hours later, when the original flag was replaced with a larger one, Joe Rosenthal of the Associated Press shot the scene without realizing he had just taken the most celebrated picture of World War II.)

The flag was on Suribachi to stay; no one doubted that. Neither did anyone doubt that there was hard fighting still ahead—the volcano was still crawling with Japs. Schrier walked over to the men whose picture had just been taken.

"We haven't time to waste around here," he said, "let's get back to work."

Even as Schrier made the remark one company below was battling more than two hundred Japanese in a honeycomb of caves partly hidden by the tangled underbrush. Trying to get the stalled attack under way, Private First Class Harold E. Benedict grabbed the only flamethrower left in the company and began scorching the cave openings. The enemy instantly concentrated their fire on him, but he continued to douse them with bursts of flame for five hours without receiving a scratch to show for the intense fire he had been under . . .

Suribachi had cost CT 28 904 casualties. (Coincidentally, this was the exact number of casualties for the entire 5th Division on D-day.) Of these, 7 officers and 202 men had been killed. On the other side, 1,231 enemy dead had been counted, hundreds more were sealed inside caves and blockhouses, and more than a thousand enemy emplacements of all kinds had been destroyed.

Working with the infantry, engineers had destroyed 165 concrete pillboxes and blockhouses—some with walls ten feet thick—had blasted 15 strong bunkers and naval-gun positions; had destroyed thousands of shells, grenades, and land mines; and had sealed 200 caves, some of them three stories high with heavy steel doors. In addition, these supporting troops evacuated hundreds of wounded marines and bulldozed 1,500 yards of roads and tank paths around the crater.

Corps took control . . . on D plus 6. Colonel Liversedge's men remained in reserve in the Suribachi area for five days picking off Japanese who dug themselves out of caves, salvaging arms and equipment, and training new replacements.

Intelligence observers and artillery spotters (including the "flash-bang" counter-battery observers) soon turned the volcano into a vital observation post. This 554-foot OP overlooked all of southern and central Iwo and proved extremely advantageous to the landing force and correspondingly hurtful to the Japanese who now were denied its use.

Marines atop Suribachi, looking to the north, could see the flash and dust of battle. Few realized what it held for them.

❀　❀　❀　❀

HOLLAND SMITH AND SECRETARY OF THE NAVY JAMES Forrestal came ashore and walked among the troops, Smith expressed a desire to climb Mount Suribachi. His aide told him he was too old. Smith fumed until Forrestal offered consolation: "Holland, the raising of that flag means a Marine Corps for the next five hundred years."

The marines on the beach were incredulous that the Secretary of the Navy should so expose himself when shells were still falling into the area. Smith also found it hard to believe: "The Secretary seemed utterly oblivious even when a shell went off a hundred yards away and wounded and killed twenty men . . . His *sangfroid* impressed us all. I could not deny the men an opportunity to see, hear and shake hands with him."

Now the 4th Division began its push northward for Motoyama No. 2 Airfield and Charley Dog Ridge. Regimental Combat Team 24 kicked off the fighting between the airfields, an area saturated with Japanese guns and ankle-deep volcanic dust; in every dune the enemy had a gun and every gun gave tongue. The attack went forward behind artillery, but after the infantry advanced, the enemy closed in from all sides. The lines literally melted away. Marines chased Japanese down long trenches, and after a while the roles would be reversed. Grenade duels were fought everywhere. Recalled Captain LaVerne Wagner (23rd Marines) of this tragicomedy: "We found ourselves in the rear of Jap pill-boxes which were still doing business on the other side . . ."

However, at this moment Kuribayashi evidently sensed his positions were being overrun, and issued these orders to his troops:

> We shall dedicate ourselves and our entire strength to the defense of the island.
> We shall infiltrate into the midst of the enemy and annihilate them.
> We shall grasp bombs, charge the enemy tanks and destroy them.
> With every salvo we will, without fail, kill the enemy.
> Each man will make it his duty to kill 10 of the enemy before dying.

After another day of fighting—proportionately the bloodiest in the history of this nation—the Marine Corps had conquered one third of Iwo Jima at a cost of 1605 dead and 5496 wounded. It took courage to lead, it took courage to follow, but it could not be done any other way.

Here, again, is Richard Newcomb.

·9· KURIBAYASHI'S LAST STAND

RICHARD NEWCOMB

The terrible two weeks began on Sunday morning, quite unspectacularly.

It was clear that the only way to take the remaining two-thirds of the island was to go up the high ground in the middle. From the relatively flat plateau, the ground broke to east and west and ran down to the shore in gullies, canyons, and arroyos. The shelling had churned them into masses of broken stone, their sides riddled with caves, holes, tunnels, the ridges broken and strewn with boulders.

On the west coast, the Fifth Division was faced with one ridge after another, each one meaning a fight up the slope and over the top, only to meet another ravine with another ridge beyond it. Japanese fire down the canyons would be murderous. The enemy would have to be driven from the high ground in the center, and even then the advance along the coast would be expensive.

The Fourth Division on the east faced a battlefield stripped of all cover. Where once the oaks had grown, there were only shattered rock, tangled brush, and defiles running to the sea like spokes from the hub of a wheel. Rising from this frozen sea of stone were Hill 382, the highest point on the island excepting Suribachi, a bald little hill someone had named Turkey Knob, and a natural bowl that quite easily took the name of the Amphitheater.

Far beyond, toward the sea, was the headquarters of Major General Sadasue Senda, and all through the rock lay his 2nd Mixed Brigade, unseen and waiting. There was a smashed radar station on top of Hill 382, and on the far bluff of the Amphitheater could be seen cave mouths and tunnel entrances. Not a gun barrel could be seen but at every turn and fold in the rock were cross-lanes of fire for machine guns and mortars, automatic weapons and rifles, light artillery, and rapid-fire cannon. Behind them were the men, some with sabres or pistols, bamboo lances, and sacks of grenades, waiting.

In the center, General Erskine took back the 21st Regiment from the Fourth Division and for the first time had all his troops then ashore under his own command. The 21st went to the rear to re-equip and rest, and the 9th went into the line. All artillery of the Corps, the Fourth and the Fifth Divisions were in place, and the remainder of the Third Division artillery was landing. The drive up the center began.

A battleship and two cruisers opened the assault, firing for twenty minutes in slow, deliberate salvos from their main batteries. The artillery followed with 1,200 rounds across the front, and carrier planes with 500-pound bombs came in just ahead of the line.

At 9:30 A.M. the men moved out, and it was as though the guns had never fired. Japanese fire sweeping across Airfield No. 2 was strong and accurate.

Twenty-six tanks were available, and there had been talk of riding the infantry across the strip on them. This idea was discarded, and the tanks lumbered out, with Ateball, Agony, and Angel at the point.

Angel and Agony were hit and flamed immediately. Ateball was stopped by a shell hit. Corporal William R. Adamson of San Jose, California, squeezed out of Agony's hatch and dropped to the ground alongside his tank. A bullet nicked his leg, and he sat in a pall of smoke from the burning machine, tearing up his pants leg to bandage the wound. From the corner of his eye he caught sight of a muzzle flash. Crawling toward Ateball, he crouched in the open, 30 yards from the muzzle of its 75, and waved wildly toward the flash. Ateball fired, again and again, and the Japanese gun was silent.

In succession, Adamson then pointed out four machine guns, a Japanese running up with a satchel charge, and 30 infantry sneaking up along a ravine. Ateball broke them all up, and a tank retriever came for Ateball. On the way it rolled over Adamson and picked him up through the escape hatch. Other tanks rolled on. By day's end, nine tanks had been knocked out.

The 1st Battalion of the 9th fought five hours and advanced 100 yards, to the foot of Hill Peter. The 2nd and 3rd made better advances, and by the end of the day the line was north of Airfield No. 2 at all points except the extreme right tip.

Erskine was not satisfied (he rarely was) and he called in Colonel Kenyon, the 9th's commander. Were the men prepared for a night attack, the General asked. The Colonel ran his arm over his sweaty red face. "They're mighty tired," he said.

The General reared back and began to talk of World War I. He told how, at Soissons, he came back from a patrol, one of four men left out of thirty-eight, and the company commander told him to go out again and throw a rock at a German machine gun so that they could spot it.

"I did what he told me," the General said. Then he turned to Captain Oscar Salgo of the reconnaissance company.

"I want you to go through the Jap lines in a night attack and blow up and burn out some of these pillboxes that are holding us up."

The Captain said he was willing to try, but which pillboxes did the General have in mind? The map showed only a few, but everybody knew there were many. The General, his eyes flinty, canceled the night attack, but he put the idea away for another time.

The Fourth Division, using the 23rd and 24th Regiments, moved off into the Meat Grinder. No one knew where the name came from, but everybody knew what it meant. It meant the area from Hill 382 down through Turkey Knob and the Amphitheater, the area where the men were ground up into meat—fresh, red meat.

They laid on the artillery, the navy gunfire, with mortar boats and LCI's firing up the draws, carrier planes plunging down in, and the LVT (A)'s firing from offshore. They sent the tanks around through the Third Division's area, because they couldn't get over the rubble in front, and armored bulldozers chewed away at the shattered rocks, trying to clear roads. And the men fought all day, and by nightfall they had made about a hundred yards.

The Fifth Division took it easy. That is, they didn't press the battle, waiting for the Third to move in the center. They took it easy, and they still had 163 casualties, with mortar and artillery fire dropping off the ridges up north. In the afternoon, the Fifth's artillery had one bright moment. Against all orders, some Japanese artillery began moving north in daylight, high up on the west coast. A plane spotted them about 3 P.M. and the Fifth's artillery enthusiastically poured on nearly 600 rounds. Three Japanese artillery pieces were smashed, and an ammunition dump was set afire. Colonel Kaido had warned against such folly. For the rest of the campaign, no more artillery moved by day.

Behind the lines, it was as though there was no dying up front. An east wind piled high surf on the east beaches, but LSM's and LST's held the beach, and trucks and cranes unloaded them. Bulldozers and Dukws waddled inland on the roads taking shape, poles went up to get the wire off the ground. Artillery cracked incessantly, and work went on under the belching muzzles. The Navy began surveying the western beaches, and Fifth Division engineers opened the first water distillation plant on the west coast, on a ledge 45 feet above the sea. Intake pipes were driven into the natural springs, and the water came out so hot it had to be cooled with sea water. But there were showers for some, and the dirt ran off the men in mud waddies.

The 31st Seabees, using some heavy equipment borrowed from the 62nd, finished blading and rolling the north-south runway on Airfield No. 1. By nightfall a strip 1,500 feet long and 150 feet wide was ready for light planes. A plane came in from the Marianas and dropped some mail. Corporal Joseph P. Whittam, twenty, of Chicago, opened his. It was a civics lesson from the Marine Corps Institute.

All day the casualties streamed to the beaches, and nine ships left for Guam. This time the cargo was men — 1,469 casualties. The Third Division opened its cemetery just off the runway of Airfield No. 1.

While the 21st Regiment rested, Corporal Leniart of the 1st Battalion made his first trip to the beach to get replacements. After the corporal's four days at the front, these men looked to him as if they'd just come off liberty in San Diego. He led them forward, 50 or 100 at a time, and turned them over to the noncoms. Once in a while he got to watch as the new men were given a BAR, or a bazooka, or a machine gun. Someone showed them how to fire a few rounds, and from then on they were "ready." They had missed the hell of D-Day, but a special kind of ordeal awaited them.

Far off to the north, Task Force 58 went in again after the Japanese mainland. The weather was very bad, and the planes, flying in from 190 miles off Tokyo, could find only secondary targets. The strike was canceled at 12:15 P.M.

Late that night, in a cave with a single bulb hanging from the roof, Baron Nishi poured a drink for himself and his aide, Okubo. During the afternoon, at Airfield No. 2, the Colonel had watched a marine run forward with a flamethrower. The Baron had ordered firing stopped, but Okubo winged the marine, and they brought him in and turned him over to the surgeons. In his pocket was a letter from his mother, in which she said she was praying for his return.

The Baron thought of his own children, and Okubo thought of the stories he had heard that the Baron was pro-American. Nishi said he wanted to question the marine for intelligence.

"If I tried to save that American, that has nothing to do with my background," the Colonel said. They talked some more, about the chances Nishi had had to stay in America and of his opportunity to avoid the Iwo Jima assignment. After Okubo went to bed, Nishi finished the bottle. The next morning he was advised that the American had died.

The second week of the Iwo Jima campaign began on Monday morning, unnoticed. In seven days of fighting the Marines had captured two-fifths of the island and paid for it with more than 8,000 casualties. (Tokyo Radio said the part of the island held by the Americans was "not more than the size of the forehead of a cat.") There was no cause, and no time, to mark this anniversary. The men who had crossed the beaches on D-Day—every hour there were fewer left at the front—could not think in terms of time as long as a week. They measured it in spans of hours: of hours still alive; of nightfall and sunrises, still alive; of short, sharp stabs of pain when the word went around, "Charley got it." "That leaves only six of us," a man would think to himself, and the skin would tighten a little more over his cheekbones, and he would look a little grayer, a little older.

And mostly they would hunch over a little more, and move forward. But when it was Harold's turn, they stopped. He was leading a rifle squad on the west coast, and they saw him fall, cut down by a swath of machine-gun fire. His own brother, Luther Crabtree, saw it, from where he was blowing up caves as a demolitions man. Private First Class William C. Erler saw it. He and Harold and Luther had been together every day since they enlisted together in Columbus, Ohio, nearly two and a half years before.

"We can't leave him out there," Erler said, and the company commander agreed to hold up a minute while they tried for the body. He shouldn't have; this had nothing to do with the battle, but he threw up a smoke barrage, and Erler and two other privates ran forward with a stretcher.

They had no trouble finding the spot; it was where the lines of fire crossed from two Japanese pillboxes, and they rolled the body onto the stretcher and raced back into the lines. Luther got there just as they arrived, and for an instant in time the war stopped for Luther. They had landed in the same assault wave eight days ago, and now Harold, his older brother, twenty-two, was dead. And Luther and Harold and Erler had never been apart before. They took the body to the rear, the smoke barrage dissipated in the light airs above the hills, and the war went on.

If you don't know about Harold Crabtree or the more than 200 other men around him who were killed or wounded that day—or maybe if you looked at it from a different angle—it was a good day on the Fifth Division front. They made about 300 yards by nightfall, and the 26th overran Japanese Wells No. 4 and 5, the last water wells the Japanese had.

Twenty LVT (A)'s of the 2nd Armored Amphibian Battalion were out most of the day, bobbing off the west coast and firing their 75-mm. guns up the draws. They knocked out at least three enemy strong points, but in the late afternoon choppy seas forced them to stop firing. The rocking guns were sending shells into Marine territory.

Up ahead, nearly 800 yards away, you could see Hill 362A, the next big objective, and during the day they had flushed some Japanese and killed them as they ran. It was the first time they had seen the enemy in the open, and it gave the men a tremendous boost in morale.

Down on Airfield No. 1 the first planes came in, two little OY-1's of the Fourth Division (VMO-4), their wheels kicking up spurts of dust as they touched down. Dirty engineers and Seabees lined the runway and cheered as the little spotter planes rolled to a stop. The Grasshoppers (Stinson Sentinels), or "Maytag Messerschmitts," stayed only a few minutes and then they took off again, to fly over Turkey Knob and the Amphitheater to spot targets for the Fourth Division. As they left, the first of the 133rd Seabees' rollers and scrapers climbed up onto the runway. After a week of fighting, and heavy casualties, and reorganization, the 133rd was ready to start on the job it had come for.

In the center of the island Colonel Kenyon's 9th Regiment opened the second day of its assault on Hill Peter. Eight bombers and fighters were out in front of the lines, their bombs falling far up ahead. The marines cursed them, and the formal language of the Third Division report said this type of support "was entirely inadequate to meet the requirements of the situation. A much larger number of aircraft employed in mass against targets holding up the advance of infantry was clearly indicated."

The 1st Battalion, Ninth Regiment did succeed in getting a flame-throwing tank around behind the hill, and a few Japanese running from a tunnel were incinerated. Petty Officer Third Class Isamu Okazaki, twenty-two, a Navy rocket gunner, came out of a bunker and was surprised to see marines about 50 yards away. A bullet hit him in the chest and he fell. Okazaki threw a grenade and killed the marine who had wounded him, and then he threw three more grenades, scattering the marines. He crawled a half mile to the field hospital under Motoyama. A surgeon sprinkled disinfectant on his wound and told him: "I can't do anything more now. Go into the cave and rest until

I can come back to you." Okazaki crawled far back into the cave and fell into a stupor. (When he came out, the battle had passed him by, and maggots and time had healed his wound. He lived by his wits among the Americans until April, when a soldier tapped him on the shoulder and took him in.)

The 9th fought all day long around Hill Peter, again using massed tanks as assault guns, but at the end of five hours there was no gain, and eleven tanks had been knocked out. Private First Class James Golden of Boston, a rifleman, did not finish the day. He was sent back to the beach in the morning, covered from head to foot with heat rash. But he didn't know anybody at the beach, and he missed his outfit. He walked back and found his squad working around the face of the hill. Shortly before noon a bullet drilled him squarely between the eyes, just under the helmet line.

The Fourth Division struck out again for Hill 382 and Turkey Knob. Colonel Lanigan's 25th, strengthened by replacements after the severe losses of the first four days, went back into the line, replacing the 24th, and ran into very strong fire from Turkey Knob and the Amphitheater. The ground was so bad tanks could not be used, and even the 75's and 37's could not get into position. But around the East Boat Basin the final nests of snipers were wiped out, and at last the beaches were clear of all close fire. General unloading began on the Fourth Division beaches, and the *Columbia Victory* arrived with artillery ammunition. Parties worked all night long moving ammunition up for the guns. Corps artillery had a record day, firing 5,652 rounds.

The 23rd worked through minefields on the taxiways at the east end of Airfield No. 2 and on the slopes around the shattered radio station lying before Hill 382.

Starting up the slope toward Hill 382, Private First Class Douglas T. Jacobson of 3/23 was seized with a frenzy. For the moment he ceased to be a rifleman and became a bazooka man. He grabbed the weapon from a man who had gone down, ran to a Japanese 20-mm. gun position and knocked it out. Running on, he destroyed a pillbox and a blockhouse with fire and demolition charges. Still he ran on, into the enemy lines, and before the fires within him subsided he had killed at least seventy-five Japanese and captured sixteen Japanese positions. Company I was a good way up the southwest slope by late afternoon, but the enemy still held the top. The 23rd had to withdraw for the night.

It was plain that the Japanese were no longer retreating. The marines were now in the main line of defense, and the Japanese had to stand. Captain Awatsu's 309th Independent Infantry Battalion, or what was left of it, stood fast. By nightfall it had ceased to exist.

The 309th had been falling back slowly since D-Day, from in front of Airfield No. 1. The 23rd now drove it to the southeast, over against Lanigan's 25th, which finished it off. Net gain for the day on the 23rd's front was 200 yards.

Off Japan, the weather was so bad before dawn that Admiral Mitscher saw he could not get into position to raid Nagoya, the day's target. For the time being, at least, Task Force 58 was through with the great showpiece raids on Japan. The force broke up, part of the carriers leaving for Ulithi. The others fueled west of Iwo Jima and set out to raid Okinawa.

For the first time that night there was no mortar fire from the sea. All thirty of the LCI (M)'s had left that day for Saipan. In a week of supporting the marines with close-range fire, only one had been damaged, by a near-miss at the beach. Their night firing, in particular, had given the marines a good feeling.

The Army's 506th Anti-Aircraft Battalion finished landing during the day and began lobbing 90-mm. shells at Kama and Kangoku Rocks off the west coast. Occasional mortar and rocket fire had been coming from there, harassing the Fifth Division troops.

In the evening the weather cleared (it had rained a little in the afternoon), and a bright moon came out. A large group of Japanese, a company or more, started down the west coast, apparently hoping to recapture the wells lost that day. Lined with concrete rings, the wells were only 25 feet deep, and the water in No. 5 was heavy with hydrogen sulphide, but they were the last ones Kuribayashi had. The marines welcomed the sight of the enemy, and those in the front line watched with great satisfaction as their artillery and destroyer fire from the sea smashed the raiding party. From now on the Japanese would have to rely on rain or stored water.

On Tuesday, the island was roaring with activity, at the front and in the rear.

Bobbie Erskine goaded the Third Division forward in the center of the line. Colonel Kenyon's 9th Regiment went after Hills Oboe and Peter again, and Doug Watson finished the job he had started the day before. Private Wilson D. Watson, twenty-four, a tall, hollow-cheeked farm boy from Alabama, had led his squad forward on Monday, brandishing a BAR and subduing pillboxes with fire and grenades. On Tuesday morning he ran to the top of a hill, firing the BAR from the hip and holding the crest alone for fifteen minutes. He was not scratched, and killed at least 60 Japanese before his platoon joined him.

At 12:40 P.M. the artillery laid down a ten-minute barrage, and suddenly the 9th Regiment was moving. Lieutenant Colonel Randall's 1st Battalion swarmed over Hill Peter, down the back slope and up

Hill Oboe. The 2nd Battalion, under Lieutenant Colonel Cushman, kept pace on the left, pushing ahead 1,500 yards. After three days of heavy fighting, the Third was coming out on the plateau, with relatively flat terrain ahead, and Airfield No. 2 was cleared.

Not so on the right. The Fourth Division, with five battalions abreast in the line, went off after a heavy barrage, including 300 rounds from the Corps' 155-mm. cannon. It was hand-to-hand fighting for the 23rd, hitting Hill 382 again and again. The top of the hill had been hollowed out and rebuilt with artillery and anti-tank gun pits. Grenades and even satchel charges were hurled up and down the slopes, into the night as well as during the day. The 23rd clawed around toward the northwest slope of the hill and made some progress. But the artillery at the top commanded the ground and forced the tanks back.

The 24th, pushing around the south of Turkey Knob and the Amphitheater, made nearly 200 yards along the east coast but accomplished little penetration of the two bastions. The 23rd, despite the fierce combat, was back at its line of departure by nightfall. The day had cost the Fourth Division 792 casualties—the worst single day it had had, or would have, in the whole campaign, excluding the first two days of slaughter across the beaches. But General Senda's 2nd Mixed Brigade was suffering too. These were mostly Kanto soldiers from around Tokyo, considered a cut below the Kyushu troops, but they were giving their best performance of the Pacific war. They still stood atop Hill 382, and late that night they sent up flares, calling for medical supplies and ammunition. Just before 1 A.M. the marines saw parachutes falling behind the hill; planes had come down from the Bonins for the last time.

The 25th had one surprise during the day. Three marines came on Superior Private Kunimatsu Kato, asleep near a cave, or pretending to be. In his hand was a stick with a white Marine sock on it: Kato, thirty, a medical corpsman with the 309th, sprang up when a marine poked him with a bayonet and readily started toward the rear. He told intelligence officers he had been on Iwo Jima fourteen months and seen at least twenty men die of malnutrition. The caves and the water gave the men colds and paratyphoid. Diarrhea, he said, had a pitiful effect on the men wasting away from poor food and water. He was glad that he had been "overpowered," and he readily agreed to try to convince other Japanese to surrender. At last he could think, too, of returning to his wife in Tamuragen, Fukushima-ken.

Not all Japanese were surrendering. The 5th Reconnaissance Company, closing out a week of hunting stragglers in the "rear" areas, had killed 515 Japanese. There were still many left, and Intelligence was revising its estimates. It now concluded that there must have been more than 20,000 Japanese on the island on D-Day, instead of the forecasts of 14,000. Enemy dead were already estimated at 5,483, though few bodies had been found. It was also said that it was still not known if General Kuribayashi himself was on the island, though he was thought to be.

On the west coast, the 27th relieved the 26th and assaulted the approaches to Hill 362A behind heavy artillery preparation. Marine guns, both division and corps, fired for thirty minutes, followed by destroyer fire, salvos from the rocket trucks, and carrier plane attacks with bombs and rockets. The advance, hard-scrabbling all day long against caves and pillboxes, carried 400 yards on the right and 500 yards along the shore. The hill was almost within reach.

During the assault, the 3rd Battalion lost a "gunny." Gunnery Sergeant William G. Walsh, twenty-two, led a platoon charge up a ridge, and they were thrown back. He led a second charge, and this time a few men made it into a trench on top. They lay there panting, and a grenade rolled in. Without an instant's pause Walsh rolled over on it. The rest of the men held the ridge and that night got his body out.

Nearly one-third of the island was now freed, and it was jammed with men and machines. Some order was beginning to emerge. The 31st Seabees moved to the west side of the island, into a foxhole camp that resembled the city dump. But the pipe-fitters tapped a hot spring and set up gang showers. The galley opened, and men no longer had to feed themselves; they were free to work.

Roadways and beach exits for the western beaches were ready to handle small craft, but Japanese fire from the north was still too strong.

Near the east coast, the Fourth Division post office opened in an abandoned cistern. Captain Emmet E. Hardin, forty-two, in private life a New York postal inspector, announced the first mail plane would leave for Saipan that night, and he was equipped to handle 100,000 V-mail letters daily for all three divisions. The troops never liked V-mail, but they wrote, and reducing the letters to microfilm was the only way the volume could have been handled.

For the first time, whole blood was moved up to company medical stations. Freshly drawn in Los Angeles, San Francisco, San Diego, and Portland, it had come all the way by plane, packed in ice, and it was welcome. A truck load rolled up to a Third Division station, and Lieutenant Commander Leo Theilen shouted, "Break it out, boys, on the double." In a few minutes the fresh scarlet blood flowed in the tents behind the sandbags. "Bless it," said Captain C. P. Archambeault of Brooklyn, a Third Division surgeon.

A Navy evacuation hospital, the first of its kind in the Pacific, set up on Purple Beach and by nightfall had two hundred beds ready. The Fourth Division Hospital, at the north edge of Airfield No. 1, had seventeen doctors working in four operating teams around the clock. The Army's 38th Field Hospital, 22 officers and 182 enlisted men, began landing. In the coming days, its six surgeons would perform 592 operations, 360 of them major surgery.

Major General James E. Chaney, head of the Army garrison force, came ashore with his staff and parts of the 147th Infantry Regiment and the 7th Fighter Command. The Fifth Division's first spotter plane landed in the afternoon, First Lieutenant Roy G. Miller piloting. He had been fired off LST 776 by Brodie gear, a giant slingshot that hurled the little Grasshoppers into the air. Ten more planes followed in the next three days (one fell into the sea before it could be fastened into the catapult), and the front-line soldiers were glad to see them. The ground crews rigged the little planes with bazookas, rockets, bombs, and the pilots flew low over the enemy lines, looking for targets—both for themselves and the artillery. Japanese fire dropped sharply when they were overhead. The enemy could not risk revealing the position of his artillery and mortars. The number of Japanese guns was shrinking fast enough. But the pilots paid for their "sport." Three of the Fifth Division's five spotters were killed. Second Lieutenant Mont Adamson, flying for the Fourth Division artillery, did twenty missions out of Airfield No. 1 and was not scratched. He died of multiple sclerosis before he was discharged.

Navy search planes, the big PBM flying boats, came in from the Marianas and began operating from three tenders off Suribachi. Planes from the *Anzio* sank a submarine a few miles west of Iwo Jima. It was the I-368, carrying *kaitens,* the one-man suicide submarines. These little subs, fastened to the deck of the regular submarine, were fired off like guided torpedoes, never to return. Japanese vied for the honor of this kind of death for the homeland. The day before, *Anzio* planes had sunk a regular submarine, the RO-43, west of Chichi Jima, and the destroyer escort *Finnegan* had bagged another *kaiten*-carrying sub, the I-370, between Iwo Jima and Saipan. The Japanese submarine force was making its last forays.

General Smith told correspondents "We expect to take this island in a few more days." He conceded that there would be heavy fighting, but he said that the Japanese were short of water and having trouble caring for their wounded. They were becoming jittery, he said.

On Wednesday, the tenth day ashore and the last day of February, the marines held less than half the island. This was the day General Harry Schmidt had predicted the battle would end.

The Third Division did make good gains in the center of the island.

The 21st began moving into the line before dawn, relieving the dawn a marine of 2/9 crumpled in a ravine, blood welling from a neat hole in his neck. Pharmacist's Mate Second Class Floyd L. Garrett, twenty-three, who had spent a good deal of time as a surgical assistant, recognized immediately that the jugular vein had been pierced. He knelt, slit the wound with a knife, laid the vein bare and clamped it. Then he stuffed the hole with gauze and motioned for the bearers. At the battalion aid station the Navy doctor, Lieutenant (j.g.) Cloyd L. Arford, whistled in admiration at the surgery.

By 9 A.M., the 9th was out and the 21st was in. Backed by its own artillery and Corps' 155's in a rolling barrage, the 21st Regiment moved forward. Almost immediately, Company I was confronted with tanks rising from the earth. These were Colonel Nishi's tanks, flushed at last from what had appeared to be hillocks. They churned forward, throwing off mounds of dirt, shrubbery, and rocks, and firing rapidly. The marines faltered in shock before the heavy fire, and for moments the battle teetered. Captain Edward V. Stephenson, who had fought at Guam with great valor, rushed forward and rallied his company. Massing flamethrowers and bazookamen, he led a counterattack that smashed the tanks. Three were destroyed on the ground, and planes caught two more of them with 20-mm. fire. Nishi now had only three tanks left.

During the morning, gains of 400 yards were made, but by noon the momentum stopped. The 21st was off again at 1 P.M., with artillery support, and the 3rd Battalion smashed through what had been the village of Motoyama. Where once General Kuribayashi had been greeted by schoolchildren, strewing flowers and waving tiny flags, there was nothing. The village had been swept clean except for the ruins of a concrete building. Beyond the village, the 21st settled in for the night. It was now firmly on high ground, having breached the center of the enemy lines, and off to the northeast could be seen the unfinished strips of Airfield No. 3.

The Fourth Division continued its assault on Hill 382, virtually surrounding it. Company A of 1/23, reaching the back slope around 2:15 P.M., began attacking from the east. The rocket trucks got in a good day, rushing up six at a time, firing double ripples of 4.5-inch rockets and retiring in less than five minutes. The heavy artillery lent support, and bazookamen blasted the fortifications. Still the hill held out, fire coming now from the east to help the enemy still inside. The fighting was extremely bitter, and Company A lost a brave man and a celebrity. Sergeant Fritz G. Truan, twenty-seven, of Cody, Wyoming, leading the assault platoon of A, as he had since D-Day, was killed during the afternoon in a burst of fire. He was billed as World Champion Cowboy, and rodeo people all over the country knew him. In 1940, he was best all-around rider at Madison Square Garden, and the next year he won $5,000 and the Sam Jackson trophy at the Pendleton Roundup. His last prize had been taken at Honolulu Stadium less than a year before, when he won the bronco-riding championship and $1,000. For the 1945 rodeo, 6,000 people stood in the darkened arena in Honolulu while Truan's riderless horse was led around the ring. Private First Class Robert L. Mather of Clinton, New York, played taps. He had been with Truan on Hill 382.

The 25th continued battering against Turkey Knob and the Amphitheater, trying to fight around north of the Knob. In desperation, the marines hauled up a 75-mm. howitzer on a Dukw, took it apart, and reassembled it at the front, to fire point-blank into the stone and concrete emplacements. Eighty-five rounds failed to destroy the fortifications but did wonders for morale. First Battalion troops, with tank support, nearly accomplished an encirclement of the Knob, but on the southeast side, Japanese high up in the ravines showered down grenades and mines and laced the cut with machine-gun fire. On the other side, to the northwest, tanks blasted at a concrete structure on top of the Knob. The Shermans' 75-mm. shells did no harm, and it was obvious a juncture could not be made around the knob. Both prongs fell back. Gain for the day—zero. Nearer the coast, 3/25 advanced easily and held up only to avert gaps in the line. In seven days, the Fourth Division had had more than 4,000 casualties, but the Japanese still held Hill 382, Turkey Knob, and the Amphitheater.

That night, General Erskine made his first request for the 3rd Regiment, nearly 3,000 fresh men, still in transports off the beach. General Harry Schmidt endorsed the request; casualties were already well over 8,000. The request was rejected by Howlin' Mad Smith, backed, for once, by Admiral Turner. It was the start of a disagreement still not resolved.

The Fifth Division, with the 27th Regiment in the line, pressed forward all day toward Hill 362A, which rose bare and sharp ahead. The 3rd Battalion reached the foot of the hill by noon, and Company I fought all the way to the crest by 4:30 P.M. but the position could not be held. During the assault up the hill, Pharmacist's Mate First Class John Harlan Willis, twenty-three, was wounded by shrapnel and ordered to the rear. He was back in a short time, and into the melee again. Running out front, he jumped into a hole and rigged a rifle to give plasma to a wounded marine. A grenade fell in the hole. Willis threw it back. He threw back seven more of them, and then his luck, far overextended, gave out. The grenade went off in his hand, killing him.

Late in the afternoon, Company H on the right, up against the

Third Division line, beat off a party of about 100 Japanese in hand-to-hand combat. But the 27th was forced to dig in for the night about 100 yards short of the top of Hill 362A. In the rear, the 26th spent the day re-equipping and resting, and the 28th, conquerors of Suribachi, began moving north.

During the day, all three Marine field hospitals, of Corps, Fourth and Fifth Divisions came into full operation. Along with the Navy and Army hospitals there were now enough beds ashore, and transfer of casualties to ships was discontinued. The four hospital LST's were released and sailed for Saipan fully loaded with casualties. In ten days they had treated 6,100 men. Toward evening, two torpedo bombers from one of the carriers sprayed the lower half of the island with DDT to prevent spread of disease by flies. Three twin-engine Navy planes and transports of the 9th Troop Carrier Squadron, USAAF, made the first air drops of medical supplies and vital parts. Thousands of marines watched and cheered as the red and green parachutes billowed down along the western beaches. Only four fell into the water, and small boats rescued three of them. In all, nearly 5 tons of supplies were dropped, saving many days over ship supply from the Marianas.

At home, President Roosevelt flew in from the meetings with Stalin and Churchill at Yalta. His aide, Jonathan Daniels, told newsmen he had never seen the President looking better. "He is in grand spirits, in great shape," Daniels said. Rumors persisted that, in fact, he was exhausted and quite unwell.

That night, the Japanese made their last attempt to recapture Wells 4 and 5. They sent down a special force, equipped with rocket guns and mortars. Not a single Japanese returned from this mission.

Admiral Ichimaru had one of his last messages from Toyoda. It was dispiriting. The Commander in Chief said the Navy would be ready for the next expected American thrust by the end of April, but that all plans depended on the outcome at Iwo.

"I regret that except for full submarine support and some air support, we cannot send reinforcements to Iwo. However, in view of over-all requirements, I earnestly hope you will maintain calm and fight staunchly by any means," Toyoda said.

Ichimaru had understood perfectly, right from the start. He had never expected reinforcements, and he had been pulling his forces back slowly, exacting the highest possible toll. The retreat had hurt morale, but it was inevitable. One man had written in his diary: "We don't fight, we just retreat. The enemy is right before our eyes and we retreat."

On the last night of the month he recorded that he had just learned that First Lieutenant Nakahara and Second Lieutenant Hanazawa had been killed on patrol. "As the saying goes, 'When one braves the dangers, death goes along hand in hand,'" he wrote. He finished in disgust: "Ordered to withdraw again."

There was no rest in the rear in the early hours of March 1. Shortly after midnight Japanese artillery, firing from new positions in the north, began shelling the west coast alongside Airfield No. 1, an area crowded with unit headquarters, supply dumps, vehicles and artillery, and the foxholes of men of many outfits.

At 2:15 A.M. a shell struck the Fifth Division's main ammunition dump, and it caught fire. Within minutes the blaze was roaring, burning flares arched into the sky, lighting it up like a Fourth of July show. Small-arms ammunition crackled, mortar shells detonated, and artillery projectiles were flying through the air. The entire southern end of the island was aroused by the wild spectacle, and at 2:38 A.M. the air-raid alarm went off. At 3 A.M. somebody tripped the gas alarm, mistaking exploding white phosphorous projectiles for gas shells. The gas alert was canceled within ten minutes, but the air alert remained until 4:30 A.M.

After the first shock, men of all units raced for the burning dump. Fifth Division service troops, disregarding the rain of explosives in the air, ran into the edges of the fire and carried out shells. Men of the Headquarters & Service Battery of the division's artillery regiment, the 13th Marines, pitched in to save the dump, and Army units helped. Major Harry Edwards and Warrant Officer Harvey Richey of the 473rd Amphibian Truck Company ran into the fire again and again and were burned many times by hot shrapnel or knocked down by explosions.

At the height of the blaze, around 5 A.M., a burning 105-mm. shell was hurled into the Corps' fire-direction center a hundred yards away. The shell detonated with a low-grade explosion, enough to set the wire lines afire, knocking out communications to the artillery. The dump of Corps telephone wire also caught fire, and nearly all of it was destroyed.

Fifth Engineers brought in bulldozers, and the drivers fearlessly pushed sand over the main dump. Gradually, with dozens of men helping, the fire was brought under control. By 7 A.M. it was out. The Fifth Division had lost 25 percent of its ammunition, but not one man was killed. In a tent near the fire, Lieutenant E. Graham Evans, a Fifth Division surgeon, had made his decision. Exhausted by endless days of operating, he had decided to stay in his cot instead of searching for a foxhole. At dawn he rolled over; the tent above him was shredded. As far as he could see the ground was littered with shell fragments, but not one man had been hit. "Foxholes are a wonderful invention," he concluded.

But the day was only beginning. The air-raid alarm had not been false. A low-flying plane, probably from the Bonins, dropped a torpedo near the destroyer *Terry* at 2:45 A.M., a few miles off Kitano Point in the north. The destroyer rang up full speed and the torpedo passed 50 feet astern. But the *Terry* pressed her luck too far. Passing the point at 7:20 A.M., about 2 1/2 miles off shore, the destroyer came under fire from a 6-inch coastal gun. Before it could get out of range, hits on the main deck and in the forward engine room killed eleven men and wounded nineteen. The battleship *Nevada* and the cruiser *Pensacola* closed in to give her protection, and the *Terry* escaped. The same day, Lieutenant Commander William B. Moore buried his dead at sea and transferred the wounded to a hospital ship; the *Terry* started for Pearl Harbor, limping on one engine.

On the Fifth Division front, the 28th went back into action for the first time since Suribachi, and it was a bloody return. The 1st and 2nd Battalions swept to the top of Hill 362A in an early morning rush, but now they were on an 80-foot cliff dropping into a ravine behind the hill. Both sides of the ravine were pocked with caves hiding Japanese riflemen, and an anti-tank ditch ran across the bottom in the middle. The only way in was around the shoulders. Company A started around the right, B around the left.

Captain Wilkins of Company A, a hero of the D-Day charge across the island, asked for volunteers. Corporal Tony Stein, cited for the Medal of Honor on D-Day, nodded and crawled out with a 20-man patrol to clear the ridge of snipers. Seven men came back. Stein was not one of them. Within the hour, mortar and gunfire killed Wilkins. He was the last original company commander in the battalion. Captain Russell J. Parsons came forward and the attack continued.

Around the other shoulder, Company B found the fire just as intense. The company commander, Captain Robert A. Wilson, was wounded and taken to the rear. For the second time, First Lieutenant Charles A. Weaver took over the company. The first time had been on D-Day, after Bobo Mears was mortally wounded assaulting a pillbox. The attack continued all day, the 3rd Battalion making good progress nearer the shore, where the ground flattened out. But somewhere down behind Hill 362A, where fire poured from the reverse cliff, and from Nishi Ridge up ahead, three other men of the 28th lay dead. One of them was Henry O. Hansen, the slim sergeant from Somerville, Massachusetts. Private Ruhl had given his life before Suribachi so that Hansen might help raise the first flag on the mountaintop.

Somewhere else in that jumble of rock and ravine, Corporal Harlon H. Block was killed. His hands had thrust the pole into the soft volcanic tuff at the top of Suribachi as the second flag went up and Joe Rosenthal snapped the famous picture.

VI Victory in the Pacific: Iwo Jima to the Conquest of Japan

Alligators, with Marines from a Coast Guard-manned invasion transport, swing past the mighty U.S.S. *Tennessee* as she pours broadsides of shells into enemy implacements on Iwo Jima. It is H-Hour and the landing craft await the signal to storm Iwo's beaches.

A wave of charging Fourth Division Marines begins an attack from the beach at Iwo as another boatload of battle-tested veterans is disgorged on the beach.

Seventh Regiment, 2nd Battalion lands on the same spot in the afternoon.

Marine rocket trucks rumble into action. (Photo by S/Sgt. Robbins)

This Marine, a member of the "Fighting Fourth Marine Division," threatens the enemy even in death on the beach. (Photo by Sgt. Bob Cooke)

Men of the floating reserve regiment attend Catholic Mass on board before their time in hell. (Photo by Lindsley)

Telephoto view from Mt. Suribachi of U.S. supplies moving in on Iwo beaches. (Photo by S/Sgt. Mark Haufman)

Looking up from Montogama Airstrip #1 toward Suribachi. (Photo by Pfc. Jack Campbell)

In the face of withering enemy fire, the Fifth Division Marine invaders of Iwo Jima work their way up the slope from Red Beach #1 toward Suribachi Yama, completely hidden in the left background by the smoke of the battle. (Photo by Dreyfuss)

Close-up of hell. (Photo by Bob Campbell)

A 37-mm. gun firing on enemy positions on the slopes of
Mt. Suribachi. (Photo by Cornelius)

Iwo Jima flame-throwers going into action.

Flame-thrower of "E" Company, Ninth Marines, goes
over the top to assault an enemy pillbox on Airfield #2.
(Photo by Christian)

Officers of the Fifth Marine Division direct the operation
of their unit from a sandbagged position on Iwo Jima.
They are, left to right, in the foreground: Brigadier General Leo D. Hermle, Assistant Division Commander; Major
General Keller E. Rockey (with phone), Division Commander; Colonel James F. Shaw, Operations Officer;
Colonel Ray Robinson, Division Chief of Staff. (Photo by
Campbell)

Private Rez Hester takes a nap while Butch, a war dog, stands guard. (Photo by Kauffman)

Hot chow, Iwo style, during one of the infrequent lulls. (Photo by Sgt. R. Scheer)

Lieutenant General Holland Smith, who commanded the
Marines in the seizure of Iwo Jima, congratulates Major
General Graves B. Erskine of La Jolla, California, com-
mander of the Third Marine Division, on the fine work
of the latter's division in breaking the backbone of the
Japanese resistance on the island.

Re-enactment scene of the flag raising on Mt. Suribachi. Left to right: Pfc. Ira H. Hayes; Pfc. Franklin R. Sously, killed in action; Sergeant Michael Strank, killed in action; Pharmacist Mate 2/C John H. Bradley; Pfc. Rene A. Gagnon; Corporal Harlon H. Block, killed in action. (Photo by Rosenthal)

Marines wade through surf over coral reef to the Okinawa beach. (Photo by H. H. Clements)

Below Shuri Castle, Marines found a Christian church whose steeple provided a sniper's nest for the Japanese. The Marines in the foreground are covering the building while a patrol comes in from the rear.

One of the Marines of a Leatherneck company driving through Japanese machine gun fire while crossing a draw, later called "Death Valley" by the men, rises from cover for a quick dash forward to another position. (Photo by Pvt. Bob Bailey)

Stretcher bearers carrying badly wounded Marine while corpsman gives plasma. (Photo by James W. Loach)

Marines pick their way through a small village where there are several dead Japanese. (Photo by McElroy)

My buddy...a Marine stands by the body of a shipmate
killed at the line. (Photo by Pfc. Bushomi)

Two miles from Naha: the battle for a ridge where "A" Company of 2nd Battalion, Fifth Marines, was held up for forty-eight hours. (Photo by Giffin)

A Marine of the First Marine Division draws a bead on a
Japanese sniper with his tommy gun as the division was
engaged in taking Wana Ridge before the town of Shuri.
(Photo by S/Sgt. Kleine)

Private First Class Galen A. Brehm, flame-thrower for the Sixth Marine Division, plays a hot lick for the inhabitants of a cave on Okinawa. (Photo by S/Sgt. D. Peakin)

Under the white flag of surrender, Japanese naval troops gather about a Marine to deliver themselves into the hands of the Americans on Okinawa as enemy resistance collapses. (Photo by Curran)

Getting their water from a Japanese well in Naha, capital of Okinawa, these Devil Dogs of the Sixth Division take their first bath in weeks. (Photo by S/Sgt. J. J. Connolly)

Marine Corporal Fenwick H. Dunn gives the candy from his K rations to an aged woman on Okinawa. The Japanese fled as Marines landed on Easter morning, abandoning the aged, infirm, and small children.

Colonel Walter L. J. Bayler, "last man off Wake Island" in December, 1941, is the first man to set foot on the island after the surrender documents were signed aboard a destroyer escort vessel. (Photo by R. O. Kepler)

As a Marine bugler plays the stirring notes of "Colors" the Stars and Stripes is hoisted to fly over Wake for the first time since its gallant defenders were overwhelmed in December, 1941. The Japanese officer at the extreme right is Rear Admiral Shigematau Sakaibara, who commanded the Wake garrison forces. (Photo by R. O. Kepler)

The Marine honor guard of the U.S.S. *Missouri* stands by as the official Japanese signing party arrives for the formal acceptance of the peace terms in Tokyo Bay. (Photo by Lt. David D. Duncan)

Marines of the Sixth Division marching on Tsingtao's Pacific road to the scene of the formal surrender of Japanese forces in the area to Major General Lemuel C. Shepherd, Jr., Division Commander, and Chinese military officials.

Marine Pfc. Clyde W. Cooksey (clinging to flagpole) cuts away the white Japanese flag of truce on the crest of Mt. Tahjma, near Sasebo, to leave only the Stars and Stripes waving over the area. (Photo by Cpl. Bob Campbell)

Repatriated Japanese military personnel brought to Kajiki from Kita Daito Shima aboard a hospital ship. Marine Private First Class Willard M. Motry stands guard.

Sergeant Michael Strank, third man from the left in that photograph, was pinned in the ravine for four hours by heavy fire. "We better send a runner to tell them where we are," he said, and knelt to draw a map in the sand. Corporal Joe Rodriguez, nineteen, faced him, leaning over as the sergeant's finger traced in the sand. Four other men bunched around, and a Japanese mortar found the range. Rodriguez remembered only the blast, and when he came to, Strank lay sprawled on his back, his arms above his head. It had been a long road for Strank, nearly six years in the Corps, from the Russells to Bougainville to the top of Suribachi. The last journey for the rough son of Czech immigrants was to Grave 7179 in Arlington National Cemetery, within sight of an heroic-sized bronze statue of six men raising a flag, one of them Michael Strank. Block, the twenty-year-old Texas oilfield worker, lay for a time in Plot 4, Row 6, Grave 912 of the Fifth Division Cemetery, near Airfield No. 1. Eventually he went home, to private burial in Weslaco, Texas.

The day had cost the Fifth Division six more officers killed, a first lieutenant and four second lieutenants, besides Captain Wilkins. The map for the day showed only the crest of Hill 362A in Marine hands.

In the center, the Third Division pounded forward from Motoyama Village, gradually turning east as the island widened. The fighting was unspectacular, but death was everywhere. Mortar shells rained down on front and "rear"; aid stations were full, and doctors moved from one table to the next, cramming a lifetime of surgery into one day. And there were not only wounded. In the afternoon a very young marine, hardly out of boyhood, wandered into an aid station 200 yards behind the line. He said he had chills and fever, but he was not ill. Or more precisely, he had not been hurt. He was frightened, and when Dr. Arford suggested that he go back to his outfit the boy began to cry. He walked about 40 feet away, toward the rear, and sat down, sobbing softly. About thirty minutes later a mortar shell exploded at his feet, blowing off his drooping head. In the aid station, corpsmen lifted another bloody marine onto the table and the doctor bent down again, scalpel in hand. The gain for the day was 500 yards, it said in the report.

The Fourth Division held back along the coast, concentrating again against Hill 382 and Turkey Knob. The hill was assaulted from the front and the sides and was nearly surrounded. At one time, Company G of 2/24 was astride the top, but still there was no quarter. The attackers fought with rifles and grenades, with flamethrowers and satchel charges. Still the defenders would not give up, even though their own fire fell on them from the ridges further east. These were the men from Kumamoto in Kyushu, an historic battlefield of the 1877

Civil War, and they would not give up. Not even when Major Kenro Anso died, burned from head to foot by a flamethrower. He led the 3rd Battalion, 145th Regiment, in defense of the hill. So great was his inspiration that at his death he was promoted two full ranks to colonel. By nightfall, the 24th and 25th had made some progress toward both objectives, but both the Hill and the Knob were still in Japanese hands. The day's toll was 374 casualties, and the Fourth Division's combat efficiency was rated at 55 percent. In eleven days of fighting it had paid 5,595 casualties for a small share of one-half of an island.

Some changes were appearing in the enemy's tactics. Japanese artillery seemed to be growing more sporadic and disorganized. Mortar fire was decreasing, and rifle fire was more discriminate. Back around Airfield No. 2, Robert Sherrod noticed that a company of marines could walk along the runways without drawing fire, but small groups drew sniper fire. The Japanese were not wasting fire. Ammunition must be running low. The most significant change of the day was not known to the marines. General Kuribayashi left the center of the island and moved to his underground headquarters in the north.

A few Korean laborers were captured during the day, and they said food and water were also low. But their word could not be trusted; they hated their conquerors, the Japanese. There was another bag of prisoners on Thursday. First Lieutenant Goro Wakatsuki, a gun-battery commander of the 8th Independent Anti-Tank Battalion, stumbled into the open below Airfield No. 2, leading 8 enlisted men. As far as he knew, they were all that was left of 180 men in the battalion. They had been hiding inside the American lines for a week, but they were exhausted and could not hold out. Wakatsuki explained that he had not escaped because he was wounded in the foot. He knew nothing of intelligence value, since the battle had long since passed by. The prisoners were put in a barbed-wire compound until they could be shipped to Guam.

During the day, Marine planes parachuted in sixty-nine sacks of mail. All of it was for the Third Division, infuriating the Fourth and Fifth Divisions. At sea, a second destroyer, the *Colhoun*, was hit by shore fire a little after 10 A.M. One man was killed and seven were wounded. The most tense moment came when the Japanese opened fire on the *Columbia Victory*, as it was moving in on the west beaches to unload ammunition. Mortar fire from Kama and Kangoku Rocks straddled the vessel, one shell falling close enough to wound a man on the fantail. The merchant ship immediately turned and headed for the open sea. "You could almost see the sweat pouring from her brow," said a Fifth Division officer. Howlin' Mad Smith was also watching. He stood with General Schmidt at Corps headquarters on the west beach. If the ammunition ship went up, the whole west coast of the island might be devastated. Thousands of marines were working there. As they watched, the second salvo fell ahead of the ship. "The next one's going to hit her square," said Smith, but neither he nor Schmidt moved. It fell astern, and by now the *Columbia Victory* was rapidly drawing out of range. Everybody went back to work.

Off to the southwest, Mitscher's carriers raided Okinawa. There was no reaction from the ground, and damage was light, but the fliers got excellent photographs for the invasion, just one month away. That night Task Force 58 headed for Ulithi; the two-week foray, in which the Navy had placed such hopes, was over. It claimed to have destroyed over 600 Japanese planes; the cost was 134 planes and the lives of 95 pilots and crewmen. The enemy still had hundreds of *kamikazes* poised for Okinawa, and some marines still say, with bitterness, that Task Force 58 might better have tended to the knitting at Iwo Jima.

※　※　※　※

THIRD DIVISION COMBAT CORRESPONDENT SERgeant Alvin Josephy joined the 2nd Battalion, 21st Marines, for the mop-up fighting on the high ground to the north. Josephy's job was to find human interest stories concerning marines under all circumstances, and the medics provided good copy. Now a senior editor of *American Heritage,* Josephy speaks of the 3rd Division push and of the death of an old friend, Sergeant Reid Carlos Chamberlain, whom we met when he escaped from The Rock.

·10· "HOW DO YOU STAY ALIVE?"

ALVIN JOSEPHY

To many of the Marines . . . ambulance drivers were the unsung heroes of our battles. They raced back and forth all day long and most of the night, taking casualties from the front-line aid stations to the beach evacuation stations. The ambulances were usually the first vehicles to follow the front-line troops into new territory. They had to keep up with the infantry and the forward aid stations. That meant that they frequently had to do the pioneering work in finding roads and trails to the front. They went through territory still held by the enemy, and often they hit mines, because they went over roads before engineers had a chance to find the mines.

Combat correspondents, who had to move around quickly from outfit to outfit, found the jeep ambulances the best means of conveyance. The drivers knew the latest positions of the front-line units and could take us speedily wherever we wanted to go. They were also up on the latest news in each outfit. They took out the wounded, and they knew who died. They picked up gossip and stories from every outfit they worked with, and they knew who the men's heroes were and who had accomplished what.

The 1st battalion aid station was nestled in a revetment at the northern end of one of the runways of the first airfield. The black sand revetment was about fifteen feet high, and the corpsmen were dug into the sand banks. They were administering dressings and plasma to several wounded men who lay in the sandy holes. The unit, under the command of Dr. Charles A. Jost, was supposedly in reserve, as was the whole battalion. But the doctors and corpsmen were as busy as if they were still in the front lines.

"Trouble is," one of the corpsmen said tiredly, "there's no place to rest on this island. Everywhere is the front."

A few minutes earlier, a stream of Jap mortar shells had landed on top of the revetment. Fragments had showered down on the men, wounding several. They were lying silently, with curious peaceful smiles on their faces, waiting to be helped into Gruggen's ambulance. They looked as if they knew they were through with Iwo.

Just after we arrived, a sudden commotion broke out on top of the revetment. Two men were standing there against the skyline. One of the doctors yelled at them: "Get the hell down. You want to draw fire?"

But the men ignored him. Then several other men appeared. The doctor began to scramble up the steep wall, muttering angrily, his face red. Suddenly there was a terrific blast on top of the revetment, and a shower of sand flew into the air. It was followed by another blast. The doctor tumbled down the slope and flung himself into a hole, swearing at the top of his lungs. The corpsmen and wounded clung to the side of the revetment, seeking shelter from another blast. After a moment, the men relaxed. Gruggen picked himself up from where he had sought safety and went over to his ambulance. He examined it quickly to see whether any fragments had hit it. The doctor who had fallen down the slope looked up bitterly. His face was covered with sand. "Damn fools," he muttered.

There was a short, sharp scream from the revetment, and a voice called weakly, "Help!"

The doctor and several corpsmen grabbed first-aid pouches and scrambled up the revetment. A moment later one of the corpsmen looked down and called for more men.

"There's a whole bunch of guys been hit up here," he shouted. "Bring up some stretchers."

Three more corpsmen struggled up the steep slope, dragging litters and first-aid kits. On top of the revetment the ground sloped away to a small tableland, covered with the shattered remains of stunted banyan trees. The two Jap shells had hit among a group of men who had been digging into the area. Torn, charred equipment lay among the blasted tree roots. A pile of helmets and shovels were punched with holes. Twelve men were lying on the ground, bleeding onto the black sand, three of them dead, the other nine wounded.

The corpsmen went to work, tying on combat dressings and giving plasma. Most of the wounded were writhing with pain. They rubbed their hands across their foreheads and groaned. One man who had been hit in the leg felt better than the others and was talkative. The doctor was dressing his leg. Every so often the doctor looked around angrily and cautioned the corpsmen to stay down.

"Did anybody escape?" the man with the wounded leg asked.

The doctor shook his head. "You sure asked for it," he said. "What the hell were you doing up here?"

"This was an artillery observation team," the wounded man said. "How can you see the Japs on this damn island if you don't stick your head up?"

The doctor didn't answer.

Slowly, the wounded men were lowered down the wall of the revetment. Gruggen took them back to the beach. A corpsman made a note of the names, ranks, and serial numbers of the men who had been evacuated. His hand was trembling, and his nose was running. He could hardly write; it seemed as if his fingers were numb from cold, and his writing looked like the jerky scrawl of a drunken man.

As he was finishing, a loud, rumbling noise approached the revetment along the open airstrip. Dr. Jost sprang to his feet and ran to the revetment's opening. A halftrack was moving along the runway, trying to stay close to the shelter of the line of embankments. Dr. Jost waved at it angrily. He cupped his hands over his mouth and shouted at the driver to stay away from the revetment. One of the corpsmen instinctively huddled against the wall of his foxhole.

"Good God!" he breathed.

The next instant, so foreseeable that not a person was shocked by it, there was a burst of earth beneath the halftrack, followed by a sharp crash. The vehicle rose slowly and turned over, settling in a cloud of dust and sand. Dr. Jost threw himself flat as debris rained through the air. The corpsmen ducked their heads and laughed hysterically at each other. What had happened seemed as inexorable as a Greek tragedy.

When the dust settled, Dr. Jost and two corpsmen raced into the open to the smoking halftrack. Five burned bodies lay among the twisted wreckage. The corpsmen extricated them and dragged them into the revetment. A mortar shell fell on the airstrip near the wrecked halftrack, and a Jap Nambu machine gun opened fire from the rocks north of the runway.

"The halftrack hit something big," one of the corpsmen said, out of breath. "Must have been a torpedo warhead."

Three of the halftrack crew were already dead. Two were still alive. Again the corpsmen went to work with bandages and plasma. The man with the book examined the wounded Marines' dog tags for their names and serial numbers. One of the injured men had his dog tags tied to the laces of his shoes, rather than around his neck. The corpsmen lifted the wounded man's foot tenderly and copied the statistics. A few minutes later another jeep ambulance arrived to take out the two men.

One of the corpsmen turned to Doctor Jost. "Well," he said, rubbing his dust-streaked face, "who's next?"

Gruggen came back to the aid station with two sailors in his ambulance.

"What are the swabbies doing here?" one of the corpsmen exclaimed.

Gruggen laughed. "They want to kill some Japs. I told them I'd give them a lift this far."

No one at the aid station thought it was funny. The sailors were in blue dungarees, with dirty white sailor caps, and had carbines over their shoulders. They seemed embarrassed.

"We're working down on the beach," one of them said. "Thought we could find some souvenirs."

"Go on, beat it, swabbies!" one of the corpsmen said angrily.

"Okay, okay," the sailor answered. He paused and smiled. "How do you stay alive on this island anyway?"

"It's luck," Gruggen said. "If Lady Luck is on your side, you stay alive. If not—" He made a motion of kissing the air with his fingers.

The sailors nodded embarrassedly and shuffled out of the revetment. They paused on the airstrip, looking at the smoking ruins of the halftrack. Then they looked around, as if trying to decide whether to go back to the beach or head for the front. They turned slowly and trudged toward the front.

Later their bodies were brought back to our cemetery. No one saw them die.

I left the aid station and made my way to the 1st battalion's companies. I moved forward beneath the protection of the wall of revetments lining the runway. In one revetment I came on a big-shouldered mortarman. He was excited and shaking and could scarcely talk. He was standing over a pile of 10-in-1 ration boxes beside a wrecked Jap plane. An M-1 rifle was over his shoulder.

"Look," he blurted, grabbing my arm. He pointed to an unexploded Jap 75 mm. shell, lying about five feet from the ration boxes. The nose of the shell was dug into the ground.

The mortarman motioned at himself. "I'm here guarding these rations," he said. "They're for the companies—up there," he pointed up the embankment. "I'm standing here when—*whoosh*—this thing comes right over my shoulder, skids across the pile of rations, and plops into the ground. I saw it—but I couldn't do anything. I stand here staring—like it's gonna go off in my face. But it don't! It's a dud!" He laughed loudly and gripped my shoulder. "How do you like that? A dud!"

We had a smoke, and he calmed down. I asked him where the companies were. He motioned up the embankment again.

"About two hundred yards ahead, dug into some bushes and sand dunes. But you gotta be careful. You gotta cross an open field. They been throwing mortars up there."

I tried to stall climbing the embankment. If I had known the terrain and what lay up there, I would have felt differently. But making the first venture into country I hadn't seen held the terrors of facing the unknown. Finally I chucked my cigarette away and climbed the embankment. The ground above looked like a desert of black sand. The field was pocked with large shellholes. About two hundred yards across the field the sand rose in precipitous dunes covered with scraggly bushes and torn banyan trees. The dunes covered one of the rows of Jap pillboxes that had been pierced by the 3d battalion's charge. Dead Marines lay in awkward positions on the ground where they had fallen during the charge. Their faces were purple and puffed, and their weapons were rusty and full of sand.

I loped across the field, zigzagging and keeping low. I heard the sharp, clear dat-dat-dat-dat of a Nambu. Halfway across, I passed a Marine running the other way. It was Reid Chamberlain, the sergeant who had come overseas after having been with the guerrillas in the Philippines. He was a runner with the 1st battalion. He was hanging onto his helmet, trying to keep it from bouncing off his head. There was a nonchalant grin on his face, as if to indicate that he had been through worse experiences.

Able (A) and Baker (B) Companies were dug into foxholes among the sand dunes and bushes across the field. The foxholes were close together around a knocked-out Jap antitank gun that poked through a concrete fort built between two dunes. The men looked as if they had just come out of a hard-fought football game. They leaned against the sides of their foxholes, exhausted and breathing heavily. Their eyes were wide open and staring, as if they could not forget the terrible sights they had seen. I recognized many friends and tried talking to them, but it was useless: They looked through me, their answers made no sense, their minds wandered. One man tried to ask me how the battle was going. He couldn't get his question out. He finished half the sentence, then repeated the last words, over and over, like a man falling asleep. But he wasn't drowsing; his mind just wouldn't function.

A sergeant crawled over and smiled good-naturedly. He stared at me a moment as though he were going to cry. Then he wiped his nose.

"Any—any mail—yet?"

I shook my head. A little later, when I was with another unit, I heard that the sergeant was killed. He was one of the best-liked men in his outfit. The man who told me that he was dead said simply: "There goes the heart of this company."

Able Company had one officer left—a captain, and he kept rubbing his hand over his face as he sat in his foxhole.

"We're in reserve," he said. "But we're still losing men. We had
two fellows hit by a mortar just a little while ago. Both good men.
As good as they come." He stared into space, dreaming.

A few minutes later a lieutenant and four enlisted men slid over
one of the sand dunes from our rear. They had carbines and rifles
and were dragging stretchers. I recognized them. They were from
the 3d battalion.

The lieutenant smiled half-heartedly at the captain.

"We're picking up our dead," he said. Then he added, "I hear we're
going into the lines again this afternoon."

The captain nodded.

The lieutenant sighed and motioned the enlisted men to follow
him. They picked their way cautiously across the clearing to the bodies that sprawled on the sand. The Nambu opened fire again. The
men stooped over, ignoring the machine gun. When they reached
the bodies, they rolled them onto the stretchers and took them back
to the safety of the revetment. They had to make several trips to pick
up all the bodies.

That afternoon the 1st and 3d battalions prepared to go back into
the lines. By evening the order hadn't come, however, and the men
dug in again for the night. No one knew the situation at the front
or why the battalions hadn't moved or where they would go, if and
when they did move. But no one cared; somebody else could worry
about all that—somebody who was running the operation. To the
men in the foxholes it was another evening alive.

The night in the sand was hideous. Land crabs crawled among the
bushes and down the dunes, scraping along the ashes and sounding
like Japs slithering toward our foxholes. Illumination flares hung
overhead, casting weird, moving shadows across the terrain. The
Japs threw mortar shells, and our artillery answered, and the sky
was filled with the whirring breath of missiles sailing back and forth
above our heads. Every so often a terrific crash sounded close by,
where a mortar shell fell among us. We dozed in turns, trying to ignore the clamor, which in our fitful dreams sounded like someone
banging doors in a house in which we were trying to sleep. The doors
were all around us, upstairs and downstairs, in the same room and
on the other side of the house. Suddenly someone slammed a door
in our face. We awoke with a start. The banging was still going on.
Sand was caving in on us from the lip of the foxhole. It was in our
mouth and our ears. We shifted our position and tried to sleep again.
The man guarding our foxhole didn't notice our stirring. He lay
silently against the edge of the foxhole, staring into the night.

The next morning before dawn the order came to move up. The 9th Marines had made gains during the two days they had pressed the attack, but they were worn out and they needed support. The 3d battalion of the 21st passed us in a line, going to the northern end of the second airfield to attack the Japs in the high ground of the center of Iwo. The men trudged silently across the dunes and past the smashed Jap pillboxes. Their rifles were on their shoulders with bayonets already fixed. Machine gunners carried the sections of their guns, leaning forward beneath their heavy metal loads. Men carrying boxes of ammunition walked beside them, quiet and business-like; one tobacco-chewing youth spat every few yards. After the machine gunners came the mortar men with their weapons. The line paused, and one of the men nodded at me. I hardly recognized him, with his black, scraggly beard and the rings of caked sand around his eyes.

"Where are we going?" he said anxiously.

Someone ahead of him turned around. "What do you care? You'll get there."

The line shoved off again. Garron, the little automatic rifleman who had killed the five Japs in the Guam jungle, walked by. "Isn't this a hell of a piece of real estate?" he called.

When the 1st battalion moved, it climbed through the rows of pillboxes, crossed the southern end of the second airfield, and went into position to the left of the 3d battalion. Here the terrain changed. The volcanic sand dunes were left behind. Instead, our men faced a wild, barren stretch of rocky ridges, cut into crags, chasms, and gulleys. It looked like the Bad Lands of the American West—or, as someone said, like hell with the fire out.

Our attack began early in the morning, following the first rolling barrage of the campaign. The shellfire ahead of our lines was thunderous. Our men squirmed into the ground and kept their heads down. The uninterrupted crashing of fire among the Jap positions made us wonder how any enemy could remain alive. For forty-nine minutes, 75, 105, and 155 mm. ground artillery shells and 5-, 6-, and 8-inch naval shells smashed among the ridges where the Japs were hiding. Then, on a time signal, the barrage lifted and moved ahead to crash down on Jap positions one hundred yards farther out. At the same time our men rose from their holes and began the attack. The riflemen, with fixed bayonets, and hand grenades hanging from their belts, ran toward the rocks. On the left the 1st battalion moved two hundred yards before the stunned Japs could recover. Then, when enemy mortar shells began falling again and bullets hit among our men, the Marines paused and sought cover. Slowly they broke into teams, and one by one rose again to attack the individual Jap positions, now all around them.

PFCs with smoke bombs and phosphorous grenades clambered among the rocks to within throwing distance of the Jap holes. As soon as they had hurled their grenades, and great puffs of smoke blanketed the walls of the ridge, flame-throwers came forward, running as fast as they could across the open. It seemed unbelievable that they could move as quickly as they did under their seventy-two-pound apparatus. Automatic riflemen and bazooka men moved up to cover the flame-throwers. The smoke drifted away from the ridge wall and cave openings were revealed, like huge black teeth in an ogre's face. As the riflemen watched each hole, the flame-thrower, completely exposed, shot his burning liquid into the cave, then turned and ran behind the protection of rocks. Other men took his place, heaving grenades or firing their bazookas, to finish the job.

Sometimes the men were pinned down among the rocks by flanking fire from other Jap positions. Sometimes the flame and bazookas and grenades didn't do the job, and tanks were called up to fire point-blank into the caves; flame-throwing tanks also took a hand. Knocked-out positions often came back to life; the Japs merely retreated into the underground tunnels, went to other holes, and then returned hours later to the cave that supposedly had been burned out.

On that day of the first rolling barrage we lost many men before we were finally stopped. Behind us by nightfall were many rocky ridges and hills covered with bodies of dead Marines. One of those ridges had been the scene of a particularly wild battle. Our men had charged to the top, using grenades and bayonets, and had engaged in a bloody hand-to-hand fight with Japs who had chosen to come out of their holes. There had been 150 mm. gun-pits on top of the ridge. The guns had been wrecked by our bombardments, and their torn, pocked barrels pointed starkly into the sky. But from the pits, entrance-ways led underground into the bowels of the ridge. Through those entrance-ways the Japs had surged to meet our charge. Our men caught them with their bayonets, clubbed them with butt strokes, threw grenades at them, and fired their BAR and Garands into their faces. During a fight in one of the gun-pits, an enemy shell had exploded, and every man in the pit—Jap and Marine—was killed.

That night, as our tired survivors dug into their holes several hundred yards ahead of the ridge, it seemed as if progress had been made. Many of the Jap positions in the high ground had fallen. We were pushing, painfully but surely, through the heart of the enemy's Iwo defenses. All we had to do was keep going. Eventually we would reach the sea—only a couple of miles to the north.

But the Japs had other ideas.

In the middle of the night they came back underground. When our men pushed out the next morning, they didn't know that the enemy was behind them. But the rear elements, coming up in reserve, discovered to their dismay that, even though the big Jap guns and mortars were being eliminated, there was no safety on Iwo so long as one uncaptured enemy remained alive. Begining that morning, the Japs in that ridge waged a struggle against our rear that was typical of fights in many supposedly secured areas.

Early in the morning Dr. Jost's aid station, still following the troops, had set up in a small amphitheater formed by the rocks at one end of the ridge. Our men were again in action up ahead, and the stretcher-bearers were bringing back a stream of wounded. A heavy Jap machine gun suddenly rattled from the side of the ridge. A man carrying a crate of ammunition had been passing by. He dropped his load of mortar shells, looked startled, and crumpled in a heap in the sand. A group of riflemen, idling across the open space, hit the dirt and wriggled behind rocks. They tried to see where the bullets were coming from, for the ridge had supposedly been freed of Japs. The men spotted an opening in the rocks and fired at it. The Jap machine gun ceased rattling. The Marines clambered out of the shellholes and crawled toward the ridge. Other men, sensing a fight, waved to each other and began to close in. Covering each other with carbines and rifles, they edged slowly toward the rocky hole.

A blaze of Jap small-arms fire came from different parts of the ridge. The bullets whistled past the men in the aid station. A corpsman looked up, bewildered, and came around the ridge to see what all the shooting was about.

"Get down!" a Marine yelled at him.

The corpsman dropped behind a rock and pushed his helmet back on his head. "Hey," he called. "Knock it off. This here's a hospital."

The men didn't appreciate the humor. They pointed down the road behind him. The corpsman turned. Four stretcher-bearers were stumbling along the road with a wounded man, hurrying to the aid station.

The corpsman cupped his hands over his mouth to try to warn the stretcher-bearers, but there was too much noise and they couldn't hear him. The Japs began to fire at them. They ran faster. Then a bullet hit one of them in the leg. He looked around wildly and crashed to the ground. The stretcher spilled on top of him. The men in front tripped as they tried to hold on to the stretcher. The Japs kept shooting into the group. The wounded stretcher-bearer jumped up again and grabbed his end of the litter. He started to drag the stretcher along, but dropped it. The man on the stretcher hung half over it, his head and shoulders dragging along the ground.

The other men half-crawled and half-ran with the stretcher until they reached the rocks. The wounded stretcher-bearer loped after them. When he reached the shelter, he fell again. It was a miracle that he had been able to stay on his feet, for the bullet had laid open his calf as if it had been hit by a meat cleaver. The man on the stretcher was stone-dead; one of the bullets from the ridge had hit him in the skull.

No one knew how many Japs were in the ridge. A supply captain, coming up from the rear, saw what was going on and radioed for tanks and demolitions men. More Marines from neighboring units gathered. They inspected the ridge from safety points behind rocks.

When the tanks arrived, the men started the step-by-step job of again cleaning out the ridge. They threw smoke bombs against the rocks and moved in with bazookas and automatic weapons. When the smoke drifted away they had to shoot fast, or a Jap would catch them from one of the many holes. The tanks hurled their 75s at every position the gunners could locate. Engineers tried to fling dynamite charges into the caves. Despite their preponderance of weapons, the Marines found that there were too many holes. They would attack one, only to be shot at from another one half a dozen feet away.

Finally flame-throwers were called. They threw long jets of flaming liquid into the holes and along the curving walls of the tunnels. The roaring flames did the trick. The Marines heard the Japs howling. A few rushed out of the caves on fire. The men shot them or knocked them down and beat out the flames and took them prisoners. When the Marines began to hear muffled explosions inside the caves, they guessed that some of the Japs were blowing themselves up with hand grenades.

Soon the flame-throwers paused. A Marine lifted himself cautiously into view. There were no shots from the caves. A Jap with his clothes in rags hunched himself out of one hole, his arms upraised. The Marines stood up behind the rocks and waved to him to come out. The Jap indicated that there were more who would like to surrender. The Marines motioned him to tell them to come out.

Almost forty scared and beaten men emerged from various holes. Some of them had round pudding faces. They grinned nervously and said they were Koreans who had been forced by the Japs to stay in the caves. They said that everyone else in the caves had either been burned to death or committed suicide.

Our men sent them to the rear. Gruggen drove some of them back in his jeep ambulance. A few of the wounded and badly burned enemy were treated at our aid station. Our men stood around sullenly while the doctors administered plasma to them—something the enemy would never have done for us.

At the ridge the Marines groped cautiously among the rocks from hole to hole, examining each entrance-way. Dead bodies, some hit by bullets and grenade fragments, some burned into frightful black lumps, lay in the holes. The smell was overwhelming, and the men turned away in disgust.

The battle of the ridge seemed over. An officer made a note to bring up demolition crews as soon as they could be spared by the front-line companies. They would seal up the holes in this troublesome ridge. The Marines gathered their casualties and drifted away. The tanks shifted into reverse and backed out. Peacefulness settled once more over the area.

But it was not for long.

Soon afterwards, Reid Chamberlain paused at the aid station. He was running a message up to Able Company, dug in among the rocks several hundred yards ahead, and he asked me to accompany him.

We began to cross the clearing which we thought had been rid of Jap sniper fire. To escape occasional mortar shells that were dropping in the open, we clung closely to the rocky walls of the ridge, intending to follow the longer semicircular, but safer, route to the company. Gruggen, whose ambulance was parked at the aid station waiting for casualties, went with us. He wanted to see the caves from which the Japs had just been burned.

We were picking our way among the stones and the burned Jap bodies when three shots rang out from the hillside. We tried to run behind some boulders. Chamberlain drew his pistol and looked hastily around. There was another shot. We heard a thud. We thought the bullet had struck the curving side of the ridge.

When we reached safe spots, we paused and looked back. Chamberlain was nowhere in sight. Gruggen and an automatic rifleman, who had been coming the other way, were crouched behind near-by rocks, their teeth clenched, their hands gripping their weapons. They were trying to find the hole from which the shots had come. We called Chamberlain but received no answer. Slowly we tried to edge back. Rifle shots cracked at us from several holes, and we ducked again.

The long, rocky ridge was once more alive with enemy. Again Marines began to gather, coming up cautiously to help us. They dashed from rock to rock and slid among the boulders, trying to seek cover from the many caves that looked out at us. We told them about Chamberlain, lying somewhere among the rocks. We formed a fire team and began crawling forward. When the Japs fired at us again, the men covering us saw where the shots were coming from. They sent a stream of automatic fire at the holes and "buttoned up" the Japs. One burly sergeant stood straight up without a helmet on and, gritting his teeth, fired his carbine from his hip, moving directly at a hole as he fired. One of the men finally reached Chamberlain's body and lifted his head. A trickle of blood flowed from behind his ear. His eyes were open, but he was dead.

There was nothing we could say or do. We felt stunned, angry, frustrated. We could have fired point-blank the rest of the day at those holes. The Japs would only have laughed at us. In an instant they had claimed one of our best men. Chamberlain's wonderful war record had ended abruptly. After so many heroic deeds, it seemed an added tragedy that he was killed while doing nothing but walking.

We crawled back and sent for flame-throwers, only to find we couldn't get any more that day; they were all busy up front. Meanwhile an outfit of the 9th Marines was moving up and pitching its bivouac on top of the ridge, which had become silent again. We hunted up the commanding officer and told him there were still Japs inside the hill. We related to him all that happened at the ridge that day. He listened concernedly but decided it was too late in the afternoon to try to root out the Japs still in the caves. He posted guards behind the rocks facing the ridge and gave them orders to keep all straggling Marines away from the holes.

That night tragedy struck again. After dark some of the Japs tried to come out of their holes. The Marine guards saw them moving among the rocks and opened fire, killing some and driving others back in. The Japs screamed and howled when they realized they were trapped, and began to commit suicide.

On top of the ridge the Marines who were dug in could hear grenades exploding in the underground caverns beneath them, as the Japs killed themselves. Suddenly, towards midnight, there was a terrific blast that rocked the whole hill. Huge boulders flew among the Marines. Some of the men were hurled into the air. Others were buried in their foxholes as hot sand poured in on them.

A flash of flame shot into the sky and there was a series of rumbles and more explosions. Rocks, dirt, and hunks of concrete showered among the startled Marines. By the light of the flames, the men dug each other out and scrambled down the ridge to safety. Stones cascaded after them in landslides that sealed up half the holes in the ridge's wall. The men took up positions behind the rocks and waited for the Japs to come out. A platoon sergeant saw two of the enemy sitting dazedly among the stones; they were carrying antipersonnel mines around their waists. He killed them as they tried to get up. Another man struggling down the slope saw other Japs trying to rush out from the holes, only to be buried in landslides; their arms and legs protruded from the dirt and rocks.

Slowly our men realized what had happened: The Japs had blown themselves up and, with them, the whole ridge. When dawn came, the Marines discovered that they had suffered only one serious casualty. Many men had been completely buried by the rocks and sulphur ashes, but companions had dug them out before they had smothered. Scouts who poked into some of the remaining holes found that the Japs had used land mines and 125-pound aerial bombs to blow up the hill.

That day our demolitions men began the tedious job of trying to seal all the cave entrances in the ridge. It soon became evident that sealing all the openings was out of the question. The men worked all day, placing charges in the mouths of more than forty caves. When they were blown, we couldn't tell but that cracks had been left through which Japs could still fire. By evening everyone felt a sense of frustration and anticipated further trouble, since there were still many caves unsealed. The demolitions men gave it up; they were needed more urgently elsewhere. Someone said: "We ought to put up a sign here; 'Pass at your own risk.'" Then we left.

A day or two later a supply unit moved into the area. The unit pitched tents and galleys, built ration piles, parked jeeps and trailers, and nonchalantly went about its business of shuttling hot food, ammunition, and water to the battalions ahead.

In the afternoon a jeep and trailer set off for the front lines with hot coffee and doughnuts. It passed the ridge and was fired on. The driver didn't wait to find out what kind of weapon was shooting at him—he knew it was something big, so he stepped on the gas and raced out of the area. On the way back he was shot at again. Jeep ambulance drivers and other supply men reported similar attacks on them. Finally a tank, lumbering over the road, was hit. The crew jumped out and hid behind some rocks.

After a while they came back and reported that an antitank gun was somewhere among the debris of the ridge. Another tank was sent up. It waited behind some rocks till the Jap gun fired and showed its position. Then the tank blasted at it with its 75. In a few moments the Jap position was a pile of smoking rubble. Automatic riflemen who moved in to catch enemy survivors found the weapon to be a 47 mm. antitank gun. The Japs had kept it concealed during all the previous fighting around the ridge.

It would seem that this should have ended the story of the ridge, but it didn't. As the battle for Iwo progressed, Jap riflemen and machine gunners continued to hang on inside the tunnels and fire out at passersby whenever good shots were presented. A wireman, stringing a telephone line between rear command posts, was shot through the head. Two cooks were winged in the arms. A whole mortar platoon was pinned down in its holes by a Jap gunner. A barber and an officer who was having his hair cut were sent running by a burst of rifle shots.

Whenever our men could spot exact positions from which Japs were firing, they tried to knock them out. With automatic rifles and bazookas, they crept among the rocks and blasted at the small holes. Then they threw dynamite charges into the slits and hoped those would do the trick.

It was an almost hopeless task. On D plus 25, the day we overran the last bit of Iwo Jima to secure the island, death was still coming from the ridge. A Jap sniper that day shot a passing corpsman through the ear.

❀   ❀   ❀   ❀

THE FINAL PUSH FOR IWO JIMA WAS TWENTY-FOUR hours away, and when it was all over Marine Corps dead numbered 5931 killed out of a total of 25,851 casualties, including 718 Navy doctors and corpsmen. Only 216 Japanese prisoners would be taken. During a momentary "lull," chaplains held their first services. Most of them had stuck with their regiments throughout the fighting, and when the opportunity for prayer presented itself marines responded eagerly. Sergeant Bob Cooke, a combat correspondent and noted peacetime Scripps-Howard columnist, described the services at the front with Cates's 4th Marine Division. "The Catholic altar was a pile of water cans, the Protestant, the radiator of a jeep. The communion rail was a mound of black volcanic gravel . . . Yet not in any of the world's great cathedrals or churches was there more sincere reverence. Men ignored heavy shells overhead. Clouds of dust from tanks and bulldozers swept the area. But the chaplain's vestments, the altar cloth, and cross gleamed through the pall of the battlefield . . ."

Here is General Holland Smith to conclude the battle.

·11· "UNCOMMON VALOR WAS A COMMON VIRTUE"

LIEUTENANT GENERAL HOLLAND M. SMITH

On March 6 we decided a coordinated attack by the whole Corps might break through. The previous day was devoted to resting our tired men and reorganizing. To prepare for the attack we employed artillery on a scale exceeding any previous effort. We laid down a devastating barrage, using all Corps and divisional artillery and

heavy guns from supporting warships. After the barrage was lifted, the
assault forces ran into unusually heavy resistance. Although most
of the enemy's large caliber guns in the immediate front had been
destroyed, enough were left in the northeastern part of the island
to resist our advances. Moreover, the rocky country made close tank
support difficult and reduced the effectiveness of our shelling. As
a result, the initial assault bogged down. We made slight gains and
could count only a number of destroyed installations and sealed-off
caves in our favor. Later in the day we attacked again, supported by
a heavy barrage, and did a little better. But by nightfall we had consolidated our line and were in a far stronger position for continued
assault.

The next day we tried something we had never attempted in the
entire Pacific war. As the preliminary artillery attack of the previous
day had little effect, we tried a night attack. The Third Division, in
the center, moved off before dawn and took the enemy by surprise.
The main objective was Hill 362C, an anchor of Kuribayashi's defense line. Another purpose was to circumvent enemy artillery fire.
Our artillery drove the Japanese into their pillboxes, but when we
advanced, their artillery, registered on their own pillboxes, came
down upon our attacking troops and inflicted many casualties. By
making a night attack we hoped to catch the enemy off guard and
reach an objective before he brought his artillery into use.

Although the Third Division did take the Japanese by surprise,
the plan was only partially successful. Before the enemy was aware
of the Marines, the 3rd Battalion, 9th Marines, had made a fair advance, but when daylight came we discovered that, in the darkness,
part of the attacking force had overrun a smaller and less important
hill, not the objective hill. The Japanese immediately guessed our
objective and hence fighting ensued. The Marines were called upon
to fight as they had never fought before. Two companies were cut
off and could not be rescued for thirty hours. Another company was
virtually cut to pieces. Doggedly the attack continued, with tanks
doing the impossible on impossible terrain, and at the end of the day
we had taken that vitally important hill.

Possession of this objective made a great change in the situation,
a change reflected immediately in our progress. On the night of March
8, Kuribayashi made a determined counterattack in the Fourth Marine
sector. This was the one attack in force he made on Iwo Jima. It was
preceded by heavy mortar, rocket and machine gun fire. The advance
started just before midnight.

As soon as the Fourth Division received the first impact of the attack, we started to pour intense artillery fire into this area, which
scattered the main body of the enemy. A number of Japanese did

get through our lines and reached the Command Post areas, where they were killed. They carried demolition charges. We learned later the object of the attack was a breakthrough to Motoyama Airfield One to wreck our planes and installations. The advance troops, having found a weak spot in our line, were to be followed by a much larger force. Thus the only counterattack on Iwo Jima that promised the Japanese any results was checked, with heavy losses for them.

On the morning of March 9, we reopened the attack in the other sectors and, while the Fifth Division recorded a slight gain, the Third Division continued to punch through the center and a six-man patrol from the 21st Regiment clambered over the last ridge dividing us from the northeast coast. To celebrate the event, they splashed in the sea in plain sight of the dumfounded Japanese manning caves on the east side of the ridge but outside the range of their guns—by now they only had small calibers left.

"We wanted to wash off the Jap dirt," one marine explained. They also scooped up a canteen of sea water and sent it back to Erskine with the famous admonition: "For inspection, not consumption."

Now the Japanese were split in two. The Third Division advanced in the footsteps of the patrol and seized the ridge overlooking the beach. Severance of the two Japanese forces was complete. One was contained in the Fourth Division sector, but the main body of survivors held the rocky area around Kitano Point in the northwest, hemmed in by the Third and Fifth Divisions. The capture of Iwo Jima was in sight.

With the reduction of enemy-held territory to two small areas occupied by only a fraction of the original garrison, resistance decreased, but we did not relax pressure. Artillery barrages, poundings by naval guns, and air strikes were maintained as a matter of routine, although shrinking enemy terrain made these assaults somewhat unmanageable. Kuribayashi was reported still alive, commanding the group in the caves at Kitano Point. He gave no indication that he would surrender, which did not surprise us overmuch.

The last enemy artillery fire fell in our lines on the morning of March 11, a few hours before we launched our final attack. The Fourth Division, with elements of the Third, jumped off in the eastern sector without any artillery preparation and by midafternoon reported all organized resistance had been eliminated. The Japanese in this pocket were well dug in among deep crevices connected with caves and tunnels, and fought desperately as their lines shrank around them. It took us five days to wipe out that pocket.

For the Kitano Point assault, the fire power of all three regiments of artillery, plus the Corps artillery, was brought to bear on that stubborn corner in a rolling barrage of exceptional intensity. This was augmented by warship fire and air attack. For nearly an hour, the rocky area was blasted, with apparently little result. The only direct route to the main enemy fortifications was a rocky gorge, 200 yards wide and 700 yards long. Entrance to the gorge was denied us by covering machine gun and rifle fire.

This was Kuribayashi's last stand. Undoubtedly he was in command and his personality was apparent in the tenacity of the defense. Although his forces had been reduced to a shadow, he suffered no lack of small arms and supplies. There was nothing to do but proceed methodically against cave after cave, pillbox after pillbox, advancing by the yard, until the enemy was wiped out.

The Third Division, on the right at Kitano Point, quickly cleared its sector, but two weeks elapsed before we finally cleaned out the area. This task fully occupied the attention of the Fifth Division after the island was declared secured and the Fifth suffered heavily. There were no suicide leaps on Iwo Jima. The Japanese fought to the end and made mopping up expensive. Kuribayashi was determined to take every last American with him.

On March 26, the Japanese made a carefully prepared sortie from their caves. This was their last counterattack, and it caused much confusion and many casualties before they were annihilated. A prisoner said that Kuribayashi was among the officers who came out, swords at their sides, to make this final demonstration, but an examination of the bodies, swords, and personal papers revealed no trace of him. Perhaps he was killed at that time; perhaps he died in one of the thousands of caves sealed by the Marines. I do not know.

The official flag raising on Iwo Jima was held at V Corps Headquarters on the morning of March 14, two days before the island was declared secured. The ceremony was attended by flag and general officers of the fleet and landing force, and Military Government Proclamation Number I, proclaiming United States sovereignty over the Volcano Islands, was published. The original flag, which had flown on Suribachi, was removed.

Tears filled my eyes when I stood at attention and saluted the flag. The ceremony marked the capture of Iwo Jima and the end of the most terrific battle in the history of the Marine Corps. The mission to take the island had been carried out successfully and I was proud, although this pride was saddened by the realization that so many brave men had given their lives to perform that mission. On a personal note, too, the ceremony was saddening, because Iwo Jima was my last combat command.

This momentous event gave pause for reflection. The amount of effort that had gone into the capture of the barren island was staggering. The Navy had put more ammunition on Iwo Jima than anywhere else in the Pacific. Marine artillery expended 450,000 shells and we used huge quantities of mortar shells, grenades, and rockets. Our air force made it the principal target this side of Japan proper. Yet, in the final analysis, it was the man on the beach with his rifle who completed the job . . .

No single chapter, no single book could describe that battle. To tell the story of Iwo Jima, I would have to tell the individual story of every man in the assault force. As Admiral Nimitz said: "Among the Americans who served on Iwo Island, uncommon valor was a common virtue."

❋ ❋ ❋ ❋

NOW THE CEMETERIES ON IWO JIMA WERE DEDICATED and the leaders of these ineffably brave men tried to put into words what each one felt. General Erskine's last remarks represented the emotions of all of them, officers and men: "Only the accumulated praise of time will pay proper tribute to our valiant dead. Long after those who lament their immediate loss are themselves dead, these men will be mourned by the Nation. They are the Nation's loss! There is talk of great history, of the greatest fight in our history, of unheard-of sacrifice and unheard-of courage. These phrases are correct, but they are prematurely employed. Victory was never in doubt. Its cost was. The enemy could have displaced every cubic inch of volcanic ash on this fortress with concrete pillboxes and blockhouses, which he nearly did, and still victory would not have been in doubt. What was in doubt, in all our minds, was whether there would be any of us left to dedicate our cemetery at the end, or whether the last marine would die knocking out the last Japanese gun and gunner. Let the world count our crosses! Let them count over and over. Then when they understand the significance of the fighting for Iwo Jima, let them wonder how few they are. We understand and we wonder—we who are separated from our dead by a few feet of earth; from death by inches and fractions of an inch. The cost to us in quality, one who did not fight side by side with those who fell, can never understand."

The Medal of Honor was awarded to twenty-seven who through their sacrifice and heroism made the victory possible: twenty-two marines and five Navy men.

And the survivors of three divisions embarked in transports to Hawaii.

In Washington, General A. A. Vandegrift, Commandant of

the Corps, was the recipient of much abuse from the press and radio. Deeply sensitive to Marine Corps losses, he speaks of the death of two close friends, and of a pilgrimage. Let us join him in these momentous post-Iwo days while the preliminaries of the next invasion, Okinawa, are under way.

·12·   "MY PRESENCE . . . COULD HAVE YIELDED VERY LITTLE"

GENERAL ALEXANDER A. VANDEGRIFT AND ROBERT B. ASPREY

Those who suffered the loss of their loved ones and those who were badly wounded should know that the possession of this hideous island saved many more thousands of lives than it cost. These lives wore a different uniform, that of American airmen, but they were American lives, they were brothers-in-arms.

Public reaction generally supported our fight. The famous Rosenthal picture of the flag raising on Mt. Suribachi stirred millions of human breasts. The postmaster general sometime later informed me that first-day cancellations of the Iwo Jima stamp broke all existing records in the main Washington post office. Telephone calls and letters by the hundreds and thousands bespoke the nation's pride in its Marines. To the few dissidents I tried to explain the gigantic issues at stake. Sometimes I was successful, sometimes not.

A few days after the initial landing I received a call late one night. A frantic woman in Chicago had heard from a friend that her son was wounded—she demanded to know how badly he was wounded as well as his present location.

"I just don't know," I told her. "I don't even know your name."

She told me her name and added, "You must know how my son is, where he is."

"I want to tell you something," I said. "My own son was badly wounded on Iwo Jima. I don't know how badly and I don't know where he is. I know he has been evacuated and is receiving excellent care, and I know the same is true of your son. If you will leave me your telephone number I will have you called the minute we get any information."

Somewhat mollified, she hung up.

I could not blame any mother for worrying or even for trying to assuage worry by abusing me or the Corps. I did resent parental influence particularly when the marine did not wish it. One case occurred in Australia after the Guadalcanal campaign. The wife of one of my young officers prevailed upon her politically powerful father to have her husband ordered home. General Holcomb asked me to look into the matter. I called the officer in and explained the situation.

"I know my wife is worried," he told me. "So are lots of other wives and mothers. I not only don't want to go home, but I sincerely ask you not to send me home."

I wrote General Holcomb:

> I could not help but congratulate him on his decision because it was, in my opinion, a very manly thing to do. I am, therefore, not returning him to the States.

At a dinner party shortly before the end of the war I was set upon by a woman saying in a loud voice, "I thought I heard someone congratulating you on the high percentage of Marines serving overseas."

I allowed as how we were proud of this particular record.

"My son isn't overseas. He is down at Camp Lejeune and is miserable. I don't see why he can't get overseas."

I learned the young marine's name. Thinking I was doing a favor, the next day I arranged his overseas orders. A week later, the war having ended, his irate father called my office—would I cancel his son's orders. The boy wished to marry and, according to the father, there was no conceivable reason for his going overseas now. I refused to consider changing the orders.

Returning to the Iwo Jima period, Mr. Forrestal did all he could to make the American public realize the value of our sacrifice. He knew what the casualty figures meant to me and to other marines and on all occasions displayed the utmost compassion at our losses. I later wrote Holland Smith:

> I personally feel that in the whole thirty-seven years of my service in the Marine Corps there has never been a finer Secretary of the Navy or one more keenly interested in the Marine Corps nor more alive to our trials and tribulations.

In late March we declared the island secure. Holland returned to Pearl Harbor from where he wrote me on March 21:

> I returned on Saturday via Guam where I spent two days. Admiral Nimitz and his staff were particularly cordial, and apparently realized what a serious fight we had on Iwo. Before leaving here in January I predicted 20,000 casualties which at that time met almost with derision.

Personal catastrophe added to the burden of these days. Bill Rupertus did not recover from the heart ailment that put him in the Bethesda hospital. Despite the best treatment, his heart continued to misbehave and in late March he faced physical retirement. Since I knew his record would still make him an asset at Quantico I wrote him offering to call him back to active duty from retirement.

Late on March 25 I was at home when Colonel Kilmartin, commanding the Marine Barracks at the Naval Gun Factory, telephoned to report Bill *in extremis*. I hastened to his side. He was dead when I arrived. The next day I received his letter thanking me for and accepting my offer to return to active duty.

Bill's death came as a low blow. After we buried him I wrote General Holcomb:

> The Marine Corps has lost one of its finest officers and I have lost one of my finest friends.

As if to acknowledge the service to the nation rendered by the Marines on Iwo Jima, I was promoted to four-star rank in early April, 1945. This made me the first four-star general on active duty in the history of the Corps. I was more than gratified by the flow of congratulatory messages which seemed to approve of the Corps's finally coming of age.

During the Iwo Jima fighting I had wanted to get to the Pacific, not only to visit the wounded and the troops who were fighting so hard but also to see something of the largest operation yet mounted in the Pacific war—Okinawa, slated for April 1.

Much as I hated to admit it, my presence in the field could have yielded very little. I held the utmost confidence in my commanders or they would not have been there. In Washington, on the other hand, I had my job—at this particular time the perennial, seemingly endless Congressional hearings attendant to the next budget. On April 8 I finally shook free of the capital.

Field Harris, assistant commandant for air, Jerry Thomas and I flew to the west coast, inspected installations in San Diego and San Francisco and proceeded to Honolulu. After conferring with Holland Smith and his staff I flew to the island of Maui to visit the splendid 4th Marine Division just returned from Iwo Jima, its fourth assault.

At the airstrip Cliff Cates silently handed me a dispatch reporting President Roosevelt's death [April 12]. I was terribly shocked. All of us in Washington knew the President was tired and undoubtedly ill but I never dreamed he was so ill. What indomitable spirit and courage this man mustered in those final weeks and days.

My gloom deepened at the sight of Cliff's diminished division.

Every inch the field commander, Cates tried to give me some idea of the fighting on those awful sands. As I talked to him and to many of his officers and men I felt a terrible gratitude made the worse because no word of mine could express it properly and fully.

We flew on to the newly established Guam headquarters of Admiral Nimitz where I inspected Bobbie Erskine's 3d Division also just recently returned from the Iwo Jima battle. I received a rude shock in Guam. To my consternation Nimitz did not think I should visit Okinawa—my main reason for making the long trip. I thought I knew what was bothering him. It was the Saipan controversy and was probably the main reason Holland Smith was sitting back in Pearl Harbor. In Nimitz' mind, I concluded, a senior Marine general by barging into Okinawa might upset the applecart of command relations. I subtly tried to quiet his fears, but at the same time I let him know I intended to visit my marines.

He countered with a suggestion to visit Iwo Jima. Recognizing a temporizing attitude and wanting to see the island anyway, I flew up the next day with Jerry and Field Harris. The commanding officer of the Army garrison unit showed us around. He had built a road up to Mt. Suribachi, the elevation on the extreme left from where the enemy poured his lethal shower on the landing marines. I later wrote General Holcomb:

> I have had the privilege of going to Iwo and standing on Suribachi, and the terrain from there just beggars description . . . I still don't see how they got ashore and having gotten ashore, I don't see how they stayed there.

A few enemy remained on the northern end of the island. We watched Army troops unseal caves and try to persuade the soldiers to surrender. Those who chose to come forth were treated well. Those who chose to die were accommodated.

❧ ❧ ❧ ❧

IWO-BASED B-29s REGULARLY STRUCK THE CITIES of Japan, and American prisoners of war could not have been more delighted. Private Martin Boyle, whom we have met, was one of a handful of marines captured when Guam fell December 10, 1941. Here he speaks of the raids, and also of the misery and degradation of those whose unhappy lot it was to be guests in the land of the Rising Sun.

·13· LIFE IN A JAPANESE POW CAMP

MARTIN BOYLE

It wasn't the dull days that bothered us . . . much, or even the ever-increasing hunger. I think what bothered us most was the long nights —especially those nights when the B-29's came over. Most of us had gotten used to the daylight raids after six months of continuous bombing, because we could see the bombers and we could see where the bombs were landing. And from the first it was obvious that the water front was not yet a priority target. The B-29's hit the high priority military targets first—the steel mills, the shipyards, the storage dumps, and the large industrial and manufacturing plants that bordered the perimeter of the Osaka-Kobe harbor complex. The big bombers were experts in picking out and destroying their targets, and before long we felt enough confidence in them to sit back and enjoy the show. But nobody was fooled, we all knew that the water front would be hit eventually, and for some reason we figured that it would come at night. And that's what made the nights different—we couldn't see the bombers, we could just hear them and we couldn't see the bombs exploding, we could just hear them, too—and we knew that every time the air raid warning siren sounded, the odds became shorter.

Most of us were pretty uneasy when we were jarred awake in the middle of the night by the wailing of the giant air raid siren that stood atop the Sumitomo warehouse two blocks from the camp. We got to know the sound well; first the whirring sound of the electric motor that set the machinery in motion—and when the big cylinders began to revolve slowly we could hear their soft and throaty sounds—then, they gathered momentum and the sound steadily increased in volume until it reached a high whining pitch; then the sound actually seemed to float away from the tall building and roll up the street like a giant tidal wave of noise. At that point, when everyone was wide awake, the piercing sound reversed itself and receded slowly back to the warehouse and we could hear it fade away—only to be replaced by the ominous rumbling of the B-29's as they approached the city.

And once wide awake, we lay on the hard *tatamis,* alert and silent, each man thinking his own thoughts as the heavy bombs pounded into the city. There was nothing to do but lie there and sweat it out, and think—think about what the bombs meant to us and what they meant to the Japanese people—and think about how it was going to be when the bombardier's aiming marks crossed on the Osaka water front.

To us, the bombers meant that the war was being driven home to the enemy and the harder the B-29's hit the quicker we could get back to normal living. They meant just about the same thing to the Japanese civilians, and even the die-hards were squirming under the steady bombings. Then the hammer struck.

. . . March, 1945. Twenty-three hundred hours, one hour·to midnight. We opened our eyes slowly, yawning and stretching, and cussing the air raid siren that had got us up. We heard the bombers approach the city from the Inland Sea and the first bombs sounded a lot different, more like big air whistles than a freight car, and they didn't even shake the building when they exploded near by.

"Holy Christ! Those things are pretty close!"

"You bet your sweet ass they are."

"Maybe we're it tonight, eh?" The voice was very quiet.

The darkness of the barracks began to drain away as a soft, reddish-orange glow filtered through the windows to light up the room.

Chasta scrambled over Mackery and me so that he could look out the window. "Hey! Something's caught on fire!" Mackery and I rolled to where we could see over Chasta's shoulder, and we looked over the barbed-wire fence toward the harbor and saw flames reflecting from the tall buildings of the water front. Then we knew that the crowded residential section directly behind us was on fire.

Mackery watched the angry reflections bounce off the buildings. "Those are incendiary bombs," he told us. "Those fires started too fast for it to be anything else."

While we were still at the window the second wave of bombers came over; they flew so low that their sleek, dark silhouettes were clearly visible to us as they flew out of the darkness and into the red glow of the fires. The B-29's attacked in tight, rigid formations, wave after wave of them, dropping thousands of tons of fire bombs—huge packages that burst into hundreds of small incendiary sticks upon contact. Thousands of fires broke out immediately and the sky turned a brilliant red, splotched by clouds of swirling smoke that almost absorbed the roar of the bombers. We crowded around the two small windows of the barracks, every man craning to get a look at the bombers. As one formation of B-29's passed overhead and disappeared another took its place, then another, and still another. Our initial reaction of elation turned to anxiety when it became apparent that the B-29's were bent on leveling the entire city. The anxiety turned back to cautious elation when it became clear that, either by accident or design, the water front was not going to be hit that night.

An hour or more after the first alarm we heard the guards scrambling around in the passageways shouting for us to get ready for a muster. We heard the mustering party go from room to room and when they got to our barracks I was surprised to see that Colonel Akami, the camp commander, was personally in charge of counting noses. He had two other officers and four or five soldiers with him, but there was no sign of either Sergeant Mabel or Sadie. The soldiers were jittery but they were doing their best to appear as calm and unruffled as Colonel Akami. The guys had elected me barracks leader, and I was in charge of the count-off; so I was standing right by the door when the colonel came in.

"Kiotsuki!" I shouted the Japanese order for attention and the dancing reflections from the nearby fires had lighted the room so much that I could see the men stiffen to a sitting position on the shelves. I reported the room number and the number of prisoners to the colonel. One of the soldiers shined a hooded flashlight on the muster board that the colonel carried, and I saw the colonel's face when he bent over to check the figures. It was the face of a tired, haggard old man, and on it was written the knowledge that the big gamble was lost and the real ordeal was just beginning.

He looked up from the board, his eyes tired, drained-looking. He needed a shave, and the little patches of gray beard reminded me that I'd never seen him without a clean shave.

"Bango," he said quietly, and his voice was very calm. But I could hardly hear it above the noise of the thundering bombers and the thump of incendiaries.

"Bango!" I shouted the order to begin the count and the old man looked sharply at me as if he detected a quaver in my voice.

The men began to count off, sharply . . . *"ichi! ni! san! shi! go! roku! shichi! hachi! kyu! ju! ju-ichi!"* The count went on and I could sense that every man was straining to shout out his number in a steady voice. Colonel Akami stood between the two tiers of shelves and took the muster as calmly as if he were in his own living room feeding his beloved cat.

After the colonel left we huddled by the windows watching the bombers. Five hours later we were still awake, and the first major fire raid on Osaka was over. The water-front buildings were still standing, but that was about all. There was no great babble of noise after the raid—the city was deathly quiet, stunned. The people didn't rush madly around trying to put out the fires mostly because they had very little to fight them with. So the flames licked away at the wood and paper buildings, and when the fires died out, the entire city was enveloped by dust and smoke that curled lazily from the ruins, and the sullen smoke cloud almost blotted out the soft gray light of the rising sun. Osaka, the second largest city in all of Japan, had suffered a mortal blow.

The ruins started at a point about three blocks from the water-front docks and warehouses and continued through the main part of the city and almost to the wooded outskirts. Wide swaths are completely burned away and in some sections only the concrete buildings were standing, and some of them were only shells. Before the dust and smoke cleared away the Japanese people began to rebuild. They searched the still warm ruins for timber, for tile, for slate, for tin, for iron braziers, for any small piece of scrap that they could salvage. They fashioned the rubble into crude shelters—and like the victims of a Mississippi River flood or a Kansas tornado, they chose to build their shelters on the same ground where their homes had once been.

Activity along the water front and all the other places where we worked had stopped, and we stayed in camp for three days while the Japanese people dug out from under. On the fourth day we went back to work. We left camp with a little apprehension because the four-teenth of March raid was not a light jab nor was it confined to mili-tary targets—it was a real smack in the chops and it had been aimed at the very doorstep of the Japanese civilians. I was with a gang that went to the Sumitomo docks that day where, surprisingly, the work-men showed no signs of antagonism toward us. Not all of them were on the job. Sam-*san,* an old guy—one of our regular civilian work bosses—was not there and the number one *hauncho* told us that he had asked for another day off so that he could continue to search for his wife and two kids. He found them that morning buried in the ruins of his shattered and burned out home. Sam returned to work that afternoon. He didn't say a word to us about his family but joined with the other Japanese civilians in giving us wide-eyed accounts of the destruction to the city. They were shocked by the extent of the damage, but they told us about it in matter-of-fact voices that pointed up their philosophy of the war—it was really no surprise, they had been expecting it all along.

When we got back to camp that night we found out that all hell had broken loose. Dr. Matsui was the officer of the day, and he had taken over the camp duty with an eye for vengeance. The unsuspect-ing *horios* who had stayed in camp on the sick, lame, and lazy list told us that Matsui was in a monumental rage. The guys thought he had gone berserk because he spent most of the day darting all over camp like a mongoose looking for prey and beat hell out of every prisoner who wasn't nimble enough to scamper out of his path as he bellowed his enraged way throughout the entire camp.

Matsui's disposition hadn't improved much by the time we returned to camp, and we knew we were in for a bad time when he ordered an early muster. It usually took about thirty minutes to hold a camp muster but Matsui didn't intend this to be an ordinary night or an ordinary routine count of prisoners. He was bent on revenge. He planned to get a little from every *horio* at Osaka #1—particularly the Americans, and more particularly, the American Marines, because Matsui hated us Marines more than anyone else simply because it was our guys who got all the credit in the Japanese papers for kicking the Nips off half the islands in the Pacific. But on that night we kind of figured that Matsui would take picks on the Army Air Force guys in the next barracks since it was the *B-ni-ju-kyu's* that had started him off on his rampage in the first place.

Anyway, we heard Matsui begin his rounds making a lot of noise as he worked his way up to us. He gave everyone a bad time as he went along but we knew that he was just warming up for our barracks. An hour later he stood outside our door, and he waited there for fifteen minutes at least. I knew he was just outside the door because I could hear him whispering to the people who were with him. I stood by the door and waited while sixty-five men sat on the shelves like so many rag-doll prizes on display in one of Keggie Collins' carnival booths. What happened next belongs in a comic opera.

The door banged open like a shot and it shook the building. Before the clapboard walls quit rattling Sergeant Mabel and Sadie the Sadist were standing at attention on either side of the door. Then Dr. Matsui stepped inside the room, marched the length of the barracks and back again to where I was standing. He turned and paraded back and forth again and this time Mabel and Sadie followed him, so close on his heels that they would have both disappeared from view if Matsui had suddenly stopped. I knew the Unholy Threesome meant business because Mabel's face was distorted by the twisted little nervous grin that always meant trouble, and Sadie had that wild look in his eye. The Japanese officer was all dressed up in his best uniform and his highly polished boots glittered in the dim light of the room; but even the high shine on his boots was overshadowed by the brightness of the big Samurai sword that he carried unsheathed. The naked sword was damned near as big as he was, and Matsui looked like a small Japanese boy all dressed up for playing soldier.

I was so surprised by the staged entrance and the military procession to the other end of the barracks and back that I stood there openmouthed. I was supposed to have hollered for attention as soon as

Matsui entered the room, but I was so shook that I forgot to do it. Matsui stopped his pacing when he got to where I was standing, and he used his free hand to cuff me alongside the ear.

"What you say when Japanese officer enter room?" he squealed. He cuffed me again and this woke me up.

"Kiotsuki!" I hollered it loud and clear, and sixty-five men froze to a sitting position, legs crossed, hands on knees, head and eyes riveted straight to the front. We had planned to throw Matsui off balance with our rapt attention to these details, but the officer didn't even look at the other men.

Matsui glowered at me through squinted, glistening eyes.

"Say again! That time not loud enough!"

"Kiotsuki!" I hollered at the top of my lungs.

Matsui turned to Sergeant Mabel. "You hear this man?" Mabel twitched his lips and shook his head in the negative.

Matsui swung around at me again. "Louder! Louder! Make all camp hear!"

I sucked in a deep breath and shook the rafters. "KIOTSUKI!" Matsui stepped closer to me. I stood at rigid attention, Japanese-style, my arms frozen tightly against my body, weaving a little bit because it's not as natural a position as the American posture of attention and it puts a strain on a man's muscles—especially when a man's standing on a pair of high, wooden clogs as I was doing.

Matsui stuck the big naked Samurai sword between my legs, and then, slowly, gently, he started to flick it with his wrist so that the sharp edge of the blade beat a steady, easy tattoo at my crotch. I tried to lock him on with a steady stare but he wouldn't have any part of that. He was staring at my crotch, rapping at it like he was trying to flick away a fly. Then he started to bring the blade up a little harder, and I fought back an urge to flinch away. I tried to think of making sergeant and shipping over in the Corps and I tried to think of a big juicy steak and a Lucky Strike . . . and I even tried to think about Lana Turner and how she wig-wagged down the street in a movie I'd seen when I was in the middle of the Pacific on Fleet maneuvers, but I couldn't think of anything but the blade between my legs. I was getting more nervous by the second since I didn't know whether the goofy pill roller was for real or only having a little fun at my expense.

Mabel and Sadie were delighted at my discomfort, and I could see that they were admiring Matsui's performance. Happily for me, Matsui tired of the fly-flicking sport although I know that he was disappointed that I hadn't moved. I guess that the big beads of sweat on my forehead must have satisfied him that I was sufficiently shaken. He put the Samurai sword back in its case and looked around for something else to do. He rubbed his hands and swaggered slowly between the shelves, and we all knew that he was playing his favorite game; we called it "eyeball," and I guess it needs a little explaining.

During the room musters the guys on the shelves were supposed to be at attention and this meant head and eyes glued to the front. The idea was to take a peek at the mustering officer when he wasn't looking and not get caught doing it. Matsui was queer for the game, and he used to play it with us every time he had the duty; we would expect at least a swat from him if we got caught moving the eyeballs a fraction of an inch.

One night when Matsui had the duty, Lashio bet another prisoner that he could get away with peeking at the Japanese officer, and when he lost the bet, Mackery and I gave him a spoonful of rice to help him cover the wager.

But there were no bets this night when Matsui started to play "eyeball" with us. He walked casually down the aisle, then suddenly whirled around looking for a roving eye. I'll say this for Matsui, he played the game fair, and when he didn't catch anyone peeking at him he climbed the studded four-by-four stanchion up to the top shelf. When he got there he took out his sword and hit all eleven men over the head with the flat side of the blade. When he climbed back down he paused at the middle tier, still hanging on to the stanchion, and whacked everyone who was within range of the sword.

When he got back on solid footing he put the sword back in its case and then wheeled and started toward me. Just as he turned, Chasta gambled on a quick peek, and Matsui caught the flicker of the moving eye. He called Chasta down from the middle shelf and made him sit on the bottom tier. Then, Matsui grabbed the top of the middle shelf and swung himself violently into the bottom bay, feet first and kicking furiously, and Chasta caught a face full of highly polished leather. This was too much. Someone laughed, and that made everyone else laugh, and Matsui almost went out of his mind trying to kick everybody at once. We didn't quit laughing until Mabel and Sadie got in the act and shut us up the hard way.

After the room quieted down, Matsui kicked Chasta once more for good measure and told him to get back on his own *tatami*. The Nip officer was breathing hard when he returned to where I was standing. He gasped for me to begin the count.

I put a strain on my vocal cords because I wanted to get this business over with before the nut killed somebody.

"*Bango!*" When I shouted the order to begin counting off I think they heard me in Kobe.

"*Ichi! Ni! San! Shi! Go!*" everyone but *go* hollered at the top of his voice.

Matsui raised his hands wearily. "No, no! You men not count loud enough."

The count started over again, and again, and again, but never loud enough for Matsui. We counted off for fifteen minutes and he stopped the count every time he heard or fancied he'd heard a flaw in Japanese diction or American volume. One time the count got up to *go-ju-shi,* fifty-four, and the knucklehead who was number fifty-four threw the next man off balance by hollering out *go-ju-yottsu,* which is another Japanese way of saying fifty-four, and the room broke up again and the Unholy Threesome went back to work on us. I think Matsui got tired so he came back to me and roared, "One more time! This time, every man count right!"

We began counting again, slow, loud, and easy when the count reached twenty-nine Matsui roared. "Stop-*u!* Stop-*u!*"

He looked up at the top shelf. "What man number *ni-ju-kyu?*"

Pappy Spencer, a lean, tough marine from the hills of Tennessee raised his hand.

"Say it again. Say *ni-ju-kyu* again." Matsui's voice was almost like syrup.

"*Ni! ju! kyu!*" Pappy shouted, pausing between each number.

Matsui smiled. "Now, say in English language."

Pappy smelled a fish. "Twenty . . . nine," he said skeptically.

"Okay. Now, you Mister Twenty-Nine, you come down here please." Matsui sounded almost human, and for a minute I thought he was going to invite Pappy uptown for a steak dinner.

Pappy climbed down from the top shelf and left the room with Mabel and Sadie. Matsui was the last one to leave and right before he went out the door he rapped me in the nose and then grinned wickedly at the other *horios* before sliding shut the door. He had good reason to be pleased with himself because he had gotten an inspiration from the number twenty-nine. Wasn't it the B-29's that had just burned out Osaka? With a fine flair for the dramatic, Matsui escorted Pappy to the guardhouse, and on the way he stopped at the other barracks and picked up every other man who sat in the twenty-nine position. When he got the men to the guardhouse he made them half-mast their drawers. When they all had their bare butts hanging out, Matsui picked up a shovel and swung it two-fisted like he would a baseball bat, and he walked up and down the line whacking at the bare butts. Sergeant Mabel and the sadistic little Sadie joined in with a garden rake and a hoe and they worked these butts over pretty good.

Pappy came back to the barracks right before lights out with a wry smile on his face. We all jumped down from the shelves and gathered around him. "What the hell happened, Pappy?" someone asked him.

Pappy didn't say anything but he still had the grin on his face. He turned his back to us and dropped his pants. His butt was chopped clean of skin and the whole thing looked like a big fat piece of raw hamburger.

Pappy could hardly walk the next morning so he reported to the sick bay. He said Dr. Matsui chuckled when he inspected the damage and then slapped some hot, gooey salve on Pappy's rear end and told him to stay in camp the rest of the day. There was some talk about reporting the incident to Colonel Akami, but we decided against it because we had never made it a practice to run to the old man every time we ran afoul of the Unholy Threesome. But Pappy's butt was another matter; no one would have thought much about the entire twenty-nine deal if the guys had come out of it with a black eye or a bruised nose or even a bloody head, but using garden tools across a man's butt was more of an indignity than punishment. Anyway, we figured out a way to bring the matter to Akami's attention without actually reporting it.

The POW in charge of the inside working details assigned Pappy to clean up the colonel's office. The plan was for Pappy to pretend to pass out in front of the old man and then the POW *hauncho* would rush in to help out and in the confusion he was to half-mast Spencer's drawers so that the colonel could see that the chewed-up butt caused Pappy to faint.

Pappy got inside the colonel's office but it didn't do any good because Akami was in Tokyo for a conference and wouldn't be back for three days. The only person in the office was Watanobi, and the little interpreter's only responsibility while the old man was away was to feed the colonel's pet cat. Now pets were a rarity in wartime Japan, because the people were having it tough enough keeping their own bellies half full much less trying to keep an animal alive. But Colonel Akami could afford to keep his cat for a pet, and I think we hated him more for this than anything else—since we suspected that part of our rations were diverted in order to keep the cat happy. The pet was a big fat arrogant animal, and we all hated it. But the colonel loved that cat, and though we didn't know anything about Akami's personal life we guessed that the cat was the only thing the old man had left.

Pappy griped more about the cat than he did his own butt, and he was really burning that night when he told us about it.

"Just imagine, that goddam cat is eating better than we are! When I was in the colonel's office I saw that big fat slob of a cat sitting right in the middle of the old man's desk, lapping away at a big bowl of milk! There was some fish and rice in another plate and the snobby bastard hadn't even eaten all of it, and when that bottle-eyed Watanobi walked in the other room I pushed the cat away and ate the fish and rice myself! I didn't get it all eaten though because Watanobi came back in and screwed the deal up, and to top it off, the little fart sat in the old man's chair and hand fed the rest of the chow to the cat! If I thought I could have gotten away with it I'd have stuffed that goddam cat right up Watanobi's ass!"

Pappy kept on raising hell about missing out on the cat's food and he passed the word all over camp. When we went to bed that night Colonel Akami had lost a lot of numbers among the *horios.*

Two or three weeks after Pappy got his butt skinned he was detailed to work in the camp galley, and a few days after that he and another prisoner were growling at each other as only two guys can growl at three o'clock in the morning.

"What really burns me up," the guy complained to Pappy as he stirred the morning's breakfast rice, "is that we have to get up at this ungodly hour just to mess around with this swill."

"Yeah, it's a hell of a note," Pappy said. He added some water to a few *daikons* that were almost lost in the bottom of the big iron cooking pot.

The other cook looked inside the soup pot. "Just look at that crap! Not even any salt to put in it. Christ! I can't even remember the last time we had any salt. If I ever see another thing that even looks like a cucumber in a bowl of water after I get out of here I swear I'll puke. What a laugh! Grab a couple of water-logged *daikons,* slice 'em up, toss 'em in hot water, and by God you still end up with hot water!"

Pappy raised both hands excitedly. "Sh! Don't move," he warned. "Turn around real slow and take a look at who just walked in."

The other man slowly turned his head. "Wow!" he murmured, "Breakfast food."

It was the colonel's cat.

"Come 'ere, Kitty. Come on, Pussy. Come on now, nice little Kitty." Pappy coaxed the cat inside the door and reached behind him for a heavy wooden mixing spoon.

The other man reached for a butcher knife. "That's right, Kitty. Come on over here like a nice little Kitty . . . come on, Kitty, nice, Kitty, Kitty, Kitty."

The two prisoners were grinning when the lugged the wooden buckets of rice and soup in the barracks a few hours later. We lined up with our bowls, and they ladled the stuff out to us. Lashio peered at his soup when he carried it back to his *tatami.* "What the hell goes here? Looks like there's more than just water in the soup this morning."

I looked at the thin layer of grease floating on top of the warm water and stuck my finger in the bowl and then tasted it. "You're right," I said, "Looks like a little meat's been thrown in for a change."

The soup was pretty tasty and everyone tried to find out what had been added.

"Knock it off you bums and pipe down!" Pappy cautioned us. "Just eat your breakfast and keep your mouths shut or we'll have every damn Jap in the joint on our ass!"

The colonel was furious and the camp was turned upside down later on in the morning when the colonel's cat turned up missing. Mabel and Sadie led a search party for it, and they even left the camp and looked all over the neighborhood, but they didn't find a trace of the beast. It was passed through the grapevine that night that both Sergeant Mabel and Sadie, as well as every guard that was on duty the night before, was severely punished for letting Colonel Akami's cat get out of the compound.

※　　※　　※　　※

WHILE THE MARINE CORPS BRACED FOR ITS LAST invasion, let us turn momentarily to a vastly different aspect of the duties performed by those marines in World War II who served as intrepid resistance fighters with the Office of Strategic Services both in Europe and the Pacific. It was the job of such as Captain Walter R. Mansfield, a linguist and demolition expert, to parachute into enemy-held territory and assist the local populace in their war against the Axis. Mansfield, much decorated in Europe for assisting Tito's partisans in their fight against the Nazis, completed his "in-fighting" mission in Yugoslavia and returned for reassignment. With the war in Europe about to be concluded, Mansfield was reassigned to duty in China, there to work with a three-man team which hoped to wreck, or considerably disrupt, a vital Japanese supply route from Peiping. One black night while his comrades were fighting on Iwo Jima, Mansfield and his team climbed into a bomber at Saipan and took off for enemy-held territory where, by prearrangement, they parachuted down to Chinese guerrillas. We meet him now on the brink of his almost private war.

·14· MARINE ON MISSION

CAPTAIN WALTER R. MANSFIELD

It was a perfect site for an ambush. There, almost at my feet, lay a stretch of the main Jap-held motor road through the famous "Corridor," the vital Jap lifeline of communications and supply from Peiping in the north to Kwelin, Hongkong, and the enemy's Southeast Asia empire, which was now rapidly crumbling.

A set of low hills, covered with shrubs and scenery, ran right down to the road. To the north, the road extended in a straight line for over 600 yards, passing over a crazy-quilt of flat, water-filled rice paddies which offered no cover on either side except two parallel ditches. Then it disappeared behind the hills. Below us was a deep cut and to our rear lay a maze of hills and more rice paddies. Intricate foot trails provided an excellent escape route.

For this ambush I had taken along the best 300 out of some 500 odd Chinese guerrillas who had been organized and trained by a small American combat team of men assigned with me by the Office of Strategic Services. With me were two American members of our team, Corporals Cedric Poland and John Owens, as well as the two most trusted Chinese interpreters, "Chee-chee" and "Susu."

Our plan was to ambush any sizeable Jap truck convoy which might come along this road. Our armament consisted of four bazookas, 40 rockets, 6 LMGs, 30 Tommy guns, 25 carbines, and several hundred "Gissimo" 7.9 mm. rifles.

I directed the riflemen to spread out and take cover in the bushes on the little hills running down to the road. Then we placed the LMGs in the hill posts where they could command the best enfilade fire. As usual we had trouble persuading the bazooka teams to get down close enough to the road so that they would not miss the target when it appeared. It was only after Corporals Poland and Owens went down with the bazooka teams that they were set. Now everything was secure. We settled down to wait in the penetrating cold of this dull, overcast day.

For two months now, we had been located in this "pocket" behind the Japanese lines in China, near the strong enemy base of Hengyang and the "Corridor," which the Japs relied upon to feed arms and supplies to their armies in the south.

. . . While the "pocket" was surrounded on all sides by Jap-held roads and territory (occupied by about 15,000 - 25,000 Japs) the intricate maze of hills and rice paddies provided an area over 20 miles square in which we could safely operate.

The Nips seldom ventured into this hinterland because they would lose their way quickly on the narrow, deceptive foot-trails which wound through the mountains, and could easily be ambushed and stampeded by much smaller guerrilla forces. Whenever a Jap force of any size was detected moving into the hills to get us, word was passed like wildfire by the Chinese so that we were never caught unaware. Most Chinese did this not because of any strong patriotic zeal. The real reason was the ancient Chinese "Paochia" system, under which each village headman would be executed by the guerrillas if he did not immediately notify them.

Nip control over the main motor road was an entirely different matter. Here they maintained a rigid patrol system to insure safe passage for their trucks. Garrisons and block-houses were set up at three-mile intervals. All bridges were guarded. Truck convoys, ranging from 30 to 90 trucks and protected by at least two tanks at the front, would usually venture out every night after dusk. Because of the constant threat of American bombers they seldom moved by day, unless the weather was bad. Today, because the sky was overcast, there was a good prospect of our intercepting a convoy.

Suddenly, we heard the rumbling exhaust of a motor, gradually growing louder. Quickly we moved into position, unlocked our pieces and got ready. Maybe this was it! About a half-minute later a lone Jap truck, about the size of a Dodge 1 1/2 - ton job, appeared around the bend and roared up toward us. I was disappointed not to see others following it.

Foo SzLing, senior Chinese officer with me, became excited, grabbed up his whistle and moved it toward his mouth. Owens and I both lunged forward and grabbed the whistle out of his hands just in time. After all the trouble I had gone to in order to stage this ambush, I was not going to see it wasted on such small fry as one lone Jap truck. We would wait for bigger game. "Chee-chee," my chief interpreter, explained our actions to Foo, who appeared distinctly unhappy over our failure to attack.

The truck passed. In the rear, were about ten Japs, quite unaware of how close they were to annihilation. A few minutes later, another truck full of supplies appeared, and I had all I could do to check our men, whose eyes gleamed at its contents.

We settled down once again to our long wait in the cold. As I sat there freezing, I thought of all the bitterness and trouble we had experienced in reaching this unpleasant location . . . It had all seemed very simple when the general officer, making the assignment, nimbly ran his fingers over the map to point out my ultimate destination. Since then I had traveled more than 800 miles overland from Kunming under difficult conditions. I was now over 200 miles east of the nearest American advance outpost in central China, which was located at Chihkiang. Between the rigors of the trip, made in coldest winter, the lack of essential supplies and food, and the difficulties in training and operating with our Chinese allies, I had been through a special kind of hell in a few months.

First, there had been the trip overland. The first 750 miles, from Kunming to Chihkiang, ran through the so-called "free China." Driving two 2 1/2-ton trucks over narrow, back-breaking roads took us seven long, exhausting days. At some points, the road wound back and forth up the side of a mountain so many times that it looked like a layer cake.

Then, we had marched overland to Wukang, Chinese Army headquarters and hopping-off point for our 200-mile trek overland through the Jap lines to the "pocket." Wukang is one of those ancient, sleepy, walled cities of interior China where everything goes on today just as it probably was 2,000 years ago. It boasts not a single wheeled vehicle, not even a cart. Everything is moved on the shoulders of coolies.

In Wukang, which had probably not seen more than a handful of white people during its entire existence, we few Americans were a curiosity. Men and women would stand at a distance, while children swept in closer to mimic. Anything we strange white people did was good for a laugh!

We began to learn some of the rigid customs and formalities which are religiously followed by all Chinese as part of the studied pattern of their everyday life—and which are essential prerequisities to getting them to act! I found that hot tea must always be served to a visitor upon his arrival, even though the "tea" consists of nothing more than a few green leaves in dirty water. A Chinese must clasp his hands together before accepting a cigarette tendered him. A host is considered most impolite if he does not walk with a departing guest beyond the threshold of the house and bow. At dinner, the guest of honor must sit in the chair facing the front door. No matter how sumptuous the meal, the host must, in accordance with polite custom, apologize for the "poor meal" he has set out for his guests. One never directly voices one's disagreement with what another Chinese has said. It must be done in a roundabout way, in order to save him face.

For a group of healthy Americans out to get things done in a hurry, it was difficult task to conform with such time-wasting procedure!

The Chinese commanding general of the 74th Army at Wukang gave me two companies of his "best troops" to escort me over the long, tortuous route through Jap lines to the "pocket." They turned out to be characteristic soldiers—as carefree and cheerful as Chinese soldiers always are. We spent three weeks steadily training them in basic infantry weapons and tactics.

Finally, my little group of about 300 men was ready to depart for the pocket. Our 2 1/2 tons of equipment (including rifles, ammo, explosives, bazookas and radio) were broken down into small bundles so that it could be borne by 70 to 80 coolies, each of whom could carry about 75 pounds a day for 20 miles. We left Wukang midst much ceremony, including a barrage of firecrackers (the Chinese have no sense of security). It was like a day at the circus!

For the next 15 days, from early morning till late afternoon each day, we marched in single file over winding, ancient stone trails which ran through rice paddies and mountains. It reminded me of pictures of the Klondike Gold Rush in Alaska—vile weather, poor food, trails covered with snow, mud and ice.

These amazing Chinese soldiers and coolies possessed nothing—absolutely nothing—in the way of bedding equipment, and very little clothing. They ate two meals a day, consisting of several bowls of rice with a few greens and, if they were lucky, a little pork. Upon camping for the night, they would gather around charcoal fires in cold rooms of the village mud huts and would huddle together under a few borrowed dirty, thin blankets. I am sure that not a single one of them ever removed or washed his clothes during the entire trip. We Americans were beginning to tighten our belts as we got used to two meals a day of rice, pork and greens.

My greatest difficulty during this trip was with our coolies rather than the Japs. The coolies were a miserable lot and for the first few nights a certain percentage would always escape during the night. This would delay the following morning's departure until some of our Chinese troops went out and forcibly rounded up a few protesting farmers into what we called our "volunteer reserve." Then I started paying the coolies $100 [yan] (about 15¢ American money) a day. They were so pleasantly dumbfounded that they stuck with me after that!

Passing through the Jap lines proved to be a relatively simple matter. The "line" consisted of a Jap-held motor road in which there were plenty of gaps which were poorly patrolled. We easily passed our entire train through one of these gaps at night, less than a quarter of a mile from 500 sleeping Japs!

Now we were in the "pocket." Guides took us over a day's winding march through the hills to the little village of Tiento, temporary headquarters of Chao SzLing, guerrilla chieftain for the area. We stored our equipment under guard in some old Chinese temples and I went to meet this leader, with whom I hoped to work in the future, and to whom I had many letters of introduction.

Chao appeared at first blush to be a most affable character—a short, wiry, energetic, smartly-dressed little man of about 40 years. He never ceased to flash his toothy smile at us, and to show off by barking out orders to the guerrilla officers who formed his immediate entourage. A Chinese Regular Army officer, he had been sent out to this territory over five months before to organize guerrillas. Now he had a group of about 1,000 men. On the following day we saw about 500 of them. They were a ragged, poor-looking lot and only about one-half possessed weapons, mostly "Gissimo" 7.9 mm. or captured Jap "Arisakas," with very little ammunition. Gradually I began to learn that they were carrying out only sporadic operations, due to lack of equipment.

For one month, we worked on a hard training program, teaching them all we knew. We set up rifle, bazooka, machine-gun and demolition ranges. Bazooka and demolitions squads were formed. Long hours of instruction were given every day. At times, it was almost unbelievably disappointing. Most of the Chinese had such poor eyes that they could not hit the side of a barn door at 100 yards! Despite these handicaps, we were able to get about 400 men (out of 1,000) whom we considered passable. Meanwhile, I was maintaining regular radio contact with American base headquarters and more supplies were beginning to pour in overland.

During this first month, we were forced to move around quite a lot, from village to village. Chinese troops usually camped in the dingy, mud huts of these primitive villages. Upon entering a town, I would try to find the best house for an operations headquarters. Usually my "office" would consist of a dark, dirty, little room in an old stone house—probably as primitive as houses were in China over a thousand years ago—with uneven, earthen floor, wood lattice window (with no glass, of course).

Outside the window of my headquarters, there were always a few polished bald Chinese heads peering silently in at the curious-looking American, fascinated by anything I might do or say. Many undoubtedly had walked over ten miles to see their first white man. At first I did not mind, but as time went on the novelty disappeared and a great temptation came to dispel them by force. I would only restrain myself when I realized that I would never be understood and that face would be lost.

Despite the unsanitary conditions which prevailed we managed to avoid most illnesses and dysentery by rigidly following the rule that all water must be boiled and all food cooked.

A meal of rice was very filling, but after a few hours, it would leave us all hungry. We missed badly those tasty things we had been used to at home (or "Shangri-la" as we called it) such as sugar, milk and cigarettes. Our only sugar consisted of a deep-brown, rough substance which closely resembled shellac in taste and smell. Milk was non-existent, and for cigarettes we smoked anything we could get our hands on, mostly vile tasting, locally made Chinese brands with flowery names such as "Red Horse," "Red Bridge" and "Precious Idea." There were also some captured Jap cigarettes and a few, good, old American ones which were rare indeed.

As time went on, I began to see our situation in better perspective. In this area called the "pocket," it was the rule of the pistol and the sword. Civil law and order existed on the surface only. A Chinese possessing a weapon and ammunition was in a position decidedly superior to the others, and when several such persons grouped together they could make their power felt in many ways.

Chao, our guerrilla commander, had taken advantage of this situation. While this group had ambushed Jap columns and trucks, their main purpose had been to capture arms and increase their power among the civilians in the community. By this time, Chao was now fairly well installed as a petty war lord, ruling by the ancient maxim that "Might is right." Weapons, not manpower, were the problem. Every Chinese civilian wanted to join our ranks so that he could be on the side which shared in the take.

Our first ambush fitted in with Chao's ideas and worked out rather well. In late February, we selected 300 of the best men for a night ambush on a Jap truck convoy to be coupled with demolition of a 75-foot wooden bridge. We picked a point on the main road where there was a hairpin turn, about one-half a mile from the bridge, and carefully scouted the area to find only a few Japs guarding the bridge.

After we started out on our 10-mile march to the ambush point, we ran smack into a Jap column and had our first healthy skirmish, which resulted in about 10 lost on both sides. We retired, returned two nights later, under ideal conditions—a beautiful moonlight night. After we had set all our men in position, we were rewarded with a 40-truck Jap convoy, which slowly labored over the road. We bazooked the third truck, then gave them everything we had. It was a pitched battle and I was disappointed at our men's inability to hold fire as they had been trained.

The results were good, however. We destroyed 14 trucks, killed about 45 Japs, captured 30 rifles, six officers' dispatch cases filled with secret papers, and a great mass of other miscellaneous equipment! The wooden bridge was destroyed, but in six days a Jap labor group rebuilt it out of beams taken from houses of a nearby town.

A month of activity had followed. From a hill near Nanyo, I was able to spot a large Jap truck dispersal area in which about 300 trucks were hidden. I arranged by radio a rendezvous with our air base at Chihkiang. Two days later seven B-25s appeared. We laid out our panels, so they could spot us, gave them an azimuth with estimated distance from our position and then talked them in on the target by means of our air-ground mike while "Chee-chee" ground away on the hand generator. It was a great thrill to talk with our own bombers, and an even greater thrill to have ringside seats when they bombed the dispersal area and destroyed about 40 trucks.

After two more fairly successful ambushes, Chao began to back down on me. Now that we were strong and had a fairly adequate supply of arms, he was no longer interested in wasting equipment on killing Japs and blowing up bridges. He was content to be the war lord of the area. Every artifice and every excuse was used to stall off each ambush I would plan. I could no longer restrain myself. We began to have words.

Finally, I took 300 of the best men and went out alone with them to carry out another ambush. We took several prisoners and on the way back located an excellent drop zone for reception of supplies to be parachuted to us.

I returned to our hideout to find the cupboard bare. Little Chao, in my absence, had moved off with his troops, lock, stock and barrel, taking every available bit of equipment! For two days, I chased him with my 300 men. Finally I caught up with him and we had a showdown which I shall never forget. After four hours of arguing back and forth, I settled with him for the return of most of the equipment and 500 men. Henceforth, I would operate separately in the northern part of the "pocket" while he operated in the south. When it came to selecting Chinese officers it was a satisfaction to see that the best of them wanted to come with me. We parted by the road, and that was the last I ever saw of the guerrilla chief, Chao SzLing.

These were some of the events which had taken place — some of the things I thought about as we waited in our ambush position by the roadside on that cold afternoon in late March, 1945. Now, for the first time, I was completely on my own. The responsibility for the success or failure of this ambush now rested solely on my own shoulders, and on the success of this first ambush might depend the future confidence of my own men. I had undertaken the job in spite of the protests of Foo SzLing, my able Chinese senior officer who felt that a daylight ambush on the main road was too risky—in fact, so risky that it had never been tried before.

We had been crouching in the cold now for over an hour, but nothing except the two Jap trucks had passed. Foo SzLing and some of the junior Chinese officers were growing restless. The men were cold, and showed it. Foo SzLing spoke to me: "Captain, I advise we turn back. About two miles down the road there is a Jap garrison. If they know we are here, they may already be circling around in back of us by some of the other trails, and be ready to cut us off."

I replied: "Let's wait another 15 minutes, Foo." Cold as I was, I hated to give up after all the trouble we had gone through to get there.

I decided to take one more look down the road through my binoculars. About a mile or so away, a small stretch of the road was visible before it disappeared again into the hills. My glasses passed over it and just as I was moving on I thought I saw something moving in the road. Quickly I swung the glasses back and could hardly believe my eyes. There, moving down the road toward us, was a group of men marching! They were still too far away in the distance for me to distinguish how many.

I handed the glasses to Foo and told him that we must now change our plans for a truck ambush and get ready to lay a personnel ambush. We had about 15 minutes in which to get ready. Our men must be moved down close to the road before the Nips rounded the last bend and swung into full view. We would let them march right on down toward us till they got about 200 feet away from a little finger of a hill which extended down to the road. Then we would hit with all we had.

We frantically changed the machine gun posts so that we would get a good enfilade fire on the proposed ambush spot. I became exasperated when Foo SzLing refused to order 50 men down to the crest of the little finger hill extending over the road because he felt it was too dangerous a position. It was only after Chee-chee, Owens, Poland and I started down for the position that he released 50 men to join us.

Now the Japs had rounded the bend and were coming down the straight stretch, about 600 yards away! For the first time I got a good look at them and was amazed. It was an almost unbelievable sight! About 100 Japs were marching four abreast in perfect formation, with no point, guard or flank—just as if they were putting on a show for Emperor Hirohito himself! Spaced behind them at 20-yard intervals were three 75 mm. horse-drawn guns, and three caissons. All the men were equipped, however, with rifles or light machine guns.

Meanwhile, we all waited tensely under cover, as they gradually drew nearer and nearer. Now they had passed through a little cut in the road about half way down to us. Our men began to sight down their rifles. Through my glasses, I could see an officer at the head of the group, his Samurai sword swinging by his side. Now, they were crossing the little road bridge about 150 yards away. In the pit of my stomach arose that same peculiar feeling which never failed to materialize just before the first shot is fired in an ambush. Foo SzLing tugged my shoulder and whispered "Chenzai, Chenzai!" (Now, now!) indicating he wanted to give the signal. "Meyo, meyo!" (No, no!) we answered. I wanted to wait until they were almost on top of us because I knew what poor shots the Chinese were.

Now I could see their faces very clearly and hear them singing— about 100 yards away—then 90—80—I raised my left arm for the signal, at the same time leveling my Tommy gun sight on the middle of the group. The whistle blew. All hell broke loose, with machine gun and small-arms fire concentrated on the group.

On the first burst we dropped about 10 men. (A group of 50 well-trained marines would certainly have knocked off at least 25 or 30, but I had learned what to expect from the Chinese.)

This was a well-trained Nip company. As we opened fire, they dashed almost simultaneously for the ditch on the other side of the road, and were out of sight. Soon all six horses dragging the heavy guns and caissons were toppled over, and there were no longer any live targets to shoot at.

The live Japs were now hiding in the ditch and waiting us out. This was smart tactics on their part. Though there was nothing to fire at, our men continued literally to pour automatic fire in the general direction of the ditch. I will never be able to understand what happens to a Chinese soldier, once firing has started. No matter how many engagements he has been in, or how much experience he has, he seems to go hog-wild on automatic fire and acts like a rookie all over again. No amount of training seems capable of changing that. Once again I became furious as I watched them wasting precious lead, hitting nothing, and disregarding our signal to cease fire.

There was only one effective way to clean out the Japs in the ditch before reinforcements arrived, and that was to get a couple of machine guns across to a house on the other side of the road, where they would have almost unobstructed fire down the ditch. I rushed two squads over. We lost three men in getting them there, but soon they paid dividends as they opened up on the ditch and knocked off another 30 or 40 Japs in a few minutes. By carefully watching for someone to move up out of the ditch, I was able to score two hits, and saw one of my targets splash back into the rice paddy.

Meanwhile, my men were getting completely out of hand. I had given the order that no bazookas were to be used because there was no target. Just then I heard a "Whoompf" followed a few seconds later by an explosion and saw a cascade rise from one of the rice paddies. Then another, and still another. Soon I got the story. One of the bazooka crew, in typical Chinese style, became excited and decided he had to get in on this. No sooner had he fired his bazooka than the other bazooka teams, thinking the order had been given to fire bazookas, opened up! This was typical of the problems we ran into every day with the Chinese.

Another example. In the midst of the firing, I noticed one of the machine gunners training his gun at what appeared to be an off-angle. I crawled up in back of him to find him aiming his Bren gun very seriously at a water buffalo down in one of the paddies, and splashing bullets all around it! Due to his poor eyesight he had mistaken the water buffalo for a Jap!

There probably were not more than 20 Japs left now out of the original 100, and most of these were huddled under the little bridge for cover. They popped out a hat on the end of a bayonet, the signal for surrender. I ordered "Cease fire!" blown, but could not quiet all our troops. Finally, realizing that time was passing (it was now almost 25 minutes since we had opened fire) and that Jap reinforcements might be brought up, I ordered the group nearest the road to scramble down to the ditch, and try to clean out the remaining Jap pocket with hand grenades. About 30 men got down into the ditch.

Soon we had grandstand seats to a running hand grenade battle between our men in one ditch and the Japs in the other. Here again I saw a touch of Chinese psychology which is almost unfathomable. In the midst of this last ditch fight, with bullets still whistling and grenades bursting, four or five of our men, attracted by the prospective loot, scrambled up onto the road and started stripping Jap bodies!

In a few minutes, the coast was clear for everyone to go down onto the road. The few remaining Japs either got away or were wiped out.

A ghastly sight awaited me—bodies lying all over the water-filled rice paddies and ditch on the other side of the road. Quickly the men went to work and spiked the gun barrels and breeches with hand grenades.

A few minutes later, a barrage of small knee-mortar fire suddenly descended on us. Nip reinforcements had arrived and were bracketing us! We quickly scrambled off the road and up the hill toward our escape route, leaving two machine gun posts to cover us.

Within two hours, we had returned to a safe point in the hills, about four miles from the road. We knew that the Japs probably would not chase us this far but just in case they tried, we rigged up a few boo-by-traps and set out a few ambush patrols at critical points.

It was a successful ambush, for a Chinese one. We had killed about 80 Japs, captured over 50 rifles, several machine guns and miscellaneous equipment (including one captain's Samurai sword, which I appropriated) and had taken two prisoners. We had lost seven men and had four more wounded [out of 300 guerrillas] . . .

※　※　※　※

NOW IT WAS TIME FOR OPERATION "ICEBERG"—OKInawa. Here was not just "another damned island" to be assaulted in the seemingly endless push westward; here was the primary objective of the concurrent drives of Admiral Nimitz from the Central Pacific and General MacArthur from the Philippines; and here too was the point at which the Imperial General Staff intended to make its "decisive" stand with all forces, including the Kamikaze—the Divine Wind. For Okinawa is only 325 miles south of Japan, and is the largest of the Ryukyu islands. Seventy miles long by eighteen wide, they are heavily wooded and mountainous in the north, with rolling farmland in the narrower southern portion. In March 1945 Okinawa became the target of targets, and its conquest—short of an assault on Japan itself—hopefully signified the last invasion of the Pacific war.

Following the seizure of the Marianas in mid-1944, the Imperial General Staff realized that the homeland was in jeopardy, and ordered Lieutenant General Watanabe to command the Ryukyu garrison which included Okinawa, Ie Shima to the northwest, and Kerama Retto to the southwest. But Watanabe became ill shortly after arriving on Okinawa and Tokyo sent down Lieutenant General Mitsuri Ushijima to replace him and organize the 32nd Army (upwards of 100,000 men) in a defense quite unlike anything previously encountered by the Marine Corps.

Ushijima was a capable and highly regarded professional, but he became ensnared in a power play between two factions. The orthodox old guard wanted him to revert to the true *bushido* battle on or near the landing beaches, while the "Kuribayashi" school (to which Ushijima himself adhered) wanted an in-depth defense with heightening resistance as the enemy penetrated inland. Although a compromise set of orders embracing the thinking of both factions was given him Ushijima, with good reason as we shall see, finalized his defense of Okinawa behind strong cross lines draw up at the southern end of the island, making no attempt to contain United States forces at the beachhead.

Ushijima's chief of staff, Major General Isamu Cho, was an engineer. Another asset in carrying out the defense preparations was a native population of 450,000 Okinawans, most of whom lived in the southern portion of the island. Cho conscripted Okinawan labor to build his fortifications extending south and east from Naha, the capital. Here he placed Lieutenant General Takeo Fujioka's 9th and 62nd Divisions, covering the area of the Hagushi beaches, and to the north Lieutenant General Tatsumi Ammiya's veteran 24th Division. Between these lines were dispersed batteries of the 1st and 23rd Medium Artillery Regiment, the 7th Heavy Artillery Regiment and the 110th Heavy Artillery Battalion. These guns ranged from 75 millimeter to 155 millimeter, and were under the command of Major General Wada. Additionally, Wada had available three machine-gun companies, four oversize anti-aircraft battalions, and three other firepower formations of mortar, antitank and rocket; of the mortars, there were 24 of 320 millimeter, 6 of 90 millemeter, and 48 of 81 millimeter; four antitank battalions each were equipped with 4.7 millimeter guns; and the rocket command was a full battalion equipped with 9-inch rockets. Ushijima, like Kuribayashi at Iwo Jima, stressed the importance of knocking out American tanks first, and to this end his orders were to bury all tanks to the turrets as fixed artillery.

The third area of defense was north of the 24th Division. Here was General Shigero Suzuki's "Bimbo Tai" (Have Nothing) command, the 44th Independent Mixed Brigade, consisting of partial brigades and Okinawan conscripts—all told, with 3500 Naval Guard troops on Motobu Peninsula, a sorely put upon little force which in December 1944 required 294 rifles, 1011 bayonets, 556 mess kits and 64 machine guns. To compound Ushijima's difficulties, the United States Army moved into Leyte and the Imperial General Staff panicked, believing Formosa was next; and despite the protests of the Okinawa commander, his crack 9th Division was transferred to Formosa.

Thus deprived of the services of his key division, Ushijima's only hope was to shift his remaining forces, and let Tokyo make of it what it would. Suzuki's 44th Independent Mixed Brigade was brought down to the eastern side of the southern part of the island, leaving only a few companies as watchdogs near Motobu; and the 24th Division was shifted around to the west side of the southern part and adjusted at its northern extremity, while the 62nd Division was adjusted slightly southward from its northern-most line.

The main defenses now extended somewhat north of Naha through Shuri Castle at the center of the island, an area of rug-ged hills, defiles and deep caves. Cho, a systematic officer, in-spected the terrain carefully and emplaced his guns so as to be mutually supporting in the cave areas. Foxholes were dug in front of the caves with connecting trenches and laterals. During a bombardment all troops in the trenches were pulled back to the caves, and when a frontal attack developed, troops were sent out through the laterals to attack American infantrymen on the flanks.

By December 1944, shortly after the 62nd Division moved into positions previously occupied by the 9th, Japanese morale never before in question, suddenly began to show signs of deterioration. American bombings had burned out most of the crops, and many of the island's farmers had been conscripted into the Japanese Army; the combined result was a poor and unsatisfying diet. "I cannot bear having a cup of tea for a meal with no side dishes," wrote a soldier. "Our health will be ruined." When Ushijima learned of the food situation, he issued a sharp reminder to the effect that his men should "display a more firm and resolute spirit, hold to the belief of positive victory, and always remember the spirit of martyrdom and of dying for the good of the country." This elevating but highly unsatisfactory-to-the-stomach speech was accepted in good grace. However, a pint and a half of sweet-potato brandy issued to the troops made the order so much easier to take. The troops were permitted to get drunk without fear of court martial, which they did, after which officers again delivered stern lectures on the virtues of dying for the Emperor.

The following month Ushijima sent Cho to Tokyo to explain the defense system on Okinawa. Although there was some dis-cussion as to why Ushijima had disregarded orders, the "new school" now held sway among the Imperial General Staff and defenses such as those at Peleliu and Iwo Jima were *de rigeur*. Moreover, by pinning down the enemy with an in-depth defense, the Divine Wind had a splendid opportunity to attack many ene-my warships and supply ships bringing reinforcements. Cho ap-parently believed a chart of American sinkings (made up after Leyte) he was shown at Imperial General Staff headquarters, which showed 1 American battleship, 6 carriers and 34 cruisers sunk by the Kamikaze Corps, for upon his return to Okinawa he circulated a report to all senior officers: "The brave, ruddy-faced warriors with white silken scarves tied about their heads, at peace in their favorite planes, dash out spiritedly to the attack. The skies are slowly brightening."

By the end of March a Japanese intelligence report, speaking of American air and submarine activity, deduced that an attack was imminent at either Okinawa or Formosa. Ushijima thereupon issued a battle plan with three primary points: no counterattacks in force, large-scale infiltration at night, and no attacks without reinforcements. Said the perspicacious Ushijima: "You cannot regard the enemy on a par with you. You must realize that material power usually overcomes spiritual power in the present war. The enemy is clearly our superior in machines. Do not depend on your spirits overcoming this enemy. Devise combat methods based on mathematical precision: then think about your spiritual power."

While the Japanese general lectured his troops, the largest invasion force ever assembled in the Pacific—some 180,000 troops, including 81,165 men of the Marine Corps—sortied from Ulithi Atoll on March 18. L-Day (D-Day) was set for April 1, 1945. With the exception of the Army's Attu landing in May 1943, this was the first combined Navy operation in which a Marine Corps officer did not have top command of the amphibious forces. For whatever reason, troop command devolved on Lieutenant General Simon Bolivar Buckner, USA. Two corps, Geiger's III Amphibious Corps (Marine) and Major General John R. Hodge's XXIV Corps (Army), comprised the major elements of the Tenth Army. Admiral Spruance, Mitcher and Turner were in command of the operation until the beachhead was established; and Admirals Deyo, Hall and Blandy commanded the support and bombardment forces. (In all, 1218 warships and train were involved.) Lastly, Generals Arnold and LeMay directed preinvasion strikes by the Strategic Air Command.

Although three Marine divisions figured in preinvasion planning—the 1st, 2nd and 6th—only the 1st and 6th Divisions actually participated in the Okinawa campaign. The 2nd Marine Division, after a diversion, returned to Saipan to prepare for the invasion of Japan. Major General F. P. Mulcahy's 2nd Marine Air Wing comprised the major elements of the Tenth Army's land-based aircraft.

After seizure of Kerama Retto on March 26 and preinvasion air strikes and bombardments by the various commands concerned, we were ready for L-Day. (Significantly, the Kamikaze Corps had already put in an appearance; of 650 Japanese planes engaged in this work, only 26 percent would be effective.) L-Day envisioned two corps landing abreast on the Hagushi beaches along the west shore and capturing airfields at Yontan and Katena. After slicing across Okinawa's girth, Geiger's marines would proceed northward to clean out Ushijima's upper breastworks, while the XXIV Corps would wheel southward to battle in the Shuri Castle - Naha area.

Thus, after much "softening," our forces stormed ashored April Fool's Day only to be greeted with profound silence. *Where was the enemy?* By noon of L-Day men and equipment had penetrated 4000 yards inland, and still not a skirmish. It was not until the third day that the 6th Division began to meet resistance, and even then there was hardly enough to make a good headline. But by that time there were other sides to the Okinawa story, and the ubiquitous John Lardner found them as he moved forward with the marines.

·15· OKINAWA ARMED WITH A PENCIL

JOHN LARDNER

By dawn of the third day ashore, the Marines I was with were ready to jump off in the final move of forty-five hundred yards, which would bring them to the eastern shore of Ishikawa Isthmus, on the opposite side of the island from where they had landed. Three battalions were going to take part in the attack. The night had been an eerie one in our dew-drenched camp on a pine-covered ridge dividing two ravines. There had not been time to flush all the ravines and caves, and we had by now heard the story of the thirteen marines who were bayoneted in their holes the night before. We watched the pink glow of a brush fire that exploding shells had started beyond the next hill. "By God, this is very mysterious. Know what I mean?" said Lieutenant Colonel Fred Beans, executive officer of the regiment, as the boys looked around desperately for something to shoot. In the matter of civilians, they showed commendable restraint, especially considering that every marine regarded Okinawans as Japs and would split no Oriental hairs whatever except to concede that these "Japs" looked very harmless and beaten down. The Okinawans we saw at first, cowering in the thatched houses of the little village of China—an apt name, since Okinawans are more like Chinese peasants than anything else—or hiding in nearby caves, were all women, old men, and children, every male civilian between sixteen and forty having been herded south by the Jap Army for labor duty.

We learned with interest from a hand radio that an airborne invasion by Japs was expected that night. Those marines who had gone to bed shivered under their blankets and ponchos; they were South Pacific fighters, unused to crisp, cool nights. Colonel Alan Shapley became concerned about a faint wailing sound up ahead of us. Finally the regiment's operations officer, Major Orville Bergren, turned from our telephone with a message. "I got the word on that noise," he said. "The second battalion has a woman and a baby with them that are hurt and crying. They wish to hell we would do something about it, because it is driving them crazy. The man that was with them got killed in the Jap fire in that little counterattack they had this evening. You know how it is. These people are scared to move by day, so they move by night and get shot up. What about it?" "Tell them to take it easy and see that the civilians are doctored, and forget it," said Shapley. "They'll be jumping off soon."

All three battalions launched their final eastbound attack at 0830 and, except for one small-fire fight on the right flank, were delayed only by the roughness of the ground. By 1100, two battalions were on the eastern beaches, and by 1130 the third was in the little coast village of Ishikawa. "Being as how we are working with the Army on this invasion and have the loan of some of their vehicles, of which they got more than there are in the city of Detroit," said Beans, who, like other marines, was never able to get over his astonishment at the Army's wealth of equipment on Okinawa, "we don't have to walk to catch up with those battalions." Then he turned to Shapley. "I'll go ahead, Colonel," he said, "and set up a new C.P. across the island, and you can follow with the other jeeps." So saying, Beans was off down the road. He returned five minutes later to recover his revolver, which he had left hanging from a branch of a pine tree. That was the kind of campaign it was.

I rode across the island in Shapley's jeep. The roads were narrow and dusty, the villages poor and dingy, but the green island around them was a fine thing to see. Some ridges were so thickly terraced for planting that it was hard to see how they remained standing. We passed across a coastal plain checkered with rice paddies and green squares of sugar cane. Potatoes, beans, garlic, onions, radishes grew everywhere. The civilians, who were now feeling easier, were walking along the roads and saluting us. Nobody returned these salutes until Shapley waved back at a jovial old gentleman with a dirty kimo-

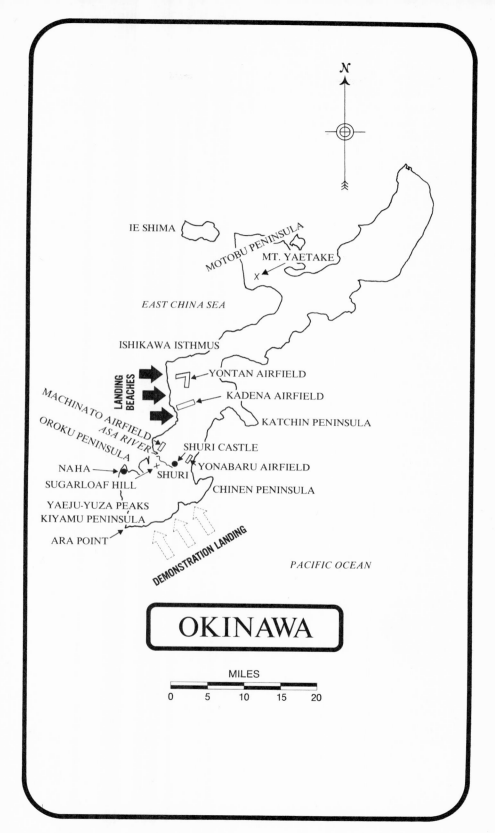

N

IE SHIMA

MOTOBU PENINSULA

MT. YAETAKE

X

EAST CHINA SEA

ISHIKAWA ISTHMUS

YONTAN AIRFIELD

LANDING BEACHES

KADENA AIRFIELD

KATCHIN PENINSULA

MACHINATO AIRFIELD

OROKU PENINSULA

ASA RIVER

SHURI CASTLE

NAHA

SHURI

YONABARU AIRFIELD

SUGARLOAF HILL

CHINEN PENINSULA

YAEJU-YUZA PEAKS

KIYAMU PENINSULA

ARA POINT

DEMONSTRATION LANDING

PACIFIC OCEAN

OKINAWA

MILES

0   5   10   15   20

no and bare feet, and then conviviality was general, with some exceptions. A truck just ahead of us was carrying five young marines and, in the uniform of the Jap labor troops, one young Okinawan who had been badly shot up that morning. Apparently his head wounds had brought on shock, headache, and nausea, for he huddled in a corner of the truck, refusing all attentions. When one of the marines, during a stop in the journey, lighted a cigarette and put it between the Okinawan's lips, he shuddered violently and pulled back after one puff. The marines watched intently.

"What do you want to treat a Jap so good for?" asked one of them, whose tow hair stuck out wildly in all directions.

"Why not?" said the man with the cigarette.

"Well, why don't they send some of them back to tell those other Japs how good we treat them?" the first man said. "Then maybe they would treat us good."

The man with the cigarette spat thoughtfully. "Why not?" he said.

"Why don't they send some of them back to tell those other Japs?" the tow-headed boy was yelling balefully as the truck moved on again.

We found Ishikawa to be a deserted village perched on a magnificent bathing beach. Colonel Beans, who had already set up a command post on a hill overlooking some rice and sugar fields, went swimming with the regimental surgeon. I wandered through the village, looking at the lights of a dozen barbecue fires that were beginning to flicker in the dusk. Pigs were roasting, and chickens. Assistant chefs were going up to the fires with handfuls of onions, garlic, and radishes. "They ought to be sticking to their rations, damn it, but I don't know what you can do about it," the doctor said to me as he came out of the sea and began to towel himself. "The main thing is if they just cook that stuff thoroughly enough. Otherwise there's going to be a lot of sick marines." The doctor was in a disgruntled frame of mind because earlier in the day a man from the regiment's weapons company, following the combat troops into Ishikawa, had been shot through the abdomen while hunting souvenirs in an area not yet searched.

"How's he coming, Doc?" asked Beans sympathetically.

"Oh, he's got a fifty-fifty chance," the doctor said gruffly.

Back at the C.P., Shapley had put a sprig of blue flowers in the buttonhole of his shirt and was outlining the day's progress to the general commanding the division. A couple of mess sergeants were cooking soup in a bucket, against the chill of the coming evening; it got cold as soon as the sun went down. Other marines were gathered around an old woman in an old black kimono, who was squatting in a corner of the camp and eating C rations with chopsticks. "I guess the

Japs didn't cut her in on those new kimonos," one marine said. A ship-ment of kimonos, just in from Japan, some lined with flaming red silk, had been found in the village. A marine gave the woman a cigarette, which she began to smoke. Apparently all older Okinawan women smoke. She was an unusual case, however, for when she had half smoked the cigarette, she threw it away and produced a long, slim opium pipe, with a tiny bowl, and got to work on that. "No kidding, this old dame startles me," said a marine. Another marine said, "I seen one of them with a pack this afternoon that I couldn't lift it myself and another guy helped me with it, and she put it on her head and she just walked away as easy as anything."

The good, rich smell of hot chicken broth filled the clean air, and the marines went up to the bucket, dipped their canteen cups in, and stood around drinking. It looked a little like a picture of a Civil War camp, with troops lounging in their high-crowned, peaked utility caps and their green utility clothes, now gray with dust.

Over in a newly dug foxhole, two Navy photographers who had just caught up with the regiment began to swap dirty pictures for souvenirs. A great many photographers are traders, and they have evolved a smooth underground commercial arrangement whereby a set of pornographic negatives is kept in some such headquarters as Guam and made available to all photographers who wish to make their own prints for trading purposes. Bidding was brisk in our camp. One sailor gave a marine twelve pictures for a little stained Japanese flag and an opium pipe. After a while everybody began to look around for a warm place to sleep.

Shapley's staff had lent me a cot and a blanket, and I spread the blanket and my poncho over me and lay thinking about infiltrators. The valleys and caves around the camp were mainly unflushed and unsearched. Pretty soon it was no longer necessary to imagine sounds or magnify little rustlings in the dark. I heard a good, substantial sound on my left, and it got closer and louder—it was something any lifetime subway passenger could immediately identify as a Jap sol-dier crawling on his hands and knees and making a slight added shuf-fling noise caused either by asthma or a knife held between his teeth. I glanced at Colonel Beans' cot and saw that he was healthily coma-tose. I reached under my bed for my canteen to use defensively, and felt my hand being nosed and then licked, in the slow, appreciative manner of a connoisseur, by something that gradually took shape in the darkness as a goat. I found in the morning that it was a white goat. It stayed with me all night, occasionally going under the cot and butting me morosely through the canvas. "It's not a matter of this goat liking you better than anybody else," said Beans when he woke up, apparently fearing that I might have derived some false vanity from the experience. "You're in a Marine camp, and goats are naturally attracted to marines. We've been having this kind of infiltration all over the Pacific. It's a wonder more of them don't get shot."

Having crossed the island, the marines now began a campaign of systematic bushwhacking through the wild and rugged northern two-thirds of Okinawa. The Fourth Regiment moved up the eastern coast in leapfrog style: the lead company of the lead battalion would turn left up the first road leading inland to search for Japs, while the next company went ahead to flush the next road, and so on till the first unit, its work done, moved up through the others to take the lead again. Warships cruised alongshore parallel to this advance, ready to lend support with their big guns in case of trouble. However, little game was found till the marines began to scour the big Motobu Peninsula, on the west shore of the island. There—as on the tiny island of Ie, off Motobu, on which Ernie Pyle was killed, almost at the end of a quick and otherwise unnoteworthy little special campaign— Japs to the number of perhaps two regiments, scattered at the time of the landing, had reformed into tight defensive pockets, and it took some fighting to break these up. The marines who had been baffled and gun-eager on landing day finally got their shooting on Motobu Peninsula. Some were killed and wounded, but not to the extent of really impressing their colleagues. One of my last memories of this phase of Okinawa is of a marine six feet three in height running up to the field hospital carrying a dead snake, perhaps eighteen inches long, by the tail. "Look at this son of a bitch!" he yelled excitedly to the medical corpsmen who were tending the wounded on litters. "He almost got me! If I hadn't been expecting something like this ever since we landed, he would of got me!"

We had heard by now that the Army, at the other end of the island, had run into one of the greatest Jap defensive battles of the war, and since the story was now there and no longer among the Marines, I went south.

❀ ❀ ❀ ❀

HARD FIGHTING FOR THE MARINE CORPS DID NOT develop until the 6th Division (under Major General Lemuel C. Shepherd) moved up to the Motobu Peninsula, where it was met by the 44th Independent Mixed. On April 12, the day President

Roosevelt died, two regiments, the 4th and the 29th, attacked a 1200-foot mountain, Yaetake. Shepherd, now fully aware that this was no peanut-sized bite, closed in front and rear with a compression movement by the 4th and 29th Marines, but Cho's breastworks stood up well. Tanks were useless in this terrain of caves and jagged peaks, and Marine offenses were halted. When cave areas were finally ascended, the Japanese simply blew themselves up. Such was the fighting at Motobu, which many strategists had written off as an "easy" campaign, over before it started . . .

One who was present with the 1st Division was famed war correspondent Ernie Pyle, the beloved champion of the GI. After two weeks of the slow-starting campaign, Pyle, looking for a story for the Scripps-Howard syndicate, decided to go over to Ie Shima and see how the Army was faring. It was there, during the operation in which the 77th took the little island northwest of Okinawa, that Pyle was killed by a sniper's bullet. The following is one of the last pieces Ernie wrote, and one of the few devoted to the men of the Marine Corps.

·16· LAST CHAPTER

ERNIE PYLE

After a short time with the headquarters of the marine regiment, I moved to a company and lived and marched with them for several days. The company was a part of the First Marine Division. I introduced myself to the company commander who took me on a half hour's walking trip around the company area before leaving me with the men. They had turned in for the night and put out perimeter defenses so that no infiltrating Japs could get through and also so that any big attack could be dealt with. The company was on a hill about 300 yards long and 100 yards wide. The men were dug in down the sides of the hill and there was a mortar platoon at the foot, all set up to throw mortars in any direction.

Our part of the island had not then been declared "secured," and we had received warning of possible attacks from sea that night. Nobody was taking any chances. "This is the most perfect defensive position we've ever had in our lives," the company commander said. "One company could hold off a whole battalion for days. If the Japs had defended these hills they could have kept us fighting for a week."

The company commander was Captain Julian Dusenbury from Claussen, South Carolina, a young man with a soft southern voice. His black hair was almost shaved and he was a little yellow from taking atabrine. He was easy-going with his men and you could tell they liked him. It happened that his twenty-fourth birthday was on April 1—the Easter Sunday we landed on Okinawa. His mother had written that she hoped he'd have a happy birthday. "That was the happiest birthday present I ever had," he said, "going through Love-day without a single casualty in the company."

Captain Dusenbury said I could have my choice of two places to spend the first night with his company. One was with him in his command post, a big, round Japanese gun emplacement made of sandbags. The Japs had never occupied it, but they had stuck a log out of it, pointing it toward the sea so that to aerial reconnaissance it looked like a gun. Captain Dusenbury and a couple of his officers had spread ponchos on the ground inside the emplacement, had hung their telephone on a nearby tree and were ready for business. There was no roof on the emplacement. It was right on top of a hill and cold and very windy.

My other choice was with a couple of enlisted men who had room for me in a little gypsylike hide-out they'd made. It was a tiny, level place about halfway down the hillside and away from the sea. They'd made a roof for it by tying ponchos to trees, and in a farmhouse they had found some Japanese straw mats which they'd spread on the ground. I chose the second of these two places, partly because it was warmer, and also because I wanted to be with the enlisted men.

My two "roommates" were Corporal Martin Clayton, Jr., of 3400 Princeton Street, Dallas, Texas, and Pfc. William Gross of 322 North Foster Street, Lansing, Michigan. Clayton was nicknamed "Bird Dog" and nobody ever called him anything else. He was tall, thin, and dark, almost Latin looking. He sported a puny little mustache he'd been trying to grow for weeks, and he made fun of it. Gross was simply called Gross. He was very quiet, and thoughtful of little things, and both of them looked after me for several days. The two of them had become very close friends, and after the war they intended to go to UCLA together to finish their education.

The boys said we could all three sleep side by side in the same "bed." So I got out my contribution to the night's beauty rest, and very much appreciated it was, too. Those marines had been sleeping every night on the ground with no cover, except for their cold, rubberized ponchos, and they had almost frozen to death. Their packs were so heavy they hadn't been able to bring blankets ashore with them. But I had carried a blanket as well as a poncho.

Our next-door neighbors, about three feet away, had a similar level spot on the hillside, and they had also roofed it with ponchos. These two men were Sergeant Neil Anderson of Coronado, California, and Sergeant George Valido of Tampa, Florida. So we chummed up and the five of us made a fire and cooked supper under a tree just in front of our "house."

Other little groups of marines had fires going all over the hillside. As we were eating, another marine came past and presented Bird Dog with a big piece of fresh roasted pig they had just cooked. Bird Dog gave me some and it sure was good after days of K rations. Several of the boys found their K rations moldy, and mine were too. They were the old-fashioned kind and we finally decided they were the 1942 rations which had been stored, probably in Australia, all this time.

Suddenly, from a few yards downhill, we heard somebody yelling and cussing, and then there was a lot of laughter. One marine had heated a ration can and, because it was pressure packed, it blew up when he pried it open and sprayed hot egg yolks over him. Usually the boys opened a can a little before heating to release the pressure so that it couldn't explode.

After supper we burned our ration boxes on the fire, brushed our teeth with water from our canteens, and then just sat talking on the ground around the fire. Other marines drifted along and after a while there were more than a dozen sitting around. We smoked cigarettes and talked of hundred things. The first topic was, as in all groups, about our surprise at no opposition to our landing. Then they got to asking me what I thought about things over here and how it compared with Europe. And when did I think the war would end? Of course, I didn't know any of the answers but it made conversation. The boys told jokes, they cussed a lot, they dragged out stories of their past blitzes, and they spoke gravely about war and what would happen to them when they finally got home.

We talked like that for about an hour, and then it grew dark and a shouted order came along the hillside to put out the fires. It was passed on and on, and the boys drifted away to their own foxholes or hillside dugouts, and Bird Dog, Gross, and I went to bed. There was nothing else to do after dark in blackout country.

That was one of the most miserable damn nights out of hundreds of miserable nights I ever spent in this war. It was too early to go to sleep, so we just lay there in the dark and talked some more. You could hear voices faintly all over the hillside. We didn't take off our clothes, of course; nobody does in the field. I did take off my boots but Bird Dog and Gross left theirs on since they had to stand watch on the field telephones from 1 till 2 A.M. The three of us lay jammed up against each other, with Bird Dog in the middle. We smoked one cigarette after another. We didn't have to hide them under the blanket since we were in a protected position where a cigarette couldn't be seen very far.

The mosquitoes started buzzing around our heads. Okinawa mosquitoes sound like flame throwers; they can't be driven off or brushed away. I got a little bottle of mosquito lotion out of my pocket and doused my face and neck, though I knew it would do no good. The other boys didn't even bother. After a while the hillside grew silent. The hours went past. By an occasional slap at the mosquitoes each of us knew the others weren't asleep.

Suddenly Bird Dog sat up and pulled down his socks and started scratching. The fleas in the grass were after him. For some strange reason I am immune to fleas. Though half the boys had red welts from hundreds of itchy little flea bites, I have never had one. But I'm the world's choicest morsel for mosquitoes. Every morning I woke up with at least one eye swollen shut.

That was the way it was all night—me with a double dose of mosquitoes and the rest with a mixture of mosquitoes and fleas. You could hear marines softly cussing all night long around the hillside. Suddenly there was a terrific outburst just downhill from us and a marine came jumping out into the moonlight, swearing and jerking at his clothes. "I can't stand these goddam things any longer," he cried. "I've got to take my clothes off."

We all laughed under our ponchos while he stood there in the moonlight and stripped off every stitch, even though it was very chilly. He shook and brushed his clothes, doused them with insect powder, and then put them back on. This unfortunate soul was Corporal Leland Taylor of 101 Francis Court, Jackson, Michigan. He was thirty-three years old and his nickname was Pop. Pop was a "character." He had a black beard and even in the front lines he wore a khaki overseas dress cap, both of which made him conspicuous. After Pop went back to bed everything was quiet for several hours, but hardly anybody was asleep. The next morning the boys on guard said that Pop must have smoked three packs of cigarettes that night. It was the same way with Bird Dog, Gross, and me.

One of the boys on guard came to wake my bedmates at a quarter to one, but they weren't asleep. I thought I might get to sleep while they were away, but I didn't. The mosquitoes were really crucifying me. The boys came back about two o'clock, took off their shoes and lay down. With my blanket over the three of us we were as warm as toast; at least we had that.

All night, without even raising our heads, we could see flashes of the big guns of our fleet across the island. They were shelling the southern part and shooting flares to light up the front lines there. Sometimes we could actually see red-hot shells, traveling horizontally the whole length of their flight, ten miles away from us, and then we saw them explode. Every so often throughout the night our own company's mortars were called upon to shoot a flare over the beach behind us, just to make sure nothing was coming in.

Once there was a distinct rustling of the bushes in front of us. Of course the first thing I thought of was a Jap, but immediately I figured a Jap wouldn't make that much noise and I decided it was one of the horses the mortar boys had commandeered, crashing through the bushes. And that's what it turned out to be.

Pop Taylor also had the Jap idea, at first. The next morning "Brady" Bradshaw, who was sleeping with Pop, said Pop shook him violently during the night to wake him up and borrow a .45, just in case. Brady laughed and laughed about it, for lying on the ground between them all the time was an arsenal of two carbines, two shotguns, and Pop's own .45.

Along about 4:30 I guess we did sleep a little from sheer exhaustion. That gave the mosquitoes a clear field. When we woke up at dawn and crawled stiffly out into the daylight my right eye was swollen shut, as usual.

All of which isn't a very warlike night to describe, but there are lots of things besides bullets that make war hell.

We started moving right after breakfast. We were to march about a mile and a half, then dig in and stay in one place for several days, patrolling and routing out the few hidden Japs in that area. We were in no danger on the march—at least we thought we weren't, and not all the marines wore steel helmets. Some wore green twill caps, some baseball caps, some even wore civilian felt hats they had found in Japanese homes. For some reason soldiers the world over like to put on odd local headgear. I've seen soldiers in Italy wearing black silk opera hats, and over here I've seen marines in combat uniform wearing panama hats. I've always enjoyed going along with an infantry company on the move, even some of the horrible moves we had to make in Italy and France. But that morning it was really a pleasant one. It was early and the air was good. The temperature was perfect and the country was pretty. We all felt that sense of ease that comes of knowing nothing too bad is ahead of you. Some of the boys were even smoking cigars.

There were always funny sights in a moving column of soldiers. Our mortar platoon had commandeered a dozen local horses to carry heavy pieces. One of the marines had tied the pack onto his horse with a Japanese obi—one of those reams of sash Japanese women wear on their backs. There he was, dirty and unshaved, leading a sorrel horse with a big bowtie of black and white silk, three feet wide, tied across its chest, and another one tied under its belly, the ends standing out on both sides.

Troops carry the oddest things when they move. One marine had a Jap photo album in his hand. One had a wicker basket. Another had a lacquered serving tray. They even had a Columbia phonograph with Jap records, strapped onto a horse. Many of them wore Japanese insignia or pieces of uniform. Later an order came out that any marine caught wearing Jap clothing would be put on burial detail. Maybe that was to keep marines from shooting each other by mistake.

There were frequent holdups ahead of us and we would stop and sit down every hundred yards or so. One marine, commenting on the slow progress, said: "Sometimes we take off like a ruptured duck, and other times we just creep along." The word was passed down the line, "Keep your eyes open for planes." About every sixth man turned his head to repeat it, and the word was sent back along the column like a wave. Toward the rear it came out: "Keep your eyes open for planes—keep your eyes open for cabbages—keep your eyes open for geisha girls."

We were walking almost on each other's heels, a solid double line of marines. Bird Dog was behind me. He said, "A column like this would be a Jap pilot's delight."

Another said, "If a Jap pilot came over the hill, we'd all go down like bowling pins." But no Japs came.

At one of our halts the word came back that we could sit down, but we were not to take off our packs. From down the line came music, a French harp and ukulele playing "You Are My Sunshine." When it was finished the marines called back request numbers. The little concert went on for five or ten minutes out there in the Okinawa fields. The harmonicist was Pfc. William Gabriel, a bazookaman from a farm on Rural Route 13, about ten miles out of Houston, Texas. He was only nineteen, but a veteran who had sustained one wound. He was a redhead and the shyest soldier I'd ever met, so bashful he could hardly talk. But he surely could make a harmonica talk. Playing with him on a sort of ukulele common to Okinawa was an officer, Lieu-

tenant "Bones" Carsters of 6023 Miramar Boulevard, Los Angeles.
It was an instrument with three strings, its head made of tightly
stretched snakeskin. It gave me the willies just to look at one.

When we started ahead again, the way was clear and that time we
went like the well-known ruptured duck and after about a mile we
arrived, all panting.

When I saw my first Jap soldiers it was midforenoon and we had
just reached our new bivouac area. The boys threw off their packs,
sat down on the ground, and took off their helmets to mop their perspiring foreheads. We were in a small grassy spot at the foot of a hill.
Most of the hillsides had caves in which household stuff was hidden.
They were a rich field for souvenir hunters, and all marines are souvenir hunters. So immediately two of our boys, instead of resting,
started up through the brush, looking for caves and souvenirs. They
had gone about fifty yards when one of them yelled, "There's a Jap
soldier under this bush."

We didn't get too excited, since most of us figured he meant a dead
Jap. But three or four of the boys got up and went up the hill. A few
moments later somebody else yelled, "Hey, here's another one.
They're alive and they've got rifles."

The boys went at them in earnest. The Japs were lying under two
bushes, with their hands up over their ears and pretending to be
asleep. The marines surrounded the bushes and, with guns pointing,
ordered the Japs out. But the Japs were too scared to move. They just
lay there, blinking.

The average Jap soldier would have come out shooting, but, thank
goodness, these were of a different stripe. They were so terrified the
marines had to go into the bushes, lift them by the shoulders and
throw them out in the open. My contribution to the capture consisted
of standing at one side and looking as mean as I could.

One Jap was small, about thirty years old. The other was just a boy
of sixteen or seventeen, but good-sized and well built. He had the
rank of superior private and the other was a corporal. They were
Japanese from Japan, and not the Okinawan home guard. They were
both trembling all over. The muscles in the corporal's jaw were twitch-
ing. The kid's face was a sickly white and he was so paralyzed he
couldn't even understand sign language.

We never knew why those two Japs didn't fight. They had good
rifles and potato-masher hand grenades. They could have stood behind their bushes and heaved grenades into our tightly packed group
and got themselves two dozen casualties, easily. The marines took
their arms. One marine tried to direct the corporal in handbook Japanese, but the fellow couldn't understand. The scared kid just stood

there, sweating like an ox. I guess he thought he was dead. Finally we sent them back to the regiment.

The two marines who flushed the Japs were Corporal Jack Ossege of Silver Grove, Kentucky, across the river from Cincinnati, and Pfc. Lawrence Bennett of Port Huron, Michigan. Okinawa was the first blitz for Bennett and these were the first Jap soldiers he'd ever seen. He was thirty years old, married, and had a baby girl. Back home he was a freight dispatcher.

The Jap corporal had a metal photo holder like a cigarette case in which were photos that we took to be of three Japanese movie stars. They were pretty, and everybody had to have a look.

Ossege had been through one Pacific blitz, but this was the first time he had ever taken Japs alive. He was an old hand at souvenir hunting and he made sure of getting a Jap rifle. That rifle was the envy of everybody; later, when we were sitting around discussing the capture, the other boys tried to buy or trade him out of it. Pop Taylor offered him $100 for it, and the answer was no. Then Taylor offered four quarts of whisky. The answer still was no. Then he offered eight quarts. Ossege weakened a little. He said, "Where would you get eight quarts of whisky?" Pop said he had no idea. So Ossege kept the rifle.

It's wonderful to see a bunch of American troops go about making themselves at home wherever they get a chance to settle down for a few days. My company dug in at the edge of a bomb-shattered village. The village was quaint and not without charm. I was astonished at its similarity to the villages of Sicily and Italy, for it didn't really seem Oriental. The houses were wooden one-story buildings, surrounded by little vegetable gardens. Instead of fences, each lot was divided by rows of shrubs or trees. The cobblestoned streets, winding and walled head-high on both sides, were just wide enough for a jeep.

A large part of the town lay shattered. Scores of the houses had been burned, and only ashes and red roofing tile were left. Wandering around, I counted the bodies of four Okinawans still in the street. Otherwise the town was deserted. The people had fled to their caves in the hillsides, taking most of their personal belongings with them. There is almost no furniture in Japanese houses, so they didn't have to worry about that.

After a few days the grapevine carried the news to them that we were treating them well, and they began to come out in droves to give themselves up. I heard one story about a hundred Okinawan civilians who had a Jap soldier among them; when they realized the atrocity stories he had told them about the Americans were untrue, our MPs had to step in to keep them from beating him.

Our company commander picked out a nice little house on a rise at the edge of town for his command post. The house was very light, fairly clean, and the floors were covered with woven straw mats. A couple of officers and a dozen men moved in and slept on the floor, and we cooked our rations over an open stone cookstove in the rear.

Then the word went around for the men of the company to plan to stay for several days. Two platoons were assigned to dig in along the outer sides of the nearby hills for perimeter defense. The boys were told they could keep the horses they had commandeered, that they could carry wooden panels out of the houses to make little doghouses for themselves, but not to take anything else. And they could have fires, except during air alerts.

They weren't to start their daily mop-up patrols in the brush until the next day, so they had the afternoon off to clean themselves up and fix up their little houses. Different men did different things. Some built elaborate homes about the size of chicken houses, with floor mats and chairs and kerosene lanterns hanging from the roof. One Mexican boy dug a hole, covered it with boards, and then camouflaged it so perfectly with brush you couldn't really see it. Some spent the afternoon taking baths and washing clothes in the river. Others rode bicycles around town, or rode their horses up and down. Some foraged around town through the deserted houses. Some went looking for chickens to cook. Some sat in groups and talked. Some just slept.

An order eventually went out against wearing Jap clothing or eating any of the local vegetables, pork, goat, beef, or fowl. But before the order came, some marines had dug up lots of Japanese kimonos out of the smashed houses and put them on while washing their single set of clothes. It was a funny sight—those few dozen dirty and unshaved marines walking around in women's pink and blue kimonos. A typical example was Private Raymond Adams of Fleason, Tennessee. He had fixed himself a dugout right on the edge of a bluff above the river, with a grand view and a nice little grassy front yard. There he had driven stakes and built a fire, over which he hung his helmet like a kettle, and he was stewing a chicken. He had taken off his clothes and put on a beautiful pink-and-white kimono.

Later a friend came along with a Jap bicycle minus one pedal, and Adams tried without much success to ride it up and down a nearby lane. If there ever is a war play about marines I hope they include one tough-looking private in a pink-and-white kimono, stewing chicken, and trying to ride a one-pedaled bicycle through a shattered Japanese village. Private Adams was married and had an eight-month-old son he had never seen. If the baby could have seen his father that day he would probably have got the colic from laughing.

When I was aboard ship somebody walked off with my fatigue and combat jackets, so I was given one of those Navy jackets lined with fleece. It was much warmer and nicer than what I'd had. On the back it had stenciled in big white letters: U.S. Navy. I wore it when I first walked through the company's defense area and later that evening, when we were sitting on the ground around a little fire warming our supper of K-rations. By that time I'd got acquainted with a good many of the boys and we felt at home with one another.

We had some real coffee which we poured into our canteen cups, and we sat around drinking it before dark. Then one of the boys started laughing and said to me, "You know, when you first showed up, we saw that big Navy stencil on your back and after you passed, I said to the others: 'That guy's an admiral. Look at the old gray-haired bastard. He's been in the Navy all his life. He'll get a medal out of this, sure as hell.'"

The originator of this bright idea was Pfc. Albert Schwab of 1743 East 14th Street, Tulsa, Oklahoma. He was a flame thrower, and flame throwers have to be rugged guys, for the apparatus they carry weighs about seventy-five pounds and also they are very apt to be shot at by the enemy. But to see Albert sitting there telling that joke on himself and me, you'd never have known he was a rugged guy at all. I'm not an admiral and I won't get any medal, but you do get a lot of laughs out of this war business when things aren't going too badly.

One morning after breakfast about a dozen of us were sitting on the mat-covered floor talking things over while sipping our coffee. Several days' accumulation of grime covered everybody. Suddenly Bones stood up and said, "I cleaned my fingernails this morning and it sure does feel good."

And then my friend Bird Dog held his own begrimed hands out in front of him, looked at them a long time, and said, "If I was to go to dinner in Dallas and lay them things up on a white tablecloth I wonder what would happen."

A good many of the Okinawan civilians wandering along the roadside bowed low to every American they met. Whether this was from fear or native courtesy I do not know, but anyhow they did it. And the Americans, being Americans, usually bowed right back.

One of my marine friends got mixed up in one of those little bowing incidents. He was Pfc. Roy Sellers, a machine gunner from Amelia,

Ohio. Roy was married and had a little girl two years old. He used to be a machinist at the Cincinnati Milling Machine Company and he played semi-pro ball too. When Roy had a beard he looked just like a tramp in a stage play. He was only twenty-seven, but looked much older; in fact he went by the nickname "Old Man."

On this occasion Old Man was trying to ride a Japanese bicycle along the bank of a little river where we camped. The ground was rough and the bicycle had only one pedal and Roy was having a struggle to keep it upright. Just then an old Okinawan, bareheaded and dressed in a black kimono and carrying a dirty sack, walked through our little camp. He wasn't supposed to be at large but it was none of our business and we didn't molest him. He was bowing to everyone, right and left, as he passed. Then he met Machine Gunner Sellers on his one-pedaled bicycle. Roy was already having his troubles, but as he came abreast of the Okinawan, he bowed deeply over the handle bars, hit a rut, lost his balance, and over he went. The Okinawan, with Oriental inscrutability, returned the bow and never looked back.

We all laughed our heads off. "Who's bowing to whom around here?" we asked. Roy denied he had bowed first, but we knew better. He decided to give his old bicycle away to somebody less polite than himself.

As our company was moving forward one day I looked down the line of closely packed marines and I thought for a moment I was back in Italy. There for sure was Bill Mauldin's cartoon character of GI Joe—the solemn, bearded, dirty, drooping, weary old man of the infantry. This character was Pfc. Urban Vachon of French-Canadian extraction, who came from Laconia, New Hampshire. He had a brother, William, fighting in Germany. Urban was such a perfect ringer for Mauldin's soldier that I asked the regimental photographer to take a picture of him to send back to the States. If you've seen it, you can prove to any disbelievers that soldiers do look the way Mauldin made them look.

We camped one night on a little hillside that led up to a bluff overlooking a small river. The bluff dropped straight down for a long way, and up there on top it was just like a little park, terraced, although it wasn't farmed, and the grass was soft and green, with small, straight-limbed pine trees dotted all over it. Looking down from the bluff, the river made a turn. Across it was an old stone bridge at the end of which was a village—or what had been a village. Now it was just a jumble of ashes and sagging thatched roofs. In every direction little valleys led away from the turn in the river—as pretty and gentle a sight as you ever saw. It had the softness of antiquity about it and the miniature charm and daintiness typical of Japanese prints. And the sad, uncanny silence that follows the bedlam of war.

A bright sun made the morning hot, and a refreshing little breeze sang through the pine trees. There wasn't a shot or a warlike sound within hearing. I sat on the bluff for a long time, just looking. I noticed a lot of the marines sitting and just looking too.

You could come from a dozen different parts of America and still find scenery on Okinawa that looked like your country at home. Southern boys said the reddish clay and the pine trees reminded them of Georgia. Westerners saw California in the green rolling hills, partly wooded, partly patchworked with little green fields. And the farmed plains looked like our Midwest.

Okinawa is one of the few places I've been in this war where our troops didn't gripe about what an awful place it was. In fact, most of the boys said they would like Okinawa if it weren't at war with us and if the people weren't so dirty. The countryside is neat and the little farms are well kept. At the time the climate was superb and the views undeniably pretty. The worst crosses to bear were the mosquitoes, the fleas, and the sight of the pathetic people.

Most of the roads on Okinawa were narrow dirt trails for small horse-drawn carts, but there were several wider gravel roads. One man aptly described it as "an excellent network of poor roads." Our heavy traffic, of course, played hob with the roads; already they were tire-deep in dust and traveling troops had masklike faces, caked with dust. Bulldozers and scrapers were constantly at work.

I've mentioned before our fears of snakes before we got to Okinawa. All the booklets given us ahead of time dwelt at length on snakes, telling us that there were three kinds of adders, all of them fatally poisonous. We were warned not to wander off the main roads, not to stop under the trees lest snakes drop on us. (As if you could fight a war without getting off the roads!) Some of the troop briefings had the marines more scared of snakes than of Japs.

I kept a close watch and made a lot of inquiries, and found that in the central part of Okinawa where we were there are practically no snakes at all. Our troops walked, poked, sprawled, and slept on nearly every square yard of the ground. And in my regiment, for one, only two snakes were seen. One was found dead; the other was killed by a battalion surgeon who coiled it into a gallon glass jar and sent it to the regimental command post as a souvenir. It was a vicious rattler, a type called habu.

Those were the only snakes I heard of. There was a rumor that in one battalion they caught and made pets of a couple of snakes, but

I didn't believe it. The local people said the island was full of snakes up until the middle thirties when some mongooses were imported which killed most of them. But we didn't see any mongooses, so we didn't know whether the story was true or not. Correspondent John Lardner said his only explanation was that St. Patrick came through here once as a tourist and took all the snakes with him.

Leland Taylor, the marine corporal known as "Pop," found four pairs of the most beautiful Japanese pajamas you ever saw in a wicker basket hidden in a cave. They were apparently brand-new, had never even been worn. They were thrilling to look at and soft to the touch. Pop carried the basket around on his arm from place to place until he could get a chance to ship them home to his wife.

One morning I wandered down to our mortar platoon and ran into a young fellow with whom I had a great deal in common. We were both from Albuquerque and we both had mosquito trouble. He was Pfc. Dick Trauth of 508 West Santa Fe Street. Both his eyes were swollen almost shut from mosquite bites, and at least one of mine was swollen shut every morning. We both looked very funny. Dick still was just a boy. He'd been nineteen months in the marines and a year overseas—a veteran of combat and still only seventeen years old. Dick wrote letters to movie stars and Shirley Temple had sent him a picture, autographed to his company just as he asked her to do. Dick was very shy and quiet and I had a feeling he must be terribly lonesome, but the other boys said he wasn't and that he got along fine.

One of the marines who drove me around in a jeep whenever I had to go anywhere was Pfc. Buzz Vitere of 2403 Hoffman Street, Bronx, New York. Buzz had other accomplishments besides jeep driving; he was known as the Bing Crosby of the Marine Corps. If you shut your eyes and didn't listen very hard you could hardly tell the difference. I first met Buzz on the transport coming up to Okinawa. He and a friend gave an impromptu concert on deck every afternoon. They would sit on a hatch in the warm tropical sun and pretty soon there would be scores of marines and sailors packed around them, listening in appreciative silence. It made the trip to war almost like a Caribbean luxury cruise.

Buzz's partner was Pfc. Johnny Marturello of 225 Livingston Street, Des Moines, Iowa. Johnny played the accordion. He was an Italian, of course, and had the Italian flair for the accordion. He sang too, but he said as a singer his name was "Frank Not-so-hotra." Johnny played one piece he composed himself—a lovely thing. He sent it to the GI Publishing Co., or whatever it was in the States, and I feel positive if it could be widely played it would become a hit. The piece is a sentimental song called "Why Do I Have to Be Here Alone?" Johnny wrote it for his girl back home, but he grinned and admitted they were "on the outs."

Johnny went ashore on Love-day and his accordion followed two days after. In his spare moments he sat at the side of the road and played for bunches of Okinawans whom the marines had rounded up. They seemed to like it. Johnny had a lot of trouble with his accordion down south in the tropical climates. Parts would warp and stick and mildew, and he continually had to take the thing apart and dry and clean it, but it was worth the trouble. It kept Johnny from getting too homesick. He knew the accordion would probably be ruined by the climate, but he didn't care. He brought it along with him from America just for his own morale. "I can always get a new accordion," Johnny said, "but I can't get a new ME."

Nearly two years back when I was with Oklahoma's Forty-fifth Division on Sicily and later in Italy, I learned they had a number of Navajo Indians in communications. When secret orders had to be given over the phone these boys gave them to one another in Navajo. Practically nobody in the world understands Navajo except another Navajo. My regiment here had the same thing. There were about eight Indians who did this special work. They were good marines and very proud of it.

There were two brothers among them, both named Joe. Their last names were different; I guess that's a Navajo custom, though I never knew it before. One brother, Pfc. Joe Gatewood, went to the Indian school in Albuquerque. In fact, our house is on the very same street, and Joe said it sure was good to see somebody from home. Joe had been out in the Pacific for three years; he had been wounded and been awarded the Purple Heart. He was thirty-four and had five children back home he wanted to see.

Joe's brother was Joe Kellwood who had also been in the Pacific three years. A couple of the others were Pfc. Alex Williams of Winslow, Arizona, and Private Oscar Carroll of Fort Defiance, Arizona, which is the capital of the Navajo reservation. Most of the boys were from around Fort Defiance and used to work for the Indian Bureau.

The Indian boys knew before we got to Okinawa that the invasion landing wasn't going to be very tough. They were the only ones in the convoy who did know it. For one thing they saw signs, and for another they used their own influence.

Before the convoy left the far south tropical island where the Navajos had been training since the last campaign, the boys put on a ceremonial dance. The Red Cross furnished some colored cloth and paint to stain their faces and they made up the rest of their Indian costumes from chicken feathers, sea shells, coconuts, empty ration cans, and rifle cartridges. Then they did their own native ceremonial chants and dances out there under the tropical palm trees with several thousand marines as a grave audience. In their chant they asked the great gods in the sky to sap the Japanese of their strength for this blitz. They put the finger of weakness on the Japs, and they ended their ceremonial chant by singing the Marine Corps song in Navajo.

I asked Joe Gatewood if they really felt their dance had something to do with the ease of our landing and he said the boys did believe so and were very serious about it, himself included. "I knew nothing was going to happen to us," Joe said, "for on the way up here there was a rainbow over the convoy and I knew then everything would be all right."

One day I was walking through the edge of a rubbled Okinawa village where marine telephone linemen were stringing wire to the tops of the native telephone poles. As I passed, one of the two linemen at the top called down rather nervously that he was afraid the wobby pole was going to break under their weight; to which one of the men on the ground, apparently their sergeant, called back reassuringly, "You've got nothing to worry about. That's imperial Japanese stuff. It can't break."

There are very few cattle on Okinawa, but there are many goats and horses. The horses are small like western ponies and mostly bay or sorrel. Most of them are skinny, but if they are well fed they are good-looking horses. They are all well broken and tame. The marines acquired them by the hundreds; our company alone had more than twenty. The boys put their heavier packs on them; more than that, they just seemed to enjoy riding them up and down the country roads. They rigged up rope halters and one marine made a bridle using a piece of bamboo for a bit. They dug up old pads and even some goatskins to use as saddle blankets. But it was surprising how many men in a company of marines didn't really know how to ride a horse.

There was one very small marine who was as nice as he could be, always smiling and making some crack. The boys said that in battle he didn't give a damn for anything. The first afternoon I joined his company he didn't know who I was and as we passed, he said very respectfully, "Good evening, colonel." I had to chuckle to myself. Later he mentioned it and we laughed about it and then he started calling me Ernie.

He was Corporal Charles Bradshaw of 526 South Holmes Avenue,

Indianapolis. Though only nineteen he was on his third campaign in the Pacific. He had had three pieces of shrapnel in him and from time to time they would try to work out through the skin. One was just about to come out of his finger.

In the Marines, Corporal Bradshaw was called "Brady" for short. Before joining up he worked on a section gang for the Pennsylvania Railroad. He usually wore one of those wide-brimmed green cloth hats instead of the regulation marine cap and he always carried a .45. It had a slightly curved 25-cent piece embedded in the handle— as he said, "to make it worth something."

In a cave Brady found two huge photograph albums full of snapshots of Japanese girls, Chinese girls, young Japs in uniform, and family poses. He treasured it as though it were full of people he knew. He studied it for hours and hoped to take it home with him. "Anything for a souvenir" could be the motto of the Marine Corps.

Another Indianapolis marine I met on Okinawa was Pfc. Dallas Rhude of 1437 East Raymond Street, who used to be a newspaperman. He worked on the Indianapolis *Times;* he started carrying it as a newsboy when he was eight, got into the editorial room as a copy boy and kept that job till he joined the Marine Corps. He was a replacement; in other words, he was in the pool from which the gaps made by casualties are filled. But since there had been very few casualties he hadn't replaced anybody yet. Dallas spent twenty-two months in Panama, was home for a little while, and now had been in the Pacific for four months. He said that the Okinawa climate sure beat Panama.

Marines may be killers, but they're also just as sentimental as anybody else. I had talked with one pleasant boy in our company but there was no little incident to write about him, so I hadn't put his name down. The morning I left the company and was saying goodby all around, I could sense that he wanted to tell me something, so I hung around until it came out. It was about his daughter, born about six weeks back. This marine was Corporal Robert Kingan of 2430 Talbot Avenue, Cuyahoga Falls, Ohio. He had been a marine for thirteen months and in the Pacific seven months. Naturally he had never seen his daughter, but he had a letter from her!

It was a V letter written in a childish scrawl and said: "Hello, daddy. I am Karen Louise. I was born February twenty-fifth at four minutes after nine. I weigh five pounds and eight ounces. Your Daughter, Karen."

And then there was a P.S. on the bottom: "Postmaster—Please rush. My daddy doesn't know I am here."

Bob didn't know whether it was his wife or his mother-in-law who wrote the letter. He thought maybe it was his mother-in-law—Mrs. A. H. Morgan—since it had her return address on it. So I put that down and then asked Bob what his mother-in-law's first name was. He looked off into space for a moment, and then started laughing. "I don't know what her first name is," he said. "I just always called her Mrs. Morgan!"

The major part of the battle was being fought by the Army—my old friends, the doughfoots. This time the marines had it easy.

Marine Corps blitzes in the Pacific had all been so bitter and the men had fought so magnificently that I had conjured up a mental picture of a marine as someone who bore a close resemblance to a man from Mars. I was almost afraid of them. I did find them confident, but neither cocky nor smart-alecky. They had fears, and qualms, and hatred for war the same as anybody else. They wanted to go home just as badly as any soldiers I've ever met. They are proud to be marines and they wouldn't be in any other branch of the service, yet they are not arrogant about it. And I found they have a healthy respect for the infantry.

One day we were sitting on a hillside talking about the infantry. One marine spoke of a certain division—a division they had fought beside—and was singing its praises. "It's as good as any marine division," he said.

"What was that you said?" a listener cut in.

The marine repeated it and emphasized it a little. Another marine stood up and called out, loudly, "Did you hear what he said? This guy says there's an army division as good as any marine division. He must be crazy. Haw, haw, haw!"

And yet other boys chimed in, arguing very soberly, and sided with the one who had praised the army division.

Before I came into the field, several marine officers asked me to try to sense just what the marine spirit is, what is its source, and what keeps it alive. In peacetime when the Marine Corps was a small outfit, with its campaigns high-lighted, everybody was a volunteer and you could understand why they felt so superior. But with the war the Marine Corps had grown by hundreds of thousands of men. It became an outfit of ordinary people—some big, some little, some even draftees. It had changed, in fact, until marines looked to me exactly like a company of soldiers in Europe. Yet that Marine Corps spirit still remained. I never did find out what perpetuated it. The men were not necessarily better trained, nor were they any better equipped; often they were not so well supplied as other troops. But a marine still considered himself a better soldier than anybody else, even though nine-tenths of them didn't want to be soldiers at all.

They were very much aware of the terrible casualties they'd had in this Pacific war. They were even proud of that too, in a way. Any argument about superiority among units was settled by citing the greatest number of casualties. Many of them even envisioned the end of the Marine Corps at Okinawa. If the marine divisions had been beaten as they were on Iwo Jima, the boys felt it would have been difficult to find enough men of Marine Corps caliber to reconstitute all the divisions. They even had a sadly sardonic song about their approach to Okinawa, the theme of which was "Goodby, Marines!"

The boys of my regiment were continuously apologizing to me because the Okinawa campaign started out so mildly. They felt I might think less of them because they didn't show me a blood bath. Nothing could have been further from the truth. I was probably the happiest American there about the way it turned out for us. I told them that kind of campaign suited me, and without exception they came back with the answer that it suited them too. I heard it said so many times that it almost became a chant: "If they could all be like this, we wouldn't mind war so much."

No, marines don't thirst for battles. I've read and heard enough about them to have no doubts whatever about the things they can do when they have to. They are o.k. for my money, in battle or out.

❧   ❧   ❧   ❧

LIEUTENANT DAVID BROWN OF THE 1ST DIVISION, whom we met at Pavuvu during the interlude before Peleliu, was killed this day. He was a sensitive young man with a brilliant talent. The following are his last letters, to a friend and to his mother, written a few hours before a sniper's bullet ended his life.

·17· "IT WAS THE FIRST I'D SEEN OF APRIL . . ."

LIEUTENANT DAVID BROWN

Okinawa Shima, Ryukyu Retto,
April 17, 1945

In your letter, which came a few days ago, you asked what I was doing on Easter morning, the day your letter was written. About twelve hours earlier it was Easter morning here, and you know by now what we were doing. Later I shall be able to say in more detail something of that April Fool's Day's experience.

One episode of our coming in will amuse you: our landing craft nearly sank! This was due to no enemy action. The boat was in faulty condition. The sea offshore was high, and the power driven pumps on the starboard side would not work. I was sitting astern and, though I had noticed much water splashing over the bowgate and gunwales into the boat, I took it for granted the boilers were functioning. After a bit one of the boys signalled that it was getting a bit deep, nearly to his knees—and at the same time the crew began to worry. We shipped a good quantity of water at that moment . . . In order to make it, we bailed with our helmets (once more proven to be the most adaptable piece of gear we carry!). Five boys bailed on each side while I grabbed a bucket, yelled something like: "Bail like hell! If the Navy can't get us in, the Marines can!" That was good for a laugh all round, and the boys worked heartily until we had regained control. The 200 lbs. medical corpsman was told to "lay to the portside to counter the list!" They were all so merry that they quite forgot their apprehension over the beach ahead. Then the sailors stirred to action and soon fixed the pumps and we went in.

That Easter morning the beach was quiet and sweet. All around were furrowed fields or patches of ripe white winter barley, and tiny bright field flowers were scattered over the light earth. It was the first I'd seen of April for two years. I cannot say much here—we had expected an Iwo Jima or something worse, and that morning we had shaken hands aboard ship with many deep misgivings. But for some reason that morning the gates of hell were yet closed. Plus je t'en dirai dès que ça sera permis!

I do not find it especially interesting—though it is, in many ways— to see a typical backward pagan civilization such as Okinawa presents. In retrospect I may find something beautiful in it. Just now, I like the scenery and am delighted with the climate, which makes me feel exhilarated for the first time in a year and a half. But I have no more than a passing or dutiful interest in any land other than my own.

Many of the homes of the natives are ruined, but it seems the people will be taken care of. They are pleasant enough, and the children are likeable and precocious. They get on well with the marines, for no service man can resist children. That in fact is strangely universal—men will kill the fathers with utmost cruelty and ruthlessness, and adopt the children! I think it was always the same, as we read in the ancient narratives of Greece or Palestine or Rome. It is malice or jealousy that provokes hate, and suspicion, and not race, in the first instance.

I am living well, and with excellent fare in every way.

David

This is just a short note to wish you belatedly a Happy Easter. I remember some of the times we've been together at Easter, and especially the one in Wilmington in 1942, when the city was so beautiful with flowers, and we visited the botanical gardens. It seems a long time since, and I regret that I have grown dull to much of the loveliness—bodily and spiritual—which I delighted in then, by God's grace.

But we pray to the dear Lord that some day, beyond this still lovely but ever decaying world, we may see the vision of all loveliness which was intimated to us in this world, with one's friends forever. That is what we profess and pray for: "The resurrection of the dead and the life of the world to come." That is what Easter means, the hope of reunion on earth and in heaven, and the vision of loveliness eternally.

David

※　※　※　※

MOTOBU PENINSULA WAS CLEANED UP BY THE END of the month. At that time General Buckner noted that the 27th

Infantry Division was understrength and worn out from the sharp fighting in the west. He sent in the 1st Marine Division and ordered the Army division to a rear area. On May 1, marines went south into the Naha-Shuri line against Japan's 24th and 62nd Divisions, a phase that was costly. Here, again, we meet the durable Private Russell Davis, speaking of the enemy's infiltration tactics and marine behavior in this first severe battle of the campaign.

·18·   FIRST ASSAULT ON NAHA-SHURI LINE

RUSSELL DAVIS

In the darkness, just inside the company perimeter, a sentry called: "Halt! Who goes there?"

Silence. And then a scrambling sound out in the darkness. Then silence again. (The password that night was "Ali Baba." The Marines used passwords with an *l* sound in them because the Japanese pronounce it *r*.)

We felt for our weapons and turned in the direction of the challenge. Off to the west there was sky glow and the muted thud of heavy antiaircraft batteries—.90's. Into the light reflected from the sky crawled Captain Tex, tilting his .45 upward to get a clip seated and worming up the bank, using only his knees for purchase. There was a loud, metallic rip as the bolt went back on somebody's Tommy gun.

"Answer up or I'll blast you," the sentry yelled.

This challenge was higher-pitched and slightly quavery, the kind a man delivered when his scalp prickled and his eyes strained into silent darkness. "What's the password?" This was screamed.

Terror bred terror. From the darkness, a quaking Midwestern voice twanged: "I forgot it. I forgot the bloody, blankety-blank password."

Whoever was out there in the darkness was scared, but he was doing the next best thing to remembering the password—he was using bad language, the sign of a marine under tension. We could almost hear him wetting his lips for another try. Then he said: "I got a message from the colonel for Captain Tex. I mean Captain—Aw, I forget his name, too. You know the captain I mean. That crazy Texas guy in Headquarters Company."

There was a sigh of released tension in the holes all around us. I could feel Murph begin to shake with silent laughter. Captain Tex bellowed: "Don't let that man through until he gives the proper password and the name of the man who gets the message. There is no crazy Texan in this sector—or anywhere."

The sentry relaxed after he heard the captain's voice, but he still sounded stern as he called: "All right, you out there. You got ten seconds to think of the password. Get it up or I'll begin to chop!"

There was a full minute of silence, and, finally, a weak and muffled voice, coming from a man who was well down in a hole or behind a wall: "Twenty thieves . . . Yeah, that's it—twenty thieves."

All through the darkness men began to laugh: "Twenty thieves," some rifleman chuckled. "How about that?"

Captain Tex's voice carried above the laughter. "Don't shoot him over twenty lousy thieves. Only a marine could be that bad in arithmetic."

"Pass, friend," the sentry said. "And hear this, you knucklehead. The password is Ali Baba—with an *l* in it. And old Ali dealt with forty thieves—not twenty. The captain, who is right over there, may have other things to say to you."

The captain stood up. This was a good moment for him, because he was a constant needler and jokester. "Young man," he began, "you have made many mistakes tonight. You forgot the password. You forgot my name. You are bad in arithmetic and have no knowledge of literature, and you can't even tell a sane man from a crazy one. What state do you come from?"

"Minnesota, sir."

"An outpost of Northern ignorance," Captain Tex said. "Now, after all this, I'll bet you've forgotten the message."

We all laughed. It was our last good laugh on Okinawa.

The messenger hadn't forgotten the message. It was the one that brought an end to the camp-out and picnic on Okinawa. The message informed us that we had been ordered south to relieve the 27th Army Division on the Naha-Shuri line. There was no longer any mystery about where the Japanese were on Okinawa: they were defending the middle of the southern part of the island, in a line running from Naha Harbor, through Shuri, and on to the Philippine Sea near Yonabaru. Here they defended stubbornly, fanatically, desperately. Here was the Japanese 32nd Army, putting up a fight-to-the-death defense, from deep caves and vaults in the ridges. On the Naha-Shuri line, the Army had been catching it. Out on the picket line, the Navy ships had been catching it from the kamikazes. The Marines had been camping out at government expense—and that couldn't last.

Murph said, "Here's where we pay for all the C-rations we ate."

"You're right," Captain Tex said. "Let's get one more good night's sleep while we can. From now on it will be bad."

We rolled from the sway of the trucks, bobbed from the jolt of them, coughed from the fumes of them, and were stained khaki by the dust of them; but we minded only one thing—the sound of guns rolling downwind from the Naha-Shuri line. We were moving south to the line, within sight of the China Sea; but the sound of the sea was lost in a mightier roar that was like the roll of drums endlessly held. The artillery was plastering the Naha-Shuri line approach, from Machinato to Wilson's Ridge. When we rounded the corners of the coral bluffs we expected to see the battlefield, but we saw only more hills and a pall of smoke far ahead. The smoke might have been hanging over an industrial city, but we knew it wasn't. It marked the place where the Japanese had decided to fight and die.

Each time a man moves up to the line, he must nerve himself against the sound of war. We were out of practice and our nerves were not in shape for the slam of the guns. When the guns slammed, some men gritted their teeth; others clenched their fists or blinked or bobbed their heads or jumped. Some men settled into a steady trembling and ducked down below the steel sides of the truck, even though we were far out of range of enemy fire.

Moving up to the line in trucks did not have the dash and color we had known when we roared into a beach in the amphibious tractors. We were amphibious men. In the truck convoy there was none of that inspired momentum that comes when a long line of small boats wheels and drives in on a defended beach. We were commuting to work from the suburbs of the war, and the job ahead would be a dangerous, slogging grind, as dull as office routine. We thought we had escaped when our beach turned out to be soft and easy; we no longer had any enthusiasm for the campaign. They were placing us in double jeopardy; and we were like men hanged for a second time after the rope broke on a first try.

The road went between twin bluffs and we had arrived at an assembly area where trucks backed and circled in a dusty clearing. The command came: "Off-load. Assemble in a column-of-twos on the road."

For the rest of the way we would walk, or perhaps crawl forward. But we would go forward. Of that every man in the First Marines was certain. We never realized the possibility of going any other way. "We go forward or we hold what we got," one colonel told me. "That's all there is to it."

The troops strung out along the right-hand side of the road and moved ahead in a column-of-twos. As first there was lurching and straggling as the men settled in against the weight of their transport packs and the discomfort of weapons and a full unit of ammunition. There was no sound but the squeak of canteen holders in cartridge belts, the slap of helmet straps or the metallic rap of a rifle butt on a box of machine-gun ammunition. Some of the older men began to breathe heavily. A few of the newer men frisked around to right and left on the roadside and sometimes stopped to look at shell cases or abandoned equipment, but they soon settled into routine march and a silence settled on the files.

A tall mortarman carried the tube, balanced on one shoulder like a log; a second man carried the bipod; a third, squat and powerful, grunted under the carrying straps as he lugged the heavy base plate. These were men from the heavy mortars. The men with the .60's swung along up ahead with the rifle companies. They didn't have as heavy loads but their ammunition was hand-carried.

Riflemen carried their weapons in every way except the way they are carried in a parade. Some had the rifles tucked under their arms, as though they were hunting upland birds. Some carried their weapons across their neck and shoulders and held onto both ends; others carried the piece over one shoulder and gripped the muzzle in one hand. The men with small carbines carried their pieces slung. BAR men shifted their long rifles from sling to shoulder to back; their assistants wore sagging belts of BAR magazines and carried an M-1 with a full "unit of fire" (ammunition allotment). Machine-gunners, mostly with light guns but a few with "heavies," toted their tripods and guns and metal boxes of ammunition and wore belted .45's. Radiomen packed their 300's and also carbines; bazooka men packed their tubes and shells; demolitionists carried bulging, dangerous packs. But the flamethrower men carried the heaviest and worst burden of all. Most of them were heavy-shouldered men. Out in front of the column prowled Tommy-gunners. The line was not close enough to make a "point" necessary, but some men had been sent out anyway to scout the front and sides. Every man carried a weapon and every man walked—that was a Marine Infantry battalion.

Down the line came the word: "Doggies coming back. Doggies coming. Here comes the Twenty-seventh back."

Before the men from the Twenty-seventh Division, Army, appeared, I saw the shoulders of the marines straighten all along the file. Weapons which had almost been dragging on the ground were raised and carried smartly, and the side straggle of the column pinched in and they formed a neater column-of-twos. Eyes turned left as the Infantry column came down the other side of the road.

The men of the Twenty-seventh did not look at the marines. They said nothing. One marine made a crack but he was silenced by other

marines. The infantrymen were quiet, dirty and dispirited, turned into zombies by days and nights on the line. The marines were thoughtful and quiet, knowing it was always possible for them to come out
the same way—if they came out at all. The two outfits passed each
other silently.

Near Machinato, our Second Battalion swung off the road and went
down toward the sea to hold a reserve area behind the First and Third
Battalions. The Battalion Three and a lieutenant and I went up to
look over the lines and to pick out a spot for an Observation Post.
We started into a destroyed village, moving down a street that was
littered with splintered panels, torn mats, up-ended farm carts and
smashed tiles. Near the end of the street was a high concrete wall.
It had been breached many times with artillery fire. The major waved
us down to a squat and we crept along the wall. We judged that we
were either on the front line or just in back of it, but there were no
troops there. The artillery fire overhead was steady.

"Wow!" the major said. He was peering arond the corner of the
wall. "Look at that!"

We crawled up behind the major and peeked over his head. I gasped
and squirmed back. Beyond the edge of the wall, the ridge ended.
There was a long roll into the valley below. Far across the valley,
beyond low hills and one east-west escarpment, was Shuri itself. The
castle and the Japanese barracks were clearly in view. There were
flashes and spurts of smoke and debris all along the Shuri Ridge.
"Look at the view," the major urged us. "This is our Observation
Post."

"You could fall right out of this village," I told him.

"But what a view!"

As he spoke, the smoke that masked Shuri ridge was split by the
flash of an exploding shell and the walls of the castle loomed. Off
beyond a coastal flat near the China Sea, Naha—largest city on the
island—smoldered like a city dump. Between Naha and the escarp-
ments in front of Shuri were rounded, grassy knobs. We studied the
ground. We were getting a preview of the country in which we would
fight our war for Okinawa. It was a frightening sight.

At nightfall we came back to our camping place—a concrete amphitheater formed by the entry to a huge burial vault. Even before
I shredded explosive to make a quick fire for my coffee, and before
I laid down my poncho for a ground cloth, a restless night had begun
on the line. Flares popped overhead and the walls of the burial vault
were frescoed with green shadows. Below in the message center we
could hear the calls coming in from the line companies:

"Illumination in G Company."

"Get some flares up over F Company."

"First Platoon of E Company reports infiltration down by the sea wall."

The company mortars fired; the battalion mortars fired; the artillery fired; the naval guns put up flares. A bad night had begun.

The major and I sat with our backs against the vault and drank our coffee. Off near the sea wall a rifle fired once. A machine gun rattled in a long-winded burst. A BAR tapped away aimlessly. Listening to it, the major said: "I remember a story about a blind shoemaker who tapped away for years while he waited for his enemy to come back. He wasn't making shoes, just making noise while he waited. That's how that sounds."

"It sounds like a symphony tuning up," I told him. "We'll be taking a part in it soon enough."

"I suppose so," the major sighed. "Let's see if we can get some sleep now."

Full spring morning had come, and though there was no heat the sun had pulled the dampness out of the earth and the hillsides were warm to sit against. We sat and watched the company which was getting ready to attack through a gap in the ridge. On either side of the gap were high sand banks; behind it was a destroyed village; out ahead were Japanese machine gunners with everything laid in on the gap.

We were waiting to see what the company commander would do about the gap. That captain had the reputation of being a wild man. They called him "'Gung Ho," "Old Blood and Guts," "Wahoo Willie" and other names to show he had more nerve than brains. He was the kind of Marine officer who did well enough as long as he never had to make a decision involving more than one choice. At that moment he was pacing up and down, just back of the gap, and he was angry.

The riflemen were plastered against the banks on either side. They were calling for mortar fire and artillery support, but nobody seemed to have any particular target in mind. The company commander didn't trust maps. When he wanted artillery support, he waved at a piece of ground and growled: "Plaster it!" He had two good decorations for bravery from other campaigns, but he couldn't read a map.

"What will the Wild One do?" I asked Ralph, the scout in that company.

"I don't know. He'd like to call for a bayonet charge. I mean if he could find somebody to stick the old cold steel into, that's what he'd do. But those Jap gunners are down in bunkers somewhere. Maybe he'll pull his pistol and go whooping through. I couldn't say."

I was wishing that the major were there to steady the company commander. The captain was pacing up and down, chewing his lip and looking wall-eyed at the gap. His platoon leader dropped back to confer with him and we could hear them.

"We just can't get through," the platoon leader told the commander. The platoon leader was down on one knee and resting his weight on his carbine. He tried to reason with the commander. "We should wait for tanks," he advised.

The captain snorted. "Tanks! Man, we gotta get through that gap. I don't know about no tanks."

Ralph said of the platoon leader: "He's a good young officer. I hope Willie doesn't get 'im killed on this thing. Willie ain't waiting for no tanks. He thinks it's not playing the game to use tanks."

The other company scout came over and sat down beside us. His name was Sam, and back in the States he had been a genuine working cowboy. "We goin' through?" he asked Ralph.

"Not in one piece we're not."

We heard the captain say, "I know there's no cover on the other side. You got to ram through there and spread out fast when you hit the other side."

He glared at the gap. He hated it. He hated any hill, river, mountain or draw that got in his way. He was a former football hero, and to him every piece of bad terrain was a tough line on the other team. He wanted to bust through it with his head and shoulder down.

The lieutenant was raising his voice, too. "There's no cover for fifty yards on the other side, Captain."

"Fifty yards!" the commander bellowed. He snorted. He was probably remembering how fast he had covered fifty yards in a football stadium. He paced up and down again, glancing over his shoulder as though he were getting ready to perform before a great crowd in the stadium.

Murph, who was watching the captain, said, "All he needs is a brass band and a few cheer-leaders."

"In his mind he hears a thousand cheers," I agreed. "He's about to do or die for old State."

"He'll die," Chief said flatly. Nobody argued that statement. The captain stopped pacing and called loudly, "I'm gonna show ya! I'm gonna drive through that hole there. I'm gonna drive through and find cover on the other side. And when I get through I want you to bring the boys through. Clear?"

"I don't think—" the lieutenant began.

"Think!" the captain yelled. *"Think?"*

"The worst possible word," Ralph said. "He hates that word. Now he'll go."

"A few machine guns holding up a whole company of Marines!" the captain said. "You got to take a few casualties in a war."

"He throws away men like they were going out of style," Ralph said. "He's going to go."

It was clear that the captain was going through the gap alone. He checked the crowd in the stands with his over-the-shoulder glance, rolled his shoulders and swung his arms, hopped a few times to loosen up his legs and pulled his pistol. He looked at his pistol, looked at the gap, and then holstered his pistol. Even he could see that it would do him no good, and it might slow him down.

The captain got down like a halfback, with his knuckles resting lightly on the blasted earth. He seemed to be listening for some phantom signal which would tell him when the ball had been snapped and he was to set off down field. It came. He drove forward—going low through the gap, weaving with his shoulders and head—faking as though he were driving through the secondary; straightening for more open field speed, and side-stepping with his knees going high. He was a big, beautifully balanced man, doing a most stupid thing.

The machine gun caught him as he side-stepped some imaginary tackler. It was a Nambu, which fired faster than a tackler could blink, and it spun the captain off balance, but he regained his feet and drove on. Then two guns went after him in tandem and he folded in the middle, stumbled and plunged forward headfirst, still churning with his legs for that extra yardage, right up until the time his nose plowed into the yellow dirt. Once he went down, he never even twitched. He had driven the last two yards stone-dead.

"Oh," Murph said. "Oh!"

The riflemen were stunned for a moment and then someone yelled and two men ran up the bank, and in a frenzy began to fire over the top. One man cursed in a very loud voice and began to run toward the gap, and others followed him. In one swirl the platoon went driving through. Only one man was hit, and he was hit lightly.

The captain had been very well liked by most of his men. As Murph and the Chief brought him back, the corpsman said, "I never seen a guy take more hits. He was a real horse."

The captain was the first man I saw killed on the Naha-Shuri line. He was one I could never forget. He died with great dash and der-ring-do. Few other men did that, even in the Marines.

❀   ❀   ❀   ❀

BY MAY 8, GENERAL SHEPHERD'S 6TH DIVISION HAD captured Machinato Airfield on the west coast and prepared to cross the Asa Kawa River over footbridges thrown up by the 6th Engineer Battalion. This same day the Kamikaze Corps registered grievous hits on elements of our naval forces: Mitscher's flagship *Bunker Hill,* the battleship *New Mexico,* two destroyers, *H. W. Hadley* and *Evans,* and an LST. As the war in Europe had drawn to a close, the Royal Navy offered its services to Admiral Nimitz; and two British warships also fell victims of the Divine Wind—carriers *Victorious* and *Formidable,* with gaping holes in their superstructures and flight decks.

Meanwhile the 6th Division, having crossed the bridges, was on high ground, with right and left flanks moving along the sea in a northerly direction and up a high slope, respectively. Shepherd received a note from one of his battalion commanders informing him that three tanks had been lost at a big hill, caved and tunneled. It was the first word of Sugar Loaf, the site that Ushijima had chosen to make his stand with 32nd Army. Here, again, is Fletcher Pratt, who takes us through to the conclusion of this campaign in which the Marine Corps suffered losses of 3,440 killed and 15,487 wounded.

·19·   SUGAR LOAF AND FINAL ASSAULT

FLETCHER PRATT

The hill had no name at that time, but it would have a grim one not long later; for the 6th Division was up against the Sugar Loaf, main western anchorage of Shuri line, where there took place a combat not exceeded for closeness and desperation by that at the Conical or Shuri Castle itself or Iwo Jima or any other. The Japs had fed the 44th Independent Mixed in to help what was left of the 62nd Division in this area. They were fresh troops, and in this part of the brigade, unlike the elements encountered in the north, there were few or no Okinawan conscripts. Sugar Loaf itself was only the outer bastion of a general position which denied our forces not only access to the rear of Shuri, but also to the river Asato and the harbor and city of Naha; hence its careful organization.

About 300 yards long, it rose abruptly from the slightly tilted plain which lay completely open. Two hundred yards south and slightly east of Sugar Loaf was another hill, the Horseshoe, with its convex side toward Sugar Loaf, and east of both a third, much larger, and slightly higher eminence called the Half Moon, which is not really a half moon at all in trace, but more like a capital H with the left leg bent. All three had received the personal attention of General Cho and were more elaborately tunneled than most hills on Okinawa. It will be clear from any consideration of the supporting Horseshoe and Half Moon hills that their convolutions included reverse slopes from which mortars could bear on the Sugar Loaf without themselves being subject to any form of attack till Sugar Loaf itself were taken and our infantry could deal with them by grenade. Beyond Half Moon the ground rose rapidly leftward to Shuri in the 1st Division's zone.

Against this Sugar Loaf position the 22nd Regiment was launched on the afternoon of 14 May, with tanks working around both flanks of the hill in support and one company each against the lower flanking eminences. The armor ran into heavy 47-mm. fire from Horseshoe and the Half Moon; part of it was disabled, the rest driven off. Three times one company reached the Sugar Loaf crest; three times they were beaten back by mortar fire from the supporting hills which the flanking companies could not approach. After dark Major H. A. Courtney, the battalion exec, detected signs of an imminent counterattack that would have been extremely hard to handle. He rallied the 20 remaining men of the company with 25 others from a supply echelon, rushed the summit once more, instructing his men to throw grenades as rapidly as possible and dig in under cover of the explosions. They made it and held the crest all night; the Jap counter was completely broken up by their close-range grenading. Courtney was killed (they gave him a posthumous Medal of Honor); in the morning one officer and 19 exhausted men, all that were left of them, had to be withdrawn.

Colonel Schneider of the regiment nevertheless planned to drive home again next morning against Sugar Loaf, while General Shepherd of the division would take some pressure off him by putting in the 29th against the Half Moon on the extreme left of the divisional area. The 1st Division beyond was still held up by the broad, but highrising gulch called Wana Draw, its sides fortified and overlooked by the guns of Shuri Castle.

The force of the Sugar Loaf position was now pretty well understood on our side, and the preliminary artillery fire for the 0800 attack, though scheduled for only fifteen minutes' duration, had not only the 6th Division's own guns in it, but also those of the Army 249th Artillery and some big pieces belonging to corps, emplaced farther back. This fire produced an unexpected dividend. General Ushijima, or Suzuki of the 44th Independent Mixed, had thought when the remnant of the Courtney command was driven down Sugar Loaf, that it was another chance like that offered by the 27th Division on 19 April and a strong local counterattack was ordered. The American artillery praparation caught these counterattackers just emerging from their holes, pinned them down, killed a good many, and took all the verve out of the movement.

With Japanese persistence the 44th Independent Mixed tried their attack anyway as soon as the fire let up, heaviest in the center against the exhausted 2nd Battalion, 22nd, but also spreading along the line to include part of the area where the 29th was working forward slowly under intense fire. The Japanese had withdrawn from some of the forward hill faces on that front to let their flanking guns fire in enfilade from the ridges the 1st Division had not yet succeeded in gaining. Attack and counterattack swayed back and forth till noon and later; by that time the 22nd had lost a couple of hundred yards, the 29th had gained maybe 700, and on both sides the men in the offensives were fought out. As soon as it grew dark enough to force our observation planes back to the fields, the Japs as usual opened up with all the guns and mortars they had, under which fire 2/22 was relieved by 3/22. More companies of the 29th were moved in, and preparations were made for a general assault by the two regiments against the Sugar Loaf - Half Moon complex, in which Sugar Loaf was to be attacked simultaneously from front and both flanks.

That day, 16 May, was the toughest of the whole campaign; the attack failed and under appalling casualties. The encirclement from the west was stopped by the fire from Horseshoe where there were still antitank guns in force. At the center the crest of Sugar Loaf was reached and on the left the outer peaks of Half Moon, but from these points not an inch of progress could be made. General Suzuki had moved nearly all remaining of the 44th Independent Mixed into the firing positions and from them mortar shells fell continuously into the hilltop foxholes, while every minute down into the twilight, the guns of Shuri poured more shells from the left rear. By night all the advance elements had to be withdrawn with no real gain reported for the day.

What was now to be done? Renew the attack; this time with the 29th carrying the ball in an effort to win the Half Moon and flank out the heaviest of the firing positions supporting Sugar Loaf, while the exhausted 22nd held its lines. *Colorado, Mississippi,* and *New York* were moved in to fire support from their big guns; the carriers flew strikes with 1,000-pound bombs against Half Moon, and under cover of support fires closer than they had been since Iwo Jima, the regiment worked forward into the northern bowl of Half Moon and scaled the precipitous crest. The men were getting a lot of fire from Shuri behind them and more from the Horseshoe; and as soon as they were on the upper slope of Half Moon they were violently counterattacked from the lateral galleries and thrown off. They attacked again; were again counterattacked; and it was not until the fourth attack in the twilight that the Japs would let them stay.

By this time the ammunition of the spearheading company was exhausted and it had so many wounded that there were not enough whole men left to get them to the rear. The crest had to be abandoned; our men now held only that northern bowl of the Half Moon. But the Japanese positions had been in fact fatally shaken, for that bowl and its adjacent caves were the most effective of the firing positions from which Sugar Loaf had been supported, and in Sugar Loaf itself the defending force was so cut down by casualties that the commander there doubted whether it could stand another day's fighting.

In this desperate case General Suzuki assembled what reserves he had behind Horseshoe and Half Moon and, as soon as dusk removed our observation planes, boldly launched them across the open to the rescue of Sugar Loaf. The inching advances had now given our forces enough points to permit ground observation, the Japs were detected forming and the fire of no fewer than twelve battalions of artillery came down redly on them in the early dark. This concentration blew the reinforcement attempt all to bits; it is doubtful whether more than a dozen men reached their destination. When the 29th attacked again on 18 May, tanks leading around both sides of Sugar Loaf, they broke through, and the long-contested hill was taken. It had cost the 6th Division alone 2,662 killed and wounded; the number of shells fired by the divisional artillery was 92,560.

The height on which Shuri stands thrusts a long curved finger out to the northwest, on the north slope of which lay that Dakeshi Town for which the 1st Division had fought so hard. South of it stands another ridge, whose southern face bore the town of Wana with Wana Draw below it; and the ridge beyond, culminating eastward in Shuri itself, is that on whose outer tentacles the Sugar Loaf positions had been organized. It may be called Shuri Ridge. While the 6th had been engaged in its climactic struggle for Sugar Loaf, the 1st Division was attempting to negotiate this Wana-Northern Shuri position, with the 7th Regiment in line on the left, the 1st on the right. The battle was less desperate than that of the 6th Division only because the surrounding conditions did not permit it to have the same character. On the front before Sugar Loaf there was no cover; no matter how heavy the supporting fire, a moment arrived when men had to stand up and run across naked ground into a level stream of bullets. Where the 1st Division was fighting there was all too much cover except in Wana Draw itself. It was never quite possible to tell whether a given little depression in the almost-vertical rock wall was a good spot to take defilade from fire, or the outer slant of one of General Cho's rifle slits, or merely a spot on which a gun above or to one side had been registered. The concerted rushes and stands against counter-attack that marked the action of the 6th did not happen here. The whole battle was a series of individualistic bushwhacking encounters between units as small as a single fire team and Japanese who behaved in quite as independent a manner.

Technically the attack of the 7th Regiment was directed at first against the north face and crest of Wana Ridge. The 1st Regiment was trying to work eastward up Wana Draw to gain the north face of Shuri Ridge. Actually, both regimental commands operated chiefly as administrative organizations, which could do little more than assign a general direction of attack to their subordinate units. On 15 May the 5th Regiment passed through the 1st and took up the work against Wana Draw. Here tanks could be and were used, but slowly, every hundred feet of ground had to be combed over, the cave entrances sought and sealed—and all the while, fire came down from above.

In this type of fighting the western edges of Wana Draw were won by 17 May and the 7th Regiment gained the crest of the ridge above. Their presence there was one of the reasons why the 6th Division's assault out southwestward carried Sugar Loaf the next day; the defenders of Shuri had too much to do in their own front yard to think about helping units on their flanks, even with fire. On 18 May the whole line heaved forward again, the 7th capturing a regimental command post. On the 19th the Japs counterattacked the 7th all day long from their lateral tunnels, taking heavy casualties in the process, and that night the 1st Regiment went back into line to relieve the 7th. On 20 and 21 May the division cleared Wana Ridge, gained the little town that was the northern outpost of Shuri and came up against a narrow neck of high ridge. Beyond, Shuri Castle itself looked down. That day the division tried to work formations across Wana Draw onto Shuri Ridge, failed to do so, and was preparing for another try the following morning.

On the east side of the island the 7th Division had just broken through along the shore at Yonabaru; it was getting heavy resistance from the hills to the south of the break-through line, but only put out security detachments in that direction, wheeling the main force of its drive rightward, with the 96th Division on its own right, up against the main Shuri mass on that side. The design was to pinch out the 77th, which had been long in line, done much hard fighting, and needed relief; but that night it began to rain.

It is an open question whether Okinawa, Eritrea in Africa, or some place in the Belgian Congo has the highest humidity in the world over a year's run, but there is no doubt that the island of the Ryukyus can put on a spectacular rainfall performance over a brief space — as much as nine inches a day. The rainy season had now arrived; and all the other rains seen by Americans on Okinawa, though heavy enough, were reduced to the status of Scotch mist. In the ordinary fields mud became ankle deep; on the alleged roads it was up to the knee and even amphitracs had difficulty. Fires could not be kept up for coffee or hot food. On the eastern flank of the island, where supply lines for the Army troops had to run back across the made tracks through the vertical ridges, it became next to impossible to keep up with the ordinary logistic requirements for a static situation, to say nothing of handling the vast quantities of extra food, ammunition, and evacuations demanded by an all-out attack.

Only on the front of the 6th Division, which had the most direct supply lines, was there much action during the week of rains that supervened. During the night of 18-19 May Suzuki made repeated counterattacks in an effort to regain his Sugar Loaf. Next morning General Shepherd moved in the 4th Regiment, his last reserve, to the relief of the 29th. The main weight of the attack was against the western flank. It early won the western eminence of Horseshoe and the marines could look down into the mortar positions that had beaten at them for so long.

This meant the jig was about up for the anchor position on the left flank of the Shuri line and no one was better aware of it than General Mitsuru Ushijima, for those protected fire positions on Horseshoe were the soul of his defense. If they were knocked out, our forces could get down into the Kokuba River valley, follow that corridor eastward to the rear of the Shuri positions, perhaps hook up with the 7th Division and surround the bulk of the Japs in their castle. The General issued preparatory orders for the evacuation of the Shuri position, but in the meanwhile called on the Naval Guard force covering the big Naha Airfield on Oroku Peninsula for a battalion to be used in a suicide attack. Rear Admiral Ota, in command of the Naval Guards, did not take at all kindly to this idea, and went so far as to radio a protest to Tokyo, but Ushijima outranked him and there was nothing to be done about it.

The battalion marched then, and was launched in attack at 2130, small groups at first, building up to the crescendo of a full-scale assault under mortar cover. It was a true banzai and, like most of them, accomplished exactly nothing; in the morning there were nearly five hundred bodies on the ground before the 4th and the Japanese resistance was broken. All the next day was spent in reducing the tunnels of the Horseshoe and by twilight that ridge was ours. Over on the left flank of the attack the Half Moon still held out, nor could even the fresh regiment reach its crests because of the fire from Shuri falling onto our men's rear. That day, 21 May, General Shepherd made the command decision to set up a defensive flank on the outer, western slope of Half Moon, swing his weight rightward, across the Asato, and clear out Naha City, for whose northern flank the river formed a moat.

The next day was spent in closing up to the stream; on that night, under the first heavy rain, patrols pushed across. They found surprisingly little resistance among houses reduced to debris, and this gave General Shepherd the idea that the place might be taken without the help of tanks, which were in any case now too much mired down to be used.

By noon the 4th was wading the stream in the little groups of an infiltration attack. Within the city there were only snipers, but just east of the place is a ridge running north and south, separating the town from what an Okinawan would consider the elegant suburb of Machishi, and this ridge was tunneled in the usual fashion. A good deal of fire issued from it, and most of the 4th was gradually drawn into a contest that was not terminated in their favor till 25 May, for although the enemy were now too weak in manpower to use the elaborate positions with the greatest effect. In the meanwhile the 29th Regiment was brought into Naha and gradually cleared it out. By 29 May the town had fallen, the division was in line facing southeastward and pushing up the peninsula between the Asato and Kokuba.

On that same day both the 1st Division and XXIV Corps had planned to renew their assault on Shuri. For the last two or three days there had been indications that the Japs were abandoning their castle under cover of poor flying weather and our inability to move tanks in rapid pursuit. Little groups of them appeared on the roads and were taken under fire; the shooting of their own guns showed a diminuendo. 29 May broke bright and clear for a wonder and at 0730 the 5th Marines jumped off in attack through mud only beginning to congeal. Now, during all those days of rain the 1st Division had been patrolling energetically, mainly in a southerly direction, and every patrol had taken fire from its left and rear, the eminence on which Tametamo's castle stood. The castle was in the 77th Division's zone, but the 1st Battalion, 1st, and its Reconnaissance Company pivoted round toward the place from a direction almost due south to get rid of that pestiferous fire. The head of the Reconnaissance Company got into a tunnel; its security detachment had just set up a machine gun above when down trail came marching sixty Japs who all fell down in three neat rows when the gun opened fire. They were the last organized group in Shuri; the 1st Battalion burst in and the long fight was won. The men of the 77th, whose attack was planned for later in the day, were more than a little annoyed . . .

As early as 18 May when the fall of the Sugar Loaf and the Conical left his flanks substantially in air, Ushijima's staff had begun to draw operation plans for a general retreat and to move the service commands (with such items as files of correspondence and the Okinawan women who served the convenience of the officers) into the southern tip of the island. There is an escarpment there, a somewhat aberrant geological formation, jutting across Okinawa where it narrows toward a point after throwing off the Oroku Peninsula to the west and the Chinen Peninsula eastward. It rises just south of the town of Itoman on the west coast, the line of hills running through Huza, just missing the town of Tomui and slanting down the east coast. All this area had been fortified by the 9th Division while it was still part of the Okinawa command, a job well done, like everything else by that division. In this area the Japanese General proposed to make his final stand.

The movement of troops and of such guns as could still be moved began on 26 May under cover of the rains and low clouds, and by the 29th there were nothing but the rear guards (one-fifth of each command) left north of the new line, except on Oraku Peninsula, where the Naval Guard troops remained to deny to the Americans the use of the big airfield, most important of all those on Okinawa.

The prospects of holding the new line for a long while cannot have looked hopeful to either Ushijima or Cho at this date. They had reorganized their formations, consolidating two of the regiments of the 24th into one (the remaining infantry regiment had but 800 men left), reducing the number of battalions in the 62nd by further consolidations, and bringing all such formations as engineers and transportation troops into the line as infantry. But the total strength now amounted to hardly as much as a division. This was insufficient for lines which, though well built, were nearly as extensive as those of Shuri, and the position was very weak in artillery, both in the effective large mortars and in machine cannon. The latter had borne the brunt of the American attacks and the former regrettably could not be moved through the mud. In fact, this mud made all progress so very slow that American spotting planes, which persisted in flying in spite of the weather, often found guns and troops on the road and called down artillery fire which destroyed them. One transport command started to march with 150 vehicles and arrived with less than 30 after being under salvos from an American battleship.

Worst of all was the state of morale within the command. The Naval Guard troops on Oroku, who had not fought except for the single battalion that conducted the banzai at the Horseshoe, were in good shape. The rest were tired out, badly beaten up and hungry, their uniforms ragged. The losses, as usual, had fallen most heavily on the best and boldest men, and in the formations remaining there was a larger proportion of the shiftless Okinawan home guards than the General cared to see. It had not been possible to make the promised issue of sweet-potato brandy on the Emperor's birthday on 29 April, and there was bitternes and whispering over this. General Ushijima had done his best to bolster the men's feelings by circulating on 20 May, just before the move to the south began, the story that an enormous landing of airborne troops had taken Yontan Airfield from the Americans and the latter's lines of communication were now gone. (As a matter of fact, this was a magnification of a radio dispatch from Tokyo which told General Ushijima that the landing would take place. It was not tried till the 24th and then there were only five planes in it. Four of them were knocked out by flak but the fifth reached ground and discharged ten Japs with demolition charges bound round their waists, who destroyed 7 planes and damaged 25 more. Yontan was out of commission for the day but this was not retaking the field.) After the troops were established in their new Yuza-Dake, Yaeju-Dake line another story was issued as an official bulletin. The troops on Okinawa had done well; they had now only to hold out till 20 June. On that date a great counter-invasion would take place near Katena Airfield, the old comrades of the 9th Division coming from Formosa and another fresh division form the China Coast under elaborate naval gunfire and airbombing cover, while a great force of parachutists struck behind the American lines and airborne troops landed to enlarge the holdings around Yontan Field.

How much of this fairy tale was believed is uncertain. Being an official order, it had almost the force of an Imperial rescript and no discussion of the matter was permissible. What Ushijima himself was really hoping for, of course, was a new series of Kamikaze attacks on the ships offshore. There had been a big one on 24-25 May in conjunction with the attempt at Yontan. Sixty-five Kamikaze and 100 Tokobetsu were in it, but their fighter cover was weak and most of the Army fliers engaged were conscripts rather than volunteers for suicide duty, a fact which caused Major General Miyoshi, commanding the units of Kyushu, to protest to Imperial headquarters that such procedures were not in accordance with the true Kamikaze spirit.

Most of them went for the picket line, the better to cover the Yontan attack. They sank the APD *Bates* and badly smashed up the APDs *Barry* and *Roper,* the destroyer escort *O'Neill,* the minesweeper *Spectacle* and the destroyers *Bright, Butler,* and *Stormes,* with one LSM. The destroyers *W. C. Cole, Cowell,* and *Guest* received lesser injuries.

The attack was thus a comparative failure and there seems to have been some heartburning in Tokyo about it, for Admiral Ugaki staged another under his personal supervision on the night of 27 May, partly to cover Ushijima's withdrawal southward and partly to demonstrate that the correct method was to throw a minor force against the American picket line while the bulk of the suiciders pushed on to the anchorages. He sent out 60 Navy and 50 Army Kamikaze this time, at night, with fairly good fighter coverage, and they did a lot of damage. The destroyer *Drexler* took two Kamikaze aboard and went down; the destroyer *Braine* also got two but survived; *Forrest* and *Shubrick* had major damage, so did the APDs *Rednour* and *Loy,* the cargo carrier *Josiah Snelling,* an LCS, a PSC, and the command ship *Dutton;* less hurt were two more transports, another PC and another LCS, the destroyer *Anthony* and the APD *Tatum;* the destroyer escort *Gilligan* was attacked by a torpedo plane that came with the Kamikaze, and was hit by a torpedo, but it failed to go off.

On our right flank the 6th Division was now north of the deep and wide Kokuba Estuary from Oroka Peninsula with its important airstrip and its control of Naha Harbor, which the Navy desperately wanted, for there were still supply problems at the front and the swinging advance that began in the last days of May gravely complicated them. As the 6th circled around Kokuba Estuary, it accordingly wheeled right to face the range of hills that runs almost north and south to seal Oroku from the main island. The 22nd Regiment was placed in line opposite these hills. The 1st Division slanted past the rear of the 22nd, reaching the coast of the East China Sea with its advance spearhead on 7 June. On the very next day it began to get supplies by water across the beaches and pushed on toward Itoman in good spirits.

Meanwhile, the question of taking Oroku had arisen all up and down the chain of command. Some time earlier it had been foreseen that such a question would ultimately come. The Marine commands concerned (III Corps and 6th Division) thought that once the land exits had been sealed off, the place should be assaulted in a regular Marine operation, from the sea, since the outer ground of the peninsula was flat and the beaches reasonably good. Tenth Army was rather of the opinion that an attack through the hills was preferable. There were hardly any amphitracs left (out of seven battalions whose normal equipment was 100 each, not one had as many as 25 in working shape), and those that were left were battered and broken. There would also be difficulties about shipping for the heavy equipment, and the Navy had enough to do with its picket line and Kamikazes without being called upon to furnish close supporting fire for a new beachhead. Still, said General Buckner, the area fell within III Corps's zone of action and if it could find the physical means, the decision as to the tactical means was one that corps could properly take. General Geiger of corps in similar fashion forward-passed the decision to General Shepherd of division, and while the discussions were going on, General Shepherd and his operations officer, the eupeptic Krulak, had been investigating possibilities. Patrols of the 22nd had found the routes into the hill mass before them intricate and subject to a good deal of the kind of fire usually encountered on Okinawa. On the other hand, our reconnaissance landing from the sea face on the night of 2 June achieved a miraculous success, getting back without losing a man to report that the beaches were not mined, everything in the northwest sector of the peninsula was lightly held or not held at all, but that the Japs were digging industriously down toward the land face and women had been moved into caves in that direction. There were enough amphitracs to carry a regiment and enough LSMs and LCMs to carry the equipment. Decision, then, for the seaborne landing—with the 4th Marines making it on the night of 3-4 June, on the tip at a place called Nishikoku.

A ridge thrown off from the island's central spine overlooks this landing spot from the south. The 4th should seize it rapidly to cover the landing of the 29th and the artillery behind. There is an island in the estuary, Ono Yama, where a two-span bridge from Naha City used to stand. The division Reconnaissance Company was to gain this simultaneously with the main landing to permit re-erection of the bridge and land transport down through Naha for purposes of subsequent supply. The remainder of the tactical plan was that as soon as the 29th landed it would work southwestward to clear the Kokuba shore and seize the long high ridge that runs southeast from Kakibana, dominating the estuary, while the 4th pushed straight in from its ridge protecting the landing, cleared the airfield, wheeled left down the southwest coast of the peninsula till it touched our lines at the base, then wheeled left again, back toward the 29th, driving the Japanese before it into a narrowing sack.

The job of assembling the supplies and troops for a divisional move that was only thirty-six hours from planning to execution was something fantastic, but it was well and thoroughly done, and the landing went off like a clockwork, two battalions of the 4th striking the beaches almost exactly on schedule at 0551 on 4 June. One battalion pushed ahead to take the inland ridge, the other leftward to gain the nose of the big ridge below Kakibana. By midmorning both were well up the slopes against opposition that was everywhere insignificant till the crests were nearly reached, when some mortar fire began to come over. All the little outcrops of the main hill were found tunneled in the best Cho manner, but all vacant—Admiral Ota had not enough men to hold both the beaches and the high ground in them where he had expected to be attacked. Ono Yama was ours by 0600; by evening there was a Bailey bridge from Naha to the island, the 29th was ashore, the lines were nearly 1,500 yards inland enclosing nearly half the airfield, and casualties were few.

It was next morning when the advance for conquest started, a peculiar battle, for if this collection of Japs lacked the artillery support those on the Shuri line had had, and if they were far too few to man all the elaborate installations, they had, to balance these, two things not met with elsewhere—so many machine guns, salvaged from wrecked planes, that a fair estimate placed their number at one for every three defenders of Oroku; and a new type of rocket, jerry-built from an 8-inch shell. The thing sounded "like a locomotive from hell." Most of them soared out to sea with that noise which led the marines to dub them "screaming meemies," but when one hit it exploded with an earth-shaking roar, usually after burying itself well in the ground, so that the physical damage was small. Very bad for the nerves, though.

That day the right flank of our lines swung forward to take all but the last corner of the airfield, while the 29th gained most of its Kokuba-dominating ridge. The night had given Admiral Ota time to recover a little from the surprise of finding marines behind him and he had rushed a good many men out into the tunneled positions. One of these nests, at the Village of Toma, on the right-center, put up a long resistance to a battalion of the 4th. It was still nothing like Sugar Loaf, the enemy fire nearly all machine gun and mortar, and gains averaged 1,000 yards.

On 6 June the 4th ran rapidly forward down the southwest coast of the peninsula with its right and the 29th made some gains to its left, but along the axial ridge at the center of the peninsula where the Japs were evidently deciding to make their main defense, there was little advance. Tanks found the ground too rough or too muddy and when they did get into action, it was discovered that the Japs had brought up a lot of 20-mm. machine cannon, almost as hard to deal with as the machine guns, because their firing ports were so small.

The 7th and 8th were days of slow advance, even on the 4th Regiment's previously fast-moving right flank. Admiral Ota had shifted some of his troops to hold off the menace of this drive, and everywhere mine fields and lack of roads made it hard to bring up armored support. On 9 June both the 29th and 4th broke through, the latter by the ingenious maneuver of using the Japs' own tunnel systems to work through bare hill crests when all the routes around and over them proved to be under fire from supporting positions. That day also the 22nd began to attack, and the squeeze was on.

It is not to be thought that the remaining four days of the fight were easy; they were days of the same crawling advance under machine gun and mortar fire, the same cave-sealing enterprises, that had marked all the rest of the Okinawa campaign. But the enemy's physical strength had been broken in the surprise and the hard fighting at the center of the peninsula (for he had lost heavily trying to move troops around and still more when the caves at the center were sealed); and on 12 June his morale broke also. Surrender flags began to appear along the line and the surviving Japs were forced out into a region of paddy fields and mudflats along the upper edge of Kokuba. Interpreters tried to get them to give up, but most answered that they requested permission from the kind Americans to commit suicide. The permission was granted as the marines on the high ground watched, dropping their guns to applaud if the suicide were sufficiently spectacular, like that of the pair who seated themselves on a quadruple demolition charge and touched off the fuse. The peninsula had cost us 1,608 casualties for one of the most neatly performed operations on Okinawa; the Japanese loss would be not far from 5,000

While this was going on, the Kamikazes came back in a new method of attack, beginning on 3 June. It was supposed to provide a steadily flowing stream of suicide planes, day and night on end for a long period, and wear out the nerves of the defenders, that old Japanese concept dating back to Guadalcanal. They lightly hit an LCI on the 3rd, a cargo vessel on the 4th; on the 5th the cruiser *Louisville*, the battleship *Mississippi*, and the destroyer *Anthony*, and did some damage to the minesweeper *Bauer*. On the 6th they crippled the latter's sister ship *Ditter* and on the 7th damaged the escort carrier *Natoma Bay*. Comparatively this was no success at all; his difficulties were beginning to catch up with Admiral Ugaki and for all this four-day attack he had been unable to get more than 20 Kamikaze and 30 Tokobetsu into the air. The Imperial Staff decided that Okinawa was now so nearly gone and the American air defense around the island had become so very civilized that it was no further use; the rest of the suicide fliers would be saved up for that invasion of the Japanese homeland which anyone with an ounce of prescience could see was in the cards.

However, the pressure was not yet off the American Fleet; on 5

June the heaviest typhoon any man in it had ever seen swept across the the ships and damaged them far more than any Kamikaze attack. The heavy cruiser *Pittsburgh* had 100 feet of her bow bodily wrenched off; on the carriers *Hornet* and *Bennington* the forward ends of the flight decks were all bent down, and of other vessels the escort carriers *Salamaua* and *Windham Bay,* the cruisers *Baltimore* and *Duluth,* the destroyers *McKee* and *Conklin,* were all so much hurt as to require major dockyard jobs. A long list of other ships, headed by the big new battleships *Alabama, Indiana,* and *Massachusetts,* and ending with no fewer than eleven destroyers, were hurt enough to go into anchorage for tender repairs. It was perhaps just as well that the Japanese Navy had been eliminated before the storm struck.

On land the gale was represented by high winds and rain that did not seem much more than normal to marines who had been under the May downpour. Under those rains the 1st Division was pressing on in its break to the coast, meeting in resistance only little pockets of Japs who made movement dangerous, the division so much hampered by problems of supply that air-drops were repeatedly asked for. By the evening of 7 June the division was in the upper end of Itoman (where a little airstrip was set up on a road so hospital planes could evacuate the wounded) and facing a small, muddy, sluggish stream called the Mukue Gawa, beyond which rose the steep outcrop of Kunishi Ridge, sheltering the town of the same name. The 7th Regiment was on the right next to the sea, with its zone of action including this ridge, which is flanked on the southwest within easy machine-gun range by another and larger ridge called the Mezado. The 1st Regiment was in line eastward, opposed to a hill bearing simply the number 69, the 5th in reserve. The ground behind was so gelatinous that the 37-mms. had not been brought forward and neither had self-propelled guns; the tanks were well behind.

That day there was an attack; the infantry of both regiments worked across the Mukue and dug in on the slopes of their respective hills, but every patrol found this was a main Japanese battle position that could not be taken without supporting weapons. The 1st Regiment was also getting fire into its flank from Yuza Ridge, most of which lay in the zone of the 96th Division, next door. 9 June was accordingly spent in improving roads, getting tanks forward and providing means for them to cross the muddy Mukue. The main attack was for the 10th, with the 1st Regiment to take Hill 69 and the outer nose of Yuza, the 7th to assault Kunishi.

That assault was a brutal business. The 96th Division was in difficulties with a similar maze of hills and could give little help against Yuza, where one company of the 1st lost 75 men out of 175. Hill 69 was only scratched at, not taken, on this day. Both regiments were in fact not up to their old battle efficiency—full of new replacements, many of them not thoroughly trained; the officers had trouble. There was a good deal of Jap antitank artillery around which, with the mud, kept the tankers from giving effective support and the Japs had so much fire on the Mukue Gawa in the 7th Regiment's zone that the men who infiltrated across it could neither be supported nor supplied.

On 11 June the 1st Regiment gained its two hills and dug in, but was now so much ahead of the formations on both flanks that it must stand. That night came an odd incident which may be taken as the first real sign of Jap breakdown. A long file of Okinawan civilians wrapped round in dirty blankets began to come through the lines of the 1st. They had almost passed the fire positions when a sharp-eyed sergeant discovered that every fifth man in the line-up was a Japanese soldier with grenades under his blanket and a demolition charge around his middle. Of course they had to turn loose the machine guns.

At Kunishi the 7th could make no progress on either 10 or 11 June. On the second night Colonel Snedeker of the regiment turned the Japs' own tactics around on them with a night attack and succeeded in getting two companies onto Kunishi crest at 0300. But after daylight broke they might as well have been in Kamchatka, for all the avenues up to their post were covered by the most intense fire, they could not advance or retreat or be supported. Later in the day the somewhat desperate device of bringing small groups of men up the slope as passengers in tanks was hit upon. It succeeded so far as bringing in a handful of reinforcements but the men on the ridge were lying out on a hot coral rock that offered the most determined resistance to digging, under constant fire from Mezado and other ridges in the rear. Air supply was not much good, the Japs getting most of the drops, and an observer from our side might have thought the battle at a standstill. It was not really so; the driblets of reinforcement kept coming in by tank, and as they did so the party on the ridge expanded inch by inch down the sides, at each few yards' gain blowing a couple more tunnels or silencing another mortar. The result was that the Japs grew gradually weaker, and after a rough three-day battle the place could be called ours by the night of 16 June.

The capture of Kunishi brought about a new distribution of forces in III Corps. The 1st Division was understrength both in numbers and in physical constitution, while Mezado loomed on its right flank, an obstacle as formidable as any yet faced. General Geiger sent the 6th Division back into battle to capture this ridge; the 5th Regiment relieved the 1st and the fresh 8th Regiment of the 2nd Division, which had been sent for as far back as the fall of Shuri, was brought into line between the 5th Regiment and the 6th Division. At the same time the boundaries of III Corps were somewhat expanded eastward to allow for the pinching out of the 96th Division, which had taken extremely heavy casualties, had fallen behind the other formations, and was also in much need of relief.

The 6th used its 22nd Regiment in the initial assault of 17 June, which reached the crest of Mezado; presently the other two regiments had to be put in, but now they and the revamped 1st Division drove forward rapidly against resistance that was everywhere crumbling into little unco-ordinated pockets. The 1st broke through to the coast on 19 June; the 6th cleared its area to the waters of the Pacific two days later, when it was announced that all organized resistance had ceased.

In those last days of Okinawa the final communication lines went out and Japanese morale, long on the teetering edge, collapsed. Surrenders, which began as a trickle, became a flood. A four-man patrol from the 6th Division captured over 150 after their officers had bowed politely, handed over their swords, shot the women with them and committed suicide. In the long run the number of prisoners came to 7,401, of whom about 4,000 turned out to be Okinawans in uniform. The counted enemy dead were 107,539; it was estimated that there were another 23,000 down in various caves. Tenth Army, after elaborately going over the Japanese records, concluded that 72,000 native Japanese troops had been killed in action with 20,000 Okinawan troops; the remaining 42,000 killed would be Okinawan civilians, though in this case and under the conditions of cave warfare it is extremely difficult to determine who is a soldier and who is not.

One of those killed on our side was Lieutenant General Simon Bolivar Buckner—in the very last act of the campaign, on 18 June, as he stood in an observation post near Mezado Ridge, when a shell dropped right on him. Of others the Army lost 4,379 killed, 17,558 wounded; the Marines 3,440 killed, 15,487 wounded; and the Navy offshore to Kamikaze and suicide boats, 4,907 killed, 4,824 wounded, for total casualties to our side of 48,025—about which it is to note that the Navy had more killed than either of the other services, despite all those caves and the hard fighting ashore. . . .

※　※　※　※

TOO, OKINAWA WAS THE BIGGEST OPERATION OF ANY for Marine aviation, which poured 12,000 men into the area in 22 shore-based squadrons, 10 carrier squadrons and an assortment of service units. Under General Francis P. Mulcahy's Tactical Air Force which included Army units were five marine air groups: MAG 31, 33, 22, 14 and 43. The big job was kamikazes.

Here is Captain John DeChant, air historian first encountered at Leyte, reviewing high points of the final days of Mulcahy's command.

·20· THE TAF AT WORK

JOHN DeCHANT

Under a bright three-quarter moon the night of May 18, two pilots of Magruder's squadron made five radar night kills between them in less than two hours.

Lieutenant Harold H. Martin, a Marine correspondent, recounted in the lingo of the night fighters how Lieutenant Robert Wellwood shot down the first three Japanese raiders.

"At the station called 'Poison,' Lieutenant Hugh Gallarneau, the old Stanford football star, began scanning the glowing dials which cast a sheen of bluish light over the radar panel at the end of the dark control van. His chick, Wellwood, was already in the air.

"Miles away at the station called 'Raccoon,' Lieutenant Jack Wilson heard his chick, Lieutenant Edward LeFaivre, report airborne.

"For a while nothing happened. On the softly glowing dials at Poison and Raccoon, only two tiny sparks of light showed where the two chicks circled, each in his orbit, in the dark above. Then, far to the northeast, toward Japan, another faint spark glowed on Gallarneau's scope. He studied it, marking its course and altitude. Bogey—unidentified aircraft. Off to the left of the board a new light glowed, querying the stranger. No answering signal came back. He was an enemy now, beyond a doubt, a target instead of a bogey. Hugh clicked on his microphone.

"'Hello, Muscles One Seven, I have a customer for you, starboard three-five-zero.'

"'One Seven to Poison. Three-five-zero. Roger and out.'

"'Hello One Seven. Target range 25 at 11 o'clock and 17,000 feet indicating 160 mph. Firewall! Poison, Out!'"

"She had altitude on me and was closing fast," Wellwood said.

"When Hugh told me to firewall, I jammed the throttle forward and started to climb. We were going fast . . . 10 miles . . . 7 miles . . . I charged my guns again, just to make sure."

"Hello One Seven," called Gallarneau. "Target range 3 at 10 o'clock starboard two-two-zero. Target crossing . . . Punch! Get him!"

Wellwood said, "When I went into my turn, I knew this was it. If Hugh had judged his vectors right and if I'd followed him as I should, I'd be coming right in on her tail. If either of us had doped off, there wouldn't be anything out there but empty sky. As I came out of my turn, I flipped my finder and peered at the little orange colored gauge on my panel. There wasn't a blip [a tiny light on the radar screen] on it. Then I got her signal. It came swimming down from up in the left-hand corner of the screen and I yelled 'Contact' so loud Hugh could have heard me even without his radio.

"I watched the blip getting bigger and bigger and coming nearer and nearer. When I thought I was close enough, I started squinting through the windscreen out into the dark. Then I saw her . . . dead ahead and 300 feet above me . . . a vague black shape in the light of the moon. I nosed up to climb a little and swung to port to get on the dark side of the moon from her, and started closing in. The twin-engine Betty didn't know I was in the sky. At 300 feet I gave the trigger a short quick squeeze. At the wing-root, between the Jap's left engine and the fuselage, I saw the white sparks flickering where the armor-piercing incendiaries were going in . . . little glints of light . . . dancing along the wing . . . like the sparklers the kids play with on the Fourth of July.

"I gave the Betty another squirt . . . the port gas-tank blew up in a red glare . . . and her right wing was gone. She went down in a tight spin. I followed a bit. She hit the water and her bombs blew up."

Five minutes later Wellwood was after a second bomber, chasing her in a graveyard spin to the left, firing as he went. The Jap kept right on going down and so did Wellwood. He reported:

"The first thing I knew, I felt my stick loose and wobbly between my knees. I was in a spin too. That scared me to death. I broke out in a cold sweat because spinning in the daytime is bad enough, but at night it's murder. I was weak as a kitten and shaking. I didn't know then what happened to the Betty and I didn't much care.

"I was fighting to get back some altitude and to get my head clear. I had vertigo so bad every time I looked out of my cockpit, the moon was whirling all over the sky. I ducked back and went on the gauges, climbing and trimming the ship. I had a little bottle of brandy the Doc issues in my pocket. A nip of that helped a lot."

Minutes later Gallarneau had another customer for him. This contact was even rougher. The bomber led him down through flak from our ships. AA punched a hole in Wellwood's wing and knocked out one of his guns. Another jammed. His radio went out.

"The Betty saw me the same time I saw her. That same blue blow-torch flame broke out from her top turret as her gunner opened fire. I bored in and sat there pouring them into her. I must have gotten the pilot because the Betty went into a tight spin to the right. I didn't follow her. She hit—a gush of flame came up—and that was all."

Radio Tokyo, which had once preened about "control of the air over Okinawa," was now muttering dire threats of a new suicide wrinkle, the Giretsu.

Past 2230 the night of May 24, that new Special Attack Corps of airborne suicide troops arrived. A Sally bomber laden with these human bombs crash-landed on Yontan, in what was termed "the most audacious and destructive attack on aviation installations in the campaign."

With the turning of the enemy Shuri line by the infantry, the land campaign had gone into its last phases. Artists at delaying the inevitable, the Japs withdrew to a final defense line on the southern tip of Okinawa, asking their air force for diversionary attacks. These came in sustained fury over a five-day period, touched off by the spectacular Giretsu raid on May 24.

That night there was a break in the bad weather which had turned the battlefields into red rivers of mud. The Japanese took quick advantage of the moonlight and clear skies. In a spider web of searchlights Lieutenants Trammel and Smurr (of 533) were directed to simultaneous kills by Gallarneau that night. A pilot named Davis of 543 shot down two Bettys. A. F. Dellamano, a lieutenant of Magruder's squadron, made three radar kills during the melee at Yontan. His last victim was a Sally bomber, believed loaded with more Giretsu, which exploded when it crashed.

Magruder's pilots continued to swing their scythes at the moon and in seven weeks they downed 35 Jap planes to lead all Marine night fighter squadrons. In spite of the hazards of night flying, only one of their pilots was lost in combat.

The three Hellcat-flying Marine night squadrons piled up a total of 68 kills in the Okinawa campaign with VMF (N) 542 adding 18 and VMF (N) 543, 15 enemy planes to those of Magruder's unit. A less spectacular but effective phase of their operations were the night heckling raids. Throughout their stay on Okinawa, the night fighter squadrons raked targets behind enemy lines on Okinawa with bomb, rocket, and machine-gun fire, and haunted northern Ryukyus installations with clocklike precision.

After the Giretsu episode, the day squadrons rode hard through bad weather and leaden skies on May 25 to turn in their best day of the Okinawa campaign. With the help of two AAF squadrons, TAF Corsairs shot down 75 planes. The Army P-47's, which had made their first kill of the campaign over Kyushu the day previously, were credited with 34 victories.

The Japanese air effort on the 25th was the high point of their attempt to divert attention from their troop withdrawals on southern Okinawa. Heavy attacks on shipping were made by what amounted to the cream of the Japanese air force. Some of the newer and faster planes which appeared were not the Kamikaze type. But the Corsair and Thunderbolt pilots made no distinction and Tojos, Tonys, Hamps, Zekes, Oscars, Irvings, Jills, Nates, Bettys, and Vals all flamed or crashed with equal facility as did one unidentified survivor of the Nazi Luftwaffe, which had black swastikas painted on its wings.

Pilots of the Death Rattler squadron made 8 kills on the 25th, raising their unit total to 105 1/2 planes in six weeks. This broke the previous record for a similar period set by VMF 215 over Rabaul.

Okinawa weather, by now as infamous in curse and song as that of the Solomons, interfered with TAF action for two days, but the Japanese came down on May 28 and lost 37 planes.

As the infantry campaign on Okinawa moved into its final weeks, the air war slumped. Except for two good scoring days on June 3 and 22, the well-mauled Japanese air force offered little further opposition. Its heavy losses to the TAF and the effects of fighter sweeps and bombing raids on enemy homeland airbases by the TAF, the Fifth Fleet, and the B29's finally cracked its offensive power. Except for sporadic raids, the remaining Japanese planes were carefully saved for the anticipated invasion of their Empire.

Command of TAF changed June 11 when Major General Louis E. Woods of the Fourth Wing replaced General Mulcahy as head of the Tenth Army's Tactical Air Force.

June 22, the last big day in the air battle for Okinawa was, oddly enough, the day after organized enemy resistance on Okinawa was declared at an end by General Geiger, then commanding the Tenth Army. [Geiger succeeded Lieutenant General Simon Buckner who was killed on June 18 by enemy artillery fire. Geiger was appointed a lieutenant general on June 9 to become the highest ranking Marine aviator in the history of the Corps.]

The aerial fracas of June 22 was marked by several headline incidents. Captain Robert Baird, VMF (N) 533, downed a Francis and a Betty, to become the first night fighter ace of the campaign. Captain Ken Walsh, Medal of Honor winner for his 20 kills in the Solomons, finally found another victim. He pushed his fast new F4U-4 in on a Zeke and splashed it for his 21st victim of the war. [The new Chance-Vought F4U-4 was first flown by marines at Okinawa in early June. It was noted for its giant four-bladed propeller and its 2300 horse-power Pratt and Whitney radial engine. Prior to its arrival, TAF Corsair squadrons had been flying Chance-Vought F4U-1D's and Goodyear FG-1's.]

The Japanese pattern of combat on June 22 was unusual. The appearance of a large number of skillful, aggressive Jap pilots flying fast fighter types made the action comparable to those over Kahili and Rabaul. Though 4 TAF pilots and 5 planes were lost, 44 enemy planes went down, with Second Wing pilots getting 32 of them.

Weirdest action of the day was that by First Lieutenant John Leaper, VMF 314, who with his wingman, Lieutenant W. L. Milne, shot down 4 planes while on early morning CAP.

Leaper had just finished his final pass at a bomber which he shot down. In the pull-out, the marine spotted a Zeke fighter making a head-on run at him. Leaper nosed around and fired 10 rounds when his ammunition gave out. The marine pulled up and over the Zeke in a split-S and closed on the Jap from behind and below. Leaper pulled up trying to buzz-saw the Zeke's tail surfaces with his propeller. shattered glass and oil on the windshield spoiled his accuracy.

Failing to connect the first time, the marine jockeyed into position and came down on top of the Jap as his propeller sawed into the enemy fighter in front of its cockpit. Simultaneously, the right pylon tank on the Corsair exploded and the Zeke disintegrated. Then the entire right wing of the F4U ripped off.

The Corsair spun violently to the right. Leaper tried to bail out, but the centrifugal force of the spin held him back. He finally risked bailing out on the wrong side. As he pulled the rip cord, his parachute split from top to bottom. The impact of the chute's opening blacked Leaper out momentarily, broke two shroud lines, and tore the dye marker off his Mae West.

While floating down in this precarious state, the marine saw another Zeke fighter diving directly at him with 6 Corsairs on its tail. Leaper avoided becoming a statistic by jerking hard on his shroud lines. This collapsed the parachute and dropped him like a brick before the Jap got close. After 4,000 feet in a free fall, he reopened the ripped parachute. It absorbed the second shock without further damage and landed Leaper safely in the water where he was picked up by a destroyer.

The defensive phase of the air battle for Okinawa was set at an end June 30. Mainly as the result of night fighter action in the last week, the TAF score reached 600 kills on that date. During the three-month period (lacking one week) squadrons of the Second Marine Air Wing had accounted for 484 1/2 planes or 81 percent of the TAF kills at Okinawa. Twenty-one new Marine aces came out of the campaign.

The air battle for Okinawa was the second most profitable of the war for Marine aviation in the actual number of kills. At least 32 different types of identified Japanese planes were shot down by Marine pilots, who maintained the startling odds of better than 120-1. Only four Marine pilots were known to have been killed in combat with planes of the Japanese Air Force.

※ ※ ※ ※

ON JUNE 22, 1945, THE ISLAND WAS SECURED, AND SIX Marine Corps divisions began to prepare for Operation "Olympic"—the invasion of the enemy homeland where more than one million Japanese troops awaited. There was no question that the next invasion, had it occurred, would be Marine Corps-led. For by now in the United States there was an uproar over the conduct of the 82-day Okinawa campaign (as there had been over Iwo); and a columnist of the stature of David Lawrence asked: "Why were the Marine Corps generals, who had had far greater experience in handling amphibious operations, not given an opportunity to carry on another type of campaign that might, perhaps, have meant larger land casualties at the outset, but in the end a quicker all-around result for the armed forces as a whole?"

Emperor Hirohito also asked a question: was there a way to get out of the war? His government under Koiso, a pro-war spirit, had collapsed, and a new government under Admiral Kentaro Suzuki had recently been formed. There were peacemakers in Tokyo, yet none knew precisely how to end the conflict. In August the atom bomb fell on Hiroshima and provided the answer; the second bomb on Nagasaki made it imperative. The Emperor dismissed General Korechika Anami, who controlled the Imperial Army, and on August 15, Japan sued for peace.

"God be thanked, I'll never have to order another man out to die!" exclaimed Admiral Halsey when the news of the Japanese capitulation reached his flagship August 15. That day Halsey received orders to "cease all offensive operations against Japan," and that same evening a Marine Corps transport, the USS

Lanier, departed Guam with the 4th Regiment, 6th Marine Division, for the occupation of Yokasuka. Here is combat correspondent Sergeant John Birch to tell of the voyage and how marines still believed there was a "gimmick" somewhere in talk of the enemy's surrender.

·21· YOKASUKA LANDING

SERGEANT JOHN BIRCH

. . . It was going to be a fast three- or four-day spurt northward. The convoy would slip into Tokyo Bay and then one fine morning the marines would race ashore, taking over Yokasuka before the Japs had a chance to throw any curves—if that was the way they were going to play, all plans were made . . .

We had been at sea about 18 hours and one of the crew said that we passed Saipan during the night. The Marianas' northernmost pin-point islands were lying ahead. It wouldn't take us long to pass them and head into the Bonins. Japan seemed within fingertip reach and tension was mounting. The marines, stripped to the waist, stayed with their weapons. They were polishing away like mad.

That night General Quarters sounded ominously. It always sounds ominously and the troops scampered to their berthing spaces to make room for the crew to reach battle stations. This business of surrender was something we had been hearing over the air on Guam. This was different. Now it was the real thing. Below, in the holds of the ship, butterflies romped in our stomachs. It was the same old, cold, eerie sensation. It made you feel lousy.

One gent, curled up on a rack, muttered:

"Surrender my foot—they'll have to prove it first."

So it went. It was definitely no picnic. The word got around that our convoy—a few transports carrying the 4th's three battalions—would rendezvous with Halsey's Third Fleet on Saturday.

The words "blackout," "rendezvous," "General Quarters," and "Third Fleet" tumbled together. They were on everyone's lips.

Lieutenant Colonel George Bell, battalion CO, was grim and full of business. From the boat deck he looked down on his men. The latter were taking exercises. It seemed that they were limbering up a lot now.

In the wardroom Col. Bell talked to his officers gathered around a table cluttered with maps, drawings, aerial views and military magazines of all sorts.

"We're going to take the naval air station at Yokasuka. We expect to be greeted by some Nips—friendly ones we've been told."

If anyone caught the humor in the remark he didn't show it. They hung on Bell's words and took notes. The war correspondents aboard took notes, too, and occasionally they shot questions at the speaker.

"How long will it take the battalion to secure the airfield?"

"We HOPE to have it secured the first day."

"Do you expect any trouble?"

"We HOPE the Japs will cooperate. We've been told they will."

"Will the ships lay off in the harbor or dock?"

"We HOPE to have some of them docked the first day."

HOPE, HOPE, HOPE. It dominated the answers. No one attempted a smile. Yet we thought at the time it was kind of funny.

The colonel went on, just as grimly as before.

"Everyone will carry a weapon. The magazine will be loaded."

Then, as though he suddenly lost his reasoning:

"The chamber will be empty!" It didn't sound right but he repeated it. "You will NOT put a slug in your chamber. Your weapon will be locked."

At this point he paused. As if struggling with an incongruity himself, he waited for it to reach the men. Then came the climax to the strange order:

"You will not fire unless fired upon."

The words were an invitation to race back over history and you came up with something that included: ". . . until you see the whites of their eyes."

Here was a realistic man. He was calling things by their right names. He wasn't taking anything for granted. Only when he was on Jap soil with his men in unquestioned control would he write the thing off. You couldn't help but feel that way about him.

On a bulletin board by his shoulder a dispatch fluttered, caught in the breeze of an electric fan. It read:

"The use of insulting epithets in connection with the Japanese as a race or as individuals DOES NOT NOW become the officers of the United States Navy. Officers of the Pacific Fleet will take steps to require all personnel under their command to observe a high standard of conduct in this matter."

Outside, the marines, sweating and bearded, practiced rifle feints. They slammed each other to the deck, practiced headlocks and grunted all their favorite oaths.

The dispatch, now in caps, read on:

"IT IS DESIRED THAT COMMANDING OFFICERS APPRISE ALL HANDS UNDER THEIR COMMAND OF THE NEED FOR PRESENTING THEMSELVES UPON ARRIVAL IN THE BEST TRADITIONS OF THE NAVAL SERVICE. STRESS PARTICULARLY PROPER UNIFORM, CLEANLINESS, SMART MILITARY BEARING AND PROPER DEPORTMENT."

The paradox was there but we didn't quite grasp it then. The excitement was too great. Japan lay almost in reach.

On Saturday, as scheduled, the fleet was spotted over the horizon at dusk and, as darkness crowded in, we hung over the rails counting the ships until they became dark, overlapping blotches on the sky line.

That night the marines went back to their weapons. Something had to happen soon. But exactly nothing happened. That was the trouble.

The next nine days stretched as a single, unending nightmare. It was as if you held a stable of pinpoint-trained thoroughbreds champing at the barrier until, weak with anticipation for the race, they lost fire and slumped into exhaustion.

The marines started to "bitch" and scuttlebutt flooded the ship like a giant wave of sea water.

Everyone had his own personal explanation for the delay. A corporal carrying a "Times Square" sign slung around his neck said: "I think they're going to kick the Emperor out! It's just taking a little time to give him the heave-ho."

Another with the voice of one carrying a message from above intoned:

"It's a trap. They're stalling. When we finally land they'll hit us with everything but the Imperial moat."

Our fast three- or four-day jaunt to the Land of the Rising Sun was a joke. It was beginning to resemble a cross-country walking contest. Now, instead of acting like marines, the troops were getting very sissified. They began playing word games, reading books and once we saw a pair of salty, tattooed characters bending over a chess board.

To make matters worse we found that we were no longer marking a circular course off the homeland. The fleet signaled that a typhoon was raging near Tokyo and our unhappy little convoy headed south. That, of course, was the wrong direction.

Personally we were beginning to wish that we never had left Guam.

The troops didn't register emotion. They remained dull and listless and spoke only in unintelligible grunts. It was rough.

Then on the afternoon of the 27th we sighted land and in a few hours rode into Sagami Wan, a sheltered bay at the mouth of Tokyo harbor. Off to our left and partially hidden by clouds lay snow-capped Fujiyama. Majestic and serene, it looked every bit of what it was cracked up to be.

Morale soared. This time we were definitely on our way. The boys whipped out the weapons again and started throwing each other all over the place, stomping on arms, legs and ears.

Then it happened once more. The ship dropped anchor and with it plummeted our morale. By this time most of us didn't know whether we were on foot or horseback.

Now Fujiyama is a very beautiful piece of real estate. No one will deny that. But try looking at it for two and one-half days, almost without let-up, as we did, and you're bound to get a little rocky.

Sometimes during those two and one-half days, we can't remember exactly when, L Day (the day we were set to hit the beach) was officially given as Thursday, August 30. Somehow the announcement didn't do anything for us and we went back to the railing and Fujiyama.

As we said earlier—the suspense was gone. The old spark had petered out.

Apparently the atmosphere was contagious because the night before the landings, Col. Bell gathered his men for a final briefing. He wasn't the same man. His voice was hard and bitter.

"Men!" he started, looking around the room to insure attention, "we're going ashore tomorrow. My instructions are the same."

He repeated the gist of his earlier words about weapons and the plan of the day.

Then he dropped the bombshell.

"When you hit the beach, Navy camera men who will land earlier will be there. They will be taking pictures. Pictures of you men landing. I don't want any of you mugging the lenses. Simply get ashore as quickly as possible and do your job."

After muttering something about "comic opera" he said, "That is all," and left the room.

This was awful. Marines hadn't been meeting cameramen when they hit a beach. They had always met cleverly concealed Nips who tried their best to keep them in the water.

We crawled into our sacks terribly embarrassed and sometime during the night the *Lanier* weighed anchor and moved into Tokyo harbor.

L Day broke warm and bright. There was hardly a ripple on the water and as the battalions scrambled into landing craft something happened.

It was like a shot in the arm. Here were marines again, headed for a shore where only Heaven knew what waited. The heavy packs were feathers on their shoulders. They joked and laughed and as the coxswains powered the craft toward a rendezvous point a few miles off shore, you were sure this was the real thing.

No one knew what would happen on the beach. You couldn't be absolutely certain. You were dealing with the Nip.

We circled interminably, the assault boats bobbing gently. We were waiting to go in and as the minutes clicked off the marines gave their gear a grim, last-minute check.

Finally the coxswain in the lead craft signaled with both hands aloft and the boats, now abreast of each other in a long line, jumped for the shore as the pilots pulled on levers.

The shore, at first faintly distinguishable, loomed larger and deeper. Figures moved into sight and then disappeared again as our craft weaved and rocked under top speed.

We crouched lower in the boat, out of habit, and waited for that breathless crunch when water gave way to sand. While we were thinking of it we heard it, and the ramp dropped quickly, spilling marines on the beach.

They raced forward, fanning around a group of hangars—one of the objectives.

Others pushed toward a series of buildings off to our left which made up part of the huge Naval Air Station on Yokasuka. Then they stopped with the abruptness with which a movie operator brings his figures to halt on the screen.

Automobiles and buses were parked all over the place. Nip drivers behind the wheels. Some of the drivers were smoking cigarets. Others scanned newspapers and magazines. Few of them paid any attention to what we were doing.

Each had the look of a resigned husband waiting for the "little woman" to finish dressing before shoving off on a bridge date for which he already was late.

That was our reception party. The vehicles were accommodations. Everything was in readiness to make our stay in Japan as pleasant as possible.

Col. Bell, standing inside a hangar, was talking with a retired Nip warrant officer who acted as interpreter for the commander of the naval air station. The commander was there too, nodding familiarly and respectfully.

A few minutes later the American flag was raised in front of the administration building.

Two or three miles farther south, the second and third battalions assigned to occupation of the Yokasuka naval base were running into the same thing.

Everything was peaceful and the Nips were doing their darndest to show that they were all for cooperation. There, too, buses, trucks and private cars complete with drivers dotted the area.

The whole thing smacked of unreality.

In the afternoon some marines relaxed in scores of immaculate barracks provided by you know who.

Others just dropped in clusters around the air strip and Navy base and munched on candy bars. Every once in a while a bus would race around a corner and a marine would pull in his feet.

Inside the city, the residents of Yokasuka went about their business as marines taking up sentry watches on street corners went about their business.

We might just as well have stood in bed for all the attention we got from the natives.

It was a very crazy beachhead.

※ ※ ※ ※

ON SEPTEMBER 2, 1945, JAPANESE DIPLOMATS SIGNED the unconditional surrender document in ceremonies aboard the crowded battleship *Missouri* in Tokyo Bay. General MacArthur signed for the Allied Powers and Fleet Admiral Nimitz for the United States. The Marine Corps was well represented. Among the distinguished witnesses was Major General William T. Clement of the old 4th Marines. He had been taken off Corregidor by submarine April 9, 1942, and had returned to fight again as commanding officer of the 1st Marine Provisional Brigade in the assault and capture of Guam. World War II was over; it had lasted 1364 days. Fighting men offered solemn prayer to the Lord.

Two days later the Marine Corps enjoyed a moment of great triumph—the return to Wake Island where Major James P. F. Devereux' 422 marines had made their epochal stand in December 1942. Liberated from a P.O.W. camp, Devereux was now en route to Washington, D.C. and a reunion with his young son. But in his place was one who had witnessed a great part of the fighting—Colonel Walter L. J. Bayler, the last man off the atoll before it was overwhelmed. His was the signal honor of being the first to step ashore September 4, 1945.

Staff Sergeant Ernie Harwell of *Leatherneck* recorded the event and its interesting sidelights.

·22· WAKE REVISITED

SERGEANT ERNIE HARWELL

The flag-raising ceremony, which once again made Wake American territory, was over in less than two minutes. In the Corps it'll be remembered forever. At 1343, Marine Brigadier General Lawson H. M. Sanderson finished reading the surrender proclamation to American and Japanese contingents.

"Prepare to raise the colors," he commanded.

Master Technical Sergeant Ralph H. Broc of Sacramento, Cal., and PFC Millard P. Moore of Tulsa, Okla., stepped forward. They began to hoist the flag as PFC George Ellis of Alliance, Ohio, sounded colors. A breeze blew in from the sea and caught the flag as it reached the top. Marines, sailors and Japanese saluted. Then, following a 21-gun tribute by the USS *Levy,* lying off-shore, General Sanderson turned the island over to Commander William Masek of the Navy.

"I accept this island proudly," said the commander. "Because this is Wake Island. Not just any island. It was here the Marines showed us how."

The general moved slowly toward the Jap naval ranks on the opposite side of the flagpole. Standing before Rear Admiral Shigematsu Sakaibara, through an interpreter he said:

"The Japanese fought bravely. Now the war is over, and there'll be peace between us."

"We are very proud for the general to take over," answered Admiral Sakaibara. "Thank you for your kind treatment of myself and my men."

The general saluted.

The surrender had been signed earlier the same day on the boat deck of the *Levy,* a destroyer escort and flagship of the three-ship convoy, which had taken the marines to Wake. At 0745, a Japanese whaleboat, carrying a white flag, put-putted out of the mist which shrouded Wake and moved alongside the DE. Admiral Sakaibara was first aboard. After saluting the ensign and the deck officer he removed a white glove and shook hands with Lieutenant Commander William G. Clarenbach of Richmond, Cal., captain of the ship. Close on the admiral's heels came three aides followed by Army Colonel Shigeharu Chikama and his aide, Massao Yoshimizu.

The naval officers were dressed in green with khaki shirts and blue ties. They wore Sam Browne belts and black puttees. A green visor cap with a yellow anchor insignia topped their uniforms. Army officers wore olive drab, khaki gloves, white, open-neck shirts, and brown puttees.

The surrendering party was escorted to the boat deck by Comdr. Clarenbach and Army Staff Sergeant Larry Watanabe, American interpreter. While they were conferring with Gen. Sanderson's chief of staff, Colonel Thomas J. Walker, Jr., of Columbia, S.C., the general came into the group. Gen. Sanderson, his face lined with a calm grimness, did not shake hands. He nodded to the Japanese delegates and told them to be seated.

He laid his tanned left hand on the shoulder of his Nisei interpreter and turned to the Japanese admiral.

"This boy," he said, "was born in US territory. He is an American citizen. Not a prisoner."

A smile broke through the admiral's stony features.

"Of course, general," he commented, "we regret that the Japanese must surrender; but we are glad it is to America."

Arranging themselves around the table to confer with the Japs were Gen. Sanderson, Col. Walker, Comdr. Masek, Commander H. E. Cross (commanding officer of the Destroyer Escort Division 11) and Lieutenant Colonel William D. Roberson. Four photographers and two movie cameramen moved around the green, felt-covered table like hunters stalking their prey. A microphone hung from above.

Comdr. Cross extracted a package of cigarets and offered one to Lieutenant (paymaster) Nakasato, who was serving as Jap interpreter. The paymaster, who wore black-rimmed glasses, accepted the cigaret but didn't inhale. Gen. Sanderson slipped on his glasses and then took a cigar from his shirt pocket. Col. Walker brought a sheaf of papers from his red brief case, and final negotiations were under way.

Already the Japs had agreed on general terms. But there were a few specific questions, written in pencil on tablet paper, which Gen. Sanderson handed the admiral. "How many buoys do you have?" and "Are they in use?" were two of the queries. These were settled, and the signing began. Gen. Sanderson handed the admiral a pen and both the original copy of the surrender and the Japanese translation.

After glancing over the Jap translation the admiral turned to his aide and questioned him.

"Why is the date not filled in? Will it be inserted?" he asked. Learning it would be, he signed. The general watched. Then he affixed his signature to both copies in a large bold hand. Eleven more copies in both Japanese and English were handed the Jap admiral.

"Why so many?" he asked.

"It is necessary," the general explained, "because of our procedure. Copies must be sent to many different headquarters."

The Jap shrugged and penned his name to the bottom of each document. Col. Walker then stamped the papers with the US Government seal, and the surrender was completed.

A discussion concerning the sending of a party ashore by the Americans took place next. Comdr. Masek pulled out a map of the island. When he did, the Japanese jumped up and pointed toward the shore line, explaining with gesticulations the location of important points. A rain blew in from the West, sending the group below to the wardroom.

Thirty-five minutes later a party of marines headed for Wake in a whaleboat. The first to step ashore was Colonel Walter L. J. Bayler of Lebanon, Pa., who on December 21, 1941, had been the last American to leave the same island. The colonel was followed ashore by a group of correspondents; and a few minutes later another boatload of marines arrived.

As they walked up the concrete steps from the pier, the first structure they saw was a white frame Japanese building, fronted by circular steps. It formerly had been a dining hall, but now was being used by the Japs as a command post. Four trucks, a 1941 station wagon, a touring car and a sedan were parked in front. Inside the hall the Nips had stacked much of their ammunition.

The Japanese who stood around the veranda in their patched uniforms were polite but steely-eyed and aloof. They told the Marines that 1250 men were left on Wake. Last supplies, they said, had been brought in by a submarine on June 21. However, half of that supply had been lost when an American sub sighted the Jap vessel and forced it to submerge.

Since the original Japanese invasion, 2000 had died of malnutrition; 1000 had been killed by air attacks and almost another 1000 had been evacuated by hospital ships. The remaining Nips were living underground, and subsisting on pumpkins, fish and rice. Many of them were emaciated.

"We must guard against sabotage," Gen. Sanderson had told the Japanese delegation at the surrender ceremony.

"There need be no worry," was the reply. "None of our men has the strength for such action."

The beleaguered Japanese had just 17 days' rations left. This condition was alleviated immediately when sailors from the *Levy* brought ashore four tons of rice and fish, plus 550 pounds of medical supplies.

The Americans had provided the Japs with movies—but didn't know it.

"We enjoyed American cinemas very much here," a Jap Army major told the group. "The films once belonged to your Marine garrison. Our sound amplifiers would not work but we did not mind."

The Jap, who spoke broken English, jotted down the names of the movies. Here is his list:

"Chicago, Dance In Honolulu, Cowboy A & B, Three People in Heaven, Lost Love, Brave Soldiers, Military Ships and Amusement of Soldiers."

Anxious to see the island, especially the old Marine encampment, the group hopped aboard a commandeered Jap truck and began a tour. Col. Bayler pointed out many spots where the small Leatherneck garrison had lived, worked and fought. The old observation tower, now staggering on three rusty legs, still stood.

"It was from there," explained Col. Bayler, "that we saw the first wave of attacking Jap planes come over the island on the morning of December 8."

Smoking a black pipe, the colonel led the group 100 yards to the left, stepping around several duds as he went.

"See those two wooden sticks over there across that tank trap?" the colonel asked. "Well, that is all that's left of our old administration building."

The Japanese, the colonel observed, had worked hard on the islands, bringing in sand and coral to build defenses. They had changed the face of the area almost completely. Off the well-kept airstrip was an underground hangar which had been built by Marine forces. Nearby stood a dugout.

Three wrecked Jap planes lay near the strong concrete revetments. In the bushes on the opposite side of the field were three of the Grumman Wildcats which had fought off the early enemy attacks.

The island still bristled with gun emplacements. A glance in any direction showed American machinery, most of it wrecked. Down the coral road from the airstrip was the former Marine industrial area. There the BOQ had been under construction when the first Jap planes roared over Wake.

All that remain today are a few toilet bowls staring bleakly into the Pacific sky.

"Were there any marines or American civilians buried on the island?"

The Japanese said yes—in two common graves. In one were 80 men. How many the other held they didn't know. Big crosses marked both graves. Atop the first mound of coral and sand was a marker which read: "Will Miles, Died July 15, 1942."

Who was Will Miles?

None of the Japs knew. The closest guess was that he had been an American civilian worker; that all the Americans had been thrown into the two graves and that Miles had been the last to die. Or perhaps as one Jap explained:

"He was the most important, so we placed his name on top of the grave."

Records of the Navy Department's Bureau of Yards and Docks carry the name of a William Miles, 57, who was on Wake at the time the island fell to the Japanese. Listed as a contractor's employee, Miles has been unreported since that time.

The plot showed signs of recent preparation. Bushes near it were freshly cut. The white paint on the posts surrounding the graves and also that on the markers was not quite dry. Evidently the Japs, expecting an early visit from American forces, had policed up the cemetery area.

When the group returned to the Jap command post to prepare for the flag-raising, correspondents asked if there was anyone left on the island who had participated in the original attack there almost four years ago.

"We have few," was the answer.

A Jap lieutenant commander dispatched a sailor to bring a man to the command post. He was Japanese Superior Seaman Tokeo Endo, a swarthy, stocky man of 31 years.

"I came ashore," he said in answer to the newsmen's queries, "in early morning of December 23. Our attacking force included four destroyers, two transports, four cruisers and one seaplane tender. We landed from a patrol vessel. The fighting was fierce—full of hand-to-hand combat—and lasted more than eight hours."

"How many men did your forces include?" he was asked.

"We had about 700. Of those we lost about 120 on landing and 60 or 70 later."

"Are you happy now that you'll be going home?"

No answer.

"Are you married?"

"Yes," he said. "But no children."

"Don't you want to see your wife?"

No answer.

The Jap said that they had taken 1600 American prisoners and moved them from Wake in two groups, the first leaving in March, 1942.

The final question put to him was, "Don't you want to return home at all?"

"I will return if ordered," was the laconic reply.

Meanwhile Gen. Sanderson had come ashore as the Japanese and American forces were gathering for the flag-raising. As the flag was hoisted into the air, Superior Seaman Endo, watching from behind the command post, looked down and scraped some coral aside with his heavy black shoe. What he was thinking no one will ever know.

What the Americans were thinking, everybody knows.

The next morning a Curtiss Commando landed at the Wake airstrip—the first plane to visit the island since its capture by the Japanese, and the first transport ever to land there. At 1000 it took off and headed for Kwajalein with Gen. Sanderson and his party.

Many more planes will land and take off from Wake. This little island which the Marines defended so stoutly is ours again.

❀ ❀ ❀ ❀

THE 6TH MARINE DIVISION DEPARTED GUAM ON October 1 for the Tientsin-Chefoo area of North China. In the fifteen-ship convoy were Major Generals Lemuel C. Shepherd and William T. Clement, who were to oversee the occupation of the Tachang and Shanghai-Chefoo airfields, and the Huangpo River area, for the link-up with the 1st Marine Division at Tientsin. The function of the occupation was to assure the release of Allied internees, disarm existing Japanese forces, maintain law and order, prevent the outbreak of disease and starvation, and accept Japanese surrenders when necessary.

At Tientsin, Major General Keller M. Rockey, who had commanded the III Amphibious Corps at Iwo Jima, accepted the surrender of General Ushida which ended Japan's eight-year war with China.

In Tsingtao it was now the afternoon of October 25, 1945, breezy and clear. A reviewing stand had been set up in the racetrack; above it rippled the flags of the United States, China, Great Britain, Russia and France. It was 2 P.M., the moment when the vanquished enemy tendered his last surrender. Three Marine generals—Rockey, Shepherd and Clement—stood at a table on the platform. Before them were 12,000 United States Marines and a battalion of massed Sherman tanks. The eloquent speeches had long since been made. General Shepherd simply glanced at General Nagamo Eiji, walked to a microphone, and stared out at the sea of olive-drab uniforms.

·23· SURRENDER AT TSINGTAO

MAJOR GENERAL
LEMUEL C. SHEPHERD, JR.

Officers and men of the Sixth Marine Division: You are about to participate in the formal surrender of the Japanese Military forces in the Tsingtao area. It is an historic event which each of you should long remember. It is the goal for which we have fought during these past four years, and I am sure the personal satisfaction each of you obtains from witnessing the local Japanese Army Commander lay down his sword in complete defeat will, in a small measure, compensate for the dangers and hardships to which you have been exposed during your service in this war.

We of the Sixth Marine Division have every reason to be proud of our accomplishments in the Pacific War and of our part in bringing victory to our cause. Melanesia, Micronesia and the Orient truly describe the scope of our contribution during the progress of the war. And in the same fashion the Crusader's sword emblazoned on our shield typifies the striking power characteristic of the Sixth Marine Division. From the initial landing of Marines in the summer of 1942 on Makin Island, through the bitter battles from Guadalcanal and Guam to the final decisive campaign on Okinawa in which our Division played such a glorious part, units of the Sixth Division have repeatedly distinguished themselves.

To have commanded this splendid body of men is the greatest honor that I shall ever receive. It is with a deep sense of humility and pride that I stand before you this day and, as your representative, receive the surrender of the enemy, for whose defeat we have fought and bled through the years.

❧   ❧   ❧   ❧

WORLD WAR II HAD COST THE UNITED STATES MARINE
Corps 86,490 dead and wounded in its victorious march across
the Pacific, with payment in blood tendered for eighty Medals
of Honor. The greatest fighting force the world has ever known
was at peace.

"Yea, though I walk through the valley of the shadow of death,
I will fear no evil: for Thou art with me . . ."

PSALMS, 23:4

INDEX

ABOUT THE EDITOR

During World War II, S. E. SMITH served in both the Atlantic and the Pacific. From 1947 - 1954 he was Rod and Gun columnist of the New York *Daily News* and thence moved to the National Broadcasting Company as a news editor and documentarian. In recent years he has been a free-lancer, writing for motion pictures, television and magazines, chiefly on military and naval subjects. He is a member of The Navy League, Marine Corps Association and the Society of Military Historians.